THIRD EDITION

Criminal Procedure

Constitution and Society

Marvin Zalman, J.D., Ph.D.

Wayne State University

Upper Saddle River, New Jersey 07458

Library of Congress Cataloging-in-Publication Data

Zalman, Marvin.
Criminal procedure: constitution and society / Marvin Zalman.—3rd ed.
p. cm.
Includes bibliographical references and index.
ISBN 0-13-089278-5
1. Criminal procedure—United States—Cases. 2. Criminal investigation—United States—Cases. 3. Civil rights—United States—Cases. I. Title.

KF9618. Z35 2002
345.73′05—dc21

2001021429

Publisher: Jeff Johnston
Executive Acquisitions Editor: Kim Davies
Editorial Assistant: Sarah Holle
Director of Production and Manufacturing: Bruce Johnson
Managing Editor: Mary Carnis
Production Liason: Adele M. Kupchik
Manufacturing Manager: Ilene Sanford
Manufacturing Buyer: Cathleen Petersen
Production Editor: Silvia Freeburg
Cover Design Coordinator: Miguel Ortiz
Creative Director: Cheryl Asherman
Marketing Manager: Ramona Sherman
Marketing Coordinator: Adam Kloza
Compositon: Clarinda Publication Services
Printing and Binding: Courier Westord

Prentice-Hall International (UK) Limited, *London*
Prentice Hall of Australia Pty. Limited, *Sydney*
Prentice-Hall Canada, Inc., *Toronto*
Prentice-Hall Hispanoamericana, S.A., *Mexico*
Prentice-Hall of India Private Limited, *New Delhi*
Prentice-Hall of Japan, Inc., *Tokyo*
Prentice-Hall Singapore Pte. Ltd.
Editora Prentice-Hall do Brasil, Ltda., *Rio de Janeiro*

10 9 8 7 6 5 4 3 2 1
ISBN 0-13-089278-5

To Greta

Contents

CHAPTER 6

WARRANTLESS SEARCHES 228

CHAPTER 7

THE RIGHT TO COUNSEL 272

Preface

Criminal procedure is a dramatic subject. Each case tells a story of conflict that pits society's vital need for the communal peace and order that makes life livable, against the right of each individual to be free from unreasonable invasions of privacy and freedom by officers of the state. Criminal procedure is also a technical subject. It encompasses many legal rules and doctrines, not all of which are perfectly logical. The drama of criminal procedure may be conveyed by a book that explores one important case, such as *Gideon's Trumpet*, Anthony Lewis' classic story of Earl Clarence Gideon's fight for the right to counsel that took his case to the United States Supreme Court. Simply studying dramatic cases limits the student's exposure to many important topics.

Every law teacher knows that the heart of American law lies in the cases. Most law texts present the subject matter either in a case-book format or in a text-book format. Each has its advantages. *Criminal Procedure: Constitution and Society* is an effort to present the best of both methods, with additional features that are uniquely tailored to social science students in Criminal Justice, Criminology, Sociology, and Political Science. The unique features of this text will make the study of criminal procedure a comprehensive educational experience.

I begin with the premise that the task confronting a social science student studying law is more difficult than that confronting a law student. The law student concentrates on the technicalities of law and is only incidentally concerned with how law fits into society. The social science student has to learn the law *and* discover how the law fits into a society that the student will confront as a police officer, probation officer, or as a lawyer. The challenge is to bring out the attributes of law and society in a way that does not overwhelm the student and is respectful of the student's intelligence yet does not water down the subject matter. This text seeks to achieve this balance with several pedagogical features that are not found in other texts.

The basic text. The longest portion of this book is devoted to presenting and explaining the core knowledge that is constitutional criminal procedure. The topics have been selected to reflect those that are of greatest interest to criminal justice students. The chapters are organized by relevant topics, with four chapters being devoted to the critical Fourth Amendment: the exclusionary rule (Chapter 3), the search warrant and essential Fourth Amendment doctrines such as plain view (Chapter 4), arrest and *Terry*-stops (Chapter 5), and a chapter devoted to warrantless searches (Chapter 6). This focus also reflects the area in which the Supreme Court has been most active in recent years. The chapters are divided into coherent sub-topics that give instructors the flexibility to cover a general area but omit specific topics within it as they see fit.

The third edition of *Criminal Procedure: Constitution and Society* has been completely revised. The number of chapters has been reduced and the content rearranged to fit into more coherent topic headings. Each line of text has been revised to ensure the greatest clarity. Throughout the text I have attempted to show that, in most areas, there has been an ongoing dialogue between the justices adhering to the Due Process Model and those adhearing to the Crime Control Model. The late Professor Herbert Packer's great organizing paradigm provides a convenient way for students to grasp the overall subject matter and each case. Thus, both in the text and in the "Case & Comments," the conflicting approaches to the law has been explicated.

It goes without saying that the purpose of education, reflected in this text, is not the rote memorization of rules, but the *understanding* of the rules. To this end the text includes not just statements of rules, but describes the facts out of which the rules emerge and the often conflicting views of the justices and the relevant historic and political factors that have influenced the decision. On occasion where a subject is overly complex (e.g., the incorporation doctrine in Chapter 2 or the automobile search doctrine in Chapter 6) I have tried to help students thread their way through the maze by providing an overview of the subject in the form of a list. On the other hand, I have with deliberation inserted a section on the theories of the exclusionary rule which presents students with an up-to-date philosophical discussion of the justification for the rule that is more abstract than the remainder of the text. Instructors who desire to challenge students are invited to cover this section, but it can be omitted without undermining a student's basic understanding of the topic.

The text includes two introductory chapters. Instructors who want to plunge directly into the substance of criminal procedure can skip these. Chapter 1 introduces basic information about law and courts that students may have learned from other courses. It also includes a more advanced section on reading cases designed to sharpen the *skills* portion of the subject, that makes most law classes among the most exciting in criminal justice programs. Many instructors, of course, have over the years developed their own approaches to introducing students to the intellectual challenge of reading cases and may wish to rely on their tried and true methods instead of using the sections in Chapter 1. The third function of Chapter 1 is to help a student see that criminal procedure is not a narrow subject or a simple matter of technical legal rules, but, instead, it is a component of a liberal arts education. Criminal procedure can be a gateway to the study of history, politics, political theory, judicial biography, and important societal currents, for all of these influence criminal procedure. Finally, Chapter 1 notes that the study of criminal procedure is the study of human rights, and may encourage students to broaden their horizons by the study of international human rights.

Chapter 2 is a detailed exploration of the historical development known as the incorporation doctrine. Some instructors may simply wish to acknowledge the fact and begin with the establishment of modern rules of criminal procedure in the 1960s. I find this a fascinating subject and a portal to help students develop an understanding of the ancient truth that rights are never handed to citizens on a silver-platter but must be fought for. In any event, the first two chapters are available for instructors who wish to explore these matters.

Case and Comments. In addition to the text, a major feature of this book is one or more "Case & Comments" in Chapters 2 through 12. Teachers who use the case method know how difficult the method can be for first year law students, let alone undergraduate students. The cases selected for the Case & Comments are the most important ones that all instructors of criminal procedure will emphasize. They have been carefully edited to provide not just a brief snippet of the holding but a fair amount of the reasoning of the justices, which, after all, is the main reason to read the cases. Furthermore, for complete understanding, in almost all of these cases relevant portions of the dissenting opinions have been included so that students can understand the law as a dialectical process.

To this familiar aspect of a case-book I have added comments that are noted by bracketed letters keyed to running comments. These are critical tools designed to assist the student, even one with no prior legal training, to read the case for himself or herself. These comments are written to achieve several goals: (1) to point out the meaning or importance of technical legal words; (2) to highlight disagreements among opposing justices; (3) to point out logical weaknesses or clever arguments; (4) to ask pointed questions of the students; (5) to highlight underlying value judgments in an opinion; (7) to indicate how the case advances or violates the doctrine of *stare decisis*.

Law in Society Sections. These sections in each chapter show the "law in action." It is too easy to view legal pronouncements about rights to mean that they are fully enjoyed. Unfortunately, there is a gap between the ideals of law and the reality of its application. Some sections, such as the accounts of police perjury, racial profiling, and prosecutorial misconduct, show criminal justice personnel at their worst. The first chapter indicates that valued constitutional rights can be treated as threats to safety and abused for political advantage. The unmet promise of equal justice shows that as a society we are not ready to pay for justice for indigents. Of course, most police officers do not commit perjury, most lawyers and prosecutors competently do their jobs, most judges do not buckle under political pressure, and most jurors do their best objectively to arrive at the proper verdict under the law. But this is not always the case and it is important to alert students to the gap between constitutional ideals and the reality on the street. Several Law in Society sections rely on social science research to indicate the complexity of the criminal process, and that simple statements or beliefs do not capture the full reality of the exclusionary rule, the use of mandatory arrest for domestic violence, or the belief that an eyewitness who is positive is therefore accurate. In these sections we get to see that innocent people confess to crimes they did not commit despite having been read their *Miranda* warnings, and see the dark side of undercover policing. By introducing information from the news and from social science research, we expand our knowledge of the social reality of the law.

Law in the States. A general course in criminal procedure inevitably stresses the provisions of the United States Constitution as interpreted by the United States Supreme Court. This is essential, since the Court took the lead of, and in a sense gave real life to, the subject with the incorporation of the Bill of Rights in the 1960s. Nevertheless, state courts have shaped criminal procedure most notably where they have departed from interpretations of the Supreme Court by granting state citizens greater individual protections. In this text, I have alerted students to the state cross-currents with Law in the States boxes that indicate areas in which there has been significant divergence. These brief inserts are an efficient way to alert students to this important complicating factor in American law, while indicating that the main thrust of constitutional criminal procedure still lies with the United States Supreme Court.

Supreme Court Justice Biographies. It is very difficult for beginning students to appreciate the extent to which constitutional law is the product of the particular men and women who have been nominated and confirmed by the Senate to sit on the nation's highest court. Many instructors utilize this knowledge to assist students in understanding the law and cases. Because of this, the text includes brief biographical sketches that highlight each of the covered justice's contributions to criminal procedure and describes the justice's general approach to the law. This unique feature of the text has been revised for this edition. In addition to adding updated information, each biography has been rewritten, made more compact, and organized into the following headings: Life and Career, Contribution to Criminal Procedure, Signature Opinion, and Assessment. Also, at least one source of information is given for each justice and where possible a comprehensive biography. An interested student can follow up an interest in this regard, and as with the Suggested Readings, an instructor who gives extra-credit assignments may wish to consider these books as candidates for book reviews.

Appendix: Summary Information about Selected Supreme Court Justices. A one line summary of the typical voting style of each justice is given. Many students have no knowledge about the justices and this "scorecard" information provides a valuable tip about the judge's orientation.

Legal Puzzles. At the conclusion of each chapter, recent cases from the U.S. Courts of Appeal are presented that indicate how some of the basic doctrines covered in the chapter have been resolved by lower courts. The answers follow in a section, so that students can quickly see how the puzzles have been resolved. These are great for generating in-class discussions, in part because the solutions to the legal questions may be unexpected. These puzzles give students greater insight into the fact that in many cases the application of legal precedent is not mechanical, but requires lower courts to do a good deal of weighing and analysis to resolve issues.

Suggested Readings. In this edition, I have added three books at the conclusion of each chapter for further reading. I have kept this list short and have selected books that I have enjoyed reading. Although a handful are designed more for instruction, quite a few of these books are pleasurable reading from which a student can derive a deeper understanding of a particular subject. As a pedagogic tool, an instructor who gives extra-credit assignments may wish to consider these books as candidates for book reviews.

Key Terms and Phrases and Expanded Glossary. At the beginning of each chapter, students are alerted to key terms and phrases, which are bolded throughout the chapter. Each term is defined in an expanded glossary, which can be used by the instructor as a pedagogic tool. A student who knows these terms will have a good grasp of the content of the text.

Relevant Excerpts of the United States Constitution. An appendix includes carefully selected portions of the Constitution that are relevant to a course on criminal procedure. This may be used by the student and instructor as a handy reference, or it may be used as a teaching tool, with certain provisions as required reading. At the very least, it is useful for students to see the Bill of Rights in its entirety.

Marvin Zalman
Wayne State University

ACKNOWLEDGMENTS

The preparation of this book has been made much easier and greatly improved thanks to the helpful criticism of colleagues in many institutions including:

Rudolph de la Torre
Los Angeles Mission College, CA

Barbara Belbot
University of Houston-Downtown, TX

Wayne Wolf
South Surburban Community College, IL

Joel Allen
Oakland Community College, MI

Donna Nicholsen
Manchester Community College, CT

Special thanks is offered to my good friend Nigel Cohen and former colleague during a sabbatical at Rutgers University, who is now a professor of criminal justice at the University of Texas—Pan American, and has graciously read every line of the text and has seen human fallibility up close. I must also acknowledge the debts owed to Professor Christopher E. Smith of Michigan State University, whose article, "Teaching the Irrelevance of Law on Criminal Procedure," in Volume 7 of the *Journal of Criminal Justice Education* stimulated me to provide more hard-hitting Law in Society sections in the second edition and in this edition.

I also owe a great debt to colleagues who reviewed the first and second editions of this text. They include: Andrew C. Blanar, John C. Conway, Jerry Dowling, Micheal Falvo, Zoltan Ferency (deceased), Robert A. Harvie, W. Richard Janikowski, Paul A. Mastriacovo, William Michalek, Andrew A. Mickle, Robert R. Reinertsen, Cliff Roberson, Cathryn Jo Rosen, Martha J. Sullivan, Donald H. Wallace, John T. Whitehead, Wayne L. Wolf, and Benjamin S. Wright. Also, several students were more than helpful in providing research assistance for earlier editions: Joyce Andries, Garth J. Milazzo and Michael J. Vasich.

The editorial staff at Pearson/Prentice-Hall has been fantastically supportive and helpful at every turn in making a large job move along very smoothly. Many thanks to acquisitions editor, Kim Davies, developmental editor, Cheryl Adam, who stayed in touch by e-mail while moving across the country (!), I'd like to thank my production editor Silvia Freeburg, and my copyeditor's Kimm Livengood and Connie Chambers.

Every writer feels some sense of guilt for the idea, right or wrong, that time spent with the book meant less time with family. Greta and Amy and Seth should know that this book could not have been written without their sustaining love.

ABOUT THE AUTHOR

Marvin Zalman began his career in criminal justice education in northern Nigeria. He and his wife Greta, then recent graduates of Brooklyn Law School, were inspired in their college years by President John F. Kennedy's challenge to young Americans: "ask not what your country can do for you, ask what you can do for your country." As Peace Corps volunteers they were assigned to Nigeria and from 1967 to 1969 were lecturers in the law faculty at Ahmadu Bello University in the city of Zaria. Zalman taught classes on criminal law and criminal procedure and decided to study these subjects in greater depth. He authored a casebook on Northern Nigerian criminal procedure and conducted a study of sentencing patterns in local criminal courts. Upon returning to the United States, he began studies in a new field of scholarship at the School of Criminal Justice at the State university of New York at Albany, from which he holds his Ph.D. degree. From 1971 to 1980 he taught at the School of Criminal Justice at Michigan State University and came to Wayne State University in Detroit, where he served as chair of the Criminal Justice Department from 1980 to 1987. From 1978 to 1980, Professor Zalman was the executive director of sentencing guideline projects for the State of Michigan and in

1984 for the State of New York. He has published research and scholarship in the areas of criminal sentencing, criminal procedure, domestic violence, prisoner's rights, and assisted suicide. He teaches classes on criminal justice policy, criminal law, the judicial process, and criminal procedure. Marvin Zalman believes passionately that constitutional criminal procedure is the most important course that criminal justice students can take because it deals with individual liberty. His parents fled to the safety of America during World War II, and he believes he owes his life to the power and decency of the United States that is embodied in its constitutional values. The message he wishes to convey is that every day, each police officer, defense lawyer, prosecutor, probation officer, and judge, who does his or her job properly keeps the promise of liberty alive.

FOREWORD

I first met Professor Marvin Zalman in the summer of 1969 when I was a twenty-two-year-old graduate student at the School of Criminal Justice at the University at Albany. Already an attorney, Marv had just come back from a stint in Nigeria as a Peace Corp volunteer and was beginning his own doctoral work in criminal justice. We have been best friends ever since. In 1990 we decided to collaborate on a book on constitutional criminal procedure. During our preliminary discussions, we seized upon a plan to create a new prototype for a legal text. Heretofore some criminal procedure texts had relied solely on case analysis as a teaching tool, whereas others had reduced the cases to minuscule excerpts and relied on the author's narrative to present legal concepts. Both methods left something to be desired. Reading cases is difficult for law students let alone undergraduates; relying solely on narrative fails to expose students to the original source material, ie., legal cases. We wanted to create a new design for teaching criminal procedure which incorporated both methods. We came up with the "Case and Comment" approach that involved presenting cases which had been carefully edited to retain their most important textual material yet retained the most significant passages so that the reasoning process of the judges could be discerned. Accompanying the cases was a running narrative, explaining legal concepts and phrases, which we believed would be an essential pedagogic tool to help students understand the meaning of a case and the legal arguments upon which it rested. Accompanying the Cases and Comments, carefully constructed narratives guided students through the intricacies of criminal procedure. In addition to combining these two teaching elements, the book blazed new trails by providing students with background information on the Supreme Court justices who wrote the decisions so that students could understand the social and political forces which guided their thinking. Another new approach was to link the cases to public policy which flowed from their legal precedents and postures. It is one thing to talk about the right to make an arrest as an abstract Fourth Amendment issue, it is another to see how case law influences the protection of women in domestic violence situations. I believed then as I do today that this method provides students with a platform to fully understand constitutional criminal procedure which is nonpareil and unmatched by any other existing text.

I believe that I was some help to Marvin in the first edition of the text, and even a little bit in the second, but now in its third edition, *CRIMINAL PROCEDURE: CONSTITUTION AND SOCIETY*, is solely a tribute to Marv's great legal scholarship. Because the book reflects his personal vision of the law and justice, I have recused myself from the title page while being honored to write these words in a foreword. As you read this text you will discover what I have known since the summer of '69, that Marvin Zalman is a legal scholar with a deep and penetrating knowledge of the law and an unbridled willingness to share it others.

Larry Siegel, Ph.D.
University of Massachusetts at Lowell

CHAPTER 1

THE MEANING AND CONTEXT OF CRIMINAL PROCEDURE

The Constitution of the United States was ordained, it is true, by descendants of Englishmen, who inherited the traditions of English law and history; but it was made for an undefined and expanding future, and for a people gathered and to be gathered from many nations and of many tongues.

—Justice Stanley Matthews, *Hurtado v. California,* 110 U.S. 516, 530–31 (1884)

CHAPTER OUTLINE

KEY TERMS AND PHRASES *(CONTINUES ON NEXT PAGE)*

Adequate and independent state grounds
Affirm
Appellate decision
Appellate opinion
Briefing a case
Burger Court
Case law
Civil rights function
Common law
Constitutionalism
Court of general jurisdiction
Court of limited jurisdiction
Crime Control Model
Democracy
Domestic tranquillity
Due Process Model
Equality
Equal Protection Clause
Facilitating function
Federalism
Hierarchy of courts
Hierarchy of law
Human rights
Judicial craft
Judicial federalism
Judicial philosophy
Judicial policy
Judicial statesmanship
Legal reasoning
Liberty
Locke, John
Order
Plain statement
Precedent
Private law

Procedural law
Public law
Rehnquist Court
Remand
Remedial law
Republicanism
Reverse
Rule of Law
Rule application
Rule making
Source of law
Substantive law
Supervisory authority
Supremacy clause
Universal Declaration of Human Rights
Warren Court

ORDER AND LIBERTY: THE MEANING OF CONSTITUTIONAL CRIMINAL PROCEDURE:

American criminal justice, a powerful engine of public safety and social control, operates under a balanced constitutional system to ensure that it does not become oppressive. This is signified by the Preamble to the United States Constitution:

> We the People of the United States, in Order to form a more perfect Union, establish Justice, insure domestic Tranquillity, provide for the common defence, promote the general Welfare, and secure the Blessings of Liberty to ourselves and our Posterity, do ordain and establish this Constitution for the United States of America.

Three aims of government stated in the preamble are relevant to criminal justice: (1) "establish Justice"—establish courts of law and other means to allow people to pursue justice when conflicts arise; (2) "insure **domestic Tranquillity**"—create the means to suppress riots, prevent crime and secure public safety or order; and (3) "secure the Blessings of Liberty to ourselves and our Posterity." Individual liberty was a revolutionary idea in the eighteenth century and to say that the guarantee of individual liberty was a central aim of government was truly something new in human affairs. **Order** and **liberty**—both necessary for a stable society—often conflict. Internal order promotes freedom, which allows people to utilize their gifts in the "pursuit of happiness," in the words of the Declaration of Independence. Yet, the stifling order of police states crushes the creative powers of individuals.

The *order–liberty tension* is resolved to a degree by the United States Supreme Court, which balances the demands for order and liberty through its interpretation of the Constitution.[1] But this tension cannot be permanently resolved. At times in American history the balance has favored the state whereas at other times individual rights and freedoms are advantaged. The Court's decisions are often controversial because it receives difficult cases with novel or unsettled issues that require it to examine fundamental constitutional policies. Cherished rights such as trial by jury, protection from unreasonable searches, and the privilege against self–incrimination are not questioned. On the other hand, hundreds of specific issues concerning the criminal trial, search and seizure, and confessions, can be decided in favor of individual liberty (the defendant) or state order (police and prosecution), and these decisions, cumulatively, can make criminal procedure law appear to be mostly "liberal" or mostly "conservative." Yet, the Court's larger goal, always, is *to preserve a society in which order is sustained and liberty is cherished.*

Criminal procedure law includes state and federal constitutions, statutes and rules, as well as the decisions of federal and state appellate courts. This branch of constitutional law establishes government power and simultaneously protects against excessive government power; that is, its rules authorize the arrest and prosecution of accused persons through the criminal justice system (deprivation of liberty) but establish procedures to ensure that the system operates fairly (guarantee of liberty). The focus of this text is on *constitutional* criminal procedure which emphasizes interpretations of the United States Constitution and the Bill of Rights by the Supreme Court.

Before 1960 criminal procedure law focused more on processing suspects than protecting their rights. It consisted largely of technical rules such as the definition of arrest powers or the conduct of a criminal trial. A few United States Supreme Court due process rulings struck down coerced confessions and checked gross violations of rights by local police. But the rights of most Americans in relation to local police and prosecutors were protected by state courts. If some states were not vigilant in protecting the liberty of its residents, there was little recourse to federal authorities. In practice, the rights of many were largely undefined and often unprotected. One author suggested that before 1960 many people would not be treated differently by the police if the Bill of Rights were repealed.[2]

During the 1960s the **Warren Court** substantially expanded the boundary of constitutional criminal procedure, increasing individuals' rights and enlarging the role of federal courts in local criminal justice. Criminal procedure then became a flashpoint of legal, constitutional, and popular controversy. Dispute about its content spilled over from the specialized world of lawyers to the larger world of politics.

Disagreements over the exclusionary rule, *Miranda* warnings, or jury verdicts in notorious cases were heated and intense. One segment of the nation is outraged when a suspected criminal is freed because police violated his or her constitutional rights; another segment applauds this demonstration of American civil liberties in action. After the O.J. Simpson murder trial in 1995, for example, many came to question trial by jury while others said that "the system works."[3]

The change in emphasis from a pro-prosecution **facilitating function** to a **civil rights function** (protecting individual rights) was so notable that the1960s era was dubbed the "due process revolution."[4] This revolution was carried out by a divided Supreme Court, with the liberal majority and conservative minority at odds over issues of federalism and the proper division between order and liberty. A more conservative Supreme Court emerged after 1969, its justices appointed by conservative Republican presidents (Richard Nixon, Ronald Reagan, and George Bush) and supported by a conservative shift in public opinion. As a result the Court has limited and qualified many of the liberal doctrines established in the 1960s. Yet, the Court has not completely eliminated such protections as the Fourth Amendment exclusionary rule or *Miranda* warnings, and the basic structure of criminal procedure in balancing order and liberty remains. Nevertheless, since 1986, when William Rehnquist became Chief Justice, the Court has become even more conservative.[5] These divisions in the Court's makeup at times led to strident accusations, with some conservative justices in the 1960s accusing their liberal brethren of setting criminals loose on society while in later decades, some liberal justices accused conservatives of trampling the essential freedoms of Americans.

The Context of Criminal Procedure

The content and direction of criminal procedure law depends upon many factors in addition to legal precedents, including public opinion, the policies of presidents and senators who appoint and ratify federal judges, and the belief systems of judges who fashion rules of criminal procedure. Therefore criminal procedure law must be studied in its social context. Knowing the context of criminal procedure helps the student better understand how and why its rules developed and the impact of the rules on police and defendants. This context includes knowledge of (1) the criminal justice system, (2) the definition and classifications of law, (3) courts, the appellate process, and federalism, (4) the basics of legal reasoning, (5) history and politics, (6) basic concepts of political theory, (7) judicial biography, (8) society and the social impact of criminal procedure, and (9) human rights.

The Criminal Justice System

Criminal justice policy is formed by all branches of government: high executive officers (e.g., the president, state governors, mayors, heads of law enforcement and correctional agencies, chief prosecutors); legislatures (by enacting criminal laws, establishing agencies and programs, and setting the budgets of criminal justice agencies), and appellate courts (by interpreting criminal legislation and by establishing legal and constitutional doctrines to guarantee fair criminal procedures). The workaday criminal justice system includes executive branch bureaucracies: police, correctional agencies, and prosecutors, who work to ensure public safety, and trial and appellate judges who adjudicate cases and who attempt to ensure that the system is fairly balanced between the needs of public safety and the rights of defendants. People not employed by the government also play important roles. Individuals assuming these roles include jurors who decide the guilt or innocence of suspects, as well as private defense attorneys, and public defenders who provide a necessary counterbalance to the executive branch. These systems and individuals, which collectively employ almost two million people and expend approximately $100 billion each year, are authorized by law to ensure justice and public safety. Criminal justice personnel perform many functions that are guided by criminal procedure law and the Constitution, such as arrest, interrogation, and search and seizure. Not all police functions are guided by law. Service activities, like giving people advice or helping them deal with interpersonal problems, have little to do with law and almost nothing to do with constitutional limitations. Also, police investigation of crime may be determined by administrative policies, ad hoc decisions, police-work traditions, and scientific-evidence gathering techniques, none of which is authorized or guided by law.

To understand the function and purpose of criminal procedure in the criminal justice system it is helpful to think of criminal justice as (1) *people* in agencies and organizations, and (2) *rules,* laws, guidelines, formal procedures, and understood ways of performing tasks. If criminal justice is people and the rules that guide them, criminal procedure falls into the second category. Criminal procedure includes state and federal statutes and rules, common law doctrines, and most importantly, constitutional law. Constitutional law includes the text of state constitutions and the U. S. Constitution and constitutional doctrines developed in law cases by state and federal appellate judges. These rules together authorize and guide the operation of the criminal justice system and limit what criminal justice agents may do. The focus of this book is on constitutional limitations, which, in turn, establish and guarantee individual rights.

Criminal procedure rules are most important in six stages of the criminal process:

1. *Police investigation* and *arrest,* which includes the process of taking an arrested person into secure custody and/or making a release decision.
2. *Pretrial screening* of complaints to determine which are factually and legally appropriate for prosecution. This stage includes important processes: the grand jury, the preliminary examination, and the bail decision.
3. *Formal charging* and taking steps to allow the suspect to make a defense. The prosecutor decides which charges to prefer under an information, or which charges to present to a grand jury.
4. *Adjudication,* the determination of guilt or innocence, may be determined by a jury or a bench trial or by the plea negotiation process.
5. *Sentencing* imposing punishment on the convicted, is a judicial decision, in which probation officers, prosecutors and defense attorneys, and in some instances victims, play roles in shaping the sentencing decision. In recent years legislatures have dominated sentencing through mandatory minimum sentences and laws requiring that a fixed percentage of a sentence be served in prison.
6. *Appellate review* by higher courts.[6]

The correctional component of criminal justice is subject to laws and regulations which include the constitutional rights of prisoners. This separate subject is not covered in criminal procedure courses. This book focuses on the first stage of the criminal process—police activities that touch on individuals' rights and liberties. Chapters 2 through 6, and 8 to 10 concern police activity, including arrest, search and seizure, interrogation and confessions, identification of suspects, and undercover work. Chapter 7 covers the right to counsel, showing that defense lawyers are critical to maintaining the balance of order and liberty. Chapter 11 concerns stages two and three, charging and the pretrial process, in which the prosecutor occupies a central role. Chapter 12 is devoted to the fourth stage, the adjudication process, where the trial judge plays the most prominent role and defense counsel and prosecutors are pivotal actors. Sentencing, the fifth stage, usually studied as part of penology, is discussed briefly in Chapter 8 in regard to the right to counsel in the correctional process. Technical matters concerning the sixth stage, the appellate process, are not emphasized in this text. Rather, it focuses on the substance of Supreme Court cases that shape constitutional criminal procedure. The last stage of the criminal process—appellate review—is, therefore, the stage in which the most important constitutional rights of suspects are formed.

Definition and Classifications of Law

As commonly understood, *law* is a body of written rules issued by legitimate government authorities designed to guide and control social action.

A common classification of law distinguishes between **private law,** which concerns private disputes and the rights of private individuals, groups, and corporations, and **public law,** which involves governmental power, and disputes between governmental departments, or between private persons or groups and government agencies.

Law is classified by its *subject matter.* Private law includes contracts, property, torts (the law of injuries), commercial law, copyright, civil procedure and the like. Public law subject matter includes constitutional law, administrative law, and tax law, as well as substantive criminal law and criminal procedure.

Law is classified by three *functions*: (1) **Substantive law** establishes and defines rights, powers, and obligations. Major areas of substantive law, for example, establish contractual obligations, property rights, or and the freedom from being intentionally or negligently harmed. Substantive criminal law defines crimes such as homicide and theft and defenses such as insanity. (2) **Procedural law** prescribes methods of enforcing substantive rights that are breached and includes rules of jurisdiction, the serving of legal process (e.g., a summons), and rules that guide the conduct of a trial. (3) **Remedial law** determines the actual benefits or "remedies" obtained by a successful party to a lawsuit. *Civil remedies* include *legal remedies* (money damages to compensate loss and punitive damages) and *equitable remedies* (injunctions or specific performances to remedy a violation of rights). Civil remedies can be imposed on police officers and departments that have been found to violate individuals' rights while they carry out their responsibilities. Exclusionary rules an important topic in criminal procedure, are treated as "remedies" for rights violations, although they are designed primarily to deter official misconduct. *Criminal law "remedies"* are the lawful punishments that may be inflicted on convicted criminals.[7] Today, in many jurisdictions, the remedy of restitution to victims of crime is authorized to be ordered by the criminal court.

Classifying criminal procedure demonstrates the complexity and imprecision of these classifications. Criminal procedure is public law that is classified as both procedural and substantive law, despite its title as "procedure." Many statutory and administrative rules of criminal procedure are designed to *facilitate* police, prosecutors, and courts as they conduct their respective functions of apprehending suspects, prosecuting defendants, and conducting trials; Thus, criminal procedure is classified as procedural law. On the other hand, to the extent that criminal procedure establishes *rights* for criminal suspects and defendants, it can be classified as substantive civil rights law.

THE SOURCES AND HIERARCHY OF LAW Law is created by differing government authorities: the legislature passes legislation (statutes or acts), appellate courts issue court decisions, the chief executive promulgates executive orders, administrative agencies create regulations, and lesser political subdivisions pass ordinances. The people can directly create law in many states by the *initiative* (voting for proposed law placed on state ballots by petition) and the *referendum* (by popular vote, a law passed by the legislature is blocked from taking effect).[8]

These laws stand in a hierarchical relationship. Laws emanating from "lower" political sources must conform to laws emanating from "higher" sources. The **hierarchy of** and **source of law** is as follows:

- *Constitution*—made by the sovereign people
- *Constitutional law*—made by supreme courts interpreting constitutions
- *Statutes*—made by legislatures (elected by the sovereign people)
- *Common law*—made by courts (popularly elected or appointed by chief executives)
- *Executive orders*—made by state governors and United States presidents
- *Ordinances*—made by units of local government (counties, cities, towns, etc.)
- *Regulations*—made by administrative agencies
- *Court rules*—made by courts and legislatures

Ordinances, for example, are subordinate and must conform to state statutes. Court made law—known as **"common law,"** or **"case law,"** or **"precedent"**—is a distinctive feature of English law and of nations that were English colonies.[9] Common law, a critical feature of criminal procedure, is discussed later in this text; *court precedents are law* and not simply interpretations of statutes.

Common law rules, created by courts in the process of deciding cases, are ultimately subordinate to statute law. A legislature may revise or abolish a common law rule on policy grounds because legislatures have a higher "rank" than courts in a republic, as the elected representatives of the sovereign people. The will of the legislature's majority more directly represents the will of the people than does the will of a court. However, a constitution is the highest form of law. Because a constitution most directly represents the will of the people, legislation must conform to it. When a person challenges legislation or state action as unconstitutional, an appellate court makes an authoritative interpretation of the Constitution, by which the challenged statute or official action is found either constitutional or unconstitutional. Because this constitutional law is based on the Constitution that was ratified by "the people," it cannot be overturned by ordinary legislation. The constitutional rulings of courts can be changed either by a constitutional amendment or by a later court overruling its earlier precedent.[10]

Every governmental officer, state and federal, swears to uphold the United States Constitution;[11] state as well as federal judges interpret and are guided by the United States Constitution. The president and Congress often justify their actions by citing the Constitution. The courts, however, have final say about the meaning of the Constitution. A state supreme court is the final authority on the meaning of a state constitution, and the United States Supreme Court has the last say on the meaning of the United States Constitution, giving it great power in shaping criminal procedure. From the beginning of the Republic, the framers saw courts playing an essential role in protecting individual liberty. In a speech to the House of Representatives in 1789, proposing the Bill of Rights, James Madison said that if the rights were adopted "into the constitution, independent tribunals of justice will consider themselves in a peculiar manner the guardians of those rights; they will be an impenetrable bulwark against every assumption of power in the legislative or executive; they will be naturally led to resist every encroachment upon rights expressly stipulated for in the constitution by the declaration of rights."[12]

Courts, the Appellate Process, and Federalism

Courts of law have two major functions: (1) **rule application**—deciding cases in accord with the law, which is primarily the function of trial courts (this includes fostering civil settlements and pleas in criminal cases), and (2) **rule making**—making law (legal precedents) by a process of interpretation, which is primarily the function of appellate courts, especially the supreme courts of the states and the United States. This section examines the law-making function of appellate courts and the place of the United States Supreme Court in criminal procedure.

THE COURT HIERARCHY The hierarchy of law, noted in the previous section, depends upon the "rank" of the law-creating agency. Likewise, the "position" of a court in the **hierarchy of courts** determines the weight of its decisions as precedent. The top court (i.e., state or federal supreme court) decides appeals from lower courts. A supreme court, by its **appellate decisions** *and* by the *reasoning* of its **appellate opinions,** establishes legal precedents that must be followed by lower courts. Below this top tier, many populous states and the federal court system maintain intermediate appellate courts. In the federal system they are known as the Courts of Appeals. There are thirteen circuits, divided into twelve geographical circuits (the Court of Appeals for the District of Columbia and the First through the Eleventh, which decide cases from federal courts located in the states and the territories) and the Federal Circuit, which handles specialized cases. The circuits have different numbers of judges because the sizes of their caseloads differ.

Trial courts are "below" ("inferior" to) appellate courts and their decisions may be appealed to and reversed by appellate ("higher" or "superior") courts. Federal trial courts are called district courts. There are ninety-four federal district courts in the states, Washington D.C. and the territories. Most states have two trial court levels: **courts of general jurisdiction** (e.g., "superior" or "circuit" courts) which try felony cases, and **courts of limited jurisdiction** (e.g., "district" or "city" courts) which try misdemeanors and hear preliminary examinations in felony cases. Court systems also include specialized courts, such as probate or family courts (that deal with matters of inheritance, child custody, and juvenile delinquency) and courts of claim (that deal with suits against the government).

Trial courts decide issues of fact and issues of law. Factual decisions, as a general rule, cannot be appealed to higher courts because a group of lay jurors (or the trial judge) are as qualified as appellate judges to sort out issues of truth and falsehood. Since the jury (or the trial judge) observe witness testimony directly, they are in a better position to assess the truth. *Issues of law,* however, can be appealed from trial courts to intermediate appellate courts (often as a matter of right) and from there to supreme courts (usually in the discretion of the high court). The basic function of appellate courts is not to retry cases or to determine if the facts were correctly decided, but to determine if the law was correctly applied. With this in mind, we turn to the appellate process and to how the courts do their work.

THE APPEAL PROCESS

An appeal occurs when the defendant in a criminal case (or either party in a civil case) requests that a court with appellate jurisdiction rule on a decision that has been made by a trial court or administrative agency.

Appellate courts receive two basic categories of cases, appeals and writs. Appeals, by far the most time-consuming and important, occur when a litigant's case receives a full-scale review after losing at the trial level (or, in several States, after losing in certain administrative proceedings).

The appeal begins when the party losing the case in the trial court, the "appellant," files a notice of appeal, usually a month or two after the trial court decision. Then within a few months the appellant files the trial court record in the appellate court. The record, often bulky, consists of the papers filed in the trial court along with a transcript of the trial testimony. Next the appellant and the opposing party, the "appellee," file briefs that argue for their respective positions. The briefs are usually followed by short oral presentations to the judge. Finally, the judges decide the case and issue a written opinion. An increasing number of courts, but still a minority, decide some appeals without written opinions.

State supreme court decisions are usually issued by the full court; intermediate court decisions are generally issued by three-judge panels. The whole decision process takes roughly a year, although it ranges from 6 months in some courts to several years in courts with large backlogs.

In making its final disposition of the case, an appellate court may—

- **"affirm,"** or uphold, the lower court ruling,
- "modify" the lower court ruling by changing it in part, but not totally reversing it,
- **"reverse,"** or set aside, the lower court ruling and not require any further court action,
- "reverse and remand" the case by overturning the lower court ruling but requiring further proceedings at the lower court that may range from conducting a new trial to entering a proper judgment,
- **"remand"** all or part of the case by sending it back to the lower court without overturning the lower court's ruling but with instructions for further proceedings that may range from conducting a new trial to entering a proper judgment.

Thus, the termination of an appellate court case may or may not be the end of the case from the perspective of the parties involved in the case. They may be required to go back to the lower court for further proceedings. If Federal law is involved, a party can petition for review in the United States Supreme Court. In criminal cases, defendants can file further petitions in a Federal court or a State court.

Source: The Bureau of Justice Statistics: *The Growth of Appeals 1973–83 Trends,* (Washington, D.C., 1985) 3.

THE ROLE OF THE UNITED STATES SUPREME COURT IN CRIMINAL PROCEDURE In this text the United States Supreme Court is the central "actor" in creating and shaping the most important rules of constitutional criminal procedure. As previously noted, James Madison conceived of the courts as "guardians" of constitutional rights. Nevertheless, when it comes to the criminal procedure rights found in the Fourth, Fifth, Sixth, and Eighth amendments, the Supreme Court did not begin to significantly play a "guardian" role until the 1940s, and became heavily involved in state criminal procedure only after 1960. The primary reason has to do with concepts of **federalism:** the proper balance of power between the United States government and the state governments. First, it is useful to understand a few basic facts about federal court jurisdiction.

FEDERAL AND SUPREME COURT JURISDICTION Courts can decide cases only if they have lawful jurisdiction to do so. Federal jurisdiction is conferred on federal courts by the United States Constitution and by congressional statutes. By a series of laws passed from 1875 to the 1990s, almost all cases decided by the Supreme Court are heard in the Court's discretion after a petitioner has filed a *writ of certiorari.* In rare instances, the Supreme Court must accept an appeal from a lower court by direct appeal. Approximately 7,000 petitions for *certiorari* are submitted to the Supreme Court each year, and of these the court selects about 100 cases to decide (the number has varied from about 80 to about 150 in the last few decades). There are no formal criteria for the Supreme Court granting a writ—it grants writs of "cert" in cases that it deems to have raised important legal or constitutional issues. Scholars have noted that the Court is more likely to grant a writ and decide a case when the United States government is a party or when a rule of law has been decided differently by different federal circuit Courts of Appeals, but these factors do not guarantee that the Supreme Court will decide to hear a case.

The Constitution and federal statutes grant jurisdiction to the Supreme Court only over *federal questions*: issues of law that concern the United States Constitution, federal legislation, or treaties made by the United States and a foreign nation. As a result, the Supreme Court can review almost all decisions of lower federal courts.[13] On the other hand, the Supreme Court has no jurisdiction over matters of state law—cases based *exclusively* on provisions of state constitutions, state legislation, or rules of state common law. The United States Supreme Court can review a case from the highest tribunal of a state *only* if it concerns a federal question. There are many complex areas of government regulation where federal laws impinge on individual and state governmental action that raise federal question issues. In the area of constitutional criminal procedure, a federal question arises in a state court when a criminal suspect or defendant claims that an action taken by a local or state officer or court violated a right protected by the Fourteenth Amendment or Bill of Rights provisions that have been applied to the states. Federal question issues that arise in state courts can also be appealed to the United States Supreme Court from lower federal courts. This occurs when a state resident files a civil claim in federal court that state officers violated her constitutional rights under the civil rights law (42 United States Code §1983), or when a state prisoner challenges the legality of confinement, on the grounds that state officers violated his constitutional rights via a writ of federal habeas corpus.

Article III of the U.S. Constitution does not directly give the Supreme Court the jurisdiction to hear federal questions that arise in state courts. Nevertheless, this power was asserted by the Supreme Court in the early Republic and is inherent in Article VI, paragraph 2: the **supremacy clause.** This clause says that where there is an issue of law that is applicable to both the federal and the state governments, federal law controls. The supremacy clause ensures that the United States will be a *united* nation, for if every state could decide the meaning of the U.S. Constitution in its own way, there would be no uniformity of constitutional doctrines.

THE SUPREMACY CLAUSE

The Constitution, and the Laws of the United States which shall be made in Pursuance thereof; and all Treaties made, or which shall be made, under the Authority of the United States, shall be the Supreme Law of the Land; and the judges in every State shall be bound thereby, any Thing in the Constitution or Laws of any State to the Contrary notwithstanding.

Source: *United States Constitution,* Article VI, paragraph 2.

There is one other infrequently used method by which the Supreme Court establishes criminal procedure rules—but only for the federal system—the **supervisory authority** or power. This power, also known as "supervisory control" or "superintending control" is deemed to be an inherent power in superior courts to compel inferior courts to act within their jurisdiction. The United States Supreme Court has explicitly affirmed that it has no supervisory power over state courts (*Victor v. Nebraska,* 1994). In exercising supervisory authority a court can establish rules not specifically required by the Constitution or the Congress, but in doing so must not violate any statute or constitutional provision.[14] In earlier years, the Supreme Court issued several significant criminal procedure rulings using its supervisory authority. The Court used its supervisory power in *Rea v. United States* (1956) to enjoin a federal narcotics officer from testifying in a state prosecution that the defendant possessed illegal drugs when the federal agent obtained the drugs by means of an unconstitutional search and seizure. This ruling put an end to the "silver platter doctrine," which existed before the Fourth Amendment's exclusionary rule was applied to the states in 1961, whereby federal agents gathered evidence illegally and then turned it over to state agents to use in state prosecutions. In 1956, the Court said that it had no constitutional authority to extend the federal exclusionary rule to the states, but it was offended by the fact that a federal officer violated federal rules. In two other noted cases, *McNabb v. United States* (1943) and *Mallory v. United States* (1957), the Supreme Court exercised its supervisory power to hold that confessions are not admissible in courts of law when obtained by federal police officers who deliberately hold suspects and do not bring them before magistrates as soon as possible. In recent years, the Supreme Court has signaled its reluctance to use, or to allow lower federal courts to use, supervisory authority to make rules of criminal procedure, holding in one case that a federal court cannot use its supervisory power to dismiss a case in which the prosecutor knowingly violated the Federal Rules of Criminal Procedure when the error was harmless, that is, when the errors would not have led the jury to a different result.

In June 2000, the Supreme Court decided *Dickerson v. United States* which held that the famous decision of *Miranda v. Arizona* (1966) was a constitutional ruling. This was a great jurisdictional battle because Congress had tried to overrule *Miranda* by statute in a 1968 law that stated that a voluntary confession was admissible in evidence even if the specific warnings of *Miranda* were not given by the police. The Court stated:

> The law in this area is clear. This Court has supervisory authority over the federal courts, and we may use that authority to prescribe rules of evidence and procedure that are binding in those tribunals. . . . However, the power to judicially create and enforce nonconstitutional "rules of procedure and evidence for the federal courts exists only in the absence of a relevant Act of Congress." . . . Congress retains the ultimate authority to modify or set aside any judicially created rules of evidence and procedure that are not required by the Constitution.
>
> But Congress may not legislatively supersede our decisions interpreting and applying the Constitution. . . . This case therefore turns on whether the *Miranda* Court announced a constitutional rule or merely exercised its supervisory authority to regulate evidence in the absence of congressional direction. *(Dickerson v. United States).*

The Court held that *Miranda* was not decided under the Court's supervisory authority but under the Constitution. As a result, (a) Congress could not override *Miranda* and (b) the *Miranda* rules apply to the states.

LAW IN THE STATES: FEDERALISM AND CRIMINAL PROCEDURE Federalism plays an important role in constitutional criminal procedure. The Supreme Court delayed applying the Bill of Rights to the states (this is known as "incorporation" and is described in the chapter 2) because it felt that it was improper for a *federal* court to interfere in state and local criminal justice. After most Bill of Rights provisions were incorporated into Fourteenth Amendment due process in the 1960s, it appeared that rules of constitutional criminal procedure would be determined exclusively by the Supreme Court because its rulings granted greater liberty and procedural protections to defendants. However, as the Court became more conservative after 1970 and began to interpret the Constitution to limit individual liberty, some state supreme courts began to interpret *their own state constitutions* to grant greater liberty to defendants. In such a case, state law controls because the issue is exclusively one of state law.

To make this clear, it is useful to think of **judicial federalism,** where there is a *federal constitutional floor*—the Fourteenth Amendment as interpreted by the U.S. Supreme Court—and a *state constitutional ceiling* wherein a state supreme court may interpret its own constitution to grant greater rights to defendants than granted by the U.S. Constitution as interpreted by the Supreme Court. The federal floor exists because the Fourteenth Amendment Due Process Clause applies to every *state,* guaranteeing that no *state* shall deprive a person of life, liberty, or property without due process of law. The Supreme Court is the final arbiter of the meaning of Fourteenth Amendment due process, and a state law or action cannot operate to give a defendant "less" due process than the Supreme Court has required by its interpretations. But in our federal system, state constitutions may be interpreted by state courts to grant a defendant a greater level of liberty on a particular issue, than would otherwise be granted by the U.S. Supreme Court in its interpretation of the Fourteenth Amendment. Because each state is a limited sovereign, it is not the business of the federal courts to tell a state that it is giving its own residents "too much" liberty. This is a matter of state policy. The only role of federal courts in criminal procedure appeals from state defendants is to determine whether or not a state court has violated a defendant's federal constitutional rights (which he/she has in addition to rights under the state constitution).

There are several reasons why a state supreme court may interpret its constitution differently from the United States Supreme Court's interpretation of a Bill of Rights provision. The wording of a state's constitution may grant greater or different individual freedoms, or may put them in positive rather than negative form. A state's constitutional history may show that its framers intended to award greater liberties, or early state legislation may have more broadly defined the meaning of rights later written into a state bill of rights. Local traditions may lead to heightened definitions of state rights, or distinctive local popular attitudes may lead a state supreme court to interpret a state constitutional provision as more favorable to liberty.[15]

A final point about this subject is that at times the United States Supreme Court is confused by whether a ruling from a state supreme court is based on the U.S. Constitution or on a state constitutional provision. State courts are competent to apply the federal Constitution, but when they do so, they are bound by precedent of the United States

Supreme Court under the Supremacy Clause. Confusion arises when state courts grant greater rights than federal law allows in a ruling (which is appealed by a prosecutor to the federal courts) whose language is not clear as to whether it is applying the rule under its own constitution (which it is free to do) or under the U.S. Constitution.

To resolve this matter the Supreme Court has announced a rule that it will not disturb a state court ruling if it is based on **adequate and independent state grounds.** In *Michigan v. Long* (1983) the Court told state supreme courts that they could ensure that the federal courts would not interfere with a state ruling granting greater rights to a defendant if the court included a **plain statement** in its judgment or opinion that the federal cases are being used only for the purpose of guidance, and do not themselves compel the result that the court has reached. However, in *Michigan v. Long,* Justice Sandra Day O'Connor's majority opinion created a presumption that when there was some doubt about the basis of a pro-defendant state court ruling, the state decided the case under the federal Constitution, and so the Supreme Court could take jurisdiction and reverse the state decision. This procedural ruling tends to favor the prosecution. Justice John Paul Stevens dissented. He argued that to preserve federalism, the Court had traditionally deferred to the state courts whenever possible, and the *Long* ruling upset this presumption and disrespected state courts. Justice Stevens said that it was an impossible task for the Court to maintain a guard over the upper limits of rights. What he did not say, but others have said, is that *Long* "reflects the Supreme Court's animosity to expansion of individual rights."[16]

In *Arizona v. Evans* (1995), Justice Ruth Bader Ginsburg, joined by Justice Stevens, forcefully attacked the *Long* doctrine. By 1995, experience had shown that the "plain statement" rule was not working. More importantly,

> The *Long* presumption, in sum, departs from the traditional understanding that "every federal court is 'without jurisdiction' unless 'the contrary appears affirmatively from the record.'" . . . And it is out of sync with the principle that this Court will avoid constitutional questions when an alternative basis of decision fairly presents itself . . . Most critically . . . the *Long* presumption interferes prematurely with state-court endeavors to explore different solutions to new problems facing modern society.

Because of the growing importance of state court opinions under the adequate and independent state grounds doctrine, in each chapter *Law in the States* boxes alert students to state supreme court rulings. These cases are drawn from a useful reference work, *State Constitutional Criminal Law,* by Professor Barry Latzer.[17] Although these insertions typically note cases that diverge from Supreme Court interpretations, in most instances state courts follow the Supreme Court's lead and interpret state constitutions in accord with federal interpretation.[18]

Basics of Legal Reasoning

This section describes the components of appellate cases and aspects of **legal reasoning** needed to provide a student with a practical guide for understanding appellate cases. The edited Supreme Court cases in this book are quite different from typical texts, making it important for first-time readers to know the basics of legal reasoning. Be forewarned that even with this introduction, reading law is a demanding intellectual task. This section begins with a "mechanical" review of **appellate opinions** and concludes with a more sophisticated analysis of legal reasoning.

THE PARTS OF A CASE: OPINIONS Turn to *Mapp v. Ohio,* found in this text in Chapter 3, on page 73. The top line gives the title of the case. The "v." stands for "versus": the appeal is an adversary contest between two parties—a fight which each side is trying to win. The battle is conducted with words and with legal ideas. *Mapp* is the "petitioner"—the party who lost the case in the court from which the case was appealed. The State of *Ohio* is the respondent—the party who is responding to the petitioner.[19]

The next line is the citation, telling readers where they can find the original printed source of the case which is excerpted here (parts of the full text of the case not useful for educational purposes have been omitted). The original report of *Mapp v. Ohio* is found in volume 367 of the United States Reports (the official reporter published by the United States Government Printing Office), beginning at page 643; in volume 81 of the Supreme Court Reports at page 1684 (published by the West Group, St. Paul), or in volume 6 of the United States Reports, Lawyer's Edition, Second Series, beginning at page 1081 (published by the Lawyer's Co–Op, now, Lexis Corporation). Next, the name of the justice who wrote the majority opinion appears. This opinion is usually the majority opinion, but on rare occasions where a clear majority cannot be mustered, it is the plurality opinion. Not every opinion is authored. *Per curiam* opinions are issued by the Court without indicating an author. Most *per curiam* opinions are brief, straightforward opinions in relatively minor cases. This is followed by the body of the majority opinion, followed by concurring and dissenting opinions, listed in order of the seniority of the justices. The majority opinion ends with a line indicating the decision.

The appellate court's decision—affirming, modifying, or reversing the lower court's decision—is contained in an essay called the "opinion" of the court. The opinion includes the reasons given by the court for its decision. The reasoning process of an opinion may be complex or simple, eloquent or plain, convincing or vapid, based on narrow legal precedent or on grand principles. Some opinions of Supreme Court justices are classics of American political rhetoric. A majority opinion is not the lone effort of the author, but has been agreed to by the justices who "sign on" to it. Often, the opinion's reasoning is a matter of compromise, as each of the justices who votes for it makes suggestions as to the proper legal basis for the decision.

An appellate case may include more than the Court's opinion. In addition, some judges may author "concurring" opinions, in which they join the *decision* or "judgment" of the court, but do so for different reasons. A justice who disagrees with the decision "dissents." A dissenting judge need not explain the dissent in a separate opinion, but it is now typical for Supreme Court justices who dissent to do so. Dissenting justices write not just to express their views. Throughout American constitutional history, many doctrines of constitutional law have been overruled by later courts. When this has happened, the later Court often looks to a dissenting opinion in an earlier case. Thus, a dissenting justice writes for the future, in the hope that in a later era his dissenting view will be adopted.

ELEMENTS OF AN OPINION: BRIEFING A CASE An appellate court opinion includes some or all of the following elements:

- the prior history of the case in the lower courts,
- the facts of the case,
- the legal issue or issues that the court is called on to decide,
- the statute or administrative rule that is relevant to the case,
- prior precedent,
- the "holding," or legal rule in the case as applied to the case facts,
- the reasoning that is essential to the resolution of the case,
- other non-essential information, known as *obiter dictum*, and
- the decision or judgment (e.g., reversed, affirmed, remanded—who won the case?).

Justices need not write these parts of the opinion in any particular order or fashion, although they are usually presented in the order listed.

Students should make notes (a "brief") of each case. They should read the entire case once, without taking notes (underlining or highlighting may be helpful). After this first reading, they should write the title, page number in the text, the year of decision, the justice who authored the opinion, and enough of the prior history of the case so it is clear how the case got to the Court. This mechanical information is not the essence of the case so it should be kept short.

There is no one way to **brief a case**—the method that works best should be used. Students should use abbreviations and short phrases, as long as they can understand them when they use the brief to study for a test. Students should then write out—*in their own words*—the most important parts of the case: those facts that are essential for the holding, the legal or constitutional issue, the essence of the reasoning used to resolve the issues, and the holding of the case and its decision. In constitutional law cases the court sometimes explicitly states the issue(s), at other times one has to read the entire case carefully to understand the actual issue. Since the student has read the case through one time, he or she will know which party won the case and have an idea of the issue and how it was resolved.

Stating the legal issue or issues in the case with precision is the key to fully comprehending the Court's reasoning. The Court often announces the issue, but at times it is only a formal issue and not the real issue. In a sense you have to understand the entire case to accurately ascertain the issue. If you think the Court's statement of the issue is accurate, do not copy it but restate it in your own words.

The Court's reasoning, which it uses to resolve the issue may include an analysis of relevant statutes or prior decisions (precedent), and appeals to history, logic, and social policy. For example, in some criminal procedure cases, the justices will, to some degree, argue that the convenience of the police in enforcing the law is a factor in the decision. In cases arising from state courts, the Court will often raise the matter of federalism. It is often difficult to determine which parts of the opinion contain essential reasoning and which contain statements that are not essential.

The *holding* of the case is a concise statement of the decision and the facts on which the decision is based. The holding is different from an abstract rule of law and from the decision. The holding is especially important because the precedent of a case is based on the holding rather than on an abstract statement of the law. The concept of the holding is related to the role of courts, for it prevents appellate courts from usurping the legislative function. A court's primary function is to decide cases, and legal rules are formulated in the context of the case's specific facts. Since only the holding is precedent, courts cannot (or should not) issue broad rules that go beyond the facts of the case. In this way, case law builds incrementally, one case after another, based on unfolding experience. A legal *doctrine* is ascertained by following a "line" of case holdings on an issue. Learning how to trace the development of case law into doctrines is an important legal skill. Appellate courts often try to clarify a ruling by explicitly stating in a case, "We hold . . ." Look for this when reading cases. The holding is more comprehensive than the decision of a case, but it is important to know who won. At times, students get so involved in the reasoning of the Court that they forget the outcome. It is useful to indicate "who won" the case in the brief.

RULES OF PRECEDENT A *precedent* is a rule of case law (the holding) that *binds* lower courts and the court which issued the precedent. A lower court decision that does not follow precedent can be reversed on appeal. Where a supreme court has not yet ruled on a particular issue, a lower court may adopt a rule that it believes is proper because there is no precedent to follow (called a *case of first impression*). But once a higher court decides a case that resolves that issue, its ruling becomes authority or precedent for the courts below it. A supreme court will generally follow its own precedent, but because American law is dynamic, in many cases, prior precedent is modified by the process of *distinguishing* the earlier precedent, and at times a court will explicitly *overrule* its own precedent and replace it with a new rule. This happens because a court changes its collective mind about the correctness or wisdom of a prior ruling. For example, when the Supreme Court announced that all indigents in felony cases were entitled to a free lawyer as a matter of the Sixth Amendment right to counsel in *Gideon v. Wainwright* (1963), it overruled a precedent, *Betts v. Brady* (1942), that had stood for two decades. The rules of precedent sustain the value of stability in the law, without making legal rules so rigid that they cannot be changed in the light of new experience.

Intermediate appellate courts set precedent for trial courts within their areas of jurisdiction. Thus, the United States Court of Appeals for the First Circuit (federal courts in Maine, New Hampshire, Massachusetts, Rhode Island, and Puerto Rico) and the Tenth Circuit (Wyoming, Utah, Colorado, Kansas, New Mexico, and Oklahoma) establish rules that apply within their geographic circuits. If the First and Tenth Circuits decide the same issue of law in different ways, it means that the rights of parties depend on where they live. An important task of the Supreme Court is to establish uniform rules when a conflict arises between circuits.

Appellate courts can modify their earlier holdings by *distinguishing* the facts of the earlier case. Opposing attorneys in a case are likely to read a precedent differently by arguing that its facts do or do not apply to the present legal controversy. It is then up to the court to make a qualitative judgment and decide whether the present case is essentially similar to the precedent or essentially different. If the court decides that the case is essentially different, it will refuse to follow the precedent, saying that it is "distinguished." A lower court can also distinguish precedent. A supreme court that modifies its earlier precedent might do so because its composition has changed and the new judges have different policy perspectives. This has clearly been the case in the realm of constitutional criminal procedure, as the Supreme Court's policy orientation shifted from conservative before the 1960s, to liberal in that decade, and back again in the following years. The process of distinguishing precedent requires great legal skill and how well it is done is a mark of a judge's craftsmanship.

Courts at times refer to "persuasive authority." For example, an Ohio Supreme Court ruling does not bind Colorado courts, but a Colorado judge may read an Ohio Supreme Court opinion and decide that its reasoning is so persuasive that it ought to be followed. The decisions of all American courts are readily available to lawyers, and so there is a good deal of cross-fertilization of legal ideas between state courts and between state and federal courts.

It should be apparent at this point that the process of precedent is not simple or mechanical. Mastering it requires close attention to the cases that you read. The main cases in this book are presented as *Case and Comments*. The comments that accompany the cases are there to help students by noting how the Court has applied the rules of precedent in the case.

LEGAL REASONING A classic work, Edward Levi's *An Introduction to Legal Reasoning,*[20] provides a concise review of what students need to know to read law with a deep understanding of the rules of the game. Perhaps the most difficult point to absorb is the simplest. Beginning students believe that law consists of fixed rules interpreted by courts in a straightforward manner. Although this may often be true at the trial court level, it does not adequately capture the way in which appellate courts, especially the United States Supreme Court, reach their decisions.

At the level of appellate decision making, law is not so much "a system of known rules" but is a *process* of "reasoning by example" or "reasoning from case to case." This is a "three-step process described by the doctrine of precedent." In the course of deciding a case, the judge reads previously decided cases that were relied on by the attorneys and that the judge found independently. The judge determines the holdings of earlier cases. The three steps, then, are as follows: "similarity is seen between cases; next the rule of law inherent in the first case is announced; then the rule of law is made applicable to the second case." This appears to be straightforward, even mechanical. It is not.

There are several reasons why the process of reasoning from case to case is not mechanical. First, the deciding judge has some freedom in determining what constitutes the holding of an earlier case, which Levi describes as an intellectual process "in which a proposition descriptive of the first case is made into a rule of law." In reviewing common law doctrines the judge "is not bound by the statement of the rule of law made by the prior judge even in the controlling case." Although judges have less freedom to re-interpret earlier holdings when their task is statutory interpretation, judges have the greatest freedom in interpreting constitutional case law, because each judge can go back to the constitutional text and argue that his or her interpretation adheres best to the intent of the framers. In any event, to nail this point down, Levi emphasized that it "is not what the prior judge intended that is of any importance, rather it is what the present judge, attempting to see the law as a fairly consistent whole, thinks should be the determining classification."

Second, the literary process of the "doctrine of dictum" forces the deciding judge "to make his own decisions" about what constituted the holding and what constituted dictum in the earlier case. The process involves "the finding of similarity or difference." There is enough play in what are considered the essential facts of an earlier case for differences of opinion to arise that must be settled by the deciding judge. One of the most difficult aspects of legal reasoning by example is that the "rules change as the rules are applied."

Third, this system of reasoning is not a closed system of pure logic but involves considerations of justice. "The problem for the law is: When will it be just to treat different cases as though they were the same? A working legal system must therefore be willing to pick out key similarities and to reason from them to the justice of applying a common classification." The introduction of ideas of justice or policy, then, may distort the pure logic of legal reasoning. Is this reasoning? "It seems better to say there is reasoning, but it is imperfect."

Fourth, the process of legal reasoning is a human process that involves litigants, lawyers, judges, and the wider community operating not only at a single point in time but over a period of history. What Levi calls the law "forum" can be thought of narrowly as a court (e.g., the United States Supreme Court) or the entire community of litigation. Litigants bring complaints to the forum which are fashioned into legal arguments by their lawyers. In all cases, but especially in public law cases, "lawyers represent more than the litigants"; they represent the aspirations of all in society who will benefit or lose from the results desired by the litigants. If litigants lose at one point in time, the forum is there for later generations of litigants to ask the Court to change its earlier rulings. "Reasoning by example shows the decisive role which the common ideas of the society and the distinctions made by experts can have in shaping the law." An idea suggested by litigants and lawyers at one time may appear strange and not be adopted by judges. But "new situations arise [and] in addition peoples' wants change." If common ideas change, a new generation of judges will more likely be in tune with them. Levi warns us that as humans even "erroneous ideas" have infused rules of law. In any event, the role of judges is critical because their decisions are law. "[J]udges after all are rulers. And the adoption of an idea by a court reflects the power structure in the community."

As a result of this, the law gains both stability and dynamism through the operation of the legal forum over time. "A controversy as to whether the law is certain, unchanging, and expressed in rules, or uncertain, changing, and only a technique for deciding specific cases misses the point. It is both." It is the process of "reasoning by example [that] will operate to change the idea after it has been adopted" depending on the needs of society developing over time.

Surely, this is rather abstract and may not be entirely understandable. Nevertheless, a student who pays close attention to what has been said about legal reasoning will see what has been said here "come to life" in the cases in this text.

CONSTITUTIONAL NORMS AND THE TWO MODELS OF THE CRIMINAL PROCESS Legal reasoning is a human process that involves common ideas held by judges. Judges are influenced by social norms—"prevailing notions of right"—and by legal and constitutional norms. Norms are less clear than legal rules and are rarely alluded to by justices in their opinions, but when a decision is not adequately explained by precedent, examining legal norms may assist in understanding the law.[21] To this degree the Constitution can be said to have an "unwritten" element. Unwritten elements of the Constitution include the two-party system of politics, the existence of state appellate courts (which are not guaranteed by the U. S. Constitution), and limiting the number of Supreme Court justices to nine. Legislation like social security is so entrenched as to have constitutional weight. When Congress disagreed with the Supreme Court, which had upheld the practice of the United States Army keeping over a hundred thousand files on suspected "subversives" (including members of Congress!) in *Laird v. Tatum* (1971), and put an end to the practice by legislation, its sense of outrage was motivated by a constitutional norm of privacy.[22]

An acute analysis of constitutional norms in criminal justice is the late Herbert Packer's "two models of the criminal process"[23]—normative abstractions that summarize two polar, but necessary, values that animate constitutional adjudication and the mundane functioning of the criminal justice system. Packer calls these the **Due Process Model** and the **Crime Control Model.** He warns that one is not "good" and the other "bad"—proponents of both models embrace constitutional values. First, they adhere to the value that underlies the ex post facto prohibition—police and prosecutors must act *only* against those who are thought to have violated specific laws, and not against behavior that may be viewed as immoral. A second shared norm is that police and prosecutors have a duty to enforce the criminal law when they have notice of crime violations. A third shared understanding "is the assumption that there are limits to the powers of government to investigate and apprehend persons suspected of committing crimes." Although there are many specific controversies about the extent to which specific constitutional doctrines actually impinge on police work, a general assumption exists "that the security and privacy of the individual may not be invaded at will." Finally, there is a shared belief "that the alleged criminal is not merely an object to be acted upon, but an independent entity" who deserves his or her day in court and may demand a trial and other procedural safeguards. This is the assumption of the adversary system, which is central to the Due Process Model but is deemphasized by the Crime Control Model.

What are the values of the Crime Control Model? First, that "the repression of criminal conduct is by far the most important function to be performed by the criminal process" because public safety is essential to personal freedom. To be effective the criminal justice system must be efficient as to those who have been lawfully apprehended. There is a premium on the speed and finality of processing. Speed "depends on informality and uniformity" (e.g., plea bargaining); "finality depends on minimizing the occasional challenge (e.g., limiting the right to appeal). The tendency is to emphasize administrative and routine functioning in criminal justice and to view the system as a conveyor belt. An attitude (not a legal rule) of Crime Control Model supporters is a "presumption of guilt"—an assumption that police and prosecutors are accurate in their decisions to arrest and apprehend suspects. Because of this attitude of confidence that the informal administrative fact-finding process has identified the right person, the remaining steps in the process can be relatively perfunctory and any restrictions on the administrative fact-finding stages are to be resisted.

"If the Crime Control Model resembles an assembly line, the Due Process Model looks very much like an obstacle course." While it values the repression of crime, it does not assume that police fact-finding is accurate. Indeed, it assumes that the criminal justice system is error-prone. Because of this, there is an "insistence on formal, adjudicative, adversary fact-finding processes in which the factual case against the accused is publicly heard by an impartial tribunal and is evaluated only after the accused has had a full opportunity to discredit the case against him." Even after a full trial, the fear of an erroneous conviction generates a desire for many avenues of appeal. "The demand for finality is thus very low in the Due Process Model." This model demands the "prevention and elimination of mistakes to the extent possible; the Crime Control Model accepts the probability of mistakes up to the level at which they interfere with the goal of repressing crime." For the Due Process Model, the "aim of the process is at least as much to protect the factually innocent as it is to convict the factually guilty." The Due Process Model is highly suspicious of those who wield power and is ideologically driven by the "primacy of the individual and the complementary concept of limitation on official power. The Due Process Model insists on *legal guilt,* whereas the Crime Control Model stresses *factual guilt.* The concept of legal guilt pervades the formal legal and trial process: no matter how "factually" guilty a person, there can be no conviction and punishment unless a court has jurisdiction, unless the prosecution occurs within the period of the statute of limitations, unless the offender is lawfully responsible (e.g., not insane). At this point, the "quixotic" presumption of innocence rises to the fore. The presumption is not the opposite of the "presumption of guilt" but is a normative principle that insists that the defendant be treated as if he or she were innocent, no matter how apparent the factual guilt. To this end, the prosecutor must prove a case beyond a reasonable doubt and the jury verdict must traditionally be unanimous. Important attributes of the Due Process Model include the emphasis on equality of treatment of all suspects and the strong belief that errors in the process invalidate convictions. The Crime Control Model strenuously disagrees with this last point and it is over this point that many disputes arise in constitutional criminal procedure. The review of Packer's two models is included in the discussion of legal reasoning because the student should remember that in addition to the formal methodology of legal reasoning, the attitudes of individual justices play an important role in the outcomes of cases, a point that is addressed in the section, *Judicial Biography and Judicial Statesmanship.*

History and Politics

Constitutional law is inseparable from social and political history: legal doctrines concerning governmental power and individual liberty were shaped by past events that reflected society's needs. This truism is brought to life at several places in this book. This chapter, for example, notes that criminal procedure doctrine shifted from a "conservative," state-interests phase before 1960, to a "liberal" **Warren Court** (1953–1969) phase, then back to a more conservative phase after 1969 during the **Burger Court** (1969–1987) and **Rehnquist Court** (1987–) eras. Keep in mind that characterizing an era, a "Court" (e.g., "the Warren Court"), or a justice as "conservative" or "liberal" is always a matter of "more or less," and not an absolute. This historic pattern (conservative–liberal–conservative) is traced in the development of search and seizure, the right to counsel, confessions, and lineups in subsequent chapters. This book also discusses, the grounding of constitutional rights in the "British liberties" claimed by rebellious colonists in the 1770s.

The historic link between African Americans' civil rights and criminal procedure rights, subjects that seem unrelated, deserves special mention. The foundation of modern criminal procedure—the Fourteenth Amendment—was ratified in 1868 as part of the post-Civil War reconstruction, to ensure that basic civil and political rights for freedmen would be guaranteed by the federal government. The promise of equality faded and died in the late nineteenth century with the rise of "Jim Crow" segregation, economic oppression, and political exclusion of African Americans. This oppression was enforced by the criminal justice system in the South, which tolerated vigilantism and Ku Klux Klan (KKK) terrorism. The violent opposition to the civil rights movement made it apparent to the Supreme Court that the racial equality required by the Constitution, and epitomized by *Brown v. Board of Education* (1954), was threatened by a "lawless" criminal justice system. For constitutional equality to grow and survive, law enforcement and criminal justice would have to be made to abide by fundamental constitutional norms. It is not surprising that many of the Supreme Court's significant criminal procedure cases involved African-American defendants victimized by state oppression. The discrepancy between American political ideals and the reality of rights violations by police and courts was an important factor in Supreme Court decisions that resulted in greater rights for all suspects, defendants, and citizens, regardless of race.[24]

Finally, constitutional law cannot be entirely separated from politics. Politics is often defined as a contest for "who gets what." Political goals include not only political office and tangible benefits (e.g., appropriations, contracts, favorable tax laws), but symbolic and ideological goods as well. The most acrimonious debates in recent American history, over issues like school prayer, abortion, gay rights, the "war on drugs," and gun control, are concerned not with tangible gains but with complex symbols which uphold a right way of life for many. There are examples in the text that link criminal procedure and politics, including information about the appointment of justices in their biographical sketches.

Political Theory[25]

Law is not a self-referential "closed system" of rules; to be fully understood and legitimate, it rests on fundamental beliefs. Behaviors are prohibited by criminal law, for example, because they violate important *social values.* Laws against the taking of human life or property violate deeply held values. Radical historic changes in values make some crimes such as heresy, obsolete. The old political crime of seditious libel would now violate profound values of free speech. Likewise, constitutional criminal procedure, which guarantees individual rights against undue government interference, reflects important *political values* that are essential to the American way of life, especially constitutionalism, the "Rule of Law," liberty, and equality.[26]

Political theory examines fundamental questions of power and obedience and asks whether government exercises its power justly. When government acts justly it improves human life through its programs and, more basically, by maintaining order and preventing crime and disorder. To do its work, government is invested with a *monopoly of force,*[27] an awesome and dangerous power delegated to criminal justice agencies. As Professor Candace McCoy noted, "Policing is a metaphor for state power; the capacity to use force is the defining characteristic of the police."[28] It is obvious that this monopoly of force must be subject to higher political and legal control. The more difficult question to answer is what yardstick determines when the constitutional controls on criminal justice become too restrictive to allow them to function effectively. To know this requires knowledge of underlying political values and institutions.

CONSTITUTIONALISM Conceptually, a nation's constitution is its permanent (or very stable) arrangements for the exercise of government power. According to Professor Glenn Tinder, "No political idea in the West has greater authority than **constitutionalism.** For more than two thousand years there has been a remarkably wide and stable consensus that government ought to be carried on within publicly known and enforceable restraints."[29] The modern concept of constitutionalism includes two ideas: limited government and the Rule of Law—"that governments exist only to serve specified ends and properly function only according to specified rules."[30] Constitutionalism implies balanced government and is antithetical to absolutism or tyranny.

In modern constitutionalism, sovereignty—the supreme power in a state—lies with the people, not with a king or an aristocracy. Popular sovereignty conveys two essential ideas: (1) **republicanism:** government is constituted for the benefit of the whole people, and not a king or a class; order should be maintained for the common good, and not to support privilege; (2) **democracy:** all citizens participate on an equal basis in government decisions, directly or by representation.

Specifically, American aspects of constitutionalism include, first and foremost, majority rule and the practice of free elections.[31] But majority rule is tempered by the legislative process, judicial independence, and the Bill of Rights. Thus, the U. S. Constitution divides power between the legislative, executive, and judicial branches; limits legislative power to an enumerated list of items; and guarantees that non-enumerated powers reside with the states or the people. To ensure that government remains deliberative and that power would not fall into the hands of a tyrant, checks and balances were erected, including bicameralism, the presidential veto, veto override by a two-thirds Congressional vote, Senate confirmation of Supreme Court justices and other high officials, and removal from office only by impeachment and conviction. The Constitution guaranteed an independent judiciary and by adding a Bill of Rights, ensured that the government, although representing the will of the majority, could not crush vital minority rights. American constitutionalism is characteristically legalistic. As the French thinker Alexis de Tocqueville (1805–1859) noted, sooner or later all political questions are reduced to legal issues in the United States.[32] It may appear logical for basic rules of criminal procedure to be made by the legislature, but our tradition is one that looks to the courts to resolve basic issues of constitutional power and liberty.[33]

THE RULE OF LAW The **Rule of Law** is neither *a* rule nor *a* law, but instead a concept of political and legal theory that holds that the government is not above the law. This means that the government conducts its business in accordance with established legal norms and procedures, and that in enforcing law the government does not exceed its legal authority. The Rule of Law stands in contrast to arbitrary rule and applies to all branches of government: a president may be subjected to a civil lawsuit while in office;[34] and legislation is declared void by courts if found to be unconstitutional; judges' constitutional rulings can be reversed only by constitutional amendment or by a later Court that interprets the constitution differently.[35] Constitutional criminal procedure advances the Rule of Law by preventing governmental abuses of power; e.g., a police officer may be sued for making an illegal arrest. The Rule of Law is obviously intertwined with constitutionalism.

Lon Fuller called the Rule of Law the "internal morality of law" and said that without it, law in any meaningful sense is impossible.[36] He suggested eight attributes of law that ensure that legal rules comport with the Rule of Law. The first is the requirement of *generality*—that there be general rules, rather than ad hoc decisions of people with government power. This obviously precludes dictatorial rule, but it also reflected in the work of Supreme Court justices who strive to fit decisions into a framework of general principles. Second, laws must be *duly promulgated*: in written form, duly passed, and published by a responsible governmental agency. Third, a vital principle of justice is that criminal laws *not be retroactive,* making criminal an act that was not against the law when committed. A fourth element is *clarity*: law must be understandable to average people. Supreme Court justices who endeavor to create "bright line" rules that can be quickly understood by working patrol officers, are in a sense trying to achieve this aspect of the Rule of Law. Fuller's fifth element is that laws should *not be contradictory.* It sometimes happens that a legislature will pass a law that contradicts an earlier one. One task of a supreme court is to ensure that rules in similar cases not be logically inconsistent. The sixth element is that law should *not require the impossible,* a hallmark of arbitrariness. Seventh, *stability*: if law changes too frequently it becomes difficult for persons to follow it. Finally, and perhaps the most important in criminal procedure, government officers must obey the legal limits on their power. The practices of the government must be *congruent* with the law as written. The glorious promises of procedural justice enshrined in the Bill of Rights can quickly become hollow and breed a terrible cynicism against government and law if they are routinely ignored.

The United States Constitution incorporates many Rule of Law concepts. Article I, sections 9 and 10, of the Constitution forbid the United States government or the government of any state from passing ex post facto laws, thus incorporating the rule against retroactive laws in the criminal law (*Calder v. Bull,* 1798). The federal Constitution and the constitution of every state has explicit rules regarding the promulgation of laws, and for the most part laws are made public. The Due Process Clause has been interpreted to support the Rule of Law. For example, a nebulous law that gives police officers too much discretion to interfere with a person's liberty will be held unconstitutional under the "void-for-vagueness" doctrine (*Papachristou v. Jacksonville,* 1972). In 1962, the Supreme Court interpreted the cruel and unusual punishment prohibition to strike down a state law that made the status of being a drug addict a crime; this ruling accorded with the idea that the Rule of Law is violated when a statute is passed which makes demands that are impossible for some persons to obey (*Robinson v. California,* 1962).

The courts, as guardians of constitutional liberties, have a central role in maintaining the Rule of Law. But the courts cannot maintain freedom if the people are not willing to fight for their rights. To a significant degree, the Rule of Law lies in "supporting institutions, procedures, and values."[37] Traditions of liberty, real political competition between the party in power and the "loyal opposition," a spirit of tolerance, the existence of interest groups who will fight vigorously in the political realm to enforce their rights, the absence of an oligarchy (an extremely lopsided distribution of wealth), a measure of political and economic stability, a vigorous political press, a literate and aware citizenry—all play a role in maintaining the Rule of Law. In this kind of society, courts can more effectively ensure that the Rule of Law continues.

LIBERTY Liberty has been the most characteristic American political ideal since colonial times.[38] The Declaration of Independence (1776) declared the purpose of government to secure the "unalienable rights" of "all men"—life, liberty, and the pursuit of happiness. The preamble to the United States Constitution (1789), includes protection of the "Blessings of Liberty" as a basic purpose of government. Liberty is guaranteed in the Fifth (1791) and Fourteenth (1868) amendments' Due Process Clauses, which declare that neither the federal government nor any state shall deprive a person of life, liberty or property without due process of law. Liberty underlies such procedural rights as bail before trial, habeas corpus, the presumption of innocence, no arrest without probable cause, and the use of judicial search warrants.

An important source of America's idea of liberty is **John Locke**'s political theory as developed in *Two Treatises of Government* (1690).[39] Locke, the leading "social contract" theorist, favored a balanced, constitutional government, based on consent, as opposed to absolute monarchy, and in it the people have the right to resist the government by force if it turns to tyranny.[40] In this political theory of popular sovereignty of free and equal men, power is held in trust by the government to be used for the common good, that is, to preserve the "lives, liberties and estates" of its members. If government rules by law, then the people have an obligation to obey the law.[41]

Throughout American history, demands for liberty have taken many forms. Nineteenth century settlers pushing westward expressed economic and personal liberty; the Civil War and the abolition of slavery was this nation's greatest test of liberty; economic liberty is sought by monied interests by seeking to limit government controls on business; the 1960s social revolution expanded the sphere of liberty in personal lifestyles. The demands for individual liberty inherent in constitutional criminal procedure are based on a value that is deeply rooted in American life and thought—and that is part of the fabric of everyday life.

EQUALITY The Constitution guarantees political **equality** and the **Equal Protection Clause** of the Fourteenth Amendment (1868) confirmed the deep seated idea of equality before the law. The value of social equality which supports political and legal equality was not so firmly entrenched, however, until the twentieth century. In colonial times, social distance between the top and bottom of society was smaller than that of Europe, but slavery and indentured servitude existed, Native Americans and women had no political rights, and class hierarchy was enforced in many spheres of life.[42] For example, John Adams' class rank at Harvard College in 1755 was determined not by his academic achievement but by his father's wealth and social standing.[43] In this light, Jefferson's statement in the Declaration of Independence that "all men are created equal" was more an Enlightenment ideal than a statement of fact.[44] Despite, or perhaps because of, this ringing statement, the growth of political equality has been a theme of American history.[45] Popular participation in government was limited in 1789 to white, male, Christian, property owners over at least the age of twenty-one. Over the next century and a half, the right to vote was extended, not without struggle, to males without property, people of all religions, former slaves and all African Americans, women, and persons over the age of eighteen. Social and economic equality has also been the focus of conflict and continues to be an issue of contemporary politics.

The Fourteenth Amendment guarantee of the "equal protection of the laws" does not prohibit all legal distinctions, only those that are unreasonable. Consequently, what constitutes "equal rights" is as much a matter of public opinion, confirmed by the political process at any given time, as it is a matter of unchanging law. Few criminal procedure cases are based on the equal protection clause, but the idea of equality has been important in expanding the right to the assistance of counsel. The Sixth Amendment guarantee did not mean, in 1791, that the state had to pay for a poor (indigent) defendant's lawyer. Nineteenth century courts often required local attorneys to represent defendants in capital cases without fee. It seemed unfair to hang a man after a trial without counsel. In the twentieth century, this informal practice was replaced by legal aid and defenders' organizations, but until 1932 the Supreme Court never ruled that a person's constitutional rights were violated by being unrepresented at trial. That year the Court seemed to say that the fair trial idea embodied in the Fourteenth Amendment Due Process Clause was violated by a state capital trial without a lawyer. Still, it was common in those days for defendants in felony cases (carrying only prison sentences) to represent themselves. This practice was not ended by the Supreme Court until 1938 in federal cases, and 1963 in state cases (see Chapter 7). These cases were not decided under the equal protection clause, but there is no doubt that they were motivated by the belief in equal justice under law. Even today indigent defendants often do not get the assistance of skilled attorneys, so that the concept of equality before the law is not one that is easily fulfilled in practice (see *Law in Society* section, Chapter 7).

Judicial Biography and Judicial Statesmanship

Brief accounts of the lives and work of Supreme Court justices who have developed criminal procedure doctrines are interspersed throughout this text. Students often view law as the mechanical product of an impersonal process. The short biographies alert readers that law is a human product. Over the long haul of American constitutional history, the

Supreme Court decides cases in accordance with popular opinion. The explanation is not that justices closely follow public opinions polls and adjust their specific decisions accordingly, nor are justices subject to direct political lobbying, but that as citizens, justices absorb information and commentary about current events that may sway their thinking. The Court is kept in line with popular opinion by the fact that justices generally share the political or ideological views of presidents who nominate them. In the final analysis, the difficult decisions made by Supreme Court justices are the sum total of their personal and professional lives. Knowledge about the justices helps the student better understand criminal procedure.

How do justices do their work? Understanding constitutional adjudication is advanced by replacing the simple idea of narrow judicial interpretation with the concept of **judicial statesmanship.** Supreme Court justices have discretion to shape the contours of the law and how they do this has a great impact on society for better or for ill. This power was used to confirm the "Jim Crow" era of repressive segregation in *Plessy v. Ferguson* (1896) and to lift the fetters of repression in *Brown v. Board of Education* (1954). For purposes of analysis, judicial statesmanship comprise of three continua: judicial philosophy, judicial policy, and judicial craftsmanship.

Judicial Philosophy—Is a justice inclined towards *judicial activism* or *judicial restraint*? The arguments for restraint are that justices who "make" law violate their constitutional authority to only decide cases, that activism overturns laws passed by democratic majorities, and that federal justices who overturn state laws upset the states-rights' understanding of federalism. The argument for activism in constitutional law is that a justice follows the Constitution to the best of his or her understanding, and that this law was passed by "the people" as a superior law. When activism results in a ruling that overturns a state law in favor of a criminal defendant, the argument is that these precious rights were placed in the Bill of Rights especially to protect individuals against majoritarian injustice. Furthermore, courts have a special duty to be guardians of rights. In the 1960s, judicial activist justices tended to be "liberal"; on the Rehnquist Court, the most activist justices pursue conservative policy goals. Justices who believe in judicial restraint are more likely to adhere strongly to prior precedent, or *stare decisis,* and are less likely to exercise judicial review.

Judicial Policy—Is the justice *liberal, middle-of-the-road,* or *conservative?* These crude labels describe only the general predilection of a judge, but can be misleading predictors of a justice's decision in a specific case. In criminal procedure the label "liberal" means that a justice more often than not votes in favor of the individual, and "conservative" that the justice more often than not votes for the state. The term should not be applied globally because a justice may, for example, be conservative on criminal issues and liberal in First Amendment issues. Even within criminal procedure, a justice can tend to favor the state on Fourth Amendment questions but lean toward the individual in Fifth Amendment issues. Although knowing the judge's predilections alerts the reader of a case to the likely outcome, it is no substitute for carefully reading the case to understand the actual logic employed by a justice in resolving the issues presented.

Judicial Craft—Judicial statesmanship rests not only on justices' decisions, but on the quality of their written opinions. Justices gain authority through well-written opinions that display a wealth of legal scholarship, a depth of judicial wisdom, and an ability to live in the minds of readers by the use of powerful or memorable phrases. One aspect of judicial craftsmanship is whether Supreme Court opinions give clear guidance to judges, lawyers, government officers, and individuals who rely on the rulings. Well-crafted opinions have a greater potential to shape a body of law and to leave a lasting legal legacy.

Law in Society: The Social Impact of Criminal Procedure

The *Law in Society* section which appears at the conclusion of each chapter of this text probes the relationship between law and contemporary society. Some sections examine social forces that changed legal doctrines. Concern over domestic violence, for example, led legislatures to eliminate the requirement that police cannot arrest for a misdemeanor not committed in the officer's presence. Other *Law in Society* sections explore social science findings, for example, whether the exclusionary rule undermines public safety. Still other sections demonstrate that the promise of fairness in constitutional criminal procedure is never entirely fulfilled. This sometimes occurs because of corruption or ignorance or human weakness among police, prosecutors, defense attorneys and judges. Even jurors are fallible and at times fail to live up to the promise of the jury system. At other times our society hypocritically espouses constitutional rights, such as the right to counsel, but with all the wealth of contemporary America, cannot find the funding to support equal justice. Abuses of constitutional rights are not the norm in America, and the *Law in Society* sections are not intended to condemn the entire criminal justice system. The great majority of police, prosecutors, defense attorneys, and judges act professionally and perform their important duties competently and within the law. However, complacency is never a proper attitude when considering liberties, and abuses in the system must be studied if they are to be corrected. In the previous brief discussion on the Rule of Law, Lon Fuller noted that the greatest way in which law fails is when there is a lack of congruence (fit) between the law as written and the actual practice. It is too much to expect perfection; but too great a gap between professed constitutional liberties and actual practice will breed cynicism, demoralization, and the collapse of our system, as Justice Louis Brandeis warned in his 1928 dissent in *Olmstead v. United States.* (See the biographical sketch of Justice Brandeis on page 27 for the quotation from this great opinion).

Criminal Procedure as Human Rights

Criminal procedure rights are **human rights.** Rights are claims created by law and enforced by courts. Human rights are a special class of rights held by a person simply by virtue of being human. They are moral rights of the highest order, grounded in the equal moral dignity of each person, that can and should be made legally binding in national, regional, or international law.[46]

After the mass deaths resulting from the Second World War II (1939–1945), international concern for human rights, including abuses committed by national criminal justice agencies, led the United Nations to adopt the **Universal Declaration of Human Rights** (UDHR) in 1948.[47] International agreements followed, establishing human rights as a matter of international law and a system of international human rights enforcement was created to allow complaints to be brought to regional enforcement organizations.[48] The agencies have not been very effective.[49] The *idea* of human rights, however, has taken root. The late 1990s have seen promising developments in the use of international criminal law to enforce human rights. These include the establishment of a permanent international criminal court (ICC) by the United Nations; the first conviction by any international court for the crime of genocide (the International Criminal Tribunal for Rwanda in the fall of 1998), an attempt by Spain to extradite Augusto Pinochet, the former Chilean dictator, from the United Kingdom to prosecute him for genocide, torture, and the deaths and disappearances of thousands of people; and the conviction of Anto Furundzija by the International Criminal Tribunal for the former Yugoslavia, based in part on his command authority, for violations of the laws of war, including torture and outrages upon personal dignity including rape.[50]

It is gratifying to know that most provisions of the U. S. Constitution's Bill of Rights (1791) have been recognized as essential elements of human rights by the world community. According to one commentator these provisions include:

- a *fair hearing* (Fifth and Fourteenth amendments) due process, and Sixth Amendment;
- a *public hearing* (Sixth Amendment);
- an *impartial and independent tribunal* (an impartial jury is required by the Sixth Amendment);
- *judicial independence*, crucial to fair criminal procedure, is guaranteed by lifetime appointment of federal judges);
- *speedy trial*—the right to be tried within a reasonable time (Sixth Amendment);
- the *presumption of innocence* (it is so basic that it was not mentioned in the Constitution or Bill of Rights but has been guaranteed by the Supreme Court, see Chapter 12;
- *notice*—the right to be informed promptly and in detail, and in a language the defendant understands, of the nature and cause of the charges (inherent in due process);
- right to *adequate time and facilities* for making a defense (a rush to judgment cannot be rationalized as a right to speedy trial—*Powell v. Alabama* [1932]);
- the right to defend oneself in court or to have the *assistance of counsel* (Sixth Amendment);
- the right to *examine witnesses* against oneself, to obtain the presence of favorable witnesses, and to examine them (Sixth Amendment and due process);
- the assistance of an *interpreter* (inherent in due process);
- the right to be *tried in one's presence* (a corollary of a due process fair hearing, see Chapter 12);
- the right to *appeal* to a higher court (the Supreme Court has stated that the right to an appeal is not guaranteed by the Constitution—*Ross v. Moffitt* [1974]).

A familiar element missing from this list is the right to trial by jury. Although the jury trial is a symbol of resistance to arbitrary conviction, it is very much a product of the Anglo-American legal system. The jury is a final trier of facts in a few common law countries: Australia, Canada, England, New Zealand, and the United States. Other countries use jurors, but these juries do not have the final power of declaring the verdict in a criminal trial. *The Universal Declaration of Human Rights* lists other criminal procedure rights that are human rights and are essential to a civilized society. For example, Article 5 states that "No one shall be subjected to *torture* or to cruel, inhuman or degrading treatment or punishment," which is borrowed from and elaborates on the Eighth Amendment. Article 9 states that "no one shall be subjected to *arbitrary arrest,* detention or exile," a right that is in essence part of the Fourth Amendment.

These rights (except trial by jury) are now deemed human rights and are included in the *Universal Declaration of Human Rights,* a tribute to America's contribution to civilization. These rights appeal to a sense of justice and transcend local cultures. They are central to other rights because democratic politics and human dignity cannot exist when government has the power to crush all opposition. A criminal justice system that adheres to human–rights principles of criminal procedure ensures a democratic form of government and a government bound by restraints of decency, which, in turn, helps ensure its legitimacy.[51]

LAW IN SOCIETY

CRIMINAL PROCEDURE AS A POLITICAL ISSUE

Politics is expected to be partisan. People participate in politics to get tangible rewards or to see views that they hold dear become public policy. They contribute to political parties and candidates who support their interests and views. Political leaders court the views of the general public through public opinion polls and listen carefully to the wants and needs of their supporters. Legislators and chief executives with the best chance of election are those who most accurately gauge the needs of the public. To get reelected, politicians must show that they delivered on their promises. Since people have different views and interests, it is normal for politicians to reflect these differences.

The law, ideally, is non–partisan. Once conflicting views of legislation are put to the vote of the majority and become law, all citizens are expected to obey it. Trial courts are expected to decide cases on the basis of known law and the facts of the case. Once a judgment has been rendered in a fair trial, the losing party is bound by the rule of the case. A losing party can appeal a lost civil judgment or criminal verdict to an appellate court on specific points of law, but the decision of the final appellate court seals the judgment. An appellate court may consider policy issues in its decision, but the ideal is that most appellate decisions are made based on legal precedent, that is, pre-existing legal rules.

The partisan and non-partisan ideals of politics and law are reflected in their methods. Politicians running for office are expected to openly support programs they favor and tell how they would vote on legislation. It is unthinkable for a judicial candidate to state how she would vote on a specific case. Candidates for judicial office, or nominees for federal judgeships testifying before the United States Senate, walk a very fine line in suggesting how they would likely vote on certain *types* of issues. They can suggest certain proclivities, but cannot say how they would vote in a specific case. It is proper and expected for partisans to call legislators and speak to them about the kind of legislation they want. Elected officials routinely receive letters, phone calls, and E-mail messages indicating support for or against proposed legislation. Organized lobbies exist to dump as many messages as they can on legislators. On the other hand, it is a violation of legal and judicial ethics, and might be a crime, for a party in a case to try to influence a judge outside the normal course of making legal arguments in written briefs and oral arguments. Although it is rare, ordinary citizens may send letters to a court in an attempt to influence the outcome of a case. Largely, this correspondence is ignored.

The non-partisan ideal of law, however, is only partly true. In reality some legal issues reflect partisan political positions. All legal rules are political in the sense that they are created by government and affect individual and group interests. But an issue or rule can be "political" in another sense when it becomes the focus of intense popular attention and dispute at a particular time, calling for a pronounced response by officials. Most rules of criminal law and criminal procedure (e.g., imprisonment for violent crime, trial by jury) are not controversial and not "political" issues. Other crime issues (e.g., legalizaton of marijuana, the death penalty) are "political" in the sense of engendering intense partisan controversy. In the 1960s, criminal procedure became a hot political issue and has ever since been an area of partisan concern. This is disturbing to people who think that all law should be nonpartisan, but the reality is that Supreme Court justices are labeled by the public and legal scholars as "conservative," "liberal," or "moderate" based on their criminal procedure rulings.

Crime Becomes a Political Issue

Crime became a national political issue in the mid–1960s, when the 1964 Republican presidential candidate, Senator Barry Goldwater of Arizona, made "violence in our streets" a viable campaign issue. By the 1968 election, the American political climate was inflamed by riots in the inner cities and by massive anti-war protests. The crime rate also increased with frightening suddenness, mainly because of the huge increase in the number of teenagers (one million each year) of the baby boom generation. The public, unaware of the age-crime relationship, blamed the crime increase on liberal "permissiveness." The era of riots and disorder was accompanied by a social revolution in mores, personal dress, sexual behavior, and drug use. Many thought the nation was disintegrating and on the brink of revolution. The assassinations of Martin Luther King, Jr., and Senator Robert Kennedy in 1968, echoing President John F. Kennedy's 1963 assassination, the outbreak of the worst ghetto riots of the decade in Detroit and Newark in 1968, and the police riot against the anti–war demonstrators at the Democratic National Convention in Chicago, made the 1968 presidential campaign seem an apocalyptic struggle for America's soul.[52]

Once crime became a major political issue, President Johnson responded to Senator Goldwater's challenge by establishing a national crime commission (1965–1967) that proposed legislation to establish significant federal funding for local criminal justice.[53] This legislation, the Omnibus Crime Control and Safe Streets Act of 1968 was favored by both Democrats and Republicans. Yet, it included a partisan provision that purported to overturn the Warren Court's *Miranda v. Arizona* (1966) decision, which required that criminal suspects be informed of their Fifth Amendment rights before questioning.[54] Indeed, the Supreme Court itself had become a political issue, reviled by many conservatives as one of the causes of all of America's troubles.

Candidate Nixon Runs Against the Supreme Court

In 1968, *law-and-order* became one of Richard Nixon's key campaign issues.[55] Nixon, a former senator and vice president of the United States from 1953 to 1961, had lost the 1960 presidential campaign to John F. Kennedy and lost an election for governor of California in 1962. He reentered the political fray in 1968 on the "law-and-order" platform. This had become a conservative catch phrase, sweeping within its purview anger against protesting anti-war students, fear of rioting by African Americans living in impoverished inner cities, latent hostility to the Warren Court's desegregation rulings and its abolition of school prayer, and a free-floating anxiety about America's direction. An author noted, "Now, more than ever before, the Court was becoming a political issue because Nixon was attacking it rather than the cancerous conditions in the black ghettos and elsewhere."[56] Nixon's law-and-order campaign had three strands: first, an attack on the liberal United States attorney general, Ramsey Clark, who was a lightning rod for conservative criticism;[57] second, a "high road" criticism of the Warren Court's activism, calling instead for "*strict construction*" of the Constitution; and third, a linking of increased crime with the Court's liberal criminal procedure rulings. In a campaign speech, Nixon said:

> A cab driver has been brutally murdered and the man that confessed the crime was let off because of a Supreme Court decision. An old woman had been murdered and robbed brutally, and the man who confessed the crime was let off because of a Supreme Court decision. . . .
>
> And I say, my friends, that some of our courts and their decisions in the light of that record have gone too far in weakening the peace forces as against the criminal forces in this country.[58]

This pledge to change the Supreme Court was made at his nomination acceptance speech to the Republican convention.

The logical connection between Supreme Court cases and increased criminal behavior is tenuous at best, but in the near-hysterical atmosphere of the late 1960s, such connections were used as powerful political symbols. Consider the following example from the Senate debate over the Omnibus Crime Control and Safe Streets Bill, proposed by the Johnson administration in 1967.

> When it came time to take up the heavy-handed set of proposals designed to reverse *Miranda v. Arizona* and a few other decisions and to strip the Supreme Court of much of its jurisdiction, Senator McClellan [of Arkansas] propped up in the rear of the Senate Chamber a huge facsimile of the FBI's crime graph. The titles of key Supreme Court decisions were marked at the peaks along the rising line, to show the embarrassing parallel between Supreme Court activity on behalf of defendants and the crime rise. As the Senators debated the bill, the graph loomed over their shoulders. Senator McClellan let it speak for itself until the last few minutes before the vote. Then he swung around, shook his fist at the chart, and bellowed: "The Supreme Court has set a low tone in law enforcement, and we are reaping the whirlwind today! Look at that chart! Look at it and weep for your country—crime spiraling upward and upward and upward. Apparently nobody is willing to put on the brakes."
>
> The vote to include the anti-Supreme Court section in the crime bill carried, 51 to 31.[59]

This attack on the Court, however irrational, touched a deep nerve in the nation. In the space of three years, the national political climate underwent a radical transformation so that what had been an area of "normal controversy" among legal and law enforcement specialists became a litmus test for the legitimacy of the Court itself. The events of those years show how the Court's decisions became a national political issue. One consequence was that the Warren Court became more cautious, handing down several rulings favorable to police.[60] Second, how Supreme Court nominees would be likely to vote on criminal issues became a critical appointment issue thereafter. Richard Nixon's election brought to the White House a policy of being "tough on crime" and this was implemented in large measure by the president nominating justices who were opposed to the criminal procedure rulings of the Warren Court.

From that day to this, Republican presidents have been careful to appoint justices with conservative views on issues of constitutional criminal procedure. When a few of their appointees (such as Justices Harry Blackmun, John Paul Stevens, or David Souter) became moderate or even liberal in deciding criminal procedure questions, this was perceived as a failure among conservative partisans. In any event, because President Nixon was able to appoint four justices in his term of office, he set the stage for reversing the liberal trend of criminal procedure cases that had been established by the more liberal Court under Chief Justice Earl Warren. And indeed, this trend proved to be popular with the general electorate. Realizing this, President Clinton, the first Democratic president to appoint a Supreme Court justice since Lyndon Johnson, generally appointed federal judges who are more accurately described as moderates than liberals.

Political scientists who study the response to rulings of the United States Supreme Court assume that constitutional law, at least at the level of the United States Supreme Court, does not fit the non-partisan ideal. For example, Professor Harry P. Stumpf has noted that Congress responds to Supreme Court rulings in four ways: by not reacting, by positively supporting Court rulings, by negative responses, and by outright hostility. Not all liberal criminal justice decisions are greeted with hostility. When the Supreme Court held that all defendants must have a lawyer in *Gideon v. Wainwright* (1963), Congress responded by creating a federal public defender system.[61] But, the larger point for a student of criminal procedure is that this branch of constitutional law is often fraught with partisanship. Many liberals and conservatives hold intensely partisan feelings about the the Supreme Court's criminal procedure doctrines, even if doctrinal changes in the law have little practical effect on criminal justice. Hence, criminal procedure has become an issue on which justices reflect judicial policy preferences, as noted in the Judicial Biography and Judicial Statesmanship section of this chapter.

SUMMARY

Criminal procedure is a branch of constitutional law that fulfills several constitutional functions of government: ensuring public safety, doing justice, and guaranteeing liberty. The demands of liberty and order are not always compatible; therefore tension sometimes arises between these functions. This tension is resolved by the United States Supreme Court which must balance the need for liberty and order. At different points in history the Court will lean more to supporting liberty or order in accord with its best view of the law and the demands of constitutional policy. At such times the Court never abandons either goal as the Constitution demands both.

Knowledge of the context of criminal procedure provides a better understanding of the subject than can be gleaned only by reading Supreme Court decisions. The context includes, first, the criminal justice system. The Supreme Court helps to make rules for the criminal justice system, along with legislatures, but criminal justice includes the people who enforce the rules. As a human process, the way criminal justice works in practice does not always accord with the dictates of the law.

Second, the context includes an understanding of the law and legal rules, as the creation of different bodies and people, including legislatures, courts, and chief executives, who are organized hierarchically according to legitimate legal and constitutional authority. In criminal procedure it is important to remember that statutes or actions of executive officers are illegal if they conflict with rules of constitutional law. Substantive law creates rights and obligations; procedural law directs officers, lawyers, and judges as how to proceed in carrying out their functions; and remedial law determines what benefits or remedies can be won by parties who prevail in law suits. Criminal procedure is procedural law in that it guides the conduct of criminal justice personnel but at the same time constitutional criminal procedure is substantive law because it creates constitutional rights of suspects and defendants.

Third, one must understand the hierarchical organization of the courts. Appellate courts exist to resolve issues of law that are challenged by parties who have not prevailed at trial, not to retry the facts of a case. The United States Supreme Court decides only federal issues but when it does, its rulings under the Constitution are superior to federal legislation and to state law (including state constitutions). State high courts can decide criminal procedure issues exclusively under their own state constitutions. When they base decisions on adequate and independent state grounds, state supreme courts can grant parties a greater level of individual rights than granted by the United States Supreme Court under the United States Constitution.

The fourth context section on the basics of legal reasoning provides the student with a guide on how to read and understand Supreme Court cases. This is an arduous, intellectual task because constitutional case law is dynamic and the rules often change as they are applied. In criminal procedure cases, the Supreme Court justices tend to lean either to the "Crime Control Model," which stresses finality, or to the "Due Process Model," which stresses the overriding need to avoid miscarriages of justice, and these orientations influence the direction of decisions in the Court.

Other contextual aspects of criminal procedure which are found in the text include *History and Politics, Judicial Biography and Judicial Statesmanship,* and *Law in Society* sections which comment on how the law works on the streets and in the courthouses. The context of political theory indicates that criminal procedure is a prime area of constitutionalism and the Rule of Law, grand concepts of government power restrained by law and courts that is a hallmark of what is civilized in Western culture. The basic political theories of liberty and equality, which are the foundations of our modern democracy, are reflected in the everyday working of criminal procedure. Lastly, it is important to remember that criminal procedure rights are not only creations of state rules but are also human rights. The underlying theme of fair treatment is owed to every person who comes within the scope of the criminal justice system which rules of criminal procedure are designed to guarantee.

FURTHER READING

Charles Rembar, *The Law of the Land: The Evolution of Our Legal System* (New York: Touchstone, 1981).

Benjamin N. Cardozo, *The Nature of the Judicial Process* (New Haven, Conn. : Yale University Press, 1921).

Bernard Schwartz, *A History of the Supreme Court* (New York: Oxford University Press, 1993).

ENDNOTES

1. In this text, "the Court" with a capital C always refers to the United States Supreme Court.
2. A. K. Pye, "The Warren Court and Criminal Procedure," *Michigan Law Review* 67: p. 249 (1968); see Alan Barth, *Law Enforcement Versus the Law* (New York: Collier Books, 1961).
3. See Jeffrey Toobin, *The Run of His Life: The People v. O. J. Simpson* (New York: Random House, 1996).
4. Fred P. Graham, *The Due Process Revolution: The Warren Court's Impact on Criminal Law* (New York: Hayden Book Co., 1970).
5. Mary Margaret Weddington and W. Richard Janikowski, "The Rehnquist Court: The Counter-Revolution That Wasn't, Part II; The Counter Revolution That Is," *Criminal Justice Review* (1997, Forthcoming).
6. Barton L. Ingraham, *The Structure of Criminal Procedure: Laws and Practice of France, the Soviet Union, China, and the United States* (New York: Greenwood Press, 1987), pp. 22–5.
7. Stanley Kinyon, *Introduction to Law Study and Law Examination in a Nutshell* (St. Paul: West Publishing, 1971), pp. 8–17.
8. See Candace McCoy, *Politics and Plea Bargaining: Victim's Rights in California* (Philadelphia: University of Pennsylvania Press, 1993), pp. 20–48.
9. Common law countries, all former English colonies, are those that have borrowed the main aspect of English judge–made law, including the United States, Canada, India, Australia, and Nigeria among others. They are distinguished from countries with other legal traditions based mainly on Roman law, called "civil law" countries; see Richard J. Terrill, *World Criminal Justice Systems: A Survey* (Cincinnati, Ohio: Anderson, 1984).
10. *U.S. Const.* Art. V.
11. *U.S. Const.* Art. VI, para. 3.
12. Helen E. Veit, Kenneth R. Bowling, and Charlene Bangs Bickford, eds., *Creating the Bill of Rights: The Documentary Record from the First Federal Congress* (Baltimore: Johns Hopkins University Press, 1991), pp. 83–4.
13. A federal court can hear issues of state law as a matter of its diversity jurisdiction (the parties reside in different states) or under "pendent jurisdiction" in which the court hears a case in which both federal and state issues are present. As a matter of judicial economy the federal court can decide the state law issue in accord with state precedents. The Supreme Court has no jurisdiction to decide a case based exclusively on state grounds, so in a very small number of cases decided by federal courts cannot be appealed to the Supreme Court.
14. *United States v. Payner,* 447 U.S. 727 (1980); *United States v. Hasting,* 461 U.S. 499 (1983); *Thomas v. Arn,* 474 U.S. 140 (1985).
15. See opinion of New Jersey Supreme Court Justice Handler in *State v. Hunt* (1982).
16. Hall, *Oxford Companion,* p. 545.
17. Barry Latzer, *State Constitutional Criminal Law* (Deerfield, Ill.: Clark Boardman Callaghan, 1995, annual updates).
18. Barry Latzer, "The Hidden Conservatism of the State Court 'Revolution'" *Judicature* 74 (1991): p.190.
19. In U.S. Supreme Court cases the parties are the petitioner(s) and the respondent(s). In some state appellate courts, the parties are labeled "appellant(s)" and "appellee(s)". Sometimes, to keep the parties clear in criminal cases the courts may designate a party as, e.g., an "appellant-defendant." Keep in mind that in U.S. Supreme Court cases, you can determine who lost the case in the last preceding court case because that party is the "petitioner" and the name of the petitioner appears first.
20. Quotations in this section are taken from pp. 1–8 in Edward Levi, *An Introduction to Legal Reasoning* (Chicago: University of Chicago Press, 1949).
21. Thomas C. Grey, "Constitutionalism: An Analytic Framework," in Pennock and Chapman, eds., *Constitutionalism,* pp. 189–209. The following discussion of constitutionalism is drawn in part from Grey's essay.
22. See Christopher Pyle, *Military Surveillance of Civilian Politics, 1967–1970* (New York: Garland Publishing, 1986).
23. Herbert L. Packer, Two Models of the Criminal Process, *University of Pennsylvania Law Review,* 113: pp. 1–68(1964); Herbert L. Packer, *The Limits of the Criminal Sanction* (Stanford University Press, 1968).
24. Robert A. Burt, *The Constitution in Conflict* (Cambridge, Mass.: Belknap Press, 1992); Richard C. Cortner, *A Mob Intent on Death: The NAACP and the Arkansas Riot Case* (Middletown, Conn.: Wesleyan University Press, 1988); James Goodman, *Stories of Scottsboro* (New York: Pantheon Books, 1994).
25. See George Sabine, *A History of Political Theory,* 3d ed. (New York: Holt, Rinehart and Winston, 1961); Alexander Hamilton, James Madison, John Jay, *The Federalist,* edited, with Introduction and Notes, by Jacob E. Cooke (Middletown, Conn.: Wesleyan University Press, 1961).
26. In this book, the term "rule of law" is capitalized when used to refer to the doctrine of legal and political theory described herein.
27. Robert Dahl, *Modern Political Analysis* (Englewood Cliffs, N.J.: Prentice-Hall, 1963), 4–13.
28. Candace McCoy, "The Cop's World: Modern Policing and the

Difficulty of Legitimizing the Use of Force," *Human Rights Quarterly* 8 (1986) pp. 270–93.

29. Glenn Tinder, *Political Thinking: The Perennial Questions,* 4th ed. (Boston: Little, Brown, 1986), p. 117.
30. Gordon J. Schochet, "Constitutionalism, Liberalism, and the Study of Politics," in J. Roland Pennock and John W. Chapman, eds., *Constitutionalism* (New York: New York University Press, 1979), p. 1.
31. Hadley Arkes, *Beyond the Constitution* (Princeton: Princeton University Press, 1990), pp. 77–9.
32. Alexis de Tocqueville, *Democracy in America,* trans. George Lawrence, ed. J. P. Mayer (Garden City, N.Y.: Anchor, 1969), pp. 99–105.
33. See Craig M. Bradley, *The Failure of the Criminal Procedure Revolution* (Philadelphia: University of Pennsylvania Press, 1993).
34. *Clinton v. Jones* (1997).
35. Compare Raoul Berger, *Government by Judiciary* (Cambridge, Mass: Harvard University Press, 1977), with R. Dworkin, "Political Judges and the Rule of Law," in *A Matter of Principle* (Cambridge, Mass.: Harvard University Press, 1985), pp. 9–32.
36. Lon Fuller, *The Morality of Law,* rev. ed., (New Haven, Conn.: Yale University Press, 1969), pp. 33–94.
37. Hall, *General Principles,* p. 27.
38. Michael Kammen, *Spheres of Liberty: Changing Perceptions of Liberty in American Culture* (Madison: University of Wisconsin Press, 1986).
39. John Locke, *Two Treatises of Government, student ed.* (Cambridge: Cambridge University Press, 1988). The first edition of *Two Treatises* first appeared in 1689–1690. See Richard Ashcraft, *Revolutionary Politics and Locke's Two Treatises of Government* (Princeton, NJ: Princeton University Press, 1986).
40. Ruth W. Grant, *John Locke's Liberalism* (Chicago: University of Chicago Press, 1987), pp. 52–3.
41. Grant, p. 199.
42. Gordon S. Wood, *The Radicalism of the American Revolution* (New York: Vintage Books, 1991).
43. Catherine Drinker Bowen, *John Adams and the American Revolution* (New York: Grosset & Dunlap, 1949).
44. A more complex interpretation is found in Gary Wills, *Inventing America: Jefferson's Declaration of Independence* (Garden City, NY: Doubleday, 1978).
45. J. R. Pole, *The Pursuit of Equality in American History.* (Berkeley: University of California Press, 1978).
46. Jack Donnelly, *Universal Human Rights in Theory and Practice* (Ithaca, NY: Cornell University Press, 1989), pp. 9–14; John Humphrey, *No Distant Millennium: The International Law of Human Rights* (Paris: UNESCO, 1989), pp. 20–1.
47. Humphrey, *No Distant Millennium,* pp. 59–71. The categories of crimes known as crimes against humanity were first declared by the London Agreement of the victorious Allies, signed on August 8, 1945. Whitney R. Harris, *Tyranny on Trial: The Evidence at Nuremberg* (Dallas: Southern Methodist University Press, 1954), p. 23; Ann Tusa and John Tusa, *The Nuremberg Trial,* pp. 84–90.
48. M. Cherif Bassiouni, ed., *The Protection of Human Rights in the Administration of Criminal Justice: A Compendium of United Nations Norms and Standards* (Irvington-on-Hudson, N.Y.: Transnational Publishers, 1994); T. Meron, ed., *Human Rights in International Law: Legal and Policy Issues* 2 vols. (Oxford: Clarendon Press, 1984); P. Sieghart, *The International Law of Human Rights* (Oxford: Clarendon Press, 1983). The optimistic view of this growth is that the idea of human rights is gaining worldwide legitimacy. The pessimistic view is that the passing of such documents reflects a deep social malaise and violations of human rights in the world, Humphrey, *No Distant Millennium,* p. 12.
49. Amnesty International, *Amnesty International Report 1995,* 41 (1995). The best established and most effective is the European Commission of Human Rights, acting under the European Convention on Human Rights and Fundamental Freedoms. Luke J. Clements, *European Human Rights: Taking a Case Under the Convention* (London: Sweet & Maxwell, 1994); L. Mikaelsen, *European Protection of Human Rights* (Germantown, Md.: Sijthoff & Noordhoff, 1980).
50. Jonathan I. Charney, "Progress in International Criminal Law?", *American Journal of International Law,* (1995) 93: pp.452–64
51. "Of course, procedural justice must contribute to the common goal of all governments, which is to further the freedom of each member of society and to secure the liberty of all. . . . Thus, criminal investigations and proceedings full of blind revenge and abhorrent to the spirit of the law are detested in western democratic societies." Wilfried Bottke, "'Rule of Law' or 'Due Process' as a Common Feature of Criminal Process in Western Democratic Societies," *University of Pittsburgh Law Review* 51 (1990) pp. 419–61, 439.
52. William H. Chafe, *The Unfinished Journey: America Since World War II, Second Edition* (New York: Oxford University Press, 1999), pp. 302–80.
53. President's Commission on Law Enforcement and Administration of Justice, *The Challenge of Crime in A Free Society* (Washington, U.S. Government Printing Office, 1967); John A. Conley, ed., *The 1967 President's Crime Commission: Its Impact 25 Years Later* (Cincinnati: Anderson, 1994).
54. Richard Harris, *The Fear of Crime* (New York: Praeger, 1968). This law became 18 U.S.C. § 3501. It was a dead letter for many years but in *Dickerson v. United States,* the Fourth Circuit Court of Appeals held that a voluntary confession was admissible even though *Miranda* warnings were not issued. The case has been appealed to the United States Supreme Court.
55. Theodore H. White devoted an entire chapter to it in *The Making of the President 1968* (New York: Atheneum Publishers,

1969): Chap. 7, "Appetite for Apocalypse: The Issue of Law–and–Order," pp. 188–223.

56. Louis M. Kohlmeier, Jr., *"God Save This Honorable Court!"* (New York: Charles Scribner's Sons, 1972), p. 79.

57. *Ibid.* p. 87.

58. The portion of the speech was quoted in F. Graham, *The Due Process Revolution,* p. 15.

59. *Ibid.*, p. 12.

60. For example, "mere evidence" of crime was now seizable by police (*Warden v. Hayden* [1967]); a "stop and frisk" power was authorized (*Terry v. Ohio* [1968]); and searches based on anonymous tips were allowed (*McCray v. Illinois* [1967]).

61. Harry P. Stumpf, *American Judicial Politics* (San Diego: Harcourt Brace Jovanovich, 1988), pp. 417–22.

JUSTICES OF THE SUPREME COURT

The Precursor Justices
Harlan I—Holmes—Brandeis—Cardozo

The "precursor" justices of the United States Supreme Court include some of the greatest who have sat on the Court. They occupied seats on the Court from 1877 (Harlan I) to 1939 (Brandeis) and for the most part decided cases in areas other than criminal procedure. Each made an important contribution to constitutional criminal procedure, especially in framing positions concerning the incorporation of the criminal justice provisions of the Bill of Rights into the Due Process Clause of the Fourteenth Amendment.

John Marshall Harlan forcefully advocated the total incorporation of the Bill of Rights into the Fourteenth Amendment, thereby anticipating the revival of this doctrine by Justice Hugo Black and its eventual adoption, albeit in its "selective" form, during the 1960s. Justices Oliver Wendell Holmes and Louis Brandeis contributed to incorporation indirectly. First, they championed First Amendment freedom of speech as fundamental to American democracy. At first dissenting against the violation of free speech by state laws, they ultimately convinced the other justices that state laws that violate free speech are unconstitutional. This amounted to the incorporation of key provisions of the First Amendment, and so "breached the wall" of the non-incorporation position. This foundation for incorporation was blocked by Justice Cardozo, who built an intellectually strong argument against incorporation in the Palko *(1938) case. That is, he defined First Amendment rights as fundamental, and therefore, as a part of due process. Fourth, Fifth, and Sixth amendment rights, however, were defined as "formal" and not worthy of incorporation.*

A profound principle of federalism, with enormous practical implications, was at play. Incorporation would undoubtedly bring the federal courts into the running of state criminal justice, and from the creation of the Republic criminal justice had been left entirely to the states. On this point, incorporation was also assisted by an important ruling, Moore v. Dempsey *(1923) championed by Justice Holmes. It held that a trial that was fundamentally unfair violated the due process clause of the Fourteenth Amendment, which prohibits any state from depriving a person of life, liberty or property without due process of law. Thus, well before the incorporation doctrine became a matter of constitutional law in the 1960s, the door to federal court interference into state criminal justice had been opened.*

John M. Harlan, I

Kentucky 1833–1911

Republican

Appointed by Rutherford B. Hayes

Years of Service: 1877–1911

Collection of the Supreme Court of the United States. Photographer: Mathew Bradey

Life and Career Harlan was the son of a prominent Kentucky attorney and of a slaveholding family. An 1850 graduate of Centre College, he studied law in his father's office. After admission to the bar in 1853, he practiced law and was politically active. During the Civil War he fought on the Union side. In 1864, he was elected attorney general of Kentucky as a Democrat, and opposed the Thirteenth Amendment. He later underwent an extreme change of views, becoming a radical Republican and an ardent supporter of African-American civil rights.

Harlan ran unsuccessfully for Kentucky governor in 1871 and 1875. At the 1876 Republican nominating convention, he swung the Kentucky delegation to Rutherford B. Hayes and was rewarded with a nomination to the Supreme Court the following year.

Contribution to Criminal Procedure Harlan's great contribution to criminal procedure was to champion the incorporation of the Bill of Rights into the Fourteenth Amendment, in order to make the federally guaranteed rights apply against state and local officers. He never succeeded in convincing the Court to incorporate any right except for the just compensation clause of the Fifth Amendment, but his efforts paved the way for the Due Process Revolution of the 1960s.

(Continued)

The importance of Harlan's dissents in *Hurtado v. California* (1884), *Twining v. New Jersey* (1908), and other cases concerning the rights of state criminal defendants under the Fifth, Sixth, and Eighth amendments, was not simply that he stood up for incorporation, often as a lone dissenter, but that his forceful dissents required the majority to formulate reasoned arguments in response to his arguments that the post–Civil War amendment fundamentally changed the nature of American federalism. To his mind, these rights were essential to citizenship. The majority opinions in these cases *agreed* that if a state were to violate the *fundamental rights* of a citizen, this would violate due process. Although the Court at that time did not view the criminal procedure rights as fundamental, a later Supreme Court used the fundamental rights formulation to selectively incorporate most of the Bill of Rights.

SIGNATURE OPINION Dissenting opinion in *Hurtado v. California* (1884). He argued that the grand jury provision of the Fifth Amendment was violated by charging a person with a felony by a prosecutor's information rather than a grand jury indictment.

ASSESSMENT In economic matters, Harlan opposed state economic regulations and favored laissez-faire procapitalist doctrines; on the other hand, he was a nationalist and so supported federal regulation, such as the Sherman Anti–Trust Act against great economic concentration. He is best known for his lone dissent in *Plessy v. Furguson* (1896), arguing against the "separate but equal" interpretation of the Equal Protection Clause that upheld the state segregation laws. Harlan, arguing that the very intent of the law was to perpetuate inequality, castigated the majority for joining Louisiana in a charade. He wrote that in the Constitution, "there is in this country no superior, dominant, ruling class of citizens. There is no caste here. Our Constitution is color–blind, and neither knows nor tolerates classes among citizens. . . . The destinies of the two races, in this country, are indissolubly linked together, and the interests of both require that the common government of all shall not permit the seeds of race hate to be planted under the sanction of the law. . . ." The "Great Dissenter," Dissenter, discerned with greater accuracy than his brethren the true nature of the American polity and its ideals.

FURTHER READING

Tinsley E. Yarbrough, *Judicial Enigma: The First Harlan* (New York: Oxford University Press, 1995).

OLIVER WENDELL HOLMES, JR.

Massachusetts 1841–1935

Republican

Appointed by Theodore Roosevelt

Years of Service: 1902–1932

Collection of the Supreme Court of the United States. Photographer: Harris and Ewing

LIFE AND CAREER Holmes was born in Boston to an established "Boston Brahmin" family, but not one of great wealth. His father was a professor of medicine at Harvard and a famous essayist. Holmes attended Harvard College in 1857. His family was devoted to the Union cause, and Holmes entered military service soon after the Civil War broke out. He was seriously wounded three times during his three years of service. He rose to the rank of captain and mustered out in the summer of 1864. His war experiences led him to see life as a struggle.

His great ambition was to become famous through his philosophical writings, but he entered the law in order to make a living. Nevertheless, while practicing law he pursued legal scholarship, editing the *American Law Review* and studying the old English cases of the common law. This resulted in a series of lectures and book, *The Common Law* (1881), which is recognized as a seminal work of legal scholarship and which did indeed make him famous. The book delved into the tangled web of old cases and demonstrated that there were coherent utilitarian reasons for seemingly irrational rules of law. In the magisterial opening phrase of *The Common Law*, "The life of the law has not been logic; it has been experience. The felt necessities of the time, the prevalent moral and political theories, intuitions of public policy, avowed or unconscious, even the prejudices which judges share with their fellow men, have a good deal more to do than the syllogism in determining the rules by which men should be governed."

After a brief appointment to the Harvard law faculty, he accepted an appointment to the Massachusetts Supreme Judicial Court (1883-1902), on which he served with distinction before his appointment to the United States Supreme Court.

Contribution to Criminal Procedure The Supreme Court heard few criminal procedure cases in his era, and so Holmes had little opportunity to write extensively on these issues. He took a conservative stance in an early Eighth Amendment case, viewing the "cruel or unusual punishment" clause as static; he advanced modern Fourth Amendment law in the *Weeks* (1914) and *Silverthorne* (1920) cases by voting for and writing in favor of the exclusionary rule. His adherence to the Rule of Law was displayed in his dissent in the *Olmstead* (1928) wiretap case. Although not as eloquent as Brandeis' dissent in that case, he stated bluntly that the government should not be above the law, even at some cost to public safety. "We have to choose, and for my part I think it is a less evil that some criminals should escape than that the government should play an ignoble part."

Signature Opinion *Moore v. Dempsey* (1923). This was a monumentally important case. Holmes had failed to convince the Court in *Frank v. Mangum* (1915) that a sham trial violates due process. When the Court's composition changed, Holmes' views became law. The importance of *Moore* was that the Supreme Court for the first time reversed a state criminal decision as a violation of due process. This opened the door to federal court intrusion into state criminal procedure, making criminal justice more civilized and uniform throughout the nation.

Assessment Holmes was one of the great Supreme Court justices, perhaps second only to Chief Justice John Marshall (1801-1835). He also stands as one of the greatest shapers of the English and American common law in its eight-hundred-year history.

Holmes' accomplishments on the Supreme Court include (along with Brandeis) the creation of modern First Amendment law, enshrining free speech as a foundation of democracy, for free government is not possible unless all ideas be allowed to compete in the "marketplace of ideas."

Further Reading

Liva Baker, *The Justice From Beacon Hill: The Life and Times of Oliver Wendell Holmes* (New York: HarperCollins, 1991).

Louis Dembitz Brandeis

Massachusetts 1856–1941

Republican

Appointed by Woodrow Wilson

Years of Service: 1916–1939

Collection of the Supreme Court of the United States. Photographer: Harris and Ewing

Life and Career Brandeis was born in Louisville, Kentucky, to a German Jewish family that sided with the Union during the Civil War. He entered Harvard Law School shortly before his nineteenth birthday, supported himself as a tutor, earned the highest grades, and spent a third year at Harvard as an instructor and graduate student. Attracted by Boston's liberal and intellectual atmosphere, he entered law practice with his classmate, Samuel Warren. They built a thriving practice representing mid-sized businesses. Brandeis developed a tremendous reputation as a thorough attorney whose success was built on a deep study of the law.

Brandeis became wealthy practicing law, but gave it up to represent the interests of laborers struggling for economic security and protection of health and safety on the job. As an unpaid mediator and attorney in labor disputes, he became a renowned defender of workers' rights in early twentieth-century America. In his victory before the conservative Supreme Court in *Muller v. Oregon* (1908), upholding a state law limiting the working hours of female laundry employees, Brandeis used an innovative written argument (or "brief"): filled with ninety-six pages of social, economic, and health facts about the damaging effects of long working hours, and only ten pages with the usual legal arguments. Since that time, this form of presentation been known as a "Brandeis Brief."

As a leading progressive who opposed monopolies, he drew the animosity of the propertied classes, but also became a key advisor to President Woodrow Wilson, who nominated him to the Supreme Court. He was appointed after a long and acrimonious confirmation debate in the Senate based mainly on his "radicalism," but also supported to some degree by anti-Semitism.

Contribution to Criminal Procedure He supported the federal exclusionary rule and the extension of federal due

(Continued)

process against the states in important cases like *Moore v. Dempsey* (1923), *Powell v. Alabama* (1932) (counsel), and *Brown v. Mississippi* (1936) (confessions).

SIGNATURE OPINION Dissent in *Olmstead v. United States* (1928). Federal agents violated a state criminal law against wiretapping. The issue was whether this was a search and seizure and, if so, whether as illegally seized evidence the wiretap evidence should be excluded. Brandeis's dissent is a classic statement of the Rule of Law:

"Decency, security, and liberty alike demand that government officials shall be subjected to the same rules of conduct that are commands to the citizen. In a government of laws, existence of the government will be imperiled if it fails to observe the law scrupulously. Our government is the potent, the omnipresent teacher. For good or for ill, it teaches the whole people by its example. Crime is contagious. If the government becomes a lawbreaker, it breeds contempt for law; it invites every man to become a law unto himself; it invites anarchy. To declare that in the administration of the criminal law the end justifies the means—to declare that the government may commit crimes in order to secure the conviction of a private criminal—would bring terrible retribution. Against that pernicious doctrine this court should resolutely set its face."

ASSESSMENT The dissents of Brandeis and Holmes in First Amendment cases ultimately persuaded the Court to hold that free speech and free press rights were so fundamental that the states could not be abridge them. This incorporation of First Amendment rights helped open the door to the later incorporation of criminal procedure rights. His work in this and many other areas rank him as one of the greatest justices.

FURTHER READING

Philippa Strum, *Louis D. Brandeis: Justice for the People* (New York: Schocken Books, 1984).

BENJAMIN NATHAN CARDOZO

New York 1870–1938

Democrat

Appointed by Herbert Hoover.

Years of Service: 1932–1938

Collection of the Supreme Court of the United States. Photographer: Harris and Ewing

LIFE AND CAREER Cardozo, born into a distinguished New York family of Sephardic Jews who emigrated to America in the mid-eighteenth century, was a brilliant student and a noted lawyer, in practice with his older brother for twenty years. Despite his personality, described as gentle, courteous, lonely, ascetic, and saintly, and his apparent lack of political involvement, his reputation as a practitioner led to a judicial appointment to New York's highest court, the Court of Appeals, on which he served from 1913 to 1932.

Cardozo's outstanding reputation as a person and a judge led to an unparalleled national clamor for his appointment as the most worthy replacement for Justice Holmes. Thus, despite the facts that he was nominally of the wrong political party, that two justices from New York (Stone and Hughes) already sat on the Court, and that a Jewish justice (Brandeis) occupied another seat, President Hoover named Cardozo to the Court.

CONTRIBUTION TO CRIMINAL PROCEDURE Cardozo was a conservative judge in criminal matters and had opposed the exclusionary rule as a judge on the New York Court of Appeals.

SIGNATURE OPINION *Palko v. Connecticut* (1938). The Supreme Court had from 1925 to 1933 incorporated several First Amendment rights; it seemed likely that the Court would next incorporate criminal procedure rights. Palko, found guilty of murder and sentenced to prison, was retried after the prosecutor appealed under state law, again found guilty, and sentenced to death. He argued that this violated the Fifth Amendment Double Jeopardy Clause and should apply to the states via due process. Cardozo's majority opinion held that the Connecticut law did not violate due process or incorporate the Double Jeopardy Clause. This was achieved by distinguishing between "fundamental" First Amendment rights and "formal" Fifth Amendment rights:

"The line of division may seem to be wavering and broken if there is a hasty catalogue of the cases on the one side and the other. Reflection and analysis will induce a different view. There emerges the perception of a rationalizing principle which gives to discrete instances a proper order and coherence. The right to trial by jury and the immunity from prosecution except as the result of an indictment may have value and importance. Even so, they are not of the very essence of a scheme of ordered liberty. To abolish them is not to violate a 'principle of justice so rooted in the traditions and conscience of our people as to be ranked as fundamental.' . . .

"We reach a different plane of social and moral values when we pass to the privileges and immunities that have been taken over from the earlier articles of the Federal Bill of Rights and brought within the Fourteenth Amendment by a process of absorption. These in their origin were effective against the federal government alone. If the Fourteenth Amendment has absorbed them, the process of absorption has had its source in the belief that neither liberty nor justice would exist if they were sacrificed. . . . This is true, for illustration, of freedom of thought and speech. Of that freedom one may say that it is the matrix, the indispensable condition, of nearly every form of freedom."

The conservative *Palko* rationale retarded the advance of the incorporation doctrine for another quarter century.

Assessment Cardozo's reputation as a great common law judge is based mainly on his work on the New York Court of Appeals. His opinions were masterpieces of judicial craft that precisely analyzed basic principles of law; his decisions were neither immobilized by precedent nor excessively experimental. His fame was enhanced by his lectures and books (especially *The Nature of the Judicial Function,* 1921), which dissected the work of the appellate judge with such penetrating candor as to add a new chapter to the philosophy of judicial realism. His Supreme Court opinions were marked by total mastery over the subject matter at hand, a graceful and fluid writing style, and a penetrating intelligence. On the Court for only five and one-half terms, he mainly supported the New Deal in economic cases and had a mixed record in civil rights cases.

Further Reading

Andrew L. Kaufman, *Cardozo* (Cambridge: Harvard University Press, 1998).

CHAPTER 2

THE CONSTITUTIONAL FOUNDATION OF CRIMINAL PROCEDURE

I cannot consider the Bill of Rights to be an outworn 18th Century "strait jacket" as the Twining *opinion did. Its provisions may be thought outdated abstractions by some. And it is true that they were designed to meet ancient evils. But they are the same kind of human evils that have emerged from century to century wherever excessive power is sought by the few at the expense of the many. In my judgment the people of no nation can lose their liberty so long as a Bill of Rights like ours survives and its basic purposes are conscientiously interpreted, enforced and respected so as to afford continuous protection against old, as well as new, devices and practices which might thwart those purposes.*

—Justice Hugo L. Black, dissenting in *Adamson v. California,* 332 U.S. 46, 89 (1947).

CHAPTER OUTLINE

KEY TERMS AND PHRASES *(CONTINUES ON NEXT PAGE)*

Bill of attainder
Bill of Rights
Checks and balances
Due process approach
Due Process Clause
Due Process Revolution
Ex post facto law
Footnote 4
Formal rights
Fundamental fairness
Fundamental rights test
Habeas corpus, writ of
Hierarchy of rights
Incorporation doctrine
Incorporation plus
Judicial independence
Judicial review
Judicial restraint

Jury independence
Jury trial
Just Compensation Clause
Law of the land
Magna Carta
Mandamus, writ of
Missouri Compromise
Non-incorporation era
Ordered liberty
Privileges or Immunities Clause
Reconstruction amendments
Selective incorporation
Separation of powers
Shocks the conscience test
Silver platter doctrine
Stare decisis
Total incorporation
Totality of circumstances
Treason Clause
Unenumerated Rights Clause

Overview of the Constitution

The Functions and Structure of the Constitution

The text of the original United States Constitution was drafted in the 1787 constitutional convention held at Philadelphia, ratified in 1788 by the states, and went into effect in 1789. It also includes twenty-seven amendments ratified between 1791 and 1992.[1] The Constitution, in a broader sense, includes constitutional law—United States Supreme Court decisions that create rules and doctrines to guide lower courts, government officers, and private persons. And, to go further, the Constitution encompasses constitutional values and traditions that form the "unwritten constitution."

The Constitution has several basic functions:

1. *Establish the government* of the United States and delegate the sovereign powers of the people to that government.
2. *Structure the government*—divide its functions into three separate branches: legislative, executive, and judicial.
3. *Limit power*—prevent tyranny by dividing sovereign power among the three branches, establishing checks and balances, limiting the legislative powers to those enumerated in the document, and sharing power between the federal and state governments.
4. *Federalism*—provide rules to guide relations between the states, and between the federal and state governments.
5. *Guarantee individual rights and liberties*—provide for the election of government officers and explicitly guarantee fundamental rights.

The government of 1789 was created by deliberation and law, not by force or conquest. The United States itself was established in a violent rebellion after 1774 as the thirteen colonies broke away from England and declared themselves a new nation. The United States was first governed by the Continental Congress during the Revolutionary War (1775–1781) under a compact that was ratified in 1781 as the Articles of Confederation.[2] Success in war brought international recognition of the United States by the Treaty of Paris (1783). By 1785, it was clear that the Articles of Confederation had created such a weak central government that the United States might fall apart or be conquered by European powers. This crisis led to the 1787 convention held in Philadelphia. The purpose of the convention was to establish a more powerful central government and ensure the existence of the United States.[3]

The 1787 Constitution consists of seven articles. Article I vests all legislative powers in the Congress, consisting of the House of Representatives and the Senate; Article II vests the executive power in the president; and Article III vests the judicial power in "one supreme Court, and in such inferior Courts as the Congress may from time to time ordain and establish." This **separation of powers** was designed to prevent tyranny by the centralization of power. To this end, the *framers* of the Constitution added various **checks and balances.** These include the presidential veto of legislation and veto override by a two-thirds vote of the House and Senate (Art. I, § 7); senatorial consent by majority vote for presidential appointment of ambassadors and judges (Art. II § 2); two-thirds Senate approval to ratify treaties made by the president (Art. II, § 2); origination of revenue bills in the House of Representatives (Art. II, § 7); bicameralism—all bills must be passed by a majority of both the House and Senate (Art. I, §7); and an independent judiciary (Art. III, §1).

The legislative role in criminal justice, at the federal and state levels, includes enacting penal codes and sentencing laws, creating and funding criminal justice agencies, enacting criminal procedure codes to guide the courts and agencies, and overseeing executive operations through legislative hearings.[4] Congress may pass laws only for the purposes enumerated by Article I, section 8, of the Constitution and under the authority of section 5 of the Fourteenth Amendment. Congress may pass general criminal laws for federal territories and for protection of federal interests, but it has no direct power to make criminal laws for the states.

The president, as chief executive,[5] participates in lawmaking by signing or vetoing bills. His constitutional duty is to "take care that the laws be faithfully executed."[6] The Constitution foresees a strong presidency, but makes it clear that the Rule of Law operates; the president has no blank check to rule as he wishes, but must execute policy through established law.[7] Policing—*law enforcement*—is an executive function. In the constitutional design it must operate within legal limits. Federal law enforcement, prosecution, and corrections are performed by executive branch departments headed by cabinet members, who are appointed by the president. In the states, law enforcement is more decentralized and includes state, county, and municipal agencies.

The federal judiciary consists of "one supreme Court, and . . . such inferior courts as the Congress may from time to time ordain and establish."[8] The Supreme Court has had fewer than and more than nine justices in the past, but a powerful custom now sets the number of justices at nine. The structure of lower federal courts has been an intense political issue in the past.[9] The federal judiciary includes intermediate appellate courts—the Courts of Appeals—divided into eleven circuits and a circuit for the District of Columbia. Federal trial courts, or district courts, exist in every state and territory; there are ninety-four judicial districts, at least one in each state. Populous states have two or more districts. There are about 180 Court of Appeals judges and over 630 district judges. Supreme Court judges are called *justices.* State judges are appointed or elected under state constitutions and laws. All judges in the United States, state and federal, as well as all state and federal legislators and other government officers, take an oath to support the United States Constitution (U.S. Const. Art VI. ¶3).

As a *federation* with dual sovereignties, and not a centralized country, the United States has a complex system of governance, creating potential for friction and power struggles. Constitutional rules created to work out federal-state and state-state conflicts are essential. Thus, the federal government can pass laws only on subjects enumerated in Article I, section 8 (e.g., regulate commerce among the states), and states cannot conduct foreign policy, engage in war, or coin money (*U.S. Const.* Art. I § 10). A state must give "full faith and credit" to the acts and judicial proceedings of another and must extradite a fleeing felon on the request of another state's governor (*U.S. Const.* Art. IV, §§ 1, 2.). In conflicts between federal law and state law, the federal law is the "supreme Law of the Land" (*U.S. Const.* Art. VI. ¶ 2).

Protecting Liberty: The 1789 Constitution

The United States Constitution established *republican* government—*for* the people—which exists to "secure the Blessings of Liberty to ourselves and our Posterity." Americans view liberty as a central purpose of government, a belief that arose out of eighteenth century Enlightenment ideas as well as from a reverence for "British liberties." The framers knew from ancient and medieval history, as well as from their own experiences, that governmental power, however necessary and beneficial, could easily turn rulers into tyrants. They drew especially on English seventeenth-century experience, a time that included two civil wars and continuous political struggle between king and Parliament that resulted in Parliamentary supremacy and a limited, constitutional monarchy. The lessons and struggles of that era shaped the 1789 Constitution and set in motion modern notions of liberty and equality that entered law and political practice.

HABEAS CORPUS Article I, section 9 prohibits Congress from suspending the **writ of habeas corpus** except when a rebellion or invasion places the existence or safety of the nation in immediate peril. Habeas corpus was a medieval English writ that required a court to order any jailer (who "had the body" of another, hence *habeas corpus*) to bring the detainee before the court to determine if the detention was legal. Habeas corpus was a prerogative writ whose power emanated directly from the king. When used by individuals against powerful aristocrats, it enhanced the king's popularity. In the seventeenth century, habeas corpus was used to challenge royal detentions. In the famous Five Knights Case of 1626, a group, who refused to pay a special tax that was levied by the king without parliamentary authority, was jailed on the king's order. The group's application for a writ of habeas corpus to challenge their jailing was denied. The knights were jailed for two years until pardoned by King James I.[10] This episode raised popular clamor against taxation without representation and against the arbitrary application of law. Parliament later strengthened the habeas corpus law and, from that time, the writ assumed a new role: allowing subjects to question the legality of arrests and detention by the state. The writ became a guarantee and symbol of liberty to ensure judicial oversight of the executive branch.[11]

JUDICIAL INDEPENDENCE Article III, section 1 of the Constitution ensures **judicial independence** from direct political control by granting lifetime appointment to federal judges (subject to impeachment) and prohibiting pay cuts. Judicial independence is enormously important to individual liberty. Royal judges, as the king's appointees, were expected to favor royal power in cases which directly affected the king's interests. In other cases they could, and usually did, rule impartially. In the seventeenth century, a famous conflict arose between Edward Coke (pronounced Cook), Chief Judge of the Court of Common Pleas from 1603 to 1613, and King James I. At a conference called to sort out the jurisdiction of various courts, Coke stated that although the king was the "fount of justice," he could not personally decide legal cases because he was not trained in law. He added that God and law were above the king. James was furious and almost sent Coke to the Tower for this expression of the Rule of Law, but Coke was protected by his father-in-law who was the king's chief minister. After several years of tension, Coke was dismissed by the king and became a member of Parliament, where he led the legislative battle against royal autocracy. Coke's monumental conflict with royal power was remembered as a testament to the importance of judicial independence. In 1701, after Parliament emerged as predominant in power over the king, the Act of Settlement guaranteed that English judges held life tenure during good behavior.[12]

THE TREASON CLAUSE The United States Constitution defines the crime of treason in the **Treason Clause** of Article III only as levying war against the United States or adhering to enemies of the United States and giving them aid and comfort (Art. III, §3).[13] Further, treason can be proved only by the testimony of two witnesses to the same overt act or by a confession in open court. Why should the Constitution be cluttered with a crime definition? The framers knew that Roman emperors and English kings often charged political opponents as traitors, in order to stifle opposition. English definitions of treason were so vague as to include any action disfavored by the king. Parliament tried to prevent this abuse by fixing the definition in the Statute of Treason (1352) in words similar to those later found in the United States Constitution's Treason Clause. The legacy of the Statute of Treasons is awareness that governments can misuse treason charges to silence political opponents, requiring a liberal policy to be set into the Constitution in an effort to prevent political manipulation of treason law. As a result, treason trials in American history are rare. In 1807, former Vice-President Aaron Burr was tried for treason for plotting to cause the western portion of the United States to secede. The trial in Richmond, Virginia, held before Chief Justice John Marshall sitting as a trial judge, was conducted impartially. Marshall ruled that the government did not prove an act of treason by two eye witnesses, and Burr was released. The dangers inherent in the treason charge were seen in the manipulation of the case by President Thomas Jefferson to eliminate Burr, a hated political opponent. "Marshall's strict reading of the Constitution and firm position on evidence put the American law of treason beyond the easy grasp of political expediency, as the Framers of the Constitution had intended."[14] This valuable precedent also displays the value of judicial independence.

OTHER PROTECTIONS OF LIBERTY Other provisions in the 1787 Constitution limited the power of *both* the federal and state governments to protect liberty, a strong reminder that the Constitution is the Constitution of the United States, (i.e., the federal and the state governments), and not of just the federal government. Article I, section 9, forbids *Congress* from passing **ex post facto laws** or **bills of attainder,** and Article I section 10, declares that "No *state* shall . . . pass any Bill of Attainder [or] ex post facto Law. . . ." Bills of attainder are criminal convictions passed by a legislature, and, in England, Parliamentary attainders dripped with political retribution and gross unfairness. Ex post facto laws are criminal statutes which punish acts that were not against the law when the acts were committed. Throughout history, tyrants have used ex post facto laws to eliminate political enemies; ex post facto legislation is now universally deemed a hallmark of unjust law.[15]

LACK OF A BILL OF RIGHTS The draft Constitution, published in the Fall of 1787, was attacked by "anti-Federalists" because it contained no **bill of rights.** The Constitution's supporters—"Federalists"—argued that it guaranteed political liberty, making a bill of rights unnecessary. The convention's failure to entertain a bill of rights was "a colossal error of judgment." The anti-Federalists, who opposed the Constitution's adoption, made the lack of a bill of rights their rallying cry during state-ratifying conventions held in 1788.[16] The Constitution was adopted by a slim majority. To mend political fences, moderate Federalists in the First Congress, led by James Madison, proposed a bill of rights in the form of constitutional amendments.

Protecting Liberty: The Bill of Rights

THE IDEA OF A BILL OF RIGHTS The English Bill of Rights of 1688 was an act of Parliament passed after its victory over King James II during the Glorious Revolution.[17] More rudimentary in its concepts of civil liberties than the later United States Bill of Rights,[18] it declared that subjects could petition the king without fear of jailing; allowed Protestants to bear arms for their defense (an echo of religious warfare); ensured freedom of speech for members of Parliament; prohibited excessive bail, excessive fines, and cruel and unusual punishments (in language borrowed a century later in the Eighth Amendment); provided for the routine empaneling of jurors; and ordered that parliaments be held frequently.

STATE BILLS OF RIGHTS, 1776–1787 The renowned *Virginia Declaration of Rights* (1776), primarily the work of George Mason (1725–1792), was adopted at a convention forming an independent state and became the fountainhead of other bills of rights. The Virginia Declaration included the rights to free exercise of religion, trial by jury in civil and criminal cases, speedy trial by a local jury, no compelled evidence against oneself, notice of criminal accusations, no excessive bail or fines or cruel and unusual punishments, and no deprivation of liberty "except by the law of the land."[19]

Virginia set the example during the Revolutionary period. By 1787, eight states added bills of rights to their constitutions. Pennsylvania added the important guarantee of free speech and free press. No single state guaranteed all the rights later found in the United States Constitution and Bill of Rights, but collectively, they laid out the panoply of rights.[20] The most important law passed by the Confederation Congress, the *Northwest Ordinance,* governing the Northwest Territories, included a bill of rights.[21] These experiments in the drafting and adopting of government plans that held assurances of civil liberties were conducted by educated leaders of society and common citizens alike and are among the most original contributions in the recorded history of self-government.[22]

CREATING THE BILL OF RIGHTS James Madison, a key delegate to the Constitutional Convention, was elected to the First Congress and proposed a bill of rights. He presented it to Congress in June 1789, in the form of amendments to the text of the Constitution. Congress, after debating and consequently modifying the amendments, voted in August to adopt twelve Amendments by a two-thirds vote of the House and the Senate, as required by Article V of the Constitution (the amending article). These twelve amendments were sent to the states for ratification in September 1789. Ten of the twelve were ratified by three-quarters of the states and went into effect on December 15, 1791; the proposed first two amendments were not adopted at that time.

It is worth noting, in light of the **incorporation doctrine,** that Madison proposed, and the House of Representatives adopted, an amendment that would have prohibited the *states* from infringing the right to trial by jury in a criminal case, religious freedoms, and the freedoms of speech and the press.[23] Madison feared that states could engage in political repression and said "that he 'conceived this to be *the most valuable amendment* in the whole list. If there was any reason to restrain the Government of the United States from infringing upon these essential rights, it was equally necessary that they should be secured against the State Governments.'"[24] Nevertheless, this amendment was removed by the Senate, probably to protect the states' interests. "Hence, the Bill of Rights as adopted imposed restrictions only upon the federal government."[25]

The phrase "bill of rights" is not formally attached to these amendments. To some all ten amendments constitute the Bill of Rights while others see only the first eight, which deal directly with individual liberties, as the Bill of Rights. An interesting feature is that Madison suggested that the proposed amendments be inserted in the appropriate place in the text of the Constitution. Instead, Congress adopted the suggestion of Roger Sherman of Connecticut, that the Amendments be added at the end of the Constitution rather than interweaved into its body.[26] Also, in what has to be the most bizarre episode in the history of constitutional amendments, the second original amendment—requiring that a congressional pay raise not take effect until after the next congressional election, although not ratified in 1791, was revived in the 1980s and was ratified by three-fourths of the states to become the Twenty-seventh Amendment in 1992.[27]

OVERVIEW OF THE BILL OF RIGHTS That the Bill of Rights is heavily concerned with criminal justice and criminal procedure is small wonder for governmental tyranny is always supported by unrestrained and unprincipled police, prosecutors, and judges. The Fourth Amendment prohibits unreasonable search and seizures; provisions of the Fifth Amendment require a grand jury for an indictment, prohibit double jeopardy and self-incrimination, and ensure due process; the Sixth Amendment guarantees an impartial jury trial, the assistance of counsel, and other rights necessary to a fair trial; and the Eighth Amendment prohibits excessive bail, excessive fines, and cruel and unusual punishments.

Other Bill of Rights freedoms guarantee a free and fair democratic political system. Of great importance are First Amendment rights of free speech, free press, peaceful assembly, and "to petition the Government for a redress of grievances" and First Amendment rights concerning religion, which forbid the government from creating a state religion and guarantee the "free exercise" of one's religion.[28] The separation of church and state was the most revolutionary aspect of the Constitution. The Second Amendment created a right to "keep and bear" arms, in relation to a "well regulated Militia"; the Third Amendment prohibited the quartering of soldiers in private homes during peace time; a Fifth Amendment clause required the government to pay "just compensation" if it confiscated private property for public use; and the Seventh Amendment guaranteed a jury trial in civil suits.

The Ninth and Tenth amendments do not guarantee specific individual rights. The Ninth Amendment simply says that just because certain rights are enumerated in the Bill of Rights it does not mean that other rights do not exist. The **Unenumerated Rights Clause** invites an active judiciary to enhance individual rights, but the Supreme Court has studiously avoided expanding rights through this amendment. The Tenth Amendment, "reserving" rights to the states and the people, has been actively litigated and has been used to either uphold or strike down federal legislation as the relative power of the federal government has waxed and waned in relation to states' rights.

DUE PROCESS The Fifth Amendment states that "No person shall . . . be deprived of life, liberty, or property, without due process of law." In some instances, legitimate government has to deprive persons of life, liberty, and property to properly function; criminal sanctions of the death penalty, imprisonment, and fines are prime examples. Also, governments must tax wealth and conscript soldiers, and create a myriad of rules that limit liberty for the common good (such as the mandatory wearing of helmets by motorcycle riders). The hallmark of procedural due process in the Anglo-American system of justice is the fair trial. Due process also exists in regular legislative procedures, in tax tribunals, and in the right of citizens to question governmental decisions by political petitioning and through lawsuits.

The power of the phrase "due process" could not be underestimated upon the British subjects of North America, who rebelled against the Crown. To them, due process summed up over 600 years of advances in procedural rights and substantive liberties since King John signed the **Magna Carta** ("great charter") in 1215 after a successful rebellion by his barons. The Magna Carta was sworn to by later kings upon their coronation and over the centuries became the greatest symbol, and often a reality, of the Rule of Law—a government ruling through law and restrained by law. It came to stand for "the idea that the law is stronger than any man, even the man called King."[29] Two "chapters" of the Magna Carta are especially relevant to criminal procedure. Chapter Forty read "To no one will we sell, to no one will we deny or delay right or justice." Its most famous and important provision was declared in Chapter Thirty-Nine: "No freeman shall be captured or imprisoned or disseised or outlawed or exiled or in any way destroyed, nor will we go against him, except by the lawful judgment of his peers or by the law of the land."[30] The barons sought to ensure that the existing system of law would be applied in a regular and fair way by the king and his justices. The term "peers" referred to nobles, but over the centuries came to include all subjects or citizens. The phrase **law of the land** was rather vague at first, but evolved into "due process of law" and the **Due Process Clauses** of the Fifth and Fourteenth amendments can be traced to the Magna Carta. The resonance of the phrase "due process" was so strong that it transcended its technical meaning as a fair trial preceded by meaningful notice of the charges against an accused and came to mean **fundamental fairness.**

JURY TRIAL **Jury trials** were part and parcel of the English inheritance and were the prime method of doing justice in colonial courts. Although not actually created by the Magna Carta, trial by jury emerged at the same time in English history. The criminal trial by jury developed out of tax inquests held by royal justices traveling on circuit whereby local knights were sworn to testify to the wealth of their neighbors. Before 1200, this inquest was used to adjudge land claims under the writ of *novel disseisin.* After the Catholic Church forbade priests to participate in trials by ordeal at the Fourth Lateran Council (1215), there was uncertainty as to how to conduct trials of serious crimes where guilt or innocence was based on circumstantial evidence. In continental Europe, courts adopted the inquisitorial procedure for the trial of heretics that the Church promulgated at the Council. In England, the government found it more convenient to rely on the twelve knights of the inquest. At first, this "jury of presentment" acted like witnesses by telling the judges what they knew about the case. In about a century, this jury grew to be the "grand jury" (or "large" jury) of twenty-three members who indicted, while the group that decided the facts became the "petit" jury (or small jury) of twelve.

Over the centuries, the English jury became seen as a check on the government. *Bushell's Case* (1670),[31] the great case establishing the principle of **jury independence,** arose when a London jury acquitted William Penn, a leading Quaker and founder of the Pennsylvania colony, of unlawful assembly (he preached in the street after a Quaker church was padlocked by government officers). The jurors were imprisoned by an angry royalist judge who deplored their leniency. On a writ of habeas corpus, Chief Judge Vaughn overruled the trial judge and held that a jury was free to reach a verdict based on the evidence; otherwise, the jury would be nothing but the government's rubber stamp.[32] Jury independence is most evolved in criminal trials. While a civil verdict may be set aside by a judge on the grounds that there is no evidence to support it, an acquittal by a jury in a criminal case is absolute (unless jury tampering occurred). It is presumed that the jury will follow the rules of law read to them in the judge's charge. Jury independence is so great that juries have the power (but not the legitimate authority) to nullify the law in their verdicts in criminal cases, although judges do not acknowledge this *sub rosa* power in their instructions to jurors.[33]

Trial by jury was so important to the framers that they guaranteed federal trials by jury in the 1787 Constitution (Art. III, § 2, ¶ 3). The anti-Federalists complained that a right for a criminal jury trial to be held "in the State where the said crimes shall have been committed" was too restrictive. As a result, a more detailed set of trial rights are found in the Sixth Amendment, including the right to counsel, far in advance of the practice in England. In 1791, this did not mean that the state had to pay for the attorney of a poor person, but that the courts could not exclude an attorney from conducting a defense. The Sixth Amendment specifies many essential attributes of a fair trial: an impartial jury, a speedy trial (shades of Chapter Forty of the Magna Carta), venue in the district where the crime occurred, the right to confront witnesses, and the right to have witnesses subpoenaed.

The Incorporation of the Bill of Rights

Overview of Incorporation

The incorporation doctrine holds that most of the rights contained in the Bill of Rights (First through Eighth Amendments) protect persons from the actions not only of the *federal* government, but also are legal protection against violations by *state* legislatures and by *state* and *local* officers. (References in this text to "the state" or to "state" officials indicates state *and* local officers as distinguished from federal officers.) More precisely, the Due Process Clause of the Fourteenth Amendment is said to "incorporate" or "absorb" specific rights in the Bill of Rights. If, for example, a state court denied an indigent defendant his or her right to a state paid lawyer, the defendant could argue (in a state or federal court) that the conviction should be reversed because the *state* court violated the Fourteenth Amendment rule that "No *state* shall . . . deprive any person of life, liberty, or property, without due process of law. . . ." That is, the right to the assistance of counsel, specifically guaranteed by the Sixth Amendment (directly applicable to the federal government), is also included in Fourteenth Amendment due process liberty.

Before the Civil War, the Supreme Court held that the Bill of Rights did *not* apply to the states. The issue was revived when the Fourteenth Amendment was ratified in 1868. It took a century of legal struggle for the Court to acknowledge that the criminal procedure liberties in the Bill of Rights applies to all government units—state and federal. This section describes the process of the incorporation of the criminal justice rights in the Bill of Rights in detail because the issue arises in many of the issues studied in this book and because it is central to understanding constitutional criminal procedure. The following chronological summary may be useful.

A SUMMARY OF INCORPORATION

1. Before the Civil War the Supreme Court held that the Bill of Rights applied only to the federal government and not to the state governments.
2. The Fourteenth Amendment, ratified in 1868, gave federal courts and Congress the power to enforce the rights of citizens against violations by state and local governments.
3. From 1884 to 1911, criminal defendants appealed unsuccessfully from state cases to the United States Supreme Court, arguing that specific Bill of Rights criminal justice provisions were binding on the states through the **Privileges or Immunities** or the Due Process clauses of the Fourteenth Amendment. The idea was supported by only one justice; the Court refused to incorporate criminal procedure rights.
4. The language and reasoning of the cases denying incorporation nevertheless opened the door to "selective" incorporation in the 1960s. The nineteenth-century Court reasoned that the Fourteenth Amendment protected only *fundamental* rights, and that criminal justice rights were *not* fundamental, or "immutable principles of justice which inhere in the very idea of free government which no member of the Union may disregard" (*Twining v. New Jersey,* 1908). (When the Court determined, in the 1960s, that such rights *were* fundamental to a free society, incorporation followed.)
5. By the end of the 1920s, several Bill of Rights protections were incorporated into the Fourteenth Amendment and applied against state governments, specifically, "just compensation" for state confiscated property under the **Just Compensation Clause** of the Fifth Amendment, and the First Amendment rights to free speech, freedom of assembly, and a free press. No criminal procedure rights were incorporated.
6. In the 1920s and 1930s, the Supreme Court began to reverse *state* criminal trials because their proceedings were fundamentally unfair, holding that they directly violated Fourteenth Amendment due process. These cases did not rule that the states violated a specific Bill of Rights provision. Many of these cases involved "lynch-mob" trials and coerced confessions.
7. In *Palko v. Connecticut* (1937), the Supreme Court appeared definitively to refuse to extend the notion of incorporation to criminal procedure rights, declaring them to be "formal" and not "fundamental."
8. In *Adamson v. California* (1947), Justice Hugo Black placed incorporation of the Bill of Rights on the "constitutional agenda," and three other justices agreed with him that the Bill of Rights should be incorporated. This marked a turning point that eventually led to incorporation.
9. In the 1950s, the Supreme Court resisted incorporation by continuing to rely on Fourteenth Amendment fundamental fairness ("all the facts and circumstances") tests to evaluate state convictions under the Due Process Clause. Such tests included the "voluntariness test" for confessions, and whether a search and seizure "shocks the conscience" of the Court.
10. Beginning with *Mapp v. Ohio* (1961), by 1969 the Supreme Court incorporated most of the criminal procedure rules in the Bill of Rights into the Fourteenth Amendment (see Table 2-1) **"Due Process Revolution".** Incorporation meant that more "liberal" federal rules overrode more "conservative" rules under state laws or constitutions.
11. In subsequent years, the Supreme Court halted the expansion of defendants' rights and has cut back several rights, but it has not "disincorporated" any rights.
12. As Supreme Court doctrines have grown more conservative since 1970, several state supreme courts have, under the "adequate and independent state grounds" doctrine, granted greater rights to defendants under more liberal interpretations of state bills of rights. For the most part, though, state criminal procedure follows the federal constitutional interpretations.

TABLE 2–1 RIGHTS, ENUMERATED IN BILL OF RIGHTS (AMENDMENTS I–VIII)

RIGHTS ENUMERATED	SELECTIVE INCORPORATION	
	DATE	**CASE**
Amendment I		
Establishment of Religion	1947	*Everson v. Board of Education*
Free Exercise of Religion	1940	*Cantwell v. Connecticut*
Freedom of Speech	1925	*Gitlow v. New York*
	1927	*Fiske v. Kansas*
	1931	*Stromberg v. California*
Freedom of Press	1931	*Near v. Minnesota*
Freedom to Peaceably Assemble	1937	*DeJong v. Oregon*
Amendment II		
Militia/Right to Bear Arms	NI	[*Presser v. Illinois,* 1886]
Amendment III		
No Quartering Soldiers	NI	
Amendment IV		
No Unreasonable Search and Seizure	1949	*Wolf. v. Colorado* (basic right)
	1961	*Mapp v. Ohio* (exclusionary rule)
Amendment V		
Grand Jury	NI	[*Hurtado v. California,* 1884]
No Double Jeopardy	1969	*Benton v. Maryland*
Due Process	NI	
No Self-Incrimination	1964	*Malloy v. Hogan*
Just Compensation for Taking Private Property	1897	*Chicago, Burlington & Quincy RR v. Chicago*
Amendment VI		
Speedy Trial	1967	*Klopfer v. North Carolina*
Public Trial	1948	In re Oliver
Impartial Jury	1966	*Parker v. Gladden*
Jury Trial	1968	*Duncan v. Louisiana*
Vicinage and Venue	NI	[implied in due process]
Notice	NI	[implied in due process]
Confrontation	1965	*Pointer v. Texas*
Compulsory Process	1967	*Washington v. Texas*
Counsel	1963	*Gideon v. Wainwright*
Amendment VII		
Jury Trial in Civil Case	NI	[*Walker v. Sauvinet,* 1875]
Amendment VIII		
No Excessive Bail	[implied]	[*Schilb v. Kuebel,* 1971]
No Excessive Fine	NI	
No Cruel & Unusual Punishment	1962	*Robinson v. California*

NI, not incorporated.

INCORPORATION TERMINOLOGY AND BASIC CONCEPTS Federalism and states' rights were the major causes of the incorporation battle. Although federal-state cooperation is important in American government, legal and political disagreements are inherent in our federal structure. States jealously guard their autonomy against federal encroachment, including federal court rulings that upset state practices. When defendants claimed that state procedures did not live up to federal standards, state prosecutors challenged these assertions in the Supreme Court. The Supreme Court's incorporation cases in the 1960s set off a political backlash fueled by federal and state politicians and judges who felt that federal power had encroached too much on the states. Indeed, since 1970, the Supreme Court has toned down the liberal/federal advances of the 1960s, thereby showing the continuing power of states' rights.

Defendants argued for incorporation because federal rules of criminal procedure were more "liberal" or more favorable to criminal defendants. There is no inherent reason for this. Still, for example, before incorporation, many states allowed judges to inform a jury that it could take into consideration the defendant's failure to testify in determining guilt or innocence. This was held *not* to violate Fourteenth Amendment due process even though federal courts were not permitted to do this under the Fifth Amendment Self-incrimination Clause. The federal view was that such comments by judges tilted the scale so much that it undermined a defendant's Fifth Amendment right to silence.

Various terms describe different kinds of incorporation and methods of incorporation. **Total incorporation** is the idea that when the Fourteenth Amendment was ratified, the "Privileges or Immunities Clause" fully and immediately applied the first eight amendments to the states. This idea was championed by Justice Black on the grounds that it reflected the intent of the Fourteenth Amendment's framers. Beyond allowing a judge to decide whether a state practice violated a Bill of Rights provision, he opposed the **due process approach** because under it federal judges acted beyond their constitutional authority. Total incorporation has not been accepted by the Supreme Court.

Selective incorporation is the historic process by which incorporation has occurred. The United States Supreme Court decides that a *specific* right in the Bill of Rights is included in the concept of Fourteenth Amendment due process "liberty" because the particular right is fundamental to the system of **"ordered liberty."** Any infringement by a state undermines "those fundamental principles of liberty and justice which lie at the base of all our civil and political institutions" (*Twining v. New Jersey,* 1908).

Incorporation plus was the position articulated by Justice Frank Murphy, dissenting in *Adamson v. California* (1947). It accurately describes the existing incorporation rule. It means that the Supreme Court has not only incorporated specific Bill of Rights provisions into the Due Process Clause of the Fourteenth Amendment, but that it will also correct state violations under the fundamental fairness concept inherent in due process. (*Adamson,* p. 124, Murphy, J., dissenting).

The *due process approach* ("fundamental fairness") was an alternative to incorporation before 1961 and is now a supplementary test. It holds that the federal courts can intervene in state criminal procedure cases under the authority of the Fourteenth Amendment, on a case-by-case basis, and not by directly applying a Bill of Rights provision to the states. It is based on the idea that due process means "fundamental fairness," as well as notice and a fair hearing. The due process approach is also known as the **totality of circumstances** test, because in order to determine if state action violated due process, a court must examine all the facts to conclude whether the procedure was fundamentally fair. The due process approach is described in different terms depending upon the issue. In pre-*Miranda coerced confessions* cases, the Court applied the *voluntariness test.* In search and seizure cases, the court fashioned a *shocks the conscience test*: a search and seizure violated the Fourth Amendment if it was conducted in such a manner as to shock the conscience of the Court. Dissatisfaction with the lack of clarity of these due process tests was one reason why the Supreme Court incorporated the more hard and fast federal rules of procedure that came in tow with incorporation.

What is the exact effect of incorporation? If one accepted the idea of early nineteenth century "contrarians"—that the Bill of Rights simply declares preexisting rights—then one could argue that incorporation cases simply set the law of constitutional criminal procedure to where it should have been at the beginning of the Republic, and that the federal Bill of Rights operates directly on the states. This, however, is not the operative theory of incorporation. Instead, the theory is that *Barron v. Baltimore* (1833) was correct in holding that the Bill of Rights was originally intended to apply only to the federal government. The Fourteenth Amendment, however, modified *Barron* so that specific fundamental rights in the Bill of Rights are applicable against the states. But it is *due process* that applies—not the amendment—directly against the state. The point is not academic, because if federal government action is controlled directly by an amendment, while a state is controlled indirectly by the amendment as filtered through the Fourteenth Amendment, the possibility exists that a criminal procedure rule, such as whether a felony jury must consist of twelve persons, can apply differently to the states. Indeed, while the Sixth Amendment has been interpreted to require a twelve-person federal jury, the Supreme Court has interpreted the "incorporated" jury provision of the Sixth Amendment as allowing fewer jurors in state felony trials (*Williams v. Florida,* 1970; *Ballew v. Georgia,* 1978).

The Non-Incorporation Era, 1791–1870

BARRON *V.* BALTIMORE AND THE NON-INCORPORATION RULE As previously noted, James Madison's proposed Bill of Rights included a provision specifically limiting the *states,* but it was dropped by the Senate. Was this a hint that the framers *intended* that the Bill of Rights *not* apply to the states? This question was answered by Chief Justice Marshall's last constitutional opinion, *Barron v. Baltimore* (1833). Barron's waterfront land was taken by Baltimore for public use.[34] He felt Maryland did not pay him enough money and sued in *federal* court, arguing that the state violated his right to just compensation under the Fifth Amendment. The Supreme Court rejected his claim, saying that Barron simply had no case in the federal courts under the Bill of Rights. The framers intended the Bill of Rights to restrict only the *federal* government, *not* state or local governments.

> The Constitution was ordained and established by the people of the United States for themselves, for their government, and not for the Government of the individual States. Each State established a Constitution for itself, and, in that Constitution, provided such limitations and restrictions on the powers of its particular government as its judgment dictated. (*Barron v. Baltimore,* 1833)

A ruling for Barron's position—allowing the federal judiciary to impose obligations on the states under the Bill of Rights—implied a stronger national government and weaker states. The country was not ready for this mode of federalism at a time when many gave their primary allegiance to their states and not to the United States.

Not all Americans accepted the *Barron* ruling. "From the 1830s until the Civil War southern states made speech and publication critical of slavery a crime. A number of leading Republicans viewed these statutes as violations of the rights of American citizens protected by the First Amendment and by other provisions of the Constitution."[35] Further, Professor Akhil Reed Amar notes that in "the fifteen years before *Barron,* a considerable number of considerable lawyers implied in passing or stated explicitly that the various provisions in the Bill did limit states." Indeed, he notes that even after *Barron* some jurists continued to contradict or even ignore the rule of *Barron.*[36] These "contrarians," basing their views on a variety of theories, believed that the Bill of Rights announced such vital and important underlying principles of justice that they had to bind all governments in America—state and federal. Although the law of the land at that time was the "nonincorporation" of the Bill of Rights, the contrary arguments help to explain how the idea of incorporation flowed into the adoption of the Fourteenth Amendment.

THE GROWTH OF FEDERAL JUDICIAL POWER Despite the ruling in *Barron,* the Bill of Rights was ultimately applied to the states. One factor was the power of the Supreme Court. When incorporation of the criminal justice amendments occurred in the 1960s, critics complained that the Court usurped its constitutional authority by making new law to fit its liberal views, instead of passively deciding cases. This complaint was about 160 years too late. The Court had begun to assert its authority as a co-equal branch of government in 1803. In *Marbury v. Madison,* the Supreme Court's most important case, the Court declared a congressional statute unconstitutional. This exercise of **judicial review,** controversial because it is not explicitly mentioned in the Constitution, established a legal precedent and expanded the Court's political authority as an *equal and coordinate branch* of government.[37]

In this odd and highly "political" case, William Marbury applied to the United States Supreme Court to issue a **writ of *mandamus*** to James Madison, secretary of state, ordering him to deliver judicial appointment papers so that Marbury could take a seat as a District of Columbia magistrate. The judicial appointment had been made by President John Adams in the last days of his Federalist administration, but the outgoing secretary of state (John Marshall) failed to deliver the appointment papers. The new Democratic-Republican administration of President Thomas Jefferson did not want a member of the opposition party to take this seat, and Madison refused to deliver the papers.

A writ of *mandamus* requires an officer to perform a clear legal duty. The Supreme Court's power to issue writs of *mandamus* was created by Congress in the Judiciary Act of 1789. Marshall's opinion stated that Marbury was entitled to the appointment and should receive his appointment papers because of the legal maxim that for every legal wrong there must be a right. Yet, the Court held that Marbury could *not* gain his right by *mandamus* in the Supreme Court because Article III of the Constitution limits the Supreme Court's *original jurisdiction* to cases "affecting Ambassadors, other public Ministers and Consuls, and those in which a State shall be a party." In all other cases, the Court has only *appellate jurisdiction.* The *mandamus* power granted by the Judiciary Act conferred original jurisdiction, and was thus inconsistent with the Constitution. The statute was declared void and of no effect, i.e., "unconstitutional." Marshall emphasized that the Court's power to nullify unconstitutional laws was general and could be applied to future cases:

> Certainly all those who have framed written constitutions contemplate them as forming the fundamental and paramount law of the nation, and consequently the

> theory of every such government must be, that an act of the legislature, repugnant to the Constitution, is void. . . .
>
> It is emphatically the province and duty of the judicial department to say what the law is. Those who apply the rule to particular cases, must of necessity expound and interpret that rule. If two laws conflict with each other, the courts must decide on the operation of each. . . . (*Marbury v. Madison,* 1803)

The power of judicial review is rarely challenged now.[38] The issue, however, is not dead and will not be as long as presidents and the Congress find their policies blocked by the Court.[39]

Other early cases solidified the Supreme Court's power over state courts under the Supremacy Clause (Art. VI, ¶ 2). These included *Fletcher v. Peck* (1810), ruling a *state* law unconstitutional because it conflicted with the "Contract Clause" (Art. I, §10), which prohibits a state from "impairing the Obligation of Contracts." *Fletcher*'s constitutional significance lay in Marshall's opinion which:

> declared categorically that the states could not be viewed as a single, unconnected sovereign power, on whom no other restrictions are imposed than those found in its own constitution. On the contrary, it is a member of the Union, and "that Union has a constitution the supremacy of which all acknowledge, and which imposes limits to the legislatures of the several states, which none claim a right to pass."[40]

Two other important cases that confirmed the Supreme Court's power were *Martin v. Hunter's Lessee* (1816) and *Cohens v. Virginia* (1821). These cases overturned the attempt by the Virginia Supreme Court to hold United States civil and criminal statutes unconstitutional. Together, these cases meant that the United States was a "real country" and not a loose federation of fully sovereign states. They confirmed the Supreme Court's authority as the final arbiter of cases arising under the Constitution. They made state governments and state courts responsible to act under the Constitution to uphold national law. The Court under Chief Justice Marshall became a legitimate wielder of power because "the Justices were able to elevate their decisions above the plane of partisan politics, to transform political issues into legal ones, and thereby to increase the political power of the Court."[41] This power, established in the early Republic, allowed the Court to play a central role in the fight to apply the Bill of Rights to the states.

THE DRED SCOTT CASE AND THE CIVIL WAR After *Barron v. Baltimore* (1833), only ratification of the Fourteenth Amendment in 1868 made "incorporation" possible. A summary of the "*Dred Scott*" case (1857) clarifies the Fourteenth Amendment. The sectional crisis between North and South over the issue of slavery which had been intensifying since the 1830s came to a head in the mid-1850s. In 1857, the Supreme Court decided the case of *Scott v. Sanford,* in which it hoped to resolve this political crisis by a judicial decision.

Scott was a slave in Missouri who had been taken by his owner to Illinois, a free state, and to free federal territories. He brought a lawsuit in federal district court suing for his freedom on the theory that once he had landed on free land his natural right to freedom came into effect and he could not be re-enslaved by a return to Missouri. The jurisdictional grounds for his suit was the "Diversity of Citizenship" Clause of the Constitution (Art. III, § 2), which allows lawsuits "between Citizens of different States" to be heard by federal courts. The Supreme Court (7–2) ruled against Scott. In a notoriously pro-slavery opinion, Chief Justice Roger Taney (1777–1864) infuriated the North and probably hastened the onset of the Civil War by ruling that the **Missouri Compromise** of 1820, which drew an East-West line between free states to the north and slave states to the south, was unconstitutional. He ruled that slave owners had a substantive due process right in their "property" and that this right could be extended to any state of the Union.

The critical point of *Scott v. Sanford* in relation to the incorporation story is that Chief Justice Taney also ruled that no person of African descent, free or slave, could be a citizen of the United States because, in his view, that was the intention of the framers. Because Scott was not a citizen, he had no jurisdiction to sue under the diversity clause. After the Civil War, this portion of the case was overturned by constitutional amendment. Section 1 of the Fourteenth Amendment, declaring that "All persons born or naturalized in the United States and subject to the jurisdiction thereof, are citizens of the United States and of the State wherein they reside", was designed to nullify the legal effect of the *Dred Scott* case.

The Civil War was fought by the Union to preserve the unity of the United States and to abolish slavery. President Lincoln, after tactical hesitation, moved the nation in this direction in 1863 by the Emancipation Proclamation and by the profoundly influential Gettysburg Address, which affirmed that the promise of equality stated in the Declaration of Independence, and of republican government by majority rule, was the moral foundation of the American polity.[42] The Union victory in 1865 confirmed that the nation was indissoluble and that slavery was dead. In light of this history, incorporation is not a narrow or technical doctrine, but instead a crucial constitutional turning point in American history. Thus, the incorporation of First Amendment rights in the 1920s and criminal justice rights in the 1960s into the Fourteenth Amendment meant that the purposes for which the Civil War was fought were finally being achieved. The country was becoming more a unified nation and less a collection of contending regions. The rights of equal political participation in, and just treatment by, all units of government were slowly being applied more uniformly to all Americans. For this to happen, when American citizens came into *federal* courts complaining that *states* had violated their rights under the Fourteenth Amendment and the provisions of the Bill of Rights, these courts had to be prepared to enforce these rights. It took the better part of a century for this to happen.

The Post-Civil War Period, 1865–1935

THE RECONSTRUCTION AMENDMENTS The Civil War (1861–1865) profoundly changed America by ending slavery, replacing a spirit of state citizenship with a sense of American nationality, and making the federal government enormously powerful.[43] The **Reconstruction amendments** constitutionally confirmed these changes by abolishing slavery (Thirteenth Amendment, 1866), solidifying national supremacy (Fourteenth Amendment, 1868), and extending voting rights to newly freed men (Fifteenth Amendment, 1870).

Section 1 of the Fourteenth Amendment is critical to the incorporation doctrine:

> All persons born or naturalized in the United States and subject to the jurisdiction thereof, are citizens of the United States and of the State wherein they reside. No State shall make or enforce any law which shall abridge the privileges or immunities of citizens of the United States; nor shall any State deprive any person of life, liberty, or property, without due process of law; nor deny to any person within its jurisdiction the equal protection of the laws.

The first sentence of Section 1 overruled the *Dred Scott* case, creating national citizenship for all. The Fourteenth Amendment made the federal government a guarantor of the rights of national citizens against action by the states, and therefore empowered federal courts to rule on whether any state action—be it a constitutional provision, statute, court ruling, or the action of a state or local official—violated the rights of its state citizens. These rights conferred on citizens were stated in broad terms and placed limitations on the power of states: (1) privileges or immunities, (2) due process, and (3) equal protection. What the rights meant in practice was for future courts to determine. The Privileges or Immunities Clause reproduced similar language in the Federalism Article of the Constitution, stating that "[t]he Citizens of each State shall be entitled to all Privileges and Immunities of Citizens in the several States" (Art. IV, § 2). This was designed basically to ensure that a state cannot discriminate against persons from another state. The Fourteenth Amendment Due Process Clause paralleled that of the Fifth Amendment, except that it specifically operated on and limited the power of the states. The language of the Equal Protection Clause was novel. Read narrowly, it means that all citizens are to be treated equally in the courts, but this is hardly a proposition that needs special constitutional emphasis. Read broadly, it seems to confirm Lincoln's goal in the Gettysburg Address: to make the Declaration of Independence "a matter of founding law, [and] put its central proposition, equality, in a newly favored position as a principle of the Constitution."[44] Section 5 of the Fourteenth Amendment gave Congress the power to enforce Fourteenth Amendment rights against the states by enacting legislation, and it did so by passing various civil rights acts, including the Ku Klux Klan Act of 1871, now found at 42 United States Code § 1983, which allows citizens to sue persons who act "under the color of law" to violate federal civil rights.

Did the framers of the Fourteenth Amendment intend it to incorporate the Bill of Rights and overturn *Barron v. Baltimore* (1833) as the first sentence overturned *Dred Scott* (1857)? Statements by the amendment's leading proponents, Representative John A. Bingham and Senator Jacob M. Howard, made in the House and Senate during the debate concerning the Fourteenth Amendment, supported this intent. Nevertheless, for a century this interpretation was refused. Some judges and scholars argued that the statements of two legislators could not be taken to be the intention of the entire Congress and the ratifying states.[45] Federalism was the more fundamental reasons for resistance to incorporation. The federal judiciary, small in number and hampered by jurisdictional limits that were not lifted for several more decades by Congress, may not have had the capacity to enforce civil rights on a recalcitrant South. In the final analysis, it was just too big a change in the federal-state relationship for the majority of the justices of the Supreme Court to accept.[46]

An important ruling confirmed the reluctance of the Supreme Court to change this state of affairs. In *The Slaughter-House Cases* (1873), the first Fourteenth Amendment case to reach the Court, a false start was made in Fourteenth Amendment jurisprudence by stating that the amendment applied only to cases involving discrimination against African Americans. This position was quickly repudiated in subsequent cases. Although the Fourteenth Amendment was created to address issues arising out of the abolition of slavery, it was written in general language applicable to all persons under United States jurisdiction, not just African Americans. On the other hand, in deciding that the common occupation of butchering was not a "privilege or immunity" protected by the Fourteenth Amendment, the Court interpreted the clause so narrowly that it was never again the basis of a Supreme Court ruling; thus, the Fourteenth

Amendment Privileges or Immunities Clause is a dead letter.[47] The Court was explicit in relying on a states' rights understanding of state-federal relations:

> Unquestionably [the "late civil war"] added largely to the number of those who believe in the necessity of a strong National government. But, however pervading the sentiment, and however it may have contributed to the adoption of the amendments we have been considering, we do not see in those amendments any purpose to destroy the main features of the general system [of federalism].[48]

The Slaughter-House Cases aborted the idea that the Privileges or Immunities Clause would be used to inaugurate *total incorporation* of the Bill of Rights.

JUSTICE HARLAN AND THE FAILURE OF INCORPORATION The selective incorporation argument was made in many appeals from 1875 to 1911, but, with one exception, the Supreme Court did not find that any of the provisions of the Bill of Rights was applicable against the states through the Due Process clause. The only provision "incorporated" was the right to "just compensation" when property is taken by the government for public use, a right that is explicitly laid against the federal government in the Fifth Amendment. *Chicago, Burlington and Quincy Railroad Company v. Chicago* (1897) did not mention or specifically overrule the holding of *Barron v. Baltimore* (1833), but it did hold that the Due Process Clause required the states to grant just compensation and that this right could be guaranteed by federal courts. A double standard clearly applied. *Property* rights were so fundamental to the American polity that state violations of the Just Compensation Clause violated the constitutional rights of property owners. *Liberty,* however, was not offended by state rules of criminal procedure that afforded criminal defendants fewer protections than would federal rules under the Bill of Rights.

In 1875, the Supreme Court held, with little discussion, that the Seventh Amendment right to a jury trial in civil cases did not apply to state courts. Saying that state trial procedure is a matter for state law, it upheld a Louisiana statute that allowed a judge, without a jury, to render verdicts in discrimination cases (*Walker v. Sauvinet,* 1875). Justice John Marshall Harlan I joined the Court two years later in 1877 and served until his death in 1911. He championed the idea of incorporation in forcefully argued dissenting opinions. Except for *Chicago Railroad* (1897), the Court never agreed with him on an incorporation question. Nevertheless, because he elevated the debate above the perfunctory level of *Walker v. Sauvinet,* the "great dissenter" forced the cases to be decided in terms which laid the foundation for incorporation of First Amendment rights in the 1920s and of criminal justice rights in the 1960s.

Justice Harlan did this by shifting the incorporation test from the framers' intent to whether or not a right was *fundamental.* Although the Court at first could not bring itself to say that most of the liberties enumerated in the Bill of Rights are fundamental, the adoption of the test allowed a later generation to see rights in a different light. The fundamental rights approach was first adopted in *Hurtado v. California* (1884), holding that a state could use a *prosecutor's information* as the formal charges in a murder trial without violating due process. In a federal case, the charges had to be by a *grand jury indictment,* as required by the Fifth Amendment. Hurtado asked the Court to make grand jury indictments obligatory on the states. Harlan's dissenting opinion reviewed centuries of common law history to argue that the common law institutions, including the grand jury, were essential to the political rights cherished by Americans. Justice T. S. Matthews' (1824–1889) majority opinion generally agreed, but gave a few reasons why the grand jury was not a guarantee of liberty, including the fact that the original grand jury operated unfairly, and that established federal and state precedent held that the Fourteenth Amendment did not apply the Bill of Rights to the states. However, he also adopted the **fundamental rights test** as a general matter:

> In the Fourteenth Amendment, by parity of reason, it refers to that law of the land in each State, which derives its authority from the inherent and reserved powers of the State, exerted *within the limits of those fundamental principles of liberty and justice which lie at the base of all our civil and political institutions. . . .* (*Hurtado* at 121, emphasis added).

The phrase—**the fundamental rights test**—became the ultimate criterion of incorporation, and gained clarity as it was applied in specific cases. Justice Matthews did say that the Supreme Court would not uphold *any* state procedure of criminal justice. Laws or government practices that are blatantly arbitrary or discriminatory would be due process violations, even though established by the democratic process, for they would constitute the "despotism of the many, of the majority."[49] To the *Hurtado* majority, an information issued by an elected prosecutor was not unfair and did not undermine "fundamental principles of liberty and justice which lie at the base of all our civil and political institutions." In short, the grand jury is not a "fundamental" right. This is still the law.

Following *Hurtado,* the Court refused to incorporate a variety of other rights, finding that none of them were fundamental. *In re Kemmler* (1890) held that state-authorized electrocution, a novel method of execution, did not violate due process and was not a question that the Court could address under the Cruel and Unusual Punishment Clause of the Eighth Amendment. In a challenge to an Illinois law forbidding private militias, the Court held that the Second Amendment applied only to the federal government (*Presser v. Illinois* (1886)). In *Spies v. Illinois* (1887), an appeal from the celebrated 1886 Haymarket bombing trial in Chicago, in which eight anarchists later found to be innocent were executed, the Supreme Court held that state jury selection procedures, even if falling below federal court standards under the impartial jury provision of the Sixth Amendment, could not be challenged because state trial procedures did not come under the Sixth Amendment through the Fourteenth Amendment.[50] Various other cases held that the Fourteenth Amendment Due Process Clause was not a proper basis to challenge the number of peremptory challenges,[51] the sufficiency of indictments (*Leeper v. Texas,* 1891, unanimous; *Hodgson v. Vermont,* 1897, unanimous), the waiver of a jury trial (*Hallinger v. Davis,* 1892), or the time of execution (*McNulty v. California,* 1893[52]). The Court also ruled that diverse state-criminal procedure practices within different areas of the same state did not violate the Equal Protection Clause of the Fourteenth Amendment, holding unanimously in *Missouri v. Lewis* (1879) that separate appellate court for specified counties did not violate equal protection. In *Maxwell v. Dow* (1900), the Supreme Court upheld a Utah eight-person felony jury. The Court had previously held that the Sixth Amendment required twelve-person federal juries, the number prescribed by the common law. Ironically, this decision was an appeal from the Utah territory (*Thompson v. Utah,* 1898). When the territory became a state, the rights of its citizens under the Constitution appeared to diminish.

In the last great case of this era, *Twining v. New Jersey* (1908), the Court ruled that the Fifth Amendment privilege against self-incrimination was not incorporated into the Fourteenth Amendment. The trial judge informed the jury that they could take into consideration of guilt or innocence a defendant's refusal to testify in his own behalf. Twining argued that the right against self-incrimination guarantees a defendant an absolute right to remain silent at trial. Allowing a judge to inform a jury that silence can be used to infer guilt undermines a defendant's absolute right to remain silent and thus violates the privilege against self-incrimination. The *Twining* majority, using fundamental rights reasoning, categorized the New Jersey rule as a "form" of procedure rather than a fundamental right. The Court made clear it was concerned with protecting states' rights, warning that if it decides that a state procedure violates the Fourteenth Amendment, "it diminishes the authority of the State, so necessary to the perpetuity of our dual form of government, and changes its relation to its people and to the Union" (*Twining,* p. 92).

ADOPTING THE DUE PROCESS APPROACH The Supreme Court not only refused to incorporate the Bill of Rights' criminal provisions, it was reluctant to rule that grossly unfair state procedures directly violated due process. The horrible reality of lynch-mob justice forced the Court to intervene in state criminal justice.[53] It considered this approach but refused to take it in *Frank v. Mangum* (1915). In a nationally notorious case, Leo Frank, a twenty-nine-year-old factory superintendent was tried in Atlanta, Georgia, for the murder of a fourteen-year-old laborer, Mary Phagan, who was found dead in the factory basement. A lynch-mob formed outside the court, and the jury clearly heard its anti-Semitic chants, threatening to kill Frank if he was acquitted.[54] After his conviction, the death sentence, and a failed appeal to the Georgia Supreme Court, Frank filed a writ of habeas corpus in federal courts.[55]

The majority in *Frank* upheld the traditional rule that a *habeas corpus* petition can be granted only for a lack of jurisdiction, not for "mere" errors at law; habeas corpus was not a substitute for a state appeal. Because the trial court had jurisdiction, Frank's argument was that mob conditions surrounding the trial resulted in deprivation of jurisdiction, a position championed by Justice Oliver Wendell Holmes. However, it was too bold a step for the majority.[56] According to Liva Baker, Holmes' dissent, "one of the most forceful he ever wrote," was "a cornerstone of the future Holmes legend."[57] Guilt or innocence was irrelevant. What mattered was the fairness of the trial: "Mob law does not become due process of law by securing the assent of a terrorized jury. We are not speaking of mere disorder, or more irregularities in procedure, but of a case where the processes of justice are actually subverted. In such a case, the Federal court has jurisdiction to issue the writ" (*Frank,* p. 347). After losing this appeal, Governor John Slaton commuted Frank's death sentence to life in prison, an act that ruined his political career. It mattered little, for a band of men invaded Frank's prison, took him away, and lynched him from a big oak tree. "His swinging body became an immediate tourist attraction."[58]

Eight years later, the Court reversed the *Frank* ruling; by that time four justices on the *Frank* majority had left the Court. *Moore v. Dempsey* (1923) arose out of post-World War I labor disturbances and the attempts of African Americans to form an agricultural worker's union. This sparked armed resistance in Phillips County, Arkansas, where as many as two hundred African Americans and five whites died. Five African Americans were tried for murder in a lynch-mob atmosphere: mobs of whites roughed-up a defense lawyer; United States Army troops stopped a lynch-mob marching on the local jail from killing the defendants; a committee appointed by the state governor promised the mob that the defendants would be found guilty; African-American witnesses were tortured; and African Americans were systematically excluded from the jury.[59] Justice Holmes, now writing for the Court's majority, held that federal habeas corpus applied:

> It certainly is true that mere mistakes of law in the course of a trial are not to be corrected in that way. But if the case is that the whole proceeding is a mask—that counsel, jury and judge were swept to the fatal end by an irresistible wave of

> public passion, and that the State Courts failed to correct the wrong—neither perfection in the machinery for correction nor the possibility that the trial court and counsel saw no other way of avoiding an immediate outbreak of the mob can prevent this Court from securing to the petitioners their constitutional rights. (*Moore v. Dempsey,* p. 91)[60]

Moore v. Dempsey did not immediately revolutionize rules of federal habeas corpus or lead to many successful appeals by state defendants.[61] But *Moore v. Dempsey* established the principle that the Court could overturn unjust state convictions that violated Fourteenth Amendment due process. In the 1930s, this led the Court to reverse state convictions in several famous and important cases. In *Powell v. Alabama* (1932), resulting from the notorious "Scottsboro Case," the Court held that due process was violated because the defendants were not allowed time to prepare a defense and, under the circumstances, were not afforded lawyers. The Scottsboro defendants were retried, found guilty, and on further appeal, the Supreme Court held that their trial was unfair because African Americans were systematically excluded from Alabama juries (*Norris v. Alabama,* 1935). In 1936, the Court ruled that a confession obtained by torture violated due process (*Brown v. Mississippi,* 1936). This trickle of cases became a stream in the 1940s and a river by the 1950s. The Court had, by that time, made state criminal justice an "agenda" on its annual dockets. Throughout this period all justices agreed that the states must adhere to civilized standards while enforcing the law. But so-called conservative justices, exemplified by Felix Frankfurter, fought against incorporation and instead decided cases under the due process approach. More liberal justices, led by Hugo Black, exposed weaknesses in the case-by-case due process approach and pushed for correcting injustices by incorporating the rules that applied to federal courts under the Bill of Rights.

As the due process approach developed into a working doctrine in criminal cases, movement continued toward the incorporation of the criminal provisions of the Bill of Rights.

The Struggle for Incorporation, 1918–1960

THE INCORPORATION OF FIRST AMENDMENT CIVIL LIBERTIES Before the Court again considered incorporating criminal procedure provisions, a momentous shift in American constitutional liberties occurred. By the 1930s, the Supreme Court, for the first time, struck down *state* laws that violated rights in the First Amendment by reading them into the Fourteenth Amendment, despite the Amendment's text that began, "*Congress* shall make no law. . . ." The free speech cases arose out of state "criminal syndicalism" laws, designed to suppress left-wing political parties, that made it a crime to advocate violence against the government, and out of federal World War I era laws making it criminal to advocate resistance to the military draft. In important *dictum* in *Gitlow v. New York* (1925), Justice Edward T. Sanford writing for the Court assumed that "freedom of speech and of the press . . . are among the fundamental personal rights and "liberties" protected by the Due Process Clause of the Fourteenth Amendment from impairment by the States." In *Fiske v. Kansas* (1927), the Court, in overturning a conviction of a person who simply carried a radical labor manifesto on his person, stated that the Kansas Criminal Syndicalism Law infringed on due process, without mentioning First Amendment free speech. Finally, *Stromberg v. California* (1931) overturned a California law making it a crime to display a red flag as an emblem of opposition to organized government. *Stromberg* held (7–2), in an opinion by Chief Justice Charles Evans Hughes, that the state law violated First Amendment free speech, which was embraced by the liberty protected by the Fourteenth Amendment. Two weeks later, in *Near v. Minnesota* (1931), with the Chief Justice again writing the majority opinion, the Court struck down a state law that allowed a judge, acting without a jury, to stop publication of a newspaper article deemed "malicious, scandalous, and defamatory." *Near* prohibited censorship and "prior restraint" of publications, and explicitly stated that the freedom of press is included in Fourteenth Amendment due process and that prior restraint strikes at the core of the First Amendment. And in January 1937, a unanimous Court ruled in *DeJonge v. Oregon* that making it a crime to participate in a peaceful political rally violated the First Amendment right of peaceful assembly via the Due Process Clause. Together, these cases clearly "incorporated" First Amendment rights.

Thus, on the next occasion in which the Court explored a challenge to a state criminal prosecution under the Fifth or Sixth amendments, the constitutional landscape was vastly different. Did the incorporation of First Amendment rights (with the free exercise of religion to soon follow) mean that the Court would be obliged to incorporate rights into the criminal procedure amendments as well?

PALKO V. CONNECTICUT (1937) This question was answered in the negative in *Palko v. Connecticut* (1937), in an 8–1 opinion authored by Justice Benjamin Cardozo, a renowned former Chief Judge of New York, whose rulings often went against criminal defendants. A jury found Frank Palko (actually, Palka; his name was incorrectly spelled in court papers) guilty of the second-degree murder of police officers. He was sentenced to life imprisonment. Under a state law, the state appealed because it believed the trial judge made erroneous rulings favorable to the defendant. The state supreme court upheld the prosecution. Palko was retried, found guilty of first-degree murder, and sentenced to death.

He appealed to the United States Supreme Court, claiming a violation of the Fifth Amendment Double Jeopardy Clause as applied to states through Fourteenth Amendment due process. Because the first jury had implicitly acquitted him of first-degree murder, he argued that the retrial for the charge was double jeopardy.[62] The Court held that the Fifth Amendment double jeopardy guarantee did not apply against the states, despite the fact that a federal prosecution would violate double jeopardy on the facts of this case.

Justice Cardozo acknowledged the First Amendment incorporation cases. So as not to be forced to incorporate the other provisions in the Bill of Rights, Justice Cardozo drew a distinction between *fundamental rights* and *formal rights.* But whereas the freedoms of speech and press were "so rooted in the traditions and conscience of our people as to be ranked as *fundamental*" and thus included in due process liberty, criminal procedure rights were merely "*formal,*" and not a part of due process liberty. To be fundamental a right had to be essential to justice and to the American system of political liberty.

> We reach a different plane of social and moral values when we pass to the privileges and immunities that have been taken over from the earlier articles of the federal bill of rights and brought within the Fourteenth Amendment by a process of absorption. . . . If the Fourteenth Amendment has absorbed them, the process of absorption has had its source in the belief that neither liberty nor justice would exist if they were sacrificed. . . . This is true, for illustration, of freedom of thought, and speech. Of that freedom one may say that it is the matrix, the indispensable condition, of nearly every other form of freedom. (*Palko v. Connecticut,* pp. 326–27)

First Amendment rights are fundamental, and applicable to the states, because political freedom rests on the free exchange of political ideas and the ability of citizens to address the government in protest. Due process and a fair trial are also essential in that justice could not be achieved without them. But to Cardozo the real question was the meaning of "due process". Was every criminal procedure in the Bill of Rights "of the very essence of a scheme of ordered liberty" and thus included in Fourteenth Amendment due process liberty?

Cardozo's answer adopted a "flexible" approach. Noting that some "right-minded men" could see the Connecticut law as an attempt to ensure that justice proceed without error, he asked:

> Is double jeopardy in such circumstances, if double jeopardy it must be called, a denial of due process forbidden to the states? The tyranny of labels . . . must not lead us to leap to a conclusion that a word which in one set of facts may stand for oppression or enormity is of like effect in every other.

Thus, a flagrant breach, such as retrying an acquitted defendant again and again on the same charge for political reasons, would amount to a due process violation. But here the "state is not attempting to wear the accused out by a multitude of cases with accumulated trials." Cardozo noted that "[t]his court has ruled that consistently with those amendments trial by jury may be modified by a state or abolished altogether." If this was so, then the Court saw no "cruelty at all, nor even vexation in any immoderate degree." In summary, the Court said that the jury, or a "technical" rule of double jeopardy, could be eliminated and a civilized system of justice would stand. This cosmopolitan view, measuring procedural justice by abstract standards of fairness was finally set aside three decades later in *Duncan v. Louisiana* (1968) which concluded that procedural rights rooted in the common law, such as the trial by jury and rules against double jeopardy, were fundamental. The *Palko* doctrine held sway for a quarter of a century before the Court began to incorporate most of the criminal procedure rights in the Bill of Rights into the Fourteenth Amendment Due Process Clause.

ADAMSON *V.* CALIFORNIA (1947) Incorporation was revived in *Adamson v. California* (1947) through the efforts of Justice Hugo Black. Adamson argued that a state trial judge's comment on his failure to take the witness stand and testify violated his Fifth Amendment right against self-incrimination, the same issue raised in *Twining v. New Jersey* (1908); Adamson lost. The case was significant because of Justice Black's forceful dissenting opinion and because three additional justices now agreed with the incorporation. With one additional vote, the criminal procedure liberties in the Bill of Rights would be applicable to the states.

On trial for murder, Adamson was on the horns of a dilemma. If he took the witness stand to testify in his defense, the prosecutor would impeach his credibility by informing the jury on cross-examination that Adamson had prior convictions for burglary, larceny, and robbery. If Adamson did not take the stand, under California law the trial judge, in summation, could tell the jury that they could allow Adamson's failure to testify to influence their decision. Under federal law, the Fifth Amendment provisions that no person "shall be compelled in any criminal case to be a witness against himself" did not allow such judicial comment on the theory that judicial comment on a defendant's silence undermined the privilege against self-incrimination.

Justice Stanley Reed's majority opinion simply relied on the precedent of *Twining* and argued that due process was not directly violated because what the judge did in this case was not a brutal or gross violation of rights as seen in the lynch-mob cases. The judge's comment was, to some jurists, logical and made the trial a fair search for truth. Justice Felix Frankfurter, a strong liberal but also a staunch supporter of **judicial restraint,** concurred and became the champion of the Court's anti-incorporation faction. He downplayed the importance of the privilege against self-incrimination, saying, "For historical reasons a limited immunity from the common duty to testify was written into the Federal Bill of Rights, and I am prepared to agree that, as part of that immunity, comment on the failure of an accused to take the witness stand is forbidden in federal prosecutions." Frankfurter argued that if the framers of the Fourteenth Amendment wanted to apply the Bill of Rights to the states, they could have done so explicitly. He challenged Justice Black's "total incorporation" idea by stressing that the Court could employ the "due process approach" to overturn atrocious state action.

Justice Black argued for "total incorporation" in his dissent. His reading of the congressional debates over the passage of the Fourteenth Amendment (much of which was reprinted in an appendix to the *Adamson* case) led him to conclude that "one of the chief objects that the provisions of the Amendment's first section, separately, and as a whole, were intended to accomplish was to make the Bill of Rights, applicable to the states." (*Adamson,* pp. 71–72, Black, J., dissenting). The three liberal justices who followed Justice Black's lead (Justices Douglas, Murphy, and Rutledge) nevertheless went beyond total incorporation to espouse "incorporation plus"—incorporation of the Bill of Rights plus the due process approach where appropriate. Justice Black opposed the due process approach because he saw the use of discretionary power by the justices as instances of judicial tyranny and a violation of the limited constitutional powers given to judges to decide cases. His position was designed not only to limit state and local government, but also to limit the discretion of federal judges. Justice Murphy, in a separate dissenting opinion, stated that, "Occasions may arise where a proceeding falls so far short of conforming to fundamental standards of procedure as to warrant constitutional condemnation in terms of a lack of due process despite the absence of a specific provision in the Bill of Rights." (*Adamson,* p. 124, Murphy, J., dissenting).

INCORPORATION TURNS THE CORNER After *Adamson,* the likelihood of the Supreme Court adopting the incorporation doctrine increased substantcially. *Adamson* changed the landscape. The Vinson and Warren Courts were divided over civil rights from 1947 to 1961, and a slim conservative majority, led by Justice Frankfurter, decided criminal cases under a due process approach. Nevertheless, lawyers began to press pro-incorporation arguments in search and seizure cases on a more hospitable Court.

The issues in *Wolf v. Colorado* (1949) were whether the federal "exclusionary rule"—not allowing prosecutors to use evidence seized in violation of the Fourth Amendment—is engrafted onto the Fourth Amendment and whether it is part of due process liberty, applicable to the states.[63] Under the *Palko* standard, Justice Frankfurter, writing for the Court, held that the *substance* of the Fourth Amendment is basic to a free society and is "therefore implicit in 'the concept of ordered liberty' and as such enforceable against the States through the Due Process Clause." But, on the narrower question of the remedy for such a wrong, the Court declined to incorporate the exclusionary rule. Several reasons were given including the facts that: there was no common law exclusionary rule; other remedies existed (e.g., civil suits against the police); and thirty states had no exclusionary rule. Justice Black surprised many by concurring in Frankfurter's opinion because the exclusionary rule was announced by the Supreme Court in 1914 and was not in the Constitution's text. Justices Murphy, Rutledge, and Douglas dissented. They believed that exclusion was the only real "remedy" because the police virtually never lost civil suits brought against them in state courts: a right without a remedy is not a true right.

State petitioners continued to seek relief from improper search and seizures. In *Rochin v. California* (1952), police broke into the home of a suspected drug seller, invaded his bedroom, scuffled with him after seeing him swallow pills, and dragged him off to a hospital where he was forced to swallow an emetic to vomit up evidence. Justice Frankfurter, writing for the Court, threw out the evidence by relying on a subjective Fourteenth Amendment due process standard: "[T]he proceedings by which this conviction was obtained do more than offend some fastidious squeamishness or private sentimentalism about combating crime too energetically. This is action that shocks the conscience." These police activities "are methods too close to the rack and the screw to permit of constitutional differentiation." The phrase created a label for the Court's due process rule in search and seizure cases: the shocks the conscience test. Justice Black concurred, but argued instead that such acts compelled a defendant to be a witness against himself, suggesting that the Fifth Amendment prohibition against self-incrimination, which should be incorporated, applied to tangible as well as to testimonial evidence.

The *Rochin* test was criticized as too vague. What shocked the conscience of appellate judges was too capricious a standard to give guidance to police officers or trial judges. It gave the Court sweeping power to inject its likes and dislikes into the Constitution. This criticism was borne out by *Irvine v. California* (1954). The justices were clearly shocked by FBI electronic eavesdropping of the bedroom of a married suspect for over a month, characterized as "repulsive" by Justice Frankfurter. Still, the majority did not incorporate the Fourth Amendment exclusionary rule and limited *Rochin* to acts of physical violence, and not to eavesdropping.

The Court signaled its growing concern with civil liberties in search and seizure by overturning the "silver platter" doctrine in *Elkins v. United States* (1960). State police officers obtained evidence of crime by means of an illegal search and seizure of defendant's home. The evidence was suppressed by a state court. Afterward, the state officers left the evidence (illegal telephone wiretapping equipment) in the safe-deposit box of a local bank where federal agents obtained it and used the evidence as the basis of a federal prosecution. The Supreme Court held that the federal exclusionary rule applied even though the federal officers did not directly engage in the illegal search and seizure. This practice undermined state efforts to exclude illegally seized evidence by encouraging federal officers "tacitly to encourage state officers in the disregard of constitutionally protected freedom." Justice Stewart's majority opinion was quite favorable to the exclusionary rule.

The Due Process Revolution and the Counterrevolution

The Due Process Revolution

By 1962, the Supreme Court's membership had changed to include five pro-incorporation liberals: Justices Black and Douglas (Roosevelt appointees), Chief Justice Earl Warren and Justice William Brennan (Eisenhower appointees), and Justice Arthur Goldberg, appointed in 1962 by President John F. Kennedy. But even before this shift, the Court opened the floodgate of incorporation cases with *Mapp v. Ohio* (1961), which held that the Fourth Amendment exclusionary rule applied to eliminate illegally seized evidence from state as well as federal trials.

After *Mapp,* virtually every year during the 1960s brought the incorporation of an additional Bill of Rights provision into Fourteenth Amendment due process. The Eighth Amendment Cruel and Unusual Punishment Clause was applied to the states in 1962. A state law made narcotics *addiction* criminal. The Court viewed addiction as a disease and held in *Robinson v. California* that the conviction and punishment of a person for a *status* such as a disease was constitutionally forbidden cruel and unusual punishment. *Robinson* opened the door for the Supreme Court to consider *state* death penalty cases in *Furman v. Georgia* (1972) and *Gregg v. Georgia* (1976). In 1962, however, *Robinson* did not attract much popular attention. The next incorporation case, *Gideon v. Wainwright* (1963), was widely publicized and quite popular. It incorporated the right to counsel in an opinion authored by Justice Black, who had argued for its incorporation in a dissent twenty-one years earlier. Over half the states provided counsel for indigent defendants by 1963. The decision appealed to the American sense of fair play: once a defendant is haled into court, he should have the same basic "equipment" to fight his fight as does the prosecutor. Congress acted to ensure that counsel would be available for indigents in federal cases, and many local bar associations and courts willingly developed systems to provide counsel. There were no dissents in *Gideon,* although some justices argued the decision should be based on the due process approach rather than incorporation.

The right against self-incrimination, the point of contention in *Twining v. New Jersey* (1908) and *Adamson v. California* (1947), was incorporated and *Twining* was overruled in 1964 in *Malloy v. Hogan* and *Murphy v. Waterfront Commission of New York Harbor. Malloy* was a five-to-four decision bringing the Fifth Amendment right against self-incrimination into the Fourteenth Amendment by allowing a witness to refuse to answer questions before a state investigatory body under the Fifth Amendment. *Murphy* unanimously held that a state witness was protected from self-incrimination in federal courts and a federal witness was protected from self-incrimination in state courts.

Other cases incorporating Bill of Rights provisions came in quick succession: *Pointer v. Texas* (1965) (Sixth Amendment Confrontation Clause); *Parker v. Gladden* (1966) (Sixth Amendment right to an impartial jury); *Washington v. Texas* (1967) (Sixth Amendment right to subpoena witnesses under the Compulsory Process Clause); *Klopfer v. North Carolina* (1967) (Sixth Amendment right to a speedy trial); and *Benton v. Maryland* (1969) (Fifth Amendment protection against double jeopardy, overruling *Palko v. Connecticut,* 1937).

The Court incorporated the Sixth Amendment right to trial by jury in *Duncan v. Louisiana* (1968). Was a jury trial required for a crime carrying a maximum penalty of two-years imprisonment? To answer this, Justice Byron White analyzed the trend of the incorporation cases and concluded that the standard of what constituted a *fundamental right,* worthy of incorporation into the Due Process Clause and made applicable against the state, had shifted considerably since the 1937 *Palko* case:

> Earlier the Court can be seen as having asked, when inquiring into whether some particular procedural safeguard was required of a State, if a civilized system could be imagined that would not accord the particular protection. . . . The recent cases, on the other hand, have proceeded upon the valid assumption that state criminal processes are not imaginary and theoretical schemes but *actual systems bearing virtually every characteristic of the common-law system* that has been developing contemporaneously in England and this country. The question thus is whether given *this kind of system* a particular procedure is fundamental—whether, that is, a procedure is necessary to an Anglo-American regime of ordered liberty. (*Duncan v. Louisiana,* 1968, emphases added)

Before 1970, rules under constitutional rights were identical, whether applied directly through the Bill of Rights in *federal* cases or through Fourteenth Amendment due process in *state* cases. This position, however, did not hold up. The Sixth Amendment guaranteed federal defendants a jury trial for crimes punishable by six months' imprisonment, but not for petty crimes. In *Baldwin v. New York* (1970), the Court allowed the crowded New York court system to deprive defendants facing six months or less in jail of the right to a jury trial, defining such offenses as "petty." For the first time, *federal and state standards for rights diverged.* In a case decided the same day, *Williams v. Florida* (1970), the Court held that the common law twelve-person jury was *not* constitutionally mandated by the Sixth Amendment, upholding a state felony conviction by a six-person jury. Justice John M. Harlan II, who opposed the incorporation doctrine, noted that flexibility could have been introduced into constitutional criminal procedure by staying with the due process case-by-case approach of *Palko, Adamson,* and *Rochin.* Now, he argued, rights guaranteed to federal defendants were being diluted in order to impose Bill of Rights protections on the states. The Court was softening the clear meaning and requirements of the Bill of Rights in federal cases; the Court has continued this trend. State felony convictions based on less than unanimous jury verdicts were upheld in *Johnson v. Louisiana* (1972) and *Apodaca v. Oregon* (1972), creating the risk that plurality juries would be far less deliberative than unanimous juries. The Court may have felt that it went far enough with these jury cases and in *Ballew v. Georgia* (1978), held that a five-person jury violated the constitutional guarantee of a jury.

At present, a few rights in the First through Eighth amendments have not been incorporated into the Fourteenth Amendment. These include indictment by grand jury, no excessive bail, jury trial in civil cases, the quartering of soldiers, and the right to bear arms as part of a militia. Reflecting on the rights excluded as a result of the selective incorporation approach, a leading commentator suggests that "perhaps it is just as well that they remain unincorporated."[64]

The due process revolution nationalized criminal justice by opening the door to federal court intervention of local and state agencies and courts, making criminal procedure somewhat more uniform. This generated enormous antagonism toward the Supreme Court and its liberal chief justice, Earl Warren, by conservative politicians and many in law enforcement. Since 1970, the Supreme Court, with a more conservative membership under Chief Justices Burger and Rehnquist, has limited the expansion of pro-defendant criminal procedure rights but has not overruled incorporation. Most Americans, while wary of defendants' rights, nevertheless have come to accept the nationalization of the Bill of Rights.

INCORPORATION AND THE WARREN COURT AGENDA: RACIAL AND POLITICAL EQUALITY. The Warren Court (1954–1969) "agenda" was comprised of decisions in four broad areas: desegregation, equal voting rights, criminal procedure, and free expression.[65] These seemingly disconnected areas are, on closer inspection, closely related by the purpose of ensuring the *equal political participation* of all, which is fundamental to the American political system. Legitimacy of majority rule is undermined without equal participation, as minorities are prevented from forming political alliances to protect their interests. Republican government—government for the people—does not work properly unless all interests and minorities can participate and be heard. The Warren Court agenda was foreshadowed by the most famous footnote in constitutional law, **Footnote 4,** in *United States v. Carolene Products Co.* (1938), which hinted that the pre-New Deal Court's agenda of protecting property rights would be replaced by a civil rights agenda. Footnote 4 suggested three areas in which the Court might strike down state laws under the Fourteenth Amendment: (1) cases involving the Bill of Rights, (2) laws that restrict the normal political process by which people can repeal undesirable legislation, and (3) laws aimed at "discrete and insular" religious, national, or racial minorities.[66]

A century after the Civil War, issues of race and regionalism continued to divide America. The goal of racial segregation was to exclude African Americans from participation in economic, social, and political life, unlike other groups who could participate to advance personal and group interests. Segregation was not merely an example of injustice but a cancer in the body of American democracy. Another legal logjam that stifled political participation were state laws that entrenched voting districts that gave rural legislators disproportionate political power at the expense of growing urban and suburban districts. These legislators refused to allow redistricting in their states and the Supreme Court had, on earlier occasions, refused to rule that this violated the Equal Protection Clause of the Fourteenth Amendment, holding in *Colegrove v. Green* (1946) (4–3) that this was a "political question" barring jurisdiction. Justice Frankfurter who wrote the majority opinion clashed with Justice Black who wrote the dissent. Finally, state officials could use libel laws in such a way as to make vibrant criticism of the political status quo very costly. The Warren Court addressed each of these.

Its "one person, one vote" cases struck down disproportionate state voting apportionment systems that gave all votes equal political power (*Baker v. Carr,* 1962; *Reynolds v. Sims,* 1964). The problem was not racial discrimination in voting but political systems that were "locked up" and controlled by a minority who benefitted from unequal voting power. The Court's First Amendment cases were designed to ensure that people could engage in a vigorous public debate without reprisal, and thus actively participate in politics. To this end, *New York Times v. Sullivan* (1964) held that for public figures to recover damages in libel suits, they had to prove that false statements were made intentionally or in reckless disregard of the truth. It is telling that in *Sullivan,* segregationist officials brought a libel suit against civil rights leaders whose full page newspaper advertisement contained minor factual errors. This suit was an attempt by the segregationists to end civil rights activism by convincing the jury to award an extremely high monetary compensation which would, in turn, be used to put civil rights organizations out of business.[67] As for the Court's racial integration agenda, the meaning of *Brown v. The Board of Education* (1954), arguably the most important case of the twentieth century, was less about schools integration and more about tearing down a system of legal repression of a "discrete and insular" minority that carried over from days of slavery. As Professor John Hart Ely put it, the larger goal of these lines of cases was to "clear the channels of political change."[68]

The Warren Court's liberal criminal procedure agenda was intimately linked to these cases. It is no coincidence that many of the most severe violations of rights occurred in cases that arose in the South and involved minority defendants. The political repression of segregation was supported by a heavy handed, often brutal, criminal justice system that too often operated outside the boundary of the Rule of Law. African Americans from the South could be certain that attempting to vote or otherwise participate in the political system in any meaningful way would be blocked by official and unofficial force by a white-dominated criminal justice system, or by terror groups who were condoned by the system. The Court rarely articulated this historical understanding in its criminal procedure cases, but it was known and undoubtedly gave its criminal procedure rulings a special urgency.[69]

The Counterrevolution

With historic regularity, revolutions produce counterrevolutions. The Warren Court had severe political critics (see the *Law in Society* section in Chapters 1 and 2), and a reaction to its rulings began in the early 1970s. Between 1969 and 1972, four justices retired and President Richard M. Nixon appointed conservative replacements. Between 1969 and 1996, twelve new justices were appointed to the Court, four by President Nixon, one by President Gerald R. Ford, three by President Ronald Reagan, two by President George Bush, and two by President Bill Clinton. The appointment of ten new justices by conservative Republicans and two by a "new," or middle-of-the-road, Democrat definitely swung the ideological makeup of the Court to the right. This section provides an overview of the shift from liberal to more-or-less conservative rulings in the period since the Due Process Revolution.

"THE COUNTERREVOLUTION THAT WASN'T": THE BURGER COURT 1969–1986[70] President Nixon's appointment of four justices led many to believe that the selective incorporation of the Bill of Rights would be overturned.[71] These fears were abetted by Chief Justice Burger's critical rhetoric attacking the *Miranda* doctrine and the *Mapp* exclusionary rule in his early cases.[72] The Burger Court did not, however, execute a reactionary return to the preincorporation era. Instead, it held the line against the expansion of rights. "In place of the expected counterrevolution, the Burger Court waged a prolonged and rather bloody campaign of guerilla warfare. It typically left the facade of Warren Court decisions standing while it attacked these decisions from the sides and underneath."[73] For example, the *Miranda* rule stands after more than thirty years of conservative criticism, but a "public safety" exception allows prewarning questions (*New York v. Quarles,* 1984), and a defendant may be subsequently questioned after first having exercised *Miranda* rights by requesting the right to remain silent (*Michigan v. Mosley,* 1975). And although the *Mapp v. Ohio* (1961) exclusionary rule was not overruled, a good-faith-reliance-on-a-defective-search-warrant exception was created (*United States v. Leon,* 1984); and illegal evidence can be used in proceedings other than the criminal trial (*United States v. Janis,* 1976—tax hearing; *United States v. Calandra,* 1974—grand jury proceedings). The Burger Court was not uniformly pro-prosecution and has extended defendants' rights on several occasions. It established, for example, a warrant requirement for entry of a house to make a felony arrest (*Payton v. New York,* 1980), and declared random automobile stops to check driver licenses to be a Fourth Amendment violation (*Delaware v. Prouse,* 1979).

One measure of the success of a Supreme Court's "agenda" over the period of a chief justice's tenure is whether or not the Court provides a coherent conceptual foundation for its decisions. In general, scholars have found the Burger Court to be lacking a coherent set of guiding principles by which decisions can be measured.[74] Professor Charles Whitebread, examining the lack of doctrinal consistency, has suggested five ways in which the Burger Court approached criminal procedure cases that account for its generally conservative rulings, while not going to the point of rolling back the Warren Court's Bill of Rights incorporation revolution. First, the Court emphasized the Crime Control Model of the criminal process and was "eager to accommodate what it perceived as legitimate needs of effective law enforcement."[75] Second, the Court established a **hierarchy of constitutional rights.** Those Sixth Amendment rights concerned with the integrity of the trial and the truth-finding process are protected more strictly than are Fifth Amendment self-incrimination issues, which in turn are given more protection than Fourth Amendment rights concerning search and seizure. Third, this hierarchy is connected with a *concern for the factual guilt or innocence* of the party whose case is before the Supreme Court. Whitebread believed that this concern distorted the Supreme Court's overriding duty to develop sound and principled general rules for the guidance of the entire court system. A fourth aspect of the Court's approach was a "jurisprudential preference for *case-by-case analysis* rather than announcing its decisions in criminal cases in rules."[76] Whitebread saw this as the most dangerous characteristic of the Court's approach. This attribute fails to give lower courts and police clear cut rules by which to guide their actions. Whitebread has predicted a spate of future cases generated by a need to determine how the narrow distinctions established by the Court are to be applied in specific instances. Fifth, the Court fostered the "new federalism" that partially closed the door to federal courts for state defendants, thus transferring significant power over criminal procedure to the state courts. For example, the Court applied a cost-benefit analysis in *Stone v. Powell* (1976) and ruled that Fourth Amendment claims, once raised and decided in state courts, could not be heard again on federal habeas corpus when the state provided a full and fair hearing. The narrowing of federal habeas corpus jurisdiction reversed a hallmark of the Warren Court opening the door of the federal courts to state defendants in *Fay v. Noia* (1963). The reimposition of procedural barriers indicated an attitude of wishing to return to an era when federal protection of constitutional rights was minimal.

THE COUNTERREVOLUTION THAT WAS: THE REHNQUIST COURT 1986-PRESENT It now seems clear that with a few exceptions, the Supreme Court from the mid 1980s to the present has taken a far more conservative stance than the Burger Court. Weddington and Janikowski write about the "counter-revolution that is."[77] The counter revolution can be seen in search and seizure decisions. Although a few Rehnquist Court rulings have upheld traditional Fourth Amendment rights, these have had little practical effect on law enforcement. For example, the Court ruled that the common law "knock and announce" procedure is required by the Fourth Amendment. This ruling has little practical effect, for the "Amendment's flexible requirement of reasonableness should not be read to mandate a rigid rule of announcement that ignores countervailing law enforcement interests" (*Wilson v. Arkansas,* 1995). On the other hand, rulings that acknowledge drug courier profiles as a basis to stop individuals (*United States v. Sokolow,* 1989), that authorize drug "bus sweeps," (*Florida v. Bostick,* 1991); that allow searches based on anonymous telephone tips (*Alabama v. White* 1990); that uphold the "protective sweep" of homes during an arrest (*Maryland v. Buie,* 1990); that permit "plain feel" pat-downs (*Minnesota v. Dickerson,* 1993); that license electronic eavesdropping without minimization procedures (*United States v. Ojeda Rios,* 1990); that sanction arrests in violation of international law (*United States v. Alvarez-Machain,* 1992); that treat a police chase as not being a "search and seizure," (*California v. Hodari D.,* 1991); and that favor full searches of containers in automobiles without warrants (*California v. Acevedo,* 1991) have substantially unshackled police from serious Fourth Amendment limitations. Many see this diminution of rights as a giving political support to an uncontrolled war on drugs and as condoning modern racism.

As for the highly controversial law of confessions, John Decker writes, "The Burger and Rehnquist Courts have more recently reflected a degree of apparent discomfort with the principles of *Miranda,* for the great majority of the opinions interpreting *Miranda* decided since the Warren Court period have not vigorously followed its lead."[78] For example, the use of undercover agents in a jail setting is allowed. While *Miranda* on its face prohibits *custodial interrogation* without Fifth Amendment warnings, the Court held that because a jailed suspect who speaks to an officer posing as a fellow inmate is *not compelled,* no warnings need be given (*Illinois v. Perkins,* 1990). The Court has also supported an aggressive campaign by federal prosecutors to disallow effective opposing defense attorneys (*Wheat v. United States,* 1988, claiming there would be a conflict of interest) and has allowed money paid to defense attorneys by drug defendants to be forfeited (*United States v. Monsanto,* 1989; *Caplin & Drysdale v. United States,* 1989).

More telling than specific conservative rulings is the Rehnquist Court's tampering with underlying doctrines. In *Arizona v. Fulminante* (1991), a majority overturned a long-standing precedent and ruled that a coerced confession could be deemed "harmless error." Thus, if police coerce a confession and a court, in error, allows such a constitutionally invalid confession to be heard by a jury, a conviction based on the coerced confession can be upheld. The Court was explicit in directing that the central purpose of a trial is to decide questions of guilt or innocence; the introduction of unconstitutional evidence is of lesser importance. Perhaps the most dramatic example of the Rehnquist Court as an activist-conservative Court, interested more in achieving the "right" result than in upholding basic principles, is *Payne v. Tennessee* (1991), which allowed victim impact statements at death penalty hearings. What has shocked commentators is that *Payne* overruled two precedents that were only four years old and, in his opinion, Chief Justice Rehnquist openly stated that precedent is not important where earlier cases were decided by close votes (*Booth v. Maryland,* 1987; *South Carolina v. Gathers,* 1989). He believed "that **stare decisis** 'is not an inexorable command' but instead a 'principle of policy.' . . . *Stare decisis* principles are at their weakest point in 'constitutional cases,' he said, because correction through legislative initiative is virtually impossible."[79] He went on to say that precedent is more important in property and contract rights than in procedural and evidentiary cases. Justice Thurgood Marshall, dissenting, noted that under the majority's theory, the Court's rulings cannot be considered "impersonal reasoned judgements" and "[p]ower, not reason, is the new currency of this Court's decisionmaking." This was a polite way of saying that the majority opinion was lawless.

Finally, the Rehnquist Court has extended the work of the Burger Court in closing the door to federal and collateral appeals. *Brecht v. Abrahamson* (1993) made it more difficult for defendants to challenge errors on habeas corpus review of constitutional error than on direct appeal. Justice Rehnquist "explained that the beyond-reasonable-doubt standard had become too costly for the government."[80] These decisions display a Court that has become hostile to the claims of defendants. What is curious, and even brilliant, is that the Court has shifted virtually every rule and underlying doctrine in favor of the state while at the same time maintaining the facade of the essential right. Thus, the *Mapp* exclusionary rule exists and the *Miranda* warnings are still required, but these general rules are shot through with exceptions.

LAW IN SOCIETY

THE ORIGINAL INTENT DEBATE—THE POLITICS OF CONSTITUTIONAL INTERPRETATION

The expansion of the incorporation doctrine in the 1960s "federalized" and "constitutionalized" much of criminal procedure, increasing the rights of criminal suspects. This liberalizing trend met political resistance, as presidents began to run campaigns critical of such rulings and appointed Supreme Court justices who favored the police and the prosecution. Conflict over constitutional issues and Supreme Court cases is a staple of modern American politics—different views about school prayer, abortion, the *Miranda* warning, term limits, whether a sitting president can be sued in a civil case, affirmative action, grandparents' rights, habeas corpus appeals in the death penalty, and sexual harassment have all been "hot button" issues that have raised popular interest and have often generated support or opposition by political figures. This kind of controversy over specific Supreme Court cases and the trend of constitutional law is part of the normal politics of the Court. The Justices do not speak out publically about this controversy but go about doing their work in the eye of the storm.[81] Yet, there was one episode where a brief speech caused two Supreme Court justices to speak out against a perceived attack, an episode that indicated that underlying constitutional doctrines are far more important than specific rulings.

By the mid-1980s, the Court had become far more conservative than it was in the 1960s. At a speech given before the American Bar Association in July 1985, former Attorney General, under President Reagan, commented on the cases decided by the United States Supreme Court during its 1984–1985 term, in the areas of federalism, criminal procedure, and religion.[82] He praised the Court for its conservative rulings and castigated it for its decisions that were not favored by the Reagan administration. There was nothing controversial about the government making its views known about the Court's work—indeed this is part of a long tradition in American politics.[83] But at the end of this speech, Meese made a few comments that generated a political firestorm. He suggested that the incorporation doctrine was fundamentally flawed, arguing that the Court's so-called liberal-activist approach violated the *only* true way to interpret the Constitution, a path that the attorney general called "a Jurisprudence of Original Intention." This speech noted that in *Barron v. Baltimore* (1833) the Supreme Court ruled that the Bill of Rights applied only to the states, and then fast-forwarded to 1925 when the Court began to incorporate the Bill of Rights, i.e., to make them apply to the states in the areas of religion and free speech, as well as in criminal procedure.

The debate over whether the justices strictly follow the Constitution or inject their policy views is hardly new. However, Meese's speech struck a raw nerve. He made incorporation seem a totally unprincipled reversal of *Barron* and completely omitted any mention of the Fourteenth Amendment (1868). He accused the Court of unprincipled decision making. "[I]t seems fair to conclude that far too many of the Court's opinions were, on the whole, more policy choices than articulations of constitutional principle."

A response soon came from unexpected quarters—two justices of the Supreme Court. In October 1985, Justices John Paul Stevens and William Brennan, obviously stung and concerned at Meese's broadside, made forceful rejoinders in very public forums. Justices rarely engage in open debate on issues before the Court and so the importance of public exchanges between the attorney general and two Supreme Court justices was not missed by the news media.[84] Justice Stevens' speech made the front page of the *New York Times,*[85] and the aggressive nature of the attorney general's speech making drew the headline: "Supreme Court: Administration Trolling for Constitutional Debate."[86] The article said that "the debate transcends crime, abortion and other specific controversies. It reaches to the heart of the courts' role in the United States in restraining majority rule."

Justice Brennan, speaking at Georgetown University in October 1985, left little doubt that he was responding to Meese:

> [C]onstitutional interpretation for a federal judge is, for the most part, obligatory. . . .
>
> There are those who find legitimacy in fidelity to what they call "the intentions of the Framers." In its most doctrinaire incarnation, this view demands that Justices discern exactly what the Framers thought about the question under consideration and simply follow that intention in resolving the case before them. It is a view that feigns self-effacing deference to the specific judgments of those who forged our original social compact. But in truth it is little more than arrogance cloaked as humility. It is arrogant to pretend that from our vantage we can gauge accurately the intent of the Framers on application of principle to specific, contemporary questions. [87]
>
> [T]he political underpinnings of such a choice should not escape notice. A position that upholds constitutional claims only if they were within the specific contemplation of the Framers in effect establishes a presumption of resolving textual ambiguities against the claim of constitutional right.[88]

Justice Brennan was saying that it is difficult or impossible to really know what the framers thought about many issues and that Meese's position, purporting to be nonpolitical, had its own political agenda, i.e., wanting the Court to rubber-stamp the positions put forward by the Reagan administration. In every case, the "Jurisprudence of Original Intention" would result in a ruling against anyone claiming a right—the government would always win.

Justice Brennan responded to the serious argument that reducing judicial power to declare government acts unconstitutional is consistent with democratic theory:

> Faith in democracy is one thing, blind faith quite another. Those who drafted our Constitution understood the difference. One cannot read the text without admitting that it embodies substantive value choices; it places certain values beyond the power of any legislature.[89]

Here, Justice Brennan reasserted the authority of the Court to determine what is, or is not constitutional, first clearly established in *Marbury v. Madison* (1803), through the mode of judicial interpretation. He also implied that liberty is a value to be generally preferred over security. Soon after, Justice Stevens weighed in before the Federal Bar Association in Chicago, directly challenging Mr. Meese's attack on the incorporation doctrine.[90]

Much of the media responded critically to the attorney general's position. A *New York Times* editorial, blasting "Mr. Meese's Contempt of Court,"[91] charged him with willfully misunderstanding the import of cases and refusing to abide by clear precedent. Leading scholars such as Herman Schwartz and Henry Steele Commager wrote critical op-ed articles against Meese's position.[92] This controversy embroiled the legal community. A leading scholar and federal judge wrote that, before 1985, the issue of originalism "was one chiefly debated by academics. . . . The academic debate has been wordy and intense, but, until recently, has largely been an in-house controversy, muffled from public audition by the buckram bindings of the law reviews. . . . All this has changed."[93]

Why should a debate about such an abstract concept as the incorporation doctrine be so controversial when it is the holdings of specific decisions that are usually of direct political significance? Legal decisions in specific cases rest on underlying theories or doctrines; a change in the underlying doctrine ultimately produces lasting changes in the outcomes of cases. The Court, as a principled institution, should base its decisions on logic and principle. Unlike presidents and the Congress, the Court does not openly make rulings based explicitly on expediency or good policy. This would openly usurp the lawmaking authority of the "political" branches of government. On the other hand, there has never been an era when justices did not infuse their opinions with policy predilections. It seems impossible to avoid such predilections. Thus, the underlying doctrines of constitutional law have political content.

What the attorney general sought to achieve by his speeches is not entirely clear. In another speech, he said that a Supreme Court decision does not necessarily bind every person. "Was he hinting that a President should defy a direct Supreme Court order that conflicts with his view of the Constitution?"[94] Meese's spokesperson said "No," but Meese had attacked a famous 1958 desegregation ruling. This smacked of a heavy-handed attempt to politicize the Court's decisions and to hint to ultraconservative voters that the Reagan Administration would have liked to reverse *Brown v. Board* (1954) the school desegregation case. It is not accidental that at that time the Reagan administration was promoting several controversial federal court appointments and may have been laying a foundation for legitimating their views. It seems no mere coincidence that Judge Robert Bork, later President Reagan's failed nominee for the Supreme Court, spoke out in favor of Attorney General Meese's points in November 1985.[95] Meese's comments drew the conservative support of William F. Buckley, Jr., who said that Meese was simply trying to lead public opinion and "he does not seek to undermine the authority of the federal court system."[96]

But many thought that this was exactly his intention. The fact that two justices felt compelled to speak out publicly against the attorney general underscores this possibility. However, the public debate soon faded from view. The public counterthrusts of Justices Brennan and Stevens deflected Meese's position from gaining popularity among a broad spectrum of Americans. With President Reagan's nomination of Justice Rehnquist to replace retiring Chief Justice Burger and the appointment of conservative Justices Antonin Scalia and Anthony M. Kennedy, a reason for perpetuating a high-visibility debate declined.[97] And with Meese embroiled in a corruption scandal upon his early retirement, little remained in the public mind about the great "original intent" debate of 1985 to 1986.[98]

Is there any validity to Meese's position? In the aftermath of this public debate, very detailed examinations of this issue by leading scholars, including a Pulitzer Prize-winning history, overwhelmingly demonstrated that it is nearly impossible to know with certainty what the framers thought about specific issues.[99] Next, a scholarly and conservative judge, in a spirited defense of judicial restraint, nevertheless distanced himself from Meese's extreme views. Judge J. Harvie Wilkinson, III, characterized Meese's position as one where the "Constitution constrains judges to 'interpret the document's words according to the intentions of those who drafted, proposed, and ratified its provisions and its various amendments."' Judge Wilkinson said in effect that this is too simple, because a judge must use the power of reason to decide cases and to avoid injecting his or her personal views into decisions. In interpreting the Constitution, a judge must examine "the document's structural principles as in its literal text, as much in the unaccountable status of judges as in the Framers' intentions."[100] Indeed, most legal scholars, working lawyers, and judges know that the real basis for legal work and dispute lies in the doctrines developed by judges, in what Professor David Strauss calls *common law constitutional interpretation,* rather than in the specific words and purported intent of the framers.[101]

This episode is a reminder that the abstract doctrines of constitutional law create "winners" and "losers" and thus generate political concern. More precisely, the major doctrines of constitutional law, like the incorporation doctrine, are the framework within which specific cases are decided. The general thrust and direction of these doctrines tend to shape the outcome of the specific cases. Therefore, the issues argued in the 'original intent debate of 1985' were of profound significance. If, indeed, Meese were able to begin a trend that led to the downfall of the incorporation doctrine, the practical effect would have been a reversal of scores of civil rights and criminal procedure decisions. Rulings on abortion and affirmative action, which have been weakened in many ways, would have collapsed. If Meese's goal of the complete elimination of the incorporation doctrine were achieved, then the Bill of Rights would no longer apply to the acts of local and state police officers. Such a result would have made a far greater change in American society than many other issues that are prominently in the public eye.

SUMMARY

The basic functions of the Constitution include: establishing and structuring the government, creating the legislative, executive and judicial branches; limiting power to prevent tyranny by establishing checks and balances, providing rules to guide relations between the states, and between the federal and state governments and guaranteeing individual rights and liberties, and provide for the election of government officers and by explicitly guaranteeing fundamental rights.

The Constitution of 1789 protected liberty by ensuring the writ of habeas corpus and judicial independence.

Individual liberties are guaranteed in law by the Bill of Rights. Important rights such as due process and trial by jury are derived from English practices and institutions.

The incorporation doctrine is the idea that the Bill of Rights applies as a limitation on state law and state and local officers. Before the Civil War, the Supreme Court ruled that the Bill of Rights applied only to the federal government. Under the Due Process Clause of the Fourteenth Amendment, a state cannot infringe the right of each person, who is both a state and a federal citizen, of the rights of due process and equal protection. Congress and the federal courts have power to enforce the Fourteenth Amendment. Over the course of a century after 1868 the argument was made that specific provisions of the Bill of Rights are also guarantees of due process. The Court accepted this concept in the 1960s and in that decade incorporated most of the criminal procedure rights in the Bill of Rights so as to require that states abide by those rights.

The federal courts, in addition to finding that a state law or practice violated a right inherent in the Bill of Rights, may also find that a state practice violated Fourteenth Amendment due process if such a practice were fundamentally unfair, as determined by examining all of the facts and circumstances of the case.

Since the due process revolution of the 1960s, the Supreme Court has become quite conservative in the area of criminal procedure. The Burger Court (1969–1986), in accord with the temper of the times that combined political conservatism with individualism, maintained the incorporation of rights but limited the expansion of most rights and created several exceptions. The Rehnquist Court (1986 – present) has accelerated this trend and has been very activist and result oriented in upholding the power of the state against individual rights except in regard to property rights.

FURTHER READING

Leonard W. Levy, *Original Intent and the Framers' Constitution* (New York: Macmillan, 1988).

Michael Kent Curtis, *No State Shall Abridge: The Fourteenth Amendment and the Bill of Rights* (Durham: University of North Carolina Press, 1986).

Akhil Reed Amar, *The Constitution and Criminal Procedure: First Principles* (New Haven: Yale University Press, 1997).

ENDNOTES

1. Michael Stokes Paulsen, "A General Theory of Article V: The Constitutional Lessons of the Twenty-seventh Amendment," *Yale Law Journal* 103: pp. 677–789 (1993)
2. Alfred H. Kelly and Winfred A. Harbison, *The American Constitution: Its Origins and Development,* 5th ed. (New York: W.W. Norton, 1976), pp. 94–106; Samuel Eliot Morison, *The Oxford History of the American People* (New York: Oxford University Press, 1965), p. 279. The Articles were drafted in 1777.
3. Jack N. Rakove, *Original Meanings: Politics and Ideas in the Making of the Constitution* (New York: Vintage Books, 1997).
4. *U.S. Const.* Art. I., §§ 2 and 3, established the Congress, consisting of the House of Representatives and Senate.
5. *U.S. Const.* Art. II, § 1.
6. *U.S. Const.* Art. II, § 3.
7. There are exceptions. The president may establish policies through executive orders. A doctrine of inherent presidential powers has been used in times of crisis. See Clinton Rossiter, *Constitutional Dictatorship: Crisis Government in the Modern Democracies* (Princeton: Princeton University Press, 1948).
8. *U.S. Const.* Art. III., § 1.
9. See Henry R. Glick , *Courts, Politics and Justice,* 2nd ed. (New York: McGraw-Hill, 1988), pp. 34–48; D. Barrow and T. Walker, *A Court Divided: The Fifth Circuit Court of Appeals and the Politics of Judicial Reform* (1988).
10. Lawyers in the *Five Knights' Case,* also known as *Darnel's Case,* based their arguments in part on the Magna Carta. See Carl Stephenson and Frederick Marcham, *Sources of English Constitutional History* (New York: Harper & Row, 1937), p. 457.
11. Duker, *Habeas Corpus,* p. 46.
12. Stephenson and Marcham, *Sources,* p. 612.
13. See J. Willard Hurst, *The Law of Treason in the United States* (Westport, Conn.: Greenwood, 1971).
14. R. Kent Newmyer, *The Supreme Court Under Marshall and Taney* (Arlington Heights, Ill.: Harlan Davidson, 1968), p. 34. See Ron Christenson, ed., *Political Trials in History* (New Brunswick: Transaction Publishers, 1991), pp. 47–50; Milton Lomask, *Aaron Burr: The Conspiracy and Years of Exile, 1805–1836* (New York: Farrar, Straus, Giroux, 1982).
15. Kermit L. Hall, ed. *The Oxford Companion to the Supreme Court* (New York: Oxford University Press, 1992), pp. 52, 270; Lon Fuller, *The Morality of Law, Revised Edition* (New Haven: Yale University Press, 1969) pp. 57–62.
16. Levy, *Original Intent,* p. 157.
17. Carl Stephenson and Frederick Marcham, *Sources of English Constitutional History* (New York: Harper & Row, 1937), pp. 599–605.
18. Bernard Schwartz , *The Great Rights of Mankind: A History of the American Bill of Rights* (New York: Oxford University Press, 1977), p. 1.
19. Rutland, *Birth of Bill of Rights,* pp. 41–48; Bernard Schwartz, *The Great Rights of Mankind: A History of the American Bill of Rights* (Madison: Madison House, 1992), pp. 67–72.
20. Schwartz, *Great Rights,* pp. 72–91; Rutland, *Birth of Bill of Rights,* pp. 49–110.
21. Schwartz, *Great Rights,* pp. 101–3; Leonard Levy, *Original Intent and the Framers' Constitution* (New York: Macmillan, 1988), pp. 145–46.
22. See Morison, *American People,* pp. 270–76.
23. Schwartz, *Great Rights,* p. 255 (Madison's proposal), 262 (House proposal).
24. Schwartz, *Great Rights,* p. 177.
25. Schwartz, *Great Rights,* p. 177.
26. Schwartz, *Great Rights,* pp. 173–4; Price Marshall, "'A Careless Written Letter': Situating Amendments to the Federal Constitution," *Arkansas Law Review,* 51: 95–115(1998).
27. Michael Stokes Paulsen, (see note 1).
28. A spirited debate over the interpretation of the Bill of Rights pits the commonly held individual-rights view of the Bill against the notion that the Bill of Rights was primarily designed to achieve structural goals of preserving a healthy democratic and republican government. See Akhil Reed Amar, *The Constitution and Criminal Procedure: First Principles* (New Haven: Yale University Press, 1997); and Akhil Reed Amar, *The Bill of Rights: Creation and Reconstruction* (New Haven: Yale University Press, 1998). For a thoughtful criticism of Amar's criminal procedure book, see Carol S. Steiker, "'First Principles' of Constitutional Criminal Procedure: A Mistake?", *Harvard Law Review,* 112:680–93 (1999).
29. Charles Rembar, *The Law of the Land: The Evolution of Our Legal System* (New York: Touchstone, 1980), p. 169.
30. Stephenson and Marcham, *Sources,* p. 121. In later reenactments of the Magna Carta when new kings ascended the throne, ten clauses were dropped, and clause 39 became clause 29.
31. Stephenson and Marcham, *Sources,* pp. 577–9.
32. Colin Rhys Lovell, *English Constitutional and Legal History* (New York: Oxford University Press, 1962), p. 407. The research of John Langbein in "The Criminal Trial Before the

Lawyers," *University of Chicago Law Review* 45:263–316 (1978), indicates that for at least a half-century after *Bushell's* Case, English judges in fact overawed and directly influenced jurors in their deliberations during criminal cases.

33. For an exhaustive study on the development of the English jury with a focus on "jury nullification," see Thomas Andrew Green, *Verdict According to Conscience: Perspectives on the English Criminal Trial Jury, 1200–1800* (Chicago: University of Chicago Press, 1985).
34. Barron owned a wharf; the city diverted streams that lowered the water level, inflicting economic loss. Hall, *Oxford Companion,* p. 65.
35. Michael Kent Curtis, "Incorporation Doctrine," in Hall, *Oxford Companion,* p. 426.
36. Amar, op. cit. The quote is on p. 145; the discussion is on pp. 145–62.
37. See Robert Lowry Clinton, Marbury v. Madison *and Judicial Review* (University of Kansas Press, 1989); and Wallace Mendelson, *Supreme Court Statecraft: The Rule of Law* and *Men* (Ames: Iowa State University Press, 1985), pp. 207–62.
38. Most constitutional scholars support the Court's judicial review power. Raoul Berger, *Congress v. The Supreme Court* (New York: Bantam Books, 1969).
39. See Alexis de Tocqueville, *Democracy in America,* ed. J.P Mayer and trans. G. Lawrence (New York: Doubleday, 1969), pp. 99–105.
40. Bernard Schwartz, *A History of the Supreme Court* (New York: Oxford University Press, 1993), p. 43, citing *Fletcher v. Peck* at p. 136.
41. G. Edward White, *The Marshall Court and Cultural Change,* abridged ed. (New York: Oxford University Press, 1991), p. 197.
42. Gary Wills, *Lincoln at Gettysburg: The Words That Remade America* (New York: Simon and Schuster, 1992), p. 263.
43. For illuminating studies of reconstruction, and the implications of America's history of slavery for criminal justice, see Eric Foner, *Reconstruction: America's Unfinished Revolution 1863–1877* (New York: Harper & Row, 1988); and Fox Butterfield, *All God's Children: The Bosket Family and the American Tradition of Violence* (New York: Alfred A. Knopf, 1995).
44. Gary Wills, *Lincoln at Gettysburg: The Words that Remade America* (New York: Simon & Schuster, 1992), p. 145.
45. See *Maxwell v. Dow* (1900), pp. 601–2. "The problem in Congress was always the same. A few Republicans would speak in support of the amendment or the pending enforcement legislation and in so doing would typically present different interpretations of the amendment's meaning: then the party as a whole would vote overwhelmingly in support of the matter at hand without the individual members identifying the interpretation they preferred. The dynamic of Congress was such that a multiplicity of views about section one would persist." William E. Nelson, *The Fourteenth Amendment: From Political Principle to Judicial Doctrine* (Cambridge: Harvard University Press, 1988), p. 148.
46. Much of the scholarship on incorporation is reviewed by Henry J. Abraham, *Freedom and the Court: Civil Rights and Civil Liberties in the United States,* 4th ed. (New York: Oxford University Press, 1982), pp. 34–41. A more recent assessment concludes that the "weight of the evidence from the Thirty-ninth Congress supports the conclusion that the Fourteenth Amendment was designed to require the states to respect all guarantees of the Bill of Rights." Michael Kent Curtis, *No State Shall Abridge: The Fourteenth Amendment and the Bill of Rights* (Durham: Duke University Press, 1986), p. 129. See also Amar, op. cit.
47. Abraham, *Freedom,* pp. 46–47. David A. J. Richards, *Conscience and the Constitution: History, Theory, and Law of the Reconstruction Amendments* (Princeton: Princeton University Press, 1993), makes a convincing argument for the idea of total incorporation based on the Privileges or Immunities Clause.
48. Quotations from the *Slaughter-House Cases* are taken from Gunther, *Constitutional Law,* p. 41.
49. Citing *Loan Association v. Topeka,* 20 Wall. 655–62, in *Hurtado,* p. 537.
50. On the Haymarket case, see Paul Avrich, *The Haymarket Tragedy* (Princeton University Press, 1984).
51. *Brown v. New Jersey* (1899): State law normally provided twenty peremptory challenges to a murder defendant and twelve to the state; either party could request a "struck jury," which seemed to allow for a summary striking of a large number of names from an initial jury roll; in such case, each party was limited to five peremptory challenges. Justice Brewer wrote for the Court and Justice Harlan concurred. *Hayes v. Missouri* (1887): that prosecution has fifteen peremptory challenges in cities with populations over 100,000 and eight in other places does not violate the Equal Protection Clause (unanimous decision).
52. Delay of execution when state changed the 30 to 60-day waiting period to 60 to 90 days was not a due process violation.
53. See Howard Smead, *Blood Justice: The Lynching of Charles Mack Parker* (New York: Oxford University Press, 1986); Walter Francis White, *Rope and Faggot* (New York: Arno Press, 1969 [1929]).
54. Liva Baker, *The Justice From Beacon Hill* (New York: HarperCollins, 1991), pp. 468–69. The trial judge believed that Frank was innocent.
55. Liva Baker, *Beacon Hill,* pp. 470–1, 478–81.
56. *Frank v. Mangum,* p. 327. Holmes was joined in dissent by Chief Justice Charles Evans Hughes.
57. Liva Baker, *Beacon Hill,* p. 479.
58. Liva Baker, *Beacon Hill,* p. 481.
59. For an excellent history of the case, see Richard C. Cortner, *A Mob Intent on Death: The NAACP and the Arkansas Riot Case* (Middletown, Conn.: Wesleyan Press, 1988).

60. Justice James McReynolds (1862–1946) dissented, joined by Justice Sutherland (1862–1942). Later, Justice Sutherland would author a very strong pro-civil rights due process opinion for the Court in the most famous mob-justice case, *Powell v. Alabama* (1932)—the "Scottsboro case."
61. E.g., Justice Holmes refused to accept a petition in the Sacco and Vanzetti case, Liva Baker, *Beacon Hill,* pp. 606–7.
62. Richard C. Cortner, *The Supreme Court and the Second Bill of Rights: The Fourteenth Amendment and the Nationalization of Civil Liberties* (University of Wisconsin Press, 1980), pp. 126–39.
63. This area of law is re-examined in Chapter 4 of this text.
64. Abraham, *Freedom,* p. 90.
65. See Archibald Cox, *The Role of the Supreme Court in American Government* (New York: Oxford University Press, 1976); Arthur J. Goldberg, *Equal Justice: The Warren Era of the Supreme Court* (New York: Farrar, Straus & Giroux, 1971).
66. See generally John Hart Ely, *Democracy and Distrust: A Theory of Judicial Review* (Cambridge: Harvard University Press, 1980).
67. Kermit Hall, ed., *The Oxford Companion to the Supreme Court of the United States* (New York: Oxford, 1992), pp. 586–7.
68. See Ely, *Democracy and Distrust.*
69. See Foner, *Reconstruction*; Dan T. Carter, *Scottsboro: A Tragedy of the American South,* rev. ed. (Baton Rouge: Louisiana State University Press, 1979); and Harvard Sitkoff, *The Struggle for Black Equality 1954–1992,* rev. ed. (New York: Hill & Wang, 1993).
70. A widely cited book edited by Vincent Blasi, *The Burger Court: The Counter Revolution That Wasn't* (New Haven: Yale University Press, 1983) made it clear that the overall record of the Burger Court was quite mixed. This was in part because several liberal and moderate justices tempered the fierce conservatism of some of the new justices. But in general, the Court tended to be more conservative on criminal justice than other issues.
71. See, for example, L. Levy, *Against the Law: The Nixon Court and Criminal Justice* (1974).
72. *Bivens v. Six Unknown Named Agents* (1971); *Harris v. New York* (1971); see M. Braswell and J. Scheb II, "Conservative Pragmatism Versus Liberal Principles: Warren E. Burger on the Suppression of Evidence, 1956–86," *Creighton Law Review* 20 (1987):789–831.
73. A. Alschuler, "Failed Pragmatism: Reflections on the Burger Court," *Harvard Law Review,* 100:1436–56, p. 1442 (1987).
74. See, for example, A. Alschuler, "Failed Pragmatism," pp. 1449–56.
75. C. Whitebread, "The Burger Court's Counter-Revolution in Criminal Procedure: The Recent Criminal Decisions of the United States Supreme Court," *Washburn Law Journal* 24: pp. 471–98, p. 471 (1985).
76. *Ibid.*, p. 472.
77. Mary Margaret Weddington and W. Richard Janikowski, "The Rehnquist Court: The Counter-Revolution That Wasn't. Part II: The Counter-Revolution That Is," *Criminal Justice Review* 21(2): pp. 231–50 (1997).
78. John F. Decker, *Revolution to the Right: Criminal Procedure Jurisprudence During the Burger-Rehnquist Court Era* (New York: Garland Publishing, 1992), p. 65.
79. Decker, *Revolution,* p. 112.
80. Weddington and Janikowski, "Counter-Revolution That Is."
81. See David M. O'Brien, *Storm Center, The Supreme Court in American Politics, 5th ed.* (New York: W.W. Norton, 2000) (the justices do not publically respond to criticism but engage in "insider" politics); David G. Savage, *Turning Right: The Making of the Rehnquist Supreme Court* (New York: Wiley, 1992).
82. This speech is reprinted in relevant part in a pamphlet: The Federalist Society, *The Great Debate: Interpreting Our Written Constitution* (Washington, D.C.: The Federalist Society, 1986), pp. 1–10.
83. Harry P. Stumpf, *American Judicial Politics, Second Edition,* pp. 428–30 (Prentice Hall, 1998)
84. There are several reasons. Commenting on specific issues before a judgment is rendered gives the appearance of bias. Commenting on philosophical approaches is often done in the course of opinion writing where the justices can give more care to saying exactly what they mean. There is little public expectation that justices will openly comment on judicial issues. And, of course, much of the Court's business is not controversial and simply does not make good news. Despite this, it is not unheard of for justices to engage in writing on general issues in scholarly legal journals, but this is usually not aimed at reaching a mass audience.
85. S. Taylor, Jr. , "Justice Stevens, in Rare Criticism, Disputes Meese on Constitution," *New York Times,* Oct. 26, 1985, p. 1 (national ed.).
86. S. Taylor, Jr., *New York Times,* 28 Oct. 1985, p. 20 (national ed.).
87. Federalist Society , *The Great Debate,* pp. 13, 14.
88. *Ibid.*, p. 15.
89. *Ibid.*, p. 16.
90. *Ibid.*, pp. 27–30.
91. *New York Times,* 26 Oct. 1986, p. IV 24 (national ed.).
92. H. Schwartz, "The Right's Attack on the Court," *New York Times,* 14 October 1985, p. 21 (national ed.); Henry Steele Commager, "Meese Ignores History in Debate with Court," *New York Times,* Nov. 20, 1985, p. 27 (Midwest ed.).
93. Louis H. Pollak, "'Original Intention' and The Crucible of Litigation," *University of Cincinnati Law Review,* 867–89, p. 867 (1989).
94. S. Taylor, Jr. , "Meese and the Storm Over the Court," *New York Times,* October 27, 1986, p. A20.
95. Federalist Society , *The Great Debate,* pp. 43–52 (speech at the University of San Diego Law School).

96. William Buckley , "Is Edwin Meese Trying to Undermine the Constitution? No., Only to Tame the Court," *Detroit Free Press,* October 30, 1986, p. 15A.
97. The impact of the "original intent" debate was heightened by the major political battle that occurred in 1987 over President Reagan's nomination of Robert Bork to fill the seat of Justice Powell and its defeat by the Senate. See John Stookey and George Watson, "The Bork Hearing: Rocks and Roles," *Judicature* 71(4):194–6 (1988); Edward J. Bloustein "Did the 'Bork Case' Change the Meaning of Our Constitution?" *Judicature* 72(3): p. 145 (1988).
98. Meese was investigated by a special prosecutor and exonerated.
99. Leonard W. Levy, *Original Intent and the Framers' Constitution* (New York: Macmillan, 1988); and Jack N. Rakove, *Original Meanings: Politics and Ideas in the Making of the Constitution* (New York: Alfred A. Knopf, 1996).
100. J. Harvie Wilkinson, III, The Role of Reason in the Rule of Law, *University of Chicago Law Review,* 779– 809, p. 802 (1989).
101. David A. Strauss, Common Law Constitutional Interpretation, *University of Chicago Law Review* 63: pp. 877–935 (1996)

JUSTICES OF THE SUPREME COURT

THE ADVERSARIES
BLACK—FRANKFURTER

It is ironic that two New Deal liberals appointed by President Franklin Roosevelt came to be bitter foes on the Supreme Court. For many years, Justices Hugo Black and Felix Frankfurter clashed over vital issues, including the incorporation of the Bill of Rights, the extent to which speech could be regulated by the government, and whether the Supreme Court should intervene to equalize the voting representation of electoral districts. In the 1940s and 1950s Frankfurter usually had the upper hand as the intellectual leader of the conservative wing of the Court. But over time, Black's dogged pursuit of a more liberal agenda bore fruit, depriving Frankfurter of imposing his views on the entire Court.

Both justices were champions of democracy, yet each took a different approach to modern government and the Court's role in it. Their disagreements, based on deeply held philosophies of judging, became a matter of personal antagonism. On the question of incorporation, Black was motivated by a strong belief that the Supreme Court must adhere as closely as possible to the strict meaning of the constitution and should not use the Due Process Clause to insert its notion of what is "reasonable" into constitutional law. He recalled that a conservative Supreme Court had done this very thing prior to the New Deal and understood that unfettered power allowed courts to be as unjust as the legislative or executive branches. Out of this, emerged the idea that the Supreme Court had to apply the Bill of Rights in a literal sense to the states. Frankfurter, although a great proponent of the philosophy of judicial restraint, came to opposite conclusions. He not only believed that the justices ought to fill out the contours of the Due Process Clause in order to achieve fundamental fairness in criminal procedure, but also believed that the Fourteenth Amendment was not intended to incorporate the Bill of Rights.

HUGO L. BLACK

Alabama 1886–1971

Democrat

Appointed by
Franklin Delano Roosevelt

Years of Service
1937–1971

Collection of the Supreme Court of the United States. Photographer: Harris and Ewing

LIFE AND CAREER The son of a country storekeeper, Hugo Black received a law degree from the University of Alabama. He practiced law in Birmingham, representing poor people, white and black, in civil cases against large corporations and in criminal matters. He also served terms as a district attorney and as a city judge, where he tried to mitigate the harsh treatment of poor people. Active in politics, he was elected to the U.S. Senate in 1926 as a populist. He was a key supporter of President Roosevelt's New Deal program, backed the "court packing" legislation to increase the size of the Supreme Court, and was Roosevelt's first choice to fill a vacancy on the Court.

CONTRIBUTION TO CRIMINAL PROCEDURE Justice Black was the chief architect of modern constitutional criminal procedure. His foremost contribution was to champion the incorporation doctrine, picking up the mantle of the first Justice Harlan, and ultimately getting the Court to agree in the 1960s that the criminal provisions of the Bill of Rights should apply to the states as a matter of Fourteenth Amendment due process. He also wrote powerful opinions against coerced confessions and took the lead in formulating the doctrine that an attorney was an absolute requirement in all criminal.

SIGNATURE OPINION *Gideon v. Wainwright* (1963) In 1942, Black dissented in *Betts v. Brady*, which held that a state felony trial in which an indigent had to defend himself or herself was fair under the Due Process Clause. He strongly believed that a fair trial is impossible if a person has to defend himself or herself, and if a person cannot afford a lawyer, one must be provided by the government without cost. Prior to *Betts* he wrote the majority opinion in *Johnson v. Zerbst* (1938) which held that in a federal felony prosecution, the assistance of counsel is essential unless the defendant knowingly and intelligently waives counsel. His persistence in pursuing this goal succeeded in *Gideon*, where the Court incorporated the Sixth Amendment right to counsel into the Fourteenth Amendment, thus requiring the states to provide counsel for indigent defendants.

Assessment Justice Black is widely recognized as one of the greatest justices, the intellectual leader of the Warren Court, and the single greatest influence on the development of modern constitutional criminal procedure. In other constitutional areas, he led the Court, along with Justice Douglas, toward an "absolutist" vision of First Amendment free speech, and he spearheaded the move to require states to reapportion voting districts to equalize the voting power of voters in different districts.

Although many of the positions he supported defined a "liberal" policy agenda, he was not so much a liberal in judicial philosophy as were other Roosevelt appointees such as Douglas, Murphy, or Rutledge. Rather, his judicial philosophy may be better described as "strict constructionist" or "constitutional fundamentalism." He believed that the Court should strictly adhere to the terms of the Constitution, which he tended to define in fairly narrow terms.

Thus, even in the incorporation area, he maintained an independent stance. He did not vote for the incorporation of the Fourth Amendment exclusionary rule in *Wolf v. Colorado* (1949) because the rule was not stated explicitly in the Constitution. He later developed the perspective that the exclusionary rule could be incorporated only if it were seen as also protecting Fifth Amendment values against self-incrimination.

Further Reading

Gerald T. Dunne, *Hugo Black and the Judicial Revolution* (New York: Simon and Schuster, 1977).

Felix Frankfurter

Massachusetts 1882–1965

Independent

Appointed by Franklin Delano Roosevelt

Years of Service: 1939–1962

Collection of the Supreme Court of the United States. Photographer: Pach Brothers Studio

Life and Career Frankfurter emigrated to America with his family from Vienna at the age of twelve and grew up in the Lower East Side Jewish ghetto in New York City. He graduated from the City College of New York and attended Harvard Law School, becoming editor of the *Harvard Law Review* on the basis of his top grades. After graduating in 1906, he worked in a large law firm for a while, but soon chose a public service career. As a protege of Henry L. Stimson, a leading Progressive, he went to Washington in 1911 when Stimson became secretary of war, forming an intellectual circle of young lawyers who befriended Justice Holmes.

In 1914, Frankfurter was appointed to the Harvard Law School faculty, a position he held until his appointment to the Court. During his tenure, he became a nationally known liberal activist who served as a labor mediator during World War I, attended the Paris Peace Conference in 1919, represented Zionist interests, co-founded the American Civil Liberties Union, contributed to *The New Republic* magazine, spoke out for the convicted anarchists Sacco and Vanzetti, and provided free counsel for the National Consumers' League. His co-authored book, *The Labor Injunction*, attacked the federal courts for stifling the labor movement. He was the co-director in 1921 of the ground-breaking Cleveland Crime Survey, a multidisciplinary social scientific study of the administration of justice. He appeared frequently before the Supreme Court on behalf of unions and other progressive causes.

As a Harvard professor, he developed a following among his students resulting from a combined passion for academic excellence and a zeal for public service. He had a close rapport with several Supreme Court justices and selected law clerks from among his students for Holmes and Brandeis. During the New Deal, he became an important advisor to President Roosevelt and placed many of his former students in important administrative and policy-shaping positions, thus enhancing his influence.

Contribution to Criminal Procedure Frankfurter's liberal policy temperament clashed with his philosophy of judicial restraint. As a result, his positions in criminal procedure were inconsistent, but must generally be counted as conservative. On this side, he staunchly opposed the total incorporation of the Bill of Rights championed by Hugo Black and favored by the liberal wing of the Court; he voted for the rule that a judge's comment on a defendant's silence does not undermine the privilege against self-incrimination; he opposed the extension of the right to counsel to all defendants in state cases; and he characterized the Fourth Amendment exclusionary rule as a mere remedy and not a constitutional rule. Nevertheless, he was sharply critical of abuses of power by the

(Continued)

police and when interpreting the flexible Due Process Clause, ruled in favor of defendants in cases involving coerced confessions and search and seizures that "shocked the conscience." In the entrapment area he favored the objective test.

Signature Opinion *Rochin v. California* (1952) The "stomach-pump" case perfectly expressed Frankfurter's judicial philosophy of restraint and respect for the authority of the states, except where the actions of local police or state courts have so grossly violated a person's right to fair treatment that a judge could exercise judgment to deem the actions as violations of due process. Frankfurter fashioned a standard—due process is violated where police action "shocks the conscience." He trusted the wisdom of the courts to determine what shocks the conscience and somehow believed such judgment would be objective and not simply private notions of what is acceptable. Justices Black and Douglas dissented, arguing that this vague standard gave judges too much power.

Assessment Frankfurter was a giant of American constitutional law, as a scholar, a public servant, and justice. He was expected to be a leading liberal on the Court, but his judicial philosophy of restraint overcame his liberal instincts. As the Court's agenda swung from economic issues to civil liberties, he failed to sense the direction of the country and the Court's special role as a guardian of liberty. Thus, he adopted cramped positions in many free speech cases and ruled against finding that seriously imbalanced state electoral districts violated the Equal Protection Clause. In supporting the school desegregation case Frankfurter played a leading liberal role, but thereafter he took a more cautious approach than did other justices. His conservative views were generally repudiated by the liberal Warren Court, although some of his rulings, including the "shocks the conscience" test, have been relied on by today's far more conservative Court.

Further Reading

Melvin I. Urofsky, *Felix Frankfurter: Judicial Restraint and Individual Liberties* (Boston: Twayne, 1991).

CHAPTER 3

THE FOURTH AMENDMENT AND THE EXCLUSIONARY RULE

This guarantee of protection against unreasonable searches and seizures extends to the innocent and guilty alike. It marks the right of privacy as one of the unique values of our civilization and, with few exceptions, stays the hands of the police unless they have a search warrant issued by a magistrate on probable cause supported by oath or affirmation.

—Justice William O. Douglas, *McDonald v. United States*, 335 U.S. 451, 453 (1948)

CHAPTER OUTLINE

KEY TERMS AND PHRASES *(CONTINUES ON NEXT PAGE)*

Attenuation rule
Balancing test
Bivens suit
Contempt of court
Contraband
Damages
Derivative evidence
Disgorgement
Exclusionary rule
Expectation of privacy
Fruit of the poisonous tree doctrine
General-reasonableness construction
General warrant
Inevitable discovery rule
Independent source rule
Injunction
Pattern and practice suit
Property theory

Particularity requirement
Reasonableness clause
Reparation
Section 1983 suit
Standing
Tort
Trespass
Warrant clause
Warrant-preference construction
Writ of assistance

The structure and content of search and seizure law is the product of several historic developments. First, the English common law ideal of the privacy of one's home solidified into a legal rule protecting that privacy against *government* invasion shortly before the framing of the Constitution (1787). Next, the framers guaranteed this right in the Fourth Amendment of the Bill of Rights (1789–1791). Then, about a century after the framing, the Supreme Court developed a remedial rule, the **exclusionary rule,** to ensure that evidence seized in violation of the Fourth Amendment's requirements would not be used in federal court to convict a person. The next major historic development in Fourth Amendment doctrine was the extension of the federal exclusionary rule to the states via the process of incorporation in *Mapp v. Ohio* (1961) (see Chapter 2). Another doctrinal shift of historic proportions occurred in the 1960s when the Court sought to replace the property-rights theory of Fourth Amendment protections with a functional theory (also known as the **balancing test**) based on individual privacy rights balanced against the legitimate requirements of law enforcement. The centerpiece of this effort was the **expectation of privacy** doctrine announced in *Katz v. United States* (1967) (see Chapter 4).

These historic developments are the focus of this chapter. Keep in mind that throughout the twentieth century the Supreme Court has been building and refining many doctrines of search and seizure law. This complex body of law is covered in Chapters 3–6.

THE COMMON LAW BACKGROUND

The old English saying that a "man's home is his castle" expresses a universally understood desire for privacy found in ancient civilizations.[1] Historian William Cuddihy's conclusion that until the year 1600, English law protected against *private,* but not *governmental* intrusion is of special importance to the development of the Fourth Amendment (1791). "By 1760, however, public opinion had inverted the relative importance that it assigned to these considerations. Promiscuous searches by the government were now recognized as more onerous than undesired visits by private persons."[2] This revolution was rooted in changed social conditions and political thought, especially the emergence of a modern political theory of liberty in the mid-eighteenth century (see Chapter 1).

This new thinking was seen in two important legal cases of the 1760s that influenced the creation of the Fourth Amendment. The first, known as *Paxton's Case* or the *Writs of Assistance Case,* arose in colonial Massachusetts and was argued and decided in 1761. The second set of cases, the *Wilkes'* cases, was a series of civil lawsuits arising out of the political persecution of John Wilkes a critic of King George III. These cases solidified a climate of opinion in the colonies that was critical of general search warrants, and led to their prohibition in the general language of the Fourth Amendment that forbids "unreasonable searches and seizures."

Up to the 1760s, most English search warrants were general warrants. A **general warrant** could be issued by a judicial or a non-judicial governmental official who did not personally have to be aware of probable cause for a search. "Promiscuously broad warrants allowed officers to search wherever they wanted and to seize whatever they wanted, with few exceptions."[3] General warrants were described as "a sort of legal pass key to all doors that places everyone's privacy at the capricious mercy of its holder."[4] Beginning with the great English jurist and Parliamentarian Edward Coke in 1642, criticism of general warrants grew in favor of specific warrants that had to specify the place to be searched and the items to be seized.[5] Nevertheless, most warrants continued to be of the general kind.

A **writ of assistance** was a type of general warrant that authorized the crown official who was issued the warrant "to command the assistance" of a peace officer or a nearby person to execute the writ. The writ allowed a search for a specific purpose and was executed in the daytime. Writs of assistance were enormously unpopular in the colonies because they were used by the British government to enforce unpopular laws. Customs officers with writs of assistance could enter warehouses and even homes to search for goods that were imported without paying the customs taxes and to collect unpaid duties. Crown impressment gangs used writs of assistance to invade private homes and public places like taverns "to kidnap able bodied men for service in the royal navy."[6] Once issued, the writ lasted for the life of the sovereign, plus six months.

After George II died, a customs officer in Massachusetts petitioned for a new writ of assistance. In February 1761, sixty-three leading Boston merchants challenged the legality of the application, presenting their case in the colony's high court before five judges, who included Chief

Justice Thomas Hutchinson. James Otis, a leading attorney, represented the merchants. He offered a learned and passionate argument: The law authorizing the writs of assistance "is against the fundamental principles of English law" and is, therefore unconstitutional and void. John Adams, a future president of the United States and then young attorney, was present and was deeply impressed by Otis' argument. In 1776, as a delegate to the Continental Congress and as a signer of the Declaration of Independence, he reflected that the movement for American independence began with the writs of assistance dispute. The Boston merchants lost their case; nevertheless, the writs continued to be unpopular and were not well-enforced because of hostile attacks on revenue collectors. To generate revenue, England passed the Townshend Act of 1767, authorizing the highest court in each American colony to issue writs of assistance to customs officers. What had been a local Massachusetts grievance, now became a major source of friction between the colonies and the mother country.[7]

The Wilkes' cases, argued in England, were a resounding political defeat of general warrants. They arose after John Wilkes (1725–1797), a British agitator, journalist, and member of Parliament, published the *North Briton,* Number 45, in 1763, a newsletter sharply critical of George III and his government. The king and Parliament tried to stifle his political attacks by charging him with seditious libel, a serious political crime. An English secretary of state issued a general warrant to officers to search for the newsletter and other writings. "Crown agents enforcing the warrants had unfettered discretion to search, seize, and arrest anyone as they pleased. They ransacked printer's shops and houses, and arrested forty-nine persons, including Wilkes, his printer, publisher, and bookseller. The officers seized his private papers for incriminating evidence after a thorough search; thousands of pages and scores of books belonging to persons associated with him were also seized."[8]

The case became a major political controversy on both sides of the Atlantic Ocean. "In the colonies, 'Wilkes and Liberty' became a slogan that patriot leaders exploited in the service of American causes."[9] Wilkes and his colleagues fought back in the courts in a series of civil lawsuits charging that the general searches were illegal. The courts upheld Wilkes and his allies. In general, the cases found that the searches were not authorized by law, were excessive, and that officers of the crown could be sued. "[T]he government paid a total of about 100,000 pounds in costs and judgments," an enormous sum at the time.[10]

In the most important of these cases, *Entick v. Carrington* (1765),[11] Lord Camden, chief justice of the Court of Common Pleas, demolished every argument put forth by the government to support the legality of the warrants. He ruled that general warrants were not authorized by act of Parliament or case law; that general warrants to search for papers were not like specific search warrants for stolen goods; and although the government had issued such warrants since the Glorious Revolution of 1688 that fact does not make the warrants legal "simply through long usage" or the previous silence of the courts. The court firmly rejected the blatantly political argument that the needs of the state took precedence over individual rights: "Political policy is not an argument in a court of law."[12] Lord Camden stressed the constitutional importance of the case and its connection to liberal political theory by noting that:

> The great end for which men entered into society was to secure their property. That right is preserved sacred and incommunicable in all instances where it has not been taken away or abridged by some public law for the good of the whole. . . . [Otherwise,] by the laws of England every invasion of private property, be it ever so minute, is a trespass *(Entick v. Carrington).*

Thus, just prior to the period of American state and federal constitution building (1776–1791), the common law had evolved to a point where general warrants were so disfavored as to be declared illegal in some cases. A person who had been arrested under a general warrant and whose home and other property had been invaded and searched by government agents, could sue executive officers who authorized general search warrants and agents who executed the warrants and recover substantial **damages** if the arrests and searches were illegal.

THE CREATION OF THE FOURTH AMENDMENT: ITS ORIGINAL AND CURRENT UNDERSTANDING

Currently, there is a lively debate among constitutional historians about the meaning of the Fourth Amendment to the framers.[13] This debate is not purely academic. If the entire body of Fourth Amendment law created by the Supreme Court since 1886 is built on a faulty notion of the original meaning of the Fourth Amendment, it could lead to substantial reconsideration. A brief outline of the arguments helps the student get a better understanding of how the Supreme Court and legal scholars perceive the structure and meaning of the Fourth Amendment.

The writs of assistance and Wilkes' controversies led most of the new states to include prohibitions against general warrants in their new state constitutions and bills of rights passed after 1776.[14] When it came time to draft a Bill of Rights to amend the new U. S. Constitution in 1789 (see Chapter 2), Representative James Madison included such a provision. His draft drew heavily on the Massachusetts provision, written by John Adams, which used the novel phrase "unreasonable search and seizure." The provision that became the Fourth Amendment was ratified in 1791:

> The right of the people to be secure in their persons, houses, papers, and effects, against unreasonable searches and seizures, shall not be violated, and no Warrants shall issue, but upon probable cause, supported by Oath or affirmation, and particularly describing the place to be searched, and the persons or things to be seized.

Unlike many of the early state bills of rights, the Fourth Amendment did not outlaw general warrants in specific terms. The modern interpretation of the amendment, stated in many cases, is that it contains two clauses: the **reasonableness clause** and the **warrant clause.** Under this construction, the ultimate test of constitutionality of any search and seizure is whether it was *reasonable.* Not all searches have to be authorized by a judicial warrant. *If* a search or arrest warrant is required, then it must meet the **particularity requirements** stated in the warrant clause.

A strong disagreement exists between more conservative and more liberal justices and scholars about the relative importance of the warrant clause. More conservative jurists, applying a **general-reasonableness construction,** have established a balancing test to determine if search and seizures are proper without a warrant and have come very close to saying that search warrants are not actually required by the Fourth Amendment. This understanding of the Fourth Amendment has been gaining ground in recent decades. The more traditional construction, favored by liberal jurists, is the **warrant-preference construction:** Warrantless searches and seizures are presumptively unreasonable, except for a narrow group of search warrant exceptions that were known at common law, namely, entries in hot pursuit, the search of mobile vehicles, and the search of a person who has just been arrested. All modern legal thinkers, nevertheless, whether favoring the "general-reasonableness" or the "warrant-preference" approaches, agree on the two-clause understanding of the Fourth Amendment.[15] Indeed, until the very recent findings of historians, it was generally believed that this two-clause construction was intended by the framers.[16] However, the most penetrating studies lead to the conclusion that the original intent of the framers and the ratifiers of the Fourth Amendment was to ban Congress from authorizing general warrants and to ban judges from issuing them—nothing more.[17]

The two-clause wording of the Fourth Amendment seems so obvious, and the needs of modern law enforcement are so pressing, that modern commentators have "read back" the modern understanding of the Fourth Amendment into perceptions of the intent of the framers. It seems inconceivable today that the framers were not concerned with warrantless searches of police officers. As Professor Thomas Y. Davies notes, however, there were no police officers in 1791, at least in the modern sense. Constables were few and were viewed as untrustworthy.[18] In the late colonial era and at the time of the framing, there was *no* discretion used in constables' decisions to make arrests or searches upon probable cause. Like any citizen, a constable could lawfully arrest or search only if the person to be arrested did in fact *committ* the crime, or if **contraband** *actually* was found; if the constable acted on suspicion or probable cause and was wrong, the constable could be sued for false imprisonment or **trespass.** Further, misconduct by an officer was, paradoxically, seen not as official misconduct, but as *personal* misconduct. As a result, the government never committed a wrongful arrest or search, and the few officers who made arrests or conducted searches almost always did so under the authorization of a warrant. "[F]raming-era common law never permitted a warrantless officer to justify an arrest or search according to any standard as loose or flexible as 'reasonableness.'"[19] There was, consequently, no pro-active policing at this period.

In light of criminal justice history, it is understandable that the Fourth Amendment was intended only to outlaw general warrants, and that the Framers were unconcerned with warrantless arrests and searches. The framers and the ratifiers were concerned *only* about the dangers of general warrants. Madison's first draft of the Fourth Amendment proposed that the "right of the people to be secure . . . against unreasonable searches and seizures, shall not be violated *by* warrants issuing without probable cause . . ."—a wording that would make the general-reasonableness construction impossible.[20]

Given the needs of a modernizing society, this original understanding, with its extremely tight rein on official discretion, soon began to erode. In the late nineteenth and early twentieth centuries, the Supreme Court began to erect modern Fourth Amendment law with the exclusionary rule at its center. Organized police departments are so actively involved in performing warrantless arrests, stops, and searches, that any Court that took Fourth Amendment values seriously would inevitably attempt to provide reasonable controls. Virtually none of the hundreds of Supreme Court Fourth Amendment cases deal with issues of general warrants. Indeed, the Supreme Court seems to have authorized, even required, general warrants for administrative searches.[21]

The historical debate is salient to modern law because the Supreme Court (or at least some of its justices) purports to base its jurisdiction and the legitimacy of its decisions on being true to the "intent of the framers." If the justices are mistaken regarding the intent of the Fourth Amendment, then the body of law they have created may be in question. Worse still, if the framers intended constables to have absolutely no authority to act "reasonably" when interfering with a person's liberty or privacy, and instead must be strictly controlled by judicial warrant, then the entire edifice of modern law enforcement could be deemed unconstitutional. Much depends on the philosophy of judging held by members of the Court. As noted in Chapter 1, justices differ along a judicial continuum philosophy from judicial activism or judicial restraint. Activist justices such as William Brennan (liberal) or William Rehnquist (conservative) have had little hesitation in accepting the words and the history of the Fourth Amendment as a mandate to fashion decisions that support their quite divergent views of constitutional policy. Two sitting justices, Antonin Scalia and Clarence Thomas, say that their decisions have to be guided by the original intent of the framers. Other justices justify particular decisions in part based on their understanding of history, although the Court's use of history has been inconsistent.[22] Assuming that Professor Davies' "authentic" reading of the Fourth Amendment challenges accepted views, "conservatives" may welcome the shrinking of the Fourth Amendment, while more "activist" jurists, comfortable with the Supreme Court's creation of a body of law to deal with the needs of individual liberty and public safety in a modern world, will not feel constrained to modify the law.[23] This is so, especially in view of the framers' concern with personal liberty.

For the student, two points are important. First, it is likely that some changes to certain Fourth Amendment doctrines may occur if the "authentic" understanding of the amendment is accepted. Thus, understanding the underlying reasons for doctrines, rather than simply memorizing the rules, is necessary because the rules may change. Second, the large body of constitutional law is kept fairly stable by the operation of stare decisis, and it is unlikely that there will be a wholesale revolution in Fourth Amendment law.[24] For that reason, the text presents the standard understanding of Fourth Amendment law, based primarily on the decisions and analyses of the Supreme Court.

DEVELOPMENT OF THE EXCLUSIONARY RULE, 1886–1921

The Fourth Amendment exclusionary rule simply says that evidence obtained by police or other governmental officers in an unconstitutional manner is not admissible in a court of law to prove the defendant's guilt. A simple outline of the rule's development is that:

1. there was no exclusionary rule at common law;
2. the text of the Fourth Amendment does not require that illegally seized evidence be excluded;
3. the Supreme Court adopted an exclusionary rule for all federal prosecutions in *Weeks v. United States* (1914);
4. the exclusionary rule was extended to state prosecutions via the incorporation doctrine in *Mapp v. Ohio* (1961); and
5. since 1971, the Supreme Court has weakened but retained the exclusionary rule in many cases, most notably in *United States v. Leon* (1984).

These legal developments show that this process not only was complicated but, as many have observed, was filled with inconsistencies.

The Supreme Court decided very few Fourth Amendment cases in the nineteenth and early twentieth centuries. It was not until Prohibition (1921–1933) that a large number of federal cases were decided, leading to a more complete body of search and seizure law. In the early cases, the Court was quite sensitive to the civil liberties values inherent in the Fourth Amendment. For example, *Ex Parte Jackson* (1878) stated, in dictum, that sealed letters sent through the mails could not be opened by postal authorities without a warrant. Because the defendant did not challenge the opening of the package in which illegal lottery tickets were mailed, the issue of exclusion did not arise. However, in the major case of *Boyd v. United States* (1886), the Supreme Court did suppress the use of evidence obtained by federal customs authorities, but did not establish a clear Fourth Amendment exclusionary rule.

Boyd v. United States was an odd case in several ways. To begin with, there was no actual search and seizure; instead, a subpoena was issued to E. A. Boyd & Co. to turn over an invoice on cases of imported glass to determine whether customs taxes had been paid. Boyd challenged the law, which required that an invoice be presented or else a court could presume that import duties had not been paid. The Supreme Court agreed with Boyd, holding that the order to produce the invoice and the law which authorized the order were unconstitutional and void. The Court created an expansive definition of a search and seizure, and conflated Fourth and Fifth amendment rights:

> The principles laid down in *[Entick v. Carrington]* affect the very essence of constitutional liberty and security. They reach farther than the concrete form of the case then before the court, with its adventitious circumstances; they apply to all invasions on the part of the government and its employes of the sanctity of a man's home and the privacies of life. It is not the breaking of his doors, and the rummaging of his drawers, that constitutes the essence of the offence; but it is the invasion of his indefeasible right of personal security, personal liberty and private property, where that right has never been forfeited by his conviction of some public offence,—it is the invasion of this sacred right which underlies and constitutes the essence of Lord Camden's judgment. Breaking into a house and opening boxes and drawers are circumstances of aggravation; but any forcible and compulsory extortion of a man's own testimony or of his

> private papers to be used as evidence to convict him of crime or to forfeit his goods, is within the condemnation of that judgment. In this regard the Fourth and Fifth Amendments run almost into each other. *(Boyd v. United States,* p. 630)

By ruling that a subpoena for a document was the equivalent of a search that infringed the Fourth as well as the Fifth amendment's right against self-incrimination, the Court avoided establishing an exclusionary rule that would apply to the illegal seizure of other items that were not written documents.

Virtually none of the points of law decided in *Boyd* are operative rules today. Business documents are no longer immune from a subpoena under the Fifth Amendment,[25] a subpoena is not a search,[26] and the melding of the Fourth and Fifth amendments is no longer considered good law (this is discussed later in the section on the theories of the exclusionary rule). Yet, *Boyd* remains an important case as the precursor to the Fourth Amendment exclusionary rule. The Supreme Court moved hesitantly toward this rule. It affirmed the traditional rule in *Adams v. New York* (1904), that "courts do not stop to inquire as to the means by which the evidence was obtained," i.e., there is no rule for excluding illegally seized evidence from a criminal trial. Despite this, the *Adams* Court stood by the earlier exclusionary ruling in *Boyd,* apparently limiting it to cases in which testimony is actually or virtually compelled (in *Boyd,* the non-production of the invoice led to an automatic finding that the tax was not paid), or invasions of a private home, or laws authorizing such things. Thus, no clear-cut Fourth Amendment exclusionary rule existed as of 1904. It *was* established a decade later in *Weeks v. United States* (1914), and rounded out by *Silverthorne Lumber Co. v. United States* (1920) and *Gouled v. United States* (1921).

The *Weeks* Court adopted a straightforward Fourth Amendment exclusionary rule, not tied to the Fifth Amendment privilege against self-incrimination. Fremont Weeks was arrested by local police without a warrant at his place of work; at the same time, a United States marshal entered Weeks's home without a warrant and "carried away certain letters and envelopes found in the drawer of a chiffonier." Weeks' demand for the return of incriminating papers before trial was denied and he was convicted in federal court for using the mails to transport lottery tickets. The Supreme Court held that all evidence seized without warrant was in violation of the Fourth Amendment and had to be returned; it could not be used against the defendant to prove his guilt.

> The effect of the Fourth Amendment is to put the courts of the United States and Federal officials, in the exercise of their power and authority, under limitations and restraints as to the exercise of such power and authority, and to forever secure the people, their persons, houses, papers and effects against all unreasonable searches and seizures under the guise of law. This protection reaches all alike, whether accused of crime or not, and the duty of giving to it force and effect is obligatory upon all entrusted under our Federal system with the enforcement of the laws. The tendency of those who execute the criminal laws of the country to obtain conviction by means of unlawful seizures and enforced confessions, . . . should find no sanction in the judgments of the courts which are charged at all times with the support of the Constitution and to which people of all conditions have a right to appeal for the maintenance of such fundamental rights. (*Weeks,* pp. 391–92).

The Court indicated, however, that its ruling was not meant to eliminate the search of a person lawfully arrested for evidence of crime, including contraband such as burglars' tools. The remedy of exclusion was inextricably tied to the constitutional right, but a deterrence rationale was also hinted at: "If letters and private documents can . . . be seized and held and used in evidence against a citizen accused of an offense [as in this case], the protection of the Fourth Amendment declaring his right to be secure against such searches and seizures is of no value, and, so far as those thus placed are concerned, might as well be stricken from the Constitution."

The constitutional basis of the exclusionary rule was confirmed and strengthened by Justice Oliver Wendell Holmes' brief opinion in *Silverthorne Lumber Co. v. United States* (1920). Frederick W. Silverthorne and his father were indicted for a federal crime and arrested at home, while federal agents entered their business offices without a warrant, and took business documents. The district court agreed with defendant's contention that their Fourth Amendment rights were violated and, on their demand, ordered the documents returned. However, the government photographed the documents and these copies were the basis of a subpoena for the original documents. Silverthorne refused to comply with the subpoena. The district court, although having found that the documents were originally procured by an unconstitutional seizure, nevertheless ordered compliance with the subpoena. On refusal, the company was fined and Silverthorne was ordered jailed until he turned over the original documents.

The Supreme Court reversed the lower court's judgment. In Holmes' words, to allow the government to seize evidence in violation of the Fourth Amendment, and then use the knowledge gained by that wrong to obtain the evidence "legally," "reduces the Fourth Amendment to a form of words." Therefore, "[t]he essence of a provision forbidding the acquisition of evidence in a certain way is that not merely evidence so acquired shall not be used before the Court but that it shall not be used at all." This is the crux of one exclusionary rule theory that will be addressed later in this text: The government cannot profit from its illegal action. As Professor William Heffernan notes, this "no use" rule was fully rights-based and went further than the present scope of the exclusionary rule, which allows illegally obtained evidence to be used to impeach a lying witness, in civil deportation cases, as a basis for framing grand jury questions, and in other areas.[27]

Holmes added one important exception to the exclusionary rule: "Of course this does not mean that the facts thus obtained become sacred and inaccessible. If knowledge of them is gained from an independent source they may be proved like any others, but the knowledge gained by the Government's own wrong cannot be used by it in the way proposed." These rules later became known as the **fruits of the poisonous tree** doctrine and the independent source exception. The rationale is that government violation of a defendant's Fourth Amendment rights does not lead to a windfall in the guise of a dismissal of the case. The government can use other evidence to convict, if that evidence is obtained by a legal route.

The final case solidifying and expanding the federal exclusionary rule was *Gouled v. United States* (1921). The United States Army suspected Gouled of defrauding it in equipment contracts. The Intelligence Department had an army private, a business acquaintance of Gouled, go to his office as an undercover agent, under the pretense of making a friendly call. While there, the private surreptitiously took documents that were used to prove the fraud. Later, a search warrant was issued and executed for additional incriminating documents. The documents were admitted into evidence over Gouled's timely objection, and he was convicted. The Supreme Court ruled that all the documents were taken in violation of the Fourth Amendment and had to be excluded from evidence. The Court held that the secret search and seizure, made by stealth while Gouled was not present, violated his Fourth Amendment rights, and that the *admission* of the documents into evidence violated his Fifth Amendment right against self-incrimination.

> In practice the result is the same to one accused of crime, whether he be obliged to supply evidence against himself or whether such evidence be obtained by an illegal search of his premises and seizure of his private papers. In either case he is the unwilling source of the evidence, and the Fifth Amendment forbids that he shall be compelled to be a witness against himself in a criminal case (*Gouled v. United States,* p. 306).

This shows that the Supreme Court still did not think in terms of an exclusive Fourth Amendment exclusionary rule, as it had in *Silverthorne,* but would rely on the Fourth and Fifth amendments in relevant cases, thereby adding confusion to the theoretical basis of the exclusionary rule.

The Court's civil liberties preference was accentuated by establishing what is known as the "mere evidence" rule. Gouled objected to the seizure of documents that (1) were his property, (2) were not contraband, and (3) tended to prove Gouled's involvement in a fraud conspiracy. The Court indicated that:

> at the time the Constitution was adopted stolen or forfeited property, or property liable to duties and concealed to avoid payment of them, excisable articles and books required by law to be kept with respect to them, counterfeit coin, burglars' tools and weapons, implements of gambling "and many other things of like character" might be searched for in home or office and if found might be seized, under search warrants, lawfully applied for, issued and executed (*Gouled v. United States,* p. 310).

From this, the Court reasoned that the suspect's property, even if it is incriminating evidence, that does not fit the category of (a) contraband, (b) instrumentalities of the crime, or (c) stolen property, may not be seized under an otherwise valid search warrant. Such "mere" evidence is absolutely protected against seizure. The Court eventually dropped this rule in *Warden v. Hayden* (1967) (Chapter 4).

Fruits of the Poisonous Tree Doctrine

Silverthorne v. United States (1920) added a necessary corollary to the exclusionary rule: evidence derived from knowledge obtained by an illegal search and seizure is not admissible. Were such **derivative evidence** admissible, police officers could violate Fourth Amendment rights with impunity, and then, after the original evidence is excluded, use information gained from the illegality to get a "legal" search warrant. *Silverthorne*'s doctrine was the basis of an obscure case decided in a brief per curiam opinion of the Supreme Court, according to Professor Heffernan.[28] In *Smith v. Ohio* (1990) two plainclothes police officers, without a warrant and without probable cause or reasonable suspicion, stopped a man exiting a convenience store carrying a brown paper grocery bag marked with the store's logo. Without identifying himself as an officer, Officer Thomas told Smith to "come here a minute." Smith kept walking but stopped when Officer Thomas identified himself as a police officer. Smith put the sack he was carrying on the hood of his car. Officer Thomas asked Smith what the bag contained. Smith did not respond. The officer reached for the bag and "rebuffed [Smith's] attempt to protect the bag, pushed [his] hand away, and opened the bag." Drug paraphernalia were found and became the basis of an arrest and conviction. The Supreme Court reversed the conviction concluding that the search was not justified on any Fourth Amendment ground. There was no basis for a self-protective stop under *Terry v. Ohio* (1967), the property was not abandoned, and there was no search incident to arrest—indeed, in *Smith,* the arrest occurred *after* the search. It is axiomatic under the Fourth Amendment that justification for searches must be provided *prior to* the search. *Retroactive justification* turns the Amendment into a sham.

The fruit-of-the-poisonous-tree metaphor was penned by Justice Frankfurter in *Nardone v. United States* (1939): what is excluded is not only the illegally seized evidence (the "poisonous tree"), but also different evidence *derived from* the illegally seized evidence (the "fruits"). Allowing the use of derivative evidence would create a rule "inconsistent with ethical standards and destructive of personal liberty." The Court in *Nardone* excluded not only the exact words overheard in a wiretap that violated a federal statute, but any information derived from the overheard conversations.

Silverthorne and *Nardone* recognize that the exclusionary rule, including the exclusion of derivative evidence, is not a windfall to the defendant—it does not lead to automatic dismissal of charges or to an amnesty on the use of other *properly obtained* evidence. The Supreme Court has recognized three exceptions to the derivative evidence exclusion: (1) evidence obtained from an independent source, (2) inevitable discovery, and (3) attenuation. One case noted that the inevitable discovery exception is an extrapolation of the independent source exception (*Murray v. United States,* 1988).

INDEPENDENT SOURCE The Supreme Court has allowed illegally seized evidence when the evidence was obtained in a constitutional manner that was entirely unconnected to the illegality—from an independent source. In *Segura v. United States* (1984), a group of police illegally entered Segura's apartment. A search warrant was later obtained based on information developed before the illegal entry took place. The Supreme Court excluded evidence in plain view during the illegal search but allowed use of evidence obtained under the search warrant—it was independent of the illegal entry. In *Murray v. United States* (1988), police illegally entered a warehouse and saw suspicious bales believed to contain marijuana. This illegal entry was not mentioned in an affidavit for a search warrant. Nevertheless, the Court allowed the use of evidence obtained by executing the warrant because it was lawfully issued on other competent evidence.

INEVITABLE DISCOVERY Illegally seized evidence is admissible if it was inevitably discovered independently of the unconstitutional action. *Brewer v. Williams* (1977) *(Williams I)* held that evidence of a murdered girl's body was excluded because it was discovered based on an unconstitutional interrogation (a so-called Christian Burial Speech, see Chapter 8). The Supreme Court, in *Nix v. Williams [Williams II]* (1984), held that this evidence was properly introduced at a retrial because a search party was within two-and-a-half miles of the body when it was found. Members of the search party were instructed to look into culverts (where the body was placed) and would have covered the area where the body was located. Thus, it inevitably would have been found, whether or not the defendant divulged its location to the police. The motivations of the police who improperly took the confession were irrelevant.

ATTENUATION Evidence derived from an illegal or unconstitutional source is allowed into evidence where, for some reason, the *link* between the initial illegality and the evidence sought to be introduced has become so *weak* or *tenuous* that the "fruit" has become "untainted." In *Nardone*, Justice Frankfurter wrote: "Sophisticated argument may prove a causal connection between information obtained through illicit wiretapping and the Government's proof. As a matter of good sense, however, such connection may have become so attenuated as to dissipate the taint." The widely cited case of *Wong Sun v. United States* (1963) clearly explicates the attenuation doctrine. Six or seven narcotics officers illegally entered the apartment of James Wah Toy behind his laundry shop at 6:00 A.M., rousted the inhabitants, and questioned Toy. Based on names given by Toy, the agents questioned several people about drug dealing. The Supreme Court excluded an exculpatory admission by Toy as well as confessions and drugs obtained from a person questioned immediately after the raid on Toy's apartment because this evidence was the "tainted" fruit of the illegal entry. On the other hand, Wong Sun had been released after arrest and he returned voluntarily several days later to make an incriminating statement. The Court held that this voluntary statement was admissible because the connection between the arrest and the statement had "become so attenuated as to dissipate the taint" (p. 491). The test for determining whether attenuation exists is: "whether, granting establishment of the primary illegality, the evidence to which instant objection is made has been come at by exploitation of that illegality or instead by means sufficiently distinguishable to be purged of the primary taint."[29]

Attenuation issues arise when a "proper" confession is made after an illegal arrest. The fact that *Miranda* warnings are given does not break the link between an illegal arrest and a confession, nor does the passage of two hours between the illegal arrest and the confession attenuate the illegality (*Brown v. Illinois,* 1975). To make *Miranda* warnings a "cure-all" for illegal police action would encourage illegal arrests and dilute the effectiveness of the *Miranda* exclusionary rule. Likewise, a six-hour delay between an illegal arrest and a confession, followed by a ten-minute meeting between the defendant and friends, did not attenuate the initial illegality despite three *Miranda* warnings (*Taylor v. Alabama,* 1982). On the other hand, evidence was allowed in *New York v. Harris* (1990). Police illegally arrested Harris at his home without a warrant, read *Miranda* rights, and obtained a confession in the house. Taken to the police station, Harris again was read his rights, signed a waiver form, and confessed. The first confession was suppressed as the fruit of an illegal police action. But the Court held the station house confession to be admissible. The Court held that Harris was legally in custody, because an illegal arrest does not deprive the court of jurisdiction to try the suspect. Therefore, "the statement, while *the product* of an arrest and being in custody, was *not the fruit* of the fact that the arrest was made in the house rather than somewhere else" (emphasis added). The Court did not use attenuation language in *Harris,* but rather saw it as a straightforward example of a case where the evidence is not a fruit of a prior illegal police action. The inconsistent 5–4 decision in *Harris* may be explained by the hostility of the majority toward the exclusionary rule. The opinion said that excluding the *first* confession vindicated the rule that made in-home arrests without a warrant unconstitutional and, thus, as for allowing in the second confession, "it does not follow from the emphasis on the exclusionary rule's deterrent value that 'anything which deters illegal searches is thereby commanded by the Fourth Amendment.'" (*New York v. Harris,* p. 20)

Attenuation depends on specific case facts. In *United States v. Ceccolini* (1984), a police officer, without any special design to investigate gambling, discovered betting slips in the defendant's flower shop by improperly looking into an envelope with cash sticking out located behind the customer counter. Ceccolini denied that gambling occurred in his place of business before a federal grand jury, but he was convicted of perjury after an employee testified about illegal gambling at his shop. The Court of Appeals ruled that the employee's statement was the fruit of the officer's original unconstitutional search and excluded the testimony. The Supreme Court reversed, finding that the link between the search and the witness's testimony had become so attenuated that the testimony could no longer be considered to be caused by the officer's unconstitutional act. The Court relied on a variety of facts: federal officials previously had the shop under suspicion and observation; several months passed between the officer telling the FBI about the slips and the initial questioning of the employee; the witness was in no way coerced or induced to testify, but did so for honorable motives; the betting slips were not used in the questioning of the witness; the officer had no intent to investigate gambling; and, in this case, the deterrent effect of excluding the evidence would be very limited. Determining whether the original illegality has become attenuated is not found by applying mechanical rules, but depends on whether, considering the totality of the circumstances, the second piece of evidence in the case would have been discovered had not the original violation taken place. If subsequent evidence is considered to be independent of the original "tainted" search and seizure then it can be used against the defendant in a court of law.

State Action Doctrine

Soon after establishing the exclusionary rule, the Court made it clear that the rule applies not to all illegally seized evidence, but only to evidence illegally seized *by the government.* The purpose of the Bill of Rights and constitutional protections is to guard individuals against the excessive, arbitrary and abusive power of the state. Aside from state illegality, courts adhere to the common law rule that they will not inquire into the source of relevant evidence, even if a private party stole evidence and turned it over to the government (*Burdeau v. McDowell,* 1921). On the other hand, if a private person acts as a proxy for the police or at their behest, then state action exists and evidence seized by them is not admissible.

In *Coolidge v. New Hampshire* (1971), the Court ruled that a private party not a suspect who voluntarily gives an item in her possession to the police when questioned about it does not thereby become a proxy for the police. Such evidence is not covered by the exclusionary rule and thus is admissible. On the other hand, in *Skinner v. Railway Labor Executives' Association* (1989) the Court held that the Fourth Amendment did apply to *private* railroad employees who were tested for alcohol or drugs immediately after a train crash, because federal regulations required mandatory testing of such employees under the federal government's interstate commerce authority. Thus, evidence of substance use obtained by the rail company was not admissible unless justified by a special Fourth Amendment doctrine.[30]

If private individuals turn over suspicious items to police agents, the police may subject the items to *only minimal investigation* before requesting a search warrant. In one such case, the FBI after being given pornographic films from an innocent, mistaken recipient, proceeded without a warrant, to screen the films in order to determine their content. This screening was held to be state action because it went beyond what the private parties saw before turning over the evidence and was determined inadmissible (*Walter v. United States,* 1980). On the other hand, in *United States v. Jacobsen* (1984), white powder discovered by Federal Express employees was chemically "field tested" and found to be cocaine by federal drug agents (DEA). The warrantless examination by DEA agents was proper because it was *not a significant expansion* of the earlier private search; thus this evidence was admissible.

The state action doctrine means that searches conducted by *any* government officer, not just by police officers acting for law enforcement purposes, fall under the protections of the Fourth Amendment. Searches by public school teachers, public hospital supervisors, probation officers, municipal building inspectors, Occupational Safety and Health Administration (OSHA) inspectors, federal mine-safety investigators, municipal fire department investigators, and customs agents must adhere to Fourth Amendment rules. Illegal searches by these personnel require the exclusion of evidence. As seen in Chapter 6, however, the Supreme Court has created the more lenient rules under the so-called "special needs doctrine" for searches and seizures conducted by different government bureaucrats. Police officers performing arrests and searches to enforce the criminal law are bound by more strict and traditional Fourth Amendment rules.

The constitutional basis of the exclusionary rule means that it does not apply to private police, even when they engage in functions that are closely related to law enforcement.[31] This seems irrational from a behavioral perspective. But the Constitution's function is to protect individual liberty against governmental overreaching, a more potent and ever-present danger to liberty than most private intrusions. However, some cases have held that off-duty police officers working as security officers, especially if in police uniform, are subject to constitutional rules.[32] In light of the enormous growth of the private security industry, some have questioned the flat rule that arrests and searches by private security agents do not amount to government action.[33]

THE FEDERALIZATION OF THE EXCLUSIONARY RULE, 1949–1963

The Movement to Incorporate

Shortly after *Adamson v. California* (1947), a movement began to incorporate the Fourth Amendment and its exclusionary rule into the Fourteenth Amendment and make them applicable to the states (Chapter 2). The issue was raised in *Wolf v. Colorado* (1949). Sheriffs' deputies in Denver, Colorado under instructions of the district attorney's office, had "definite information" concerning an abortion performed by Dr. Wolf. They "went to the office of Wolf without a warrant and took him into custody and there they took possession of . . . his day books of 1944 and 1943 up to the time of the arrest. They were records of patients who consulted him professionally." These records were introduced in evidence and used to convict Dr. Wolf, who received a twelve- to eighteen-month prison sentence. The Colorado Supreme Court held the evidence admissible, although the search was illegal.[34] Had this been a federal search, it clearly would have violated the Fourth Amendment and the evidence ruled inadmissible under *Weeks*. The Fourth Amendment, however, did not bind local or state police and courts at that time.

The United States Supreme Court held, in an opinion by Justice Frankfurter, that (1) the Fourth Amendment *is* "incorporated," but (2) the exclusionary rule is *not* "incorporated." That is, "in a prosecution in a State court for a State crime the Fourteenth Amendment does not forbid the admission of evidence obtained by an unreasonable search and seizure" (*Wolf v. Colorado,* p. 33).

As to the first holding Justice Frankfurter wrote:

> Unlike the specific requirements and restrictions placed by the Bill of Rights (Amendments I to VIII) upon the administration of criminal justice by federal authority, the Fourteenth Amendment did not subject criminal justice in the States to specific limitations. The notion that the "due process of law" guaranteed by the Fourteenth Amendment is shorthand for the first eight amendments of the Constitution and thereby incorporates them has been rejected by this Court again and again, after impressive consideration. . . .
>
> Due process of law thus conveys neither formal nor fixed nor narrow requirements. It is the compendious expression for all those rights which the courts must enforce because they are basic to our free society. But basic rights do not become petrified as of any one time, even though, as a matter of human experience, some may not too rhetorically be called eternal verities. It is of the very nature of a free society to advance in its standards of what is deemed reasonable and right. Representing as it does a living principle, due process is not confined within a permanent catalogue of what may at a given time be deemed the limits or the essentials of fundamental rights.
>
> The security of one's privacy against arbitrary intrusion by the police—which is at the core of the Fourth Amendment—is basic to a free society. It is therefore implicit in "the concept of ordered liberty" and as such enforceable against the States through the Due Process Clause. The knock at the door, whether by day or by night, as a prelude to a search, without authority of law but solely on the authority of the police, did not need the commentary of recent history to be condemned as inconsistent with the conception of human rights enshrined in the history and the basic constitutional documents of English-speaking peoples.
>
> Accordingly, we have no hesitation in saying that were a State affirmatively to sanction such police incursion into privacy it would run counter to the guaranty of the Fourteenth Amendment. (*Wolf v. Colorado,* pp. 27– 28)

This elegant language, interspersed among paragraphs that disparage the incorporation doctrine, incorporates the underlying rule of the Fourth Amendment. However, the Court's majority refused to impose the exclusionary rule on the states via incorporation:

> But the ways of enforcing such a basic right raise questions of a different order. How such arbitrary conduct should be checked, what remedies against it should be afforded, the means by which the right should be made effective, are all questions that are not to be so dogmatically answered as to

preclude the varying solutions which spring from an allowable range of judgment on issues not susceptible of quantitative solution.

In *Weeks v. United States,* this Court held that in a federal prosecution the Fourth Amendment barred the use of evidence secured through an illegal search and seizure. This ruling was made for the first time in 1914. It was not derived from the explicit requirements of the Fourth Amendment; it was not based on legislation expressing Congressional policy in the enforcement of the Constitution. The decision was a matter of judicial implication. Since then it has been frequently applied and we stoutly adhere to it. But the immediate question is whether the basic right to protection against arbitrary intrusion by the police demands the exclusion of logically relevant evidence obtained by an unreasonable search and seizure because, in a federal prosecution for a federal crime, it would be excluded. As a matter of inherent reason, one would suppose this to be an issue as to which men with complete devotion to the protection of the right of privacy might give different answers. When we find that in fact most of the English-speaking world does not regard as vital to such protection the exclusion of evidence thus obtained, we must hesitate to treat this remedy as an essential ingredient of the right. The contrariety of views of the States is particularly impressive in view of the careful reconsideration which they have given the problem in the light of the *Weeks* decision. (*Wolf v. Colorado,* pp. 28–29)

Justice Frankfurter emphasized that the *basic* Fourth Amendment right, now applicable against state as well as federal encroachment, was protected by the "remedies" of civil lawsuits in all states whether or not they had adopted their own exclusionary rules. As of 1949, sixteen states had adopted the *Weeks* exclusionary doctrine as a matter of local law, while thirty-one had rejected it. What was not "incorporated" was the *Weeks* exclusionary rule.

It is instructive that Justice Black, the leading proponent of incorporation, joined the majority because he felt that "the federal exclusionary rule is not a command of the Fourth Amendment but is a judicially created rule of evidence which Congress might negate," i.e., is not a constitutional *requirement.* This placed Justice Black in a seemingly incongruous position in terms of judicial philosophy, as a judicial activist who also adhered strongly to his view of originalism, or following the original intent of the framers. He believed that the Fourteenth Amendment was intended to make the Fourth Amendment automatically applicable to the states. The original Fourth Amendment itself did not include an exclusionary rule. His position in *Wolf* would be consequential in the decision of *Mapp v. Ohio* (1961).

Three liberal justices, Douglas, Murphy, and Rutledge, dissented in *Wolf,* arguing for incorporation of the exclusionary rule. They argued that civil lawsuits and criminal prosecutions against police and prosecutors are virtually never successful, especially if the person alleging an unconstitutional search had a criminal record. This reality meant that, for all practical purposes, the Fourth Amendment was a right without a remedy. Justice Frank Murphy noted that in states that followed the *Weeks* doctrine, police are carefully trained in the law of search and seizure; whereas the subject was virtually ignored in states without the exclusionary rule. "The conclusion is inescapable that but one remedy exists to deter violations of the search and seizure clause. That is the rule which excludes illegally obtained evidence" (*Wolf v. Colorado,* p. 44).

Three years after *Wolf,* the Supreme Court did suppress evidence obtained in a state search and seizure, in *Rochin v. California,* 1952, not via *Weeks*'s automatic Fourth Amendment exclusion rule, but under the more flexible due process rule of the Fourteenth Amendment. Los Angeles police officers, believing that Rochin was dealing drugs, invaded his home without a warrant, went up the stairs, and forced open a door to his bedroom. "Inside they found [Rochin] sitting partly dressed on the side of the bed, upon which his wife was lying. On a 'night stand' beside the bed the deputies spied two capsules. When asked 'Whose stuff is this?' Rochin seized the capsules and put them in his mouth. A struggle ensued, in the course of which the three officers 'jumped upon him' and attempted to extract the capsules. The force they applied proved unavailing against Rochin's resistance. He was handcuffed and taken to a hospital. At the direction of one of the officers a doctor forced an emetic solution through a tube into Rochin's stomach against his will. This 'stomach pumping' produced vomiting. In the vomited matter were found two capsules which proved to contain morphine."

Given this outrageous police action, the justices, for different reasons, unanimously agreed that the evidence should not be admissable. Justice Frankfurter's majority opinion did not apply *Weeks,* but instead excluded the evidence where the totality of circumstances "shocked the conscience" of the appellate court. Justice Frankfurter believed the shocks-the-conscience test was an objective standard that would guide lower courts. Justice William Douglas, concurring in the decision, disagreed strongly with the philosophy of the shocks-the-conscience test. As with any due process test that rests on the "totality of the circumstances," the application of the rule could differ from one judge to another. As he saw it, unlike the "unequivocal, definite and workable rule of evidence" of the *Weeks* exclusionary rule, the rule fashioned in *Rochin* "turn[s] not on the Constitution but on the idiosyncrasies of the judges who sit here" (*Rochin v. California,* p. 179).

The validity of Justice Douglas' criticism was proven in *Irvine v. California* (1954). Local police, suspecting Irvine of illegal bookmaking, secretly entered his home and, without a judicial search warrant, wired the entire house for sound, including the bedroom. The police listened in on all the private conversations of Irvine and his wife for many weeks, and testified to what they heard at Irvine's trial. Irvine was convicted based on this evidence. Justice Robert Jackson's majority opinion stated: "Few police measures have come to our attention that more flagrantly, deliberately, and persistently violated the fundamental principle declared by the Fourth Amendment . . ." (*Irvine v. California,* p. 132). The Supreme Court, nevertheless, held that the evidence should not be excluded. The *Weeks* exclusionary rule did not apply to the states, and the majority refused to apply the *Rochin* shocks-the-conscience test because the facts of *Rochin* included the element of *coercion* not found in the *Irvine* case. This was too much for Justice Frankfurter who dissented on the grounds that *Rochin* did apply. "The holding of the case is that a State cannot resort to methods that offend civilized standards of decency and fairness" (*Irvine v. California,* p. 144). The subjectivity of the shocks-the-conscience test was exposed when the majority in *Irvine* did not find such a flagrant violation of Fourth Ammendment privacy to "shock the conscience." In a spirited dissent Justice Douglas called again for the incorporation of the exclusionary rule saying, "The search and seizure conducted in this case smack of the police state, not the free America the Bill of Rights envisaged" (*Irvine v. California,* p. 149).

As the 1950s wore on, more states adopted the exclusionary rule by court action, most notably the California Supreme Court.[35] The tide in favor of reversing *Weeks* was "halting but seemingly inexorable."[36] A harbinger was *Elkins v. United States* (1960). Soon after *Weeks* (1914), an end-run around the exclusionary rule arose called the "silver-platter" doctrine: if state or local police seized evidence of a federal crime by an illegal search and seizure, the evidence was admissible in a federal trial as long as the federal officers did not participate in the illegal search. This, of course, put a premium on "pious perjury," or winking at the truth.

The Supreme Court signaled its unhappiness with this in *Rea v. United States* (1956). The Court exercised its supervisory authority to enjoin a federal narcotics agent, who had illegally seized marijuana which was excluded from a federal prosecution by a district judge, from testifying about the marijuana in a state prosecution. This eliminated a federal-to-state "silver platter."

In *Elkins,* the Supreme Court put an end to the state-to-federal transfer of illegally seized evidence. Justice Stewart, writing for the majority in a 5–4 decision, noted that the basis of the silver-platter doctrine was eroded once *Wolf v. Colorado* (1949) held that *substantive* Fourth Amendment rights applied against the states. The four dissenting justices complained that the Court was interfering with states' rights. In reply, Justice Stewart wrote, "The very essence of a healthy federalism depends upon the avoidance of needless conflict between federal and state courts." Thus, in states with state exclusionary rules, the silver-platter doctrine undermined *state* policy. *Elkins* was decided not on constitutional grounds, but on "the Court's supervisory power over the administration of criminal justice in the federal courts" (p. 216). Justice Stewart's strong defense of the exclusionary rule presaged the decision in *Mapp v. Ohio* (1961).

Incorporating the Exclusionary Rule

The due process revolution of the 1960s was initiated by *Mapp v. Ohio*. The movement is associated with a five-justice majority of the Warren Court in the 1960s. It is worth noting that Justice Tom Clark, who wrote the opinion of the Court, more often than not voted for the state.

Two years after *Mapp,* in *Ker v. California* (1963), the Court fully "federalized" the exclusionary rule, saying that the "standard of reasonableness is the same under the Fourth and Fourteenth Amendments." Essentially, state courts would have to abide by the United States Supreme Court's exclusionary rule interpretations. The Court noted that it had no supervisory authority over the states, only the jurisdiction to interpret the Constitution, and said that *Mapp* "implied no total obliteration of state laws relating to arrests and searches in favor of federal law. *Mapp* sounded no death knell for our federalism." On the other hand, "Findings of reasonableness, of course, are respected only insofar as consistent with federal constitutional guarantees." In practice this meant that state search and seizure law had to conform to Supreme Court-determined *minimum* constitutional standards; but under the adequate and independent state grounds concept, a state could expand a suspect's rights in a search and seizure case (see Chapter 2).

In 1965, the Supreme Court held, in *Linkletter v. Walker,* that the exclusionary rule was not retroactive to state cases decided prior to *Mapp;* its effect was prospective only. This decision was important later when the theory of the exclusionary rule was reconsidered. Applying the Court's pragmatic approach to determining if a constitutional rule should be applied retroactively, the 7–2 majority opinion stated that "*Mapp* had as its prime purpose the enforcement of the Fourth Amendment through the inclusion of the exclusionary rule within its rights. This, it was found, was the *only effective deterrent to lawless police action.* Indeed, all of the cases since *Wolf* requiring the exclusion of illegal evidence have been based on the necessity for an effective *deterrent* to illegal police action. . . . We cannot say that this purpose would be advanced by making the rule retrospective" (*Linkletter v. Walker,* pp. 636–37, emphasis added).

The Warren Court's positive approach to the exclusionary rule was underscored by its application of the rule to a

• CASE & COMMENTS •

Mapp V. Ohio
367 U.S. 643, 81 S.Ct. 1684, 6 L.Ed.2d 1081 (1961)

MR. JUSTICE CLARK delivered the opinion of the Court.

[Cleveland police officers went to Mrs. Mapp's home on a tip that a suspected gambler involved in a bombing was residing there. She refused to let them enter without a warrant. The police broke in after a three-hour wait. There was a scuffle for a piece of paper that the police waved, but no warrant was ever produced. Mrs. Mapp and her daughter were handcuffed and confined to a bedroom while the police ransacked the house (looking into all rooms and into her personal papers and photograph albums). The police found obscene books in a trunk in the basement belonging to a roomer who was no longer living in the house. At trial, the alleged warrant was never produced. Mrs. Mapp was convicted for possession of obscene books seized during a search of her home. **[a]** The Ohio courts acknowledged that the books and pictures were "unlawfully seized during an unlawful search of [her] home, * * *" but still allowed the evidence to be used, relying on *Wolf v. Colorado* (this volume).]

[a] This case was appealed to the Supreme Court primarily on First Amendment (free speech) grounds. The Fourth Amendment issue was added perfunctorily. The dissent accused the majority of "reaching out" to settle an issue that was not fully briefed.

I.

Seventy-five years ago, in *Boyd v. United States* 1886, considering the Fourth and Fifth Amendments as running "almost into each other,"on the facts before it, this Court held that the doctrines of those Amendments **[b]**

> "apply to all invasions on the part of the government and its employees of the sanctity of a man's home and the privacies of life. * * * "

[b] Notice that Justice Clark begins by quoting the *Boyd* view that exclusion depends on the Fourth and Fifth amendments together, rather than on the *Weeks* exclusionary rule. He does so for an important tactical reason, and not simply to provide a full history of this area of law.

The Court noted that

> "constitutional provisions for the security of person and property should be liberally construed. . . . It is the duty of courts to be watchful for the constitutional rights of the citizen, and against any stealthy encroachments thereon."

* * * Concluding, the Court specifically referred to the use of the evidence there seized as "unconstitutional."

Less than 30 years after *Boyd,* this Court, in *Weeks v. United States (1914),* stated that

> "the Fourth Amendment . . . put the courts of the United States and Federal officials, in the exercise of their power and authority, under limitations and restraints. * * *

Specifically dealing with the use of the evidence unconstitutionally seized, the Court concluded:

> "If letters and private documents can thus be seized and held and used in evidence against a citizen accused of an offense, the protection of the Fourth Amendment declaring his right to be secure against such searches and seizures is of no value, and, so far as those thus placed are concerned, might as well be stricken from the Constitution. * * *

Finally, the Court in that case clearly stated that use of the seized evidence involved "a denial of the constitutional rights of the accused." . . . Thus, in the year 1914, in the *Weeks* case, this Court "for the first time" held that "in a federal prosecution the Fourth Amendment barred the use of evidence secured through an illegal search and seizure." * * *

There are in the cases of this Court some passing references to the *Weeks* rule as being one of evidence. But the plain and unequivocal language of *Weeks*—and its later paraphrase in *Wolf*—to the effect that the *Weeks* rule is of constitutional origin, remains entirely undisturbed. * * * **[c]**

[c] This states unequivocally that the exclusionary rule is a constitutional rule. The Supreme Court no longer accepts this theory of the exclusionary rule. The change involves changes of national politics

II.

[In *Wolf v. Colorado* (1949), the Court first considered the applicability of the Fourth Amendment against the states, and] after declaring that the "security of one's privacy against arbitrary intrusion by the police" is "implicit in 'the concept of ordered liberty' and as such enforceable against the

• CASE & COMMENTS •

States through the Due Process Clause," * * * and announcing that it "stoutly adhere[d]" to the *Weeks* decision, [nevertheless] the Court decided that the *Weeks* exclusionary rule would not then be imposed upon the States as "an essential ingredient of the right." * * *

and judicial policy. The change is traced in the next section.

[Since 1949, a majority of the states have adopted the exclusionary rule and federal courts no longer allow into evidence items that were illegally seized by state officers.]

It, therefore, plainly appears that the factual considerations supporting the failure of the *Wolf* Court to include the *Weeks* exclusionary rule when it recognized the enforceability of the right to privacy against the States in 1949, while not basically relevant to the constitutional consideration, could not, in any analysis, now be deemed controlling.

III.

* * * Today we once again examine *Wolf*'s constitutional documentation of the right to privacy free from unreasonable state intrusion, and, after its dozen years on our books, are led by it to close the only courtroom door remaining open to evidence secured by official lawlessness in flagrant abuse of that basic right, reserved to all persons as a specific guarantee against that very same unlawful conduct. We hold that all evidence obtained by searches and seizures in violation of the Constitution is, by that same authority, inadmissible in a state court.

IV.

Since the Fourth Amendment's right of privacy has been declared enforceable against the States through the Due Process Clause of the Fourteenth, it is enforceable against them by the same sanction of exclusion as is used against the Federal Government. * * * **[d]** In short, the admission of the new constitutional right by *Wolf* could not consistently tolerate denial of its most important constitutional privilege, namely, the exclusion of the evidence which an accused had been forced to give by reason of the unlawful seizure. To hold otherwise is to grant the right but in reality to withhold its privilege and enjoyment. * * *

[d] The "same sanction" phrase is critically important to the entire incorporation doctrine. It means that the United States Constitution must be interpreted identically for state as well as for the federal government. Since the Constitution is the "supreme law of the land," the practical effect of incorporation is that the Supreme Court makes specific rules for state courts and law enforcement.

V.

Moreover, our holding that the exclusionary rule is an essential part of both the Fourth and Fourteenth Amendments is not only the logical dictate of prior cases, but it also makes very good sense. There is no war between the Constitution and common sense. Presently, a federal prosecutor may make no use of evidence illegally seized, but a State's attorney across the street may, although he supposedly is operating under the enforceable prohibitions of the same Amendment. **[e]** Thus the State, by admitting evidence unlawfully seized, serves to encourage disobedience to the Federal Constitution which it is bound to uphold. * * * "[The] very essence of a healthy federalism depends upon the avoidance of needless conflict between state and federal courts." * * * **[f]**

[e] This refers not to the "silver-platter" doctrine, eliminated in *Elkins v. United States* (1960), but to the incongruity of uneven enforcement of constitutional rights.

[f] It appears that even with the elimination of the silver-platter doctrine, Justice Clark feared that allowing different search and seizure rules would cause tension between state and federal officers.

Federal-state cooperation in the solution of crime under constitutional standards will be promoted, if only by recognition of their now mutual obligation to respect the same fundamental criteria in their approaches. "However much in a particular case insistence upon such rules may appear as a technicality that inures to the benefit of a guilty person, the history of the criminal law proves that tolerance of shortcut methods in law enforcement impairs its enduring effectiveness." * * * Denying shortcuts to only one of two cooperating law enforcement agencies tends naturally to breed legitimate suspicion of "working arrangements" whose results are equally tainted. * * *

There are those who say, as did JUSTICE (then Judge) CARDOZO, that under our constitutional exclusionary doctrine "[the] criminal is to go free because the constable has blundered." * * * In some cases this will undoubtedly be the result. **[g]** But, * * * "there is another consideration—the imperative of judicial integrity." The criminal goes free, if he must, but it is the law that sets him free. Nothing can destroy a government more quickly than its failure to observe its own laws, or worse, its disregard of the charter of its own existence. * * *

[g] The arguments in favor of and opposed to the exclusionary rule, and the various theories of the exclusionary rule, are considered in a later section.

The ignoble shortcut to conviction left open to the State tends to destroy the entire system of constitutional restraints on which the liberties of the people rest. * * * [W]e can no longer permit that right to remain an empty promise. * * *

• CASE & COMMENTS •

Reversed and remanded.

MR. JUSTICE BLACK, concurring.

[JUSTICE BLACK noted that in *Wolf,* he stated that "the federal exclusionary rule is not a command of the Fourth Amendment but is a judicially created rule of evidence which Congress might negate."]

* * *

I am still not persuaded that the Fourth Amendment, standing alone, would be enough to bar the introduction into evidence against an accused of papers and effects seized from him in violation of its commands. **[h]** For the Fourth Amendment does not itself contain any provision expressly precluding the use of such evidence, and I am extremely doubtful that such a provision could properly be inferred from nothing more than the basic command against unreasonable searches and seizures. Reflection on the problem, however, in the light of cases coming before the Court since *Wolf,* has led me to conclude that when the Fourth Amendment's ban against unreasonable searches and seizures is considered together with the Fifth Amendment's ban against compelled self-incrimination, a constitutional basis emerges which not only justifies but actually requires the exclusionary rule. * * *

[h] Justice Black's vote in favor of the exclusionary rule is the crucial fifth majority vote. His rationale makes it clear why Justice Clark's argument included *Boyd*'s theory that the Fourth and Fifth amendments operate in conjunction to exclude evidence. It is worth noting that the Fifth Amendment basis of the exclusionary rule, while still alluded to, had become obsolete by the 1960s, as the search and seizure exclusionary rule was treated exclusively as a Fourth Amendment issue.

[JUSTICE DOUGLAS concurred, expanding on the facts of the case and emphasizing the inability of any method other than exclusion to deter police illegalities.]

[JUSTICE STEWART expressed no opinion on the search and seizure issue; he would have reversed the conviction on First Amendment grounds.]

MR. JUSTICE HARLAN, whom MR. JUSTICE FRANKFURTER and MR. JUSTICE WHITTAKER join, dissenting.

In overruling the *Wolf* case the Court, in my opinion, has forgotten the sense of judicial restraint which, with due regard for *stare decisis,* is one element that should enter into deciding whether a past decision of this Court should be overruled. **[i]** Apart from that I also believe that the *Wolf* rule represents sounder Constitutional doctrine than the new rule which now replaces it. * * *

[i] Examine the material on judicial statesmanship in Chapter 1.

II

Essential to the majority's argument against *Wolf* is the proposition that the [exclusionary] rule of *Weeks* * * * derives not from the "supervisory power" of this Court over the federal judicial system, but from Constitutional requirement. This is so because no one, I suppose, would suggest that this Court possesses any general supervisory power over the state courts. Although I entertain considerable doubt as to the soundness of this foundational proposition * * * I shall assume, for present purposes, that the *Weeks* rule "is of constitutional origin."

At the heart of the majority's opinion in this case is the following syllogism: (1) the rule excluding in federal criminal trials evidence which is the product of an illegal search and seizure is "part and parcel" of the Fourth Amendment; (2) *Wolf* held that the "privacy" assured against federal action by the Fourth Amendment is also protected against state action by the Fourteenth Amendment; and (3) it is therefore "logically and constitutionally necessary" that the *Weeks* exclusionary rule should also be enforced against the States.

This reasoning ultimately rests on the unsound premise that because *Wolf* carried into the States, as part of "the concept of ordered liberty" embodied in the Fourteenth Amendment, the principle of "privacy" underlying the *Fourth Amendment,* * * * it must follow that whatever configurations of the Fourth Amendment have been developed in the particularizing federal precedents are likewise to be deemed a part of "ordered liberty," and as such are enforceable against the States. For me, this does not follow at all. **[j]**

[j] What follows is the non-incorporation view that had been part of Fourteenth Amendment jurisprudence since *Hurtado v. California* (1884). Justice Harlan's strenuous dissent is indeed a cry for stare decisis, for the majority

It cannot be too much emphasized that what was recognized in *Wolf* was not that the Fourth Amendment *as such* is enforceable against the States as a facet of due process, * * * but the principle of privacy "which is at the core of the Fourth Amendment." * * * It would not be proper to expect or impose any precise equivalence, either as regards the scope of the right or the means of its implementation, between the requirements of the Fourth and Fourteenth Amendments. For the Fourth, unlike what was said in *Wolf* of the Fourteenth, does not state a general principle only; it is

• CASE & COMMENTS •

a particular command, having its setting in a pre-existing legal context on which both interpreting decisions and enabling statutes must at least build. **[k]**

* * * Since there is not the slightest suggestion that Ohio's policy is "affirmatively to sanction * * * police incursion into privacy" * * * what the Court is now doing is to impose upon the States not only federal substantive standards of "search and seizure" but also the basic federal remedy for violation of those standards. For I think it entirely clear that the *Weeks* exclusionary rule is but a remedy which, by penalizing past official misconduct, is aimed at deterring such conduct in the future. **[l]**

I would not impose upon the States this federal exclusionary remedy. The reasons given by the majority for now suddenly turning its back on *Wolf* seem to me notably unconvincing.

[JUSTICE HARLAN then put forth several reasons for not extending the exclusionary rule to the states: (1) that many states have voluntarily adopted the exclusionary rule does not determine a constitutional question; (2) "the preservation of a proper balance between state and federal responsibility in the administration of criminal justice" *Constitutionally* forbids the federal courts from developing solutions for perceived problems of state law enforcement; (3) procedural symmetry between the federal system and the states is not required by the Constitution; and (4) the purported analogy between the exclusion of involuntary confessions under the Fourteenth Amendment and search and seizure cases is spurious.]

decision in *Mapp* was genuinely revolutionary, by overturning the theory of the relationship between the Bill of Rights and the Fourteenth Amendment.

[k] This sentence implies a knowledge about the history of searches and warrants in the era of the framing that might, in light of more recent scholarship, be in error.[37]

[l] A dissent always is a call to the future. As the personnel of the Supreme Court changed and the Court adopted a more activist-conservative stance, Justice Harlan's view of the nature of the exclusionary rule has become the accepted view of the Court. This will be discussed below in the section on the theories of the exclusionary rule.

civil forfeiture of an automobile which state liquor control officers stopped and searched because it was "low in the rear, quite low." Upon inspection, the officers found thirty-one cases of liquor. The Court in *One 1958 Plymouth Sedan v. Pennsylvania* (1965) agreed with the state trial judge, who found that the stop was made without probable cause. In applying the exclusionary rule, it noted that forfeitures are quasi-criminal procedures in which the penalty is often more onerous than a criminal sentence.

The exclusionary rule was subjected to judicial and political criticism during the remaining years of the Warren Court (to 1969). In fact, liberal Warren Court decisions regarding criminal suspects became a major issue in the 1968 presidential campaign. After his election, President Nixon sought to nominate justices who would reverse these decisions (see Chapter 2). Thus, within a decade of *Mapp,* a "counterattack" to erode the exclusionary rule began.

UNDERMINING THE EXCLUSIONARY RULE

After 1972, the Court's new conservative majority had a guarded, if not outrightly hostile, attitude toward the exclusionary rule. Chief Justice Burger, for example, called for its total overruling in a dissent in *Bivens v. Six Unknown Agents* (1971), stating that the *only* foundation for the rule was the *deterrence of police illegality.* The Court has never overruled the exclusionary rule, but since 1974 it has limited its application. The move to limit the rule was first applied in *United States v. Calandra* (1974), when a majority of six justices held that a grand jury question could be based on information obtained from an unconstitutional search and seizure. Justice Lewis Powell's majority opinion specified reasons that would thereafter be the foundation for the Court's exclusionary rule decisions:

1. In determining whether to apply the exclusionary rule to a proceeding the Court must *balance* the cost to the law enforcement process (e.g., grand jury proceedings) against the benefits of the rule.
2. The *use* of illegally seized evidence against a suspect does not violate his Fourth Amendment rights. The Fourth Amendment violation "is *fully accomplished*" when the illegal search and seizure occurs. Thus, the application of the exclusionary rule is not a question of a violation of a person's constitutional rights, but is pragmatic evaluation of the proper scope of the rule.

3. The "purpose of the exclusionary rule is not to redress the injury to the privacy of the search victim."
4. The "rule's prime purpose is to *deter future unlawful police conduct* and thereby effectuate the guarantee of the Fourth Amendment against unreasonable searches and seizures."
5. "In sum, the rule is a judicially created remedy designed to safeguard Fourth Amendment rights generally through its deterrent effect, rather than a personal constitutional right of the party aggrieved."

Justice Brennan, joined by Justices Douglas and Marshall, dissented vigorously at this "downgrading" of the exclusionary rule, but to no avail.

Stone v. Powell (1976) indicates the Supreme Court's lower opinion of the exclusionary rule by limiting the scope for challenging it via a federal writ of habeas corpus. *Stone* held that if a person convicted in a state court already had a full and fair opportunity to litigate a Fourth Amendment claim in the state courts, he or she has no right to reopen the issue in federal habeas corpus proceedings. Justice Powell noted that the rule was a judicially created means of enforcing Fourth Amendment rights, rather than a right itself; that it rests primarily on the theory of deterrence of police misconduct rather than "the imperative of judicial integrity"; and that the rule "deflects the truthfinding process and often frees the guilty." The Court has not limited federal habeas corpus review as to any other constitutional guarantee.

Chief Justice Burger, who had called for overruling the exclusionary rule in *Bivens,* conceded to accepting the continued existence of the rule, but in its weakened form. He stated that "the exclusionary rule has been operative long enough to demonstrate its flaws. The time has come to modify its reach, even if it is retained for a small and limited category of cases." This may reflect that a majority of the Court felt constrained by *stare decisis* and uneasy with dismantling an important protection for a fundamental constitutional right. Chief Justice Burger thus shifted his ground to push for limitation of the exclusionary rule rather than its elimination.[38]

On the reasoning of *Calandra* and *Stone v. Powell,* the Court has held that the exclusionary rule does not apply to the Internal Revenue Service in a civil tax proceeding (*United States v. Janis,* 1976) or to deportation hearings (*I.N.S v. Lopez-Mendoza,* 1984). These rulings undercut the viability of *One 1958 Plymouth Sedan,* although that decision was never overruled. More recently, the Court declined to apply the exclusionary rule to parole revocation in *Pennsylvania Board of Probation and Parole v. Scott* (1998). Parole officers, without a warrant, entered the home of a parolee whom they believed possessed weapons in violation of parole conditions. The state courts ruled that the warrantless search of a parolee's home violated the Fourth Amendment because "illegal searches would be undeterred when officers know that the subjects of their searches are parolees and that illegally obtained evidence can be introduced at parole hearings." The United States Supreme Court, in a 5–4 decision, reversed the Pennsylvania Supreme Court. Justice Clarence Thomas' majority opinion, referring to the rule as a "grudgingly taken medicant,"[39] reviewed the Court's approach to the exclusionary rule in cases since *Calandra* and noted that the rule now applies only in criminal trials, and even there with some exceptions. Four Justices dissented. Justice John Paul Stevens endorsed the view made by Justice Potter Stewart in a journal article that the "rule *is* constitutionally required, not as a 'right' explicitly incorporated in the fourth amendment's prohibitions, but as a remedy necessary to ensure that those prohibitions are observed in fact."[40] Justice David Souter, in dissent, noted that parole revocation proceedings often serve the same function as criminal trials.

Illegally obtained evidence also is used to impeach the credibility of a defendant who testifies by showing that her testimony is contradicted by the illegally seized evidence. The Court initially disallowed such use, at least when the defendant was not questioned about the evidence on direct examination (*Agnello v. United States,* 1925). This rule was weakened by a 1954 decision which allowed a prosecutor to introduce illegally seized evidence of an old drug transaction in an effort to rebut a defendant's assertion on direct examination that he had never sold narcotics. This was tangential to the issue of illegally seized evidence in regard to the charged offense (*Walder v. United States,* 1954). The Burger Court ruled that an improperly obtained confession could be used to impeach a defendant (*Harris v. New York,* 1971), and on similar reasoning, effectively overruled *Agnello* in *United States v. Havens* (1980). In *Havens,* a T-shirt with a pocket especially sewn in to hold drugs was illegally seized at an airport. Havens, tried for importing drugs on the testimony of his fellow traveler, denied drug activity on direct examination and denied any connection with the T-shirt that was introduced on cross-examination to impeach his testimony. The Supreme Court held this use of the illegal evidence proper because the government did not "smuggle in" the evidence, but instead the cross-examination was reasonably suggested by defendant's direct examination. In his majority opinion, Justice White emphasized the importance of arriving at the truth in criminal trials, the dangers of allowing a constitutional shield to be "perverted into a license to use perjury," and the belief that the use of illegally seized evidence for impeachment would not undermine the deterrent effect of the exclusionary rule. The Court later limited this use of illegally seized evidence to impeach only the defendant and not other witnesses, out of concern that expanded impeachment use would create a premium to obtain evidence in violation of the Constitution and weaken its deterrent effect (*James v. Illinois,* 1990).

Good Faith Exceptions

To date the most powerful attack on the exclusionary rule has been the allowance of illegally seized evidence to be introduced in the trial to prove the defendant's guilt. Unlike *Calandra* and similar cases, where tainted evidence was used in peripheral proceedings,—the so-called good faith exception cases—the Court has reasoned that the introduction of such evidence in the "case-in-chief" would not undermine the exclusionary rule's deterrent effect. These cases confirm the Court's present view, which modifies the original theory of the exclusionary rule: it is not a constitutional rule but is a judicially created remedy designed to deter police from violating Fourth Amendment rights.

The good faith exception was first adopted in principle in *Michigan v. DeFillippo* (1979). Detroit Police stopped DeFillippo on suspicion and arrested him for violating a 1976 ordinance that required stopped persons to give their identity to the police. A search incident to the arrest disclosed illegal drugs on his person. Michigan appellate courts later declared the ordinance unconstitutionally vague and suppressed the evidence. The United States Supreme Court, in an opinion by Chief Justice Burger, held that the evidence could be introduced because the ordinance, although unconstitutional, did not undermine the probable cause requirement and because the police followed a then-valid ordinance in good faith. The stage was set for a major reassessment and limitation of the exclusionary rule in *United States v. Leon* (1984).

Leon was followed by *Illinois v. Krull* (1987), which held that the exclusionary rule does not apply where the police violate a person's rights in good faith reliance on a statute. Chicago police officers, under an Illinois regulatory statute, searched cars and records of an automobile wrecking yard without a search warrant. The statute was declared unconstitutional by a federal court. On appeal, the Supreme Court, applying the reasoning of *Leon,* found that because similar regulatory search schemes had been held constitutional in the past, the officers relied on the law in good faith. *Krull* differs from the *DeFillippo* case. In *DeFillippo,* the statute was voided because its vague wording violated the Fourteenth Amendment Due Process Clause, while in *Krull,* the constitutional infirmity was a violation of the Fourth Amendment. For this reason, the decision was closer in *Krull* (5–4), with Justice Sandra Day O'Connor writing the dissent, joined by Justices Brennan, Marshall, and Stevens. Justice O'Connor noted that the Fourth Amendment was originally designed to constrain the legislature. She minced no words: "[l]egislatures have, upon occasion, failed to adhere to the requirements of the Fourth Amendment." She also disagreed with the majority as to whether a legislature could be deterred by the application of the exclusionary rule in a case such as this one. "Providing legislatures a grace period during which the police may freely perform unreasonable searches in order to convict those who might otherwise escape provides a positive incentive to promulgate unconstitutional laws." Justice O'Connor's experience as a leader of the Arizona Senate seems to have provided the insight that, for political gain, legislators at times have decided to intentionally pass laws that violate individual rights.

Two instructive cases display instances in which the good faith exception makes sense and instances in which it does not. In *Massachusetts v. Sheppard* (1984), a companion case to *Leon,* a police officer filed a homicide search warrant affidavit on a form to search for controlled substances. Because it was Sunday, the courts were closed and the officer could not find the proper form.The officer and the magistrate modified the form, but, still, the search warrant erroneously authorized a search for controlled substances yet did not incorporate the affidavit. The warrant was executed and the detective along with other officers searched Sheppard's residence for items listed in the affidavit. They discovered several incriminating pieces of evidence and entered them into evidence. The Court held that in this case, the police objectively relied in good faith on a defective warrant. This is an instance in which a good faith reliance exception avoids a patently absurd conclusion. It is worth noting that Justice Stevens, concurring in the decision, felt that the warrant and affidavit were in fact quite specific and that the magistrate and the police officers were fully aware of their contents. Thus, he believed there simply was no Fourth Amendment defect and that the majority manufactured one in order to make new law.

A more disturbing case is *Arizona v. Evans* (1995). Evans was stopped by a Phoenix police officer for driving the wrong way on a one-way street. A computer check indicated an outstanding misdemeanor warrant; he was arrested and marijuana was discovered. However, the arrest warrant against Evans had, in actuallity, been quashed seventeen days prior to his arrest. An error in the *court* clerk's office resulted in the information not being conveyed to the sheriff's office to remove the arrest notation from the law enforcement computer database. The Arizona Supreme Court excluded the evidence because there was no basis for the arrest and the "application of the exclusionary rule would 'hopefully serve to improve the efficiency of those who keep records in our criminal justice system.'" On appeal by the state, the United States Supreme Court reversed. Chief Justice Rehnquist, writing for the Court, believed that Evans had no complaint because the wrong condemned by the

• CASE & COMMENTS •

United States v. Leon
468 U.S. 897, 104 S.Ct. 3405, 82 L.Ed.2d 677 (1984)

JUSTICE WHITE delivered the opinion of the Court.

This case presents the question whether the Fourth Amendment exclusionary rule should be modified so as not to bar the use in the prosecution's case in chief of evidence obtained by officers acting in reasonable reliance on a search warrant issued by a detached and neutral magistrate but ultimately found to be unsupported by probable cause. **[a]** To resolve this question, we must consider once again the tension between the sometimes competing goals of, on the one hand, deterring official misconduct and removing inducements to unreasonable invasions of privacy and, on the other, establishing procedures under which criminal defendants are "acquitted or convicted on the basis of all the evidence which exposes the truth."* * *

[a] JUSTICE WHITE states the issue *and* establishes a "judicial methodology", – the "balancing test" – to resolve the issue. The choice assists in producing the desired outcome. The dissent utilizes a different analytic framework to reach its contrary result.

I

[Local police obtained a "facially valid" search warrant from a state judge based on information from a confidential informant "of unproven reliability." A stakeout revealed suspected drug dealing at a house, and a car parked outside belonged to Leon, a previously convicted drug dealer. A search warrant affidavit was prepared by an experienced drug enforcement officer and reviewed by several assistant prosecutors. A warrant was issued by a state judge. The warrant was executed and drugs were found. On this evidence, Leon and others were indicted in a federal District Court for drug dealing. They moved to suppress evidence and challenged the constitutionality of the search warrant. The federal judge, overturned the warrant—the informant's reliability was not established and probable cause of drug sales was not independently established. The court stated that the case was a close one and that the officers acted upon the warrant in the good faith belief that it was based upon probable cause. The federal Court of Appeals upheld the District Court. The case is decided on the understanding that the search warrant was not valid under the Fourth Amendment and in effect that the search violated Leon's Fourth Amendment rights.]

We have concluded that, in the Fourth Amendment context, the exclusionary rule can be modified somewhat without jeopardizing its ability to perform its intended functions. Accordingly, we reverse the judgment of the Court of Appeals.

II

Language in opinions of this Court * * * has sometimes implied that the exclusionary rule is a necessary corollary of the Fourth Amendment, * * * [or] the conjunction of the Fourth and Fifth Amendments. [*Mapp v. Ohio*] **[b]** * * * These implications need not detain us long. The Fifth Amendment theory has not withstood critical analysis or the test of time, * * * and the Fourth Amendment "has never been interpreted to proscribe the introduction of illegally seized evidence in all proceedings or against all persons." * * *

[b] JUSTICE WHITE sets the stage for his opinion and deflects a major argument of the dissent by dismissing the precedential value of *Mapp* as a constitutional rule by relying on later cases. JUSTICE WHITE, a long-standing critic of *Mapp,* is now able to use precedents he helped create to weaken its effect. This is typical judicial strategy in the Supreme Court.

A

The Fourth Amendment contains no provision expressly precluding the use of evidence obtained in violation of its commands, and * * * the use of [unlawfully seized evidence] "work[s] no new Fourth Amendment wrong." * * * The wrong condemned by the Amendment is "fully accomplished" by the unlawful search or seizure itself, * * * and the exclusionary rule is neither intended nor able to "cure the invasion of the defendant's rights which he has already suffered." The rule thus operates as "a judicially created remedy designed to safeguard Fourth Amendment rights generally through its deterrent effect, rather than a personal constitutional right of the party aggrieved." * * *

Whether the exclusionary sanction is appropriately imposed in a particular case is "an issue separate from the question whether the Fourth Amendment rights of the party seeking to invoke the rule were violated by police conduct." * * * **[c]** Only the former question is currently before us, and it must be resolved by weighing the costs and benefits of preventing the use in the prosecution's case-in-chief of inherently trustworthy tangible evidence obtained in reliance on a search warrant issued by a detached and neutral magistrate that ultimately is found to be defective.

[c] In some areas of law, the remedy is part of the right. A complete definition of crime includes the penalty (the public's "remedy," not the personal remedy of the injured party). For Fourth Amendment violations, however, the Court

• CASE & COMMENTS •

The substantial social costs exacted by the exclusionary rule for the vindication of Fourth Amendment rights have long been a source of concern. **[d]** * * * "[U]nbending application of the exclusionary sanction to enforce ideals of governmental rectitude would impede unacceptably the truth-finding functions of judge and jury."* * * Particularly when law enforcement officers have acted in objective good faith or their transgressions have been minor, the magnitude of the benefit conferred on such guilty defendants offends basic concepts of the criminal justice system. * * * Indiscriminate application of the exclusionary rule, therefore, may well "generat[e] disrespect for the law and administration of justice." * * * Accordingly, "[a]s with any remedial device, the application of the rule has been restricted to those areas where its remedial objectives are thought most efficaciously served." * * *

B

[This section reviews cases in which the Court has "demoted" the exclusionary rule, including *Stone v. Powell* (1976); *United States v. Calandra,* (1974); and *United States v. Janis,* (1976), the attenuation cases, the impeachment cases, and the retroactivity cases. **[e]**

III

A

* * *

* * * To the extent that proponents of exclusion rely on its behavioral effects on judges and magistrates, * * * their reliance is misplaced. [f] First, the exclusionary rule is designed to deter police misconduct rather than to punish the errors of judges and magistrates. Second, there exists no evidence suggesting that judges and magistrates are inclined to ignore or subvert the Fourth Amendment or that lawlessness among these actors requires application of the extreme sanction of exclusion.

* * *

[M]ost important, we discern no basis, and are offered none, for believing that exclusion of evidence seized pursuant to a warrant will have a significant deterrent effect on the issuing judge or magistrate. **[g]** * * * [A]s neutral judicial officers, they have no stake in the outcome of particular criminal prosecutions. * * * Imposition of the exclusionary sanction is not necessary meaningfully to inform judicial officers of their errors. * * *

B

If exclusion of evidence obtained pursuant to a subsequently invalidated warrant is to have any deterrent effect, therefore, it must alter the behavior of individual law enforcement officers or the policies of their departments. One could argue that applying the exclusionary rule in cases where the police failed to demonstrate probable cause in the warrant application deters future inadequate presentations or "magistrate shopping" and thus promotes the ends of the Fourth Amendment. Suppressing evidence obtained pursuant to a technically defective warrant supported by probable cause also might encourage officers to scrutinize more closely the form of the warrant and to point out suspected judicial errors. **[h]** We find such arguments speculative and conclude that suppression of evidence obtained pursuant to a warrant should be ordered only on a case-by-case basis and only in those unusual cases in which exclusion will further the purposes of the exclusionary rule.

We have frequently questioned whether the exclusionary rule can have any deterrent effect when the offending officers acted in the objectively reasonable belief that their conduct did not violate the Fourth Amendment. "No empirical researcher, proponent or opponent of the rule, has yet been able to establish with any assurance whether the rule has a deterrent effect * * *" **[i]** But even assuming that the rule effectively deters some police misconduct and provides incentives for the law enforcement profession as a whole to conduct itself in accord with the Fourth Amendment, it cannot be expected, and should not be applied, to deter objectively reasonable law enforcement activity.

indicates that the public's remedy of exclusion is not an essential part of the right. See the section below on theories of the exclusionary rule.

[d] The exclusionary rule is "put on the defensive," stressing its costs, limits, and status as a "mere" remedy rather than as a constitutional right. The extent of social costs involved in the exclusionary rule is an empirical question still open to much debate. Phraseology is important. The "imperative of judicial integrity" of liberal justices becomes the "ideal of governmental rectitude" to conservative justices. The phrases convey different meanings.

[e] Constitutional cases do not stand in isolation; JUSTICE WHITE's recitation of these cases shows that support for a strong exclusionary policy has been eroded.

[f] This can be challenged by arguing that the purpose of the Bill of Rights is to protect individual rights against violations by all government officers.

[g] By way of analogy, judges have immunity from lawsuit for errors made on the bench but are subject to reversal on appeal as a way of correcting their errors and deterring them from not following precedent. Why should magistrates not be concerned when their warrants are overturned as improper?

[h] Does the majority make highly selective factual assumptions? Justice White here brushes aside the educative function of the law, that is, the idea that over the long run the law is effective through educating police officers.

[i] See the *Law in Society* section on the effects of the Exclusionary Rule.

• CASE & COMMENTS •

* * *

This is particularly true, we believe, when an officer acting with objective good faith has obtained a search warrant from a judge or magistrate and acted within its scope. In most such cases, there is no police illegality and thus nothing to deter. * * * **[j]**

[j] What does Justice White imply by "no police illegality"? Can rights be violated with no one responsible? Having ruled that the exclusionary rule does not apply to magistrates, this impossibility may result. Perhaps he meant that the police did not commit a crime or actionable tort in nevertheless violating Leon's rights.

C

* * *

Suppression * * * remains an appropriate remedy if the magistrate or judge in issuing a warrant was misled by information in an affidavit that the affiant knew was false or would have known was false except for his reckless disregard of the truth. * * * The exception we recognize today will also not apply in cases where the issuing magistrate wholly abandoned his judicial role. * * * Nor would an officer manifest objective good faith in relying on a warrant based on an affidavit "so lacking in indicia of probable cause as to render official belief in its existence entirely unreasonable." * * * Finally, depending on the circumstances of the particular case, a warrant may be so facially deficient—*i.e.,* in failing to particularize the place to be searched or the things to be seized—that the executing officers cannot reasonably presume it to be valid. * * * **[k]**

[k] Here, Justice White stresses that the good faith reliance-on-the-warrant exception is not a blank check to the police. Four cases are set out where the exclusionary rule should apply even if an officer relies on a warrant. Thus, the "good faith exception" is less than a clear-cut rule and more of a guideline. This kind of pronouncement by the Court is likely to produce a good amount of confusion as lower courts hand down divergent rulings on similar factual circumstances.

* * *

JUSTICE BLACKMUN, concurring.

* * *

* * * [T]he Court has narrowed the scope of the exclusionary rule because of an empirical judgment that the rule has little appreciable effect in cases where officers act in objectively reasonable reliance on search warrants. * * * **[l]**

What must be stressed, however, is that any empirical judgment about the effect of the exclusionary rule in a particular class of cases necessarily is a provisional one. By their very nature, the assumptions on which we proceed today cannot be cast in stone. To the contrary, they now will be tested in the real world of state and federal law enforcement, and this Court will attend to the results. If it should emerge from experience that, contrary to our expectations, the good-faith exception to the exclusionary rule results in a material change in police compliance with the Fourth Amendment, we shall have to reconsider what we have undertaken here. The logic of a decision that rests on untested predictions about police conduct demands no less.

[l] Justice Blackmun's concurrence is unusually frank about the flexibility of this area of law. The majority and the dissent strive to establish firm rules and Fourth Amendment methodologies. This less partisan stance recognizes that the pendulum can swing as to the exclusionary rule. The concurrence is also a warning to police that widespread Fourth Amendment violations will be the impetus for the Court to once again expand the scope of the exclusionary rule.

* * *

JUSTICE BRENNAN, with whom JUSTICE MARSHALL joins, dissenting.

Ten years ago in *United States v. Calandra,* 414 U.S. 338 (1974), I expressed the fear that the Court's decision "may signal that a majority of my colleagues have positioned themselves to reopen the door [to evidence secured by official lawlessness] still further and abandon altogether the exclusionary rule in search-and-seizure cases" (dissenting opinion). **[m]** Since then, in case after case, I have witnessed the Court's gradual but determined strangulation of the rule. It now appears that the Court's victory over the Fourth Amendment is complete. * * *

[m] This strong language may be discounted in part as a tactic, but it *is* a way of reaching beyond the majority to stir a wider audience and future generations in the hope that a different Court might overturn this decision.

* * *

The majority ignores the fundamental constitutional importance of what is at stake here. * * * [W]hat the Framers understood [in 1791] remains true today—that the task of combating crime and convicting the guilty will in every era seem of such critical and pressing concern that we may be lured by the temptations of expediency into forsaking our commitment to protecting individual liberty and privacy. It was for that very reason that the Framers of the Bill of Rights insisted that law enforcement efforts be permanently and unambiguously restricted in order to preserve personal

• CASE & COMMENTS •

freedoms. * * * **[n]** [T]he sometimes unpopular task of ensuring that the government's enforcement efforts remain within the strict boundaries fixed by the Fourth Amendment was entrusted to the courts. * * * If those independent tribunals lose their resolve, however, as the Court has done today, and give way to the seductive call of expediency, the vital guarantees of the Fourth Amendment are reduced to nothing more than a "form of words." * * *

[n] Justice Brennan in effect accuses the majority of "selling out" the Constitutional rights of citizens because fear of crime was a popular political issue to the Presidents who appointed them. Do you agree?

I

* * *

A

[JUSTICE BRENNAN restated the majority argument here: the exclusionary rule is a mere judicial remedy designed to deter police illegality; the constitutional wrong is complete when the police invade a person's constitutionally protected privacy; and thus there is no constitutional violation if unconstitutionally seized evidence is admitted into evidence.]

Such a reading appears plausible, because, * * * the Fourth Amendment makes no express provision for the exclusion of evidence secured in violation of its commands. * * * [M]any of the Constitution's most vital imperatives are stated in general terms and the task of giving meaning to these precepts is therefore left to subsequent judicial decisionmaking in the context of concrete cases. **[o]** The nature of our Constitution, as CHIEF JUSTICE MARSHALL long ago explained, "requires that only its great outlines should be marked, its important objects designated, and the minor ingredients which compose those objects be deduced from the nature of the objects themselves." * * *

[o] It could be argued that this point applies more to an open textured right such as "due process" than to more narrowly focused rights such as the Fourth Amendment.

A more direct answer may be supplied by recognizing that the Amendment, like other provisions of the Bill of Rights, restrains the power of the government as a whole; it does not specify only a particular agency and exempt all others. The judiciary is responsible, no less than the executive, for ensuring that constitutional rights are respected.

* * * Once that connection between the evidence-gathering role of the police and the evidence-admitting function of the courts is acknowledged, the plausibility of the Court's interpretation becomes more suspect. * * * The Amendment therefore must be read to condemn not only the initial unconstitutional invasion of privacy—which is done, after all, for the purpose of securing evidence—but also the subsequent use of any evidence so obtained.

The Court evades this principle by drawing an artificial line between the constitutional rights and responsibilities that are engaged by actions of the police and those that are engaged when a defendant appears before the courts. **[p]** According to the Court, the substantive protections of the Fourth Amendment are wholly exhausted at the moment when police unlawfully invade an individual's privacy and thus no substantive force remains to those protections at the time of trial when the government seeks to use evidence obtained by the police.

[p] Justice Brennan characterizes the majority's doctrine as an artificial line between constitutional rights and responsibilities. All legal doctrine involves line drawing. Do you think he provides a better rationale for the exclusionary rule as a constitutional right?

I submit that such a crabbed reading of the Fourth Amendment * * * rests ultimately on an impoverished understanding of judicial responsibility in our constitutional scheme. For my part, "[t]he right of the people to be secure in their persons, houses, papers, and effects, against unreasonable searches and seizures" comprises a personal right to exclude all evidence secured by means of unreasonable searches and seizures. The right to be free from the initial invasion of privacy and the right of exclusion are coordinate components of the central embracing right to be free from unreasonable searches and seizures.

* * *

B

* * *

* * * [T]he Court since *Calandra* has gradually pressed the deterrence rationale for the rule back to center stage. * * * [JUSTICE BRENNAN then reviewed the cost-benefit analysis utilized by the majority.] * * *

• CASE & COMMENTS •

* * * To the extent empirical data are available regarding the general costs and benefits of the exclusionary rule, it has shown, on the one hand, as the Court acknowledges today, that the costs are not as substantial as critics have asserted in the past, * * * and, on the other hand, that while the exclusionary rule may well have certain deterrent effects, it is extremely difficult to determine with any degree of precision whether the incidence of unlawful conduct by police is now lower than it was prior to *Mapp.* * * * The Court has sought to turn this uncertainty to its advantage by casting the burden of proof upon proponents of the rule. * * *

* * * [B]y basing the rule solely on the deterrence rationale, the Court has robbed the rule of legitimacy. A doctrine that is explained as if it were an empirical proposition but for which there is only limited empirical support is both inherently unstable and an easy mark for critics. **[q]** The extent of this Court's fidelity to Fourth Amendment requirements, however, should not turn on such statistical uncertainties. * * * Rather than seeking to give effect to the liberties secured by the Fourth Amendment through guesswork about deterrence, the Court should restore to its proper place the principle framed 70 years ago in *Weeks* that an individual whose privacy has been invaded in violation of the Fourth Amendment has a right grounded in that Amendment to prevent the government from subsequently making use of any evidence so obtained.

***

[q] This is a strong point. Should basic rights depend on measured effectiveness? If so, could a tyrant fail to uphold rights and then demand that they be abolished because they don't "work." Does this critique properly apply to a "remedy"?

Fourth Amendment is fully accomplished by the unlawful seizure itself, and the use of the "fruits" of a past unlawful search or seizure does not introduce a new Fourth Amendment violation. The Court noted that the exclusionary rule is designed to deter unconstitutional *police* activity, and not errors made by judges or personnel in judicial bureaucracies. It reasoned that there is no reason to believe that the exclusionary rule will deter errors by court clerks. Unlike police who are "zealous" in their desire to "get" suspects, court clerks "have no stake in the outcome of particular criminal prosecutions." This reasoning seems as wrongheaded as the application of the exclusionary rule in a case like *Sheppard.* This seems to have been recognized in Justice O'Connor's concurring opinion, expressing some concern that widespread computer errors might undermine individual rights. Justice Stevens dissented on the grounds that the text and the history of the Fourth Amendment indicates a more majestic goal of protecting individual privacy and liberty from encroachment from *any* part of the government. *Arizona v. Evans* (1995), perhaps a limited ruling, shows that rights can be lost from the negligent maintenance of modern technology as they can from more direct state action.

The Supreme Court has not approved an exclusionary rule exception for using illegally obtained evidence based on a police officer's good faith observations leading to a warrantless stop, arrest, or search. According to Professors Whitebread and Slobogin, the Court has deliberately avoided this issue.[41] Although there surely are instances when police arrest or search without probable cause, but do so in objective good faith, the inherent human subjectivity that tends to make every person a "biased judge" about his or her own actions would make such an exception a more risky proposition for individual rights than allowing the use of unconstitutional evidence obtained by the officer's good faith reliance on the judgment of the legislature or a judge.

Standing

Another rule that diminishes the exclusionary rule is **standing.** Not every defendant who is implicated by incriminating evidence is allowed to challenge the means by which it was seized. The concept of "standing to sue" is that a person must have a sufficient stake in a legal controversy in order to obtain a judicial resolution. Standing in constitutional cases is predicated on Article III of the Constitution, which confers jurisdiction on the Supreme Court and federal courts only in "cases or controversies." A person making a constitutional claim has "standing" only if the person has a right to begin with, i.e., a legal basis for the controversy. The Court has held that simply because evidence is introduced in a trial against a person does not give that person a Fourth Amendment right to challenge the constitutionality of the search and seizure. The Fourth Amendment standing doctrine grew out of the older concept that Fourth Amendment rights are based on property interests and that one had to have some level of property interest to assert a personal

LEON IN THE STATES

According to Professor Latzer, the following states have approved of the Leon rule by court action or statute: Arkansas, California, Indiana, Kansas, Kentucky, Louisiana, Missouri, Ohio, South Dakota, Texas, Utah, Virginia, and Wyoming. "The courts of several states have cast doubt upon the good faith concept without actually rejecting *Leon*": Arizona, Florida, Georgia, Illinois, Minnesota, Mississippi, North Carolina, Washington, Wisconsin. States which have repudiated Leon include: Connecticut, Idaho, Michigan, New Jersey, New Mexico, New York, Pennsylvania, and Vermont.

Barry Latzer, State Constitutional Criminal Law, § 2.11–14.

In *Connecticut v. Marsala,* the Connecticut Supreme Court, rejecting the application of the *Leon* good faith reliance on a warrant rule under the state constitution, suggested that *Leon* exaggerated the "costs" of the exclusionary rule and held that they were not so substantial as to overcome the benefits of the exclusionary rule. More critically, the Connecticut court rejected the idea that the Fourth Amendment is separate from the exclusionary rule. "The exclusionary rule places no limitations on the actions of the police. The fourth amendment does."[42]

claim against an alleged illegal search and seizure, i.e., to have standing.

Rules of standing have become more flexible than resting on a strict property basis, but are still restrictive. The position most favorable to defendants, yet never adopted by the Court, is the "target" theory. The target theory states that any defendant "against whom the search was directed," the "target," would have standing to challenge the constitutionality of the means by which the evidence was obtained. The Court has rejected this approach on the theory "that Fourth Amendment rights are personal rights which, like some other constitutional rights, may not be vicariously asserted." (*Alderman,* p. 174). Were it otherwise, a "target" could vicariously assert the rights of a victim of a search, possibly to the detriment of the person who had standing. As an expanded standing rule would expand the exclusionary rule, and as the present Court views the exclusionary rule as a "cost," it has stated that any incremental deterrent value in allowing a "target" to invoke the exclusionary rule "would justify further encroachment upon the public interest in prosecuting those accused of crime and having them acquitted or convicted on the basis of all the evidence which exposes the truth." (*Alderman,* p. 175)

In *Jones v. United States* (1960), petitioner was convicted of drug possession after being discovered by agents who entered an apartment with a warrant. The district and circuit courts held that Jones had no standing to challenge the warrant because he did not own the apartment and was a guest there. The Supreme Court reversed and held that Jones did have standing. It rejected technical property law classifications as the basis of standing and instead held that a defendant had standing to make a Fourth Amendment challenge when he was "legitimately on the premises."

After *Katz v. United States* created the "expectation of privacy doctrine" in 1967 (see Chapter 4), another basis for standing was created—that a person has a subjective and objective expectation of privacy in a premises. *Katz* logically would tend to expand Fourth Amendment standing, but the Court has not applied *Katz* in recent cases—indeed, it has narrowed the scope of standing, thus further restricting the applicability of the exclusionary rule.

In *Rakas v. Illinois* (1978), police stopped a car on suspicion of it having been involved in a recent robbery. Two women, including the owner, were in the front seat, and two men in the rear seat when the car was stopped. A warrantless search produced a sawed-off rifle and rifle shells. They were introduced in evidence to convict Rakas, one of the men in the car. The state courts ruled that Rakas, who did not claim ownership or possession of the guns and shells, had no standing to challenge the constitutionality of the automobile search. The Supreme Court agreed and refused to expand the rule of *Jones.* Indeed, it narrowed the rule. Essentially, Rakas argued that he had standing because he was legitimately in the car. Justice Rehnquist, writing for a five-justice majority, noted that the concept of standing added little to the analysis of the case. The real issue was whether the search violated the personal Fourth Amendment rights of the defendant, and that has to be determined by examining the facts of the case. The majority in *Rakas* stated that the phrase—"legitimately on the premises"—is too broad. Instead, a court must examine the defendant's connection with the premises. A casual visitor to an apartment, for example, has no standing to challenge a search, while an overnight guest does have standing. Justice White, dissenting, stated that the flaw in the majority opinion was that, "[t]he distinctions the Court would draw are based on relationships between private parties, but the Fourth Amendment is concerned with the relationship of one of those parties to the government."

Since *Rakas,* the Court has generally limited standing and, thus, has limited the exclusionary rule. In *Rawlings v. Kentucky* (1980), the Court held that Rawlings had no standing to challenge a search of a companion's purse, even though Rawlings claimed that the illegal drugs in the bag belonged to him. In *Jones,* the Supreme Court held that possession of the object of a possessory crime conferred standing. In *Rawlings* and a companion case, *United States v. Salvucci* (1980), this rule of automatic standing in possession cases was explicitly overruled. One reason for the *Jones* rule, that a defendant who claimed standing had to assert possession of contraband, has been reversed in order to preserve a defendant's Fifth Amendment interests, thus providing a reason to overrule the automatic standing rule.

In *Minnesota v. Olson* (1990), the Court affirmed the state court, which held that a defendant had standing in an apartment he did not own, to which he had no key, at which he had no possessions except extra clothes in a bag, and where he slept on the floor, but where he had indefinite permission to stay and had the right to allow or deny visitors entry. This holding appears to broaden *Jones* somewhat and creates standing for overnight guests. "To hold that an overnight guest has a legitimate expectation of privacy in his host's home merely recognizes the everyday expectations of privacy that we all share. . . . From the overnight guest's perspective, he seeks shelter precisely because it provides him with privacy, a place where he and his possessions will not be disturbed by anyone but his host and those his host allows inside" (*Minnesota v. Olson* [1990]).

Business occupants, however, are on a different footing. In *Minnesota v. Carter* (1998), police entered an apartment on a tip that illicit drug business was being conducted there and found two men bagging cocaine. They were from out of town and "had come to the apartment for the sole purpose of packaging the cocaine. [They] had never been to the apartment before and were only in the apartment for approximately 2 1/2 hours. In return for the use of the apartment, [they] had given [the renter] one-eighth of an ounce of the cocaine." On these facts the Court held that the defendants had no standing to challenge the police search.

> Property used for commercial purposes is treated differently for Fourth Amendment purposes than residential property. . . . And while it was a "home" in which respondents were present, it was not their home. Similarly, the Court has held that in some circumstances a worker can claim Fourth Amendment protection over his own workplace. . . . But there is no indication that respondents in this case had nearly as significant a connection to Thompson's apartment as the worker in *O'Connor* had to his own private office. . . .
>
> If we regard the overnight guest in *Minnesota v. Olson* as typifying those who may claim the protection of the Fourth Amendment in the home of another, and one merely "legitimately on the premises" as typifying those who may not do so, the present case is obviously somewhere in between. But the purely commercial nature of the transaction engaged in here, the relatively short period of time on the premises, and the lack of any previous connection between respondents and the householder, all lead us to conclude that respondents' situation is closer to that of one simply permitted on the premises. We therefore hold that any search which may have occurred did not violate their Fourth Amendment rights. (*Minnesota v. Carter,* pp. 90–91)

Justice Ruth Bader Ginsburg dissented, arguing that the decision undermines the security of short-term guests and anyone that a home owner or renter invites "into her home to share in a common endeavor, whether it be for conversation, to engage in leisure activities, or for business purposes licit or illicit, that guest should share his host's shelter against unreasonable searches and seizures."

According to Professor Heffernan, the Supreme Court's theory of standing is inconsistent with its theory of the exclusionary rule: "Using highly implausible arguments, [the Court] has continued to insist simultaneously on irreconcilable points: that exclusion's sole function is to deter the police, and that the opportunity to seek suppression must be limited to those complaining of violations of their own rights."[43] That is, the exclusionary rule is said not to be a personal right, but to challenge evidence one must assert one's personal rights under the Amendment. What is unmistakable is that the Court's restrictive standing rule is tied to its distaste for the exclusionary rule. A practical concern raised by Justice White in *Rakas* is the fear that lax standing rules, like the rule not allowing passengers to argue Fourth Amendment issues, "invites police to engage in patently unreasonable searches every time an automobile contains more than one occupant. Should something be found, only the owner of the vehicle, or of the item, will have standing to seek suppression, and the evidence will presumably be usable against the other occupants." (*Rakas,* pp. 168–69). While he doubted that most police officers would take advantage of the rule in this way, the larger point is that constitutional rules designed to protect individual liberty should not be structured in such a way as to give police the opportunity to skirt constitutional dictates.

Alternative Remedies

The King's officers who invaded the homes of John Wilkes and his associates in the 1760s were sued in English common law courts, found liable for trespass, and assessed considerable money damages. The colonials who challenged writs of assistance were, in effect, seeking injunctions to prevent the Crown from issuing general search warrants. When the Bill of Rights was ratified, it is likely that the framers assumed that violations of privacy by the government would lead to such lawsuits, which in turn would embarrass the government into reversing and preventing such abuses. As dissenting justices in *Wolf v. Colorado* and the majority in *Mapp v. Ohio* noted, however, police officers were almost never held responsible for violating individuals' Fourth Amendment rights. *Mapp* was predicated in part on the belief that *Weeks'* exclusionary rule was the best way of deterring police breach of rights. More recently, exclusionary rule critics have argued that alternate remedies are preferable. This section briefly reviews the alternative or parallel remedies to exclusion which fall into four general categories:

1. civil law suits,
2. injunctions against police action,
3. criminal prosecution of police officers, and
4. administrative measures.

Remedies are central to the law and to the legitimacy of government's promise to do justice. The foundation of federal judicial power, *Marbury v. Madison* (1803), stated that:

> The very essence of civil liberty certainly consists in the right of every individual to claim the protection of the laws, whenever he receives an injury.
>
> * * *
>
> The government of the United States has been emphatically termed a government of laws, and not of men. It will certainly cease to deserve this high appellation if the laws furnish no remedy for the violation of a vested right.[44]

As Professor Cornelia Pillard stated, "According to Marbury's ideal, legal rights are not mere precatory or aspirational statements, but remediable claims, redressable in courts, for violations of law."[45] In blunt terms, constitutional rights become meaningless platitudes unless officers and the state are held accountable and made to pay if and when their acts trample on the rights of individuals.

Civil Lawsuits for Damages

STATE COMMON LAW TORT SUITS A person alleging that an arrest or a search occurred without probable cause can sue the offending police officer for an intentional **tort** such as false imprisonment or trespass. Private lawsuits against government units or agents were at one time blocked by the common law doctrine of "sovereign immunity" that was inherited from England. States have lifted sovereign immunity in part, but actual rules differ in different states. In a Florida case, for example, a sheriff's deputy gratuitously beat a suspect in handcuffs during a booking procedure and the injured person sued the deputy and the Volusia County Sheriff's Department. Under Florida law, the deputy could be held liable for a civil battery if he acted within the scope of his employment. The department could be liable only if the deputy's acts exceeded the scope of his employment. Florida law was structured so that either the agency could be held liable, or the deputy, but not both.[46]

STATE CONSTITUTIONAL TORTS: STATE OFFICERS IN STATE COURT In addition to shoe-horning a constitutional violation into the shape of a common-law tort, some states' courts, following the federal example, have established distinct state constitutional torts: a direct cause of action for damages for violation of a constitutional right against a government or individual defendants. Unlike a state common-law tort, which is designed to vindicate personal interests, a constitutional tort "reinforces the moral accountability of the state and vindicates the reliance interest of the people; . . . [it] holds the government responsible as an agent of the people."[47] At the present time, nine states have recognized civil damages suits under their constitutions (a few with special conditions), nine state appellate courts have suggested that such lawsuits are proper under certain circumstances, and seven have rejected the idea.[48] For example, the New York Court of Appeals, that state's highest court, established a right to sue for a constitutional tort based on a violation of the search and seizure clause of the New York constitution. In that case, state police and local law enforcement officials embarked on a five-day "street sweep" in which every nonwhite male found in and around the City of Oneonta was stopped and interrogated for a reported crime.[49]

SECTION 1983: THE CIVIL RIGHTS ACT: STATE OFFICERS IN FEDERAL COURTS Most civil rights lawsuits against municipal police officers are conducted in federal court under the Civil Rights Act of 1871, which is found in Title 42 *United States Code,* section 1983, and are commonly known as **Section 1983 lawsuits.** This right of action in federal courts against state and local officers was created by Congress after the Civil War, under the authority of the Fourteenth Amendment in order to counteract Ku Klux Klan terrorism against African Americans. Such a lawsuit is based on a violation of a person's federal statutory or constitutional rights by persons "acting under the color of state law" or custom. The law was not much used for a century. After the Supreme Court held that a Fourth Amendment violation stated a Section 1983 claim in *Monroe v. Pape* (1961), thousands of Section 1983 suits proliferated. In *Monroe,* Chicago police officers without a warrant entered the plaintiff's home at night, rousted his family, and arrested and detained the plaintiff for ten hours without probable cause before his release. The history and wording of Section 1983 prevents lawsuits against state governments. In 1978, the Court, on reexamining the history of the statute, extended Section 1983 lawsuits to cases against municipal governments, making such suits more attractive to plaintiffs; however, such suits are limited to situations in which the officer acted pursuant to a municipal policy.[50]

***BIVENS* SUITS:** FEDERAL OFFICERS IN FEDERAL COURTS The Supreme Court in *Bivens v. Six Unknown Named Agents* (1971) held for the first time that there is a federal constitutional tort remedy for violations of constitutional rights by federal agents. Prior to that time, a person whose only remedy was a civil suit had to pursue a doubly anomalous suit against such officers under state common law torts. The Civil Rights Act of 1871 (creating Section 1983 suits) applied only against local officers. The facts in *Bivens* demonstrate that the only remedy for the wrongs done to him was a civil lawsuit for money damages. Webster Bivens was arrested at home by federal narcotics agents who searched his Brooklyn apartment "from stem to stern" and was strip-searched at booking. He was never prosecuted, so exclusion of evidence was a meaningless remedy and because it was unlikely that he would again be arrested, an injunction suit made no sense. His suit for damages, based on an illegal arrest and search and seizure, was thrown out of federal court because no such cause of action existed in federal law. If Bivens sued in state court, the federal government might have tried to remove the case to federal court where it would be dismissed on jurisdictional grounds. So, Bivens appealed to the Supreme Court, urging the creation of a federal tort remedy. The Supreme Court agreed with Bivens, in effect finding that the fundamental rule of a legal remedy for every legal wrong outweighed the doctrine of sovereign immunity that had previously blocked a federal constitutional tort. The Court noted that the underlying interests in a federal suit were more serious than a trespass suit under state law, and that after the creation of the expectation of privacy doctrine in *Katz v. United States* (1967), Fourth Amendment violations are deemed to be based on *constitutional* interests, and not simply on *property* rights that undergird one's right to be free of a civil trespass.

In addition to these standard avenues of redress, lawyers may seek other remedies that exist in state or federal common law. A startling example was a ruling by a Reagan-appointed federal trial judge that allowed the Los Angeles Police Department to be sued in August 2000, under the RICO (Racketeer Influenced and Corrupt Organizations) Act in the notorious Ramparts Division scandal. The scandal involved anywhere from a dozen to seventy officers systematically arresting at least one hundred innocent people, planting incriminating evidence on them, giving perjured testimony, improperly using Immigration officials in making arrests, and physically assaulting people without cause. The RICO law was first established to attack organized crime families, but has been extended to other organizations that use illegal means to further its goals and interfere with interstate commerce. The benefit to the plaintiffs in the suit is that the RICO statute of limitations is ten years and it allows triple damages. The potential damages to Los Angeles were put at $100 million.[51]

Injunctions

Injunctions are not common remedies for Fourth Amendment violations. An **injunction** is a judicial order that either (1) commands a defendant to perform a particular act, (2) prohibits specified activity, or (3) orders a defendant to cease wrongful activity from continuing. Injunctions may be granted by a court where plaintiffs can prove that rights violations are *persistent* and repeated and that an injunction is the *only effective remedy.* Injunctions are enforced by the judicial power of **contempt,** which can include fines or jail for disobedience.

The Supreme Court has been reluctant to uphold federal injunctions against local police departments. It struck down an injunction against the Los Angeles Police Department that prohibited the use of chokeholds in *Los Angeles v. Lyons* (1983), which were not specifically prohibited or authorized by departmental regulations. "At the time *Lyons* was decided, the chokehold had caused the deaths of over a dozen persons; by 1991, twenty-seven people had died as a result of this restraint technique. The Court dismissed the suit, holding that in order to have standing to sue for an injunction, the plaintiff must show that he is likely to be a future victim of that same technique."[52] In *Rizzo v. Goode* (1976), the Court reversed a federal injunction against the Philadelphia Police Department's cumbersome procedural process for investigating citizens' complaints about the use of excessive force. The Court reasoned that complainants had failed to demonstrate that the existing policy resulted in *routine and persistent* patterns of excessive force and civil rights violations. These cases demonstrate that the Supreme Court believes it is unwise for federal courts to become involved in close judicial supervision of police departments' administration. It is deemed more judicious in such cases for the administrative and political process to bring about policy changes in police departments.

A prohibitory injunction was issued by a lower federal court and upheld on appeal by the Fourth Circuit in *Lankford v. Gelston* (1966) against a local police department that had been conducting a "dragnet" type search. Police officers searching for the killers of fellow police officers had, over a three-week period, entered three hundred houses based on anonymous tips and without legal justification. Because there were no arrests, the exclusionary rule could not be used to deter the officers, and the police activity was flagrant and persistent. Under these circumstances, the injunction was justified.[53]

Criminal Prosecution

STATE PROSECUTIONS Criminal prosecutions of police officers for acts committed in the line of duty are rare and limited to egregious cases, typically involving the death of a suspect.[54] It is difficult to obtain such a conviction if the defense attorney convinces the jury that the officers acted reasonably to enforce the law or if the victim suffered little or no personal injury. A notable example was the acquittal, in February 2000, of four New York City Street Crime Unit police officers of the murder of Amadou Diallo, an African immigrant, who was shot nineteen times as he reached for his wallet. Professor James Fyfe, an expert who more often testifies against police, testified that the facts showed that the officers believed Diallo had a gun and acted properly. A juror said the prosecution had not proved that the officers acted criminally.[55]

The past decade has been rife with notorious prosecutions of police officers, including the trial and first acquittal of Los Angeles police officers for beating Rodney King, a speeding motorist, which was videotaped and played to a national audience.[56] In Detroit, police officers were convicted and imprisoned for the beating death of Malice Green.[57] Three white suburban Pittsburgh police officers were acquitted of manslaughter in the asphyxiation death of an African-American motorist, Jonny Gammage.[58] These sporadic prosecutions are a proper response to the specific cases, but they have an impact on systemic errors or abuse only if they spark reforms. In the aftermath of the Louima case, for example, New York City bowed to pressure and agreed to federal monitoring of the way in which officers accused of abuse are investigated and disciplined.[59]

FEDERAL PROSECUTIONS OF LOCAL POLICE OFFICERS A federal civil rights law originally enacted in 1866 authorizes federal prosecution of local officers who, acting under color of local law or custom, deprive a person of rights under the Constitution (18 U.S.C. § 242). The Supreme Court has held that a conviction requires a purpose to deprive a person of a specific constitutional right.[60] In recent decades, federal prosecutors have become more active in investigating and prosecuting crimes by local police. Federal civil rights prosecutions have included several high profile cases, e.g., the second trial of the police officers involved in the Rodney King beating and the trial of officers in the sexual brutalization of Haitian immigrant Abner Louima by New York City police officers. If the sexual torture inflicted on Louima was perpetrated by a private person all bystanders would justly be horrified. But the additional concern in a civil rights violation was captured by the words of the federal judge who sentenced the police officer to thirty years imprisonment: "Short of intentional murder, one cannot imagine a more barbarous *misuse of power* than Volpe's."[61] Misuse of power undermines trust in the government, makes people—especially the poor and dispossessed—skeptical of protection by the criminal justice system, and makes people believe that honest police officers are actual or potential rights-violators.

Administrative Remedies

Ideally, violations of constitutional rights should rarely, if ever, occur. External legal sanction, such as the exclusionary rule or civil suits, may control police behavior to some extent, but they are *reactions to past violations*—they encourage future compliance through punishment which has had limited effectiveness (see *Law in Society* section of this chapter). Non-judicial and administrative methods, therefore, are essential to encourage police to adhere to the Rule of Law. Methods for making police more understanding of the people they police and more mindful of rights include community policing, civilian review boards,[62] a police ombudsman,[63] accreditation of police departments,[64] civilianizing many roles in police departments,[65] tightening rules on the use of lethal force,[66] cultural diversity and sensitivity training,[67] higher standards for police recruits,[68] training in Asian martial arts,[69] and similar improvements. Better academy and in-service training in constitutional law is important. Jerome Skolnick and James Fyfe, leading police scholars, urge that the conditions under which there is a *duty* to use legitimate force be rethought and made more clear, to emphasize that *"The primary job of the police is to protect life."*[70]

If constitutional mandates like the Fourth Amendment are to be regularly obeyed by police officers, the impetus must come more from within police departments. For example, William Bratton, the innovative former New York City police commissioner, made obedience to the Constitution a key goal for the NYPD.[71] Policies that reward police with raises, promotions, and other advances if they follow constitutional guidelines are likely to guarantee stronger compliance with constitutional norms than external penalties. Police departments' internal review units clearly have a vital role to play.

Professor Christopher Slobogin, a leading criminal procedure scholar, has proposed that the exclusionary rule be abolished in favor of a legal-administrative program with the following features:

> An administrative agency would be responsible for bringing and assessing Fourth Amendment claims. The claims would be heard by a judge in proceedings that are streamlined in

> much the way most administrative proceedings are. Plaintiffs who prevail would receive liquidated damages amounting to a percentage of the typical field officer's salary (say, somewhere between one percent and five percent). The individual officer would be personally liable for the damages unless he or she acted in good faith, in which case the police department would be financially responsible. Variants of the damages remedy, such as class actions and injunctions, would also be available through the court. Appeals could be taken to the normal appellate court.[72]

Regardless of whether or not a state would adopt such a system, it indicates that many are searching for workable alternatives. In fact, one promising alternative approach has been passed by Congress.

PATTERN AND PRACTICE REVIEW A federal law passed as part of the Violent Crime Control and Law Enforcement Act of 1994, has brought the weight of the Department of Justice (DOJ) to bear on finding non-judicial solutions to police violations of constitutional rights. Title 42 U.S.C. § 14141 prohibits *governmental authorities* from engaging in a "pattern or practice of conduct by law enforcement officials" that deprives persons of constitutional rights. When the Attorney General has reasonable cause to believe that a violation has occurred, the Justice Department is authorized to sue for equitable and declaratory relief "to eliminate the pattern or practice." DOJ monitoring is not triggered by isolated incidents of unlawful acts but by conditions where unlawful acts have virtually become "standard operating procedure." The law is an attempt to find a better way to respond to situations like the Rodney King beating than to civil and criminal cases aimed at specific officers.

As of 1999, two police departments, Pittsburgh, Pennsylvania, and Steubenville, Ohio, have entered **pattern and practice** consent decrees for excessive force, improper searches and seizures, and false arrest. Nine other agencies were being investigated. The principal provisions of the consent decrees in those departments imposed requirements in the areas of police "training, the receipt and investigation of referrals and complaints concerning improper police behavior; and the development and maintenance of an early warning system." Although enforcement of Section 14141 is in its earliest stages, this "new remedy for police misconduct" seems to offer a substantial improvement over traditional tort remedies.[73]

Arguments Against the Exclusionary Rule

The discussion of exclusionary rule theories in the next section is related to the controversial policy question of whether the exclusionary rule should be abolished. To understand why this issue continues to be raised, it is useful to briefly review the battery of criticisms that have been leveled against the rule.

1. A civil lawsuit against offending police officers for a Fourth Amendment violation is a true remedy. It acts directly against the offending party and it is a traditional legal remedy for injuries. In contrast, the exclusion of evidence is not a liability that is necessarily felt by the officer: it causes a loss to a third party (the people, who lose an opportunity to truthfully adjudicate a criminal case), may give the victimized person a windfall in the guise of not being convicted, and still does not directly compensate the person whose rights were violated.
2. The exclusionary rule suppresses relevant evidence that tends to prove the defendant's guilt. Enforcing the Fourth Amendment in this way means, in the classic adage of Justice (then Judge) Cardozo, that "The criminal is to go free because the constable has blundered. . . ."[74] The cost to society of this is that the truth-finding attributes of the criminal trial are weakened, a crime goes unavenged, and a criminal is set free, perhaps to reoffend. This is in contrast to Fifth and Sixth amendment exclusionary rules that suppress confessions or lead to dismissals for lack of effective counsel where those errors might lead to the conviction of *innocent* defendants.
3. The exclusionary rule has no deterrent effect on Fourth Amendment violations where nothing is seized. In such cases, only the alternative remedies of civil lawsuits of criminal prosecution will vindicate the person whose rights were violated.
4. The actual deterrent effect of the exclusionary rule will never be known (see *Law in Society* section, this chapter). However, there are logical reasons why the exclusionary rule is not well suited to be an effective deterrent: (a) the impact of exclusion is directly felt by the prosecutor "rather than the cop," (b) police know and count on the fact that the rule is rarely applied, (c) judges are reluctant to find a Fourth Amendment violation when they know that evidence points to guilt (hindsight biasing).[75]
5. Although the "cost" of the exclusionary rule is worth paying in excluding evidence from the "case-in-chief" where it is likely to have the greatest effect, it need not be imposed where it will have limited effect, i.e., impeachment, grand jury questions, civil cases, deportation, parole revocation. It can be disregarded even in the trial to prove guilt where the officer reasonably and in good faith relied on the Fourth Amendment judgment of another official, such as a magistrate or the legislature because it will have limited deterrent effect.[76]

6. The exclusionary rule encourages of police perjury. Very few rogue police officers manufacture or plant evidence on innocent suspects, but many officers "shade the truth" when testifying in court, especially in possession cases. (See *Law in Society* section, Chapter 4). Not only is this a negative consequence for a sense of fairness in the courts, but police know that they can reduce the effectiveness of the exclusionary rule by their own success in undermining it.[77]
7. Any police sanctioning that occurs as a result of the exclusion of evidence, occurs indirectly when the prosecutor complains to police administrators, who relay such complaints down the chain of command; and such sanctioning tends to be offset by the praise and recognition that officers receive for making good arrests that are not outrageous.[78]
8. The doctrinal attacks on the exclusionary rule made by Justice Frankfurter in *Wolf v. Colorado* (1949) and by Justice Harlan dissenting in *Mapp v. Ohio* (1961), appear to have been triggered by powerful federalism concerns—Federalism and Judicial Activism—a traditionalist sense that the Supreme Court should not upset established modes of procedure in the states. Prior to the push to incorporate the exclusionary rule, there seems to have been little of the heated debate that erupted after *Wolf.* When the exclusionary rule became a politicized political issue in the 1960s, the conservative justices who were thereafter appointed tended to launch a strenuous attack on the rule, whether in federal or state cases, as instances of selective activism, as seen in opinions by Justices Burger, White, Powell, and Thomas in *Bivens v. Six Unknown Named Agents* (1971), *United States v. Calandra* (1974), *Stone v. Powell* (1976), *United States v. Leon* (1984), and *Pennsylvania Board of Probation* and *Parole v. Scott* (1998).

All the information provided about the development of the exclusionary rule, alternative remedies, and criticisms of the rule now provide a background to consider the ultimate question of whether the rule must be retained as a constitutional matter.

THEORIES OF THE EXCLUSIONARY RULE

The Supreme Court developed the exclusionary rule by reasoning from case to case and in response to arguments put forward by defendants and prosecutors in the legal "forum" (see Chapter 1), rather than by laying out a theoretically coherent plan. Different reasons, therefore, have been offered to justify the rule, leading to confusion. This section describes several of the theories used to justify the exclusionary rule. These justifications are intertwined with arguments in favor of and opposed to the existence of the rule.

No theory for (or against) the exclusionary rule is entirely coherent. The present state of the law is paradoxical, which can be seen in a brief overview of the rule's development:

1. From 1914 to 1974, the Court justified the rule as one required by the Constitution and applicable to legislatures, executive agencies (i.e., the police), and courts in cases like *Weeks* (1914), *Elkins* (1960), and *Mapp* (1961).
2. Since 1974, in cases like *Calandra* (1974) and *Leon* (1984), the Court has ruled that the exclusionary rule is *not* required by the Constitution, but is a judicially created remedy designed to deter Fourth Amendment violations by police only. (A minority of justices before 1974 argued that the rule was not constitutionally required, and a minority of justices after 1974 believe that it is.)
3. If the exclusionary rule is not a constitutional rule, then the Court's jurisdiction to create it in *Weeks* rested on supervisory authority, which applied only to federal cases. This idea casts doubt on the legitimacy of *Mapp* and the application of the rule to state courts. (This argument does not threaten *Rochin* (1952), which was based explicitly on the Fourteenth Amendment Due Process Clause.)
4. Were the existence of the exclusionary rule to come squarely before the Court, a variety of theoretical arguments could support its continued existence. (a) For example, the Court could modify the incorporation theory, going back to Justice Harlan's dissent in *Mapp,* and assert that only the core of the Fourth Amendment rule is applied to the states through the more flexible Fourteenth Amendment rule, allowing different rules for federal and state cases. This would require overruling *Ker v. California* (1963) and would revive the problematic silver-platter doctrine. (b) Or, the Court could dispose of a direct challenge to *Mapp* as it did with a direct challenge to *Miranda* in *Dickerson v. United States* (2000), by stating that however the present Court would have decided *Mapp* in 1961, principles of *stare decisis* (precedent) require that a rule that has been heavily relied on be maintained if its core meaning has not been eroded. (c) Finally, the Court could return to a renewed *Weeks-Mapp* understanding that the exclusionary rule is required by the logic of the Fourth Amendment, if one agrees with Professor William Heffernan that "[W]ithout an exclusionary principle, the Amendment collapses on itself."[79] The discussion in this section borrows heavily from articles by Professor Heffernan, who supports the exclusionary rule, and Professor Slobogin who believes it should be abolished—who delineate the following theories.

DETERRENCE THEORY All punitive and remedial systems have some general deterrent effect; thus, even if the exclusionary rule is based on non-consequentialist reasons, it would still likely deter some misconduct by police and magistrates. Nevertheless, since *Calandra,* the Supreme Court has made deterrence the sole rationale for the exclusionary rule, and since *Leon* has applied it only to police misconduct. As a result, where deterrence is thought minimal, the rule does not apply.[80] Because deterrence is a utilitarian rationale, its legitimacy turns primarily on whether it is effective. This has been the subject of a huge debate and is the focus of this chapter's *Law in Society* section. The following theories are based on non-consequential ideas and principles.

FIFTH AMENDMENT THEORY *Boyd* (1886) excluded evidence from an invoice based on the idea that the "Fourth and Fifth Amendments run almost into each other." Both amendments concern privacy rights, and most critically, the Fifth Amendment was seen to explicitly require exclusion by its words ("No person . . . shall be compelled in any criminal case to be a witness against himself. . . .), whereas the words of the Fourth Amendment do not explicitly command exclusion. Although *Weeks* explicitly rested on the Fourth Amendment, several cases thereafter relied on the *Weeks* Fourth + Fifth formula (*Gouled,* 1921), and Justice Black's crucial fifth vote in *Mapp* was based on this theory. It may have made sense because, in many of the early exclusionary rule cases, including *Weeks,* the items taken were letters or other documents. Nevertheless, the Court discarded the theory in *Andresen v. Maryland* (1976), which held that business records could be seized with a warrant, and this was confirmed by Justice White's comment in *Leon:* "The Fifth Amendment theory has not withstood critical analysis or the test of time."[81] The idea that a search compels the disclosure of evidence would make searches impossible, because "the Fifth Amendment excludes all compelled testimony, whether or not it was obtained by police who had probable cause."[82] This could not have been contemplated by the Fourth Amendment.

PROPERTY THEORY *Weeks* (1914) and *Silverthorne* (1920), among other cases, seem to rest on the idea that a defendant rather than the state has a greater property right over evidence illegally seized by the state. There are some inconsistencies with this theory. If the successful defendant requests the return of contraband, the request will be denied even if the evidence is suppressed.[83] The mere evidence rule of *Gouled* (1921) indicates that the government has a possessory interest superior to the defendant-owner in contraband, fruits of crime, and instrumentalities. Under existing forfeiture laws, all sorts of "innocent" items used in the commission of crime may be forfeited. The Court has undermined *Boyd* and has allowed the seizure of papers. All these examples undermine a strong property basis for the exclusionary rule. The final straw is the "expectation of privacy" doctrine of *Katz v. United States* (1967), which attempted, and partially succeeded, to recast the foundation of Fourth Amendment jurisprudence. By making nontangible information "seized" by electronic eavesdropping the subject of the Fourth Amendment, property was displaced, if not eliminated, as a theoretical basis of the exclusionary rule. The *Katz* philosophy was confirmed and strengthened by the abolition of the mere evidence rule in *Warden v. Hayden* (1967), under which Fourth Amendment principles (balancing law enforcement needs against individual privacy) outweigh property interests in determining whether the government may seize evidence.

STATUS QUO ANTE THEORY The exclusionary rule positions the parties where they would have been had the Constitution been followed. This is a strong, common sense, and ethical rationale. It also explains the inevitable discovery exception to the fruits of the poisonous tree doctrine: Because the police would have legally obtained the evidence in any event, they should not be placed in a difficult position because an unconstitutional search did happen. Professor Slobogin claims that the theory has holes because it does not result in the return of contraband and it cannot restore the "ruptured privacy" of the person subjected to an illegal search and seizure. His idea that the rule is not logically applied because it does not allow the introduction of evidence where the police *could have* lawfully obtained the evidence seems specious, and does not meet the deeper objections posed by Professor Heffernan. This theory blends into the last, and the most normative-ethical consideration, which is now reviewed. A conclusion as to the last theory will determine whether or not the exclusionary rule should be considered a necessary, constitutional rule. As Professor Heffernan shows, although he agrees with this point made by the Court and Professor Slobogin, it does not encompass the entire issue.

THE IMPERATIVE OF JUDICIAL INTEGRITY/RULE OF LAW The basic issue is whether the exclusionary rule is constitutionally required. The *Calandra-Leon* thesis is no, because (a) the rule is not explicit in the language of the amendment; (b) the purpose of the Fourth Amendment is to prevent unreasonable government intrusions into the *privacy* of one's person, house, papers, or effects; (c) the invasion of privacy is *fully accomplished* by the original search without probable cause; and (d) the *use* of evidence illegally seized works no new Fourth Amendment wrong but is only a derivative use of the product of past unlawful search and seizure. Because the exclusionary rule, which has been created by the Supreme Court to deter police illegality, reaches only the derivative use of the evidence and not the Fourth Amendment wrong, it is not constitutionally required.

Justice Brennan, dissenting in *Calandra,* provided the following answer to these arguments: (a) the justices who established the exclusionary rule made no mention of deterrence as a rationale but fashioned an enforceable remedy to give content and meaning to the Fourth Amendment's guarantees; (b) as judges have no direct power over the police, a remedy has to be feasible; (c) one goal of the exclusionary rule was to ensure that the courts would not be tainted by partnership in official lawlessness; (d) another goal of the exclusionary rule was to assure the people that the government would not profit from its lawless behavior; (e) the exclusionary rule is consistent with the Rule of Law; (f) *Linkletter v. Walker* (1965), the non-retroactivity case, can be explained pragmatically as taking into account state reliance on the precedent of *Wolf v. Colorado* (1949), and the possible "wholesale release of innumerable convicted prisoners" (*U.S. v. Calandra* [1974] pp. 355–61).

Professor Slobogin dismisses a variety of formulations for the judicial integrity/Rule of Law theory. For example, regarding the argument that an illegal search and seizure is a nullity and cannot be used at all, he points out that the Supreme Court, under some circumstances, allowed the use of illegally seized evidence for impeachment during the era when the rule was viewed as a constitutional requirement; therefore, it could not have been seen as a nullity (*Walder v. U.S.,* 1954). Also, *Mapp* was held not to be retroactive, implying that it is not an absolute constitutional right.[84] He concludes that none of the theories in support of the exclusionary rule "provide grounds for concluding that it is appropriate as a remedy in the typical case."

Professor Slobogin's position and numerous other arguments may have been answered by Professor Heffernan's thorough analysis of the *Calandra-Leon* thesis, which takes into account the structure and functions of remedies in light of the multiplicity of interests protected by the Fourth Amendment. Most commentators on the exclusionary rule discuss remedies without thinking through their different levels and goals. Heffernan demonstrates that there are three types and goals of remedies. *First-party remedies* aim at **reparation** to restore the injured party to his position before the injury occurred. *Second-party* remedies have the goal of **disgorgement** to place the wrongdoer in no better position than the one he occupied prior to his wrongful conduct. *Third-party* remedies aim at *deterrence* of future wrongdoing to the benefit of the general public. In practice, these types and goals of remedies may overlap in a single case, and may be mutually supportive or at odds with one another. All three rationales have been used by the Supreme Court to support the exclusionary rule.

Next, Professor Heffernan notes that Fourth Amendment cases indicate that the amendment protects three distinct rights: liberty, property, and privacy—not just privacy. He agrees with the Court's doctrine that once the *privacy* rights of a suspect have been breached by a wrongful search and seizure, it is irreversible. However, if exploitation of the privacy interest is obtained by violating a defendant's property or liberty interests, these are *ongoing violations* that can be repaired by a return of the property or a freeing of the defendant. The government cannot insist on holding onto illegally seized evidence in order to determine if it discloses incriminating information, for that would allow seizures before probable cause is obtained. "Absent exclusion, all personal property is held on a probationary basis: government agents can seize personal property at will, inspect it, and return it only if it is found not to provide evidence of a crime."[85] The internal logic of the Fourth Amendment cannot allow this kind of *retroactive legitimation.* If the exclusionary rule were totally eliminated, police could choose to violate Fourth Amendment rights in specific cases they deem important and be willing to pay the price in a tort action if it came to that. Thus, Heffernan believes that Justice Holmes and the Court had it right in *Silverthorne* (1920). Whatever the framers thought about exclusion as a remedy, the Court in *Weeks* and *Silverthorne* intuited that the exclusionary principle "emerges from an analysis of the internal logic of the Amendment itself."[86] Professor Heffernan asks the reader to consider the obscure case of *Smith v. Ohio* (1990) discussed previously in the section on the fruits of the poisonous tree doctrine. Without the logic of exclusion, police, without probable cause or reasonable suspicion, could stop people and search them; a court confronted with such a scenario would have to accept evidence obtained in this way. To Heffernan, the logic of exclusion lies in the interplay of privacy and the Fourth Amendment protected interests of property and liberty. That is, the "fully accomplished" invasion of a suspect's privacy interests was accomplished by a simultaneous invasion of the suspect's property or liberty interests which can be redressed by returning the property or releasing the suspect. Should the government not be able to retain the information, which lies at the heart of the invasion of privacy interests? After all, instead of first obtaining probable cause, the government violated property rights and subsequently found probable cause. This is a wrong that calls for the second-party remedy of disgorgement. Heffernan concludes, then, by conceding that exclusion cannot remedy the privacy violation via a first party-remedy, and that the public pays a high cost in the third-party remedy, but he finds that the aim of the second-party type of remedy (disgorgement) is met by exclusion.

To make the point, he raises a hypothetical question: If the police were to enter a home and seize computer diskettes suspected of containing criminal information, but which are encrypted, should the government be allowed to hold the diskettes in order to break the code if the owner sues for their return? Professor Heffernan suggests that this attempt to cause irreparable harm to the suspect's privacy interest requires their return. Further, the internal logic against retroactive justification overrides the historical reality that the framers did not consider exclusion, because without the exclusionary rule the Amendment collapses on itself.[87] In sum, the Supreme Court was correct in establishing the exclusionary rule as a constitutional rule in *Weeks* and in extending it to the states in *Mapp* as a constitutional requirement.

LAW IN SOCIETY

Costs and Benefits of the Exclusionary Rule

Since 1974, the Supreme Court has confronted two empirical issues concerning the exclusionary rule: its deterrent effect and its costs in lost convictions. Both issues have been used in arguments for and against the rule, so that studies and findings have been examined with partisan intensity. In the course of examining these empirical questions, the Supreme Court has used and, on occasion, misused social science data. This section reviews some of the findings on these sensitive issues.

In order to understand human behavior, social scientists first attempt to accurately measure behavior systematically and with quantitative precision to the greatest extent possible. Statistical tests are applied to data to determine the extent to which the collected data (a sample) reflects actual behavior (the universe). These rigorous attempts to quantify knowledge contrast with the human tendency to generalize: to make overly broad conclusions about human behavior based on a small number of personal experiences or on the basis of a few stories heard from others or from external sources.

The Deterrent Effect of the Exclusionary Rule

CALANDRA V. UNITED STATES (1974) "adopted the view that the primary rationale for the federal exclusionary rule is the factual premise that suppression of illegally seized evidence will deter the police from conducting illegal searches."[88] Only a few studies of the exclusionary rule had been published by 1974. The most prominent, by Dallin Oaks, appeared to show that the exclusionary rule had no effect on police behavior in several cities.[89] Oaks's *data* did *not* conclusively show whether the exclusionary rule deterred police misconduct. Rather, his stated *personal opinion* was that the rule failed to deter and should be abolished. According to Thomas Davies, "the Oaks study has probably established something of a record for being widely cited as empirical support for a finding it did not really claim to make."[90]

Proponents of the exclusionary rule were fearful that the Supreme Court would use a finding of no deterrence to abolish the rule. For example, in his *Bivens* dissent, Chief Justice Burger stated: "If an effective alternative remedy is available, concern for official observance of the law does not require adherence to the exclusionary rule." This would be especially troublesome if the Court made constitutional law based on flawed research. Indeed, Oaks's research conclusion, if not his data, was flawed in that he believed the exclusionary rule failed simply because Fourth Amendment violations continued to occur after the *Mapp* decision. This was a conceptual failure: The more appropriate question was whether the number and rates of such violations increased, decreased, or remained level after *Mapp.* Oaks failed to make these comparisons.[91]

In *United States v. Janis* (1976), a careful and exhaustive review of the deterrence research in Justice Harry Blackmun's majority opinion finally put to bed the deterrence issue. The issue in *Janis* was whether the exclusionary rule would be extended to federal IRS civil tax assessment hearings to exclude illegally seized evidence. A strong finding about the deterrent effect could sway the Court to extend the rule or to abolish it. Justice Blackmun's honest review of the research literature concluded that there is *no conclusive evidence that the rule has or does not have a deterrent effect:* "The final conclusion is clear. No empirical researcher, proponent or opponent of the rule, has yet been able to establish with any assurance whether the rule has a deterrent effect even in the situations in which it is now applied." (*Janis,* fn. 22.) The way in which the Court applied this equivocal and correct empirical conclusion is interesting. Justice Blackmun said that even if the exclusionary rule has a strong deterrent effect "the additional marginal deterrence provided" by extending the rule to federal civil tax proceedings "surely does not outweigh the *cost to society* of extending the rule to that situation" (*Janis,* pp. 453–54, emphasis added). The majority in *Janis* clearly did not want to extend the exclusionary rule and so its analysis had a "heads I win, tails you lose" quality, by switching the focus of inquiry from deterrence to the costs of the exclusionary rule.

Nevertheless, the Court's conclusion in *Janis* in regard to the empirical research is supported by Professor Davies' most thorough review of the issue.[92] The problem is not so much that of poor research designs, but of the special difficulty of defining and studying legal deterrence. According to Davies, "it is quite unlikely that there will be any rigorous measurement of the rule's specific deterrent effect in terms of how often illegal searches have been prevented."[93] This problem arose partly because the research community paid little attention to the exclusionary rule when criminal justice research made it clear that the rule was a minor factor in the total disposition of cases. Thus, studies on the effectiveness of deterrence and on its "costs" were left to policy-relevant studies that framed the issue narrowly.[94]

The Educative Effect of the Exclusionary Rule

Another empirical question is whether the exclusionary rule has had a broad educative effect. Proponents have not been able to establish this by rigorous empirical research, but there is some anecdotal evidence that because of the rule, police are now trained in the law, police and prosecutors seriously discuss search and seizure rules, and the police community generally takes the Fourth Amendment more seriously than it did before *Mapp.*[95] A study comparing drug, weapons, and gambling arrests in nineteen cities before and after *Mapp* appears to indicate that *Mapp* had a decided effect in six cities, no effect in ten cities, and an intermediate effect in three.[96] This suggests "that Mapp's impact largely has been mediated by differentials in attitudes and styles among police and civic leaders. . . . [T]he police are likely to behave differently in a city where the chief almost openly encourages evasion of a Supreme Court decision than in one where the chief insists on obedience."[97]

This is supported by the observational study of police by law professor Richard Uviller, who noted that honest police officers bring to their work an "innate sense of limits" that prevails "over the broad license allowed by law" in many situations.[98] Too often the "legal focus" portrays police as overly aggressive, overly zealous, and filled only with a "crime control" mentality. Uviller's closely observed police officers display a good deal of common sense, decency, and a real desire to operate within the limits of the law, even if they are not always precisely correct about the operative rules. This perspective is one that suggests that, over the long run, police behavior actually will become more law-abiding. One may also speculate that as Burger and Rehnquist Court decisions are more favorable to the police, it is easier for police to obey rules of constitutional criminal procedure. A more cynical possibility may be that successful evasion of the exclusionary rule is a factor in police acquiescence to the rule. All these factors may be at play simultaneously. In any event, to bring police behavior into line with constitutional norms requires practical training for police officers. Where the law does place limits on what the police may do, departments are well advised to include some training into the reasons for these limits.

Costs of the Exclusionary Rule

The Court, in its anti-exclusionary rule mood, tended to emphasize the costs of lost convictions in broad terms. Justice White's concurrence in *Illinois v. Gates* (1983) is an example of poorly reviewing social science studies, in contrast to Justice Blackmun's more precise review of the deterrence studies. For example, his broad conclusion—"We will never know how many guilty defendants go free as a result of the rule's operation"[99]—is wrong. To make matters worse, he quoted a misleading National Institute of Justice (NIJ) study that reported: "prosecutors rejected approximately 30 percent of all felony drug arrests because of search and seizure problems."[100] As we shall see, this was a gross exaggeration of the costs of the exclusionary rule.

Unlike deterrence, which is inherently difficult to measure, lost cases can be more precisely measured. Because the total number of arrests and the number of cases dismissed owing to search and seizure errors can be obtained from prosecution and court records, the proportion of "lost cases" can be calculated. Several research studies are in general agreement that the "costs" of the exclusionary rule are not great. In almost all instances, the percentage of cases dropped because the proportion search and seizure problems is *less than one percent:*

1. *Forst, Lucianovic, and Cox* (1974)—arrests in Washington, D.C.: prosecutors rejected 168 out of 17,534 arrests (1 percent) for all kinds of due process problems, including but not limited to, search and seizure violations.
2. *Brosi* (1977)—prosecutors declined to issue complaints for all types of due process errors in 1 percent of the cases in Washington, D.C., 2 percent in Cobb County, Georgia, 2 percent in Salt Lake City, 4 percent in Los Angeles, and 9 percent in New Orleans.[102]
3. *Forst et al.* (1977 and 1978)—due process violations led to dismissals in less than 1 percent of arrests in six cities, 2 percent in Los Angeles and 6 percent in New Orleans.[103]
4. *General Accounting Office* (1979)—case attrition in federal prosecutions: prosecutors declined to accept 46 percent of all cases; 6.6 percent of the declined cases were rejected for legal violations overall, 0.4 percent of all cases were declined because of illegal searches.[104]
5. *Nardulli* (1983)—reviewed 7,500 cases in nine counties in three states; motions to suppress physical evidence filed in fewer than 5 percent of the cases and were successful in 0.69 percent of the cases; motions to suppress illegal confessions or identifications were filed in 2 percent of the cases and successful in 4 percent of these; some defendants were convicted even after the evidence was suppressed; in the entire sample, 46 out of 7,500 cases were lost (less than 0.6 percent) because of the three exclusionary rules combined.[105]

6. *Feeney et al.* (1983)—nine out of 885 nonconvictions (1 percent) were lost due to illegal searches; since about half of the arrests resulted in nonconvictions, 0.5 percent of the cases in Jacksonville and San Diego were lost because of the exclusionary rule.[106]
7. *Uchida and Bynum* (1991)—seven cities: 1.4 percent of all defendants (19 out of 1,355) in cases based on search warrants were granted motions to suppress.[107]

Despite the virtually unanimous conclusion that about one percent or less of cases are lost because of the rule, Justice White claimed in *Gates* that 30 percent of the cases were lost due to excluded evidence. He based this on a federal study of California case processing, and repeated the figure put forward in the solicitor general's brief. Davies notes that the NIJ study was seriously flawed and that the 30 percent figure is grossly misleading. First, the NIJ study showed that 4.8 percent of *all rejected* felony cases are lost because of search and seizure problems. This in no way indicates the cost of the exclusionary rule—it does not show what proportion of cases are lost due to the rule; it instead shows that *among those cases that prosecutors rejected,* 4.8 percent were lost due to the exclusionary rule. This is meaningless because the percentage calculated in this way can change dramatically depending on changes in the other reasons for dismissals. When the NIJ data of lost cases are calculated against a *base figure of total arrests,* those lost due to the exclusionary rule drop to about 0.8 percent, more in line with the other studies. As for the 30 percent figure, it was drawn from a sample of 150 drug cases from two local prosecutors' offices in Los Angeles, which was not at all representative, for, as Davies indicates, between 1978 and 1982 statewide, California prosecutors rejected 2.4 percent of felony drug arrests because of illegal searches.

Further, the studies show that the number of cases rejected on Fourth Amendment grounds in *serious violent felonies* is lower, about 0.2 percent of all arrests, and somewhat higher for drug offenses. Davies makes the point that many such rejected arrests in drug cases may not be those of carefully planned raids, but rather are arrests on suspicion where drugs are found and the probable cause basis is very weak to begin with. Thus, unlike the inconclusive result of the exclusionary rule's deterrent effect, research findings of its costs firmly show that fewer than one percent of arrests are lost because of the exclusionary rule. In half of these lost cases, *convictions are still obtained* because of other evidence.

Do these findings mean that the costs are low? This is a normative issue. The figures show that the exclusionary rule is not subverting law enforcement efforts. Yet, its effect may still be unacceptably high to some. "Indeed, some critics have taken the position that *even one lost arrest* is an excessive cost."[108] Thus, when Justice White had to confront this new evidence, he stated that "the small percentages with which [the researchers] deal mask a large absolute number of felons who are released because the cases against them were based in part on illegal searches or seizures" (*United States v. Leon,* 1984, fn. 6). Of course, in a country with a population of 260 million, virtually any small percentage will generate large numbers. I would tend to agree with Uchida and Bynum, quoting Van Duizend and colleagues, "that the 'exclusionary rule, though seldom invoked, serves as an incentive for many police officers to follow the limits imposed by the Fourth Amendment as defined in their jurisdictions."[109] Thus, the exclusionary rule debate presents an interesting case history of the use and misuse of social science data in the judicial decision-making process.

The Effectiveness of Tort Remedies

Another aspect of the exclusionary rule debate is the effectiveness of tort suits against the police. The evidence is generally that they do not provide strong control over police misbehavior, including police brutality. Empirical studies of *Bivens* suits, for example, disclose that they virtually never lead to findings of police officer liability.

> Government figures reflect that, out of approximately 12,000 *Bivens* claims filed between 1971 and 1985, *Bivens* plaintiffs actually obtained a judgment that was not reversed on appeal in only four cases. While similar figures have not been systematically kept since 1985, recoveries from both settlements and litigated judgments continue to be extraordinarily rare. According to one estimate, plaintiffs obtain a judgment awarding them damages in a fraction of one percent of *Bivens* cases and obtain a monetary settlement in less than one percent of such cases. The low rate of successful claims indicates that, notwithstanding *Bivens,* federal constitutional violations are almost never remedied by damages. The low success rate of these claims also reflects that the courts are processing a tremendous amount of *Bivens* litigation. When analyzed by traditional measures of a claim's "success"—whether damages were obtained through settlement or court order—*Bivens* litigation is fruitless and wasteful, because it does not provide the remedies contemplated by the decision, and it burdens litigants and the judicial system.[110]

While recovery in other kinds of tort cases against the police may not be quite so nonexistent, they are hard to obtain and monetary claims are low. In a study based on telephone interviews with civil rights attorneys in southern California, a variety of reasons were given for the lack of success[111]:

- Civil rights attorneys are unwilling to take weak cases;
- witnesses with past criminal records are not credible to jurors;
- police have a qualified immunity defense for acts taken in good faith;
- municipalities provide the costs of defense and pay for any settlement in cases won by plaintiffs;
- it is more difficult for plaintiffs to discover facts in the hands of defendants in these cases compared to other civil litigation;
- defendants can tie up plaintiffs, who tend to have limited resources, with interlocutory appeals in § 1983 suits;
- the "blue curtain" of silence makes police witnesses very reluctant to testify;
- police perjury is rampant (see *Law in Society* section in Chapter 4);
- jurors almost always believe the police.

As a result, the likely deterrent effect of lawsuits on police *brutality* is very low. Commissions on police brutality report that many cases of abuse are committed by officers who are repeat offenders, indicating that departments do a poor job of sanctioning officers with a history of excessive violence. Many cities in the last decade have paid out multiples of millions of dollars in tort damages for police brutality, and the numbers do not appear to have substantially diminished. Although there seems to be a slight, growing public interest in police brutality in the early 21st century, there is virtually no political pressure for police departments to abide by the Constitution.[112] As Professor Canon noted in his study of police departments that follow warrant procedure, much depends on the attitudes of the police chief. "The chief and higher-ranking supervisors establish the tone and culture within a police department. If the upper ranks do not enforce violations of department policy, there will be no curb on officers' misconduct out on the street." Chiefs who are concerned with the legal conduct of their officers can affect policy and action by the selection of field training officers, by their own disciplinary decisions, by the emphasis given to legal issues in academy and in-service training, and by having records of tort cases become part of an officer's file and be taken into account in promotions.[113] All such measures should not lead to demoralization of police officers or overdeterrence so that police shy away from performing their difficult jobs effectively. But there are examples, such as William Bratton's tenure as New York City police commissioner, that, to paraphrase Justice Tom Clark, there is no war between effective policing and law-abiding policing.

SUMMARY

The structure and content of search and seizure law is the product of history. English common law came to protect the privacy of one's home against *government* invasion shortly before the framing of the Constitution (1787) in the *Writs of Assistance* case and the *Wilkes* cases. They held that general warrants are illegal and that a victim of a general warrant could sue the government for damages.

The Fourth Amendment was intended to eliminate the government's use of general search warrants. In the founding era, police had no power to conduct warrantless arrests or searches based on probable cause; a warrant was required. Nevertheless, modern constitutional interpretation authorizes warrantless arrests and searches upon probable cause under the general-reasonableness construction of the Fourth Amendment. The warrant-preference construction holds that warrants are required except in hot pursuit, vehicle searches and search incident to arrest.

The Fourth Amendment exclusionary rule states that illegally seized evidence may not be introduced into evidence in a trial. It was established in *Weeks v. United States* (1914) and *Silverthorne Lumber Co. v. United States* (1920). The rule was based on the Constitution and stated that illegally seized evidence shall not be used at all. The rule applies only to government officers, not to illegal searches by private individuals. Evidence derived from illegally seized evidence cannot be introduced into evidence (fruits of the poisonous tree doctrine), despite an illegal search, even though evidence of the crime may be introduced if it is obtained from an independent source, by inevitable discovery, or because the link between the primary illegality and the evidence seized has become attenuated.

The Supreme Court incorporated the exclusionary rule (extended it to the states) in *Mapp v. Ohio* (1961), after having refused to do so in *Wolf v, Colorado* (1949) and *Rochin v. California* (1952). In the latter case, the Court excluded evidence that was seized by methods that "shocked the conscience." This was a due process, "totality of the circumstances," test, and criticism of its subjectivity was a factor in the *Mapp* decision. The basis of *Mapp* was that the exclusionary rule is required by the Fourth Amendment and that exclusion is the best deterrent of police misbehavior.

After *Mapp,* a more conservative Supreme Court eroded the exclusionary rule. It upheld the use of illegally seized evidence to impeach a witness in *United States v. Calandra* (1974), which modified the theoretical basis of the exclusionary rule. It became viewed as a judicially created remedy designed to safeguard Fourth Amendment rights generally through its deterrent effect on future unlawful police conduct, rather than a personal constitutional right of the party aggrieved. This concept was expanded by *United States v. Leon* (1984), which allowed the introduction of illegally seized evidence for the proof of guilt where the evidence was obtained by police officers in the "good faith" reliance on a statute or search warrant. It also held that the exclusionary rule does not apply to unconstitutional acts committed by the judiciary.

In order to challenge evidence taken in violation of the Fourth Amendment, a party must have standing, that is, the party must have suffered a personal invasion of privacy rights rather than suffered actual harm because of the invasion of the privacy rights of another person. In *Rakas v. Illinois* (1978), the Court held that a passenger of an automobile does not have such a personal right. A personal interest to raise a Fourth Amendment challenge does not depend on the defendant's strict property right but in his level of interest in a place; thus, overnight guests in an apartment have standing, but persons invited into an apartment for business purposes do not have standing.

Aside from the exclusionary rule, individuals whose Fourth Amendment rights have been violated have other potential sources of relief. These include lawsuits against the police officer or the department. Different types of tort lawsuits include: state common law tort suits, state constitutional torts wherein state officers are sued in state courts, Section 1983–civil rights suits against state and local officers and municipalities (but not state governments) in federal courts, and *Bivens* suits against federal officers in federal courts. For violations that are likely to persist against specific individuals, injunctions that prohibit the illegal police activity from recurring are available, but the Supreme Court generally disfavors injunctions. Federal and state criminal prosecutions are also brought against police officers, but are typically reserved for the most egregious violations involving unnecessary violence. Police departments can improve their record of abiding by the law by adopting better recruitment, training, and supervision procedures and by other administrative measures. Congress passed Title 42 U.S.C. § 14141 in 1994, allowing the Department of Justice to bring suits against police departments to correct violations by means such as improved hiring, training, and complaint procedures where a pattern or practice of conduct by law enforcement officials that deprives persons of Constitutional rights has been proven.

The exclusionary rule remains controversial. Arguments against it include: it is not a true remedy against the offending officer; it suppresses relevant evidence of crime and thus thwarts the truth finding goal of the criminal trial; it has little or no deterrent effect; it leads to police perjury; and it undermines the authority of the states to fashion their own rules of criminal procedure.

Fourth Amendment law has been confused because there are overlapping and conflicting theories of the exclusionary rule. These include the idea that the rule is required by the Constitution; that it is only a judicially created rule designed to deter police from violating individual's rights; that it is based on the Fifth Amendment privilege against self-incrimination; that it is based on property rights; that it is based on returning the parties to their original position; that once breached privacy rights can never be repaired; and that violations of privacy interests involve property or liberty violations that should be repaired under a theory of disgorgement. Each of these theories has at least one weakness. Thus, there is some level of policy choice open to jurists in deciding how to justify the exclusionary rule.

LEGAL PUZZLES

How Have Courts Decided These Cases?

3–1. Two roofers accidentally damaged siding on a house they were re-roofing. Paige, the owner, had told them earlier to go into a work room in a detached garage if they needed anything. The roofers went into the garage looking for sections of siding. Not finding them in the workroom, a roofer lifted himself into an attic space and saw a scale and several packages, which appeared to be drugs. The roofer called his father, the owner of the roofing company and a deputy sheriff. The father arrived without a warrant and determined the substance to be marijuana. He informed an assistant district attorney, who told a narcotics detective to return to the property and examine the substance. He did so, and without a warrant the detective entered the attic and confirmed the marijuana by its odor. Paige, who had returned home, was then arrested, and the marijuana was seized. Was the warrantless search, or seizure, by the detective an extension of the initial private search? *U.S. v. Paige,* 136 F.3d 1012 (5th Cir. 1998).

3–2. Fultz, a homeless man, was suspected of a robbery. Detectives went to a home where he had stayed off and on. The owner said that Fultz, who was last seen twenty-four hours before, had left his belongings in a box in the garage, and gave the officers permission to search the house but did not give consent to search Fultz's belongings. The officers went through Fultz's belongings in the garage, opened a cardboard box, and found a sawed-off gun, introduced to convict Fultz of possessing an unregistered firearm. Did Fultz have standing to challenge the search of a cardboard box? *U.S. v. Fultz,* 146 F.3d 1102 (9th Cir. 1998).

3–3. Francis, a probationer, signed a contract with Louisiana Home Detention Services, Inc. (LHD), a private company designated by the State of Louisiana to monitor individuals placed in home incarceration, allowing the warrantless search of his home if LHD employees had probable cause to believe he possessed contraband. This condition was never imposed by a court. After a traffic stop, police inquired of LHD and developed probable cause to believe Francis possessed drugs in his home. LHD employees and police went to Francis' address and requested entry. Francis said the house belonged to his girlfriend. She refused to allow entry, but did so after being told that the officers would enter whether she consented or not. The court held that warrantless entry was not consensual and that the contract provision allowing entry on probable cause was illegal because the condition was not imposed by a judge. Is the search legal because the officers relied on the contract in good faith? *U.S. v. Francis,* 183 F.3d 450 (5th Cir. 1999).

3–4. Allen was approached while boarding an inter-city bus by police officers who asked if they could search his bag. He consented, and marijuana was found in his knapsack. Officers went through the bus and found a duffel bag that no passenger claimed. Allen denied owning the duffel bag. The bag was opened, without a warrant, and crack cocaine, plus information identifying Allen as the owner, were found. The district court found that the duffel bag was not abandoned. Thus, its search was unconstitutional. The officer testified that if she thought the duffel bag belonged to Allen, she would have requested a K-9 dog to sniff the duffel bag. She had never brought a trained dog onto a bus before. The dog used at that location had been successful in identifying drugs at the undercarriage of the bus in the past, but not in individual luggage. Was the crack cocaine found in the duffel bag admitted into evidence on the basis of inevitable discovery? *U.S. v. Allen,* 159 F. 3d 832 (4th Cir. 1998).

ANSWERS TO LEGAL PUZZLES

3–1 NO. The initial search of the attic was by private parties and not directed by the police (Paige did not challenge the search by the father-deputy). The search by the detective was not a Fourth Amendment intrusion because he was invited by private parties who had discovered what might be drugs, under circumstances that lessened Paige's expectation of privacy because they were foreseeable. Although Paige lost his expectation of privacy in his property, he retained a possessory interest in it, protected by the Fourth Amendment. His Fourth Amendment right was violated because the seizure of the marijuana was intended to be permanent and to test the entire batch, and thus went beyond the scope of the private search.

3–2 YES. He had an expectation of privacy in his closed containers. The homeowner had no authority to consent to a search of an area in which she did not share and had been given no permission to go through. "Although certain types of containers—suitcases, valises, purses, and footlockers, for instance—do command high expectations of privacy, this does not mean that other types of containers in which people store their personal belongings command no expectation of privacy. . . . As a practical matter, Fultz's boxes *were* his suitcases or valises or footlockers. After all, such containers are used to store personal belongings. Courts recognize that people have the highest expectations of privacy in these containers not because of what they look like or because of what they cost, but presumably because of what they contain."

3–3. NO. The officers did not have a subjective good faith belief that the contract authorized the search. Officer Judice (who made the traffic stop) testified that he did not believe the contract allowed the search.

3–4. NO. There is no showing that the officer would have used the dog. The officer stated that she would have brought in the dog if Allen claimed ownership of the bag—the predicate for the officer's dog use—but Allen never claimed the bag. "A finding of inevitable discovery necessarily rests on facts that did not occur. However, by definition the occurrence of these facts must have been likely, indeed 'inevitable,' absent the government's misconduct," and that is not shown in this case.

FURTHER READING

J. David Hirschel, *Fourth Amendment Rights* (Lexington, Mass: Lexington Books, 1979).

Richard C. Cortner, *The Supreme Court and the Second Bill of Rights: The Fourteenth Amendment and the Nationalization of Civil Liberties* (Madison: University of Wisconsin Press, 1981).

H. Richard Uviller, *The Tilted Playing Field: Is Criminal Justice Unfair?* (New Haven.: Yale University Press, 1999).

ENDNOTES

1. William J. Cuddihy, *The Fourth Amendment: Origins and Meaning, 602–1791* (Doctoral Dissertation), pp. xc–xciv; Susan Ford Wiltshire, *Greece, Rome, and the Bill of Rights,* (Norman: University of Oklahoma Press, 1992), pp. 146–49.
2. Cuddihy, p. c.
3. Leonard W. Levy, *Original Intent and the Framers' Constitution* (New York: Macmillan Publishing Co. 1988), p. 224.
4. Cuddihy, p. cii.
5. Ibid., pp. 200 et seq.

6. Levy, p. 226.
7. Levy, pp. 222–29; Catherine Drinker Bowen, *John Adams and the American Revolution* (New York: Grosset & Dunlap, 1950), pp. 208–19. See also Cuddihy, pp. 757–825; M. H. Smith, *The Writs of Assistance Case* (Berkeley: University of California Press, 1978).
8. Levy, p. 229.
9. Levy, p. 230.
10. Levy, p. 231.
11. 95 Eng. Rep. 807; C. Stephenson and F. Marcham, *Sources of English Constitutional History* (New York: Harper, 1937) pp. 705–10.
12. C. R. Lovell, *English Constitutional and Legal History* (New York: Oxford University Press, 1962), p. 454.
13. These include Akhil Reed Amar, *The Constitution and Criminal Procedure: First Principles* (New Haven, Yale University Press, 1997); Gerard V. Bradley, The Constitutional Theory of the Fourth Amendment, *DePaul Law Review* 38(4):817–872 (1989); Cuddihy, note 1; Thomas Y. Davies, Recovering the Original Fourth Amendment, *Michigan Law Review* 98(3): pp. 547–750 (1999); Levy, note 3; Tracey Maclin, The Complexity of the Fourth Amendment: A Historical Review, *Boston University Law Review* 77:925–74 (1997).
14. Cuddihy, note 1, pp. 1231 1358; Davies, note 13, pp. 668–93.
15. Davies, pp. 557–60; much recent scholarship is cited in note 9, p. 557.
16. Amar, note 13, pp 1–45; Professor Amar's scholarship is refuted in detail by Professor Davies, note 13.
17. Bradley, note 13, p. 843–49; Davies, note 13.
18. Davies, note 13, p. 577.
19. Davies, note 13, p. 578, pp. 620–29, 632–34, 660–64.
20. Bradley, note 13, p. 827, (emphasis to Madison's text added by Professor Bradley). Davies does not believe that the change of wording conveyed a two-clause understanding, pp. 719–22.
21. *Camara v. Municipal Court* (1967).
22. Macklin, note 13, pp. 926–27.
23. These are the responses of Professor Bradley, note 13, pp. 865–72 and Professor Davies, note 13, pp. 747–50.
24. *Planned Parenthood v. Casey*, 505 U.S. 833 (1992); Dickerson v. U.S. (2000).
25. *Wilson v. U.S.* (1911) (corporation); *Bellis v, U.S.* (1974) (partnership); *Fisher v. U.S.* (1976) (individual tax records); *U. S. v. Doe* (1984) (single proprietor);
26. *Hale v. Henkel* (1906); *Fisher v. U.S.* (1976); *Andresen v. Maryland* (1976); *U.S. v. Jacobsen,* p. 113 (1984).
27. William C. Heffernan, Foreword: The Fourth Amendment exclusionary rule as a Constitutional Remedy, *Georgetown Law Journal* 88(5): pp. 799–878 (2000), p. 812.
28. Heffernan, note 27, pp. 838–40.
29. Citing Maguire, *Evidence of Guilt,* 221 (1959).
30. See the section on the "special needs doctrine" in Chapter 6.
31. In re *Christopher H.,* 227 Cal. App. 3d 1567, 278 Cal. Rptr. 577 (1991); *People v. Toliver,* 60 Ill. App. 3d 650, 377 N.E. 2d 207 (1978).
32. *State v. Berry,* 391 So. 2d 406; op. at 396 So.2d 880 (La. 1980). *Alston v. United States,* 518 A.2d 439 (D.C.Ct. App. 1986): in Washington, D.C., private security guards are licensed as either Special Police Officers with "the same powers as a law enforcement officer to arrest without warrant" or as Security Officers who only have the arrest power of private citizens. The former were held bound by the Fourth Amendment.
33. John M. Burkoff, "Not So Private Searches and the Constitution," *Cornell Law Review,* 66: p. 627 (1981); Lynn M. Gagel, "Comment: Stealthy Encroachments upon the Fourth Amendment: Constitutional Constraints and Their Applicability to the Long Arm of Ohio's Private Security Forces," *University of Cincinnati Law Review* 63: p. 1807(1995).
34. *Wolf v. People,* 117 Colo. 279; 187 P.2d 926 (1947); *Irvine v. California* (1952), p. 133.
35. *People v. Cahan,* 44 Cal. 2d 434, 282 P. 2d 905 (1955).
36. *Elkins v. United States* (1960), p. 218
37. See Cuddihy, note 1; Davies, note 13.
38. For a detailed examination of Justice Burger's thinking over time on this issue, see M. Braswell and J. Scheb II, "Conservative Pragmatism versus Liberal Principles: Warren E. Burger on the Suppression of Evidence, 1956–86," *Creighton Law Review* 20 (1987): pp. 789–831.
39. *United States v. Janis* (1976), p. 454, n. 29.
40. Potter Stewart, The Road to *Mapp v. Ohio* and Beyond: The Origins, Development and Future of the Exclusionary Rule in Search-and-Seizure Cases, *Columbia. Law Review* 83: pp. 1365–1404 (1983), p. 1389.
41. Charles H. Whitehead and Christopher Slobogin, *Criminal Procedure: An Analysis of Cases and Concepts, Fourth Edition* (New York: Foundation Press, 2000), p. 33.
42. 216 Conn. 150, 165; 579 A.2d 58, 65, citing Potter Stewart, The Road to *Mapp v. Ohio* and Beyond: The Origins, Development and Future of the Exclusionary Rule in Search-and-Seizure Cases, 83 *Columbia Law Review* pp. 1392–93 (1983), p. 1365.
43. Heffernan, p. 859.
44. *Marbury v. Madison,* p. 137, 163 (1803).
45. Cornelia T.L. Pillard, Taking Fiction Seriously: The Strange Results of Public Officials' Individual Liability Under *Bivens, Georgetown Law Journal* 88: pp. 65–105, p. 69 (1999).
46. *McGhee v. Volusia County,* 679 So.2d 729 (Fla. 1996).
47. T. Hunter Jefferson, Note: Constitutional Wrongs and Common Law Principles: The Case for the Recognition of State Constitutional Tort Actions against State Governments, *Vanderbilt Law Review* 50: pp. 1525–76, pp. 1549–50 (1997).
48. Jefferson, p. 1534.

49. *Brown v. New York,* 89 N.Y.2d 172, 674 N.E.2d 1129, 652 N.Y.S.2d 223, 75 A.L.R. 5th 769 (1996).
50. *Monell v. Department of Social Services* (1978); cities have "deeper pockets" than individual officers.
51. Henry, Weinstein, Judge Oks Use of Racketeering Law in Rampart Suits; Scandal: LAPD Can Be Sued as a Criminal Enterprise, He Rules. The Decision Could Triple the City's Financial Liability for Mistreatment of Citizens, Experts Say, *Los Angeles Times,* Aug. 29, 2000, p. A1; David Rosenzweig, L.A. Seeks to Appeal Racketeering Ruling; Rampart: the City Asks Judge's Permission to Challenge His Decision That the LAPD Can Be Sued under RICO Law, *Los Angeles Times,* Aug. 31, 2000, p. B3.
52. Alison L. Patton, Note: The Endless Cycle of Abuse: Why *42 U.S.C. § 1983* Is Ineffective in Deterring Police Brutality. *Hastings Law Journal* 44: pp. 753–808 (1993), pp. 766–67.
53. *Lankford v. Gelston,* 364 F.2d 197 (4th Cir. 1966).
54. In 1990, a local jury in Tyler, Texas, convicted three white police officers of the killing of Loyal Garner, Jr., an African-American man with no prior criminal history, while he was held in jail for alleged drunk driving, P. Applebome and R. Suro, "Texas Slaying: A Tale of Two Counties," *New York Times,* May 11, 1990, p. 1.
55. Jan Hoffman, Police Reformer Draws on His Experience, *New York Times,* Feb. 24, 2000, p. B2; Somini Sengupta, The Diallo Case: The Jurors; 2 Jurors Defend Diallo Acquittal, *New York Times,* Feb. 27, 2000, t1, p.1; Winnie Hu, The Diallo Case: the Deliberations; When Case Was Weighed, Prosecution Was Wanting, Juror Says, *New York Times,* Feb. 28, 2000, p. B5.
56. M. Zalman and M. Gates, "Rethinking Venue in Light of the 'Rodney King' Case: An Interest Analysis," *Cleveland State Law Review* 41(2) (1993): pp. 215–277.
57. J. Wilson, "Ex-Cops Get Prison, Budzyn, Nevers are remorseful over death," *Detroit Free Press,* Oct. 13, 1993.
58. Robyn Meredith, Jurors Acquit White Officer In the Death Of Black Driver, New York Times, Nov. 14, 1996, p. A20.
59. William K. Rashbaum, A Reversal On Oversight Of the Police, *New York Times,* July 7, 2000, p. B1.
60. *United States v. Screws* (1945).
61. Joseph P. Fried, Volpe Sentenced to a 30-year Term in Louima Torture, *New York Times,* Dec. 14, 1999, p. A1.
62. Edward Littlejohn, The Civilian Police Commission: A Deterrent of Police Misconduct, *Detroit Journal of Urban Law* 59:5 (1981).
63. Suggested in Whitebread and Slobogin, note 41, p. 65.
64. J. H. Skolnick and J. J. Fyfe, *Above the Law: Police and the Excessive Use of Force* (New York: Free Press, 1993), pp. 243–45.
65. Skolnick and Fyfe, *Above the Law,* pp. 255–57.
66. D. Johnston, "Reno Tightening Rules on Use of Lethal Force by Federal Agents," *New York Times,* Oct. 18, 1995, p. A13.
67. M. Newman, "Training for Trust; a Course for Police Recruits Examines How They Judge and Are Judged," *Pittsburgh Post-Gazette,* April 10, 1996, p. B1.
68. Editorial, "Higher Standards for Police Recruits," *New York Times,* Nov. 28, 1995, p. A14 (nat. ed.).
69. J. McKinnon, "Police Add Japanese Martial Art to Skills," *Pittsburgh Post-Gazette,* Jan. 23, 1996, p. B1.
70. Solnick and Fyfe, *Above the Law,* pp. 239–245.
71. William Bratton and Peter Knobler, Turnaround: How America's Top Cop Reversed the Crime Epidemic (New York: Random House, 1998), pp. 241–44.
72. Christopher Slobogin, Why Liberals Should Chuck the Exclusionary Rule, *University of Illinois Law Review* 1999: pp. 363–446, pp. 405–06 (1999).
73. Debra Livingston, Police Reform and the Department of Justice: An Essay on Accountability, *Buffalo Criminal Law Review* 2: pp. 815–857 (1999).
74. *People v. Defore,* 242 N.Y. 13, 21, 150 N.E. 585, 587 (1926).
75. Slobogin, note 72, p. 372–76.
76. Heffernan, note 27, p. 826.
77. Slobogin, note 72, p. 376, n. 40.
78. Slobogin, note 72, pp. 378–79.
79. Heffernan, note, 27 p. 840.
80. Slobogin, note 68, pp. 424, citing *U.S. v. Havens* (1980), *U.S. v. Janis* (1976).
81. Slobogin, note 72, pp. 425–27.
82. Slobogin, note 72, p. 427.
83. Fed. Rules of Criminal Procedure 41(e). Heffernan, note 27, p. 813, notes that several lower courts in the 1920s did return contraband, and that the issue never reached the Supreme Court.
84. Slobogin, note 72, pp. 435–36.
85. Heffernan, note 27, p. 837.
86. Heffernan, note 27, p. 838.
87. Heffernan, note 27, pp. 832–40, 848–60. It should be apparent that the full complexity of Professor Heffernan's argument cannot be fully specified in this text.
88. Thomas Davies, "A Hard Look at What We Know (and Still Need to Learn) about the 'Costs' of the Exclusionary Rule: The NIJ Study and Other Studies of 'Lost' Arrests," *American Bar Foundation Research Journal* 1983: pp. 611–90, p. 626.
89. Dallin Oaks, "Studying the Exclusionary Rule in Search and Seizure," *University of Chicago Law Review* 37(1970): p. 665.
90. Davies, "A Hard Look," p. 628.
91. This criticism is raised by Donald Horowitz, who is generally not an advocate of an activist judiciary. See D. Horowitz, *The Courts and Social Policy* (Washington, D.C.: Brookings Institution, 1977), pp. 224–25.
92. Davies, "A Hard Look."
93. *Ibid.*, p. 619.

94. For example, D. Oaks, "Studying the Exclusionary Rule in Search and Seizure," *University of Chicago Law Review* 37(1970): p. 665; J. Spiotto, "Search and Seizure: An Empirical Study of the Exclusionary Rule and Its Alternatives," *Journal of Legal Studies* 2(1973): p. 243. These were sharply criticized by Davies, "A Hard Look," pp. 627–28.
95. Davies, "A Hard Look," p. 630.
96. Bradley C. Canon, "Testing the Effectiveness of Civil Liberties Policies at the State and Federal Levels: The Case of the Exclusionary Rule," *American Politics Quarterly* 5(1)(1977): pp. 57–82.
97. *Ibid.*, p. 71.
98. H. R. Uviller, *Tempered Zeal* (Chicago: Contemporary Books, 1988), p. 131.
99. *Illinois v. Gates,* p. 257.
100. National Institute of Justice, *The Effects of the Exclusionary Rule: A Study in California* (Washington, D.C.: U.S. Dept. of Justice, 1982).
101. B. Forst, J. Lucianovic, and S. Cox, *What Happens After Arrest: A Court Perspective of Police Operations in the District of Columbia* (Washington, D.C.: U.S. Dept. of Justice, Law Enforcement Assistance Administration, 1978).
102. K. Brosi, *A Cross City Comparison of Felony Case Processing* (Washington, D.C.: U.S. Dept. of Justice, Law Enforcement Assistance Administration, 1979).
103. B. Forst, et al., *Arrest Convictability as a Measure of Police Performance* (Washington, D.C.: U.S. Dept. of Justice, National Institute of Justice, 1982).
104. Report of the, *Impact of the Exclusionary Rule on Federal Criminal Prosecutions* (Washington, D.C.: U.S. General Accounting Office, 1979).
105. P. Nardulli, "The Societal Cost of the Exclusionary Rule: An Empirical Assessment," *American Bar Foundation Research Journal* 1983: pp. 585–609.
106. F. Feeney, F. Dill, and A. Weir, *Arrests Without Conviction: How Often They Occur and Why* (Washington, D.C.: U.S. Dept. of Justice, National Institute of Justice, 1983).
107. Craig D. Uchida and Timothy S. Bynum, Search Warrants, Motions to Suppress and "Lost Cases:" The Effects of the Exclusionary Rule in Seven Jurisdictions, *Journal of Criminal Law and Criminology* 81(4): pp. 1034–66 (1991).
108. Davies, "A Hard Look," p. 679.
109. Uchida and Bynum, p. 1065, quoting from R. Van Duizend, L. Sutton, & C. Carter, *The Search Warrant Process: Preconceptions, Perceptions, and Practices* (1986), p. 106
110. Pillard, note 45, p. 66 (footnotes excluded).
111. Patton, note 52, pp. 755–67. See John L. Burris, *Black vs. Blue* (New York: St. Martin's Press, 1999).
112. Patton, note 52, pp. 767–779.
113. Patton, note 52, pp. 780–90, drawing heavily on the Christopher Commission Report, issued after the Los Angeles riots following the Rodney King beating case.

JUSTICES OF THE SUPREME COURT

Roosevelt's Liberals
Douglas—Murphy—Jackson—Rutledge

Franklin Roosevelt appointed no justices during his first term in office and yet ended up appointing more justices (nine) than any president except Washington, thanks in large part to his unprecedented four terms in office. Roosevelt's primary goal was to name individuals who would support New Deal legislation on economic and labor issues. For a half century, a conservative Supreme Court had, on behalf of the wealthy, more or less restricted the ability of the democratic branches of government to pass legislation to improve working conditions and on behalf of the interests of workers, farmers, and the lower middle class.

The ascendancy the Roosevelt administration during the great economic crisis of the 1930s finally led to a liberalization of the bench. As the Supreme Court reduced its role in passing on the wisdom of economic legislation, a new wave of civil rights cases began to press forward for hearing. The civil liberties cases of the 1940s and 1950s included freedom of speech, freedom of the press, religious freedom, freedom of conscience regarding loyalty issues, and criminal procedure. It was not a foregone conclusion that justices who were liberal on economic matters would also be liberal on civil rights and criminal procedure questions. Four of Roosevelt's appointees—Black, Douglas, Murphy, and Rutledge—were "liberal" in favoring the incorporation of the Bill of Rights into the Fourteenth Amendment. They tended to vote for criminal defendants and, when joined by Frankfurter and Jackson, placed limits on local police officers whose actions were found to have violated the Due Process Clause of the Fourteenth Amendment.

Justices Douglas, Rutledge, and Jackson have been ranked as "near great" and Justice Murphy as average by a poll of scholars, but Murphy's originality in criminal procedure stands as a real contribution to criminal jurisprudence, as it defined the actual position taken during the due process revolution of the 1960s.

William O. Douglas

Connecticut 1898–1980

Democrat

Appointed by
Franklin Delano Roosevelt

Years of Service:
1939–1975

Collection of the Supreme Court of the United States. Photographer: Harris and Ewing

Life and Career Douglas grew up poor in Yakima, Washington; he was six years old when his father, a Presbyterian missionary, died. He was an excellent student, but contracted polio, and to strengthen his legs took long, strenuous hikes into the mountains. He became a lifelong naturalist and hiker. He entered Whitman College in 1916, served briefly in the Army during World War I, and taught school for a few years before entering law school. He graduated second in his class at Columbia Law School, practiced briefly at a Wall Street law firm, and then taught at Columbia and Yale law schools, gaining recognition as a top financial law expert.

Douglas joined President Roosevelt's New Deal administration in 1934, to work on the Securities and Exchange Commission (SEC), a new watchdog agency designed to regulate the stock market. He became a member of the SEC in 1936 and its chairman in 1937. First known as anti-business, Douglas built bridges to the business world and tried to stimulate internal reform in the stock exchange to minimize governmental intrusion. He became an adviser to the president and was Roosevelt's fourth nominee to the Court at the young age of thirty-nine.

He authored thirty-two books in his lifetime, traveled to all parts of the world where he made efforts to meet with ordinary people, and was a frequent speaker on issues of foreign policy and the environment. He was a staunch environmentalist long before it was a popular issue, and in the 1950s he began to speak out for the recognition of communist China and for internationalism.

CONTRIBUTION TO CRIMINAL PROCEDURE Despite his enormous output of cases, he wrote relatively few criminal procedure opinions. He was, however, the most liberal justice and consistently voted for the "incorporation plus" doctrine. His solid liberal vote on criminal issues under five chief justices was a critical element in the due process revolution.

SIGNATURE OPINION Griffin v. California (1965) A defendant in a state trial did not take the stand. The judge instructed the jury that he had a right to remain silent but that the jury could take his failure to deny or explain facts in the case into consideration in determining whether the facts are true, although his silence did not create a presumption of guilt. The Court held that the federal rule against such comment was based on the Fifth Amendment privilege against self-incrimination, and that it therefore applied to the states via the Due Process Clause of the Fourteenth Amendment. "For comment on the refusal to testify is a remnant of the 'inquisitorial system of criminal justice,' which the Fifth Amendment outlaws. It is a penalty imposed by courts for exercising a constitutional privilege." *Griffin* in effect overruled the specific holding of the important anti-incorporation case of *Adamson v, California* (1947).

ASSESSMENT Douglas served longer than any other justice: thirty-six years. He was steeped in the philosophy of Legal Realism, which held that a judge's policy preferences were the prime determiner of the judge's decisions. His outspoken activism made him one of the most controversial justices. He was extremely hard working, and wrote a large number of opinions (many on antitrust and economic issues), but wrote them very quickly. Although all who knew him acknowledged his brilliance, he was accused of writing opinions that did not precisely spell out the doctrinal foundation. This can be seen in his opinion in *Douglas v. California* (1963), which held that a convicted person has a firm right to one appeal.

In addition to his contributions to the law of business regulation, Douglas helped to advance an absolutist concept of free speech, with his dissent in *Dennis v. United States* (1951), arguing against the conviction of Communist Party leaders for advocating the violent overthrow of the government (his dissent became the law in the 1970s). He wrote, "Free speech has occupied an exalted position because of the high service it has given our society. Its protection is essential to the very existence of a democracy." He is most famous for establishing the right of privacy in the *Griswold v. Connecticut* (1965) contraception law opinion, and basing the right on values that are basic to the First, Fourth, and Fifth amendments of the Bill of Rights. *Griswold* laid the foundation for the *Roe v. Wade* (1973) abortion rights ruling.

FURTHER READING

Stephen L. Wasby, ed., *"He Shall Not Pass This Way Again": The Legacy of Justice William O. Douglas* (Pittsburgh: University of Pittsburgh Press, 1990).

FRANK MURPHY

Michigan 1890–1949

Democrat

Appointed by
Franklin Delano Roosevelt

Years of Service:
1940–1949

Collection of the Supreme Court of the United States. Photographer: Pach Brothers Studio

LIFE AND CAREER Frank Murphy, a native of Michigan, obtained his undergraduate and law degrees from the University of Michigan. He had an extensive public career prior to his appointment to the Court serving as an Army officer in World War I; a federal assistant prosecutor; a judge of the Detroit Recorder's Court; mayor of Detroit from 1930 to 1933, when he gained national fame for innovative attempts to ease the burden of the Great Depression; governor general of the Philippines from 1933 to 1937, on a presidential appointment; governor of Michigan from 1937 to 1939, during which time he refused to order the violent suppression of automobile workers' sit down strikes; and attorney general of the United States from 1939 to 1940, when he established the civil rights division. His vigor and compassion made him a leading political figure and even a potential presidential candidate, despite the fact that he was Catholic, a handicap at that time.

CONTRIBUTION TO CRIMINAL PROCEDURE In other criminal procedure cases, Murphy voted in favor of the defendant's right to counsel in every case; wrote a majority opinion that

(Continued)

struck down the systematic exclusion of day-laborers from juries; and dissented in cases that allowed the government to wiretap and electronically eavesdrop without a warrant. With one exception, he sided with the defendant in coerced confessions cases.

Signature Opinion Dissent in *Adamson v. California* (1947). The majority held that the Fifth Amendment is not incorporated into the Fourteenth Amendment. Justice Black dissented, arguing for total incorporation. Justice Murphy's dissent best anticipated the due process revolution of the 1960s, by establishing the "incorporation plus" concept that supported both the incorporation of the Bill of Rights into the Fourteenth Amendment *and* the independent use of the due process clause to strike down unfair governmental action. "Occasions may arise where a proceeding falls so far short of conforming to fundamental standards of procedure as to warrant constitutional condemnation in terms of a lack of due process despite the absence of a specific provision in the Bill of Rights."

Assessment Justice Murphy was, with Justice Douglas, the most liberal justice on the Court in the 1940s. He dissented in the case upholding the removal of Japanese Americans from their homes to relocation centers during World War II. He wrote many pro-worker opinions in the field of labor law. His consistently favored the expansion of First Amendment rights, opposed racial segregation, favored gender equality, and generally supported the underdog.

Murphy was not a great legal stylist or a profound legal thinker and has been rated an average justice by scholars. He probably delegated more drafting to his law clerks than other justices. He brought to the Court his extensive experience in public life and "a great heart attuned to the cries of the weak and suffering." His unwavering commitment to civil liberties strengthened the "solid minority" of criminal procedure liberals in the Stone and Vinson Courts and helped pave the way to the due process revolution.

Further Reading

J. Woodford Howard, Jr., *Mr. Justice Murphy: A Political Biography* (Princeton: Princeton University Press, 1968).

Robert H. Jackson

New York 1892–1954

Democrat

Appointed by
Franklin Delano Roosevelt

Years of Service:
1941–1954

Collection of the Supreme Court of the United States. Photographer: Harris and Ewing

Life and Career Robert Jackson developed a reputation as the most skillful government litigator in Washington, D.C., in the heady days of the New Deal. Yet his formal educational background consisted only of high school and a year at Albany Law School. He trained for the law as an apprentice in a law office and opened his own practice in Jamestown, New York, in 1913. Over the next twenty years, he developed a prosperous practice and became a respected attorney in his region.

Treasury Secretary Morgenthau persuaded Jackson to join the New Deal administration in 1934 as general counsel for the Bureau of Internal Revenue. His reputation soared by winning complex cases for the government. He was appointed assistant attorney general in charge of the Antitrust Division in 1936 and argued ten cases for the government before the Supreme Court. He won the important case upholding the Social Security Act on broad grounds that made the laws easier to administer. He supported President Roosevelt's "court packing" plan. He became solicitor general in 1938, where he "showed a remarkable insight into both basic governmental policy and the tactics of advocacy." His service as attorney general from January 1940 to mid-1941 was marked more by careful legal advice than by administrative innovations. His most brilliant achievement was his Attorney General's Opinion justifying President Roosevelt's controversial "lend-lease" program in the dark days before America's entry into World War II, whereby fifty overage destroyers were transferred to the British navy in return for military bases in Bermuda.

Contribution to Criminal Procedure He generally joined Justice Frankfurter in opposing incorporation. His votes were mixed; in some Fourth Amendment cases he was quite critical of abusive police work, but he was not as consistently liberal as Justices Black, Douglas, Murphy, or Rutledge. He believed in judicial restraint and was a strong proponent of federalism. Thus, in state confessions cases he often voted to uphold the confession under the Due Process Clause, especially where a very serious crime was charged, unless the police action made it perfectly clear that the confession was obtained involuntarily.

Signature Opinion *Johnson v. U.S.* (1948). Police standing outside a hotel room smelled opium and entered without a warrant. In holding that this was a violation of the Fourth Amendment, Justice Jackson issued the classic statement about the value of a search warrant: "The point of the Fourth Amendment, which often is not grasped by zealous officers, is not that it denies law enforcement the support of the usual inferences which reasonable men draw from evidence. Its protection consists in requiring that those inferences be drawn by a neutral and detached magistrate instead of being judged by the officer engaged in the often competitive enterprise of ferreting out crime."

Assessment He generally was liberal on civil rights issues, writing the decisive compulsory flag salute opinion (holding that requiring school children to salute the flag violated First Amendment rights). In substantive criminal law, he wrote a ringing affirmation of the common law principle that the government cannot create a legislative definition of a serious crime, such as theft, without the element of criminal intent (*mens rea*).

He was a great stylist, and many of his opinions are filled with interesting and quotable passages. His was interested in the improvement of criminal justice and chaired the American Bar Association special committee on the administration of criminal justice. He interrupted his service as a justice for over a year after World War II to serve as the chief American prosecutor at the Nuremberg War Crimes Tribunal trials of the top Nazi leaders. In this role, he made an abiding contribution to international law and the development of human rights.

Further Reading

Glendon Schubert, ed. *Dispassionate Justice: A Synthesis of the Judicial Opinions of Robert H. Jackson* (Indianapolis: Bobbs-Merrill, 1969)

Wiley B. Rutledge

Iowa 1894–1949

Democrat

Appointed by
Franklin Delano Roosevelt

Years of Service:

1943–1949

Collection of the Supreme Court of the United States. Photographer: Harris and Ewing

Life and Career Rutledge was the son of a fundamentalist Baptist minister who preached in Kentucky, Tennessee, and North Carolina. A biographer notes that "although in later life he became a Unitarian, his father's fervor was reflected in his zeal for justice and right." He graduated from the University of Wisconsin in 1914, taught school for a few years, and nearly died from tuberculosis. He recovered and received his LL.B. degree from the University of Colorado in 1922. After two years of law practice in Boulder, he became a law professor, and then dean of the University of Iowa College of Law in the 1930s. He developed a reputation as an inspiring teacher and civic activist.

Moved by the plight of the poor and unemployed during the Great Depression, he spoke out publicly against the Supreme Court's rulings that struck down New Deal legislation. As one of the few academics to support President Roosevelt's "court packing" scheme in 1937—a stance that led several Iowa state legislators to threaten to withhold law school salaries in reprisal—Rutledge came to the attention of the Roosevelt administration. He was appointed to the United States Court of Appeals for Washington, D.C., in 1939 and served for four years before his nomination to the Supreme Court.

Contribution to Criminal Procedure Rutledge joined Justice Black to be a member of the Court's liberal bloc in the 1940s in favor of incorporating the Bill of Rights in *Adamson* (1947), helping to make incorporation a respectable, if controversial, position. Indeed, he joined the more liberal "incorporation plus" position with Justices Murphy and Douglas.

Signature Opinion *Brinegar v. United States* (1949). Writing for the majority in upholding an automobile search of a bootlegger, Justice Rutledge stated the classical definition of probable cause that has been oft-repeated by the Court: "In

(Continued)

dealing with probable cause, however, as the very name implies, we deal with probabilities. These are not technical; they are the factual and practical considerations of everyday life on which reasonable and prudent men, not legal technicians, act. . . . Requiring more would unduly hamper law enforcement. To allow less would be to leave law-abiding citizens at the mercy of the officers' whim or caprice."

Assessment Rutledge's tenure on the Court was marked by a fierce dedication to the principles of liberty. His most famous opinion, a dissent in the *Yamashita* (1946) case, acknowledged the authority of the United States to try the former Japanese commander of the Philippines accused of authorizing or allowing atrocities by his troops, but dissented bitterly that the proceeding was characterized by none of the hallmarks of due process. He agreed with the Court in another case that a naturalized citizen could not have his citizenship revoked merely because he had belonged to the Communist Party at the time of his naturalization.

Further Reading

Landon G. Rockwell, "Justice Rutledge on Civil Liberties," *Yale Law Journal* 59:27 (1949).

CHAPTER 4

Essential Fourth Amendment Doctrines

These [Fourth Amendment rights], I protest, are not mere second-class rights but belong in the catalog of indispensable freedoms. Among deprivations of rights, none is so effective in cowing a population, crushing the spirit of the individual and putting terror in every heart. Uncontrolled search and seizure is one of the first and most effective weapons in the arsenal of every arbitrary government. And one need only briefly to have dwelt and worked among a people possessed of many admirable qualities but deprived of these rights to know that the human personality deteriorates and dignity and self-reliance disappear where homes, persons and possessions are subject at any hour to unheralded search and seizure by the police.

—Justice Robert Jackson, dissenting in *Brinegar v. United States,* 338 U.S. 160, 180–81 (1949)

CHAPTER OUTLINE

KEY TERMS AND PHRASES

Anticipatory warrant
Balancing of interests
Beeper
Consent search
Controlled delivery
Curtilage
Enhancement device
Extraterritorial
Inventory and return
Knock and announce rule
Magistrate
Media ride-along
Neutral and detached magistrate
No-knock warrant
Open fields
"Plain feel" rule
Plain view
Probable cause
Secret informant
Telephonic warrant
Thermal imaging
Two-pronged test
Undercover agent

INTRODUCTION

This chapter presents five basic areas of Fourth Amendment law: the search warrant, the expectation of privacy doctrine, probable cause, the plain view doctrine, and consent searches. Fourth Amendment analysis has an interlocking quality—that is, several issues are often considered simultaneously in the same case. This makes it difficult for a beginning student to follow a Fourth Amendment case because one has to know *all* the law before understanding *any* of it! To add to the complexity, Fourth Amendment doctrines have developed chronologically, and have at times been fully or partially reversed as the justices have given close attention to various issues or have determined to advance certain preset agendas. Finally, as seen in Chapter 3, there are several competing theories at work in this area, and different justices may utilize different theories in the same case. In any event, each of these doctrinal areas—search warrant, expectation of privacy, probable cause, plain view, and consent—are presented here as isolated topics for ease of study.

THE SEARCH WARRANT

Rationale and Values Supporting a Search Warrant

> The presence of a search warrant serves a high function. Absent some grave emergency, the Fourth Amendment has interposed a magistrate between the citizen and the police. This was done not to shield criminals nor to make the home a safe haven for illegal activities. It was done so that an objective mind might weigh the need to invade that privacy in order to enforce the law. The right of privacy was deemed too precious to entrust to the discretion of those whose job is the detection of crime and the arrest of criminals. (*McDonald v. United States, 1948,* pp. 455–56)

Chapter 3 noted that Supreme Court justices construe the Fourth Amendment in two ways. Under the "general-reasonableness construction," a search is constitutional simply if it is reasonable; the "warrant-preference construction" holds that search and seizures are presumed unreasonable unless authorized by a judicial warrant except for a few well-established exceptions that allow warrantless searches. The latter construction has frequently led the Court to express a *preference for the search warrant.* To ensure that officers apply to magistrates for warrants, the Court has at times eased the strict requirements of probable cause. In *United States v. Ventresca* (1965), for example, the issue was whether hearsay was sufficient to establish probable cause and support a warrant to search a house for an illegal liquor distillery. The Court made it clear that in a close case, if the search was conducted under a warrant, the Court would lean in favor of upholding the search: "A grudging or negative attitude by reviewing courts toward warrants will tend to discourage police officers from submitting their evidence to a judicial officer before acting." Of course, this does not mean that a magistrate must automatically grant a warrant simply on request (*Ventresca,* pp. 108–09). A search occurring without a warrant has been a reason given by the Supreme Court to find the search illegal. In the seminal case of *Katz v. United States* (1967), although federal agents had facts that might have persuaded a magistrate to grant a warrant to listen to conversations in a telephone booth via a microphone, and despite the fact that the search was objectively reasonable and limited to single conversations about illegal betting information from a racetrack, the Supreme Court found that the evidence was obtained in violation of the Fourth Amendment.

This stated preference for a search warrant is based on three factors: the long history of warrant use, the Fourth Amendment's text, and the policy and values that underlie the amendment. The values sought to be protected are highly prized by Americans: personal autonomy, privacy, security, and freedom. The policy of the Amendment is to protect these values by establishing procedures that place the decision in the hands of the courts whether to invade a person's liberties for law enforcement purposes and to do so as infrequently as possible. The rationale was best expressed by Justice Robert Jackson:

> The point of the Fourth Amendment, which often is not grasped by zealous officers, is not that it denies law enforcement the support of the usual inferences which reasonable men draw from evidence. Its protection consists in requiring that those inferences be drawn by a **neutral and detached magistrate** instead of being judged by the officer engaged in the often competitive enterprise of ferreting out crime. Any assumption that evidence sufficient to support a magistrate's disinterested determination to issue a search warrant will justify the officers in making a search without a warrant would reduce the Amendment to a nullity and leave the people's homes secure only in the discretion of police officers. (*Johnson v. United States* [1948], pp. 13–14)

In *Johnson,* an experienced federal narcotics officer smelled burning opium coming from a closed hotel room in Seattle, Washington. He demanded entry and found one person in the room in possession of opium. The Court noted: "At the time entry was demanded the officers were possessed of evidence which a magistrate might have found to be probable cause for issuing a search warrant." The evidence was nevertheless excluded because the officer invaded Anne Johnson's room without first submitting his evidence to the judgment of a judicial officer.

In deciding who should have priority in determining whether probable cause exists, the Supreme Court does not place the judge above the police officer because of any belief that the judge is more intelligent or more expert than the officer, or simply because of the traditional use of warrants. The policy is wrapped up in Justice Jackson's memorable phrase "a neutral and detached magistrate." This conveys that the magistrate is part of the judicial branch, detached from "the government" (i.e., the executive branch) and, therefore, not part of the apparatus that seeks to prosecute the suspect. Further, the judge is neutral in the case. The officer is a partisan who is "engaged in the often competitive enterprise of ferreting out crime." Because the officer is a partisan, he or she is likely to judge a case in his or her own favor and find that probable cause exists. This does not suggest that the officer is dishonest, but that human nature is such that a partisan virtually always sees things his or her way. The judge is formally neutral—an arbiter between the police and prosecution on the one side, and the defendant on the other. It is because the magistrate is neutral that he or she is more likely to exercise balanced judgment.

Obtaining a search warrant from a judge is less efficient than allowing police to make a decision to enter a home on their own assessment of probable cause to search. This adds a cost to public safety-a cost that the Framers felt was necessary to maintain liberty. Skeptics may question whether the warrant practice, in fact, adds that much protection. It is worth noting that severe invasions by the FBI and other police agencies did occur for political reasons during the Cold War, and that the courts were not as active as Congress and public opinion in ending such gross abuses.[1] Also, warrant procedure does not absolve police and prosecutors from fairly evaluating the facts and making their own probable cause decisions before applying for a warrant. But if the police make a patently ridiculous application for a warrant, or a patently ridiculous warrantless search, then the job of the magistrate is to deny the warrant application or throw out the evidence. Yet, at times, pressure can cause a magistrate to blunder. This was the case when Judge Kathleen Kennedy-Powell ruled that Los Angeles Police detectives Mark Fuhrman and Philip Vannatter were justified in vaulting over the wall of O.J. Simpson's estate in the early morning hours of June 13, 1994 without a search warrant because they claimed that they feared for his safety.[2] This was a patently weak reason because ex-husbands are typically prime suspects in spouse killings and Fuhrman had been called to the Simpson residence earlier to investigate a wife-beating. As lawyer-novelist Scott Turow noted, "If veteran police detectives did not arrive at the gate of Mr. Simpson's home thinking he might have committed these murders, then they should have been fired."[3] Ironically, Judge Kennedy-Powell's case-saving ruling backfired. When Fuhrman's perjurious, racist statements later came out, the jury might have also questioned his truthfulness about the entry and search of Simpson's home and grounds.

To add to the skepticism, there is some concern that magistrates tend to rubber-stamp warrant requests. Despite all this, law Professor Richard Uviller, after observing police for a year, reflects on the value of search warrants.

> It's easy to say that the whole routine is a sham: magistrates are not actually neutral or detached but just as closely associated with the prosecution as the cops; they don't really read the affidavits, many of those exercising the authority would not know the difference between probable cause and potato chips, much less the complexities of the law regarding the reliability of third-party informants who supply the hearsay on which the cop's belief may be founded.
>
> However much truth there may be in such assertions, it has always seemed to me that the real values of the search warrant procedure are: (1) It makes the officer pause in his pursuit and reflect on whether he has a good reason to go into someone's private space; (2) it requires him to make a record of his reasons, recording what he knows about the case before he makes the move; and (3) his recorded reasons stand immutably for review by a knowledgeable judge after the fact, at trial, and again on appeal, if the search is challenged. In the enforced hesitation, recorded articulation, and prospect of true review, the objectives of the Fourth Amendment are well served.[4]

A Neutral and Detached Magistrate

The Supreme Court has decided several revealing cases on the ground of whether the actions of a magistrate or another governmental officer rose to the standards of a "**neutral and detached magistrate.**" In *Coolidge v. New Hampshire* (1971), the state *attorney general,* an executive branch officer, personally took charge of a murder investigation. An archaic statute made him a justice of the peace and, as such, he issued a search warrant to himself. Over the dissents of three justices, who viewed this action as "harmless error," the Supreme Court ruled that it violated the fundamental Fourth Amendment premise that warrants must issue from a neutral and detached magistrate. What was important was not that the statute *called* the Attorney General a "justice of the peace," but that *in fact* he was not a "detached" judicial officer; he was the chief investigator and prosecutor in the case.

Shadwick v. City of Tampa (1972) also shows that formal title is less important than the actual situation of the officer issuing a warrant. Here, the Supreme Court upheld a law and practice that allowed a *municipal court clerk* to issue arrest warrants for municipal ordinance violations. The clerk met two tests: (1) he was capable of determining whether probable cause existed as to ordinance violations, such as impaired driving or breach of the peace, and (2) he was neutral and detached in that he was not under the authority of the prosecutor or police but worked in the judicial branch, subject to the supervision of the municipal court judge. Thus, under limited circumstances, a valid warrant can be issued by a person who is not a lawyer or a judge.

The Supreme Court has ruled that a magistrate is not neutral or detached if he receives not a salary but rather gets a *fee,* even a small one, for each warrant that is issued. In *Connally v. Georgia* (1977), the magistrate received five dollars for each search warrant issued but nothing if a warrant is denied. The *possibility* of personal, financial gain is sufficient to violate the due process and Fourth Amendment rights of suspects, whatever the actual disposition of the magistrate. On the other hand, the actions of a magistrate can cause the magistrate to lose the element of neutrality in a specific case. This was held to occur in *Lo-Ji Sales, Inc. v. New York* (1979) (emphasis added). An overly helpful town justice, rather than simply issuing a search warrant for the seizure of films from an adult bookstore, also joined police officers and prosecutors on a six-hour raid of the premises, determining at the scene whether there was probable cause to seize various materials. In determining that the warrant was improper, a unanimous Court said, "The Town Justice did not manifest that neutrality and detachment demanded of a judicial officer when presented with a warrant application for a search and seizure." This loss of "detachment" was not, according to the Court, a matter of subjective intent but was inferred from the objective fact that the town justice "allowed himself to *become a member, if not the leader, of the search party* which was essentially a police operation." Yet, despite the objective nature of the rule, it is easy to imagine that a judge who works too closely with the prosecutors will come to see himself/herself as a member of the "prosecution team" rather than a neutral and detached magistrate in a subjective sense.

The principle of the neutral and detached magistrate led the Supreme Court to invalidate a portion of the 1968 electronic eavesdropping law that allowed the president of the United States to authorize electronic eavesdropping for a "national security" purpose without a warrant (*United States v. United States District Court* 1972). The Court ruled that even if the President was exempt from particular procedural requirements of the statute, he was still required to seek "judicial approval prior to initiation of a search or surveillance" under the Fourth Amendment. The Court reasoned that dangers to free speech and political liberty are of great concern in national security cases, that such issues are not too difficult for judges to understand, and that national security would not be compromised by requiring the President to seek prior judicial approval for electronic eavesdropping. Since 1978, under the Foreign Intelligence Surveillance Act, warrants for electronic eavesdropping for national security purposes are issued by a special court drawn for each case from among sitting federal judges.[5]

Obtaining a Search Warrant

The Fourth Amendment requires that "no Warrant shall issue but upon probable cause supported by Oath or affirmation. . . ." In order to obtain a search warrant, law enforcement officers must: (1) present a written affidavit to a magistrate which requests that a warrant be issued, (2) swear under oath that the information in the affidavit is truthful, and (3) convince the magistrate that the information sworn to establishes probable cause to believe that a search warrant is justified. The magistrate should question the officer requesting the warrant about the circumstances of the case and must be personally satisfied that the evidence constitutes probable cause. The oath signifies that the officer takes responsibility for the facts alleged.[6]

The affidavit, or sworn statement, is presented to the court at an *ex parte* hearing, i.e., a hearing with only one party present. Such a procedure normally would violate due process but is allowed out of necessity and is hemmed in with other safeguards, such as the return on the warrant, which requires the officer to report on the execution of the warrant. The magistrate usually questions only the affiant but may require additional witnesses to testify before being satisfied

STATE OF MICHIGAN

SS SEARCH WARRANT AND AFFIDAVIT

COUNTY OF WAYNE

TO THE SHERIFF OR ANY PEACE OFFICER OF SAID COUNTY: Wayne; Police Officer Phillip Melon.

Affiant, having subscribed and sworn to an affidavit for a Search Warrant, and I having under oath examined affiant, am satisfied that probable cause exists.

THEREFORE, IN THE NAME OF THE PEOPLE OF THE STATE OF MICHIGAN, I command that you search the following described please:

18793 Colorado, a one story brick building, bearing the name O'Grady's Collision, located in the City of Detriot, County of Wayne, State of Michigan, and to seize, secure, tabulate and make return according to law the following property and things:

1. A 1-1984 Chevrolet Nova, Blue, VIN#1FABPO758EW236587, bearing license plate #241-LUS
2. Any stolen vehicles or parts of stolen vehicles
3. Any and all other vehicles belonging to Stephen Switzerland and Warren Switzerland
4. Any repair orders, estimates or other paperwork relating to the repair of vehicles.

The following facts are sworn to by affiant in support of the issuance of this Warrant:

Affiant is a member of the Detriot Police Department, assigned to the Commercial Auto Theft Section. Affiant on January 19, 1988 and January 20, 1988 executed search warrants on this location and seized a stolen vehicle, a 1984 Chevrolet, 241-LUS. Affiant while conducting an investigation in regards to this stolen vehicle discovered that the vehicle had been falsely reported stolen in order to collect the insurance monies from Mackinac Insurance Company. On March 24, 1988, a warrant for Attempted OMUFP 0/100 (Obtaining Money under False Pretenses over $100) were obtained against Irwin Schmidlopp (Owner of the 1984 Chevrolet Nova) and for Stephen Switzerland (Owner of O'Grady's Collision). During the investigation it was discovered that persons would obtain insurance through the Mackinac Agency for vehicles that they did not own and then a claim would be submitted to the insurance company and an adjuster would arrive at O'Grady's Collision (an unlicensed motor vehicle repair facility). The insurance company would then issue a check to O'Grady's Collision and the insured party for the repair of this vehicle. One vehicle, a 1985 Oldsmobile, was repaired at least three times by O'Grady's listing three different owners when in fact, none of these alleged owners ever owned the vehicle or got into an accident with this 1985 Oldsmobile. All three checks were co-issued to O'Grady's Collision and all three checks, totaling about $15,000.00, were cashed by Stephen Switzerland through his account at First of America. Affiant on March 29, 1988, observed the 1984 Chevrolet, belonging to defendant, Irwin Schmidlopp, still inside this location. Affiant believes that estimates and bills and receipts will be found inside this location to show further schemes and frauds committed by these suspects to defraud the insurance companies.

Phillip Melon
Affiant

Subscribed and sworn to before me and issued under my hand this 30 th day of March, 1988

Approved:

John Carter
Assistant Prosecuting Attorney
P91234

Jane Ellis
Judge of 36th District Court, Wayne County, Michigan, and a Magistrate

that there is sufficient evidence. The law enforcement agency applying for a warrant should keep all evidence and records of its application; if the warrant is challenged, the loss of such information would weigh heavily against the agency. Also, if a jurisdiction allows the agency to make a new warrant application to a different magistrate if an initial request is turned down, then the evidence submitted in the first application must be submitted in the second application.

The *classes of evidence* that may be searched and seized under a warrant are spelled out in the Federal Rules of Criminal Procedure: "A warrant may be issued under this rule to search for and seize any (1) property that constitutes evidence of the commission of a criminal offense; or (2) contraband, the fruits of crime, or things otherwise criminally possessed; or (3) property designed or intended for use or which is or has been used as a means of committing a criminal offense; or (4) person for whose arrest there is probable cause, or who is unlawfully restrained." (F.RC.P., Rule 41[b]).

The typical affidavit and warrant for a search need not be lengthy; they are often only one or two pages long. What is important is that the affidavit state sufficient evidence to suggest probable cause and that the warrant give clear directions to the executing officers. In some jurisdictions, a warrant is issued without attaching the affidavit; in others the warrant incorporates the affidavit. This is the practice in Detroit, Michigan, from which a warrant and affidavit are included (with names and identifying information changed) as an example of what is required to establish probable cause.

TELEPHONIC WARRANTS Modern technology makes it possible to reduce the time between requesting a search warrant and receiving authorization if large distances between the police officers and the court make the normal affidavit process cumbersome. In 1970, California enacted legislation to allow **telephonic warrants** and, according to Professor Geoffrey Alpert, another eight states and the federal government have followed suit.[7] Under F.R.C.P. Rule 41(c)(2), a federal magistrate may issue a warrant on oral testimony given over a telephone "[i]f the circumstances make it reasonable to dispense, in whole or in part, with a written affidavit." The magistrate must record the "duplicate original warrant" prepared by the officer or have a stenographic or longhand verbatim record made. In either case, the caller is immediately placed under oath by the magistrate.

Professor Alpert suggests that the advent of telephonic warrants may cast doubt on the validity of certain warrantless arrests as it becomes easier for police to get judicial permission to conduct searches when distance or time would otherwise impede them. For such an ideal situation to occur, which simultaneously ensures effective law enforcement while protecting individual liberty, officers must be aware of the procedure and courts must be structured to accept warrants. This would require that police routinely have recording devices available to record their oral requests.[8] Most important, it requires police to have knowledge of the procedure and their willingness to use it; however, both may be lacking. For example, in the O. J. Simpson murder trial, Detective Mark Fuhrman was asked on cross-examination "why the detectives did not try to secure a warrant by telephone."[9] A commentator noted that "while judges are available by phone, many police detectives simply don't use that procedure; Detective Mark Fuhrman testified in the preliminary hearings that he has never used telephonic warrants."[10] Another commentator noted that in Colorado, telephonic warrants are obtained in an hour and a half.[11]

Particularity

The Fourth Amendment requires that a warrant "particularly describ[e] the place to be searched, and the persons or things to be seized." To do this, an officer making out an affidavit must investigate to ensure that the place is accurately described. In addition to a street number, for example, it is wise to add a description of the premises in case of a mistake that might render the search to be illegal. For example, police planned a drug raid at a house located at the corner of Short and Adkinson Streets. The warrant incorrectly listed the place to be searched as "325 Atkinson Street" when in fact it was 325 Short Street. The affidavit also described the house as a single residence with silver siding and red trim on the south side of the street. Despite the error regarding the address, the search was held valid and the description met the particularity requirement because the "test for determining the sufficiency of the description of the place to be searched is whether [it] is described with sufficient particularity as to enable the executing officer to locate and identify the premises with reasonable effort, and whether there is any reasonable probability that another premise might be mistakenly searched."[12]

The Supreme Court confirmed that mistakes in a warrant do not violate the Fourth Amendment if they are "reasonable." In *Maryland v. Garrison* (1987), police obtained "a warrant to search the person of Lawrence McWebb and 'the premises known as 2036 Park Avenue third floor Apartment.' " Diligent police investigation did not reveal that there was another apartment on the third floor. When executing the warrant, police officers encountered McWebb downstairs and required him to walk up to the third floor. He opened the only apartment door, which led to a vestibule. Garrison was standing there and doors to both Garrison's and McWebb's apartments were open; the police did not, at that time, know that there were two apartments. They entered Garrison's apartment and seized drugs in **plain view.** As soon as they were told that it was not McWebb's apartment, they left. The Supreme Court ruled that the police did not know and could not reasonably have known that there were two apartments on the third floor. Consequently, their mistake did not invalidate an otherwise valid warrant. "[S]ufficient probability, not certainty, is the touchstone of reasonableness under the Fourth Amendment. . . ."

The goal of the "things to be seized" particularity requirement is that "nothing is left to the discretion of the officer executing the warrant" (*Marron v. United States* 1927). Nonetheless, reasonable latitude is allowed. If police investigation shows that heroin is being sold from a particular location, then the warrant can specify that police search for and seize "a quantity of drugs." It is important that the police investigate the situation to the greatest extent feasible and make a good faith effort to know in advance what is likely to be discovered in the place to be searched. The plain view doctrine (discussed later in this chapter) necessarily creates an expansion of what items the police may lawfully seize from a premises. A valid search warrant is one of the basic ways in which police are legitimately in a premises; once there legitimately, they may seize all contraband in plain view, even if it is unrelated to the object of the search warrant.

Stanford v. Texas (1965) dealt with a search warrant authorizing police to search Stanford's San Antonio home to seize "books, records, pamphlets, cards, receipts, lists, memoranda, pictures, recordings and other written instruments concerning the . . . operations of the Communist Party of Texas. . . ." In actions eerily reminiscent of *Entick v. Carrington* (1765), officers spent almost five hours in Stanford's home, taking over a thousand books from his small business and his personal library. Books seized included some by alleged radical authors such as "Karl Marx, Jean Paul Sartre, Theodore Draper, Fidel Castro, Earl Browder, Pope John XXIII, and MR. JUSTICE HUGO L. BLACK." Many of Stanford's private documents and papers, "including his marriage certificate, his personal insurance policies, his household bills and receipts, and files of his personal correspondence," were seized. Ironically, no "records of the Communist Party" or any "party lists and dues payments" were found. The Court held that this was a general warrant and violated the Fourth and Fourteenth amendments, and added that when the things to be seized are books "and the basis of their seizure is the ideas which they contain," this implicates the First Amendment, and particularity must "be accorded the most scrupulous exactitude." Noting the historic continuity between this case and the earliest days of the American republic, Justice Stewart concluded by stating that "the Fourth and Fourteenth amendments guarantee to John Stanford that no official of the State shall ransack his home and seize his books and papers under the unbridled authority of a general warrant—no less than the law 200 years ago shielded John Entick from the messengers of the King."

Anticipatory Warrants

The United States Supreme Court has not ruled on **anticipatory warrants,** but such warrants have been authorized by F.R.C.P., Rule 41(a) since 1991 and are a useful tool for law enforcement.[13] In the standard case, police have probable cause to believe that contraband is *already* in a specified place when a warrant application is made. In an ongoing investigation, however, police may have good reason to believe that contraband or seizable evidence *will be* found in a specified place on the condition that another event, usually a delivery, occurs. A search warrant issued on such a basis *anticipates* the existence of facts that will make a search and seizure lawful. Given the need for such anticipation in drug crimes and in some federal white collar crimes, allowing anticipatory warrants encourages the use of the search warrant over warrantless searches based on exigent circumstances.[14]

A federal warrant may issue "for a search of property or for a person either within or outside the district if the property or person is within the district when the warrant is sought but might move outside the district before the warrant is executed." This includes two situations: First, where the suspect or contraband is anticipated to be in the district in the future, and second, where the suspect or contraband is currently in the district but may move out before the warrant is executed.[15] If the warrant is issued by a federal magistrate, federal law enforcement officers may execute it anywhere in the United States.

The amended rule facilitates **controlled deliveries.** If law enforcement becomes aware that illicit drugs or other contraband are in transit, they may *delay* the movement of the goods long enough to obtain a warrant, and then follow the delivery of the package to its destination. At that point, law enforcement agents will have probable cause to arrest the recipient of the package and to search the package. Without more evidence, however, this situation does not give agents probable cause to search the *place* to which the suspected package was delivered.[16]

This creates some extra hazards for unconstitutional searches. Therefore, when police or prosecutors request, and magistrates issue, anticipatory warrants, they have to be careful about four issues:[17]

1. the basis for probable cause
2. the degree of certainty that a seizable item will be delivered to a specified location
3. the specificity of the place to be searched
4. the appropriate scope of the warrant.

The basis of probable cause in a controlled delivery is often established by a reasonable seizure made by customs or mail officials who establish that goods are contraband drugs or child pornography. In cases where probable cause is established by an informant, the reliability of the informant should be subject to the rule of *Illinois v. Gates* (1983).

The goal of controlled deliveries is to identify the persons engaged in the criminal transaction and to view a completed crime in order to establish a basis for prosecution. For this to occur, the goods must be delivered to their "final" destination. In a controlled delivery scenario, a magistrate can be certain of the actual delivery. But an affidavit should include corroborating information to support an observed or uncontrolled delivery. Professor James Adams argues that "exercise of the officer's discretion will have to be objectively reasonable under all the circumstances" and that the "good faith" exception should *not* apply to such situations.[18]

When the final destination of the contraband is not previously known, it may be impossible to meet the Fourth Amendment requirement that the place to be searched be particularly described. A search under this condition must be based either on (1) an anticipatory warrant that authorizes police to search the "ultimate location," (2) an application for a telephone warrant or a telephone call to the magistrate with information before entering the premises, or (3) entrance of the premises under exigent circumstances. If an exigency does not exist, or if it is impractical to telephone the magistrate, the first option is the only one that makes controlled deliveries worth the effort. In that case, several courts have stated that the police should have as little discretion in determining the place, or the "ultimate location," as possible.[19]

Because the simple delivery of controlled substances does not establish probable cause to search a premises, the *scope of the search* following the controlled delivery depends on the extent of the information that the police have before they initiate the search. To be sure that officers do not write affidavits for anticipatory searches that are subterfuges for officers to enter and to "create" plain view, "affidavits in support of such warrants should demonstrate probable cause to believe additional evidence is on the premises and should specify the nature of that additional evidence."[20]

Challenging a Search Warrant Affidavit

After a search warrant has been executed, a defendant may challenge the constitutionality of the warrant, for example, by raising the issue of whether a secret informant was reliable.[21] A different question is whether a defendant can challenge the truthfulness of the affidavit. The officer submitting the warrant is an affiant—he swears to the truthfulness of the information in the warrant. What if the officer lies? The Supreme Court held (7–2) in *Franks v. Delaware* (1978), that a challenge to an affidavit is possible, but is limited to certain situations. The basic holding of *Franks* is that if a defendant can show that police injected lies into an affidavit, then the defendant is entitled to a hearing to present evidence to void the warrant. A more complete statement of the *Franks* rule is: (1) where a defendant makes a substantial preliminary showing, (2) that a false statement, knowingly and intentionally, or with reckless disregard for the truth, was included by an affiant in his affidavit for a search warrant (3) if the alleged false statement was necessary to the finding of probable cause, (4) then the Fourth Amendment requires that a hearing be held at the defendant's request so that he might challenge the truthfulness of factual statements made in the affidavit; (5) if at such hearing the defendant established, by a preponderance of the evidence, the allegation of perjury or reckless disregard (6) with the affidavit's false material set to one side, the affidavit's remaining content was insufficient to establish probable cause (7) then the search warrant has to be voided and the fruits of the search excluded to the same extent as if probable cause was lacking on the face of the affidavit. This is an exacting standard and precludes the frequent challenge to affidavits.

In this rape case, two detectives swore in an affidavit that they contacted Jerome Franks' co-workers about relevant evidence and "did have personal conversation with both these people." On that basis, a warrant was issued and executed. Police found clothes which implicated Franks and found a knife similar to one described by the victim. Franks claimed that he had a consensual sexual encounter and the knife, which was displayed to the jury, was never established to be the knife described by the victim. After the warrant was executed, the defense attorney requested a hearing at which he would call Franks' co-workers to testify that they never spoke personally to the detectives and that "although they might have talked to another police officer, any information given by them to that officer was 'somewhat different' from what was recited in the affidavit." The Delaware courts denied the hearing and the United States Supreme Court reversed.

In finding for Franks, Justice Blackmun reviewed the several competing values that were involved in the case. The arguments *against* ever allowing a hearing to challenge an affidavit included: (1) it magnifies the use of the exclusionary rule which is only a judicially created remedy and not a personal right, (2) the swearing to the affidavit sufficiently protects privacy, as does perjury prosecutions for a tiny number of falsified affidavits, (3) the magistrate can ferret out the truth at the warrant application, (4) allowing a post-affidavit hearing undermines the magistrate's authority, (5) the issue of an affidavit's truthfulness is collateral to the question of the defendant's guilt, (6) the truth of statements in an affidavit are often beyond the complete control of the officer since the affidavit may include hearsay, and (7) Justice Rehnquist, dissenting, also stressed the value of finality—that legal proceedings must come to an end at some point and should not be dragged on.

Against these objections, Justice Blackmun raised the following points: (1) "[A] flat ban on impeachment of veracity could denude the probable-cause requirement of all real meaning.", (2) A one–sided *ex parte* hearing is not entirely sufficient to block the introduction of perjury, (3) Alternative sanctions such as a perjury prosecution, administrative discipline, contempt, or a civil suit are relatively weak threats and thus not adequate to deter an officer bent on lying, (4) "[A]llowing an evidentiary hearing, after a suitable preliminary proffer of material falsity, would not diminish the importance and solemnity of the warrant-issuing process.", (5) A hearing to determine if an affidavit is truthful in no way interferes with the truth-finding aspects of the criminal case, (6) Given the requirements on the defendant to obtain a hearing, the right to challenge an affidavit will be infrequent and will not waste judicial resources, (7) The exclusionary rule should be applied to evidence obtained by means of police perjury.

Execution of the Search Warrant

Search warrants can become stale and must be executed as quickly as possible because the criminal evidence may be moved or in some other way destroyed or lose its character as contraband. F.R.C.P. Rule 41(c)(1) authorizes the magistrate to specify the time period within which the search must be carried out, within an outer limit of ten days. Similar rules exist in every state. Because nighttime searches create a greater intrusion on privacy and raise the risk of greater violence born of confusion, the federal rules specify: "The warrant shall be served in the daytime, unless the issuing authority, by appropriate provision in the warrant, and for reasonable cause shown, authorizes its execution at times other than daytime."[22] Not every state requires that a magistrate authorize a nighttime entry, leaving such a determination in the discretion of law enforcement officers.

The common law rule that officers must *announce their presence* before entering and state that they have a warrant—the **knock and announce rule**—is designed to (1) reduce the potential for violent confrontations, (2) protect individual privacy by minimizing the chance of forced entry into the dwelling of the wrong person, and (3) prevent a physical invasion of privacy by giving the occupant time to voluntarily admit the officers.[23] However, when officers have reason to believe, based on specific facts, that prior announcement of entry would produce immediate violence or an attempt to destroy all the evidence, they may dispense with the announcement.[24] This is a well-litigated area, and if it is proved that the police were unreasonable in failing to announce their entry, then the evidence will be excluded as a result of a Fourth Amendment violation. It may seem odd that the constitutionality of this requirement was not resolved until fairly recently. The issue has been addressed by four United States Supreme Court cases.

In *Ker v. California* (1963), police had sufficient probable cause to believe that Ker possessed marijuana in his home. They went to the building manager and obtained a passkey to Ker's apartment, and without obtaining a warrant entered the apartment without knocking. The United States Supreme Court upheld the search and seizure on the grounds that the police entered for the purpose of arresting Ker and not to search. (This is no longer constitutional; see *Payton v. New York* [1979], Chapter 5). As for the unannounced entry, the Court noted that "the lawfulness of these arrests by state officers for state offenses is to be determined by California law [which] permits peace officers to break into a dwelling place for the purpose of arrest after demanding admittance and explaining their purpose." A judicially created exception in California allowed police to enter without announcement "in order to prevent the destruction of contraband" and the California courts in *Ker* held that the circumstances of the case fit the exception. The failure to knock and announce "was therefore lawful." As a result, the Supreme Court did not have to directly confront the constitutionality of the knock and announce issue.

That opportunity finally arose in *Wilson v. Arkansas* (1995). Petitioner Sharlene Wilson made a series of narcotics sales to an informant acting at the direction of the Arkansas State Police at the home that Wilson shared with Bryson Jacobs. At one sale, Wilson produced a semiautomatic pistol and waved it in the informant's face threatening to kill her if she turned out to be working for the police. Based on the information supplied by the informant, police obtained a warrant to search the house and to arrest Wilson and Jacobs. The affidavits stated that Jacobs had previously been convicted of arson and firebombing. The warrant did not authorize an unannounced entry.

> The search was conducted later that afternoon. Police officers found the main door to petitioner's home open. While opening an unlocked screen door and entering the residence, they identified themselves as police officers and stated that they had a warrant. Once inside the home, the officers seized marijuana, methamphetamine, valium, narcotics paraphernalia, a gun, and ammunition. They also found petitioner in the bathroom, flushing marijuana down the toilet. Petitioner and Jacobs were arrested and charged with delivery of marijuana, delivery of methamphetamine, possession of drug paraphernalia, and possession of marijuana. (*Wilson v. Arkansas,* 1995)

The Arkansas Supreme Court upheld the search and seizure and specifically found that the Fourth Amendment does not include a rule that police must knock and announce. A unanimous United States Supreme Court reversed that decision.

Because the text of the Fourth Amendment does not include a knock and announce rule, it is possible to argue that the rule is not engrafted onto the Amendment. The opinion by Justice Clarence Thomas, one of the two strong "originalist" justices (along with Antonin Scalia), took a different tack. "In evaluating the scope of this right, we have looked to the traditional protections against unreasonable searches and seizures afforded by the common law at the time of the framing." In other words, the Court has engrafted a rule onto the text of the Fourth Amendment so long as it existed in the common law of England prior to the framing of the Constitution. This was justified by the idea that because the basic rule of the Fourth Amendment is that searches be reasonable (the "general-reasonableness construction"), what was reasonable to the Framers can be determined by the existing common law rules in the late eighteenth century. Also significant was the fact that the new states, shortly after July 4, 1776, passed "reception" statutes making the English common law the law of the state up until the date of the statute. Justice Thomas produced a noted case from the early seventeenth century, *Semayne's Case* (1603), and several prominent English commentators to establish that "At the time of the framing, the common law of search and seizure recognized a law enforcement officer's authority to break open the doors of a dwelling, but generally indicated that he first ought to announce his presence and authority." Furthermore, the "common-law knock-and-announce principle was woven quickly into the fabric of early American law." In all, the Court's opinion surmised that the Framers thought that the "knock and announce" rule was part of the "reasonableness" analysis of the Fourth Amendment.

The Court did not pass on the constitutionality of the actual search in this case. It noted that there were exceptions to the "knock and announce" rule under a variety of circumstances:

- a threat of physical violence
- a suspect escapes from an officer and retreats to his dwelling
- a demand to open was refused
- reason to believe that evidence would likely be destroyed if advance notice were given.

The case was remanded to the Arkansas courts to determine if any exception permitted the search and seizure in this case.

It appears that *Wilson v. Arkansas* does not create a major impediment to unannounced entry when it can be justified by the circumstances. The Supreme Court has made it clear, nevertheless, that the circumstances allowing a constitutional unannounced search must be justified in each case. In *Richards v. Wisconsin* (1997), police obtained a search warrant to enter a hotel room of a man suspected of dealing drugs. The magistrate deleted the "no-knock" part of the application. The warrant was executed at 3:40 A.M. by a police officer dressed as a maintenance man who knocked on Richards' door. With the chain still on the door, Richards cracked it open, saw a uniformed officer standing behind the disguised officer, and quickly slammed the door closed. After waiting two or three seconds, the officers began kicking and ramming the door to gain entry to the locked room. Richards was caught trying to escape through the window. Cash and cocaine were found hidden in plastic bags above the bathroom ceiling tiles. The trial court allowed the introduction of the evidence, because the officers could have concluded that Richards knew they were police officers and that he might try to destroy evidence or try to escape. The judge emphasized that the easily disposable nature of the drugs the police were searching for further justified their decision to identify themselves as they crossed the threshold instead of announcing their presence before seeking entry.

The Wisconsin Supreme Court affirmed and held that when police officers execute a warrant to search for drugs, the circumstances automatically raise exigent circumstances. In other words, the Wisconsin Court held that police never have to knock and announce in a drug case. The United States Supreme Court unanimously rejected this categorical rule. It found that a blanket no-knock exception had two flaws: Some warrants for drugs might be executed at a house where the occupants, at the time of the search, were not involved in the drug trade; and such an exception would soon negate the rule as it would be applied to all other crimes. The Court also specified the evidentiary standard to support a **no-knock warrant**: "a reasonable suspicion that knocking and announcing their presence, under the particular circumstances, would be dangerous or futile, or that it would inhibit the effective investigation of the crime by, for example, allowing the destruction of evidence." (*Richards v. Wisconsin,* p. 394) Applying this standard, the Supreme Court found that the no-knock entry into Richards' hotel room did not violate the Fourth Amendment because as soon as the door was opened, Richards was aware that police sought entry. Any further delay would have been unreasonable under the circumstances.

The rules concerning the execution of no-knock searches were further refined in *United States v. Ramirez* (1998). The Court unanimously held that police officers are not held to a higher standard than "reasonable suspicion" when the execution of a no-knock warrant results in damage to property. A reliable, confidential informant told federal agents that a dangerous prisoner, who escaped from a county jail in Oregon, where he had been sent to testify in a case, was hiding in the home of Hernan Ramirez. A "no-knock" warrant was obtained to search Ramirez' home for the prisoner.

> In the early morning of November 5, approximately 45 officers gathered to execute the warrant. The officers set up a portable loud speaker system and began announcing that they had a search warrant. Simultaneously, they broke a single window in the garage and pointed a gun through the opening, hoping thereby to dissuade any of the occupants from rushing to the weapons the officers believed might be in the garage.

Ramirez, awakened by this, thought his house was being burglarized and took his pistol and fired it into the ceiling of his garage. He dropped the gun when he realized the besiegers were police officers. Ramirez was indicted for being a felon in possession of firearms. The federal district court granted his motion to suppress evidence regarding the weapon possession; it found that the Fourth Amendment had been violated because there were "insufficient exigent circumstances" to justify the police officer's destruction of property in their execution of the warrant. The Ninth Circuit Court of Appeals affirmed, holding that property destruction accompanying a no-knock entry required more than a "mild" exigency.

The Supreme Court unanimously reversed. It held that there is no higher standard for a "no-knock" entry when property damage occurs as part of the entry. While noting that excessive property damage created during an entry could amount to a Fourth Amendment violation, the breaking of a single pane of glass, in this case, was reasonable.

Inventory and Return

After a search is executed, the officers must complete an **inventory and return.** This is a statutory requirement. F.R.C.P. Rule 41(d) states that the "return shall be made promptly and shall be accompanied by a written inventory of any property taken." The inventory must be made in the presence of a "credible person other than the applicant for the warrant or the person from whose possession or premises the property was taken." This is a valid practice that ensures the regularity of the search and seizure process and protects police officers from charges of theft.

The detail in an inventory and return can be examined in this excerpt from and FBI Agent's Affidavit an Inventory of the Search of the Unabomber's Cabin.

> "Your affiant, Special Agent (S.A.) Donald J. Sachtleben, Federal Bureau of Investigation, states as follows: 1. I, S.A. Donald J. Sachtleben, have been a Special Agent for twelve years. I graduated from the F.B.I. Hazardous Devices School and the F.B.I. Post Blast School. I have investigated bombing cases for 10 years and taught classes on the investigation of improvised explosive devices (I.E.D.). I have participated in the on scene investigation of bombing cases. ***
>
> 5. In order to construct a pipe bomb, one needs either a commercially manufactured explosive or an improvised explosive, a casing, a device to detonate the explosive, and a power source for the detonating device. During the search I observed materials from which all of these could be made. In particular, during the search I observed the following:
>
> 1. Ten three-ring binders. . . .
> 2. Pipes that appear to be galvanized metal, copper and plastic. Four of the copper pipes had plates affixed to one end, which is one of the first steps in the construction of a pipe bomb. . . .
> 3. Containers containing powders labeled as "KClO3" (potassium chlorate), "NaClO3" (sodium chlorate), "Sugar", "Zinc", "Aluminum", "Lead", and "Silver Oxide." Necessary ingredients in the preparation of explosives include an oxidizer and a fuel. Sugar, zinc, aluminum, lead and silver oxide all can serve as fuels, and potassium chlorate can be oxidizers. . . .
> 4. Solid cast ingots, one of which is labeled aluminum. . . . Aluminum can be used as an additional fuel and a catalyst in an explosive mixture.
> 5. C cell batteries and electrical wire. . . .***

The importance of police honesty and accuracy in the search warrant process cannot be overstated. The *Law in Society* section in this chapter deals with police perjury. On September 29, 1999, four Denver SWAT officers were sent to execute a no-knock warrant at 3738 High Street, a two-story home; it was the wrong house. Instead of executing the warrant, the officers who broke in executed forty-five-year-old Mexican, migrant laborer, Ismael Mena, father of nine, when he raised a gun as the police entered his bedroom. The SWAT officers were exonerated after a close examination of their response. But the officer who swore out the affidavit, Joseph Bini, was charged with perjury and faces a six-year term if convicted. He was charged with "'unlawfully and knowingly' lying on a search warrant affidavit." He claimed in the affidavit that "he personally observed an informant make his or her way on foot to the house" at 3738 High Street. Based on the affidavit, an assistant district attorney reviewed and signed the warrant and a county judge read and signed the warrant. But, in fact, the drug deal took place at 3742 High Street, a single-story home. Bini dropped the informant off four blocks from the house. The district attorney believed "[The informant] attempted to determine the address by counting the houses down the alley and up the front on this particular block. He apparently miscounted the houses and wrote the address down wrong." As a result, a man died and Denver paid Mena's family $400,000 to settle legal claims and the police chief was fired. On recommendations from a panel, Denver police will have only three days instead of ten days to serve no-knock warrants, more training will be provided, and experienced police supervisors will evaluate and approve no-knock raids. Denver's mayor said he thinks "the public can expect to see a decrease in the number of no-knock raids" as a result of the tighter guidelines. But it took an unnecessary death to achieve that result.[25]

REVOLUTIONIZING THE FOURTH AMENDMENT

For many years, Fourth Amendment law was tied to property concepts, especially the idea that a search and seizure involved a *physical trespass* onto a person's "*constitutionally protected area.*" This concept was based on traditional practice and on the words of the Fourth Amendment, protecting "persons, houses, papers and effects" from unreasonable search and seizure. Yet, this thinking created problems when the Supreme Court in *Olmstead v. United States* (1928) held that wiretapping did not constitute a search and seizure. This withdrew constitutional protection from a vital area of privacy and caused many to understand that the Fourth Amendment protected vital *interests* rather than property alone. It was not until 1967 that the Court revisited and overruled *Olmstead,* but to do so it had to establish an entirely new doctrine, because protecting such intangible privacy was not compatible with the "constitutionally protected area" doctrine.

Modernizing Search and Seizure Law

In 1967 and 1968, the Supreme Court "revolutionized" Fourth Amendment law in four cases that upset established doctrines and opened the door for a freewheeling mode of search and seizure interpretation. *Katz v. United States* (1967) was the centerpiece of this revolution. It broke away the law of search and seizure from its traditional mooring in property law. In its stead, issues were now to be decided more explicitly on a **balancing of interests** deemed central to the Fourth Amendment: The need for effective law enforcement versus the protection of privacy and liberty based on the notion of the "expectation of privacy." *Katz* was followed by *Warden v. Hayden* (1967), which abolished the "mere evidence" rule of *Gouled v. United States* (1921), on the reasoning that the rule: (1) Did not serve a defendant's legitimate privacy interest; (2) was based on outmoded property concepts; and (3) hampered the legitimate law enforcement interests of the state. Next came *Camara v. Municipal Court* (1967) and its companion case *See v. City of Seattle* (1967), which appeared to expand Fourth Amendment rights of individuals by requiring a warrant for administrative searches that did not directly enforce the criminal law. But to make such a program workable, the Court watered down the Fourth Amendment particularity requirement. Last, *Terry v. Ohio* (1968), for the first time, upheld a state deprivation of liberty as constitutional although it was based on a lesser standard of evidence than probable cause: a standard that came to be known as "reasonable suspicion." (*Terry* is discussed in Chapter 5).

Each of these cases worked a major change in search and seizure law in its own right. Together they set loose a mode of interpretation by which the Court has shaped Fourth Amendment doctrines to its liking, without much constraint from established precedent, thereby making search and seizure law dynamic and contentious. *Flexibility* of interpretation is the hallmark of these cases. The ability of the justices to achieve the law enforcement and administrative ends they desired was also achieved by shifting from a warrant-preference to a general-reasonableness construction of the Fourth Amendment. The four cases were generated by novel problems. Each required a solution that was possible only by changing old law. In order to maintain doctrinal coherence, the Court produced new theories and ways of examining Fourth Amendment problems that would have unforseen consequences. The four revolutionary decisions were not inherently liberal or conservative—two of them explicitly expanded the powers of the state (*Warden* and *Terry*) while the other two (*Katz* and *Camara*) formally expanded the rights of individuals. In their larger effects, the cases were "liberal" in that they brought a larger measure of police work within constitutional oversight, but "conservative" in permitting a flexible approach that made it easier for the Court to water down traditional Fourth Amendment standards. It is ironic that the liberal Warren Court laid a foundation of flexible interpretation—an approach that was resisted by relatively "conservative" justices like John M. Harlan II—that was adapted by the politically conservative Burger and Rehnquist Courts to expand the powers of the state against the individual.

Creating the Expectation of Privacy Doctrine

Modern conditions generate problems that require novel legal thinking. As noted above, electronic communication by telegraph, telephone, and by wireless communication—unknown to the Framers in 1791—led to invasions of privacy by police that did not have the appearance of a traditional search and seizure, with the police pounding at the door and physically searching a place. The Supreme Court ruled in *Olmstead v. United States* (1928) that wiretapping did not constitute a search because there was no physical trespass and no tangible evidence was taken. This ruling was deeply disturbing because wiretapping and electronic eavesdropping by the government is an obvious intrusion into the lives of individuals. A federal statute soon placed some controls on telephone wiretapping, but not on "bugging"—electronic eavesdropping by means of a wireless listening device. Over the next few years, the Court grappled with the question while the application of traditional Fourth Amendment concepts produced weirdly inconsistent results. *Goldman v. United States* (1942), for example, held that placing an electronic listening device *against* a wall was not a trespass, and therefore, under *Olmstead,* was not a search and seizure under the Fourth Amendment. Dissatisfied with the notion of leaving individuals open to government spying, the Court in *Silverman v. United States* (1961) held that *tacking* a mike into a wall was a physical trespass and thus a search and seizure subject to the rules of the Fourth Amendment. These were contradictory cases because the underlying invasion of privacy—listening in on and recording private conversations—was the same. Such incoherence led the Court to overrule *Olmstead* in *Katz* by breaking with the past and creating a new doctrine.

• CASE & COMMENTS •

Katz v. United States

389 U.S. 347, 88 S.Ct. 507, 19 L.Ed.2d 576 (1967)

MR. JUSTICE STEWART delivered the opinion of the Court.

[Katz was convicted of the federal crime of interstate transmission of wagering information by telephone. **[a]** The evidence, words spoken by Mr. Katz, was overheard by agents who placed an electronic listening device outside a telephone booth. The microphone was not physically driven into the booth. Katz entered at the same booth the same time each day (after a race track closed) and agents activated the microphone only when Katz was in the phone booth. No search warrant was obtained to place the device. A recording of the incriminating words spoken by Katz into the telephone was introduced into evidence.]

[a] Because the police knew where and when Katz would transmit betting information, there was no exigency and obtaining a search warrant would not have extended the investigation.

* * * In affirming his conviction, the Court of Appeals rejected the contention that the recordings had been obtained in violation of the Fourth Amendment, because "[t]here was no physical entrance into the area occupied by [the petitioner]." We granted certiorari in order to consider the constitutional questions thus presented.

The petitioner has phrased those questions as follows: **[b]**

[b] The way an issue is phrased is critical in appellate strategy. The choice of an issue can determine the outcome of a case. Here, the attorneys framed their issues to fit existing legal categories. However, Justice Stewart looked at this issue in a revolutionary way.

> "A. Whether a public telephone booth is a constitutionally protected area so that evidence obtained by attaching an electronic listening recording device to the top of such a booth is obtained in violation of the right to privacy of the user of the booth."
>
> "B. Whether physical penetration of a constitutionally protected area is necessary before a search and seizure can be said to be violative of the Fourth Amendment to the United States Constitution."

We decline to adopt this formulation of the issues. In the first place, the correct solution of Fourth Amendment problems is not necessarily promoted by incantation of the phrase "constitutionally protected area." **[c]** Secondly, the Fourth Amendment cannot be translated into a general constitutional "right to privacy." That Amendment protects individual privacy against certain kinds of governmental intrusion, but its protections go further, and often have nothing to do with privacy at all. Other provisions of the Constitution protect personal privacy from other forms of governmental invasion. But the protection of a person's *general* right to privacy—his right to be let alone by other people—is, like the protection of his property and of his very life, left largely to the law of the individual States.

[c] The attorneys "incanted" this phrase because that is the way the Supreme Court had analyzed the problem in the past.

Because of the misleading way the issues have been formulated, the parties have attached great significance to the characterization of the telephone booth from which the petitioner placed his calls. The petitioner has strenuously argued that the booth was a "constitutionally protected area." The Government has maintained with equal vigor that it was not. But this effort to decide whether or not a given "area," viewed in the abstract, is "constitutionally protected" deflects attention from the problem presented by this case. **[d]** For the Fourth Amendment protects people, not places. What a person knowingly exposes to the public, even in his own home or office, is not a subject of Fourth Amendment protection. * * * But what he seeks to preserve as private, even in an area accessible to the public, may be constitutionally protected. * * *

[d] These sentences are often repeated as the core concept of *Katz.* Do these pithy phrases solve all search and seizure issues before

• CASE & COMMENTS •

The Government stresses the fact that the telephone booth from which the petitioner made his calls was constructed partly of glass, so that he was as visible after he entered it as he would have been if he had remained outside. But what he sought to exclude when he entered the booth was not the intruding eye—it was the uninvited ear. He did not shed his right to do so simply because he made his calls from a place where he might be seen. **[e]** No less than an individual in a business office, in a friend's apartment, or in a taxicab, a person in a telephone booth may rely upon the protection of the Fourth Amendment. One who occupies it, shuts the door behind him, and pays the toll that permits him to place a call is surely entitled to assume that the words he utters into the mouthpiece will not be broadcast to the world. To read the Constitution more narrowly is to ignore the vital role that the public telephone has come to play in private communication.

The Government contends * * * that the activity of its agents * * * should not be tested by Fourth Amendment requirements, for the surveillance technique they employed involved no physical penetration of the telephone booth. * * * It is true that the absence of such penetration was at one time thought to foreclose further Fourth Amendment inquiry, * * * for that Amendment was thought to limit only searches and seizures of tangible property. But "[t]he premise that property interests control the right of the Government to search and seize has been discredited."* * * [O]nce it is recognized that the Fourth Amendment protects people—and not simply "areas"—against unreasonable searches and seizures it becomes clear that the reach of that Amendment cannot turn upon the presence or absence of a physical intrusion into any given enclosure.

We conclude that the underpinnings of *Olmstead* and *Goldman* have been so eroded by our subsequent decisions that the "trespass" doctrine there enunciated can no longer be regarded as controlling. **[f]** The Government's activities in electronically listening to and recording the petitioner's words violated the privacy upon which he justifiably relied while using the telephone booth and thus constituted a "search and seizure" within the meaning of the Fourth Amendment.

[The Court went on to hold that there was no exception to the Fourth Amendment warrant requirement in this case and that therefore the evidence of conversations "seized" in the phone booth was inadmissible.]

MR. JUSTICE HARLAN, concurring.

* * * The question * * * is what protection [the Fourth Amendment] affords to those people. Generally, as here, the answer to that question requires reference to a "place." **[g]** My understanding of the rule that has emerged from prior decisions is that there is a twofold requirement, first that a person have exhibited an actual (subjective) expectation of privacy and, second, that the expectation be one that society is prepared to recognize as "reasonable." * * *

* * *

MR. JUSTICE BLACK, dissenting.

* * *

Tapping telephone wires, of course, was an unknown possibility at the time the Fourth Amendment was adopted. **[h]** But eavesdropping (and wiretapping is nothing more than eavesdropping by telephone) was * * * "an ancient practice which at common law was condemned as a nuisance. . . ." * * * There can be no doubt that the Framers were aware of this practice, and if they had desired to outlaw or restrict the use of evidence obtained by eavesdropping, I believe that they would have used appropriate language to do so in the Fourth Amendment. * * *

The Fourth Amendment protects privacy only to the extent that it prohibits unreasonable searches and seizures of "persons, houses, papers, and effects." No general right is created by the Amendment so as to give this Court the unlimited power to hold unconstitutional everything which affects privacy. Certainly the Framers, well acquainted as they were with the excesses of governmental power, did not intend to grant this Court such omnipotent lawmaking authority as that. The history of governments proves that it is dangerous to freedom to repose such powers in courts.

* * *

the courts? To be successful, a legal doctrine must assist lawyers and judges in resolving future cases logically and efficiently.

[e] The Court seems to "update" the Constitution to fit new inventions not conceived of in 1791. Is this updating true to the goals and intent of the 1791 amendment? Does the *Katz* ruling apply to mobile phone conversations made in public?

[f] The Court overrules *Olmstead* and *Goldman,* and replaces the trespass doctrine with the "expectation of privacy" doctrine. Overruling a prior case is unusual. When it occurs, it is often preceded by a series of cases that show problems with the application of a doctrine. As a result, cases begin to narrow the scope of a doctrine and thus to "erode" it. *Silverman* did not so much erode *Olmstead* and *Goldman* as highlight their problems.

[g] Note that Justice Harlan's point modifies Justice Stewart's statements that the decision must turn on what *a person* seeks to keep private. Although written in a concurrence, Justice Harlan's addition of an objective element has become the operative rule of *Katz,* as later cases demonstrate.

[h] Is Justice Black more true to the Constitution by applying it as it would have been applied in 1791? If James Madison were sitting on the Court instead of Hugo Black, would he vote with the majority? Does the majority undermine constitutional adjudication by appealing to the underlying values in the Fourth Amendment? Or does the majority enhance the Constitution by its expanded view of the Fourth Amendment? Why is Justice Black concerned with granting "omnipotent lawmaking authority" to the Supreme Court?

Application of the Expectation of Privacy Doctrine

Katz has substantially changed the way in which the Court analyzes Fourth Amendment issues, and many cases have been decided based on the Court's belief that a government intrusion amounts to an invasion of a subjective and objective expectation of privacy. Additionally, *Katz* appears to apply except when the Court rules otherwise. Therefore, the Court has not only formally held that the Fourth Amendment protects property as well as privacy interests (*Soldal v. Cook County* 1992), but in several cases when dissenting justices believed that the *Katz* doctrine favored the defendant, the majority has ruled in favor of the state (e.g., *Rakas v. Illinois* 1978). Any reference to the *Katz* doctrine now means that the expectation of privacy is a combination of Justice Stewart's *subjective* and Justice Harlan's *objective* tests: Fourth Amendment protection is extended to what a person seeks to preserve as private *and* to what "society is prepared to recognize as 'reasonable.'"

MAINTAINING PROPERTY INTERESTS AFTER KATZ After *Katz,* the Court made it clear that the Fourth Amendment continues to protect property interests. In *Soldal v. Cook County* (1992), a mobile home park took action to evict Soldal and his mobile home from its property and utilities. The mobile home park owner called the Sheriff's deputies and alerted them to stand by in the event that the eviction might lead to violence. The employees of the park pushed Soldal's trailer into a road causing major property damage. The park did not act in accordance with law. There was no invasion of Soldal's *privacy,* as the employees never entered Soldal's trailer, but his property was damaged. Although the officers did not physically assist in the eviction, the Court held that their presence established governmental action. Soldal sued the Sheriff's department under 42 U.S.C. § 1983. The government argued that without a *Katz*-like violation to privacy rights, there was no Fourth Amendment wrong. This argument was firmly rejected: *Katz* protects *both* privacy and property rights. According to Justice White, although there was *no search,* there was a *seizure*—a "meaningful interference with an individual's possessory interests in that property." Because "[w]hat matters is the intrusion on the people's security from governmental interference," this case fell within the Fourth Amendment.

EXPECTATION OF PRIVACY IN DWELLINGS It goes without saying that each individual has a subjective expectation of privacy in one's dwelling and that society upholds this expectation. At times, the Supreme Court has leaned in favor of a defendant's rights for this reason. For example, in *Payton v. New York* (1979), the Court ruled that an arrest warrant must be obtained in order to forcibly enter a home to arrest a person. The "physical entry of the home is the chief evil against which the wording of the Fourth Amendment is directed."[26] The protection of the home applies to apartments, offices, garages, and temporary dwellings, such as hotel rooms. This has been confirmed in cases where the Court has denied landlords and hotel keepers the right to consent to police searches of the rooms of tenants (*Chapman v. California,* 1961; *Stoner v. California,* 1964). The protection of home privacy was a key reason for the Court's modification of the hot pursuit doctrine to disallow warrantless home entry for relatively minor offenses. (*Welsh v. Wisconsin,* 1984)

When the core area of the home is involved, even a relatively conservative Court has scrupulously protected Fourth Amendment rights by maintaining the warrant and probable cause requirements. A person has no expectation of privacy in his public movements and, thus, no warrant was required when police placed an electronic **beeper** in a drum containing chloroform to monitor a suspected drug manufacturer driving along public streets (*United States v. Knotts,* 1983). On the other hand, a suspect's Fourth Amendment rights were violated when, without a warrant, agents traced a drum into the home of a suspect and noted its movement in the home (*United States v. Karo,* 1984). In a similar vein, while there is no Fourth Amendment protection of "**open fields,**" the Court has taken the common-law concept of the **curtilage**—the area immediately surrounding a house—and given it constitutional protection (*United States v. Dunn,* 1987; *Oliver v. United States,* 1984). Still, the Court has strained to not apply the curtilage idea to police observations of back yards from low-flying fixed-wing airplanes and helicopters. (*California v. Ciraolo,* 1986; *Florida v. Riley,* 1989)

Nevertheless, certain dwellings are not clothed with Fourth Amendment protection. No matter how closely attached a prisoner becomes to his or her prison cell, "a prison shares none of the attributes of privacy of a home." Although prisoners retain certain constitutional rights, such as freedom of religion, freedom from cruel and unusual punishment, and due process, "society is not prepared to recognize as legitimate any subjective expectation of privacy that a prisoner might have in his prison cell; . . . the Fourth Amendment proscription against unreasonable searches and seizures does not apply within the confines of the prison cell." The practical consequence of this is that prison authorities are allowed under the Constitution to make random shakedown searches of prisoners' cells (*Hudson v. Palmer,* 1984). Similarly, the Court, over a strong dissent, allowed a probation officer to enter a *probationer's home* without a warrant and on less than probable cause (*Griffin v. Wisconsin,* 1987). The Court implied that a probationer's criminal status imposes a lower expectation of privacy at home than unconvicted persons. An arrest in a home cannot lead to the search of the entire premises (*Chimel v. California,* 1969); but an arrest in a house allows police to make a "protective sweep" to be sure other persons are not present (*Maryland v. Buie,* 1990).

MEDIA RIDE ALONG In *Wilson v. Layne* (1999), the Court held it "a violation of the Fourth Amendment for police to bring members of the media or other third parties into a home during the execution of a warrant when the presence of the third parties in the home was not in aid of the execution of the warrant." A proper arrest warrant was issued to United States Marshals to enter a home in Rockville, Maryland, to arrest Dominic Wilson, a dangerous fugitive. Unbeknownst to the police, it was the home of the fugitive's parents. The arrest warrant was executed at 6:45 A.M., much to the surprise of the parents. After discovering that Dominic was not at the house, the arrest team departed. The team "was accompanied by a reporter and a photographer from the *Washington Post,* who had been invited by the Marshals to accompany them on their mission as part of a Marshal's service ride-along policy." The reporter took numerous photographs but none were published. The reporter was in the living room and observed a scuffle and the handcuffing of Mr. Wilson, who was wearing briefs. The reporters did not assist in executing the warrant. The Wilsons brought a civil lawsuit for money damages against the Marshal's service for violating their Fourth Amendment right of privacy by bringing reporters into their home.

The Court found that the warrant was supported by probable cause and its execution, aside from bringing along the reporters, did not violate the Wilson's Fourth Amendment rights. The government tried to justify the **media ride-along** by arguing that: media presence promotes accurate reporting and crime fighting; the presence of third parties minimize police abuses and protect the suspects; and the police should be allowed to determine if these law enforcement interests are advanced by the ride-along.

The Court found these reasons unpersuasive. Even if reasonable, these factors promote *general* interests and are not sufficient to overcome the *specific* constitutional right held by the Wilsons. The Court did not refer to *Katz* or the expectation of privacy in *Wilson*; instead it emphasized the "the importance of the right of residential privacy at the core of the Fourth Amendment," a "centuries-old principle of respect for the privacy of the home." Beyond this, the Court did not reason except to say that, "Were such generalized 'law enforcement objectives' themselves sufficient to trump the Fourth Amendment, the protections guaranteed by that Amendment's text would be significantly watered down." *Wilson* shows a trend of the modern Court to emphasize the expectation of privacy in the home but not to apply the *Katz* doctrine to the fullest extent in other areas of law enforcement practice.

EXPECTATION OF PRIVACY IN ONE'S BODY Obtaining physical evidence from within a person's body raises Fourth Amendment questions which have been answered by closely examining the severity of the intrusion and the law enforcement interests. Factors include the risk to safety or health in the procedure, the extent of control used on the person's body, and the effect on the suspect's personal dignity. Forced *surgery* to remove a bullet lodged in a robbery suspect was held to violate his Fourth Amendment rights because the expectation of privacy in one's bodily integrity is great (*Winston v. Lee,* 1985). Taking *blood* in a medical setting to determine a driver's blood alcohol level after a fatal accident has been upheld; it presents virtually no health risk and is so routine as to involve a minimal interference with Fourth Amendment dignity interests (*Schmerber v. California,* 1966). Lower courts have also perceived a greater privacy interest in bodily integrity in cases involving body cavity searches and strip searches.[27]

A person's observable physical characteristics, such as one's voice or handwriting, are not "seized" if someone testifies to them at a trial or if a person's description is taken by police in an investigation (*United States v. Dionisio,* 1973; *United States v. Mara,* 1973). Requiring a person to participate in a line-up does not violate one's Fourth or Fifth amendment rights (*United States v. Wade,* 1967).

The Supreme Court has held that *urine collection and testing* intrudes upon expectations of privacy that society has long recognized as reasonable. "There are few activities in our society more personal or private than the passing of urine. Most people describe it by euphemisms if they talk about it at all. It is a function traditionally performed without public observation; indeed, its performance in public is generally prohibited by law as well as social custom." The Court noted that the expectation of privacy is not only rooted in the traditional dictates of modesty, but also in the fact that the chemical analysis of urine, like that of blood, can reveal a host of medical facts about a person. Although urine testing by state agencies in order to detect drugs or alcohol is protected by the Fourth Amendment, the collection is allowed under certain conditions (*Skinner v. Railway Labor Executives' Association,* 1989). (See Chapter 6.) In contrast, private business is not restricted in this practice by the Fourth Amendment because there is no state action.

EXPECTATION OF PRIVACY IN AUTOMOBILES There is a lesser expectation of privacy in an automobile than in a home (*California v. Carney,* 1985). The Supreme Court has found that at common law mobile vehicles could be stopped without a warrant and has generally extended this exception into the Fourth Amendment "automobile exception" (*Carroll v. United States,* 1925). Yet, the Court has applied the expectation of privacy doctrine to the stopping of automobiles by United States Border Patrol Officers, and later to all police agencies, and has found that the stopping of an automobile is a seizure, and that it can cause annoyance or fright. Therefore, a warrantless stop of a vehicle must be justified by reasonable suspicion or probable cause of a traffic violation or crime (*United States v. Brignoni-Ponce,* 1975; *Delaware v. Prouse,* 1979). On the other hand, because a stop at a fixed checkpoint does not produce the same anxiety as that associated with being stopped by a roving patrol, the expectation of privacy is less and the stop need not be justified by particularized suspicion. (*United States v. Martinez-Fuerte,* 1976; *Mich. Dept. of State Police v. Sitz,* 1990)

EXPECTATION OF PRIVACY IN PROPERTY AND EFFECTS The Supreme Court has held that a *footlocker* is protected by a subjective and objective expectation of privacy. Police had probable cause to believe that a footlocker contained marijuana, had arrested its possessor, and had the luggage in custody. Opening the footlocker violated Chadwick's Fourth Amendment rights and the evidence was suppressed. The police should have sought a search warrant from a magistrate (*United States v. Chadwick,* 1977). The Court has further extended the expectation of privacy to soft baggage that was squeezed by a Border Patrol agent. A bus traveling from California to Arkansas stopped at a Border Patrol checkpoint in Texas, and the agent boarded the bus to check the immigration status of its passengers. After reaching the back of the bus, having satisfied himself that the passengers were lawfully in the United States, the agent began walking toward the front. Along the way, he squeezed the soft luggage which passengers had placed in the overhead storage space above the seats. He squeezed a green canvas bag belonging to passenger Steven Dewayne Bond and noticed that it contained a "brick-like" object later identified as methamphetamine. The Supreme Court held that this physical examination was a search. Bond exhibited an actual expectation of privacy by using an opaque bag and placing that bag directly above his seat. The agent's manipulation of the bag went beyond that tolerated by society:

> When a bus passenger places a bag in an overhead bin, he expects that other passengers or bus employees may move it for one reason or another. Thus, a bus passenger clearly expects that his bag may be handled. He does not expect that other passengers or bus employees will, as a matter of course, feel the bag in an exploratory manner. But this is exactly what the agent did here. We therefore hold that the agent's physical manipulation of petitioner's bag violated the Fourth Amendment. (*Bond v. United States,* 2000)

On the other hand, the Court has come close to stating that a person has no expectation of privacy in the *odor of drugs* emanating from a piece of luggage in a public area if detected by a trained drug sniffing canine (*United States v. Place,* 1983). There is no expectation of privacy in *abandoned property* such as *trash* left in opaque plastic bags at curbside. It may be seized and searched without a warrant. The general public does not believe that a person expects trash to be kept private because the bags can be opened by children playing, by animals, or by scavengers (*California v. Greenwood,* 1988). The same result occurs under the older property theory: Once people abandon property, they lose all control over it.

The Court has held that by depositing money in banks, people expose financial information in *bank records* to strangers such as bank employees, and thus, Congress may require that large cash or other transactions be reported to federal agencies without showing particularized suspicion. One's banking records can be subpoenaed by the government under the Bank Secrecy Act. (*California Bankers Association v. Schultz* (1974); *United States v. Miller,* 1976)

EXPECTATION OF PRIVACY IN BUSINESS RECORDS AND COMMERCIAL PROPERTY As noted in Chapter 3, the Court has held that business records are not protected by the Fifth Amendment and thus are subject to seizure with a proper search warrant (*Andresen v. Maryland,* 1976). Business premises are protected by the Fourth Amendment (*Hale v. Henkel,* 1906; *See v. City of Seattle,* 1967). If commercial property is open to the public, such as a retail store, a police agent may enter the premises and observe or purchase suspected items, and such an entry and purchase is not a search and seizure (*Maryland v. Macon,* 1985). Although warrants are required for commercial health or safety inspections under the *Camara–See* doctrine, they require a lesser standard of evidence than the traditional probable cause standard (*Marshall v. Barlow's, Inc.,* 1978). Some commercial properties are subject to warrantless inspections, although retaining expectations of privacy, because of the nature of the business or the special risks that the business creates (e.g., mining). (*Donovan v. Dewey,* 1981). (See Chapter 6)

Demise of the Mere Evidence Rule

As noted in Chapter 3, the "mere evidence" rule of *Gouled v. United States* (1921) limited what police could seize in a search to the *fruits* of crime (*i.e.,* loot), *weapons* used in a crime, and *contraband.* Items not falling into these categories were "mere" evidence and could not be seized. *Gouled* derived the rule from its reading of the common law, and it is clear that the rule was based on the owner's property rights. The reason for extinguishing the doctrine in *Warden v. Hayden* (1967) was related to the thinking in *Katz* and exemplifies the modern Court's instrumental approach which balances the interests of the state and the individual.

Now, instead of determining the property which the police may seize on the basis of technical property rights, the Court analyzes the nature of the *interests:* the individual's desire for property, liberty, and privacy balanced against the government's need to successfully prosecute crimes. The tipping of the balance rests on the justices' views of whose rights are more just and logical.

In *Warden v. Hayden,* police were informed of the robbery of taxi company offices. Cab drivers followed the robber to a house and called the dispatch office, which gave police the location of the house and a description of the robber. Officers knocked and were allowed into the house by the defendant's wife. Officers proceeded through the house looking for the robber, money, and weapons. One "officer was attracted to an adjoining bathroom by the noise of running water, and discovered a shotgun and a pistol in a flush tank; another officer who, . . . 'was searching the cellar for a man or the money' found in a washing machine a jacket and trousers of the type the fleeing man was said to have worn." Bennie Joe Hayden "was found in an upstairs bedroom feigning sleep" and was arrested. The Supreme Court held the entry and search of the house a valid "hot pursuit" warrantless search. (see Chapter 6). The issue was whether the jacket and trousers—mere evidence—were admissible as they could not be classified as loot, weapons, or contraband. Justice Brennan, writing for the majority, rejected the mere evidence rule "as based on premises no longer accepted as rules governing the application of the Fourth Amendment." He pointed out that the rule "was a reaction to the evils of the use of the general warrant in England and the writs of assistance in the Colonies, and was intended to protect against invasions of 'the sanctity of a man's home and the privacies of life.'" He went on to demolish every basis for the rule: textual, the privacy interest, and property interests:

> Nothing in the language of the Fourth Amendment supports the distinction between "mere evidence" and instrumentalities, fruits of crime, or contraband. . . . Privacy is disturbed no more by a search directed to a purely evidentiary object than by a search directed to an instrumentality, fruit, or contraband. . . . Indeed, the distinction is wholly irrational, since, depending on the circumstances, the same "papers and effects" may be "mere evidence" in one case and "instrumentality" in another.
>
> The premise that property interests control the right of the Government to search and seize has been discredited. Searches and seizures may be "unreasonable" within the Fourth Amendment even though the Government asserts a superior property interest at common law. We have recognized that the principal object of the Fourth Amendment is the protection of privacy rather than property, and have increasingly discarded fictional and procedural barriers resting on property concepts. . . . (*Warden v. Hayden,* 1967)

He noted that *Katz,* by holding that intangible evidence comes within the purview of the Fourth Amendment, in effect abolished the property/trespass basis for legitimate police searches and seizures. Conversely, *Katz* protected "fruits," instrumentalities, contraband, and the like if their seizure violated a person's reasonable expectation of privacy. In sum, police can seize *any* property that is logically related to proving the crime as long as it was lawfully seized. (Once the noncontraband evidence has served its evidentiary purpose, it should be returned to its owner.)

Several liberal justices were uncomfortable with a ruling that completely eliminated a personal protection. Justice Fortas, joined by Chief Justice Warren, concurred. He would have modified the mere evidence rule by simply adding 'clothing worn during a crime' to seizable items. Justice Douglas dissented, wanting to keep the greatest scope of protection for individual privacy.

The Modern Administrative Search Doctrine

The Court's previous position contended that searches into homes and businesses by governmental administrative officers such as health, fire, or housing inspectors, for purposes of enforcing regulations, did not come under the Fourth Amendment. In the few cases when homeowners or business proprietors refused to allow agents to enter without a warrant, they were convicted of minor crimes and fined. The Supreme Court upheld such convictions, by a narrow 5–4 margin, in *Frank v. Maryland* (1959). The majority felt that the warrant process was not meant to apply to essentially noncriminal actions. The *Frank* dissent argued that the Fourth Amendment limits not only privacy intrusions by police enforcing the penal code, but extends to all state action.

Frank was overruled in the leading administrative search cases, *Camara v. Municipal Court* (1967) and *See v. City of Seattle* (1967), which played an important role in reconceptualizing Fourth Amendment doctrine. These cases expanded the scope of Fourth Amendment coverage, while concurrently allowing a more flexible view of the Amendment's particularity requirement. This reasoning was instrumental in the development of *Terry v. Ohio* (1968) and to later diminution of strict constitutional protections under the "special needs" doctrine (see Chapter 6).

Camara and *See* were based on the principle that Fourth Amendment protections apply against *all* arbitrary government intrusions, whether carried out by a police officer or other government agent, for the purpose of criminal law enforcement or public administration, and whether the intrusion is in a home or a business establishment. The *Camara* majority deemed that *Mapp v. Ohio* (1961), which incorporated the exclusionary rule, ushered in a new era that changed the operative constitutional norms. Thus, even if administrative searches are less hostile and intrusive than police searches for criminal evidence, the Court in *Camara* could not agree that Fourth Amendment interests were peripheral. "[E]ven the most law-abiding citizen has a very tangible interest in limiting the circumstances under which the sanctity of his home may be broken by official authority, for the possibility of criminal entry under the guise of official sanction is a serious threat to personal and family security." Furthermore, an occupant's refusal to admit an administrative inspector could lead to a criminal penalty. Nor was the Court impressed by the fact that inspections were held at reasonable times and that they had to be reasonable, even if conducted without a warrant. Therefore, the Court ruled that administrative searches of the kind conducted in *Camara* and *See,* if not based on consent, had to be authorized by a warrant.

This, however, created a problem. Most administrative inspection programs are based not on particularized probable cause of a safety hazard in a particular home or business, but on administrative assessments that houses or businesses in an *entire neighborhood* should be entered and inspected. If a municipality had to get particularized probable cause for each house in the neighborhood, the inspection program would fail. The constitutional issue, then, was how to make the administrative warrant requirement both feasible and in accordance with the particularity requirement of the Fourth Amendment's warrant clause.

The Court solved the problem with a *flexible* interpretation by analyzing the constitutionality of administrative *warrants* under the *reasonableness* clause, rather than the warrant clause. It then applied the *balancing test* to find that area-wide administrative searches were reasonable because they were based on long accepted practice and the need for public health and safety, and were less intrusive than police searches for criminal evidence. Justice White's majority opinion reasoned:

> Having concluded that the area inspection is a "reasonable" search of private property within the meaning of the Fourth Amendment, it is obvious that "probable cause" to issue a warrant to inspect must exist if reasonable legislative or administrative standards for conducting an area inspection are satisfied with respect to a particular dwelling. Such standards, which will vary with the municipal program being enforced, may be based upon the passage of time, the nature of the building (*e.g.,* a multi-family apartment house), or the condition of the entire area, but they will *not* necessarily *depend upon specific knowledge* of the condition of the *particular* dwelling. It has been suggested that so to vary the probable cause test from the standard applied in criminal cases would be to authorize a "synthetic search warrant" and thereby to lessen the overall protections of the Fourth Amendment. But we do not agree. The warrant procedure is designed to guarantee that a decision to search private property is justified by a reasonable governmental interest. But *reasonableness is still the ultimate standard.* If a valid public interest justifies the intrusion contemplated, then there is probable cause to issue a suitably restricted search warrant. Such an approach neither endangers time-honored doctrines applicable to criminal investigations nor makes a nullity of the probable cause requirement in this area. It merely gives full recognition to the competing public and private interests here at stake and, in so doing, best fulfills the historic purpose behind the constitutional right to be free from unreasonable government invasions of privacy. (*Camara v. Municipal Court,* 1967, pp. 538–39, emphasis added)

More conservative Justices Clark, Harlan, and Stewart dissented. It is clear that the liberal majority, in order to extend the reach of the Fourth Amendment, had to water down the meaning of probable cause and particularity and in effect uphold general warrants, the very thing that the Fourth Amendment was designed to avoid. In the future, reliance on the general-reasonableness construction would be used to modify doctrines. The "stop and frisk" ruling of *Terry v. Ohio* (1968) and the "special needs" cases, for example, expanded the scope of governmental intrusiveness.

Entry into Premises by Undercover Agents

In *Gouled v. United States* (1921), Army investigators sent a "secret agent" into Gouled's office, not by means of a trespass or burglary, but by false pretenses. Is this kind of entry a search under the Fourth Amendment? The Supreme Court resolved the issue in two cases decided on the same day in 1966. There is no Fourth Amendment right of privacy against "inviting" a person who is a secret government agent into the home.

Lewis v. United States (1966) dealt with the common situation of a narcotics agent being invited into a home to conclude an illicit drug transaction after having misrepresented his intentions. The Fourth Amendment was not violated since Lewis had converted his home "into a commercial center to which outsiders are invited for purposes of transacting unlawful business." Thus, whether one applies the older property basis or the modern expectation of privacy basis of Fourth Amendment rights, there is no constitutional violation in this scenario. The Court warned that entry gained by invitation did not give the **undercover agent** the right to conduct a general search of the premises. In *Lewis,* the Court also expressed its concern for the practical needs of law enforcement:

> Were we to hold the deceptions of the agent in this case constitutionally prohibited, we would come near to a rule that the use of undercover agents in any manner is virtually unconstitutional *per se.* Such a rule would, for example, severely hamper the Government in ferreting out those

> organized criminal activities that are characterized by covert dealings with victims who either cannot or do not protest. A prime example is provided by the narcotics traffic. (*Lewis v. United States,* p. 210, footnote omitted)

In *Hoffa v. United States* (1966) national Teamster Union president James Hoffa was convicted of bribing jurors in an earlier trial. Evidence of the jury tampering was offered by Edward Partin, a teamster union official who was in trouble with the law, and who was present in Hoffa's hotel apartment during the earlier trial. He had assisted Hoffa while simultaneously reporting on the jury tampering to federal agents. Partin went to Hoffa's apartment as a government agent; in return for his spying, state and federal criminal charges against him were dropped and Partin's wife was paid $1,200 out of government funds. Hoffa argued that Partin's entry into the apartment violated his Fourth Amendment right to privacy and was an illegal "search" for verbal evidence. The Court agreed that Hoffa had a Fourth Amendment right to privacy in the hotel apartment, and that entry could have been made both by a trespass and, as in *Gouled,* by trickery. What Hoffa relied on was the protection offered by the place. Thus, if Partin had opened a desk drawer or a filing cabinet and stolen incriminating evidence, this would have intruded into Hoffa's constitutionally protected area. The same result would occur by applying the *Katz* expectation of privacy analysis. However,

> It is obvious that [Hoffa] was not relying on the security of his hotel suite when he made the incriminating statements to Partin or in Partin's presence. Partin did not enter the suite by force or by stealth. He was not a surreptitious eavesdropper. Partin was in the suite by invitation, and every conversation which he heard was either directed to him or knowingly carried on in his presence. The petitioner, in a word, was not relying on the security of the hotel room; he was relying upon his misplaced confidence that Partin would not reveal his wrongdoing. . . .
>
> Neither this Court nor any member of it has ever expressed the view that the Fourth Amendment protects a wrongdoer's misplaced belief that a person to whom he voluntarily confides his wrongdoing will not reveal it. (*Hoffa v. United States,* p. 302)

The Fourth Amendment does not protect a person against false friends.

A related question is whether there is any Fourth Amendment protection when a "false friend" wears a concealed microphone on his body to transmit and/or record incriminating conversations. The Supreme Court has consistently ruled that this practice is not prohibited by the Fourth Amendment. When a person "invites" an undercover agent to speak with him voluntarily, the effect of the recording device is to improve the accuracy of the agent's testimony against the defendant. The Court has so held, both before and after *Katz,* and the federal electronic eavesdropping law has confirmed this rule as a matter of federal law.[28]

Extraterritorial Application of the Fourth Amendment

The question of whether the Fourth Amendment applies to searches by American officers in foreign countries—whether it has **extraterritorial** effect—is not, strictly speaking, a question of expectation of privacy. It is related, however, in that both issues relate to the *scope* of the Amendment's application. The Supreme Court held in *United States v. Verdugo-Urquidez* (1990) that the Fourth Amendment does not have any effect when United States officers search the premises of an alien in a foreign country even if the alien is arrested and is on American soil in federal custody at the time of the search, and the purpose of the search is to obtain evidence for the conviction of the alien of a federal crime.

Verdugo-Urquidez, a reputed drug dealer, was arrested in Mexico by Mexican officers at the request of American authorities and charged in federal court for the kidnapping and murder of a Drug Enforcement (DEA) special agent. A raid of Verdugo's home in Mexico was carried out by a joint Mexican Police–DEA task force and the evidence obtained was used exclusively by the DEA to prosecute Verdugo. No approval was sought from United States Attorneys or magistrates for the raid. The Ninth Circuit Court of Appeals held that a warrant was required for such a search. Although the warrant would be of no legal validity in Mexico, it would "define the scope of the search" for American authorities.

In rejecting this argument, Chief Justice Rehnquist, writing for the majority, noted that the Fourth Amendment had never been extended to protect aliens on foreign soil. The fact that Verdugo was in custody on American soil at the time of the raid is a "fortuitous circumstance" that should not dictate the outcome of the case. Foreign relations activities may have influenced the *Verdugo-Urquidez* decision. At the time the case was being considered, the United States invaded Panama to rid that country of its military dictator, Manuel Noriega, who was under federal indictment for drug dealing. Noriega surrendered to United States forces and was transported to the United States for trial. Chief Justice Rehnquist noted that the United States had employed its armed forces over two hundred times on foreign soil. "Application of the Fourth Amendment to those circumstances could significantly disrupt the ability of the political branches to respond to foreign situations involving our national interest." The Court clearly thought it would be bad policy to impose the burden or concern on the president and members of Congress "as to what might be reasonable in the way of searches and seizures conducted abroad" before authorizing such actions.

Justice Brennan, dissenting, noted that in recent years the extraterritorial reach of American criminal law against foreign nationals has been increasing under United States drug laws, antitrust laws, securities laws, antiterrorist and piracy laws, and other statutes. If the United States can extend its criminal law overseas, then the Fourth Amendment should "travel with" American agents who go abroad to exercise criminal jurisdiction. The dissenters saw a "sufficient connection" between Verdugo-Urquidez and the United States by the facts of the case.

PROBABLE CAUSE AND THE FOURTH AMENDMENT

The Fourth Amendment states that warrants must be issued on **probable cause,** and this standard has been used as the touchstone of all Fourth Amendment action, including arrests, warrantless searches, and warrants. Until *Terry v. Ohio* (1967), a forcible police interference with liberty, property, or privacy on less than probable cause violated the Fourth Amendment. *Terry's* flexible interpretation, first applied to field interrogation, introduced the lower evidentiary standard of reasonable suspicion.

The Concept of Evidence Sufficiency

Liberty is a fundamental precept in American political life. At its most basic level it implies that a person's freedom of movement, privacy, or property must not be stopped or interfered with by the government unless the government can first show a need to interfere that is justified by law. In Fourth Amendment terms, a police officer must have evidence to support a stop, arrest, or search *before* the search takes place. The best way for a police agent to do this is to obtain a warrant. If a warrantless stop, arrest, or search is challenged, the officer must convince a court that he or she had a sufficient level of evidence to lawfully interfere with the defendant's liberty interests. In other areas where the criminal justice or legal process interferes with liberty, other levels of evidence sufficiency are required. This is illustrated in Table 4–1. The concept of evidence sufficiency is therefore a latent part of due process and helps to ensure fundamental fairness.

Defining Probable Cause

Probable cause is defined as *known facts that could lead a reasonably prudent person to draw conclusions about unknown facts,* and is a standard of *evidence* that triggers official action. It is also referred to as *reasonable cause.* Because the evidence standard of *Terry v. Ohio* is commonly known as "reasonable suspicion", it is useful to use these terms precisely. Evidence is any kind of proof offered to establish the existence of a fact. Evidence may be (a) the *testimony* of a witness as to what was heard, seen, smelled, tasted, or felt; or (b) *physical items* such as documents, drugs, or weapons. Physical evidence is sometimes called *real evidence.*

Probable cause is one of several standards of evidence that trigger and justify intrusive governmental action. Table 4–1 displays a hierarchy of evidentiary standards. These standards pertain to the *sufficiency* or *weight* of evidence rather than to its admissibility. In general, the greater the impact of a legal action on an individual, the more stringent is the evidentiary standard.

Probable cause is the legal standard for a wide variety of police and legal decisions in the pretrial criminal process: Arrest, search and seizure, a magistrate authorizing a charge in an initial hearing shortly after arrest, a magistrate's bindover decision after a preliminary hearing, and the formal charging of a criminal defendant by a prosecutor's information or by an indictment by a grand jury voting a "true bill" against a suspect. (In some states, the grand jury or bindover decision might be subjected to the slightly more rigorous "prima facie case" standard). Probable cause to *arrest* a person consists of facts that would lead a prudent person to believe that a crime has been committed and that the suspect has committed it. Probable cause to *search* a place and seize evidence consists of facts that would lead a prudent person to believe that "seizable" items (*i.e.,* contraband, the fruits of a crime, instrumentalities used to commit a crime, or evidence of criminality) are or soon will be located at a particular place.

The line between probable cause and the lesser reasonable suspicion standard is a fine one. *Terry* (1967) did not use the term "reasonable suspicion" but upheld a temporary "stop"—a lesser intrusion than an arrest—where an officer believed that "criminal activity is afoot" based on *articulable facts,* taken together with logical inferences from those facts. A mere hunch does not support reasonable suspicion. Reasonable suspicion will be explored at greater length in Chapter 5. At this point, note that the standard has been applied, not only to the stops of individuals, but to search and seizure situations, and in order to understand several cases it is necessary to distinguish between probable cause and reasonable suspicion.

Probable cause is not only a lower "weight" of evidence than that needed for civil or criminal verdicts, but it also relies on less stringent rules guiding the admissibility of evidence. Thus, probable cause may be established on the basis of *hearsay evidence;* it is up to the magistrate to weigh the hearsay to determine whether it is plausible and genuine on the one hand, or farfetched or even fabricated on the other.

TABLE 4–1 STANDARDS OF EVIDENCE SUFFICIENCY

STANDARD	MEANING	LEGAL CONSEQUENCE
Proof beyond a reasonable doubt	No actual and substantial doubt must be present; not a vague apprehension or imaginary doubt; not absolute certainty	Conviction of guilt in a criminal trial
Clear and convincing evidence	Higher than a preponderance of evidence; need not be conclusive	Hold a person without bail under preventive detention; involuntary civil commitment; establish civil fraud; prove a gift
Preponderance of the evidence	Evidence reasonably tending to prove the essential facts in a case; the greater weight of the evidence	Verdict for the plaintiff in a civil litigation
Prima facie case	Evidence good and sufficient on its face to prove a fact or group of facts	Evidence that makes out the plaintiff's or prosecutor's case at trial and is strong enough to prevent a directed verdict for the defendant; in some jurisdictions, a prima facie case is required as the basis for indictment instead of probable cause
Substantial evidence on the whole record	Such evidence that a reasonable mind might accept as adequate to support a conclusion	Judicial review upholding administrative agency action
Probable cause	Known facts that would lead a reasonably prudent person to draw a conclusion about unknown facts	Lawful arrest; reasonable search and seizure; judicial determination to hold a suspect after an initial inquiry; bindover by magistrate after preliminary examination; prosecutor's information; indictment after grand jury deliberations
Reasonable suspicion	Facts that would lead an experienced police officer to believe that a crime has been, is, or is about to be committed	Stop, pat-down search of outer clothing, and brief questioning of a person
None or "mere" suspicion	Whimsy; randomness; mere suspicion	Observation and surveillance of person by police or government agent that does not amount to harassment or otherwise unduly interfere with the reasonable expectation of privacy

Probable Cause Based on Informers' Tips

An officer/affiant seeking a search warrant swears to the magistrate that the information presented is true. Where the officer affirms that he or she saw things or smelled odors (common in drug cases) that would lead a prudent person to believe that contraband is located at a specific place, the magistrate can directly question the officer to be sure of the accuracy of the evidence. Likewise, information given to an officer or magistrate by a victim of a crime is usually considered to be honest and accurate.

However, much criminal activity—especially illicit drug trading—is conducted in secret, and officers or blameless victims simply cannot get access to the criminal behavior. Often, the only way for law enforcement agencies to detect and prosecute such crimes is by using undercover agents to infiltrate the worlds of drug trafficking, organized crime, and white-collar crime. These **secret informants** are themselves often involved in criminal activity. Professors Robert Reinertsen and Robert Bronson state, "Informants are generally unsavory types, engaged in marginal activities that involve betrayal of others. Nonetheless, despite their negative image, informants play such a large and important role in law enforcement efforts that they cannot be ignored."[29] The common terms—snitch, fink, stool pigeon—attests to the negative image and reality of informants. They rarely aid the police out of altruistic motives. More likely, they are being paid, given a promise of prosecutorial leniency, or even rewarded with illicit drugs. Law enforcement agencies are caught in a dilemma. Knowing the risk of receiving unreliable information when using criminal informants, agencies establish policies regarding informants' recruitment, control, and payment. On the other hand, the need to maintain absolute secrecy of informants' identities, recognized by the Supreme Court, means that bureaucratic oversight is necessarily limited (*Rovario v. United States,* 1957). The proper use of informants depends in large measure on the honesty and mature judgment of the law enforcement officers who control them.[30]

Magistrates play an important role in screening out fabrications by informants. When magistrates receive affidavits for search warrants based on information supplied by unnamed informants, they have good reason to be cautious and to examine the affidavit with special care. Some of the fiercest Fourth Amendment battles in the Supreme Court have arisen over probable cause based on information supplied by secret informants. Liberal justices, emphasizing individual rights, have tended to be critical of using informants to determine the existence of probable cause; conservative justices, emphasizing efficient law enforcement, have tended to be more accepting. The case of *Spinelli v. United States* illustrates judicial feeling on the use of informers.

The *Aguilar—Spinelli* "two-pronged test" to obtaining a warrant based on an informer's hearsay includes: (1) a *veracity,* or truthfulness, prong—showing that the informant is

• CASE & COMMENTS •

Spinelli v. United States

393 U.S. 410, 89 S.Ct. 584, 21 L.Ed.2d 637 (1969)

MR. JUSTICE HARLAN delivered the opinion of the Court.

[William Spinelli was convicted of the federal crime of interstate travel in aid of racketeering; specifically, of illegal bookmaking. The government proved that he went to St. Louis, Missouri, from a nearby Illinois suburb to conduct an illegal gambling operation. The Supreme Court granted certiorari in order to clarify the rules concerning search warrants spelled out in an earlier case, *Aguilar v. Texas,* 378 U.S. 108 (1964). Spinelli challenged the constitutionality of the warrant that authorized a search. The Supreme Court reversed his conviction.]

In *Aguilar* a search warrant had issued upon an affidavit of police officers who swore only that they had "received reliable information from a credible person and do believe" that narcotics were being illegally stored on the described premises. While recognizing that the constitutional requirement of probable cause can be satisfied by hearsay information, **[a]** this Court held the affidavit inadequate for two reasons. First, the application failed to set forth many of the "underlying circumstances" necessary to enable the magistrate independently to judge of the validity of the informant's conclusion that the narcotics were where he said they were. Second, the affiant-officers did not attempt to support their claim that their informant was "'credible' or his information 'reliable.'" **[b]** The Government is, however, quite right in saying that the FBI affidavit in the present case is more ample than that in *Aguilar.* [I]t contain[s] a report from an anonymous informant [and] a report of an independent FBI investigation which is said to corroborate the informant's tip. We are then required to delineate the manner in which *Aguilar*'s **two-pronged test** should be applied in these circumstances.

[a] The basic hearsay-use rule is mentioned in passing.

[b] The Court stated a two-prong rule in negative terms, i.e., "what the police failed to do" in *Aguilar.* Restate the two-pronged test positively, in your own words. Does the second prong have two elements?

[The affidavit, when reduced to its essential information, contained four facts: **[c]**

1. that for four of the five days he was followed, Spinelli crossed into Missouri from Illinois at about noon, went to the same apartment house about 4:00 p.m., and was seen to enter a particular apartment
2. that there were two telephones in the apartment listed under another's name
3. that Spinelli had a reputation as a bookmaker and gambler among law enforcement agents, including the affiant
4. that a "confidential reliable informant" told the FBI agent that Spinelli was operating a gambling operation with the telephones in the apartment.]

[c] Which of these facts, standing alone, raise a reasonable suspicion that Spinelli was a "bookie"? Do they become more suspicious when taken together? If you were a magistrate, would you allow the police to enter the apartment to search for evidence of crime?

There can be no question that the last item mentioned, detailing the informant's tip, has a fundamental place in this warrant application. Without it, probable cause could not be established. The first two items reflect only innocent-seeming activity and data. Spinelli's travels to and from the apartment building and his entry into a particular apartment on one occasion could hardly be taken as bespeaking gambling activity; and there is surely nothing unusual about an apartment containing

• CASE & COMMENTS •

two separate telephones. Many a householder indulges himself in this petty luxury. **[d]** Finally, the allegation that Spinelli was "known" to the affiant and to other federal and local law enforcement officers as a gambler is but a bald and unilluminating assertion of suspicion that is entitled to no weight in appraising the magistrate's decision. *Nathanson v. United States,* (1933).

So much indeed the Government does not deny. Rather, * * * the Government claims that the informant's tip gives a suspicious color to the FBI's reports detailing Spinelli's innocent-seeming conduct and that, conversely, the FBI's surveillance corroborates the informant's tip, thereby entitling it to more weight. * * * **[e]** We believe, however, that the "totality of the circumstances" approach * * * paints with too broad a brush. Where, as here, the informer's tip is a necessary element in a finding of probable cause, its proper weight must be determined by a more precise analysis.

The informer's report must first be measured against *Aguilar*'s standards so that its probative value can be assessed. If the tip is found inadequate under *Aguilar,* the other allegations which corroborate the information contained in the hearsay report should then be considered. At this stage as well, however, the standards enunciated in *Aguilar* must inform the magistrate's decision. He must ask: Can it fairly be said that the tip, even when certain parts of it have been corroborated by independent sources, is as trustworthy as a tip which would pass *Aguilar*'s tests without independent corroboration? * * * **[f]**

Applying these principles to the present case, we first consider the weight to be given the informer's tip when it is considered apart from the rest of the affidavit. It is clear that a [magistrate] could not credit it without abdicating his constitutional function. Though the affiant swore that his confidant was "reliable," he offered the magistrate no reason in support of this conclusion. **[g]** Perhaps even more important is the fact that *Aguilar*'s other test has not been satisfied. The tip does not contain a sufficient statement of the underlying circumstances from which the informer concluded that Spinelli was running a bookmaking operation. We are not told how the FBI's source received his information—it is not alleged that the informant personally observed Spinelli at work or that he ever placed a bet with him. Moreover, if the informant came by the information indirectly, he did not explain why his sources were reliable. **[h]** In the absence of a statement detailing the manner in which the information was gathered, it is especially important that the tip describe the accused's criminal activity in sufficient detail so that the magistrate may know that he is relying on something more substantial than a casual rumor circulating in the underworld or an accusation based merely on an individual's general reputation.

The detail provided by the informant in *Draper v. United States* (1959), provides a suitable benchmark. While Hereford, the FBI's informer in the case, did not state the way which he had obtained his information, he reported that Draper had gone to Chicago the day before by train and that he would return to Denver by train with three ounces of heroin on one of two specified mornings. Moreover, Hereford went on to describe, with minute particularity, the clothes that Draper would be wearing upon his arrival at the Denver station. **[i]** A magistrate, when confronted with such detail, could reasonably infer that the informant had gained his information in a reliable way. Such an inference cannot be made in the present case. Here, the only facts supplied were that Spinelli was using two specified telephones and that these phones were being used in gambling operations. This meager report could easily have been obtained from an off-hand remark heard at a neighborhood bar.

* * * We conclude, then, that in the present case the informer's tip—even when corroborated to the extent indicated—was not sufficient to provide the basis for a finding of probable cause. * * * [I]t needed some further support. * * * All that remains to be considered is the flat statement that Spinelli was "known" to the FBI and others as a gambler. **[j]** But just as a simple assertion of police suspicion is not itself a sufficient basis of probable cause, we do not believe it may be used to give additional weight to allegations that would otherwise be insufficient.

The affidavit, then, falls short of the standard set forth in *Aguilar, Draper,* and our other decisions that give content to the notion of probable cause. * * * [W]e do not retreat from the established propositions that only the probability, and not a prima facie showing, of criminal activity is the standard of probable cause; that affidavits of probable cause are tested by much less rigorous standards than those governing the admissibility of evidence at trial; * * * that * * * magistrates are not to be

[d] Reputation is, in ordinary life, a kind of hearsay that guides the behavior of most people. Why does the Court, upholding the *Nathanson* rule, virtually banish the use of a person's reputation when other kinds of hearsay may be used to establish probable cause?

[e] Probable cause is a standard of the *weight* of evidence, so Justice Harlan assumes that an informer's testimony is always less weighty than an officer's or a victim's and thus needs a special framework for analysis, that is, the two-pronged test, designed to inquire into the truthfulness of the informant as well as the weight of the evidence. In other cases, the "totality of the circumstances" approach is sufficient, but not here. What does Justice Harlan mean by saying that it "paints with too broad a brush"?

[f] If the tip does not support probable cause, then it may be corroborated by other evidence obtained by police investigation; this is evidence that supports the main conclusion that there is probable cause to believe there is evidence of crime in a place.

[g] For a magistrate to accept an affiant's bald assertion and act as a "rubber stamp" is placed on the level of a constitutional error.

[h] This suggests that because informers have reasons to lie or rely on weak hearsay, the FBI agents should have been more critical of their informants and should have demanded better information from them. Even if the informer does not lie, how can the police officer or magistrate determine the accuracy of hearsay based on hearsay?

[i] Why were *Draper*'s *details* so important? None of Hereford's details, except that Draper would be carrying heroin, were inherently

• CASE & COMMENTS •

confined * * * by restrictions on the use of their common sense; * * * and that their determination of probable cause should be paid great deference by reviewing courts. **[k]** But we cannot sustain this warrant without diluting important safeguards that assure that the judgment of a disinterested judicial officer will interpose itself between the police and the citizenry.

MR. JUSTICE WHITE, concurring.

* * * The tension between *Draper* and the *Nathanson-Aguilar* line of cases is evident from the course followed by the majority opinion. * * * **[l]** The *Draper* approach would reasonably justify the issuance of a warrant in this case, particularly since the police had some awareness of Spinelli's past activities. The majority, however, while seemingly embracing *Draper,* confines that case to its own facts. Pending full scale reconsideration of that case, on the one hand, or of the *Nathanson-Aguilar* cases on the other, I join the opinion of the Court. * * *

[JUSTICES BLACK, FORTAS, and STEWART dissented; JUSTICE MARSHALL took no part in the case.]

suspicious. What did the details indicate about Hereford's relationship with Draper? How do *Draper*'s details differ from *Spinelli*'s?

[j] In short, the police cannot simply say "trust me." Probable cause has to be *proved,* even though the standard of proof is low.

[k] These statements indicate that Justice Harlan does not want to unduly hamper law enforcement in obtaining warrants.

[l] The concurrence points out a flaw in the *Spinelli* opinion: the corroborating details in *Draper* and *Spinelli* are logically similar. The *Spinelli* opinion, then, seems to be a policy statement favoring close scrutiny of informers' tips rather than a "natural" reading of the information. Justice White's questioning of *Spinelli* was significant fourteen years later in *Illinois v. Gates.*

truthful because he was used successfully in the past or because the tip is so strong that it is inherently believable; and (2) a *basis-of-knowledge* prong—showing that the facts were obtained by the informant in a manner that is sufficiently reliable to establish probable cause. The facts that support the prongs must be strong enough to convince the magistrate making an independent determination that the informant had a real basis for knowing about the criminal activity. Any weaknesses in the information provided by the informant can be strengthened by the police gathering corroborating information. *Spinelli* shows how a magistrate should critically evaluate information presented in an affidavit.

Conservative Revisions

A task of the Supreme Court, to lay down clear rules for the guidance of lower court judges and government officers, seems to have been fulfilled in *Spinelli* when the Court clarified a line of informers' tip decisions begin with *Nathanson v. United States* (1933) with relatively clear procedural guides for resolving probable cause issues. *Spinelli* exemplified the Warren Court's penchant for establishing structured rules in its cases. This would soon change with the advent of the Burger Court as conservative activism replaced liberal activism.

Chapter 2 refers to Professor Charles Whitebread's overview of the five elements of the Burger Court's criminal procedure jurisprudence:[31]

- a crime control orientation
- a hierarchy of constitutional values with Sixth Amendment trial rights on a higher plane than Fourth Amendment rights
- a preference for case-by-case analysis rather than establishing general rules
- a tendency to uphold the prosecution side if the Court believes in the defendant's factual guilt
- and the denial of federal jurisdiction from state cases.

These tendencies were clearly at work in *Illinois v. Gates,* which upset the *Aguilar-Spinelli* rule after fourteen years during which there was little criticism of the two-prong test.

• CASE & COMMENTS •

Illinois v. Gates

462 U.S. 213, 103 S.Ct. 2317, 76 L.Ed.2d 527 (1983)

JUSTICE REHNQUIST delivered the opinion of the Court.

Respondents Lance and Susan Gates were indicted for violation of state drug laws after police officers, executing a search warrant, discovered marihuana and other contraband in their automobile and home. * * * The Illinois Supreme Court * * * held that the affidavit submitted in support of the State's application for a warrant to search the Gateses' property was inadequate under this Court's decisions in *Aguilar v. Texas,* 378 U.S. 108 (1964) and *Spinelli v. United States* [this volume] (1969).

We granted certiorari to consider the application of the Fourth Amendment to a magistrate's issuance of a search warrant on the basis of a partially corroborated anonymous informant's tip. * * *

* * *

II

* * * On May 3, 1978, the Bloomingdale Police Department received by mail an anonymous handwritten letter which read as follows: **[a]**

> "This letter is to inform you that you have a couple in your town who strictly make their living on selling drugs. They are Sue and Lance Gates, they live on Greenway, off Bloomingdale Rd. in the condominiums. Most of their buys are done in Florida. Sue his wife drives their car to Florida, where she leaves it to be loaded up with drugs, then Lance flys down and drives it back. Sue flys back after she drops the car off in Florida. May 3 she is driving down there again and Lance will be flying down in a few days to drive it back. At the time Lance drives the car back he has the trunk loaded with over $100,000.00 in drugs. Presently they have over $100,000.00 worth of drugs in their basement.
>
> "They brag about the fact they never have to work, and make their entire living on pushers.
>
> "I guarantee if you watch them carefully you will make a big catch. They are friends with some big drugs dealers, who visit their house often.
>
> "Lance & Susan Gates
> "Greenway
> "in Condominiums"

[a] What motivates such an anonymous letter? Motives like envy or revenge might enhance the reliability of such a letter; on the other hand, a false, incriminating letter could be written as a prank or as a means to harass someone. The police and the magistrate did not rely exclusively on the letter to initiate the search.

The letter was referred by the Chief of Police * * * to Detective Mader, who decided to pursue the tip. Mader learned * * * that an Illinois driver's license had been issued to one Lance Gates, residing at a stated address in Bloomingdale. He contacted a confidential informant, whose examination of certain financial records revealed a more recent address for the Gateses, and he also learned from a police officer assigned to O'Hare Airport that "L. Gates" had made a reservation on Eastern Airlines Flight 245 to West Palm Beach, Fla., scheduled to depart from Chicago on May 5 at 4:15 P.M.

Mader then made arrangements with an agent of the Drug Enforcement Administration for surveillance of the May 5 Eastern Airlines flight. The agent later reported to Mader that Gates had boarded the flight, and that federal agents in Florida had observed him arrive in West Palm Beach and take a taxi to the nearby Holiday Inn. They also reported that Gates went to a room registered to one Susan Gates and that, at 7 o'clock A.M. the next morning, Gates and an unidentified woman left the motel in a Mercury bearing Illinois license plates and drove northbound on an interstate highway frequently used by travelers to the Chicago area. In addition, the DEA agent informed Mader that the license plate number on the Mercury was registered to a Hornet station wagon owned by Gates. The agent also advised Mader that the driving time between West Palm Beach and Bloomingdale was approximately 22 to 24 hours.

Mader signed an affidavit setting forth the foregoing facts, and submitted it to a judge of the Circuit Court of Du Page County, together with a copy of the anonymous letter. The judge of that court thereupon issued a search warrant for the Gateses' residence and for their automobile. The judge, in deciding to issue the warrant, could have determined that the *modus operandi* of the Gateses had been substantially corroborated. As the anonymous letter predicted, Lance Gates had flown from Chicago to West Palm Beach late in the afternoon of May 5th, had checked into a hotel room

• CASE & COMMENTS •

registered in the name of his wife, and, at 7 o'clock A.M. the following morning, had headed north, accompanied by an unidentified woman, out of West Palm Beach on an interstate highway used by travelers from South Florida to Chicago in an automobile bearing a license plate issued to him. **[b]**

At 5:15 A.M. on March 7, only 36 hours after he had flown out of Chicago, Lance Gates, and his wife, returned to their home in Bloomingdale, driving the car in which they had left West Palm Beach some 22 hours earlier. **[c]** The Bloomingdale police were awaiting them, searched the trunk of the Mercury, and uncovered approximately 350 pounds of marihuana. A search of the Gateses' home revealed marihuana, weapons, and other contraband. * * *

The Illinois Supreme Court concluded—and we are inclined to agree—that, standing alone, the anonymous letter * * * would not provide the basis for a magistrate's determination that there was probable cause to believe contraband would be found in the Gateses' car and home. **[d]** The letter provides virtually nothing from which one might conclude that its author is either honest or his information reliable; likewise, the letter gives absolutely no indication of the basis for the writer's predictions regarding the Gateses' criminal activities. Something more was required. * * *

* * *

[The evidence was suppressed by the Illinois courts, all holding that probable cause was not made out under the *Aguilar-Spinelli* test.]

* * * The Illinois Supreme Court, like some others, apparently understood *Spinelli* as requiring that the anonymous letter satisfy each of two independent requirements before it could be relied on. * * * According to this view, the letter, as supplemented by Mader's affidavit, first had to adequately reveal the "basis of knowledge" of the letterwriter—the particular means by which he came by the information given in his report. Second, it had to provide facts sufficiently establishing either the "veracity" of the affiant's informant, or, alternatively, the "reliability" of the informant's report in this particular case.

The Illinois court, alluding to an elaborate set of legal rules that have developed among various lower courts to enforce the "two-pronged test," found that the test had not been satisfied. First, the "veracity" prong was not satisfied because, "[t]here was simply no basis [for] conclud[ing] that the anonymous person [who wrote the letter to the Bloomingdale Police Department] was credible." * * * The court indicated that corroboration by police of details contained in the letter might never satisfy the "veracity" prong, and in any event, could not do so if, as in the present case, only "innocent" details are corroborated. * * * In addition, the letter gave no indication of the basis of its writer's knowledge of the Gateses' activities: [it] * * * failed to provide sufficient detail to permit such an inference. Thus, it concluded that no showing of probable cause had been made. **[e]**

We agree with the Illinois Supreme Court that an informant's "veracity," "reliability," and "basis of knowledge" are all highly relevant in determining the value of his report. We do not agree, however, that these elements should be understood as entirely separate and independent requirements to be rigidly exacted in every case, which the opinion of the Supreme Court of Illinois would imply. Rather, as detailed below, they should be understood simply as closely intertwined issues that may usefully illuminate the commonsense, practical question whether there is "probable cause" to believe that contraband or evidence is located in a particular place.

III

This totality-of-the-circumstances approach is far more consistent with our prior treatment of probable cause than is any rigid demand that specific "tests" be satisfied by every informant's tip. **[f]** Perhaps the central teaching of our decisions bearing on the probable-cause standard is that it is a "practical, nontechnical conception." * * * "In dealing with probable cause, * * * as the very name implies, we deal with probabilities. These are not technical; they are the factual and practical considerations of everyday life on which reasonable and prudent men, not legal technicians, act." * * *

* * * [P]robable cause is a fluid concept—turning on the assessment of probabilities in particular factual contexts—not readily, or even usefully, reduced to a neat set of legal rules. * * *

[b] Is the level and type of specificity in the letter similar to or different from that given by Hereford in *Draper?* Although the travel plan stated in the letter was mostly corroborated, does that dissolve doubts about the fact that Officer Mader had no idea who wrote the letter?

[c] Can you think of any legitimate explanations for this travel plan that may cast doubt on its suspicion? Does the existence of any legitimate explanation negate probable cause?

[d] The Court is wary of information from anonymous tips—yet it does not close the door on the use of such information.

[e] Did the close match between the Gates's travels and the letter establish the veracity or truthfulness of the anonymous letter writer? If so, was it veracity regarding the Gates's peculiar travel patterns or veracity as to their drug dealing?

[f] "Totality of the circumstances" was proposed to the Court by the prosecution in *Spinelli* but rejected by the Court at that time. What factors caused the Court to shift gears?

• CASE & COMMENTS •

"Informants' tips, like all other clues and evidence coming to a policeman on the scene, may vary greatly in their value and reliability." Rigid legal rules are ill-suited to an area of such diversity. "One simple rule will not cover every situation." * * *

Moreover, the "two-pronged test" directs analysis into two largely independent channels—the informant's "veracity" or "reliability" and his "basis of knowledge." **[g]** There are persuasive arguments against according these two elements such independent status. Instead, they are better understood as relevant considerations in the totality-of-the-circumstances analysis that traditionally has guided probable-cause determinations: a deficiency in one may be compensated for, in determining the overall reliability of a tip, by a strong showing as to the other, or by some other indicia of reliability. * * *

[Justice Rehnquist suggests that an unusually reliable informant should be believed when on occasion he fails to state the basis of knowledge regarding a prediction of crime.] * * *

[g] Justice Harlan, a noted conservative, offered a reason in *Spinelli* for why a weakness in one prong should not be made up in another: even a "reliable" informant may, at times, obtain information from a weak hearsay source. Also, if probable cause is a practical, "nontechnical" search for information, why is reputation evidence not used?

* * *

We also have recognized that affidavits "are normally drafted by nonlawyers in the midst and haste of a criminal investigation. Technical requirements of elaborate specificity once exacted under common law pleadings have no proper place in this area." * * * Likewise, search and arrest warrants long have been issued by persons who are neither lawyers nor judges, and who certainly do not remain abreast of each judicial refinement of the nature of "probable cause." * * * **[h]** The rigorous inquiry into the *Spinelli* prongs and the complex superstructure of evidentiary and analytical rules that some have seen implicit in our *Spinelli* decision, cannot be reconciled with the fact that many warrants are—quite properly,—issued on the basis of nontechnical, common-sense judgments of laymen applying a standard less demanding than those used in more formal legal proceedings. Likewise, given the informal, often hurried context in which it must be applied, the "built-in subtleties," * * * of the "two-pronged test" are particularly unlikely to assist magistrates in determining probable cause.

[h] This analysis is belied by a recent article that shows that police agencies prefer the two-prong rule reviewed at the conclusion of this case. Is Justice Rehnquist setting his sights too low regarding the mental capabilities of lay magistrates and police officers?

* * *

[Justice Rehnquist urged that courts not review the facts of magistrates' probable cause decisions, but pay them great deference. He also argued that if courts continue to scrutinize affidavits according to the two-prong test, police will stop using warrants and will turn more to warrantless searches.]

Finally, the direction taken by decisions following *Spinelli* poorly serves "[t]he most basic function of any government": "to provide for the security of the individual and of his property." * * * **[i]** If, as the Illinois Supreme Court apparently thought, that test must be rigorously applied in every case, anonymous tips would be of greatly diminished value in police work. * * *

* * * [W]e conclude that it is wiser to abandon the "two-pronged test" established by our decisions in *Aguilar* and *Spinelli.* In its place we reaffirm the totality-of-the-circumstances analysis that traditionally has informed probable-cause determinations. * * *

[i] Is this a "constitutional" reason or a "policy" reason? Can such a division be neatly made? Does this seem as if the Court is interpreting the Constitution in a way that achieves a desired result?

* * *

JUSTICE BRENNAN's dissent also suggests that "[w]ords such as 'practical,' 'nontechnical,' and 'common sense,' as used in the Court's opinion, are but code words for an overly permissive attitude towards police practices in derogation of the rights secured by the Fourth Amendment." * * * **[j]** [N]o one doubts that "under our Constitution only measures consistent with the Fourth Amendment may be employed by government to cure [the horrors of drug trafficking];" * * * but this agreement does not advance the inquiry as to which measures are, and which measures are not, consistent with the Fourth Amendment. "Fidelity" to the commands of the Constitution suggests balanced judgment rather than exhortation. The highest "fidelity" is not achieved by the judge who instinctively goes furthest in upholding even the most bizarre claim of individual constitutional rights, any more than

[j] Justice Brennan, a result-oriented liberal, argues in his dissent that Justice Rehnquist's opinion is result-oriented. In reply, Justice Rehnquist makes the valid point that different justices (and different people) genuinely view constitutional rules differently.

it is achieved by a judge who instinctively goes furthest in accepting the most restrictive claims of governmental authorities. The task of this Court, as of other courts, is to "hold the balance true," and we think we have done that in this case.

IV

Our decisions applying the totality-of-the-circumstances analysis outlined above have consistently recognized the value of corroboration of details of an informant's tip by independent police work. * * *

* * *

The showing of probable cause in the present case was * * * compelling. * * * **[k]** Even standing alone, the facts obtained through the independent investigation of Mader and the DEA at least suggested that the Gateses were involved in drug trafficking. In addition to being a popular vacation site, Florida is well known as a source of narcotics and other illegal drugs. * * * Lance Gates' flight to Palm Beach, his brief, overnight stay in a motel, and apparent immediate return north to Chicago in the family car, conveniently awaiting him in West Palm Beach, is as suggestive of a prearranged drug run, as it is of an ordinary vacation trip.

In addition, the judge could rely on the anonymous letter, which had been corroborated in major part by Mader's efforts. * * *

Finally, the anonymous letter contained a range of details relating not just to easily obtained facts and conditions existing at the time of the tip, but to future actions of third parties ordinarily not easily predicted. The letterwriter's accurate information as to the travel plans of each of the Gateses was of a character likely obtained only from the Gateses themselves, or from someone familiar with their not entirely ordinary travel plans. If the informant had access to accurate information of this type a magistrate could properly conclude that it was not unlikely that he also had access to reliable information of the Gateses' alleged illegal activities. Of course, the Gateses' travel plans might have been learned from a talkative neighbor or travel agent; under the "two-pronged test" developed from *Spinelli,* the character of the details in the anonymous letter might well not permit a sufficiently clear inference regarding the letterwriter's "basis of knowledge." But, as discussed previously, * * * probable cause does not demand the certainty we associate with formal trials. It is enough that there was a fair probability that the writer of the anonymous letter had obtained his entire story either from the Gateses or someone they trusted. And corroboration of major portions of the letter's predictions provides just this probability. It is apparent, therefore, that the judge issuing the warrant had a "substantial basis for * * * conclud[ing]" that probable cause to search the Gateses' home and car existed. The judgment of the Supreme Court of Illinois therefore must be

Reversed.

[JUSTICE WHITE, concurred in the judgment, on grounds that the corroboration in this case supplied information to support both the basis of knowledge and the veracity prongs of the *Aguilar-Spinelli* rule, which he would not abandon.]

JUSTICE BRENNAN, with whom JUSTICE MARSHALL joins, dissenting.

* * *

I

The Court's current Fourth Amendment jurisprudence, as reflected by today's unfortunate decision, patently disregards Justice Jackson's admonition in *Brinegar v. United States* (1949):

> "[Fourth Amendment rights] are not mere second-class rights but belong in the catalog of indispensable freedoms. Among deprivations of rights, none is so effective in cowing a population, crushing the spirit of the individual and putting terror in every heart. Uncontrolled search and seizure is one of the first and most effective weapons in the arsenal of every arbitrary government. * * *
>
> "But the right to be secure against searches and seizures is one of the most difficult to protect. Since the officers are themselves the chief invaders, there is no enforcement outside of court." * * * (dissenting opinion).

[k] Do you agree with Justice Rehnquist that this evidence is "compelling"? Or is it a close call? When deciding to intrude into a person's home and car, should magistrates lean toward restraint? If the warrant were not issued in this case, how much additional investigation would the Bloomingdale Police Department have to do after the Gates' return to make a stronger case for probable cause? Given the Court's allowance of a corroborated anonymous letter as the basis of probable cause, does this create a risk that a dishonest police officer will be tempted to have an "anonymous" letter submitted in a hard to crack case?

• CASE & COMMENTS •

In recognition of the judiciary's role as the only effective guardian of Fourth Amendment rights, this Court has developed over the last half century a set of coherent rules governing a magistrate's consideration of a warrant application and the showings that are necessary to support a finding of probable cause. * * *

In order to emphasize the magistrate's role as an independent arbiter of probable cause and to ensure that searches or seizures are not effected on less than probable cause, the Court has insisted that police officers provide magistrates with the underlying facts and circumstances that support the officers' conclusions. * * *

* * *

* * * Properly understood, therefore, *Spinelli* stands for the proposition that corroboration of certain details in a tip may be sufficient to satisfy the veracity, but not the basis of knowledge, prong of *Aguilar.* As noted, *Spinelli* also suggests that in some limited circumstances considerable detail in an informant's tip may be adequate to satisfy the basis of knowledge prong of *Aguilar.*

* * *

Until today the Court has never squarely addressed the application of the *Aguilar* and *Spinelli* standards to tips from anonymous informants. Both *Aguilar* and *Spinelli* dealt with tips from informants known at least to the police. * * * And surely there is even more reason to subject anonymous informants' tips to the tests established by *Aguilar* and *Spinelli.* By definition nothing is known about an anonymous informant's identity, honesty, or reliability. * * *

To suggest that anonymous informants' tips are subject to the tests established by *Aguilar* and *Spinelli* is not to suggest that they can never provide a basis for a finding of probable cause. **[I]** It is conceivable that police corroboration of the details of the tip might establish the reliability of the informant under *Aguilar*'s veracity prong, as refined in *Spinelli,* and that the details in the tip might be sufficient to qualify under the "self-verifying detail" test established by *Spinelli* as a means of satisfying *Aguilar*'s basis of knowledge prong. The *Aguilar* and *Spinelli* tests must be applied to anonymous informants' tips, however, if we are to continue to ensure that findings of probable cause, and attendant intrusions, are based on information provided by an honest or credible person who has acquired the information in a reliable way. * * *

[I] What sort of fact would verify the basis of knowledge in an anonymous tip? Perhaps a verifiable reference to criminal activity that would not be known to an average person?

II

* * *

* * * But of particular concern to all Americans must be that the Court gives virtually no consideration to the value of insuring that findings of probable cause are based on information that a magistrate can reasonably say has been obtained in a reliable way by an honest or credible person. I share JUSTICE WHITE's fear that the Court's rejection of *Aguilar* and *Spinelli* and its adoption of a new totality-of-the-circumstances test, * * * "may foretell an evisceration of the probable-cause standard. * * *" * * *

[JUSTICE STEVENS dissented on the grounds that probable cause did not exist. At the time the magistrate issued the warrant, he did *not* know that Lance and Sue Gates had driven twenty-two hours nonstop from West Palm Beach to Bloomingdale, a suspicious activity in light of the anonymous letter. All he knew was that they had left the Palm Beach area and were heading north. This fact differed from the anonymous letter's prediction that stated that Sue would fly back to Illinois while Lance drove. To JUSTICE STEVENS, the discrepancy was critical because it indicated: (1) that the Gateses' willingness to leave their house unattended should have been interpreted as indicating that it did not contain drugs; (2) that their activity was not as unusual as if they had left separately, Therefore, the search of their house was improper.]

It is interesting that the nine justices came up with four different analyses of the facts:

1. the majority found probable cause to exist under the new totality test
2. Justice White found probable cause to exist under the two-pronged test
3. Justices Brennan and Marshall found no probable cause under either test
4. Justice Stevens found no probable cause because of discrepant facts.

In any event, *Gates* was a constitutionally important decision that significantly shifted the criminal procedure balance in favor of the state, a result that has been criticized by some legal commentators.[32] An interesting study published in 2000, examining the practices of six Atlanta area police academies, shows that the departments train their officers in the *Aguilar-Spinelli* two-pronged test rather than the open-ended *Gates* totality test. Two reasons were given by the training officers: (1) they felt that prosecutors and courts were likely to demand adherence to the two-pronged or a similar test, and (2) "almost all of the instructors stated that they did not believe a majority of their recruits could master the intricacies of an open-ended standard such as the *Gates* standard."[33] This is contrary to the main reason given by Justice Rehnquist for the majority opinion. This would not be the first time that police practice did not agree with legal speculation.

PLAIN VIEW AND RELATED DOCTRINES

Plain view is a useful doctrine for police officers. It allows *seizures* of evidence without a warrant when the police are *already* lawfully in a place or have made a *lawful search.*

GATES IN THE STATES

*According to Professor Latzer, the "*Gates *rule has been widely approved on state constitutional grounds"—citing cases of twenty-six states that have applied the totality of circumstances analysis. Several states have rejected Gates in favor of retaining the* Aguilar-Spinelli *rule.*

The New York Court of Appeals (that state's highest court) in *People v. Griminger* (1988) held that evidence introduced into state courts, obtained as a result of search warrants based on the hearsay of confidential informants (whether issued by federal or state magistrates), must make a minimal showing of the informant's reliability. In explicitly requiring that the *Aguilar-Spinelli* two-pronged test be used, the Court rejected several of the arguments put forth in *Illinois v. Gates.* The New York Court disagreed with the idea that police would be less likely to apply for warrants merely because the State continued to apply the *Aguilar-Spinelli* test. The Court of Appeals disagreed with the idea that the two-pronged test was hypertechnical. Instead,

> *the more structured "bright line"* Aguilar-Spinelli *test better serve[s] the highly desirable "aims of predictability and precision in judicial review of search and seizure cases", and . . . "the protection of the individual rights of our citizens are best promoted by applying State constitutional standards."*[34]

The facts in *Griminger* demonstrate the need for caution in accepting hearsay warrants. Federal Secret Service agents arrested a counterfeiting informant, who, while under arrest, accused Griminger of keeping large quantities of drugs in his home. An agent prepared a federal affidavit stating that "a confidential informant known as source 'A' . . . observed 150 to 200 pounds of marijuana in defendant's bedroom and adjacent attic. . . . Although the agent did not personally know the counterfeiting suspect, his affidavit said that the undisclosed informant was 'a person known to your deponent.' The agent also omitted the fact that the informant was under arrest when he provided this information." On the basis of this affidavit, a federal magistrate issued a warrant and a subsequent search of Griminger's home turned up "10 ounces of marijuana, over $ 6,000 in cash and drug-related paraphernalia." The lower state courts found that the Secret Service agent had not established the reliability of the informant. These facts indicate the dangers in a rule that makes it easy for police to rely on any arrested person as an informant. They support New York's skepticism: "Our courts should not 'blithely accept as true the accusations of an informant unless some good reason for doing so has been established.' "[35]

Barry Latzer, *State Constitutional Criminal Law*, § 3.13.

This section also examines the related "open fields" doctrine and the use of enhancement devices.

Plain View

The simple idea that a police officer can seize contraband lying about in a public place is so obvious that it has rarely been litigated. In *Cardwell v. Lewis* (1974), the Court articulated the principle that there is no Fourth Amendment privacy interest in material or possessions that are exposed to public scrutiny. In this case, a car owned by a murder suspect was in a public parking lot; the police scraped a bit of paint from a fender to be used as evidence. The court found no constitutional violation: "where probable cause exists, a warrantless examination of the exterior of a car is not unreasonable under the Fourth and Fourteenth Amendments."

It is a different matter for police to seize material from inside a place that is protected by the Fourth Amendment. Professors Whitebread and Slobogin assert, correctly, that a police officer who saw marijuana through a house window while standing on a sidewalk could not enter and seize the evidence, although in a factual sense it was in "plain view."[36] As the Supreme Court stated in *Agnello v. United States* (1925): "Belief, however well-founded, that an article sought is concealed in a dwelling house furnishes no justification for a search of that place without a warrant." In such a case, the officer would have to obtain a warrant to enter lawfully.

PRIOR JUSTIFIED SEARCH The basic rules of plain view were established in *Coolidge v. New Hampshire* (1971). In that case, Justice Stewart, writing for a plurality, made clear the ancillary or "piggy-back," nature of the doctrine:

> What the "plain view" cases have in common is that the police officer in each of them had a *prior justification* for an intrusion. . . . The doctrine serves to supplement the prior justification—whether it be a warrant for another object, hot pursuit, search incident to lawful arrest, or some other legitimate reason for being present unconnected with a search directed against the accused—and permits the warrantless seizure. (*Coolidge v. New Hampshire,* p. 466, emphasis added)

Under *Katz*, a plain view seizure of property is justified on the ground that there is no reasonable expectation of privacy in items that are contraband or the clear evidence of crime; police have a legitimate interest, not blocked by the Fourth Amendment, to take such items.

Nevertheless, it must be stressed that the *first rule* of plain view is that there must be a *lawful intrusion.* In *Coolidge,* Justice Stewart noted:

> But it is important to keep in mind that, in the vast majority of cases, *any* evidence seized by the police will be in plain view, at least at the moment of seizure. The problem with the "plain view" doctrine has been to identify the circumstances in which plain view has legal significance rather than being simply the normal concomitant of any search, legal or illegal. (*Coolidge v. New Hampshire,* p. 466, emphasis in original)

Police cannot "create" plain view by taking advantage of an illegal search. Justice Stewart put it this way: "[P]lain view alone is never enough to justify the warrantless seizure of evidence." It would destroy Fourth Amendment protections to allow the police to search at will, or without a warrant where a warrant is otherwise required, and to rationalize a seizure because an unearthed item is seen to be contraband or evidence of criminality.

IMMEDIATELY APPARENT *Coolidge* established a *second rule* of plain view—the "immediately apparent" rule. The police in Coolidge conducted a warrantless search of an automobile suspected to contain fibre evidence and sought to justify it because the car itself was "in plain view." The cars were obviously in plain view, but vacuumed microscopic particles certainly were not. Justice Stewart said, "Of course, the extension of the original justification is legitimate only when it is *immediately apparent* to the police that they have evidence before them; the "plain view" doctrine may not be used to extend a general exploratory search from one object to another until something incriminating at last emerges." The rule that the evidence in plain view must be immediately apparent as contraband is another way of saying that *probable cause* must exist to secure the evidence at the moment of seizure.

As with all probable cause decisions, absolute certainty is not required. For example, in *Texas v. Brown* (1983), a police officer looked into an automobile at night with a flashlight at a routine traffic license checkpoint and saw an opaque, green party balloon knotted about one-half inch from the tip. The Supreme Court ruled that he had probable cause to believe that the balloon contained illegal drugs because it was known that this was a common way for drug dealers to carry their wares. The Court thus allows the police some leeway for making an inference in determining whether it was immediately apparent that drugs were in the car.

PLAIN FEEL Plain view is not limited to matters viewed by eyesight, but applies to evidence known to any of the senses. In *Minnesota v. Dickerson* (1993), police lawfully stopped Dickerson outside a known drug house when his overall behavior created a reasonable suspicion that he carried drugs. An officer, following the rule of *Terry* (1968), patted down the outside of Dickerson's jacket to check for weapons. He testified that "I felt a lump, a small lump, in the front pocket. I examined it with my fingers and it slid and it felt to be a lump of crack cocaine in cellophane." The officer then retrieved a small plastic bag with crack cocaine from Dickerson's pocket.

Dickerson raised two plain view issues. First, must the police *visually observe* an item for it to be in plain view? The Court answered that plain "view" applies to any seizable item apparent to any of the senses.

> To this Court there is no distinction as to which sensory perception the officer uses to conclude that the material is contraband. An experienced officer may rely upon his sense of smell in DWI stops or in recognizing the smell of burning marijuana in an automobile. The sound of a shotgun being racked would clearly support certain reactions by an officer. The sense of touch, grounded in experience and training, is as reliable as perceptions drawn from other senses. "Plain feel," therefore, is no different than plain view and will equally support the seizure here. (*Minnesota v. Dickerson* (1993), pp. 369–70, quoting trial judge)

Two arguments to the contrary were used by the Minnesota Supreme Court to reject this so-called **"plain feel" rule:** (1) that the sense of touch is inherently less immediate and less reliable than the sense of sight, and (2) that the sense of touch is far more intrusive into personal privacy. The United States Supreme Court, noting that the facts in *Terry* (1968) allowed the sense of touch to be used for pat-down searches, disagreed.

The *Dickerson* case required the resolution of a second issue; whether what the officer felt was *immediately apparent* as crack cocaine. Justice White's close examination of the facts led to the conclusion that the officer "overstepped the bounds" of the limited search authorized by *Terry* because he *continued to explore* Dickerson's outer pocket after determining that it contained no weapon. The *Terry* rule overlapped with the immediacy/probable cause rule: "If . . . the police lack probable cause to believe that an object in plain view is contraband without conducting some further search of the object—*i.e.,* if "its incriminating character [is not] 'immediately apparent,'" . . . the plain-view doctrine cannot justify its seizure."[37] Here, because the officer had to slide the object in the pocket around, it was *not* immediately apparent as contraband and was not admissible as evidence in a trial.

INADVERTENCE *Coolidge* stated a *third* plain view rule, that the officer must come across incriminating evidence *inadvertently.* This rule, supported by a plurality of four justices and not a majority in *Coolidge,* was overturned by the Court in *Horton v. California* (1990). Justice Stewart, in *Coolidge,* thought that without the rule of inadvertence, police could simply dispense with a search warrant whenever they had reason to believe that contraband was located in a premises. This, of course, is not the case. But *Horton*'s facts made it reasonable to dispense with the inadvertence rule.

Justice Stevens, writing for the majority in *Horton,* stated that the inadvertency requirement served no purpose in protecting individual rights and could frustrate legitimate searches. The police had probable cause to believe that Horton committed a robbery and that he had the stolen property (three specifically described rings) and weapons (an Uzi machine gun, a .38 caliber revolver, and a stun gun) in his home. A warrant affidavit mentioned both the robbery proceeds and the weapons, but the magistrate's warrant mentioned only the stolen property. When executing the warrant, an officer saw and seized the weapons but did not find the stolen property. Because the officer had prior knowledge of the weapons, they were not seized inadvertently, and Horton argued that the evidence should be suppressed. The Supreme Court disagreed.

The Court's majority concluded that the rule adds nothing to protect an individual's right to privacy. First, an officer's anticipation that evidence would be present does not damage the individual as long as the officer is legitimately present. Second, the inadvertence requirement itself does not prevent a search from becoming a general search or prevent a particular warrant from becoming a general warrant. If the police go beyond the terms of a valid warrant or exceed the limits of a warrantless search, the evidence will be inadmissible as a violation of the Fourth Amendment particularity requirement. A second protection is not needed. On the other hand, if a search is within the scope of a warrant, the Court reasoned that the individual's privacy has already been legitimately invaded and that no additional right against seizure is needed other than the "immediately apparent" requirement.

Justice Brennan, dissenting in *Horton* and joined by Justice Marshall, noted that under the constitutional scheme of the Fourth Amendment, if an officer fails to mention in an affidavit an item known to be in a place and then seizes it anyway, this is per se unreasonable. Furthermore, the inadvertent discovery requirement enhances possessory interests. Finally, the lack of an inadvertency requirement would lead to an increase in the number of *pretext searches.* He cited several state cases where this had happened, but noted that the entry in Horton did not seem to be a pretext to seize the guns. Given the fact that the Court has since ruled that a pretextual stop is not unconstitutional as long as an officer has a valid basis to search or make an arrest, this argument is no longer satisfactory.[38]

Several of the plain view issues are explored in *Arizona v. Hicks.*

• CASE & COMMENTS •

Arizona v. Hicks

480 U.S. 321, 107 S.Ct. 1149, 94 L.Ed.2d 347 (1987)

Justice SCALIA delivered the opinion of the Court.

In *Coolidge v. New Hampshire* (1971), we said that in certain circumstances a warrantless seizure by police of an item that comes within plain view during their lawful search of a private area may be reasonable under the Fourth Amendment. * * * [The issue] in the present case [is] whether this "plain view" doctrine may be invoked when the police have less than probable cause to believe that the item in question is evidence of a crime or is contraband.

I

[Police entered an apartment without a warrant to search for a person who shot a bullet through the floor, injuring a man in the apartment below.] **[a]** They found and seized three weapons, including a sawed-off rifle. * * *

[a] The three standard exigency exceptions to the warrant requirement are hot pursuit, automobile search, and search incident to arrest. The fact that the Court upheld the entry in *Hicks* means that a general exigency category exists, based on reasonableness.

One of the policemen, Officer Nelson, noticed two sets of expensive stereo components, which seemed out of place in the squalid and otherwise ill-appointed four room apartment. Suspecting that they were stolen, he read and recorded their serial numbers—moving some of the components, including a Bang and Olufsen turn-table, in order to do so—which he then reported by phone to his headquarters. On being advised that the turntable had been taken in an armed robbery, he seized it immediately. It was later determined that some of the other serial numbers matched those on other stereo equipment taken in the same armed robbery, and a warrant was obtained and executed to seize that equipment as well. Respondent was subsequently indicted for the robbery.

[On a suppression motion, the state trial court and court of appeals held that the view of the serial numbers was an additional search, unrelated to the exigency of search for the shooter, impliedly rejecting the idea that the actions were justified by the plain view doctrine. The evidence was suppressed. The state appealed]

II

* * * We agree that the mere recording of the serial numbers did not constitute a seizure. * * * In and of itself * * * it did not "meaningfully interfere" with respondent's possessory interest in either the serial number or the equipment, and therefore did not amount to a seizure. * * *

Officer Nelson's moving of the equipment, however, did constitute a "search" separate and apart from the search for the shooter, victims, and weapons that was the lawful objective of his entry into the apartment. Merely inspecting those parts of the turntable that came into view during the latter search would not have constituted an independent search, because it would have produced no additional invasion of respondent's privacy interest. But taking action, unrelated to the objectives of the authorized intrusion, which exposed to view concealed portions of the apartment or its contents, did produce a new invasion of respondent's privacy unjustified by the exigent circumstance that validated the entry. **[b]** This is why * * * the "distinction between 'looking' at a suspicious object in plain view and 'moving' it even a few inches" is much more than trivial for purposes of the Fourth Amendment. It matters not that the search uncovered nothing of any great personal value to the respondent—serial numbers rather than (what might conceivably have been hidden behind or under the equipment) letters or photographs. A search is a search, even if it happens to disclose nothing but the bottom of a turntable.

[b] Justice Scalia recognized that the thin line between observing and recording a serial number and moving an object to see the serial number is nevertheless an important behavioral boundary line.

III

The remaining question is whether the search was "reasonable" under the Fourth Amendment.

* * * [W]e reject, at the outset, the * * * position * * * that because the officers' action directed to the stereo equipment was unrelated to the justification for their entry into respondent's apartment, it was *ipso facto* unreasonable. That lack of relationship *always* exists with regard to action validated

• CASE & COMMENTS •

under the "plain view" doctrine; where action is taken for the purpose of justifying entry, invocation of the doctrine is superfluous. * * * **[c]**

We turn, then, to application of the doctrine to the facts of this case. "It is well established that under certain circumstances the police may *seize* evidence in plain view without a warrant," *Coolidge v. New Hampshire* * * * (plurality opinion) (emphasis added). Those circumstances include situations "[w]here the initial intrusion that brings the police within plain view of such [evidence] is supported . . . by one of the recognized exceptions to the warrant requirement. * * * It would be absurd to say that an object could lawfully be seized and taken from the premises, but could not be moved for closer examination." It is clear, therefore, that the search here was valid if the "plain view" doctrine would have sustained a seizure of the equipment.

There is no doubt it would have done so if Officer Nelson had probable cause to believe that the equipment was stolen. **[d]** The State conceded, however, that he had only a "reasonable suspicion," by which it means something less than probable cause. * * *

We now hold that probable cause is required. To say otherwise would be to cut the "plain view" doctrine loose from its theoretical and practical moorings. The theory of that doctrine consists of extending to nonpublic places such as the home, where searches and seizures without a warrant are presumptively unreasonable, the police's longstanding authority to make warrantless seizures in public places of such objects as weapons and contraband. And the practical justification for that extension is the desirability of sparing police, whose viewing of the object in the course of a lawful search is as legitimate as it would have been in a public place, the inconvenience and the risk—to themselves or to preservation of the evidence—of going to obtain a warrant. **[e]** Dispensing with the need for a warrant is worlds apart from permitting a lesser standard of *cause* for the seizure than a warrant would require, *i.e.,* the standard of probable cause. No reason is apparent why an object should routinely be seizable on lesser grounds, during an unrelated search and seizure, than would have been needed to obtain a warrant for that same object if it had been known to be on the premises.

[There are some searches allowable] on less than probable cause * * * where * * * the seizure is minimally intrusive and operational necessities render it the only practicable means of detecting certain types of crime. * * * No special operational necessities are relied on here, however—but rather the mere fact that the items in question came lawfully within the officer's plain view. That alone cannot supplant the requirement of probable cause.

The same considerations preclude us from holding that, even though probable cause would have been necessary for a *seizure,* the *search* of objects in plain view that occurred here could be sustained on lesser grounds. A dwelling-place search, no less than a dwelling-place seizure, requires probable cause, and there is no reason in theory or practicality why application of the "plain view" doctrine would supplant that requirement. * * * **[f]** [T]o treat searches more liberally would especially erode the plurality's warning in *Coolidge* that "the 'plain view' doctrine may not be used to extend a general exploratory search from one object to another until something incriminating at last emerges." * * * In short, whether legal authority to move the equipment could be found only as an inevitable concomitant of the authority to seize it, or also as a consequence of some independent power to search certain objects in plain view, probable cause to believe the equipment was stolen was required. **[g]**

* * *

For the reasons stated, the judgment of the Court of Appeals of Arizona is

Affirmed.

JUSTICE O'CONNOR, with whom THE CHIEF JUSTICE and JUSTICE POWELL join, dissenting.

The Court today gives the right answer to the wrong question. The Court asks whether the police must have probable cause before either seizing an object in plain view or conducting a full-blown search of that object, and concludes that they must. I agree. In my view, however, this case

[c] Here, the defendant argued that the police could seize only items in plain view that related to the shooting; such an argument would destroy the practical value of the plain view doctrine and would not adhere to its logic. Note that both the defense and the prosecution make extreme arguments to the Court in this case.

[d] Note how the case turns on the level of evidence sufficiency.

[e] Notice the *practical* justification for the plain view rule.

[f] To the dissent, lifting the stereo is not a search but a "cursory inspection." But the majority fears that to allow police to rummage in a home beyond their lawful purpose, to *create* plain view, opens a theoretic rift in the plain view doctrine that can have negative, practical consequences.

[g] Justice Scalia is a "conservative" justice. His decision here is conservative in the sense of "nonactivist"—adhering to an established link between a house search and the probable cause

• CASE & COMMENTS •

presents a different question: whether police must have probable cause before conducting a cursory inspection of an item in plain view. **[h]** Because I conclude that such an inspection is reasonable if the police are aware of facts or circumstances that justify a reasonable suspicion that the item is evidence of a crime, I would reverse the judgment of the Arizona Court of Appeals, and therefore dissent.

[A *Coolidge* requirement is that for evidence to be within the "plain view" exception,] it must be "immediately apparent" to the police that the items they observe may be evidence of a crime, contraband, or otherwise subject to seizure. * * *

The purpose of the "immediately apparent" requirement is to prevent "general exploratory rummaging in a person's belongings." If an officer could indiscriminately search every item in plain view, a search justified by a limited purpose—such as exigent circumstances—could be used to eviscerate the protections of the Fourth Amendment. * * *

* * *

* * * When a police officer makes a cursory inspection of a suspicious item in plain view in order to determine whether it is indeed evidence of a crime, there is no "exploratory rummaging." Only those items that the police officer "reasonably suspects" as evidence of a crime may be inspected, and perhaps more importantly, the scope of such an inspection is quite limited. In short, if police officers have a reasonable, articulable suspicion that an object they come across during the course of a lawful search is evidence of crime, in my view they may make a cursory examination of the object to verify their suspicion. If the officers wish to go beyond such a cursory examination of the object, however, they must have probable cause. **[i]** This distinction between a full-blown search and seizure of an item and a mere inspection of the item * * * [is] based on their relative intrusiveness. * * *

* * *

standard. "Conservative" is also used to mean prolaw enforcement (and "liberal" to mean prodefendant) rulings. These dual uses of the terms *conservative* and *liberal* cause some confusion.

[h] The dissent turns on a fine, factual distinction not on a fundamental disagreement with established doctrines; much case law turns on such distinctions.

[i] The dissenters are aware that their approach could undermine constitutional protections if taken too far. They are not hostile to constitutional protection of individual liberty, but believe their rule does not endanger liberty.

Open Fields

The Fourth Amendment protects the privacy, liberty, and property interests of "persons, houses, papers and effects against unreasonable searches and seizures." Does Fourth Amendment protection extend to landed property? The answer depends upon the location of the land in relation to a house. As a general rule, what is referred to as "open fields" in Fourth Amendment law does *not* come under the protection of the Amendment, whereas areas close to the house—known as the curtilage—are protected. As a result, police do not need a warrant to go onto "open fields" and any contraband found there may be seized in plain view. In other words, a government intrusion upon an open field in not a "search" in the constitutional sense.

The rule was stated tersely by Justice Holmes in *Hester v. Unites States* (1924): The "special protection accorded by the Fourth Amendment to the people in their 'persons, houses, papers, and effects,' is not extended to the open fields. The distinction between the latter and the house is as old as the common law." After *Katz,* the question arose as to whether this distinction still stood under a modernized, nonproperty interpretation of the Fourth Amendment, or whether expectation of privacy analysis would extend Fourth Amendment protection to so-called open fields. The Court dealt with this issue in *Oliver v. United States* (1984). In two consolidated cases, the essential facts were that police officers, without warrants or consent, went into the lands owned by defendants and discovered marijuana patches. The privately owned fields were posted with "No Trespassing" signs. One site was highly secluded, over a mile from the defendant's house, and a gate to the fields was locked. To reach the other site, officers had to walk a path between the defendant's house and a neighbor's house. In one case, the lower court upheld the search; in the other the evidence was suppressed.

Justice Powell's majority opinion provided several reasons for upholding the open fields rule. First, the explicit language of the Fourth Amendment "is not extended to the open fields." Second, open fields are not "effects" within the meaning of the Fourth Amendment. Significantly, a first draft of the Fourth Amendment included a protection of "other property" along with persons, houses, and papers. The change in wording confirms the idea that "effects" refers to personal property. Third, the majority felt there was no expectation of privacy in open fields that society is prepared to recognize as reasonable, i.e., *Katz* had not changed the open fields rule. Several factors support this conclusion. First, open land is put to uses, such as the cultivation of crops, which are not the kinds of intimate activities that occur in homes that have historically called for strong privacy protection. Fourth, "as a practical matter these lands usually are accessible to the public and the police in ways that a home, an office, or commercial structure would not be." Rural land may be fenced and posted with "No Trespassing" signs, but these do not effectively keep hikers or hunters off the land. They certainly do not provide the same kind of psychological barrier that apartment and house doors and windows provide. Also, "the public and police lawfully may survey lands from the air." Fifth, the common law distinction between open fields and the curtilage supports the idea that the Framers did not intend to extend Fourth Amendment protection to open fields:

> At common law, the curtilage is the area to which extends the intimate activity associated with the "sanctity of a man's home and the privacies of life," * * * and therefore has been considered part of the home itself for Fourth Amendment purposes. Thus, courts have extended Fourth Amendment protection to the curtilage; and they have defined the curtilage, as did the common law, by reference to the factors that determine whether an individual reasonably may expect that an area immediately adjacent to the home will remain private. * * * Conversely, the common law implies, as we reaffirm today, that no expectation of privacy legitimately attaches to open fields. (*Oliver v. United States,* p. 180)

Sixth, a defendant's *property interest,* such as ownership or leaseholding, that is violated by police committing a trespass to land, no longer decides the case under *Katz.* "The existence of a property right is but one element in determining whether expectations of privacy are legitimate."

The Court also provided practical reasons for supporting the open fields doctrine. An argument was made that in each case where police trespass on real estate and discover contraband, the courts should conduct a factual inquiry to discover whether the land and its uses come within the open fields rule. The Court rejected this. Under a case-by-case approach, "police officers would have to guess before every search whether landowners had erected fences sufficiently high, posted a sufficient number of warning signs, or located contraband in an area sufficiently secluded to establish a right of privacy. The lawfulness of a search would turn on '[a] highly sophisticated set of rules, qualified by all sorts of ifs, ands, and buts and requiring the drawing of subtle nuances and hairline distinctions . . . .' " A bright-line rule better serves law enforcement and ensures that constitutional rights will uniformly be enforced.

Justice Marshall, joined by Justices Brennan and Stevens, wrote a spirited dissent. He felt, first, that provisions that "identify a fundamental human liberty" should "be shielded forever from government intrusion" and so should be interpreted in an expansive manner "to lend them meanings that ensure that the liberties the Framers sought to protect are not undermined by the changing activities of government officials." Next, he argued that if, as the majority believed, the Fourth Amendment offered no protection to real property, then the protection extended to the curtilage is inconsistent. Again, the objective expectation of privacy is seen in laws that allow the prosecution of trespassers. Posting and fencing is a clear way in which owners announce their expectation of privacy and it is understood by all. Finally, the dissent disagreed with the majority that the uses to which property owners put lands are not the sort of activities that society deems worthy of privacy:

> The uses to which a place is put are highly relevant to the assessment of a privacy interest asserted therein. * * * If, in light of our shared sensibilities, those activities are of a kind in which people should be able to engage without fear of intrusion by private persons or government officials, we extend the protection of the Fourth Amendment to the space in question, even in the absence of any entitlement derived from positive law. * * *
>
> Privately owned woods and fields that are not exposed to public view regularly are employed in a variety of ways that society acknowledges deserve privacy. Many landowners like to take solitary walks on their property, confident that they will not be confronted in their rambles by strangers or policemen. Others conduct agricultural businesses on their property. Some landowners use their secluded spaces to meet lovers, others to gather together with fellow worshippers, still others to engage in sustained creative endeavor. Private land is sometimes used as a refuge for wildlife, where flora and fauna are protected from human intervention of any kind. Our respect for the freedom of landowners to use their posted "open fields" in ways such as these partially explains the seriousness with which the positive law regards deliberate invasions of such spaces, * * * and substantially reinforces the landowners' contention that their expectations of privacy are "reasonable." (*Oliver v. United States,* pp. 191–92)

The curtilage concept expands the Fourth Amendment definition of a house to a certain "reasonable" amount of land around a house. This gives the constitutional protections of the Fourth Amendment some "breathing room" and prevents the open fields exception from allowing police to tightly surround a house or creep up to windows to peer in or eavesdrop. Are these rules based on common sense?

Curtilage

Whether criminal evidence discovered on a person's property is suppressed depends on whether it is part of the curtilage or the open fields. *Oliver* described the curtilage, an old English term, as the area under the eaves of the main house, small structures near the main house; such as a shed, smokehouse, or garage; and the area around a house. The yard of a typical suburban home is a curtilage; the wall around O.J. Simpson's Brentwood house described its curtilage, and before Detective Mark Fuhrman could enter he had to have a warrant or enter under a warrant exception. In *United States v. Dunn* (1987), a warrant was issued on the basis of facts obtained from the following property:

> Respondent's ranch comprised approximately 198 acres and was completely encircled by a perimeter fence. The property also contained several interior fences, constructed mainly of posts and multiple strands of barbed wire. The ranch residence was situated 1/2 mile from a public road. A fence encircled the residence and a nearby small greenhouse. Two barns were located approximately 50 yards from this fence. The front of the larger of the two barns was enclosed by a wooden fence and had an open overhang. Locked, waist-high gates barred entry into the barn proper, and netting material stretched from the ceiling to the top of the wooden gates.
>
> . . . [L]aw enforcement officials made a warrantless entry onto respondent's ranch property. [They] crossed over the perimeter fence and one interior fence. Standing approximately midway between the residence and the barns, the DEA agent smelled what he believed to be phenylacetic acid, the odor coming from the direction of the barns. The officers approached the smaller of the barns—crossing over a barbed wire fence—and, looking into the barn, observed only empty boxes. The officers then proceeded to the larger barn, crossing another barbed wire fence as well as a wooden fence that enclosed the front portion of the barn. The officers walked under the barn's overhang to the locked wooden gates and, shining a flashlight through the netting on top of the gates, peered into the barn. They observed what the DEA agent thought to be a phenylacetone laboratory. The officers did not enter the barn. At this point the officers departed from respondent's property, but entered it twice more . . . to confirm the presence of the phenylacetone laboratory. (*Dunn v. United States,* pp. 297–98)

The Court ruled that the barn was *not* within the curtilage, and the police officers violated no Fourth Amendment expectation of privacy when they went up to the barn and observed an illegal drug factory inside.

OVERFLIGHT CASES If the curtilage itself is normally open to view, police may observe it from a public vantage point such as a road. What they may not do is physically invade the curtilage itself to encroach on the *zone of privacy* that one expects to have around a dwelling. In several cases that the Framers surely could not have contemplated, the Supreme Court considered the extent to which the curtilage protection applied to airspace above premises. The *Katz* doctrine provided no protection against the warrantless *aerial surveillance* by police of a backyard where marijuana was growing. The Court in *California v. Ciraolo* (1986) upheld the police action, saying that the defendant's expectation of privacy in his backyard was not one that society was prepared to honor. The owner had surrounded the backyard, which also contained a swimming pool, with a six-foot outer fence and a ten-foot inner fence. Police could not observe the backyard to confirm an anonymous tip, so they hired a private airplane and buzzed the suburban backyard to gather visual evidence with the naked eye from about one thousand feet. The Court reasoned that the yard was *exposed to the public* in that it was subject to the gaze of the crews and passengers in commercial airliner overflights. In effect, the search was held to be within the open fields category. Justice Powell, in a stinging dissent, accused the Court of failing to uphold its role as a guardian of rights by allowing a "stealthy encroachment" on rights by the remote intrusion of commercial overflights. He noted that the curtilage was entitled to similar protections as a home and that the use of a private airplane to peer down into Ciraolo's backyard, pool and all, was similar to the use of listening devices by law enforcement officers.

The Court, on the same day, in *Dow Chemical v. United States* (1986), upheld an aerial search of two thousand acres of commercial property by an airplane equipped with a sophisticated camera that could magnify its pictures to detect pipes a half inch thick from twelve hundred feet. Even if the government officers could not physically go onto the commercial complex, the warrantless overflight was not a search and seizure. Thus, *Dow Chemical* upheld the concept of an industrial curtilage but, as in *Ciraolo,* held it did not protect property from aerial surveillance while using ordinary camera resolution.

The Court continued this approach in *Florida v. Riley* (1989). A four-justice plurality upheld the surveillance of a partially covered greenhouse in a residential backyard from a helicopter hovering four hundred feet above ground. Justice White reasoned that this flight did not violate any law or regulation, and any member of the public with a helicopter could have legally hovered above Riley's property and observed the contents of the greenhouse. This reasoning was not satisfactory to Justice O'Connor who concurred only in the judgment. She thought that the Court relied too heavily on police compliance with Federal Aviation Administration

(FAA) regulations and suggested that if lower overflights were sufficiently rare, even if they were in FAA compliance, in such a case, the householder would have a reasonable expectation of privacy. Justice Brennan dissented (joined by Justices Marshall and Stevens), arguing that by not taking into account the difficulty and lengths to which the police must go in making an "open fields" aerial search, the Court was ignoring the "the very essence of *Katz*."

In these cases, areas that are within the curtilage and nominally protected by the Fourth Amendment were, in fact, opened up to warrantless police surveillance under reasoning that stretched the traditional categories of open fields and narrowed the protection of the curtilage. The fact that conservative justices such as Lewis Powell and Sandra Day O'Connor were bothered by the decisions shows the malleability of constitutional concepts, and suggests the extent to which the Court's decisions are influenced by result-oriented jurisprudence.

Enhancement Devices

Is the plain view doctrine limited to items that are immediately apparent as contraband to a police officer's senses—unaided by any **enhancement devices?** At first blush, it may seem logical to think that if the police must resort to technology to determine whether or not evidence is contraband or incriminating, then it is not immediately apparent as such and can be obtained only after a warrant is obtained. This logic seemed to be at work in regard to the vacuuming for microscopic evidence in *Coolidge v. New Hampshire* (1971). Similarly, in *Katz* and other surreptitious electronic eavesdropping cases, private conversations that are obtained via enhancement devices that amplify the aural sense are protected by the Fourth Amendment. Such information is within the individual's zone of constitutionally protected privacy.

This is an area of law that the Supreme Court has not fully visited. It has ruled on the use of "beepers," which are radio transmitters, (usually battery-operated) that emit periodic signals. They allow government agents to trace the movement of a car or other object in which the beeper is surreptitiously placed. As noted previously in two cases involving beepers, the Court has ruled that there is no constitutional impediment to the government using such a device to enhance the senses (e.g., visual observation) if the device does not infringe an expectation of privacy. In *United States v. Knotts* (1983), agents placed a beeper in a five-gallon can of chloroform to track an automobile on public streets. A person traveling in an automobile has no reasonable expectation of privacy in his movements from one place to another, and so the use of the beeper was held not to constitute a search. In *United States v. Karo* (1984), the Court ruled that detecting motion with the use of beepers *inside a person's house* equated to a search and required a prior warrant. Because the Fourth Amendment is clearly violated by an agent secretly entering a house to verify that a drum of ether is inside, the use of the beeper to establish that fact is the legal equivalent. Justice White expressed the policy that: "Indiscriminate monitoring of property that has been withdrawn from public view would present far too serious a threat to privacy interests in the home to escape entirely some sort of Fourth Amendment oversight." For this kind of

OVERFLIGHT CASES IN THE STATES

Professor Latzer's treatise indicates that almost all the state courts that have considered the airplane or helicopter overflight issue under their state constitutions have agreed with the approach taken by the United States Supreme Court. These include Colorado, Hawaii, Kentucky, New York, Oregon, Tennessee, Washington, and possibly Florida. California has made an interesting distinction. The California Supreme Court held in 1985 that under the California Constitution's search and seizure provision, a warrantless flight sixteen hundred feet over the defendant's back yard violates an owner's reasonable expectation of privacy in the home and curtilage. The court said that the reasonableness of an individual's expectation of privacy is not defined solely by technological progress (*People v. Cook,* 1985)[39]. On the other hand, in *People v. Mayhoff* (1986),[40] the California Supreme Court did not apply this rule to airplane overflights of open fields looking for illegal cultivation of marijuana. Three reasons to distinguish *Mayhoff* from *Cook* were offered: (1) the open fields doctrine provides an initial justification for the search, (2) unlike *Cook,* there is less chance that open fields overflights will pry on innocent activities occurring within a legitimate zone of privacy, and (3) law enforcement interests are stronger where aerial surveillance of remote areas may be the only feasible way of discovering illegal cultivation.

Barry Latzer, *State Constitutional Criminal Law,* § 3.6.

in-house tracking to be constitutional, a warrant must be obtained.

In *Texas v. Brown* (1983), the Court said that it was "beyond dispute" that an officer "shining his flashlight to illuminate the interior of [a] car trenched upon no right secured . . . by the Fourth Amendment." Citing *United States v. Lee* (1927), the Court also found no constitutional objection to "the use of a marine glass or a field glass. It is not prohibited by the Constitution." Flashlights and field glasses are in such common use that allowing their use may be explained by the fact that they are common devices used everyday in ordinary situations. However, the Court has also found no Fourth Amendment impediment to more high-tech devices. In *Dow Chemical* (1986), the Court upheld a warrantless aerial surveillance of a two thousand-acre chemical manufacturing facility, heavily secured against entry on the ground but partially exposed to visual observation from the air, by the Environmental Protection Agency, to check emissions from the facility's power plant. The "EPA employed a commercial aerial photographer, using a standard floor-mounted, precision aerial-mapping camera, to take photographs of the facility from altitudes of 12,000, 3,000, and 1,200 feet." In upholding this level of surveillance as not protected by the Fourth Amendment, the Court noted that "The photographs at issue in this case are essentially like those commonly used in mapmaking. Any person with an airplane and an aerial camera could readily duplicate them." With the end of the Cold War, "spy satellites" are now commercially available and have been used by "mining companies, mapmakers, geologists, city planners, ecologists, farmers, hydrologists, road makers, journalists, land managers, disaster-relief officials and others seeking to monitor the planet's changing face. The global market in such imagery is expected to reach as high as $5 billion by 2004."[41] The implications are that there are virtually no limits to aerial surveillance by the police for law enforcement purposes.

An area of high-tech searching on which the Supreme Court has not ruled is **thermal imaging** (heat sensing). Thermal imaging is a widely used technology and federal cases have been decided in which police agencies have detected indoor marijuana cultivation from heat emitted by high-wattage halide lamps. As of 1999, four federal circuits have upheld this use of thermal imaging by police without judicial warrants, while two circuits have disagreed. These courts have struggled to find a consistent Fourth Amendment rationale for their decisions. For example, the subjective privacy prong of the *Katz* doctrine states that a person who takes steps to protect his or her privacy may be accorded Fourth Amendment protection. Courts upholding the warrantless searches stated that no steps were taken by growers to conceal heat emissions from houses. Courts on the other side of the issue relied on the idea that "the pertinent inquiry is not whether there is an expectation of privacy in the escaping heat, but whether there is an expectation of privacy in the activities within the home that generated the heat."[42] One court generated a "waste heat" theory which reasoned that because thermal imaging detected the differences in temperature at the surface of the house and the outside, it did not detect heat inside the house and thus was similar to the *Greenwood* (1987) abandoned trash case; i.e., a person has no expectation of privacy in "abandoned" heat. However, a homeowner has control over abandoning trash, while "a homeowner has no choice whether heat dissipates from his home."[43] Other courts have used the analogy of the use of trained dogs to sniff illicit drugs, which have been thus far upheld by the Supreme Court (*United States v. Place,* 1983), in that no interior search takes place. However, unlike the dog sniff which identifies only illegal substances, thermal imaging can identify excess heat from a home which may be produced by innocent uses. One case involved thermal energy emitted by a dehumidifier.[44] Thermal imaging by police without prior judicial warrants could lead to general or area searches, with police then targeting all "excess heat emitters." Another theory used inconsistently by the courts to support prewarrant thermal imaging, taken from a factor raised in *Dow Chemical,* is that thermal imaging does not disclose "intimate details." The Supreme Court has never defined what would constitute protected intimate details and such inquiry may divert courts from the proper inquiry of whether the police activity is a search.[45] Also, the Court appears to have disregarded this factor in *Irvine* (1954), the month-long police bugging of the bedroom of a married couple, which was held not to violate due process. And, the factual premise may be wrong, as one of the courts questioning thermal imaging suggested that it "would not be extremely 'difficult to identify (if not, strictly speaking, to watch) two people making love in the privacy of their darkened bedroom.'"[46] As this brief review shows, a variety of Fourth Amendment theories can generate difficulty in resolving Fourth Amendment questions, especially when new investigative technology does not fit older theories of law.

CONSENT SEARCHES

"The consent-based procedure is the bread and butter of the criminal justice system."[47] To an astonishing degree, criminal suspects plead guilty, confess to crime, allow police into their homes, and meekly submit to arrests rather than go to jury trial, stay mum, refuse to allow police entry without a warrant, and forcibly resist arrest. What is surprising about the first three scenarios is that suspects *give up* their constitutional rights to trial, self-incrimination, and privacy, which are guaranteed by the Sixth, Fifth and Fourth amendments. (There are different legal requirements for relinquishing Fourth Amendment rights on the one hand, and Fifth and Sixth amendment rights on the other;

these are addressed later.) Constitutional law has, for many years, allowed defendants to give up these rights under certain conditions. (Not all rights can be voluntarily set aside. The law will not allow a person to give up his or her rights to due process [Fifth and Fourteenth Amendments] or against cruel and unusual punishment [Eighth Amendment] under any conditions. No court would uphold a contract by which a person sold himself into slavery [Thirteenth Amendment].)

Police favor **consent searches** and stops because they do not have to worry about a suspect's constitutional rights. A person may have an absolute constitutional right to refuse to stop or to open the door to his or her home or automobile trunk when requested to do so by a police officer—it is of no matter. Once he or she admits the officer, he or she is lawfully in the premises and if contraband is observed in plain view, it may be seized and the possessor arrested for possession. "[A] search authorized by consent is wholly valid."[48] If the person consented to stop and to be searched, then it does not matter that the police officer had no probable cause to arrest or reasonable suspicion to stop.

Voluntariness Requirement

The one absolute requirement of a valid consent to give up one's Fourth Amendment rights is that the consent must be voluntary. If any threat or force is used to obtain consent, it is invalid. An arrested person can never give valid consent to a search because the person is by definition forcibly detained and in the custody of the police—any lawful search incident to arrest is made forcibly.[49] To voluntarily give up one's rights, one must be free to do so, both physically and psychologically. The following cases help to define the voluntariness requirement by example.

In *Amos v. United States* (1921), two federal "revenuers" looking for untaxed whiskey came to Amos's house without a warrant. He was not there and his wife opened the door. They told her "that they were revenue officers and had come to search the premises 'for violations of the revenue law'; that thereupon the woman opened the store and the witnesses entered, and in a barrel of peas found a bottle containing not quite a half-pint of illicitly distilled whisky, which they called 'blockade whisky'." A unanimous Court summarily dismissed the contention that the officers were let in voluntarily because they demanded entry under government authority. A similar case is *Bumper v. North Carolina* (1968). Bumper, a murder suspect not yet arrested, "lived with his grandmother, Mrs. Hattie Leath, a 66-year-old Negro widow, in a house located in a rural area at the end of an isolated mile-long dirt road." Four officers came to the house and told Mrs. Leath that they had a search warrant. In response, she allowed them to search the house and a weapon was discovered. It was later determined that there never was a search warrant. The Supreme Court held that Mrs. Leath, who did not appear from her testimony to have been at all intimidated, nevertheless did not give valid consent to the warrantless search:

> A search conducted in reliance upon a warrant cannot later be justified on the basis of consent if it turns out that the warrant was invalid. The result can be no different when it turns out that the State does not even attempt to rely upon the validity of the warrant, or fails to show that there was, in fact, any warrant at all.
>
> When a law enforcement officer claims authority to search a home under a warrant, he announces in effect that the occupant has no right to resist the search. The situation is instinct with coercion—albeit colorably lawful coercion. Where there is coercion there cannot be consent.
>
> We hold that Mrs. Leath did not consent to the search, and that it was constitutional error to admit the rifle in evidence against the petitioner. (*Bumper v. North Carolina,* pp. 549–50)

The coercion of law is not assumed simply from the fact that police officers ask a person if they may enter. However, if officers falsely claim to have a warrant or *demand* entry as if the law required it, then they are acting under *color of law* and this is coercive. But if a police officer *asks* a person in a nonthreatening manner if he or she may enter a home, or speak with a person, or view a briefcase or the trunk of a car, and the person agrees, then the person voluntarily relinquishes his or her Fourth Amendment right to privacy. It does not matter whether the officer views the person as a suspect.

A basic rule is that the burden of proof is on the government to prove consent:

> When a prosecutor seeks to rely upon consent to justify the lawfulness of a search, he has the burden of proving that the consent was, in fact, freely and voluntarily given. This burden cannot be discharged by showing no more than acquiescence to a claim of lawful authority. (*Bumper v. North Carolina,* pp. 548–49)

Thus, every legal contest over the existence of the voluntariness of a consent search delves into the facts of the case. A good example is *Schneckloth v. Bustamonte* (1973). Officer James Rand, on routine patrol in Sunnyvale, California, stopped a car containing six men at 2:40 A.M. when he observed that its license plate light and a headlight were burned out. The driver did not have a driver's license. The officer asked the men to step out of the car.

> [A]fter two additional policemen had arrived, Officer Rand asked Alcala if he could search the car. Alcala replied, "Sure, go ahead." Prior to the search no one was threatened with arrest and, according to Officer Rand's uncontradicted testimony, it "was all very congenial at this time." Gonzales testified that Alcala actually helped in the search of the car, by opening the trunk and glove compartment. (*Schneckloth v. Bustamonte,* p. 220)

Officer Rand found three crumpled checks that had been stolen from a car wash. The checks were introduced into evidence against one of the passengers. Based on these facts, the Supreme Court held that the search was voluntary. The Court made it clear that consent is determined by all the facts and circumstances of the case. There is no formula by which a court can automatically determine if consent to search was voluntary. The only rule is that "the Fourth and Fourteenth Amendments require that a consent not be coerced, by explicit or implicit means, by implied threat or covert force. For, no matter how subtly the coercion was applied, the resulting 'consent' would be no more than a pretext for the unjustified police intrusion against which the Fourth Amendment is directed." (*Schneckloth,* p. 228)

In Chapter 5, many cases are presented where the validity of a personal search turns on whether the person was arrested, *Terry*-stopped, or gave consent. The basic case presented here is *United States v. Mendenhall* (1980). The defendant deplaned at the Detroit Metropolitan Airport. She was observed by two DEA agents, who thought her conduct appeared to be "characteristic of persons unlawfully carrying narcotics." They approached Mendenhall, identified themselves as federal agents, and asked to see her identification and airline ticket. The name on her driver's license, Sylvia Mendenhall, and that on the ticket, Annette Ford, did not match. When asked why, she replied she "just felt like using that name." One agent then specifically identified himself as a narcotics agent and Mendenhall "became quite shaken, extremely nervous. She had a hard time speaking." Ms. Mendenhall was then asked if she would accompany the agents to offices just fifty feet away. Once there, she was asked if she would allow a search of her person and handbag. She was told she had the right to decline if she desired. She responded: "Go ahead." A female police officer was called, who, before conducting the search, asked Ms. Mendenhall if she consented to the search; she replied that she did. Heroin was found in her undergarments and she was arrested.

Judge Stewart's plurality opinion held that Mendenhall had consented to the initial stop, going to the office, and the search of her person. There was no arrest until the heroin was found. The force of a *Terry* stop was not applied. The reasoning begins with the rule that not every police-citizen encounter is a seizure of the person, i.e., a Fourth Amendment intrusion that requires reasonable suspicion or probable cause to be lawful. The test that distinguishes between a consent stop and a seizure is whether, in view of all the facts and circumstances, a reasonable person would believe that he or she is not free to leave; "a person is 'seized' only when, by means of physical force or show of authority, his freedom of movement is restrained." They concluded that Ms. Mendenhall could have walked away from the agents at any point. Here, no grabbing or touching occurred. The agents were not in uniform and no weapons were displayed. The initial encounter occurred in public. They asked, but did not demand, to see her identification.

Justice White (joined by Brennan, Marshall, and Stevens) dissented. They believed that Ms. Mendenhall was not free to leave once DEA agents stopped her and asked for her identification. Although three concurring justices thought that a drug courier profile had established reasonable suspicion, the plurality and dissent agreed that the officers had no basis to forcibly stop the respondent. Neither the plurality nor the dissent delves into the possibility that Ms. Mendenhall subjectively believed that she had lost her freedom of movement. The plurality opinion briefly considers, and dismisses, this approach: "It is additionally suggested that the respondent, a female and a Negro, may have felt unusually threatened by the officers, who were white males. While these factors were not irrelevant, . . . neither were they decisive, and the totality of the evidence in this case was plainly adequate to support the District Court's finding that the respondent voluntarily consented to accompany the officers to the DEA office." (*Mendenhall,* p. 558)

Third-Party Consent

The general rule is when two or more persons share a room or common area, one person may voluntarily consent to a search of the *common area* by the police. If evidence is found that incriminates the other party, it may be admitted in evidence. The prosecution must show by a preponderance of the evidence that a person who gave consent had actual authority to consent.

In the leading case on third-party consent searches, *United States v. Matlock* (1974), police searched a house, including the bedroom, with the consent of Mrs. Graff, who was living with Matlock. Evidence of a robbery was found and admitted to prove guilt. The fact that the couple was not married was irrelevant for Fourth Amendment purposes to negate consent. The authority of a third party to consent to the search depends not on property law concepts or on rules of evidence that apply in a trial, "[b]ut rests rather on mutual use of the property by persons generally having *joint access or control* for most purposes, so that it is reasonable to recognize that any of the coinhabitants has the right to permit the inspection in his own right and that the others have assumed the risk that one of their number might permit the common area to be searched" (*United States v. Matlock*). Similarly, a roommate who shares a duffel bag may consent to its search. (*Frazier v. Cupp* 1969)

In contrast to *Matlock,* the Court held in *Stoner v. California* (1964) that a hotel clerk did not have authority to consent to a police search of a guest's room. The Court said, "It is important to bear in mind that it was the petitioner's constitutional right which was at stake here, and not the night clerk's or the hotel's." Although *Stoner* was decided before the "expectation of privacy" principle of *Katz* (1967) was enunciated, as a rule of thumb it seems that only persons with an expectation of privacy over an area may consent to a search. *Stoner* was preceded by *Chapman v. California* (1961), which held that a landlord may not give consent to a police search into a tenant's apartment or house, even though the landlord has a general right of entry for normal inspection purposes.

Matlock and *Stoner* were clarified, extended, and harmonized in *Illinois v. Rodriguez* (1990). Police were given consent to enter a house by a person, who in reality, did not possess common authority over the premises; however, the police *reasonably believed* that she had common authority and possession of the place. The Court held that the entry was reasonable under the Fourth Amendment. A woman complained to Chicago police that the respondent had beaten her. The police took her from her mother's apartment to the respondent's apartment, where she let them in with a key that she had. On the drive to the respondent's apartment, she referred to his apartment as "our" place. The officers did not know that she had moved out a month earlier, had removed her clothing, did not invite friends there, was never in the house when respondent was not there, did not contribute to the rent, and did not have her name on the lease. Instead of characterizing the case as one of a valid waiver of Fourth Amendment rights, the proper question is "whether the right to be free of *unreasonable* searches has been *violated.*" The Court noted that in making probable cause decisions, police and magistrates do not violate Fourth Amendment rights if they make reasonable mistakes. By analogy, a reasonable mistake in a consent case does not violate the individual's Fourth Amendment rights. Thus, *Rodriguez* answers a question left open by *Matlock* and extends the authority of police to enter a place under third-party consent. The Court differentiated *Stoner,* which is still good law, by indicating that the case does not mean that apparent authority can never be the basis for a third-party search, only that the police must have a reasonable basis to believe that a third party has authority over a place. Ordinarily, motel clerks do not have general authority to enter a guest's room outside of normal cleaning and maintenance functions. On the other hand, when a woman with a key to an apartment claims that her boyfriend beat her, there is no reason why the police should not believe that she lives in the apartment. Justice Marshall dissented in *Rodriguez,* (joined by Brennan and Stevens), urging the theory that because entry into a home without a warrant is presumptively unreasonable, police cannot dispense with the rights of person where that person has not limited his expectation of privacy by sharing his home with another. Under this analysis, the reasonableness of the police officers' action is irrelevant. He stressed that the police should have obtained a warrant in this situation and that the warrant requirement should not be dropped to prevent inconvenience to police officers.

Knowledge of One's Rights

Sylvia Mendenhall was told that she had a right to not be searched. Is knowledge of one's Fourth Amendment rights a constitutional requirement for a consent search?

The Court held in *Ohio v. Robinette* (1996) that a police officer who asks a stopped motorist, after warning the driver, if he or she may search the car and receives voluntary consent, need not inform the driver, under the Fourth Amendment, that the driver is "free to go." The Court noted that in *Schneckloth* it "rejected a *per se* rule very similar to" the

• CASE & COMMENTS •

Schneckloth v. Bustamonte

412 U.S. 218, 93 S.Ct. 2041, 36 L.Ed.2d 854 (1973)

MR. JUSTICE STEWART delivered the opinion of the Court.

It is well settled under the Fourth and Fourteenth Amendments that a search conducted without a warrant issued upon probable cause is "*per se* unreasonable . . . subject only to a few specifically established and well-delineated exceptions." **[a]** It is equally well settled that one of the specifically established exceptions to the requirements of both a warrant and probable cause is a search that is conducted pursuant to consent. The constitutional question in the present case concerns the definition of "consent" in this Fourth and Fourteenth Amendment context.

I

[Bustamonte was tried on] a charge of possessing a check with intent to defraud. *** [At 2:40 A.M., Officer Rand stopped a car with a headlight and a license plate light burned out. The driver had no

[a] Justice Stewart, author of the *Coolidge* opinion, was a staunch proponent of the warrant-preference construction of the Fourth Amendment, a "liberal" approach. Yet, where the warrant does not apply, as in consent searches, he demonstrates a leaning that does not

• CASE & COMMENTS •

driver's license. Bustamonte and Joe Alcala were among the five passengers. Only Alcala had a driver's license. He said the car belonged to his brother. At the officer's request, all the passengers exited the car. Two other officers arrived.] Officer Rand asked Alcala if he could search the car. Alcala replied, "Sure, go ahead." Prior to the search no one was threatened with arrest and, according to Officer Rand's uncontradicted testimony, it "was all very congenial at this time." Gonzales testified that Alcala actually helped in the search of the car, by opening the trunk and glove compartment. *** [The police found stolen checks in the trunk that were used to convict the respondent of possessing a check with intent to defraud.]

[The evidence was held admissible by the California courts on the ground that the consent to search was voluntarily given. A federal District Court denied a writ of habeas corpus, but the federal court of appeals held that consent was a waiver of Fourth and Fourteenth amendment rights and that the state had to prove that respondent knew he had a right to refuse to have his vehicle searched. The court of appeals remanded the case to the district court for factual findings, at which point the case was taken by the Supreme Court to determine whether knowledge of one's rights is required for a valid consent search].

extend a defendant's rights to their furthest extent.

II

*** [A] search conducted pursuant to a valid consent is constitutionally permissible [and] is wholly valid. ***

The precise question in this case, then, is what must the prosecution prove to demonstrate that a consent was "voluntarily" given. **[b]** And upon that question there is a square conflict of views. *** [The federal court of appeals] concluded that it is an essential part of the State's initial burden to prove that a person knows he has a right to refuse consent. The California courts have followed the rule that voluntariness is a question of fact to be determined from the totality of all the circumstances, and that the state of a defendant's knowledge is only one factor to be taken into account in assessing the voluntariness of a consent. ***

[b] The issue of the case was not precisely stated in the opening paragraph. Here it is precisely stated in a way that shows that different courts disagree as to the conclusion. What is the issue?

B

*** [We] agree with the courts of California that the question whether a consent to a search was in fact "voluntary" or was the product of duress or coercion, express or implied, is a question of fact to be determined from the totality of all the circumstances. **[c]** While knowledge of the right to refuse consent is one factor to be taken into account, the government need not establish such knowledge as the *sine qua non* of an effective consent. As with police questioning, two competing concerns must be accommodated in determining the meaning of a "voluntary" consent—the legitimate need for such searches and the equally important requirement of assuring the absence of coercion. In situations where the police have some evidence of illicit activity, but lack probable cause to arrest or search, a search authorized by a valid consent may be the only means of obtaining important and reliable evidence. *** **[d]** [In] cases where there is probable cause to arrest or search, but where the police lack a warrant, a consent search may still be valuable. If the search is conducted and proves fruitless, that in itself may convince the police that an arrest with its possible stigma and embarrassment is unnecessary, or that a far more extensive search pursuant to a warrant is not justified. In short, a search pursuant to consent may result in considerably less inconvenience for the subject of the search, and, properly conducted, is a constitutionally permissible and wholly legitimate aspect of effective police activity.

[c] The Court states its decision at the outset: Knowledge of the right to refuse to consent is not constitutionally required. The remainder of the opinion goes to justify the conclusion.

[d] Justice Stewart praises the practical benefits of consent both as a boon to police and as a way to protect the innocent. Does this prove that consent without knowledge of one's rights is constitutional?

But the Fourth and Fourteenth Amendments require that a consent not be coerced, by explicit or implicit means, by implied threat or covert force. **[e]** For, no matter how subtly the coercion were applied, the resulting "consent" would be no more than a pretext for the unjustified police intrusion against which the Fourth Amendment is directed. ***

[e] This simply reiterates the basic rule that a consent stop or search must be voluntary.

The approach of the Court of Appeals *** would, in practice, create serious doubt whether consent searches could continue to be conducted. [Except for rare cases,] *** where there was no

• CASE & COMMENTS •

evidence of any coercion, explicit or implicit, the prosecution would nevertheless be unable to demonstrate that the subject of the search in fact had known of his right to refuse consent. **[f]**

The very object of the inquiry—the nature of a person's subjective understanding—underlines the difficulty of the prosecution's burden under the rule applied by the Court of Appeals in this case. Any defendant who was the subject of a search authorized solely by his consent could effectively frustrate the introduction into evidence of the fruits of that search by simply failing to testify that he in fact knew he could refuse to consent. ***

One alternative that would go far toward proving that the subject of a search did know he had a right to refuse consent would be to advise him of that right before eliciting his consent. **[g]** That, however, is a suggestion that has been almost universally repudiated by both federal and state courts, and, we think, rightly so. For it would be thoroughly impractical to impose on the normal consent search the detailed requirements of an effective warning. Consent searches are part of the standard investigatory techniques of law enforcement agencies. They normally occur on the highway, or in a person's home or office, and under informal and unstructured conditions. The circumstances that prompt the initial request to search may develop quickly or be a logical extension of investigative police questioning. The police may seek to investigate further suspicious circumstances or to follow up leads developed in questioning persons at the scene of a crime. These situations are a far cry from the structured atmosphere of a trial where, assisted by counsel if he chooses, a defendant is informed of his trial rights. **[h]** *** And, while surely a closer question, these situations are still immeasurably far removed from "custodial interrogation" where, in *Miranda v. Arizona,* we found that the Constitution required certain now familiar warnings as a prerequisite to police interrogation. ***

Consequently, we cannot accept the position of the Court of Appeals. ***

***

In short, neither this Court's prior cases, nor the traditional definition of "voluntariness" requires proof of knowledge of a right to refuse as the *sine qua non* of an effective consent to a search. ***

C

It is said, however, that a "consent" is a "waiver" of a person's rights under the Fourth and Fourteenth Amendments. The argument is that by allowing the police to conduct a search, a person "waives" whatever right he had to prevent the police from searching. **[i]** It is argued that under the doctrine of *Johnson v. Zerbst,* to establish such a "waiver" the State must demonstrate "an intentional relinquishment or abandonment of a known right or privilege."

But these standards were enunciated in *Johnson* in the context of the safeguards of a fair criminal trial. Our cases do not reflect an uncritical demand for a knowing and intelligent waiver in every situation where a person has failed to invoke a constitutional protection. *** **[j]**

***

*** [T]he Court has evaluated the knowing and intelligent nature of the waiver of trial rights in trial-type situations, such as the waiver of the privilege against compulsory selfincrimination before an administrative agency or a congressional committee, or the waiver of counsel in a juvenile proceeding.

***

And in *Miranda v. Arizona,* [this volume], the Court *** made it clear that the basis for decision was the need to protect the fairness of the trial itself [because of the inherently coercive atmosphere of police custody]. *** **[k]**

There is a vast difference between those rights that protect a fair criminal trial and the rights guaranteed under the Fourth Amendment. Nothing, either in the purposes behind requiring a "knowing" and "intelligent" waiver of trial rights, or in the practical application of such a requirement suggests that it ought to be extended to the constitutional guarantee against unreasonable searches and seizures.

[f] In these paragraphs, Justice Stewart indicates a concern that the knowledge-of-rights requirement would end or seriously diminish the number of consent searches. Is this fear realistic? If so, is it too high a price to pay for the knowledge-of-rights rule?

[g] Would it have been inconvenient for Officer Rand to say to Alcala, "May I open the trunk? you have a right to refuse."? This was said in *Mendenhall.* If the officer had provided a written waiver form, would *that* have been impractical? Is the real concern that such statements or actions would reduce the number of consent searches?

[h] In what ways is questioning a suspect in custody different from requesting consent to search?

[i] *Johnson v. Zerbst* (1938) is presented in Chapter 7 on the Right to Counsel.

[j] Recall that the Burger Court established a hierarchy of rights, placing fifth and sixth Amendment rights above fourth Amendment rights. This section of *Schneckloth* is a prime example. Students often have difficulty in initially grasping the point that a requirement for one constitutional right does not necessarily apply to another right.

[k] Having stated that the knowledge-of-rights requirement is essential to processes such as confessions and waivers of trial, the

• CASE & COMMENTS •

A strict standard of waiver has been applied to those rights guaranteed to a criminal defendant to ensure that he will be accorded the greatest possible opportunity to utilize every facet of the constitutional model of a fair criminal trial. Any trial conducted in derogation of that model leaves open the possibility that the trial reached an unfair result precisely because all the protections specified in the Constitution were not provided. A prime example is the right to counsel. For without that right, a wholly innocent accused faces the real and substantial danger that simply because of his lack of legal expertise he may be convicted. *** **[l]**

The protections of the Fourth Amendment are of a wholly different order, and have nothing whatever to do with promoting the fair ascertainment of truth at a criminal trial. Rather, *** the Fourth Amendment protects the "security of one's privacy against arbitrary intrusion by the police. . . ." ***

Nor can it even be said that a search, as opposed to an eventual trial, is somehow "unfair" if a person consents to a search. While the Fourth and Fourteenth Amendments limit the circumstances under which the police can conduct a search, there is nothing constitutionally suspect in a person's voluntarily allowing a search. The actual conduct of the search may be precisely the same as if the police had obtained a warrant. And, unlike those constitutional guarantees that protect a defendant at trial, it cannot be said every reasonable presumption ought to be indulged against voluntary relinquishment. **[m]** We have only recently stated: "[It] is no part of the policy underlying the Fourth and Fourteenth Amendments to discourage citizens from aiding to the utmost of their ability in the apprehension of criminals." *** Rather, the community has a real interest in encouraging consent, for the resulting search may yield necessary evidence for the solution and prosecution of crime, evidence that may ensure that a wholly innocent person is not wrongly charged with a criminal offense.

***

E

Our decision today is a narrow one. We hold only that when the subject of a search is not in custody and the State attempts to justify a search on the basis of his consent, the Fourth and Fourteenth Amendments require that it demonstrate that the consent was in fact voluntarily given, and not the result of duress or coercion, express or implied. Voluntariness is a question of fact to be determined from all the circumstances, and while the subject's knowledge of a right to refuse is a factor to be taken into account, the prosecution is not required to demonstrate such knowledge as a prerequisite to establishing a voluntary consent. ***

MR. JUSTICE MARSHALL, dissenting. [Justices Douglas and Brennan also dissented]

*** [T]oday the Court reaches the curious result that one can choose to relinquish a constitutional right—the right to be free of unreasonable searches—without knowing that he has the alternative of refusing to accede to a police request to search. I cannot agree, and therefore dissent.

I

I believe that the Court misstates the true issue in this case. That issue is not, as the Court suggests, whether the police overbore Alcala's will in eliciting his consent, but rather, whether a simple statement of assent to search, without more, should be sufficient to permit the police to search and thus act as a relinquishment of Alcala's constitutional right to exclude the police. This Court has always scrutinized with great care claims that a person has forgone the opportunity to assert constitutional rights. I see no reason to give the claim that a person consented to a search any less rigorous scrutiny. **[n]** Every case in this Court involving this kind of search has therefore spoken of consent as a waiver. ***

B

*** Freedom from coercion is a substantive right, guaranteed by the Fifth and Fourteenth Amendments. **[o]** Consent, however, is a mechanism by which substantive requirements, otherwise applicable, are avoided. [Unlike exigency exceptions to the warrant requirement, in consent searches] *** the needs of law enforcement are significantly more attenuated, for probable cause to search may be

Court now goes on to explain why.

[l] This is the crux of the issue in this case and it is similar to the debate over the exclusionary rule: errors in Fifth and Sixth amendment rights can lead to the conviction of innocent parties. Errors in the Fourth Amendment may lead to the exclusion of physical evidence which clearly proves that the suspect is guilty.

[m] Is Justice Stewart saying that it is fair for the police to take advantage of the ignorance of suspects? Can this be correct? Should standards of fairness be less refined in criminal justice than in other settings (like the proverbial used-car salesperson)?

[n] The majority in effect establishes a verbal distinction between a "waiver" (which applies to the Fifth and Sixth amendments) and consent (which applies to the Fourth Amendment). The distinction did not make sense to Justice

• CASE & COMMENTS •

lacking but a search permitted if the subject's consent has been obtained. **[p]** Thus, consent searches are permitted, not because such an exception to the requirements of probable cause and warrant is essential to proper law enforcement, but because we permit our citizens to choose whether or not they wish to exercise their constitutional rights. Our prior decisions simply do not support the view that a meaningful choice has been made solely because no coercion was brought to bear on the subject.

[The majority mistakenly rests its holding on the convenience of the police, a factor that is not relied on in the search incident to arrest or automobile search rationales. Furthermore, it is too easy for the police to demand entry to search without the overt use of force and for courts to uphold these as consent searches.] *** I cannot believe that the protections of the Constitution mean so little.

II

My approach to the case is straightforward and, to me, obviously required by the notion of consent as a relinquishment of Fourth Amendment rights. I am at a loss to understand why consent "cannot be taken literally to mean a 'knowing' choice." In fact, I have difficulty in comprehending how a decision made without knowledge of available alternatives can be treated as a choice at all.

*** I would therefore hold, at a minimum, that the prosecution may not rely on a purported consent to search if the subject of the search did not know that he could refuse to give consent. ***

***

*** [T]here are several ways by which the subject's knowledge of his rights may be shown. [These include the defendant affirmatively showing he knew of his rights by responses to questions, the defendant indicating knowledge of rights by actions, such as a prior refusal to allow a search, or the police informing the defendant of his rights.]***

The Court's assertions to the contrary notwithstanding, there is nothing impractical about this method of satisfying the prosecution's burden of proof. ***

***

I must conclude, with some reluctance, that when the Court speaks of practicality, what it really is talking of is the continued ability of the police to capitalize on the ignorance of citizens so as to accomplish by subterfuge what they could not achieve by relying only on the knowing relinquishment of constitutional rights. Of course it would be "practical" for the police to ignore the commands of the Fourth Amendment, if by practicality we mean that more criminals will be apprehended, even though the constitutional rights of innocent people also go by the board. But such a practical advantage is achieved only at the cost of permitting the police to disregard the limitations that the Constitution places on their behavior, a cost that a constitutional democracy cannot long absorb. ***

Marshall. Does it make sense to you?

[o] Justice Marshall suggests that a lack of voluntary consent may occur even when there is no coercion. Can you think of any examples? Is this separation of consent from coercion psychologically feasible? Does it make sense as a legal rule?

[p] This is the crux of Justice Marshall's dissent. He sees consent as a freedom that an individual has to give up her constitutional rights, and as such should be narrowly construed. This disagrees sharply with Justice Stewart's view that consent is a law enforcement tool that should be maximally supported.

Ohio ruling that a driver had to be told that he is "free to go" before a valid consent to search the vehicle of a driver about to be released. It reiterated the rule that "voluntariness is a question of fact to be determined from all the circumstances."

Scope of Consent

"Dade County police officer, Frank Trujillo, overheard . . . Enio Jimeno, arranging what appeared to be a drug transaction over a public telephone. Believing that Jimeno might be involved in illegal drug trafficking, Officer Trujillo followed his car. The officer . . . pulled Jimeno over to the side of the road in order to issue him a traffic citation [for making an illegal turn]. Officer Trujillo told Jimeno that he had been stopped for committing a traffic infraction. The officer went on to say that he had reason to believe that Jimeno was carrying narcotics in his car, and asked permission to search the car. He explained that Jimeno did not have to consent to a search of the car. Jimeno stated that he had nothing to hide and gave Trujillo permission to search the automobile. After Jimeno's spouse, respondent Luz

> Jimeno, stepped out of the car, Officer Trujillo went to the passenger side, opened the door, and saw a folded, brown paper bag on the floorboard. The officer picked up the bag, opened it, and found a kilogram of cocaine inside."
>
> "The Jimenos were charged with possession with intent to distribute cocaine in violation of Florida law" (*Florida v. Jimeno,* 1991, pp. 249–50).

The Florida Supreme Court ruled that the officer had to receive specific consent to open the container. The United States Supreme Court reversed, holding that under the Fourth Amendment the scope of a consent search depends on whether the search was reasonable. In this case, the search was reasonable because, according to Chief Justice Rehnquist, the "scope of a search is generally defined by its expressed object," Jimeno "did not place any explicit limitation on the scope of the search," and a "reasonable person may be expected to know that narcotics are generally carried in some form of a container." He stressed that Jimeno could have limited the scope of the search, and concluded with the policy expressed in Schneckloth, that "The community has a real interest in encouraging consent, for the resulting search may yield necessary evidence for the solution and prosecution of crime. . . ."

Justice Marshall, dissented, joined by Justice Stevens. He noted that under the Court's precedent, there is a lesser expectation of privacy in cars, but a heightened expectation of privacy in the content of closed containers. These "distinct privacy expectations . . . do not merge when the individual uses his car to transport the container." Also, the way in which "reasonableness" is used by the majority could lead to absurd or unacceptable results. After all, if "a reasonable person may be expected to know that drug couriers frequently store their contraband on their persons or in their body cavities" then consent to search a car could lead to a body-cavity search. Jimeno, in fact, did not consent to a search of the envelope and the Court should interpret rights expansively and interpret limitation of rights (such as consent) narrowly. Marshall reiterated his conclusion in *Schneckloth.*

LAW IN SOCIETY

POLICE PERJURY AND THE FOURTH AMENDMENT

A decade ago, police perjury was the "the dirty little secret of our criminal justice system."[50] Now it is common knowledge, thanks in large part to the exposed perjury of Detective Mark Fuhrman in the O.J. Simpson murder trial.[51] A law professor reports that his students frequently interrupt classroom hypotheticals involving illegal police conduct with statements such as, "What if the police just lie about what happened?"[52] And this, indeed, is the critical point. People in all walks of life, from presidents of the United States on down, have been known to lie, and it is necessary for society to prosecute business fraud, for professional organizations to investigate and sanction falsehoods by its members, and so forth. "What distinguishes police officers is their unique power—to use force, to summarily deprive a citizen of freedom, to even use deadly force, if necessary—and their commensurately unique responsibilities—to be the living embodiment of the 'law' in our communities, as applied fairly to every member."[53] If police officers routinely commit perjury about the legality of arrests or searches and routinely get away with it, then the true result is not a personal benefit (a good arrest record) or even a misguided belief that this enhances public safety—it effectively destroys the basic constitutional rights of every person who is subject to such illegal action and threatens the rights of the rest of us (including cops) who have not yet been framed by police lies. This kind of perjury occurs most frequently in drug enforcement.

It is important to begin with Professor Morgan Cloud's observation that not "all police officers lie under oath, or that most officers lie, or that even some officers lie all the time."[54] An insightful article by Professor Andrew McClurg notes a profound paradox: (1) "Most police officers are honorable, moral persons," and (2) "Many of these same police officers lie in the course of their official duties." Any resolution of the problem of police perjury requires understanding the pressures that proliferate police perjury.

The kind of police perjury most likely to undermine Fourth Amendment rights occurs when (1) a police officer thinks that a defendant was in possession of contraband or incriminating evidence, (2) the officer obtained the evidence by an unconstitutional act, and (3) in a suppression hearing the officer "embellishes" the truth by testifying so as to make it appear as if the stop, arrest, or search was performed in a constitutional manner. "Routine" perjury is a greater threat to rights than more outrageous action, such as planting evidence on innocent persons or "booming" (illegally breaking into homes without a warrant or pretense of legality),[55] because most cops, being honorable, draw the line at such "over-the-top" behavior. But they will "shade" the truth, if they view constitutional rights as "mere technicalities"—as impediments to effective law enforcement. Professor Richard Uviller, who spent a year observing an New York Police Department street crimes unit, notes that like most people, "cops were raised with a strong sense of justice, and they naturally apply it when the occasion arises."[56]

Scholars who have studied this issue believe that routine perjury in regard to the seizure of incriminating evidence began as a result of the federalization of the exclusionary rule in *Mapp v. Ohio* (1961). A frequently cited 1971 article by Irving Younger, a former prosecutor and judge, noted that before *Mapp,* police easily testified to making illegal stops and finding contraband—"This had the ring of truth." After *Mapp,* judges suppressed evidence obtained in this way. Police officers then discovered "that if the defendant drops the narcotics on the ground, after which the policeman arrests him, then the search is reasonable and the evidence is admissible." After this, "dropsy" testimony increased enormously.[57] Younger's observations were substantiated by a before-after empirical study of police testimony in misdemeanor narcotics arrests showing that the percent of arrests where narcotics were "hidden on the body" dropped from about twenty-five percent of all arrests to about five percent, while "dropsie" cases, which accounted for about ten percent to fifteen percent of arrests before *Mapp,* increased to forty-one percent for narcotics officers.[58]

"Routine" perjury is close to impossible for defense lawyers, prosecutors, or judges to detect because they are so simple:

> Lying about search and seizure matters "was part of everyday police work" according to a former New York City police officer interviewed for an article announcing that cops in New York must now go to school to learn to tell the truth. The Mollen Commission cataloged a "litany" of manufactured search and seizure tales uncovered by its investigation:
>
> For example, when officers unlawfully stop and search a vehicle because they believe it contains drugs or guns, officers will falsely claim in police reports and under oath that the car ran a red light (or committed some other traffic violation) and that they subsequently saw contraband in the car in plain view. To conceal an unlawful search of an individual who officers believe is carrying drugs or a gun, they will falsely assert that they saw a bulge in the person's pocket or saw drugs and money changing hands. To justify unlawfully entering an apartment where officers believe narcotics or cash can be found, they pretend to have information from an unidentified civilian informant or claim they saw the drugs in plain view after responding to the premises on a radio run. To arrest people they suspect are guilty of dealing drugs, they falsely assert that the defendants had drugs in their possession when, in fact, the drugs were found elsewhere where the officers had no lawful right to be.[59]

A Harvard Law School conference held shortly after the verdict in the O.J. Simpson case concluded: "There are no national studies or statistics on police perjury, and there is considerable disagreement on how widespread the problem is."[60] Nevertheless, a great deal of anecdotal evidence from police commissions and others indicate that police perjury is widespread.[61] A study of Chicago police asked them: "In your experience, do police officers ever shade the facts a little (or a lot) to establish probable cause when there may not have been probable cause in fact?"—sixteen officers responded "yes" and five responded "no."[62] Of course, the actual number is unknown because "[b]y their very nature, successful lies will remain undetected, and we would expect a perjurer to attempt to conceal his crime".[63] Former Kansas City and San Jose police chief and Hoover Institution research fellow, Joseph D. McNamara, estimated "that *hundreds of thousands* of law-enforcement officers commit felony perjury every year testifying about drug arrests." He based this estimate on the fact that about one million drug arrests a year are for possession, not selling; that hundreds of thousands of police swear under oath that the drugs were in *plain view* or that the defendant gave *consent* to a search; and that: "This may happen occasionally but it defies belief that so many drug users are careless enough to leave illegal drugs where the police can see them or so dumb as to give cops consent to search them when they possess drugs."[64]

"Routine" perjury has serious consequences. First, there is the danger that police fabrication will lead to the charging or conviction of innocent persons. In some cases, the police have convinced themselves, against the evidence, that the victim of their lies was guilty. Well known cases include Richard Jewell, suspected of bombing Olympic Park at the 1996 Atlanta Olympics, and Rolando Cruz, who was on death row in Illinois—but there are many others.[65]

Second, the frequent commission of "pious perjury" creates an enabling atmosphere that allows a minority of "rogue cops" to go "over-the-top" by planting evidence on innocent people or booming. There is no way of knowing whether such abuses are widespread. Commission reports and the anecdotes of police and lawyers do *not* indicate that such practices are routine. Nevertheless, when such cases do occur, they are reported and quite a few have appeared in the last decade:

- Philadelphia's 39th District scandal where six "rogue cops" planted evidence on many innocent people, including a grandmother who pestered them with questions when they came looking for her grandson, and spent two years in prison for her verbal challenges; the city paid out at least seven million dollars and fourteen hundred cases were reviewed.[66]
- Perjury convictions of cops in the mid-1990's NYPD 30th Precinct scandal in which wrongful arrests and booming was connected to police participation in illegal drug sales.[67]
- Convictions of five New York State Troopers who faked fingerprint evidence in thirty cases and lifted fingerprints from a corpse and planned to plant it on anyone charged with the crime.[68]

- Perjury to cover up a police ring that systematically shook down drug dealers in Hartford, Connecticut.[69]
- The conviction of Eufrasio G. Cortez, a California narcotics Officer of the Year, who admitted that he stole a half-million dollars from drug busts, committed perjury thirty times, beat suspects on twenty occasions, and used false statements in search warrants one hundred times over a fifteen-and-a-half-year police career.[70]

Third, the practice cannot be kept hidden and eventually leads to a loss of public confidence in the police. As a result; jurors become skeptical of police testimony which undermines fair prosecutions; minorities become less willing to call the police for protection; and the public is less interested in law enforcement as a career.[71]

Fourth, the practice undermines the morale and diminishes the sense of pride felt by honest officers.[72] When police lie to cover their corruption, the professional self-esteem of honest cops is injured. Professor Uviller sensed in honest cops "a sense of betrayal by the corrupt members who have demeaned the Job and made it harder for the rest to convince the public of their probity."[73]

Fifth, the practice leads to corrupt police work, including the use of drugs by undercover officers who then lie to the jury about such practices. East Texas police officer and FBI undercover agent, Kim Wozencraft finally told the truth about routinely planting evidence, using drugs with suspects, and lying about it in court. She was convicted of perjury, served time, and later resumed her life as a novelist and editor of *Prison Life* magazine.[74]

Sixth, perjury by police forces honest cops into the risky role of being "whistle blowers" and suffering consequences, or joining the "blue-wall of silence" and tolerating the corruption around them. Officer Michael McEvoy of the Arlington Heights, Illinois Police Department "blew the whistle" on a case of police perjury and would have been fired by his chief, but the Arlington Heights Board of Fire and Police Commissioners reinstated McEvoy when his account was substantiated by a third officer.[75] It is not implausible to believe that a number of whistle blowers were not as lucky as Officer McEvoy.

Seventh, the practice drives a wedge between judges who occasionally suppress evidence and police who become angry at judges who do not accept their lies. Judge Joseph Q. Koletsky of Hartford, Connecticut, threw out evidence of a crime after the testimony of arresting police was clearly contradicted by physical evidence. Detectives told a plausible story of stopping a suspect next his truck and arresting him when he reached behind him and finding cocaine in a search incident to arrest. Spilled powder cocaine in the cab of the truck supported the defendant's testimony that the officers simply drew guns and arrested him in his truck. After the evidence was suppressed, the detectives insisted that they did the right thing. "It's a bad decision, but what can you do?" Officer Murzin said. "Some people live in the real world and some people don't."[76] In the real world, people with power can lie and get away with it. In a more famous case, federal judge Harold Baer suppressed evidence in a New York City drug bust. He had been a member of the Mollen Commission on Police Corruption and expressed skepticism of the police in his decision. After media coverage, it quickly became a national issue during the 1996 Presidential campaign. In an unusual move, the judge ordered a second hearing, heard more testimony, and decided that the search and seizure was lawful.[77]

Finally, and most important, police perjury diminishes liberty and undermines the constitutional order. In addition to the growing subcultural belief that the Constitution is an impediment to be overcome, judicial acceptance of police perjury undermines the very rationale given for the exclusionary rule: deterrence of police illegality.

An important reason why police perjury is pervasive is that it is in large measure condoned by the courts. According to Alan Dershowitz, "A judge in Detroit after listening on one day to more than a dozen 'dropsy' cases . . . chastised the police for not being more 'creative,' but nonetheless accepted their testimony."[78] Professor Cloud gives five reasons why judges accept police perjury:

1. It can be difficult to determine if a witness is lying.
2. Judicial dislike of the exclusionary rule.
3. The cynical belief that "most defendants in the criminal justice system are guilty," and "even if they are innocent of these specific crimes, [they] are guilty of something." Therefore, "it is not too disturbing that evidence will not be suppressed."
4. They assume that criminal defendants will commit perjury and so distrust the testimony of suspects.
5. Tact. "Judges simply do not like to call other government officials liars—especially those who appear regularly in court. It is distasteful; it is indelicate; it is bad manners."[79]

To this list Professor McClurg adds that "judges do not want to generate adverse publicity that portrays them as being 'soft on crime;' especially, "elected judges are afraid of jeopardizing their chances of reelection."[80]

Numerous proposals have been made to deal with this issue. Many involve modifying legal rules and procedures, including:

- Eliminate the exclusionary rule
- Eliminate the exclusionary rule for violent crimes but not for crimes like drug possession
- Expand the use of judicial warrants to all nonexigent searches and seizures while narrowing the exigency exception

- Admit polygraphs of witnesses in suppression hearings
- Make probable cause more flexible to allow common sense judgments
- Permit impeachment of police testimony through proof of bias and motive to lie, and by allowing evidence of the prevalence of the blue wall of silence
- Allow judges to order discovery and allow cross-examination where there is an initial showing of police perjury in a suppression hearing.[81]

Some of these proposals are implausible, but some may have a limited impact on police perjury. Institutional changes have been proposed. Skolnick and Fyfe propose major changes in police departments and a move toward community policing as a way to ameliorate the problem.[82] Professor McClurg believes that "[w]e cannot rely with confidence on external actors or institutions to control police lying," and that "[p]olice lying will be substantially reduced only when more police officers come to view it as an unacceptable practice."[83] He believes that police perjury is so pervasive because of the contradiction between the fact that most police officers are moral persons and that many will commit "routine" perjury which causes cognitive dissonance, and to reduce the tension, the officers rationalize their behavior by coming to believe that lying is moral behavior.[84] To deal effectively with police perjury, he proposed a system of police academy training and on-the-street mentoring to show that the end-justifies-the-means reasoning that supports perjury is short-sighted and injurious, and to fortify the initial decency that rookies bring to the academy before it becomes hardened into cynicism.[85] The details of this interesting proposal are beyond the scope of this section. Clearly it can work only if the head of the law enforcement agency and the political leadership of the municipality support this.

To sum up, "routine" police perjury is pervasive and it seriously threatens the existence of Fourth Amendment rights. As noted in Chapter 1, the most important aspect of the Rule of Law is "congruence": "The practices of the government must be *congruent* with the law as written. The glorious promises of procedural justice enshrined in the Bill of Rights can quickly become hollow and breed a terrible cynicism against government and law if they are routinely ignored." Such cynicism is widespread and it is vital that judges, and more important, that the police, take rights seriously.

SUMMARY

The Supreme Court has expressed a preference for the search warrant over warrantless searches. The most important reason is that a warrant places the judgment of a detached and neutral judicial officer between the police and the citizen in deciding whether probable cause exists to effect a search. A judicial officer who receives fees from warrants issued or who becomes too closely attached to the police search effort is not a neutral and detached magistrate. To obtain a search warrant, an officer must present a written affidavit to a magistrate and swear to the truth of the facts in an *ex parte* hearing that purports to show probable cause. If authorized by statute, a warrant can be obtained by telephone. The place to be searched must be precisely described, but a reasonable mistake in describing the place will not make the search illegal. Search warrants for materials protected by the First Amendment must describe the materials exactly. Statutes provide for anticipatory warrants that authorize police to seize evidence from places which do not contain the contraband at the time the warrant is issued, but reasonably expect the contraband to be delivered to the location. A defendant can obtain a hearing to challenge an executed search warrant in cases where he or she can make out a preliminary showing that the officer who made out the warrant intentionally lied about material facts or made statements in the warrant with reckless disregard for the truth. Search warrants must be executed within ten days of issuance. The Fourth Amendment requires that police officers knock and announce their presence when executing a warrant; the knock and announce element can be set aside by a magistrate in a "no-knock" warrant where potential danger to officers or loss of evidence is likely if the police knock and announce. However, a blanket no-knock policy violates the Fourth Amendment. After a warrant is executed, the officer must specify each item seized on an inventory and a copy must be presented to the person whose premises were searched.

In the 1960s, search and seizure law was modernized by creating the expectation of privacy doctrine under *Katz v. United States,* eliminating the mere evidence rule, and utilizing the general-reasonableness construction of the Fourth Amendment to weaken the particularity requirement to support administrative search warrants and to authorize investigative stops on less than probable cause as in *Terry* (1968). Together these changes made Fourth Amendment interpretation more flexible. The expectation of privacy doctrine held that the Fourth Amendment protected that which a person seeks to keep private and that which society is prepared to recognize as reasonable. Property interests are still protected by the Fourth Amendment but the Court looks to the subjective and objective expectation of privacy balanced against the needs of effective law enforcement. The expectations given the greatest weight are those of the privacy of the home and bodily integrity. Under *Camara v. Municipal Court* (1967) a non-police government employee who seeks to enter a home without the consent of the owner to enforce an administrative ordinance must have a judicial warrant; such a warrant, however, need not have all the characteristics of a criminal search warrant and, indeed, in some ways resembles a general warrant. The Fourth Amendment does not prohibit the use of undercover agents who are invited into homes and private areas under false pretense; such an agent cannot conduct a general search of the premises, but can testify as to any criminal activity that occurs in his presence. The Fourth Amendment does not apply to searches and seizures conducted by American agents in foreign countries, even though they are intended to gather evidence to be used to prosecute suspects in United States courts.

Probable cause is defined as known facts that could lead a reasonably prudent person to draw conclusions about unknown facts. It is a standard of evidence sufficiency that allows a law enforcement official to arrest a person, obtain a warrant, or perform a warrantless search. Probable cause may be based on hearsay. When the hearsay is provided by a secret informant, the Supreme Court has required magistrates to examine the affidavits carefully. Under the older *Aguilar-Spinelli* two-pronged test, the magistrate had to be convinced that the officer's affidavit supplied credible information about the informant's veracity and his or her basis of knowledge. The Court in *Illinois v. Gates* (1983) replaced the two-prong test with a totality-of-the circumstances-test which it applied to an anonymous tip so that a deficiency in one prong can be compensated for by a strong showing as to the other, or by some other indicia of reliability in determining the overall reliability of a tip.

The plain view doctrine allows the seizure of contraband when a police officer who makes the seizure is lawfully in the place (by a warrant or by virtue of being in a public place) and the illegal nature of the thing seized is immediately apparent. The "immediately apparent" rule is, in effect, a rule of probable cause. A police officer cannot create plain view by illegally entering a premises or by manipulating evidence beyond that authorized by the purpose of the officer's mandate. A plain view seizure can be based on any of the senses, not only on sight. Open fields are not protected by the Fourth Amendment; evidence seized by officers who trespass on open land is admissible. The curtilage is the area and buildings immediately surrounding a house, and is protected by the Fourth Amendment to the extent that the expectation of privacy in the area is secured. Airplane and helicopter flyovers may lawfully obtain evidence of what is visible in a curtilage, even if fenced, because commercial overflights have eliminated the expectation of privacy from the air. Ordinary devices, such as flashlights and field glasses, that enhance the senses do not undermine the "immediately apparent" rule. The use of an enhancement device such as a beeper, without a warrant, that detects movement within a home and suggests criminal activity, violates the Fourth Amendment.

A person may consent to relinquish his Fourth Amendment right to privacy to a law enforcement officer. An officer who seeks consent to search need have no reasonable suspicion or probable cause to do so. An officer need not inform a person, when requesting consent to search, that the person has a constitutional right to refuse. Facts and circumstances of a consent encounter must show that the consent was voluntary. The burden of proof is on the government to show voluntariness. Entry under the pretense of having a search warrant negates consent. A person who shares a common area with another may give consent to the police to search. Landlords or hotel keepers cannot give consent for a criminal search. Police may rely on consent given by a person who reasonably appears to have shared control over an area, even if, in fact, the person has no authority or control over an area. Consent to search an area, such as a car, gives police the right to open containers located in the area.

LEGAL PUZZLES

HOW HAVE COURTS DECIDED THESE CASES?

4–1. Omaha police received information from the DEA in Los Angeles that Africa Sweeney would arrive by airplane with illegal drugs. Officers approached Sweeney at the Omaha airport and he consented to speak with them. Sweeney had a ticket made out in another name. Police informed Sweeney they suspected him of transporting drugs. He consented to be searched and nothing was found. At the baggage claim, Sweeney was acting nervously and was evasive about which luggage was his. Sweeney asked to use the restroom. He was accompanied there by officers, was pat-searched, and told not to lock the door or flush the toilet. Despite the instruction, Sweeney locked the door upon entering the stall, was told to unlock the door, and was observed through the gap between the stall door and the wall of the stall. As Sweeney unlocked the door, an officer saw him drop his airline ticket between his legs and flush the toilet. The officer entered the stall and retrieved the ticket from the toilet. Did the observation of Sweeney in the bathroom stall violate his reasonable expectation of privacy? *United States v. Delaney,* 52 F.3d 182 (8th Cir. 1995)

4–2. A search warrant was issued by a magistrate to search the home of Lauren Eric Wilhelm to search for marijuana. It was based on a detective's affidavit made out on the day he received a telephone call from an anonymous caller. The detective did not know the caller and did not meet with him or her. All the information known to the police was revealed in the affidavit which stated, in full:

> On 3–7–94 applicant received information from a reliable source who is a concerned citizen, a resident of Iredell County, a mature person with personal connections with the suspects and has projected a truthfull [*sic*] demeanor to this applicant. Informant stated to applicant the directions to this residence and the directions have been confirmed to be true by the applicant through surveillance on this date. The informant described the substance he/she believed to be marijuana and the informants [*sic*] description is consistent with the applicants [*sic*] knowledge of marijuana. Informant described transactions between residents and patrons that purchase marijuana at this residence and his/her descriptions of these actions are consistent with applicants [*sic*] knowledge of how marijuana is packaged and sold. Informant has personally observed residents selling marijuana at this residence within the last 48 hours. Informant also observed a quanity [*sic*] of un-sold marijuana at this residence within the last 48 hours.

Was the warrant properly issued under the totality of circumstances of *Illinois v. Gates* and *Alabama v. White? United States v. Wilhelm,* 80 F.3d 116 (4th Cir. 1996)

4–3. A woman attacked by a knife-wielding stranger at 2:00 A.M. in her apartment fought off the assailant and cut her hands. Her next door neighbor, Daniel Turner, heard the noise and called police. The next morning, while investigating, police noticed blood on Turner's windowsill. Further blood stains and a knife matching that described by the attack victim led police to begin to suspect Turner. Turner signed a written consent for the police to look in his apartment for all evidence of the assault. During a ninety-minute search of Turner's apartment, police found videotapes containing sexually explicit material and saw Turner's computer monitor screen suddenly turn on. The computer "desktop" disclosed a photograph of a nude woman with light-colored hair similar to that of the assault victim. The officer sat at the computer and searched its files, locating photographs of nude blonde women in bondage, text concerning rape and/or bondage, and files with names such as "young" and "young with breasts." He opening one such file and viewed what he believed was child pornography. On the advice of the district attorney, the officer copied files onto a floppy disk and closed down and seized the computer. Turner did not know his computer files had been subjected to the search until it was completed. Turner was charged with one count of possessing child pornography. Did Turner consent to a search of his computer files? Was the child pornography file found in plain view? *United States v. Turner,* 169 F. 3d 84 (1st Cir. 1999)

4–4. An arrest warrant was issued against Patrick Elie, a former Haitian cabinet member, in Washington for an assault against Ms. Preval-Belot, First Secretary of the Haitian Embassy in Washington, D.C. Several local police officers and federal agents went to Elie's hotel to arrest him. Elie was "considered armed and dangerous." The officers, with guns drawn, confronted Elie in the hotel restaurant, ordered him to the ground, and handcuffed and searched him for weapons. After being helped to his feet, and prior to any police questioning, Elie stated that he was a diplomat. Elie was asked if he had weapons. He answered affirmatively and was asked if he wanted them to be secured by either hotel management or the police. Elie elected to have the officers secure and inventory his property. Under the facts and circumstances, did Elie voluntarily consent to a search of his hotel room? *United States v. Elie,* 111 F.3d 1135 (4th Cir. 1997)

ANSWERS TO LEGAL PUZZLES

4–1. NO. An occupant of a toilet stall in a public restroom may have a reasonable expectation of privacy against clandestine police surveillance of the interior of the stall, but it is not absolute. The officer's observation of Sweeney in the restroom did not violate any legitimate expectation of privacy. There was no clandestine or surreptitious police surveillance of Sweeney in the airport restroom. At the time Sweeney asked to use the restroom, he was the subject of a lawful investigative stop. The officer who escorted Sweeney to the stall was standing in a position where he had a legal right to be. Also, the officer specifically instructed Sweeney not to lock the door or flush the toilet. Sweeney was aware that an officer was standing just outside the stall to ensure compliance with those instructions. Given these circumstances, Sweeney had no subjective expectation of privacy in the stall.

4–2. NO. There was no corroboration of the tip in this case, as was done in *Gates* and *White.* The affidavit relied on an unnamed informant and provided no indication of his or her truthfulness or reliability. The officer's assessment of the informant's credibility was conclusory.

4–3. NO, NO. A consensual search may not exceed the scope of the consent given and the scope is generally defined by its expressed object. In this case, an objectively reasonable person would have understood that the police intended to search only in places where an intruder hastily might have disposed of any physical evidence of the attempted rape immediately after it occurred; for example, in places where a fleeing suspect might have tossed a knife or bloody clothing. Therefore, the court rejected the state's argument that the sexually suggestive image which suddenly came into "plain view" on the computer screen rendered Turner's computer files "fair game" under a consent search simply because the assault had a sexual component (e.g., the attacker attempted to tie her hands). The detectives never told Turner they were investigating a sexual assault or an attempted rape.

4–4. YES. It is appropriate to consider the characteristics of the accused (e.g., age, maturity, education, intelligence, experience) as well as the conditions under which the consent to search was given (e.g., the officer's conduct, the number of officers present, the duration, location, and time of the encounter). Elie was intelligent, well-educated, and familiar with the criminal justice system and its consequences. He had significant law enforcement responsibilities with the Haitian Government. Elie was forty-six years old, spoke fluent English, held an advanced degree in chemistry, and was aware of his *Miranda* rights. As for the conduct of the officers, the incident occurred during the middle of the afternoon in a hotel lobby and was not of inordinate duration. Any tension created by the initial arrest, when Elie was confronted at gunpoint, ordered to the floor, and handcuffed, had been defused by the time Elie consented to the search.

FURTHER READING

Fred P. Graham, *The Due Process Revolution: The Warren Court's Impact on the Criminal Law* (New York: Hayden Book Co., 1970)

Craig M. Bradley, *The Failure of the Criminal Procedure Revolution* (Philadelphia: University of Pennsylvania Press, 1993)

Barbara J. Shapiro, *"Beyond Reasonable Doubt" and "Probable Cause": Historical Perspectives on the Anglo-American Law of Evidence* (Berkeley: University of California Press, 1991)

ENDNOTES

1. Under Director J. Edgar Hoover (1925 through 1972), the FBI often acted as would a secret police agency in a totalitarian state. See Richard Gid Powers, *Secrecy and Power: The Life and Times of J. Edgar Hoover* (New York: Free Press, 1987); Athan G. Theoharis and John Stuart Cox, *The Boss: J. Edgar Hoover and the Great American Inquisition* (Philadelphia: Temple University Press, 1988). In recent years the FBI has matched its technical proficiency with a serious dedication to the rule of law.
2. B. Drummond Ayres Jr., The Simpson Case: the Law; For Judge, a Case Where Circumstances Outweigh Safeguards, *New York Times,* July 8, 1994, p. A14.
3. Scott Turow, "Policing the Police: The D.A.'s Job" p. 190, in Jeffrey Abramson, ed. *Postmortem: The O.J. Simpson Case* (Basic Books, 1996).
4. H. R. Uviller, *Tempered Zeal* (Chicago: Contemporary Books, 1988), pp. 125–26.
5. Jim McGee and Brian Duffy, Someone to Watch Over Us, *Washington Post,* June 23, 1996, p. W9.
6. Commentary to *Federal Rules of Criminal Procedure,* 1987–88 Educational Edition (St. Paul: West Publishing Co., 1987), p. 129, quoting *United States ex rel., Pugh v. Pate,* 401 F.2d 6 (7th Cir. 1968).
7. Geoffrey P. Alpert, Telecommunications in The Courtroom: Telephonic Search Warrants, *University of Miami Law Review* 38:625–35, p. 626 (1996); the states are: Arizona, Montana, Nebraska, New York, Oregon, South Dakota, Utah, Washington, and Wisconsin.
8. Alpert, p, 630.
9. P. Pringle, "Officer Explains Search of Simpson's Property Police Say They Saw Blood, Feared a Life at Stake," *Dallas Morning News,* July 6, 1994, p. A1.
10. S. Estrich, "Who's on Trial, O.J. or Cops?" *USA Today,* Sept. 22, 1994, p. 13A.
11. Walter Gerash, "Next Two Days Critical for Simpson Hearing," *Rocky Mountain News,* July 6, 1994, p. A33.
12. *Lyons v. Robinson,* 783 F.2d 737 (8th Cir. 1985), citing *United States v. Gitcho,* 601 F.2d 369, 371 (8th. Cir. 1979).
13. James A. Adams, "Anticipatory Search Warrants: Constitutionality, Requirements, and Scope," *Kentucky Law Journal* 79 (1991):681–733, p. 687, n. 19.
14. Ibid., pp. 705–706, note 67.
15. Ibid., pp. 695–97.
16. Ibid., pp. 698–99.
17. Ibid., pp. 709–10.
18. Ibid., pp. 715, 727–29.
19. Ibid.
20. Ibid., pp. 720–21.
21. *Spinelli v. United States* (1969); *Illinois v. Gates* (1983).
22. *Federal Rules of Criminal Procedure,* R. 41(C)(1).
23. *United States v. Ruminer,* 786 F.2d 381 (10th Cir. 1986).
24. *Ker v. California* (1963).
25. Information from the *Denver Post,* Feb. 4, 2000, July 18, 2000 and the *Denver Rocky Mountain News,* Feb. 5, 2000, Feb. 6, 2000, March 14, 2000, June 28, 2000.
26. *Payton,* pp. 585–86, citing *United States v. United States District Court,* p. 313.
27. See *Ward v. County of San Diego,* 791 F.2d 1329 (9th Cir. 1986); *Stewart v. Lubbock County,* 767 F.2d 153 (5th Cir. 1985).
28. *On Lee v. United States* (1952); *Lopez v. United States* (1963); *United States v. White* (1971) (plurality opinion); 18 U.S.C. § 2511 (2) (c) & (d).
29. Robert R. Reinertsen and Robert J. Bronson, "Informant Is a Dirty Word," in J.N. Gilbert, ed., *Criminal Investigation: Essays and Cases* (Columbus: Merrill Publishing Co.), pp. 99–103.
30. Reinertsen and Bronson, "Informant." p. 99.
31. C. Whitebread, "The Burger Court's Counter-Revolution in Criminal Procedure: The Recent Criminal Decisions of the United States Supreme Court," *Washburn Law Journal* 24 (1985):471–98.
32. See Wayne R. LaFave, "Fourth Amendment Vagaries (of Improbable Cause, Imperceptible Plain View, Notorious Privacy, and Balancing Askew)," *Journal of Criminal Law and Criminology* 74 (1983):1171–1224.
33. Corey Fleming Hirokawa, Making The "Law of the Land" the Law on the Street: How Police Academies Teach Evolving

Fourth Amendment Law, *Emory Law Journal* 49(1):295–334, pp. 319–20 (2000).

34. People v. Griminger, 71 N.Y.2d 635, 640, 524 N.E.2d 409, 412, 529 N.Y.S.2d 55 (1988).
35. *Griminger*, 71 N.Y. at 639, citing People v Rodriguez, 52 NY2d 483, at 489 (1981).
36. Charles H. Whitebread and Christopher Slobogin, *Criminal Procedure: An Analysis of Cases and Concepts, Fourth Edition* (New York: Foundation Press, 2000) , p. 225.
37. *Dickerson v. Minnesota* (1993).
38. *Whren v. United States* (1996), see Chapter 5.
39. 41 Cal.3d 373, 21 Cal. Rptr. 499, 710 P.2d 299 (1985).
40. 42 Cal.3d 1302, 233 Cal. Rptr. 2, 729 P.2d 166 (1986).
41. William J. Broad, Ideas & Trends; We're Ready for Our Close-Ups Now, *New York Times,* Jan. 16, 2000, Sec. 4, p. 4.
42. T. Wade McKnight, Comment: Passive, Sensory-Enhanced Searches: Shifting the Fourth Amendment "Reasonableness" Burden, *Louisiana Law Review,* 59: 1243–68, pp. 1253–54 (1999).
43. McKnight, p. 1255.
44. McKnight, p. 1257.
45. McKnight, pp. 1258–59.
46. McKnight, p. 1257, n. 110, citing *United States v. Cusumano,* 67 F.3d 1497, 1504 and n.11 (10th Cir. 1995).
47. F.J. Remington, D.J. Newman, E.L. Kimball, M. Melli and H. Goldstein, *Criminal Justice Administration, Materials and Cases* [First Edition] (Indianapolis: Bobbs-Merrill, 1969). p. 32.
48. *Schneckloth v. Bustamonte* (1973), p. 222.
49. In *Davis v. United States* (1946) the Supreme Court upheld a conviction in which evidence was obtained from a locked room by an arrested person upon the demand of government agents. The evidence consisted of rationing stamps which were public property and which the defendant-proprietor was required by law to keep. The opinion stressed that this decision would not apply to private property.
50. Morgan Cloud, "The Dirty Little Secret," *Emory Law Journal* 43(1994):1311–49, p. 1311.
51. Scott Turow, "Simpson Prosecutors Pay for Their Blunders," *N.Y. Times,* Oct. 4, 1995, p. A21; *Larry King Live,* 9:00 PM ET, CNN, Aug. 28, 1995, Transcript No. 1524–2, "Will O.J. Testify?" (Guests: Alan Dershowitz, Simpson Defense Attorney; Bill Hodes, Professor of Law, Indiana University). David Margolick, "Forget O. J.—The Question Becomes: Is Fuhrman the Question?" *N.Y. Times,* Sept. 10, 1995, § 4, p. 2; Carl Rowan, "Fuhrman Tips the Scale at Simpson Trial," *Chicago Sun-Times,* Sept. 10, 1995, editorial sec., p. 39. Charles L. Lindner, "The Simpson Trial; When You Can't See the Forest for the Leaf," *Los Angeles Times,* Sept. 3, 1995, p. M1.
52. Andrew J. McClurg, "Good Cop, Bad Cop: Using Cognitive Dissonance Theory to Reduce Police Lying," *University of California at Davis Law Review* 32: 389–453, p. 398 (1999).
53. David N. Dorfman, "Proving the Lie: Litigating Police Credibility," *American Journal of Criminal Law* 26: pp. 462–503 (1999).
54. Cloud, "Secret," p. 1313, footnote omitted.
55. George James, "Officer Admits Illegal Apartment Entries," *N.Y. Times,* Jan. 10, 1996, p. B6. He claimed the precinct's most senior officers raided and searched a building without first obtaining a warrant, and "[i]t was kind of implied that this was what they wanted." This account was hotly denied by Commissioner Bratton who claimed that it was not corroborated, Barbara Ross and Wendell Jamieson, "Bratton Slams Dirty 30 Sgt.," *Daily News* (New York), Jan. 12, 1996, p. 10.
56. H. Richard Uviller, *Tempered Zeal* (Chicago: Contemporary Books, 1988), p. 158.
57. Irving Younger, "The Perjury Routine," *The Nation,* pp. 596–97 (1967), cited in Cloud, "Secret," p. 1317; as a judge he noted the problem in *People v. McMurtry,* 314 N.Y.S.2d 194 (Crim. Ct. 1970).
58. Sarah Barlow, "Patterns of Arrests for Misdemeanor Narcotics Possession: Manhattan Police Practices 1960–62," *Criminal Law Bulletin* 4(1968):549–81. See Paul Chevigny, "Comment," *Criminal Law Bulletin* 4(1968):581.
59. McClurg, pp. 398–99, footnotes omitted.
60. Sarah Terry, "Experts Try to Pin Down Extent of Police Misconduct," *N.Y. Times,* Nov. 19, 1995, § 1, p. 33.
61. See Joseph D. Grano, "A Dilemma for Defense Counsel: *Spinelli-Harris* Search Warrants and the Possibility of Police Perjury," *University of Illinois Law Forum* 1971(1971):405, 409, cited in Cloud, "Secret," p. 1312, n. 4. Other legal commentators cited in Cloud include: Alan Dershowitz, *The Best Defense,* pp. xxi–xxii (1982); Comment, "Police Perjury in Narcotics 'Dropsy' Cases: A New Credibility Gap," *Georgetown Law Journal* 60(1971):507. Professors Cloud, McClurg (pp. 396–404), and Dorfman (pp. 460–62) review all these materials and they all believe that these kinds of practices are routine.
62. Myron W. Orfield, Jr., "The Exclusionary Rule and Deterrence: An Empirical Study of Chicago Narcotics Officers," *University of Chicago Law Review* 54:1016–69 (1987), pp. 1050–51.
63. Cloud, "Secret," p. 1313, footnote omitted.
64. Joseph D. McNamara, "Law Enforcement; Has the Drug War Created an Officer Liars' Club?" *Los Angeles Times,* Feb. 11, 1996, p. M1.
65. McClurg, pp. 417–419; Daniel Jeffreys, "Last Hope on Death Row: Call McCloskey; He Gave up a Lucrative Career in Business to Help People Wrongly Imprisoned. He Has Saved Four Lives: So Far." *The Independent,* January 3, 1996, p. 4.
66. Don Terry, "Philadelphia Shaken by Criminal Police Officers," *N.Y. Times,* Aug. 28, 1995, p. A1; Barbara Whitaker, "Philadelphia Still Reeling From Police Scandal Officials Review More than 1,400 Arrests Made by Six Officers Charged with Theft, Framing Suspects," *Dallas Morning News,* Sept. 3, 1995, p. 14A.
67. "Officer Is Acquitted in Theft and Perjury," *N.Y. Times,* Jan. 26, 1996, p. B3 (Officer Stephen Setteducato. Earlier, Officer John Arena was cleared by a federal jury in Manhattan). *N.Y. Times,* Jan. 5, 1996, p. B2. Seth Faison, "In Plea Deal, Officer Agrees To Give Details Of Corruption," *N.Y. Times,* May 24, 1994, p. B1. George James, "Officer Admits Illegal Apartment Entries,"

N.Y. Times, Jan. 10, 1996, p. B6. He claimed the precinct's most senior officers raided and searched a building without first obtaining a warrant, and "[i]t was kind of implied that this was what they wanted." This account was hotly denied by Commissioner Bratton who claimed that it was not corroborated, Barbara Ross and Wendell Jamieson, "Bratton Slams Dirty 30 Sgt.," *Daily News* (New York), Jan. 12, 1996, p. 10.

68. "Ex-Trooper Admits a Plot to Falsify Fingerprints," *N.Y. Times,* Dec. 29, 1995, p. B5; "Prosecutor Tries to Make Trooper Talk on Tampering," *N.Y. Times,* Jan. 4, 1996, p. B5.
69. Lynne Tuohy, "Grand Juror Details Police Abuse of Power; 6 Arrests Made, More Expected; Police Corruption Probe Leads to Six Arrests in Hartford," *Hartford Courant,* Dec. 2, 1993, p. A1; "Police Arrested in Corruption Probe; State Trooper, Hartford Officer in Custody After 9-month Inquiry; State, Hartford Officer Taken into Custody," *Hartford Courant,* Dec. 1, 1993, p. A1.
70. Victor Merina, "Officers Marked Sobel for Death, Jury Told; Trial: Ex-deputy Says He and Colleagues Wanted to Eliminate the Sheriff's Sergeant When They Learned He Secretly Cooperated with Prosecutors," *Los Angeles Times,* Mar. 21, 1992, p. B1.
71. Joe Sexton, "Jurors Question Honesty of Police," *N.Y. Times,* Sept. 25, 1995, p. B3.; McClurg, pp. 419–23.
72. H. Richard Uviller, *Tempered Zeal* (Chicago: Contemporary Books, 1988), p. 115.
73. Uviller, *Tempered Zeal,* pp. 12–13.
74. Keith Kachtick, "Rush to Justice," *Texas Monthly,* Jan. 1996, p. 56.
75. Marco Buscaglia, "Board Clears Officer of Misconduct Charges," *Chicago Tribune,* Jan 5, 1996, p. 2 (Metro Nwest).
76. Matthew Kauffman, "Judge Doubts City Officers' Account of Arrest," *Hartford Courant,* Feb. 6, 1996, p. A3 (Statewide Section).
77. Dorfman, p. 471, n. 73; McClurg, pp. 406–11.
78. Alan Dershowitz, "Police Tampering: How Often, Where" *Buffalo News,* Feb. 21, 1995, p. 3.
79. Cloud, "Secret," pp. 1321–24, footnotes omitted.
80. McClurg, p. 405.
81. The many sources of these proposals is found in Dorfman. The last proposal is that of Prof. Dorfman.
82. Jerome K. Skolnick & James J. Fyfe, *Above the Law: Police and the Excessive Use of Force* (New York; Free Press, 1993).
83. McClurg, p. 410.
84. McClurg, pp. 412–15, 424–29.
85. McClurg, pp. 412–13, 428–53.

JUSTICES OF THE SUPREME COURT

STALWART CONSERVATIVES, 1938–1962
REED—VINSON—BURTON—MINTON—WHITTAKER

These five justices, appointees of Presidents Franklin D. Roosevelt, Henry S. Truman, and Dwight D. Eisenhower, were instrumental in delaying the implementation of the due process "incorporation" revolution of the 1960s. They were uniformly conservative in their criminal procedure rulings, both in denying the validity of the incorporation argument and in construing the due process clause narrowly. For the most part, legal commentators rank these justices as not especially distinguished: Their visions of the Court's role tended to be cramped, and they failed to explain their positions with intellectual force. They typically followed the lead of justices with more manifest abilities, especially Frankfurter and Harlan II. These justices displayed basic legal competence but little independence in their decisions. They did not write opinions with great skill, which is critical to the shaping of the law.

This group of justices, with Justice Clark, formed a majority of the Court from 1949 to 1953 (excluding Justice Whittaker, who sat from 1957 to 1962). From 1953 to 1962, a combination of centrist and less dyed-in-the-wool conservatives kept the Court from breaching the Palko *doctrine until Justice Clark's decision in* Mapp. *With Justice Frankfurter's retirement and replacement by Justice Arthur Goldberg in 1962, the Court took a decidedly liberal turn that marked the Warren Court of the 1960s.*

STANLEY F. REED

Kentucky 1884–1980
Democrat

Appointed by Franklin Delano Roosevelt

Years of Service:
1938–1957

Collection of the Supreme Court of the United States. Photographer: Harris and Ewing

LIFE AND CAREER Justice Reed held B.A. degrees from Kentucky Wesleyan College and Yale University and studied law at the Sorbonne, Columbia University, and the University of Virginia without graduating. He completed legal studies by reading law in a Kentucky lawyer's office and practiced from 1910 to the 1920s. He entered government service under President Hoover but remained in the attorney general's office as a faithful New Dealer under President Roosevelt. As solicitor general from 1935, he argued some of the key New Deal cases before the Supreme Court and developed a high reputation for legal craftsmanship. He was President Roosevelt's second appointment to the Supreme Court.

CONTRIBUTION TO CRIMINAL PROCEDURE He was a stalwart supporter of Justice Frankfurter and helped to block the movement toward incorporation, applying the criminal provisions of the Bill of Rights to the states.

SIGNATURE OPINION *Adamson v. California* (1947) Reed's majority opinion in *Adamson* kept the Court's anti-incorporation position intact. Adamson was tried for murder; he did not take the stand in his own defense, knowing that if he did so, prior convictions for burglary, larceny, and robbery would have been introduced into evidence to impeach him. California law allowed the judge to comment on the defendant's silence to the jury. Writing for the majority, Reed relied on a long train of cases, including *Twining v. New Jersey* (1908) for the proposition that the Self-Incrimination Clause was not a fundamental right incorporated into the Due Process Clause of the Fourteenth Amendment. He relied on the *Palko* case, noting that this ruling allowed the states to pursue their own criminal procedure policies unfettered by rules under the Bill of Rights which had limited the federal government. "It accords with the constitutional doctrine of federalism by leaving to the states the responsibility of dealing with the privileges and immunities of their citizens except those inherent in national citizenship."

In addition, Justice Reed made it clear that he did not entirely disapprove of the practical impact of a judge telling a jury that they could take the defendant's refusal to testify into account in weighing the evidence, even though by 1947 a majority of the states had abolished the practice by statute or state constitutional rule. Adamson argued that this placed a penalty on his right to silence under the California constitution and shifted the burden of proof from the government to himself. Justice Reed, to the contrary, noted: "[W]e see no reason why comment should not be made upon his silence. It seems quite natural that when a defendant has opportunity to deny or explain facts and determines not to do so, the prosecution should bring out the strength of the evidence by commenting upon defendant's failure to explain or deny it. The prosecution evidence may be of facts that may be beyond the knowledge of the accused. If so, his failure to testify would have little if any weight. But the facts may be such as are necessarily in the knowledge of the accused. In that case a failure to explain would point to an inability to explain."

ASSESSMENT Justice Reed's record was "liberal" in regard to New Deal economic issues. He was a strong believer in judicial restraint, and feared what he called "krytocracy" or government by judges. He was a judicial conservative vote in many civil liberties areas and voted consistently with Justice Frankfurter's bloc. On the question of school desegregation, he had consistently voted against segregated facilities under the "separate but equal" doctrine but was at first reluctant to overturn the doctrine in *Brown v. Board of Education* (1954). After Chief Justice Vinson died during deliberations, Chief Justice Earl Warren persuaded Reed to join a unanimous Court in overruling *Plessy v. Ferguson* (1896).

FURTHER READING

John D. Fassett, *New Deal Justice: The Life of Stanley Reed of Kentucky* (New York: Vantage, 1994)

FRED M. VINSON
Kentucky 1890–1953
Democrat

Appointed Chief Justice
by Harry S. Truman

Years of Service:
1946–1953

Collection of the Supreme Court of the United States. Photographer: Harris and Ewing

LIFE AND CAREER Vinson, born in Kentucky, was educated at Kentucky Normal School and Centre College, where he excelled in athletics and received a law degree. Vinson practiced law from 1911 to 1931. Elected to the House of Representatives in 1924, he rose to a position of power on the Ways and Means Committee and, as loyal ally to Roosevelt, was instrumental in developing New Deal tax and coal programs. He was appointed to the United States Circuit Court for the District of Columbia in 1938, but resigned during World War II to become director of economic stabilization and later director of war mobilization. He developed a strong friendship with President Truman who appointed him secretary of the treasury.

Vinson's public philosophy, including his theory of the Supreme Court's role, was shaped by these momentous events. He believed the federal government needed the power to solve the enormous problems threatening the nation. He was pragmatic and, while serving in all three branches, had participated in the process of big government winning the greatest war in history and taming the worst political-economic crisis in the life of the United States. He had faith born of experience that American political institutions and the American public had the judgment to successfully resolve competing interests for the public good.

CONTRIBUTION TO CRIMINAL PROCEDURE In 1946, a liberal bloc of four justices (Black, Douglas, Murphy, and Rutledge) came close to inaugurating the incorporation of the Bill of Rights. Vinson opposed this action and, during his tenure, the number of justices opposed to incorporation increased as Murphy and Rutledge were replaced by Clark and Minton. Also, Justices Frankfurter and Jackson, while of a more liberal temperament and more willing to find for defendants under the Due Process Clause, were opposed to the incorporation doctrine.

SIGNATURE OPINION Although Vinson voted in favor of the federal government in its heavy-handed repression of American communists in loyalty cases during the cold war, he drew a line at the use of the courts to stifle traditional rights. The right to bail came up in *Stack v. Boyle* (1951). Pre-trial bail was set at fifty thousand dollars each for leaders of the American Communist Party on trial for the theoretical advocacy of the violent overthrow of the government. Writing for the Court, Vinson held that the bail was excessive because it was set at a figure higher than reasonably calculated to giving adequate assurance that the defendant would return to stand trial and submit to sentence. He wrote: "This traditional right to freedom before conviction permits the unhampered preparation of a defense, and serves to prevent the infliction of punishment prior to conviction. Unless this right to bail before trial is preserved, the presumption of innocence, secured only after centuries of struggle, would lose its meaning."

ASSESSMENT Vinson believed in judicial restraint. Having seen a conservative Supreme Court subvert the political will at the beginning of the New Deal, Vinson consistently voted to uphold the power of government in civil liberties (in loyalty oath and Communist conspiracy cases), in economic affairs, and in criminal law. He was appointed Chief Justice in part to calm several personal antagonisms that had developed among more brilliant justices, but his lack of constitutional vision and craft made him an ineffective chief justice.

FURTHER READING

Melvin I. Urofsky, *Division and Discord: The Supreme Court Under Stone and Vinson, 1941–1953* (Columbia: University of South Carolina Press, 1997)

HAROLD BURTON

Ohio 1888–1965
Republican

Appointed by
Harry S. Truman

Years of Service:
1945–1958

Collection of the Supreme Court of the United States. Photographer: Harris and Ewing

LIFE AND CAREER Harold Burton was born in Jamaica Plain, Massachusetts, educated at Bowdoin College and Harvard Law School, and practiced law in the West before settling in Cleveland. His political career included service in the Ohio House of Representatives from 1929, election to mayor of Cleveland in 1935—serving two terms—and election to the Senate in 1941. Although a Republican mayor, he cooperated with the national government, a position taken by few midwestern Republicans. Although sometimes critical of the Democratic administration, Burton was supportive of the economic and social policies of the New Deal and was supportive of the entry of the United States into the United Nations. These positions made Burton an acceptable Republican nominee by a Democratic president. Again, as with all of Truman's nominees, the president and Senator Burton were friends; Burton had been a member of Truman's committee to investigate wartime fraud.

CONTRIBUTION TO CRIMINAL PROCEDURE Burton was a stalwart conservative in opposing the incorporation doctrine. In confessions cases, he was unwilling to use the Due Process Clause to exclude confessions that the Court's majority found coercive. On the other hand, he was in the minority in a case that held that a person who was electrocuted and lived could be executed a second time without violating any constitutional provision, including the fundamental fairness aspect of due process.

SIGNATURE OPINION *Rovario v. United States* (1957). Writing for a 6–1 majority, Justice Burton held that the identity of a secret undercover informant must be made known to the defendant during a trial for heroin possession where the informer had taken a material part in bringing about Rovario's possession of the drugs, had been present with Rovario while the crime occurred, and might have been a material witness as to whether Rovario knowingly transported the drugs. He ruled that the so-called "informer's privilege" is in reality the government's privilege to withhold from disclosure the identity of persons who furnish information of violations of law to officers charged with enforcement of that law. This "privilege" assists effective law enforcement by encouraging people to inform about crime, but where it conflicts with fundamental fairness, it must give way to the defendant's rights to a fair trial. In effect, where a conviction depends upon the disclosure of the identity of a secret informant, the government must either divulge the informant's identity or dismiss the prosecution. *Rovario* indicates that the stalwart conservatives in criminal procedure, while tending to favor the prosecution, adhered to fundamental standards of a fair trial.

ASSESSMENT On the Court, Burton's conservative positions on civil liberties were close to those of Justice Reed. As Chief Justice Vinson, Sherman Minton, and Tom Clark were appointed, they joined to form what seemed to be a voting bloc that upheld the government's loyalty oath programs.

FURTHER READING

Mary Frances Berry, *Stability, Security, and Continuity: Mr. Justice Burton and Decision-Making in the Supreme Court, 1945–1958* (Westport, Conn.: Greenwood Press, 1978)

SHERMAN MINTON

Indiana 1890–1965
Democrat

Appointed by
Harry S. Truman

Years of Service:
1949–1956

Collection of the Supreme Court of the United States. Photographer: Harris and Ewing

LIFE AND CAREER Sherman Minton was born in Indiana, graduated at the head of his class at Indiana University, studied law at Yale University, and returned home to practice law while engaging in local politics. In 1933, he was appointed counselor to that state's Public Service Commission. He played a significant role in developing a state version of the New Deal and was elected in 1934 to the Senate, where he was a staunch supporter of the Roosevelt Administration. His legal knowledge and militant manner in debate led to his rise to a Senate leadership role in which he supported Roosevelt's "court packing" plan. He was an internationalist, a position that was not too popular in the Midwest; and Minton lost his Senate seat in 1940. He worked as a presidential assistant for the next year and was appointed to the United States Court of Appeals for the Seventh Circuit (Indiana, Illinois, and Wisconsin) in 1941. It was Minton's good fortune to be seated next to another freshman senator, Harry Truman, in 1934. They became and remained good friends, which was a key element in each of Truman's appointments to the Supreme Court.

CONTRIBUTION TO CRIMINAL PROCEDURE As a stalwart conservative on criminal matters, Minton joined the Frankfurter-led bloc to halt any advance toward incorporation.

SIGNATURE OPINION He wrote the majority opinion in *United States v. Rabinowitz* (1950), which established the rule that a search incident to arrest could justify the search of the entire premises; a rule that stood until overturned by the *Chimel* decision in 1969. He wrote: "What is a reasonable search is not to be determined by any fixed formula. The Constitution does not define what are "unreasonable" searches and, regrettably, in our discipline we have no ready litmus-paper test. The recurring questions of the reasonableness of searches must find resolution in the facts and circumstances of each case." In *Rabinowitz,* Justice Minton viewed the search as reasonable because the search and seizure were incident to a valid arrest; the place of the search was a business room to which the public was invited; the room was small and under the immediate and complete control of respondent; the search did not extend beyond the room used for unlawful purposes; and the possession of the forged stamps was a crime. The Court was clearly influenced by the Crime Control Model of criminal justice: "A rule of thumb requiring that a search warrant always be procured whenever practicable may be appealing from the vantage point of easy administration. But we cannot agree that this requirement should be crystallized into a *sine qua non* to the reasonableness of a search. . . . The judgment of the officers as to when to close the trap on a criminal committing a crime in their presence or who they have reasonable cause to believe is committing a felony is not determined solely upon whether there was time to procure a search warrant. Some flexibility will be accorded law officers engaged in daily battle with criminals for whose restraint criminal laws are essential."

ASSESSMENT Minton replaced liberal Justice Rutledge and was thought by most observers at the time to be in the liberal mold. However, he fit very closely into the Vinson-Reed-Burton camp; as a New Dealer, he acquiesced to Congress in economic matters, but in civil rights issues, he had the most conservative record voting for the government even more than Chief Justice Vinson. As a judicial conservative, he strongly maintained that the Court had no special obligation to support civil rights and that the Court had no power to legislate.

FURTHER READING

Harry L. Wallace, "Mr. Justice Minton: Hoosier Justice on the Supreme Court," *Indiana Law Journal* 34:145–205 (1959)

CHARLES E. WHITTAKER

Missouri 1901–1973
Republican

Appointed by Dwight D.
Eisenhower

Years of Service:
1957–1962

Collection of the Supreme Court of the United States. Photographer: Abdpm Dapid Ackad

LIFE AND CAREER Charles Whittaker was born and raised on a modest Kansas farm, where he trapped small animals and tracked game to supplement his family's income. He attended the University of Kansas City Law School at night while working as a clerk in a law firm, graduating in 1924. From then until 1954 (as partner from 1930), he practiced law in the same firm, which represented many large corporations doing business in Missouri, first as a litigator and later as an advisor to the firm's large business clients. He was active in bar association activities and became president of the Missouri State Bar Association. In 1954, he was appointed by President Eisenhower as a federal district judge and, in 1956, as a judge to the United States Court of Appeals for the Eighth Circuit. He was known for his hard work and efficiency as a judge and established conservative credentials in ruling that a tenured professor in a private university could be dismissed for refusing to answer questions asked by a congressional committee and the University's Board of Trustees about possible Communist Party affiliations. He was selected to replace Justice Reed, as President Eisenhower was seeking a conservative Republican judge.

CONTRIBUTION TO CRIMINAL PROCEDURE Justice Whittaker strove to put aside ideological considerations and decide cases on their merits alone. This led to a somewhat inconsistent position. While he voted for the defendant in a number of cases, he also opposed the incorporation of the Fourth Amendment exclusionary rule in *Mapp v. Ohio* (1961).

SIGNATURE OPINION *Draper v. United States,* 358 United States 307 (1959). Writing for a 6–1 majority, Whittaker ruled that probable cause existed to arrest Draper based on evidence given by a known reliable informant. An officer was told that Draper, a known drug peddler in Denver, would return by train from Chicago with a supply of heroin. The informant described to the officer the clothing that Draper would be wearing (a light-colored raincoat, brown slacks and black shoes). The Court held that probable cause existed because the officer, having corroborated every factual element about Draper, except the possession of drugs, when he detrained, "had 'reasonable grounds' to believe that the remaining unverified bit of [the informant's] information—that Draper would have the heroin with him—was likewise true."

ASSESSMENT On the Court, Justice Whittaker aligned himself with such conservative justices as Frankfurter, Harlan, Clark, Burton, and Stewart to maintain a slim majority in several civil liberties and criminal procedure cases. Unlike these conservative justices, he never was able to articulate a coherent philosophy of judging by which to guide his opinions. Thus, when he did rule in favor of defendants, his votes appeared to be based more on emotional factors of sympathy than on a firm understanding of the role of the federal judiciary. It would appear that he did not outgrow his position as a district court judge who could achieve success in applying the law; as a Supreme Court justice, it is necessary to expound the contours of the Constitution in novel and difficult cases. It is possible that Justice Whittaker's abilities were overtaxed, for he apparently put in an enormous number of hours and worried substantially about the cases. He fell ill in March 1962, apparently exhausted from his work. He resigned from the Court that year and accepted a position as a legal advisor to the General Motors Corporation.

FURTHER READING

Barbara B. Christensen, "Mister Justice Whittaker: The Man on the Right," *Santa Clara Law Review* 19:1039–62 (1979).

CHAPTER 5

ARREST AND STOP UNDER THE FOURTH AMENDMENT

Because the strongest advocates of Fourth Amendment rights are frequently criminals, it is easy to forget that our interpretations of such rights apply to the innocent and the guilty alike.

—Justice Thurgood Marshall in *United States v. Sokolow,* 490 U.S. 1, 11 (1989)

CHAPTER OUTLINE

KEY TERMS AND PHRASES *(CONTINUES ON NEXT PAGE)*

Arrest
Arrest warrant
Body cavity search
Booking
Brevity requirement
Bright-line rule
Citizen arrest
Custodial arrest
Custody
De novo review
Drug courier profile
False arrest
Field interrogation
"Fleeing felon" rule
Frisk

Illegal arrest
In personam jurisdiction
In presence rule
Internal Passport
Inventory search
Investigative stop
Least intrusive means
Merchant's privilege
Mistaken arrest
Mixed question of law and facts
Police officer expertise
Pretext search
Protective sweep
Radio bulletin
Reasonable force
Roadblock
Scope of search incident to arrest
Search incident to arrest
Seizure of the person
Sobriety checklane
Source city
Stop
Stop and frisk
Strip search
Sui generis
Terry stop
Vagrancy statute

OVERVIEW OF THE LAW OF PERSONAL DETENTION

The physical detention of a person by a police officer is a drastic event even if it is a routine police activity. It is stressful to the person intercepted, whether justified or not; for some it may be psychologically traumatic. To a police officer, even the most routine act of detaining a person may quickly escalate into a life-threatening episode, although firearms are not used in 99.8 percent of all arrests and in only 5.1 percent of arrests are weapons of any type used, displayed, or threatened by police. Indeed, in 84 percent of all arrests, police use no tactics at all—persons simply submit to arrest.[1] Despite this, the law of detention considers all seizures to be forcible in the sense that they are not consensual encounters.

Arrests and Investigative Stops

The law classifies the detention of a person in several ways. The most important distinction in the cases that follow is between lawful and illegal detentions. Because liberty has priority in American constitutional law, all detentions by officers of the state must be justified by legal standards. In the past, there was one dividing line between a lawful or unlawful detention—whether probable cause existed to make an **arrest.** For example, in *Henry v. United States* (1959), two federal agents investigating interstate thefts of whiskey had some suspicion, but no clear indication, that two men they had observed in a neighborhood during daylight hours were involved. The agents observed the men loading a few boxes into a car, followed them for a short period, and then stopped the car. "The agents searched the car, placed the cartons (which bore the name 'Admiral' and were addressed to an out-of-state company) in their car, took the merchandise and [the men] to their office and held them for about two hours when the agents learned that the cartons contained stolen radios. They then placed the men under formal arrest." The Supreme Court reversed the conviction and ruled that the arrest took place when the car was stopped. At that point, the two men were forcibly detained (although they offered no resistance) and the Court ruled that the police needed to have probable cause to lawfully stop the car.

Since *Terry v. Ohio* (1968), the older rule has been qualified. Now there is a lesser type of detention known simply as a **stop** (or **investigative stop**) that can be predicated on a lesser standard of evidence which is typically called "reasonable suspicion." Under constitutional law, both arrests and stops are Fourth Amendment "seizures." Seizures may be lawful, if justified by probable cause or reasonable suspicion, or illegal if an arrest or stop is made on a hunch.

Another important distinction compares seizures to police-citizen encounters that are not detentions (i.e., not a **seizure of the person** under the Fourth Amendment). The latter category falls into two groups: (1) consensual encounters, where a person voluntarily agrees to talk to officers, or even allows a purse or piece of luggage to be searched, and (2) situations in which an officer observes a person in a public place. Both kinds of encounters "intrude[] upon no constitutionally protected interest," (*United States v. Mendenhall,* 1980, p. 552) A police officer need establish *no* level of evidence sufficiency to observe a person in public, but cases have arisen when the person observed was running and was followed by police in various ways.

The cases which have shaped the law of detention arise in two ways. In some instances, a person will sue the police in a civil action for money damages for a wrongful arrest or seizure, often in the nature of a wrongful death action. More often, the legality of a seizure is challenged because a search following the detention produced contraband or evidence derived from a search following an illegal seizure is the "fruit" of a "poisonous tree" and may be suppressed under the exclusionary rule.

This chapter will review arrests, stops, and consent encounters in detail. At the outset, a few brief distinctions and definitions provide useful guideposts:

- When arrested, a person is in the **custody** of the police and relinquishes his or her freedom; the person will frequently be taken to a police station for booking and may be jailed during the pretrial process; the arrest is executed for the purpose of initiating a criminal prosecution. In contrast, a stop confers limited powers in the police to detain a person; it is temporary and not designed to initiate a criminal prosecution but to give an officer a brief time to question the person to determine if suspicious circumstances are, in fact, innocent.
- An arrested person may be thoroughly searched for weapons and for incriminating evidence. A person held briefly under a ***Terry* stop** may be subjected only to a brief pat-down of outer clothing to determine if he or she is armed.
- If a person is properly stopped based on reasonable suspicion, but the personal search is too intrusive or the person is held for too long a time, the officer has overstepped the bounds and has, unlawfully, turned the stop into an arrest. Likewise, a consensual encounter may escalate into an investigative stop or an arrest if the encounter becomes coercive. It then becomes a Fourth Amendment seizure, justified only by the requisite level of evidence.

These preliminary guideposts do not include the full definitions of each subject.

Legal categories are, at times, created by the Supreme Court to fit the needs of an ordered society. In *Terry v. Ohio* (1968), the Court created a new legal category, the investigative stop, for the purpose of bringing police practice within the scope of judicial control. The Court believed that the function was necessary to police work, and, when conducted properly, balanced the needs of law enforcement with individual liberty. In addition to the major categories of arrest and investigative stop, the Court has had to consider other kinds of detention, which only partially fit into the arrest and stop categories, and has, up to a point, made special rules to deal with them. Two examples are detentions for investigative purposes and detention while executing a search warrant.

Detention to Investigate

Detention for investigation of a crime raises several search and seizure issues. A well-established rule is that a person's *physical characteristics,* such as fingerprints, are not protected by the expectation of privacy and, therefore, may rightfully be obtained during an investigation. The one-time taking of a voiceprint (*United States v. Dionisio,* 1973) or a handwriting sample (*United States v. Mara,* 1973) for grand jury investigations, or the required appearance at a lineup or trial so that the appearance of a suspect may be viewed, is not a Fourth Amendment seizure. The Court has extended this principle to the scraping of a dried blood sample from a suspect's finger (*Cupp v. Murphy,* 1973) and the taking of blood samples from suspected drunk drivers under reasonable circumstances (*Breithaupt v. Abram,* 1957; *Schmerber v. California,* 1966).

An issue that has not been fully resolved is whether police may briefly but forcibly (i.e., on demand) detain a person one time for fingerprinting even though a specific suspicion has not fallen on that individual. The issue has arisen twice, in which the Supreme Court held the particular detentions unreasonable Fourth Amendment violations, but has held open the possibility of such detention being lawful. In *Davis v. Mississippi* (1969), police rounded up twenty-five African-American teenagers to collect fingerprint samples attempting to match those found at the scene of a crime. These mass arrests, justified only by a witness's statement that the offender was black, were not authorized by a judicial warrant. The detentions did not focus on a specific group of persons on whom some suspicion fell and involved a second fingerprinting session and interrogations; this violated the Fourth Amendment. Yet, the Court, in dictum, stated that brief detention for fingerprinting may be reasonable because: (1) fingerprinting does not intrude into a person's thoughts or belongings, (2) fingerprints can be obtained briefly during normal business hours and need be taken only once, and (3) fingerprints are an inherently reliable means of identification. In *Hayes v. Florida* (1985), a majority of the Court, again in dictum, suggested that fingerprinting at the scene of a crime would be permissible. In this case, however, the Court found that fingerprinting at the station house was impermissible because the defendant was forcibly taken to the station house without probable cause. Justices Brennan and Marshall's opinion sharply differed from the Court's dictum that on-site fingerprinting without a warrant or probable cause would be permissible.

The Court categorically stated that the police have no authority to detain persons at will and take them to the police station—without probable cause, reasonable suspicion, or consent—to investigate a crime. In *Dunaway v. New York* (1979), Rochester police were told by an informant that Dunaway was involved in a murder and robbery. Without gaining more evidence, the detective in charge ordered officers to "pick up" Dunaway and "bring him in" for questioning. At that point, there was not sufficient evidence to obtain an arrest warrant. The defendant was not told he was under arrest, but he would have been restrained if he had attempted to leave. During the subsequent interrogation, Dunaway made incriminating statements; he was eventually convicted of murder. The Court refused to extend the *Terry* principle to allow taking a person into custody against whom there may be reasonable suspicion of crime. Dunaway could have been briefly detained where he was found and questioned. The actions of the police—taking him to the station—created an arrest that was not justified by probable cause or consent.

Detention and Search During the Execution of a Search Warrant

In *Michigan v. Summers* (1981), Detroit police officers, while executing a search warrant at a house for narcotics, encountered Summers walking down the front steps of his house. They asked for his assistance in entering the house and detained him while searching. After discovering narcotics in the basement and determining that Summers owned the house, they arrested him. In a search incident to the arrest, an envelope with 8.5 grams of heroin was found in Summers' pocket. Although the police did not have probable cause to believe that Summers was carrying drugs before the arrest, the seizure was nevertheless upheld. It was deemed constitutional under the stop and frisk doctrine, with the Court findings that there was reasonable suspicion for the stop and justified by finding drugs in his house, which was searched under the authority of a lawful search warrant.

Summers is general authority for the rule that police may detain homeowners or others present while executing a search warrant. The individual's significant right to liberty is outweighed by law enforcement needs in this situation. On the other hand, the length of the detention is limited by the time it takes to search the house; the police have no reason to extend the detention because they seek evidence from the search of the premises and not the person detained. The warrant establishes the right of the police to be present. The *Summers* rule promotes positive policies. Giving police "unquestioned command of the situation" as a matter of routine is likely to minimize harm to the police and the residents. By controlling the person temporarily during the search, the officers minimize the risk of harm to themselves that may be caused by sudden violence or frantic efforts to conceal or destroy evidence. Detaining the resident facilitates the orderly completion of the search with minimal damage to property, because the owner can open locked doors and cabinets. Detention in the person's own home also avoids the public stigma and inconvenience of being taken to the police station. Further, there is a legitimate law enforcement interest in preventing the flight of a person in the event that incriminating evidence is found.

In the *Summers* case, Summers was searched only after contraband was found in the house and it was established that he was the homeowner. This established probable cause. *Summers* did not create a rule that allows police to automatically search anyone present in a premises during the execution of a warrant. In *Ybarra v. Illinois* (1979), police had a valid warrant to search a bar and a bartender for drugs, but not the patrons. When police entered the bar, they announced to about a dozen patrons that they would all be frisked for weapons. In Ybarra's case, the officers found a cigarette pack that was not immediately seized. A few moments after the "frisk" for weapons, an officer returned to Ybarra, a patron in the bar, retrieved the cigarette pack from his pants pocket, and found packets of heroin inside. The Supreme Court overturned Ybarra's conviction. There was no probable cause to search Ybarra or any patrons, so the search warrant did not justify the intrusion. Nor were there any grounds to arrest Ybarra simply because he was a patron in a bar where drugs were sold since there was no indication that he participated in purchases. "[A] person's mere propinquity to others independently suspected of criminal activity does not, without more, give rise to probable cause to search that person." Further, the Court held that the police had no reasonable suspicion to frisk the patrons; from the patrons' presence and their passive behavior when the raid was announced, there was no reasonable suspicion to believe they were armed and presently dangerous. Dissenting justices argued that the seizure of heroin was the result of an appropriate frisk for weapons. The majority replied: "The 'narrow scope' of the *Terry* exception does not permit a frisk for weapons on less than reasonable belief or suspicion directed at the person to be frisked, even though that person happens to be on premises where an authorized narcotics search is taking place."

ARREST

Defining a Fourth Amendment Seizure and Arrest

The Supreme Court has offered two definitions for a search and arrest. In *United States v. Mendenhall* (1980), the Court said: "a person has been 'seized' within the meaning of the Fourth Amendment only if, in view of all of the circumstances surrounding the incident, a reasonable person would have believed that he was not free to leave." A person can be arrested even though not physically touched by the officer. Also, there are no words that have to be spoken to effect an arrest: Neither an announcement that a person is under arrest, nor a description of a crime for which a person is arrested, nor a reading of *Miranda* warnings (a popular misconception). Examples of personal seizure offered by the Court in *Mendenhall* include: "the threatening presence of several officers, the display of a weapon by an officer, some physical touching of the person of the citizen, or the use of language or tone of voice indicating that compliance with the officer's request might be compelled."

The terms of the *Mendenhall* definition, depending on how they are defined, do not necessarily encompass every situation. The Court has amended the *Mendenhall* definition in *California v. Hodari D.* (1991) to mean that a seizure (and hence an arrest) occurs only when an assertion and intent to arrest is followed by *submission* of the arrested party. This definition evolved as the result of an officer chasing a youth who, while running, threw away some crack cocaine. By holding that Hodari was not seized or arrested, and by disregarding the subjective element of the *Mendenhall* definition (believed he was not free to leave), *Hodari D.* resulted in the introduction of the "abandoned" contraband in evidence. The *Hodari D.* decision is controversial and will be reviewed later in this chapter.

A Fourth Amendment seizure can occur in a variety of ways. In *Tennessee v. Garner* (1985), the Court ruled that when a person is shot by the police, he or she is considered to be arrested: "there can be no question that apprehension by the use of deadly force is a seizure subject to the reasonableness requirement of the Fourth Amendment." A **roadblock** set up intentionally to intercept a driver fleeing from the police becomes the instrument of an arrest if the driver plows into it (*Brower v. Inyo County,* 1989). This becomes an arrest because there has been an "intentional acquisition of physical control." Thus, "a roadblock is not just a significant show of authority to induce a voluntary stop, but is designed to produce a stop by physical impact if voluntary compliance does not occur." Finally, a person, after hearing that a warrant has been issued for his arrest, and voluntarily surrenders to the police, is seized for purposes of the Fourth Amendment (*Albright v. Oliver* 1994, Justice Ginsburg, concurring). In each of these cases, there was an intent on the part of the police to gain custody of the suspect and actual custody. If either element is absent, there is no seizure. Thus, in *California v. Hodari D.* (1991), although a police officer was chasing the youth, the officer had not yet physically stopped him before he threw away some crack cocaine; there was no arrest because there was no physical detention. In *County of Sacramento v. Lewis* (1998), there was no seizure when a motorcycle passenger was thrown into the path of an oncoming police car that was giving high-speed chase through a residential neighborhood. There was no arrest or seizure because it was not the intention of the officer to apprehend the motorcycle driver or the passenger by hitting them. The Court held "that high-speed chases with no intent to harm suspects physically or to worsen their legal plight do not give rise to liability under the Fourteenth Amendment, redressible by an action under § 1983." Because there was no search or seizure, the Fourth Amendment did not cover this case.

The Consequences of An Arrest

When a person is "captured" the person is in the **custody** of state officers. This custody, defined and guided by law, is justified by its ultimate goal. "The purpose of an arrest at common law, in both criminal and civil cases, was 'only to compel an appearance in court.'"[2] The judicial process will put the suspect, now a defendant, through various "screens" (initial appearance, preliminary hearing, grand jury) to determine whether to charge the person with a crime and, if charged, to adjudicate the person's guilt. Because of this goal, many people believe that a "real" arrest does not occur until certain administrative formalities occur at the police station, such as: fingerprinting and identification; **"booking,"** or entering the fact of the arrest in a formal record which reveals if the arrested person has a criminal history; and filling out court papers to further process the suspect. The law, however, does not consider these formalities but defines arrest as occurring at the moment that a police officer significantly interferes with a person's liberty and takes him or her into custody. The lawfulness of an arrest, therefore, is determined by what happens at the moment of the seizure.

Once arrested, a suspect loses his or her freedom of movement and most other rights of personal privacy. The suspect may be intimately searched and have personal items taken from his or her possession (*United States v. Robinson* 1973). The "search incident to arrest" is a major exception to the Fourth Amendment warrant requirement and is examined in detail in a later section.

Arrested persons have no right to prevent police officers from observing their movements and activities. In *Washington v. Chrisman* (1982), the Court announced a clear rule: "[I]t is not 'unreasonable' for a police officer, as a matter of routine, to monitor the movements of an arrested person, as his judgment dictates, following an arrest. The officer's need to ensure his own safety—as well as the integrity of the arrest—is compelling." In this case, a campus police officer arrested an apparently underage student for possession of alcoholic beverages. He followed the student to his dormitory room in order to retrieve identification. As the officer stood outside the door of the room, he observed suspicious behavior of a roommate, entered, and saw marijuana seeds. The Court ruled that the officer had a right to follow the arrested student into the room to maintain secure custody; any motivation the officer had for observing the room in addition to keeping the arrested person under custody was irrelevant.

Because the contraband was in plain view, and the officer was lawfully in the room, the marijuana was lawfully seized.

Probable Cause to Make an Arrest

Probable cause to arrest, as with probable cause to search, can be determined by a magistrate on an arrest warrant affidavit. Most arrests, however, are made without warrants and in such cases the officer must make a probable cause determination. Probable cause was defined in *Beck v. Ohio* (1964):

> Whether that arrest was constitutionally valid depends in turn upon whether, at the moment the arrest was made, the officers had probable cause to make it—whether at that moment the *facts and circumstances within their knowledge and of which they had reasonably trustworthy information were sufficient to warrant a prudent man in believing that the petitioner had committed or was committing an offense.* (*Beck v. Ohio,* p. 91, emphasis added)

Police officers in a squad car saw William Beck driving his car and stopped him without a warrant. An officer later testified that he knew what Beck looked like and had heard reports that Beck had a record and was involved in gambling, but did not refer to a specific informant to provide more solid information about Beck's business. A search of the car was fruitless, so Beck was transported to a police station; a search of his person revealed betting slips in his shoe. The Supreme Court ruled this arrest illegal. At the time the police stopped the car, the officers did not have a level of evidence that would have satisfied a magistrate that Beck was then transporting betting slips. Beck's appearance and prior record were not "inadmissible or entirely irrelevant upon the issue of probable cause. But to hold that knowledge of either or both of these facts constituted probable cause would be to hold that anyone with a previous criminal record could be arrested at will." Thus, hearsay can be used to support probable cause, but it must be more reliable than simple rumors. The *F.R.C.P.* Rule 4(b), for example, provides: "The finding of probable cause may be based upon hearsay evidence in whole or in part."

The Court also made it clear, as with cases in which search warrants are based on informers' tips, that ultimately a court (either in issuing a warrant or in determining after the fact that a warrantless arrest was legal) must be given facts to determine probable cause:

> We may assume that the officers acted in good faith in arresting the petitioner. But "good faith on the part of the arresting officers is not enough." If subjective good faith alone were the test, the protections of the Fourth Amendment would evaporate, and the people would be "secure in their persons, houses, papers, and effects," only in the discretion of the police. (*Beck v. Ohio,* p. 97)

Thus, the probable cause standard for arrest is objective, not subjective.

In a typical case, probable cause is established by the officer's observation of a crime in progress or by the report of an eyewitness. In *Peters v. New York* (1968), a companion case to *Terry* (1968), a police officer observed two men in his apartment building tip-toeing in the hallway. In the twelve years he had been living there, Officer Lasky had never seen these men. The men were still there when the officer had completed a phone call. When he approached them, they fled. He apprehended Peters, who gave no satisfactory reason for his actions. Lasky searched him and found burglar's tools. The Court ruled that "It is difficult to conceive of stronger grounds for an arrest, short of actual eyewitness observation of criminal activity." While Lasky did not actually see Peters trying to jimmy a lock, the other evidence supplied probable cause: facts that would lead a prudent person to believe that Peters was engaged in an attempt to break and enter. In *Chambers v. Maroney* (1970), a light-blue compact station wagon carrying four men was stopped by police on the evening of May 20, 1963, in North Braddock, Pennsylvania, about one hour after the robbery of a Gulf service station and about two miles from the station. Chambers, one of the men in the car, was wearing a green sweater and there was a trench coat in the car:

> Two teen-agers, who had earlier noticed a blue compact station wagon circling the block in the vicinity of the Gulf station, then saw the station wagon speed away from a parking lot close to the Gulf station. About the same time, they learned that the Gulf station had been robbed. They reported to police, who arrived immediately, that four men were in the station wagon and one was wearing a green sweater. [The station attendant] told the police that one of the men who robbed him was wearing a green sweater and the other was wearing a trench coat. A description of the car and the two robbers was broadcast over the police radio.

This is a typical example of police obtaining probable cause from a reliable (and non-secret) informant. It is hearsay, but is fully reliable. Of course, such information would never be mistaken for absolute proof of a crime. In rare cases, the initial information may be given as a misguided prank or out of malice. Also, in many cases, facts are garbled and eyewitness identification of key facts may be wrong, especially about the identity of an offender (see Chapter 9 on Identification.) But, in most cases, felony arrest scenarios are initiated in this way.

Probable cause must focus on a specific individual. In *Johnson v. United States* (1948), an officer standing outside an apartment smelled burning opium in the hallway, but was not sure who occupied the place. The officer knocked and announced his presence. Anne Johnson opened the door and the officer told her "to consider yourself under arrest." The

Supreme Court held that the entry into the home without a warrant was a Fourth Amendment violation. Further, the arrest itself was illegal because "the arresting officer did not have probable cause to arrest [Johnson] until he had entered her room and found her to be the sole occupant." Another common problem confronting police is whether probable cause exists to arrest a person who is in close proximity to another person who is lawfully arrested.

Mere proximity to a person committing a crime does not create probable cause. For example, in *DiRe v. United States* (1948), an informer, Reed, told investigators that he was going to buy counterfeit ration coupons from one "Buttitta at a named place in the City of Buffalo, New York." Agents followed a car driven by Buttitta which had DiRe in the front passenger seat and Reed in the back seat. DiRe was not known to the agents. The car was stopped and Buttitta and DiRe were arrested. After the arrest, counterfeit ration coupons were found on DiRe's person. This evidence was held to be illegally obtained. The agents did not have probable cause to believe that DiRe was involved in the crime. Reed had not named DiRe and at the time the car was stopped, "the only person who committed a possible misdemeanor in the open presence of the officer was Reed, the Government informer who was found visibly possessing the coupons." The police suspicion against Buttitta was based on the word of their informant, Reed. "But the officer had no such information as to Di Re. All they had was his presence, and if his presence was not enough to make a case for arrest for a misdemeanor, it is hard to see how it was enough for the felony of" possessing illegal coupons with knowledge that they were counterfeit. The Court also dismissed the argument that there was a conspiracy simply because DiRe was in the car.

In contrast to *DiRe* is *Ker v. California* (1963) (see Chapter 4). By their own observations and the word of an informer, police had probable cause to believe that George Ker was dealing marijuana from his house. The Court held that the police entered lawfully. After entering, an agent saw George Ker sitting in the living room, Diane Ker emerge from the kitchen, and "through the open doorway a small scale atop the kitchen sink, upon which lay a "brick-like—brick-shaped package containing the green leafy substance which he recognized as marijuana." The Court conceded that the police did not have probable cause to arrest Diane Ker when they entered the apartment. But it ruled that viewing the marijuana in plain view established probable cause to believe that she was involved in the illicit business with her husband. This was not simply guilt by association, but a rational inference. Unlike DiRe, who might not have known that the ration coupons he held were counterfeited, Diane Ker had to know that there was marijuana in the kitchen, and given the probable cause that police had that George Ker was illegally dealing, it was a rational inference that she was "in joint possession with her husband." This amounted to probable cause to believe that she was "committing the offense of possession of marijuana in the presence of the officers."

JUDICIAL DETERMINATION OF PROBABLE CAUSE

If an arrest warrant is not used, then the police officer's probable cause determination must be reviewed by a judge or magistrate as soon as possible. A Florida procedure allowed a person to be arrested on a prosecutor's bill of information and held for a month before being brought before a magistrate. This was struck down as a Fourth Amendment violation in *Gerstein v. Pugh* (1975):

> [A] policeman's on-the-scene assessment of probable cause provides legal justification for arresting a person suspected of crime, and for a brief period of detention to take the administrative steps incident to arrest. Once the suspect is in custody, however, the reasons that justify dispensing with the magistrate's neutral judgment evaporate. There no longer is any danger that the suspect will escape or commit further crimes while the police submit their evidence to a magistrate. And, while the State's reasons for taking summary action subside, the suspect's need for a neutral determination of probable cause increases significantly. The consequences of prolonged detention may be more serious than the interference occasioned by arrest. Pretrial confinement may imperil the suspect's job, interrupt his source of income, and impair his family relationships. Even pretrial release may be accompanied by burdensome conditions that effect a significant restraint on liberty. When the stakes are this high, the detached judgment of a neutral magistrate is essential if the Fourth Amendment is to furnish meaningful protection from unfounded interference with liberty. Accordingly, we hold that the Fourth Amendment requires a judicial determination of probable cause as a prerequisite to extended restraint on liberty following arrest. (*Gerstein v. Pugh,* pp. 113–14)

The rule of *Gerstein* is hardly unusual. The federal government and every state has a rule that requires police to bring arrested persons to a magistrate in a timely manner for initial processing.[3]

The Supreme Court clarified the time period for which a person can be held in *County of Riverside v. McLaughlin* (1991). The majority, in an opinion by Justice O'Connor, ruled that, as a general matter, if an arrested person is brought before a magistrate within forty-eight hours, the requirements of the Fourth Amendment are met. The Court noted that the county's rule that a person must be arraigned within two days (excluding weekends and holidays) could result in being held for five days if arrested at the end of a week, or up to seven days over a Thanksgiving holiday. The Court made it clear that the forty-eight-hour rule is not inflexible. If a person can be brought before a magistrate sooner but the police hold off in order to gather additional evidence, this may constitute a Fourth Amendment violation. On the other hand, a delay of more than forty-eight hours may be justified in a case of "bona fide emergency or other extraordinary circumstance." Liberal dissenting justices (per Justice Marshall) argued that the proper constitutional rule is that a person must be brought before a magistrate "immediately upon completion of the 'administrative steps incident to arrest.'" An interesting dissent was filed by the conservative Justice Scalia. He opted for a twenty-four-hour time period based on his "originalist" research that found that such a time period was common in the late eighteenth and early nineteenth centuries.

In the past, lengthy post-arrest detention without recourse to a magistrate was used to force confessions out of suspects. Such a practice tempts police to abuse their control over a suspect. The rules of *Gerstein* and *Riverside County* rightfully make constitutional what is now standard practice.

USE OF SECONDARY INFORMATION A police officer may depend on a reliable informant to establish probable cause to arrest. An informant could be an impartial witness, a victim, or an "undercover" informant who works for the police or receives lenient treatment in return for information about crimes such as drug sales.[4] This is closely related to the use of third-party informants in order to establish probable cause to obtain a search warrant, (which is discussed in Chapter 4).

In this era of high mobility and instantaneous communications, it is necessary for police to rely on the **radio bulletins** or computer notifications from other police departments as a basis for probable cause to arrest. In *Whitely v. Warden* (1971), the Court ruled that police may rely on a radio bulletin from another police department informing them that an arrest warrant has been issued to make an arrest. But in *Whitely,* the original arrest warrant was defective—it was not based on probable cause. As a result, the arrest was illegal and the evidence seized in a search incident to the arrest was not admissible. The clear implication of *Whitely,* however, was that the officers who made the arrest reasonably relied upon the radio bulletin and should not be held civilly liable for the arrest. They acted reasonably even if there was no probable cause for the original arrest warrant. In *Arizona v. Evans* (1995) (see Chapter 3, the section on good faith reliance on a warrant), the police computer information that Isaac Evans, who was stopped for driving the wrong way on a one-way street, had an outstanding warrant was false. Because the information was based on *court* records rather the police system, a marijuana cigarette discovered in the search was not suppressed because the exclusionary rule did not apply to courts. The merits of *Arizona v. Evans* (1995) aside, the case points to the need for accuracy in police records in order to prevent unconstitutional searches. Justice O'Connor, concurring, stressed that the rule of the case did not apply to police record-keeping systems. She expressed some concerns that widespread computer errors might undermine individual rights.

THE FELONY/MISDEMEANOR RULE The traditional rules for felony and misdemeanor arrests by law enforcement officers differ. Under common law rules, a police officer may arrest a person for a felony when he or she has probable cause to believe that a crime has been committed and that the arrestee is the perpetrator.[5] For a misdemeanor arrest to be lawful, however, the misdemeanor must have been committed in the officer's *presence.* The reason for this distinction, apparently, is that the public safety requires swift arrests for more serious crimes. Because petty crimes are often the result of squabbles between individuals, an arrest based on a complainant's say-so may result in instances of false arrest and legally sanctioned harassment. The general rule for a lawful misdemeanor arrest is that the victim must first obtain an arrest warrant from a judge via a formal complaint. In recent years, this rule has come under severe criticism because it has prevented police from making arrests in cases of domestic violence. Legislatures have rethought the case and virtually all have modified their rules (see *Law in Society* section in this chapter). Statutes have also modified the misdemeanor arrest rule for traffic related misdemeanors not observed directly by a police officer.[6]

CITIZEN ARRESTS A mistaken arrest by a police officer that is nevertheless based on probable cause does not lead to personal, civil liability for the tort of false arrest because the officer acted reasonably. The basic rule for **citizen arrests**—arrests by non-police "civilians"—is more stringent. A private citizen who arrests another is held strictly accountable for any errors made during the arrest; if an individual arrests another person under the mistaken belief that the arrested person committed a felony, then the arresting individual may be successfully sued for the tort of **false arrest.** This is so even if the citizen's actions are reasonable. This rule places a high premium on individual liberty to be free from unwarranted interference. The relaxation of the rule for law enforcement officers is evidence of a policy that seeks to encourage officers to be less fearful of the consequences of their acts so that they will not shirk their duty. This recognized the difficulties that confront law enforcement officers when hard decisions must be made with little time for reflection and under circumstances of heightened stress. This common law rule has the greatest effect on security guards; they cannot arrest a person for theft, for example, without the threat of liability unless they are actually correct. "Unless the owner has given consent, a security guard's search of private property will generally constitute a trespass. And arrests or detentions not authorized by state law generally will expose a security guard to civil and criminal liability for false imprisonment and, if force is involved, for assault."[7] On the other hand, "most states have codified a **'merchant's privilege'** that allows store investigators, and in some instances other categories of private security personnel, to conduct brief investigatory detentions that would be tortious or criminal if carried out by ordinary citizens."[8]

Consequences of Illegal and Mistaken Arrests

A Court obtains jurisdiction in a criminal case when the defendant is physically brought before the court (a form of ***in personam* jurisdiction**). The established rule is that a court does not lose jurisdiction if the defendant was brought to the court by illegal means. In *Frisbie v. Collins* (1952), the Supreme Court refused to interfere with a conviction although police officers from southwest Michigan traveled to Chicago to arrest the defendant. Because their jurisdiction did not extend to Illinois, technically they may have been in violation of the federal kidnaping law! In *United States v. Crews* (1980), a person was arrested without probable cause, charged with a robbery, and thereafter put on trial. The Court ruled that the mere fact that an accused's presence at his or her prosecution is the result of an illegal arrest does not require the suppression of the identification of his or her face as the fruit of the **illegal arrest.**

The Supreme Court more recently upheld this rule in *United States v. Alvarez-Machain* (1992). The defendant, a citizen of Mexico, was indicted by the United States for participating in the kidnaping and murder of Enrique Camarena-Salazar, a United States DEA agent. Federal authorities had Dr. Alvarez-Machain abducted in Mexico, at gun point, from his office in Guadalajara, Mexico and transported to the United States for trial. The federal court of appeals affirmed the dismissal of the indictment on the grounds that the defendant's illegal seizure violated a United States-Mexico extradition treaty. The Supreme Court reversed and held that under the authority of *Frisbie v. Collins* and earlier cases, the trial court had jurisdiction. Chief Justice Rehnquist ruled that the treaty did not specify the only way that one country could gain custody over the citizen of the other country. Also, it was deemed irrelevant that the action of the United States government may have violated international law. Justice Stevens, in a strong dissent and joined by Justices Blackmun and O'Connor, referred to the majority's opinion as "monstrous."[9] The opinion was criticized as a violation of international law.[10]

The most important consequence of an illegal arrest is that evidence obtained as a result of an illegal arrest, being the "fruit of the poisonous tree," is subject to the exclusionary rule and may be suppressed on a proper motion by the defendant. Because of this, the legality of an arrest is a matter of great practical importance when contraband or other incriminating evidence is discovered in a subsequent search. This consequence occurs in many cases discussed in this chapter.

The constitutional law regarding a **mistaken arrest** follows common law doctrines: If an arrest is made by police who act reasonably and with probable cause but arrest the wrong person, the proper remedy is the release of the detained person. The police officer is not subject to civil liability because the officer acted in a reasonable manner. Any search conducted pursuant to the arrest is valid insofar as it discovered any contraband. The rule reflects the idea that probable cause does not require certainty. In *Hill v. California* (1971), police had probable cause to arrest Hill when two men, driving Hill's car, were arrested for a robbery and implicated Hill. The police verified Hill's automobile ownership, description, and association with one of the informants. They went to Hill's motel room to arrest him. A man fitting Hill's description opened the door to the motel room. He was arrested despite the fact that he produced identification indicating he was Miller. The Court held that the arrest of Miller was supported by probable cause; he could not satisfactorily explain why he was in Hill's room and his personal identification could have been fabricated. This probable cause was based upon reasonable facts and circumstances, not the subjective good faith of the police; as a result, contraband seized during the arrest was admissible. Because it can be difficult to ascertain the true motives of police, the distinction between an illegal and a mistaken arrest turns on the objective reasonableness of the police behaviors, not on subjective motives.

The Use of Force

"The criminal justice process rests basically on force, the authority of the state to use raw power, properly and appropriately applied, to apprehend, detain, try, and imprison. The basis of force pervades and colors the whole criminal justice system."[11] The force of the system may be mute, as in prison walls; or symbolized by the judge's robe and the patrol officer's uniform; it may be mostly held in reserve; but when consent and compliance fail, the system, and especially the police, are required to use physical power to carry out its functions. The use of force is problematic because liberty is primary in the American constitutional scheme, but it is justified by its ends and means, the goal of enforcing public law, and by its proper and appropriate application. The common law of arrest translates this last point into a simple rule: the force used to effect an arrest must be reasonable; it must not be excessive. But what is **reasonable force?** Few guidelines exist: One guideline is that the force must be commensurate with the resistance offered by a person whom the police try to arrest. If a person resists with nondeadly-force, then the police may use nonlethal force to subdue him. If a person resists with deadly force, then the police can reply in kind.

THE FLEEING FELON RULE Under the English common law, a police officer could use deadly force to subdue and arrest a "fleeing felon" even though the felon had not used deadly force. Presumably because most common law felonies were punishable by death, their seriousness tended to increase the likelihood that felons were dangerous to the life of others. The fleeing felon rule served as a substitute for the executioner! In America the **"fleeing felon" rule** has been controversial and seriously criticized in the decades since 1960, as the use of the death penalty decreased and many felonies are no longer dangerous to life. By 1980, most states had modified the fleeing felon rule by statute, and many police departments altered their policies so that deadly force could be used only when a suspect presented clear evidence of violent intentions. These states felt that a blanket rule allowing police to shoot at any fleeing felon was excessive.

The issue came before the Supreme Court, giving it a rare opportunity to discuss the police use of force from a constitutional perspective in *Tennessee v. Garner* (1985). The Court modified the fleeing felon rule as a matter of constitutional law and held, in an opinion by Justice Byron White, that

> The use of deadly force to prevent the escape of all felony suspects, whatever the circumstances, is constitutionally unreasonable. It is not better that all felony suspects die than that they escape. Where the suspect poses no immediate threat to the officer and no threat to others, the harm resulting from failing to apprehend him does not justify the use of deadly force to do so. (*Tennessee v. Garner* 1985, p. 11)

The fleeing felon rule violated the Fourth Amendment rather than the Due Process Clauses of the Fourteenth Amendments. This creates a flat rule: a statute that allows police to shoot-to-kill *any* fleeing felon is void. A due process rule would have subjected the issue to painstaking case-by-case analysis. Deadly force against a fleeing felon is still allowed where reasonable: "Where the officer has probable cause to believe that the suspect poses a threat of serious physical harm, either to the officer or to others, it is not constitutionally unreasonable to prevent escape by using deadly force." Thus, the Court in *Garner* upheld the common law framework: Determining the legality of the use of force by police is based on what was reasonable under all the facts and circumstances of a case; all the Court did was to announce that as a matter of the Constitution, a flat use-of-deadly-force rule in all fleeing felon circumstances was unreasonable.

Justice O'Connor dissented, joined by Chief Justice Burger and Justice Rehnquist. A teenager of average height was shot and killed by a police officer while trying to get over a fence after running from a non-violent house burglary. "[T]he officer fired at the upper part of the body, using a 38-calibre pistol loaded with hollow point bullets, as he was trained to do by his superiors at the Memphis Police Department. He shot because he believed the boy would elude capture in the dark once he was over the fence. The officer was taught that it was proper under Tennessee law to kill a fleeing felon rather than run the risk of allowing him to escape."[12] The youth died of the gunshot wound. On his person was ten dollars and jewelry he had taken from the house. Justice O'Connor pointed out that no matter how regrettable were the consequences of this case, because of the facts and circumstances, it was not unreasonable for an officer to shoot at a fleeing burglar at night since it was not known whether the burglar was armed nor what had happened in the burglarized house. "With respect to a particular burglary, subsequent investigation simply cannot represent a substitute for immediate apprehension of the criminal suspect at the scene." Her opinion reflects a position that is more willing to accord discretion to the police than that of the majority.

It is not always clear whether a legal doctrine has any "real-world" effect. *Tennessee v. Garner* is a positive example which stimulated police departments to modify policies and practices that have had life-saving effects, not only for suspects but also for police. The leading police scholars Jerome Skolnick and James Fyfe write:

> When police have started their attempts to develop policy with the principle that good policing in any situation consists of the actions that best meet the primary police responsibility to protect life, the results have been remarkably successful. Deadly force policies that, in both philosophy and substance, emphasize the sanctity of life over the need to apprehend suspects have reduced killings by police—and the backlash that often follows—without negative effects on the safety of citizens or the safety and effectiveness of officers.[13]

Federal cases dealing with excessive use of force by state officers arise as civil actions under 42 U.S.C. Sec. 1983, and *Graham v. Connor* (1989) issued rules to regulate these lawsuits. When a person is seized, the issue of excessive force must be decided under the more specific Fourth Amendment rather than the more general concept of Fourteenth Amendment substantive due process. Important consequences flow from this. First, the question of whether excessive force was used is to be decided by *objective factors*—the officer's motive is irrelevant. "An officer's evil intentions will not make a Fourth Amendment violation out of an objectively reasonable use of force; nor will an officer's good intentions make an objectively unreasonable use of force constitutional." (*Graham v. Connor,* p. 397) Second, the " 'reasonableness' of a particular use of force must be judged from the perspective of a *reasonable officer on the scene,* rather than with the 20/20 vision of hindsight. . . . The calculus of reasonableness must embody allowance for the fact that police officers are often forced to make split-second judgments—in circumstances that are tense, uncertain, and rapidly evolving—about the amount of force that is necessary in a particular situation." (*Graham v. Connor,* p. 396, emphases added) *Graham* was remanded for reconsideration.

The facts of *Graham* raise a controversial issue. Did the police officers, despite their crude language, act reasonably? Officer Connor stopped Graham a half-mile from a crowded convenience store in Charlotte, North Carolina, after seeing him hastily enter and then leave. Connor did not know that Graham, a diabetic, was driven to the store by a friend so he could buy orange juice to counteract an insulin reaction. Graham left the store because of a long line and asked his friend to take him to another friend so he could get sugar. When stopped, Graham told Connor about the insulin reaction. Connor told him to wait until he returned to the store to discover what happened and to call for backup forces. Graham was handcuffed, his pleas for sugar were ignored by one officer who said, "I've seen a lot of people with sugar diabetes that never acted like this. Ain't nothing wrong with the M. F. but drunk. Lock the S. B. up." Graham passed out twice. He asked an officer to look into his wallet for a diabetic decal and was told to "shut up." A friend brought some orange juice to the patrol car for Graham but the officers refused to let him have it. After discovering that nothing criminal occurred at the convenience store, the police drove Graham home and released him. Graham sustained a broken foot, cuts on the wrist, a bruised forehead, and an injured shoulder.

Brower v. Inyo County (1989) established that a roadblock can be an instrument of force and a means of arrest. Was there excessive force in this case? Brower stole a car and eluded the police in a high-speed, twenty-mile chase. A police roadblock was set up consisting of an eighteen-wheel tractor-trailer blocking both lanes of a road behind a curve, with a police car's headlights pointing at the oncoming traffic. The case was remanded. If police action is related to injury or death by negligence, as in *County of Sacramento v. Lewis* (1998), in which a police car, engaged in a high-speed chase of a motorcycle, ran into and killed the passenger who had been thrown from the vehicle, and there is no seizure, then any constitutional issue of police liability under 42 U.S.C. § 1983 is determined by Fourteenth Amendment substantive due process. The Court ruled that the proper standard of liability is whether the police officer's action shocked the conscience—the due process standard created in *Rochin v. California* (1952).

THE ARREST WARRANT REQUIREMENT

The need to obtain an **arrest warrant,** and the form the warrant takes, are determined by the circumstances and settings under which the suspect is to be taken into custody. This section reviews the law that pertains to arresting suspects (1) in public, (2) in their own homes, and (3) in the homes of third parties. It also reviews the question of detaining and searching persons while executing a search warrant.

• CASE & COMMENTS •

United States v. Watson
423 U.S. 411, 96 S.Ct. 820, 46 L.Ed.2d 598 (1976)

MR. JUSTICE WHITE delivered the opinion of the Court.

This case presents questions under the Fourth Amendment as to the legality of a warrantless arrest. * * *

I

[A reliable informant, Khoury, informed postal inspectors that Watson would furnish stolen credit cards. Acting under their instructions, Khoury arranged a meeting with Watson five days later in a restaurant.] Khoury had been instructed that if Watson had additional stolen credit cards, Khoury was to give a designated signal. The signal was given, the officers closed in, and Watson was forthwith arrested. [No stolen credit cards were found on Watson, but some were found in his automobile. The court of appeals ruled that the arrest was a violation of the Fourth Amendment because there was no arrest warrant and no exigency; consequently, evidence obtained from the search of Watson's automobile and seizure of the credit cards had to be excluded as the fruits of an illegal arrest.]

• CASE & COMMENTS •

II

* * *

Contrary to the Court of Appeals' view, Watson's arrest was not invalid because executed without a warrant. **[a]** Title 18 U.S.C. sec. 3061(a)(3) expressly empowers the * * * Postal Service to authorize Postal Service officers and employees "performing duties related to the inspection of postal matters" to

> "make arrests without warrant for felonies * * * if they have reasonable grounds to believe that the person to be arrested has committed or is committing such a felony."

* * * Because there was probable cause in this case to believe that Watson had violated [the law], the inspector and his subordinates, in arresting Watson, were acting strictly in accordance with the governing statute and regulations. The effect of the judgment of the Court of Appeals was to invalidate the statute as applied in this case and as applied to all the situations where a court fails to find exigent circumstances justifying a warrantless arrest. **[b]** We reverse that judgment.

Under the Fourth Amendment, the people are to be "secure in their persons, houses, papers, and effects, against unreasonable searches and seizures,* * * and no Warrants shall issue, but upon probable cause. * * *" **[c]** Section 3061 represents a judgment by Congress that it is not unreasonable under the Fourth Amendment for postal inspectors to arrest without a warrant provided they have probable cause to do so. This was not an isolated or quixotic judgment of the legislative branch. Other federal law enforcement officers have been expressly authorized by statute for many years to make felony arrests on probable cause but without a warrant. * * * **[d]**

* * * [T]here is nothing in the Court's prior cases indicating that under the Fourth Amendment a warrant is required to make a valid arrest for a felony. Indeed, the relevant prior decisions are uniformly to the contrary.

> "The usual rule is that a police officer may arrest without warrant one believed by the officer upon reasonable cause to have been guilty of a felony . . . ." * * * **[e]** Just last Term, while recognizing that maximum protection of individual rights could be assured by requiring a magistrate's review of the factual justification prior to any arrest, we stated that "such a requirement would constitute an intolerable handicap for legitimate law enforcement" and noted that the Court "has never invalidated an arrest supported by probable cause solely because the officers failed to secure a warrant." *Gerstein v. Pugh* [this volume] * * *

The cases construing the Fourth Amendment thus reflect the ancient common-law rule that a peace officer was permitted to arrest without a warrant for a misdemeanor or felony committed in his presence as well as for a felony not committed in his presence if there was reasonable ground for making the arrest. * * * This has also been the prevailing rule under state constitutions and statutes. * * * **[f]**

The balance struck by the common law in generally authorizing felony arrests on probable cause, but without a warrant, has survived substantially intact. It appears in almost all of the States in the form of express statutory authorization. * * * [The American Law Institute's *Model Code of Pre-arraignment Procedure* in 1975 adopted] "the traditional and almost universal standard for arrest without a warrant."

* * * Congress has plainly decided against conditioning warrantless arrest power on proof of exigent circumstances. Law enforcement officers may find it wise to seek arrest warrants where practicable to do so, and their judgments about probable cause may be more readily accepted where backed by a warrant issued by a magistrate. * * * **[g]** But we decline to transform this judicial preference into a constitutional rule when the judgment of the Nation and Congress has for so long been to authorize warrantless public arrests on probable cause rather than to encumber criminal prosecutions with endless litigation with respect to the existence of exigent circumstances, whether it was practicable to get a warrant, whether the suspect was about to flee, and the like.

Watson's arrest did not violate the Fourth Amendment, and the Court of Appeals erred in holding to the contrary.

[a] This, of course, cannot be the end of the inquiry. Because the Court of Appeals invalidated the statute on the basis of its reading of the Constitution, the Supreme Court must confront the constitutional issue.

[b] Would *you* require the police to get a judical arrest warrant in investigations where they have plenty of time to get one?

[c] Does this "judgment by Congress" violate the plain words of the Fourth Amendment?

[d] In *Entick v. Carrington* (1765) the English Court said that an illegal practice does not become legal simply because it has been practiced for a long time. Is this Justice White's point? If not, what is the meaning of the fact that for years statutes, cases and law enforcement practice have allowed warrantless arrests?

[e] Is the need for law enforcement efficiency a *constitutional* reason? What are the legitimate needs of law inforcement? Could this include the total elimination of arrest warrants?

[f] The majority assumes that the Fourth Amendment absorbed common law practice. Another perspective is that the Amendment was designed to change common law practices in the direction of expanding the protection of individual liberties.

[g] Does the majority make arrest warrants totally discretionary, allowing police to completely avoid prior judicial authorization for arrests?

• CASE & COMMENTS •

* * *

MR. JUSTICE POWELL, concurring.

* * * Today's decision is the first square holding that the Fourth Amendment permits a duly authorized law enforcement officer to make a warrantless arrest in a public place even though he had adequate opportunity to procure a warrant after developing probable cause for arrest. **[h]**

On its face, our decision today creates a certain anomaly. There is no more basic constitutional rule in the Fourth Amendment area than that which makes a warrantless search unreasonable except in a few "jealously and carefully drawn" exceptional circumstances. * * * On more than one occasion this Court has rejected an argument that a law enforcement officer's own probable cause to search a private place for contraband or evidence of crime should excuse his otherwise unexplained failure to procure a warrant beforehand. * * * **[i]**

Since the Fourth Amendment speaks equally to both searches and seizures, and since an arrest, the taking hold of one's person, is quintessentially a seizure, it would seem that the constitutional provision should impose the same limitations upon arrests that it does upon searches. Indeed, as an abstract matter an argument can be made that the restrictions upon arrest perhaps should be greater. **[j]** A search may cause only annoyance and temporary inconvenience to the law-abiding citizen, assuming more serious dimension only when it turns up evidence of criminality. An arrest, however, is a serious personal intrusion regardless of whether the person seized is guilty or innocent. Although an arrestee cannot be held for a significant period without some neutral determination that there are grounds to do so, * * * no decision that he should go free can come quickly enough to erase the invasion of his privacy that already will have occurred. * * * Logic therefore would seem to dictate that arrests be subject to the warrant requirement at least to the same extent as searches.

But logic sometimes must defer to history and experience. **[k]** [Justice Powell then goes on to argue that historical practice shows that the Fourth Amendment was not intended to require arrest warrants and that to adopt such a rule would severely hamper law enforcement].

* * *

MR. JUSTICE MARSHALL, with whom MR. JUSTICE BRENNAN joins, dissenting.

* * *

There is no doubt that by the reference to the seizure of persons, the Fourth Amendment was intended to apply to arrests. * * *

The Court next turns to history. It relies on the English common-law rule of arrest and the many state and federal statutes following it. There are two serious flaws in this approach. First, as a matter of factual analysis, the substance of the ancient common-law rule provides no support for the far-reaching modern rule that the Court fashions on its model. Second, as a matter of doctrine, the longstanding existence of a Government practice does not immunize the practice from scrutiny under the mandate of our Constitution.

The common-law rule was indeed as the Court states it. * * * To apply the rule blindly today, however, makes [little] sense * * * without understanding the meaning of * * * words in the context of their age. For the fact is that a felony at common law and a felony today bear only slight resemblance, with the result that the relevance of the common-law rule of arrest to the modern interpretation of our Constitution is minimal.

* * * Only the most serious crimes were felonies at common law, and many crimes now classified as felonies under federal or state law were treated as misdemeanors. * * * **[l]**

* * * To make an arrest for any of these crimes [misdemeanors] at common law, the police officer was required to obtain a warrant, unless the crime was committed in his presence. Since many of these same crimes are commonly classified as felonies today, however, under the Court's holding a warrant is no longer needed to make such arrests, a result in contravention of the common law.

Thus the lesson of the common law, and those courts in this country that have accepted its rule, is an ambiguous one. Applied in its original context, the common-law rule would allow the warrantless

[h] It is interesting that a practice could exist for centuries before being challenged legally. There was greater acceptance of the legal status quo in the past and a higher level of litigation today.

[i] What is the anomaly? Has the majority opinion simply failed to confront a basic issue?

[j] Do you agree? If so, is it not more important that police get arrest warrants when they can than search warrants? Which are more important?

[k] Is this too easy an out? Having directly confronted the issue of the constitutional text, is Justice Powell evasive? Or is he saying, in effect, that the Constitution is what the justices say it is?

[l] Most common law felonies were capital crimes. Justice Marshall suggests that the common law rule that allowed arrest of felonies on probable cause without warrant should be restricted to violent crimes punishable with death, life or

• CASE & COMMENTS •

arrest of some, but not all, of those we call felons today. Accordingly, the Court is simply historically wrong when it tells us that "[t]he balance struck by the common law in generally authorizing felony arrests on probable cause, but without a warrant, has survived substantially intact." As a matter of substance, the balance struck by the common law in accommodating the public need for the most certain and immediate arrest of criminal suspects with the requirement of magisterial oversight to protect against mistaken insults to privacy decreed that only in the most serious of cases could the warrant be dispensed with. This balance is not recognized when the common-law rule is unthinkingly transposed to our present classifications of criminal offenses. Indeed, the only clear lesson of history is contrary to the one the Court draws: the common law considered the arrest warrant far more important than today's decision leaves it.

extremely long terms, and not to the kind of fraud involved in this case. Do you think this is a better rule than the rule of the majority?

* * * [T]he Court's unblinking literalism cannot replace analysis of the constitutional interests involved. **[m]** While we can learn from the common law, the ancient rule does not provide a simple answer directly transferable to our system. Thus, in considering the applicability of the common-law rule to our present constitutional scheme, we must consider *both* of the rule's two opposing constructs: the presumption favoring warrants, as well as the exception allowing immediate arrests of the most dangerous criminals. The Court's failure to do so, indeed its failure to recognize any tension in the common-law rule at all, drains all validity from its historical analysis.

* * *

[m] Justice Marshall in effect says that justices must engage in constitutional reasoning to "tinker" with fixed rules. In doing so, he seems to produce a rule closer to the intent of the framers than the rule of the majority. The majority, on the other hand, seems to leave unchanged the established rule, but this produces a result that is not what the framers would have been pleased with.

Arrest in Public

Watson upheld the authority of the police to arrest felons in public places without a warrant. It left several questions unresolved; the most important of which was whether an arrest warrant was necessary to enter a home in order to make an arrest. This question was answered four years later in *Payton v. New York* (1980).

Arrest in the Home

Payton v. New York (1980) held that absent an exigency, police were required to have an arrest warrant to enter a person's home to make an arrest. Police had probable cause to believe that Payton committed a murder and robbery. Around 7:30 A.M., six officers went to Payton's apartment without an arrest warrant, intending to arrest him. Lights were on and music was heard in the apartment, but there was no response to their knock on the metal door. About thirty minutes later, the police used crowbars to break open the door and enter the apartment. No one was there, but a .30-caliber shell casing in plain view was seized and admitted into evidence at Payton's murder trial. Payton moved to suppress the shell casing as the product of an illegal arrest.

The majority (*per* Justice Stevens) held that entering the home to make a routine felony arrest without a warrant violated the Fourth Amendment. The government argued that the Fourth Amendment was designed only to prevent "general warrants," and not to require warrants when the police had probable cause to arrest. The Court replied, "the evil the Amendment was designed to prevent was broader than the abuse of a general warrant. Unreasonable searches or seizures conducted without any warrant at all are condemned by the plain language of the first clause of the Amendment."

Was this ruling consistent with *Watson* which overlooked the literal words of the Amendment? The Court did not disturb the *Watson* rule but instead *distinguished* arrests made in the home from arrests made in public places: "[H]owever, . . . [a] greater burden is placed . . . on officials who enter a home or dwelling without consent. Freedom from intrusion into the home or dwelling is the archetype of the privacy protection secured by the Fourth Amendment." The "right of a man to retreat into his own home and there be free from unreasonable governmental intrusion" stands at the very core of the Fourth Amendment. *Payton* is one of several post-*Katz* cases that places a special emphasis on the privacy of the home rather than treating all "expectations of privacy" the same. The majority supported its position with common-law history and trends among the states: a "long-standing, widespread practice is not immune from constitutional scrutiny. But neither is it to be lightly brushed aside." As for the concern by law enforcement that the rule would undermine public safety, the Court made it clear that the police may enter a home without a warrant when there is an exigency.

Justice White dissented, joined by Chief Justice Burger and Justice Rehnquist, giving four reasons to uphold the rule that had allowed police to enter a house without a warrant to make an arrest: the rule was limited to felonies and did not apply to misdemeanors, the privacy of the resident was protected by the "knock and announce" rule, the arrest had to be made in the daytime, and such arrest was lawful only if supported by "stringent probable cause." These are rather weak arguments since the dissent restates conditions that would exist in any event. If pushed to the extreme, such arguments could totally eliminate the requirement for arrest warrants for home arrests, just as *Watson* had, in effect, destroyed any constitutional underpinning for arrest warrants in public places.

The difference between the *Watson* and *Payton* decisions is, at one level, explained by the factual difference between an arrest in public and in one's home. Yet, there is enough similarity in these cases to illustrate how "middle-of-the-road" or "swing" justices influence Supreme Court decision making. In these cases, two consistently liberal justices, Brennan and Marshall, voted for a warrant in both *Watson* and *Payton.* Similarly, three staunch conservatives, Justices White and Rehnquist and Chief Justice Burger, voted against the warrant in both cases. The different outcomes in the two cases may be explained by the thinking of the three "swing" justices—Stewart, Blackmun and Powell—who voted against a warrant in *Watson* (1976) but in favor of a warrant in *Payton* (1980). The swing justices were joined by Justice Stevens, who was appointed to the Court between the two cases. Thus, the facts alone did not explain the different holding in *Watson* and *Payton.* Rather, the attitudes of the justices who evaluated those facts were decisive. The pre-exisitng leanings in favor of or against law enforcement of the "conservative" and "liberal" justices made their votes unresponsive to the differing facts of *Watson* and *Payton.* The justices with less ideological leanings concerning this issue were able to evaluate the cases differently. This "political" way of evaluating the work of the Supreme Court has some power, but it must be noted that justices do not automatically vote in a "liberal" or "conservative" way in each case. This kind of analysis shows that at some level, justices' personalities, temperaments, life experiences, and belief systems come into play in fashioning the rules and doctrines of constitutional law.

EXIGENT CIRCUMSTANCES *Payton* held that police may enter the suspect's home to make an arrest without a warrant when exigent circumstances exist. The Supreme Court has been highly protective of the expectation of privacy in one's home and has narrowly viewed police claims that they have entered under an "exigency." For example, in *Welsh v. Wisconsin* (1984) (see Chapter 6), police entered a suspect's home without a warrant or consent in "hot pursuit" of a person suspected in a non-jailable, first-time, civil driving-under-the-influence offense traffic. The police tried to justify the entry on an exigency basis: that the blood alcohol level of a suspected drunk driver was decreasing over time. The Court found that this "exigency" simply did not outweigh the sanctity of the home.

In *Minnesota v. Olson* (1990), police made a warrantless entry into an apartment in which Olson was a guest, and discovered incriminating evidence. The Court first held that under *Rakas v. Illinois,* Olson had a legitimate expectation of privacy (See Chapter 3). Did the police breach that privacy by entering without a warrant? In this case, the crime—a robbery and murder—was far more serious than in *Welsh.* The Minnesota Supreme Court applied "*Dorman* analysis" to find, under a "totality of the circumstances approach," that there was no exigency in the case at hand. Under *Dorman* a court considers:

- whether the offense is a grave offense—particularly a crime of violence
- whether the suspect is reasonably believed to be armed
- whether the showing of probable cause connecting the defendant to the offense is more than minimal
- whether the police have strong reason to believe that the suspect is in the premise being entered
- whether there is a likelihood that the suspect will escape if not swiftly apprehended.[14]

In this case, Olson was not clearly identified as the driver of a car involved in a robbery and murder. The only link was a few papers found in the car and identified by an unverifiable, anonymous tip. The police did not rush to arrest him when they learned of his identity and knew that he was in the apartment with women who called the police. They had sufficient time to obtain a warrant. The apparent danger of violence or escape was low in light of the police actions. The Minnesota court found, under these circumstances, that no exigency existed and suppressed the incriminating evidence. The United States Supreme Court upheld this fact-based application of the *Payton* rule and the lower court's suppression of the evidence. In Olson, there was no hot pursuit of a dangerous felon nor a situation in which the destruction of incriminating evidence was imminent.

ARRESTS AND SEARCHES IN THE HOMES OF THIRD-PARTY Is a *search warrant* needed to arrest a person who is in the home of a third party, or is an arrest warrant for the suspect sufficient? In *Steagald v. United States* (1981), police obtained an arrest warrant for Lyons. Two days later, they proceeded to Steagald's home, in which they believed Lyons was hiding. Outside the premises, they stopped and frisked Steagald and his acquaintance, Gaultney, and then entered the home to look for Lyons. Lyons was not present, but the police observed cocaine in plain sight. Based on that observation, a search warrant was obtained, and large quantities of cocaine were found in the house. The Supreme Court held that the initial intrusion into the home was unconstitutional. There was neither an exigency, a search warrant, nor consent to authorize or allow entry into the home of a third party to look for Lyons: A warrant to arrest a person does not give officers the right to enter the home of a third party who knows the person named in the arrest warrant. Even if the officers had a reasonable belief that the suspect was in the house, that belief was not "subjected to the detached scrutiny of a judicial officer." The privacy interests of a homeowner superseded the authority of the police to enter under these circumstances.

SEARCH INCIDENT TO ARREST

The police have the authority to conduct a warrantless search of a person for weapons and evidence whenever a person is lawfully arrested upon probable cause for any crime. An arrest always creates an exigency—the risk of injury to the officer and the likelihood of destruction of evidence. A magistrate's warrant is not needed to conduct such a search. Under the warrant-preference construction of the Fourth Amendment, the **search incident to arrest** is one of three well-accepted warrant exceptions; the other two are entries into homes in hot pursuit and automobile searches.

Scope of the Search Incident to Arrest

The question of the **scope or extent of a search incident to arrest** proceeds in two directions, essentially: toward and away from the arrested person. First, how intrusively of the body and clothing of the arrested person is the officer authorized to be? *Chimel v. California* (1969), which dealt with the search of the area surrounding an arrest, implied that the search of the individual may be extremely thorough, but the point was clarified in 1973 in *United States v. Robinson.* Officer Jenks of the Washington, D.C. Police Department saw Robinson driving an automobile and knew that Robinson's driver's license had been revoked four days earlier. Having reason to believe that Robinson was driving without a license, Jenks stopped Robinson and cited him for driving without a license. Under Washington D.C. law, driving without a license was a crime for which a person could be brought into custody at a police station. According to police department procedures, Officer Jenks patted down Robinson's clothing. "He felt an object in the left breast pocket of the heavy coat" Robinson was wearing, could not tell what it was, and reached into the pocket and pulled out a "crumpled up cigarette package." The officer opened it and found fourteen gelatin capsules of heroin.

Writing for the Court, Justice Rehnquist distinguished between the search that may be made of the *person* and a search of the *area under his control* following a lawful arrest, the issue in *Chimel.* Unlike the area of control rule which had varied over time, courts have consistently upheld the right of the police to thoroughly search a person incident to arrest in order to secure and preserve evidence of crime and "to disarm the suspect in order to take him into custody." These reasons are in force when a police officer has probable cause and makes a **"custodial arrest."** When a person is taken into custody, a *Terry* pat-down does not offer the officer sufficient protection against weapons that may be concealed and could be used during the transport to a police station. The arrest was considered proper and the search was allowed under the Fourth Amendment, making the evidence admissible.

Four dissenting judges argued that an arrest for a traffic violation does not raise suspicion of drug possession and that the extent of the search must be limited by the nature of the crime. The majority, however, refused to limit the authority of the police in such a manner. "A police officer's determination as to how and where to search the person of a suspect whom he has arrested is necessarily a quick *ad hoc* judgment which the Fourth Amendment does not require to be broken down in each instance into an analysis of each step in the search. The authority to search the person incident to a lawful custodial arrest, while based upon the need to disarm and to discover evidence, does not depend on what a court may later decide was the probability in a particular arrest situation that weapons or evidence would in fact be found upon the person of the suspect." The Court thus created a **bright-line rule**—this means that police do not have to weigh each arrest situation on the street to guess whether this particular crime justifies a particular level of search. The constitutional rule is that the police may conduct a thorough search of the person upon arrest, without having to account for whether the search was related to the crime or the circumstances of the arrest.

If there is no custody arrest, there is no basis for the thorough search incident to arrest allowed in *Robinson.* Thus, a *Terry* stop, designed for a brief on-the-street interrogation, does not justify a full custody search—only a brief pat-down of the outer clothing for weapons. This limitation came into play in *Knowles v. Iowa* (1998). An Iowa police officer stopped an automobile driver for speeding, issued the driver a citation rather than arresting him and, with neither the driver's consent nor probable cause, conducted a full automobile search that revealed a bag of marijuana and a "pot pipe." Iowa statutes allow an officer either to arrest a person for a traffic offence and bring the person before a magistrate, or allow "the far more usual practice of issuing a citation in lieu of arrest or in lieu of continued custody after an initial arrest." The statutes also authorize officers to make a full custody search of a stopped car, even though a citation has been issued. The Supreme Court held that the search, in this case, violated the Fourth Amendment, even though authorized by state law. The two rationales for the *Robinson* search incident to arrest rule are not strongly supported here. "The threat to officer safety from issuing a traffic citation . . . is a good deal less than in the case of a custodial arrest." As for the second rationale: "Nor has Iowa shown the second justification for the authority to search incident to arrest—the need to discover and preserve evidence. Once Knowles was stopped for speeding and issued a citation, all the evidence necessary to prosecute that offense had been obtained. No further evidence of excessive speed was going to be found either on the person of the offender or in the passenger compartment of the car." The Court also rejected Iowa's contention that a full-blown search of the car might turn up evidence of another, undetected crime.

Chimel deals with the other "direction" of the scope of a search incident to arrest—how far *away* from the arrested individual may the search be conducted? Although the right to conduct a warrantless search incident to arrest has never been questioned, the Supreme Court had, over a half-century period from 1914 to 1969, issued an inconsistent string of rulings on the scope question. In *Chimel v. California* (1969), the Supreme Court sought to finally resolve the issue by handing down a clear statement concerning the proper extent of boundaries of warrantless searches around the person following an arrest.

• CASE & COMMENTS •

Chimel v. California

395 U.S. 752, 89 S.Ct. 2034, 23 L.Ed.2d 685 (1969)

MR. JUSTICE STEWART delivered the opinion of the Court.

This case raises basic questions concerning the permissible scope under the Fourth Amendment of a search incident to a lawful arrest.

* * * Late [one] afternoon * * * three police officers arrived at the * * * home of the petitioner with a warrant authorizing his arrest for [a] burglary. * * * The officers knocked on the door, identified themselves to the petitioner's wife, and asked if they might come inside. She ushered them into the house, where they waited 10 or 15 minutes until the petitioner returned home from work. **[a]** When the petitioner entered the house, one of the officers handed him the arrest warrant and asked for permission to "look around." The petitioner objected, but was advised that "on the basis of the lawful arrest," the officers would nonetheless conduct a search. No search warrant had been issued.

Accompanied by the petitioner's wife, the officers then looked through the entire three-bedroom house, including the attic, the garage, and a small workshop. In some rooms the search was relatively cursory. In the master bedroom and sewing room, however, the officers directed the petitioner's wife to open drawers and "to physically move contents of the drawers from side to side so that [they] might view any items that would have come from [the] burglary." **[b]** After completing the search, they seized numerous items—primarily coins, but also several medals, tokens, and a few other objects. The entire search took between 45 minutes and an hour.

[Items seized during the search were admitted in evidence against Chimel at a criminal trial.] * * *

[The Court assumed that the arrest was valid.] This brings us directly to the question whether the warrantless search of the petitioner's entire house can be constitutionally justified as incident to that arrest. The decisions of this Court bearing upon that question have been far from consistent, as even the most cursory review makes evident.

[Dictum in *Weeks v. United States* (1914) referred in passing to a well-known exception to the warrant requirement: "to search the person of the accused when legally arrested."] That statement

[a] Why did the officers wait for Chimel to return home before searching the home? If Chimel's wife had refused them entry and they arrested Chimel outside his house would a search of his house be just as reasonable? Justified? Could they have demanded entry under the arrest warrant?

[b] A magistrate specifies the things to be searched in a search warrant. By searching without a warrant or under an arrest warrant, does an officer potentially have a greater scope to search than if a search warrant had been obtained?

• CASE & COMMENTS •

made no reference to any right to search the *place* where an arrest occurs. * * * Eleven years later the case of *Carroll v. United States* (1925), brought the following embellishment of the *Weeks* statement:

> "When a man is legally arrested for an offense, whatever is found upon his person *or in his control* which it is unlawful for him to have and which may be used to prove the offense may be seized and held as evidence in the prosecution." * * * (Emphasis added.)

> [Another 1925 case, *Agnello v. United States,* "still by way of dictum" said:] **[c]**

> "The right without a search warrant contemporaneously to search persons lawfully arrested while committing crime and to search the place where the arrest is made in order to find and seize things connected with the crime as its fruits or as the means by which it was committed, as well as weapons and other things to effect an escape from custody, is not to be doubted." * * *

[c] The words "in his control" and "search the place" could logically apply to the actions of the police in Chimel's house.

And in *Marron v. United States* (1927), two years later, the dictum of *Agnello* appeared to be the foundation of the Court's decision, [where agents with a search warrant to seize liquor and a still also seized a ledger. **[d]** The ledger was seized as incident to the arrest of the illicit producers at the still.] The Court upheld the seizure of the ledger by holding that since the agents had made a lawful arrest, "[t]hey had a right without a warrant contemporaneously to search the place in order to find and seize the things used to carry on the criminal enterprise." * * *

[d] The earlier statements about the area of a search incident to arrest were dictum because they were not necessary to resolve the issue. The Marron decision could be seen as relating more to the question of whether the Fourth Amendment particularity requirement was met.

That the *Marron* opinion did not mean all that it seemed to say became evident, however, a few years later in *Go-Bart Importing Co. v. United States* (1931), and *United States v. Lefkowitz* (1932). * * * [In these cases the Supreme Court limited the *Marron* ruling to situations where the things seized incident to arrest "were visible and accessible and in the offender's immediate custody."] * * * [I]n *Lefkowitz,* * * * the Court held unlawful a search of desk drawers and a cabinet despite the fact that the search had accompanied a lawful arrest. * * * **[e]**

[e] Is the *Lefkowitz* decision consistent with the words of the *Go-Bart* opinion?

The limiting views expressed in *Go-Bart* and *Lefkowitz* were thrown to the winds, however, in *Harris v. United States,* decided in 1947. * * * [Harris] was arrested [on an arrest warrant] in the living room of his four-room apartment, and in an attempt to recover two canceled checks thought to have been used in effecting the forgery, the officers undertook a thorough search of the entire apartment. Inside a desk drawer they found a sealed envelope marked "George Harris, personal papers." The envelope, which was then torn open, was found to contain altered Selective Service documents, and those documents were used to secure Harris' conviction for violating the Selective Training and Service Act of 1940. **[f]** The Court rejected Harris' Fourth Amendment claim, sustaining the search as "incident to arrest." * * *

[f] Perhaps the brief deviation of *Harris* from the *Go-Bart* rule had to do with the view, immediately after World War II, that draft dodging not a result of being a conscientious objector, was viewed as treachery and cowardice.

Only a year after *Harris,* however, the pendulum swung again. In *Trupiano v. United States,* [1948], [the Court invalidated the seizure of evidence at an illegal distillery made without a search warrant but pursuant to arrests.] The opinion stated:

* * *

> "A search or seizure without a warrant as an incident to a lawful arrest has always been considered to be a strictly limited right. It grows out of the inherent necessities of the situation at the time of the arrest. But there must be something more in the way of necessity than merely a lawful arrest." * * *

In 1950, two years after *Trupiano,* came *United States v. Rabinowitz,* the decision upon which California primarily relies in the case now before us. **[g]** In *Rabinowitz,* federal authorities * * * [armed with an arrest warrant, arrested the defendant] at his one-room business office. At the time of the arrest, the officers "searched the desk, safe, and file cabinets in the office for about an hour and a half," * * * and seized 573 stamps with forged overprints. * * * The Court held that the search in its entirety fell within the principle giving law enforcement authorities "[t]he right 'to search the place where the arrest is made in order to find and seize things connected with the crime * * *' " * * * The test, said the Court, "is not whether it is reasonable to procure a search warrant, but whether the search was reasonable." * * * **[h]**

[g] Two of the most liberal justices, Frank Murphy and Wiley Rutledge, died in 1949 and were replaced by more conservative justices, Tom Clark and Sherman Minton.

* * * [The *Rabinowitz*] doctrine, however, at least in the broad sense in which it was applied by the California courts in this case, can withstand neither historical nor rational analysis.

[h] On a sheet of paper, trace the zig-zag of the Court's rulings on the scope of the search incident to arrest.

• CASE & COMMENTS •

* * *

[The Court then noted that the line of cases supporting the *Rabinowitz* rule was quite wavering. Furthermore, the historic background of the Fourth Amendment was the strongly felt abuses of general warrants, hated by the American colonists, implying that] * * * the general requirement that a search warrant be obtained is not lightly to be dispensed with, and "the burden is on those seeking [an] exemption [from the requirement] to show the need for it * * *" * * *

Only last Term in *Terry v. Ohio* (1968), we emphasized that "the police must, whenever practicable, obtain advance judicial approval of searches and seizures through the warrant procedure," * * * and that "[t]he scope of [a] search must be 'strictly tied to and justified by' the circumstances which rendered its initiation permissible." * * *

A similar analysis underlies the "search incident to arrest" principle, and marks its proper extent. When an arrest is made, it is reasonable for the arresting officer to search the person arrested in order to remove any weapons that the latter might seek to use in order to resist arrest or effect his escape. **[i]** Otherwise, the officer's safety might well be endangered, and the arrest itself frustrated. In addition, it is entirely reasonable for the arresting officer to search for and seize any evidence on the arrestee's person in order to prevent its concealment or destruction. And the area into which an arrestee might reach in order to grab a weapon or evidentiary items must, of course, be governed by a like rule. A gun on a table or in a drawer in front of one who is arrested can be as dangerous to the arresting officer as one concealed in the clothing of the person arrested. **[j]** There is ample justification, therefore, for a search of the arrestee's person and the area "within his immediate control"—construing that phrase to mean the area from within which he might gain possession of a weapon or destructible evidence.

[i] The dual purposes of the search incident to arrest of the person are extended to the search of the immediate area around the arrest.

[j] The search of a closed drawer is consistent with *Lefkowitz* (1932).

There is no comparable justification, however, for routinely searching any room other than that in which an arrest occurs—or, for that matter, for searching through all the desk drawers or other closed or concealed areas in that room itself. Such searches, in the absence of well-recognized exceptions, may be made only under the authority of a search warrant. The "adherence to judicial processes" mandated by the Fourth Amendment requires no less.

* * *

It is argued in the present case that it is "reasonable" to search a man's house when he is arrested in it. But that argument is founded on little more than a subjective view regarding the acceptability of certain sorts of police conduct, and not on considerations relevant to Fourth Amendment interests. **[k]** Under such an unconfined analysis, Fourth Amendment protection in this area would approach the evaporation point. It is not easy to explain why, for instance, it is less subjectively "reasonable" to search a man's house when he is arrested on his front lawn—or just down the street—than it is when he happens to be in the house at the time of arrest. * * * Thus, although "[t]he recurring questions of the reasonableness of searches" depend upon "the facts and circumstances—the total atmosphere of the case," * * * those facts and circumstances must be viewed in the light of established Fourth Amendment principles.

[k] The *Chimel* case is evaluated through the lens of the warrant-preference construction of the Fourth Amendment, rather than the general-reasonableness construction.

* * *

[The Court noted that the *Rabinowitz* rule creates the possibility for "pretext" arrests, where the police deliberately attempt to arrest a suspect at home so as to avoid the necessity to obtain a search warrant, especially where probable cause does not exist. Thus, in effect, police could operate as if they had general warrants.]

Rabinowitz and *Harris* have been the subject of critical commentary for many years and have been relied upon less and less in our own decisions. **[l]** It is time, for the reasons we have stated, to hold that on their own facts, and insofar as the principles they stand for are inconsistent with those that we have endorsed today, they are no longer to be followed.

Application of sound Fourth Amendment principles to the facts of this case produces a clear result. The search here went far beyond the petitioner's person and the area from within which he might have obtained either a weapon or something that could have been used as evidence against

[l] The justices, if so inclined, pay attention to critiques of the law by law professors, practicing lawyers, and lower court judges, and strive to make the law consistent if this audience points out inconsistencies.

• CASE & COMMENTS •

him. There was no constitutional justification, in the absence of a search warrant, for extending the search beyond that area. The scope of the search was, therefore, "unreasonable" under the Fourth and Fourteenth Amendments, and the petitioner's conviction cannot stand.

Reversed.

[Justice Harlan concurred.]

[Justice White wrote an elaborate dissenting opinion, joined by Justice Black. The gist of the dissent was that the broad search-incident-to-arrest rule of *Rabinowitz* was correct because the searches conducted under it must adhere to a general rule of reasonableness. In this case, the search was reasonable because the arrest alerted Mrs. Chimel, and she would have been in a position to get rid of incriminating evidence after the police had left the house.]

In *New York v. Belton* (1981), the Court brought together the automobile search exception to the search warrant (discussed in Chapter 6) with the search incident to arrest rationale in order to uphold a search of a person's jacket pocket in a stopped automobile. A lone New York State trooper stopped a speeding car on the New York Thruway; discovered that none of the four men in the car owned it or were related to the owner, smelled burnt marijuana, and saw an envelope on the floor of the car characteristic of those containing marijuana. The trooper ordered the men out of the car, searched each, and then searched the passenger compartment of the car. The trooper found a jacket belonging to Belton, one of the occupants. He unzipped one of the pockets and discovered cocaine. The Supreme Court noted that the issue of the case relied on two doctrines: "the proper scope of a search of the interior of an automobile incident to a lawful custodial arrest of its occupants." The *Belton* case, upholding the legality of the search, was somewhat inconsistent with other automobile search rulings at the time of its decision. However, its holding is better explained by viewing the case primarily as one resting on the search incident to arrest rule.

Some questioned the wisdom of a bright-line rule that whenever "a policeman has made a lawful custodial arrest of the occupant of an automobile, he may, as a contemporaneous incident of that arrest, search the passenger compartment of that automobile." Was *Chimel* stretched because the suspects were not near the interior of the car when the search was actually made? *Belton* was not a bizarre extension of *Chimel* because the officer was outnumbered by four arrestees and, even though he had secured them outside the car, he could not be certain that one of them would not bolt for the car and find a concealed weapon. *Belton*'s bright-line holding precludes the argument that under some circumstances a search incident to arrest at a vehicle is unreasonable, as, for example, when two police officers arrest a sole driver.

The Protective Sweep Exception

Maryland v. Buie (1990) established the **protective sweep** warrant exception under the Fourth Amendment based on the reasonable suspicion standard of *Terry* (1968). Justice White, in his majority opinion, defined a protective sweep as "a quick and limited search of a premises, incident to an arrest and conducted to protect the safety of police officers or others. It is narrowly confined to a cursory visual inspection of those places in which a person might be hiding." He noted that *Michigan v. Long* (1983), in a sense, authorized a "frisk" of an automobile for weapons. Analogously, the protective sweep is like a "frisk" of a house to search for persons other than the arrested person who might endanger the officers.

In *Buie,* two robbers, one wearing a red running suit, held up a pizza parlor and fled. An arrest warrant was obtained that day against Jerome Buie and his alleged accomplice, Lloyd Allen. Buie's house was placed under surveillance. Two days later, the arrest warrant was executed by seven officers who entered the house after verifying that Buie was home. They knew that the robbery had been committed by a pair of men and could not be sure that Buie was alone in the house. Upon entering, the officers "fanned out through the first and second floors." A corporal shouted down to the basement, and Buie, hiding there, surrendered. A detective, who then entered the basement "in case there was someone else down there," spotted the red running suit laying on a stack of clothes in plain view and seized it. If the detective's entry into the basement was an improper intrusion on Buie's expectation of privacy, then the running suit would be inadmissible as evidence.

The central issue in *Buie* was the standard of evidence needed by police to go beyond the room in which the person sought was arrested: (i) probable cause, (ii) reasonable suspicion or (iii) no evidence at all? When police enter a house under an arrest warrant, hot pursuit (as in *Warden v, Hayden,* 1967), or another valid exigency (as in *Arizona v. Hicks,* 1987) to arrest a person, they may obviously go throughout the house looking for the person and may open closet doors and look into places where the suspect might reasonably hide. Once the person has been seized, the arrest warrant has been executed and/or the exigency is at an end. At that point, the underlying expectation of privacy in the home comes into play. In *Buie,* the prosecution argued for position (iii)—that under a general reasonableness balancing test, police should be permitted to conduct a protective sweep whenever they make an in-home arrest for a violent crime. The Maryland courts and the United States Supreme Court disagreed, adhering to the concept that under the Fourth Amendment, Buie had an expectation of privacy in those remaining areas of his house. After all, if the police wanted to conduct a search of the house for evidence they would have to obtain a search warrant *(Chimel v. California).* On the other hand, the Maryland courts had ruled that for officers to go beyond the place of arrest in a home, they were required to have probable cause to believe that other persons were present.

The Supreme Court instead opted for position (ii) and ruled that the Fourth Amendment permits a protective sweep if the searching officer possesses a reasonable belief based on "specific and articulable facts which, taken together with the rational inferences from those facts, that the area swept harbors an individual posing a danger to the officer or others." The Maryland decision was reversed and the case remanded.

The Court reasoned that Jerome Buie's expectation of privacy in his home did not immunize other rooms from entry. The balancing approach of Fourth Amendment analysis found in *Terry* and other cases shows a basic concern for officers' safety by allowing them to frisk potentially armed suspects. The protective sweep, similarly, is designed to protect the arresting officers by allowing them "to take steps to assure themselves that the house in which a suspect is being or had just been arrested is not harboring other persons who are dangerous and who could unexpectedly launch an attack." The risk of danger in a home arrest is as great as, if not greater than, an on-the-street or roadside investigatory encounter. "A frisk occurs before a police-citizen confrontation has escalated to the point of arrest. A protective sweep, in contrast, occurs as an adjunct to the serious step of taking a person into custody for the purpose of prosecuting him for a crime. Moreover, unlike an encounter on the street or along a highway, an in-home arrest puts the officer at the disadvantage of being on his adversary's 'turf.' An ambush in a confined setting of unknown configuration is more to be feared than it is in open, more familiar surroundings."

Under this reasoning, the Court made two rules in *Buie.* First, the Court held "that there must be articulable facts which, taken together with the rational inferences from those facts, would warrant a reasonably prudent officer in believing that the area to be swept harbors an individual posing a danger to those on the arrest scene." In other words, a protective sweep must be based on reasonable suspicion. But the Court also held "that as an incident to the arrest the officers could, as a precautionary matter and without probable cause or reasonable suspicion, look in closets and other spaces immediately adjoining the place of arrest from which an attack could be immediately launched." Thus, the "sweep" of the entire house is differentiated from an "adjoining space" search. Justice White also emphasized the *limits* of the protective sweep:

- its purpose is only to protect the arresting officers if justified by the circumstances
- it may extend only to a cursory inspection of those spaces where a person may be found
- it is not a full search of the premises
- it is limited to that period necessary to dispel the reasonable suspicion of danger "and in any event no longer than it takes to complete the arrest and depart the premises."

Justice Brennan, joined by Justice Marshall, dissented, stating that the narrow *Terry* exception has swallowed the general rule that searches are reasonable only if based on probable cause. He argued that the majority's characterization of a protective sweep as a "minimally intrusive" search akin to a *Terry* frisk "markedly undervalues the nature and scope of the privacy interests involved." As he saw it, a protective sweep was not far removed from a full-blown search that was not allowed in *Chimel.* "A protective sweep would bring within police purview virtually all personal possessions within the house not hidden from view in a small enclosed space. Police officers searching for potential ambushers might enter every room including basements and attics; open up closets, lockers, chests, wardrobes, and cars; and peer under beds and behind furniture. The officers will view letters, documents and personal effects that are on tables or desks or are visible inside open drawers; books, records, tapes, and pictures on shelves; and clothing, medicines, toiletries and other paraphernalia not carefully stored in dresser drawers or bathroom cupboards. While perhaps not a "full-blown" or "top-to-bottom" search, a protective sweep is much closer to it than to a "limited patdown for weapons."

Thus, the *Buie* protective sweep holding, while concerned primarily with officers' safety, does operate in tandem with the plain view rule to allow the seizure of contraband or clear evidence in the open. The limitations of *Arizona v. Hicks* (1987) clearly come into play—police should not use the protective sweep as an excuse to hunt for evidence by moving items around. Also, the "adjoining area" rule could possibly be used to extend every in-home arrest into a protective sweep, but this would violate the spirit of Justice White's opinion.

Searching at the Station House

INVENTORY SEARCH When an arrested person is brought to a police lockup or a jail for booking, it is standard practice for an officer to go through and inventory every item of property that the person has. In *Illinois v. Lafayette* (1983), Ralph Lafayette was arrested for disturbing the peace. He was taken to the Kankakee police station where, in the process of booking him, a warrantless search of his shoulder bag, made for the purpose of inventorying his possessions, turned up amphetamine pills. The Illinois Appellate Court ruled that the privacy interest in an item of personal luggage like a shoulder bag during an **inventory search** is greater than that in an automobile inventory search, and suppressed the evidence of the drugs. The United States Supreme Court reversed.

In the Court's opinion, Chief Justice Burger ruled that an inventory search does not rest on probable cause, so the lack of a warrant is immaterial. The inventory search constitutes a well-defined exception to the warrant requirement: It "is not an independent legal concept but rather an incidental administrative step following arrest and preceding incarceration." The justification of the inventory in Lafayette's shoulder bag depended on the balancing of his privacy interests in the bag versus the government's interests. The Court found that the state's interests outweighed those of the individual—the inventorying of all items in a person's possession is therefore a reasonable search under the Fourth Amendment. The Illinois Supreme Court's ruling was reversed and the plain view seizure of the amphetamines upheld.

The government and individual interests that support the conclusion that a station house inventory search is reasonable include:

1. Protecting the arrestee's property from theft by police officers
2. Protecting police from false claims of theft by the arrested person ("A standardized procedure for making a list or inventory as soon as reasonable after reaching the station house not only deters false claims but also inhibits theft or careless handling of articles taken from the arrested person.")
3. Accurately determining the identity of the arrested person
4. Ensuring the safety of all persons in jail ("Dangerous instrumentalities—such as razor blades, bombs, or weapons—can be concealed in innocent-looking articles taken from the arrestee's possession.")

Chief Justice Burger stated that "The governmental interests underlying a stationhouse search of the arrestee's person and possessions may in some circumstances be even greater than those supporting a search immediately following arrest." He dismissed the suggestion of the Illinois court that it was feasible in such situations to secure the property of arrestees in secure lockers and thus preserve their individual rights of privacy.

LAFAYETTE IN THE STATES

"Massachusetts permits inventory searches, but demands adherence to written guidelines explicit enough to guard against the possibility that police officers may exercise discretion in opening closed containers."

Thea Rostad was stopped while driving for speeding and swerving, and arrested for driving without a license by a Belchertown police officer. At the police station an "officer unzipped and opened the defendant's handbag and inventoried its contents, which included bags and packets containing drugs." This was done pursuant to a written policy that read: "[t]he officer-in-charge or an officer designated by him shall search the arrestee and make an inventory of all items collected. The arrestee shall be asked to sign the inventory list." The Supreme Judicial Court of Massachusetts held this inventory search to violate Article 14 of the Massachusetts Declaration of Rights, which requires probable cause for all searches. An inventory exception is allowed for reasons given in federal cases, but any inventory must be conducted under specific written regulations. "[W]e do not agree that the written policy of the Belchertown police, . . . was specific or 'obvious' enough. More precisely, perhaps, we do not agree that the policy was explicit enough to guard against the possibility that police officers would exercise discretion with respect to whether to open closed wallets and handbags as part of their inventory search." *Commonwealth v. Rostad,* 410 Mass. 618, 574 N.E.2d 381 (1991)

Barry Latzer, *State Constitutional Criminal Law,* § 3:22.

In dictum, the Chief Justice referred to whether or not a person can be ordered to disrobe at the station house: "Police conduct that would be impractical or unreasonable—or embarrassingly intrusive—on the street can more readily—and privately—be performed at the station. For example, the interests supporting a search incident to arrest would hardly justify disrobing an arrestee on the street, but the practical necessities of routine jail administration may even justify taking a prisoner's clothes before confining him, although that step would be rare."

WARRANTLESS STATIONHOUSE SEARCH FOR EVIDENCE An inventory search is not a search for evidence of a crime. If such evidence does turn up in plain view, it may be seized. The Supreme Court has held that evidence, such as a locked footlocker that is in police custody following an arrest, cannot be opened by the police without having obtained a search warrant (*United States v. Chadwick,* 1977). The Court has held that if the police have probable cause to believe that the clothing worn by an arrested person contains evidence of a crime, such as paint chips from the scene of a burglary, the police may, without a warrant, require the person in a lockup to exchange his clothing for other clothing. Such a seizure can be made at the time of the inventory or, as in *United States v. Edwards* (1974), ten hours after the defendant was locked up. The Supreme Court found that the time delay was reasonable because the police waited until morning, when a substitute set of clothing could be purchased. The *Edwards* case fell within the search incident to arrest exception and made clear that when a person is in a police lockup or jail, the exigency that supports the search incident to arrest (i.e., destruction of evidence) may continue for considerable periods of time.

A warrantless search was also upheld in *Cupp v. Murphy* (1973). The search and seizure consisted of police at a police station taking dry blood scrapings from the finger of a man who voluntarily appeared at a police station after the strangulation death of his wife. When the police noticed the stain and the man held his hands behind his back, an exigency arose because he might have destroyed evidence. *Cupp* is problematic because at the time the blood was scraped from the individual's finger there was no formal custodial arrest. In that case, the police had only reasonable suspicion that the person murdered his wife, but their action was a very limited intrusion, and the evidence was the kind that could be readily destroyed. Under these circumstances, the search and seizure was constitutional.

STRIP SEARCHES The Supreme Court has not dealt with the issue of whether the **strip search** of a person held in jail on a relatively minor crime or offense is reasonable. In *Bell v. Wolfish* (1979), the Court ruled on many conditions of confinement of pretrial detainees that also housed convicted prisoners awaiting transportation or serving short sentences. Detainees who were held in a federal jail on serious federal charges were required to expose their body cavities for visual inspection as a part of a strip search conducted after every contact visit with a person from outside the institution. The practice was justified by correctional authorities "not only to discover but also to deter the smuggling of weapons, drugs, and other contraband into the institution." The Supreme Court applied the general reasonableness construction of the Fourth Amendment in upholding this practice as reasonable. "A detention facility is a unique place fraught with serious security dangers. Smuggling of money, drugs, weapons, and other contraband is all too common an occurrence."

On the other hand, lower federal and state courts have held blanket strip search, or **body cavity search,** regulations and practices unreasonable for minor crimes. The Seventh Circuit Court of Appeals, in *Mary Beth G. v. City of Chicago* (1983),[15] described strip searches as "demeaning, dehumanizing, undignified, humiliating, terrifying, unpleasant, embarrassing, repulsive, signifying degradation and submission." A City of Chicago policy in force from 1952 to 1980 required all females who were detained to be subjected to a strip search regardless of the charges while all males were patted down. In four consolidated cases, women had been subjected to strip searches after arrests for having outstanding parking tickets, failing to produce a driver's license, and disorderly conduct. The Court of Appeals for the Seventh Circuit found these searches to be within the search incident to arrest exception to the warrant requirement and relied on the *Bell v. Wolfish* balancing test to determine whether these strip searches were reasonable. The government's primary justification for the strip searches was to prevent the women from bringing weapons or contraband into the jail. The specific holding of *Wolfish* did not apply to the Chicago cases because the essential facts differed: in *Mary Beth G.,* the plaintiffs "are minor offenders who were not inherently dangerous and who were being detained only briefly while awaiting bond." Further, *Wolfish* "does not validate strip searches in detention settings *per se.*" After carefully weighing the competing interests, the Seventh Circuit held that the strip searches in Chicago bore an insubstantial relationship to security needs and, when balanced against the plaintiff's privacy interests, could not be considered reasonable.[16] Despite such rulings, municipal police departments in many places have continued to use strip and body cavity searches in inappropriate situations and have lost substantial lawsuits as a result. Some departments have instituted regulations to utilize these searches when reasonable. "Two states, New Jersey and Tennessee, have passed statutes requiring a search warrant or consent in order to perform a visual body cavity search." In neither state have police departments complained that these laws made their lockups unsafe.[17]

STOP AND FRISK

This section explores the establishment and characteristics of the second major category of personal seizure: the investigative stop.

Establishing the Constitutional Authority to Stop

Arrest law is rooted in common law cases going back hundreds of years. Virtually no law existed regarding the temporary stopping of individuals by the police in order to obtain information, although organized police forces exercised this power as a matter of custom since their inception in the nineteenth-century. In the 1960s, state statutes and cases began to define the so-called **"stop and frisk"** power. These laws generated constitutional challenges that soon landed on the Supreme Court's doorstep. The basic rules were formulated in *Terry*.

Terry was handed down during an explosive moment in American history—an extended period of intense racial conflict that boiled over into hundreds of inner-city riots that lasted from 1964 to 1972 reaching its highest pitch in the summers of 1967 and 1968. The central irritant fueling this unrest was episodes between largely all-white police forces and mostly young, male African Americans who felt that the promises of the civil rights movement were not being fulfilled.[18] Given the overheated political climate of 1968, some commentators suggest that the liberal Warren Court justices voted to extend the powers of the police in part as a way of mollifying the bitter attacks on the Court by the police establishment and many conservatives in Congress following the 1966 decision in *Miranda v. Arizona*.[19] Journalist Fred Graham, in this skeptical vein, noted that "[t]he Supreme

• CASE & COMMENTS •

Terry v. Ohio
392 U.S. 1, 88 S.Ct. 1868, 20 L.Ed.2d 889 (1968)

MR. CHIEF JUSTICE WARREN delivered the opinion of the Court.

This case presents serious questions concerning the role of the Fourth Amendment in the confrontation on the street between the citizen and the policeman investigating suspicious circumstances.

Petitioner Terry was convicted of carrying a concealed weapon. * * * Officer McFadden testified that while he was patrolling in plain clothes in downtown Cleveland [one] afternoon * * * his attention was attracted by two men, Chilton and Terry, standing on the corner of Huron Road and Euclid Avenue. * * * [H]e was unable to say precisely what first drew his eye to them. However, he testified that he had been a policeman for thirty-nine years. * * * [H]e had developed routine habits of observation over the years[;] * * * he would "stand and watch people or walk and watch people at many intervals of the day." **[a]** He added: "Now, in this case when I looked over they didn't look right to me at the time."

* * * [Officer McFadden saw them pace up and down the block five or six times each, pausing frequently to look into the window of a jewelry store and to confer.] After this had gone on for 10 to 12 minutes, the two men walked off together [following a third]. * * *

* * * He testified that * * * he suspected the two men of "casing a job, a stick-up," and that he considered it his duty as a police officer to investigate further. **[b]** He added that he feared "they may have a gun." * * * Deciding that the situation was ripe for direct action, Officer McFadden approached the three men, identified himself as a police officer and asked for their names. At this point his knowledge was confined to what he had observed. * * * When the men "mumbled something" in response to his inquiries, Officer McFadden grabbed petitioner Terry, spun him around * * * and patted down the outside of his clothing. In the left breast pocket of Terry's overcoat Officer McFadden felt a pistol. * * * At this point, * * * the officer ordered all three men to enter Zucker's store. As they went in, he removed Terry's overcoat completely [and] removed a .38-caliber revolver from the pocket. * * * [Pat-downs of Chilton and Katz produced a gun on Chilton but not on Katz.] The officer testified that he only patted the men down to see whether they had weapons, and that he did not put his hands beneath the outer garments of either Terry or Chilton until he felt their guns. * * *

[a] The case does not indicate that Terry and Chilton were African Americans and the third who joined them, Katz, was a white male.

[b] Is Officer McFadden's suspicion based on facts? Are they reasonable? Is there probable cause to arrest the petitioners on the basis of what he saw? For what crime?

• CASE & COMMENTS •

I

* * * Unquestionably petitioner was entitled to the protection of the Fourth Amendment as he walked down the street in Cleveland. * * * The question is whether in all the circumstances of this on-the-street encounter, his right to personal security was violated by an unreasonable search and seizure.

* * * [T]his question thrusts to the fore difficult and troublesome issues regarding a sensitive area of police activity[:] * * * the power of the police to "stop and frisk"—as it is sometimes euphemistically termed—suspicious persons. * * *

[The police claim the needed authority to deal with street encounters and that the brief detention of a "stop and frisk" not amounting to arrest should not be governed by the Fourth Amendment. **[c]** The defendant argues that unless the police have probable cause to arrest, they have no power under the Fourth Amendment to forcibly detain a person temporarily or to **frisk** them.]

In this context we approach the issues in this case mindful of the limitations of the judicial function in controlling the myriad daily situations in which policemen and citizens confront each other on the street. * * *

The exclusionary rule has its limitations, however, as a tool of judicial control. It cannot properly be invoked to exclude the products of legitimate police investigative techniques on the ground that much conduct which is closely similar involves unwarranted intrusions upon constitutional protections. **[d]** Moreover, in some contexts the rule is ineffective as a deterrent. Street encounters between citizens and police officers are incredibly rich in diversity. They range from wholly friendly exchanges of pleasantries or mutually useful information to hostile confrontations of armed men involving arrests, or injuries, or loss of life. Moreover, hostile confrontations are not all of a piece. Some of them begin in a friendly enough manner, only to take a different turn upon the injection of some unexpected element into the conversation. Encounters are initiated by the police for a wide variety of purposes, some of which are wholly unrelated to a desire to prosecute for crime. **[e]** Doubtless some police **"field interrogation"** conduct violates the Fourth Amendment. But a stern refusal by this Court to condone such activity does not necessarily render it responsive to the exclusionary rule. Regardless of how effective the rule may be where obtaining convictions is an important objective of the police, it is powerless to deter invasions of constitutionally guaranteed rights where the police either have no interest in prosecuting or are willing to forgo successful prosecution in the interest of serving some other goal.

Proper adjudication of cases in which the exclusionary rule is invoked demands a constant awareness of these limitations. The wholesale harassment by certain elements of the police community, of which minority groups, particularly Negroes, frequently complain, will not be stopped by the exclusion of any evidence from any criminal trial. Yet a rigid and unthinking application of the exclusionary rule, in futile protest against practices which it can never be used effectively to control, may exact a high toll in human injury and frustration of efforts to prevent crime. **[f]** No judicial opinion can comprehend the protean variety of the street encounter, and we can only judge the facts of the case before us. Nothing we say today is to be taken as indicating approval of police conduct outside the legitimate investigative sphere. Under our decision, courts still retain their traditional responsibility to guard against police conduct which is overbearing or harassing, or which trenches upon personal security without the objective evidentiary justification which the Constitution requires. When such conduct is identified, it must be condemned by the judiciary and its fruits must be excluded from evidence in criminal trials. * * *

* * * **[g]** [W]e turn our attention to the quite narrow question posed by the facts before us: whether it is always unreasonable for a policeman to seize a person and subject him to a limited search for weapons unless there is probable cause for an arrest. * * *

II

Our first task is to establish at what point in this encounter the Fourth Amendment becomes relevant. That is, we must decide whether and when Officer McFadden "seized" Terry and whether and when he conducted a "search." * * * It must be recognized that whenever a police officer accosts an

[c] The police argument is revolutionary as a point of arrest law. They ask for constitutional authority for "field interrogation"—a well-established practice.

[d] Just because a legal process is abused does not mean that it should be abolished.

[e] Terry invokes the exclusionary rule to have the gun suppressed, claiming that the initial stop was not based on probable cause and thus was unconstitutional. Does it matter to the resolution of this case that in some other cases individuals who are stopped by the police without justification will not be able to invoke the exclusionary rule because nothing was seized and the individual released?

[f] *Terry* was decided in the midst of the "long hot summers" from 1964 to 1972, during which major riots by disaffected African Americans occurred in hundreds of cities, often with loss of life and major property damage. Tensions between largely all-white police forces and minority communities were at a fever pitch throughout this period.

[g] Note that the issue is couched in the terms of the Fourth Amendment: seizure and probable cause.

• CASE & COMMENTS •

individual and restrains his freedom to walk away, he has "seized" that person. And it is nothing less than sheer torture of the English language to suggest that a careful exploration of the outer surfaces of a person's clothing all over his or her body in an attempt to find weapons is not a "search." * * * It is a serious intrusion upon the sanctity of the person. * * * **[h]**

[h] Thus, by stopping and frisking Terry, Officer McFadden seized and searched him. Note that the frisk is defined as a limited search for one purpose only.

* * * This Court has held in the past that a search which is reasonable at its inception may violate the Fourth Amendment by virtue of its intolerable intensity and scope. * * * The scope of the search must be "strictly tied to and justified by" the circumstances which render its initiation permissible. * * *

* * * We therefore reject the notions that the Fourth Amendment does not come into play at all as a limitation upon police conduct if the officers stop short of something called a "technical arrest" or a "full-blown search."

[The next question is whether this seizure and search were unreasonable, that is, whether the officer's action was justified at its inception and whether it was reasonably related in scope to the circumstances that justified the interference in the first place.]

III

* * * [W]e deal here with an entire rubric of police conduct—necessarily swift action predicated upon the on-the-spot observations of the officer on the beat—which historically has not been, and as a practical matter could not be, subjected to the warrant procedure. **[i]** Instead, the conduct involved in this case must be tested by the Fourth Amendment's general proscription against unreasonable searches and seizures.

[i] *Terry* here solidifies the "general-reasonableness" construction of the Fourth Amendment.

Nonetheless, the notions which underlie both the warrant procedure and the requirement of probable cause remain fully relevant in this context. * * * **[j]** [I]n justifying the particular intrusion the police officer must be able to point to specific and articulable facts which, taken together with rational inferences from those facts, reasonably warrant that intrusion. The scheme of the Fourth Amendment becomes meaningful only when it is assured that at some point the conduct of those charged with enforcing the laws can be subjected to the more detached, neutral scrutiny of a judge who must evaluate the reasonableness of a particular search or seizure in light of the particular circumstances. **[k]** And in making that assessment it is imperative that the facts be judged against an objective standard: would the facts available to the officer at the moment of the seizure or the search "warrant a man of reasonable caution in the belief" that the action taken was appropriate? * * * Anything less would invite intrusions upon constitutionally guaranteed rights based on nothing more substantial than inarticulate hunches, a result this Court has consistently refused to sanction. * * * And simple "'good faith on the part of the arresting officer is not enough.' * * * If subjective good faith alone were the test, the protections of the Fourth Amendment would evaporate, and the people would be 'secure in their persons, houses, papers, and effects,' only in the discretion of the police." * * *

[j] This is the key rule governing "stops.'

[k] If a stop is challenged in court, the police officer must provide *articulable facts* to show that she had a good reason to make the stop. Note that this paragraph does not use the words "probable cause" or "reasonable suspicion."

[The Court noted that the police have an interest to prevent and detect crime that necessitates temporary stops of individuals to inquire into suspicious circumstances.]

The crux of this case, however, is not the propriety of Officer McFadden's taking steps to investigate petitioner's suspicious behavior, but rather, whether there was justification for McFadden's invasion of Terry's personal security by searching him for weapons in the course of that investigation. **[l]** * * * Certainly it would be unreasonable to require that police officers take unnecessary risks in the performance of their duties. American criminals have a long tradition of armed violence, and every year in this country many law enforcement officers are killed in the line of duty. * * *

[l] The Court turns its attention to the frisk, and devotes more attention to this subject than to the stop.

In view of these facts, we cannot blind ourselves to the need for law enforcement officers to protect themselves and other prospective victims of violence in situations where they may lack probable cause for an arrest. * * *

We must still consider, however, the nature and quality of the intrusion on individual rights which must be accepted if police officers are to be conceded the right to search for weapons in situations where probable cause to arrest for crime is lacking. Even a limited search of the outer

• CASE & COMMENTS •

clothing for weapons constitutes a severe, though brief, intrusion upon cherished personal security, and it must surely be an annoying, frightening, and perhaps humiliating experience. **[m]** Petitioner contends that such an intrusion is permissible only incident to a lawful arrest, either for a crime involving the possession of weapons or for a crime the commission of which led the officer to investigate in the first place. However, this argument must be closely examined.

* * * [Terry] says it is unreasonable for the policeman to [disarm a suspect] until such time as the situation evolves to a point where there is probable cause to make an arrest. When that point has been reached, petitioner would concede the officer's right to conduct a search of the suspect for weapons, fruits or instrumentalities of the crime, or "mere" evidence, incident to the arrest.

There are two weaknesses in this line of reasoning, however. First, it fails to take account of traditional limitations upon the scope of searches, and thus recognizes no distinction in purpose, character, and extent between a search incident to an arrest and a limited search for weapons. **[n]** The former, although justified in part by the acknowledged necessity to protect the arresting officer from assault with a concealed weapon, * * * is also justified on other grounds, and can therefore involve a relatively extensive exploration of the person. A search for weapons in the absence of probable cause to arrest, however, must, like any other search, be strictly circumscribed by the exigencies which justify its initiation. * * * Thus it must be limited to that which is necessary for the discovery of weapons which might be used to harm the officer or others nearby, and may realistically be characterized as something less than a "full" search. * * *

* * * [Second,] [a]n arrest is a wholly different kind of intrusion upon individual freedom from a limited search for weapons, and the interests each is designed to serve are likewise quite different. An arrest is the initial stage of a criminal prosecution. It is intended to vindicate society's interest in having its laws obeyed, and it is inevitably accompanied by future interference with the individual's freedom of movement, whether or not trial or conviction ultimately follows. **[o]** The protective search for weapons, on the other hand, constitutes a brief, though far from inconsiderable, intrusion upon the sanctity of the person. It does not follow that because an officer may lawfully arrest a person only when he is apprised of facts sufficient to warrant a belief that the person has committed or is committing a crime, the officer is equally unjustified, absent that kind of evidence, in making any intrusions short of an arrest. Moreover, a perfectly reasonable apprehension of danger may arise long before the officer is possessed of adequate information to justify taking a person into custody for the purpose of prosecuting him for a crime. * * *

Our evaluation of the proper balance that has to be struck in this type of case leads us to conclude that there must be a narrowly drawn authority to permit a reasonable search for weapons for the protection of the police officer, where he has reason to believe that he is dealing with an armed and dangerous individual, regardless of whether he has probable cause to arrest the individual for a crime. The officer need not be absolutely certain that the individual is armed; the issue is whether a reasonably prudent man in the circumstances would be warranted in the belief that his safety or that of others was in danger. * * * And in determining whether the officer acted reasonably in such circumstances, due weight must be given, not to his inchoate and unparticularized suspicion or "hunch," but to the specific reasonable inferences which he is entitled to draw from the facts in light of his experience. * * *

IV

* * * We think * * * a reasonably prudent man would have been warranted in believing petitioner was armed and thus presented a threat to the officer's safety while he was investigating his suspicious behavior. * * * **[p]** We cannot say [Officer McFadden's] decision at that point to seize Terry and pat his clothing for weapons was the product of a volatile or inventive imagination, or was undertaken simply as an act of harassment; the record evidences the tempered act of a policeman who in the course of an investigation had to make a quick decision as to how to protect himself and others from possible danger, and took limited steps to do so.

[m] In this case Officer McFadden placed his hands on Terry's coat (the frisk) simultaneously with the stop. He did not have probable cause to believe Terry was armed. Terry was arrested *after* the frisk disclosed a gun. Thus, the case facts do not fit the rules of a 'search incident to arrest.'

[n] The Court draws a fairly clear distinction between a full search after arrest and a limited frisk (pat down) after or accompanying a stop.

[o] The Court slips back to explaining and justifying a stop and compares it to a full custody arrest. This analysis of the stop is interleaved with that of the frisk, making it difficult to untangle the two issues.

[p] The general rules laid down in the case are applied to the specific facts. The Court concludes that Terry's seizure was based on more than a hunch.

• CASE & COMMENTS •

* * *

* * * [q] The sole justification of the search in the present situation is the protection of the police officer and others nearby, and it must therefore be confined in scope to an intrusion reasonably designed to discover guns, knives, clubs, or other hidden instruments for the assault of the police officer.

[q] The Court reemphasizes the limited scope of the frisk.

* * *

V

* * * We merely hold today that where a police officer observes unusual conduct which leads him reasonably to conclude in light of his experience that criminal activity may be afoot and that the persons with whom he is dealing may be armed and presently dangerous, where in the course of investigating this behavior he identifies himself as a policeman and makes reasonable inquiries, and where nothing in the initial stages of the encounter serves to dispel his reasonable fear for his own or others' safety, he is entitled for the protection of himself and others in the area to conduct a carefully limited search of the outer clothing of such persons in an attempt to discover weapons which might be used to assault him. Such a search is a reasonable search under the Fourth Amendment, and any weapons seized may properly be introduced in evidence against the person from whom they were taken.

Affirmed.

MR. JUSTICE HARLAN, concurring.

* * *

* * * [I]f the frisk is justified in order to protect the officer during an encounter with a citizen, the officer must first have constitutional grounds to insist on an encounter, to make a *forcible* stop. * * * I would make it perfectly clear that the right to frisk in this case depends upon the reasonableness of a forcible stop to investigate a suspected crime. [r]

[r] Justice Harlan's point is that officers need have no additional probable cause or reasonable suspicion to believe that the person stopped is armed; a legal frisk is justified solely by the legality of the stop. As with his concurrence in *Katz,* Justice Harlan's point came to be accepted by later cases as part of the *Terry* rule.

Where such a stop is reasonable, however, the right to frisk must be immediate and automatic if the reason for the stop is, as here, an articulable suspicion of a crime of violence. Just as a full search incident to a lawful arrest requires no additional justification, a limited frisk incident to a lawful stop must often be rapid and routine. There is no reason why an officer, rightfully but forcibly confronting a person suspected of a serious crime, should have to ask one question and take the risk that the answer might be a bullet. * * *

* * *

MR. JUSTICE DOUGLAS, dissenting.

I agree that petitioner was "seized" within the meaning of the Fourth Amendment. I also agree that frisking petitioner and his companions for guns was a "search." But it is a mystery how that "search" and that "seizure" can be constitutional by Fourth Amendment standards, unless there was "probable cause" to believe that (1) a crime had been committed or (2) a crime was in the process of being committed or (3) a crime was about to be committed. [s]

[s] Justice Douglas, perhaps the most liberal member of the Warren Court, is here the most conservative justice by adhering to established rules of law.

* * * If loitering were in issue and that was the offense charged, there would be "probable cause" shown. But the crime here is carrying concealed weapons; and there is no basis for concluding that the officer had "probable cause" for believing that that crime was being committed. * * * [A] magistrate would, therefore, have been unauthorized to issue [a warrant], for he can act only if there is a showing of "probable cause." We hold today that the police have greater authority to make a "seizure" and conduct a "search" than a judge has to authorize such action. We have said precisely the opposite over and over again. [t]

[t] By changing the rules that guide police on-the-street- detention, the Court has imposed on magistrates the duty to uphold police stops short of traditional arrests.

* * *

To give the police greater power than a magistrate is to take a long step down the totalitarian path. Perhaps such a step is desirable to cope with modern forms of lawlessness. But if it is taken, it should be the deliberate choice of the people through a constitutional amendment. * * *

* * *

Court has never conceded that it intentionally compensates for a tough decision on one point by handing down a soft ruling on another, but its actions occasionally give that impression . . . ."[20] Thus, after *Miranda,* the Court upheld the use of informers and electronic eavesdropping, dropped the mere evidence restriction on searches, and authorized stop and frisk on less than probable cause. This does not prove that the Court acted from narrow political motives, but it does fuel the kind of speculation that surrounds the most-watched court in the country.

TERRY AND VAGRANCY LAWS: CLOSING A LEGAL LOOPHOLE While *Terry* can be viewed as a conservative turn for the decidedly liberal Warren Court, several years later, in *Papachristou v. City of Jacksonville* (1972), the more conservative Burger Court took a "liberal" stance in restricting the use of overly broad or vague **vagrancy statutes.** These laws had for centuries given police in England and the United States a "cover" to stop and question individuals who merely appeared suspicious but against whom no probable cause to arrest existed.[21] Vagrancy laws were used not only to question persons suspected of crime, but to control and harass social deviants and poor people as well. A destructive aspect of these laws was their use as "cover" charges: a police officer ensured against a lawsuit for false arrest by charging a person stopped with "vagrancy." The Supreme Court, by openly recognizing the field-interrogation power of the police in *Terry,* and by shutting down the abusive extremes of overbroad vagrancy laws in *Papachristou,* eliminated a source of hypocrisy in police work and in theory brought this area of police activity under judicial scrutiny.

After *Papachristou,* the states could continue to rely on loitering laws but tended to narrowly tailor them to specifically target disruptive behavior such as prowling around homes, streetwalking prostitution, and on-the-street drug sales. The change worked by *Papachristou* was that now citizens could turn to the courts to determine if such specifically targeted laws met due process criteria.

The Supreme Court has applied the stop-and-frisk doctrine in a variety of cases in the years following *Terry.* While some cases have limited the power of police officers to stop, most have expanded the investigative stop doctrine beyond a strict reading of *Terry.* Most commentators believe that a rough balance between pro-police rights and individual rights established in the Burger Court years has given way to a legal regime that decidedly favors police in the Rehnquist Court. The mostly Republican-appointed Court has been charged with creating a "drug exception" to the Fourth Amendment linked to the nation's "war on drugs."[22]

In the cases that follow, the Court often has had to determine whether police action constituted an arrest, a *Terry* stop, or a consensual encounter, and if a seizure, if the seizure was justified by probable cause or reasonable suspicion. Instead of organizing the cases in a purely chronological fashion, they are presented, somewhat artificially, by the source of reasonable suspicion and the place in which the stop occurs.

The Sources of Reasonable Suspicion

HEARSAY At first it seemed that the novel *Terry* rule, allowing a Fourth Amendment seizure on less than probable cause but on "reasonable suspicion," had to be based on the personal observations of an experienced police officer. *Terry* stated: "in determining whether the officer acted reasonably in such circumstances, due weight must be given, not to his inchoate and unparticularized suspicion or 'hunch,' but to the specific reasonable inferences which he is entitled to draw from the facts in light of his experience." Nevertheless, the Court soon established that reasonable suspicion can be based upon reliable hearsay.

In *Adams v. Williams* (1972), a person known to Police Sgt. John Connolly approached him at 2:15 A.M. in a high crime area and told him that an individual in a nearby car was carrying narcotics and had a gun at his waist. Sgt. Connolly approached the car, tapped on the driver's window, and asked the occupant to open the door. Williams, who was alone in the car, rolled down the window instead, and the officer reached in and seized a loaded gun from Williams's waistband. Based on the discovery of the gun, Connolly arrested Williams for illegally possessing a weapon, searched him, and discovered drugs that were admitted into evidence. Unlike Officer McFadden in *Terry,* who personally saw suspicious behavior, Sgt. Connolly did not personally see the gun or corroborate this fact before simultaneously stopping and frisking (i.e., searching and seizing). The Court expressly ruled that reliable hearsay may be the basis of an officer's investigative stop, which occurred when Sgt. Connolly tapped on the window and demanded that the occupant step out.

Adams v. Williams also extended the *Terry* ruling in several other ways. It extended the stop-and-frisk authority to crimes of possession. Some felt that it should be limited to violent crimes or thefts. This extension has made warrantless police action a potent tool in the "war on drugs" and has also been at the center of the bitter controversy over racial profiling (see Law in Society section, Chapter 6). *Adams* is not a perfect precedent for the proposition that a frisk does not need to be supported by independent reasonable suspicion, but if an officer has reasonable suspicion that a person stopped is armed, the officer may frisk before asking any questions.

ANONYMOUS TIPS The Court in *Adams* noted that "[t]his is a stronger case than obtains in the case of an anonymous telephone tip." Such a situation was resolved by the Court in *Alabama v. White* (1990). At 3:00 P.M., Montgomery,

Alabama, police received "a telephone call from an anonymous person, stating that Vanessa White would be leaving 235-C Lynwood Terrace Apartments at a particular time in a brown Plymouth station wagon with the right taillight lens broken and that she would be going to Dobey's Motel and would be in possession of about an ounce of cocaine inside a brown attache case." The police did not know Vanessa White or what she looked like, but they corroborated the facts (except that White was not carrying an attaché case) and stopped White in her car shortly before she reached Dobey's Motel. The officers told her she was stopped because she was suspected of carrying cocaine and they obtained consent to look into a locked, brown attaché case that was in the car. They found drugs in the attaché case.

The Supreme Court held (6–3) that "the tip, as corroborated by independent police work, exhibited sufficient indicia of reliability to provide reasonable suspicion to make the investigatory stop." The decision was assisted to some extent by the ruling in *Illinois v. Gates* (see Chapter 4) when the Court approved a totality of circumstances approach to determining whether an anonymous informant who supplied probable cause for a search warrant was reliable, truthful, and had a basis of knowledge. In *White,* the Court applied this approach to find that the totality of circumstances apparently indicated that the informant was so familiar with Vanessa White's movements as to be reliable and truthful and have a basis of knowledge. In the course of its opinion, the Court made an important distinction between probable cause and reasonable suspicion. Reasonable suspicion not only is a lesser quantum of proof, but it is also *less reliable.* "[R]easonable suspicion can arise from information that is less reliable than that required to show probable cause." This language gives police ample leeway to stop individuals without great concern that the information supplied is unreliable.

Justice Stevens's brief dissent saw these facts differently. "An anonymous neighbor's prediction about somebody's time of departure and probable destination is anything but a reliable basis for assuming that the commuter is in possession of an illegal substance." He suggested that White may have been a room clerk at the motel and offered a much more troubling suggestion—that in cases like this, the tipster could be another police officer who has a "hunch" about a person. This is not mere surmise, but it is a technique used by corrupt police, as noted in a book on the subject:

> "There happened to be money missing on a job they went on, and the guy who lost the money came into the precinct bitching. It was a set-up job. It wasn't a real radio run. They [police] had *dropped a dime* on the guy. They had called 911 themselves and then responded to the bogus call to get inside the building . . . ."[23]

The Supreme Court has more recently limited the acceptance of anonymous information in a unanimous decision that rejected an anonymous tip that presented only general information (*Florida v. J. L.* 2000). After an anonymous caller reported to the Miami-Dade Police that a young black male standing at a particular bus stop and wearing a plaid shirt was carrying a gun, officers went to the bus stop and saw three black males, one of whom, respondent J. L., was wearing a plaid shirt. Apart from the tip, the officers had no reason to suspect any of the three of illegal conduct. The officers did not see a firearm or observe any unusual movements. One of the officers frisked J. L. and seized a gun from his pocket. J. L., who was then almost sixteen years of age, was charged under state law with carrying a concealed firearm without a license and possessing a firearm while under the age of eighteen. The Court distinguished *Alabama v. White* by noting that although the tip itself in *White* did not amount to reasonable suspicion, once "police observation showed that the informant had accurately predicted the woman's movements, . . . it become reasonable to think the tipster had inside knowledge about the suspect and therefore to credit his assertion about the cocaine" (*Florida v. J. L.*). Justice Ginsburg, in her majority opinion, called *White* a "borderline" decision.

> The tip in the instant case lacked the moderate indicia of reliability present in *White* and essential to the Court's decision in that case. The anonymous call concerning J. L. provided no predictive information and therefore left the police without means to test the informant's knowledge or credibility. That the allegation about the gun turned out to be correct does not suggest that the officers, prior to the frisks, had a reasonable basis for suspecting J. L. of engaging in unlawful conduct. The reasonableness of official suspicion must be measured by what the officers knew before they conducted their search. All the police had to go on in this case was the bare report of an unknown, unaccountable informant who neither explained how he knew about the gun nor supplied any basis for believing he had inside information about J. L. If *White* was a close case on the reliability of anonymous tips, this one surely falls on the other side of the line (*Florida v. J. L.*)

POLICE BULLETIN The *Terry* basis of reasonable suspicion was also expanded in *United States v. Hensley* (1985). *Hensley* made it clear that police may detain a suspect based on information contained in a flyer or bulletin they receive from another jurisdiction. If the flyer has been issued on the basis of articulable facts supporting a reasonable suspicion that the wanted person has committed an offense (rather than probable cause), then it justifies a stop to check identification, to pose questions to the person, or to detain the person briefly while attempting to obtain further information. As a result, *Hensley* held that stops not only may be made to prevent a *future* crime or stop *ongoing* offenses, as was the case in *Terry,* but also can be used to inquire about *past* criminal acts. Justice O'Connor maintained that although the crime prevention rationale and the exigency present in *Terry* did not exist in *Hensley,* the ability to stop a suspect for questions based on reasonable suspicion promotes the government interest of solving crime and prevents the chance that a suspect might flee.

Terry on the Streets

In several post-*Terry* cases, the Court found that the police interfered with liberty without reasonable suspicion violating the liberty rights of individuals. Such was the case in *Sibron v. New York* (1968), a companion case to *Terry* designed to draw the line between legal and illegal stops. An NYPD patrol officer noticed Sibron "hanging around" a street corner for many hours in the late afternoon and evening where drug sales were believed to occur and he was seen talking to known drug addicts. Sibron went into a diner and, as he was eating pie and drinking coffee, was ordered outside by the officer. The officer had seen no evidence of a drug sale but approached Sibron saying "You know what I am after," reached into Sibron's pocket, and found a packet of heroin. The Court held that this seizure was not based on reasonable suspicion and, therefore, was an unreasonable and unconstitutional stop. There were no articulable objective facts to establish drug dealing or possession. It was also clear that the officer was not "frisking" Sibron for a weapon but simply searching for drugs. The drugs were suppressed as the product of an illegal search and seizure.

IDENTIFICATION AND LOITERING LAWS The next set of cases involve state statutes designed to control on-the-street behavior, rather than straightforward applications of a police officer's *Terry* powers. The Court has held that the police do not have a generalized power to obtain personal identification from a person in the context of a statute that empowered police to obtain the identification of a person abroad on the street. In *Brown v. Texas* (1979), officers saw Brown and a man in an alley in El Paso, in a high crime area, at 12:45 P.M. The officer testified that the situation "looked suspicious, but he was unable to point to any facts supporting that conclusion. There is no indication in the record that it was unusual for people to be in the alley." When asked for identification, Brown angrily refused to give it. He was arrested, jailed, and upon conviction, fined twenty dollars for violating a Texas statute that made it a crime for a person to intentionally refuse to report his name and address to a police officer who has lawfully stopped the person and requested such information. The Court ruled that the application of the statute violated the Fourth Amendment because the police had no grounds for stopping Brown in the first place. This leaves open the question of whether a person who refuses to answer a question as to his identity on a valid *Terry* stop can be convicted for failure to talk. The Court noted that the mere fact that the area was frequented by drug users was not reasonable suspicion to stop Brown.

The Court went a step beyond *Brown v. Texas* in favor of individual liberty in *Kolender v. Lawson* (1983), a case decided on the grounds that a California statute violated due process. The California statute required persons who loiter or wander on the streets to identify themselves and to account for their presence when a peace officer requests. Edward Lawson was detained or arrested on approximately fifteen occasions while walking between March 1975 and January 1977 under this statute. He was prosecuted twice and convicted once. He brought a civil suit to have the law declared unconstitutional. The California courts limited the application of the statute only to instances where a police officer "has reasonable suspicion of criminal activity sufficient to justify a *Terry* detention." The Supreme Court ruled, that even as so construed, the statute still violated the Fourteenth Amendment in that it was "void-for-vagueness." This doctrine states that a law that is not sufficiently definite, so that ordinary people are unable to understand what conduct is prohibited violates due process. The essential fault with such a law is that it either defines a crime or gives police authority in such an open-ended fashion, without standards, that it encourages arbitrary and discriminatory enforcement of the law. The California statute left police with virtually complete discretion to determine whether the suspect offered "credible and reliable" identification. Because the law contained no such standards, it raised the possibility of arbitrary enforcement, a violation of due process of law. This may be discerned from the facts: An African-American man, a business consultant in his mid-thirties who wore his hair in dread locks, was arrested fifteen times within two years for simply walking about (see *Law in Society* section, Chapter 6). Justice O'Connor, writing for the majority, commented on the values that underpin these rules: "Our Constitution is designed to maximize individual freedoms within a framework of ordered liberty."

Justice Brennan, although concurring in the decision, disagreed with the due process basis of the majority's holding. He argued that even if the defect in the California law were cured to define which kinds of identification were acceptable, *any* law requiring citizens to identify themselves in the absence of a criminal act is in violation of the Fourth Amendment: "Merely to facilitate the general law enforcement objectives of investigating and preventing unspecified crimes, States may not authorize the arrest and criminal prosecution of an individual for failing to produce identification or further information by a police officer." Justices

White and Rehnquist dissented on the ground that a person who is given actual notice of the application of the statute cannot challenge it on the grounds of vagueness because they are apprized of the impact of the law.

A distinguishing hallmark of American life is that there is no general requirement that citizens carry official identification at all times, unlike many democratic and tolerant nations that require its citizens to carry "internal passports." However reasonable might be the general requirement that Americans carry identification at all times, this would generate outrage because of the powerful cultural norms of individuality and freedom that mark the American character. The American aversion to an **internal passport** system helps to explain a specific ruling like *Kolender v, Lawson.*

The Court again confronted a loitering statute in *City of Chicago v. Morales* (1999). The city of Chicago enacted a "gang congregation" ordinance, with criminal penalties, that prohibited loitering together in any public place by two or more people if at least one individual was a "criminal street gang member." The ordinance defined "loitering" as remaining in any one place with no apparent purpose. A police officer who observed what he or she reasonably believed was loitering under the ordinance was required to order all of the persons to disperse. A failure to disperse was a violation of the criminal provisions of the ordinance. The Chicago Police Department promulgated guidelines to prevent arbitrary or discriminatory enforcement of the ordinance. These confined arrest authority to designated gang squad officers, established detailed criteria for determining street gangs and membership, and limited enforcement only to high gang-activity but publicly undisclosed enforcement areas. The Court struck down the ordinance on vagueness grounds under the Due Process Clause.

The ordinance was vigorously enforced and thus affected thousands of persons—42,000 had been arrested for violating the ordinance over a three-year period. Justice Stevens, a Chicago native, writing for the majority, noted that the assertion of the ordinance—gang violence that imperils safety and disrupts normal street life—is not in dispute. On the other hand, as *Papachristou* made clear, a person has a right to "loiter"—i.e., "to remove from one place to another according to inclination" is "an attribute of personal liberty" protected by the Constitution. In what ways did this ordinance specifically violate the Fourteenth Amendment? The ordinance was unclear about terms like "disperse" and leaving the "locality." What exactly would a purported gang member have to do to "disperse?" For example, how quickly did they have to move and how far would he have to go? Next, the ordinance did not adequately define "loitering" with the specificity seen in ordinances that targeted drug dealing or prostitution, and so it "necessarily entrusts lawmaking to the moment-to-moment judgment of the policeman on his beat," citing *Kolender.* Finally, the ordinance could apply to essentially peaceful activity and not to underlying activities that are dangerous. In sum, the ordinance violated the Due Process Clause.

FLEEING FROM THE POLICE Among the most hotly contested post-*Terry* cases have been those concerning scenarios in which a police officer follows or chases a person. *Michigan v. Chesternut* (1988) held that police "intrusion" did not amount to an illegal detention and search. Chesternut, standing on a Detroit street corner, began to run when he saw a police car drive near. The patrol car turned the corner and followed to see where he was going. The car quickly caught up with him and drove alongside for a short distance. The officers noticed Chesternut discard packets from his right-hand pocket which they retrieved, and found pills that one officer who was trained as a paramedic identified as codeine. Chesternut was arrested, searched, and drugs were found on his person. The Michigan courts held that this was an "investigatory pursuit" that amounted to a seizure under *Terry.* Thus, simply running away from a police car does not raise reasonable suspicion for the police to give chase.

A unanimous Supreme Court reversed, holding that the police conduct of driving alongside the defendant did not constitute a stop or a Fourth Amendment seizure. The police used no flashers or siren, drew no weapons, nor ordered the defendant to stop. The car was not operated in an aggressive way to block Chesternut's course or otherwise control his speed or movement. "While the very presence of a police car driving parallel to a running pedestrian could be somewhat intimidating, this kind of police presence does not, standing alone, constitute a seizure. . . . The police therefore were not required to have 'a particularized and objective basis for suspecting [Chesternut] of criminal activity,' in order to pursue him." *Chesternut* is an example of the rule that police need no evidentiary basis for observing on-the-street-behavior, even if the observation becomes obvious.

In *California v. Hodari D.,* the police did not simply follow, but clearly chased, a person on foot. Is a police chase such a significant interference with personal liberty as to require that police have reasonable suspicion at the onset of the chase? To bring about a satisfactory result, the Court had to revise the *Mendenhall* definition of a seizure.

A commentator saw *Hodari D.* as the "culmination of a struggle between two factions of the Supreme Court," and a victory by the group led by conservative Justices Kennedy and Scalia. If the *Mendenhall* Court meant what it said when it proposed that a seizure is to be measured by the reasonable understanding of the individual, then the majority in *Hodari D.* created a new rule when it added a "physical restraint" element to Fourth Amendment seizures.[24] A year

• CASE & COMMENTS •

California v. Hodari D.

499 U.S. 621, 111 S. Ct. 1547, 113 L.Ed.2d 690 (1991)

JUSTICE SCALIA delivered the opinion of the Court.

Late one evening in April 1988, Officers Brian McColgin and Jerry Pertoso were on patrol in a high-crime area of Oakland, California. They were dressed in street clothes but wearing jackets with "Police" embossed on both front and back. Their unmarked car proceeded west on Foothill Boulevard, and turned south onto 63rd Avenue. **[a]** As they rounded the corner, they saw four or five youths huddled around a small red car parked at the curb. When the youths, [including Hodari D.], saw the officers' car approaching they apparently panicked, and took flight. * * *

[a] Does a group of huddled teenagers provide grounds to arrest them? To forcibly stop them under *Terry?*

The officers were suspicious and gave chase. **[b]** McColgin remained in the car * * *; Pertoso left the car [and chased on foot]. Hodari [emerged from an alley and did not see] Pertoso until the officer was almost upon him, whereupon he tossed away what appeared to be a small rock. A moment later, Pertoso tackled Hodari, handcuffed him, and radioed for assistance. Hodari was found to be carrying $130 in cash and a pager; and the rock he had discarded was found to be crack cocaine.

[b] Do you think that a teen who runs from the sight of a cop should be chased? If caught should he be arrested? Subjected to field-interrogation?

In the juvenile proceeding brought against him, Hodari moved to suppress the evidence relating to the cocaine. The court denied the motion without opinion. The California Court of Appeal reversed, holding that Hodari had been "seized" when he saw Officer Pertoso running towards him, that this seizure was unreasonable under the Fourth Amendment, and that the evidence of cocaine had to be suppressed as the fruit of that illegal seizure. The California Supreme Court denied the State's application for review. We granted certiorari. * * *

As this case comes to us, the only issue presented is whether, at the time he dropped the drugs, Hodari had been "seized" within the meaning of the Fourth Amendment. **[c]** If so, respondent argues, the drugs were the fruit of that seizure and the evidence concerning them was properly excluded. If not, the drugs were abandoned by Hodari and lawfully recovered by the police, and the evidence should have been admitted. (In addition, of course, Pertoso's seeing the rock of cocaine, at least if he recognized it as such, would provide reasonable suspicion for the unquestioned seizure that occurred when he tackled Hodari. * * *).

[c] California conceded that the flight of the youths upon seeing the police was not in itself reasonable suspicion for a *Terry* stop. Although Justice Scalia thought the point was arguable, he was bound by this concession. The issue was left open for a later case.

We have long understood that the Fourth Amendment's protection against "unreasonable . . . seizures" includes seizure of the person. * * * From the time of the founding to the present, the word "seizure" has meant a "taking possession." * * * For most purposes at common law, the word connoted not merely grasping, or applying physical force to, the animate or inanimate object in question, but actually bringing it within physical control. **[d]** A ship still fleeing, even though under attack, would not be considered to have been seized as a war prize. * * * To constitute an arrest, however—the quintessential "seizure of the person" under our Fourth Amendment jurisprudence—the mere grasping or application of physical force with lawful authority, whether or not it succeeded in subduing the arrestee, was sufficient. * * *

[d] Is the chase of a sailing ship on the high seas a good analogy for a police officer chasing a youth through a city neighborhood?

To say that an arrest is effected by the slightest application of physical force, despite the arrestee's escape, is not to say that for Fourth Amendment purposes there is a *continuing* arrest during the period of fugitivity. If, for example, Pertoso had laid his hands upon Hodari to arrest him, but Hodari had broken away and had *then* cast away the cocaine, it would hardly be realistic to say that that disclosure had been made during the course of an arrest. * * * The present case, however, is even one step further removed. It does not involve the application of any physical force; Hodari was untouched by Officer Pertoso at the time he discarded the cocaine. His defense relies instead upon the proposition that a seizure occurs "when the officer, by means of physical force *or show of authority,* has in some way restrained the liberty of a citizen." *Terry v. Ohio,* (emphasis added). Hodari contends (and we accept as true for purposes of this decision) that Pertoso's pursuit qualified as a "show of authority" calling upon Hodari to halt. The narrow question before us is whether, with respect to a show of authority as with respect to application of physical force, a seizure occurs even though the subject does not yield. We hold that it does not.

The language of the Fourth Amendment, of course, cannot sustain respondent's contention. The word "seizure" readily bears the meaning of a laying on of hands or application of physical force to restrain movement, even when it is ultimately unsuccessful. ("She seized the purse-snatcher, but he

• CASE & COMMENTS •

broke out of her grasp.") It does not remotely apply, however, to the prospect of a policeman yelling "Stop, in the name of the law!" at a fleeing form that continues to flee. That is no seizure. **[e]** Nor can the result respondent wishes to achieve be produced—indirectly, as it were—by suggesting that Pertoso's uncomplied-with show of authority was a common-law arrest, and then appealing to the principle that all common-law arrests are seizures. An arrest requires *either* physical force (as described above) *or,* where that is absent, *submission* to the assertion of authority. * * *

[e] As *Watson* demonstrated, a strict reading of the language of the Constitution does not always bind the Court. Is it *reasonable* to view a chase as a seizure if the police officer is close to the person running and is likely to capture him?

We do not think it desirable, even as a policy matter, to stretch the Fourth Amendment beyond its words and beyond the meaning of arrest, as respondent urges. Street pursuits always place the public at some risk, and compliance with police orders to stop should therefore be encouraged. * * *

Respondent contends that his position is sustained by the so-called *Mendenhall* test, . . . "A person has been 'seized' within the meaning of the Fourth Amendment only if, in view of all the circumstances surrounding the incident, a reasonable person would have believed that he was not free to leave." * * * In seeking to rely upon that test here, respondent fails to read it carefully. It says that a person has been seized "only if," not that he has been seized "whenever"; it states a *necessary,* but not a *sufficient* condition for seizure—or, more precisely, for seizure effected through a "show of authority." *Mendenhall* establishes that the test for existence of a "show of authority" is an objective one: not whether the citizen perceived that he was being ordered to restrict his movement, but whether the officer's words and actions would have conveyed that to a reasonable person. Application of this objective test was the basis for our decision in the other case principally relied upon by respondent, *Chesternut,* * * * where we concluded that the police cruiser's slow following of the defendant did not convey the message that he was not free to disregard the police and go about his business. **[f]** We did not address in *Chesternut,* however, the question whether, if the *Mendenhall* test was met—if the message that the defendant was not free to leave *had* been conveyed—a Fourth Amendment seizure would have occurred. * * *

[f] The facts of *Hodari D.* are the exact opposite. Is this not a concession by Justice Scalia? Perhaps the point is clouded by the use of the double negative.

[This case is like the chase in *Brower v. Inyo County* (1989): there was no arrest until Brower crashed into the roadblock.]

In sum, assuming that Pertoso's pursuit in the present case constituted a "show of authority" enjoining Hodari to halt, since Hodari did not comply with that injunction he was not seized until he was tackled. The cocaine abandoned while he was running was in this case not the fruit of a seizure, and his motion to exclude evidence of it was properly denied. We reverse the decision of the California Court of Appeal, and remand for further proceedings not inconsistent with this opinion.

JUSTICE STEVENS, with whom JUSTICE MARSHALL joins, dissenting.

The Court's narrow construction of the word "seizure" represents a significant, and in my view, unfortunate, departure from prior case law construing the Fourth Amendment. * * * [T]he Court now adopts a definition of "seizure" that is unfaithful to a long line of Fourth Amendment cases. Even if the Court were defining seizure for the first time, which it is not, the definition that it chooses today is profoundly unwise. **[g]** In its decision, the Court assumes, without acknowledging, that a police officer may now fire his weapon at an innocent citizen and not implicate the Fourth Amendment—as long as he misses his target.

[g] If a police officer, without probable cause or reasonable suspicion, fired a gun at you and missed, in a civil suit against the officer should you be able to claim a violation of your Fourth Amendment rights?

For the purposes of decision, the following propositions are not in dispute. First, when Officer Pertoso began his pursuit of respondent, the officer did not have a lawful basis for either stopping or arresting respondent. * * * Second, the officer's chase amounted to a "show of force" as soon as respondent saw the officer nearly upon him. * * * Third, the act of discarding the rock of cocaine was the direct consequence of the show of force. * * * Fourth, as the Court correctly demonstrates, no common-law arrest occurred until the officer tackled respondent. * * * Thus, the Court is quite right in concluding that the abandonment of the rock was not the fruit of a common-law arrest.

It is equally clear, however, that if the officer had succeeded in touching respondent before he dropped the rock—even if he did not subdue him—an arrest would have occurred. **[h]** * * * In that event (assuming the touching precipitated the abandonment), the evidence would have been the fruit of an unlawful common-law arrest. The distinction between the actual case and the hypothetical case is the same as the distinction between the common-law torts of assault and battery—a touching

[h] Should constitutional rights turn on whether the officer "tagged" the fleeing youth?

• CASE & COMMENTS •

converts the former into the latter. Although the distinction between assault and battery was important for pleading purposes, * * * the distinction should not take on constitutional dimensions. The Court mistakenly allows this common-law distinction to define its interpretation of the Fourth Amendment.

At the same time, the Court fails to recognize the existence of another, more telling, common-law distinction—the distinction between an arrest and an attempted arrest. As the Court teaches us, the distinction between battery and assault was critical to a correct understanding of the common law of arrest. * * * ("An arrest requires either physical force . . . *or,* where that is absent, *submission* to the assertion of authority"). However, the facts of this case do not describe an actual arrest, but rather, an unlawful *attempt* to take a presumptively innocent person into custody. Such an attempt was unlawful at common law. **[i]** Thus, if the Court wants to define the scope of the Fourth Amendment based on the common law, it should look, not to the common law of arrest, but to the common law of attempted arrest, according to the facts of this case.

[i] This challenges the accuracy and completeness of Justice Scalia's common law analysis—an especially sharp attack because Justice Scalia, as an originalist, relies heavily on the common law.

The first question, then, is whether the common law should define the scope of the outer boundaries of the constitutional protection against unreasonable seizures. Even if, contrary to settled precedent, traditional common-law analysis were controlling, it would still be necessary to decide whether the unlawful attempt to make an arrest should be considered a seizure within the meaning of the Fourth Amendment, and whether the exclusionary rule should apply to unlawful attempts.

I

The Court today takes a narrow view of "seizure," which is at odds with the broader view adopted by this Court almost twenty-five years ago. * * *

* * * Significantly, in the *Katz* opinion, the Court repeatedly used the word "seizure" to describe the process of recording sounds that could not possibly have been the subject of a common-law seizure. * * *

[Justice Black's literal reading of the Fourth Amendment in *Katz,* arguing that the *words* of the Fourth Amendment did not apply to eavesdropping, was rejected by the Court.]

The expansive construction of the word "seizure" in the *Katz* case provided an appropriate predicate for the Court's holding in *Terry v. Ohio* * * * As a corollary to the lesser justification for the stop, the Court necessarily concluded that the word "seizure" in the Fourth Amendment encompasses official restraints on individual freedom that fall short of a common-law arrest. Thus, *Terry* broadened the range of encounters between the police and the citizen encompassed within the term "seizure," while at the same time, lowering the standard of proof necessary to justify a "stop" in the newly expanded category of seizures now covered by the Fourth Amendment. * * *

The decisions in *Katz* and *Terry* unequivocally reject the notion that the common law of arrest defines the limits of the term "seizure" in the Fourth Amendment.* * * The Court mistakenly harkens back to common law, while ignoring the expansive approach that the Court has taken in Fourth Amendment analysis since *Katz* and *Terry.*

II

The Court fares no better when it tries to explain why the proper definition of the term "seizure" has been an open question until today. In *Terry,* in addition to stating that a seizure occurs "whenever a police officer accosts an individual and restrains his freedom to walk away," * * * the Court noted that a seizure occurs "when the officer, by means of physical force or show of authority, has in some way restrained the liberty of a citizen. . . ." * * * **[j]** The touchstone of a seizure is the restraint of an individual's personal liberty "*in some way.*" * * * (emphasis added). Today the Court's reaction to respondent's reliance on *Terry* is to demonstrate that in "show of force" cases no common-law arrest occurs unless the arrestee *submits.* * * * That answer, however, is plainly insufficient given the holding in *Terry* that the Fourth Amendment applies to stops that need not be justified by probable cause in the absence of a full-blown arrest.

[j] This reading of *Terry* provides a reasoned basis for the dissent. What neither the majority nor dissent can openly say is that the justices have some leeway to read common law and constitutional precedent in ways that support their policy views.

* * * Examples of seizures [in *Mendenhall*] include "the threatening presence of several officers, the display of a weapon by an officer, some physical touching of the person of the citizen, or

• CASE & COMMENTS •

the use of language or tone of voice indicating that compliance with the officer's request might be compelled." * * * The Court's unwillingness today to adhere to the "reasonable person" standard, as formulated by JUSTICE STEWART in *Mendenhall,* marks an unnecessary departure from Fourth Amendment case law.

* * *

Even though momentary, a seizure occurs whenever an objective evaluation of a police officer's show of force conveys the message that the citizen is not entirely free to leave—in other words, that his or her liberty is being restrained in a significant way. * * *

* * *

before *Hodari D.,* a leading scholar accepted as an established rule that "[w]hen a cop accosts a citizen on the street, the constitutional standard for measuring whether a seizure occurs is whether—in light of the totality of the circumstances—a reasonable person would feel free to leave the scene."[25] Professor Maclin saw this as a matter of commonsense reality: "In the typical street encounter, few persons, if any, feel free to ignore or leave the presence of a police officer who has approached and questioned them. . . . [T]he average individual who is approached by a police officer does not feel free to leave."[26] The implication of a pure *Mendenhall* rule plus "what everyone knows about being approached by the police" was that a police officer who "rushes" an individual without reasonable suspicion has seized that person; and if the person flees and tosses away contraband, its seizure is the product of an illegal search and seizure. The *Hodari D.* modification allows the tossed contraband to be taken and used as "abandoned" property.

The unresolved issue in *Hodari D.,* whether mere flight from the sight of a police officer alone established reasonable suspicion for an officer to give chase, was settled in favor of the police in *Illinois v. Wardlow* (2000). A four-car police caravan was cruising through a "high crime neighborhood" looking for on-the-street drug deals. Sam Wardlow was standing alone and holding an opaque bag; he made eye contact with an officer in the last car and "fled." Two officers in the car watched Wardlow run through a gangway and an alley and eventually cornered him on the street. One officer exited his car, stopped Wardlow, "and immediately conducted a protective pat-down search for weapons because in his experience it was common for there to be weapons in the near vicinity of narcotics transactions. During the frisk, Officer Nolan squeezed the bag respondent was carrying and felt a heavy, hard object similar to the shape of a gun. The officer then opened the bag and discovered a .38-caliber handgun with five live rounds of ammunition. The officers arrested Wardlow."

The Court emphasized the rule of *Brown v. Texas* (1979)—the simple presence of a person in a high crime area does not give officers reasonable suspicion to stop a person. On the other hand, the Court ruled that unprovoked flight from the police, as a "commonsense judgment[] and inferences about human behavior," and in the totality of circumstances, constitutes reasonable suspicion. The Court did not say that flight is a *per se* factor that always established reasonable suspicion. While simple, unprovoked flight tends to be a basis of reasonable suspicion, under this view, the officer may also take into account other factors, such as the belief that a neighborhood is a high crime area. Four justices in *Wardlow D.*—Stevens, Souter, Ginsburg, and Breyer—concurred in part and dissented in part. The concurring opinion kept alive the idea that under some conditions flight will not be viewed as reasonable suspicion for a stop.

The ruling creates some tension with another rule of *Terry:* that a person against whom the police do not have reasonable suspicion may refuse to talk to the officer and, citing *Bostick,* "any 'refusal to cooperate, without more, does not furnish the minimal level of objective justification needed for a detention or seizure.'" Now, if a police officer, with no reasonable suspicion, approaches a person on the street to ask if the person will consent to talk to the officer and the person "flees," this could invoke reasonable suspicion. Much would depend on the facts of such a scenario. Also, *Wardlow* does not fully define what is meant by flight. Thus, it is unclear whether in a *Wardlow* scenario, if the person, after looking at an officer, got on a bicycle and rode away or entered a taxi and drove off, or entered the building he was standing in front of, if this would constitute flight.[27] Resolution of such issues will be decided in future cases. *Wardlow* clearly expands the actual authority of police to control the streets.

HODARI D. IN THE STATES

"As for the Hodari D. test for seizures—actual submission to authority, or application of physical force—some state high courts swiftly repudiated it." States rejecting the *Hodari D.* test include Connecticut, Hawaii, Louisiana, Minnesota, New Hampshire, New Jersey, New York, Pennsylvania, and West Virginia. States that have adopted the *Hodari D.* test for a seizure are: Florida, Idaho, Illinois, Maryland, Nebraska, Texas and Washington.

Shreveport and Louisiana State Police conducted a drug sweep of an area code-named "Operation Thor." Its objective was to reclaim certain high-crime areas from drug trafficking and gang-related activities. The sweep began at around 10:30 P.M. when approximately ten to twelve marked police vehicles carrying twenty to thirty officers converged on Roby's Arcade. As officers approached, they observed Tucker and another man standing huddled together by a parked car outside the arcade. When the two men noticed the approaching police cars, they quickly broke apart and began to leave the scene. As they did, Officer Wilson stopped his car and began to get out while simultaneously ordering the two men to "halt" and "prone out." One of the men laid down immediately. Tucker, however, moved several steps toward the rear of the arcade and tossed away a plastic bag. He then obeyed the police command and laid down. The bag was retrieved and found to contain forty-seven rolled marijuana cigarettes.

Was Tucker seized when ordered to "prone out" or did he abandon the property without being seized? Under Art. 1, sect. 5 of the Louisiana Constitution, that state's high court held that Tucker was seized: It "is only when the citizen is *actually stopped* without reasonable cause or when a stop without reasonable cause is *imminent* that the 'right to be left alone' is violated, thereby rendering unlawful any resultant seizure of abandoned property. *State v. Tucker,* 626 So.2d 707, 710–11 (La. 1993)"[28]

Barry Latzer, *State Constitutional Criminal Law,* § 3:23.

Terry on the Road

Many cases that have applied the *Terry* doctrine and have developed auxiliary rules for interpreting the police "stop and frisk" authority have arisen in automobile stop situations. Issues that deal specifically with the extent of a search of an automobile based on probable cause are dealt with in Chapter 6 in the section on the automobile exception to the search warrant requirement.

SCOPE OF A *TERRY* STOP AND FRISK Most *Terry* cases that take place when persons are stopped in and around cars involve a "frisk" of the *person. Michigan v. Long* (1983) held that when police stop a person without arresting him, they may look around the *area* of the stop—a quick and cursory examination—allowing, in a manner of speaking, a "visual frisk" of the immediate surroundings of the stop. Sheriffs' deputies stopped a speeding and erratically driven car. The driver pulled into a ditch and exited the car to meet the officers at the rear of the car with the door left open. The driver, Long, did not respond to a request to produce identification. Long began to walk back to the car but was stopped and frisked. No weapons were found. The deputies saw a hunting knife on the floorboard of the driver's side of the car. One deputy peered into the car with a flashlight and saw something protruding from under the armrest on the front seat. He knelt in the vehicle and lifted the armrest, saw an open pouch on the front seat, and upon flashing his light on the pouch, determined that it contained what appeared to be marijuana. Long was arrested and a search of the car's trunk revealed seventy-five pounds of marijuana.

The Court held the search constitutional and justified by the principles of *Terry.* One reason for this rule is that "investigative detentions involving suspects in vehicles are especially fraught with danger to police officers." Thus, to protect their safety, police officers who stop cars may engage in a cursory examination of the passenger areas of the vehicle to look for weapons in those areas in which a weapon may be placed or hidden when they have a reasonable belief based on articulable facts that the suspect poses a danger. This is analogous to the rule of *Chimel v. California* concerning the scope of a search incident to arrest.

INFERENTIAL REASONING AND REASONABLE SUSPICION The rule of *Terry* that defines reasonable suspicion is that "in justifying the particular intrusion the police officer must be able to point to specific and articulable facts which, taken together with *rational inferences from those facts,* reasonably warrant that intrusion."[29] This important part of the *Terry* doctrine was clarified and extended in *United States v. Cortez* (1981). U.S. Border Patrol officers, alerted by distinctive footprints and tiretracks in a sparsely settled area of desert thirty miles north of the Mexican border, deduced that a truck capable of holding eight to twenty persons would approach from the east and stop between

2 A.M. and 6 A.M. near milepost 122 on Highway 86. As the officers surveyed the road on a particularly bright moonlit night, a camper passed traveling west and then returned approaching from the east at about the time it would take to return from milepost 122. The camper was stopped and illegal aliens were found on board. The Court unanimously held that this stop was based on reasonable suspicion. In the course of his opinion, Chief Justice Burger established a structure for reasonable suspicion analysis:

> Courts have used a variety of terms to capture the elusive concept of what cause is sufficient to authorize police to stop a person. Terms like "articulable reasons" and "founded suspicion" are not self-defining; they fall short of providing clear guidance dispositive of the myriad factual situations that arise. But the essence of all that has been written is that the totality of the circumstances—the whole picture—must be taken into account. . . .
>
> The idea that an assessment of the whole picture must yield a particularized suspicion contains two elements, each of which must be present before a stop is permissible. First, the assessment must be based upon all the circumstances. The analysis proceeds with various objective observations, information from police reports, if such are available, and consideration of the modes or patterns of operation of certain kinds of lawbreakers. From these data, a trained officer draws inferences and makes deductions—inferences and deductions that might well elude an untrained person.
>
> The process does not deal with hard certainties, but with probabilities. . . .
>
> The second element contained in the idea that an assessment of the whole picture must yield a particularized suspicion is the concept that the process just described must raise a suspicion that the particular individual being stopped is engaged in wrongdoing. (*United State v. Cortez,* pp. 417–18)

Note that *Cortez* continues to support the concept of **police officer expertise** that was a basis of finding reasonable suspicion in the *Terry* case.

BREVITY REQUIREMENT Another stop-and-frisk case that arose from an automobile stop clarified a very important *Terry* rule: A legal detention must be reasonably *brief.* In *United States v. Sharpe* (1985), a United States Drug Enforcement Agency (DEA) agent patrolling a road under surveillance for suspected drug trafficking noticed an overloaded pickup truck with an attached trailer being followed closely by a Pontiac. After following the two vehicles for twenty miles, the officer decided to make an investigatory stop and radioed the South Carolina Highway Patrol for assistance. When the DEA agent and the state police officer indicated that the two vehicles were to pull over, the Pontiac did so but the truck continued along the road in an attempt to evade the state police. The driver of the Pontiac was detained for twenty minutes while the DEA agent followed the truck, approached it after it was stopped, smelled marijuana in it, and returned to the detained Pontiac. While the Court found that the officer had reasonable suspicion to make the initial stop, at issue was whether a twenty-minute detention was too long under the *Terry* doctrine because it violated the **brevity requirement** for stops. The Supreme Court held that whether a stop is too long (and thus becomes an arrest) depends not only on the length of time of the stop but also the surrounding circumstances. The question is whether the length of time employed was reasonable. In *Sharpe,* the delay occurred because of the evasive action of the driver of the truck. The Court found that because the police acted diligently to ascertain the facts without creating unnecessary delays, *Terry* was not violated. Note that a twenty-minute stop was sufficiently long so that a special reason had to be supplied to justify it. *Terry* stops are supposed to be just long enough for an officer to ask questions to determine, based on objective factors, whether there is probable cause to arrest or no basis for further detention.

AUTHORITY TO STOP AN AUTOMOBILE A patrol officer in *Delaware v. Prouse* (1979) made a "routine" stop of the car, explaining, "I saw the car in the area and wasn't answering any complaints, so I decided to pull them off." Prior to the vehicle stop, he did not observe any traffic or equipment violations nor any suspicious activity. He made the stop merely to check the driver's license and registration. The officer did not act pursuant to any standards, guidelines, or procedures pertaining to document spot checks as defined by his department or the state attorney general. During the stop the officer smelled marijuana and made an arrest and seizure.

Lower courts had split on whether this kind of stop, without reasonable suspicion or probable cause, violated the Fourth Amendment. The Supreme Court, holding this kind of stop and seizure unconstitutional, was not writing on a blank slate. Four years earlier it decided in *United States v. Brignoni-Ponce* (1975) that Border Patrol agents conducting roving patrols near the international border violated the Fourth Amendment by stopping vehicles at random. Although intercepting illegal aliens was important, the Court felt that to stop cars—not at the border or at fixed checkpoints—but on roads within one hundred miles of the Mexican border, without establishing reasonable suspicion was unconstitutional. The reasons are that such stops interfere with freedom of movement, are inconvenient and time-consuming, and may create substantial anxiety for a driver who is pulled over for no apparent reason. In contrast, a motorist does not feel the same anxiety at a roadblock or fixed checkpoint where it is observed that every motorist goes through the same drill. The Court dismissed the arguments that an automobile stop is an administrative search or that people have a lesser expectation of privacy in a car than in a home:

> An individual operating or traveling in an automobile does not lose all reasonable expectation of privacy simply because the automobile and its use are subject to government regulation. Automobile travel is a basic, pervasive, and often necessary mode of transportation to and from one's home, workplace, and leisure activities. Many people spend more hours each day traveling in cars than walking on the streets. Undoubtedly, many find a greater sense of security and privacy in traveling in an automobile than they do in exposing themselves by pedestrian or other modes of travel. Were the individual subject to unfettered governmental intrusion every time he entered an automobile, the security guaranteed by the Fourth Amendment would be seriously circumscribed. . . . (*Delaware v. Prouse,* pp. 662–63)

The stop in *Prouse* was unconstitutional and the evidence had to be suppressed.

An important related issue is whether a police officer can stop a car based on reasonable suspicion of a traffic offense when the *true motive* of the officer is to search for drugs—the **pretext search** issue. This question is highly contentious because police departments, especially those astride busy highways, "earn" billions of dollars in drug asset forfeitures of cars and cash and so have an incentive to stringently enforce traffic laws. The question has become politically explosive because it has been shown that this practice been accompanied with "racial profiling" that disproportionately targets minorities (See *Law in Society* section, Chapter 6).

A unanimous Supreme Court resolved the pretext search issue in favor of the police in *Whren v. United States* (1996) by making it clear that an automobile stop and arrest is valid whenever the police have objective evidence of probable cause of a traffic violation. On a June evening,

> plainclothes vice-squad officers of the District of Columbia Metropolitan Police Department were patrolling a "high drug area" of the city in an unmarked car. Their suspicions were aroused when they passed a dark Pathfinder truck with temporary license plates and youthful occupants waiting at a stop sign, the driver looking down into the lap of the passenger at his right. The truck remained stopped at the intersection for what seemed an unusually long time—more than 20 seconds. When the police car executed a U-turn in order to head back toward the truck, the Pathfinder turned suddenly to its right, without signalling, and sped off at an "unreasonable" speed. The policemen followed, and in a short while overtook the Pathfinder when it stopped behind other traffic at a red light. They pulled up alongside, and Officer Ephraim Soto stepped out and approached the driver's door, identifying himself as a police officer and directing the driver, petitioner Brown, to put the vehicle in park. When Soto drew up to the driver's window, he immediately observed two large plastic bags of what appeared to be crack cocaine in petitioner Whren's hands. Petitioners were arrested, and quantities of several types of illegal drugs were retrieved from the vehicle. (*Whren v. United States,* pp. 808–09)

Whren argued that the stop was not "really" for the traffic infractions—that the traffic stop was a pretext for searching for drugs. The Supreme Court has ruled that the standard for Fourth Amendment review is objective, rather than subjective, placing examination of the officer's motives off limits. Whren tried another tack. He pointed out that D.C. police regulations "permit plainclothes officers in unmarked vehicles to enforce traffic laws 'only in the case of a violation that is so grave as to pose an immediate threat to the safety of others.'" In light of these regulations, he suggested a rule for a valid auto stop for a traffic violation: (a) the officer must have probable cause that the traffic infraction occurred, and (b) the stop must be one that "a police officer, acting reasonably, would have made. . . for the reason given."

The Court refused to establish this rule. It noted that in cases dealing with inventory searches, administrative searches, maritime searches, and searches incident to arrest, the motives of the officer are irrelevant as long as there is an objective legal standard—probable cause—to support the intrusion. The only cases in which the Court has balanced the interests of a defendant against the state to find that probable cause is not a sufficient standard are cases involving:

> searches or seizures conducted in an extraordinary manner, unusually harmful to an individual's privacy or even physical interests—such as, for example, seizure by means of deadly force, [*Tennessee v. Garner* (1985)], unannounced entry into a home, [*Wilson v. Arkansas* (1995)], entry into a home without a warrant, [*Welsh v. Wisconsin* (1984)], or physical penetration of the body, [*Winston v. Lee* (1985)]. The making of a traffic stop out-of-uniform does not remotely qualify as such an extreme practice, and so is governed by the usual rule that probable cause to believe the law has been broken "outbalances" private interest in avoiding police contact. (*Whren v. United States,* p. 818)

Another 1996 case involving field interrogation connected with an automobile search, *Ornelas v. United States* (1996), clarified the *standard of review* of *Terry* issues on appeal. In the early morning hours of a December day in Milwaukee, an experienced detective spotted a 1981 two-door Oldsmobile with California license plates in a motel parking lot. He determined that the car was registered to Ornelas, who had checked into the motel with another man, at 4:00 A.M., without making reservations. "The car attracted [the detective's] attention for two reasons: because older model, two-door General Motors cars are a favorite with drug couriers because it is easy to hide things in them; and because California is a 'source State' for drugs." To confirm this "profile" information, a check of the DEA's "Narcotics and Dangerous Drugs Information System (NADDIS), a federal database of known and suspected drug traffickers" revealed that both names of the motel guests appeared as known or suspected drug dealers.

When the two men got in the car, they were approached by two officers and asked if they could search the car. The driver agreed, but the Government conceded that a reasonable person would not have felt free to leave, so this was an investigatory stop. The officer who looked into the car had searched approximately two thousand cars for drugs over a period of nine years. "He noticed that a panel above the right rear passenger armrest felt somewhat loose and suspected that the panel might have been removed and contraband hidden inside. . . . [He] dismantled the panel and discovered two kilograms of cocaine." Was there reasonable suspicion to stop the men and probable cause to remove the panel? The District Court ultimately answered each question in the affirmative.

The basis for the judge's decision that reasonable suspicion existed to stop the men was that "the model, age, and source-State origin of the car, and the fact that two men traveling together checked into a motel at 4 o'clock in the morning without reservations, formed a drug-courier profile and that this profile together with the NADDIS reports gave rise to reasonable suspicion of drug-trafficking activity; in the court's view, reasonable suspicion became probable cause when [the officer] found the loose panel." Although the Supreme Court remanded the case to the Court of Appeals to review the District Court's decision, Chief Justice Rehnquist, a native of Milwaukee who had moved to warmer Arizona, noted that the specific local facts may guide courts. "For example, what may not amount to reasonable suspicion at a motel located alongside a transcontinental highway at the height of the summer tourist season may rise to that level in December in Milwaukee." He also noted that Milwaukee's pleasant summer climate drops to an average daytime temperature of thirty-one degrees in December, making it "a reasonable inference that a Californian stopping in Milwaukee in December is either there to transact business or to visit family or friends." *Ornelas* also indicates that the use of drug courier profiles is now pervasive in American policing.

Ornelas is important for establishing the standard of review of a magistrate's reasonable suspicion or probable cause decision by an appellate court. Every reasonable suspicion or probable cause decision consists of two parts: (1) a determination of the "historical facts" of the case that are relevant to deciding the issue, and (2) a **"mixed question of law and facts"** that applies the facts to the case to determine whether, under a standard of objective reasonableness, they amount to reasonable suspicion or probable cause, as the case may be. In *Ornelas,* the Seventh Circuit Court of Appeals reviewed the magistrate's decision *deferentially,* meaning that an appellate court would overturn a reasonable suspicion decision only for *clear error.* The Supreme Court held that this was an error. Although the appellate court must be deferential to the trial court's finding of the historical facts as to the ultimate determination of reasonable suspicion, a more strict standard of review is called for: **de novo review,** in which the appellate court independently evaluates the facts and draws its own conclusion as to whether reasonable suspicion existed. In making its conclusion, however, the appellate court should evaluate the facts from the perspective of "an objectively reasonable police officer."

The Court gave several reasons for this ruling. A policy of "sweeping deference" would allow different magistrates to come to different reasonable suspicion conclusions on essentially the same facts. "Such varied results would be inconsistent with the idea of a unitary system of law." Because probable cause and reasonable suspicion decisions turn on combinations of facts, *rules* of what constitutes these standards emerge from the cases. "Independent review is therefore necessary if appellate courts are to maintain control of, and to clarify, the legal principles." *De novo* review will, in turn, benefit police officers by "unify[ing] precedent" to provide a defined "set of rules" as to what constitutes reasonable suspicion or probable cause in a given situation. Indeed, appellate courts apply a less stringent standard of review. Although the Court's decision on the standard of review is one that is favorable to defendants, Professor George Thomas has noted that, in reality, the Court's *Ornelas* standard is not far removed from one of deference because "the crucial part of making a *Terry* determination is not the law but the facts."[30]

CONTROLLING PEOPLE IN THE STOPPED AUTOMOBILE The Supreme Court has given police almost complete control to either order the driver and passengers to remain in the automobile when it is stopped or to order the driver and passengers out. The primary rationale in these case is the safety of the officer.

In *Pennsylvania v. Mimms* (1977), an automobile was stopped for an expired license plate. On ordering the driver out, the officer noticed a bulge under the driver's sports jacket; a frisk produced a loaded revolver in Mimms's waistband. Balancing the interests of individual privacy against the safety of law enforcement officers, the Court noted that many police officers are killed during routine traffic stops. Against this, the added intrusion of requiring that a driver exit the car momentarily is so minimal that it hardly rises to the level of a "petty indignity"; at most it is a mere inconvenience that cannot prevail against legitimate concerns for the officer's safety. The *Mimms* ruling was unanimous; given its basis in the safety of the officer and that the officer had a Fourth Amendment basis for stopping the automobile, it was consistent with *Prouse.*

In *Maryland v. Wilson* (1997), the rule of *Mimms* was extended to passengers. Police stopped a speeding automobile—a rental car with no regular license plate. The officer ordered the driver and the passengers to exit the car. There was no legal suspicion that the passengers were engaged in any illegal activity. As Wilson, a passenger, got out of the car an amount of crack cocaine fell to the ground. Maryland's highest court suppressed the evidence on the ground that the police had no authority to order passengers out of the car; the court viewed the order to exit as a Fourth Amendment personal seizure. The Supreme Court, in an opinion by Chief Justice Rehnquist, reversed the Maryland ruling. The *Mimms* rationale—the officer's safety—applied equally to passengers. Indeed, additional persons in the car increases the danger to the police. Despite the lack of probable cause or reasonable suspicion against the passenger, and the fact that a passenger has a greater liberty interest than the driver, as a practical matter the passenger is already stopped by the police detaining the vehicle. This case is analogous to *Michigan v. Summers* (1981), which states that police may temporarily detain a person whose home is being searched under a search warrant.

Justice Stevens dissented, arguing that statistics show no greater danger to police from passengers in stopped cars; the decision intrudes on personal liberty without solid reason.

Justice Kennedy dissented, saying, "Traffic stops, even for minor violations, can take upwards of 30 minutes. When an officer commands passengers innocent of any violation to leave the vehicle and stand by the side of the road in full view of the public, the seizure is serious, not trivial." This decision plus *Whren* (pretextual stops) "puts tens of millions of passengers at risk of arbitrary control by the police." When the *Wilson* rule is combined with the decision of *Wyoming v. Houghton* (1999) (see Chapter 6), that allows the police to search the handbag of a passenger when there is probable cause to search the automobile, the control of an officer over a stopped automobile is close to complete.

Terry in Tight Places

The nature of a stop was explored in *Immigration and Naturalization Service v. Delgado* (1984). With the consent of a factory owner, United States Immigration and Naturalization Service (INS) officers who were looking for illegal immigrants walked through a factory, briefly questioning workers at their work stations and, if reasonable, asking to see immigration papers. Agents were posted at the exits of the factory. Were the illegal workers *seized* within the meaning of the Fourth Amendment? The Court said "no," noting that "police questioning, by itself, is unlikely to result in a Fourth Amendment violation." In this case, the workers were not free to leave, but the "detention" was caused not by the police but by the workers' normal employment requirements. The Court held that the agents were simply questioning people and that these encounters were consensual. Justices Brennan and Marshall dissented, arguing instead that the show of authority by the immigration officials was sufficiently substantial to "overbear the will of any reasonable person." Based on this show of authority, reasoned the dissenters, the factory workers were forcibly stopped within the meaning of *Terry.*

The use of drug courier profiles at airports (discussed later) has spawned similar practices at bus and train stations. In *Florida v. Bostick* (1991), the Supreme Court confirmed its sharp swing toward supporting police practices in regard to on-the-street encounters in *Hodari D.,* decided two months earlier. In this case:

> Two [Broward County sheriff's] officers, complete with badges, insignia and one of them holding a recognizable zipper pouch, containing a pistol, boarded a bus bound from Miami to Atlanta during a stopover in Fort Lauderdale. Eyeing the passengers, the officers admittedly without articulable suspicion, picked out the defendant passenger and asked to inspect his ticket and identification. The ticket, from Miami to Atlanta, matched the defendant's identification and both were immediately returned to him as unremarkable. However, the two police officers persisted and explained their presence as narcotics agents on the lookout for illegal drugs. In pursuit of that aim, they then requested the defendant's consent to search his luggage. (*Florida v. Bostick,* pp. 431–32)

Cocaine was found in the bag. Before they began this encounter, the officers had no reasonable suspicion or probable cause to believe that Terrance Bostick was carrying drugs. The issue was whether Bostick consented to the search or whether he was seized. Six members of the Court, joining Justice O'Connor's opinion, held that Bostick consented. The legal test applied by the case was the *Mendenhall* test: "Our cases make it clear that a seizure does not occur simply because a police officer approaches an individual and asks a few questions. So long as a reasonable person would feel free to disregard the police and go about his business, . . . the encounter is consensual and no reasonable suspicion is required" (*Florida v. Bostick* [internal quotation marks modified]). It is curious that the Court cited *Hodari D.* for this proposition rather than relying exclusively on *Mendenhall.* The Court's majority in these cases appears to have selected a different theory in each case to ensure the decision would favor law enforcement: under *Hodari D.,* one who flees is not seized; under *Mendenhall-Bostick* one who relents, consents. This seems to create a "heads-I-win, tails-you-lose" rule, with the police holding the coin.

The Court in *Bostick* based its holding on the following facts: Bostick was told he had a right to refuse; the pouched gun was never removed nor did the officers ever point it at Bostick or use it in a threatening manner; and Bostick agreed to open his bag. Bostick argued that the cramped confines of the bus compelled an "agreement" to the search. The Court disagreed relying on *INS v. Delgado* (1984), where factory workers could not walk away from interrogating agents because they were at their place of work, as precedent.

> The present case is analytically indistinguishable from *Delgado.* Like the workers in that case, Bostick's freedom of movement was restricted by a factor independent of police conduct—i.e., by his being a passenger on a bus. Accordingly, the "free to leave" analysis on which Bostick relies is inapplicable. In such a situation, the appropriate inquiry is whether a reasonable person would feel free to decline the officers' requests or otherwise terminate the encounter. (*Florida v. Bostick,* p. 436)

The Court also ruled that the "reasonable person" standard "presupposes an innocent person."

Justice Marshall, joined by Justices Blackmun and Stevens, had harsh words for the police practice. He likened police bus station sweeps to the hated "general warrants" that were seen by the British "Redcoats" as effective law enforcement measures.

> These sweeps are conducted in "dragnet" style. The police admittedly act without an "articulable suspicion" in deciding which buses to board and which passengers to approach for interviewing. By proceeding systematically in this fashion, the police are able to engage in a tremendously high volume of searches. See, *e.g., Florida v. Kerwick,* (single officer employing sweep technique able to search over 3,000 bags in nine-month period). The percentage of successful drug interdictions is low. See *United States v. Flowers,* (sweep of 100 buses resulted in seven arrests). (*Florida v. Bostick* [footnotes and citations omitted], pp. 441–42)

The dissenters believed that the technique is inherently coercive.

> To put it mildly, these sweeps "are inconvenient, intrusive, and intimidating." They occur within cramped confines, with officers typically placing themselves in between the passenger selected for an interview and the exit of the bus. Because the bus is only temporarily stationed at a point short of its destination, the passengers are in no position to leave as a means of evading the officers' questioning. Undoubtedly, such a sweep holds up the progress of the bus. Thus, this "new and increasingly common tactic," burdens the experience of traveling by bus with a degree of governmental interference to which, until now, our society has been proudly unaccustomed. See, *e.g., State ex rel. Ekstrom v. Justice Court,* (Feldman, J., concurring) ("The thought that an American can be compelled to 'show his papers' before exercising his right to walk the streets, drive the highways or board the trains is repugnant to American institutions and ideals"). (*Florida v. Bostick* [citations omitted], p. 442)

Most scholarly commentators agree with the dissent in *Bostick* and refer to the decisions in this case and *Hodari D.* as the "no seizure" rule. Professor Gerald Ashdown, for example, writes: "Hardly anyone who is confronted and questioned by armed officers, asked for identification and permission to search, believes he is free to do much of anything, certainly not to refuse to answer or to walk away. Anyone with a lick of sense knows that doing these things will only aggravate the situation and cause him more trouble."[31]

AUTOMOBILE CHECKLANES In *Delaware v. Prouse* (1979), discussed above, the Court held that a car cannot be stopped while proceeding in traffic unless an officer has specific suspicion to believe that it was engaged in a traffic violation or criminal act. *Prouse* distinguished on-the-road stops from those at roadblocks or fixed checkpoints contending that motorists do not feel the same anxiety because they observe other motorists going through the same drill. The Supreme Court specifically upheld sobriety checklanes in *Michigan Department of State Police v. Sitz* (1990). Drivers stopped at such points are not implicated in a Fourth Amendment seizure. Chief Justice Rehnquist noted in his majority opinion that drunk driving is a serious national problem resulting in approximately twenty-five thousand deaths annually. This, of course, is not the constitutional reason for the Court's ruling because the seriousness of crime is not a reason for eliminating the privacy rights of suspects and innocent citizens alike.

In deciding that **sobriety checklanes** are constitutional, and not a violation of a person's reasonable expectation of privacy, the Court relied on border search-fixed checkpoint cases: *United States v. Ortiz* (1975) and *United States v. Martinez-Fuerte* (1976). Those cases compared the subjective and psychological level of intrusion of fixed checkpoints on the highway as compared to stops made by roving patrols. Since at the fixed checkpoint the motorist sees other vehicles being briefly detained and sees the visible indicia of the police officers' authority, "he is much less likely to be frightened or annoyed by the intrusion" (*Ortiz,* quoted in *Martinez-Fuerte*). These findings were applied to the Michigan sobriety checklane situation: "Here, checkpoints are selected pursuant to the guidelines, and uniformed police officers stop every approaching vehicle. The intrusion resulting from the brief stop at the sobriety checkpoint is for constitutional purposes indistinguishable from the checkpoint stops we upheld in *Martinez-Fuerte.*" (*Sitz*)

In *Sitz,* the Court also considered an issue arising in *Brown v. Texas* (1979). That case established a Fourth Amendment balancing test that included as a factor the *effectiveness* of the governmental intrusion. Sitz sought to prove that sobriety checklanes are an ineffective method to deal with the problem of drunk drivers and did not outweigh the Fourth Amendment intrusion involved. The Court stated that the "passage from *Brown* was not meant to transfer from politically accountable officials to the courts the decision as to which among reasonable alternative law enforcement techniques should be employed to deal with a serious public danger. . . . [F]or purposes of Fourth Amendment analysis, the choice among such reasonable alternatives remains with the governmental officials who have a unique understanding of, and a responsibility for, limited public resources, including a finite number of police officers" (*Sitz*).

Justice Stevens, dissenting, disagreed with the Court's finding that sobriety checklanes are essentially the same as border checklanes. Sobriety checklanes, for example, occur at night, are not at fixed checkpoints but are set up quickly to effect the element of surprise, and are less standardized than a review of registration papers, for the officer must visually assess the sobriety of the driver.

In a very important ruling, *City of Indianapolis v. Edmond,* the Court decided (6–3) in November 2000, that a roadblock whose primary purpose was general law enforcement and the detection of ordinary criminal wrongdoing, and not traffic safety, was a violation of the Fourth Amendment. The police in Indianapolis set up roadblocks identified as narcotics checkpoints, detained drivers for about two to three minutes, examined drivers' licenses and registrations, and had a narcotics-detection dog walk around the vehicle. In finding this practice unconstitutional, the Court distinguished the reasoning of pretext stops (*Whren*), of brief check-point stops for purposes of detecting alcohol-impaired drivers or illegal aliens (*Sitz*; *Martinez-Fuerte*), and special needs (*Von Raab*). The City argued that all other checkpoint stops upheld by the Court employed arrests and criminal prosecutions in pursuit of other goals. In a statement that captured the deep policy concerns of the Court, Justice O'Connor, in her majority opinion, replied:

> If we were to rest the case at this high level of generality, there would be little check on the ability of the authorities to construct roadblocks for almost any conceivable law enforcement purpose. Without drawing the line at roadblocks designed primarily to serve the general interest in crime control, the Fourth Amendment would do little to prevent such intrusions from becoming a routine part of American life. (*City of Indianapolis v. Edmond,* 2000)

After a raft of cases that have expanded the ability of police in actuality to stop virtually any car and to control the passengers and examine all containers, the Court was faced with a line, which if crossed, might have made the total surveillance of anyone walking abroad subject to inspection. First, in a brief by the National League of Cities, the Supreme Court was told that many cities were prepared to initiate narcotics checkpoints depending on the outcome of *Edmond.* What was left unsaid was that a ruling favorable to the government in *Edmond* could have opened the door to virtually unrestricted on-the-street surveillance with drug-sniffing dogs and with highly intrusive electronic and thermal sensing devices that penetrated the clothing of individuals. It is noteworthy that the three most conservative

IN THE STATES: *SITZ* ON REMAND

When the *Sitz* case was returned to the Michigan courts for retrial, they held that sobriety checklanes violated the Michigan Constitution and that state's supreme court agreed: "Because there is no support in the constitutional history of Michigan for the proposition that the police may engage in warrantless and suspicionless seizures of automobiles for the purpose of enforcing the criminal law, we hold that sobriety checklanes violate art 1, § 11 of the Michigan Constitution." The opinion recalled that Michigan had been one of the first states to adopt the exclusionary rule. It noted that the Michigan search and seizure provision should be read as similar to federal law unless there is a compelling reason to deviate, but the compelling reason standard is not "a conclusive presumption artificially linking state constitutional interpretation to federal law." Turning to the specific issue, the court concluded, quite contrary to the reasoning of the United States Supreme Court, that it retained the right to determine what constituted reasonable searches under state law:

> *This Court has never recognized the right of the state, without any level of suspicion whatsoever, to detain members of the population at large for criminal investigatory purposes. Nor has Michigan completely acquiesced to the judgment of "politically accountable officials" when determining reasonableness in such a context. In these circumstances, the Michigan Constitution offers more protection than the United States Supreme Court's interpretation of the Fourth Amendment.*

Sitz v. Michigan Dept. of State Police, 443 Mich. 744, 506 N.W.2d 209 (1993).

justices—Rehnquist, Scalia, and Thomas—dissented, but that swing justices—O'Connor and Kennedy—voted to declare such practices unconstitutional.

Terry at the Airport: Drug Stops and Drug Courier Profiles

The typical scenario in most of the cases in this section that we have already addressed in *United States v. Mendenhall* (1980) (discussed in detail in the section on consent in Chapter 4), is that Drug Enforcement Agency (DEA) agents ask to speak with a person at an airport. In such cases, DEA agents or local police regularly scan airports and other transportation hubs for people who may be transporting illegal drugs. These cases differ from those in which agents have been tipped off by informants that a specific courier is arriving at an airport. Instead, the officers approach a person on a hunch that he or she looks like the sort of person who carries drugs (often young people of college age) or based on a person fitting a "profile" of variables that seem to be characteristic of people who carry drugs. The following cases focus in on the question of whether the facts in the case amounted to a voluntary consent encounter, a *Terry* search, or an arrest. They also show the Court moving toward accepting the "drug courier profile" as a constitutional basis for an investigative stop.

The **drug courier profile** was developed in the early 1970s by a single DEA agent, Paul Markonni, working out of the Detroit Metropolitan Airport, who borrowed the idea from an airplane hijacker profile developed in the late 1960s. The use of the drug profiles has spread to airports throughout the nation.[32] "Because even local police officers now receive high quality training by the DEA, street level drug interdiction programs have resulted in surprisingly few complaints of individual police officer misconduct, such as unjustified, armed threats or arbitrary harassment."[33] Stephen Hall briefly describes how they are used:

> One or more DEA agents (or other law enforcement officers) observe individuals at an airport for characteristics that match the profile. Agents single out an individual as a match, approach the suspect, and identify themselves as law enforcement officers. They then ask the suspect's name and destination. If the Agents are still suspicious, they usually ask the suspect to accompany them to another location for further questioning. At this point, agents ask the suspect to consent to a search of his person, luggage or both.[34]

In *Mendenhall* (1980), the young woman who deplaned was politely approached by DEA agents and asked to accompany them to a room. After some discussion, she agreed to be searched by a female officer in private and drugs were found on her person. *Mendenhall* can be read for three purposes. First, given the variety of opinions, it demonstrates the difficulty of sorting out the facts to determine whether they amounted to a consent encounter or a personal seizure. Second, it shows the concern of the cases on drug courier profiles. Third, it confirms and establishes the test for a seizure as a reasonable person believing that she was not free to leave in view of all of the circumstances surrounding the incident. Although the *Mendenhall* test was modified to fit the contours of the chase in *Hodari D.,* it was, and still is, the standard that is applied in airport scenarios.

The stop of Ms. Mendenhall at the Detroit Metropolitan Airport was triggered by her supposedly fitting the characteristics of such a drug courier profile, leading to a favorable discussion of the device by Justice Powell. He referred to "highly skilled agents" carrying out a "highly specialized law enforcement operation" being assigned to the Detroit airport "as part of a nationwide program to intercept drug couriers transporting narcotics between major drug sources and distribution centers in the United States." He noted, "During the first 18 months of the program, agents watching the Detroit Airport searched 141 persons in 96 encounters. They found controlled substances in 77 of the encounters and arrested 122 persons."[35] Despite this endorsement, neither the lead opinion nor the concurrence in *Mendenhall* was based on a blank acceptance of the profile. The tone of Justice White's dissent was less enthusiastic: "the Government sought to justify the stop by arguing that Ms. Mendenhall's behavior had given rise to reasonable suspicion because it was consistent with portions of the so-called 'drug courier profile,' an informal amalgam of characteristics thought to be associated with persons carrying illegal drugs."[36] Although the majority in *Mendenhall* held that the encounter did not violate the Fourth Amendment, it did so on the basis of consent. *Mendenhall* did not constitutionalize the drug courier profile.

Reid v. Georgia (1980), a brief *per curiam* decision handed down a month after *Mendenhall,* found an airport encounter to violate the Fourth Amendment and indicated some skepticism about accepting the profile as a basis of a *Terry* stop. The government gave the following basis for the stop: Reid arrived in Atlanta from Fort Lauderdale, Florida, a principal place of origin of cocaine sold elsewhere in the country. He "arrived in the early morning, when law enforcement activity is diminished." The passengers left the plane in single file and proceeded through the concourse. Reid was observed occasionally looking backward in the direction of another man who was further back in the line. Reid and the other man carried similar shoulder bags. "When they reached the main lobby of the terminal, the second man caught up with the petitioner and spoke briefly with him. They then left the terminal building together." The government argued they were trying to conceal the fact that they were traveling together and that the lack of checked baggage was suspicious. The Court did not accept this argument and concluded that as a matter of law these innocent facts, which described the activity of many air travelers, could not establish reasonable suspicion of drug transport.

In *Florida v. Royer* (1983), the Supreme Court found that an airport seizure was a Fourth Amendment violation, but the justices could not agree on a reason. A young man was approached by two county narcotics officers at the Miami International Airport because he purportedly fit a drug courier profile: He had purchased a one-way ticket to New York City, was carrying two American Tourister suitcases that appeared to be heavy, was casually dressed, appeared pale and nervous, paid for his ticket in cash with a large number of bills, and wrote only a name on the airline identification tag. The officers identified themselves and asked Royer if he had a "moment" to speak with them. He said yes. Without oral consent, he produced his ticket and a driver's license upon request. He explained a discrepancy between his name and the name "Holt" written on the baggage tag by saying that a friend named Holt had made the reservations. The officers did not return the ticket or license but asked Royer to accompany them to a room forty feet away. In the small office, Royer was told that he was suspected of transporting narcotics and was asked if he would consent to a search of the suitcases. Without orally responding, Royer produced a key, opened the baggage, and marijuana was found. These events took about fifteen minutes.

A majority of justices found that by holding onto Royer's ticket and driver's license, the officers had, in effect, arrested him without probable cause. When police officers retain these important documents, a reasonable person could not believe that he is free to leave. Thus, when Royer went along with the police to the room, he could not consent but had to follow or give up his ticket and license! Holding these documents was the equivalent of a show of force.

Did the facts of *Royer* establish reasonable suspicion to temporarily detain the traveller to briefly question him to confirm or dispel the suspicion? Only four justices in the majority thought so. Thus, *Royer* was not precedent for a drug courier profile in itself constituting reasonable suspicion, but it indicated that many of the justices were leaning in that direction. In any event, a majority felt that the police actions in obtaining the key to Royer's luggage went beyond that justified by a *Terry* stop. This was not a frisk for weapons, but a search for evidence. Justice Powell, notably, did not join the plurality opinion that found support for reasonable suspicion. Justice Brennan, concurring, thought that the majority was wrong to comment on its belief that reasonable suspicion existed because the acts of the officers in detaining Royer went beyond the brief detention called for by *Terry.* Four justices (Burger, Blackmun, Rehnquist, and O'Connor) believed that the acts of the police officers were reasonable and would have upheld the encounter as based on consent.

The next airport search case, *United States v. Place* (1983), held the search to be unconstitutional because the agents detaining Place violated the *brevity requirement* of *Terry.* Place aroused the suspicions of DEA agents at the Miami International Airport and they briefly detained him for questioning. He agreed to a search of his luggage, but because his airplane was departing, the search had to be postponed. The agents called ahead to LaGuardia Airport in New York City, where another team of DEA agents observed Place when he arrived. Their suspicions were also aroused and they detained him by telling him that they believed he was carrying narcotics. Place did not consent to a search of his luggage. The agents seized the bags, giving Place information as to where they could be retrieved. The bags were then sent to Kennedy Airport, where a trained narcotics detection dog indicated the presence of drugs. This process took ninety minutes. After the positive identification, as it was Friday afternoon, the bags were held until Monday, when a search warrant was obtained and drugs were found in the bags.

As Place was detained, not on probable cause but at best on reasonable suspicion, the extent of the detention must be "minimally intrusive of the individual's Fourth Amendment interests." By holding a person's luggage, the person is *detained* by the police although the person is technically free to go. "[S]uch a seizure can effectively restrain the person since he is subjected to the possible disruption of his travel plans in order to remain with his luggage or to arrange for its return." Thus, the seizure of luggage at the airport effectively "seizes" a person. Indeed, the *Terry* brevity principle was violated simply by the length of the detention of Place's luggage. Justice O'Connor noted:

> Although the 90-minute detention of respondent's luggage is sufficient to render the seizure unreasonable, the violation was exacerbated by the failure of the agents to accurately inform respondent of the place to which they were transporting his luggage, of the length of time he might be dispossessed, and of what arrangements would be made for return of the luggage if the investigation dispelled the suspicion. In short, we hold that the detention of respondent's luggage in this case went beyond the narrow authority possessed by police to detain briefly luggage reasonably suspected to contain narcotics.

The Court commented favorably on the canine sniff as an important investigative technique. As a general matter, it appears that when police have reasonable suspicion of drug possession they can *briefly* detain luggage to ascertain whether drugs are present by use of a trained dog.

> A "canine sniff" by a well-trained narcotics detection dog, . . . does not require opening the luggage. It does not expose

> noncontraband items that otherwise would remain hidden from public view, as does, for example, an officer's rummaging through the contents of the luggage. Thus, the manner in which information is obtained through this investigative technique is much less intrusive than a typical search. Moreover, the sniff discloses only the presence or absence of narcotics, a contraband item. Thus, despite the fact that the sniff tells the authorities something about the contents of the luggage, the information obtained is limited. This limited disclosure also ensures that the owner of the property is not subjected to the embarrassment and inconvenience entailed in less discriminate and more intrusive investigative methods. In these respects, the canine sniff is **sui generis.** We are aware of no other investigative procedure that is so limited both in the manner in which the information is obtained and in the content of the information revealed by the procedure. Therefore, we conclude that the particular course of investigation that the agents intended to pursue here—exposure of respondent's luggage, which was located in a public place, to a trained canine—did not constitute a "search" within the meaning of the Fourth Amendment.

This does not resolve all constitutional questions about the use of trained dogs in drug detection, but it indicates that the Court views the technique with favor.

The constitutionality of drug courier profiles was finally upheld in *United States v. Sokolow* (1989). Sokolow was forcibly stopped by DEA agents at the Honolulu airport because he fit the following profile elements: he paid $2,100 for two airplane tickets from a roll of $20 bills; he traveled under a name that did not match the name under which his telephone number was listed; his original destination was Miami, a **source city** for illicit drugs; he stayed in Miami for only forty-eight hours even though a round-trip flight from Honolulu to Miami takes twenty hours; he appeared nervous during his trip; and he checked none of his luggage. He wore the same black jumpsuit with gold jewelry on both his outgoing and returning trips. A canine sniff indicated the presence of drugs, and over a thousand grams of cocaine were found in his carry-on luggage.[37]

The Court confirmed the rule that a suspect fitting a drug courier profile raises the mere suspicion of the agent to the level of reasonable suspicion that allows a *Terry* stop. The majority held that the profile elements in this case amounted to reasonable suspicion. Although each of the facts separately are not indicative of criminality, *taken together* they were out of the ordinary and amounted to reasonable suspicion. For example, Justice Rehnquist wrote, "While a trip from Honolulu to Miami, standing alone, is not a cause for any sort of suspicion, here there was more: surely few residents of Honolulu travel from that city for 20 hours to spend 48 hours in Miami during the month of July." Second, the Court ruled explicitly that reasonable suspicion may be established even though each articulable element of suspicion is innocent. It is not necessary that there also be evidence of ongoing criminal activity to establish reasonable suspicion, as the lower court had held. Finally, the majority also ruled that it was not necessary for the officers to use the "**least intrusive means** available to verify or dispel their suspicions that he was smuggling narcotics," for example, by approaching the suspect and speaking with him, rather than forcibly detaining him. Justice White in *Florida v. Royer* did say that officers must use the least intrusive means reasonably available to verify or dispel their suspicion, but he was referring to the length of time to hold the suspect, not to the technique used. The "least intrusive" rule "would unduly hamper the police's ability to make swift on-the-spot decisions—here, respondent was about to get into a taxicab—and it would require courts to 'indulge in "unrealistic second-guessing"' " (*Sokolow*).

Justice Marshall offered a spirited attack on the drug courier profiles in *Sokolow* but failed to convince a majority that they are flawed. He noted that the *Terry* rule in many cases required evidence of ongoing criminality—such as taking evasive action, "casing" a store, using an alibi, or the word of an informant—to trigger the reasonable suspicion standard. No such indicator of criminality existed in this case. Next, he warned that the mechanistic application of a profile would "dull the officer's ability and determination to make sensitive and fact-specific inferences 'in light of his experience.'" Most telling, he observed that what constituted profile factors seemed to shift from case to case. Citing specific cases, previously decided by lower courts, he pointed out that the profile has been held to be established by:

- The fact that the suspect was the first to deplane, or the last to deplane, or got off in the middle
- That the suspect purchased a one-way ticket or a round-trip ticket
- That the suspect took a nonstop flight or that the suspect changed planes
- That the suspect had one shoulder bag or that the suspect had a new suitcase
- That the suspect was traveling alone or that the suspect was traveling with a companion
- That the suspect acted too nervously or that he acted too calmly.

Justice Marshall demonstrated that the majority's belief that drug courier profiles are sufficiently stable and reliable to authorize investigatory stops, is belied by the cases that show that the elements of the profile may shift from case to case.

There is little research on the effectiveness of these profiles, but a sampling of records by a reporter at the New

York, Miami, and Houston airports indicates "a success rate of about fifty–fifty." A DEA spokesperson conceded that innocent persons are stopped as often as guilty ones, adding, "It's not a science, . . . [i]t's a technique." The story noted that those stopped under a profile are often handcuffed and held for several hours, including being taken to a hospital for x-rays, before being released. The story also suggested that African Americans and Hispanics are stopped more frequently, although the DEA does not keep records of airport stops that can confirm these observations. Finally, it was also noted that drug courier profiles are used on highways, in train stations, and on interstate buses, although less frequently than in airports.[38]

Most scholarly commentators are skeptical or critical about these profiles. A primary reason is given by Justice Marshall: "no uniform drug courier profile exists throughout the nation. Instead, agents create their own individual profiles based on their own professional experiences and observations."[39] A trial court noted that the profile consists of "anything that arouses the agent's suspicion."[40] Professors Janikowski and Giacopassi point out that unlike the FAA "skyjacker profile," which was formulated and tested by psychologists and was tested on 500,000 passengers yielding 1,406 stops and sixteen arrests, "there is some concern as to whether a profile truly exists or whether the profile is, in reality, a loose and malleable compilation of characteristics based on experiential knowledge of the drug trade and the exigencies of the situation."[41] A highly detailed analysis of the use of the profiles by Morgan Cloud, predating *Sokolow,* confirms Justice Marshall's analysis that the profiles are not predictive; he concludes that by relying on the profiles, the courts are abdicating their constitutional responsibilities.[42]

LAW IN SOCIETY

ARREST AND DOMESTIC VIOLENCE

A significant policy debate concerns the rules for arresting wife batterers. Domestic violence is a serious problem: "[S]urveys in 1995 and 1996 estimated that anywhere between one million and four million women a year experience violence at the hands of their partners."[43] About half of all women who are murdered "were killed by either a husband, ex-husband, common law husband, or boyfriend."[44] Studies that sort out instances of female self-defensive violence estimate that women are the perpetrators of domestic violence in only four to ten percent of all cases.[45] Aside from individual physical and psychological injury, a lax criminal justice system strengthens cultural norms that tolerate these assaults, which in turn perpetuates the social and political subjugation of women.[46] The criminal justice response to domestic violence is therefore a weather vane of gender equality, and arrest policies are a critical component of the criminal justice response. The key issues are:

1. What role is played by police discretion in responding to domestic violence?
2. How did the misdemeanor arrest rule contribute to lax domestic violence enforcement?
3. Does arrest deter domestic violence?
4. Is the proper police response to domestic violence mandatory or discretionary arrest?
5. What are the strengths and limits of arrest as a response to domestic violence?

Changing Norms and Laws About Domestic Violence

At ground zero in the early 1970s, by the mid-1980s forty-nine states and the District of Columbia had enacted legislation to provide legal remedies to the victims of domestic violence. These included judicial protection orders, shelters for battered women, and diversion programs for offenders subjected to prosecution.[47] The police community shifted from a policy of separating couples and non-arrest in domestic fights in the late 1960s,[48] to a law enforcement approach by the mid-1970s.[49] In 1984, the United States Attorney General's *Task Force on Family Violence* said, "Family violence should be recognized and responded to as a criminal activity."[50] Women's and the victims' rights groups "were particularly vocal in their support of a more punitive approach. . . ."[51] These changes were caused primarily by "the rise of the new feminist movement, gathering force from about 1970 and affecting virtually every aspect of American life and thought, including the law. . . . [T]he ideological basis of the new feminism, in general, has been gender equality in most spheres of life. As a legal and political phenomenon, feminism has without doubt 'empowered' women. As an empowered group, women forced society at large to shake off the selective social vision that formerly took little notice of the physical abuse of spouses."[52]

The early models for dealing with domestic violence, such as protection orders,[53] were not fully effective but did "increase police responsiveness to the requests of battered women for assistance."[54] In the 1970s, the first mandatory arrest laws were resisted by police officers who were reluctant to arrest spouse beaters.[55] In order to push police into enforcing these laws, several successful civil lawsuits were won against police departments. *Nearing v. Weaver* (1983)[56] held that by failing to enforce the Oregon mandatory arrest statute, police violated the specific legal duty they owed to Nearing to arrest her estranged husband after repeated incidents of threats, harassment, and beatings, and numerous calls by Nearing to the police to enforce a restraining order.[57] Another early case, *Thurman v. City of Torrington,*[58] was the first case in which a federal court held that police handling of domestic violence cases differently from other assaults is gender-based discrimination and violates the Fourteenth Amendment Equal Protection Clause.[59]

Impediment to Change: Police Discretion and Domestic Violence

Legal rules define probable cause, the use of force, the scope of a search incident to arrest, and when a warrant is required for an arrest. Yet, no common law or constitutional doctrine guides the vital question of discretion: When is it proper for a law enforcement officer to arrest or not arrest a suspect? Total enforcement of criminal law is impossible; police discretion in making arrest decisions is inevitable for several reasons:[60] some laws (e.g., disorderly conduct) are vague or open-ended;[61] police departments are understaffed; and enforcing every minor offense to the maximum extent may be excessively rigid and unfair. Police discretion typically is exercised by the lowest-ranking officers, with minimal guidance from supervisors—a "low visibility" practice that often undermines the equal application of the law. Ideally, police use discretion to arrest all serious offenders and to mitigate the harshness of the crime according to "common sense," but it does not always work so nicely.[62] Discretion can also breed unfairness if it is shaped by inappropriate "common sense" values.[63] Thus, a response to a domestic call—whether arrest, avoidance, lecturing, clinical-type counseling, or judgmental intervention—was not a matter of deliberate policy, but depended on the individual police officer's beliefs about the rightness of wife beating.[64] In this, the police reflected the larger society that traditionally condoned wife beating to such an extent that it was not considered a criminal act by many.[65] Yet, the crimes committed by a wife beater "include assault and/or battery, aggravated assault, intent to assault or to commit murder, and, in cases where the woman is coerced sexually, rape."[66] The combination of traditional views and police discretion has thus discouraged the arrest of batterers. Even mandatory arrest laws may not result in more arrests—a point borne out in a study by Professor Kathleen Ferraro, observing arrest patterns by Phoenix police officers in domestic cases under a mandatory arrest law. She found that police discretion shaped how officers assessed the existence of probable cause, leading to questionable no-probable-cause decisions. Police discretion remains and is influenced by legal, ideological, practical, and political factors, even when a department adopts a mandatory arrest policy.[67] Thus, the existence of police discretion means that changes in behavior require changes in fundamental social thinking on the part of police officers and more attention to control of discretion by high ranking supervisors.

Impediment to Change: Warrantless Misdemeanor Arrests

The common law rule is that an officer cannot make a misdemeanor arrest unless it occurs in his presence. This rule prevented officers from making domestic violence arrests in "the largest category of calls received by police each year"[68]: Two-thirds of domestic violence cases are classified as misdemeanors. A battering victim would have to file a complaint and get a judicial warrant to have the beater arrested, a situation that virtually never occurred.[69] When this problem became apparent in the first wave of feminist criticism, the states quickly responded and dropped the in-presence requirement for misdemeanor arrests in domestic violence cases. "Statutes in 47 states and the District of Columbia now authorize or mandate warrantless, probable cause arrest for crimes involving domestic violence. This is a significant departure from the common law."[70] Officers could now arrest if probable cause exists to believe (1) that the suspect has committed a misdemeanor involving domestic violence, or (2) that the suspect has committed a misdemeanor and there is reason to believe that the suspect presents a continuing danger if not immediately arrested.[71] This legal change is especially important because forty-two percent of the victims of "simple assaults" suffered physical injury, compared to thirty-six percent of women who reported felony crimes in domestic violence. This may be because the display of a weapon without any physical injury raises the crime to a felony.[72]

The Minneapolis Experiment and the Replication Experiments

In 1984, a report of a Minneapolis police experiment conducted by Professors Lawrence Sherman and Richard Berk showed that arresting a batterer produced lower levels of official reports of domestic violence than giving the parties on-the-spot mediation or simply separating the couple. The report, suggesting that arrest alone deterred spousal abuse, caused a sensation. Among criminologists it raised questions because it went against substantial research evidence that specific programs generally do not measurably deter crime.[73] The report had a tremendous impact on police policies for two reasons. First, one of the authors publicized the research in the news media otherwise broadcasting the findings to the general public and police chiefs.[74] Second, these publications fit the temper of the time; they likely accelerated a trend toward the arrest of batterers that was already under way.[75]

Because of the controversial nature of the findings, and the importance of the policy issue, the National Institute of Justice funded several replications of the Minneapolis experiment in the late 1980s in Charlotte, Colorado Springs, Miami, Milwaukee and Omaha. The results of these experiments unleashed a new barrage of controversy. The most important result is that there was no simple deterrent effect of arrest on domestic violence recidivism. Sherman summarized the paradoxical and contradictory findings in four "policy dilemmas":

1. Arrest reduces domestic violence in some cities but increases it in others
2. Arrest reduces domestic violence among employed people but increases it among unemployed people
3. Arrest reduces domestic violence in the short run but can increase it in the long run
4. Police can predict which couples are most likely to suffer future violence but our society values privacy too highly to encourage preventive action.[76]

It would be incoherent and unconstitutional to fine tune an arrest policy that mandates arrests of employed batterers but not those without a job! What Professor Sherman proposed was to repeal mandatory arrest laws but allow warrantless misdemeanor arrests, and encourage police departments to develop local policies. He also recommended the creation of special units and policies to focus on chronically violent couples.[77]

A Response to the Replication Studies

Joan Zorza, in an article critical of the replication studies, supports mandatory arrest of batterers while pointing out the limitations of relying on arrest alone to deal with a deep-seated behavioral problem. She noted that the arrest studies were conducted in isolation of what arrest could accomplish as part of a coordinated response.[78] The National Council of Juvenile and Family Court Judges, for example, has proposed a detailed and coordinated effort to deal with domestic violence.[79] Zorza also suggested that batterers should not be released sooner than others charged with assault and that police should arrest when they have probable cause (or obtain arrest warrants for absent abusers). If findings show that unemployed batterers are least deterred by arrest, then court programs should seek employment for them, but not at the expense of services and employment opportunities for victims of violent crime. Zorza concludes by saying that the "real implication of the police replication studies are that a coordinated community response is what is needed to best eliminate domestic violence."[80] But even with coordinated policies, the policy debate over mandatory arrest laws continues.

Mandatory Arrest Laws and Policies

AGAINST MANDATORY ARREST First, the deterrent effect of a mandatory arrest policy is far from proven; any effect seems to be temporary. Mandatory arrest ignores the wide range of behavior that falls within the definition of domestic violence and may amount to overkill. If the arrested partner is acquitted, the abused spouse will feel let down and the incident might spark further violence. Even the goal of immediate protection may be short-lived as an arrested partner is likely to be released shortly on bond or recognizance. Again, this may place the victim in a worse situation. Mandatory arrest increases the probability of abuse of the process by police officers or by a vindictive spouse. Some advocates for battered women oppose mandatory arrest on the belief that it "further erodes victims' self-esteem and contributes to their sense of helplessness by usurping their control." Others are concerned that women will lose economic support.[81]

There is no guarantee that an arrest would lead to a close prosecutor-victim interaction that will increase the determination and awareness of the victim. Finally, a mandatory arrest policy assumes that relationships are always power relationships, where the woman is essentially powerless and requires strong external intervention.[82] Instead, Carol Wright proposes a wide range of options, including discretionary arrest, victim assistance techniques, mediation programs, shelters and other social programs, a comprehensive legislative framework, and publicity to give domestic abuse victims a better awareness of all their options.[83]

FOR MANDATORY ARREST[84] Rates of arrest in domestic violence are so low, often because police fail to find probable cause and thus discourage victims from pressing charges, that mandatory arrest laws are needed to counteract police bias and send a message that arrest is the appropriate response to battering. Further, mandatory arrest laws do not strip police officers of all discretion. Mandatory arrest relieves police officers from the inappropriate role of family counselors. It also removes the decision to arrest from the victim's control, where the victim's fear and a power imbalance in the relationship are likely to cause the victim to not opt for arrest. Thus, mandatory arrest laws may empower victims by giving them the courage to call the police in the first place. Studies that show increased violence after arrest may be flawed.

Marion Wanless notes that as of 1996, sixteen states and the District of Columbia have adopted mandatory arrest laws. States with such laws have seen a sharp increase in arrests for domestic violence. This shows that "In states with the laws, police take domestic violence seriously."[85] In a close examination of these laws, she notes that not all mandatory arrest laws are the same. By their terms, they pose three levels of arrest threshold: low, moderate, and high. In high-threshold states, mandatory arrest is required only when a condition such as injury occurs, unless the officer believes that the victim will be protected from further injury. This undermines the mandatory arrest rule. Wanless recommends laws with moderate thresholds: Arrest is mandatory arrest where injury has occurred, there is a risk for continued danger, or a dangerous weapon was used.[86]

Still, even this strong proponent of mandatory arrest laws concludes that "Mandatory arrest, without more, may also be insufficient to protect victims."[87] Even in a system with vigorous prosecution of batterers and a full array of sentencing and social intervention options, the police play a critical role as gatekeepers, shunting domestic violence cases to the criminal justice system or the social service system, or leaving them as private matters.

Conclusion

This section has explored the powerful tradition of arrest discretion and discussed how in an area of particular concern to the public, domestic violence, it has come under legal attack. Because old habits die hard, we see there are several legal avenues that women have used to remind the criminal justice system that its obligations to protect the personal safety of people do not end at the doorstep of the home. Arrest of batterers has been subject to social science inquiry, yielding complex results. Policy must be developed without final evidence of what arrest can achieve. In any event, using arrest without prosecution as a method of social control raises due process questions. Thus, a policy of mandatory, or at least preferred, arrest, followed by vigorous prosecution and well-thought-out court and probation programs seems to be the best approach to dealing with the distressing issue of domestic abuse.

SUMMARY

The personal detention of a person by a police officer may be legal or illegal. Legal detentions or seizures under the Fourth Amendment fall into two categories: arrests supported by probable cause or investigative stops supported by reasonable suspicion. In addition, a person may consent to engage in an encounter with a law enforcement agent, for which the officer requires no level of evidence. Police have no right to detain persons at will to investigate without a level of suspicion. A lawful arrest authorizes an officer to take a person into custody to begin a process of prosecution. An officer who has only reasonable suspicion may temporarily detain a person for brief questioning to confirm or dispel the suspicion. A person in a premises may be detained during the time a search warrant is executed. An arrested person may be subjected to a thorough search for evidence of crime or weapons. A person briefly detained for an investigatory stop may only be subjected to a "frisk": a brief pat-down of outer clothing to detect the presence of a weapon.

Two definitions of "seizure" arrest issued by the Supreme Court are: 1. An arrest occurs when a person believes he or she is not free to leave (*Mendenhall*), and 2. When physically stopped (*Hodari D.*). A person who is fleeing from a police officer intent on stopping him is not seized until the instant the person is physically stopped. An arrested person loses his right to privacy and may be kept in view of police at all times. An officer must have probable cause *before* making an arrest. Probable cause is an objective standard supported by facts, not on the good faith of an officer. Proximity to a crime alone does not establish probable cause. Every warrantless arrest is subjected to a probable cause determination by a judicial officer soon after an arrest; typically within forty-eight hours. Probable cause can also be based on direct observation of an officer, hearsay, or reports from other police departments. Misdemeanor arrests can be made only for offenses committed in the officer's presence; except that in most states, by statute, misdemeanor arrests can be made on probable cause in domestic violence cases. A court does not lose jurisdiction of a case if an officer makes an illegal arrest. Evidence seized during an illegal arrest is inadmissible; but evidence obtained during an arrest based on probable cause that was in fact mistaken is admissible. A "citizen arrest" may be made on probable cause but if mistaken, the person making the arrest is strictly liable for the tort of false arrest. Police may use reasonable force to effect an arrest and deadly force where it is reasonable. The common law rule allowing an officer to shoot to kill a fleeing felon violates the Fourth Amendment because it is excessive and unreasonable.

The Fourth Amendment does not require an arrest warrant for a lawful arrest that is made in a public place, even if the police have had time to obtain the warrant. On the other hand, police must have an arrest warrant to enter a person's home to arrest him or her unless the entry is justified by an exigency. An exigency is not created merely because the crime for which the arrest is made was a serious crime. Police cannot rely on an arrest warrant to enter the home of a third party to arrest a person—such an entry has to be justified with a search warrant.

A person arrested for a crime that authorizes the officer to take the person into custody may be thoroughly searched for weapons and for evidence. The evidence from a search incident to arrest need not pertain to the crime for which a person was arrested. A police officer who stops a speeding car and issues a citation rather than making an arrest has no justification to search the car. When a person is arrested, the police may search the area within the person's immediate control for weapons or evidence but may not go beyond to search a house or other premises. When police enter a premises and arrest a person, they may look into the adjoining room, without any evidentiary basis, to look for another person who could injure the officers. However, for them to conduct a protective sweep of the entire premises to look for a confederate of the arrested person, they must have reasonable suspicion to believe that another person is in the house. Police may conduct an inventory of all an arrested person's belongings at a police lockup or jail; this is not a Fourth Amendment search for evidence but an administrative procedure designed to promote safety and deter theft and false claims of theft of the prisoner's goods. A search incident to arrest may be made at the police station. Pretrial detainees held in a jail may be subjected to strip and body cavity searches when reasonable.

The Court has recognized the law enforcement power to briefly detain suspects who are reasonably believed to be involved in criminal activity in order to question them about their suspicious activity and to frisk them for weapons. The standard of evidence for such "stop and frisks" is "reasonable suspicion," a lesser standard than probable cause to believe that a crime has been committed and that the suspect committed it. Reasonable suspicion can be based on an officer's expertise in drawing inferences from observed facts, on an informant's hearsay, from a verified and reliable anonymous call, or from a police bulletin. Reasonable suspicion is based on a totality of the circumstances, including inferences from facts. An investigatory stop must be brief and nonintrusive.

A person cannot be stopped on the street simply for identification under an indefinite vagrancy statute or because he or she is standing in a high crime neighborhood. A gang loitering ordinance that makes it a crime for a gang member to simply "loiter" and not "disperse" when so ordered violates the void-for-vagueness doctrine of the Fourteenth Amendment. A person who is chased by a police officer is not seized until the person is physically caught, and any property that the person throws away before being caught has been abandoned and is not protected by the Fourth Amendment expectation of privacy. A person who flees from a police officer without provocation establishes reasonable suspicion for an investigatory stop.

Automobile drivers cannot be stopped at random on the highway by police for a registration and license check without probable cause or reasonable suspicion of a crime or a motor vehicle violation. When a person is stopped in a car for an investigatory stop, officers may visually scan the interior of the car for weapons. There is no Fourth Amendment violation if an officer who stops a car for an existing traffic offense did so for the purpose of searching for drugs—a pretext search is constitutional. A drug courier profile can be the basis for making a stop of a person in an automobile. The standard for appellate review of a reasonable suspicion or probable cause determination is *de novo* review that independently evaluates the facts and not deference to the magistrate's decision. Once a car is stopped the officer may, for his own safety, order the driver and passengers to exit the automobile.

When police officers accost a person in a nonthreatening manner in a space where the person would not ordinarily be free to move about, such as at a factory workstation or in an inter-city bus, that fact alone does not turn a consensual encounter into a seizure. A person stopped for an open automobile sobriety checklane is not seized for Fourth Amendment purposes. Police who accost a person at an airport and ask to speak to him or her about drug transportation do not seize such a person unless they detain the passenger's ticket or luggage for more than a few moments. A sniff of luggage by a trained for narcotics dog is not a Fourth Amendment search. A person who gets off an airplane from Florida on an early morning flight and looks behind him for a companion does not fit a drug courier profile. A drug courier profile may be based on a series of innocent facts that, when taken together, allow an officer to draw a reasonable conclusion that the person is a drug courier. Police have reasonable suspicion to stop a person who fits a drug courier profile.

LEGAL PUZZLES

How Have Courts Decided These Cases?

5–1. A woman called 911 about noon to report she had been beaten. Police soon arrived and found a severely beaten and bloodied woman, who identified her husband as the beater. She said that her husband was dealing drugs and suspected her of going over to the FBI. She said he left with three other men. The police went to the husband's house and surrounded it with an eight member SWAT team dressed in black fatigue uniforms and armed with shotguns, rifles, and submachine guns. An inner and outer police perimeter was set up and the entire area was cordoned off. The husband and other men in the house saw the police. The police telephoned the house and ordered the men to leave the house, one by one, backwards out the back door. When the men exited the house, they were physically handcuffed and taken into custody. The police had no arrest warrants. (i) Did the arrest take place in the house or outside the house? (ii) Did an exigency exist to allow a warrantless arrest? (*Sharrar v. Felsing,* 128 F.3d 810 [3rd Cir. 1997])

5–2. Police armed with an arrest warrant staked out the apartment of Henry, also known as "Roach", at 9:30 A.M. Late that morning, Henry's fiancee emerged from the apartment and told the police that he was inside and that there was no one else in the apartment with him. At 1:30 P.M., Henry stepped from the apartment into the internal hallway of the building leaving the door ajar behind him. An officer immediately placed Henry under arrest and radioed for backup. A number of officers arrived from their posts outside the building, physically subdued Henry, and handcuffed him. At this point, Henry's co-defendant was outside the building peering into the hallway through a window and officers heard Henry tell the co-defendant that "they got me." Five officers then went into the apartment with Henry and conducted a "security check." In the bedroom, two bags of a white powdery substance were found which later proved to be heroin. At the suppression hearing the officers testified an informant said that Henry's "boys" might be with him. Did the police have grounds to conduct a protective sweep of the apartment? (*United States v. Henry,* 48 F.3d [D.C. Cir. 1995])

5–3. A border patrol agent driving south on a highway near Alpine, Texas, about 80 miles north of the Mexican border and four miles north of a fixed border checkpoint, turned north to follow a Toyota 4-Runner covered in wet mud, although there had been no rainfall in the area in the previous weeks. The agent thought the driver, Jones, looked like a tourist. A blue tarpaulin was draped over something in the rear cargo area of the 4-Runner. The agent followed the car, at times tail-gating to view the license plate. Jones continually glanced back at the agent. [Jones was driving with his headlights on.] The car was stopped and marijuana was found. Do these facts constitute reasonable suspicion to stop the 4-Runner? (*United States v. Jones,* 149 F.3d 364 [5th Cir. 1998])

5–4. A patrol officer in Memphis stopped a car for speeding. The driver, Robinson, had no license and he accompanied the officer to the patrol car to do a license check. Owens, the passenger, was questioned separately; the two men gave inconsistent answers about their names and the car ownership. The officer called for backup (which arrived shortly), a drug sniffing dog, and for a stolen car check. Fourteen minutes into the stop, Robinson admitted that his driver's license had been suspended, a fact confirmed by a police communication five minutes later. Robinson was then arrested for driving without a license. The normal procedure of having the driver-owner sign permission to drive to the passenger was not possible because the car ownership was not certain. Robinson then said that Owens was the owner but the officers elected to await the results of the vehicle registration check. About twenty-nine minutes into the stop, the officers received information that Robinson had a cocaine possession charge, that the registered owner, Kenneth Allen, had several criminal charges, and an NCIC indication that the vehicle has not been reported stolen. The officers still waited for the results of the vehicle registration check rather than permit Owens to drive away, because they believed that stolen cars did not always appear on the NCIC database. At fifty minutes into the stop, while the officers were still waiting for the results of the vehicle registration check, the canine unit arrived. Drugs, guns, and money were discovered in the car. Treating the initial stop as a *Terry* stop, and the detention of Owens as justified by reasonable suspicion, did the fifty minute length of detention turn the stop into an arrest? (*United States v. Owens,* 167 F.3d 739 [1st Cir. 1999])

ANSWERS TO LEGAL PUZZLES

5–1. (i) IN THE HOUSE; (ii) NO. (i) "[W]hen a SWAT team surrounds a residence with machine guns pointed at the windows and the persons inside are ordered to leave the house backwards with their hands raised, an arrest has undoubtedly occurred. There was a clear show of physical force and assertion of authority. No reasonable person would have believed that he was free to remain in the house. . . . Under these circumstances the arrests occurred inside [the] home." (ii) "There is an insufficient basis . . . to hold . . . that exigent circumstances existed as a matter of law. There [was no] "hot pursuit," a fear that the suspects would flee, or a fear that evidence would be destroyed. . . . [A]t most, the police believed that the suspects posed a danger because [the wife] said she had been hit with a gun. The mere possession of a gun, which as far as the officers knew had been used only once and then against [the] wife, no matter how grievous a crime, does not necessarily show exigent circumstances. The police have not satisfactorily explained why, when the house was completely surrounded by an armed SWAT team, they could not secure the premises while they went to procure an arrest warrant, especially in light of the fact that [a] Municipal Court Judge . . . was sitting on the bench at the police station during this entire episode. The issue of exigent circumstances in these circumstances would be one for the jury."

5–2. YES. Although *Buie* concerned an arrest made in the home, its principles are fully applicable when the arrest takes place just outside the residence. That the police arrested the defendant outside rather than inside his dwelling is relevant to the question of whether they could reasonably fear an attack by someone within it. The officers' exact location, however, does not change the nature of the appropriate inquiry: Did articulable facts exist that would lead a reasonably prudent officer to believe a sweep was required to protect the safety of those on the arrest scene?

5–3. NO. (1) The stop occurred eighty miles from the border and there "are far too many places between Alpine, Texas, and the Texas-Mexico border for a vehicle to pick up fresh mud virtually any time of the year . . . There are numerous ranch roads in the area that cross spring-fed creeks that flow year-round. . . . In short, there is simply nothing suspicious about a muddy 4 Runner traveling in an area where one should expect most vehicles to have some mud on them." (2) "The fact that Jones was driving with his lights on may indicate that he crossed the border or picked up illegal aliens on this side of the border before dawn. However, the fact that Jones was driving northbound on Highway 118 with his lights on at 7:00 A.M. five miles south of Alpine, Texas, is just as consistent with him being a tourist who left Big Bend National Park before dawn. Indeed, the latter possibility is far more likely, since, as noted by Agent Barrera, Jones looked like a tourist." (3) "Barrera had it on good authority that smugglers had recently engaged in the practice of using tourists or tourist-looking persons to bootleg illegal aliens, because they looked less suspicious. In other words, what was suspicious about Jones is that he looked like an unsuspicious tourist. A factual condition which is consistent with the smuggling of illegal aliens in a particular area, will not predicate reasonable suspicion, if that factual condition occurs even more frequently among the law abiding public in the area."

5–4. NO. The fifty-minute detention was a lengthy one, and in some circumstances would establish a *de facto* arrest, but long duration does not by itself transform an otherwise valid stop into an arrest. The period of detention was reasonable: the officers spent twenty minutes ascertaining whether Robinson had a valid driver's license. Only after arresting Robinson did the officers face the problem of whether to permit Owens to drive a car that he did not own. They diligently pursued a means of investigation that would dispel their suspicions. They initiated a number of computer checks on the car and its occupants and reasonably awaited the results.

FURTHER READING

Lawrence P. Tiffany, Donald M. McIntyre, Jr., and Daniel L. Rotenberg, *Detection of Crime* (Boston: Little, Brown, 1967)

William Ker Muir, Jr., *Police: Streetcorner Politicians* (Chicago: University of Chicago Press, 1977)

Human Rights Watch, *Shielded From Justice: Police Brutality and Accountability in the United States* (New York: Human Rights Watch, 1998)

ENDNOTES

1. Joel H. Garner and Christopher D. Maxwell, Measuring the Amount of Force Used By and Against the Police in Six Jurisdictions, in United States Office of Justice Programs, *Use of Force by Police,* pp. 31–33 (Washington: Nat'l. Inst. Of Justice, Oct. 1999).
2. *Albright v. Oliver* (1994), Justice Ginsburg, concurring, citing Blackstone.
3. *Fed. R. Crim. Pro.,* Rule 5(a).
4. *Draper v. United States* (1959); *McCray v. Illinois* (1967).
5. These rules may not, as is commonly believed, be traceable to the old English common law but may be relatively modern developments of the late eighteenth and the nineteenth centuries. See Thomas Y. Davies. Recovering the Original Fourth Amendment, *Michigan Law Review* 98(3):547–750, pp. 634–42, 724–26 (1999).
6. See J. Bradley Ortins, District of Columbia Survey: Warrantless Misdemeanor Arrest for Drunk Driving Found Invalid in Schram v. District of Columbia, *Catholic University Law Review* 34:1241–54 (1985).
7. David A. Sklansky, The Private Police, *UCLA Law Review* 46:1165–1287 (1999), p. 1183.
8. Sklansky, Private Police, p. 1184.
9. The case ended badly for the United States. Dr. Alvarez-Machain was acquitted of murder and torture in the Los Angeles Federal District Court in December 1992. The judge threw out the case, calling the prosecution's case the "wildest speculation." Another man was convicted. The incident caused much resentment of the United States in Mexico. As a result of the incident, the Clinton Administration has promised Mexico that it will not engage in any cross-border kidnapping of Mexican citizens pending a revised extradition treaty. Dr. Alvarez-Machain sued federal law enforcement officials for $20 million in damages for kidnapping, torture, and false imprisonment. "Mexican Can Sue U.S.," *New York Times,* Feb. 23, 1997, sec. 1. p. 1.
10. Michael J. Glennon, International Kidnapping: State-sponsored Abduction: a Comment on *United States v. Alvarez-Machain, American Society of International Law Newsletter* 86:746 (October, 1992).
11. F.J. Remington, D.J. Newman, E.L. Kimball, M. Melli and H. Goldstein, *Criminal Justice Administration, Materials and Cases* [First Edition] (Indianapolis: Bobbs–Merrill, 1969). p. 20.
12. Garner v. Memphis Police Department, 710 F.2d 240 (6th Cir. 1983).
13. Jerome H. Skolnick and James J. Fyfe, *Above the Law: Police and the Excessive Use of Force* (New York: Free Press, 1993), p. 246.
14. *Dorman v. United States,* 435 F.2d 385, 392–93 (D.C. Cir. 1970).
15. 723 F.2d 1263 (7th Cir. 1983).
16. Robin Lee Fenton, Comment: the Constitutionality of Policies Requiring Strip Searches of All Misdemeanants and Minor Traffic Offenders, *University of Cincinnati Law Review* 54: 175–89 (1985), pp. 180–81.
17. William J. Simonitsch, Comment: Visual Body Cavity Searches Incident to Arrest: Validity Under the Fourth Amendment, *University of Miami Law Review* 54:665–88 (2000), pp. 681–82.

18. D. Caute, *The Year of the Barricades: A Journey Through 1968* (New York: Harper & Row, 1988).
19. However, one biographer read *Terry* at face value as a balancing of law enforcement needs against privacy rights. G. Edward White, *Earl Warren: A Public Life* (New York: Oxford University Press, 1982), pp. 276–78.
20. F. Graham, *The Due Process Revolution: The Warren Court's Impact on Criminal Law* (New York: Hayden Book Co., 1970), pp. 22–23.
21. P. Chevigny, *Police Power: Police Abuses in New York City* (New York: Pantheon, 1969).
22. M. Lippman, "The Drug War and the Vanishing Fourth Amendment," *Criminal Justice Journal* 14(1992):229–308.
23. M. McAlary, *Buddy Boys: When Good Cops Turn Bad* (New York: Putnam's, 1987), p. 87.
24. T. J. Devetski, "Fourth Amendment–Protection Against Unreasonable Seizure of the Person: The New (?) Common Law Arrest Test for Seizure," *Journal of Criminal Law & Criminology* 82 (1992):747–72.
25. T. Maclin, "Book Review: Seeing the Constitution from the Backseat of a Police Squad Car," *Boston University Law Review* 70(1990):543–91, p. 550 (emphasis added).
26. Maclin, "Book Review," p. 550.
27. Marvin Zalman, Fleeing From the Fourth Amendment, *Criminal Law Bulletin* 36(2):129–47 (2000).
28. Citing *State v. Belton,* 441 So.2d 1195, 1199 (La. 1983) (emphasis added).
29. *Terry v. Ohio,* p. 21.
30. George C. Thomas, III, *Terry v. Ohio* in the Trenches: A Glimpse at How Courts Apply "Reasonable Suspicion," *St. John's Law Review* 72: 1025–41, p. 1032 (1998).
31. G. G. Ashdown, "Drugs, Ideology, and the Deconstitutionalization of Criminal Procedure," *West Virginia Law Review* 95(1992):1–54, p. 22 (paragraph breaks ignored).
32. M. Cloud, "Search and Seizures by the Numbers: The Drug Courier Profile and Judicial Review of Investigative Formulas," *Boston University Law Review* 65(1985):843–921, pp. 844–45, 847–48; S. E. Hall, "A Balancing Approach to the Constitutionality of Drug Courier Profiles," *University of Illinois Law Review* 1993:1007–1036, pp. 1009–1010.
33. S. Guerra, "Domestic Drug Interdiction Operations: Finding the Balance," *Journal of Criminal Law & Criminology* 82 (1992):1109–61, p. 1114.
34. Hall, "A Balancing Approach," p. 1010.
35. *United States v. Mendenhall* (1980), p. 562 (Powell, J., concurring).
36. *United States v. Mendenhall* (1980), pp. 567–68 (White, J., dissenting).
37. A warrant was initially obtained to search the shoulder bag, which yielded documents pointing to drug trafficking; a warrant was then obtained to search the carry-on bag, and the cocaine was found.
38. Lisa Belkin, "Airport Anti-Drug Nets Snare Many People Fitting 'Profiles,'" *New York Times,* Mar. 20, 1990, p. 1.
39. Hall, "A Balancing Approach," pp. 1010–11.
40. Cases cited in Hall, "A Balancing Approach," p. 1011, n. 35.
41. W. R. Janikowski and D. J. Giacopassi, "Pyrrhic Images, Dancing Shadows, and Flights of Fancy: The Drug Courier Profile as Legal Fiction," *Journal of Contemporary Criminal Justice* 9(1993):60–69.
42. Cloud, "Search and Seizures by the Numbers," note 32.
43. Betsy Tsai, Note: the Trend Toward Specialized Domestic Violence Courts: Improvements on an Effective Innovation, *Fordham Law Review* 68:1285 (2000), p. 1292, citing The Commission on Domestic Violence, Statistics (visited Oct. 15, 1999) <http:www.abanet.org/domviol/stats.html>
44. E. S. Buzawa and C. G. Buzawa, *Domestic Violence: The Criminal Justice Response* (Newbury Park, Calif.: Sage, 1990), p. 20.
45. J. Zorza, "Must We Stop Arresting Batterers?: Analysis and Policy Implications of New Police Domestic Violence Studies," *New England Law Review* 28(1994):929–90, p. 931.
46. Buzawa and Buzawa, *Domestic Violence,* p. 20.
47. Lerman, "Statute."
48. Richard J. Gelles and Murray A. Straus, *Intimate Violence* (New York: Touchstone, 1989), p. 114. The earlier training manual is International Association of Chiefs of Police, *Training Key 16: Handling Disturbance Calls* (Gaithersburg, Md.: International Association of Chiefs of Police, 1967).
49. International Association of Chiefs of Police, *Training Key 245: Wife Beating* (Gaithersburg, Md.: International Association of Chiefs of Police, 1976): "The officer who starts legal action may give the wife the courage she needs to realistically face and correct her situation."
50. Gelles and Straus, *Intimate Violence,* p. 166; United States Attorney-General's Task Force on Family Violence, *Report* (Washington, D.C.: U.S. Dept. of Justice, 1984).
51. A. Binder and J. Meeker, "The Development of Social Attitudes Toward Spousal Abuse," in E. S. Buzawa and C. G. Buzawa, eds, *Domestic Violence: The Changing Criminal Justice Response* (Westport, Conn.: Auburn House, 1992) pp. 3–19, p. 82. See generally, F. J. Weed, *Certainty of Justice: Reform in the Criminal Justice Movement* (New York: Aldine de Gruyter, 1995).
52. M. Zalman, "The Courts' Response to Police Intervention in Domestic Violence," in E. S. Buzawa and C. G. Buzawa, eds, *Domestic Violence: The Changing Criminal Justice Response* (Westport, Conn.: Auburn House, 1992), pp. 79–110, p. 82.
53. They are also known as restraining orders, protective orders, or temporary restraining orders, Lerman, "Statute," pp. 76–120; see Comment in Gary Brown, Karin A. Keitel, and Sandra E. Lundy, "Starting a TRO Project: Student Representation of Battered Women," *Yale Law Journal* 96(1987):1985–2020.
54. Hart, State Codes, p. 24 (footnotes omitted).
55. Ruth Gundle, "Civil Liability for Police Failure to Arrest: *Nearing v. Weaver,*" *Women's Rights Law Reporter* 9(3&4): 259–265, pp. 259–60 (1986), p. 262. Injunction suits were brought: *Bruno v. Codd,* 90 Misc.2d 1047, 396 N.Y.S.2d 974

(Sup Ct. Special Term 1977), *rev'd in part, appeal dismissed in part,* 64 A.D.2d 582, 407 N.Y.S.2d 165 (1978), *aff'd,* 47 N.Y.2d 582, 393 N.E.2d 976, 419 N.Y.S.2d 901 (1979) (class action; consent decree entered to enforce protection orders); *Scott v. Hart,* No. C–76–2395 (N.D., Cal. filed Nov. 24, 1976); *Raguz v. Chandler,* No. C–74–1064 (N.D. Ohio, filed Nov. 20, 1974). These cases are discussed in Gundle, "Civil Liability," pp. 261–262; Case Comment, Carolyne R. Hathaway, "Gender Based Discrimination in Police Reluctance to Respond to Domestic Assault Complaints," *Georgetown Law Review* 75(1986):667–91, pp. 676–77. Their effectiveness is limited to a single individual or municipality.

56. 295 Or. 702, 670 P.2d 137 (1983).
57. *DeShaney v. Winnebago County* (1989).
58. 595 F. Supp. 1521 (D. Conn 1984).
59. Case Comment in Hathaway, "Gender Based Discrimination," p. 669.
60. American Bar Association, *Standards Relating to The Urban Police Function* (1972), p. 116; J. Goldstein, "Police Discretion Not to Invoke the Criminal Process: Low-Visibility Decisions in the Administration of Justice," in G. Cole, *Criminal Justice: Law and Politics,* 5th ed. (Pacific Grove, Calif.: Brooks/Cole, 1988), pp. 83–102, from *Yale Law Journal* 69:543–94; William Ker Muir, Jr., *Police: Streetcorner Politicians* (Chicago: University of Chicago Press, 1977).
61. Indeed, legislatures at times assume that laws they pass will not be strictly enforced by the police, see M. Zalman, "Mandatory Sentencing Legislation: Myth and Reality," in M. Morash, *Implementing Criminal Justice Policies* (Beverly Hills, Calif.: Sage, 1982), pp. 61–69.
62. Muir, *Police,* pp. 101–25; Goldstein, "Police Discretion," pp. 94–97.
63. K. C. Davis, *Discretionary Justice: A Preliminary Inquiry* (Baton Rouge: Louisiana State University Press, 1969), pp. 3, 5.
64. Muir, *Police,* pp. 57, 82–100.
65. Lloyd Ohlin and Michael Tonry, "Family Violence in Perspective," in Ohlin and Tonry, eds. *Family Violence* (Chicago: University of Chicago Press, 1989), pp. 1–18. A 1970 survey found that 25% of the male respondents and 17% of the females approved of a husband slapping his wife under certain circumstances. Irene H. Frieze and Angela Browne, "Violence in Marriage," in Ohlin and Tonry, eds., *Family Violence,* p. 165.
66. Del Martin, *Battered Wives, Revised, Updated* (San Francisco: Volcano Press, 1981), pp. 87–88.
67. K. J. Ferraro, "Policing Women Battering," *Social Problems* 36(1) (1989):61–74.
68. J. Zorza, "The Criminal Law of Misdemeanor Domestic Violence," *Journal of Criminal Law and Criminology* 83(1992): 46–72, p. 46.
69. A national victimization survey found that one-third of battered spouses were victims of the felonies of rape, robbery, or aggravated assault, while two-thirds were victimized by misdemeanor simple assaults. Patrick A. Langan and Christopher A. Innes, *Bureau of Justice Statistics Special Report: Preventing Domestic Violence Against Women* (Washington, D.C.: U.S. Dept. of Justice, 1986).
70. B. Hart, "State Codes on Domestic Violence: Analysis, Commentary and Recommendations," *Juvenile and Family Court Journal* 43(1992):1–81, p. 63.
71. Lisa G. Lerman, "Statute: A Model State Act: Remedies for Domestic Abuse," *Harvard Journal on Legislation* 21(1984): 61–143, pp. 126–27. Illinois has adopted such a provision.
72. Langan and Innes, *Bureau of Justice Statistics Special Report.* Lisa G. Lerman, "Expansion of Arrest Power: A Key to Effective Intervention," *Vermont Law Review* 7(1982):59–70, pp. 64–65.
73. The research involved an experimental design and the type of intervention was determined randomly and before the police entered the house so that there would be no exercise of discretion; the sample was quite small. It was conducted by Lawrence W. Sherman and Richard A. Berk and published in the *Police Foundation Reports* (1984). A scholarly journal article was also published: L. Sherman and R. Berk, "The Specific Deterrent Effects of Arrest for Domestic Violence," *American Sociological Review* 49(2) 261–72 (1984). The authors were cautious in drawing policy conclusions but despite such cautions, the findings were widely publicized and "caught fire" with the relevant public of police administrators and state legislators.

    The Minneapolis report, L. Sherman's replication report, and a general analysis of these issues is found in L. Sherman, *Policing Domestic Violence: Experiments and Dilemmas* (New York: Free Press, 1992).
74. R. Lempert, "Humility Is a Virtue: On the Publicization of Policy-Relevant Research," *Law & Society Review* 23(1989): 146–161.
75. Zorza, "Arresting Batterers," pp. 935–36.
76. Sherman, *Policing,* p. 19.
77. Sherman *Policing,* pp. 22–24.
78. Zorza, "Arresting Batterers," p. 985.
79. S. Herrell and M. Hofford, *Family Violence: Improving Court Practice* (Reno: National Council of Juvenile and Family Court Judges, 1990).
80. Zorza, "Arresting Batterers," p. 985 (emphasis added).
81. Marion Wanless, Notes: Mandatory Arrest: a Step Toward Eradicating Domestic Violence, but Is it Enough? *University of Illinois Law Review* [1996]:533–75, pp. 548–50.
82. Comment (Carol Wright), "Immediate Arrest in Domestic Violence Situations: Mandate or Alternative," *Capital University Law Review,* 14(1985):243–68, pp. 254–59.
83. *Ibid.,* pp. 261–267.
84. See Wanless, "Mandatory Arrest."
85. Wanless, p. 559.
86. Wanless, p. 558.
87. Wanless, p. 562.

JUSTICES OF THE SUPREME COURT

THOUGHTFUL CONSERVATIVES
CLARK—HARLAN II—STEWART—WHITE

Justices Tom Clark, John Marshall Harlan II, Potter Stewart, and Byron White, were appointed by presidents (Truman, Eisenhower, and Kennedy) with differing political philosophies. Nevertheless, these four justices exhibited several similarities. On criminal procedure issues, all were conservative in that they generally opposed incorporation; they tended to find for the prosecution. On the other hand, all were receptive to the civil rights claims of African Americans. Clark, as a key architect of President Truman's anti-Communist loyalty oath program, was fiercely opposed to easing the application of these rules. Each of these justices were thorough and thoughtful in his review of cases, and each had at times ruled in support of criminal defendants in significant cases.

Among these justices, John Harlan ranks as the most acute legal thinker. Known as a lawyer's justice, he carefully crafted opinions without ambiguity to be applied by practicing lawyers and trial judges. Potter Stewart was the most centrist of these justices in criminal procedure matters. He dissented in Miranda v. Arizona *(1966), but his opinions in such cases as* Chimel v. California *(1969) (reach-and-lunge rule) and* Coolidge v. New Hampshire *(1971) (warrant preference interpretation) were quite liberal. His opinion in* Katz v. United States *(1967) was the keystone in modernizing Fourth Amendment law.*

Justice White may have been a surprise; nominated by a liberal president, he quickly joined the conservative wing of the Court on many issues, especially criminal procedure. In this regard, he stands in sharp contrast to Kennedy's other appointee, Arthur Goldberg. Justice White's influence on the Court was enhanced by his lengthy tenure and his practice of at times shifting to the center of the Court so as to occupy the pivotal middle ground.

TOM C. CLARK

Texas 1899–1977
Democrat

Appointed by
Harry Truman

Years of Service:
1949–1967

Collection of the Supreme Court of the United States. Photographer: Harris and Ewing

LIFE AND CAREER The son of a Dallas lawyer, Clark served in the United States Army during World War I, graduated from the University of Texas Law School, and practiced in his father's law firm from 1922 to 1927. Thereafter, he held appointed posts as civil district attorney and assistant (criminal) district attorney for Dallas. His involvement in politics led to his appointment to the U.S. Justice Department in 1937, where he worked on a variety of issues including war claims, antitrust, the evacuation of Japanese Americans from the West Coast to camps during World War II, and war frauds. In 1943, he was appointed assistant attorney general and headed the antitrust and the criminal divisions.

He supported Harry Truman for the vice-presidential nomination in 1944 and was appointed by Truman as attorney general in 1945. Clark was a vigorous attorney general, instituting 160 antitrust cases, supporting civil rights actions designed to end racial segregation, and playing a key role in developing President Truman's anti-Communist loyalty oath program, generated by Cold War fears of internal subversion.

In 1967, Justice Clark resigned from the Court as a gesture of paternal love when his son, Ramsey Clark, was appointed by President Johnson as attorney general. That would have created a conflict of interest would have arisen in every Supreme Court case involving the United States government. For the next decade of his life, he actively participated as a judge in the various federal circuits and contributed to numerous programs designed to enhance the quality of the American judiciary.

CONTRIBUTION TO CRIMINAL PROCEDURE He more often than not voted in favor of the state in this area. For example, he dissented in *Miranda v. Arizona* (1966). He dissented in a case that held that probable cause could not be based on a person's general reputation (*Beck* 1964); he dissented in a case that excluded evidence seized from a second person pursuant to an illegal arrest of a first person (*Wong Sun* 1963); and he joined Justice Minton's decision in *Rabinowitz* (1950). Nevertheless, he wrote the majority opinion in the breakthrough incorporation decision of *Mapp v. Ohio*. On the other hand, he was a staunch supporter of fair trials, as seen in his opinions finding constitutional error because of excessive pretrial publicity.

SIGNATURE OPINION *Mapp v. Ohio* (1961). Why did a generally conservative justice on criminal matters support the incorporation of the exclusionary rule? In a revealing interview after retirement, Clark told a seminar of students that as a young lawyer, he defended his cook's son against a Prohibition charge (possessing liquor) after Dallas police simply entered the accused's room, ripped open a mattress, and gave the bottle of liquor they found to federal agents. Clark was shocked that police could do this. Thus, although as a justice he was loath to curb the legitimate power of police officers, the facts of *Mapp* were excessive. To Justice Clark, the exclusionary rule, applied to the states as well as the federal government, simply made sense, and as he wrote in *Mapp*, "there is no war between the Constitution and common sense."

ASSESSMENT Clark replaced the staunch liberal justice, Frank Murphy, in 1949, tilting the Vinson Court in a more conservative direction. Clark generally joined justices Reed, Frankfurter, Jackson, and Burton, although he was somewhat more liberal than Chief Justice Vinson. During the 1950s, he supported the government in antitrust and loyalty cases, where his experiences as attorney general shaped his approaches, thus taking a liberal stance in the first area and a conservative stance in the latter. His positions on First Amendment, voting district reapportionment, and racial segregation issues were in sync with the liberal Warren Court.

FURTHER READING

Richard Kirkendall, "Tom C. Clark," in *The Justices of the United States Supreme Court, 1789–1969*, edited by Leon Friedman and Fred L. Israel, vol. 4, pp. 2665–95 (New York: Chelsea House, 1969).

JOHN M. HARLAN II

New York 1899–1971
Republican

Appointed by
Dwight D. Eisenhower

Years of Service:
1955–1971.

Collection of the Supreme Court of the United States. Photographer: Harris and Ewing

LIFE AND CAREER The grandson of a Supreme Court justice by the same name, John Harlan was viewed as a "progressive Republican" when appointed. He was born in Chicago, educated at private schools, and served briefly in World War I. He received his bachelor's degree from Princeton in 1920, was a Rhodes Scholar at Oxford, and completed his legal studies at New York Law School in 1924. He practiced law in New York with a prestigious Wall Street law firm up until his appointment to the Second Circuit Court of Appeals in early 1954. However, his background also included years of public service. He prosecuted a former United States attorney general for corruption when he was as an assistant United States attorney in the 1920s, acted as a special prosecutor for New York State in a major investigation of municipal graft in the 1930s, directed a critical unit of experts advising the commanding general of the Eighth Air Force on bombing operations in Europe during World War II, and was chief counsel of an organized crime investigation for the state of New York in the early 1950s. After less than a year on the Second Circuit Court of Appeals, he was nominated by President Eisenhower to the Supreme Court.

CONTRIBUTION TO CRIMINAL PROCEDURE He opposed incorporation and dissented in *Mapp* and *Miranda*; he believed the federal government should be held to higher standards of procedural regularity under the Bill of Rights than states under the Fourteenth Amendment. He was generally conservative and voted for the state, but not slavishly so. Thus, he concurred on extending the right to counsel to all felony defendants (*Gideon* 1963); he concurred in extending the right to counsel to juveniles (*In re Gault* 1967) and in *Katz v. United States* (1967). He dissented in *United States v. White* (1971), arguing that police agents should not be able to wear body-mikes without a prior judicial warrant.

SIGNATURE OPINION *Spinelli v. United States* (1969). His opinion upheld the two-prong test for determining when the hearsay evidence of a confidential informant can amount to probable cause for a search warrant. Harlan closely examined the facts put forth by the FBI and penetrated the affidavit's veneer of certainty to show that the agency was, in effect, asking for a blank check on its decision. The opinion highlights the vital importance of judicial scrutiny of police affidavit requests to the preservation of Fourth Amendment privacy and liberty.

ASSESSMENT Justice Harlan developed a close intellectual friendship with Justice Frankfurter; with Frankfurter's resignation in 1962, Harlan took on the mantle of the chief spokesperson for judicial restraint and traditional judicial conservatism. During the entire period of the due process revolution, Justice Harlan wrote the most exhaustive and penetrating dissents against the incorporation doctrine.

Justice Harlan was "a lawyer's judge"—he closely examined cases and often based decisions on fine factual distinctions rather than upon broad generalizations, and his opinions reflected a concern to give lawyers and judges clear guidance in applying the rules of the case. He had a profound respect for judicial precedent and felt the Court should interfere as little as possible into the political workings of both state and federal government. His incorporation dissents noted that "the American federal system is itself constitutionally ordained, that it embodies values profoundly making for lasting liberties in this country. . . ." He was skeptical about the ability of courts to ensure true liberty by their rulings, believing that liberty "can rise no higher or be made more secure than the spirit of a people to achieve and maintain it." He also believed that federalism encouraged differences between the states and that it was not the role of the Supreme Court to eradicate these differences by applying the Bill of Rights as a steamroller over variations of state procedure.

FURTHER READING

Tinsley E. Yarbrough, *John Marshall Harlan: Great Dissenter of the Warren Court* (New York: Oxford University Press, 1992)

POTTER STEWART

Ohio 1915–1986
Republican

Appointed by
Dwight D. Eisenhower

Years of Service:
1958–1981

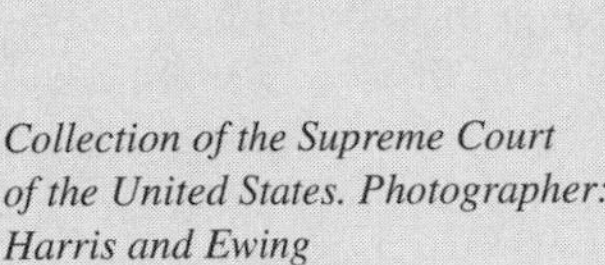

Collection of the Supreme Court of the United States. Photographer: Harris and Ewing

LIFE AND CAREER Born into a politically active Republican Ohio family with "a strong tradition of public service," Stewart was educated at the Hotchkiss School, Yale University (where he was a Phi Beta Kappa), and Yale Law School, where he generally supported the New Deal. He served as a deck officer on an oil tanker during World War II, which put him in contact with men of a different background than he would meet at Yale or in corporate law practice. He practiced law in his hometown of Cincinnati from 1946 to 1954. His political activity (he was twice elected to the Cincinnati City Council), and his support for Dwight Eisenhower for the Republican presidential nomination in 1952 against Ohio Senator Robert Taft led President Eisenhower to name him to the Sixth Circuit Court of Appeals in 1954 at the young age of 39. His reputation as an excellent judge led to his nomination to the Supreme Court in 1958.

CONTRIBUTION TO CRIMINAL PROCEDURE Although known as a middle-of-the-road justice who did not automatically side with either liberal or conservative justices, Justice Stewart wrote a large number of Fourth Amendment opinions for the Supreme Court that often tended to expand defendants' rights. On the "liberal or pro-defendant" side were *Vale v. Louisiana* (1970) (a doorstep arrest does not authorize a general search of a premises) and *Coolidge v. New Hampshire* (1971) (supporting the warrant preference construction of the Fourth Amendment). On the pro-prosecution side, Stewart opposed incorporation, dissented in *Miranda v. Arizona,* and wrote the majority opinion in *Schneckloth v. Bustamonte* (1973), holding that the police need not warn suspects of their Fourth Amendment rights before requesting consent to search.

Justice Stewart had a talent for turning a pithy phrase that encapsulates a rule, and wrote logical, well-organized opinions. This was seen in his most important Fourth

Amendment opinion, *Katz v. United States* (1967), where his emblematic statement—"For the Fourth Amendment protects people, not places"—nicely summed up the major shift in Fourth Amendment jurisprudence from its foundations in property law to its new basis on an expectation of privacy.

SIGNATURE OPINION His majority opinion in *Chimel v. California* (1969), ended the long zigzag course of opinions on the scope of a search incident to arrest; it confirmed that while officers may reasonably search the area within the immediate control of an arrested suspect to seize weapons and contraband, they may not use the arrest as an excuse to search a premises without a warrant.

ASSESSMENT His approach to constitutional law was cautious and restrained. His middle of the road votes made him a "swing justice" in many areas. His judicial philosophy appeared to be that a judge should first defer to legislative and executive branch authority, but not hesitate to exercise judicial review in order to maintain essential procedural safeguards and prevent abuses of power. Justice Stewart favored narrow rulings and preferred that cases be resolved on the specific facts when necessary. He was a lone dissenter in the case that held school prayer to violate the First Amendment but voted for free speech in censorship cases. On the death penalty, he held it to be unconstitutional as applied in 1972, but voted to uphold revised death penalty laws in 1976 that incorporated the element of guided discretion. He decided a very large number of criminal procedure cases. Ultimately, it was not possible to classify Justice Stewart simply as a liberal or conservative or as an activist or passivist judge.

FURTHER READING

Tinsley E. Yarbrough, "Justice Potter Stewart: Decisional Patterns in Search of Doctrinal Moorings," in *The Burger Court: Political and Judicial Profiles,* edited by Charles M. Lamb and Stephen C. Halpern, pp. 375–406 (Urbana: University of Illinois Press, 1991)

BYRON R. WHITE

Colorado 1917–
Democrat

Appointed by
John F. Kennedy.

Years of Service:
1962–1993

Collection of the Supreme Court of the United States. Photographer: Joseph Bailey

LIFE AND CAREER Byron White's youth was filled with hard work in the beet fields of rural Colorado and on railroad section crews. He was an excellent student and outstanding athlete in high school and at the University of Colorado, where he was elected to Phi Beta Kappa, graduated first in his class in 1938, and attracted national attention as a star tailback (nicknamed "Whizzer") on Colorado's unbeaten football team. He also won varsity letters in basketball and baseball. Between 1938 and 1942, White spent a year at Oxford University as a Rhodes Scholar (where he met Ambassador Joseph Kennedy's son, John), was the highest paid professional football player in America, and began law school. While serving as a naval intelligence officer in the South Pacific during World War II, he again met John Fitzgerald Kennedy. White completed his law degree at Yale after the war, clerked for Chief Justice Fred Vinson (1946–1947), and while in Washington, had numerous opportunities to meet with freshman Congressman John Kennedy of Massachusetts. In 1947, he returned to Colorado and the private practice of law.

In 1959, White led the Colorado organization on behalf of Kennedy's efforts to gain the Democratic presidential nomination. He was appointed deputy United States attorney general in 1961, and won recognition as an able administrator, effectively acting as "chief of staff" of the Justice Department. During the tense days in May 1961, when Attorney General Robert Kennedy dispatched four-hundred federal marshals to Alabama to protect freedom riders, White calmly and competently supervised the marshals and deputies. In this position, he ably screened candidates for federal judgeships.

CONTRIBUTION TO CRIMINAL PROCEDURE White was generally conservative on criminal procedure issues; he dissented strongly in *Escobedo* (1964) and *Miranda* (1966) and was clearly opposed to the incorporation of the Fourth Amendment exclusionary rule. On occasion, he could decide in favor of the defendant. In *Duncan v. Louisiana* (1968), however, he effectively ended the *Palko* (1937) approach to fundamental rights and write that if a Bill of Rights procedure is fundamental to the *American* system of justice, it ought to be incorporated.

His pro-government rulings include the late 1980s ruling that a helicopter overflight of a backyard at four-hundred feet is not a search; there is no expectation of privacy in abandoned trash; an indicted defendant may waive his right to counsel and be interrogated without his attorney present; and government forfeiture of funds to prevent paying an attorney does not violate the right to counsel. On the other hand, in *Arizona v. Fulminante* (1991), he led a liberal coalition in holding that a confession was coerced, and dissenting against a new rule that a coerced confession can be harmless error.

SIGNATURE OPINION His most significant Fourth Amendment opinion was *United States v. Leon* (1984), which held admissible evidence obtained without probable cause by a police officer relying in good faith on a faulty judicial warrant. *Leon* was the first clear exception to the *Mapp v. Ohio* (1961) exclusionary rule and a significant victory for conservative justices opposed to the expansion of the rights of criminal suspects. *Leon*'s reasoning relied heavily on a balancing analysis and to some extent on shaky empirical research.

ASSESSMENT He was generally a middle-of-the-road or swing justice. In the 1960s, he supported governmental authority over individual liberty in cases involving the investigation of Communists and other groups. On the other hand, his votes on the civil rights of minorities usually favored integration, school busing and affirmative action. White has puzzled commentators because of his apparent lack of a clear judicial philosophy. Thus, despite his generally strong support for civil rights and "one man one vote," he has on occasion ruled inconsistently. Some inconsistent decisions can be explained by his concern with the specific factual and procedural contours of each case.

FURTHER READING

Dennis J. Hutchinson, *The Man Who Once Was Whizzer White: A Portrait of Byron R. White* (New York: Free Press, 1998)

CHAPTER 6

Warrantless Searches

[T]he most basic constitutional rule in this area is that "searches conducted outside the judicial process, without prior approval by judge or magistrate, are per se *unreasonable under the Fourth Amendment—subject only to a few specifically established and well-delineated exceptions." . . . In times of unrest, whether caused by crime or racial conflict or fear of internal subversion, this basic law and the values that it represents may appear unrealistic or 'extravagant' to some. But the values were those of the authors of our fundamental constitutional concepts.*

—Justice Potter Stewart in *Coolidge v. New Hampshire,* 403 U.S. 443, 455 (1971)

CHAPTER OUTLINE

KEY TERMS AND PHRASES

Actual border
Actual mobility
Automobile search
Border
Border search
Controlled delivery
"Crime scene investigation" exception
Exigency exception
Fixed checkpoint
Hot pursuit
Impoundment
In loco parentis
Inventory search
Pervasively regulated industry
Roving patrol
"Special needs" doctrine
Warrantless search

INTRODUCTION

Warrantless searches are of enormous practical importance to police work. Despite the Supreme Court's preference for a search warrant, warrantless searches are more common, especially **automobile searches.** Every warrantless search, conducted without prior judicial review, is subject to judicial review after the fact. Nevertheless, a search based on an officer's assessment of probable cause is more likely to be arbitrary than one subjected to the warrant process.

This text has already discussed several kinds of warrantless searches: plain view, consent, search incident to arrest, and the *Terry* "stop and frisk." Each is based on a different rationale and is held to different legal standards. An item "seized" in plain view involves no Fourth Amendment interest or expectation of privacy because the officer is in public or is lawfully in the place from which the "plain view" occurs. The Fourth Amendment is not burdened by a consent search because the person has voluntarily given up the right of privacy. An officer seeking consent can exploit a person's ignorance of personal rights and can seek consent to search, even without probable cause or reasonable suspicion. The Fourth Amendment, however, is relevant when imposing the absolute standard to which all warrantless searches are held: they must be deemed *reasonable.* Thus, for example, consent must be truly voluntary and an item in "plain view" must be immediately apparent as contraband.

In contrast, a warrantless search incident to arrest is upheld as valid even though it directly interferes with a person's Fourth Amendment rights. The state's interest in the officer's security and preventing the destruction of evidence overrides the individual's right to a warrant at the time of the arrest. This exception, unlike other exceptions, is held to the stringent Fourth Amendment evidentiary standard of probable cause. The search incident to arrest is known as an **exigency exception.** The exigency exceptions to the warrant requirement include (i) **hot pursuit** entries, (ii) the "automobile exception," (iii) search incident to arrest, and (iv) miscellaneous exigencies that impinge on Fourth Amendment interests (e.g., the home entry in *Arizona v. Hicks* to look for a shooter; firefighters entering a premises to extinguish a fire; police seizure of evidence from a person that can be easily destroyed). To be legal, each requires the warrantless search to be based on probable cause. Exigency exceptions are compatible with the warrant-preference construction of the Fourth Amendment:

> Thus the most basic constitutional rule in this area is that "searches conducted outside the judicial process, without prior approval by judge or magistrate, are *per se* unreasonable under the Fourth Amendment—subject only to a few specifically established and well-delineated exceptions." The exceptions are "jealously and carefully drawn," and there must be "a showing by those who seek exemption . . . that the exigencies of the situation made that course imperative." (*Coolidge v. New Hampshire,* pp. 454–55)

These warrant exceptions were assumed to have existed under common law and are not viewed as undermining the warrant requirement. The warrant-preference construction warns against creating new categories of exceptions. Recently, however, the Court has created controversy in this area, especially in regard to automobile searches and the "special needs" doctrine, which are reviewed in this chapter. This chapter also reviews other kinds of non-exigency warrantless searches: inventory searches, warrantless administrative searches, and **border searches.**

To reiterate, the basic rule that justifies all warrantless searches under the Fourth Amendment is *reasonableness.* Beyond this basic requirement, the exigency exceptions require the prior existence of probable cause. Some warrantless searches dispense with probable cause and rely on reasonable suspicion (e.g., *Terry* stops, searches of the baggage of public school students by teachers, fire inspectors returning to the site of a non-suspicious blaze to determine its origins). Other warrantless searches require no probable cause or reasonable suspicion (e.g., automobile inventory searches). And still others dispense with particularized suspicion against a specific person (e.g., automobile sobriety checklanes).

HOT PURSUIT AND OTHER EXIGENCY SEARCHES

Hot pursuit occurs when a dangerous criminal suspect is being chased by police and is seen entering his own home, a public building, the residence of a third party, or some other location that is cloaked with a Fourth Amendment expectation of privacy. Because the suspect presents a danger to society in that he may flee or harm someone, as well as the possibility that evidence may be destroyed, police officers want to enter the premises immediately to make an arrest and search for weapons and contraband without a warrant. The immediacy of the situation makes obtaining a search or arrest warrant unworkable and absurd. A greater danger to the public and to the police might develop if the police cordoned off a house; it certainly gives a suspect an opportunity to destroy evidence. Evidence seized in a warrantless search that follows a hot pursuit entry into a premises is admissible in criminal trials.

Warden v. Hayden (1967), the case that eliminated the mere evidence rule (see Chapter 4), is the leading hot pursuit case. In this case, taxi cab drivers followed Hayden to a house after he had robbed the taxi company office and they transmitted the information to the taxi dispatcher, who in turn relayed the information to the police. Police officers arrived at Hayden's home "within minutes" of receiving the call, knocked on his door, and entered when the door was opened by the suspect's wife. A search of the house for the suspect turned up incriminating evidence which would be admissible in evidence only if the initial entry was lawful. The Supreme Court, holding the entry and search to be constitutional, explained the basis of the hot pursuit exception to the warrant requirement:

> The Fourth Amendment does not require police officers to delay in the course of an investigation if to do so would gravely endanger their lives or the lives of others. Speed here was essential, and only a thorough search of the house for persons and weapons could have ensured that Hayden was the only man present and that the police had control of all weapons which could be used against them or to effect an escape. (*Warden v. Hayden,* pp. 298–99)

From the facts and rulings of *Warden,* several legal principles of the hot pursuit exception can be derived. *First,* the hot pursuit warrant exception, as an exigency exception, must be based on *probable cause* to believe that the persons who have just entered the premises have committed a felony or are dangerous to the safety of others. *Second,* hot pursuit may be based either on the officer's personal observations or on reliable *hearsay. Third,* the pursuit need not be immediate; there may be *a short time lapse* between the suspect's entry into the house and the arrival of the police. The *fourth* rule concerns the *scope* of the search pursuant to the hot pursuit entry. "The permissible scope of search must, . . . at the least, be as broad as may reasonably be necessary to prevent the dangers that the suspect at large in the house may resist or escape" (*Warden v. Hayden,* p. 299). In other words, until the offender is found, the police may *search the entire premises* for the suspects, weapons, and evidence of the crime. However, once the offender is apprehended, the police may not search beyond the limits of a search incident to an arrest.

Most hot pursuits proceed from public property onto private property. *United States v. Santana* (1976) established a *fifth* rule: The pursuit *may* begin on *private* property. Officers had reliable information that the suspect was in possession of marked money from a heroin buy. As the police approached the house, Ms. Santana was standing in the doorway to her house holding a paper bag. She retreated to a vestibule, where the police seized her. In a brief struggle, heroin packets fell from the bag and were lawfully seized by the police. Here, although the pursuit technically began on private property, the Court held that for Fourth Amendment purposes, it was a public place. The *Santana* ruling, however, does not allow the police to enter a house where there is no exigency and thereby "create" one.

The *sixth* rule, established by *Welsh v. Wisconsin* (1984), concerns the *gravity of the offense:* Police may enter a premises without a warrant in hot pursuit only for *serious crimes.* A minor offense cannot generate an exigency that overrides the Fourth Amendment rule that police must obtain an arrest warrant in order to arrest a suspect in his or her home (*Payton v. New York,* 1980). The offense in this case was a civil infraction of driving while intoxicated (DWI). Welsh's erratic driving resulted in his car careening off a road and into a ditch on a rainy night. A witness saw the apparently intoxicated driver walk off into the night and called the police, who arrived at Welsh's nearby home within the hour. They entered the house without a warrant or the consent of Welsh's stepdaughter, found Welsh in bed, arrested him, and took him to the police station, where he refused to submit to a breath analysis test. The refusal could result in a license revocation only if the arrest was legal, and this, in turn, depended on the legality of the forcible, warrantless home entry. The state's only rationale for a constitutional entry was hot pursuit.

The Wisconsin Supreme Court upheld the warrantless entry because of the need to prevent physical harm to the offender and the public, and to prevent the destruction of the blood alcohol evidence. The United States Supreme Court reversed, discounting the weak public safety reasoning because the offender was in bed and thus not a threat to anyone. Preservation of evidence is a basis of the hot pursuit exigency, but the Court held "that an important factor to be considered when determining whether any exigency exists is the gravity of the underlying offense for which the arrest is being made." Under Wisconsin law, the underlying offense in this case—first offense DWI—was a noncriminal violation subject to a $200 fine. Justice Brennan, writing for the majority, noted that a warrantless entry into a home is presumptively unreasonable and the burden is on the government to prove that an exigency makes a warrantless entry reasonable. The Court felt that a hot pursuit entry for a minor crime is presumptively unreasonable and difficult for the government to rebut.

The Court found that the entry and search in this case violated the Fourth Amendment because (1) "there was no immediate or continuous pursuit of the petitioner from the scene of a crime," (2) Welsh had arrived home and abandoned his car so there was little remaining threat to the public safety, and (3) the exigency of ascertaining Welsh's blood-alcohol level was outweighed by the fact that first-offense DWI was classified as a civil offense. The majority believed that this would be "unreasonable police behavior that the principles of the Fourth Amendment will not sanction."

Justice White's dissent noted that a warrantless entry into a home is as serious for a person wanted for a serious felony as for a minor crime, and therefore an exigency exists whenever the state's interest is to ensure personal safety and preserve evidence. The warrantless intrusion into Welsh's bedroom promoted the "valid and substantial state interests" of prosecuting drunk driving. He also suggested that police are better served by bright-line rules so that what constitutes a serious offense—justifying hot pursuit—is not open to interpretation. The dissent also urged the Court to defer to the State's judgment as to the seriousness of the offense.

Welsh does not indicate what constitutes a non-serious crime, outside of the civil offense of first-time DWI punishable by a fine. Justice Brennan implied that a simple bright-line division between felonies and misdemeanors is not the proper line between serious and non-serious offenses. Even if the *Welsh* rule does not apply only to civil offenses punishable by a fine, the case itself does not establish the serious—non-serious criterion. Perhaps, then, it is the penalty, such as imprisonment for thirty days or six months. Possibly, hot pursuit is not proper for some non-violent felonies, but is for some violent misdemeanors. Another uncertainty left by *Welsh* is whether the hot pursuit exception for minor crimes applies in premises other than the home.

The Supreme Court has held, in *Minnesota v. Olson* (1990), that being wanted for a serious felony does not in itself create an exigency. Police suspected that Olson, a murder suspect, was in a house and they entered without a warrant. Their hot pursuit justification for the warrantless entry was undercut by several factors: the suspect was thought to be the driver of a get-away car and not the shooter; the police had already recovered the murder weapon; there was no suggestion of danger to persons with the suspect; the entry occurred a day after the murder-robbery; and three or four police squads surrounded the house, which was secured. *Minnesota v. Olson* demonstrates that the finding of an exigency is a factual determination made by a court assessing all of the circumstances of the case.

OTHER EXIGENCIES The hot pursuit exception to a warrant requirement is an example of a more general rule that police may enter a premises or conduct a search without a warrant when exigent circumstances justify the search or intrusion. The exigent circumstance may be an imminent threat to the life or safety of people that no police officer should ignore. In *Arizona v. Hicks* (1987) (see Chapter 4), the officer properly entered an apartment to search for a man who had shot a bullet through the floor into another apartment, injuring a person, and creating an obvious and continuing threat to life and safety. In *Hicks,* there was probable cause to believe that a person had committed a felony. There was no hot pursuit as such, but the entry met all the reasonableness criterion of an exigency exception.

Warrantless entry into homes by government agents who are not police officers enforcing the criminal law must also be supported by a real exigency. Firefighting, discussed later, is a prime example (*Michigan v. Tyler,* 1978; *Michigan v. Clifford,* 1984). Other cases deal with situations wherein probable cause exists to believe a suspect has committed a crime and an immediate search is essential or evidence of the crime will be destroyed. In such a case, the nature of the search must be reasonable and the intrusion on privacy interests minimal. An unconscious driver, in *Schmerber v. California* (1966) was arrested for drunk driving in the context of a fatal accident that generated reasonable cause of a vehicular homicide. The key evidence would quickly be lost because the blood alcohol level drops over time. The Court upheld this warrantless search for blood alcohol, noting that taking blood by medical workers in this case is not dangerous, is routine, is not very invasive or humiliating, and is likely to produce highly accurate evidence.

Other cases upheld warrantless searches as reasonable because of the exigency that evidence might be destroyed. In these cases, privacy rights were minimal and the cases did not precisely fit the search incident to arrest warrant exception. *United States v. Edwards* (1974) involved taking potentially incriminating paint chips from the clothing of a police lockup inmate who was ordered to exchange his clothing for jail issue. *Cupp v. Murphy* (1973) (discussed in Chapter 5), upheld the removal of what was apparently dried blood from the finger of a potential murder suspect, who had not been arrested, at a police station.

REJECTING THE HOMICIDE CRIME SCENE INVESTIGATION EXCEPTION The Supreme Court rejected the opportunity to develop a new **crime scene investigation exception** to the warrant requirement. A police officer was killed in a drug raid in the Tucson, Arizona, apartment of Rufus Mincey, who was apparently shot by the slain officer. The officers who were present went quickly through the apartment, located other persons, called for emergency assistance, and refrained from further investigation of the place. Ten minutes later, homicide investigators arrived and arranged for the removal of the fatally injured officer and the suspects, and then secured the apartment. They then proceeded to gather evidence.

> Their search lasted four days, during which period the entire apartment was searched, photographed, and diagrammed. The officers opened drawers, closets, and cupboards, and inspected their contents; they emptied clothing pockets; they dug bullet fragments out of the walls and floors; they pulled

> up sections of the carpet and removed them for examination. Every item in the apartment was closely examined and inventoried, and 200 to 300 objects were seized. In short, Mincey's apartment was subjected to an exhaustive and intrusive search. No warrant was ever obtained. (*Mincey v. Arizona* (1978), p. 389)

Much evidence was obtained which was introduced and used to convict Mincey of homicide and drug possession. The Arizona Supreme Court held such a warrantless search to be reasonable under the Fourth Amendment when conducted to investigate "the scene of a homicide—or of a serious personal injury with likelihood of death where there is reason to suspect foul play" as long as "the purpose [is] limited to determining the circumstances of death and the scope [does] not exceed that purpose. The search must also begin within a reasonable period following the time when the officials first learn of the murder (or potential murder)."

The Supreme Court unanimously held that this warrantless search violated the Fourth Amendment. It rejected numerous arguments that were advanced by the state to support the search. First, although Mincey was a suspect, he retained some reasonable expectation of privacy in his home. To allow him to be stripped of all rights of home privacy "would impermissibly convict the suspect even before the evidence against him was gathered." The state also argued that in light of Mincey's arrest, the further intrusion into his privacy by the crime scene search "was constitutionally irrelevant. But this claim is hardly tenable in light of the extensive nature of this search. It is one thing to say that one who is legally taken into police custody has a lessened right of privacy in his person. . . . It is quite another to argue that he also has a lessened right of privacy in his entire house" (*Mincey v. Arizona,* p. 391). The Supreme Court also rejected the exigency rationale. The police may enter the scene of a violent crime, look about, secure the location and seize contraband items in plain view. But, "a four-day search that included opening dresser drawers and ripping up carpets can hardly be rationalized in terms of the legitimate concerns that justify an emergency search" (*Mincey v. Arizona,* p. 392). The Court also rejected the idea that special promptness was required to search the scene of a homicide, suggesting that an exception for that crime would lead to a blanket crime scene warrant exception and the argument that dispensing with a warrant would be more efficient. There was no suggestion that a search warrant could not have been easily and conveniently obtained. The last argument, that the exception was confined by the guidelines laid out by the Arizona courts, was belied by the extensive search that was conducted.

The Supreme Court unanimously adhered to its *Mincey* ruling in a *per curiam* opinion, reversing a West Virginia case in which police conducted a warrantless, thorough, sixteen-hour homicide investigation of a cabin that had been leased to a couple in a West Virginia state park. (*Flippo v. West Virginia,* 1999)

THE AUTOMOBILE EXCEPTION

An Overview of Vehicle Search Rules

The stop and search of mobile vehicles by police raises a variety of constitutional issues, some of which are discussed in Chapters 4, 5, and 8.

1. *Stopping:* Under what legal standards may an officer order a mobile vehicle to stop? (See *Delaware v. Prouse* (1979), Chapter 5)
2. *Pretext Stops:* May an officer stop a car with objective reasonable suspicion or probable cause of a traffic violation if the true, subjective reason for the stop is to search for drugs when there is no legal basis to stop the car for that reason? (See *Whren v. United States* (1996), Chapter 5)
3. *Stop and Frisk:* May an officer enter an automobile to frisk a suspect or inspect the interior? (See *Adams v. Williams* (1972); *Michigan v. Long* (1983), Chapter 5)
4. *Control of Driver and Passengers:* May an officer order the driver and passengers to remain in or exit the vehicle? (See *Pennsylvania v. Mimms* (1977); *Maryland v. Wilson* (1997), Chapter 5)
5. *Knowledge and Consent:* Need an officer inform a driver that he or she is free to go before obtaining consent to search a vehicle? (See *Schneckloth v. Bustamonte* (1973); *Ohio v. Robinette* (1996), Chapter 4)
6. *Scope of Consent:* Does consent to search a car include consent to search a container in the car? (See *Florida v. Jimeno* (1991), Chapter 4)
7. *Questioning:* Must an officer read *Miranda* warnings before questioning a stopped motorist? (See *Berkemer v. McCarty* (1984); *Pennsylvania v. Muniz* (1990), Chapter 8)
8. *Automobile Exception: Search of Vehicle:* What is the scope of an officer's authority to look into or to search a stopped mobile vehicle without a warrant? (See *United States v. Ross* (1982) Chapter 6)
9. *Automobile Exception: Search of Containers:* What is the scope of an officer's authority to look into or to search closed areas or closed containers in a stopped mobile vehicle without a warrant? (See *California v. Acevedo* (1991), Chapter 6)
10. *Check Lanes:* What limits exist for stopping and searching mobile vehicles and questioning the driver and passengers at roadside check lanes? (See *Michigan Department of State Police v. Sitz* (1990), Chapter 5)

11. *Impounded Vehicles:* What rules guide the *inventory search* of impounded vehicles? (See *Florida v. Wells* (1990), Chapter 6)

These are only general issues; many additional specific questions have arisen in relation to them. Clearly, then, an "automobile search" is, in its totality, a complex legal field. Indeed, the development of various car search rules over the last three decades has been one of the most confusing and most contentious areas of criminal procedure. Most prominent legal scholars have sharply criticized the Supreme Court for ruling in automobile search cases irrespective of Fourth Amendment principles. They accuse the Court of twisting principles to ensure that police officers can search automobiles almost at will. Thus, one scholar has stated: "Although the Court has described warrantless searches as presumptively invalid, more than twenty seemingly haphazard exceptions to the warrant clause in fact have swallowed the warrant requirement."[1] The relentless pressure by police to search cars is driven by the "war on drugs" and by the fact that police departments can augment their budgets by the forfeiture of automobiles found to be transporting illegal drugs.[2] The constitutional debate has recently become an explosive law enforcement and political issue as the practice of racial profiling has been exposed (see *Law in Society*, this chapter).

Professor David Steinberg has classified the constitutional law of automobile searches into three broad categories: (1) the automobile, or mobile vehicle, exception to the warrant clause; (2) cases concerning whether a warrant is required before police can open a closed container found in an automobile, and (3) groups of cases in which the police "do not rely on the automobile exception at all." This third category includes search incident to arrest (see *New York v. Belton* (1981), Chapter 5), inventory search, plain view search (see *Texas v. Brown* (1983), Chapter 4), consent, and fixed checkpoint searches. The discussion of the "automobile exception," narrowly defined, usually focuses on the first two categories. However, in the "real world" of policing, the totality of rules and exceptions come together to produce a powerful regime of rules that makes it possible for a police officer to search virtually any car that he or she has a mind to stop. Driving is a pervasive activity in America and it is nearly impossible for anyone to drive without violating some motor vehicle law, including speeding, driving over a line, changing lanes without signaling, inoperative taillight, headlights not on one-half hour after sunset to one-half hour before sunrise "and at such other times as atmospheric conditions render visibility as low as or lower than is ordinarily the case during that period," and an excessively loud muffler.[3] Therefore, a police car following a vehicle is likely to spot a violation at some point and on stopping that car, can utilize one of the various automobile search rules to engage in some level of lawful search. This potential—and reality—of pervasive stopping of black and Hispanic drivers in large numbers on pretextual grounds has led Professor David Harris to claim that "Indeed, it is no exaggeration to say that in cases involving cars, the Fourth Amendment is all but dead."[4]

The Automobile Exception

The Supreme Court has upheld warrantless searches of automobiles for two reasons:

> Our first cases establishing the automobile exception to the Fourth Amendment's warrant requirement were based on the automobile's "ready mobility," an exigency sufficient to excuse failure to obtain a search warrant once probable cause to conduct the search is clear. . . . *Carroll v. United States* (1925). More recent cases provide a further justification: the individual's reduced expectation of privacy in an automobile, owing to its pervasive regulation. (*Pennsylvania v. Labron,* 1996)

Early on, the Supreme Court applied the "automobile" exception to a boat, and lower courts have applied the rule to searches of such mobile vehicles as train roomettes, airplanes, ferries, and houseboats (*United States v. Lee,* 1927).[5]

Carroll v. United States (1925) is the foundation case for the automobile exigency exception. Chief Justice William Howard Taft wrote:

> The guaranty of freedom from unreasonable searches and seizures by the Fourth Amendment has been construed, practically since the beginning of the government, as recognizing a difference between a search of a store, dwelling house or other structure in respect of which a proper official search warrant readily may be obtained, and a search of a ship, motor boat, wagon or automobile for contraband goods, where it is not practicable to secure a warrant, because the vehicle can be quickly moved out of the locality or jurisdiction in which the warrant must be sought. (*Carroll v. United States,* p. 153)

The *Carroll* rule requires that (1) police have probable cause to believe the vehicle contains contraband, and (2) there is a "mobility exigency"—the vehicle will be driven off if it is not immediately seized. It is a common-sense observation that if a police officer has probable cause to search an automobile, but must leave the scene to obtain a warrant, any contraband will quickly be removed. As will be seen, this exception has been expanded in a variety of ways.

The second rationale for a warrantless automobile search, a *lesser expectation of privacy* than exists in homes or in luggage, was explained in *California v. Carney:*

> However, although ready mobility alone was perhaps the original justification for the vehicle exception, our later cases

have made clear that ready mobility is not the only basis for the exception . . . .

Even in cases where an automobile was not immediately mobile, the lesser expectation of privacy resulting from its use as a readily mobile vehicle justified application of the vehicular exception. In some cases, the configuration of the vehicle contributed to the lower expectation of privacy; for example we held in *Cardwell v. Lewis* (1974) that, because the passenger compartment of a standard automobile is relatively open to plain view, there are lesser expectations of privacy. But even when enclosed "repository" areas have been involved, we have concluded that the lesser expectations of privacy warrant application of the exception. We have applied the exception in the context of a locked car trunk, a sealed package in a car trunk, a closed compartment under the dashboard, the interior of a vehicle's upholstery, or sealed packages inside a covered pickup truck.

These reduced expectations of privacy derive not from the fact that the area to be searched is in plain view, but from the pervasive regulation of vehicles capable of traveling on the public highways. As we explained in *South Dakota v. Opperman* (1976), an inventory search case:

> "Automobiles, unlike homes, are subjected to pervasive and continuing governmental regulation and controls, including periodic inspection and licensing requirements. As an everyday occurrence, police stop and examine vehicles when license plates or inspection stickers have expired, or if other violations, such as exhaust fumes or excessive noise, are noted, or if headlights or other safety equipment are not in proper working order."

The public is fully aware that it is accorded less privacy in its automobiles because of this compelling governmental need for regulation. Historically, "individuals always [have] been on notice that movable vessels may be stopped and searched on facts giving rise to probable cause that the vehicle contains contraband, without the protection afforded by a magistrate's prior evaluation of those facts." In short, the pervasive schemes of regulation, which necessarily lead to reduced expectations of privacy, and the exigencies attendant to ready mobility justify searches without prior recourse to the authority of a magistrate so long as the overriding standard of probable cause is met. (*California v. Carney,* pp. 391–92)

To the extent that the automobile exception rests on the mobility rationale, it is a traditional, common-law based and common-sense exigency exception to the warrant requirement that easily fits into the warrant-preference construction of the Fourth Amendment. The lesser expectation of privacy rationale, however, strains against the common-sense exigency basis for dispensing with a warrant. Professor Steinberg states "This argument makes no sense. Under this line of reasoning, a state could eviscerate Fourth Amendment protections simply by heavy regulation of an activity or location." Also, although houses are "regulated extensively by building codes," police cannot search them without a warrant.[6] This seems to point to a policy preference on the part of the Supreme Court's majority to simply give police a virtually free hand when searching in and around an automobile. This is the conclusion drawn by Professor Harris who believes that the Court is motivated by "the desire that the police have wide latitude to investigate and the safety of the officers while they carry out these duties. The reduced expectation of privacy inherent in vehicles often plays a justifying role, but only in support of the other two reasons."[7] This motivation is revealed throughout the automobile search cases.

THE MOBILITY FACTOR In *Coolidge v. New Hampshire* (1971), a plurality of the Court ruled that the exception does not apply to *immobilized* vehicles. The defendant was arrested for murder. Two days later, his car was impounded by police and searched pursuant to a search warrant which was later declared to be defective. The police argued that the search was nevertheless constitutional under the automobile search exception. The Court rejected this argument, holding that the exception does not apply simply because an automobile was searched:

> The word "automobile" is not a talisman in whose presence the Fourth Amendment fades away and disappears. And surely there is nothing in this case to invoke the meaning and purpose of the rule of *Carroll v. United States*—no alerted criminal bent on flight, no fleeting opportunity on an open highway after a hazardous chase, no contraband

THE AUTOMOBILE WARRANT EXCEPTION IN THE STATES

"A substantial majority of the states have approved the automobile exception as a matter of state constitutional law." Approximately twenty-nine states were identified as having automobile search warrant rules that closely matched the United States Supreme Court's interpretation of the Fourth Amendment in regard to automobile searches.

Nine states were identified as having automobile search rules that, in some respect, tended to favor the individual: Connecticut, Hawaii, Indiana, New Hampshire, New Mexico, Pennsylvania, Utah, Vermont and Washington.

Barry Latzer, *State Constitutional Criminal Law,* § 3:28

> or stolen goods or weapons, no confederates waiting to move the evidence, not even the inconvenience of a special police detail to guard the immobilized automobile. In short, by no possible stretch of the legal imagination can this be made into a case where "it is not practicable to secure a warrant," . . . and the "automobile exception," despite its label, is simply irrelevant. (*Coolidge v. New Hampshire,* pp. 461–62)

To the consternation of legal scholars, the Court has not strictly held to this aspect of *Coolidge* and in many cases invoked the automobile exception to uphold the search of a parked automobile where mobility was not a factor. *Coolidge* seemed to say that the mobility exigency was based on **actual mobility**—the immediate, or almost immediate, possibility that the car would be driven away. More recently, the Court seems to have diluted this rationale by leaning toward the potential mobility of the vehicle. Thus, in *Pennsylvania v. Labron* (1996), the Court upheld the search of a car belonging to a suspect who had been arrested for a drug transaction. There was no confederate to take the car away and a warrant could have been obtained. The Pennsylvania Supreme Court ruled that a warrant was required, but this was reversed by the United States Supreme Court, stating: "If a car is *readily* mobile and probable cause exists to believe it contains contraband, the Fourth Amendment thus permits police to search the vehicle without more" (*Pennsylvania v. Labron,* p. 940, emphasis added). The weakening of the mobility factor has also been seen in the time frame of the exigency, both before and after the search.

TIME FRAME OF THE EXIGENCY Part of the Court's reasoning in *Coolidge* was that the automobile was searched two-and-a-half weeks after the police had probable cause. The time frame of the exigency seems to overlap with the mobility factor. However, the Court has expanded the time frame beyond a point when it can reasonably be said that an exigency exists. The foundation for this approach was laid in a Prohibition Era case of the same vintage as *Carroll*—*Husty v. United States* (1927). A reliable informant told a prohibition officer that Husty, a previously convicted bootlegger, had "had two loads of liquor in automobiles of a particular make and description, parked in particular places on named streets." The agent proceeded to the car, although he had sufficient time to obtain a warrant. He saw Husty and two other men get into the car. At that point, the agent approached and the two other men fled. The car was searched and contraband found. In response to the argument that the agents had sufficient time to obtain a warrant, Justice Harlan Fiske Stone reasoned: The agent "could not know when Husty would come to the car or how soon it would be removed. In such circumstances we do not think the officers should be required to speculate upon the chances of successfully carrying out the search, after the delay and withdrawal from the scene of one or more officers which would have been necessary to procure a warrant" (*Husty v. United States,* p. 701). Under these circumstances an actual exigency existed.

But four decades later, the Supreme Court moved the time frame into the potential exigency concept and beyond. It can be argued that once an automobile is stopped by police who have probable cause that it contains contraband, the police can uphold the constitutional values of the Fourth Amendment by securing the vehicle until a warrant has been obtained. The Supreme Court rejected this argument in *Chambers v. Maroney* (1970): "For constitutional purposes, we see no difference between on the one hand seizing and holding a car before presenting the probable cause issue to a magistrate and on the other hand carrying out an immediate search without a warrant. Given probable cause to search, either course is reasonable under the Fourth Amendment." Justice White held that this is so, even given the Court's stated preference for a warrant, because it is not clear whether it is a greater intrusion on a person's liberty to be held at the roadside awaiting a warrant or to have one's car searched. Justice Harlan, dissenting, thought that the search was more intrusive, because it could lead to a criminal conviction, and because a person with nothing to hide would give police consent to search the car. On the other hand, forcing police to obtain a warrant to search a stopped vehicle can create unnecessary risks and burdens on law enforcement. In *Chambers,* the police seized the car at night with four robbery suspects inside. Under these circumstances, it was neither practical nor safe for the officers to conduct the search on the roadside; consequently, the car was impounded and searched at the police station. Even at that point, however, the warrant rule was not imposed, apparently because the car had not been impounded and it was, in theory, possible for a confederate or a stranger to enter the automobile. As a practical matter, the *ad hoc* impoundment in *Chambers* has been replaced by more routine police practices of impounding all seized vehicles and subjecting them to a detailed inventory search. *Chambers* demonstrates that the Court ignored the mobility rationale of *Carroll* even before establishing the lesser expectation of privacy rationale for automobile searches.

Chambers can be explained by the important factor that the police officer's safety made it reasonable for the officer to take the car to the station house instead of searching it on the road at night; there was a real exigency when the car was first seized. But in *Texas v. White* (1975), the Court allowed the search of a vehicle at the station house, although there was, at best, a potential exigency when the car was seized. White was arrested at 1:30 P.M. while attempting to pass fraudulent checks at a drive-in window of a bank, after police had a

CHAMBERS v. MARONEY IN THE STATES

"In State v. Miller,[8] the Connecticut Supreme Court rejected on state constitutional grounds the *Chambers* tow-and-search rule. Miler was taken into custody as he exited an automobile that matched the vehicle described by a witness to a supermarket robbery. After he was transported to the police station, defendant's car was towed to a police department garage, where the police secured it and conducted a warrantless search which revealed a .357 Smith and Wesson revolver in the trunk. Miller was convicted of criminal possession of a weapon.

"The issue . . . was 'whether the state constitution prohibits a warrantless automobile search supported by probable cause but conducted while the automobile is impounded at a police station.' The court first noted a strong state constitutional policy in favor of warrants. . . . It then rejected 'the fiction that the legitimate safety concern that may necessitate towing an automobile from the site of its seizure to the police station also provides justification for the warrantless search of that automobile at the station.' Next, the court rebuffed the state's contention that privacy interests in an automobile are invaded to the same extent by a warrantless search at the scene of its seizure as by a warrantless search at the police station.

> We tolerate the warrantless-on-the-scene automobile search only because obtaining a warrant would be impracticable in light of the inherent mobility of automobiles and the latent exigency that that mobility creates. . . . If the impracticability of obtaining a warrant no longer exists, however, our state constitutional preference for warrants regains its dominant place in that balance, and a warrant is required."

Barry Latzer, *State Constitutional Criminal Law,* § 3:28

report of a similar incident at another bank earlier that day by a person matching White's description. He was ordered to park his car and was observed by a bank employee and an officer attempting to stuff something between the seats. White was driven to the station house while another officer drove his car there. After thirty to forty-five minutes of questioning, White refused to consent to a search of his car, but the officers proceeded to search it anyway. During the search, four wrinkled checks corresponding to those White had attempted to pass at the first bank were discovered. The Court, in a brief *per curiam* opinion, upheld the search on this reading of *Chambers:* "police officers with probable cause to search an automobile on the scene where it was stopped could constitutionally do so later at the station house without first obtaining a warrant." Justice Thurgood Marshall, dissenting (joined by Justice Brennan), took the majority to task for misreading the holding of *Chambers.* The facts in *Chambers* included a nighttime stop of a car with four suspected armed robbers, a clearly perilous scenario. "*Chambers* simply held [the station house search] to be the rule when it is *reasonable* to take the car to the station house in the first place" (*Texas v. White,* p. 69, emphasis added). By ignoring these facts, the Court has moved to a *per se* rule that allows a search, after the fact, of a probable cause seizure of a car.

Chambers and *Texas v. White* clearly betoken the weakening of the mobility exigency rule of *Carroll.* It is useful to note that these cases occurred just prior to the time that the Supreme Court recognized the inventory search which will be discussed later. A routine inventory search is not an exigency search and serves other constitutional interests than those of a probable cause search. Nevertheless, as a functional matter, if not as a matter of constitutional law, routine inventory searches, in effect, allow the seizure of all contraband found in a car that is searched well after an arrested person has been taken into custody. In any event, although the second rationale—a lesser expectation of privacy—has been a vital element in the Court's expansion of the power of police to search cars, the softening of the mobility exception has also been a factor. The Court's willingness to authorize warrantless automobile searches in parked cars is demonstrated in *California v. Carney* (1985).

WHAT IS AN AUTOMOBILE? *California v. Carney* (1985) gave a precise *definition* of an "automobile" for Fourth Amendment purposes. Carney lived in a fully mobile motor home. Police, suspicious that he was trading drugs for sex, had his motor home under surveillance while it was parked in a downtown San Diego public parking lot not far from the courthouse. They observed a youth enter the vehicle and stay there for an hour and a quarter. The youth emerged, was stopped by the police, and he told them that he received marijuana in return for allowing Carney sexual contact. The police and the youth went to the motor home, knocked, and after Carney stepped out, entered it without a warrant and seized illegal drugs.

Carney argued that because this vehicle was also his home, it had to be given the same Fourth Amendment protection as a stationary home, that is, the police could not search it without obtaining a warrant. The Supreme Court disagreed, holding that such a van is a mobile vehicle, subject to similar licensing and regulation requirements as an automobile; therefore, the reasonable (i.e., objective) expectation of privacy in a van is equivalent to what one expects in an automobile, not a home. These factors brought the van under the exigency exception to the warrant requirement: "Our application of the vehicle exception has never turned on the other uses to which a vehicle might be put."

Justice Stevens dissented in *Carney* on the grounds that there was no exigency. He urged the Court to rule that the automobile exception should not apply to a parked vehicle where there is time to obtain a warrant, but only to vehicles in motion along the highway. The majority refused to adopt this restriction. In both *Coolidge* and *Carney,* there was time to obtain a warrant. In *Coolidge,* however, the seizure was preceded by a two-week investigation and the vehicle was in full police control, while in *Carney,* the surveillance of the van lasted for a little over an hour. Thus, the police had ample time to plan their action in *Coolidge,* while the police in *Carney* acted with less preparation or planning, although they apparently had the ability to obtain a warrant. In *Coolidge,* the car was taken to the police station, while in *Carney,* the mobile home was in a public parking lot. In *Coolidge,* neither the defendant nor anyone associated with him had access to the car, while Carney was in his vehicle and could have driven it away if he was not arrested. The Court stated in *Carney,* "[T]he respondent's motor home was readily mobile. Absent the prompt search and seizure, it could readily have been moved beyond the reach of the police."

The Supreme Court is clearly reluctant to add any qualification or addition to the automobile exigency rule that benefits defendants. In *Maryland v. Dyson* (1999), police had advance warning, amounting to probable cause, that a specific vehicle would come into the jurisdiction with illegal drugs. An intermediate Maryland appellate court ruled that because the police had time to obtain a warrant, there was no exigency and a search warrant was required. The Court, in a *per curiam* opinion, reversed. "[U]nder our established precedent, the 'automobile exception' has no separate exigency requirement." On the other hand, the Court has added embellishments to the automobile search rule in order to uphold the warrantless entry into an automobile, such as the VIN rule.

THE VIN RULE The Supreme Court demonstrated its creativity in allowing a police entry into a vehicle in *New York v. Class* (1986) by fabricating a limited right of intrusion into a car without probable cause in order to view a vehicle identification number (VIN) not viewable from outside the car. Police stopped a car for speeding. The driver produced a registration certificate and proof of insurance but no driver's license. The officer could not see the VIN on the dashboard so he "reached into the interior of the car to move some papers obscuring the area of the dashboard where the VIN is located in all post-1969 models. In doing so, the officer saw the handle of a gun, and respondent was promptly arrested." As a valid VIN entry, the gun was in plain view and thus admissible. The Court reasoned that the VIN is needed to protect safety and property and is required by federal regulations to be in a place that can be easily read by someone standing outside the automobile. Combining the special requirements of the VIN with the lesser expectation of privacy in an automobile, the Court felt justified in creating a warrant exception authorizing such an entry without probable cause to believe there was contraband in the car. *Class* created a limited police power, because police cannot enter a vehicle if the VIN is observable from the car's exterior, and newer model cars are designed to make it impossible to cover the VIN. The case illustrates the Court's creativity in engineering a rule to fit a particular situation, and that does not violate the basic rule that a search must be objectively reasonable, which favors the police.

SEIZURE OF A CAR SUBJECT TO FORFEITURE In *Florida v. White* (1999), officers observed Tyvessel Tyvorus White make cocaine deliveries in his car in July and August 1993 and, for inexplicable reasons, did not arrest him. Under the Florida Contraband Forfeiture Act, his car was subject to forfeiture. Several months later, White was arrested at his workplace on charges unrelated to the cocaine delivery. Police officers went to the employer's parking lot where White's car was parked and seized it without a warrant. A subsequent inventory search disclosed cocaine. The Florida Supreme Court ruled the warrantless seizure unconstitutional. The United States Supreme Court reversed and offered two reasons for upholding the warrantless seizure: (1) Although the police had no probable cause to believe the car contained contraband, "they certainly had probable cause to believe that the vehicle *itself* was contraband under Florida law," and the mobility rationale applies to the warrantless seizure of contraband in a mobile vehicle and the mobile vehicle itself; (2) "[O]ur Fourth Amendment jurisprudence has consistently accorded law enforcement officials greater latitude in exercising their duties in public places." The Court treated the owner's private property as a public place for Fourth Amendment purposes and concluded that "the Fourth Amendment did not require a warrant to seize respondent's automobile . . . ." (*Florida v. White,* pp. 565–566.)

Justice Stevens dissented in *White,* joined by Justice Ginsburg. Under *Soldal v. Cook County* (1992), the Fourth Amendment protects property as well as privacy interests. There was no exigency here. White had been arrested and there was sufficient time to obtain a search warrant. The car is not inherent contraband, such as drugs or firearms, so its seizure is not required to preserve public safety. A "warrant application interjects the judgment of a neutral decision-maker, one with no pecuniary interest in the matter." Justice Stevens found it "particularly troubling . . . not that the State provides a weak excuse for failing to obtain a warrant either before or after White's arrest, but that it offers us no reason at all" and concluded that "the officers who seized White's car simply preferred to avoid the hassle of seeking approval from a judicial officer." The simple convenience of officers was deemed too feeble a reason to override Fourth Amendment rights. Although the majority did not disavow the warrant requirement, "its decision suggests that the exceptions have all but swallowed the general rule."

Searches of Containers in Mobile Vehicles

In the 1970s and 1980s, the most hotly contested issue in automobile search cases was the *scope* of a search of closed areas and containers found in mobile vehicles. The "container" cases demonstrate that visions of constitutional interpretation are shaped by ideology. On the one side stood liberal-moderate justices Brennan, Marshall, and Stevens, who urged the Court to require warrants to search mobile containers that had been secured by police, a position supported by the warrant-preference construction of the Fourth Amendment and informed by the Due Process Model of Criminal justice (see Chapter 1). On the other side stood a growing conservative majority on the Court. They found the Crime Control Model of criminal justice more congenial and, despite some doctrinal difficulties, ultimately ruled that under the general-reasonableness construction of the Fourth Amendment, warrants are not needed to open closed areas and containers in automobiles if there is probable cause to believe that the containers contain contraband.

SEARCH OF CONTAINERS NOT IN AUTOMOBILES In *Carroll v. United States* (1925), the Supreme Court held that when the automobile exception comes into play, officers could search any part of the car in which the contraband could reasonably be found. The officer's determination of what to search was coextensive with that of a magistrate. In *Carroll,* an agent determined that the back seat of the roadster was hard and began to tear up the seat cushion. Thus, the destruction of parts of the car within which contraband was reasonably held was allowed.

In contrast to this aspect of the *Carroll* case, *United States v. Chadwick* (1977) held that a person's "effects" are given full constitutional protection. A container, out of the context of the automobile exception, cannot lawfully be opened by an officer unless the officer has a warrant, even if the officer has probable cause to believe that the container contains contraband. *Chadwick* involved a **controlled delivery** of the kind upheld in *United States v. Van Leeuwen* (1970), where police temporarily seized a suspicious package without a warrant in order to give them time to continue investigating, to corroborate their suspicion and to obtain a warrant to search the package. In *Chadwick,* Amtrak officials in San Diego became suspicious when two persons, one of whom fit the profile of a drug trafficker, loaded a footlocker that was unusually heavy for its size and leaking talcum powder (used to mask the odor of marijuana) on a Boston-bound train. Federal narcotics agents in Boston were on hand two days later when the footlocker arrived. They had no arrest or search warrant, but a trained dog signaled the presence of a controlled substance inside the trunk. Three persons took possession of the footlocker and loaded it into the trunk of a car. At that moment, the agents arrested the three men and seized the footlocker. An hour and a half later in the federal building, the agents obtained the key to the footlocker, opened it, and found large amounts of marijuana. The brief contact with a car did not turn this into an automobile search case. The Court also found that under the facts of the case, a warrantless search of the footlocker could not be justified as a search incident to arrest.

The Supreme Court, in a 7–2 opinion authored by Chief Justice Burger, held that this warrantless search violated the Fourth Amendment. Although the agents had probable cause to believe that the footlocker contained illicit drugs, it was protected by the warrant clause, which "makes a significant contribution to [the] protection" against unreasonable searches and seizures. As early as 1878, the Supreme Court had said that "[l]etters and sealed packages . . . are as fully guarded from examination and inspection, except as to their outward form and weight, as if they were retained by the parties forwarding them in their own domiciles" (*Ex Parte Jackson,* 1878). Important privacy interests are at stake when a person sends a locked trunk to another place, both subjective and reasonable (socially objective). There is a constitutional expectation of privacy in such a container.

The *Chadwick* Court distinguished a footlocker (an "effect") from an automobile. Although a footlocker is mobile, it is afforded *greater* Fourth Amendment protection because it is not subjected to the pervasive government regulation of an automobile. Furthermore, once the footlocker's general mobility was ended and it was secured in the Boston federal building under the exclusive control of the police, there was no exigency that required an on-the-spot search without a warrant. "With the footlocker safely immobilized, it was unreasonable to undertake the additional and greater intrusion of a search without a warrant" (*United States v. Chadwick,* 1977).

THE SEARCH OF MOBILE CONTAINERS IN AUTOMOBILES If *Chadwick* is to be logically followed, it seems that when police search an automobile under the automobile exigency exception and they discover a container that does not immediately indicate that it holds contraband (the hardness of the back seat of the roadster in *Carroll* indicated bottles of whiskey), they should seize the container and apply to a magistrate for a search warrant. The court followed this mode of analysis in *Arkansas v. Sanders* (1979). Police, acting on probable cause supplied by a reliable informant's tip that the respondent would arrive at an airport with drugs, followed the suspect, who carried a suitcase, and saw him enter a taxi cab. The police followed the cab for several blocks and pulled it over. Without asking permission, they took the suitcase from the cab, opened it, and found over nine pounds of marijuana. The Supreme Court held that although the police had probable cause to believe the suitcase contained drugs, and although they were justified in stopping the taxi and seizing the suitcase, the suitcase could not be opened and searched without a search warrant because the mobility exigency regarding the suitcase had ended. The *Sanders* decision was a straightforward application of *Chadwick:*

> [W]e hold that the warrant requirement of the Fourth Amendment applies to personal luggage taken from an automobile to the same degree it applies to such luggage in other locations. Thus, insofar as the police are entitled to search such luggage without a warrant, their actions must be justified under some exception to the warrant requirement other than that applicable to automobiles stopped on the highway. (*Arkansas v. Sanders,* p. 766)

The *Sanders* rule, however, proved to be unstable and short-lived. The five justices in the majority included liberal and moderate justices (Justice Powell authored the opinion, joined by Brennan, Stewart, White, and Marshall). Justices Blackmun and Rehnquist dissented on the grounds that *Chadwick* was not correctly decided, and even if it were, a container which police had probable cause to believe held contraband in a mobile vehicle should be subject to the rules of *Carroll* (1925) and *Chambers v. Maroney* (1970); i.e., the police should be able to open it on the spot without a warrant. The dissent stressed the "untoward costs on the criminal justice system of this country in terms of added delay and uncertainty" caused by the *Chadwick-Sanders* rule. Quite significantly, two concurring justices (Chief Justice Burger and Justice Stevens) argued that the situation in *Sanders* was *not* an automobile exigency search, thus clouding an understanding of the scope of a search of containers found in a mobile vehicle.

Sanders was followed by *New York v. Belton* (1981), which held that a police officer who had probable cause to *arrest* a suspect after stopping his automobile acquired the right to search the interior compartment of the automobile (see Chapter 5). In *Belton,* a New York State Trooper stopped a speeding car, ordered the driver and three passengers out, found that none had a vehicle registration, and smelled marijuana in the vehicle. He arrested all four occupants, secured them with handcuffs, searched them individually, and returned to the car to pick up an envelope marked "Supergold." He unzipped a pocket of a black leather jacket which was laying on the back seat of the car and found that it contained cocaine, which was introduced into evidence. The Supreme Court held that "when a policeman has made a lawful custodial arrest of the occupant of an automobile, he may, as a contemporaneous incident of that arrest, search the *passenger compartment* of that automobile." And, as an extension of that rule, the Court stated that "the police may also examine the *contents of any containers* found within the passenger compartment, for if the passenger compartment is within reach of the arrestee, so also will containers be within his reach" (emphasis added). This language seemed to undermine the *Chadwick-Sanders* rule.

The apparent inconsistency between *Belton* and *Chadwick-Sanders* can be explained by *Belton*'s specific facts, and the search incident to arrest rationale for the search. One police officer arresting four men at the side of a state highway could reasonably be in danger that one of them would run to the car to seize a weapon or evidence in the passenger compartment. This is factually distinguishable from several officers arresting individuals in possession of a locked footlocker, where there is no ready chance that they could overwhelm the officers and flee. The Court, however, preferred not to establish a rule that tracked the precise extent of the exigency, but rather established a "bright-line" rule to give better guidance to police officers in fast-moving street situations. Thus, *Belton* was a confusing precedent because its absolute language in support of a container search in a car was undercut by its facts. While it did not clarify the authority of officers to search closed containers in a motor vehicle, it seemed to be at odds with *Chadwick-Sanders.*

The issue was further confused by the Court's fractured decision in *Robbins v. California* (1981). Police stopped a station wagon traveling erratically; an officer smelled marijuana smoke when Robbins emerged, searched Robbins, and found a vial of liquid. The officer then searched the interior of the car and found marijuana. The police officers then opened the tailgate of the station wagon and raised the cover of a recessed luggage compartment, in which they found two packages wrapped in green opaque plastic. The police unwrapped the packages and discovered a large amount of marijuana in each. The issue was whether the opening of the two packages violated the Fourth Amendment. The Supreme Court, in a plurality opinion by Justice Stewart, held this an unreasonable search and seizure on the authority of *Chadwick* and *Sanders*: (1) the outward appearance of the package did not undermine Robbins' expectation of privacy; (2) there was no constitutional difference between a footlocker (a "worthy" container) and a plastic bag or package (an "unworthy" container). Concurring Justices Powell and Chief Justice Burger, however, expressed reservations about the decision and suggested a line of reasoning that would soon undermine the *Chadwick-Sanders* rule, namely that "when the police have probable cause to search an automobile, rather than only to search a particular container that fortuitously is located in it, the exigencies that allow the police to search the entire automobile without a warrant support the warrantless search of every container found therein."

BRIGHT-LINE RULES FOR THE SCOPE OF AUTOMOBILE EXCEPTION SEARCHES This reasoning undermined the strength of *Robbins* as a precedent. In the following year Justice Stewart retired and was replaced by the more conservative Justice O'Connor which allowed reconsideration of the doubts raised in *Robbins.* Indeed, the Court overturned *Robbins* the next year in *United States v. Ross* (1982). In *Ross* and *California v. Acevedo* (1991), a conservative tide on the Court swept away the *Chadwick-Sanders* rule in two waves, finally establishing the bright-line rule that allowed police to search automobiles and *any* closed compartments or containers in them without a search warrant whenever probable cause existed to believe that contraband was in the car generally *or* in a specific container. Their rules are simple. *Ross* holds that when police have probable cause to believe that contraband is located in a automobile, they may, under the automobile exception, open any closed container in the car that may logically hold the contraband; this overrules *Robbins. Acevedo* holds that when an officer has probable cause to believe that a specific container located in a car contains contraband, the officer may, upon lawfully stopping the car and gaining access to its interior, open the container. This overrules *Sanders* but not *Chadwick,* because *Chadwick* was not treated as an automobile exception case.

The facts in *Ross* were that a known reliable informant telephoned a police detective and told him that an individual known as "Bandit" was selling narcotics kept in the trunk of a "purplish maroon" Chevrolet Malibu parked at a specific street location, that the informant had just observed "Bandit" complete a sale, and that "Bandit" had told him that additional narcotics were in the trunk. A police car drove to the street address, saw a maroon Malibu parked there, did a computer check, and discovered that the car was registered to Albert Ross, who fit the informant's description and who used the alias "Bandit." The officers drove through the neighborhood twice but did not observe anyone matching Ross' description. They returned five minutes later and saw the maroon Malibu being driven off by a man matching the informant's description. The officers stopped the car and ordered Ross out of the car. Officers observed a bullet on the front seat so they searched the interior of the car and found a pistol in the glove compartment, whereupon they arrested and handcuffed Ross. A detective took Ross' keys, opened the trunk, and found a closed brown paper bag. When opened, the bag was found to contain a number of glassine bags containing a white powder that was later determined to be heroin. At the station house, the car trunk was searched without a warrant and a zippered red leather pouch found and opened. It contained thirty-two hundred dollars in cash.

Ross squarely presented the issue of the scope of an automobile search wherein police had probable cause to believe that contraband was located somewhere in the car or the trunk, but not in a specific bag or container. On the one hand, the *Carroll* case allowed police to rip open upholstery on the side of the road to get at the contraband. On the other hand, *Chadwick* pointed to a rule that the container can be seized and held (but not opened) until a search warrant was obtained. The Court opted for the *Carroll* approach. The details of *Ross* did not include the facts of *Sanders,* in that police had probable cause to believe that there was contraband in a container located in a moving car, but no probable cause to believe that there was contraband elsewhere in the car. For the time being, *Chadwick* controlled *Sanders*-type situations.

The Court advanced several reasons for its decision. It noted that from the *Carroll* case in 1925 up to *Chadwick* (1977), decisions of lower courts and the Supreme Court never questioned the right of police to open bags of suspected contraband found in lawfully stopped cars. The practical benefits of the *Carroll* rule would be largely nullified by not allowing police to open closed containers reasonably suspected of housing contraband because illegal materials are usually secured to be kept out of sight. Also, *Carroll* did not increase the scope of a lawful search, but instead "merely relaxed the requirements for a warrant on grounds of practicability." (*Henry v. United States* (1959), p. 104) thus, a search warrant allowing a search for contraband implies that officers may open containers in the premises that could logically hold the kind of contraband sought.

> When a legitimate search is under way, and when its purpose and its limits have been precisely defined, nice distinctions between closets, drawers, and containers, in the case of a home, or between glove compartments, upholstered seats, trunks, and wrapped packages, in the case of a vehicle, must give way to the interest in the prompt and efficient completion of the task at hand. (*United States v. Ross,* p. 821)

This rule applies to all containers; the Court upheld the concept of *Robbins* that a constitutional distinction between "worthy" and "unworthy" containers was improper, as long as the container shielded its contents from plain view. Finally, because a search under the automobile exception was as valid as a search incident to arrest or a search under a warrant, the suspect loses the expectation of privacy to the same extent as in these cases which allow the opening of "some containers." In conclusion, the "scope of a warrantless search of an automobile . . . is not defined by the nature of the container in which the contraband is secreted [but] by the object of the search and the places in which there is probable cause to believe that it may be found" (*United States v. Ross,* p. 824). The majority stated that it rejected the precise holding in *Robbins,* but upheld the specific holding in *Sanders,* although it rejected some of its reasoning.

Justice Marshall dissented, joined by Justices Brennan and White, harshly accusing the Court of "repeal[ing] the Fourth Amendment warrant requirement itself" and "utterly disregard[ing] the value of a neutral and detached magistrate." The specific reasoning to support this view was, first, a reiteration of the value of a search warrant and the effect of the warrant process on the officers who had to write an affidavit justifying the search. Next, in many of the automobile exception cases there was an actual exigency that reasonably justified police in advance of a warrant. Fourth Amendment principles are undermined when the automobile exigency exception is applied to every search of an automobile, even when the suspect is arrested and there is not a reasonable likelihood that another person will get to the car. Ignoring this difference is a sleight-of-hand. A decision based on Fourth Amendment principles must apply the *Chadwick* rule to a search of an automobile when the exigency is at an end. Finally, the majority's ruling in *Ross* is inconsistent with the rule of *Sanders.* Prophetically, Justice Marshall stated that "This case will have profound implications for the privacy of citizens traveling in automobiles."

A decade later, the Court dropped the other shoe and, in *California v. Acevedo* (1991), overruled *Arkansas v. Sanders* (1979). Between 1982 and 1991, the composition of the Court had become considerably more conservative, with Justice Rehnquist becoming Chief Justice upon the retirement of Chief Justice Burger, the addition of Justices Scalia, Kennedy, and Souter to the Court, and the retirement of Justices Powell and Brennan. Justice Blackmun, who had dissented in *Sanders,* now had the opportunity to bury that decision in his majority opinion, and was joined by Chief Justice Burger and Justices O'Connor, Kennedy, and Souter. Justice Scalia concurred with the majority. Justices White, Stevens, and Marshall dissented.

In *Acevedo,* marijuana lawfully seized by the DEA in Hawaii was shipped to Officer Coleman of the Santa Ana, California, Police Department. He set up a controlled, Federal Express pick up, to one Jamie Daza, who picked up the package at 10:30 A.M. on a certain day. Daza, package in hand, was followed to his apartment. At 11:45 A.M., Daza left the apartment and dropped the marijuana container's wrapping into a trash bin. Officer Coleman left the scene to get a search warrant. At 12:30 P.M., respondent Charles Steven Acevedo arrived. He entered Daza's apartment, stayed for about ten minutes, and emerged carrying a brown paper bag that appeared full. Other officers observing the scene noticed that the bag was the size of one of the wrapped marijuana packages sent from Hawaii. Acevedo walked to a silver Honda in the parking lot, placed the bag in the trunk of the car, and started to drive away. Fearing the loss of evidence, officers in a marked police car stopped him. They opened the trunk and the bag, and found marijuana. The California Court of Appeals suppressed the marijuana on the basis of *Chadwick* (instead of *Ross*) because the officers had probable cause to believe that the paper bag contained drugs but lacked probable cause to suspect that Acevedo's car itself otherwise contained contraband.

The reasons given for allowing a warrantless search of a closed container in an operative vehicle, which had become immobilized and the driver taken into custody, began with an observation on *Ross*: that where police have probable cause to believe that contraband is located in a car but have not pinpointed a specific container, "that the time and expense of the warrant process would be misdirected if the police could search every cubic inch of an automobile until they discovered a paper sack, at which point the Fourth Amendment required them to take the sack to a magistrate for permission to look inside." The majority forthrightly noted:

> that a container found after a general search of the automobile and a container found in a car after a limited search for the container are equally easy for the police to store and for the suspect to hide or destroy. In fact, we see no principled distinction in terms of either the privacy expectation or the exigent circumstances between the paper bag found by the police in *Ross* and the paper bag found by the police here. Furthermore, by attempting to distinguish between a container for which the police are specifically searching and a container which they come across in a car, we have provided only minimal protection for privacy and have impeded effective law enforcement. (*California v. Acevedo,* p. 574)

Put this way, it seems clear that the fine line between *Sanders-Acevedo* (specific probable cause) cases and *Carroll-Ross* (general probable cause) cases is a thin one—that it would be better for the cases to be decided consistently—either all containers can be opened by the police or all containers should be held until a magistrate has ruled on the police officer's assessment of probable cause. Which way was best? The path chosen by the majority was based, first, on its stated assumption that the *Ross* rule provided "minimal protection for privacy" because in the *Chadwick-Sanders* situation the suspicious package is seized and held for a warrant in any event. Next, the Court noted that the clear theoretical distinction is not always clear to a police officer searching a car in the field. If some doubt exists about probable cause in an automobile search case applying to the whole car or the container, then a defendant would invariably assert the latter and seek the protection of *Chadwick-Sanders,* causing unneeded litigation. Also, police might try to circumvent that rule by needlessly searching an entire car to make it seem as if the *Ross* rule operates when they have probable cause to believe that the contraband is located in a container. Further, the opening of a container is less physically intrusive than a full search of an automobile: "If destroying the interior of an automobile is not unreasonable, we cannot conclude that looking inside a closed container is." To these reasons, Justice Blackmun was critical of the fact that the dichotomy between the two automobile search rules has created confusion in the lower courts and impeded effective law enforcement. "The *Chadwick-Sanders* rule is the antithesis of a 'clear and unequivocal' guideline." The Court overruled *Sanders* and stated that it had returned all automobile search cases to the basic rule of *Carroll.*

Justice Stevens' dissent was unusual in that it specifically referred to the Court relying "on arguments that conservative judges have repeatedly rejected in past cases." Justices are aware of the ideological leanings of their colleagues and themselves, but it is another thing to mention this in an opinion. Because a dissent is the justice's personal statement, such dissents are often more freewheeling or idiosyncratic than a majority opinion, which reflects the judgment of each justice who joins the opinion. By stating that conservative justices in the past supported the *Sanders* rule, Justice Stevens suggested that the *Acevedo* majority are extremists. The opinion begins with an exposition on constitutional policy favoring the use of warrants and reminding that "[t]he Fourth Amendment is a restraint on Executive power." The burdens of obtaining warrants "are outweighed by the individual interest in privacy that is protected by advance judicial approval." He then argued that *Ross* and *Chadwick-Sanders* were not inconsistent; *Ross* applied to the scope of an automobile search, whereas *Sanders* applied to the search of all closed containers, whether found in automobiles or not. He also noted, as did Justice Marshall dissenting in *Ross,* that "[t]he Court does not attempt to identify any exigent circumstances that would justify its refusal to apply the general rule against warrantless searches."

Justice Stevens challenged three specific points made by Justice Blackmun. First, the majority claimed that the existence of the *Chadwick-Sanders* rule and the *Ross* rule was confusing and anomalous. Justice Stevens recited cases that seemed to have no difficulty in distinguishing between the two, and so disagreed as to the confusion. Regarding the anomaly, he posed the matter in an interesting way: "To the extent there was any 'anomaly' in our prior jurisprudence, the Court has 'cured' it at the expense of creating a more serious paradox. For, surely it is anomalous to prohibit a search of a briefcase while the owner is carrying it exposed on a public street yet to permit a search once the owner has placed the briefcase in the locked trunk of his car" (*California v. Acevedo,* p. 598). Justice Stevens thought that making the automobile search rules the same by *eliminating* the warrant requirement in both was the worse solution because the person had the same expectation of privacy in the container, whether found in or out of a car.

Second, he disagreed that the *Chadwick-Sanders* rule does not protect any significant interest in privacy. "Every citizen clearly has an interest in the privacy of the contents of his or her luggage, briefcase, handbag or any other container that conceals private papers and effects from public scrutiny. . . . Under the Court's holding today, the privacy interest that protects the contents of a suitcase or a briefcase from a warrantless search when it is in public view simply vanishes when its owner climbs into a taxicab. Unquestionably the rejection of the *Sanders* line of cases by today's decision will result in a significant loss of individual privacy." The third argument of the majority opinion was that the rules impede effective law enforcement. Justice Stevens noted that the Court cited no authority for its contentions and stated that, even if true, it was "in any event, an insufficient reason for creating a new exception to the warrant requirement." This last point, of course, is an expected statement for one who leans toward the Due Process Approach; a proponent of the Crime Control Model of criminal justice would disagree.

Ross and *Acevedo* are significant cases because, by a single bright-line rule, they resolved the tangled legal threads on the scope of automobile and sealed container searches. To the dissenting justices, these cases seriously undermine Fourth Amendment rights and give the police carte blanche to search cars. Each majority opinion, however, mandates that there must be a clear connection between probable cause and the scope of a search. Doctrinally, *Ross* and *Acevedo* do not grant police unbridled searching power; for example, police cannot search the locked trunk of a car if its driver is arrested for driving under the influence of alcohol or a controlled substance. However, the real fear may be that lenient rules will be applied by the police as license to use their discretion to search, guided only by their common sense and innate sense of decency, and that when police step over the legal line, lower court judges will excuse such behavior.

The *Ross* rule was extended to automobile passengers in *Wyoming v. Houghton.*

Automobile Inventory Searches

An inventory search of an impounded motor vehicle is a form of administrative search upheld by the Supreme Court as reasonable under the Fourth Amendment. It is designed to

• CASE & COMMENTS •

Wyoming v. Houghton

526 U.S. 295, 119 S.Ct. 1297, 143 L. Ed. 2d 408 (1999)

JUSTICE SCALIA delivered the opinion of the Court.

This case presents the question whether police officers violate the Fourth Amendment when they search a passenger's personal belongings inside an automobile that they have probable cause to believe contains contraband.

In the early morning hours *** a Wyoming Highway Patrol officer stopped an automobile for speeding and driving with a faulty brake light. There were three passengers in the front seat of the car: David Young (the driver), his girlfriend, and respondent. While questioning Young, the officer noticed a hypodermic syringe in Young's shirt pocket. He left the occupants under the supervision of two backup officers as he went to get gloves from his patrol car. Upon his return, he instructed Young to step out of the car and place the syringe on the hood. The officer then asked Young why he had a syringe; with refreshing candor, Young replied that he used it to take drugs. **[a]**

[a] Suppose you are driven to classes by a friend and the car is stopped for speeding. The officer orders your friend out of the car and notices a single marijuana cigarette on the floor. Should the officer be able to search your backpack which is sitting on the back seat? Should it matter if you claim the backpack as your property?

[The two female passengers were ordered out of the car. Asked for identification, Houghton falsely identified herself as "Sandra James." In light of Young's admission, the officer searched the passenger compartment of the car for contraband, and found a purse on the back seat which Houghton claimed as hers. He removed her wallet containing her driver's license. When the officer asked her why she had lied about her name, she replied: "In case things went bad." The officer then removed a brown pouch and a black wallet-type container. Houghton denied that the pouch was hers, and claimed ignorance of how it came to be there. It contained drug paraphernalia and a syringe with 60 ccs of methamphetamine. The officer also found fresh needle-track marks on Houghton's arms. He placed her under arrest. The trial court denied Houghton's motion to suppress evidence obtained from the purse as the fruit of a Fourth Amendment violation. She was convicted of felony possession of methamphetamine. The trial court held that the officer had probable cause to search the car for contraband, and, by extension, any containers therein that could hold such contraband.]

[The Wyoming Supreme Court, reversing the conviction, ruled that where an officer has probable cause to believe that contraband is somewhere in a lawfully stopped car, the officer may search all containers in the car *except* containers that the officer knows or should know is a personal effect of a passenger who is not suspected of criminal activity, "*unless* someone had the opportunity to conceal the contraband within the personal effect to avoid detection."]

II

* * *

*** [I]n the present case [] the police officers had probable cause to believe there were illegal drugs in the car. **[b]** *Carroll v. United States* (1925) *** held that "contraband goods concealed and illegally transported in an automobile or other vehicle may be searched for without a warrant" where probable cause exists.

[b] Notice that the specific exigency reasoning of *Carroll* is not mentioned.

We have furthermore read the historical evidence to show that the Framers would have regarded as reasonable (if there was probable cause) the warrantless search of containers *within* an automobile. **[c]** In *Ross* we upheld as reasonable the warrantless search of a paper bag and leather pouch found in the trunk of the defendant's car by officers who had probable cause to believe that the trunk contained drugs. ***

[c] As an "originalist", Justice Scalia justifies Fourth Amendment rulings by "finding" what he thinks the Framers would have ruled rather than interpreting principles.

Ross summarized its holding as follows: "If probable cause justifies the search of a lawfully stopped vehicle, it justifies the search of *every part of the vehicle and its contents* that may conceal the object of the search." (emphasis added). **[d]** And our later cases describing *Ross* have characterized it as applying broadly to *all* containers within a car, without qualification as to ownership.***

[d] This logically includes Houghton's purse.

* * *

In sum, neither *Ross* itself nor the historical evidence it relied upon admits of a distinction among packages or containers based on ownership. When there is probable cause to search for contraband

• CASE & COMMENTS •

in a car, it is reasonable for police officers—like customs officials in the Founding era—to examine packages and containers without a showing of individualized probable cause for each one. **[e]** A passenger's personal belongings, just like the driver's belongings or containers attached to the car like a glove compartment, are "in" the car, and the officer has probable cause to search for contraband *in* the car.

Even if the historical evidence, as described by *Ross,* were thought to be equivocal, we would find that the balancing of the relative interests weighs decidedly in favor of allowing searches of a passenger's belongings. Passengers, no less than drivers, possess a reduced expectation of privacy with regard to the property that they transport in cars, which "travel public thoroughfares." ***

In this regard—the degree of intrusiveness upon personal privacy and indeed even personal dignity—the two cases the Wyoming Supreme Court found dispositive differ substantially from the package search at issue here. **[f]** *United States v. Di Re* (1948), held that probable cause to search a car did not justify a body search of a passenger. And *Ybarra v. Illinois,* (1979), held that a search warrant for a tavern and its bartender did not permit body searches of all the bar's patrons. These cases turned on the unique, significantly heightened protection afforded against searches of one's person. ***

Whereas the passenger's privacy expectations are, as we have described, considerably diminished, the governmental interests at stake are substantial. **[g]** Effective law enforcement would be appreciably impaired without the ability to search a passenger's personal belongings when there is reason to believe contraband or evidence of criminal wrongdoing is hidden in the car. As in all car-search cases, the "ready mobility" of an automobile creates a risk that the evidence or contraband will be permanently lost while a warrant is obtained. In addition, a car passenger—unlike the unwitting tavern patron in *Ybarra*—will often be engaged in a common enterprise with the driver, and have the same interest in concealing the fruits or the evidence of their wrongdoing. **[h]** A criminal might be able to hide contraband in a passenger's belongings as readily as in other containers in the car,—perhaps even surreptitiously, without the passenger's knowledge or permission. ***

To be sure, these factors favoring a search will not always be present, but the balancing of interests must be conducted with an eye to the generality of cases. To require that the investigating officer have positive reason to believe that the passenger and driver were engaged in a common enterprise, or positive reason to believe that the driver had time and occasion to conceal the item in the passenger's belongings, surreptitiously or with friendly permission, is to impose requirements so seldom met that a "passenger's property" rule would dramatically reduce the ability to find and seize contraband and evidence of crime. [Litigation would increase over the issue of whether the police officer should have believed a passenger's claim of ownership.] We think they militate in favor of the needs of law enforcement, and against a personal-privacy interest that is ordinarily weak.

* * *

We hold that police officers with probable cause to search a car may inspect passengers' belongings found in the car that are capable of concealing the object of the search. The judgment of the Wyoming Supreme Court is reversed.

[Justice Breyer concurred.]

JUSTICE STEVENS, with whom JUSTICE SOUTER and JUSTICE GINSBURG join, dissenting.

* * *

*** In the only automobile case confronting the search of a passenger defendant—*United States v. Di Re,* (1948)—**[i]** the Court held that the exception to the warrant requirement did not apply (addressing searches of the passenger's pockets and the space between his shirt and underwear, both of which uncovered counterfeit fuel rations). In *Di Re,* as here, the information prompting the search directly implicated the driver, not the passenger. Today, instead of adhering to the settled distinction between drivers and passengers, the Court fashions a new rule that is based on a distinction between

[e] While this is so, *Ross* did not involve passengers, and so the shaky "originalist" analysis aside, it does not establish direct precedent for a rule that allows an officer to open a container (a woman's purse) that is not likely to belong to the driver. In any event, while following the bright-line rule of *Ross* to a logical conclusion, Justice Scalia does not ask whether the *Ross* rule *ought to* extend to a passenger's purse.

[f] *DiRe* is central to Justice Steven's dissent. The majority does not overrule *DiRe* but instead distinguishes it, so that the rule of *DiRe* still exists, but so too does the rule of *Houghton.*

[g] Given the control that the police had over the car in this case (the driver arrested, the car subject to impoundment) and in most similar cases, have references to "ready mobility" become a smokescreen that simply allows the police to search a car and all its contents simply because it is a car? Would obtaining a warrant simply be inconvenient?

[h] The real difference between the majority and the dissenters seems to be that the majority imposes a *per se,* bright-line rule allowing no *Ross* exception for the belongings of a passenger. The dissent would allow the search of a passenger's bag if an officer had probable cause that her "container" held contraband. Justice Scalia suggests that such a rule would lessen the number of valid seizures from automobiles and enmesh police in on-the-street, fine-tuned adjudications of probable cause.

[i] See *DiRe* in Chapter 5. In that case an informer was riding in the car and would have seen the driver pass contraband to DiRe.

• CASE & COMMENTS •

property contained in clothing worn by a passenger and property contained in a passenger's briefcase or purse. **[j]** In cases on both sides of the Court's newly minted test, the property is in a "container" (whether a pocket or a pouch) located in the vehicle. Moreover, unlike the Court, I think it quite plain that the search of a passenger's purse or briefcase involves an intrusion on privacy that may be just as serious as was the intrusion in *Di Re.*

Even apart from *Di Re,* the Court's rights-restrictive approach is not dictated by precedent. **[k]** For example, in *United States v. Ross* (1982), we were concerned with the interest of the driver in the integrity of "his automobile," and we categorically rejected the notion that the scope of a warrantless search of a vehicle might be "defined by the nature of the container in which the contraband is secreted," . . . "Rather, it is defined by the object of the search and the places in which there is probable cause to believe that it may be found." We thus disapproved of a possible container-based distinction between a man's pocket and a woman's pocketbook. ***

Nor am I persuaded that the mere spatial association between a passenger and a driver provides an acceptable basis for presuming that they are partners in crime or for ignoring privacy interests in a purse. Whether or not the Fourth Amendment required a warrant to search Houghton's purse, at the very least the trooper in this case had to have probable cause to believe that her purse contained contraband. The Wyoming Supreme Court concluded that he did not.

Finally, in my view, the State's legitimate interest in effective law enforcement does not outweigh the privacy concerns at issue. **[l]** I am as confident in a police officer's ability to apply a rule requiring a warrant or individualized probable cause to search belongings that are—as in this case—obviously owned by and in the custody of a passenger as is the Court in a "passenger-confederate[']s" ability to circumvent the rule. Certainly the ostensible clarity of the Court's rule is attractive. But that virtue is insufficient justification for its adoption. Moreover, a rule requiring a warrant or individualized probable cause to search passenger belongings is every bit as simple as the Court's rule; it simply protects more privacy.

* * *

[j] If *DiRe* is still good law and the search of Houghton's purse is constitutional, could an officer lawfully zip open a "fanny pack" worn by a passenger on a belt?

[k] It is true that *Ross* is not direct precedent for the search of a passenger's bag, but the "object" of the search in *Ross* was drugs located somewhere in the car, not in a specific container, so the majority's extension of *Ross* to a passenger's belongings is logical. Further, Justice Stevens, the author of the *Ross* opinion, did not specifically mention a pocket or pocketbook in that opinion. The *Ross* case made no reference to *DiRe,* so it seems that Justice Stevens overreaches in explaining what *Ross* said as opposed to what he now thinks it should have said in light of the scenario of examples like *DiRe* and *Houghton.*

[l] Ultimately, the majority and dissenters are separated by their adherence to the "Due Process" or "Crime Control" model of criminal justice (see Chapter 1). Justice Stevens would impose the obligation on the officer to ensure there was probable cause to believe Houghton's purse contained contraband, and favors the liberty of the individual over the convenience of the officer.

perform a *caretaking* function. An inventory is a list of *all* items found in an impounded car or in the possession of the person taken into custody. In order to inventory the items in a car, it must be searched.

A constitutional automobile inventory requires that the car's **impoundment** be proper. Statutes and local ordinances govern the power of police to impound cars for sound reasons: to remove vehicles involved in accidents so as to permit the uninterrupted flow of traffic or to preserve evidence, to remove damaged cars from the highways, to tow away automobiles which violate parking ordinances, to impound cars after the driver has been arrested, to impound automobiles subject to forfeiture, and the like. An inventory of the property of a person who has been taken into custody is legally proper only if the underlying arrest is legal. A car may be impounded in an unsecured private lot of a local garage (*Cady v. Dombrowski,* 1973) (rural area; lot seven miles from the police station) or in an impoundment lot operated by a municipality. (*South Dakota v. Opperman,* 1976)

A judicial warrant is not needed to justify an inventory search. It does not fall under the automobile search exception. Probable cause or reasonable suspicion of contraband is

HOUGHTON IN THE STATES

As of August 2000, six states have followed *Wyoming v. Houghton*: Arkansas, Georgia, Nebraska, Ohio, South Dakota, and Wisconsin. *Houghton* has been rejected by Washington, in *State v. Parker* (1999) on the basis of Art. I. section 7 of the state constitution, and not under the Fourth Amendment. In three consolidated cases, police stopped a car and arrested the driver; in each the personal effects of non-arrested passengers were searched and police knew the items searched belonged to the passengers. The Washington Supreme Court held that the search of the purses and jackets of the respondents violated the state constitution. "[V]ehicle passengers hold an independent, constitutionally protected privacy interest. This interest is not diminished merely upon stepping into an automobile with others."[9] The Washington court specifically adopted the reasoning of the Wyoming Supreme Court in *Houghton v. State,*[10] that had been reversed by the United States Supreme Court, on Fourth Amendment grounds, in *Wyoming v. Houghton* (1999).

not needed to trigger an inventory search—thus, evidentiary standards are irrelevant. An inventory search is the opposite of an exigency search—it must be conducted under standardized rules and regulations so that each inventory search is as much like another as possible. Inventory searches are constitutionally reasonable because of their unique functions and attributes. In addition to inventory searches carried out on impounded vehicles, inventory searches are routinely performed on the personal effects of an arrested person who is placed into a police lockup or a jail cell (see Chapter 5).

An inventory search is not a search for evidence of crime, but if contraband is discovered during the course of an inventory search, it may be admitted into evidence against the possessor in a criminal prosecution because the police had a right to conduct the inventory, making it a plain view seizure.

REASONS FOR THE INVENTORY SEARCH The purposes of automobile inventory and the inventory of a person taken into custody are similar and overlap. First, the routine listing protects the owner's property against theft or careless handling by the police while it remains in police custody. Second, the inventory protects the police against false claims or disputes over lost or stolen property. Third, it protects the police from potential danger. Additionally, the inventory helps determine whether a vehicle has been stolen (*South Dakota v. Opperman,* 1976). As for the inventory of the person in custody, "arrested persons have also been known to injure themselves—or others—with belts, knives, drugs, or other items on their person while being detained. Dangerous instrumentalities—such as razor blades, bombs, or weapons—can be concealed in innocent-looking articles taken from the arrestee's possession" (*Illinois v. Lafayette,* p. 646). In *Lafayette,* the Court added: "It is immaterial whether the police actually fear any particular package or container; the need to protect against such risks arises independently of a particular officer's subjective concerns. Finally, inspection of an arrestee's personal property may assist the police in ascertaining or verifying his identity." The danger rationale is likely to be rare in automobile inventories, but in the unusual event that explosives or weapons are stolen from an impounded car, the consequences can be serious. It has been suggested that opening a vehicle containing explosives can increase the risk to the officers.[11] The Court has ruled that these administrative "interests outweighed the individual's Fourth Amendment interests" (*Colorado v. Bertine,* p. 372).

In *Cady v. Dombrowski* (1973), Justice Rehnquist explained that "Local police officers . . . frequently investigate vehicle accidents in which there is no claim of criminal liability and engage in what, for want of a better term, may be described as community caretaking functions, totally divorced from the detection, investigation, or acquisition of evidence relating to the violation of a criminal statute."

SCOPE OF AN INVENTORY SEARCH The cases generally show that an inventory search can be extremely thorough. In *South Dakota v. Opperman* (1976), the Supreme Court upheld the inventory of items in the unlocked glove compartment of an automobile. In *Michigan v. Thomas* (1982), the Court upheld the inventory search of a car's locked trunk, the space under the front seat and under the dashboard, and the opening of air vents under the dashboard where a loaded revolver was found. The Court rejected the argument that the search of the air vents was improper because that is not a place where personal items are normally stored. In *Florida v. Meyers* (1984), the Court, in a brief *per curiam* opinion upheld, without explanation, a second inventory search of an automobile made eight hours after the car was first searched and impounded. In *Illinois v. Lafayette* (1983), a police lockup inventory case (see Chapter 5), the police searched a purse-type shoulder bag belonging to a person taken into custody; the Supreme Court held that the police were under no obligation to place it in a secure box or locker, even if this was less intrusive than the inventory search. "The reasonableness of any particular governmental activity does not necessarily or invariably turn on the existence of alternative 'less intrusive' means" (*Illinois v. Lafayette*, p. 647).

The issue of the scope of an inventory was revisited in *Colorado v. Bertine* (1987) to determine if *United States v. Chadwick* (1977)—holding warrantless searches of closed trunks and suitcases to violate the Fourth Amendment—modified inventory searches. *Bertine* reaffirmed the *Opperman* decision. A van was impounded after the driver was arrested for driving under the influence. The van's contents were subjected to a detailed inspection and inventory in accordance with local police procedures. The officer then opened a closed backpack and found drugs. The Supreme Court found that the search was legal and the drugs admissible in evidence. Chief Justice Rehnquist, for the majority, said that an inventory search is made for regulatory reasons and is not a search for criminal evidence. There was no proof that the police acted in bad faith for the sole purpose of investigation, and the police department's regulations mandated the opening of closed containers and the listing of their contents. Justice Marshall, dissenting, argued that, in fact, the procedures were not standardized thereby making the action a criminal search rather than an inventory. He wrote that the search was conducted in a "slipshod" manner that undermined the purposes of an inventory procedure, and that the rule of *Chadwick* should apply to a backpack.

THE NECESSITY OF STANDARDIZED RULES It seems that Supreme Court doctrine has evolved from allowing an ad hoc inventory when made for inventory purposes (*Cady v. Dombrowski,* 1973) to a rule that requires that a police department have in place standardized inventory rules and procedures in order for an inventory search to be constitutional (*Florida v. Wells,* 1990).

In *Colorado v. Bertine* (1987), the Court has emphasized the importance of written, standardized procedures to guide the inventory search. No such procedures apparently existed in *Cady v. Dombrowski* (1973), which involved the warrantless search of a car for the express purpose of finding the weapon in the private vehicle of a drunk driver who was a police officer. The inventory search was upheld because it was clearly performed for administrative purposes and not as a search for criminal evidence. A driver involved in a fairly serious single-car accident was taken into custody in the evening for drunk driving in a rural Wisconsin town. He stated that he was a Chicago police officer. The Wisconsin officers believed that Chicago police officers were required, by regulation, to carry their service revolvers at all times; they looked into the passenger compartment and glove box but found no service revolver. A towtruck arrived and removed the disabled car to a garage seven miles from the police station, where it was left unguarded. Dombrowski, the driver, was hospitalized after lapsing into a coma. Hours later, after midnight, an officer went to the car to search for Dombrowski's police weapon. The officer testified that the effort to find the revolver was "standard procedure in our department." He opened the trunk of Dombrowski's car and did not find a gun but did find his police uniforms, a Chicago police baton with his name imprinted on it, and fresh blood that was introduced into evidence to convict Dombrowski of first-degree murder. Under these circumstances, the Court treated this search as a valid administrative search and not as a search for criminal evidence. "Where, as here, the trunk of an automobile, which the officer reasonably believed to contain a gun, was vulnerable to intrusion by vandals, we hold that the search was not 'unreasonable' within the meaning of the Fourth and Fourteenth Amendments" (*Cady v. Dombrowski,* p. 448).

From the somewhat loose procedure upheld in *Dombrowski,* the Court has moved to a position that asserts that for an inventory search to be constitutionally reasonable it must be authorized by (i) departmental policy and regulations that establish standard procedures, or (ii) established routine. The rationale is that one inventory search is conducted like another, and that the procedure actually produces an inventory—a list. An important goal is to limit the discretion of the officer as to the manner in which the inventory is to be conducted. "The individual police officer must not be allowed so much latitude that inventory searches are turned into 'a purposeful and general means of discovering evidence of crime'" (*Florida v. Wells,* 1990, citing *Colorado v. Bertine,* 1987).

Florida v. Wells (1990) is an example of an officer turning a routine inventory into a search for evidence because he overstepped administrative regulations. Wells was stopped for speeding and arrested for DUI after an officer smelled alcohol on his breath. An inventory search of the car revealed two marijuana cigarette butts in an ashtray and a locked suitcase in the trunk. There was *no* departmental inventory policy. The officer used his discretion to order the suitcase forced open and large quantities of marijuana in a plastic bag were found. The Supreme Court agreed with the Florida Supreme Court that the evidence should be suppressed as a Fourth Amendment violation, because the police department had no inventory policy at all. In the course of his majority opinion, Chief Justice Rehnquist said:

> A police officer may be allowed sufficient latitude to determine whether a particular container should or should not be opened in light of the nature of the search and characteristics of the container itself. Thus, while policies of opening all containers or of opening no containers are unquestionably permissible, it would be equally permissible, for example, to allow the opening of closed containers whose contents officers determine they are unable to ascertain from examining the containers' exteriors. The allowance of the exercise of judgment based on concerns related to the

> purposes of an inventory search does not violate the Fourth Amendment. (*Florida v. Wells,* p. 4)

This quote was treated as dictum by some of the justices, so the precise question of the limits on an officer's discretion on which containers to open has not been finally resolved. Four concurring justices disagreed with this statement and felt that the officer should not have such discretion, i.e., that an inventory policy should order an officer to open all containers or none. Justice Brennan expressed concern that "police may use the excuse of an 'inventory search' as a pretext for broad searches of vehicles and their contents."

BORDER SEARCHES

Every sovereign nation has a right to control its **borders** to determine who or what shall come into or exit the country, to collect customs, and to control smuggling. To enforce this plenary power, a country may search entering persons and luggage. As a general rule, the Fourth Amendment does not apply to searches and seizures at the border of the United States. As Justice Rehnquist noted in *United States v. Montoya de Hernandez* (1985):

> Since the founding of our Republic, Congress has granted the Executive plenary authority to conduct routine searches and seizures at the border, without probable cause or a warrant, in order to regulate the collection of duties and to prevent the introduction of contraband into this country. . . . This Court has long recognized Congress' power to police entrants at the border.[12]

United States v. Ramsey (1977) described border searches as "reasonable" simply because a person or item enters into the country from outside, without any regard to the existence of probable cause or recourse to a judicial warrant. In practice, any automobile or passenger entering the United States at the Canadian or Mexican border, or any international traveler entering at an international seaport or airport, may be searched at random by customs officers. Such a practice, of course, would be intolerable and blatantly unconstitutional if it were conducted by law enforcement officers within the United States.

In recent decades, as the United States has dealt with mounting problems of drug importation, illegal aliens, and foreign terrorists, issues concerning border searches have proliferated. Along with thorny political and law enforcement issues, the constitutional law in this area has become complex, primarily because the Supreme Court has had to resolve issues arising out of variations on the location of the "border" search and specific kinds of intrusions. The cases deal with five types of border searches:

1. at the **actual border**;
2. at a **fixed checkpoint** miles from the border;
3. **roving patrols** by the Border Patrol up to 100 miles from the border
4. search of international mail; and
5. boarding ships in open waters.

SEARCHES AT THE ACTUAL BORDER For *routine searches* by customs officers, the general rule is alive and well—any person seeking entry may be stopped and searched without probable cause or reasonable suspicion. In 1999, a customs officer stopped an Algerian national at the small Port Angeles, Washington, checkpoint on the United States-Canadian border on a *hunch.* Explosives were discovered in the wheel well of the Algerian's car.[13]

For *non-routine border searches,* the Fourth Amendment requires the *reasonable suspicion* standard to justify search and detention. In *United States v. Montoya de Hernandez* (1985), Rosa Elvira Montoya de Hernandez arrived in Los Angeles on a flight from Bogota, Colombia. An experienced customs agent thought she was smuggling drugs by having swallowed drug-filled balloons. An airline refused to return her to Colombia because she did not have a proper visa. As a result, she was held without a warrant in a locked room for sixteen hours, during which she "refused all offers of food and drink, and refused to use the toilet facilities." She "exhibited symptoms of discomfort consistent with 'heroic efforts to resist the usual calls of nature.'" Ultimately, a court order was obtained and a medical examination determined the existence of a foreign substance in her rectal canal. Subsequently, she "passed 88 balloons containing a total of 528 grams of 80 percent pure cocaine hydrochloride."

The Supreme Court found that the customs officer had reasonable suspicion to believe she was smuggling drugs and this was sufficient grounds for the court order and the body cavity search. She said she came to Los Angeles to purchase merchandise for her husband's store. However, because she arrived from a "source city" for drugs, could not speak English, and did not have family or friends in the United States, her explanation was questionable. She had not scheduled appointments with merchandise vendors nor made hotel reservations. Even though she carried $5,000 in cash (mostly $50 bills), she did not have a billfold nor did she possess checks, waybills, credit cards, or letters of credit, and, she did not recall how her ticket was purchased. She told an implausible story that she "planned to ride around Los Angeles in taxicabs visiting retail stores such as J. C. Penney and K-Mart in order to buy goods for her husband's store with the $ 5,000." These articulable facts "clearly supported a reasonable suspicion that respondent was an alimentary canal smuggler."

Was the sixteen-hour detention without a warrant and the dealy in summoning medical personnel "reasonably related in scope to the circumstances which justified it initially?" The Court rejected a hard-and-fast time limit as to what is reasonable. In this case, Ms. Montoya refused to be X-rayed, falsely claiming to be pregnant. The alternatives were to hold her for observation or allow her into the interior of the country.

Justice Brennan dissented, joined by Justice Marshall. He felt that more intrusive border detentions and searches are constitutionally reasonable only if authorized by a judicial officer upon probable cause of criminality. There was no exigency in this case and a warrant could have been obtained at the outset. The majority replied that "not only is the expectation of privacy less at the border than in the interior, . . . [but] the Fourth Amendment balance between the interests of the Government and the privacy right of the individual is also struck much more favorably to the Government at the border."

STOPS AND SEARCHES AT FIXED CHECKPOINTS Permanent or fixed checkpoints may be located up to one-hundred miles from the United States boundary and the Supreme Court has applied standard Fourth Amendment reasoning to fixed checkpoint searches, employing the concepts of administrative searches, stop and frisk, and arrest. The rule is that suspicion is not needed to *stop* a vehicle at a fixed checkpoint, but that *probable cause* is required to *search* a car that has been stopped.

A checkpoint at San Clemente, California, was well marked and warned motorists a mile in advance that they would have to slow down or stop. At that location, a "point" agent visually screened all northbound traffic. Standing between two lanes of traffic, the agent directed some cars to a secondary inspection area where the driver and passengers were questioned for three to five minutes. If the stop produced proof that the passengers were illegal aliens, they were arrested and returned to Mexico. In *United States v. Martinez-Fuerte* (1976), a detected illegal alien challenged a conviction on the basis that the stop was without reasonable suspicion, probable cause, or a warrant and, therefore, violated the Fourth Amendment. The Court agreed "that checkpoint stops are 'seizures' within the meaning of the Fourth Amendment," but they are a reasonable and valid governmental response to a valid problem. A requirement that the stops be based on reasonable suspicion "would be too impractical because the flow of traffic tends to be too heavy to allow the particularized study of a given car that would enable it to be identified as a possible carrier of illegal aliens." The intrusion of these stops "is quite limited" and involve only a brief detention during which a few questions must be answered. "Neither the vehicle nor its occupants are searched, and visual inspection of the vehicle is limited to what can be seen without a search." Unlike a roving patrol, checkpoint stops involve less discretion, and notice of the checkpoint is clearly given to those approaching it; checkpoints do not create the same concern or fear that may be generated during a stop along a road by a patrol car. As a result, no evidentiary requirement is necessary for a fixed checkpoint stop.

On the other hand, the Supreme Court held unanimously in *United States v. Ortiz* (1975) that during such a checkpoint stop, a trunk of a car cannot be opened (i.e., searched) unless the officers have *probable cause* to believe that contraband or illegal aliens are present in the closed area. The Court reasoned that Fourth Amendment considerations come to the fore when the brief stop at the checkpoint, miles from the border, moves beyond a brief visual inspection and the asking of a few questions (a seizure) to a more intrusive search by customs officials. The Court noted that many reasonable factors could be taken into account by the Border Patrol officers to determine probable cause, including "the number of persons in a vehicle, the appearance and behavior of the driver and passengers, their inability to speak English, the responses they give to officers' questions, the nature of the vehicle, and indications that it may be heavily loaded." No such factors were apparent in *Ortiz,* and the Court found the search to be unconstitutional.

STOPS AND SEARCHES BY ROVING CUSTOMS PATROLS Given the difficulties involved in enforcing customs and immigration rules along our extensive borders, Congress authorized the Border Patrol to conduct roving patrols along the roads and in off-road areas within one-hundred air miles of the border. Roving patrol *stops* by the Border Patrol are more intrusive than checkpoint stops and, therefore, *United States v. Brignoni-Ponce* (1975) held they must be justified with *reasonable suspicion.* An officer must be "aware of specific articulable facts, together with rational inferences from those facts, that reasonably warrant suspicion" that a vehicle contains illegal aliens. Four years later, the reasoning in *Brignoni-Ponce* led the Court to extend the same right to drivers throughout the United States in *Delaware v. Prouse* (1979). The Court expanded that thinking in *Almeida-Sanchez v. United States* (1973) and held that the *search* of an automobile by Border Patrol officers is a greater intrusion on personal privacy, thus mandating the need for *probable cause* before a search is constitutional. The majority was concerned that allowing roving patrol searches up to one-hundred miles from the border would destroy the Fourth Amendment rights of local residents.

INSPECTIONS AND INVESTIGATION OF INTERNATIONAL MAIL *United States v. Ramsey* (1977) held that customs officials may inspect incoming mail from outside the United States if they have *reasonable suspicion* to believe the mail contains contraband. While examining a sack of international mail from Thailand, a customs inspector noticed eight bulky envelopes bound for four different locations in the Washington, D.C., area. The addresses apparently had been typed on the same typewriter. He felt and weighed the envelopes and determined that they contained items other than paper. He opened the envelopes and in each found plastic bags containing heroin placed between cardboard. A warrant was then obtained and the presence of heroin reconfirmed. The packages were resealed and delivered, which ultimately led to the arrest of the defendant.

The Court held that the more exacting probable cause standard was not required to justify opening the mail under the Fourth Amendment because (1) the federal statute that guided this action imposes a less stringent requirement than that of 'probable cause' required for the issuance of warrants, and (2) mail inspection is justified by the greater authority that the government has to make stops at the border. Justice Stevens dissented in *Ramsey,* joined by Justices Brennan and Marshall. He argued that the 1866 statute which authorized mail stops was intended to apply to large packages and that until 1971, the post office opened mail only in the presence of the addressee or under the authority of a court order supported by probable cause.

CONTROLLED DELIVERIES In *Illinois v. Andreas* (1983), the Supreme Court ruled that an initial inspection of international shipments that discloses contraband may lead to a "controlled delivery" to suspects in the interior of the country. These persons may be arrested and the container searched without a warrant when they take possession of the delivered contraband. In *Andreas,* customs agents found marijuana in a table shipped from India, repackaged it, and had police officers posing as delivery men convey it. The defendant accepted the package and was arrested less than an hour later as he exited his house. The warrantless arrest and search was justified by the initial customs inspection which found contraband thus creating a lesser expectation of privacy. Resealing the package does not function to revive or restore the lawfully invaded privacy rights. After the first inspection, the contraband was, in effect, in plain view. The lapse of time during which the police could not see the defendant did not reinstate his privacy rights. The Court stated that perfect controlled deliveries are not always possible. The arrest and search was not unreasonable because there was a "substantial likelihood" that the contents of the container were not changed.

BOARDING AND SEARCHING SEAGOING VESSELS Under Federal law in force continuously since 1790, Coast Guard and customs officers may, without a warrant or reasonable articulable suspicion of criminal activity, hail, stop, and board any vessel located in waters that provide ready access to the open sea for the purpose of inspecting the ship's manifest and other documents. In contrast, automobiles may not be stopped without probable cause or reasonable suspicion of a traffic violation or crime (*United States v. Brignoni-Ponce,* 1975; *Delaware v. Prouse,* 1979). This rule for ships was held to be reasonable in *United States v. Villamonte-Marquez* (1983) because at sea, it is impossible to establish the equivalent of border checkpoints or roadblocks which produce less potential fear to automobile drivers. While checkpoints could be established in ports, smugglers could easily avoid ports by anchoring at obscure points along the shore or by transferring cargo to other vessels. Also, the documentation requirements for vessels are different and more complex than automobile licensure, and information about the ship's registry and travel manifests cannot be known without boarding to inspect documents. The intrusion on a ship's Fourth Amendment interests is limited, constituting "a brief detention while officials come on board, visit public areas of the vessel, and inspect documents." In *Villamonte-Marquez,* a forty-foot sailboat named the *Henry Morgan II* was packed with tons of marijuana and the odor gave customs officials plain view authority to search. Justice Brennan, joined by Justice Marshall, dissented in *Villamonte-Marquez,* arguing that as a practical matter, ships in a channel can be funneled into a checkpoint area that allows the uniform checking of documents of all ships.

Special Needs and Regulatory Searches

This section reviews warrantless searches by government officers and by police under a variety of rubrics other than the standard enforcement of criminal law.

The "Special Needs" Doctrine

The so-called **"special needs" doctrine** evolved as a result of a series of cases in the 1980s in which searches were conducted by governmental officers who are *not* police officers (with one exception) and were *not* conducting searches to enforce the criminal law. In each case, the search by a government officer was deemed constitutional although none of them required a warrant, some of them dispensed with the probable cause requirement, and some of them were based on no particularized suspicion at all. The special needs cases are prime examples of cases decided under the general-reasonableness construction of the Fourth Amendment. The Court has said that these searches were conducted for "special needs beyond the normal need for law enforcement." The special needs doctrine is also a basis of the drug testing cases discussed below.

The "special needs" doctrine originated in *New Jersey v. T.L.O.* (1985); which involved the vice principal's examination of a high school student's purse in an attempt to enforce a no-smoking rule. This case provides a sound example of how legal doctrines evolve. When Justice White wrote the majority opinion in *T.L.O.,* he intended to justify the Court's belief that a warrantless search of a public school student's purse, while protected by the Fourth Amendment, was reasonable on the basis of reasonable suspicion alone. In the course of his opinion, he wrote in Footnote 2 that "the special needs of the school environment require assessment of the legality of such searches against a standard less exacting than that of probable cause." Also, Justice Blackmun, concurring with the majority decision, wrote that "Only in those exceptional circumstances in which special needs, beyond the normal need for law enforcement, make the warrant and probable-cause requirement impracticable, is a court entitled to substitute its balancing of interests for that of the Framers" (*New Jersey v. T.L.O.,* p. 351). Justice White employed ordinary usage designed to indicate that a school search was different from a police officer's warrantless search of a suspected felon. Justice Blackmun's use of the phrase seems a somewhat more deliberate attempt to formulate a new legal rule, but the words "exceptional circumstances" seem to be what differentiates a police search of a criminal suspect from a school search conducted to enforce a no-smoking rule. Yet, he did not call any greater attention to the phrase. At this point *T.L.O.* could be viewed as a lone exception to the warrant and probable cause requirements—perhaps indicating a rule for school searches only.

The analysis undertaken by Justice White in *T.L.O.* was not formulaic—he did not preconceive a special needs "category" and then fit school bag searches into the category. Inductively, he sought to understand how the actualities of school life in the 1980s blend with the rules of Fourth Amendment law. In *T.L.O.,* a fourteen-year-old, public high school student caught smoking in a lavatory by a teacher—in violation of school rules—was taken to a vice principal who ordered her to open her purse. The vice principal found a pack of cigarettes, which confirmed the student's violation of a school rule; he also found a pack of rolling papers. However, this did not establish probable cause to believe that she possessed marijuana, because some teens roll their own tobacco cigarettes. It did, however, create a reasonable suspicion that she possessed marijuana. A further search of the purse disclosed a small amount of marijuana, a pipe, plastic bags, many one-dollar bills, an index card with a list of students who owed T.L.O. money, and two letters that implicated her in selling marijuana. T.L.O. was later prosecuted and this evidence was admitted into juvenile delinquency proceedings.

The Court first decided that the Fourth Amendment applies to a public school—the search of the purse by a vice principal constituted state action. The Court rejected the notion that high school students have no privacy rights because of the **in loco parentis** doctrine—that the teachers have the authority of parents. This old-fashioned concept makes no sense in a world of large, bureaucratic public schools in which teacher-employees "act in furtherance of publicly mandated educational and disciplinary policies." The state argued that public school students had no reasonable expectation of privacy in school because they are supervised continuously—an expectation of privacy is incompatible with maintaining a sound educational environment; and a child has a minimal interest in bringing any items of personal property into the school. If the Court agreed with this reasoning, then public schools across America could institute school searches at will. The Court rejected this reasoning after examining the reality of school students:

> Students at a minimum must bring to school not only the supplies needed for their studies, but also keys, money, and the necessaries of personal hygiene and grooming. In addition, students may carry on their persons or in purses or wallets such nondisruptive yet highly personal items as photographs, letters, and diaries. Finally, students may have perfectly legitimate reasons to carry with them articles of property needed in connection with extracurricular or recreational activities. In short, school children may find it necessary to carry with them a variety of legitimate, noncontraband items, and there is no reason to conclude that they have necessarily waived all rights to privacy in such items merely by bringing them onto school grounds. (*New Jersey v. T.L.O.,* p. 339)

Following the decision that a student has an expectation of privacy, the next issue was whether schools have an interest in maintaining discipline through the enforcement of school rules. The Court quickly answered this question in the affirmative. More specifically, because the vice principal engaged in a Fourth Amendment search, was he bound by the warrant and probable cause requirements? "The warrant requirement, in particular, is unsuited to the school environment: requiring a teacher to obtain a warrant before searching a child suspected of an infraction of school rules (or of the criminal law) would unduly interfere with the maintenance of the swift and informal disciplinary procedures needed in the schools." The Court also rejected the probable cause standard, which is not an irreducible requirement of a valid search. Instead, the Court upheld a school search of a student's bag based on reasonable suspicion to believe that the student had violated a rule. This decision was rendered based on application of the general-reasonableness construction of the Fourth Amendment to the specific facts of a school search.

Two years after *T.L.O.,* the Supreme Court expanded its ruling in three decisions in which searches by government officers who were not police officers, or police officers enforcing a regulatory law, were upheld; in none of the cases were the searches justified by a warrant or probable cause. None of the cases involved public school searches. The first of these, *O'Connor v. Ortega* (1987), a civil suit, focused on the thorough search of the office, desk, and filing cabinet of a psychiatrist employed by a state hospital. He was suspected of improprieties in the acquisition of a computer and charges were brought against him for sexual harassment of female hospital employees and inappropriate disciplinary action against a resident. The search was ordered by the executive director of the state hospital; it constituted state action and Dr. Ortega had a reasonable expectation of privacy in his office. But, an expectation of privacy can be overcome if a governmental interest outweighs an individual's privacy interests under the Fourth Amendment balancing test. The Supreme Court found the search to be justified and cited administrative search cases. In her majority opinion justifying the search, Justice O'Connor relied heavily on the incipient rule in Justice Blackmun's *T.L.O.* concurrence, stating:

> In sum, we conclude that the "special needs, beyond the normal need for law enforcement make the . . . probable-cause requirement impracticable," (BLACKMUN, J., concurring in judgment), for legitimate work-related, noninvestigatory intrusions as well as investigations of work-related misconduct. (*O'Connor v. Ortega,* p. 725)

Now Justice Blackmun's formulation was applied to a new situation—legitimate work-related inspections whether non-investigatory or for the investigation of misconduct. His phrase was on the way to becoming a *doctrine.* Indeed, a concurring opinion by Justice Scalia was more explicit:

> While as a general rule warrantless searches are *per se* unreasonable, we have recognized exceptions when "special needs, beyond the normal need for law enforcement, make the warrant and probable-cause requirement impracticable. . . ." *New Jersey v. T. L. O.,* (BLACKMUN, J., concurring in judgment). (*O'Connor v. Ortega,* p. 732)

Notice that Justice Scalia refers to the single example of *T.L.O.* in the plural, ("we have recognized exceptions"), thereby giving that case greater heft and suggesting wider application. It is also noteworthy that both Justice O'Connor and Justice Scalia, in their quote from Justice Blackmun's sentence in *T.L.O.,* exclude the opening words: "Only in those exceptional circumstances in which . . ." This may or may not have been deliberate. Perhaps a doctrine known as the "exceptional circumstances" doctrine would include in its terms the concept that it should be rarely employed, whereas more types of searches by government officers could be justified by "special needs."

The development of a "special needs" doctrine continued in *Griffin v. Wisconsin* (1987). The Supreme Court upheld a probation officer's search of a probationer's home without a warrant—under a state law allowing such a search—when the probationer was suspected of having guns in his apartment. The argument was that there had to be reasonable grounds for searching Griffin's home. The Court made it clear that the search of the home of a probationer was reasonable simply because state regulations allowed such a search—probation officers needed no evidence of a rule violation to make such an entry. Justice Scalia, writing for the majority, relied heavily on the "special needs" concept:

> A probationer's home, like anyone else's, is protected by the Fourth Amendment's requirement that searches be "reasonable." Although we usually require that a search be undertaken only pursuant to a warrant (and thus supported by probable cause, as the Constitution says warrants must be), see, e. g., *Payton v. New York* (1980), we have permitted exceptions when "special needs, beyond the normal need for law enforcement, make the warrant and probable-cause requirement impracticable." *New Jersey v. T.L.O.* (1985) (BLACKMUN, J. concurring in judgment). (*Griffin v. Wisconsin,* p. 873)

The creation of a new doctrine requires a certain amount of maneuvering. Strictly speaking, neither *T.L.O.* nor *O'Connor v. Ortega,* which was also cited by Justice Scalia, applied to a house. Many cases like *Payton* have powerfully stated that the protection of the home is a core concern of the Fourth Amendment. Yet, a careful—indeed a brilliant—justice such as Antonin Scalia glided over the point.

The Court also relied on "special needs" combined with the **pervasively regulated industry** warrant exception to administrative search warrants in *New York v. Burger* (1987). This allows evidence found in plain view during a *police* inspection of automobile junk shops to be admitted. A state statute required vehicle dismantlers to maintain records of cars in their junkyards and to allow police or motor vehicle inspectors to examine the records during working hours. Failure to produce records was a misdemeanor. NYPD officers, who were part of a team that conducted five to ten junk shop inspections daily, inspected Burger's junkyard. Burger did not produce any records. The police copied down the VINs of several vehicles and discovered that several were stolen. They had no warrant nor did they have reasonable suspicion to believe that the cars were stolen. Burger was charged with possession of stolen automobiles and operating as an unregistered vehicle dismantler.

Justice Blackmun, writing for the majority, justified the warrantless search for several reasons. First, "the owner or operator of commercial premises in a 'closely regulated' industry has a reduced expectation of privacy" because the government interest in regulating the business is substantial. The warrantless inspection was necessary to uphold the regulatory requirements and the regulation provided an adequate substitute for a warrant by being made pursuant to the law, by being narrow in scope, and by limiting the inspecting officers' discretion. Next, the statute was not a pretext for criminal searches without a warrant, because a state can address a major social problem both through the administrative system and penal sanctions. Finally, Justice Blackmun ruled that it was not constitutionally significant that the inspections were carried out by police officers because they have many duties besides criminal law enforcement.

Burger was the first special needs case that involved searches by police (writing down the VIN) that seemed designed to pursue criminal prosecution. If the Court's statement that "a State can address a major social problem both by way of an administrative scheme and through penal sanctions" were taken to logical extremes, then the *Burger* decision could destroy the warrant requirement by redefining criminal investigations as "administrative inquiries" and by adding a regulatory mechanism to certain crimes (e.g., civil drug rehabilitation centers; civil commitment for sexual offenders). However, since 1987, there has been no indication that either the Court or society has moved in this direction.

What many laypersons may fail to recognize is that these cases are not really an application of exisitng law but the creation of new law. The justices take care to couch their language in such a way as to make the outcome of the case seem to rely "naturally' upon earlier precedent and overlook any problems in the reasoning process. As is often the case in the development of legal doctrines, a court decides a case when the facts do not precisely fit earlier precedent. In the written opinion explaining the decision of the case, the court finds *a phrase* in an earlier case that seems to provide an explanation for the decision. By using the phrase in subsequent cases, it becomes solidified into a doctrine or theory that clarifies the past decision and then becomes a category used to decide future cases. This produces the appearance that the system of common law reasoning is more inductive than deductive.[14] By organizing the cases under a doctrine, the Court attempts to offer a consistent and satisfactory explanation to lower court judges and police officers who must decide novel cases.

These special needs cases highlighted the difference between conservative (Crime Control Model) justices and liberal (Due Process Model) justices. They disagree on different aspects in the cases. In *T.L.O.,* Justices Brennan and Marshall agreed that, in general, the search of a student's purse or bag may be conducted without a search warrant, but they believed that the search had to be based on probable cause, rather than on the lesser standard of reasonable suspicion. Justice Blackmun's dissents in *Ortega* and *Griffin* show him becoming a "swing" justice. In *O'Connor v. Ortega,* writing for himself and Justices Brennan, Marshall, and Stevens, Blackmun argued that there were no special needs to search the doctor's office. The adult workplace is unlike the school setting in which teachers and principals must act swiftly to maintain order and enforce school rules. In a doctor's office, if the hospital director suspects that an employee is engaged in conduct that includes a criminal violation, and there is no exigent circumstances, that "seems to be exactly the kind of situation where a neutral magistrate's involvement would have been helpful in curtailing the infringement upon Dr. Ortega's privacy" (*O'Connor v. Ortega,* p. 742). The same four justices dissented in *Griffin v. Wisconsin,* with Justice Blackmun arguing that the entry into a probationer's home should be justified by a warrant in nonexigent circumstances, but one based on less than probable cause. He especially stressed the traditional protection given to the home by the Fourth Amendment. On the other hand, Justice Blackmun wrote the majority opinion in *New York v. Burger* (1987) while Justice O'Connor, who had united with the majority in other "special needs" cases, joined Justice Brennan's dissent. Justice Brennan was critical of the Court's rationale that the New York "chop shop" law was a narrowly tailored administrative regulation of a "pervasively regulated" business. Perhaps most disturbing is that the law "authorizes searches intended solely to uncover evidence of criminal acts." Moreover, the liberal justices dissenting in the special needs cases saw this as an assault on fundamental rights. This sentiment is captured in Justice Thurgood Marshall's statement:

> In the four years since this Court, in *T.L.O.,* first began recognizing "special needs" exceptions to the Fourth Amendment, the clarity of Fourth Amendment doctrine has been badly distorted, as the Court has eclipsed the probable-cause requirement in a patchwork quilt of settings: public school principals' searches of students' belongings, *T.L.O.;* public employers' searches of employees' desks, *O'Connor;* and probation officers' searches of probationers' homes, *Griffin.* Tellingly, each time the Court has found that "special needs" counseled ignoring the literal requirements of the Fourth Amendment for such full-scale searches in favor of a formless and unguided "reasonableness" balancing inquiry, it has concluded that the search in question satisfied that test. I have joined dissenting opinions in each of these cases, protesting the "jettison[ing of] . . . the only standard that finds support in the text of the Fourth Amendment" and predicting that the majority's "Rohrschach-like 'balancing test'" portended "a dangerous weakening of the purpose of the Fourth Amendment to protect the privacy and security of our citizens." *T.L.O., supra,* at 357–358 (opinion of Brennan, J.) (*Skinner v. Railway Labor Executives' Association* (1989), p. 639, footnote omitted)

The liberal justices would prefer that the Court apply the traditional Fourth Amendment analysis to each case rather than substituting the "finding" of "special needs." Given the elasticity of the special needs logic and the potential for a large number of privacy intrusions exercised by modern government, this Fourth Amendment category bears special watching.

Administrative Searches and Criminal Justice

The administrative search case of *Camara v. Municipal Court* (1967) (see Chapter 4) added flexibility, and modernized search and seizure law. The general rule after *Camara* is that administrative searches must be supported by an administrative search warrant. This rule applies to inspections of commercial establishments (*See v. Seattle* 1967) unless the warrantless entry is of a "pervasively regulated" industry, such as liquor stores or gun dealers. Inspectors can enter these businesses without a warrant during normal business hours, if permitted by regulations (*Colonnade Catering v. United States* 1970; *United States v. Biswell,* 1972). The regulations do not allow inspectors to employ force to enter these premises, but dealers who bar inspectors can lose their license. The Supreme Court required area warrants for inspections under OSHA—this type of regulation is relatively new and does not transform all industries that are monitored for safety and health into "pervasively regulated" industries. (*Marshall v. Barlow's, Inc.* 1978).

An interesting warrant exception exists for inspections under the Mine Safety and Health Act (*Donovan v. Dewey* 1981). Unannounced mine inspections are needed because safety and health problems are more pervasive in mining than in most other industries. The Court applied the reasonableness standard to uphold this aspect of the mine safety law. The law: (1) reduces inspector discretion by mandating inspections of *all* mines, (2) specifies safety standards so the inspector knows what to look for in advance and does not have to go on a "fishing expedition," and (3) forbids forcible entry. Under these circumstances, Justice Marshall ruled that "the statute's inspection program, in terms of the certainty and regularity of its application, provides a *constitutionally adequate substitute for a warrant.*"

Fire Inspections

Determining the cause of a blaze involves a post-fire inspection, which is conducted for both administrative and criminal investigation purposes. Rules for these kinds of searches were established in *Michigan v. Tyler* (1978) and *Michigan v. Clifford* (1984):

Rule 1. "A burning building creates an exigency that justifies a warrantless entry by fire officials to fight the blaze."

Rule 2. "Moreover, . . . once in the building, officials need no warrant to *remain* for 'a reasonable time to investigate the cause of a blaze after it has been extinguished.'"

Rule 3. "Where, however, reasonable expectations of privacy remain in the fire-damaged property, additional investigations begun after the fire has been extinguished and fire and police officials have left the scene, generally must be made pursuant to a warrant or the identification of some new exigency."

Rule 4. "If the primary object [of a renewed search] is to determine the cause and origin of a recent fire, an administrative warrant will suffice. To obtain such a warrant, fire officials need show only that a fire of undetermined origin has occurred on the premises, that the scope of the proposed search is reasonable and will not intrude unnecessarily on the fire victim's privacy, and that the search will be executed at a reasonable and convenient time."

Rule 5. "If the primary object of the [renewed] search is to gather evidence of criminal activity, a criminal search warrant may be obtained only on a showing of probable cause to believe that relevant evidence will be found in the place to be searched."

Rule 6. "If evidence of criminal activity is discovered during the course of a valid administrative search [or during the initial firefighting], it may be seized under the 'plain view' doctrine. . . . This evidence then may be used to establish probable cause to obtain a criminal search warrant."

In *Michigan v. Tyler,* a fire broke out in a furniture store at midnight. At 2:00 A.M., just as the fire fighters were "watering down smoldering embers," fire inspectors arrived to determine the cause, and they seized two plastic containers of flammable liquid. A police detective arrived at 3:30 A.M. and took photographs of the suspected arson. Shortly thereafter, the police investigator abandoned the investigation because the smoke and darkness made careful observation of the crime scene impossible. The fire inspectors returned briefly at 8:00 A.M. after the fire had been fully extinguished and the building was empty. They left and returned with the police investigator at 9:30 A.M. During this search, they discovered more evidence of arson: pieces of tape on a stairway with burn marks and pieces of carpet suggesting a fuse trail. The investigators left to obtain tools, returned, and seized the incriminating evidence. Three weeks later, an investigator with the state police arson section returned to take pictures. All the entries were made without consent or warrants.

The Court held that the Fourth Amendment applied to post-fire searches, noting that a magistrate must not be a "rubber stamp" when issuing an administrative search warrant: The magistrate must ensure that the investigation does not stray beyond reasonable limits. The magistrate's role is to prevent undue harassment of property owners and to keep the inspection to a minimum.

Applying the post-fire search rules to the facts of *Tyler,* the Court held that the warrantless entry and search immediately after the fire was proper (Rules 1 and 2). The search at 9:30 the next morning was construed by the Court as a *continuation of the search* begun a few hours before: that search was cut off owing to the smoke and darkness and "[l]ittle purpose would have been served by their remaining in the building, except to remove any doubt about the legality of the warrantless search and seizure later that same morning." The photographs taken by the state police investigator, however, were not admissible without a warrant: Too much time had elapsed and suspicion accrued.

Michigan v. Clifford involved an early-morning house fire. Fire fighters arrived on the scene at 5:40 A.M., extinguished the blaze, and left the scene shortly after 7:00 A.M. One hour later, a police fire investigator received an order to investigate. Because he was working on other cases, he did not arrive on the scene until 1:00 P.M. When he arrived, a work crew hired by the owner was boarding up the house and pumping water out of the basement. Clifford was out of town on a vacation and was communicating about the situation through a neighbor and Clifford's insurance agent. After the work crew departed, the investigators entered the basement of the house without obtaining consent or an administrative warrant and quickly found evidence of arson (a strong odor of fuel and a crock pot attached to a timer set for 3:45 A.M. which stopped at 4:00 A.M.). This evidence was seized and marked. The officer proceeded through the remainder of the house, much of which was still intact, and seized other suspicious evidence.

The Supreme Court held this seizure to be a Fourth Amendment violation. The owner, by hiring a crew to board up and pump out his house clearly maintained an expectation of privacy in his home. Therefore, before entry, the officer should have obtained an *administrative* search warrant: The time lapse meant there was no longer an exigent circumstance. Once the officer found incriminating items in the basement, it was necessary to halt the search and take the evidence to a magistrate to seek a *criminal* search warrant. Thus, all the evidence was inadmissible.

In sum, fire officials have the right to enter burned premises immediately after a fire in an attempt to determine the cause of a fire. Owners or residents, however, do not lose their right to privacy; more extensive, long-term investigations and searches must be accompanied by a warrant.

Drug Testing

Increased awareness of the personal and social costs of alcohol and illicit-drug abuse has made them prime domestic issues. Governmental agencies and private employers, including major league sports franchises, have turned to random or mandatory drug testing as a way to deter drug use and identify users. The pervasiveness and visibility of drug testing assured court challenges. The Supreme Court dealt with the question in several cases. Drug testing is a complex area of law in which the Court's reasoning is based on a combination of expectation of privacy analysis, the administrative search doctrine, and "special needs" reasoning. Drug testing by *private* businesses is not a Fourth Amendment concern, just as searches in *private* schools do not infringe on a constitutional right of privacy; drug testing by government agencies, on the other hand, comes under the Fourth Amendment.

In *Skinner v. Railway Labor Executives' Association* (1989), the Court upheld regulations mandating drug testing of all on-site railway employees after any major accident. As noted in Chapter 3, the testing by the railway industry was treated as state action because it was required by law. In *National Treasury Employees Union v. Von Raab* (1989), the Court upheld the testing of all United States Customs Service officers who (1) are directly involved in drug interdiction or the enforcement of drug laws, (2) are required to carry firearms, or (3) handle classified material that would be useful to drug smugglers and could be relinquished through the bribery or blackmail of drug-dependent employees.

The cases involved multiple issues. First, jurisdiction in *Skinner* and *Von Raab* had to pass the *Katz* doctrine: Taking and testing blood and urine samples intruded on reasonable expectations of privacy. Second, what standards were needed to ascertain the constitutionality of this kind of on-the-spot search? The Court applied the "special needs" doctrine to find these drug-testing programs *reasonable* within the contours of the Fourth Amendment, even though no warrant was required and no level of individualized suspicion was needed to trigger drug testing. Third, the linchpin of the holdings in *Skinner* and *Von Raab* was that the purposes of these laws tend to fall more within the sphere of administrative searches than traditional criminal law enforcement. Thus, in *Von Raab,* Justice Kennedy wrote for the majority, "where a Fourth Amendment intrusion served special governmental needs, beyond the normal need for law enforcement, it is necessary to balance the individual's privacy expectations against the Government's interests to determine whether it is impractical to require a warrant or some level of individualized suspicion in the particular context." Thus, in deciding these cases, the Court had to determine whether the governmental interests involved were legitimate and weighty enough to dispense with both the warrant requirement and the individualized suspicion requirement (whether in the form of probable cause or reasonable suspicion).

Skinner's finding of reasonableness was based on several points: (i) preserving the life and safety of train passengers is important; (ii) the employees subjected to the testing program are involved in safety-sensitive tasks; (iii) the absolute prohibition of alcohol and drug use while on the job is a reasonable requirement; and (iv) the usual sanction for on-the-job intoxication is dismissal and not criminal prosecution.

The Court found that the warrant requirement would add little to further the aims of the drug-testing program because the tests were standardized. Also, the fact that blood alcohol levels are eliminated at a constant rate requires swift testing and creates an exigency. Citing *Camara,* Justice Kennedy noted that the reasonableness of eliminating the warrant requirement is strongest when the burden of obtaining a warrant is likely to undermine the governmental purpose for the testing. Furthermore, the Court noted that, like school officials and hospital administrators in *T.L.O.* (1985) and *O'Connor v. Ortega* (1987), railway supervisors have little familiarity with the Fourth Amendment; it would be unreasonable to impose on them the requirement of seeking a judicial search warrant when a serious train accident has occurred.

The next issue in *Skinner* was whether there must be a *particularized suspicion* against specific railroad employees after an accident before they could be tested. The regulations imposed a flat rule requiring that every on-site employee be tested. The Court concluded that mandatory and comprehensive testing was constitutional for the following reasons:

1. blood and urine testing, although they are Fourth Amendment searches, are *relatively limited encroachments* on the expectations of privacy of the railway employees because they are job- and safety-related requirements in a pervasively regulated industry
2. the testing is relatively *limited in time,* intrusiveness, and ancillary risk
3. the *government's interest* in testing without individualized suspicion is *compelling* because it is not easy for supervisors to spot individuals who have used a drug and are still under its influence
4. a mandatory testing and dismissal rule has a *greater deterrent effect* than a weaker mandatory testing policy
5. an *accident scene is chaotic* and it may be extremely difficult for supervisors to sort out who is to be tested and who is not to be tested on the basis of individualized suspicion
6. the fact that drug tests are not, in themselves, conclusive proof of impairment does not solely render the program unconstitutional because the statistical evidence obtained from mandatory, across-the-board testing is very useful to the railway industry in *assessing the causes* of accidents.

The balance of interests in *National Treasury Employees Union v. Von Raab* (1989) differed in several respects. The Customs Service testing program was not triggered by a particular negative incident but was required for hiring or promotion into sensitive posts. The governmental interest was not proposed to prevent on-the-job impairment as a direct result of alcohol or drug use. Instead, the interest was to ensure that customs officers in drug enforcement positions who carried firearms would, in effect, *lead drug-free lives.* The government argued that drug-addicted customs agents are targets for bribery and cannot carry out their functions in a positive way (i.e., they may be sympathetic to the goals of drug traffickers). Furthermore, government employees in sensitive jobs (i.e., employees of the United States Mint, military or intelligence officers, customs officers) "have a diminished expectation of privacy in respect to the intrusions occasioned by" their positions.

Agreeing with these arguments, Justice Kennedy, again writing for the majority, held that a warrant would serve no useful purpose in such a program. A warrant serves to alert an individual that an intrusion authorized by law and limited in scope by a neutral magistrate will occur. But the Customs Service testing program is known to all prospective candidates, and is standard and of limited intrusion. Thus, a warrant would not add any information or protection. Furthermore, "[w]e have recognized before that requiring the Government to procure a warrant for every work-related intrusion would conflict with the common-sense realization that government offices could not function if every employment decision became a constitutional matter" (internal quotation marks omitted). For these reasons, the Court also found that an individualized suspicion requirement—probable cause or reasonable suspicion—made no sense in this context. The Court also dismissed the argument that individuals could fool the program by temporarily abstaining from drugs: Such attempts were uncertain because drug residues could be detected long after actual use.

The majority could not decide whether the third rationale for testing—the protection of classified information—was constitutionally reasonable. The Court could not determine, based on the evidence presented, whether the Customs Service rules really had the desired effect. It also questioned whether testing for this program was reasonably limited to employees who were likely to gain access to sensitive information. It remanded the case to the lower courts for further deliberation on this issue.

Justice Marshall, joined by Justice Brennan, dissented in both *Skinner* and *Von Raab* on the grounds that "special needs" analysis was flawed (referring to the Court's "shameless manipulability of its balancing approach")—the elimination of individualized suspicion violated the Fourth Amendment rights of the employees in these cases. The dissenters viewed the Fourth Amendment intrusions in a more serious light than did the majority justices, and found the governmental interests less compelling. Justice Marshall did not believe that the need for individualized suspicion against an employee before testing would undermine these agencies' programs. He accused the majority of submitting to popular pressure generated by public hysteria over the drug problem and giving away precious rights.

Justices Scalia and Stevens concurred in *Skinner* but dissented in *Von Raab.* Justice Scalia's dissent noted that the factual predicate for the two cases differed. In *Skinner,* the government gave evidence to show that a substantial number of train accidents were caused by intoxicated railroad employees. In *Von Raab,* on the other hand, "neither the frequency of use nor connection to harm is demonstrated or even likely. In my view the Customs Service rules are a kind of immolation of privacy and human dignity in symbolic opposition to drug use." Justice Scalia noted that the government did not supply even one example in which the purported state interest of preventing bribe-taking, poor intentions, unsympathetic law enforcement, or the compromise of classified information was endangered by drug use. He pointed out weaknesses in the government's argument, such as the fact that the use of drugs by an officer does not necessarily mean the officer would be hostile or indifferent to drug enforcement. Referring to the petitioner's reasons as "feeble," Justice Scalia noted that the commissioner of the United States Customs Service, in announcing the testing program, stated that it would "set an important example in our country's struggle with this most serious threat to our national health and security." In effect, Justice Scalia agreed with Justice Marshall's point, at least in regard to the customs officers' testing, that these programs were unnecessarily sacrificing constitutional freedoms as a result of public and political pressure.

DRUG TESTING OF HIGH SCHOOL ATHLETES The issue of mandatory drug testing was revisited in *Vernonia School District 47J v. Acton* (1995). The Court upheld a policy of *mandatory* drug testing of *all* students involved in interscholastic athletic programs. Constitutionally, *Vernonia* is similar to *Skinner* and *Von Raab* in that it found that Fourth Amendment searches were constitutionally proper without a warrant and without any level of individualized suspicion. It is noteworthy that *Vernonia* went beyond *T.L.O.*, which held that a search of a student's belongings required *individualized* suspicion of wrongdoing, including the violation of a school rule.

Justice Scalia, writing for a six-justice majority, gave several reasons for finding unwarranted blanket searches, not based on individual suspicion, to be reasonable:

1. Drug use had become evident and was believed to be widespread. The school district was concerned, among other things, that student athletes using drugs were prone to injury.
2. Urine testing constitutes a Fourth Amendment search.
3. The actual privacy interests of student athletes, however, are "negligible." Public schools have "custodial and tutelary responsibility for children"; students are subject to physical examinations and vaccinations for health purposes; and "school sports are not for the bashful," as the athletes bathe in communal showers.
4. The intrusion is limited. The school personnel who collect the urine samples do not directly observe the function; all student athletes are subject to testing; laboratories reveal only the presence of illicit drugs and not other health information; the results are known only by a limited group of school personnel; and results are not turned over to police.
5. The state's interest is very important because drug use is especially harmful to youngsters.

As a result, the district need not base its testing on individualized suspicion. The state is not required to select the "least intrusive" method of search—it can balance the practicalities and select this method. The Court noted that focusing on "troublesome" students for testing could lead to arbitrary testing decisions.

Justice Ginsburg, concurring, noted that the decision does not determine whether routine testing of all public school students in a school or a district, not just those enrolled in interscholastic athletics, is allowable.

A spirited dissent in *Vernonia* was written by Justice O'Connor, joined by Justices Stevens and Souter. Justice O'Connor focused on one issue: the *lack of individualized suspicion.* The Court's decision means that millions of student athletes, the "overwhelming majority" who have given school officials "no reason whatsoever to suspect they use drugs at school, are open to an intrusive bodily search." Her study of the history of the Fourth Amendment shows that the Framers were concerned with general searches, not only with general warrants. "[M]ass, suspicionless searches" are unreasonable in the criminal law enforcement context,[15] and each "special needs" case that dispenses with individualized suspicion has to advance a "sound reason[] why such a regime would likely be ineffectual under the usual circumstances. . . ." Additionally, individualized suspicion is put aside in cases where program failures can put the lives and safety of many people at risk. In a close factual analysis of the Vernonia District's policy, she discounted the costs. Therefore, the district cannot simply decide to discard individualized suspicion; without specific and compelling reasons to show that eliminating individualized suspicion is reasonable, the requirement is constitutionally necessary.

A speculative analysis of the *Vernonia* opinions offers glimpses of the justices' constitutional norms, their views of political theory, and even their personal backgrounds. Justice O'Connor gave the following reason for her dissent:

> Searches based on individualized suspicion also afford potential targets considerable control over whether they will, in fact, be searched because a person can avoid such a search by not acting in an objectively suspicious way. And given that the surest way to avoid acting suspiciously is to avoid the underlying wrongdoing, the costs of such a regime, one would think, are minimal. (*Vernonia School District v. Acton*, p. 667)

This logical, deterrence-based argument connects the Fourth Amendment's probable cause and, more broadly, its individualized suspicion requirement to a political philosophy of individualism. The Constitution balances public safety against individual liberty. The Framers essentially have forced later generations of Americans to take risks in regard to public safety by trusting its citizens to make their own personal decisions to be law-abiding. Perhaps this strong leaning toward individualism can be explained, in part, by her upbringing. Justice O'Connor "spent her early years on the Lazy B ranch doing the chores expected of a child growing up on a ranch—driving tractors, fixing fences, branding cattle. Sandra learned to be independent at an early age."[16]

In contrast, Justice Scalia's majority opinion can be seen as statist. The democratic majority of the Vernonia District formulated a school policy that emphasizes public control of all students, under the pain of penalty, rather than individual self-control. Justice Scalia's opinion refers positively to the fact that teachers in private schools "stand *in loco parentis* over the children entrusted to them." This is not entirely necessary to decide the opinion. This part of his opinion was most likely inserted to support authority-based reasoning in this and later cases. We can speculate that Justice Scalia's comfort with an authoritarian regime of drug testing is not entirely unrelated to the fact that he attended high school at a Catholic military academy.[17] Finally, to return to Justice O'Connor's dissent, she writes: "Blanket searches, because they can involve 'thousands or millions' of searches, 'pose a greater threat to liberty' than do suspicion-based ones, which 'affect one person at a time,'" citing her dissent in *Illinois v. Krull* (1987). As we suggest in Chapter 3, this concern by a conservative justice may have been generated by her experience as a state legislator.

DRUG TESTING OF POLITICAL CANDIDATES The Supreme Court finally drew the line at mandatory drug testing which a Georgia law required of every candidate for state office. In *Chandler v. Miller* (1997), libertarian candidates for statewide offices challenged the law as an infringement of their Fourth Amendment rights. The Supreme Court, in an 8–1 opinion authored by Justice Ginsburg, agreed. This search was not based on individualized suspicion but was "relatively noninvasive" by permitting a candidate to provide a urine specimen in the office of his or her private physician. The results are given to the candidate, who controls further dissemination of the report. The core issue was whether the certification of drug testing required before a person's name could be placed on a ballot was a "special need" that overrides the basic requirements of the Fourth Amendment.

> Nothing in the record hints that the hazards respondents broadly describe [i.e., drug addicted candidates] are real and not simply hypothetical for Georgia's polity. The statute was not enacted, as counsel for respondents readily acknowledged at oral argument, in response to any fear or suspicion of drug use by state officials. (*Chandler v. Miller,* p. 319)

The testing program was simply too weak to identify or to deter candidates who violate anti-drug laws. In contrast to programs designed to deal with the real dangers of illicit drug testing challenged in *Skinner, Von Raab,* and *Vernonia,*

> What is left, after close review of Georgia's scheme, is the image the State seeks to project. By requiring candidates for public office to submit to drug testing, Georgia displays its commitment to the struggle against drug abuse. The suspicionless tests, according to respondents, signify that candidates, if elected, will be fit to serve their constituents free from the influence of illegal drugs. But Georgia asserts no evidence of a drug problem among the State's elected officials, those officials typically do not perform high-risk, safety-sensitive tasks, and the required certification immediately aids no interdiction effort. The need revealed, in short, is symbolic, not "special," as that term draws meaning from our case law. (*Chandler v. Miller,* pp. 321–22)

Chief Justice Rehnquist, the lone dissenter, found no infringement on a personal right and, displaying his pro-state philosophy, wrote, "Nothing in the Fourth Amendment or in any other part of the Constitution prevents a State from enacting a statute whose principal vice is that it may seem misguided or even silly to the members of this Court."

LAW IN SOCIETY:

RACIAL PROFILING AND CONSTITUTIONAL RIGHTS

No discussion of law enforcement and constitutional rights is complete without acknowledging the pernicious and continuing role played by race and racism. The scope of these topic spans the historic injustices of slavery and the Jim Crow Era, the effects of race on the judicial process, and all aspects of police brutality.[18] This section focuses on a narrower, but hardly inconsiderable, problem: racial profiling—unequal law enforcement based on skin color and the propensity of police officers to stop individuals who are black or Hispanic in circumstances under which a white person would not be stopped. Racial profiling is an old and pervasive practice, known and endured within minority communities, that has become a major political issue only since 1998. In the black community, the practice was half-jokingly referred to as DWB—Driving While Black—a phrase that has since become mainstream.[19] Analysis suggests that seemingly neutral constitutional doctrines have contributed to racial profiling.

Awareness of racial profiling in the larger community had been low. A computer search of newspapers for the terms "racial profiling" or "driving while black" resulted in twenty-one stories using these terms from 1990 to 1995. The number increased to 269 in 1998 and over 1,000 in 1999.[20] Books on the topic have recently appeared including a 1999 volume by civil rights attorney, John L. Burris, and journalist Kenneth Meeks' *Driving While Black,* which relates specific incidents and gives readers practical advice about how to respond to profiling.[21] The issue has escalated, and in political science jargon, it has been placed on the political agenda.

The Prevalence of Racial Profiling

Do police, in fact, violate the Fourth Amendment rights of racial minorities in greater proportion to whites when stopping, arresting, or searching them? Until recently, the evidence for racial profiling was largely anecdotal. The official statistics indicated a direct correlation between the rate of arrests for *serious crimes* and the rate of commission for both black and white suspects; i.e., that there was no systematic discrimination in arrest practices.[22] The higher rates of African Americans arrested reflected higher crime rates generated by poverty and repression; a phenomenon noted by the distinguished scholar W. E. B. DuBois as early as 1899.[23] But the lack of discrimination in major crime arrests failed to examine on-the-street police behavior where persons were stopped and released or arrested and cited for traffic offenses. In this sphere, anecdotes of racial profiling—large numbers of innocent minority men and women detained on streets, in airports, bus terminals, and train stations, and stopped in their cars—were plentiful.

> Fifteen years before defending O. J. Simpson, Johnnie Cochran "was driving down Sunset Boulevard in his Rolls-Royce with two of his children in the back seat. Suddenly, he saw police lights flashing in the rear-view mirror, and pulled over. 'Get out with your hands up,' a police officer commanded over a bullhorn. 'I knew not to make any quick moves, especially with my kids in the car,' Mr. Cochran recalled, 'and I got out of the car and I looked back and I saw the police officers had their guns out.' His children started to cry. Then, as Mr. Cochran watched incredulously, the police began searching the car. They soon found his badge from the District Attorney's office, where he was then the third-highest ranking official. Realizing they had made what could be a career-ending mistake, they muttered quick, embarrassed apologies and sped away."[24]

There is no official record of Cochran's stop. The incident lives on only in memory.

Newark Judge Claude Colman was arrested in a New Jersey Bloomingdale's while Christmas shopping because earlier in the day a black man who bore no resemblance to Judge Colman had tried to use a stolen credit card. Colman was handcuffed, led through the crowd, chained to a wall, and prevented from calling a lawyer.[25]

A black, Los Angeles psychologist leaves his work identification badge on during his drive home from work—just in case he is pulled over by police, he wants the officer to see he is a professional, not a criminal.[26]

African American Don Jackson, a former police officer, was documenting police discrimination while driving in Long Beach, California. He was stopped by police and during questioning was pushed through a plate glass window. The incident was filmed by NBC News.[27]

Two former students of the author, both lawyers and African-American men, have recounted being stopped in their cars by police for no reason—one was driving with his white wife in Los Angeles; the other was returning a video, with his child properly secured in a rear child-seat, while driving from Detroit into Grosse Pointe, Michigan, a wealthy white suburb.

"Filemon B. Vela is a federal judge, but a Border Patrol agent recently mistook him for an illegal immigrant or a drug smuggler. Mr. Vela and three aides were driving on an isolated road when the agent pulled them over. Why? Because, the agent explained, there were too many people in the car."[28]

"Nearly every contemporary black writer tells similar stories. In *Parallel Time: Growing Up in Black and White* (1994), Brent Staples, a member of the editorial board of the *New York Times,* recounts numerous incidents of stereotyping that he encountered as a college graduate and since. . . . Harvard philosopher Cornel West writes in *Race Matters* (1993) of being stopped 'on false charges of trafficking in cocaine while driving to Williams College and of "being stopped three times in my first ten days in Princeton for driving too slowly on a residential street with a speed limit of twenty-five miles per hour.[29]

While a large number of anecdotes do provide powerful evidence they cannot show that the stopping was disproportionate, and some African-American men can claim they have never been subjected to racial profiling.[30] Until 1998, there was no statistical evidence to support this wealth of anecdotes indicating that blacks and Hispanics were stopped in far greater numbers than whites in comparable situations. Now, quantitative evidence of systematic racial profiling exists. There are three sources of data, all discussed in a December 1999 article by Professor David Harris.[31] The first two sources extracted data from two lawsuits against state police in New Jersey and Maryland, which claimed racial profiling on the New Jersey Turnpike and on I-95. The third was conducted by Professor Harris using data from four Ohio cities.

The New Jersey and Maryland studies were conducted by Dr. John Lamberth of Temple University. In order to conclude that minorities were disproportionately stopped, he had to discover: (1) the rate at which blacks were being stopped, ticketed, and/or arrested on the relevant part of the highway, and (2) the percentage of blacks among travelers on that same stretch of road. The second question was answered by teams counting cars on the road and tabulating the apparent race of drivers and occupants. "The teams observed each car that they passed or that passed them, noted the race of the driver, and also noted whether or not the driver was exceeding the speed limit." Data were recorded on 42,000 cars for the New Jersey study. Arrest and stop data were supplied by the police agencies. The New Jersey study found (1) that black and white drivers violated the speed limits at almost exactly the same rate, (2) blacks were 73.2 percent of those arrested but constituted only 13.5 percent of all drivers, and (3) blacks were 35 percent of all drivers stopped while accounting for 13.5 percent of drivers or passengers. Dr. Lamberth concluded that the odds of these results occurring by chance was "substantially less than one in one billion" and that "it would appear that the race of the occupants and/or drivers of the cars is a decisive factor" for arrests and stops.

Similar findings surfaced in the Maryland I-95 study. Observations of 6,000 cars showed that "the percentages of blacks and whites violating the traffic code were virtually indistinguishable." Blacks constituted 17.5 percent of the population violating the traffic code but more than 72 percent of those stopped and searched. "The disparity between 17.5 percent black and 72 percent stopped includes 34.6 standard deviations. Such statistical significance, Lamberth said, 'is literally off the charts.'" He concluded that "While no one can know the motivation of each individual trooper in conducting a traffic stop, the statistics presented herein, . . . show without question a racially discriminatory impact on blacks . . . from state police behavior along I-95. The disparities are sufficiently great that taken as a whole, they are consistent and strongly support the assertion that the state police targeted the community of black motorists for stop, detention, and investigation. . . ."[32]

Professor Harris obtained Municipal Court records from four Ohio counties in which the cities of Akron, Columbus, Dayton, and Toledo were located. This gave the race of persons arrested for traffic offenses. Any findings of racial disparity were conservative because these data did not include stops in which there was either no action taken or merely simple warnings given, and Hispanics were tabulated as white. Arrest figures were compared with census data on the percentage of whites and blacks of driving age in the four counties. The percentage for blacks was reduced by 21 percent to account for the fact that 21 percent of black households do not own a vehicle. A likelihood ratio was computed to determine whether blacks received tickets in numbers that are out of proportion to their presence in the estimated driving population. The "likelihood ratios for Akron, Dayton, Toledo, and Franklin County [Columbus], Ohio, all either approach or exceed 2.0. In other words, blacks are about twice as likely to be ticketed as nonblacks." Thus, for the first time, quantitative evidence exists to show that in six localities studied thus far, there is statistically significant evidence to show that drivers are being stopped on the highways because they are members of a racial minority.

These findings have apparently been confirmed by the most recent evidence—91,000 pages of internal state records released by New Jersey on November 27, 2000—indicating that over a period of ten years, eight out of every ten automobile searches carried out by New Jersey state troopers involved cars driven by blacks and Hispanics, who constituted 13 percent of all drivers. Of all cars stopped, 30 percent yielded some kind of contraband, whereas 70 percent of those stopped were completely innocent. Furthermore, the records indicated that the New Jersey police were trained in-on-the-road drug interdiction by the federal Drug Enforcement Agency and Department of Transportation in a program called Operate Pipeline, which has trained more than 25,000 officers in 48 states. Despite claims by the DEA that it did not teach racial profiling, critics argue that the agency is in denial about what amounts to racial profiling.[33]

Motivations for Racial Profiling

In the past, motives for racial profiling surely included harassment for its own sake, as well as social and political repression. It is probably the case that these motives have entirely disappeared as official policy today and are relatively rare among individual police officers, although it would be foolish to entirely discount the existence of simple racism among some.

> A 1988 investigation of the Reynoldsburg, Ohio, police department established that a group of officers identified themselves as a "SNAT" team, standing for "strategic" or "special nigger arrest team." At best, SNAT was a crude and offensive joke. At worst, the interviews suggested that a number of Reynoldsburg police officers, referring to themselves as the SNAT team, intentionally discriminated against blacks."[34]

As for racially discriminatory police action, it is worth remembering that only since about 1970 has there begun to be a reasonable promise of equal treatment in American society. After centuries of slavery, legal segregation, and bitter resistance to the civil rights movement, it is small wonder that deep and indelible traces of discrimination remain in the mental reactions of white Americans.[35] Police action before 1970 occurred against a background of what Professor William Julius Wilson calls "historic discrimination." Things have changed, but instead of true equality, a more complex social situation has emerged, which Wilson characterizes as "contemporary discrimination."[36] Policing now occurs in a different social matrix. Economically, a substantial black middle class has emerged, but a substantial black underclass persists.[37] Political participation of African Americans has increased but has "not led to equality with whites commensurate to that achieved in civil status."[38] Residential segregation remains high.[39] And closer to our inquiry, "there has been a steady increase in support among white Americans for principles of racial equality, but substantially less support for policies intended to implement principles of racial equality."[40]

Against this backdrop of progress in race relations, the criminal justice picture is fraught with powerful negative examples, including the "demonization" of blacks as criminals by presidential candidate George Bush in 1988 in the notorious Willie Horton advertisement;[41] the mass hysteria in Boston when Charles Stuart, who murdered his wife and later committed suicide, falsely claimed that she had been killed by a black assailant, thereby unleashing mass stops of black men in Boston for weeks;[42] and in New York City in the late 1990s, the brutalization of Abner Louima by NYPD officer Justin Volpe and the nearly successful attempt to cover up the sordid incident;[43] the killing of Ahmadou Diallo by four members of the NYPD street crimes unit, even though legally justified;[44] and the killing of Patrick Dorismond, an unarmed African-American man who was approached without cause by a sting officer trying to sell drugs.[45] These cases indicate that white America is too quick to jump on evidence of black criminality, real or fabricated, which is uncomfortably close to a "presumption of guilt" against all African Americans. This aura of black criminality, acting on the minds of many police officers, when combined with the police propensity to react negatively to real or perceived slights to their authority, and stimulated by the "war on drugs," creates a situation that increases the likelihood of racial profiling.

This complex reality helps to explain a paradox: the existence of racial profiling by police officers who see nothing wrong in what they are doing. The reason is understandable: White police officers (and perhaps some minority officers as well) seem to believe that race is a proxy for crime. Even though most of the people they stop in drug interdiction teams at airports and bus stations are innocent, and even though the vast majority of people who live in urban poverty areas are law abiding ("roughly 97.9 percent of the national population of blacks and 99.5 percent of the national population of whites in any given year will not be arrested for committing a crime"[46]), the fact that rates of serious crime are higher among African Americans has been used inaccurately to "criminalize blackness."[47] It seems that police are overgeneralizing, a problem noted by all who focus on the issue. Legal scholar-critics of racial profiling acknowledge that there are cases in which the police legitimately use a variety of factors that include the suspect elements of race and place, and do not suggest a blanket rule that ties the hands of the police.[48] This is miles away from scruffily dressed undercover agents who roughly stopped a vacationing, African-American school teacher, six months pregnant, at midday in the Baltimore, Maryland, Amtrak station. The drug interdiction teams were supposed to be looking for "what they call the 'Yo girls,' young black women with long fingernails and hair weaves who carry Fendi bags."[49] The officers acted in a racially discriminatory way by not making fine discriminations in the factors of their supposed profile. Because they could get away with it, their drug interdiction profile had been reduced to the factor of skin color.

What is especially illogical about these policies is that while the crime rate for serious felonies is tragically higher among poor minority communities, there is little evidence that this is true for drug crimes. National statistics indicate that "The percentages of drug *users* who are black or white are roughly the same as the presence of those groups in the population as a whole."[50] This suggests that drug sellers are more proportionate to the racial mix of users, i.e., the racial mix of society, but insofar as police overly target minorities, their drug arrest statistics tend to reflect police policies and practices rather than drug-selling activity.

Racial Profiling and the Law

Racial profiling is wrapped up with the Supreme Court's stop-and-frisk and automobile search cases since *Terry v. Ohio*. With a few exceptions, the cases have almost all tended to expand the discretion of police officers to a point where as a practical matter, police can target any car and legally stop it, and target most persons and get them to place themselves into the temporary custody of the officer. The totalitarian nightmare that police officers can stop anyone at any time for any reason does not exist for most white Americans, but is very close to a palpable reality for most African Americans and Hispanics. Police on the prowl for drugs and for the profits of drug asset forfeitures can and do stop cars the occupants of which often are completely innocent. A prominent Detroit attorney, Dennis Archer, then president of the Michigan Bar Association, was stopped by drug cops fifteen years ago, while driving a Cadillac Seville. This was before he was elected to the state Supreme Court and before he became mayor of Detroit. And it has happened several times in recent years to his son, Dennis Archer, Jr., also an attorney. He was stopped in the Detroit suburb of Royal Oak in a Jeep that matched the one used in a robbery. The initial stop was clearly supported by reasonable suspicion, but it took the white officers who handcuffed Archer and his female companion fifteen minutes to determine that she was an assistant county prosecutor, although she had asked them immediately to check her hand bag.[51]

Under the automobile search cases, a car can be stopped on a pretext, the driver and passengers ordered out, and the interior carefully inspected; if any evidence of crime on the driver's part is uncovered, the passengers can be searched. All can be questioned without *Miranda* warnings. Police can ask stopped drivers for consent to search without ever indicating their rights, and the subjective sense of intimidation is legally irrelevant if no arrest has been made. Even if a driver refuses to consent, the car can be held until a drug sniffing dog is brought onto the scene. And while the Supreme Court has limited the time of a stop, students tell of far longer waits on the side of the road. "The upshot is that officers are free to exercise a vast amount of discretion when they decide who to stop."[52] Even if one were to cling to the view that the Court's doctrine adequately protect one's reasonable expectation of privacy, Professor Tracey Maclin, examining the issue of racial profiling agrees that a "huge gap exists between the law as theory and the law that gets applied to black males on the street."[53]

The Political Reaction to Racial Profiling

To date, the legal response to racial profiling by lower courts has been disappointing, as courts have tended to uphold stops made on the basis of actions occurring in "high crime neighborhoods," rather than allowing closer inquiry into the motives and methods of police. [54] Recommendations for better police racial sensitivity training alone has also fallen short of the mark.[55] Racial profiling has had a great and harmful impact on society, on law enforcement, and on the criminal justice system. It has caused "deep cynicism among blacks about the fairness and legitimacy of law enforcement and courts." It has created a corrosive ends-justify-the-means mentality in law enforcement. It has generated skeptical jurors who disbelieve the testimony of police officers. It has fueled the skyrocketing imprisonment of black men for drug crimes as serious felonies have steadily declined. It has distorted the way in which law-abiding minorities act and dress, made them wary of police, and has caused them to question such life-affirming programs as mandatory seat belt laws because such laws gives police one more reason to stop a car. The distrust bred by racial profiling undermines efforts to establish and entrench community policing.[56]

After years of obscurity, the issue has burst onto the political scene. On August 26, 2000, a rally in front of the Lincoln Memorial on the thirty-seventh anniversary of Martin Luther King, Jr.'s march on Washington drew tens of thousands of demonstrators and national news coverage meant to focus on the issue of racial profiling. One participant said that "The exhaustive news coverage of the rally . . . accomplished much in educating the public to the problem of profiling and brutality."[57] The rally occurred at a time of unprecedented political action. Representative John Conyers of Michigan introduced a bill to require police departments to gather data on the race of persons stopped. The bill initially passed in the House but was killed in the Senate by the opposition of police groups; however, it is likely to be reintroduced.[58] Similar laws have been passed in North Carolina and Connecticut, and have been introduced in Arkansas, Rhode Island, Pennsylvania, Illinois, Virginia, Massachusetts, Ohio, New Jersey, Maryland, South Carolina, Oklahoma, and Florida.[59] A racial profiling information act was passed by both houses of the California legislature but was vetoed by Governor Gray Davis.[60]

Legal action in New Jersey and Maryland has required the collection of race data on stops by state troopers. The Michigan State Police decided to follow suit,[61] as have the Washington State police and the Seattle Police Department. But foot-dragging in the Seattle plan will not require officers to record their own race, an important factor in assessing the nature of racial profiling.[62] Numerous newspaper stories gathered in August 2000 show racial profiling to be a prominent issue in St. Louis; Greensboro, North Carolina; Arlington, Texas; Milwaukee; Los Angeles; Cleveland; and San Diego. Racial profiling was detected among the police force of Michigan State University.[63] It is too early to tell whether this activity will begin to reduce the practice of racial profiling, while Fourth Amendment law leaves so much power in the hands of police, but it is certainly a step in the right direction.

However, it would be a mistake to think that racial profiling has been generated simply by racial misperceptions and the lingering effects of racism. The prime generator of police stops of motorists and travelers has been the "war on drugs." If police perceptions are wrong about the greater propensity of minorities to carry drugs, then their profiling activity is failing to deter drug transportation. Steven Landsburg, commenting on an economic study of racial bias in automobile searches, notes that a study of stops on a stretch of I-95 in Maryland showed that both one-third of whites and blacks stopped were found to be carrying drugs, but that blacks were three and one-half times as likely as whites to be stopped.[64] He argued that if blacks are aware of racial profiling and still are discovered carrying drugs in equal proportion, they may be more likely to be carrying drugs in the first place. This seems to make racial profiling "rational." But the much larger number of white travelers means that a police focus on black drivers "makes it easier for white drug carriers to slip through the net." Continuing this economic analysis, Landsburg argues that if the police were motivated by racism, they would crack down further on black drivers to a point where very few would be caught with drugs. "Instead we see equal conviction rates, which suggests that the police concentrate on stopping blacks right up to the point where it helps them increase their conviction rates and no further." But this policy, while boosting police arrest rates, does not maximize deterrence because racial profiling "advertises to whites that they have little to fear from the police, which emboldens more whites to carry drugs. And because there are so many white people around, this effect can be quite large."[65] This analysis suggests that the "war on drugs" can be fought more effectively by eliminating racial profiling and training police, again to use the word correctly and ironically, to be more discriminating, i.e., to focus on the more likely drug dealers. The economic analysis fails to consider the cynical conclusion that legal but constitutionally dangerous policies that have undermined the actual expectation of privacy of African Americans will continue to be unleashed on the young and the poor, while effective treatments for the drug scourge may lie elsewhere.

Summary

Warrantless searches are routine and of enormous practical importance to police work, despite the Supreme Court's preference for a search warrant. Each type of warrantless search is based on a unique rationale. Every warrantless search must meet the minimum constitutional requirement for reasonableness. Exigency exceptions to the warrant requirement are lawful only if police have probable cause to believe that contraband is present; they include hot pursuit entries, the "automobile exception," search incident to arrest, and miscellaneous exigencies that impinge on Fourth Amendment interests. They are compatible with the warrant-preference construction of the Fourth Amendment.

Hot pursuit occurs when a dangerous criminal suspect is being chased by police and is seen entering a premises that is cloaked with Fourth Amendment protection. An exigency exists that allows the police to enter without a warrant. A constitutional hot pursuit entry must be accompanied by probable cause, may be based on hearsay, may occur a few minutes after the suspect has entered a premises, may begin on private property outside the premises, authorizes the police to search an entire premises to find the suspect, and is limited to chases of suspects of serious crimes.

Automobile searches constitute another exigency exception to the search warrant requirement based on the exigency of mobility and on the lesser expectation of privacy accorded to people in cars. In addition to the automobile exigency exception, an automobile search involves several other warrantless search rules, including consent, plain view, stop and frisk, and pretext searches. The Supreme Court appears to allow warrantless automobile searches even when cars are immobilized and the suspect is in custody, as long as the car is potentially mobile. Any operative motor vehicle is an automobile for purposes of the exception, even if it is a person's home. The automobile exception applies even if police have time to obtain a warrant. A car subject to forfeiture may be seized from a public area without warrant.

A "container"—whether a footlocker or a closed paper bag—is an effect and thus protected by Fourth Amendment privacy rights. If police arrest a person and have probable cause to believe there is contraband in a closed container, a warrant must be obtained to open the container (unless it is subject to a search incident to arrest). However, after some case development, the Supreme Court has held that when police have probable cause to believe that contraband is located in a automobile, they may open any closed container, under the automobile exception, located in the car that may logically hold the contraband (*United States v. Ross* 1982). When an officer has probable cause to believe that a specific container located in a car contains contraband, the officer may, upon lawfully stopping the car and gaining access to its interior, open the container (*California v. Acevedo,* 1991). *Ross* was extended to passengers: police officers with probable cause to search a car may inspect passengers' belongings found in the car which are capable of concealing the object of the search (*Wyoming v Houghton*, 1999).

An automobile inventory search is a regulatory search based on a routine policy to make an inventory of items contained in all cars that are impounded by police for traffic or other violations. No probable cause is required. The main purposes for making an inventory are to protect the owner's property against theft or careless handling by the police, to protect the police against false claims or disputes over lost or stolen property, and to protect the police from potential danger. Inventory searches must be made routinely and under proper standards and procedures that limit the discretion of the officer. Officers conducting inventory searches may look into an unlocked glove compartment, a locked trunk, the space under the front seat and under the dashboard, and the opening of air vents under the dashboard, as well as the open area. Any contraband found in the course of an inventory search is seized in plain view and is admissible in evidence.

A border search is based on a nation's sovereign power to control entry and egress of people and goods, and requires no warrant or probable cause. In addition to a search at the actual border, this area of law covers roving patrols and fixed checkpoints. In general, there is a lesser expectation of privacy at the border, but both aliens and citizens retain some Fourth Amendment protections. At the border, or its functional equivalent, a person may be detained and searched at random, but the search must be reasonable. Reasonable suspicion must exist before border agents may subject a person to a body-cavity search. Border agents operating fixed checkpoints or roving patrols must have probable cause to search parties who have been stopped under reasonable suspicion by roving patrols, or no suspicion at fixed checkpoints. Reasonable suspicion of contraband is required before international mail can be searched. Because of the well-established rules for ships, the complex nature of ships' documents, and the special difficulties of stopping sea-going vessels, government agents may stop and board vessels for document inspections without warrants or reasonable suspicion.

Searches by government employees infringe on Fourth Amendment interests but may be allowed without a warrant or probable cause if they are conducted for "special needs beyond the normal need for law enforcement." This has been applied to a public school teacher searching the bag of a student who is reasonably suspected of violating a school no-smoking rule; the search of the office of a physician hired by a state hospital and suspected of violating rules; the warrantless search of the home of a probationer for violating a condition of probation (no reasonable suspicion required); and a *police* inspection of automobile junk shops without a warrant under a regulatory law.

An administrative search warrant may be foregone for searches of pervasively regulated industries (such as gun and liquor dealers) or safety inspections of mines. OSHA safety inspections require warrants.

Firefighters who enter a premises to extinguish a fire intrude on an expectation of privacy but may do so because the fire creates an exigency. They may stay after the fire is extinguished to investigate the cause of a blaze. If the firefighters leave the site of a fire that retains an expectation of privacy, they must obtain an administrative warrant before returning to determine the cause and origin of a recent fire and must obtain a criminal search warrant if they are suspicious of arson.

Drug testing by government agencies intrudes on a reasonable expectation of privacy but may be upheld if special needs beyond the normal need for law enforcement make it reasonable. The Supreme Court has upheld the drug testing of railway workers after a crash without individualized suspicion, the drug testing of Customs Service officers who were in drug enforcement positions and who carried firearms, and the testing of high school varsity athletes. The Court found that the required testing of candidates for state office without particularized suspicion did not meet the criteria of special needs.

LEGAL PUZZLES

LEGAL PUZZLES: HOW HAVE COURTS DECIDED THESE CASES?

6–1. A confidential informant told a DEA agent that Jimmy Hogan was selling methamphetamine and marijuana at the automobile plant where he worked, and that Hogan brought the drugs to the plant in his white, 1990 Dodge pickup truck. The DEA agents obtained a warrant to search Hogan's house and truck a day before the informant said that Hogan would be bringing drugs to the plant. The affidavit did not mention another vehicle. A search of the house turned up a small amount of marijuana. Hogan was arrested and refused to give consent to search his Oldsmobile sedan. A dog sniff indicated drugs were in the car. The DEA seized the car, obtained a warrant, and found a half-pound of marijuana and a quarter-pound of methamphetamine in the Oldsmobile. Was the automobile properly seized under the automobile exception? *United States v. Hogan,* 25 F.3d 690 (8th Cir. 1994)

6–2. Alberto Rodriguez was arrested at his place of work on suspicion of possessing cocaine. He was allowed to lock his tools and remove his work coveralls. Rodriguez was then taken to the sheriff's lockup, where a thorough search was conducted and an address book was found in his possession. Pursuant to a general procedure, a deputy photocopied each page of Alberto's address book, which contained the phone number of a coconspirator. Was the address book properly seized? *United States v. Rodriguez,* 995 F.2d 776 (7th Cir.), *cert. denied* 114 S.Ct. 648 (1993)

6–3. Barnett was under surveillance by DEA agents for manufacturing methamphetamine. Barnett had been previously arrested eight times and had been previously sentenced for eighteen drug violations. When he was arrested in the present case, the DEA agents had no warrant. Seven or eight agents appeared at the door of Barnett's home with guns drawn. He was arrested and handcuffed, and the officers holstered their guns. An officer advised Barnett of his *Miranda* rights. An agent then said, "Mike, we are just going to look around and take you down to the Marshfield Police Station, okay?" Barnett replied, "Okay." Barnett was not informed he had a right to refuse the search. Did Barnett validly consent to a search of his home? *United States v. Barnett,* 989 F.2d 546 (1st Cir.), *cert. denied* 114 S.Ct. 148 (1993)

6–4. Border Patrol agents stopped Rodolfo Venzor-Castillo's car on suspicion of transporting illegal aliens. The stop took place on a summer afternoon on a road believed to be used by smugglers to avoid a fixed checkpoint located 235 miles from the U.S.-Mexican border. The road was not a direct route from the border and passed through thirteen New Mexico towns and cities between the nearest border point of entry and the location of the stop. The agent observed four or five occupants seated upright and as the car approached, then he saw the passengers in the back seat slide down. The car appeared to be heavily loaded, with its undercarriage close to the road surface, causing the tail pipe to drag on the road when the car hit bumps. The vehicle was a large, older model Cadillac, which the agent often found to be favored by illegal alien smugglers. Was the stop a lawful border search? *United States v. Venzor-Castillo,* 991 F.2d 634 (10th Cir. 1993)

ANSWERS TO LEGAL PUZZLES

6–1. NO. The car was seized without a warrant. The automobile exception requires that the police have probable cause to believe the vehicle that was stopped contains contraband. Probable cause did not exist to stop and search the Oldsmobile, which was not named in the warrant. All the information the agents possessed indicated that Hogan transported drugs to work in his truck and that the truck was the sole vehicle he drove to and from work. At most, the agents had a hunch that the drugs from the house or truck might be in the Oldsmobile. The prerequisite to a valid search under the automobile exception, however, is probable cause, not a supposition.

6–2. YES. The court determined that the search at the sheriff's lockup was not an inventory search but a search incident to arrest. Alberto was searched immediately upon arriving at his initial place of detention.

6–3. YES. Written consent is not essential to the establishment of a valid consensual search. It is not essential that the officers first inform the consenting party of the right to withhold consent although knowledge of the right to withhold consent is a factor to be considered in assessing voluntariness. Notwithstanding the inherently unnerving effect of having numerous officers arrive at one's door with guns drawn, Barnett was no "newcomer" to law enforcement encounters. Being advised of his *Miranda* rights put Barnett on notice that he could refuse to cooperate. In these circumstances, Barnett's will was not overborne, nor was his capacity for self determination critically impaired.

6–4. NO. Federal regulations allow Border Patrol agents to search any vehicle for illegal aliens without a warrant within a reasonable distance, which is defined as within one hundred air miles from the border. This car was stopped more than one hundred miles from the border at a time when legitimate tourist travel was greater than at other times of the year. The agent lacked specific information that the defendant's vehicle had recently crossed the border. The agent, therefore, lacked reasonable suspicion to believe that the Cadillac was engaged in illegal alien smuggling.

FURTHER READING

Randall Kennedy, *Race, Crime, and the Law* (New York: Pantheon Books, 1997).

Leonard W. Levy, *A License to Steal: The Forfeiture of Property* (Chapel Hill: The University of North Carolina Press, 1996).

James F. Simon, *The Center Holds: The Power Struggle Inside the Rehnquist Court* (New York: Simon & Schuster, 1995).

ENDNOTES

1. David E. Steinberg, "The Drive Toward Warrantless Auto Searches: Suggestions From A Back Seat Driver," *Boston University Law Review* 80(2):545–575 (2000).
2. Marvin Zalman, "Judges in Their Own Case: A Lockean Analysis of Drug Asset Forfeiture," *Criminal Justice Review*, 21(2):197–230 (1996); Eric Blumenson & Eva Nilsen, "Policing for Profit: The Drug War's Hidden Economic Agenda," *University of Chicago. Law Review* 65:35 (1998).
3. David Harris, "Car Wars: The Fourth Amendment's Death on the Highway," *George Washington Law Review* 66:556–91 (1998), pp. 560–61.
4. Harris, Car Wars, p. 556.
5. *United States v. Whitehead*, 849 F.2d 849 (4th Cir,. 1988); *United States v. Nigro*, 727 F.2d 100 (6th Cir. 1984); *U.S v. Boynes*, 149 F.3d 208 (3rd Cir. 1998); *United States v. Albers*, 136 F.3d 670 (9th Cir. 1998).
6. Steinberg, "Back Seat Driver," p. 549.
7. Harris, "Car Wars," pp. 566–67.
8. 227 Conn. 363, 630 A.2d 1315 (1993).
9. State v. Parker, 139 Wn.2d 486, 496, 987 P.2d 73, 79 (1999).
10. 956 P.2d 363 (Wyo. 1998).
11. Charles Whitebread and Christopher Slobogin, *Criminal Procedure: An Analysis of Cases and Concepts, Fourth Edition* (New York: Foundation Press, 2000), p. 309.
12. See *Carroll v. United States* (1925); *United States v. 12 200–Foot Reels of Film* (1973).
13. Robin Wright, "Bin Laden Tie Seen in Border Arrest," *Los Angeles Times*, December 19, 1999, Sec. A; p. 25.
14. See Edward Levi, *An Introduction to Legal Reasoning* (Chicago: University of Chicago Press, 1949, 1961).
15. *Ybarra v. Illinois* (1979).
16. Nancy Maveety, "*Justice Sandra Day O'Connor: Strategist on the Supreme Court*" (Lanham: Rowman & Littlefield, 1996), pp. 12–13.

17. David A. Schultz and Christopher E. Smith, *The Jurisprudential Vision of Justice Antonin Scalia* (London: Rowman & Littlefield, 1996), p. xiii.
18. See generally, Randall Kennedy, *Race, Crime, and the Law* (New York: Pantheon Books, 1997).
19. Henry Louis Gates, Jr., "Thirteen Ways of Looking at a Black Man," *New Yorker*, Oct. 23, 1995, cited in Kennedy, *Race, Crime*, pp. 151–52.
20. Lexis search in "newsgroup" news file; search: "racial profiling or driving while black and police and date = [year]."
21. John L. Burris (with Catherine Whitney), *Blue vs. Black: Let's End the Conflict Between Cops and Minorities* (New York: St. Martin's Press, 1999); Kenneth Meeks, *Driving While Black: Highways, Shopping Malls, Taxicabs, Sidewalks* (New York: Broadway Books, 2000).
22. M. Tonry, *Malign Neglect-Race, Crime, and Punishment in America* (New York: Oxford University Press, 1995), p. 70.
23. Tonry, *Malign Neglect*, pp. 52–56.
24. K. B. Noble, "A Showman in the Courtroom, for Whom Race is a Defining Issue," *New York Times*, Jan. 20, 1995, p. A27.
25. Cited in Tonry, *Malign Neglect*, pp. 50–51.
26. A. Wallace and S. Chavez, "Understanding the Riots Six Months Later; Separate Lives/Dealing with Race in L.A.; Can We All Get Along?", *Los Angeles Times*, Nov. 16, 1992, p. JJ–1.
27. T. Maclin, "'Black and Blue Encounters'—Some Preliminary Thoughts About Fourth Amendment Seizures: Should Race Matter?" *Valparaiso University Law Review* 26:243–79 (1991) p. 254.
28. Jim Yardley, "Some Texans Say Border Patrol Singles Out Too Many Blameless Hispanics," *New York Times*, Jan. 26, 2000, p. A17.
29. Tonry, *Malign Neglect*, p. 51.
30. Bill Johnson, The Answer to Driving while Black is Not More Racial Profiling, *Detroit News,* July 30, 1999, p. A12.
31. David A. Harris, "The Stories, the Statistics, and the Law: Why 'Driving While Black' Matters," *Minnesota Law Review* 84:265–326 (1999).
32. Harris, "The Stories," pp. 277–81.
33. David Kocieniewski and Robert Hanley, "Racial Profiling was the Routine," New Jersey Finds, *New York Times*, Nov. 28, 2000, p. A1; David Kocieniewski, New Jersey Argues that the U.S. Wrote the Book on Race Profiling, *New York Times*, Nov. 29, 2000, p. A1.
34. *Murphy v. Reynoldsburg*, 1991 WL 150938 (Ohio Ct. App. 10th App. Dist. Franklin Co., 1991); *Murphy v. Reynoldsburg*, 65 Ohio St. 3d 356, 604 N.E.2d 138 (1992).
35. See H. Sitkoff, *The Struggle for Black Equality, 1954–1992, Revised Edition* (New York: Hill and Wang, 1993); P. Finkelman, "The Crime of Color," *Tulane Law Review* 67(1993): 2063–2112; S. Walker, *Popular Justice* (New York: Oxford University Press, 1980); L. Friedman *Crime and Punishment in American History* (New York: P[illegible]ic Books, 1993); C. R. Mann, *Unequal Justice: A Matter of Color* (Bloomington: Indiana University Press, 1993).
36. W. J. Wilson, *The Truly Disadvantaged* (Chicago: University of Chicago Press, 1987).
37. G. J. Jaynes and R. M. Williams, Jr., *A Common Destiny: Blacks and American Society* (Washington, D.C.: National Academy Press, 1989), pp. 6, 274.
38. *Ibid.*, p. 258.
39. *Ibid.*, pp. 88–91.
40. *Ibid.*, p. 117.
41. Tonry, *Malign Neglect*, pp. 10–12; D. C. Anderson, *Crime and the Politics of Hysteria: How the Willie Horton Story Changed American Justice* (New York: Times Books, 1995).
42. Anderson, *Crime and the Politics of Hysteria*, pp. 8–9.
43. David Barstow and Kevin Flynn, "Officer Who Broke the Code of Silence Defies Labels," *New York Times*, May 15, 1999, p. B1.
44. Jodi Wilgoren and Ginger Thompson, "After Shooting, an Eroding Trust in the Police," *New York Times*, February 19, 1999, p. A1.
45. Bob Herbert, "In America—The Mud-Slingers," *New York Times*, March 20, 2000, p. A23.
46. Developments in the Law—"Race and the Criminal Process," *Harvard Law Review* 101 (1988): 1472–1641, p. 1508.
47. Harris, "The Stories," pp. 291–94.
48. Johnson, "Decision to Detain," pp. 218–219.; R. Kennedy, "Race, Crime and the Law," pp. 153–63.
49. Meeks, *Driving While Black*, pp. 63–67.
50. Harris, "The Stories," p. 296, emphasis added, citing 1997 United States Dept. of Health and Human Services data from the National Household Survey on Drug Abuse.
51. Robyn Meredith, "Near Detroit, a Familiar Sting in Being a Black Driver," *New York Times*, July 16, 1999, p. A10.
52. Harris, "The Stories," p. 318, see pp. 310–20.
53. Maclin, "Black and Blue Encounters," p. 252.
54. S. L. Johnson, "Race and the Decision to Detain a Suspect," *Yale Law Journal* 93:214–58 (1983); Maclin, "Black and Blue Encounters," pp. 268–79; Developments—"Race and the Criminal Process," p. 1519.
55. D. E. Georges Abeyie, "Symposium: Law Enforcement and Racial and Ethnic Bias," *Florida State University Law Review* 19:717–26 (1992), pp. 718–19; R. A. Carter, "Point of View: Improving Minority Relations," *FBI Law Enforcement Bulletin* 64(1995):14–17.
56. Harris, "The Stories," pp. 298–309.
57. Cindy Loose and Chris L. Jenkins, "Rallying to 'Redeem the Dream'; Rights' Leaders Target Racial Profiling," *Washington Post*, August 27, 2000, p. C1.
58. Harris, "The Stories," pp. 319–21.
59. Ibid., pp. 321–22.
60. Miguel Bustillo and Carl Ingram, "Bill on Racial Profiling Scrapped," *Los Angeles Times*, Aug, 25, 2000, Part A1, p. 3.

61. David Shepardson, Police Track race of Drivers: It's to Show Motorists are not Ticketed Based on Skin Color, *Detroit News*, July 26, 1999, p. C1.
62. Susan Paynter, "Race-Profile Issue Means 'You Have to Have Faith'," *Seattle Post-Intelligencer*, August 25, 2000, p. B1; Kimberly A. C. Wilson, New Dispute Erupts on Race Profiling Issue; Police Officers Won't Have to Record Own Ethnic Background, *Seattle Post-Intelligencer*, August 24, 2000, p. A1.
63. Eric Lacy, Michigan State U. report examines racial profiling, *The State News* via U-Wire, August 7, 2000.
64. The study is John Knowls, Nicola Persico, and Petra Todd, "Racial Bias in Motor Vehicle Searches: Theory and Evidence" (Cambridge, MA: National Bureau of Economic Research, 1999).
65. Steven E. Landsburg, "The Crazy Incentives of the Drug War," *Slate Magazine*, August 14, 2000.

JUSTICES OF THE SUPREME COURT

WARREN COURT LIBERALS
WARREN–GOLDBERG–FORTAS

The liberal reputation of the Warren Court (1954–1969) rests primarily on its work in four major areas: destroying legalized racial segregation, mandating equal voting power through the apportionment of voting districts so that each voter's vote was of approximately equal weight, expanding First Amendment rights, and incorporating most of the criminal procedure provisions of the Bill of Rights. The last achievement, in fact, began in 1961 with Mapp v. Ohio, *and gathered momentum only with the appointment of Justice Goldberg upon the retirement of Justice Frankfurter. The incorporation cases often, but not invariably, hinged on the votes of a slim majority—Warren, Black, Douglas, Brennan, and Goldberg (and Fortas after him). This is not surprising to constitutional scholars, because important constitutional innovations often embody one side of a large conflict of ideals of the society. The competing ideals of liberty and security are both essential, so the law of criminal procedure is bound to exhibit some tension and shift. The adoption of a competing ideal in a particular case is less a matter of "right and wrong" in a factual sense than a value choice between the approaches and a response to differing perceived needs of the nation at a given time. This may explain why American electoral politics, policy choices, and constitutional doctrines are subject to broad swings over the decades; there may be no other way to maintain peaceful continuity in a nation so vast and so varied.*

EARL WARREN

California 1891–1974

Republican

Appointed Chief Justice by Dwight D. Eisenhower

Years of Service: 1953–1969

Collection of the Supreme Court of the United States. Photographer: Abdon Daoud Ackad

LIFE AND CAREER The son of a Norwegian immigrant railroad car inspector, Warren received his undergraduate and law degrees from the University of California, Berkeley. After army service in World War I, he entered public service and became district attorney (prosecutor) of Alameda County (Oakland, California) in 1925. His vigorous prosecution of corrupt politicians and organized crime helped to elevate him to California's attorney general in 1938. In that role, he backed the relocation of Japanese Americans from their homes to internment camps for the duration of World War II. He was elected Governor of California in 1943, and he ran for vice president of the United States in 1948 on the losing Republican ticket with Thomas Dewey of New York. (His support of a rule that allowed Dwight Eisenhower to win the nomination of the Republican party led to his appointment as Chief Justice in 1953.)

CONTRIBUTION TO CRIMINAL PROCEDURE After his first two terms on the Court, Warren became a critical liberal vote, and with the appointment of Goldberg to replace Frankfurter in 1962, the way was clear to accomplish the "due process revolution" by which most of the criminal provisions of the Bill of Rights were incorporated. His important majority opinions include *Terry v. Ohio* (1967) (stop and frisk); *Sherman v. United States* (1958) (entrapment); and *Klopfer v. North Carolina* (1967) (incorporating the Sixth Amendment right to a speedy trial). Earl Warren, a tough prosecutor, knew well how such public servants could abuse their great powers of office to overwhelm the will of the individual.

SIGNATURE OPINION *Miranda v. Arizona* (1966) is the case that revolutionized the law of confessions. Warren characteristically devoted relatively little space to the discussion of the precedents that would ordinarily be critical to justify a decision and instead devoted the lion's share of the opinion to documenting the numerous ways that law enforcement officers "subjugated the individual to the will of his examiner." The decision in *Miranda* spelled out practical rules and their application for police and prosecutors, an approach that has been derided by critics as judicial legislation. *Miranda* was characteristic of his activism and liberalism, and his willingness to ignite controversy if he believed his position was the fair course to take.

ASSESSMENT Warren is ranked a great chief justice, not because he had a brilliant legal mind or because of his judicial craft in writing opinions, but for his leadership. He was a progressive with strong streaks of moralism and populism, and a superb administrator who knew how to motivate people and get things done. He is most remembered for his masterful ability to take a divided Court on the monumental issue of school segregation and steer it to a unanimous opinion in *Brown v. Board of Education* (1954), a feat considered to be the hallmark of judicial statesmanship. During an oral argument, he often cut through technical presentations to ask lawyers if the position they were supporting was fair, a question some saw as unsophisticated. However, this approach provided the framework for rulings that transformed American politics, law enforcement, and society. Under Warren the Supreme Court was marked by activism, liberalism, and populism. It outlawed racial segregation, ended unrepresentative voting districts in the states, extended First Amendment rights, and vigorously upheld antitrust laws.

Further Reading

Bernard Schwartz, *Super Chief: Earl Warren and His Supreme Court—A Judicial Biography,* Unabridged Edition (New York: New York University Press, 1983).

ARTHUR J. GOLDBERG

Illinois 1908–1990

Democrat

Appointed by John Fitzgerald Kennedy

Years of Service: 1962–1965

Collection of the Supreme Court of the United States. Photographer: Abdon Daoud Ackad

LIFE AND CAREER The youngest of eleven children of Russian immigrants, Goldberg was educated in Chicago public schools and received his bachelor's and law degrees from Northwestern University, graduating first in his law school class. He practiced law in Chicago until World War II and, in 1938, began to practice labor law. During the war, he served in the Office of Strategic Services in charge of labor espionage behind enemy lines.

After the war, he became a leading labor lawyer and, in 1948, became general counsel for the United Steelworkers Union. He played a central role in the merger of the American Federation of Labor and the Congress of Industrial Organizations (AFL-CIO), becoming the group's general counsel. In 1957, he led the fight to expel the crime-ridden Teamster's Union from the labor body. Through this work and his excellent reputation as a negotiator, Goldberg gained national prominence. He became an adviser to Senator John F. Kennedy in his 1960 bid for the presidency and was selected by President Kennedy to be Secretary of Labor, where he played an active role in settling several major strikes. In 1962, he was nominated by Kennedy to replace Justice Frankfurter.

In 1965, President Lyndon Johnson persuaded Justice Goldberg to resign his seat to become Ambassador to the United Nations in the hope that his negotiating skills would help in bringing a speedy end to the Vietnam War.

CONTRIBUTION TO CRIMINAL PROCEDURE Despite his short period of service on the Court, Goldberg's appointment created a liberal majority on the Court and thus inaugurated the due process revolution of applying the Bill of Rights to the states in criminal procedure.

SIGNATURE OPINION *Escobedo v. Illinois* (1964), the confessions case that held that police refusal of a lawyer's request to see a client violated the right to counsel; a confession obtained under those conditions was inadmissible in court. *Escobedo,* a breakthrough case, paved the way to *Miranda v. Arizona* (1966).

ASSESSMENT Goldberg was a liberal who believed that the Court has a legitimate problem-solving role and an important role in democracy by imposing Constitutional–majoritarian restraints to protect minority rights. He was a creative justice and established himself as the leading liberal spokesperson on a wide variety of explosive civil rights issues. In *Griswold v. Connecticut* (1965), the "contraceptive" case that established a framework for abortion rights, Goldberg concurred on the intellectually daring position that the rarely used Ninth Amendment should be the basis for removing criminal penalties against physicians who dispense, and married persons who seek, contraception advice. He argued that the Court should look to the "traditions and [collective] conscience of our people" to discover which rights are fundamental and beyond the reach of the legislature. He also opposed the death penalty, arguing in 1963 that the Court should decide its constitutionality, an issue that the Court did not confront until the 1970s. He took a bold approach to civil rights, urging the Court to go beyond declaring discriminatory laws unconstitutional, and requiring the states to act affirmatively to guarantee civil rights, a position shared by only two other justices.

Further Reading

Stephen J. Friedman, "Arthur Goldberg," in *The Justices of the United States Supreme Court, 1789–1969,* edited by Leon Friedman and Fred L. Israel, vol. 4, pp. 2977–2990 (New York: Chelsea House,1969).

ABE FORTAS

Tennessee 1910–1982

Democrat

Appointed by Lyndon Johnson

Years of Service: 1965–1969

Collection of the Supreme Court of the United States. Photographer: Harris and Ewing

LIFE AND CAREER A native of Memphis and the son of a poor tailor, Fortas graduated from Southwest College and Yale Law School. At Yale, he came to the attention of Professor William O. Douglas, who brought Fortas to Washington during the New Deal. Fortas was a tough and brilliant government lawyer; at age of 32, as under secretary of the interior, he argued unsuccessfully against the removal of Japanese Americans from the West Coast.

After World War II, he went into private law practice in Washington, D.C. The firm of Arnold, Porter and Fortas developed a reputation for effectively representing large corporations and for courageously defending the civil liberties of persons hounded by the government during the anticommunist hysteria of the late 1940s and early 1950s. Fortas skillfully represented Texas Congressman Lyndon Johnson, under charges of election fraud, in a notorious 1948 Senate primary election vote recount that secured Johnson a Senate seat. Fortas, thereafter, became a close advisor to Johnson.

As a private lawyer, Fortas took several *pro bono* cases that significantly changed criminal law and procedure. *Durham v. Unites States* (District of Columbia Court of Appeals [1954] later reversed) made a major change in the insanity defense in Washington, D.C. He argued for the defendant in *Gideon v. Wainwright* (1963), playing an important role in advancing the incorporation doctrine and expanding the right to counsel.

Fortas was nominated by President Johnson to be chief justice after Earl Warren announced his *prospective* retirement in 1968. Johnson did not seek a new term because of the intense politics surrounding the Vietnam war. As a result, Republicans in the Senate blocked Fortas' appointment, and he eventually withdrew it. During the nomination process, the press discovered that Fortas was a major presidential advisor while sitting on the bench and that he was receiving an annual payment of $20,000 from a family foundation of a businessman who had gone to prison for stock manipulation. Again, under intense public scrutiny and abetted by inside pressure from the President Nixon's Attorney General John Mitchell, Fortas resigned in 1969, although he had done nothing illegal.

CONTRIBUTION TO CRIMINAL PROCEDURE As a Warren Court liberal, Fortas voted for the incorporation doctrine and for the expansion of suspects' and defendants' procedural rights in several important cases, providing the crucial fifth majority vote in *Miranda v. Arizona* (1966). He had a special interest in the rights of juvenile delinquents, a novel area for the Court, and his majority opinion in *Kent v. United States* (1966) held that a juvenile is entitled to a hearing under the Due Process Clause before a delinquency case can be transferred from juvenile court into the adult criminal system.

SIGNATURE OPINION *In re Gault* (1967) made major changes in the way that juvenile court proceedings would henceforth be conducted. Before being adjudged delinquent, juveniles were entitled to many of the same procedural guarantees afforded to adults, including counsel, notice, the confrontation of witnesses, cross-examination, a written transcript, and appellate review. Fortas's opinion was powerful because it recognized that a benevolent governmental purpose can mask oppression in practice, and emphasized that the procedural rights of the Constitution are critical to the legitimacy of American courts, even special courts designed to help juveniles and not merely to punish. No matter how noble the goal of the state, Due Process Clause applies whenever a person, including a minor, is stripped of life, liberty, or property.

ASSESSMENT Fortas was a solid liberal in all civil rights areas, but unlike most liberal justices, in antitrust matters he was not opposed to big business and usually did not vote against corporate mergers. His resignation allowed an additional appointment by President Nixon, thus shifting the center of gravity of the Court from a liberal to a moderate-conservative stance in the area of criminal procedure.

Further Reading

Laura Kalman, *Abe Fortas: A Biography* (New Haven: Yale University Press, 1990)

CHAPTER 7

THE RIGHT TO COUNSEL

It is a fair summary of history to say that the safeguards of liberty have frequently been forged in controversies involving not very nice people.

—Justice Felix Frankfurter, dissenting in *United States v. Rabinowitz*, 339 U.S. 56, 69 (1950)

CHAPTER OUTLINE

KEY TERMS AND PHRASES *(CONTINUES ON NEXT PAGE)*

Actual imprisonment rule
Appointed counsel
Asset forfeiture
Assigned counsel
Assize
Authorized imprisonment rule
Conflict of interest
Continuance
Counsel, Right to
Critical stage
Deficient performance
Dossier
Formal charge rule
Indigent
Multiple representation

Parallel right
Prejudice the case
Pro bono publico
Pro se defense
Public defender
Recoupment
Retained counsel
Self-representation
Special circumstances rule
Standby counsel
Waiver of counsel

INTRODUCTION

A defense lawyer stands next to her criminal client in court. Both face judge and jury while awaiting verdict. The defendant will suffer the penalty for a guilty verdict, but their standing together is a powerful reminder that the attorney is the defendant's surrogate—the lawyer "stands in the defendant's shoes." The attorney owes the client an undivided duty of representation, within the law, marked by "warm zeal." The attorney is cloaked with the attorney-client privilege that preserves a criminal client's right against self-incrimination and without which adequate representation and a fair trial are impossible.

There are four federal constitutional sources of the **right to counsel:** the Sixth Amendment, the Due Process Clauses (Fifth and Fourteenth amendments), the Fourteenth Amendment Equal Protection Clause, and the Fifth Amendment right against self incrimination. Additionally, a *state* by statute or by its state constitution can grant the assistance of counsel in proceedings beyond those guaranteed by the United States Constitution.

The Sixth Amendment states that *"In all criminal prosecutions the accused shall enjoy the right . . . to have the assistance of counsel for his defence."*[1] The structure and wording of the Amendment convey important lessons. First, the amendment includes seven other distinct trial rights (e.g., the right to confront hostile witnesses). By placing the right to counsel *last,* the amendment indicates that trial rights have little meaning without the presence of a forceful advocate to make the rights effective. As Justice William Douglas wrote, "Of what value is the constitutional guaranty of a fair trial if an accused does not have counsel to advise and defend him?"[2] The right benefits *society* by guaranteeing that the adversary system of justice remains robust and fair. Next, the right to the *assistance* of counsel means that the defendant must be consulted by counsel and allowed to make important strategic decisions. Finally, the words "in all criminal prosecutions" reveal the amendment's limits: it does not guarantee counsel until a defendant is formally charged nor after a sentence is rendered. A constitutional right to counsel during police interrogation, upon appeal or during probation revocation hearings, must be based on other constitutional or statutory provisions.

The Supreme Court has filled some gaps in the right to counsel through the fundamental fairness concept of the Fifth and the Fourteenth amendment Due Process Clauses. Thus, for example, in some (but not all) probation violation hearings, due process mandates the appointment of a lawyer. Due process was important in guaranteeing counsel in some state trials before the Sixth Amendment was incorporated in 1963 by *Gideon v. Wainwright.*

The Equal Protection Clause plays a smaller part in the right to counsel. It ensures that the attendant cost of justice, such as filing fees, be waived for **indigent** persons, whether for trials or appeals. Under certain circumstances, benefits such as a trial transcript must be provided to an indigent free of charge on appeal. The combined force of due process and equal protection was held to guarantee a lawyer for a convicted defendant's first appeal as of right.

Police investigation or arrest does not trigger the Sixth Amendment right to counsel. There is no right to a lawyer during a pre-indictment lineup and undercover agents can infiltrate the lives of suspects who are not formally charged with crimes. What about the famous right to counsel that is read to suspects as a part of their *Miranda* warnings (*Miranda v. Arizona,* 1966)? This is a special right to counsel established by the Supreme Court under the *Fifth* Amendment to protect the right against self-incrimination when a suspect is subjected to custodial interrogation by police.

Before the mid-twentieth century, the Sixth Amendment right to counsel meant that no court or statute could abolish a defendant's right to be represented in court by a paid, licensed lawyer of his choosing. This right was affirmed in 1791 because the common law of England did not allow legal representation in all criminal cases. In the nineteenth century, however, it was constitutionally acceptable for a poor person to defend himself or herself without a lawyer in a felony trial and with whatever help the judge was disposed to grant. In complex or death penalty cases, judges would order local lawyers to represent indigent defendants for no charge, **pro bono publico,** but the practice was not uniform. Thus, the development of the right to counsel has centered on the practical issue of whether the state would make the right absolute by requiring the state to compensate a lawyer for a person who is too poor to pay.

Before tracing constitutional developments of the right to counsel, we examine the function of a criminal lawyer in the adversary system.

The Role and Importance of Lawyers in the Adversary System

Lawyers play a key role in fair criminal trials where truth emerges from the clash of evidence provided by prosecution and defense. The trial is a technical and intimidating process. The criminal attorney is trained in the rapidly changing and intricate substantive criminal law, criminal procedure, rules of evidence, and techniques for the conduct of trials. In addition to trial advocacy, an attorney directs the pretrial investigation and protects the defendant's rights in legally complex pretrial hearings. Motions for bail, discovery, suppression of illegally obtained evidence, change of venue in notorious cases, and the conduct of plea negotiations require experienced attorneys. Plea bargaining is quite adversarial. Attorneys who prepare negotiated cases as if they were going to trial learn strengths and weaknesses of the case and are in a position to back up a negotiating position with a resort to trial if needed. The adversarial nature of American trials pervades the entire adjudication process and makes even routine cases dependent on the abilities of trained and professional advocates. A defendant without a lawyer is at a severe disadvantage.

To highlight the importance of lawyers in common law trial systems, compare the role of lawyers in continental Europe's "civil law" systems. In France, for example, the trial is primarily conducted by the president (chief judge) of the **assize** (felony) court. Moreover, the French judiciary is more active than English or American judges in investigating and developing a file (**dossier**) in order to judicially determine the facts of the case. Unlike the American trial where the lawyers call witnesses, in French felony trials "the president can still order the appearance of anyone to the trial that may be of assistance, or he can request that new or additional evidence be brought to him. The president's mission during the trial is to see that all avenues are explored with the aim of discovering the truth."[3] The common law trial judge is not specially trained to lead investigations and, resting on eight hundred years of tradition, acts more as a *referee.* It is the attorney who "decides what theory of defence to pursue, what witnesses to call, what evidence to adduce, what strategy to follow, and what arguments to make."[4] The positive side of this is that the Anglo-American defense lawyer is better situated to expose governmental arbitrariness against an individual. The negative aspect is that if the defense lawyer is incompetent, the defendant stands a greater likelihood of being wrongfully convicted. American lawyers focus on presenting evidence to the jury. The European system seeks the truth by concentrating its truth-finding mechanism in the hands of trained professionals. Through the process of a trial, these professionals compile all relevant evidence into a single file and sift through it, in order to form a conclusion about what happened. The accusatorial or adversarial system searches for the truth by having two sides present their best evidence and attempt to discredit each other. The merits and weaknesses of these systems have been debated for centuries.[5] Since the adversary system cannot be abolished without constitutional amendment, improvements will come by increasing attorney competence and by reforming procedures (e.g., allowing defense access to evidence obtained by police). A fair adversary system requires both the state and the defendant to have generally matched resources.

Common Law Roots of Legal Representation

The extensive use of lawyers in criminal cases is a relatively recent development. From the misty beginnings of the common law jury trial in thirteenth-century England to the mid-eighteenth century, lawyer assistance was virtually unknown and, in some instances, forbidden by law. A criminal trial in early common-law England was a "long argument" between the defendant and a private accuser, and rarely by counsel for the crown.[6] Initially, there were no lawyers; and when professional attorneys emerged, they did not appear in court to try cases directly, but instead to advise defendants. The role of Royal prosecutor was established in the sixteenth century to prosecute treason cases against enemies of the crown.[7] In 1695—shortly after the 1688 "Glorious Revolution"—England allowed legal representation of defendants who were charged with treason. Nevertheless, state prosecutors were not used in common criminal cases, and lawyers were barred from defending persons charged with felonies. Oddly, lawyers were allowed to defend misdemeanants. These rules seem bizarre today because defendants' rights are well established; but the rule was originally established to give an advantage to the Crown in cases where the stability of the realm was at stake.[8] Disallowing counsel struck the great legal scholar, William Blackstone, as unjust in 1769, and it did not surprise him that the rule was often breached by English judges in practice.[9] Parliament dropped the rule in 1836, forty-five years after the United States Bill of Rights guaranteed the right to counsel.

In contrast to England, colonial America embraced the use of attorneys in criminal trials, as exemplified by the career of John Adams as a criminal defense lawyer. In the celebrated Boston Massacre case, Adams, although a member of the pro-liberty party, vigorously defended and won acquittals for the British soldiers who fired in self-defense on a large, stone-throwing mob of zealous patriots.[10] This famous case shows that the framers viewed the right to counsel favorably, even if not intending to provide free lawyers for indigent defendants. Many state constitutions included guarantees of counsel in criminal cases.[11] Still, despite the right to counsel guarantee of the Bill of Rights, most indigent defendants represented themselves. The right to counsel existed for only those who could afford a lawyer. When poor defendants tried their own cases, ideally, the judge took special care to provide some advice to ensure that they did not completely ruin their defense. In death penalty cases, judges often ordered a lawyer to donate services free of charge as a professional obligation.

THE DEVELOPMENT OF THE RIGHT TO COUNSEL TO 1961

The rapid growth of urban populations and bureaucratic, multi-judge courts in the twentieth century required that providing lawyers for indigents in an ad hoc fashion be replaced with more formal legal aid and defender systems. As this ensued, the Supreme Court began a journey to define the right to counsel and, ultimately, to apply the Sixth Amendment right to the states by incorporating the right into the Fourteenth Amendment Due Process Clause. The constitutional journey began with one of the most celebrated trials in American history, the infamous "Scottsboro" case. In *Powell v. Alabama* (1932), the Court found that under certain circumstances state courts had to provide criminal defendants with free counsel.

Powell v. Alabama: The Scottsboro Case

Nine African-American teens, arrested after a fistfight with several white boys on a freight train rolling through Alabama in 1931, were falsely accused of rape by two white women passengers. The teens were tried for a capital crime in Scottsboro, Alabama. Thus began one of the great trial sagas in American history. It did not end until the last of the defendants was released from prison decades later.[12] The "Scottsboro boys" were tried three times in a climate dripping with racism; sentenced to death; gained national notoriety; grew to maturity in prison; were saved by appeals, stays of execution, and commutations; and twice saw their cases go before the United States Supreme Court.[13]

The first trials were three one-day affairs held on successive days. Eight of the teens were sentenced to death. The Alabama Supreme Court affirmed seven of the capital sentences. The United States Supreme Court accepted the case and reversed the convictions in November, 1932. Justice George Sutherland's majority opinion in *Powell v. Alabama* (1932), held that the defendants' due process rights were violated. Although Hugo Black, a Roosevelt appointee, is rightly credited with advancing the constitutional right to counsel, his way was paved by Sutherland's opinion. A recent biographer complains that Sutherland, an anti-New Deal conservative, has been unfairly overlooked for his positive accomplishments by liberal scholars.[14] It is worth commenting, in light of Justice Sutherland's contribution, that due process rights and fundamental fairness are valued by people across the political spectrum.

The issue in *Powell* was whether the defendants' *due process* rights were violated by the denial of the right to counsel, "with the accustomed incidents of consultation and opportunity of preparation for trial." Prior to 1932, the Supreme Court had not incorporated any criminal procedure rights. Appeals from state defendants were rare—the only avenue was a federal writ of habeas corpus claiming the defendant was illegally detained because the state violated Fourteenth Amendment due process rights. The Supreme Court first upheld such a claim less than a decade before in *Moore v. Dempsey* (1923), holding that a trial occurring in a mob atmosphere is no trial at all (see Chapter 2). This was not the precise basis of *Powell,* but Justice Sutherland did note that the atmosphere surrounding the trials was one of "tense, hostile and excited public sentiment."

Sutherland's opinion first reviewed the record and concluded that the "defendants were not accorded the right of counsel in any substantial sense," and, second, concluded that the lack of counsel violated the defendants' right to Fourteenth Amendment due process. Justice Black later claimed that the case "incorporated" the Sixth Amendment right to counsel into due process, but a close reading of the opinion shows otherwise.

How were the defendants represented in the Scottsboro case? The transcript indicated that lawyers for the defendants examined and cross-examined witnesses and made arguments. On this basis, the Alabama Supreme Court ruled that Ozie Powell and the other youths were represented by counsel. How did the United States Supreme Court conclude otherwise? Justice Sutherland noted that the defendants, young and poor strangers in Scottsboro, were not asked if they had access to lawyers. They were not given much time to contact their families in other states to arrange for counsel:

> It is hardly necessary to say that, the right to counsel being conceded, a defendant should be afforded a fair opportunity to secure counsel of his own choice. Not only was that not done here, but such designation of counsel as was attempted was either so indefinite or so close upon the trial as to amount to a denial of effective and substantial aid in that regard. (*Powell v. Alabama,* p. 53)

Indeed, an examination of the trial transcript disclosed that none of the lawyers was willing to definitely be a lawyer for a specific defendant. For example, Mr. Steven Roddy, a Tennessee lawyer, was asked by the court whether he intended to appear for the defendants. Roddy answered that he was not really hired although he "would like to appear along with counsel that the court might appoint."[15] Ultimately, no single lawyer was appointed for all the defendants, nor was each defendant appointed individual counsel. Instead, the trial judge "appointed *all* the members of the bar for the purpose of arraigning the defendants" and continued that arrangement for the trial when neither Roddy nor any of the local lawyers would stand up to be *the* attorney of record.[16] The white lawyers were obviously unwilling to vigorously defend the African-American teens. In the critical period before trial when a lawyer could have organized an investigation into the facts and marshaled legal arguments, no one focused on this task. This lack of resolution and focus clearly offended Justice Sutherland:[17]

> It is not enough to assume that counsel thus precipitated into the case thought there was no defense, and exercised their best judgment in proceeding to trial without preparation. Neither they nor the court could say what a prompt and thoroughgoing investigation might disclose as to the facts. No attempt was made to investigate. No opportunity to do so was given. Defendants were immediately hurried to trial. . . . Under the circumstances disclosed, we hold that defendants were not accorded the right of counsel in any substantial sense. To decide otherwise, would simply be to ignore actualities. (*Powell v. Alabama,* p. 58)

Justice Sutherland turned to another point. Did this lack of counsel violate the defendants' federal due process rights? He reviewed the history of the right to counsel in the original states: twelve established the right to counsel when no such right existed in England, showing its importance. In death penalty cases, some *colonies* required the appointment of defense counsel as was the law in Alabama in 1931.

Justice Sutherland addressed the incorporation issue. He reasoned, first, that because the right to counsel was found in the Bill of Rights, and because *Hurtado v. California* (1884) held that the federal courts could not encompass a right in the Bill of Rights (grand jury) to the states via the Fourteenth Amendment Due Process Clause, *Hurtado* would bar Powell's claim if the case "stood alone." But *Hurtado* did not stand alone. *Chicago, Burlington & Quincy R. Co. v. Chicago* (1897) held that the states, as a matter of Fourteenth Amendment due process, had to grant just compensation when the state took private property for public use, even though a Just Compensation Clause existed in the Fifth Amendment. Furthermore, "freedom of speech and of the press are rights protected by the Due Process Clause of the Fourteenth Amendment, although in the First Amendment, Congress is prohibited in specific terms from abridging the right."[18] Therefore, a right found in the Bill of Rights as a proscription on the federal government, could also exist as a **parallel right,** within the concept of due process. This "parallel right" approach is clearly not the "total incorporation" under the Privileges or Immunities Clause desired by the first Justice Harlan or Hugo Black, nor is it the modern approach of "selective incorporation." Yet, it seems clear that Sutherland was influenced by the "fundamental rights" reasoning of *Twining v. New Jersey* (1908) (see Chapter 2).

Is assistance of counsel a fundamental right as a component of a *fair trial?* At minimum, due process requires notice, a fair hearing, and a competent tribunal. The philosopher Hadley Arkes suggests that Justice Sutherland was concerned with basic principles: "To begin at the root, the purpose of a trial was to do justice, to punish the guilty and vindicate the innocent. The central task was to make reasoned discriminations between the innocent and the guilty and arrive at verdicts that were substantially just."[19] Justice Sutherland then wrote the classic passage explaining the vital importance of a fully committed defense attorney in a criminal case.

> What, then, does a hearing include? Historically and in practice, in our own country at least, it has always included the right to the aid of counsel when desired and provided by the party asserting the right. The right to be heard would be, in many cases, of little avail if it did not comprehend the right to be heard by counsel. Even the intelligent and educated layman has small and sometimes no skill in the science of law. If charged with crime, he is incapable, generally, of determining for himself whether the indictment is good or bad. He is unfamiliar with the rules of evidence. Left without the aid of counsel he may be put on trial without a proper charge, and convicted upon incompetent evidence, or evidence irrelevant to the issue or otherwise inadmissible. He lacks both the skill and knowledge adequately to prepare his defense, even though he had a perfect one. He requires the guiding hand of counsel at every step in the proceedings against him. Without it, though he be not guilty, he faces the danger of conviction because he does not know how to establish his innocence. If that be true of men of intelligence, how much more true is it of the ignorant and illiterate, or those of feeble intellect. If in any case, civil or criminal, a state or federal court were arbitrarily to refuse to hear a party by counsel, employed by and appearing for him, it reasonably may not be doubted that such a refusal would be a denial of a hearing, and, therefore, of due process in the constitutional sense.[20]

With this, the Court easily ruled that the Fourteenth Amendment due process rights of the Scottsboro defendants were violated, and a new trial was required.

What was *Powell*'s significance as legal precedent? Did the states have to provide a lawyer for every indigent defendant in every felony trial? Or was the scope of its application narrower? The outcome makes it clear that the decision was based on facts and circumstances.

> All that it is necessary now to decide, as we do decide, is that in a capital case, where the defendant is unable to employ counsel, and is incapable adequately of making his own defense because of ignorance, feeble mindedness, illiteracy, or the like, it is the duty of the court, whether requested or not, to assign counsel for him as a necessary requisite of due process of law. . . .[21]

As a Due Process Clause precedent, *Powell,* became known as the **special circumstances rule:** due process requires counsel in cases, where "special circumstances" exist.

After *Powell:* Toward Incorporation

Six years after *Powell,* Justice Hugo Black forcefully made the assistance of counsel in a *federal* case—*directly* applying the Sixth Amendment, uncluttered by states' rights or special circumstances considerations—an *absolute* right. *Johnson v. Zerbst* (1938) resulted from two soldiers, on leave in South Carolina, being convicted of passing counterfeit currency. They were tried without the assistance of counsel. This case shows why a lawyer is necessary. The defendants presented a defense that was inartful at best and one that a jury could read as an evasion of guilt. Johnson misused his time by attempting to answer minor, possibly prejudicial, statements by the prosecutor (*e.g.,* that he was a "hoodlum from New York"). Johnson also failed to challenge the evidence and neglected to raise legal challenges that could have mitigated the crime or won an acquittal.

Justice Black's majority opinion secured two important constitutional rules. First, it held for the first time that a federal felony trial conducted without a defense lawyer, unless properly waived, is a *jurisdictional violation.* It is not a mere technical mistake, but an infringement of the Sixth Amendment that deprives the court of "the power and authority to deprive an accused of his life or liberty " (*Johnson,* p. 463).

> "This is [a] safeguard[] . . . deemed necessary to ensure fundamental human rights of life and liberty. [It is an] essential barrier[] against arbitrary or unjust deprivation of human rights. The Sixth Amendment stands as a constant admonition that if the constitutional safeguards it provides be lost, justice will not 'still be done'" (*Johnson v. Zerbst,* p. 462).

Second, the case specified the rules for **waiver of counsel.** There is a *presumption against the waiver* of such a fundamental right. Even if the defendant silently goes along with the conduct of a trial without complaining about the lack of counsel, his or her silence does not amount to a waiver. A waiver is defined as "an *intelligent relinquishment or abandonment of a known right or privilege.*" For a waiver to be constitutional, the defendant must *know* that he or she has right to counsel and *voluntarily* give it up knowing that the a right to claim it exists. The Supreme Court later required trial judges to carefully investigate waivers of counsel and make a *written record* of any waivers.[22] "Presuming waiver from a silent record is impermissible. The record must show . . . that an accused was offered counsel but intelligently and understandably rejected the offer." (*Carnley v. Cochran,* 1962). These rules became the standard for all Fifth and Sixth amendment waivers, including waivers of the right to remain silent, after having been read one's *Miranda* warnings.

Betts v. Brady (1942), decided a decade after *Powell,* was a setback to the incorporation of the Sixth Amendment. *Betts* confirmed the *special circumstances* rule of *Powell.* Betts, a farm hand, was indicted for non-capital robbery. Not having the money to hire a lawyer, he asked the judge for **appointed counsel** at his arraignment. The judge refused, saying that the Carroll County court appointed counsel for indigent defendants only in prosecutions for murder and rape. Betts pleaded not guilty and defended himself in a nonjury trial before the judge.

> At his request witnesses were summoned in his behalf. He cross-examined the State's witnesses and examined his own. The latter gave testimony tending to establish an alibi. Although afforded the opportunity, he did not take the witness stand. The judge found him guilty and imposed a sentence of eight years (*Betts v. Brady,* p. 457).

The issue before the Supreme Court, sharpened by Betts's explicit request for a lawyer, was (as in *Powell*) whether a *state* felony trial conducted without defense counsel was a deprivation of Fourteenth Amendment due process liberty. The majority, in an opinion by Justice Owen Roberts, clearly rejected "incorporation"—the "Sixth Amendment of the national Constitution applies only to trials in federal courts." Relying on *Palko v. Connecticut* (1938), it refused to apply the rule of *Johnson* to state cases. The Court found that the *Sixth Amendment* right to counsel is not *in* the Due Process Clause. Instead, the contours of the Due Process Clause, insofar as the clause required the appointment of a lawyer for an indigent in a state case, were set out in *Powell.* The Court dealt with Betts's petition as a "pure" due process issue, which must decide, on an "appraisal of the totality of facts in a given case," whether a trial without defense counsel is "a denial of fundamental fairness, shocking to the universal sense of justice" (*Betts v. Brady,* p. 462).

Applying *Powell,* Justice Roberts concluded that *special circumstances* did not exist in Betts's case. Therefore, due process did not require the state to appoint counsel. The case was not complicated: did Betts commit a robbery? He put alibi witnesses on the stand and the issue for the judge was a simple matter of witness credibility. Unlike the *Scottsboro* defendants, Betts was "not helpless, but was a man forty-three years old, of ordinary intelligence, and [able] to take care of his own interests on the trial of that narrow issue. He had once before been in a criminal court, pleaded guilty to larceny and served a sentence and was not wholly unfamiliar with criminal procedure."[23] None of the racism and lynch-mob atmosphere of *Powell* surrounded this run-of-the-mill case. In affirming Betts's uncounseled conviction of a non-capital felony, the majority was satisfied that its conclusion did not violate "natural, inherent, and fundamental principles of fairness." First, uncounseled defense was a common practice to "those who have lived under the Anglo-American system of law." Most states then provided an attorney at no charge to the defendant in noncapital cases only at the discretion of the court, and not as a mandatory right. At that time, the provision of counsel was seen as a legislative or political issue, not as a fundamental right. Furthermore, Maryland law required the appointment of counsel if special circumstances existed. The Supreme Court worried that a flat rule would burden states with the cost of providing counsel even in "small crimes tried before justices of the peace" and in "trials in the Traffic Court."

Justice Black's spirited dissent, joined by Justices Douglas and Murphy, urged incorporation of the Sixth Amendment right to counsel into the Fourteenth Amendment. Failing that, he argued that Justice Sutherland's logic in *Powell*—that it is difficult for any layperson to adequately defend oneself in a criminal trial—means that a felony trial conducted without defense counsel is *always* unfair and a due process violation. Justice Black sought to extend *Johnson* to state cases. Black, a former populist Senator, emphasized the greater risks of unjust conviction to poor people. "A practice cannot be reconciled with 'common and fundamental ideas of fairness and right,' which subjects innocent men to increased dangers of conviction merely because of their poverty. . . . Denial to the poor of the request for counsel in proceedings based on charges of serious crime has long been regarded as shocking to the 'universal sense of justice' throughout this country."[24]

Justice Black was later vindicated in *Gideon v. Wainwright* (1963). In the two decades following *Betts,* the Court undermined the special circumstances test by finding that special circumstances existed in many instances. The Court held that counsel was required by due process in all death penalty trials (1948), in all capital case arraignments, and in cases involving an unsworn defendant who wishes to make a statement (1961).[25] Justice Stanley Reed revealed that the Court was divided as to noncapital cases but that several justices felt "the Due Process Clause . . . requires counsel for all persons charged with serious crimes. . . ."[26] These cases paved the way to *Gideon.*

The Equal Protection Approach

Griffin v. Illinois (1956) opened the door to a new theory on which to base rights connected to the right to counsel. The Court held that, under the Fourteenth Amendment *Equal Protection Clause,* indigent defendants are entitled to a *trial transcript* in order to facilitate appeals. Under Illinois procedure then in effect, to obtain a full appeal of a criminal conviction a defendant had to furnish the appellate court with a bill of exceptions or report of proceedings at the trial certified by the trial judge. The state agreed that "it is sometimes impossible to prepare such bills of exceptions or reports without a stenographic transcript of the trial proceedings." Free transcripts were provided at county expense to indigent defendants sentenced to death. "In all other criminal cases defendants needing a transcript, whether indigent or not, must themselves buy it." Under these circumstances, four justices, in an opinion written by Justice Black, held that a free transcript must be provided. Justice Frankfurter, concurring specially, added that the ruling in *Griffin* should not be applied retrospectively. The plurality opinion did not rule that trial transcripts had to be provided to indigent defendants in all cases: only where the effect was to deny indigents a right to appeal because of their poverty. Although the Constitution did not mandate appellate courts, once appeals were universally required, appellate review could not be administered in a manner that discriminated against the poor.

The dissent, by Justice Burton (joined by Justices Minton, Reed and Harlan), expressed a concern for federalism. A free transcript was a fine thing, but it should be provided by the states as they saw fit, and not required by federal constitutional law. They expressed concern that an equal protection ruling would lead to "leveling"—the abolition of all laws that had *any* disparate economic impact on the rich and the poor (e.g., a sales tax).

Justice Black's opinion in *Griffin* seems designed to undermine the *Betts* special circumstances rule with the flat requirement of counsel. He wrote: "There can be no equal justice where the kind of *trial* a man gets depends on the amount of money he has." If *Griffin* implied that it is the justice system's duty to eliminate the differences between the rich and the poor so as to ensure equal justice, and if people with the means had an absolute right to counsel, should not a lawyer be provided for indigents? As it turned out, the Equal Protection Clause was *not* the platform for the rule requiring trial counsel. However, it was the basis, combined with due process, for the Court's holding in *Douglas v. California* (1963), entitling an indigent to a free lawyer on a first appeal (which is not, strictly speaking, part of the criminal prosecution as defined in the Sixth Amendment).

The *Griffin* equality principle was the foundation of rulings that benefitted indigent persons: eliminating filing fees in criminal appeals and state postconviction/habeas corpus hearings;[27] and ensuring the right on appeal to free transcripts of preliminary hearing records, lower court habeas corpus hearings, and local ordinance violation trials.[28] By 1970, it appeared to be an absolute rule requiring that an indigent who was involved in the criminal process be given any benefit that a wealthier person could afford. Still, the more conservative Burger Court placed a significant limit on this line of cases when applied to counsel on discretionary appeals, an issue addressed after reviewing *Gideon.*

GIDEON V. WAINWRIGHT AND ITS AFTERMATH

In *Gideon v. Wainwright,* the Supreme Court guaranteed the right to counsel to all *state* felony defendants by incorporating the Sixth Amendment into Fourteenth Amendment due process.

• CASE & COMMENTS •

Gideon v. Wainwright
372 U.S. 335, 83 S.Ct. 792, 9 L.Ed.2d 799 (1963)

MR. JUSTICE BLACK delivered the opinion of the Court. **[a]**

[Gideon, charged with breaking into a pool hall, a felony, demanded (because of his indigency) and was refused appointed counsel. He conducted his own defense.] He made an opening statement to the jury, cross-examined the State's witnesses, presented witnesses in his own defense, declined to testify himself, and made a short argument "emphasizing his innocence to the charge contained in the Information filed in this case." The jury returned a verdict of guilty, and petitioner was sentenced to serve five years in the state prison. [The Court characterized the facts as similar to *Betts v. Brady* (this text) and set the case for review to reconsider the *Betts* rule because of the "continuing source of controversy and litigation in both state and federal courts" that the *Betts* rule presented.]

* * * Upon full reconsideration we conclude that *Betts v. Brady* should be overruled.

We have construed [the Sixth Amendment] to mean that in federal courts counsel must be provided for defendants unable to employ counsel unless the right is competently and intelligently waived. [JUSTICE BLACK reviewed *Betts v. Brady,* noting that it held the Sixth Amendment right of counsel not fundamental, and thus not incorporated into the Due Process Clause of the Fourteenth Amendment.]

We accept *Betts v. Brady*'s assumption, based as it was on our prior cases, that a provision of the Bill of Rights which is "fundamental and essential to a fair trial" is made obligatory upon the States by the Fourteenth Amendment. We think the Court in *Betts* was wrong, however, in concluding that the Sixth Amendment's guarantee of counsel is not one of these fundamental rights. Ten years before *Betts v. Brady,* this Court, after full consideration of all the historical data examined in *Betts,* had unequivocally declared that "the right to the aid of counsel is of this fundamental character." *Powell v. Alabama.* * * * While the Court at the close of its *Powell* opinion did by its language, as this Court frequently does, limit its holding to the particular facts and circumstances of that case, its conclusions about the fundamental nature of the right to counsel are unmistakable. * * *

* * * The fact is that in deciding as it did—that "appointment of counsel is not a fundamental right, essential to a fair trial"—the Court in *Betts v. Brady* made an abrupt break with its own well-considered precedents. In returning to these old precedents, sounder we believe than the new, we but restore constitutional principles established to achieve a fair system of justice. **[b]** Not only these precedents but also reason and reflection require us to recognize that in our adversary system of criminal justice, any person haled into court, who is too poor to hire a lawyer, cannot be assured a fair trial unless counsel is provided for him. This seems to us to be an obvious truth. Governments, both state and federal, quite properly spend vast sums of money to establish machinery to try defendants accused of crime. Lawyers to prosecute are everywhere deemed essential to protect the public's interest in an orderly society. Similarly, there are few defendants charged with crime, few

[a] Justice Black had the pleasure of writing the opinion in a landmark decision overruling a case in which he strenuously dissented two decades before.

[b] Justice Black seems to be stretching a fair reading of the "older precedent" of *Powell v. Alabama* by viewing it as having guaranteed the right of counsel to indigents in *all* felony cases. Compare this reading of precedent to that made in the concurrence by Justice Harlan.

• **CASE & COMMENTS** •

indeed, who fail to hire the best lawyers they can get to prepare and present their defenses. That government hires lawyers to prosecute and defendants who have the money hire lawyers to defend are the strongest indications of the widespread belief that lawyers in criminal courts are necessities, not luxuries. The right of one charged with crime to counsel may not be deemed fundamental and essential to fair trials in some countries, but it is in ours. From the very beginning, our state and national constitutions and laws have laid great emphasis on procedural and substantive safeguards designed to assure fair trials before impartial tribunals in which every defendant stands equal before the law. This noble ideal cannot be realized if the poor man charged with crime has to face his accusers without a lawyer to assist him. * * *

The judgment is reversed. * * * **[c]**

[c] The case was remanded and Earl Clarence Gideon was tried again in Panama City, Florida , this time represented by counsel. Anthony Lewis' celebrated book, *Gideon's Trumpet,* recounts the second trial. Gideon's lawyer, Fred Turner, prepared the case carefully by thoroughly reviewing the facts and observing the pool hall. His skillful cross-examination of the lead prosecution witness raised the real possibility that the teen who had identified Gideon as the criminal was himself the burglar. Gideon was acquitted.

[JUSTICES DOUGLAS and CLARK concurred in separate opinions].

MR. JUSTICE HARLAN, concurring.

I agree that *Betts v. Brady* should be overruled, but consider it entitled to a more respectful burial than has been accorded, at least on the part of those of us who were not on the Court when that case was decided.

I cannot subscribe to the view that *Betts v. Brady* represented "an abrupt break with its own well-considered precedents." * * * In 1932, in *Powell v. Alabama,* * * * a capital case, this Court declared that under the particular facts there presented—"the ignorance and illiteracy of the defendants, their youth, the circumstances of public hostility * * * and above all that they stood in deadly peril of their lives" * * *—the state court had a duty to assign counsel for the trial as a necessary requisite of due process of law. It is evident that these limiting facts were not added to the opinion as an afterthought; they were repeatedly emphasized, * * * and were clearly regarded as important to the result.

Thus when this Court, a decade later, decided *Betts v. Brady,* it did no more than to admit of the possible existence of special circumstances in noncapital as well as capital trials, while at the same time insisting that such circumstances be shown in order to establish a denial of due process. The right to appointed counsel had been recognized as being considerably broader in federal prosecutions [*Johnson v. Zerbst*], but to have imposed these requirements on the States would indeed have been "an abrupt break" with the almost immediate past. The declaration that the right to appointed counsel in state prosecutions, as established in *Powell v. Alabama,* was not limited to capital cases was in truth not a departure from, but an extension of, existing precedent.

The principles declared in *Powell* and in *Betts,* however, have had a troubled journey throughout the years. * * *

[More and more capital and noncapital cases found "special circumstances," even in doubtful instances.] The Court has come to recognize, in other words, that the mere existence of a serious criminal charge constituted in itself special circumstances requiring the services of counsel at trial. In truth the *Betts v. Brady* rule is no longer a reality. **[d]**

[d] Justice Harlan correctly points out that in the twenty years between *Betts* and *Gideon,* many narrow decisions began to shift toward granting the right to counsel in more and more cases. He posits a less absolutist view of constitutional rights and constitutional change than does Justice Black. In Justice Harlan's view, the meaning of constitutional provisions can change gradually over time to take into account new social realities. This was anathema to Justice Black who strenuously rejected what he saw as judicial lawmaking.

This evolution, however, appears not to have been fully recognized by many state courts, in this instance charged with the front-line responsibility for the enforcement of constitutional rights. To continue a rule which is honored by this Court only with lip service is not a healthy thing and in the long run will do disservice to the federal system.

The special circumstances rule has been formally abandoned in capital cases, and the time has now come when it should be similarly abandoned in noncapital cases, at least as to offenses which, as the one involved here, carry the possibility of a substantial prison sentence. (Whether the rule should extend to *all* criminal cases need not now be decided.) This indeed does no more than to make explicit something that has long since been foreshadowed in our decisions.

[JUSTICE HARLAN then stated his disagreement with the majority over the incorporation question, stating that in his opinion, the *Gideon* decision falls under the Fourteenth Amendment only, and not the Sixth.]

On these premises I join in the judgment of the Court.

Does *Gideon* Apply to Misdemeanor Trials?

Earl Clarence Gideon had a *felony* trial. Did the *Gideon* precedent apply to an indigent charged with a *misdemeanor?* The Court dealt with the issue a decade later. In *Argersinger v. Hamlin* (1972), the majority found no constitutional basis for distinguishing between a misdemeanor and a felony for purposes of **assigned counsel** for indigents. It held that counsel was required by the Sixth Amendment in misdemeanor cases where a defendant is actually sentenced to imprisonment. The Court reserved the issue of whether counsel is constitutionally required in cases involving *imprisonment as an authorized punishment,* but the defendant does not actually lose liberty.

Justice Powell, dissenting in *Argersinger,* urged the Court to choose a due process middle course between the state's rule denying appointed counsel in all cases where the penalty was less than six months incarceration, and the majority's approach of requiring counsel if a defendant was to spend even one day in jail. He would have allowed the trial court, in its discretion, to appoint counsel when required by special circumstances (such as the complexity of an issue), but not require the states to shoulder the costs of providing counsel in each and every case, no matter how straightforward and simple the issues.

The issue reserved in *Argersinger* was decided in a case concerning a shoplifter, who was convicted without a lawyer and fined a fifty dollars, although the law authorized a jail term. In *Scott v. Illinois* (1979), the Court held that *Argersinger* meant that **actual imprisonment** differs from a penalty of a fine or a threat of jailing and that, therefore, "the Sixth and Fourteenth Amendments to the United States Constitution require only that no indigent criminal defendant be sentenced to a term of imprisonment unless the State has afforded him the right to assistance of appointed counsel in his defense." The mere fact that one is being tried under a statute that authorizes incarceration does not automatically guarantee counsel. Justice Brennan, dissenting, argued that *Argersinger* required appointment of counsel if there is actual incarceration *or* if the crime charged is punishable by more than six months in prison. He thus urged the Court to adopt an "**authorized imprisonment**" rather than an "actual imprisonment" rule.

Scott injects an illogical element into the Sixth Amendment: a person charged with a felony must have a lawyer even if not sentenced to prison although counsel is not required for a similar misdemeanor defendant. Justice Powell, concurring, expressed some concern that the "actual imprisonment" rule would lead judges to guess in advance of the trial what the likely outcome would be and thus distort the judicial process. He concurred because he thought the Court should substitute the flexible due process rule rather than the rigid Sixth Amendment requirement to misdemeanor trials.

When Does the Right to Counsel Attach? Pretrial: The Critical Stage and Formal Charge Rules

Gideon did not resolve all issues concerning the right to counsel. The Sixth Amendment, now applicable to state as well as federal felony trials, applies to "all criminal prosecutions." What proceedings are included in a Sixth Amendment *criminal prosecution?* The answer is found in the **critical stage** doctrine developed by the Court. Counsel is required at a pretrial proceeding if it is one in which factual determinations can be made that could determine the outcome of the case and in which a lawyer plays a significant role.

ARRAIGNMENT The critical stage doctrine was developed prior to *Gideon.* A unanimous Court in *Hamilton v. Alabama* (1961) ruled that, under Alabama law, an arraignment in a capital case was a critical stage because it was the only point in the criminal process at which a defendant could raise an insanity defense without the approval of the trial judge. Other important motions had to be made at arraignment: pleas in abatement, motions to quash based on systematic exclusion of one race from the grand jury, or on the ground that the grand jury was otherwise improperly drawn. "Available defenses may be as irretrievably lost, if not then and there asserted, as they are when an accused represented by counsel waives a right for strategic purposes"

ARGERSINGER IN THE STATES

"California, in *Mills v. Municipal Court,*[29] criticized the *Argersinger* rule for requiring a trial judge to attempt to predict at the outset of a criminal prosecution whether or not imprisonment may be an appropriate sanction without access to the most relevant sentencing material, such as the defendant's prior record. *Mills* thought the better approach was to offer counsel to all, and permit on-the-record waivers by any defendant."

Barry Latzer, *State Constitutional Criminal Law,* § 5.4.

(*Hamilton,* p. 54). If an arraignment is a simple formality where no important decision is made (such as arranging for bail), then the lack of counsel is not a due process or Sixth Amendment violation. Otherwise, a defendant must be represented by an attorney.

PRELIMINARY EXAMINATION In *Coleman v. Alabama* (1970), the Supreme Court ruled that a preliminary examination is a critical stage requiring assistance of counsel. Under Alabama law, the defendant was not required to raise a defense, but if he was without counsel to cross-examine prosecution witnesses, any testimony taken was inadmissible at trial. The Alabama courts saw this as a fair rule that prevented the lack of counsel from causing **prejudice to the defendant's case.** Yet, Justice Brennan's majority opinion noted that (1) a lawyer's skilled cross-examination of witnesses can expose fatal weaknesses in the prosecution case that will lead a magistrate to dismiss; (2) cross-examination of witnesses may establish a basis for impeaching witnesses at the trial; (3) trained counsel can use the hearing as a way of discovering prosecution information that can prove helpful in devising a defense strategy; and (4) counsel can be influential in making arguments for bail or for a psychiatric examination. "The inability of the indigent accused on his own to realize these advantages of a lawyer's assistance compels the conclusion that the Alabama preliminary hearing is a 'critical stage' of the State's criminal process at which the accused is 'as much entitled to such aid [of counsel] . . . as at the trial itself'" (*Coleman,* p. 10).

POLICE INVESTIGATION No court has ever held that a lawyer must accompany police in conducting interviews or in gathering physical evidence of a crime. A lawyer has no traditional role to play during investigation, and any problems with the evidence may be derived from discovery or cross-examination. Counsel is not required in investigative hearings, such as grand jury and legislative hearings,[30] or when taking fingerprints, handwriting samples, or voice exemplars.[31]

CUSTODIAL INTERROGATION In *Miranda v. Arizona* (1966), the Supreme Court ruled that police interrogation that was conducted while a suspect was in custody raised a sufficient level of compulsion to become a potential violation of the suspect's right against self-incrimination under the Fifth Amendment, requiring warnings that include a right to counsel. This right is included under the *Fifth* Amendment and is *not* part of Sixth Amendment critical stage analysis (see Chapter 8).

LINEUP IDENTIFICATION The Supreme Court has held that a Sixth Amendment right to counsel applies to *postindictment* lineup identifications (*United States v. Wade,* 1967), but *not* to preindictment showups (*Kirby v. Illinois,* 1972). The basis for this distinction was that the laying of a **formal charge,** by indictment or information, brought the Sixth Amendment into play. The Court in *Kirby* said that the initiation of a prosecution is not a "mere formalism" for it is "then that a defendant finds himself faced with the prosecutorial forces of organized society, and immersed in the intricacies of substantive and procedural criminal law." Nevertheless, in *United States v. Ash* (1973) the Court held that counsel was *not* required under the Sixth Amendment during a postindictment *photographic display* because, since the defendant was not present, there is not the kind of confrontation that was contemplated in *Wade.* The dissent in *Ash* reasoned that the same suggestibility which can taint a lineup can taint a photographic identification, and an attorney can play the same role of preventing or observing the suggestive acts (see Chapter 9).

PRISON ADMINISTRATIVE DETENTION Four prison inmates were suspected of murdering another prisoner. They were held in administrative detention for ninety days during the investigation and were indicted for the murder nineteen months after the crime. The federal court of appeals held that they were entitled to counsel during the period of detention. The Supreme Court reversed in *United States v. Gouveia* (1984), holding that the *formal charges* rule of *Kirby* applied to prison as well as to non-prison settings: there is no right to counsel until the accused has been formally charged.

Are the "formal charge" cases and the "critical stage" cases in conflict? From an ideological perspective, the critical stage cases were decided by a more liberal Court. Beginning in *Kirby,* a more conservative Court has attempted to limit the right of counsel. It seems logical to rule that if counsel plays an important role in preventing or observing suggestive behaviors during a postindictment lineup, the same role is played during a preindictment lineup or a photographic identification. On one hand the majority in *Gouveia,* citing *Kirby,* stated that all cases in which the Supreme Court held that the Sixth Amendment right to counsel attached before trial "have involved points of time at or after the initiation of adversary judicial criminal proceedings—whether by way of formal charge, preliminary hearing, indictment, information, or arraignment." On the other hand, concurring and dissenting justices in *Gouveia* noted that *Kirby*'s language "does not foreclose the possibility that the right to counsel might under some circumstances attach prior to the formal initiation of judicial proceedings."[32] They suggested that functional critical stage reasoning provides a better rule than the formalistic line-drawing of *Kirby.* Thus, lower courts should determine if, for *all practical purposes,* a person has been charged with a crime and whether a lawyer can provide substantial assistance, even though formal charges have not been laid.

When Does the Right to Counsel Attach? Postconviction and Other Processes

Important criminal justice processes occur *after conviction* in the correctional system and in other proceedings that affect the rights of convicted persons. If a procedure is part of the Sixth Amendment criminal prosecution, *Gideon* applies and counsel is absolutely required. Otherwise, if counsel is required at all, it must be through the more flexible "facts and circumstances" approach of due process.

SENTENCING AND DEFERRED SENTENCING *Mempa v. Rhay* (1967) involved a sentencing hearing following a deferred sentence with probation. The Court held that counsel was required under the Sixth Amendment. Justice Marshall, for the majority, stated that the Sixth Amendment right to counsel applied to sentencing: it was part of the "criminal prosecution." Sentencing included deferred sentencing that involved the revocation of conditional liberty. The Court announced a broad principle: "appointment of counsel for an indigent is required at every stage of a criminal proceeding where substantial rights of a criminal accused may be affected." But, in subsequent years, the Court has refused to extend this logic to probation and parole revocations and prison disciplinary hearings, which apply to convicted persons.

PROBATION AND PAROLE REVOCATION The Supreme Court ruled in *Gagnon v. Scarpelli* (1973) (probation) and *Morrissey v. Brewer* (1972) (parole) that "Probation revocation, like parole revocation, is not a stage of a criminal prosecution, but does result in a loss of liberty." (*Gagnon,* p. 782). As a result, neither probation nor parole could be revoked without a formal, due process hearing that required notice, disclosure of evidence, an opportunity to be heard, a neutral hearing body, and written statements of the fact finders. In neither case was counsel required by the Sixth Amendment. Should counsel be *required* as a matter of due process fundamental fairness? Under due process the Court might have ruled that counsel is either never or always required in revocation hearings. Instead, more flexible due process rules were applied. The Court did not address the issue in *Morrissey* but took it up the next year in *Gagnon,* where it refused to specify rules under which counsel would be required, but offered guidelines:

> Presumptively, . . . counsel should be provided in cases where, after being informed of his right to request counsel, the probationer or parolee makes such a request, based on a timely and colorable claim (i) that he has not committed the alleged violation of the conditions upon which he is at liberty; or (ii) that, even if the violation is a matter of public record or is uncontested, there are substantial reasons which justified or mitigated the violation and make revocation inappropriate, and that the reasons are complex or otherwise difficult to develop or present. In passing on a request for the appointment of counsel, the responsible agency also should consider, especially in doubtful cases, whether the probationer appears to be capable of speaking effectively for himself. (*Gagnon v. Scarpelli,* pp. 790–91)

Gagnon thus resurrected the *Betts v. Brady* special circumstances test.

PRISON DISCIPLINARY HEARINGS Prisoners have even fewer procedural rights in disciplinary hearings than do probationers or parolees facing revocation, since they have much less freedom to lose than probationers or parolees. In *Wolff v. McDonnell* (1974), the Court required a due process hearing before an inmate could be subjected to major institutional forms of discipline involving losses of liberty, such as placement in solitary confinement or a loss of good time. But the dangerous reality of prisons, when combined with the lesser liberty interest of prisoners, led the Court to conclude that inmates had no absolute right to confront and cross-examine witnesses and were, therefore, at the mercy of the prison hearing officer's discretion. As for counsel, the Court, after reviewing its ruling in *Gagnon,* said, "At this stage of the development of these procedures we are not prepared to hold that inmates have a right to either **retained** or appointed counsel in disciplinary proceedings" (emphasis added). Thus, whereas a probationer facing revocation has a right to the assistance of retained counsel, a prisoner has no Fourteenth Amendment right to paid lawyer's presence in an administrative prison disciplinary hearing. In the interests of inmate safety and prison security, a prison may legitimately bar all attorneys from disciplinary hearings.

TERMINATION OF PARENTAL CUSTODY *Lassiter v. Department of Social Services* (1981) held that in civil proceedings where parents might have their parental rights over their children permanently severed, due process did not entitle the parents to an absolute right to counsel. The appointment of an attorney was left to the discretion of the judge on a case-by-case basis. The Court relied on the formal logic of the misdemeanor trial cases: indigents have an inalienable right to counsel only in those proceedings which result in the *actual* loss of personal liberty. The dissenting justices were appalled that greater rights were granted to a shoplifter jailed for a few months than to a parent faced with the total and irrevocable termination of all rights of custody and visitation. Justice Blackmun, dissenting in *Lassiter,* also pointed out that the legal issues in a parental termination hearing are neither simple nor easily defined and, therefore, require the assistance of counsel for such a procedure to be fair.

PSYCHIATRIC EXPERT WITNESS The case-by-case approach was applied in *Ake v. Oklahoma* (1985), where the Court held that a psychiatrist must be provided for an indigent defendant whenever insanity is reasonably raised as an issue. The holding was based on a combination of equal protection and due process reasoning. According to Justice Marshall, "[m]eaningful access to justice has been the consistent theme of these cases. . . . [A] criminal trial is fundamentally unfair if the State proceeds against an individual defendant without making certain that he has access to the raw materials integral to the building of an effective defense."

SUMMARY COURT MARTIAL *Middendorf v. Henry* (1976) held that a summary court-martial was not a criminal prosecution within the meaning of the Sixth Amendment. Under due process, a defendant is not constitutionally entitled to counsel in a summary court-martial where the maximum penalty could not exceed thirty days' confinement. In addition, analysis of the summary court-martial's function demonstrated that, unlike special and general courts-martial where counsel was provided, in summary proceedings the goal is to exercise justice promptly for purposes of discipline. The proceeding, informal and conducted by one officer has none of the trappings of a courtroom. Justice Rehnquist noted that the potential of confinement was not a controlling factor in not labeling the proceeding a criminal prosecution because it occurred within the special context of the military community.

JUVENILE DELINQUENCY TRIALS The Court held in *In re Gault* (1967), that a juvenile delinquency adjudication is not a criminal trial within the contemplation of the Sixth Amendment. Yet, under the Due Process Clause, the Court held that an adjudication of juvenile delinquency, that may result in commitment to an institution, is so much like an adult criminal trial that the provision of counsel was essential. If the child or parents could not afford counsel, the state was required to appoint a lawyer to represent the child.

Limitations on the Right to Counsel

RIGHT TO CHOOSE RETAINED COUNSEL The right to retain one's own counsel for a criminal defense is not absolute. "Regardless of his persuasive powers, an advocate who is not a member of the bar may not represent clients (other than himself) in court. Similarly, a defendant may not insist on representation by an attorney he cannot afford or who for other reasons declines to represent the defendant. Nor may a defendant insist on the counsel of an attorney who has a previous or ongoing relationship with an opposing party, even when the opposing party is the government." (*Wheat v. United States* 1988, p. 159). In *Wheat,* the Court held that a trial court could deny a defendant the counsel of his choice if, according to the district court's opinion, the representation carried a substantial possibility of a **conflict of interest**. This ruling subordinates the right to counsel to that of a fair adversary trial. Here, the court was concerned that **multiple representation** of three drug-sale defendants in separate trials by the same lawyer would undermine the lawyer's ability to cross-examine his clients. Thus, even though the defendants were willing to waive their right to a trial free of conflict of interest, the Court refused to accept their waivers. Four dissenting justices agreed that the right to select a lawyer is not absolute, but they would recognize a presumption in favor of a defendant's counsel of choice. In a stinging dissent, Justice Stevens characterized the Court's rule in *Wheat* as paternalistic and said, "This is not the first case in which the Court has demonstrated 'its apparent unawareness of the function of the independent lawyer as a guardian of our freedom.'"

PAYMENT AND ASSET FORFEITURE Two 1989 decisions upheld Congressional acts which allow prosecutors to freeze assets of suspected organized crime and drug dealers "before trial [and] without regard to whether the person will have enough money left to hire a lawyer."[33] The **asset forfeiture** law, used aggressively by federal prosecutors, was thought to undermine the Sixth Amendment right to adequate representation. *Caplin & Drysdale v. United States* was a suit by a law firm for its legal fees, which had been placed in escrow before trial, and which the government tried to seize after their client's conviction. In *United States v. Monsanto*, pretrial freezing of assets forced the defendant to rely on a **public defender.** The Supreme Court, 5–4, found both practices to be constitutional.

The forfeiture law made assets that were proceeds of crime government property from the commission of the crime. Since illegal assets were declared government property, a defendant's payment to her lawyer was, in effect, spending someone else's (i.e., the government's) money. Relying on *Wheat v. United States,* the Court said that "a defendant may not insist on representation by an attorney he cannot afford." The law created some exemptions to this rule (owners of stolen property and some innocent retailers), but none for attorneys' fees.

Four dissenting justices felt that the constitutional requirement of adequate representation required the Court to create an exemption for legal fees so that the alleged proceeds of a crime could be used for lawyers. They argued that pretrial asset freezing would "undermine the adversary system as we know it" because it gives the Government "an intolerable degree of power over any private attorney who takes on the task of representing a defendant in a forfeiture case." It allows prosecutors to

> use the forfeiture weapon against a defense attorney who is particularly talented or aggressive on the client's behalf—the attorney who is better than what, in the Government's view, the defendant deserves. The spectre of the Government's

> selectively excluding only the most talented defense counsel is a serious threat to the equality of forces necessary for the adversarial system to perform at its best. (*Caplin & Drysdale v. United States,* 1989).

MEANINGFUL ATTORNEY-CLIENT RELATIONSHIP *Morris v. Slappy* (1983) held that the Sixth Amendment does not guarantee a meaningful relationship between defendant and appointed counsel. A deputy public defender represented Slappy at a preliminary hearing and supervised an extensive investigation in his rape prosecution. Shortly before trial, the deputy public defender was hospitalized for emergency surgery and a senior trial attorney from the public defender's office was assigned to the case. Slappy claimed that the attorney did not have enough time to prepare the case and moved for a **continuance.** The newly assigned attorney stated that he was prepared and that a further delay would not benefit him in presenting the case. The trial court denied Slappy's motion, the trial continued, and Slappy was found guilty by a jury on three counts. During a second trial of counts left unresolved in the first trial, Slappy refused to cooperate with or even speak to his attorney; the jury returned a guilty verdict on the other counts. The federal appeals court, in a federal habeas corpus action, held that the Sixth Amendment includes the right to a meaningful attorney-client relationship.

The Supreme Court reversed, and held that under the circumstances of this case, there was no Sixth Amendment violation by the trial court refusing to grant a continuance when the attorney himself did not want one. The Court rejected the novel idea that an indigent defendant is guaranteed a "meaningful" relationship with assigned counsel; furthermore, an indigent defendant does not have an unqualified right to the appointment of counsel of his or her own choosing. Justice Brennan, while concurring in the decision, noted that lower federal courts have recognized the importance of a defendant's relationship with his attorney, so that a defendant with *retained* counsel was seen to have "a qualified right to continue that relationship." The qualified right is not the guarantee of "rapport" between client and attorney. Rather, according to Justice Brennan, where an attorney has put sufficient work into case so that she has become knowledgeable of its intricacies, a court should take into account the length of delay before allowing another attorney to try the case.

RECOUPMENT OF COSTS The governmental unit that pays for indigent assigned counsel may constitutionally seek to recoup the costs of the defense whenever the defendant has the means to pay. According to *Fuller v. Oregon* (1974), a **recoupment** law does not violate the Equal Protection Clause providing it allows the indigent person to claim all the exemptions granted to other judgment debtors in the state's civil code and does not require payment if the defendant remains or again becomes indigent. The *exemption* of indigents who are *acquitted* was deemed a rational distinction in the law. Dissenting justices felt that recoupment would have a "chilling effect" on the right to counsel; an indigent defendant would decline to accept free counsel knowing that he or she may have to repay the costs of the defense. However, Justice Stewart thought this unlikely because of the protections in the statute ensuring that an indigent cannot be compelled to pay. The Court also noted that defendants whose financial status places them just above the poverty line may have to go into debt in order to pay the costs of a criminal defense. "We cannot say that the Constitution requires that those only slightly poorer must remain forever immune from any obligation to shoulder the expenses of their legal defense, even when they are able to pay without hardship."

The Right to Counsel on Appeal

"[E]very state and the federal system provide some means of review to defendants in criminal cases. However, according to a long line of Supreme Court opinions, there is no constitutional mandate that states provide any type of review process for defendants convicted in their criminal courts."[34] If so, does this mean that there is no right to counsel on appeal? The appellate process is not included within the wording of the Sixth Amendment's "criminal prosecution." The Supreme Court has analyzed the question of the right to counsel on appeal in state courts under the Fourteenth Amendment and has applied a functional analysis. It has concluded that counsel is required on first appeals as of right, but is not required for subsequent, discretionary appeals.

RIGHT TO COUNSEL ON FIRST, MANDATORY APPEAL *Douglas v. California* (1963) held that the Fourteenth Amendment guarantees a defendant the right to representation of counsel on a first, mandatory appeal. By the mid-twentieth century, every state had, by its own laws, granted a convicted criminal defendant the right to one mandatory appeal. Not every state guaranteed counsel for indigents to prepare and argue the appeal as of right. In *Douglas,* a California rule allowed the appellate court to review the trial record and decide, for the defendant, whether an attorney would serve any useful purpose. Indigent defendants, convicted of robbery and assault with intent to commit murder, petitioned the state court of appeal for assistance of counsel. This request was denied by the district court of appeal, which made "an independent investigation of the record" and determined that appointing a lawyer for the defendants would not be "of advantage to the defendant or helpful to the appellate court." The California Supreme Court upheld this procedure. In contrast, the "federal courts must honor [a defendant's] request for counsel [on first appeal] regardless of what they think the merits of the case may be; and 'representation in the role of an advocate is required.'"

The United States Supreme Court overturned the California procedure as invidious discrimination against persons too poor to hire a lawyer to assist them on appeal. It paraphrased *Griffin v. Illinois:* "For there can be no equal justice where the kind of an appeal a man enjoys "depends on the amount of money he has." A person with means will present his or her case to the appellate court with "the full benefit of written briefs and oral argument by counsel." A person who cannot afford a lawyer has to rely on a judge to review the record without the benefit of partisan legal analysis and argument. "Any real chance he may have had of showing that his appeal has hidden merit is deprived him when the court decides on an *ex parte* examination of the record that the assistance of counsel is not required." Under this circumstance, the majority held that counsel must be provided. The majority muddied the equal protection basis of its holding by stating: "When an indigent is forced to run this gantlet of a preliminary showing of merit, the right to appeal does not comport with fair procedure." Fairness is the due process test. Thus, the loosely written majority opinion seemed to base its decision both on due process and equal protection.

The opinion was careful to note that the guarantee of counsel on appeal did not apply to second, discretionary appeals, such as writs of habeas corpus or petitions for certiorari. Also, the majority acknowledged that a state can allow differences based on wealth as long as it does not draw pernicious lines between the rich and the poor. For example, an indigent granted counsel cannot insist on the most highly paid lawyer available.

The dissenting opinion of Justice Harlan zeroed in on the looseness of the majority opinion. Noting that the majority appeared to rely on both equal protection and due process grounds, Justice Harlan concluded that the Equal Protection Clause is not the proper basis for a holding. "[I]ts application to cases like the present one can lead only to mischievous results." He believed the issue had to be judged under the Due Process Clause and felt that California's procedure for determining the need for appellate counsel did not violate due process.

Turning first to equal protection analysis, he pointed out that the state does not deny appeals to indigents. All laws create distinctions and any distinction which has a monetary effect will inevitably affect less wealthy persons more harshly. For example, a uniform sales tax, a state university tuition, municipal water fees determined by the amount used, and standard criminal fines or fixed bail for specific offenses are all more easily paid by those with greater wealth. If the Equal Protection Clause prevented such a result, it would either stymie all lawmaking or require the ruthless leveling of all persons to a condition of equality. Therefore, the "Equal Protection Clause does not impose on the States 'an affirmative duty to lift the handicaps flowing from differences in economic circumstances.'"

Justice Harlan then addressed the issue of

> whether or not the state rule, as applied in this case, is consistent with the requirements of fair procedure guaranteed by the Due Process Clause. . . . The State's responsibility under the Due Process Clause is to provide justice for all. Refusal to furnish criminal indigents with some things that others can afford may fall short of constitutional standards of fairness. The problem before us is whether this is such a case.

His analysis noted that "appellate review is in itself not required by the Fourteenth Amendment." Thus, whether California's "rules with respect to the appointment of counsel" are unconstitutionally arbitrary or unreasonable has to be determined *"in the context of the particular appellate procedure that it has established."* In this context, appellate review appears simple: "the kinds of questions that may arise on appeal are circumscribed by the record of the proceedings that led to the conviction; they do not encompass the large variety of tactical and strategic problems that must be resolved at the trial." Therefore, the California procedure guarantees the defendant "full consideration of his appeal" when a judge or clerk reviews the pauper's case as opposed to an assigned attorney. Justice Harlan pointed out that the United States Supreme Court does not grant free counsel to indigents who petition the Court for writs of certiorari.

Finally, Justice Harlan thought there was nothing special about a first appeal being granted as a matter of right. Fairness should dictate that an indigent be granted free counsel in both mandatory and discretionary appeals or in neither: "Nor can it well be suggested that having appointed counsel is more necessary to the fair administration of justice in an initial appeal taken as a matter of right, which the reviewing court on the full record has already determined to be frivolous, than in a petition asking a higher appellate court to exercise its discretion to consider what may be a substantial constitutional claim." This admission was not followed by the conservative majority that decided, in the next significant case, that counsel was not required in discretionary appeals.

RIGHT TO COUNSEL ON SECOND, DISCRETIONARY APPEALS A decade later, a more conservative Supreme Court refused to extend the guarantee of counsel to second, discretionary appeals. *Ross v. Moffitt* (1974) consolidated two cases from North Carolina, involving two defendants found guilty at trial who had pursued their one appeal as of right with state appointed counsel, and whose convictions were upheld. One defendant requested counsel to assist him in pursuing a discretionary habeas corpus writ to the state supreme court and the other was denied court-appointed counsel to prepare a petition for a writ of certiorari to the United States Supreme Court. North Carolina trial courts denied their request for state paid lawyers. The state court of appeals reversed, ruling that counsel was beneficial to a person seeking discretionary review, and therefore: "As long as the state provides such procedures and allows other convicted felons to seek access to the higher court with the help of retained counsel, there is a marked absence of fairness in denying an indigent the assistance of counsel as he seeks access to the same court. . . . The same concepts of fairness and equality, which require counsel in a first appeal of right, require counsel in other and subsequent discretionary appeals."

The Supreme Court reversed this decision in an opinion by Justice Rehnquist who borrowed heavily from Justice Harlan's dissent in *Douglas* and curiously turned the decision on its head. Unlike Justice Harlan, who thought that equal protection was a weak argument and that due process was the real issue, Justice Rehnquist quickly dismissed the due process argument and focused his attention on equal protection. He noted at the outset that "'Due process' emphasizes fairness between the State and the individual dealing with the State, regardless of how other individuals in the same situation may be treated. 'Equal protection,' on the other hand, emphasizes disparity in treatment by a State between classes of individuals whose situations are arguably indistinguishable."

The due process basis of a right to counsel for indigents pursuing a discretionary appeal was collapsed into an equal protection issue. According to Justice Rehnquist, since there is no constitutional right to an appeal, and since a convicted defendant pursuing a second appeal seeks to upset his prior determination of guilt, the fact that an appeal procedure has been authorized by the state, "does not automatically mean that a State then acts unfairly by refusing to provide counsel to indigent defendants at every stage of the way. . . . Unfairness results only if indigents are singled out by the State and denied meaningful access to the appellate system because of their poverty. That question is more profitably considered under an equal protection analysis."

Justice Rehnquist pointed out that the "Fourteenth Amendment 'does not require absolute equality or precisely equal advantages.' . . . It does require that the state appellate system be 'free of unreasoned distinctions." A state rule that effectively cut off an indigent's right to pursue a discretionary appeal would violate due process, since there is no reasonable basis for allowing a person of average means to pursue a writ. Nonetheless, "[t]he question is not one of absolutes, but one of degrees." The Court examined the procedures in detail and concluded that North Carolina's procedure did not create an "unreasoned distinction" in allowing a wealthier person with a lawyer to pursue a writ while not providing counsel for an indigent petitioner. It said that the defendant had already "received the benefit of counsel in examining the record of his trial and in preparing an appellate brief on his behalf for the state Court of Appeals." As a result, the defendant

> will have, at the very least, a transcript or other record of trial proceedings, a brief on his behalf in the Court of Appeals setting forth his claims of error, and in many cases an opinion by the Court of Appeals disposing of his case. These materials, supplemented by whatever submission respondent may make *pro se,* would appear to provide the Supreme Court of North Carolina with an adequate basis for its decision to grant or deny review (*Ross v. Moffitt,* 1974).

Thus, since the "raw materials" needed to evaluate the case are before the appellate court in a discretionary appeal, no unfairness results from an indigent petitioner pursuing a writ without the benefit of an attorney. This conclusion is fortified by noting that the purpose of discretionary appeals "is not whether there has been 'a correct adjudication of guilt' in every individual case, . . . but rather whether 'the subject matter of the appeal has significant public interest,' [or] whether 'the cause involves legal principles of major significance to the jurisprudence of the State.'" Thus, even if the Supreme Court believes that a lower court decision was incorrect, it may deny certiorari if the case does not raise an important issue of legal policy.

The majority opinion, noting that counsel may be useful to a defendant pursuing a discretionary appeal, argued that a discretionary appeal is not as demanding as a trial or a first appeal. "The duty of the State under our cases is not to duplicate the legal arsenal that may be privately retained by a criminal defendant in a continuing effort to reverse his conviction, but only to assure the indigent defendant an adequate opportunity to present his claims fairly in the context of the State's appellate process." At any rate, a state could, by statute, provide free counsel to indigents pursuing discretionary appeals.

Justice Douglas, at the twilight of his career, dissented in *Ross* on the equity and fairness grounds specified in *Douglas.* He quoted from *Douglas v. California* that the "same concepts of fairness and equality, which require counsel in a first appeal of right, require counsel in other and subsequent discretionary appeals." But that belief, so resonant to an older generation, failed to convince a newer generation of justices that the constitution required state and local governments to pay for counsel in the context of discretionary appeals.

THE RIGHT TO COUNSEL FOR DISCRETIONARY APPEAL BY INDIGENT DEATH ROW INMATES *Murray v. Giarratano* (1989) held that under *Ross* indigent death-row inmates seeking postconviction review of their death sentences, after their first appeals, had no Fourteenth

ROSS V. MOFFITT IN THE STATES

"The Colorado Constitution provides a broader right to assigned counsel than does the federal Constitution for discretionary appeals to the state's highest court.[35] *People v. Valdez*[36] reasoned that since defendants have a right derived from the state constitution to petition the state supreme court for certiorari, they therefore have 'a right to obtain counsel and to rely upon such counsel's skill for the purpose of preparing and filing that application.' "[37]

Barry Latzer, *State Constitutional Criminal Law,* § 5.7.

Amendment right to counsel at the expense of the state. The majority was unmoved by the petitioner's three arguments that were seen as valid by four dissenting justices: (1) death-row inmates are under greater emotional stress than other inmates and thus less able to write adequate legal briefs; (2) Virginia's law postponed some issues normally heard at first appeal to the postconviction proceedings, thus making these second appeals more like first appeals for death-row inmates; and (3) "a grim deadline imposes a finite [time] limit on the condemned person's capacity for useful research." In rejecting these arguments, the Court emphatically limited the right to counsel on Fourteenth Amendment equal protection and due process grounds in procedures other than the trial. While indigents retain the same basic rights as wealthier persons, there are limits to what the state must do to remedy the infirmities in the justice system caused by economic inequality.

THE RIGHT TO SELF-REPRESENTATION

The Sixth Amendment right to the assistance of counsel has, from the beginning of the Republic, coexisted with a criminal defendant's seemingly contradictory right of self-representation. Before the Supreme Court constitutionalized the right of a defendant to proceed ***pro se***—in one's own behalf—federal statutes and the laws of thirty-six states upheld such a right.[38] There is no sure way to know the extent of *pro se* defense; one expert estimated that approximately fifty such trials occurred in 1997. A survey in one jurisdiction indicates that civil litigants are more likely to represent themselves than are criminal defendants and that the number of *pro se* defendants is rising.[39]

Self-Representation and the Waiver of Counsel

Self-representation reflects the American value of self-reliance and the distrust of lawyers, but also may conflict with the right to a fair trial. Some defend themselves in notorious, political trials, in order to publicize their point of view. Angela Davis, an African-American communist and philosophy instructor was tried in California for abetting murder in the Soledad Brothers case and won an acquittal in 1972. She represented herself, but had substantial assistance. Jack Kevorkian, the well-known proponent and practitioner of physician-assisted suicide, was acquitted three times when ably defended by counsel, but was convicted of murder when he sought to defend himself.[40] *Pro se* defense is more likely to occur when a defendant becomes frustrated with the actual or perceived incompetence of assigned counsel or a public defender, or when a defendant sharply disagrees with the legal strategy of counsel. Also, a defendant may request self-representation with the underhanded intention of causing delay or a mistrial by asking for a lawyer once the trial has begun.

Several problems arise as a result of self-representation. The obvious one is that a *pro se* defendant may cause a mockery of justice. A prime example is that of Colin Ferguson, who, claiming to have acted out of a sense of "black rage," shot and killed six and wounded nineteen commuters on a Long Island Railroad car in 1993. In 1993, the Supreme Court ruled, in *Godinez v. Moran*, that the standard of competency to waive counsel is the same as the standard to stand trial—a rational and factual understanding of the proceedings. Under this standard, Ferguson was allowed to dismiss his well-known "radical" lawyers, Ronald Kuby and the late William Kunstler, who wanted him to plead insanity and who correctly predicted that the trial would become a circus.[41] Against overwhelming evidence, Ferguson, who was articulate and spoke clearly, claimed that an unknown white man did the shooting; asked to subpoena President Clinton; claimed without any evidence that the jury he helped pick was biased;[42] and blandly cross-examined surviving shooting victims who then testified that Ferguson shot them.[43] He told jurors that "There were 93 counts to that indictment, 93 counts only because it matches the year 1993. If it had it been 1925, it would have been a 25-count indictment."[44] His standby counsel, Alton Rose, sitting while Ferguson made it impossible for an insanity defense to succeed, could "only watch in silence from the defense table, where he often slumps, clasping his head as if trying to prevent it from splitting apart in frustration."[45] A person who avidly watched the televised trial said, "I know it's the way the legal system works, but the way we let this guy carry on [made] buffoons out of all of us."[46]

A problem with *pro se* defense is that it may require a judge to intervene and tell the defendant that he has made an error and instruct him as to how to proceed. This creates the appearance of bias to the jury and may make it difficult for the judge to be completely impartial in ruling on trial motions. In these instances, it falls to the trial judge, while inquiring into a waiver of the right to counsel, to discover whether the defendant has the legal knowledge to conduct a trial and whether his or her actions are likely to cause costly delays, a mistrial, and/or a subsequent appeal.

Judges treat the desire to waive counsel as an unusual and extreme step. If a defendant expresses a desire to defend *pro se,* the judge personally informs the defendant "of the many procedural complications of representing oneself, that he will be given no special treatment, and that waiving counsel is generally unwise."[47] In the colloquy with the defendant, the judge takes pains to ensure that the waiver is *voluntary,* that it is *unequivocal* and *express,* that it is *knowing* and *intelligent,* and that the defendant is *mentally able* to make the waiver. The verbal exchange between the judge and the defendant is placed on the *record.* If, after all this, the defendant meets the minimum standard of competency and continues to insist on self-representation, the judge has no right to deny this a constitutional right.

Faretta v. California

In *Faretta v. California* (1975), the Supreme Court decided, 6–3, that the Sixth Amendment established a right to self-representation and set down guidelines for *pro se defense.* Justice Stewart, writing for the majority, said that the issue "is whether a State may constitutionally hale a person into its criminal courts and there force a lawyer upon him, even when he insists that he wants to conduct his own defense" (*Faretta,* p. 807). Faretta, who had previously defended himself in court, was charged with grand theft. He felt that his assigned counsel in the Los Angeles Superior Court was too burdened with a high caseload to adequately assist him. The trial judge, after questioning Faretta about the hearsay rule and the law regarding challenges to potential jurors, ruled that Faretta had no constitutional right to self-representation. The trial was conducted with appointed counsel.

The core of the decision was the basic significance of the Sixth Amendment's text:

> The Sixth Amendment does not provide merely that a defense shall be made for the accused; it grants to the accused personally the right to make his defense. It is the accused, not counsel, who must be "informed of the nature and cause of the accusation," who must be "confronted with the witnesses against him," and who must be accorded "compulsory process for obtaining witnesses in his favor." Although not stated in the Amendment in so many words, the right to self-representation—to make one's own defense personally—is thus necessarily implied by the structure of the Amendment. The right to defend is given directly to the accused; for it is he who suffers the consequences if the defense fails.
>
> . . .
>
> The counsel provision supplements this design. It speaks of the "assistance" of counsel, and an assistant, however expert, is still an assistant. The language and spirit of the Sixth Amendment contemplate that counsel, like the other defense tools guaranteed by the Amendment, shall be an aid to a willing defendant—not an organ of the State interposed between an unwilling defendant and his right to defend himself personally. To thrust counsel upon the accused, against his considered wish, thus violates the logic of the Amendment. In such a case, counsel is not an assistant, but a master; and the right to make a defense is stripped of the personal character upon which the Amendment insists. It is true that when a defendant chooses to have a lawyer manage and present his case, law and tradition may allocate to the counsel the power to make binding decisions of trial strategy in many areas. . . . This allocation can only be justified, however, by the defendant's consent, at the outset, to accept counsel as his representative. An unwanted counsel "represents" the defendant only through a tenuous and unacceptable legal fiction. Unless the accused has acquiesced in such representation, the defense presented is not the defense guaranteed him by the Constitution, for, in a very real sense, it is not his defense . . . (*Faretta,* pp. 819–21).

The majority did not find that the right to counsel announced in *Gideon v. Wainwright* was inconsistent with the right to self representation: "Personal liberties are not rooted in the law of averages. The right to defend is personal" (*Faretta,* p. 834).

On the other hand, self-representation is not a license. The judge, while taking the waiver to counsel, has to be convinced that the defendant has ability to conduct the trial and is obligated to ensure that the defendant possesses the *minimal qualifications* to conduct the trial. "A defendant need not himself have the skill and experience of a lawyer in order competently and intelligently to choose self-representation." (*Faretta,* p. 835). Therefore, a judge cannot deny self-representation to a defendant simply because the defendant does not have an *expert knowledge* of criminal law and procedure. As the record in the case showed "that Faretta was literate, competent, and understanding, and that he was voluntarily exercising his informed free will," the trial judge was in error in denying him the right to represent himself, even if he did not have expert knowledge of hearsay rules (*Faretta,* pp. 835–36).

Chief Justice Burger, dissenting in *Faretta* (pp. 836–46), saw the basic right as the Sixth Amendment *right to a fair trial.* The entire justice system and the people at large have a stake in a fair and competent trial system. "That goal is ill-served, and the integrity of and public confidence in the system are undermined, when an easy conviction is obtained due to the defendant's ill-advised decision to waive counsel." Furthermore, the dissent saw the majority opinion as undermining the authority of the trial judge who should retain final discretion on this question, because the judge "is in the best position to determine whether the accused is capable of conducting his defense."

Standby Counsel

The practice of the judge appointing **standby counsel** to assist a *pro se* defendant was upheld by the Supreme Court in *McKaskle v. Wiggins* (1984). Justice O'Connor ruled that a defendant's Sixth Amendment rights are not violated when standby counsel is appointed, even over the defendant's objection. To ensure that standby counsel does not overwhelm the defendant's personal right to make a defense, Justice O'Connor specified two rules to guide the conduct of such counsel and to determine when the attorney might have undermined the defendant's rights.

> "First, the *pro se* defendant is entitled to preserve *actual control* over the case he chooses to present to the jury. . . . If standby counsel's participation over the defendant's objection effectively allows counsel to make or substantially interfere with any significant tactical decisions, or to control the questioning of witnesses, or to speak *instead* of the defendant on any matter of importance, the *Faretta* right is eroded.
>
> "Second, participation by standby counsel without the defendant's consent should not be allowed to destroy the *jury's perception that the defendant is representing himself.* The defendant's appearance in the status of one conducting his own defense . . . exists to affirm the accused's individual dignity and autonomy."[48]

Dissenting justices suggested that this two-pronged rule actually gives trial justices little guidance on how to restrain standby counsel from taking over the case from the self-represented defendant. Also, the dissenters sharply differed with the majority about whether the activity of standby counsel in this case (including over fifty interventions in a three-day trial precipitating some disagreements that were observed by the jury) amounted to a violation of the *Faretta* self-representation right.

Four reasons support the regular appointment of standby counsel. (1) If a *pro se* defendant, purposely or out of confusion, decides during trial to ask for a lawyer, there will be no delay—standby counsel will be able to immediately continue the case. (2) Standby counsel, by providing expert advise, helps the *pro se* defendant "exercise his right of self-representation more effectively and begins to level the playing field in the courtroom."[49] (3) Standby counsel can assist "a defendant of questionable mental or emotional fortitude," who still meets the low appointment standard of *Godinez v. Moran* (1993), in making a meaningful defense and thus maintain the fairness of the judicial process.[50] (4) Standby counsel eliminates the need for a judge to give the appearance of bias by giving the defendant practice pointers during the trial.

However, some problems may occur from the use of standby counsel. As *McKaskle v. Wiggins* noted, when standby counsel interferes too strongly, the defendant may feel that his or her right to self-representation is infringed. Also, it is unwise for a court to appoint as standby counsel the lawyer whom the defendant dismissed. Finally, "hybrid representation," where both the defendant and standby counsel appear before the jury, should be disallowed. It causes confusion in the jury's mind and may prejudice defendant's case. To correct this, Marie Williams suggests that (a) standby counsel be appointed in every *pro se* defense, (b) the jury be instructed as to the constitutionality and nature of standby counsel, and (c) that hybrid representation not be allowed except when the defendant is cross-examining the victim and when the defendant takes the stand to testify.[51]

THE EFFECTIVE ASSISTANCE OF COUNSEL

In 1970, the Supreme Court clarified that the Sixth Amendment assistance of counsel guarantee in criminal cases means the *effective* assistance of retained and appointed counsel (*McMann v. Richardson*). *Strickland v. Washington* (1984) began to define the constitutional standards of effective assistance.

Applying the *Strickland* Test

Strickland's rules apply not only to felony trials and death penalty sentencing proceedings, but also at plea bargaining.[52] The Court did not definitively rule out the application of *Strickland* to ordinary sentencing, but it hinted that a Sixth Amendment effective assistance rule did not apply. Sentencing proceedings are often informal. They often involve standardless discretion for which criteria of effective assistance are hard to ascertain. Capital sentencing, on the other hand, "is sufficiently like a trial in its adversarial format and in the existence of standards for decision" so the two-pronged test applies.

PROOF OF INEFFECTIVE ASSISTANCE *United States v. Cronic* (1984) ruled that ineffective assistance of counsel is not to be inferred. A defendant convicted of mail fraud claimed ineffective assistance of counsel because (a) the lawyer was inexperienced; (b) the charge was serious; (c) the facts were complex; (d) the time to investigate was limited to thirty days; and (e) some witnesses were inaccessible. The *Strickland* standard puts the *burden of proof* on the convicted

• CASE & COMMENTS •

Strickland v. Washington
466 U.S. 668, 104 S.Ct. 2052, 80 L.Ed.2d 674 (1984)

JUSTICE O'CONNOR delivered the opinion of the Court.

* * *

I

A

[Respondent, Washington, was found guilty and sentenced to death for a crime spree that included three murders, torture, kidnapping, and theft. He confessed to the police. Against the advice of his experienced, assigned defense lawyer, Washington waived a jury trial and pleaded guilty, telling the judge that he accepted responsibility for his acts. Against counsel's advice, once again, Washington also waived an advisory jury on the death penalty issue.]

[*Case history:* after his trial, conviction and sentence to death, Washington appealed as of right to the Florida Supreme Court which upheld his conviction. He then brought a collateral appeal in state courts on ineffective assistance of counsel grounds; the issue was heard by a trial judge who ruled that counsel was effective and this ruling was upheld on appeal by the Florida Supreme Court. Washington then filed a petition for a writ of habeas corpus in federal district court, which held an evidentiary hearing and found for the state. This denial was appealed to the United States Court of Appeals for the Fifth Circuit, which remanded for further hearings. This decision was then vacated by Unit B of the former Fifth Circuit, now the Eleventh Circuit, which reheard the case *en banc,* and reversed the District Court and remanded the case for new factfinding under the newly announced standards. Florida then petitioned the United States Supreme Court, which reversed the Court of Appeals, finding that the federal district court was correct in denying the writ of habeas corpus.]

* * *

In preparing for the sentencing hearing, counsel spoke with respondent about his background. He also spoke on the telephone with respondent's wife and mother, though he did not follow up on the one unsuccessful effort to meet with them. He did not otherwise seek out character witnesses for respondent. **[a]** *** Nor did he request a psychiatric examination, since his conversations with his client gave no indication that respondent had psychological problems. ***

[a] Character witnesses testify only about a defendant's general reputation and rarely make negative statements. Judges are less likely to be impressed by character witnesses than are juries.

Counsel decided not to present and hence not to look further for evidence concerning respondent's character and emotional state. That decision reflected trial counsel's sense of hopelessness about overcoming the evidentiary effect of respondent's confessions to the gruesome crimes. *** It also reflected the judgment that it was advisable to rely on the plea colloquy for evidence about respondent's background and about his claim of emotional stress: the plea colloquy communicated sufficient information about these subjects, and by foregoing the opportunity to present new evidence on these subjects, counsel prevented the State from cross-examining respondent on his claim and from putting on psychiatric evidence of its own.

Counsel also excluded from the sentencing hearing other evidence he thought was potentially damaging. He successfully moved to exclude respondent's "rap sheet." *** Because he judged that a presentence report might prove more detrimental than helpful, as it would have included respondent's criminal history and thereby undermined the claim of no significant history of criminal activity, he did not request that one be prepared. ***

At the sentencing hearing, counsel's strategy [stressed Washington's remorse, his acceptance of responsibility, the stress that he claimed he was under at the time of the crime spree, and his apparently clean prior criminal record.] The State put on evidence and witnesses largely for the purpose of describing the details of the crimes. Counsel did not cross-examine the medical experts who testified about the manner of death of respondent's victims.

[The trial judge found that the aggravating circumstances outweighed the mitigating circumstances and sentenced Washington to death.]

• CASE & COMMENTS •

* * *

B

*** Respondent challenged counsel's assistance in six respects. He asserted that counsel was ineffective because he failed to move for a continuance to prepare for sentencing, to request a psychiatric report, to investigate and present character witnesses, to seek a presentence investigation report, to present meaningful arguments to the sentencing judge, and to investigate the medical examiner's reports or cross-examine the medical experts. **[b]** In support of the claim, respondent submitted 14 affidavits from friends, neighbors, and relatives stating that they would have testified if asked to do so. He also submitted one psychiatric report and one psychological report stating that respondent, though not under the influence of extreme mental or emotional disturbance, was "chronically frustrated and depressed because of his economic dilemma" at the time of his crimes. **[c]**

[b] Part I A indicates that the defense lawyer had a tactical reason for his failures to take these actions.

[c] Would this evidence convince you that a spree killer does not deserve the death penalty?

[Florida courts found Washington's six claims to be groundless: (1) there was no legal basis for seeking a continuance; (2) state psychiatric examinations of Washington disclosed no mental abnormalities; (3) character witnesses would not have rebutted aggravating circumstances and would have added no mitigating circumstances; (4) a presentence report would have brought out the respondent's prior criminal record, which was otherwise kept out of the proceedings; (5) counsel presented an "admirable" argument for the respondent in light of the overwhelming nature of the aggravating circumstances; and (6) cross-examination of the state's psychiatric witnesses could have led the prosecution, on rebuttal, to undermine Washington's claim that he was under stress when he went on his crime spree.]

*** [T]he trial court concluded that respondent had not shown that counsel's assistance reflected any substantial and serious deficiency measurably below that of competent counsel that was likely to have affected the outcome of the sentencing proceeding. The court specifically found: "[A]s a matter of law, the record affirmatively demonstrates beyond any doubt that even if [counsel] had done each of the *** things [that respondent alleged counsel had failed to do] at the time of sentencing, there is not even the remotest chance that the outcome would have been any different. The plain fact is that the aggravating circumstances proved in this case were completely *overwhelming*. ***" ***

The Florida Supreme Court affirmed the denial of relief. *** [Washington then filed a federal habeas corpus action in a federal district court. Upon dismissal he appealed. The federal court of appeals remanded the case to the district court to determine whether counsel was ineffective in this case on the grounds that he did not investigate every plausible line of defense. The state of Florida challenged this ruling to the Supreme Court.]

II

*** The right to counsel plays a crucial role in the adversarial system embodied in the Sixth Amendment, since access to counsel's skill and knowledge is necessary to accord defendants the "ample opportunity to meet the case of the prosecution" to which they are entitled. *** **[d]**

[d] The right to counsel is placed in the context of the right to a fair trial; thus it serves the interests of society while benefitting the individual defendant.

*** That a person who happens to be a lawyer is present at trial alongside the accused, however, is not enough to satisfy the constitutional command. The Sixth Amendment recognizes the right to the assistance of counsel because it envisions counsel's playing a role that is critical to the ability of the adversarial system to produce just results. An accused is entitled to be assisted by an attorney, whether retained or appointed, who plays the role necessary to ensure that the trial is fair.

For that reason, the Court has recognized that "the right to counsel is the right to the effective assistance of counsel." *** **[e]**

[e] Part II of Justice O'Connor's opinion lays down general rules before moving on to the specific issues that arise in this case.

*** The benchmark for judging any claim of ineffectiveness must be whether counsel's conduct so undermined the proper functioning of the adversarial process that the trial cannot be relied on as having produced a just result. [This principle also applies to capital sentencing proceedings because they are similar to trials in having one of two results, but it does not apply to ordinary sentencing proceedings which can result in an array of different sentences.]

• CASE & COMMENTS •

III

A convicted defendant's claim that counsel's assistance was so defective as to require reversal of a conviction or death sentence has two components. **[f]** First, the defendant must show that counsel's **performance was deficient.** This requires showing that counsel made errors so serious that counsel was not functioning as the "counsel" guaranteed the defendant by the Sixth Amendment. Second, the defendant must show that the deficient performance prejudiced the defense. This requires showing that counsel's errors were so serious as to deprive the defendant of a fair trial, a trial whose result is reliable. Unless a defendant makes both showings, it cannot be said that the conviction or death sentence resulted from a breakdown in the adversary process that renders the result unreliable.

[f] Here, the Court establishes a "two-prong" test for the effective assistance of counsel.

A

[T]he proper standard for attorney performance is that of reasonably effective assistance. *** When a convicted defendant complains of the ineffectiveness of counsel's assistance, the defendant must show that counsel's representation fell below an objective standard of reasonableness. **[g]**

[g] The burden of proof is on the convicted defendant to prove that her lawyer was ineffective.

More specific guidelines are not appropriate. The Sixth Amendment refers simply to "counsel," not specifying particular requirements of effective assistance. It relies instead on the legal profession's maintenance of standards sufficient to justify the law's presumption that counsel will fulfill the role in the adversary process that the Amendment envisions. *** The proper measure of attorney performance remains simply reasonableness under prevailing professional norms.

*** Counsel's function is to assist the defendant, and hence counsel owes the client a duty of loyalty, a duty to avoid conflicts of interest. *** From counsel's function as assistant to the defendant derive the overarching duty to advocate the defendant's cause and the more particular duties to consult with the defendant on important decisions and to keep the defendant informed of important developments in the course of the prosecution. Counsel also has a duty to bring to bear such skill and knowledge as will render the trial a reliable adversarial testing process. *** **[h]**

[h] In this section, the Court gives only the general idea of what constitutes effective (or deficient) performance by a criminal defense lawyer. As a result, deficient performance must be determined from case-by-case decisions of the Supreme Court or federal courts of appeal.

These basic duties neither exhaustively define the obligations of counsel nor form a checklist for judicial evaluation of attorney performance. In any case presenting an ineffectiveness claim, the performance inquiry must be whether counsel's assistance was reasonable considering all the circumstances. Prevailing norms of practice as reflected in American Bar Association standards and the like *** are guides to determining what is reasonable, but they are only guides. No particular set of detailed rules for counsel's conduct can satisfactorily take account of the variety of circumstances faced by defense counsel or the range of legitimate decisions regarding how best to represent a criminal defendant. Any such set of rules would interfere with the constitutionally protected independence of counsel and restrict the wide latitude counsel must have in making tactical decisions. ***

Judicial scrutiny of counsel's performance must be highly deferential. It is all too tempting for a defendant to second-guess counsel's assistance after conviction or adverse sentence, and it is all too easy for a court, examining counsel's defense after it has proved unsuccessful, to conclude that a particular act or omission of counsel was unreasonable. *** [A] court must indulge a strong presumption that counsel's conduct falls within the wide range of reasonable professional assistance. *** There are countless ways to provide effective assistance in any given case. Even the best criminal defense attorneys would not defend a particular client in the same way. ***

[Intense scrutiny of lawyers' performances by appellate courts would produce a flood of ineffectiveness challenges that would make lawyers less willing to represent criminal defendants and undermine trust between attorney and client.]

*** A convicted defendant making a claim of ineffective assistance must identify the acts or omissions of counsel that are alleged not to have been the result of reasonable professional judgment. The court must then determine whether, in light of all the circumstances, the identified acts or omissions were outside the wide range of professionally competent assistance.

• CASE & COMMENTS •

* * *

B

An error by counsel, even if professionally unreasonable, does not warrant setting aside the judgment of a criminal proceeding if the error had no effect on the judgment. *** The purpose of the Sixth Amendment guarantee of counsel is to ensure that a defendant has the assistance necessary to justify reliance on the outcome of the proceeding. Accordingly, any deficiencies in counsel's performance must be prejudicial to the defense in order to constitute ineffective assistance under the Constitution. **[i]**

In certain Sixth Amendment contexts, prejudice is presumed. Actual or constructive denial of the assistance of counsel altogether is legally presumed to result in prejudice. *** Prejudice in these circumstances is so likely that case-by-case inquiry into prejudice is not worth the cost. ***

One type of actual ineffectiveness claim warrants a similar, though more limited, presumption of prejudice. In *Cuyler v. Sullivan,* [446 U.S. 335 (1980)], the Court held that prejudice is presumed when counsel is burdened by an actual conflict of interest. In those circumstances, counsel breaches the duty of loyalty, perhaps the most basic of counsel's duties. *** Prejudice is presumed only if the defendant demonstrates that counsel "actively represented conflicting interests" and that "an actual conflict of interest adversely affected his lawyer's performance." *** **[j]**

Conflict of interest claims aside, actual ineffectiveness claims alleging a deficiency in attorney performance are subject to a general requirement that the defendant affirmatively prove prejudice. *** Attorney errors come in an infinite variety and are as likely to be utterly harmless in a particular case as they are to be prejudicial. They cannot be classified according to likelihood of causing prejudice. Nor can they be defined with sufficient precision to inform defense attorneys correctly just what conduct to avoid. Representation is an art, and an act or omission that is unprofessional in one case may be sound or even brilliant in another. Even if a defendant shows that particular errors of counsel were unreasonable, therefore, the defendant must show that they actually had an adverse effect on the defense.

[i] *Prejudice* is used here to describe the second prong: whether counsel's performance substantially contributed to the guilty verdict or sentence of death. It does not mean "discrimination" in this context.

[j] The Court describes two cases of automatic prejudice: (1) no assistance of counsel and (2) conflict of interest, followed by analysis of cases where *actual* prejudice has to be determined by examining the facts of the case.

* * *

[The defendant cannot argue that his or her conviction would likely not have occurred because the jury would have nullified the law. The prejudice prong must be assessed on the basis of assuming that a conscientious jury would have applied legal standards impartially.]

*** When a defendant challenges a conviction, the question is whether there is a reasonable probability that, absent the errors, the factfinder would have had a reasonable doubt respecting guilt. When a defendant challenges a death sentence such as the one at issue in this case, the question is whether there is a reasonable probability that, absent the errors, the sentencer *** would have concluded that the balance of aggravating and mitigating circumstances did not warrant death. **[k]**

In making this determination, a court hearing an ineffectiveness claim must consider the totality of the evidence before the judge or jury. Some of the factual findings will have been unaffected by the errors, and factual findings that were affected will have been affected in different ways. Some errors will have had a pervasive effect on the inferences to be drawn from the evidence, altering the entire evidentiary picture, and some will have had an isolated, trivial effect. Moreover, a verdict or conclusion only weakly supported by the record is more likely to have been affected by errors than one with overwhelming record support. Taking the unaffected findings as a given, and taking due account of the effect of the errors on the remaining findings, a court making the prejudice inquiry must ask if the defendant has met the burden of showing that the decision reached would reasonably likely have been different absent the errors. **[l]**

[In Part V, the Court applied the standards announced in Parts II and III to the facts of the case. The majority concluded that the conduct of Washington's lawyer was adequate and was not the cause of the death penalty sentence.]

JUSTICE MARSHALL, dissenting.

[k] The appellate court deciding the prejudice prong of an ineffective assistance case must ask whether the outcome would likely have differed if the attorney had not made the errors which established deficient performance under the first prong.

[l] A "facts and circumstances" or "totality of the evidence" standard is open-ended; it is the antithesis of a "bright-line" rule. As with the deficient-performance prong, standards will develop incrementally as the courts decide specific cases.

• CASE & COMMENTS •

* * *

I

A

My objection to the performance standard adopted by the Court is that it is so malleable that, in practice, it will either have no grip at all or will yield excessive variation in the manner in which the Sixth Amendment is interpreted and applied by different courts. To tell lawyers and the lower courts that counsel for a criminal defendant must behave "reasonably" and must act like "a reasonably competent attorney," is to tell them almost nothing. In essence, the majority has instructed judges called upon to assess claims of ineffective assistance of counsel to advert to their own intuitions regarding what constitutes "professional" representation, and has discouraged them from trying to develop more detailed standards governing the performance of defense counsel. In my view, the Court has thereby not only abdicated its own responsibility to interpret the Constitution, but also impaired the ability of the lower courts to exercise theirs. **[m]**

[m] If Justice Marshall is correct, is it possible to specify good lawyering? Should Washington's lawyer have performed each of the six acts not done?

* * *

B

I object to the prejudice standard adopted by the Court for two independent reasons. First, it is often very difficult to tell whether a defendant convicted after a trial in which he was ineffectively represented would have fared better if his lawyer had been competent. Seemingly impregnable cases can sometimes be dismantled by good defense counsel. On the basis of a cold record, it may be impossible for a reviewing court confidently to ascertain how the government's evidence and arguments would have stood up against rebuttal and cross-examination by a shrewd, well-prepared lawyer. The difficulties of estimating prejudice after the fact are exacerbated by the possibility that evidence of injury to the defendant may be missing from the record precisely because of the incompetence of defense counsel. In view of all these impediments to a fair evaluation of the probability that the outcome of a trial was affected by ineffectiveness of counsel, it seems to me senseless to impose on a defendant whose lawyer has been shown to have been incompetent the burden of demonstrating prejudice. **[n]**

[n] In other words, Justice Marshall would eliminate the prejudice prong entirely. Any indication that a lawyer did something at trial that fell below proper practice standards would mean an automatic reversal and a new trial even if the evidence of a defendant's guilt is overwhelming and the error was not gross incompetence.

Second and more fundamentally, the assumption on which the Court's holding rests is that the only purpose of the constitutional guarantee of effective assistance of counsel is to reduce the chance that innocent persons will be convicted. In my view, the guarantee also functions to ensure that convictions are obtained only through fundamentally fair procedures. The majority contends that the Sixth Amendment is not violated when a manifestly guilty defendant is convicted after a trial in which he was represented by a manifestly ineffective attorney. I cannot agree. Every defendant is entitled to a trial in which his interests are vigorously and conscientiously advocated by an able lawyer. **[o]** A proceeding in which the defendant does not receive meaningful assistance in meeting the forces of the State does not, in my opinion, constitute due process.

[o] Justice Marshall was the most experienced trial attorney sitting on the bench in 1984. As an African-American lawyer challenging racial segregation in southern courts in the 1930s, 1940s, and 1950s, he often worked under extremely hostile circumstances. Should his experience give his views special weight?

* * *

STRICKLAND V. WASHINGTON IN THE STATES

"With few exceptions, state constitutional case law nearly always utilizes the *Strickland* test or a close approximation. . . . Three states—Hawaii, Massachusetts and Maine—offer state constitutional tests that differ from *Strickland's,* especially in the language of the prejudice prong."

Barry Latzer, *State Constitutional Criminal Law,* §

The test given by the Hawaii Supreme Court is: "The defendant has the burden of establishing ineffective assistance of counsel and must meet the following two-part test: 1) that there were specific errors or omissions reflecting counsel's lack of skill, judgment, or diligence; and 2) that such errors or omissions resulted in either the withdrawal or substantial impairment of a potentially meritorious defense." [*State v. Aplaca,* 837 P.2d 1298 (1992)] *Aplaca* ruled that "the decision not to conduct a pretrial investigation of prospective defense witnesses cannot be classified as a tactical decision or trial strategy." Thus, a lawyer must almost always conduct a pretrial investigation of the facts. The Massachusetts Supreme Judicial Court applied the ineffective assistance of counsel rule to ordinary (i.e., non-capital) sentencing, and held that a defendant who was deprived of effective assistance of counsel at sentencing is entitled to a new sentencing hearing. [*Commonwealth v. Lycus,* 406 Mass. 135; 546 N.E.2d 159 (1989)]

complainant to prove that her lawyer's assistance was ineffective. Cronic raised a set of relevant factors, but could not point to any *specific action* by his lawyer that showed deficient performance. If Cronic's position were accepted, the Court could find ineffective assistance even though the lawyer's performance was flawless. None of the factors in the case, alone or in combination, deprived Cronic of a fair trial: relevant evidence was supplied and the government's evidence cross-examined. The Court also noted in *Cronic* that the test of adequate performance did not require that the lawyer perform flawlessly in a trial. "When a true adversarial criminal trial has been conducted—even if defense counsel may have made demonstrable errors—the kind of testing envisioned by the Sixth Amendment has occurred."

EXAMPLE OF INEFFECTIVE ASSISTANCE An example of deficient performance is found in *Kimmelman v. Morrison* (1986). The defense lawyer in a rape prosecution failed to object to the introduction of illegally seized evidence, filed a late motion for the suppression of evidence, and did not ask for discovery of police reports that would have indicated that the seizure of evidence was arguably unconstitutional. The attorney's excuse was that he believed it was the state's responsibility to turn over all relevant evidence. Since there is no such general obligation, the Supreme Court ruled that the lawyer's failure to take normal and routine steps before trial to obtain relevant evidence was inexcusable negligence, amounting to deficient performance.[53]

EFFECTIVE ASSISTANCE AND TRUTH The attorney's obligation to maintain the integrity of the trial process and to elicit the truth can appear to conflict with the specific obligation to provide the best defense. It is fundamental to the adjudication process that evidence cannot be fabricated. A lawyer has no obligation to support a defendant with false testimony. In *Nix v. Whiteside* (1986), a defendant charged with murder claimed self-defense. He told his lawyer that he did not actually see a gun in his assailant's hand, but believed it was there. He wanted to testify that he saw "something metallic" because a jury would be more likely to believe the assailant had a gun. Counsel told Whiteside that as a matter of law, it was not necessary for the defendant to see a gun to prove self-defense, and made it clear that if Whiteside perjured himself, the lawyer would indicate this to the judge. Whiteside was convicted and argued that the lawyer's advice was ineffective assistance. The Supreme Court ruled that as there is no right, constitutional or otherwise, to testify falsely; therefore, the lawyer's assistance was not deficient.

Conflict of Interest

Multiple representation occurs when a retained or assigned attorney represents two or more codefendants. In *Cuyler v. Sullivan* (1980), two attorneys, DiBona and Peruto, represented three defendants. DiBona was primarily responsible for Sullivan's trial, while Peruto, responsible for the trial of Sullivan's codefendants, advised DiBona in the Sullivan trial. The Supreme Court held that this constituted multiple representation, but the multiple representation did *not,* in itself, violate an attorney's obligations to adequately defend and to give full and complete attention to the client's defense. Multiple representation, therefore, is not automatically a *conflict of interest.* This rule takes economic realities of providing counsel into consideration. As Justice Stevens said in *Burger v. Kemp* (1987), "Particularly in smaller communities where the supply of qualified lawyers willing to accept the demanding and unrewarding work of representing capital prisoners is extremely limited, the defendants may actually benefit from the joint efforts of two partners who supplement one another in their preparation. Moreover, we generally presume that the lawyer is fully conscious of the overarching duty of complete loyalty to his or her client."

A *conflict of interest* arises when, in the circumstance of multiple representation, an attorney renders *less effective assistance to one client out of consideration for the interests of the other client.* It is a long-standing rule that where a conflict of interest is shown to exist, the defendant has established ineffective assistance of counsel per se and need not show that the conflict of interest prejudiced the case (*Glasser v. United States,* 1942). A trial judge is not obligated to hold a hearing into the possibility of a conflict of interest in every case of multiple representation (*Cuyler v. Sullivan,* 1980). However, should an assigned attorney raise a *timely objection* to multiple representation on the grounds that it constitutes a conflict of interest, the trial judge is required to hold a hearing to make certain that there is no genuine conflict before the trial can proceed (*Holloway v. Arkansas,* 1978).

A conflict of interest can be difficult to prove, as the defendant "must demonstrate that an actual conflict of interest adversely affected his lawyer's performance." (*Cuyler v. Sullivan,* 1980). *Burger v. Kemp* (1987) is an example where the *possibility* of a conflict of interest does not amount to the ineffective assistance of counsel under *Strickland.* Burger first argued that his lawyer, in an appellate brief, failed to raise as a death penalty mitigation that Burger was less culpable for the killing than a codefendant. The Supreme Court rejected this contentions because (a) the lesser culpability defense was raised and rejected at trial; (b) Burger actually killed the victim; (c) the Georgia Supreme Court found his acts to be "inhuman;" and (d) lower courts found that it was not deficient performance by the attorney to forgo this avenue on appeal. Burger next claimed that the lawyer failed to obtain a plea bargain resulting in a life sentence. However, the facts indicated that the defense lawyer attempted to obtain a plea, but the prosecutor simply refused to agree to a plea bargain. Finally, Burger claimed that the lawyer failed to bring out mitigating circumstances at the death penalty sentencing hearing. The omission of some mitigating information was deemed a tactical decision by the lawyer, designed to keep the defendant off the stand and thereby keep aggravating information from the court. Over the vigorous dissent of four justices, the Supreme Court held in this case that there was no deficient performance or conflict of interest.

LAW IN SOCIETY: THE UNMET PROMISE OF EQUAL JUSTICE

Gideon v. Wainwright, Argersinger v. Hamlin, and *Strickland v. Washington* guarantee a competent attorney for every defendant facing a serious criminal charge—even if the defendant is too poor to pay for legal services. A legal guarantee "on the books" is only as good as its enforcement. The promise of equal justice is meaningless if the lawyers, courts, county commissions, state legislators, and governors —and ultimately the American people—fail to implement it substantially. Have the legal community and responsible government units responded to the guarantee of equal justice?

Providing Lawyers for Indigent Defendants[54]

In one way they have—by ensuring that a lawyer always represents an indigent client at public expense. Indigent defense is provided through three mechanisms, which may coexist in some jurisdictions.

ASSIGNED COUNSEL Private lawyers are assigned to defend specific indigent clients and the fees are paid by either the state or the county. Assignments are usually made by bar associations, other such organizations, or by judges. Fees are usually capped. Lawyers are assigned to both trial and appellate cases. As of 1986, assigned counsel systems operate in fifty-two percent of the nation's counties.

PUBLIC DEFENDER OFFICES Indigents are represented by a public or private nonprofit organization with full or part-time staff attorneys and support personnel, including investigators, paralegals, social workers and secretaries. Some states have statewide appellate defender offices. The last national survey indicated that trial public defenders' offices operate in thirty-seven percent of the nation's counties.

CONTRACT ATTORNEYS Under this system, a jurisdiction enters into a contract with an attorney, a group of attorneys, or a bar association to provide representation for some or all indigent defendants. This system is often used to provide counsel for misdemeanor defendants; it was available in eleven percent of all counties in 1986. It is believed that the number of jurisdictions using public defender and contract systems has grown in the last fifteen years.

Yet, in significant ways, serious failings exist in the provision of *competent* counsel. The problem is not the general malpractice of criminal attorneys. Proper criminal defense work is an expensive, labor-intensive, expert undertaking. The problem is that in an era of unparalleled prosperity, in too many places, indigent defense is underfunded and as a result, gross injustices, including the conviction of innocent people of serious crimes, has grown. Sadly, America's people and its governmental servants have grown increasingly insensitive in the last few decades to the promise for equal justice.

The Expense of Private Criminal Defense

The cost of retaining a private defense lawyer to begin with can become huge. A survey by journalists of 1996 indigent cases in Houston, Texas found that retained lawyers "often can earn $ 25,000 to $ 75,000 to defend a felony case, depending on the complexity of the case and the probability that it will go to trial. Several top criminal defense attorneys acknowledged that fees for complex, high-profile cases can run into the hundreds of thousands of dollars."[55]

- A car service dispatcher in Queens, New York, who was charged with felonious assault in 1995, claimed self-defense. A seasoned attorney charged $15,000 and hired an investigator at $50 an hour to find witnesses. The dispatcher was found guilty of a lesser charge "and probably avoided prison time." His father mistakenly believed that the money would be returned if his son was found not guilty.[56]
- In the notorious Wenatchee, Washington witch hunt, police officer Robert Perez accused Pentecostal Minister Robert Roberson, his wife Connie, and more than forty parishioners of conducting orgies with children. The case ultimately collapsed after several poor and mentally retarded parishioners were imprisoned. Attorney Robert Van Siclen, who volunteered to defend Mr. Roberson, estimated the case cost his firm $100,000. He planned to sue the county in an effort to recoup the cost of defending the six week trial.[57]
- Karen and Jeffrey Wilson, a paralegal and a high school teacher respectively, were charged with child abuse when their seven-month-old son, Brock, was treated for a head injury. They spent $60,000 in legal fees to regain custody of Brock who was taken from them by the social service department. Charges were dismissed by the family court.[58]
- Between January and March 2000, Representative Earl Hilliard spent $37,500 in legal fees, out of the $40,000 that he raised for his re-election campaign, to defend himself against an ethics investigation into his previous race.[59]
- An injured trucker, accused of perpetrating criminal workers' compensation fraud, spent more than $100,000 in attorneys fees fighting criminal allegations. The trucker was vindicated.[60]
- In late 1999, seven big vitamin companies pleaded guilty to price fixing and agreed to pay $1.05 billion in damages. The attorneys' fees were estimated at $122 million.[61]
- Linda Tripp, whose Maryland charges for wiretapping in the Whitewater/Lewinsky scandal were ultimately dismissed, ran up legal bills of about $750,000. A defense fund has been set up to help her pay these charges.[62]
- Monica Lewinsky, the White House intern and a central figure in the scandal that led to the impeachment of President Clinton, was represented by top lawyers Plato Cacheris and Jacob Stein, who charge hourly billing rates in the range of $400 per hour. At the time she hired this team it was predicted that, "she'll likely owe more than $300,000 to her first legal team, led by William Ginsburg" whom she dismissed. [63]
- President Clinton's bill for legal services in the impeachment and the trial on the impeachment exceeded $10 million. To pay these bills, President Clinton created a legal defense fund to receive private donations.[64]
- Murder cases are in a special league. "'In a murder case, practically every defendant is indigent,' says Larry Hammond, a criminal lawyer in Phoenix, Arizona. 'They may not have started that way, but for anyone other than the super-rich, they will be indigent before the case is over.'" Dale Bertsch, an anesthesiologist accused of murdering his ex-wife, in a case with no physical evidence against him, was quoted fees in the $250,000 range. Hammond took the case for the sum total of Bertsch's liquidated assets, which came to about $160,000. He could not pay for an evidentiary hearing, which would have required $50,000, or a mock jury for $30,000. Dr. Bertsch was convicted.[65]
- As for the "super-rich," O. J. Simpson, whose net worth before his trial was said to be $10 million, took out a $3 million credit line on his Brentwood home, spent $100,000 for a jury consultant, paid a fee of $100,000 a month for twelve months to Robert Shapiro, and paid Johnnie Cochran, Jr., "a large flat fee," to mention only the lead attorneys.[66]

Funding for Indigent Defense

The under-funding of indigent criminal defense makes a mockery of the constitutional ideal of equal justice. The "largely hospitable funding environment" for indigent defense of the 1960s has given way to "public outcry over the neglect of . . . crime victims" and a steering of "resources toward law enforcement and away from indigent defense."[67] The late chief judge David Bazelon, of the Washington, D.C., United States Court of Appeals, wrote in 1984 that the "battle for equal justice is being lost in the trenches of the criminal courts," as the poor, uneducated, and unemployed are being represented all too often by "walking violations of the sixth amendment."[68]

In all jurisdictions, the amounts paid to assigned counsel are significantly below what retained counsel charge. As of May 2000, New York State had not raised assigned attorney fees in fourteen years.[69] In 1999, the federal Criminal Justice Act, which since 1964 has provided funding for assigned counsel in federal cases, set a *maximum* fee of $ 60 per hour for in court time and $ 40 per hour for out of court time, far below going rates for retained lawyers.[70] Virginia places a cap of $845 on the amount an attorney can receive for representing a defendant on a murder charge, but its General Assembly has approved a twenty-four percent increase in fees, effective July 1, 2001. "That level of funding will keep Virginia at or near the bottom of the rankings for payment of court-appointed attorneys' fees."[71]

As for public defender's offices, in most places, the caseloads of public defenders are so high, because of underfunding, as to diminish the ability of defenders to perform at the best of their abilities. There is no survey that assesses the total picture in the United States, but there is substantial evidence of real under-funding of indigent defense.

> . . . Across the nation, the bulk of criminal justice funds go to the police, prosecutors and jails. Only *2.3%* of the seventy-four billion dollars spent on the justice system in 1990 went to pay for attorneys *for indigent defendants* while *7.4% went to the prosecution.* However, the number of defendants unable to afford an attorney had risen dramatically, from forty-eight percent in 1982 to *eighty percent* today. *Public defenders handle over 11 million* of the *13 million cases* which are tried annually. Yet, as of 1990, the United States Department of Justice found that nationally, public defenders are receiving less than one-third of the resources provided to the prosecution. *Prosecutors' offices received $5.5 billion dollars* from federal, state, local, county and municipal governments as opposed to the *$1.7 billion provided for public defense* by the same government sources. Moreover, defense lawyers are further overwhelmed by additional resources provided to prosecutors including a great deal of investigatory work by law enforcement which are officially classified as "police expenditures."[72]

- An assistant public defender in the western U.S. admitted to doing an inadequate job in open court. She testified that she had collapsed in court and her health was seriously threatened by a caseload of 2,000 cases per year. She resigned from the Public Defender's Office, saying that she was "actually doing the defendants more harm by just presenting a live body than if they had no representation at all."[73]
- A New Orleans' public defender, representing 418 clients in the first seven months of 1991 and with seventy cases pending trial, obtained a court ruling that his excessive caseload precluded effective representation to the clients. "Not even a lawyer with an 'S' on his chest," the judge ruled, "could handle this docket."[74]
- In 1992, New Jersey eliminated $2.9 million budgeted to the Department of the Public Advocate to pay for counsel in cases where a conflict of interest barred the public defender. This left indigent defendants jailed without an attorney to represent them. The public advocate resigned "in disgust" to protest the budget reductions.[75]
- A late 1980s survey showed an annual starting salary of $24,259 for public defenders and an average salary of $34,787 for a defender with five years' experience. This may not have improved by the late 1990s as the legal profession has become "saturated."[76]

The Crisis in Death Penalty Cases

The most acute problem is that the most serious cases, involving capital punishment, are among the most severely affected by underfunding and incompetent attorneys.

- George Alec Robinson, charged with capital murder in Virginia, was vigorously defended by two appointed attorneys who worked a combined total of 600 hours. Robinson was found guilty, but was spared death by the electric chair. The attorneys submitted a bill of approximately $55,000 at prevailing rates for private clients. During this trial, the attorneys neglected their private practices and even their personal lives under the pressure of having the responsibility for a man's life. The State of Virginia paid them $573—each. "The two lawyers subsequently removed their names from the list of attorneys willing to accept appointments. They joined an increasing number of experienced attorneys nationwide who are no longer willing to provide their services at such great personal and financial sacrifice."[77]
- Calvin Jerold Burdine was released by a federal court from a Texas prison after spending sixteen years on death row. His lawyer had no cocounsel and slept through substantial portions of his trial. The Texas Court of Criminal Appeals did not think that this constituted ineffective assistance of counsel. Burdine's case was one of several of Texas prisoners on death row whose lawyers slept during their trials. Then Governor George Bush of Texas vetoed a bill in 1999 to improve the quality of legal representation of poor defendants, expressing satisfaction with the Texas justice system.[78]
- Frederico Martinez-Macias, a common laborer convicted of a double murder, was defended by a court-appointed attorney who was paid $11.84 an hour but did no legal research to correct his erroneous view about key evidence and failed to call an alibi witness who would have placed Martinez-Macias miles away from the crime. After being sentenced to death, a Washington firm took his case pro bono. Full investigation established his innocence.[79] The pro bono lawyers invested about $1 million dollars of billable hours, spent $11,599 for psychological testimony, and found eyewitnesses who did not identify Martinez-Macias at the murder scene.[80] other cases like this exist.[81]
- Attorney Mike Williams, a small town Alabama lawyer, was assigned a capital murder case of James Wyman

Smith. Williams was given no money for an investigator and estimated that he received $4.98 per hour to prepare for the defense. Another Alabama solo practitioner, Wilson Meyers, submitted an itemized bill for $13,399 to the trial court, which reduced the amount to $4,128. The court agreed that Mr. Meyers had put in the time, but called the fees too excessive. After paying his investigator and paralegal, Mr. Meyers netted $5.05 an hour on this case. As a result, earnest lawyers like Mike Williams, who learn the ropes of doing three or four death cases, drop out because of the financial burden, leaving inexperienced or incompetent lawyers to take such cases.[82]

- Some lawyers are forced to take assigned capital cases or face contempt of court. They may put in about fifty hours on death penalty cases when, according to experts, adequate preparation requires 500 to 1,000 hours.[83]

Causes of Ineffective Counsel

What is the cause for the diminished funding for indigent defense?

- Tough on crime attitudes "Providing free attorneys to accused criminals is probably one of the government's least popular functions. In recent years, 'victim's rights' movements have become increasingly popular. Many politicians, being sensitive to public opinion, are concerned with appearing to be 'tough on crime.' Citizens and politicians alike often have little understanding of or sympathy for the needs of the adversary system, at least insofar as it requires a strong defense advocate. Defense attorneys are often seen as obstacles to justice. . . ."[84]
- Rising caseloads From 1982 to 1984, there was a forty percent increase in caseloads for the nation's indigent defense systems. A 1990 study, commissioned by Chief Justice Rehnquist, concluded that the most pressing problem for federal courts was the unprecedented number of federal drug prosecutions. In 1964, federal courts made 16,000 compensated appointments of counsel under the Criminal Justice Act of 1964. By 1993, that number rose to 89,000 indigent appointments in federal courts.[85]
- Diminishing governmental resources "Recently, many local governments, the primary locus of funding of defense services, have seen their resources dwindle, as tax-cutting measures are passed by the electorate and federal funds for local programs are cut."[86]
- Greater demands on defense attorneys Prosecutors have either limited or eliminated plea bargaining for certain crimes, have increased the number of charges filed against defendants, and have charged more serious crimes. All of this requires greater defense efforts. New crimes and harsher penalties passed by legislatures require defense attorneys to spend time learning the law, developing appellate challenges to the new provisions, and offering a more dogged defense against higher penalties.[87]

Solving the Problem of Ineffective Counsel

Several steps can be taken to solve the problem of the ineffective assistance of counsel, including:

- Modify the rule of *Strickland v. Washington* to make it easier for courts to find ineffective assistance of counsel.
- Improve the efficiency of public defenders offices by the widespread use of advanced technology for managing information in complex cases, in case-tracking, and for information exchange.[88]
- Reengineer the role of chief public defenders from that of narrow and defensive managers to be spokespersons for the need for adequate funding for indigent defense. This may include developing better relations with legislators, prosecutors, police, corrections, the media, and community groups in an effort to advocate the need for indigent defense and to sponsor community crime prevention programs.[89]
- Tie the expenditure of indigent defense (all systems) to a percentage of funding of public prosecution, at a suggested rate of seventy-five percent.[90]
- Public defenders' offices negotiate reasonable caseload limits with courts and funding agencies.
- Require minimum experience before assigning major cases.[91]
- Eliminate the practice of judges compelling attorneys to take major cases on a pro bono basis.[92]
- Finance indigent defense in part with a portion of court fees.
- Reduce the enforcement component of the "war on drugs," with its draconian punishments for low level crimes, and replace this with more treatment options.

Until such practical solutions are implemented, the promise of the Constitution—equal justice under law—will go unfulfilled.

SUMMARY

The right to the assistance of counsel in a criminal prosecution is guaranteed by the Sixth Amendment. It is fundamental to the proper conduct of criminal trials and the adversary system of justice. In other proceedings, a right to counsel has been guaranteed by the Due Process and Equal Protection Clauses of the Fourteenth Amendment as well as the Fifth Amendment right against self-incrimination. Defense counsel is more important in common-law trials than in trials under the European civil law system. The actual use of lawyers in trials was a late common law development.

Prior to its incorporation into the Fourteenth Amendment in *Gideon v. Wainwright* (1963), the Sixth Amendment right applied only to federal prosecutions. Under federal law, a defendant had to be represented and could waive counsel only if it specifically appeared on the record that the defendant did so knowingly and voluntarily (*Johnson v. Zerbst,* 1938). In state cases, lack of counsel violated a defendant's Fourteenth Amendment due process right to a fair trial only when special circumstances existed: e.g., death penalty, defendant's immaturity or ignorance, complex issues, or an atmosphere of prejudice (*Powell v. Alabama,* 1932). *Griffin v. Illinois* (1956) held that under the Fourteenth Amendment Equal Protection Clause, in which the state allows certain legal benefits to those who can afford it, the state must provide at no cost benefits, such as transcripts for appeals, to indigent defendants.

Gideon v. Wainwright (1963) incorporated the Sixth Amendment right to counsel into the Fourteenth Amendment Due Process Clause. The right to counsel was later applied to all misdemeanor cases in which the defendant was actually imprisoned. The Sixth Amendment right to counsel extends to all critical stages (preliminary examination, capital arraignment, sentencing), but not to postconviction correctional processes (probation revocation, parole revocation, or prison disciplinary hearings). The Sixth Amendment requires appointment of a psychiatric expert where necessary to decide an insanity issue.

In proceedings which are not Sixth Amendment prosecutions, counsel is authorized by the Due Process Clause in some proceedings (probation and parole revocations, juvenile delinquency adjudication), but not in others (prison discipline, parental rights termination, summary court martial). In probation revocation hearings courts have discretion to appoint counsel to indigents where special circumstances exist, but in juvenile adjudication counsel must be provided.

Courts can prevent persons who are not licensed in the practice of law from serving as counsel and can bar an attorney from representing a person where the court believes there will be a conflict of interest. A federal forfeiture statute that allows the confiscation of attorney fees before trial does not violate the Sixth Amendment right to counsel. The Sixth Amendment does not guarantee a meaningful relationship between a defendant and assigned counsel. When counsel is provided without cost to an indigent defendant, the state has a right to seek compensation at a later time when the defendant has obtained the money to repay the costs.

Counsel is guaranteed on a first appeal under the Due Process and Equal Protection Clauses (*Douglas v. California,* 1963). The Court limited the extension of this rule in *Ross v. Moffitt* (1974) so that counsel is not constitutionally required for indigent litigants pursuing discretionary second appeals or habeas corpus proceedings, as long as the state allows indigent prisoners to pursue such appeals.

The right to representation at a criminal trial is personal, and a defendant has a right to waive the assistance of counsel and conduct a defense *pro se* (*Faretta v. California* 1975). A waiver requires the trial judge to closely examine the defendant to be sure he or she understands the benefits of counsel and waives appointed counsel voluntarily, and to be sure that the defendant has the minimum skills needed to conduct a reasonable defense. The court cannot disqualify a *pro se* defense because the defendant does not have expert knowledge of the law or of the trial process. In instances of *pro se* defense, the court may appoint standby counsel over the defendant's objection.

The Sixth Amendment requires that the assistance afforded to a defendant be effective. The basic rules of effective assistance are, first, that the attorney's conduct must be reasonable, or not deficient, according to the prevailing standards of practicing attorneys in the locality and, second, that if the attorney's performance was deficient, this must have prejudiced the defendant's case so that the conviction was a result of the deficient performance. The complaining defendant has the burden of proving ineffective assistance. Ineffective assistance will not be presumed. It is not deficient performance to refuse to assist a client in committing perjury. In cases involving a real conflict of interest, ineffective assistance is presumed, but the mere fact that an attorney represented two clients is not in itself a conflict of interest. If an attorney raises a reasonable possibility of a conflict of interest, a trial judge must hold a hearing to inquire into the matter.

LEGAL PUZZLES

How Have Courts Decided These Cases?

7–1. Hansen, charged with furnishing alcohol to a minor, had requested court-appointed counsel. The state court inquired into his financial status at a preliminary hearing, granted the request in part, determined that Hansen was entitled to counsel, and ordered that if he paid $1,000 prior to the omnibus hearing, the court would appoint a public defender to represent him. Hansen appeared without counsel and without having paid the $1,000 to entitle him to a public defender, claiming that he did not have the money. He refused to waive his right to counsel. At trial, Hansen refused to accept the representation offered by the public defender even though the trial judge strongly encouraged Hansen to accept her assistance. Hansen proceeded *pro se,* and the public defender acted as standby counsel. Did Hansen waive his right to counsel by having the ability to contribute $1,000 and refusing to do so? *Hansen v. Passer,* 13 F.3d 275 (8th Cir. 1994).

7–2. Savage was on trial for murder. Citing a conflict of interest with his court-appointed attorney, Savage requested the right to defend himself. The trial judge noted that Savage's severe speech impediment might cause him considerable difficulty in presenting his own defense, but, finding that the appellant had made a knowing and intelligent waiver of his right to counsel, reluctantly granted the motion, discharged Savage's court-appointed attorney, and appointed an investigator to assist the appellant with the preparation of his defense. Savage handled the pretrial part of his case competently. A standby counsel was appointed. After some time, citing conflicts, Savage moved to have the standby counsel removed. The judge refused on the ground that Savage's speech impediment was so severe that it would effectively preclude him from being able to articulate his defense to a jury. Standby counsel presented the entire case to the jury, although Savage retained many rights as a co-counsel. Was Savage's right to self-representation under *Faretta v. California* violated? *Savage v. Estelle,* 924 F.2d 1459 (9th Cir. 1990).

7–3. After three trials, Poyner was convicted of five counts of capital murder and sentenced to death. The victims were women killed in robbery sprees. Poyner confessed that he chose only women as his victims because women are afraid of guns and are easier to rob than men. He said that he killed his victims to keep them from identifying him, (during previous jail terms fellow prisoners said they wished they had killed their robbed victims).

Poyner claimed ineffective assistance of counsel in the penalty phases: failure to investigate, develop, and present psychiatric evidence of his psychological condition as a mitigating factor. Dr. Deitz filed an affidavit that indicated that Poyner could be a serial killer driven by various psychological conditions. Poyner argued that had his counsel and psychiatrists investigated and put on evidence of these conditions, the jury might have believed that Poyner was driven by a motive other than the simple expediency of preventing his robbery victims from identifying him—a mitigating factor.

Before trial, Poyner was subjected to a wide range of psychological evaluations over a two-week period, family members were interviewed, and a psychiatrist was hired by the defense counsel to evaluate Poyner. No evidence of the specific conditions that would meet Dr. Deitz's serial killer profile was uncovered. All the psychological evidence was presented to the jury. Does this amount to ineffective assistance of counsel? *Poyner v. Murray,* 964 F.2d 1404 (4th Cir. 1992).

7–4. Ostrander, a successful young businessman, was accused by his fifteen-year-old sister-in-law of molesting her on several occasions beginning when she was thirteen. He was charged in a six-count indictment with three counts of carnal knowledge of a minor, two counts of sexual battery, and one count of sodomy. He had two attorneys. They told Ostrander that they worked out a plea agreement with the prosecutor under which Ostrander would plead guilty to four of the six charges and the Commonwealth would agree that the sentences would run concurrently, that his sentence would be "capped" at three to five years, that the Commonwealth would not oppose work release, and that Ostrander's receiving work release was guaranteed. The plea otherwise would expose Ostrander to a twenty-year maximum sentence.

Ostrander pled guilty and was sentenced to twelve years in prison. Within days of sentencing, he discovered not only that had he not been approved for work release, but also that he was ineligible for work release as a matter of law because of the nature of his offense. Did this constitute ineffective assistance of counsel? *Ostrander v. Green,* 46 F.3d 347 (4th Cir. 1995).

ANSWERS TO LEGAL PUZZLES

7–1. NO. To waive the right to counsel, the accused must make a voluntary, knowing, and intelligent waiver and must be fully advised of the dangers and disadvantages of self-representation before waiving the right. No such waiver appears on the record in this case. Even assuming Hansen was capable of paying $1,000, the prepayment requirement does not transform this case into one where the defendant was found capable of obtaining private counsel.

7–2. NO. In this case, the jury did not perceive Savage as representing himself. Rather, Savage appeared before it as would have any criminal defendant represented by counsel. A denial of *Faretta* rights is permissible under *McKaskle v. Wiggins* if an accused is not "able and willing to abide by rules of procedure and courtroom protocol." Savage was not able to meet this test because the state trial court concluded that because of his extreme stutter, Savage was physically incapable of presenting his case to the jury. It made this conclusion only after Savage's inability to communicate orally to the jury and to the court was demonstrated again and again over the course of several months. Savage admitted that the greater the tension, the worse his stutter became. The court noted that this decision did not deny the right to communicate to the jury with the assistance of a sign language interpreter or some other mechanical or nonmechanical means of rapid communication.

7–3. NO. Poyner's claim is not so much against counsel as against the psychiatrists who were not experienced or imaginative enough to recognize that Poyner might have been motivated by sexual sadism, the crime-spree killer phenomenon, or some other psychological disorder that might support an argument that Poyner's killings were motivated by more than just a desire to evade capture and prosecution for robbery. Each of Poyner's trial attorneys thereafter put their psychiatrist on the stand and competently elicited the results of the evaluations. The mere fact that his counsel did not shop around for a psychiatrist willing to testify to the presence of more elaborate or grave psychological disorders does not constitute ineffective assistance.

7–4. YES. Under the specific standard of *Hill v. Lockhart,* the defendant must show merely that there is a reasonable probability that he would not have pled guilty and would have insisted on going to trial under the facts. Lower courts erroneously applied the more restrictive *Strickland* prejudice rule. Ordinarily, an attorney need not advise her client of the myriad of "collateral consequences" of pleading guilty. However, where the client asks for advice about a "collateral consequence" and relies upon it in deciding whether to plead guilty, the attorney must not grossly misinform his or her client about the law.

FURTHER READING

James Goodman, *Stories of Scottsboro* (New York: Pantheon Books, 1994).

Anthony Lewis, *Gideon's Trumpet* (New York: Vintage Books, 1964).

David J. Bodenhamer, *Fair Trial: Rights of the Accused in American History* (New York: Oxford University Press, 1992).

ENDNOTES

1. In England and Canada, and in colonial and early Republican United States, the word was spelled "defence." The modern American spelling is "defense."
2. *Bute v. Illinois* (1948), p. 678.
3. R. Terrill, *World Criminal Justice Systems* (Cincinnati, Ohio: Anderson, 1984), pp. 149–50.
4. D. Karlen, in collaboration with G. Sawyer and E. Wise, *Anglo-American Criminal Justice* (New York: Oxford University Press, 1967), p. 176.
5. J. Frank, "The 'Fight' Theory Versus the 'Truth' Theory," in *Courts on Trial: Myth and Reality in American Justice* (New York: Atheneum, 1963), pp. 80–102. For a more recent and thoughtful critique, see L. Weinreb, *Denial of Justice: Criminal Process in the United States* (1977).
6. *Faretta v. California* (1975), quoting Holdsworth, *History of English Law*; C. Rembar, *The Law of the Land* (New York: Simon and Schuster, 1980), p. 181; L. Levy, *Origins of the Fifth Amendment* (New York: Oxford University Press, 1968), p. 19.
7. C. Bowen, *The Lion and the Throne: The Life and Times of Sir Edward Coke (1552–1634)* (Boston: Little, Brown, 1956), pp. 139–59, 190–217, 253–73, detailing prosecution by Attorney General Coke against Essex, Raleigh, and the Gunpowder Plot conspirators (Guy Fawkes).
8. C. Rembar, *Law of the Land,* pp. 383–84.
9. W. Blackstone, *Commentaries on the Laws of England, Volume 4—Of Public Wrongs (1769)* (Chicago: University of Chicago Press, 1979, facsimile of First Edition), pp. 349–50.
10. Hiller B. Zobel, *The Boston Massacre* (New York: W.W. Norton, 1970).
11. *Powell v. Alabama* (1932), citing the right to counsel in the first constitutions of Maryland, Massachusetts, New Hampshire, New York, Pennsylvania, Delaware, New Jersey, and Connecticut (not adopted until 1818) and statutes of North Carolina and South Carolina and later constitutions of Georgia and Rhode Island.
12. Two excellent histories of the Scottsboro case are D. T. Carter, *Scottsboro: A Tragedy of the American South,* rev. ed. (Baton Rouge: Louisiana State University Press, 1979) and J. Goodman, *Stories of Scottsboro* (New York: Pantheon Books, 1994). The narrative of the case is taken from these sources.
13. The second appeal to the United States Supreme Court, *Norris v. Alabama* (1934) held that the exclusion of African Americnas from juries violated the defendants' right to equal protection under the Fourteenth Amendment.
14. H. Arkes, *The Return of George Sutherland: Restoring a Jurisprudence of Natural Rights* (Princeton: Princeton University Press, 1994).
15. *Ibid.*
16. *Ibid.,* emphasis added.
17. Hadley Arkes, *The Return of George Sutherland: Restoring A Jurisprudence of Natural Rights,* (Princeton: Princeton University Press, 1994) p. 265.
18. He cited *Gitlow v. New York* (1925), *Stromberg v. California* (1931), and *Near v. Minnesota* (1931).
19. Arkes, *Return of George Sutherland,* p. 268.
20. *Powell v. Alabama,* pp. 68–69.
21. *Ibid.,* p. 71.
22. *Von Moltke v. Gillis* (1948).
23. *Betts v. Brady,* p. 472.
24. *Betts v. Brady,* p. 476 (paragraph break disregarded).
25. *Bute v. Illinois* (1948); *Hamilton v. Alabama* (1961); *Ferguson v. Georgia* (1961).
26. *Uveges v. Pennsylvania* (1948).
27. *Smith v. Bennett* (1961); *Burns v. Ohio* (1959).
28. *Roberts v. Lavallee* (1967); *Gardner v. California* (1969); *Mayer v. Chicago* (1971).
29. *Mills v. Municipal Court for San Diego Judicial District* (1973) 10 Cal 3d 288, 110 Cal Rptr 329, 515 P2d 273.
30. *In re Groban* (1957) (dictum).

31. *Davis v. Mississippi* (1969); *Gilbert v. California* (1967); *United States v. Dionisio* (1973).
32. Justice Stevens in *Gouveia* cited *Escobedo v. Illinois* (1964) as an example of the Supreme Court finding the right to counsel prior to formal charges.
33. Linda Greenhouse, "High Court Backs Seizure of Assets in Criminal Cases," *New York Times,* June 22, 1989, p. 1.
34. David Rossman, "'Were There No Appeal': The History of Review in American Criminal Courts," *Journal of Criminal Law and Criminology,* 81(3):518–566 (1990), p. 519.
35. *People v. Valdez,* (1990, Colo) 789 P2d 406.
36. Ibid.
37. Ibid. p. 408.
38. Marie Higgins Williams, Comment: The Pro Se Criminal Defendant, Standby Counsel, and the Judge: A Proposal for Better Defined Roles, *University of Colorado Law Review,* 71: 789–818 (2000), pp. 795–97.
39. Williams, p. 793, n. 28, citing a past-president of the National Association of Criminal Defense Lawyers.
40. Ron Christenson, ed., *Political Trials in History* (New Brunswick: Transaction Publishers, 1991), pp. 91–93; Williams, pp. 789–90.
41. J. T. McQuiston, "Suspect in L.I.R.R. Killings Ruled Competent for Trial," *New York Times,* Dec. 10, 1994, §1, p.28. They became standby counsel, but later resigned when Ferguson's antics became intolerably bizarre, J. T. McQuiston, "Adviser to L.I.R.R. Suspect Threatens to Quit," *New York Times,* Feb. 7, 1995, p. B8.
42. J. T. McQuiston, "L.I.R.R. Defendant Helps Pick Jury, Then Says It Is Biased," *New York Times,* Jan. 24, 1995, p. B4.
43. J. T. McQuiston, "In the Bizarre L.I.R.R. Trial, Equally Bizarre Confrontations," *New York Times,* Feb, 5, 1995, § 13LI, p. 1.
44. D. Van Biema, "A Fool for a Client; Accused L.I.R.R. Killer Colin Ferguson is Defending Himself, and That May Be Something of a Crime," *Time,* Feb. 6, 1995, p. 66.
45. J. Hoffman, "Hapless Lawyer, Thankless Job; Colin Ferguson's Adviser Sees Reputation and Practice Suffer," *New York Times,* Feb. 14, 1995, p. B1.
46. P. Marks, "Relief That the Book Is Closed on a Looking-Glass Trial," *New York Times,* Feb. 19, 1995, § 1, p. 46.
47. Williams, p. 801.
48. *McKaskle v. Wiggins* (1984) (emphasis added).
49. Williams, p. 805.
50. Ibid.
51. Ibid., pp. 809–815.
52. *Hill v. Lockhart* (1985).
53. The Supreme Court did not have enough evidence to determine whether the deficient performance prejudiced the case and remanded it to the lower courts to determine whether prejudice occurred.
54. Information in this section is taken from Spangenberg Group, *Indigent Defense and Technology: A Progress Report* (Bureau of Justice Assistance, NCJ 179003, Nov. 1999).
55. Bob Sablatura, "Study confirms money counts in county's courts; Those using appointed lawyers are twice as likely to serve time," *Houston Chronicle,* October 17, 1999, p. A1.
56. "I Think You Get All the Justice You Can Afford," *Time,* June 19, 1995, pp. 46–47.
57. Gregg Herrington, "Sex Ring Attorney Looks to Civil Trial," *The Columbian,* Dec. 15, 1995, p. A2; T. Egan, "Pastor and Wife Are Acquitted on All Charges in Sex-Abuse Case," *New York Times,* Dec. 12, 1995, p. A11; D. Nathan, "Justice in Wenatchee," *New York Times,* Dec. 19, 1995, p. A19.
58. D. West, "Cleared of Child Abuse, but the Anguish Lingers," *New York Times,* Oct. 19, 1995, p. A12.
59. Bulletin Broadfaxing Network, The Bulletin's Frontrunner, April 26, 2000 "Legal Fees Reduce Hilliard's Warchest To $149; Blames Racism For His Problem."
60. "CHSWC Okays New Study on Drug Costs," *Workers' Comp Executive,* December 1, 1999, Vol. 9, No. 22.
61. David Lawsky, "$1 Billion Settlement Reported in Vitamin Suit," *Toronto Star,* November 4, 1999, Business Section.
62. Del Quentin Wilber (*Baltimore Sun*), "Tripp seeks help paying lawyers," *Des Moines Register,* November 18, 1999, p.12.
63. Jill Abramson, "The Nation: The Price of Being Lewinsky; Dream Team, Nightmare Tab," *New York Times,* June 7, 1998, Sec. 4, p. 3.
64. Don Van Natta Jr., "Fewer Donations Coming In For Clinton Defense Fund," *New York Times,* August 13, 1999, p. A12, col 5.
65. "I Think You Get All the Justice You Can Afford," *Time,* June 19, 1995, pp. 46–47.
66. E. Gleick, "Rich Justice, Poor Justice," *Time,* June 19, 1995, p. 39.
67. Kim Taylor-Thompson, "Effective Assistance: Reconceiving the Role Of the Chief Public Defender," *Journal of the Institute for the Study of Legal Ethics* 2:199–220 (1999), p. 200.
68. David Bazelon, quoted in R. Klein, "The Emperor *Gideon* Has No Clothes: The Empty Promise of the Constitutional Right to Effective Assistance of Counsel," *Hastings Constitutional Law Quarterly* 13(1986):625–93, p. 656.
69. Editorial, "Judicial Reforms in Albany," *New York Times,* May 26, 2000, p. A22 (nat.ed.).
70. Martha K. Harrison, Note: Claims For Compensation: The Implications of Getting Paid When Appointed under the Criminal Justice Act, *Boston University Law Review* 79: 553–76 (1999), p. 555, n. 15.
71. Alan Cooper, Appointed Lawyer's Low Fee Ruled No Bar to Fair Trial, *Richmond Times Dispatch,* May 5, 2000, p. B3.
72. R. Marcus, "Racism in Our Courts: The Underfunding of Public Defenders and Its Disproportionate Impact Upon Racial Minorities," *Hastings Constitutional Law Quarterly* 22(1994): 219–67, pp. 228–29 (footnotes omitted, emphasis added).
73. S. Mounts, "The Right to Counsel and the Indigent Defense System," *New York University Review of Law & Social Change* 14(1986):221–41, p. 221, citing *Cooper v. Fitzharris,* 551 F.2d 1162, at 1163, n.1 (9th Cir. 1977).

74. R. L. Spangenberg and T. J. Schwartz, "The Indigent Defense Crisis Is Chronic," *Criminal Justice,* Summer 1994, p. 13, citing *State v. Peart,* 621 So. 2d 780 (La. 1993).
75. Spangenberg and Schwartz, citing *National Law Journal,* Aug. 20, 1992, p. 3.
76. R. L. Spangenberg, "We Are Still Not Defending the Poor Properly," *Criminal Justice,* pp. 11–13+ (Fall 1989), p. 12.
77. S. E. Mounts and R.J. Wilson, "Systems for Providing Indigent Defense: An Introduction," *New York University Review of Law & Social Change,* 14(1986):193–201, p. 194, citing *Washington Post,* June 25, 1984, p. D1.
78. Ross E. Milloy, "Judge Frees Texas Inmate Whose Lawyer Slept at Trial," *New York Times* , March 2, 2000, p. A20; Paul Duggan, "George W. Bush: The Record in Texas; Attorneys' Ineptitude Doesn't Halt Executions," *Washington Post,* May 12, 2000, p. A1 .
79. S. Bright, "Counsel for the Poor: The Death Sentence Not for the Worst Crime but for the Worst Lawyer," *Yale Law Journal* 103(1994):1835–83, pp. 1838–39.
80. A. Cohen, "The Difference a Million Makes," *Time,* June 19, 1993, p. 53.
81. "Another Wrongly Convicted Man," Indianpolis Star, Feb. 10, 2000, p. A21; Bright, "Counsel for the Poor."
82. Sarta Rimer, "Questions of Death Row Justice for Poor People in Alabama," *New York Times,* March 1, 2000, p. A1.
83. Sarta Rimer, Ibid. March 1, 2000, p. A1.
84. Mounts and Wilson, "Systems for Providing Indigent Defense," pp. 200–201.
85. Spangenberg and Schwartz, "The Indigent Defense Crisis," p. 14; J. J. Cleary. "Federal Defender Services: Serving the System or the Client?" *Law and Contemporary Problems* 58 (1995):65–80, p. 65.
86. Mounts and Wilson, "Systems for Providing Indigent Defense," pp. 200–201.
87. Spangenberg and Schwartz, "The Indigent Defense Crisis."
88. Spangenberg Group, 1999.
89. Taylor-Thompson, "Effective Assistance: Reconceiving the Role."
90. Ibid., pp. 207–08.
91. Jo Becker, "Rules set for death row lawyers," *St. Petersburg* (Fla.) *Times,* Oct. 30, 1999, p. 5B.
92. Stafford Henderson Byers, "Delivering Indigents' Right to Counsel While Respecting Lawyers' Right to Their Profession: a System "Between a Rock and a Hard Place," *St. John's Journal of Legal Commentary* 13:491–526 (1999).

JUSTICES OF THE SUPREME COURT

Enduring Liberals
Brennan–Marshall

When William Brennan was appointed by President Eisenhower and Thurgood Marshall by President Johnson, the Supreme Court was representative of the ascendant liberal ideology of the day. Their backgrounds, experiences, and beliefs about the Court's role well-suited them to play a role in expanding the rights of society's outcasts. As justices with long tenures, their careers coincided with a long swing of the political pendulum, from liberal to conservative, that has marked American politics since the 1960s. The careers of Justices Brennan and Marshall exemplify an important institutional aspect of the Supreme Court. Presidents nominate individuals who represent the political aspirations of the day, but with life tenure, justices who sit for several decades can extend their philosophies over time. This places the Court somewhat above the political passions of the period and offers a form of stability. The disadvantage is that at times it makes the Court unresponsive to the needs and demands of the polity.

The resignation of Justices Goldberg, Fortas, and Warren between 1965 and 1970 led to a change in the Court's composition that reflect and possibly accelerated a shift toward a conservative mood in some issues. This has persisted since 1970 as ten nominees of Republican Presidents Nixon, Ford, Reagan, and Bush have moved the Court progressively to the right. Democratic President Carter had no opportunity to nominate a justice, and President Clinton has carefully selected moderate rather than liberal justices.

Thus, for two decades, Justices Brennan and Marshall, the enduring liberals, penned more than a normal share of dissents in many criminal procedure cases. At times, their dissents expressed outrage and dire warnings that conservative justices were subverting constitutional rights. Less frequently, they joined with at least three moderate justices to rule in favor of the defendant. For the most part, their dissents after 1970 were written not so much for the present, but for the future, in the hope that a new generation of justices will be more open to defendants' claims.

William J. Brennan, Jr.

New Jersey 1906–1997

Democrat

Appointed by Dwight Eisenhower

Years of Service: 1956–1990

Collection of the Supreme Court of the United States. Photographer: Robert Oakes

Life and Career The son of an Irish immigrant who became a political leader in Newark, New Jersey noted for integrity and efficiency, William Brennan grew up in comfortable circumstances. He graduated from the Wharton School of the University of Pennsylvania with honors and was in the top ten percent of his class at Harvard Law School in 1931. He practiced law with a prestigious Newark firm specializing in labor issues for corporate clients. During World War II, he was a labor productivity troubleshooter for the undersecretary of war, rising to the rank of colonel. After the war, he became associated with the judicial reform efforts of New Jersey's renowned Chief Justice Arthur Vanderbilt and as a result was appointed a trial judge. He rose to become an associate justice of the New Jersey Supreme Court and came to the attention of U.S. Attorney General Brownell at a conference on judicial administration where he sat in for Vanderbilt. The next year when a vacancy appeared on the Court, Brennan fit the requirements of being a Catholic, an easterner, and a nominal Democrat acceptable to Republicans. The only senator to vote against his confirmation to the Supreme Court was Joseph McCarthy, the demagogic communist-hunter who may have been angered by Brennan's earlier public criticism of "McCarthyism."

Contribution to Criminal Procedure Justice Brennan wrote few criminal procedure majority opinions in the 1960s, although he consistently voted for incorporation and defendants' rights. Under a more conservative Court, he authored many criminal procedure dissents, as in *Leon* (1984) (good faith exception to exclusionary rule), *Gates* (1983) (abolishing the *Spinelli* two-prong test for reliability of informant), *Calandra* (1974) (use of illegally obtained evidence in grand jury is constitutional), *Florida v. Riley* (1989) (helicopter overflights not a search subject to Fourth Amendment warrant requirement), *Hampton* (1976) (no entrapment if government agent supplies illegal drug), *Mosley* (1975) (reinterrogation allowed after a suspect claims right to silence), *Ash* (1973) (*Wade* lineup rule does not apply to photographic identification), *Kuhlman v. Wilson* (1986) (passive jail informant does not violate a suspect's right to counsel under the *Massiah* doctrine), and other cases.

In many dissents, he was outspokenly critical of the majority, often accusing it of ignoring facts or twisting precedent simply to arrive at a desired outcome—the same charge of result-oriented jurisprudence that was hurled at the activist Warren Court during the 1960s. In reaction to the curtailment of defendants' rights, Justice Brennan called on state court judges to apply their own state constitutions to afford more rights to suspects than were granted under the current reading of the Bill of Rights. This indeed has been a growing trend and is an ironic twist for a justice who championed federal rights in the 1960s.

Signature Opinion Dissenting opinion in *Illinois v. Gates* (1983). In this *tour de force,* Justice Brennan directly attacked the ideological basis of the conservative Court's criminal procedure rulings as "code words for an overly permissive attitude toward police practices in derogation of the rights secured by the Fourth Amendment."

Assessment He was called "a towering figure in modern law who embodied the liberal vision of the Constitution as an engine of social and political change" and many commentators referred to the Warren Court as the "Brennan Court," so great was the influence of his prolific opinions and his ability to gain majorities for his opinions. He strongly influenced all the major areas of the Warren Court's liberal agenda, including free speech, free press, separation of church and state, voting apportionment, school busing, and criminal procedure.

Further Reading

Kim Isaac Eisler, *Justice For All: William J. Brennan, Jr., and the Decisions That Transformed America* (New York: Simon and Schuster, 1993).

Thurgood Marshall

New York 1908–1991

Democrat

Appointed by Lyndon Johnson

Years of Service: 1967–1991

Collection of the Supreme Court of the United States. Photographer: Joseph Lavenburg

Life and Career Thurgood Marshall had one of the most distinguished and significant legal careers in American constitutional history. Born in Baltimore into a middle-class family, the great-grandson of a slave graduated from Lincoln University (Chester, Pennsylvania) and was first in his class at Howard University Law School. From 1933 to 1938, he was the counsel for the National Association for the Advancement of Colored People (NAACP) in Baltimore, and from 1938 to 1960, he was the chief counsel of the Legal Defense Fund, the legal organization spun off from the NAACP to defend the civil rights of African Americans in a then legally segregated society. As such, he led the legal battle to overturn segregation laws and thus played a central role in the Civil Rights movement. He appeared before the Supreme Court thirty-two times and won thirteen of the sixteen cases in which he was the principal attorney. His most significant victories were *Shelly v. Kramer* (1948), which declared restrictive covenants on real estate deeds unenforceable in the courts, and *Brown v. Board of Education* (1954), the most important case of the twentieth century, which overturned the "separate but equal doctrine" and outlawed school segregation. In 1961, President Kennedy named Marshall to the Court of Appeals for the Second Circuit, and in 1965, President Johnson named him as the solicitor general, the chief federal attorney to argue cases before the Supreme Court.

Contribution to Criminal Procedure As the Court moved steadily to the right after 1970, Marshall, along with Brennan and, on occasion Blackmun and Stevens, dissented in most criminal procedure cases. His opinions were often trenchant and eloquent denunciations of what he saw as the Court's conservative majority oppressively misreading of the Bill of Rights and seeking to dismantle constitutional protections. In *Schneckloth v. Bustamonte* (1973) (knowledge of rights not required to give valid consent to search), for example, he stated "I have difficulty in comprehending how a decision made without knowledge of available alternatives can be treated as a choice at all."

Along with Justice Brennan, he held that the death penalty is a flat violation of the cruel and unusual punishment clause of the Eighth Amendment and voted to overturn each capital punishment case, a position adopted by Blackmun a few months before his retirement. On occasion, he wrote a majority opinion for a unanimous Court as in the ruling that a brief roadside stop of a motorist for a traffic violation does not constitute the kind of custodial interrogation that triggers the need for *Miranda* warnings (*Berkemer v. McCarty,* 1984).

SIGNATURE OPINION Concurring opinion in *Batson v. Kentucky* (1986). Although the Court's majority issued a "liberal" decision, that the exclusion of a juror on account of race in a single trial could be challenged, Marshall moved beyond the frontiers of the decision and argued that use of peremptory challenges during voir dire perpetuates the potential for discrimination and should be eliminated altogether.

ASSESSMENT Marshall was a staunch supporter of civil rights. He consistently voted throughout the Burger Court era and into the Rehnquist Court era to uphold liberal positions that were staked out during the 1960s. He dissented powerfully in cases that limited the scope of school integration orders to districts that had practiced deliberate discrimination. Marshall was often an engaging, blunt, and humorous speaker, but issued critical dissents. He was sharply critical of his successor on the bench, Clarence Thomas. Nevertheless, Thurgood Marshall exuded great warmth and when he retired, he was praised by his colleagues. Even those who did not agree with him respected his convictions, accomplishments, and fierce candor.

Further Reading

Michael E. Davis and Hunter R. Clark, *Thurgood Marshall: Warrior at the Bar, Rebel on the Bench,* Updated and Revised Edition (New York: Citadel Press, 1994).

CHAPTER 8

INTERROGATION AND THE LAW OF CONFESSIONS

The Constitution of the United States stands as a bar against the conviction of any individual in an American court by means of a coerced confession. There have been, and are now, certain foreign nations with governments dedicated to an opposite policy: governments which convict individuals with testimony obtained by police organizations possessed of an unrestrained power to seize persons suspected of crimes against the state, hold them in secret custody, and wring from them confessions by physical or mental torture. So long as the Constitution remains the basic law of our Republic, America will not have that kind of government.

—Justice Hugo Black, *Ashcraft v. Tennessee,* 322 U.S. 143, 155 (1944)

CHAPTER OUTLINE

KEY TERMS AND PHRASES

Admission
Bright-Line rule
Compulsion
Confession
Cruel Trilemma
Exculpatory
Immunity
Inculpatory
Interrogation
Involuntary Confession
Privilege
Real evidence
Self-incrimination
Supervisory authority
Testimonial evidence
Third Degree
Voluntariness test

INTRODUCTION

Questioning suspects and witnesses are vital techniques of police investigation.[1] This chapter examines the interrogation of suspects in order to obtain **admissions** or **confessions** of guilt. A major focus is on rules of *Miranda v. Arizona* (1966) under the Fifth Amendment privilege against self-incrimination and the interpretive cases following *Miranda.* In addition to protection against undue police pressure guaranteed by the Fifth Amendment, persons are also protected against coercive police tactics by the Due Process Clause. Prior to the *Miranda* decision, the Supreme Court decided many state cases under the Fourteenth Amendment that held **involuntary confessions** to be inadmissible into evidence. The due process involuntary confessions rule still exists as a back-stop to *Miranda* protections. Finally, the chapter looks at the Sixth Amendment rule, established in *Massiah v. United States* (1964), that a person who has been formally charged with a crime cannot be questioned, openly or surreptitiously, without the presence of her lawyer.

The Privilege Against Self-Incrimination

All persons questioned by police have a general obligation to cooperate and to answer questions truthfully (*Brogan v. United States,* 1998). A witness who does not agree to testify in a trial or before a grand jury, for example, may be subpoenaed, and a witness who has information material to the prosecution of a pending indictment, accusation or complaint for a crime, or a criminal investigation before a grand jury, may be confined as a material witness if a judge believes the person will flee.[2]

The law recognizes several **privileges** that exempt a person from providing information to lawful authority, including the privileges of religious, medical, or legal practitioners not to divulge information given in professional confidence. The privilege against **self-incrimination** was a product of English common law and was enshrined in the Fifth Amendment: "No person . . . shall be compelled in any criminal case to be a witness against himself. . . ." (This text uses the term "right" against self-incrimination interchangeably with the "privilege" against self-incrimination.) "The privilege is widely regarded as both fundamental to human liberty and venerable in the history of the development of civil rights."[3] Today, it is clearly related to modern notions of the right to privacy and is consonant with the essential constitutional rules that the *burden of proof* of guilt rests on the prosecution, and that guilt must be proven beyond a *reasonable doubt.* These rules are mainstays of the adversary system of justice. The privilege against self-incrimination stands in sharp contrast to brutal measures of ancient Rome and medieval and early modern continental Europe where torture was a lawful tactic that could be employed by judges to obtain evidence of serious crime.[4] But it also contrasts with far more civilized European criminal justice system today that many view as more effective in getting at the truth.[5] Nevertheless, in the American system of justice the privilege:

> reflects many of our fundamental values and most noble aspirations: our unwillingness to subject those suspected of crime to the **cruel trilemma** of self-accusation, perjury or contempt; our preference for an accusatorial rather than an inquisitorial system of criminal justice; our fear that self-incriminating statements will be elicited by inhumane treatment and abuses; our sense of fair play which dictates a fair state-individual balance by requiring the government to leave the individual alone until good cause is shown for disturbing him and by requiring the government in its contest with the individual to shoulder the entire load; our respect for the inviolability of the human personality and of the right of each individual to a private enclave where he may lead a private life; our distrust of self-deprecatory statements; and our realization that the privilege, while sometimes a shelter to the guilty, is often a protection to the innocent. (*Murphy v. Waterfront Commission of New York Harbor,* 1964, p. 55, internal references and quotation marks omitted)

The privilege has several elements and requirements that must be met before a person can properly claim its protection. Where the privilege does apply, it is an *absolute* bar to government questioning. Unlike Fourth Amendment law, there is no "balancing test" to determine whether the state or the individual will prevail if a person has a Fifth Amendment right. If the state wishes to achieve its legitimate goal to gather information in an inquiry or to further prosecution, and it believes that an individual who claims the privilege has relevant information, it cannot force the person to testify but has to grant immunity from prosecution or forego the testimony. If immunity from prosecution is granted and the witness continues to refuse to testify, the courts have power "to compel testimony . . . by use of civil contempt and coerced imprisonment. *Shillitani v. United States* (1966)." (*Lefkowitz v. Turley,* 1973)

In 1964, the Supreme Court incorporated the Fifth Amendment right against self-incrimination. Since that date, the privilege applies equally to federal, state, and local officers. "The Fourteenth Amendment secures against state invasion the same privilege that the Fifth Amendment guarantees against federal infringement—the right of a person to remain silent unless he chooses to speak in the unfettered exercise of his own will, and to suffer no penalty . . . for such silence." (*Malloy v. Hogan,* 1964, p. 8)

NATURAL PERSONS The privilege against self-incrimination is a personal right limited to protecting only the *natural individual* from being compelled to testify or produce personal records. An "artificial person," such as a corporation or its officers, may not claim the privilege (*Wilson v. United States,* 1911). A single proprietor has to produce documents, such as tax records or ledgers, in response to a subpoena, even if they are incriminating; he or she is simply not protected by the privilege against self-incrimination (*United States v. Doe,* 1984). The Fifth Amendment does not prevent the government from subpoenaing business records from a partner or partnership (*Bellis v. United States,* 1974), or tax records created by an individual and delivered to the person's attorney (*Fisher v. United States,* 1976). The Court has reasoned that these kinds of business records are made voluntarily.

COMPULSION Voluntary statements, no matter how incriminating, are not protected by the privilege. A person who admits to a friend that he robbed a store has made a voluntary statement and has no Fifth Amendment protection preventing the friend from divulging this information to the police. The same applies to a person who makes an incriminating statement to an undercover agent or into a lawfully placed secret electronic eavesdropping device.

The state, however, cannot *coerce* or compel a criminal suspect to testify at his trial. A corollary is that it violates a defendant's Fifth Amendment rights for a judge to comment to the jury on his silence because this creates state pressure to forego the exercise of one's right (*Griffin v. California,* 1965). A defendant could have a defense conducted by counsel entirely by cross-examination. An ordinary witness in a trial or grand jury hearing is not deemed under compulsion and so need not be given warnings as to their Fifth Amendment rights (*United States v. Monia,* 1943). If a witness makes an incriminating statement during his or her testimony, the statement has been made voluntarily. Therefore, it is the responsibility of a witness to claim the privilege, or it will be lost. On the other hand, "Testimony given in response to a grant of legislative **immunity** is the essence of coerced testimony. In such cases there is no question whether physical or psychological pressures overrode the defendant's will; the witness is told to talk or face the government's coercive sanctions, notably, a conviction for contempt" (*New Jersey v. Portash,* 1979). Therefore, grand jury testimony compelled by a grant of immunity could not be used later in a trial to impeach the witness's credibility.

The simple fact that a police officer asks a person questions is not Fifth Amendment **compulsion.** Police compulsion, discussed later, requires the reading of *Miranda* warnings and occurs in instances where a person is in custody.

INCRIMINATION Although the words of the Fifth Amendment state that the privilege applies "in any criminal case," it is not limited to criminal *prosecutions.* "The Amendment not only protects the individual against being involuntarily called as a witness against himself in a criminal prosecution but also privileges him not to answer official questions put to him in any other proceeding, civil or criminal, formal or informal, where the answers might incriminate him in future criminal proceedings" (*Lefkowitz v. Turley,* 1973). In *Lefkowitz,* architects refused to testify or sign waivers of immunity before a grand jury inquiry into bribery. The state then attempted to apply a law that would have barred them from receiving government contracts. The Court held that "A waiver secured under threat of substantial economic sanction cannot be termed voluntary."

A police officer was called to testify in an Attorney General's inquiry into fixing traffic tickets under the threat of losing his job. His testimony was held to be compelled, and the statement could not be used against him in a later prosecution for conspiracy (*Garrity v. New Jersey,* 1967). Similarly, a police officer subpoenaed to appear before a grand jury investigating police bribery and corruption refused to testify or to waive immunity, and, as a result, was discharged from his position for this refusal. The Supreme Court held that his discharge was unconstitutional because it was based on his "refusal to waive a constitutional right" (*Gardner v. Broderick,* 1968).

The costs that were threatened or imposed by the state in these cases came under the Fifth Amendment privilege because they were *punitive,* even though they did not involve the loss of liberty. In *Allen v. Illinois* (1986), the Supreme Court held (5–4) that the non-punitive loss of liberty is not protected by the privilege. Allen, charged with a sexual assault in Illinois, was ordered by the judge to submit to psychiatric examinations. The criminal charges were dropped, and the state proceeded against him under the Sexually Dangerous Persons Act. Allen claimed that the testimony of psychiatrists should be disallowed because he was not informed of his right against self-incrimination or right to counsel before the examinations. The Court held the psychiatric testimony to be admissible because the proceedings were essentially civil, rather than criminal, and the statements that Allen made to the psychiatrists did not lead to any criminal penalty. This decision has been criticized because it "is insensitive to the reality of the commitment system."[6] A person committed under the act may be held indefinitely; a petition is triggered only by criminal charges; a prior sexual crime is a predicate to the petition; the hearing has many criminal trial rights including a jury trial; the state must prove the person's sexual dangerousness beyond a reasonable doubt; the place of treatment is a psychiatric center located at a prison; and the center also houses convicts needing psychiatric care. Despite all this, the majority held that the Fifth Amendment did not apply to the questioning.

Incrimination refers only to incrimination in American courts. Aloyzas Balsys was subpoenaed by the Justice

Department to determine whether he committed perjury in his immigration application to the United States. He claimed that he had been hiding in Lithuania during World War II, but there was suspicion that he had been involved in Nazi-sponsored persecution. Since the statute of limitations on perjury had expired, Balsys could not be prosecuted in the United States. Balsys claimed correctly that any answers he provided could be the basis of prosecution in other countries, including Lithuania or Germany. The Supreme Court held that the terminology of the Fifth Amendment, "any criminal case," apparently broader than the words of the Sixth Amendment ("in all criminal prosecution"), nevertheless refers to American procedures, as do the other clauses of the Fifth Amendment (grand jury, double jeopardy, due process, just compensation). (*Balsys v. United States,* 1998)

TESTIMONY The Fifth Amendment privilege protects testimony, that is, evidence that is given by a live witness to a tribunal or police officer (or the transcript of a missing witness) who conveys information based on what the witness knows or believes he knows. Evidence is testimonial when it is of a "communicative nature" (*Schmerber v. California,* 1966). To be considered testimonial a "communication must itself, explicitly or implicitly, relate a factual assertion, or disclose information" that expresses "the contents of an individual's mind" (*Doe v. United States,* 1988). Testimony may not be directly self-incriminating, but when a witness speaks, the witness reveals something about his or her mental process to the listener; in a sense, the witness opens up his or her mind and psychological process to the scrutiny of the listener as well as providing facts that can lead to investigation, indictment, and incrimination. Thus, any witness who testifies is potentially open to the possibility that the statements will lead the listener to infer that the witness has admitted to a fact that is incriminating. In this way, even if a witness does not clearly confess to a crime, the witness may make admissions that are incriminating. It follows that all witnesses are entitled to raise the privilege against self-incrimination in those settings where the privilege applies. But this privilege applies only to **testimonial evidence.**

Physical evidence, also called real evidence, no matter how incriminating, is not protected by the privilege against self-incrimination. Justice Holmes ruled that a suspect has no right to prevent the court, jury, or witnesses from viewing the suspect's face and person (*Holt v. United States,* 1910). The physical evidence rule allows the government to "compel a person to reenact a crime; shave his beard or mustache; try on clothing; dye her hair; demonstrate speech or other physical characteristics; furnish handwriting samples, hair samples, or fingerprints; have her gums examined; or take a blood-alcohol, breathalyser, or urine test."[7] A suspect or defendant can be photographed or measured, have tattoos and scars examined, and be required to stand in a lineup. In *Schmerber v. California* (1966), the Court sustained the compulsory blood sample taken by medical personnel in a reasonable manner because there was reason to believe that the defendant was driving while intoxicated (DWI) and was responsible for a fatal automobile crash. The blood-taking did not invade the defendant's Fourth Amendment privacy interests (see Chapter 3), nor was the blood and its alcohol level a Fifth Amendment communication, although it was incriminating. Taking blood does not force a defendant to testify against himself or herself. In *Schmerber,* Justice Brennan distinguished blood evidence from a "lie detector" session. A lie detector is aimed, in part, at gathering physiological attributes, but "may actually be directed to eliciting responses which are essentially testimonial. To compel a person to submit to testing in which an effort will be made to determine his guilt or innocence on the basis of physiological responses whether willed or not, is to evoke the spirit and history of the Fifth Amendment. . . ." Thus, police departments uniformly give *Miranda* warnings before administering polygraph examinations.

THE ACT OF PRODUCING EVIDENCE Several federal courts of appeal have held although "the contents voluntarily produced papers are not protected by the Fifth Amendment, the act of producing such documents is protected . . . if the act itself is both testimonial and incriminating."[8] This is so because production exposes the producer to four potentially incriminating facts in regard to the paper: its existence, authenticity, possession, and the belief that the documents match the terms of a subpoena (*Fisher v. United States,* 1976). The Supreme Court has not established a bright-line rule that protects compelled production of records by the privilege against self-incrimination. Each case must be resolved on its own facts. Where a court determines that production itself is incriminating, the individual may still have to produce the records but may be personally shielded from criminal prosecution, but immunity is not automatic (*United States v. Doe,* 1984).

Certainly the oddest and most dramatic act-of-production case is *Baltimore Department of Social Services v. Bouknight* (1990). The Baltimore City Department of Social Services (BCDSS) removed an infant, Maurice, from his mother, Jacqueline Bouknight, on suspicion of child abuse. He was returned to her a few months later, under various conditions. Eight months later, fearing for Maurice's safety, juvenile court ordered his return to BCDSS custody. Jacqueline Bouknight refused to turn over the boy. A diligent search by police and relatives failed to produce him. Bouknight was held in contempt of court for failing to produce Maurice and was jailed. She challenged this in the United States Supreme

Court on the ground that the compelled production of Maurice might tend to incriminate her.

The Supreme Court held that Bouknight had no Fifth Amendment claim based on anything that the physical condition of Maurice might disclose. Her act-of-control argument was that "her implicit communication of control over Maurice at the moment of production might aid the State in prosecuting Bouknight." The Court ruled that even if the production of the boy were testimonial, it still did not give her the right to refuse the order, "because she has assumed custodial duties related to production [of Maurice] and production is required as a part of a noncriminal regulatory scheme." Therefore, the Court did not directly answer the question whether the Fifth Amendment would protect Bouknight against prosecution if she complied with the order and produced Maurice, and the production indicated child abuse. Having lost her case, Jacqueline Bouknight remained in custody for contempt of court for seven and a half years, one of the longest terms for contempt in United States history. She was released in October 1995. The judge who ordered the release said that continued imprisonment was no longer an effective tool to force the information from her. Her lawyers called Bouknight a hero of civil disobedience, but the judge who had held her in contempt expressed fears that the child might be dead.[9]

Confessions Law Before *Miranda*

English and American state courts first developed a common-law "rule of evidence which precludes the use at trial of involuntary statements," in about the 1780's. Police could question suspects, and incriminating statements could be used in evidence against them as long as the statements were not "induced by force, threat of force, or promise of leniency from a person in authority, for if it has been so obtained, it is considered 'involuntary' and excluded."[10] In 1912, the English Courts advanced the protection offered to a suspect from coercive interrogation by establishing the so-called *Judges' Rules* for the guidance of police officers. The *Judges' Rules* stated that before asking a person about to be charged with a crime if he or she wished to say anything in answer to the charges, that person should be told "You are not obliged to say anything unless you wish to do so, but whatever you say will be taken down in writing and may be given in evidence."[11] A failure to give the warning would render a statement improper and it could be excluded from consideration at trial. While the *Judges' Rules,* of course, had no legal effect in American states, they were well known to American jurists and established the idea that it is proper to inform a suspect of his basic right against self-incrimination.

The **voluntariness test** was established in each American state by the late nineteenth century. The Supreme Court, in *Bram v. United States* (1897), held that coerced confessions in *federal* cases were guided by the Fifth Amendment right against self-incrimination, and the test applied to determine whether a confession violated one's right against self-incrimination was essentially the voluntariness test. In both state and federal law, therefore, coerced or involuntary confessions were excluded from evidence but no warning requirement was yet established. In this era, the criminal justice Amendments of the Bill of Rights had not yet been incorporated, and so, the Fifth Amendment rule of *Bram* did not apply to the states. In practice, state courts were often reluctant to exclude confessions even when there was compelling evidence of coercion. As a result, defendants whose confessions were the product of coercion began to turn to the federal courts, claiming that such practices violated their Fourteenth Amendment rights in that their liberty had been deprived without due process. From 1936 until 1966, the Supreme Court decided more than thirty confessions cases from the states under the Due Process Clause. In 1964, the Fifth Amendment self-incrimination rule was incorporated, paving the way to *Miranda v. Arizona* (1966). A brief review of the due process voluntariness test helps us appreciate the significance of the "*Miranda* revolution."

In *Brown v. Mississippi* (1936), the first Supreme Court case to review a confession obtained by state or local officers, three African-American men confessed to committing a murder after they were subjected to torture during their interrogation by the local sheriff and others. Their treatment included being hung by a rope to a tree, being let down, and being hung again, and whipping "with a leather strap with buckles on it" that cut their backs to pieces. After resisting these tortures over three days, they were told that it would continue until they signed a confession dictated by a deputy. The Supreme Court held that confessions obtained by such physical torture was "not consistent" with Fourteenth Amendment due process of law, rendering the trial and conviction void because it "is a mere pretense where the state authorities have contrived a conviction resting solely upon confessions obtained by violence" (*Brown v. Mississippi* 1936). Thus, *Brown*'s legal foundation was not a specific Bill of Rights provision but the "fair trial" idea of the Fourteenth Amendment Due Process Clause, first adopted by the Court in *Moore v. Dempsey* (1923) (see Chapter 2).

This due process/fair trial approach toward involuntary confessions initiated by the *Brown* ruling was not limited to physical torture. The Court soon applied the voluntariness test to lesser forms of coercion. The basic question was whether, under the facts and circumstances of the case, a particular confession was *voluntary*? was it made of the defendant's *free will*? was it obtained by police interrogation tactics that overcame the defendant's will? In case after case, the Supreme Court moved inexorably toward *more refined* standards. In *Ashcraft v. Tennessee* (1944), for example, the police did not beat the defendant but questioned him "in relays" for *thirty-six hours* with no interruption until he confessed to murdering his wife. The Supreme Court held that the long period of straight questioning was itself sufficient coercion so that his statements were not voluntary but compelled. Justice Black cited the Wickersham Commission's report of 1930 that condemned this kind of police behavior, known as the **third degree,** "as a secret and illegal practice."[12] The "third degree," common in that era, ranged from severe questioning to police beatings of suspects to force confessions out of them. The Court, by granting certiorari in a stream of state confessions cases, was enforcing the involuntary confession rule in order to cause police departments to adopt more civilized methods of investigation. "An opinion in a coerced confessions case, *Chambers v. Florida* (1940), clearly acknowledged that the federal government had a duty to guarantee fair trials in state as well as federal courts."[13]

Other practices held to undermine the defendant's will and induce involuntary confessions in violation of the Fourteenth Amendment, included:

- defendant moved to secret places so that family, lawyers, or friends could not contact him, *Chambers v. Florida* (1940), *Ward v. Texas* (1942)
- defendant kept naked for several hours, *Malinski v. New York* (1945)
- defendant told by a state-employed psychiatrist that the doctor was there to help him and would provide medical assistance, thus gaining the defendant's confidence and incriminating information, *Leyra v. Denno* (1954)
- suspect, a young African-American, told that he would be handed over to a lynch mob, *Payne v. Arkansas* (1958)
- defendant, in his cell, told by a police officer (a childhood friend of the defendant) over a period of time, that the officer would lose his job if he did not get a statement, *Spano v. New York* (1959)
- vigorously interrogation of a mentally defective or insane suspect, *Blackburn v. Alabama* (1960); *Culombe v. Connecticut* (1961)
- using "truth serum," *Townsend v. Sain* (1963); and
- defendant told that her children's welfare assistance would be cut off and her children taken from her if she failed to cooperate with the police, *Lynumn v. Illinois* (1963).

Most of the justices were appalled by these police excesses, but as a court of law the Supreme Court could not directly outlaw them. However, using its due process jurisdiction, the Court progressively expanded the scope of what constituted coercion in the hope that police departments would refrain from engaging in these improper methods. Due process was appropriate to this task because it embodies "fundamental fairness," an elastic concept that, ideally, entrusts the Court to combine the community's "highest values with operating realities, to fashion a rule." In skillful hands, the "due process approach" allows the law to grow incrementally in response to specific problems while not making a radical break with the past.

PROBLEMS WITH THE VOLUNTARINESS RULE On the other hand, the due process approach also injects a level of *subjectivity* into the law that produces other problems. These problems created a growing dissatisfaction with the Supreme Court's confessions cases under the voluntariness test and, ultimately, led the Court to decide *Miranda* in the way that it did. A problem that made the due process voluntariness test unsatisfactory to many in the legal community was that it produced no clear guidance for lower courts and police. Rather than a clear-cut or **bright-line rule** stating how an interrogation should be conducted to avoid being found unconstitutional, police and judges were given a list of examples of what had been found improper in the past. Professor Richard Cortner commented:

> Adhering to the fair trial approach to the Due Process Clause, the Court followed a meandering and ofttimes puzzling course in state criminal cases during the 1950s. . . . [T]he Court's performance under the Due Process Clause was such as to involve it in unpredictable intrusions into the state criminal process on the basis of standards nowhere satisfactorily articulated—with the result that serious federal-state strains developed.[14]

This due process/totality of the circumstances approach to coerced confessions made it seem that the Court was engaging in *ad hoc,* case-by-case decision making, rather than following a firm constitutional policy. In different cases, the Court suggested three different constitutional policies for the due process voluntariness test: "(1) ensuring that convictions are based on *reliable evidence;* (2) *deterring improper police conduct;* or (3) assuring that a defendant's confession is the product of his *free and rational choice.*"[15] As the Court shuttled between these rationales, commentators, lawyers, and trial judges were left in confusion. In such early cases as *Brown* and *Ashcraft,* all three elements coincided: excessive police conduct overpowered the suspect's will and raised real doubts about the accuracy of the confession. In some later cases, the Court seemed to focus primarily on the *reliability* or accuracy of confessions. *Lyons v. Oklahoma* (1944) ruled that a confession would be upheld if the state "employed a fair standard in adjudicating common law in voluntariness claims" as long as it appeared that the confession was *true.* But in other cases, the Court set aside convictions, even where the confession's truthfulness was substantially corroborated, because the police misconduct was too great (*Watts v. Indiana,* 1949). Without signaling a clear intention to do so, the Court seemed to be shifting toward a *police conduct* test, concerned less with the accuracy of the confession or the voluntariness with which it was made and more with controlling egregious police conduct. In *Rogers v. Richmond* (1961), for example, the Court struck down a seemingly accurate and voluntary confession because the police tricked the suspect into thinking they were going to arrest his ailing wife for questioning. Although the Court did not use the *Rogers* case as a vehicle for sharply limiting police interrogation, it was clear that these varying purposes could produce inconsistent results in different cases. The lack of clarity of the rules or underlying purposes in its due process cases, led the Court to search for bright-line confessions rules that gave the police greater guidance.

THE FEDERAL "TIME" TEST A bright-line rule was established in *McNabb v. United States* (1943) and applied later in *Mallory v. United States* (1957). If a suspect arrested by federal officers was not brought before a magistrate without "unnecessary delay," as required by the Federal Rules of Criminal Procedure, a confession obtained was inadmissible. *McNabb* stated that an important goal of the universal rule that arrested persons be brought to a judicial officer without delay was to lessen the opportunity for police coercion. "For this procedural requirement checks resort to those reprehensible practices known as the 'third degree' which, though universally rejected as indefensible, still find their way into use. It aims to avoid all the evil implications of secret interrogation of persons accused of crime." This rationale was repeated in *Mallory* which also noted that an important function of the judge at the initial appearance is to inform a suspect of his or her rights.

The dangers inherent in the police practice of holding suspects in custody without bringing them to a judge were highlighted shortly before the *Miranda* decision in *Davis v. North Carolina* (1966). Elmer Davis, Jr., an African American with low mental functioning who had escaped from a prison camp, was held as a suspect in a rape-murder for *sixteen days* in a police lockup cell measuring six by ten feet and questioned every day in order to obtain a confession. A written station-house order instructed police not to allow anyone to have contact with Davis. Only after confessing was he taken before a magistrate, despite the state rule requiring that an arrested person be brought before a magistrate within a reasonable period of time. The Supreme Court ruled his confession to be involuntary.

An important limitation of the *McNabb-Mallory* rule is that it applied only to *federal* law enforcement officers and agencies because it was not based on the Fourteenth Amendment due process doctrine of "fundamental fairness." It was, instead, a *per se* rule based on the Supreme Court's inherent **supervisory authority** over lower *federal* courts and *federal* law enforcement. The "time test" was an indication that the justices were displeased by heavy-handed police actions in obtaining confessions, a concern that would animate the *Miranda* decision.

RIGHT TO COUNSEL The secrecy of police interrogation was a major concern. Without representation by counsel, the defendant is alone and vulnerable to improper police tactics. In two cases of the late 1950s, a minority of the justices challenged voluntary confessions on the grounds that the defendants' requests for attorneys were denied. Nevertheless, the decisions in *Crooker v. California* (1958) and *Cicenia v. LaGay* (1958) held that a mere denial to see one's attorney was not itself a due process violation. This position began to erode in *Spano v. New York* (1959), when four concurring justices argued that the defendant had a right of access to counsel and noted that he had been formally charged by indictment before confessing. The *Gideon v. Wainwright* (1963) decision a few years later, incorporating the right to counsel at trial, accelerated the pressure to view police interrogation as a critical stage. Moreover, in 1964, the Court in *Massiah v. United States* held that indicted defendants who had already obtained counsel could not be secretly taped or questioned by the police without the consent of the defendant's lawyer.

The turning point in the move to overtake the voluntariness test with a more determinate rule came in *Escobedo v. Illinois* (1964), which ruled that a pre-indictment suspect had a Sixth Amendment right to counsel during police interrogation, but only if the lawyer had been hired before the interrogation began. The *Escobedo* case has been called "enigmatic" because its holding was based on a dense set of facts, and it was not clear which of these facts would be crucial in extending the right to counsel in later cases.[16] For example, in *Escobedo,* a lawyer was hired by the family of a murder suspect; he made repeated attempts over a period of three or four hours to see his client at the police station; at one point, Escobedo and his lawyer made eye contact; the police refused to allow them to meet. There was no coercion under the voluntariness test, but the confession was declared unconstitutional. Which of these factors was critical to the holding of the case?

The Court's opinion also muddied the Sixth Amendment basis for its holding by injecting Fifth Amendment concerns: "[w]ithout informing him of his absolute right to remain silent in the face of this accusation, the police urged him to make a statement." *Escobedo* was an important case, but it was clearly not the final word on a firm rule for the guidance of police interrogation. In addition to the fact-specific nature of the holding, basing a right to counsel at police interrogation on the Sixth Amendment was problematic because the Sixth Amendment applies to the "criminal prosecution" which does not commence until formal charges have been preferred against a defendant. The *Escobedo* case left many questions unanswered, and the Supreme Court expected it would receive appeals, over a period of years, designed to clarify the ambiguities of the case. Instead of a trickle, it received a flood of cases and within two years startled the legal community with its monumental *Miranda* decision. *Miranda* took a new turn and, "decid[ing] to answer all of the questions at once," placed state confessions law firmly on a Fifth Amendment foundation.[17]

THE *MIRANDA* DECISION

The *Miranda* rule was not in itself an "incorporation case." The recently incorporated rights to counsel and privilege against self-incrimination, in a sense, gave the Supreme Court an impetus to forge a new approach and a definitive rule in an area of law that had bedeviled it for three decades. As it turned out, the Fifth Amendment, not the Sixth Amendment, provided the constitutional foundation for the *Miranda* rule. *Miranda* was, for a time, one of the most severely criticized cases in the Court's history referred to by some as a "self-inflicted wound." Many in the legal community were offended by the unprecedented and legislative-like style of the ruling, while police officials and conservative politicians denounced the Court for its pro-defendant ruling.[18]

Miranda was retried for rape and convicted in 1967 on the testimony of his common law wife that he had told her about the crime. He was later paroled but continued to get into criminal trouble. Ernesto Arturo Miranda was stabbed to death on January 31, 1976, in the restroom of a cheap bar in Phoenix, Arizona, after a fistfight. Police caught the man who had assailed Ernest and read him his *Miranda* warnings.[19]

• CASE & COMMENTS •

Miranda v. Arizona

384 U.S. 436, 86 S.Ct. 1602, 16 L.Ed.2d 694 (1966)

[The Supreme Court consolidated four cases. None of the suspects were fully informed of their constitutional rights, although some were informed of their right to remain silent. **[a]** In *Miranda v. Arizona,* the defendant confessed to a rape after being interrogated for two hours at a police station. In *Vignera v. New York,* the defendant made an oral admission to police questions about a robbery an the afternoon and made a written confession to a prosecutor in the evening. In *Westover v. United States* the defendant was arrested in the evening and interrogated about a robbery by local police. He was interrogated again the next day by FBI agents from 9 a.m. to 2:00 p.m. when he confessed. No warnings were given until noon. In *Stewart v. California* the defendant was interrogated nine times over five days by the police, and was held incommunicado until he confessed. He was then taken before an examining magistrate. There was no evidence of threats or violence in any of these cases. The majority opinion discussed the facts of the cases after fifty pages of constitutional analysis.]

[a] The facts in these cases, except perhaps for *Stewart,* would not have led the Supreme Court to declare these confessions unconstitutional under the voluntariness test.

MR. CHIEF JUSTICE WARREN delivered the opinion of the Court.

The cases before us raise questions which go to the roots of our concepts of American criminal jurisprudence: the restraints society must observe consistent with the Federal Constitution in prosecuting individuals for crime. **[b]** More specifically, we deal with the admissibility of statements obtained from an individual who is subjected to custodial police interrogation and the necessity for procedures which assure that the individual is accorded his privilege under the Fifth Amendment to the Constitution not to be compelled to incriminate himself.

[b] The factual setting for the ruling (custodial police interrogation) and the constitutional basis for the decision (the Fifth Amendment privilege) are stated simply and precisely.

* * *

We start here, as we did in *Escobedo,* **[c]** with the premise that our holding is not an innovation in our jurisprudence, but is an application of principles long recognized and applied in other settings. * * *

[c] This is disingenuous. As the dissents make plain, this case was clearly an innovation in the law.

* * *

Our holding ***briefly stated is this: the prosecution may not use statements, whether **exculpatory** or **inculpatory,** stemming from custodial interrogation of the defendant unless it demonstrates the

• CASE & COMMENTS •

use of procedural safeguards effective to secure the privilege against self-incrimination. **[d]** By custodial interrogation, we mean questioning initiated by law enforcement officers after a person has been taken into custody or otherwise deprived of his freedom of action in any significant way. As for the procedural safeguards to be employed, unless other fully effective means are devised to inform accused persons of their right of silence and to assure a continuous opportunity to exercise it, the following measures are required. Prior to any questioning, the person must be warned that he has a right to remain silent, that any statement he does make may be used as evidence against him, and that he has a right to the presence of an attorney, either retained or appointed. The defendant may waive effectuation of these rights, provided the waiver is made voluntarily, knowingly and intelligently. If, however, he indicates in any manner and at any stage of the process that he wishes to consult with an attorney before speaking there can be no questioning. Likewise, if the individual is alone and indicates in any manner that he does not wish to be interrogated, the police may not question him. The mere fact that he may have answered some questions or volunteered some statements on his own does not deprive him of the right to refrain from answering any further inquiries until he has consulted with an attorney and thereafter consents to be questioned.

[d] It is unusual, but not unheard of, for the Court to summarize a case at the beginning. This long paragraph is an outline of *Miranda*'s rules, more fully analyzed in Part III. The statute-like statement of the rules drew the fire of many legal commentators; they accused the Court of engaging in "judicial legislation" rather than deciding the case by resolving a narrow issue based on precedent.

I

*** [All the cases here] share salient features—incommunicado interrogation of individuals in a police-dominated atmosphere, resulting in self-incriminating statements without full warning of constitutional rights. **[e]**

An understanding of the nature and setting of this in-custody interrogation is essential to our decisions today. The difficulty in depicting what transpires at such interrogations stems from the fact that in this country they have largely taken place incommunicado. From extensive factual studies undertaken in the early 1930s, including the famous Wickersham Report to Congress by a Presidential Commission, it is clear that police violence and the "third degree" flourished at that time. In a series of cases decided by this Court long after these studies, the police resorted to physical brutality—beatings, hanging, whipping—and to sustained and protracted questioning incommunicado in order to extort confessions. ***

[e] The specific facts of the interrogation in each of the four cases are almost irrelevant to the decision, except for interrogation in secret and the lack of warnings. The relevant facts do not include physical or psychological coercion. This segues into a discussion of interrogation techniques found in police manuals.

* * *

Again we stress that the modern practice of in-custody interrogation is psychologically rather than physically oriented. *** ["T]his Court has recognized that coercion can be mental as well as physical, and that the blood of the accused is not the only hallmark of an unconstitutional inquisition". *** **[f]** Interrogation still takes place in privacy. Privacy results in secrecy and this in turn results in a gap in our knowledge as to what in fact goes on in the interrogation rooms. A valuable source of information about present police practices, however, may be found in various police manuals and texts which document procedures employed with success in the past, and which recommend various other effective tactics. ***

[f] The Court's skeptical attitude toward police interrogation conducted with brutality or extreme psychological pressure under the voluntariness test is transferred to the existence of *secret* interrogation under the *Miranda* rules.

The officers are told by the manuals that the "principal psychological factor contributing to a successful interrogation is privacy—being alone with the person under interrogation." ***

To highlight the isolation and unfamiliar surroundings, the manuals instruct the police to display an air of confidence in the suspect's guilt and from outward appearance to maintain only an interest in confirming certain details. **[g]** The guilt of the subject is to be posited as a fact. The interrogator should direct his comments toward the reasons why the subject committed the act, rather than court failure by asking the subject whether he did it. Like other men, perhaps the subject has had a bad family life, had an unhappy childhood, had too much to drink, had an unrequited desire for women. The officers are instructed to minimize the moral seriousness of the offense, to cast blame on the victim or on society. These tactics are designed to put the subject in a psychological state where his story is but an elaboration of what the police purport to know already—that he is guilty. Explanations to the contrary are dismissed and discouraged. * * *

[g] Are these practices outrageous? If not, are they akin to "high pressure sales tactics" designed to get the suspect to say things that would otherwise remain unsaid?

• CASE & COMMENTS •

* * *

When the techniques described above prove unavailing, the texts recommend they be alternated with a show of some hostility. One ploy often used has been termed the "friendly-unfriendly" or the "Mutt and Jeff" act. ***

The interrogators sometimes are instructed to induce a confession out of trickery. **[h]** The technique here is quite effective in crimes which require identification or which run in series. In the identification situation, the interrogator may take a break in his questioning to place the subject among a group of men in a line-up [and to coach a witness to identify the suspect] . ***A variation on this technique is called the "reverse line-up":

> "The accused is placed in a line-up, but this time he is identified by several fictitious witnesses or victims who associated him with different offenses. It is expected that the subject will become desperate and confess to the offense under investigation in order to escape from the false accusations."

[h] Is it ethical to engineer false accusations against a suspect if it is the only way to get a "guilty" person to confess? What if the suspect is in fact not guilty? Should there be some limits to such trickery?

* * *

From these representative samples of interrogation techniques, the setting prescribed by the manuals and observed in practice becomes clear. **[i]** In essence, it is this: To be alone with the subject is essential to prevent distraction and to deprive him of any outside support. The aura of confidence in his guilt undermines his will to resist. He merely confirms the preconceived story the police seek to have him describe. Patience and persistence, at times relentless questioning, are employed. To obtain a confession, the interrogator must "patiently maneuver himself or his quarry into a position from which the desired objective may be attained." When normal procedures fail to produce the needed result, the police may resort to deceptive stratagems such as giving false legal advice. It is important to keep the subject off balance, for example, by trading on his insecurity about himself or his surroundings. The police then persuade, trick, or cajole him out of exercising his constitutional rights.

[i] These examples from police manuals are not scientifically drawn random samples of police activity; nevertheless, there is no reason to disbelieve that they are uncommon. In your opinion, are they *inherently* coercive.

* * *

In the cases before us today, given this background, we concern ourselves primarily with this interrogation atmosphere and the evils it can bring. ***

In these cases, we might not find the defendants' statements to have been involuntary in traditional terms. **[j]** Our concern for adequate safeguards to protect precious Fifth Amendment rights is, of course, not lessened in the slightest. *** The fact remains that in none of these cases did the officers undertake to afford appropriate safeguards at the outset of the interrogation to insure that the statements were truly the product of free choice.

It is obvious that such an interrogation environment is created for no purpose other than to subjugate the individual to the will of his examiner. This atmosphere carries its own badge of intimidation. To be sure, this is not physical intimidation, but it is equally destructive of human dignity. ***Unless adequate protective devices are employed to dispel the compulsion inherent in custodial surroundings, no statement obtained from the defendant can truly be the product of his free choice.

[j] The Court here puts the finishing touch on its argument: the Fifth Amendment forbids compelled testimony; secret police interrogation is inherently compelling; safeguards are required in order to "dispel" compulsion.

* * *

[Part II of the opinion reviewed the history of the right against self-incrimination in English and American law, and its incorporation into the Fourteenth Amendment in *Malloy v. Hogan,* (1964), which established the constitutional jurisdiction for the Court to apply the Fifth Amendment to the states.]

III

Today, then, there can be no doubt that the Fifth Amendment privilege is available outside of criminal court proceedings and serves to protect persons in all settings in which their freedom of action is curtailed in any significant way from being compelled to incriminate themselves. We have concluded that without proper safeguards the process of in-custody interrogation of persons suspected or accused of crime contains inherently compelling pressures which work to undermine the

• CASE & COMMENTS •

individual's will to resist and to compel him to speak where he would not otherwise do so freely. In order to combat these pressures and to permit a full opportunity to exercise the privilege against self-incrimination, the accused must be adequately and effectively apprised of his rights and the exercise of those rights must be fully honored.

It is impossible for us to foresee the potential alternatives for protecting the privilege which might be devised by Congress or the States in the exercise of their creative rule-making capacities. **[k]** Therefore we cannot say that the Constitution necessarily requires adherence to any particular solution for the inherent compulsions of the interrogation process as it is presently conducted. Our decision in no way creates a constitutional straitjacket which will handicap sound efforts at reform, nor is it intended to have this effect. We encourage Congress and the States to continue their laudable search for increasingly effective ways of protecting the rights of the individual while promoting efficient enforcement of our criminal laws. However, unless we are shown other procedures which are at least as effective in apprising accused persons of their right of silence and in assuring a continuous opportunity to exercise it, the following safeguards must be observed.

[k] The Court's suggestion that other protective techniques could replace the warnings became an extremely controversial point. Later, critics used this statement to argue that *Miranda* warnings are not rules required by the constitution.

At the outset, if a person in custody is to be subjected to interrogation, he must first be informed in clear and unequivocal terms that he has the right to remain silent. **[l]** For those unaware of the privilege, the warning is needed simply to make them aware of it—the threshold requirement for an intelligent decision as to its exercise. More important, such a warning is an absolute prerequisite in overcoming the inherent pressures of the interrogation atmosphere. ***

[l] The first two warnings state the gist of the right against self-incrimination. What reasons are given for requiring them? Do you find the reasons convincing?

The Fifth Amendment privilege is so fundamental to our system of constitutional rule and the expedient of giving an adequate warning as to the availability of the privilege so simple, we will not pause to inquire in individual cases whether the defendant was aware of his rights without a warning being given. ***

The warning of the right to remain silent must be accompanied by the explanation that anything said can and will be used against the individual in court. This warning is needed in order to make him aware not only of the privilege, but also of the consequences of foregoing it. It is only through an awareness of these consequences that there can be any assurance of real understanding and intelligent exercise of the privilege. Moreover, this warning may serve to make the individual more acutely aware that he is faced with a phase of the adversary system—that he is not in the presence of persons acting solely in his interest.

The circumstances surrounding in-custody interrogation can operate very quickly to overbear the will of one merely made aware of his privilege by his interrogators. **[m]** Therefore, the right to have counsel present at the interrogation is indispensable to the protection of the Fifth Amendment privilege. ***

[m] The right to request counsel is *not* based on the Sixth Amendment but is required to protect Fifth Amendment rights.

* * *

In order fully to apprise a person interrogated of the extent of his rights under this system then, it is necessary to warn him not only that he has the right to consult with an attorney, but also that if he is indigent a lawyer will be appointed to represent him. Without this additional warning, the admonition of the right to consult with counsel would often be understood as meaning only that he can consult with a lawyer if he has one or has the funds to obtain one. ***

Once warnings have been given, the subsequent procedure is clear. If the individual indicates in any manner, at any time prior to or during questioning, that he wishes to remain silent, the interrogation must cease. **[n]** At this point he has shown that he intends to exercise his Fifth Amendment privilege; any statement taken after the person invokes his privilege cannot be other than the product of compulsion, subtle or otherwise. Without the right to cut off questioning, the setting of in-custody interrogation operates on the individual to overcome free choice in producing a statement after the privilege has been once invoked. If the individual states that he wants an attorney, the interrogation must cease until an attorney is present. At that time, the individual must have an opportunity to confer with the attorney and to have him present during any subsequent questioning. If the individual cannot obtain an attorney and he indicates that he wants one before speaking to police, they must respect his decision to remain silent.

[n] This consequence follows from the fact that one's Fifth Amendment right to be free of compelled testimony is absolute. In constitutional theory, at least, when a suspect is asked by the police to talk, he or she can "just say no." The right to cut off interrogation indicates that the Court feared that

• CASE & COMMENTS •

This does not mean, as some have suggested, that each police station must have a "station house lawyer" present at all times to advise prisoners. ***

If the interrogation continues without the presence of an attorney and a statement is taken, a heavy burden rests on the government to demonstrate that the defendant knowingly and intelligently waived his privilege against self-incrimination and his right to retained or appointed counsel. **[o]** *** Since the State is responsible for establishing the isolated circumstances under which the interrogation takes place and has the only means of making available corroborated evidence of warnings given during incommunicado interrogation, the burden is rightly on its shoulders.

An express statement that the individual is willing to make a statement and does not want an attorney followed closely by a statement could constitute a waiver. But a valid waiver will not be presumed simply from the silence of the accused after warnings are given or simply from the fact that a confession was in fact eventually obtained. ***

in practice police would disregard the suspect's rights and continue questioning. Do you think this level of distrust is justified?

[o] Two waiver rules are included here: the burden of proof of a voluntary waiver is on the state, and the state must produce some proof of a waiver.

* * *

The warnings required and the waiver necessary in accordance with our opinion today are, in the absence of a fully effective equivalent, prerequisites to the admissibility of any statement made by a defendant. **[p]** No distinction can be drawn between statements which are direct confessions and statements which amount to "admissions" of part or all of an offense. The privilege against self-incrimination protects the individual from being compelled to incriminate himself in any manner; it does not distinguish degrees of incrimination. Similarly, for precisely the same reason, no distinction may be drawn between inculpatory statements and statements alleged to be merely "exculpatory." If a statement made were in fact truly exculpatory it would, of course, never be used by the prosecution. In fact, statements merely intended to be exculpatory by the defendant are often used to impeach his testimony at trial or to demonstrate untruths in the statement given under interrogation and thus to prove guilt by implication. These statements are incriminating in any meaningful sense of the word and may not be used without the full warnings and effective waiver required for any other statement. In *Escobedo* itself, the defendant fully intended his accusation of another as the slayer to be exculpatory as to himself.

[p] This paragraph closes potential loopholes in the *Miranda* rules. A suspect might be led to say things he *thinks* will clear him (*exculpatory* statements) but which instead lead to independent evidence of guilt. These too are covered by the *Miranda* warnings.

The principles announced today deal with the protection which must be given to the privilege against self-incrimination when the individual is first subjected to police interrogation while in custody at the station or otherwise deprived of his freedom of action in any significant way. **[q]** It is at this point that our adversary system of criminal proceedings commences, distinguishing itself at the outset from the inquisitorial system recognized in some countries. ***

Our decision is not intended to hamper the traditional function of police officers in investigating crime. ***

[q] This makes the critical point that the Fifth Amendment privilege, thought by the dissenters to apply only at judicial-like hearings, applies prior to formal charges in the context of interrogation in police custody.

* * *

In dealing with statements obtained through interrogation, we do not purport to find all confessions inadmissible. Confessions remain a proper element in law enforcement. Any statement given freely and voluntarily without any compelling influences is, of course, admissible in evidence. *** There is no requirement that police stop a person who enters a police station and states that he wishes to confess to a crime, or a person who calls the police to offer a confession or any other statement he desires to make. **[r]** Volunteered statements of any kind are not barred by the Fifth Amendment and their admissibility is not affected by our holding today.

[r] Some contemporary critics in law enforcement felt that *Miranda* would eliminate police interrogation of suspects

* * *

[Part IV presented policy arguments in favor of the warnings requirement, noting that warnings were required in England and many Commonwealth nations, and were routinely given by FBI agents and military police without any loss of effective law enforcement. Part V applied the general rules of the decision to the four specific consolidated cases and in each held that the Fifth Amendment tights of the defendants had been violated.]

• CASE & COMMENTS •

[Justices Clark (concurring in *Stewart v. California*), Harlan, and White; each wrote dissenting opinions.]

MR. JUSTICE WHITE, with whom MR. JUSTICE HARLAN and MR. JUSTICE STEWART join, dissenting. ***

I

The proposition that the privilege against self-incrimination forbids in-custody interrogation without the warnings specified in the majority opinion *** has no significant support in the history of the privilege or in the language of the Fifth Amendment. ***The rule excluding coerced confessions matured about 100 years [after the privilege against self-incrimination did,] "but there is nothing in the reports to suggest that the theory has its roots in the privilege against self-incrimination. . . ." ***[s]

[s] The dissent's historical criticism is weakened by the fact that the Supreme Court applied the right against self-incrimination to confessions in *Bram*. The essence of the dissent's argument is that the majority has superseded the case-by-case voluntariness test which asked whether *this* defendant's will was overborne by the interrogation tactic, with the general rule of the warnings.

* * *

*** [T]he Fifth Amendment privilege was . . . extended to encompass the then well-established rule against coerced confessions *** [in] *Bram v. United States* ***

* * *

Bram, however, itself rejected the proposition which the Court now espouses. The question in *Bram* was whether a confession, obtained during custodial interrogation, had been compelled. ***[T]he Court declared that:

> "***the mere fact that the confession is made to a police officer, while the accused was under arrest in or out of prison, or was drawn out by his questions, does not necessarily render the confession involuntary; but, as one of the circumstances, such imprisonment or interrogation may be taken into account in determining whether or not the statements of the prisoner were voluntary" ***

* * *

III

*** Rather than asserting new knowledge, the Court concedes that it cannot truly know what occurs during custodial questioning, because of the innate secrecy of such proceedings. [t] It extrapolates a picture of what it conceives to be the norm from police investigatorial manuals, published in 1959 and 1962 or earlier, without any attempt to allow for adjustments in police practices that may have occurred in the wake of more recent decisions of state appellate tribunals or this Court. But even if the relentless application of the described procedures could lead to involuntary confessions, it most assuredly does not follow that each and every case will disclose this kind of interrogation or this kind of consequence. Insofar as appears from the Court's opinion, it has not examined a single transcript of any police interrogation, let alone the interrogation that took place in any one of these cases which it decides today. *** [T]he factual basis for the Court's premise is patently inadequate.

[t] Justice White accuses the majority of fabricating the constitutional element of coercion by assuming that the police manuals describe an undeviating reality in every confession situation, without proof of coercion in each specific case.

* * *

*** [E]ven if one assumed that there was an adequate factual basis for the conclusion that all confessions obtained during in-custody interrogation are the product of compulsion, the rule propounded by the Court would still be irrational, for, apparently, it is only if the accused is also warned of his right to counsel and waives both that right and the right against self-incrimination that the inherent compulsiveness of interrogation disappears. [u] But if the defendant may not answer without a warning a question such as "Where were you last night?" without having his answer be a compelled one, how can the Court ever accept his negative answer to the question of whether he wants to consult his retained counsel or counsel whom the court will appoint? *** The Court apparently realizes its dilemma of foreclosing questioning without the necessary warnings but at the same time permitting the accused, sitting in the same chair in front of the same policemen, to waive his right to consult an attorney. ***

[u] Justice White argues that there is a logical flaw in the opinion. If the station house atmosphere is inherently coercive, then it is logically impossible for suspects to voluntarily waive their rights in that atmosphere, even after being

• CASE & COMMENTS •

*** By considering any answers to any interrogation to be compelled regardless of the content and course of examination and by escalating the requirements to prove waiver, the Court not only prevents the use of compelled confessions but for all practical purposes forbids interrogation except in the presence of counsel. That is, instead of confining itself to protection of the right against compelled self-incrimination the Court has created a limited Fifth Amendment right to counsel—or, as the Court expresses it, a "need for counsel to protect the Fifth Amendment privilege." *** The focus then is not on the will of the accused but on the will of counsel and how much influence he can have on the accused. Obviously there is no warrant in the Fifth Amendment for thus installing counsel as the arbiter of the privilege.

informed of their rights. The majority assumes that armed with information, a suspect will be able to make an informed and non-compelled choice whether or not to speak.

In sum, for all the Court's expounding on the menacing atmosphere of police interrogation procedures, it has failed to supply any foundation for the conclusions it draws or the measures it adopts.

IV

* * *

In some unknown number of cases the Court's rule will return a killer, a rapist or other criminal to the streets and to the environment which produced him, to repeat his crime whenever it pleases him. **[v]** As a consequence, there will not be a gain, but a loss, in human dignity. The real concern is not the unfortunate consequences of this new decision on the criminal law as an abstract, disembodied series of authoritative proscriptions, but the impact on those who rely on the public authority for protection and who without it can only engage in violent self-help with guns, knives and the help of their neighbors similarly inclined. ***

[v] There is always a trade-off between security and liberty in criminal procedure; Justice White sees little gain in civil liberties by limiting the power of the police in this area.

Nor can this decision do other than have a corrosive effect on the criminal law as an effective device to prevent crime. A major component in its effectiveness in this regard is its swift and sure enforcement. The easier it is to get away with rape and murder, the less the deterrent effect on those who are inclined to attempt it. This is still good common sense. ***

* * *

AN INTERPRETATION OF MIRANDA Critics saw *Miranda* as a revolutionary break with the older rule. It could, however, be seen as an extension of the voluntariness test that previously was the rule both for federal law enforcement under the Fifth Amendment rule of *Bram* and for state and local police under the Fourteenth Amendment Due Process Clause. Therefore, the underlying rationale of the Fifth Amendment and due process is the same: forbidding compelled testimony. Since the voluntariness test had itself evolved over time from outlawing torture to finding that certain psychological pressure tactics were unconstitutional, it is not unreasonable to see *Miranda* as continuing the progressive civilizing approach of the confessions exclusionary rule, by getting at the source of undue compulsion. Hence, if the Court was correct that modern police interrogation is so highly manipulative as to amount to coercion, *Miranda* can be seen as a conservative ruling in that it preserved police interrogation. A logical extension of the voluntariness test could have led the Court to rule that all secret interrogation is unconstitutional. The effect of such a rule would have been like the *Massiah* rule, discussed at the end of this chapter, forbidding all questioning of a suspect without a lawyer present.

There is an irony to the aftermath of *Miranda.* The Court wished to replace the mass of case-specific rules under the voluntariness test with one bright-line rule for determining whether or not a confession was constitutional. It was not to be. *Miranda* was followed by an explosion of cases that litigated its meaning. In the two sections that follow, these cases are divided into two groups. The next section examines the very constitutional basis of *Miranda.* These cases were made possible by the rapid shift of the Supreme Court from one that followed the "due process approach" in the 1960s to a more conservative "crime control" court in the years that followed. Most of the justices appointed by Presidents Nixon, Reagan and Bush were hostile, or at best lukewarm, toward the *Miranda* rule. As was the case in regard to the Fourth Amendment exclusionary rule, the *Miranda* decision was not overruled, but it was declared not to be a constitutional rule. This led some to argue that if that was the case then the Court had no legitimate authority to impose a non-constitutional rule on the states. This issue was resolved in *Dickerson.* The section, "Interpreting *Miranda,*" examines cases that amplified the meaning of many of *Miranda*'s rules.

MIRANDA AS A CONSTITUTIONAL RULE

Attacking the Constitutional Basis of *Miranda*

The liberal majority that decided *Miranda* was roundly criticized for it in the 1968 presidential campaign and was succeeded by a pro-prosecution, centrist-to-conservative Court,[20] as Justices Warren, Fortas, Black, and Harlan were replaced by Justices Burger, Blackmun, Powell, and Rehnquist by 1972.[21] Many wondered whether the *Miranda* decision would be overruled. *Miranda*'s burial was hinted at in *Harris v. New York* (1971) which held that a confession obtained without complete *Miranda* warnings could nevertheless be introduced into evidence, not to prove guilt, but to *impeach* the credibility of the defendant whose testimony contradicted his confession. This suggested that a *Miranda*-deficient confession was not truly a constitutional violation and that a lower level of respect would be given to the words of *Miranda* than to the Constitution. Justice Brennan, dissenting, quoted a passage from *Miranda* that clearly rebutted the decision of *Harris:*

> The privilege against self-incrimination protects the individual from being compelled to incriminate himself in *any* manner . . . [S]tatements merely intended to be exculpatory by the defendant are often used to *impeach* his testimony at trial. . . . These statements are incriminating in any meaningful sense of the word and *may not be used without the full warnings* and effective waiver required for any other statement. (*Miranda v. Arizona,* 1966, quoted in *Harris v. New York* (1971) (emphasis added)

Chief Justice Burger, author of the majority opinion, avoided the logic of this statement by treating it as mere *dictum* that "was not at all necessary to the Court's holding [in *Miranda*] and cannot be regarded as controlling." In contrast to a *Miranda* error, a "pure" self-incrimination situation arises when a grand jury witness is required to speak under a grant of immunity. This is direct Fifth Amendment compulsion, and it violates the privilege against self-incrimination for the state to use the compelled grand jury statements to impeach the witness later at a trial (*New Jersey v. Portash,* 1979). In *Harris,* the Court began to chip away at the underlying theory of the *Miranda* warnings as constitutional rules.

Michigan v. Tucker (1974), continuing to undermine *Miranda,* went beyond *Harris* by providing the conceptual framework that has contained the spread of the *Miranda* ruling and was later used to roll it back. warnings were given to Tucker (he was right to appointed counsel) before the was handed down. Tucker gave police information to a witness who incriminated Tucker. Nothing that Tucker said was used against him, but evidence *derived* from his statement, the fruit of the poisonous tree, was used against him. Because the interrogation occurred prior to the *Miranda* decision (which was held not to be retroactive), eight justices, including several liberals, concurred that the conviction should not be reversed.

The importance of *Tucker* was in Justice Rehnquist's reasoning. He divided *Miranda* into two components, asking "whether the police conduct complained of directly infringed upon respondent's right against compulsory self-incrimination or whether it instead violated only the prophylactic rules developed to protect that right." *Miranda* was a "new doctrine" that allowed the exclusion of confessions for reasons other than non-voluntariness. "To supplement this new doctrine and to help police officers conduct interrogations without facing a continued risk that valuable evidence would be lost, the Court in *Miranda* established a set of specific protective guidelines, now commonly known as the *Miranda* rules." Then came the lynchpin of his argument:

"The [Miranda] Court recognized that these procedural safeguards were not themselves rights protected by the Constitution but were instead measures to insure that the right against compulsory self-incrimination was protected" (Michigan v. Tucker, p. 444, emphasis added). He deduced that the Miranda majority did not view the warnings as constitutional from these words in Miranda v. Arizona (p. 467): "We cannot say that the Constitution necessarily requires adherence to any particular solution for the inherent compulsions of the interrogation process as it is presently conducted."

Was this correct? Justice Rehnquist omitted portions of the quotation. Three sentences after these words, Chief Justice Warren, in Miranda, wrote, "However, unless we are shown other procedures which are at least as effective in apprising accused persons of their right of silence and in assuring a continuous opportunity to exercise it, the following safeguards must be observed" (emphasis added). The mandatory nature of the warnings requirement, or some equivalent protection, plus the statement that the Constitution requires the protections, makes it plausible that the Warren Court majority did not intend to separate the Miranda Fifth Amendment right from the warnings. Nevertheless, the Tucker majority employed the classic device of analyzing prior precedent (as described by Professor Levi in Chapter 1 of this text).

The majority in *Tucker* concluded that the police did not violate Tucker's historic right against compulsory self-incrimination "but rather failed to make available to him the ıl measure of procedural safeguards associated with that right since *Miranda*." There was no heavy handed coercion here. Did a violation of the *Miranda* warnings require exclusion of the derivative evidence? The Court noted that Tucker's statements could not be admitted at his trial. It then made an analogy to the Fourth Amendment exclusionary rule which allows the use of illegally seized evidence in proceedings other than the trial, since (1) the exclusionary rule is not itself a constitutional rule, but a court made protective device, and (2) the ancillary use of such evidence has a lower deterrent effect on police misconduct. The Court extended this logic to the law of confessions.

In this way, *Miranda* was not overruled, but it was "reduced in rank," so to speak. A violation of the Self-Incrimination Clause *itself* does not allow the Court to balance liberty against the needs of effective law enforcement: where testimony is compelled, it cannot be used in any form. By ruling that the *Miranda* warnings are not in themselves constitutional rights but merely protective remedies, a less than direct violation of the *Miranda* rule gives the Court leeway to balance the interests of the state and the suspect and allow the use of statements taken in violation of the *Miranda* warnings. The Court held that given the inadvertent nature of the violation in this case excluding the fruits of Tucker's voluntary statements would not deter police misconduct.

A majority of the Court, thereafter, continued to view the *Miranda* warnings as procedural safeguards and not as constitutional rights in themselves. In *Oregon v. Elstad* (1985), police arrested a teenage burglary suspect in his home and in response to a question—interrogation prefaced by no *Miranda* warnings—he made a quick admission: "Yes, I was there." Later that day, at the police station, proper *Miranda* warnings were given followed by a waiver of rights and a confession. The initial statement was inadmissible because no warnings were given. The Court ruled that the fruit-of-the-poisonous-tree doctrine did not bar the second confession: it was not "tainted" as a result of the prior illegal admission. Justice O'Connor noted that:

> a procedural *Miranda* violation differs in significant respects from violations of the Fourth Amendment, which have traditionally mandated a broad application of the "fruits" doctrine. The purpose of the Fourth Amendment exclusionary rule is to deter unreasonable searches, no matter how probative their fruits. . . .
>
> The *Miranda* exclusionary rule, however, serves the Fifth Amendment and sweeps more broadly than the Fifth Amendment itself. It may be triggered even in the absence of a Fifth Amendment violation. (*Oregon v. Elstad* [1985])

Therefore, a *Miranda* default does not necessarily carry other constitutional implications. The majority felt that if the first admission had been coerced under the voluntariness test, that might have invalidated a later confession.

Justice Brennan dissented strongly. He argued that the *Elstad* example was a classic ploy designed to break a suspect's will. The first question might have been asked of eighteen-year-old Michael Elstad to "soften him up" into a confessing mood making him more willing to waive his rights and talk at the police station since the "cat was out of the bag." The majority and the dissenters clearly differed as to whether *Miranda* was a constitutional rule. Justice Brennan believed that "*Miranda* clearly emphasized that warnings and an informed waiver are essential to the Fifth Amendment privilege itself."

Despite this, the Burger and Rehnquist Courts did not overrule *Miranda* but has kept its application within narrow bounds. After arguing that the case should be overruled, Chief Justice Burger signaled his willingness to abide by *Miranda* in 1980: "The meaning of *Miranda* has become reasonably clear and law enforcement practices have adjusted to its strictures; I would neither overrule *Miranda,* disparage it, nor extend it at this late date" (*Rhode Island v. Innis,* 1980, concurring). The reasons for this turnabout were (1) a concern that overruling *Miranda* "at this late date" might be misread by some police officers as a withdrawal of the Court's concern, thus, tacitly condoning abusive police tactics, (2) a desire, for symbolic purposes, not to make it seem as if the Court was retracting individual liberties, and, perhaps most important (3) a realization by 1980 that *Miranda* was not hampering police in obtaining confessions.

The Public Safety Exception

The doctrinal foundation laid in *Harris, Tucker,* and *Elstad* bore full fruit in *New York v. Quarles* (1984), a case that created a "public safety" exception to *Miranda.* By creating an explicit exception to *Miranda* based on a balancing test, the Court confirmed its view that the *Miranda* warnings were not constitutionally required even if a coerced confession itself violated the Fifth Amendment privilege. The *Quarles* decision implied that *Miranda* could be overruled if the Court found, for example, that other methods prove adequate to lessen the coercive atmosphere of custodial interrogation and adequately protect Fifth Amendment rights. This concern was alive in *Miranda* jurisprudence for a decade and a half and was finally put to rest in 2000 in *Dickerson v. United States.*

The facts in *Quarles* are that at 12:30 A.M. two police officers were approached by a woman who told them that she had just been raped by a black male whom she described as wearing a jacket with the name "Big Ben" printed in yellow letters on the back. She told the officers that the man had just entered an A & P supermarket located nearby and that he was carrying a gun. The officers spotted the man in the supermarket and arrested him after a brief chase through the aisles. When frisked, the man, Benjamin Quarles, was wearing an empty shoulder holster. After handcuffing him, Officer Kraft asked him where the gun was. Quarles nodded in the direction of some empty cartons and responded, "the gun is over there." Officer Kraft then retrieved a loaded .38–caliber revolver from a carton, formally placed Quarles under arrest, and read him his *Miranda* rights from a printed card. Quarles said that he would be willing to answer questions. When Officer Kraft asked him if he owned the gun and where he had purchased it, Quarles answered that he did own it and that he had purchased it in Miami.

The New York courts, at every level, excluded Quarles' initial statement and the gun from evidence in the trial because he had not been read *Miranda* warnings before the question was asked, and also excluded the statement about the ownership and purchase of the gun as being derived from an illegal interrogation. The Supreme Court agreed that the brief scenario in *Quarles* constituted custodial interrogation by police, a situation that calls for warning a suspect of his rights under *Miranda* for any statement to be admissible in evidence. Nevertheless, the Court (6–3) reversed the New York Court of Appeals (that state's highest court) and remanded the case for further proceedings.

The basis of the Court's holding was that "this case presents a situation where concern for public safety must be paramount to adherence to the literal language of the prophylactic rules enunciated in *Miranda*." The Court thus injected something like the Fourth Amendment balancing test and an exigent-circumstances exception into a Fifth Amendment area. Were *Miranda* a constitutional rule, this would not be permissible for "the Fifth Amendment's strictures, unlike the Fourth's, are not removed by showing reasonableness" (*Quarles,* p. 653, n. 6), i.e., the Fifth Amendment is absolute. The key to the holding, then, is that the *Miranda warnings* themselves are not an essential part of the Fifth Amendment—are not themselves constitutional rules. "The prophylactic *Miranda* warnings therefore are 'not themselves rights protected by the Constitution but [are] instead measures to insure that the right against compulsory self-incrimination [is] protected.' Requiring *Miranda* warnings before custodial interrogation provides 'practical reinforcement' for the Fifth Amendment right" (*Quarles,* p. 654, citing *Michigan v. Tucker*) and would "reduce the likelihood that the suspects would fall victim to constitutionally impermissible practices of police interrogation."

Justice Rehnquist, writing for the majority, made a subtle statement that indicated an attitude dismissive of Quarles' claim. While acknowledging that the case came within the four corners of *Miranda,* he also wrote: "In this case we have before us no claim that respondent's statements were *actually compelled* by police conduct which overcame his will to resist. Thus the only issue before us is whether Officer Kraft was justified in failing to make available to respondent the procedural safeguards associated with the privilege against compulsory self-incrimination since *Miranda*" (*Quarles,* pp. 654–55). This is odd, first, because if *Miranda* applies (i.e., if there is custodial interrogation) there is by definition a coercive atmosphere, which provides Fifth Amendment compulsion. Second, as Justice Marshall emphasized in the dissent, Quarles was handcuffed when asked where the gun was weakening the conclusion that there was a real threat to public safety and increasing the belief that the suspect was in a coercive atmosphere.

In any event, the Court held that:

> on these facts there is a 'public safety' exception to the requirement that *Miranda* warnings be given before a suspect's answers may be admitted into evidence, and that the availability of that exception does not depend upon the motivation of the individual officers involved. In a kaleidoscopic situation such as the one confronting these officers, where spontaneity rather than adherence to a police manual is necessarily the order of the day, the application of the exception which we recognize today should not be made to depend on . . . the subjective motivation of the arresting officer. Undoubtedly most police officers, if placed in Officer Kraft's position, would act out of a host of different, instinctive, and largely unverifiable motives—their own safety, the safety of others, and perhaps as well the desire to obtain incriminating evidence from the suspect. (*New York v. Quarles,* pp. 655–56)

The holding was criticized by three dissenting justices who differed sharply in their view of the constitutional basis of the warnings. Because the "Court in *Miranda* determined that custodial interrogations are inherently coercive . . . [it] therefore created a *constitutional presumption* that statements made during custodial interrogations are compelled in violation of the Fifth Amendment and are thus inadmissible in criminal prosecutions" (*New York v. Quarles,* Marshall, J. dissenting, p. 683, emphasis added). The dissent also chided the majority for substituting its view of whether a threat to public safety existed. Each New York court that reviewed the facts believed there was no threat to public safety: the store was deserted in the middle of the night; there was no indication that Quarles had a confederate who might take the gun and turn it on the police; the police were certain that the gun was in the immediate area of the arrest, Quarles was handcuffed; and "the arresting officers were sufficiently confident of their safety to put away their guns." The majority ruled that a threat to public safety depended on objective factors rather than "the subjective motivation of the arresting officer." Still, Justice Marshall said that the New York courts had so ruled and archly noted that members of the majority in another case said they would defer to the fact finding of the state courts. Without saying so directly, Justice Marshall was saying that the more conservative judges were picking and choosing rules to fit the outcome they wanted to achieve.

A last point worth noting about *Quarles* was raised by Justice O'Connor who concurred in the majority opinion and, in essence, cast her vote against the public safety exception. Her concern was that "In my view, a "public safety" exception unnecessarily blurs the edges of the clear line heretofore established and makes *Miranda*'s requirements more difficult to understand." This would lead to inconsistent rulings. As a result, she would have excluded Quarles' answer to Officer Kraft's question but would have allowed the gun to be used in evidence. The majority opinion acknowledged Justice O'Connor's concern that the bright-line rule of always giving the warnings would "to some degree [] lessen the desirable clarity of that rule. . . . The exception will not be difficult for police officers to apply because in each case it will be circumscribed by the exigency which justifies it. We think police officers can and will distinguish almost instinctively between questions necessary to secure their own safety or the safety of the public and questions designed solely to elicit testimonial evidence from a suspect." The majority believed that adding some slight confusion to the law was worth the price of increasing public safety, especially when dealing with a rule—the *Miranda* warnings—that supposedly were not, in themselves, constitutional rules.

Rehabilitating *Miranda*

CONGRESS ATTACKS *MIRANDA* A backlash in Congress shortly after the *Miranda* decision set the stage for the Court's last word on the constitutional stature of the confessions case more than 30 years later. In 1968, Congress passed a Crime Control Act that established the federal criminal justice agency (now the National Institute of Justice) and included in its Title II "the most sweeping attack on the Supreme Court since Franklin Roosevelt tried to expand its membership in 1937"[23]—a law which purported to overrule *Miranda* and a few other defendant's rights cases that angered conservative senators. The statute, codified as 18 *U.S.C.* §3501, basically says that in any federal prosecution a confession "shall be admissible in evidence if it is voluntarily given." Under the law, being advised of one's right to remain silent is not required for a confession to be admissible, but is only one factor to be taken into account to determine if the confession is voluntary. Under accepted doctrines of American constitutionality, Congress may, by statute, reverse judge-made law that is not based on the Constitution. But, when the Supreme Court establishes a constitutional doctrine by its interpretation of a constitutional provision, the only way in which that can properly be modified is by the court itself (e.g., *Gideon v. Wainwright* overruling *Betts v. Brady*) or by constitutional amendment (e.g., the first sentence of the Fourteenth Amendment "overruled" the *Dred Scott* case). Congress could legitimately "overrule" *Miranda* (for federal prosecutions only) and roll back the law to the case-by-case voluntariness rule only if the decision was *not* a "constitutional" ruling.

NON-APPLICATION OF §3501 Why had §3501 not arisen in any case until the 1990s? Since the passage of the statute, U.S. Attorneys General, Republican and Democrat, have understood that the law directly pitted the power of Congress against the authority of the Court. They exercised restraint and refused to invoke the law in the rare cases in which a defendant won an appeal on the grounds of a *Miranda* violation, not wishing to raise the specter of conflict between two branches of government. After the Supreme Court established the *Tucker* doctrine—that *Miranda* warnings are only prophylactic rules developed to protect the underlying Fifth Amendment right—a foundation was created for overruling *Miranda* on this basis, or using it to energize §3501. The Court did not do this leading some critics to argue that the Court was imposing a non-constitutional rule on the states via its supervisory power and, thus, illegitimately

THE PUBLIC SAFETY EXCEPTION IN THE STATES

Most states appear to have adopted the public safety exception. However, in its application, some courts have found that it does not always apply.

MINNESOTA A police officer arrested Hazley and without reading *Miranda* warnings asked him who he was and who he was with. Hazley replied and the answer was incriminating because it connected him to a robber. The trial court admitted the statement under the public safety exception. The Court of Appeals of Minnesota held that this did not come under the public safety exception even though the police had reason to believe that one of the robbers carried a gun. "Missing accomplices cannot be equated with missing guns in the absence of evidence that the accomplice presents a danger to the public 'requiring immediate action by the officers beyond the normal need expeditiously to solve a serious crime.'" *State v. Hazley* (Minn. App. 1988)[22] asserting "the power of constitutional amendment." They urged that *Miranda* be overruled, although other scholars have defended the ruling.[24] In fact, the Supreme Court had occasion to interpret a part of §3501 in *United States v. Alvarez-Sanchez* (1994) (holding that a rule that made voluntary confession admissible if made within six hours of initial custody applied to federal charges) without raising the constitutional conflict because this portion of the act modified the *McNabb-Mallory* rule which had been based on the Supreme Court's supervisory power and not on an interpretation of the Constitution. In *Davis v. United States* (1994), Justice Scalia, a critic of Miranda, testily noted in a case that refused to apply the section that "This is not the first case in which the United States has declined to invoke §3501 before us" . . . and warned that he would raise §3501, even if not raised by the government, "when a case that comes within the terms of this statute is next presented to us." Thus, critics who looked forward to overruling *Miranda* were seeking an opportunity to bring §3501 before the Court.

DICKERSON: REHABILITATING MIRANDA This opportunity finally arose in 2000. Charles Dickerson was indicted for bank robbery and related crimes. He moved to suppress a statement he had made to FBI agents on the ground that he had not received *Miranda* warnings. The district court granted the motion to suppress because of technical errors in warning Dickerson and specifically ruled that the confession was otherwise voluntary. The federal prosecutors appealed this ruling to the Court of Appeals for the Fourth Circuit, reputed to be the most conservative federal court of appeals in the nation. At this point, the Clinton Administration, through a letter from Attorney General Janet Reno to Congress, asserted that insofar as §3501 sought to overrule *Miranda,* it was unconstitutional. An interesting feature of the case was that the Washington Legal Foundation, a conservative public interest group, entered the case as amicus curiae, and its attorney, Professor Paul Cassell, a former prosecutor who helped to formulate a critical review of *Miranda* under President Reagan's Attorney General, Edwin Meese, submitted arguments against *Miranda.*[25] This was not a chance happening. Professor Cassell, described as "an indefatigable, ideologically driven young law professor at the University of Utah" has made a career of trying to get the courts to use §3501 to overrule *Miranda.* "For seven years, Cassell filed such briefs in one or two cases a year, primarily in the District of Utah or in the Fourth Circuit. These were his current and former stomping grounds and two of the most inviting venues legally, based on controlling Federal precedents in those regions."[26] *Dickerson v. United States* (2000) was an ideal vehicle. When the Court of Appeals for the Fourth Circuit held (2–1) that "Congress, pursuant to its power to establish the rules of evidence and procedure in the federal courts, acted well within its authority in enacting §3501, [and] §3501, rather than *Miranda,* governs the admissibility of confessions in federal court," and the opinion was upheld by a majority of the entire Fourth Circuit court, the stage was set for a showdown over *Miranda.*

In a 7–2 opinion for the Court, Chief Justice Rehnquist wrote:

> We hold that *Miranda,* being a constitutional decision of this Court, may not be in effect overruled by an Act of Congress, and we decline to overrule *Miranda* ourselves. We therefore hold that *Miranda* and its progeny in this Court govern the admissibility of statements made during custodial interrogation in both state and federal courts. (*Dickerson v. United States,* 120 S. Ct. 2329–30)

How did the majority square this definitive holding with its longstanding view that the *Miranda* warnings were only protective rules and not of constitutional weight? The Court relied on two modes of reasoning. First, it said that it has always applied *Miranda* as a constitutional rule, "although we concede that there is language in some of our opinions that supports the view" that *Miranda* is not a constitutional rule. Several reasons were given to support the view of *Miranda* as a constitutional rule. One seems circular: *Miranda* is constitutional because it was applied to three state cases and has been applied thereafter to many state cases. Another reason cites the *Miranda* case itself which stated that it was giving "concrete constitutional guidelines" to law enforcement. Another reason adopted the argument of the dissenters in *Tucker:* the warnings required by *Miranda* have not been superseded by other methods of securing a suspect's right to remain silent in the coercive atmosphere of a police station. What of cases like *Quarles* and *Harris* that have created exceptions to *Miranda?* The answer was (i) that the Court had also broadened the scope of *Miranda* in a couple of cases and (ii) that a rule can be constitutional and have exceptions:

> These decisions illustrate the principle—not that *Miranda* is not a constitutional rule—but that no constitutional rule is immutable. No court laying down a general rule can possibly foresee the various circumstances in which counsel will seek to apply it, and the sort of modifications represented by these cases are as much a normal part of constitutional law as the original decision. (*Dickerson v. United States,* p. 2335)

The Court dealt with the rule of *Oregon v. Elstad* that stated: "the *Miranda* exclusionary rule . . . serves the Fifth Amendment and sweeps more broadly than the Fifth Amendment itself." The Court recast this statement to mean it "does not prove that *Miranda* is a nonconstitutional decision, but simply recognizes the fact that unreasonable searches under the Fourth Amendment are different from unwarned interrogation under the Fifth Amendment." (*Dickerson,* p. 2335)

The second basis for *Dickerson* is precedent.

> Whether or not we would agree with *Miranda*'s reasoning and its resulting rule, were we addressing the issue in the first instance, the principles of *stare decisis* weigh heavily against overruling it now. See, e.g., *Rhode Island v. Innis,* (1980) (Burger, C. J., concurring in judgment) ("The meaning of *Miranda* has become reasonably clear and law enforcement practices have adjusted to its strictures; I would neither overrule *Miranda,* disparage it, nor extend it at this late date"). While *stare decisis* is not an inexorable command, particularly when we are interpreting the Constitution, even in constitutional cases, the doctrine carries such persuasive force that we have always required a departure from precedent to be supported by some special justification.
>
> We do not think there is such justification for overruling *Miranda. Miranda* has become embedded in routine police practice to the point where the warnings have become part of our national culture. While we have overruled our precedents when subsequent cases have undermined their doctrinal underpinnings, we do not believe that this has happened to the *Miranda* decision. If anything, our subsequent cases have reduced the impact of the *Miranda* rule on legitimate law enforcement while reaffirming the decision's core ruling that unwarned statements may not be used as evidence in the prosecution's case in chief. (*Dickerson v. United States,* p. 2336, internal citations and quotations omitted)

The Court concluded its opinion with one of the original criticisms of the voluntariness approach, that it "is more difficult than *Miranda* for law enforcement officers to conform to, and for courts to apply in a consistent manner."

The two most conservative justices, Scalia and Thomas, dissented. Justice Scalia's opinion states that the majority opinion did not say directly that the rule of §3501 (allowing the use of a voluntary confession even if warnings were not given) was unconstitutional, because the "Justices whose votes are needed to compose today's majority are on record as believing that a violation of *Miranda* is *not* a violation of the Constitution." He, pinpointed a rather uncomfortable aspect of the case, that it appears that several of the justices, including Chief Justice Rehnquist, made an about face. Thus, he noted that the Court used phrases like "*Miranda* is a constitutional decision," "*Miranda* is constitutionally based," *and Miranda* has "constitutional underpinnings," without saying "that custodial interrogation that is not preceded by *Miranda* warnings or their equivalent violates the Constitution of the United States." "[The majority] cannot say that, because a majority of the Court does not believe it. The Court therefore acts in plain violation of the Constitution when it denies effect to this Act of Congress" (*Dickerson,* pp. 2337–38). The dissent sees a fundamental violation of constitutional principle. Chief Justice Rehnquist's adroit opinion, on the other hand, can be seen as a mature reflection of the fact that constitutional government can be based on understandings—constitutional norms—that develop over time and has also been read as a signal to Congress that it cannot tread lightly on an area within the preserve of the Supreme Court's authority. After years of doubt as to the viability of the *Miranda* rule, the question appears to have been put to rest.

Voluntariness after *Miranda*

Miranda v. Arizona did not eliminate the due process voluntariness test. Even if *Miranda* warnings are read to a suspect, police interrogation may still be coercive and overbear the suspect's will. In such a case, a confession is inadmissible under the Fourteenth Amendment because it is coerced. Additionally a coerced confession cannot be used to impeach the defendant should he chose to testify.

A blatant example of involuntariness occurred in *Mincey v. Arizona* (1978). The Supreme Court remanded the case on Fourth Amendment grounds, examined *Miranda*-deficient statements taken from the defendant; in anticipation of their use to impeach Mincey's testimony, the Court ruled on the voluntariness of the statements. Mincey, an injured suspect, was brought to the intensive care unit of a hospital in critical condition. He was heavily medicated when asked by Detective Hust, "Did you shoot anyone?" It seemed clear to the Court that Mincey's reply, "I can't say, I have to see a lawyer," was evidence of a clear desire not to speak. Yet, he was pressed by the detective and made an incriminating statement.

> It is hard to imagine a situation less conducive to the exercise of "a rational intellect and a free will" than Mincey's. He had been seriously wounded just a few hours earlier, and had arrived at the hospital "depressed almost to the point of coma," according to his attending physician. Although he had received some treatment, his condition at the time of [Detective] Hust's interrogation was still sufficiently serious that he was in the intensive care unit. He complained to Hust that the pain in his leg was "unbearable." He was evidently confused and unable to think clearly about either the events of that afternoon or the circumstances of his interrogation, since some of his written answers were on their face not entirely coherent. Finally, while Mincey was being questioned he was lying on his back on a hospital bed, encumbered by tubes, needles, and breathing apparatus. He was, in short, "at the complete mercy" of Detective Hust, unable to escape or resist the thrust of Hust's interrogation. (*Mincey v. Arizona,* pp. 398–99)

Despite the fact that Mincey had made some coherent statements, the Court concluded:

> It is apparent from the record in this case that Mincey's statements were not "the product of his free and rational choice." . . . To the contrary, the undisputed evidence makes

> clear that Mincey wanted *not* to answer Detective Hust. But Mincey was weakened by pain and shock, isolated from family, friends, and legal counsel, and barely conscious, and his will was simply overborne. Due process of law requires that statements obtained as these were cannot be used in any way against a defendant at his trial. (*Mincey v. Arizona,* pp. 401–02)

Thus, the state could not use Mincey's statements for impeachment purposes.

The Supreme Court held (5–4) a confession to be involuntary in *Arizona v. Fulminante* (1991). Fulminante, in federal prison for a weapons offense, was suspected of having murdered his stepdaughter. He was befriended by another inmate, Anthony Sarivola, a former police officer who became a paid informant for the FBI. Masquerading as an organized crime figure, Sarivola promised to protect Fulminante against violence from other inmates if they discovered he had killed his daughter, but only if he told Sarivola whether he committed the crime. Fulminante admitted the crime to Sarivola who later testified at Fulminante's murder trial. The Supreme Court, in what Justice White for the majority called a close question, affirmed the Arizona Supreme Court's decision that "[T]he confession was obtained as a direct result of extreme coercion and was tendered in the belief that the defendant's life was in jeopardy if he did not confess. This is a true coerced confession in every sense of the word." Both courts drew on common knowledge of the fact that prisoners are known to assault and even murder child abusers and, thus, could conclude that Fulminante spoke out of fear for his life.

When a defendant raises the issue of a coerced confession under the Due Process Clause at trial, he must be allowed to introduce evidence of "the physical and psychological environment in which the confession was obtained." Therefore, even if a court determines in a pre-trial hearing that a confession is voluntary, a jury may disagree and find that the confession was involuntary, or decide not to give it great weight (*Crane v. Kentucky,* 1986). Innocent suspects have been known to make voluntary confessions, which they later regret, and it would be impossible for a defendant making such a claim to be able to prove it if evidence of the confession environment were excluded.

INTERPRETING *MIRANDA*

Miranda v. Arizona (1966) spawned scores of cases that interpreted each particular rule that together make up the decision. For the most part, the rulings ensured sufficient flexibility to ensure that the rules would not be overly restrictive on the police, although several areas of law strengthened protections for defendants.

Adequacy of Warnings

The four warnings that are read to a suspect prior to interrogation need not be read in the *precise words* found in the *Miranda* case, but they must adequately convey the *substance* of each warning (*California v. Prysock,* 1981). Randall Prysock, a minor, was arrested for murder and declined to talk to his interrogator, Police Sergeant Byrd. His parents were called and spoke with Randall, and he agreed to talk. Sergeant Byrd informed Randall and his parents in a taped procedure of his rights: that incriminating evidence would be used against him, to remain silent, to have a lawyer present before and during questioning and, as a juvenile, to have his parents present. As for providing free counsel to an indigent, Sergeant Byrd said: "You all, uh,—if,—you have the right to have a lawyer appointed to represent you at no cost to yourself." The Supreme Court majority found that "[i]t is clear that the police in this case fully conveyed to respondent his rights as required by *Miranda.*" Justice Stevens's dissented because, as the California courts found, the warning failed to inform Prysock "that the services of a free attorney were available *prior* to the impending questioning." It was more likely that Prysock would have decided not to talk until he had a lawyer had the warning been clearer.

The Court again, in *Duckworth v. Eagan* (1989) refused (5–4) to find somewhat "nonstandard" language in the warnings given to a defendant to be inadequate. Eagan was told, as part of otherwise complete *Miranda* warnings, that:

> You have a right to talk to a lawyer for advice before we ask you any questions, and to have him with you during questioning. You have this right to the advice and presence of a lawyer even if you cannot afford to hire one. *We have no way of giving you a lawyer, but one will be appointed for you, if you wish, if and when you go to court.* If you wish to answer questions now without a lawyer present, you have the right to stop answering questions at any time. You also have the right to stop answering at any time until you've talked to a lawyer. (*Duckworth v. Eagan,* 1989, emphasis added)

Chief Justice Rehnquist, for the majority, noted that the warnings as a whole "touched all of the bases required by *Miranda.*" The additional phrase that a lawyer will be appointed "if and when you go to court" merely informs the suspect of the normal routine of how lawyers are appointed. He also noted that under *Miranda,* lawyers need not be producible on call, nor do police stations need to have attorneys on the premises at all times to advise suspects.

Justice Marshall, for the dissenters, thought the warnings given here would mislead the average suspect into believing that only suspects who could *afford* lawyers could have one immediately; others "not so fortunate" must wait. Also, "a warning qualified by an 'if and when' caveat still fails to give a suspect any indication of when he will be taken to court. Upon hearing the warnings given in this case, a suspect would likely conclude that no lawyer would be provided until trial" (*Duckworth v. Eagan,* 1989, Marshall, J. dissenting). The dissents in *Prysock* and *Eagan* aimed at making *Miranda* protections clear and unambiguous to defendants, even to the point of *expanding* the content of the required warnings. The majority opinions adhere closely to the precise contours of *Miranda.*

The Supreme Court has not added new warnings or *additional information* to the four basic warnings (*Colorado v. Spring,* 1987). Spring was questioned twice while in jail, about two months apart, first by federal agents and a second time by Colorado officers. Complete warnings were administered both times, and Spring signed waiver forms. The federal agents questioned Spring about a firearms violation. They knew he was a homicide suspect and asked him, during the questioning, if he had ever shot anyone. "Spring admitted that he had 'shot [a] guy once'" and that statement was used in evidence against him. The Supreme Court held it was not necessary, under *Miranda,* for the federal officers to tell Spring that they knew he was a murder suspect or that he would later be approached by Colorado officers about that crime. "The Constitution does not require that a criminal suspect know and understand every possible consequence of a waiver of the Fifth Amendment privilege. . . . Here, the additional information could affect only the wisdom of a *Miranda* waiver, not its essential voluntary and knowing nature." Justice Marshall, dissenting, saw this as a psychological ploy designed to undermine Spring's will to remain silent. Under these circumstances, he argued, a failure to give the suspect additional information nullified the voluntary, knowing, and intelligent nature of the waiver of rights making the confession unconstitutional.

The Waiver of Rights

Miranda v. Arizona (1966) held that if a confession is obtained, "a *heavy burden* rests on the Government to demonstrate that the defendant *knowingly* and *intelligently* waived his privilege against self incrimination and his right to retained or appointed counsel." The Court allowed an oral waiver, but stated that "a valid waiver will not be presumed simply from the silence of the accused after warnings are given or simply from the fact that a confession was in fact eventually obtained."

The "heavy burden" of proving a voluntary waiver was met in *North Carolina v. Butler* (1979). Butler was read his rights and refused to sign a waiver form. The officer told him that he did not have to speak or sign the form but that he wanted to talk to Butler. Butler replied, "I will talk to you but I am not signing any form." Justice Stewart ruled that this constituted a valid waiver:

> An express written or oral statement of waiver of the right to remain silent or of the right to counsel is usually strong proof of the validity of that waiver, but is not inevitably either necessary or sufficient to establish waiver. The question is not one of form, but rather whether the defendant *in fact* knowingly and voluntarily waived the rights delineated in the *Miranda* case. As was unequivocally said in *Miranda* mere silence is not enough. That does not mean that the defendant's silence, coupled with an understanding of his rights and a course of conduct indicating waiver, may never support a conclusion that a defendant has waived his rights. (*North Carolina v. Butler,* 1979, emphasis added)

The majority found, after examining the facts and circumstances, that the defendant had knowingly and voluntarily waived his rights. The minority view, expressed by Justice Brennan for three dissenting justices, interpreted *Miranda* to require an *affirmative waiver* and, therefore, considered Butler's confession invalid. While an affirmative waiver, such as signing a *Miranda* form, is the normal practice today, *Butler* indicates that where the state meets its heavy burden of proving a voluntary waiver, a verbal agreement to speak can constitute a waiver of rights. *Butler* is an example of the Court's reluctance to expand the specific rules of *Miranda.*

The "heavy burden" was not met in *Tague v. Louisiana* (1980), where the state produced no evidence to show that the defendant knowingly or voluntarily waived his rights. In *Butler,* the *record* indicated that the full complement of warnings was read and that the defendant understood them. In *Tague,* the arresting officer who testified at the hearing to suppress the confession could not recall whether the defendant understood his rights. Without a record, it was an error to *presume* that the suspect understood the warnings.

Connecticut v. Barrett (1987) held that a suspect can *partially waive Miranda* rights. After warnings were read to him, Barrett said he was willing to talk to the police but would not sign a statement without a lawyer present. As a general rule, questioning should have ceased. In this case, however, Barrett was very clear that he was willing to talk about the crime but wanted to see a lawyer only about whether he should *sign* a statement, and he repeated this at his trial. The Supreme Court held his incriminating statements admissible. Here, his "affirmative announcements of his willingness to speak with the authorities" overrode his limited request for a lawyer. This is an exceptional case and the general rule is that a request for a lawyer ends a confession session.

Termination and Resumption of Questioning

> Once warnings have been given, the subsequent procedure is clear. If the individual indicates in any manner, at any time prior to or during questioning, that he wishes to remain silent, the interrogation must cease. At this point he has shown that he intends to exercise his Fifth Amendment privilege; any statement taken after the person invokes his privilege cannot be other than the product of compulsion, subtle or otherwise. Without the right to cut off questioning, the setting of in-custody interrogation operates on the individual to overcome free choice in producing a statement after the privilege has been once invoked. (*Miranda v. Arizona,* pp. 473–74)

Chief Justice Warren, an experienced former prosecutor, knew it was quite common for interrogating officers to badger suspects—to continue questioning them even after they invoke their right to remain silent. Although the passage may seem clear on its face, the Supreme Court later thought that it is ambiguous:

> This passage . . . does not state under what circumstances, if any, a resumption of questioning is permissible. The passage could be literally read to mean that a person who has invoked his "right to silence" can never again be subjected to custodial interrogation by any police officer at any time or place on any subject. Another possible construction of the passage would characterize "any statement taken after the person has invoked his privilege" as "the product of compulsion" and would therefore mandate its exclusion from evidence, even if it were volunteered by the person in custody without any further interrogation whatever. Or the passage could be interpreted to require only the immediate cessation of questioning, and to permit a resumption of interrogation after a momentary respite. (*Michigan v. Mosley,* 1975, pp. 101–02)

Richard Mosley was arrested for a robbery. During questioning at Detroit police headquarters, after having been read his rights, Mosley said he did not want to talk about the case, whereupon questioning ceased. Some time later, at 6:00 P.M., Mosley was taken from his fourth-floor cell to the homicide division on the fifth floor of the same building. He was read his rights, agreed to talk, and made an incriminating statement that led to evidence that was used to convict him of a homicide. The Supreme Court ruled that Mosley's second statement was admissible at trial. Justice Stewart fashioned a facts-and-circumstances rule that allow the police to question a defendant who has invoked his rights about an entirely *different crime* after a *lapse of time.* Mosley's statement was admissible in evidence because he was properly warned and *never requested a lawyer* and, when he asked that questioning cease, his request was honored. The mere fact that he once terminated the interrogation did not bar requestioning for a different criminal act.

TERMINATION AND RESUMPTION TENNESSEE IN THE STATES

Melvin Crump, an escapee from a Department of Corrections work detail was arrested for a murder at about 1:00 P.M. He was handcuffed, placed in the back seat of a patrol car, *Mirandized,* and asked if he wished to talk. He said that he did not. The officer terminated questioning and told Crump that he was wanted for murder. Other officers arrived and were informed that Crump, after hearing warnings, refused to talk. For the next few hours, Crump was taken "on a ride through north Nashville to retrace his escape route, with the hope of 'learning something that deals with the homicide.'" At the location of a car robbery connected to the homicide, officers asked Crump if he had taken anything from the car. He admitted to doing so. The officers told Crump that this connected him to the homicide. At this point his emotions changed, and he looked upset. When they returned to the police station, Crump made a confession. The "trial court found that Crump's right to cut off questioning and remain silent was not 'scrupulously honored,'" under *Mosley.*

The Tennessee Supreme Court agreed. "Thirty minutes after responding to Miranda warnings with 'I don't have anything to say,' he was taken on a 30 to 45-minute drive and questioned while retracing the route of his escape. This clearly constituted an impermissible resumption of in-custodial interrogation, which caused the admissions made by Crump during the drive to be inadmissible." Noting that the Tennessee constitutional self-incrimination provision is "more protective of individual rights than the test of voluntariness under the Fifth Amendment," the Tennessee court distinguished *Mosley* and ruled that the violation in this case was of constitutional magnitude and the confession was suppressed. (State v. Crump, 1992)[27]

Invoking the Right to Counsel

> [A]n individual held for interrogation must be clearly informed that he has the right to consult with a lawyer and to have the lawyer with him during interrogation. . . . This warning is an absolute prerequisite to interrogation. No amount of circumstantial evidence that the person may have been aware of this right will suffice to stand in its stead. (*Miranda v. Arizona,* pp. 471–72)

Once a defendant claims a desire to see an attorney, questioning must stop. The Supreme Court has generally interpreted this requirement favorably for suspects.

For example, in *Smith v. Illinois* (1984), an eighteen-year-old robbery suspect, while in custody, was read the required *Miranda* warnings. Told he had a right to consult with a lawyer and have a lawyer present while being questioned, he replied, *"Uh, yeah. I'd like to do that."* The officer did not stop, but continued to advise Smith of his rights and asked, "Do you wish to talk to me at this time without a lawyer being present?" Smith replied, *"Yeah and no, uh, I don't know what's what really."* To this, the officer said, "*Well. You either have [to agree] to talk to me this time without a lawyer being present* and if you do agree . . . you can stop at any time you want to." Smith replied, "All right. I'll talk to you then" and subsequently confessed.

The Court found that Smith *invoked his right to counsel* by his first statement in a clear and unambiguous way. While the statements made after the first request for counsel may have been ambiguous, the Court held that "[w]here nothing about the request for counsel or the circumstances leading up to the request would render it ambiguous, all questioning must cease" (*Smith v. Illinois,* 1984). The Court also ruled that "an accused's postrequest responses to further interrogation may not be used to cast retrospective doubt on the clarity of the initial request itself. Such subsequent statements are relevant only to the distinct question of waiver." Justice Rehnquist, writing for three dissenters, believed that the interrogation had not yet begun but that police were still in the process of giving Smith his warnings. He noted that Smith had not been badgered. Justice Rehnquist felt that the *Miranda* warning process should be examined in its totality. The holding of *Smith v. Illinois,* however, demonstrates that invocation of the right to counsel is defined strictly by the Supreme Court.

NONLEGAL ADVISORS The Court's strict posture regarding requests for *counsel* is not extended to requests for help from other individuals or officials. In *Fare v. Michael C.* (1979), a juvenile in custody asked to see his probation officer during a murder interrogation. Justice Blackmun held that a request for a probation officer was not equivalent to a *Miranda* request for an attorney. "The *per se* aspect of *Miranda* [was] based on the unique role the lawyer plays in the adversarial system of criminal justice. . . ." A probation officer is a state employee who is a peace officer and does not act unequivocally on behalf of the suspect. Justice Marshall dissented (joined by Justices Brennan and Stevens), reinterpreting *Miranda* to say that questioning should stop whenever a juvenile requests an adult who is obligated to represent his or her interests. He suggested that it is unrealistic to expect a juvenile to call for a lawyer; it is more likely for a youth to turn to parents or an other adult, such as a welfare worker, as the only means of securing legal counsel. However reasonable this point is, the Court was not willing to *expand Miranda* rights.

THIRD-PARTY INVOLVEMENT What happens if third parties—such as parents, friends, or relatives—request an attorney for suspects being held by the police, even though the accused themselves have not invoked their *Miranda* rights? The Court has ruled that this is not an invocation of Fifth Amendment rights by the suspect personally, and any confession made while an attorney is trying to contact the suspect does not violate this *Miranda* rule.

In *Moran v. Burbine* (1986), Brian Burbine was arrested for breaking and entering and was suspected of an earlier murder. After his arrest, his sister called the public defender's office to obtain assistance of an attorney. A staff attorney, Allegra Munson, called the police department. Once advised that Burbine was in custody, she told the police that she was representing him in the event he was questioned or placed in a lineup. The unidentified officer told Munson that Burbine would not be questioned that night. An hour later, however, police did *Mirandize* and question Burbine who waived his rights and ultimately made incriminating statements.

Burbine raises the issues of waiver and the right to counsel. Regarding waiver, Justice O'Connor, for the majority, held that "[e]vents occurring outside of the presence of the suspect and entirely unknown to him surely can have no bearing on the capacity to comprehend and knowingly relinquish a constitutional right." Even the officer's deception of attorney Munson, whether inadvertent or not, unethical or not, does not change the fact that Burbine knowingly and intelligently waived his rights. The Court refused to add a requirement to *Miranda* that the police must inform a defendant of attempts of an attorney to reach him, citing grave practical problems that such a requirement would raise.

That someone had procured counsel for Burbine before he was questioned did not change the complexion of his rights. Justice O'Connor stated:

> the suggestion that the existence of an attorney-client relationship itself triggers the protections of the Sixth Amendment misconceives the underlying purposes of the right to counsel. The Sixth Amendment's intended function is not to wrap a protective cloak around the attorney-client relationship for its own sake any more than it is to protect

> a suspect from the consequences of his own candor. Its purpose, rather, is to assure that in any "criminal prosecutio[n]" the accused shall not be left to his own devices in facing the " 'prosecutorial forces of organized society.' " (*Moran v. Burbine,* p. 430)

Also, since Burbine had not yet been charged by a grand jury or by information, the Sixth Amendment right to an attorney did not yet apply. The majority refused to apply *Escobedo v. Illinois* which had come to be reinterpreted as a case having focused more on the right against self-incrimination than the right to counsel, in effect, making the *Escobedo* rule a dead letter.

TERMINATION AND RESUMPTION OF QUESTIONING The Supreme Court more strictly protects the rights of suspects who invoke the right to counsel than those who terminate questioning without asking for the assistance of counsel. In *Edwards v. Arizona* (1981), Robert Edwards was arrested for robbery, burglary, and murder. Questioned at the police station after being given proper *Miranda* warnings, he told the officers that he wanted to "make a deal," but the police terminated the discussion when he said, "I want an attorney before making a deal." The next day, detectives came to the lockup and reinterrogated him. After playing him a taped statement of an alleged accomplice, Edwards agreed to talk as long as it was not tape-recorded, and he implicated himself in the crime. The Supreme Court reversed his conviction. Although a person may validly waive rights, Justice White, for the majority, held:

> when an accused has invoked his right to have counsel present during custodial interrogation, a valid waiver of that right cannot be established by showing only that he responded to further police-initiated custodial interrogation even if he has been advised of his rights. We further *hold* that an accused, such as Edwards, having expressed his desire to deal with the police only through counsel, is not subject to further interrogation by the authorities until *counsel has been made available* to him, *unless the accused himself initiates* further communication, exchanges, or conversations with the police. (*Edwards v. Arizona* [1981], emphasis added)

Oregon v. Bradshaw (1983) dealt with the issue of the suspect initiating further questioning. In this case, interrogation ceased after Bradshaw requested counsel. The Court held that it was properly initiated by Bradshaw's question made in the trip between the police station and jail, *"Well, what is going to happen to me now?"* Bradshaw was again read his rights, and, in a "general conversation," Bradshaw agreed to take a lie detector test. The next day, Bradshaw took a lie detector test which was preceded by *Miranda* warnings and that resulted in an incriminating admission. A four-justice plurality said that Bradshaw's question, although ambiguous, "evinced a willingness and a desire for a generalized discussion about the investigation." A four-justice dissent, written by Justice Marshall, found the interpretation placed on Bradshaw's words by the plurality to be preposterous:

> If respondent's question had been posed by Jean-Paul Sartre before a class of philosophy students, it might well have evinced a desire for a "generalized" discussion. But under the circumstances of this case, it is plain that respondent's only "desire" was to find out where the police were going to take him. (*Oregon v. Bradshaw,* p. 1055)

The Supreme Court, in *Davis v. United States* (1995), held that in order to invoke the protection of *Edwards,* the request for counsel must be made *clearly.* Naval investigators suspected that Robert L. Davis beat another sailor to death with a pool-cue. Davis was arrested, advised of his rights under military law, and waived his rights to remain silent. An hour and a half into the interview, Davis said, *"Maybe I should talk to a lawyer."* The Navy investigators said:

> We made it very clear that we're not here to violate his rights, that if he wants a lawyer, then we will stop any kind of questioning with him, that we weren't going to pursue the matter unless we have it clarified is he asking for a lawyer or is he just making a comment about a lawyer, and he said, "No, I'm not asking for a lawyer," and then he continued on, and said, "No, I don't want a lawyer." . . . (*Davis v. United States,* p. 455)

The investigators took a short break and then reminded Davis of his rights to remain silent and to counsel. They continued the interview for another hour, and at that point Davis said, "I think I want a lawyer before I say anything else." . . . Questioning then ceased. An incriminating statement was made after Davis said "Maybe I should talk to a lawyer." The Court held that the statement was admissible and that Davis's rights under *Edwards* were not violated.

Analytically, there are three possible options to determine if the statement invoked counsel: (1) any mention of counsel, however ambiguous, invokes counsel; (2) the *Edwards* protection is invoked if the suspect's request meets a "threshold" standard of clarity; or (3) whenever a suspect mentions a lawyer, questioning must cease, but interrogators may ask "narrow questions designed to clarify the earlier statement and the [suspect's] desires respecting counsel." The Court selected the second option.

Noting that *Edward*'s prohibition on questioning is not itself a constitutional right but, like the *Miranda* rule, a protection for the Fifth Amendment, Justice O'Connor, writing for the Court, held that "after a knowing and voluntary waiver of the *Miranda* rights, law enforcement officers may continue questioning until and unless the suspect clearly requests an attorney." Justice O'Connor said that asking "clarifying questions" (option number three), while good police practice, is not required. *Davis* upholds the bright-line rule of *Edwards* by not forcing interrogating officers "to make difficult judgment calls about whether the suspect in fact wants a lawyer even though he hasn't said so, with the threat of suppression if they guess wrong."

Although the *Bradshaw* plurality seemed to strain in order to rule in favor of the state, and *Davis* burdens a suspect's *Edwards'* rights, for the most part, the Supreme Court has interpreted the *Edwards* "bright-line rule" in favor of suspects.

For example, in *Michigan v. Jackson* (1986), the Court held that a suspect invokes the right to counsel at a formal arraignment where the suspect tells a judge that he wants a lawyer. Police officers present at Jackson's arraignment were bound by the *Edwards* rule and could not lawfully interrogate him simply by reading him his *Miranda* warnings. And, in *Arizona v. Roberson* (1988), the Court held that once a suspect asked to see a lawyer before speaking, this knowledge applied not only to the officer who first *Mirandized* the suspect, but to every officer in the same agency. This is a necessary corollary to the *Edwards* rule since it would be too easy for police officers to sidestep *Edwards* by claiming ignorance of an invocation of rights. Justice Stewart noted that "[C]ustodial interrogation must be conducted pursuant to established procedures, and those procedures in turn must enable an officer who proposes to initiate an interrogation to determine whether the suspect has previously requested counsel." In a well-run police department, an officer who questions a suspect should know which other officers had previously questioned him and be apprised of any request for counsel.

Support for the *Edwards* rule continued in *Minnick v. Mississippi* (1990). A suspect invoked the right to counsel during an interrogation, was allowed to consult with a lawyer, and was thereafter interrogated without counsel present. He made an admission during the second interrogation. The Court held, in an opinion by Justice Kennedy, that simply allowing the suspect to confer with counsel does not satisfy *Edwards.* A suspect who asks to speak to a lawyer is demanding a right to have a lawyer *present* during interrogation. Unless a subsequent uncounseled conversation is *initiated* by the suspect, as required by *Edwards,* the police cannot reinterrogate. The Court emphasized that a different standard would dilute the clarity of *Edwards*'s bright-line rule; it could create confusion whereby a suspect would gain *Edwards* protection at several points during custody by invoking the right to counsel, and then lose it after conferring with an attorney. Justice Kennedy stated several benefits of maintaining the *Edwards* rule. It prevents the police from badgering suspects; it conserves judicial resources that would be expended in making factually complex voluntariness determinations; it avoids the burden on officials to determine when a consultation with counsel is sufficient to create a waiver; and it avoids counsel delaying meetings with clients so as to preserve their *Edward*'s protections.

Justice Scalia dissented, joined by Chief Justice Rehnquist. He stressed that both *Miranda* and *Edwards* were prophylactic and not constitutional rules, and that *Edwards* sets a higher standard for waiver of rights than that of *Johnson v. Zerbst* (1938). He believed that the Court in *Minnick* established an irrebuttable presumption (i.e., virtually a firm rule) against waiving the right to counsel. Instead, he would allow the state to prove—after an invocation of the right to counsel and after counsel has been provided—that a confession was made knowingly and voluntarily.

Defining Custody

> By custodial interrogation, we mean questioning initiated by law enforcement officers after a person has been taken into custody or deprived of his freedom of action in any significant way. (*Miranda v. Arizona,* p. 444)

The Supreme Court has expanded *Miranda*'s definition of *police custody* beyond the station house. The basic question is: Does the setting in which a confession is given create the compulsion contemplated by the Fifth Amendment that brings the *Miranda* requirement and its exclusionary rule into play? That is, is the interrogation setting coercive? This eliminates the Sixth Amendment "focus" or "target" test of *Escobedo* and grand jury procedure which forbids questioning the *target* of investigation. This is appropriate because the Fifth Amendment does not forbid interrogation, but looks instead to see whether the questioning is accompanied by compulsion.

HOME Thus, for example, being questioned in one's own *home* may be custodial depending upon the facts. There was custody in *Orozco v. Texas* (1969) when police entered the defendant's house at 4:00 A.M. and questioned him while he was under arrest, not free to leave, and surrounded by police officers. On the other hand, in *Beckwith v. United States* (1975), although Beckwith was the target of a criminal tax investigation, the IRS agents came to his home, politely requested admittance during the daytime, and gave him time to finish dressing. The interview was conducted in a friendly and relaxed manner at Beckwith's dining room table. He was not pressed to answer questions and was told at the beginning of the interview that he had a right to refuse to answer questions. On these facts, the interview was held not custodial and *Miranda* warnings did not have to be given. This was so even though Beckwith, as a target of an investigation, could have legally refused to answer questions had he been subpoenaed.

PRISON *Mathis v. United States* (1968) seems to hold that *all* interrogation of inmates that occur in *prison* must be preceded by *Miranda* warnings. IRS agents interviewed Mathis in *prison* without issuing *Miranda* warnings, about tax issues *unrelated* to his prison conviction. Based on his *custody status,* the Supreme Court found a *Miranda* violation and overturned his conviction. Justice White, dissenting, believed that the underlying rationale of *Miranda* "rested not on the mere fact of physical restriction but on a conclusion that coercion—pressure to answer questions—usually flows from a certain type of custody, police station interrogation" of a suspect. Since Mathis was in familiar surroundings when questioned, even though confined, Justice White felt he was under no pressure to talk.

POLICE STATION Interrogation in a police station does not become custodial merely because of the location—it depends instead on the circumstances of the interrogation atmosphere. The majority in *Oregon v. Mathiason* (1977) found no custody or significant curtailment of freedom of action when a suspect voluntarily complied with a police request that he come to the station house for an interview. Carl Mathiason, a parolee, was identified as a probable burglar. A police officer left a card at Mathiason's residence asking him to call. At Mathiason's convenience, a meeting was held at a police station. The officer shook Mathiason's hand when he came to the station, and they met in a closed office with the officer sitting across a desk. The officer falsely told Mathiason that his fingerprints were found, whereupon he confessed. *Miranda* warnings were then read and another confession was taken. The Court concluded that Mathiason was not in custody before he confessed, and so no *Miranda* warnings had to be read. The Court said that "Any interview of one suspected of a crime by a police officer will have coercive aspects to it, simply by virtue of the fact that the police officer is part of a law enforcement system which may ultimately cause the suspect to be charged with a crime." One can think of this kind of pressure as a kind of "background radiation" that attaches to police officers and is different from the heightened compulsion that occurs when a person is taken into custody. Justice Marshall dissented. He felt that Mathiason's freedom of movement was curtailed in a true sense, and that he was in custody even though not formally placed under arrest. The Court reached the same result in *California v. Behler* (1983) on similar facts, except the defendant was not a parolee, and he went voluntarily to the police station to tell the police that he was at the scene of a homicide.

The test for what constitutes custody is an *objective* determination of whether the suspect was under arrest or otherwise deprived of freedom in any significant way. This is demonstrated by *Stansbury v. California* (1994) which ruled that "an officer's subjective and undisclosed view concerning whether the person being interrogated is a suspect is irrelevant to the assessment whether the person is in custody." A police detective investigating the abduction and rape-murder of a ten-year-old girl questioned Robert Stansbury, one of two ice cream truck drivers who the girl had spoken to on the day of her killing. Stansbury was not read *Miranda* warnings because the detective thought the other driver was the likely suspect. During the questioning, Stansbury described a borrowed car he drove on the night of the murder that was similar to a description of the car given by a witness. This aroused the officer's suspicion. The questioning continued. When Stansbury admitted to prior convictions for rape, kidnapping, and child molestation, the officer terminated questioning and another officer advised Stansbury of his rights. It is true that the officer *focused* on Stansbury as a suspect *before* he was read his *Miranda* warnings. However, Stansbury had no way of reading the officer's mind, and the officer did not convey, by word or deed, to Stansbury that he was not free to leave. Under the objective standard, therefore, Stansbury was not yet in custody, and his incriminating statements were admissible.

PROBATION INTERVIEW The Supreme Court held in *Minnesota v. Murphy* (1984) that a *probation interview* is not custody for *Miranda* purposes. This is the case, even though a probationer is *legally* required to attend probation interviews and that a condition of probation is that he answer all questions truthfully. The probationer was not under arrest nor was his freedom of movement seriously restrained. By extension, interviews or interrogations conducted in other constrained environments are not deemed the equivalent of the coercive atmosphere of police station questioning. In this case, Murphy's probation officer planned, in advance, to ask him about previous crimes designed to elicit incriminating information, gave Murphy no prior warning of such questions, and had no observer present to guard against abuse or trickery. He admitted to previously committing a rape and murder, and the statement to the probation officer was admissible in his first-degree murder trial.

The reason Murphy's statement was not compelled is that, except for the *Miranda* situation, the Fifth Amendment privilege against self-incrimination is *not self-executing.* Incriminating statements are not automatically excluded simply because a person makes them to a listener. With the exception of a police custodial interrogation situation, in which a person must be informed of his rights, a person must *claim* the privilege in order to rely on it. Once a person utters an incriminating statement, it is presumed voluntary, and the listener can tell what he or she heard to prosecutorial authorities (or anyone else) and may testify in court as to what was heard.

Murphy claimed that the probation condition that required truthful answers to the probation officer's questions amounted to compulsion. The Court disagreed. The probationer is in a similar situation as a witness subpoenaed before a grand jury. Both are legally compelled to attend, to answer truthfully, and they are not granted immunity. The probation conditions did not deprive Murphy of his Fifth Amendment rights. He could have refused to answer the questions that could have incriminated him. Murphy claimed that he feared revocation of probation if he did not answer. There was no proof, however, that Minnesota law or practice punished a probationer who claimed the protection of the Fifth Amendment.

TRAFFIC STOPS A motorist stopped for a moving violation, whether a misdemeanor or felony, such as speeding or operating under the influence of drugs or alcohol, is certainly detained for the time it takes to write a ticket or proceed to an arrest. Writing for a nearly unanimous Court in *Berkemer v. McCarty* (1984), Justice Marshall held that "persons temporarily detained pursuant to" police roadside stops of vehicles for traffic violations "are not 'in custody' for the purposes of *Miranda.*" Such stops do not significantly restrain the freedom of movement of persons to such an extent as to deprive them of their will as contemplated by *Miranda,* for two simple reasons. First, "detention of a motorist pursuant to a traffic stop is presumptively temporary and brief." Second, the stop occurs in public so that the motorist does not feel completely at the mercy of the police. Thus, although the motorist is detained, these factors "mitigate the danger that a person questioned will be induced 'to speak where he would not otherwise do so freely'" (*Berkemer v. McCarty,* quoting *Miranda*). The stopped motorist is far less likely, under this reasoning, to be coerced into giving up Fifth Amendment rights.

McCarty was stopped by a trooper who saw his car weaving in traffic. After he failed a field sobriety test, he was told he would be taken into custody. Asked if he had taken any intoxicants, McCarty said that "he had consumed two beers and had smoked several joints of marijuana a short time before." At the jail, McCarty was again asked questions and gave incriminating answers. At no time were *Miranda* warnings read. All of McCarty's statements were admitted into evidence.

Berkemer v. McCarty, in addition to holding that *Miranda* warnings need not be given during temporary traffic stops, also held that once a motorist has been arrested or has been placed in custody on felony or traffic misdemeanor charges, *Miranda* warnings must be read prior to interrogation. The Court equated traffic misdemeanors and felonies in order to uphold the "simplicity and clarity of the holding of *Miranda.*" An exception from warnings for traffic misdemeanors would create confusion and the potential for endless litigation. For example, some crimes escalate from misdemeanors to felonies depending on the number of prior DUI convictions, while in other situations it is not clear at the time of the vehicle stop whether a driving offense is a misdemeanor or felony. An accident (misdemeanor) could become a vehicular homicide if an injured passenger later dies. Thus, admissions made by McCarty on the roadside were admissible, but those made at the police station were inadmissible.

Pennsylvania v. Muniz (1990) further clarified the application of *Miranda* when a driver is stopped for driving while intoxicated (DUI) and is ordered to undergo a field sobriety test. (1) The Supreme Court held that *Miranda* warnings were not required simply for stopping a driver for DUI. The fact that the driver's *speech is slurred,* however incriminating, does not come under *Miranda* because physical inability to articulate words is not testimonial evidence. (2) Similarly, ordering a driver to perform and videotaping standard physical sobriety tests—the horizontal gaze nystagmus test, the walk-and-turn test, and the one leg stand test—are not testimonial. An officer orders a DUI suspect to perform the tests in "carefully scripted instructions as to how the tests were to be performed. These instructions were not likely to be perceived as calling for any verbal response and therefore were not 'words or actions' constituting custodial interrogation." As a result, *Miranda* warnings are not required. (3) Furthermore, an officer can ask a driver's name, address, height, weight, eye color, date of birth, and current age. The Court held that answers to these questions are admissible under a *"routine booking question" exception* to *Miranda.* Biographical data which is needed to complete booking or pretrial services and which is requested for record-keeping purposes only is reasonably related to police administrative concerns. (4) In this case, Muniz made unsolicited, incriminating statements that he had been drinking while the officer read him another carefully prepared script concerning the nature of Pennsylvania's implied consent law and a request to submit to a Breathalyzer test. The only questions asked of Muniz were whether he understood the instructions and whether he wished to submit to the test. "These limited and focused" questions were a part of legitimate police procedure and were not designed or likely to be perceived as calling for an incriminating response." Therefore, Muniz's statements that he had drinking were admissible.

The Court held that *Miranda* warnings were required only as to one question posed by the officer: "Do you know what the date was of your sixth birthday?" This was held to be testimonial interrogation. Muniz gave an incoherent response, which implied that he was intoxicated, which was not admissible because the question was asked before *Miranda* warnings were administered. Justice Brennan, for the majority, reasoned that the *content* of the answer allowed the police officer to infer that the driver's mental state was confused.

This was not physical evidence—the physical status of Muniz's brain merely described the way in which the inference from the answer was incriminating. Because the incriminating inference was drawn from a testimonial act rather than a physical fact, the question confronted the suspect with the classic "trilemma" of self-incrimination, perjury, or contempt. Chief Justice Rehnquist disagreed on this point, claiming that Justice Brennan's assumption about human behavior was wrong. Given the nature of the question to Muniz, which was basically to check how well he could add the number six to his date of birth, there was no real incentive for Muniz to lie and commit perjury. In this view, the question was closer to the physical tests and the "booking questions" that did not violate the Fifth Amendment in this case.

The Nature of Interrogation

Miranda v. Arizona (1966) applies to custodial **interrogation.** *Rhode Island v. Innis* (1980) ruled that:

> *Miranda* safeguards come into play whenever a person in custody is subjected to either *express questioning* or its *functional equivalent.* That is to say, the term "interrogation" under *Miranda* refers not only to express questioning, but also to any words or actions on the part of the police (other than normally attendant to arrest and custody) that the police should know are reasonably likely to elicit an incriminating response from the suspect. (*Rhode Island v. Innis,* emphasis added)

The functional equivalent of express interrogation can be discovered from the facts and circumstances of cases.

Police arrested Innis at 4:30 A.M. on suspicion of murdering a taxicab driver with a shotgun. They advised him of his rights. He said he wanted to speak with a lawyer, terminating any interrogation. Innis was placed in the back of a patrol car and driven to the station. On the way to the station, Officer Gleckman spoke to Officer McKenna about the shotgun, saying there was a school for handicapped children in the area "and God forbid one of them might find a weapon with shells and they might hurt themselves." McKenna agreed and suggested that they should continue to search for the shotgun. At that point, Innis interrupted the conversation, stating that he could lead the officers to the gun, which he did. This incriminating statement and the shotgun were admitted into evidence to convict him.

Was this exchange the functional equivalent of interrogation? Justice Stewart, writing for the majority, said no. He characterized the comments as only a few offhand remarks that the police could not have known would suddenly move Innis to make a self-incriminating response. A lengthy and more pointed "harangue" might become interrogation, but not the conversation here. The Court suggested that an example of a functional equivalent of interrogation is a "reverse lineup" where the police plant a "witness" in the lineup room to vocally accuse the suspect of a fictitious crime in order to induce him to confess to the actual crime. The Court added an important embellishment to its "functional equivalent" rule:

> But, since the police surely cannot be held accountable for the unforeseeable results of their words or actions, the definition of interrogation can extend only to words or actions on the part of police officers that they *should have known* were reasonably likely to elicit an incriminating response. (*Rhode Island v. Innis*)

To go further, police knowledge includes not only the likely effect of words on a hypothetical person, but also on a suspect with *known weaknesses or susceptibilities.*

Justice Marshall, who concurred with the definition of "interrogation" but dissented from its application to the facts of the case, picked up on this embellishment. He noted that appeals to the decency and the honor of the suspect are classic interrogation ploys and that "[o]ne can scarcely imagine a stronger appeal to the conscience of a suspect." Justice Stevens, also dissenting, suggested a different definition of interrogation: "any statement that would normally be understood by the average listener as calling for a response is the functional equivalent of a direct question, whether or not it is punctuated by a question mark." This definition focuses on the intention of the officers, to some degree, while the majority's rule, on the other hand, "focuses primarily upon the perceptions of the suspect, rather than the intent of the police."

The *Innis* definition was applied in *Arizona v. Mauro* (1987). William Mauro was arrested for the murder of his son after turning himself in at a local K-Mart store. He refused to make statements without a lawyer present and he was not questioned. Police interviewed Mrs. Mauro at the station. She insisted on speaking with her husband and was allowed to after some resistance on the part of the police. She was told that an officer would be present, and a tape recorder was placed prominently on the table. Mr. Mauro told his wife not to answer questions until a lawyer was present. At trial, the taped conversation was admitted into evidence to refute Mauro's insanity defense.

The Court held (5–4), in an opinion by Justice Powell, that the recording of the conversation was not the functional equivalent of interrogation under *Miranda* or *Innis.* The police did not send Mrs. Mauro in to speak with her husband, and the presence of the officer during their conversation was not improper. The mere possibility that a suspect in custody will incriminate himself under these circumstances does not amount to interrogation. "[T]he actions in this case were far less questionable than the 'subtle compulsion' that we held *not* to be interrogation in *Innis.* . . . Officers do not interrogate a suspect simply by hoping that he will incriminate himself."

Justice Stevens, for the dissenters, reasoned that the police used a "powerful psychological ploy" when they allowed Mrs. Mauro's to speak to her husband—it was bound to generate some discussion after he had manifested a clear desire to remain silent. The legitimacy of the police presence is irrelevant to this finding, for on the witness stand, the police captain admitted that one reason for allowing the meeting was to obtain statements that could "shed light on our case." Also, a police detective testified that a standard police technique used to get juveniles to talk is to bring their parents into the police station. It is interesting to note that in both the *Innis* and the *Mauro* cases, the state supreme courts believed that interrogation, or its functional equivalent under *Miranda,* had occurred.

Colorado v. Connelly (1986) is a classic example of noninterrogation. Francis Connelly, a chronic schizophrenic, traveled from Boston to Denver because the "voice of God" commanded him to do so. He approached a police officer on a downtown Denver street "and, *without any prompting,* stated that he had murdered someone and wanted to talk about it." Connelly was immediately informed of his rights, but he insisted he wanted to speak. He gave a confession on the street, after two additional *Miranda* warnings, and appeared at that point to be mentally normal. Connelly's confession was held valid because it was a *purely voluntary statement* not barred by the Fifth Amendment.

The Use of Deception

Police are allowed to employ deception during interrogation, and the literature reports frequent instances of police deceitfully telling suspects that a confederate lied or that a fingerprint or blood test put them at the crime scene when that is not the case. The idea is that a truly guilty party may at that point confess, while a truly innocent person will deny such charges. A risk is that police lying, combined with forceful and prolonged interrogation, has also led innocent people to confess (see *Law in Society*). Deception should not extend to express lies about the law.

Illinois v. Perkins (1990) upheld the use of a jail "plant"—an undercover agent—to obtain an incriminating statement from a suspect. The police discovered, through state prisoner Charlton, that Perkins admitted to committing a murder. Shortly after discovering this, Perkins was transferred to a jail on an unrelated aggravated battery charge. An undercover agent, posing as an escaped convict, was admitted to the jail and placed in the same cell as Charlton and Perkins. The undercover officer won Perkins's confidence by suggesting they escape from the jail together, and he *initiated* Perkins's narration of the crime by asking him whether he had ever "done someone." Perkins then recounted the events of the murder in detail which the agent later testified to in Perkins' murder trial. Of course, as Justice Kennedy dryly noted, the officer did not give Perkins *Miranda* warnings before the conversation. The Illinois courts held that because Perkins was *in correctional custody,* and the agent's statement was *indirect interrogation,* under *Innis, Mathis v. United States* (1968) required that *Miranda* warnings be given.

The Supreme Court (8–1) disagreed. It held that the conversation was *not* interrogation because the essential *Miranda* ingredients of a "police-dominated atmosphere" and compulsion were missing. Perkins had no idea he was speaking to a police officer, and "[c]oercion is determined from the perspective of the suspect." The Court reasoned that for the purposes of *Miranda,* Perkins was not in custody. "We reject the argument that *Miranda* warnings are required whenever a suspect is in custody in a technical sense and converses with someone who happens to be a government agent. . . . [W]here a suspect does not know that he is conversing with a government agent, [mutually reinforcing psychological pressures that weaken a suspect's will] are not present."

Finally, Justice Kennedy noted that a certain amount of deception by law enforcement officers is allowed under *Miranda* as long as the deception does not become coercive. "Ploys to mislead a suspect or lull him into a false sense of security that do not rise to the level of compulsion or coercion to speak are not within *Miranda's* concerns." The Court distinguished *Mathis* by noting that in that case, the defendant knew he was questioned by law enforcement officers. The majority opinion distinguished *Perkins* from *United States v. Henry* (1980) and *Maine v. Moulton* (1985) (discussed later) which were decided under the *Massiah* Sixth Amendment right to counsel rule. Those cases involved undercover agent-suspect interactions after the suspects had been *formally charged* and had attorneys. In *Perkins,* no charges had been filed on the subject of the interrogation so the Sixth Amendment did not come into play. *Perkins* allows the use of a valuable investigation tool, although law enforcement should be vigilant about abuses that can occur in using inmates as snitches.

CONFESSIONS AND PSYCHIATRIC EXAMINATIONS

Criminal defendants may have to submit to a psychiatric examination to determine whether they have the capacity to stand trial and to provide information when the defendant claims the insanity defense. They may also be required to have a psychiatric evaluation for special proceedings, such as in the administration of "sexual psychopath" laws (see *Allen v. Illinois,* 1986). When the judge *orders* a psychiatric examination, this is legal compulsion that may trigger the Fifth Amendment privilege against self-incrimination.

Miranda protections, therefore, are applicable to psychiatric testimony that is used at *sentencing hearings.* In

Estelle v. Smith (1981), a court ordered Ernest Smith to submit to a psychiatric examination in order to determine his competency to stand trial for murder. No *Miranda* warnings were read, nor was there a lawyer present during the examination. After Smith was convicted, Dr. Grigson, the psychiatrist who examined Smith at the pretrial hearing to determine competency, testified at a death penalty hearing that Smith would be a future danger to society. Smith claimed that this use of pretrial evidence, taken without a lawyer present, violated his Sixth Amendment right to counsel and Fifth Amendment self-incrimination protection, and that the psychiatrist's entire testimony should not have been allowed in the death penalty hearing. The Supreme Court agreed with Smith in a unanimous decision authored by Chief Justice Burger:

> When Dr. Grigson went beyond simply reporting to the court on the issue of competence and testified for the prosecution at the penalty phase on the crucial issue of respondent's future dangerousness, his role changed and became essentially like that of an agent of the State recounting unwarned statements made in a postarrest custodial setting. During the psychiatric evaluation, respondent assuredly was "faced with a phase of the adversary system" and was "not in the presence of [a] perso[n] acting solely in his interest." (*Estelle v. Smith* [1981], quoting in part from *Miranda v. Arizona*)

The Court noted that compelling a defendant to submit to a competency examination does not violate his or her rights as long as the evidence is used only for the issue of whether the defendant is competent to stand trial.

QUESTIONING AFTER FORMAL CHARGING: THE SIXTH AMENDMENT

Miranda—based on the Fifth Amendment privilege against self-incrimination—applies after a criminal suspect is taken into custody. Once the suspect is *formally charged*—by indictment, by a prosecutor's information, or by a magistrate's bindover after a preliminary examination—the legal picture changes. At this point, the criminal *prosecution* begins and the Sixth Amendment right to counsel "attaches." Once charged, different and more stringent constraints on police questioning and eavesdropping apply. Post-indictment statements obtained by the police surreptitiously, or in disregard of the defendant's right to counsel, are excluded from the trial.

This rule was established in *Massiah v. United States* (1964). Winston Massiah, a crew member on a ship from South America, was charged in New York with transporting cocaine into the United States, *indicted,* and released on bail. While on bail, Massiah's codefendant, one Colson, agreed to cooperate with the government. A listening device was placed in Colson's car and transmitted evidence of Massiah making incriminating statements. A government agent testified to the incriminating statements at Massiah's trial. The Supreme Court held that introducing the testimony violated Massiah's Sixth Amendment right to counsel. The Court said that counsel has long been considered essential during the pretrial stages and held that secretly obtaining incriminating statements from an indicted defendant interfered with his right to legal representation.

Justice Stewart's majority opinion repeated his views in *Spano v. New York* (1959), a pre-*Miranda* confession case decided on the voluntariness test, that obtaining a confession from an indicted defendant without notifying an attorney "might deny a defendant 'effective assistance of counsel at the only stage when legal aid and advice would help him'" (*Massiah,* quoting *Spano*). Justice White, dissenting, believed there was no interference with Massiah's right to counsel. Unlike the Canon of Professional Ethics that prevents an *attorney* from interviewing an opposing party, there is no ethical restriction on *investigators* contacting a defendant. "Law enforcement may have the elements of a contest about it, but it is not a game" (*Massiah v. United States,* p. 213, White, J. dissenting). Justice White's view failed to acknowledge that once the investigator speaks to or overhears a suspect and gets incriminating statements, the value of a lawyer's advice is nullified.

The *Massiah* area of law deals with similar functional issues to those that arise under *Miranda,* including the definition of interrogation and the validity of a waiver. Such questions arose in the notorious "Christian Burial Speech" case of *Brewer v. Williams* (1977). Williams, incidentally, was retried and found guilty. The Supreme Court upheld the second conviction under the doctrine of inevitable discovery in *Nix v. Williams* (1984) (*Williams II,* see Chapter 3).

THE *MASSIAH* RIGHT AFTER *BREWER V. WILLIAMS*

The Supreme Court found in favor of defendants in *Michigan v. Jackson* (1986). A defendant who requests a lawyer at arraignment has invoked his right to counsel, and police may not initiate interrogation until counsel has been made available to the suspect. This seemed to extend the rule of *Edwards v. Arizona* (1981) (a questioned suspect who asks for a lawyer under *Miranda* cannot be interrogated without counsel present). However, in subsequent cases, the Court shrunk this extension of a defendant's Sixth Amendment rights.

Patterson v. Illinois (1988) resolved an issue not completely answered in *Brewer v. Williams.* It held that an indicted defendant who is read *Miranda* warnings may validly waive his right to counsel. Under some circumstances, then, a charged defendant can speak to police without an attorney

• CASE & COMMENTS •

Brewer v. Williams
430 U.S. 387, 97 S.Ct. 1232, 51 L.Ed.2d 424 (1977)

MR. JUSTICE STEWART delivered the opinion of the Court.

I

*** [Robert Williams, a mental hospital escapee, turned himself in to Davenport, Iowa, police for the murder of a ten-year-old girl at a Des Moines YMCA on December 26, 1968. **[a]** He was arrested, formally arraigned (charged) for the crime, and advised of his rights by the judge, who noted that Williams was represented by attorney McKnight in Des Moines and attorney Kelly in Davenport. McKnight spoke to Williams on the phone, in the presence of Des Moines police detective Leaming. He informed Williams that Des Moines officers would drive to Davenport, pick him up, and they would not interrogate him or mistreat him. He warned Williams not to talk to the officers about the crime. When Detective Leaming picked up Williams, Kelly, the Davenport lawyer, was denied a request to ride back to Des Moines with them. Kelly repeated to Detective Leaming that Williams was not to be questioned on the ride back.]

[a] Which of the facts are essential to the holding of the case?

[On the 160-mile ride to Des Moines, Williams expressed no desire to be interrogated without his lawyer present; he said he would tell the whole story at the end of the trip. Leaming knew Williams was a deeply religious former mental patient and engaged him in a general discussion. Soon after the trip began, Leaming delivered the so-called] "Christian burial speech." Addressing Williams as "Reverend," the detective said: **[b]**

[b] Was the speech made deliberately by Detective Leaming to elicit incriminating evidence or just to pass the time?

> "I want to give you something to think about while we're traveling down the road . . . . Number one, I want you to observe the weather conditions, it's raining, it's sleeting, it's freezing, driving is very treacherous, visibility is poor, it's going to be dark early this evening. They are predicting several inches of snow for tonight, and I feel that you yourself are the only person that knows where this little girl's body is, that you yourself have only been there once, and if you get a snow on top of it you yourself may be unable to find it. And, since we will be going right past the area on the way into Des Moines, I feel that we could stop and locate the body, that the parents of this little girl should be entitled to a Christian burial for the little girl who was snatched away from them on Christmas [E]ve and murdered. And I feel we should stop and locate it on the way in rather than waiting until morning and trying to come back out after a snow storm and possibly not being able to find it at all."

Williams asked Detective Leaming why he thought their route to Des Moines would be taking them past the girl's body, and Leaming responded that he knew the body was in the area of Mitchellville—a town they would be passing on the way to Des Moines. **[c]** Leaming then stated: "I do not want you to answer me. I don't want to discuss it any further. Just think about it as we're riding down the road."

[c] The call for silence allows Leaming's speech to work on Williams's mind.

As the car approached Grinnell, a town approximately 100 miles west of Davenport, Williams asked whether the police had found the victim's shoes. When Detective Leaming replied that he was unsure, Williams directed the officers to a service station where he said he had left the shoes; a search for them proved unsuccessful. As they continued towards Des Moines, Williams asked whether the police had found the blanket, and directed the officers to a rest area where he said he had disposed of the blanket. Nothing was found. The car continued towards Des Moines, and as it approached Mitchellville, Williams said that he would show the officers where the body was. He then directed the police to the body of Pamela Powers.

* * *

[This evidence was introduced and used to convict Williams of murder. The Iowa courts ruled that Williams waived his right to counsel, but the lower federal courts, on a writ of habeas corpus, ruled the evidence inadmissible on the alternative grounds of denial of assistance of counsel, a *Miranda* violation, and that his statements were involuntary.]

• CASE & COMMENTS •

II

B

*** [*Miranda v. Arizona* does not apply to this case.] For it is clear that the judgment before us must in any event be affirmed upon the ground that Williams was deprived of a different constitutional right—the right to the assistance of counsel. **[d]**

This right, guaranteed by the Sixth and Fourteenth Amendments, is indispensable to the fair administration of our adversary system of criminal justice. [It is a] vital need at the pretrial stage. ***

*** Whatever else it may mean, the right to counsel granted by the Sixth and Fourteenth Amendments means at least that a person is entitled to the help of a lawyer at or after the time that judicial proceedings have been initiated against him—"whether by way of formal charge, preliminary hearing, indictment, information, or arraignment." ***

There can be no doubt in the present case that judicial proceedings [by arraignment] had been initiated against Williams before the start of the automobile ride from Davenport to Des Moines. *** **[e]**

There can be no serious doubt, either, that Detective Leaming deliberately and designedly set out to elicit information from Williams just as surely as—and perhaps more effectively than—if he had formally interrogated him. Detective Leaming was fully aware before departing for Des Moines that Williams was being represented in Davenport by Kelly and in Des Moines by McKnight. Yet he purposely sought during Williams' isolation from his lawyers to obtain as much incriminating information as possible. Indeed, Detective Leaming conceded as much when he testified at Williams' trial. *** **[f]**

The circumstances of this case are thus constitutionally indistinguishable from those presented in *Massiah v. United States.* ***

That the incriminating statements were elicited surreptitiously in the *Massiah* case, and otherwise here, is constitutionally irrelevant. *** Rather, the clear rule of *Massiah* is that once adversary proceedings have commenced against an individual, he has a right to legal representation when the government interrogates him. ***

[d] The extension of the right to counsel at the arraignment, as a *critical stage* was established in *Hamilton v. Alabama* (1961) (see Chapter 7).

[e] Does this seem obvious? If so, how could Justice Blackmun, dissenting below, seriously disagree? Should the Supreme Court wink at blatant violations of rights for the investigation of horrible crimes?

[f] This clarifies the basis of *Massiah*: it was based, essentially, on the lack of counsel, not that an agent secretly listened in on a conversation between Massiah and Colson.

III

The Iowa courts recognized that Williams had been denied the constitutional right to the assistance of counsel. **[g]** They held, however, that he had waived that right during the course of the automobile trip from Davenport to Des Moines. ***

[The Iowa courts applied a totality of circumstances test to ascertain whether Williams waived his right to counsel. The federal courts held that this was the wrong standard under the constitutional guarantee to counsel: there must be an affirmative waiver.]

* * *

The [lower federal courts] were also correct in their understanding of the proper standard to be applied in determining the question of waiver as a matter of federal constitutional law—that it was incumbent upon the State to prove "an intentional relinquishment or abandonment of a known right or privilege." *** **[h]** We have said that the right to counsel does not depend upon a request by the defendant, ***and that courts indulge in every reasonable presumption against waiver. *** This strict standard applies equally to an alleged waiver of the right to counsel whether at trial or at a critical stage of pretrial proceedings. ***

We conclude, finally, that the Court of Appeals was correct in holding that, judged by these standards, the record in this case falls far short of sustaining petitioner's burden. It is true that Williams had been informed of and appeared to understand his right to counsel. **[i]** But waiver requires not merely comprehension but relinquishment, and Williams' consistent reliance upon the advice of counsel in dealing with the authorities refutes any suggestion that he waived that right. [He spoke to both the Des Moines and Davenport attorneys numerous times before the trip.] Throughout, Williams was advised not to make any statements before seeing McKnight in Des Moines, and was

[g] Federal courts, and ultimately the Supreme Court, have the final say as to standards and doctrines under the United States Constitution.

[h] This is as much a right to counsel case as an interrogation case. The rules of the Sixth Amendment are deemed to apply strictly.

[i] The state had the burden of proof that Williams voluntarily waived his right to counsel. The facts of the case prove otherwise to the majority. Compare this

• CASE & COMMENTS •

assured that the police had agreed not to question him. His statements while in the car that he would tell the whole story *after* seeing McKnight in Des Moines were the clearest expressions by Williams himself that he desired the presence of an attorney before any interrogation took place. But even before making these statements, Williams had effectively asserted his right to counsel by having secured attorneys at both ends of the automobile trip, both of whom, acting as his agents, had made clear to the police that no interrogation was to occur during the journey. Williams knew of that agreement and, particularly in view of his consistent reliance on counsel, there is no basis for concluding that he disavowed it.

paragraph to Justice White's reasoning in his dissent. Would formally informing Williams of his rights have allowed him to properly waive the Sixth Amendment counsel protection?

Detective Leaming proceeded to elicit incriminating statements from Williams. Leaming did not preface this effort by telling Williams that he had a right to the presence of a lawyer, and made no effort at all to ascertain whether Williams wished to relinquish that right. The circumstances of record in this case thus provide no reasonable basis for finding that Williams waived his right to the assistance of counsel.

The Court of Appeals did not hold, nor do we, that under the circumstances of this case Williams *could not,* without notice to counsel, have waived his rights under the Sixth and Fourteenth Amendments. It only held, as do we, that he did not.

IV

The crime of which Williams was convicted was senseless and brutal, calling for swift and energetic action by the police to apprehend the perpetrator and gather evidence with which he could be convicted. **[j]** No mission of law enforcement officials is more important. Yet, "[d]isinterested zeal for the public good does not assure either wisdom or right in the methods it pursues." *** Although we do not lightly affirm the issuance of a writ of habeas corpus in this case, so clear a violation of the Sixth and Fourteenth Amendments as here occurred cannot be condoned. The pressures on state executive and judicial officers charged with the administration of the criminal law are great, especially when the crime is murder and the victim a small child. But it is precisely the predictability of those pressures that makes imperative a resolute loyalty to the guarantees that the Constitution extends to us all.

[j] The biggest difference between the majority and dissenting justices is that the majority refuses to "bend the rules" of constitutional rights to gain a conviction in a terrible crime. Compare the remarks of Chief Justice Burger.

The judgment of the Court of Appeals is affirmed.

It is so ordered.

[Justices Marshall, Powell, and Stevens concurred in separate opinions.]

MR. CHIEF JUSTICE BURGER, dissenting. **[k]**

The result in this case ought to be intolerable in any society which purports to call itself an organized society. It continues the Court—by the narrowest margin—on the much-criticized course of punishing the public for the mistakes and misdeeds of law enforcement officers, instead of punishing the officer directly, if in fact he is guilty of wrongdoing. It mechanically and blindly keeps reliable evidence from juries whether the claimed constitutional violation involves gross police misconduct or honest human error.

[k] This sounds a bit like a "tough on crime" speech by a politician. Have rights swung too far to favor suspects? Or could the Court end up eliminating individual rights if motivated by a desire to structure rules of constitutional criminal procedure to always favor the state?

* * *

[Further in his opinion the CHIEF JUSTICE argued that the exclusionary rule should not apply to nonegregious police conduct.]

MR. JUSTICE WHITE, with whom MR. JUSTICE BLACKMUN and MR. JUSTICE REHNQUIST join, dissenting.

* * *

Respondent relinquished his right not to talk to the police about his crime when the car approached the place where he had hidden the victim's clothes. **[l]** Men usually intend to do what they do, and there is nothing in the record to support the proposition that respondent's decision to talk was anything but an exercise of his own free will. Apparently, without any prodding from the officers, respondent—who had earlier said that he would tell the whole story when he arrived in Des

[l] Can this logic be used to make legal any incriminating statement except those obtained by torture? Do you believe that Williams was

• CASE & COMMENTS •

Moines—spontaneously changed his mind about the timing of his disclosures when the car approached the places where he had hidden the evidence. However, even if his statements were influenced by Detective Leaming's above-quoted statement, respondent's decision to talk in the absence of counsel can hardly be viewed as the product of an overborne will. The statement by Leaming was not coercive; it was accompanied by a request that respondent not respond to it; and it was delivered hours before respondent decided to make any statement. Respondent's waiver was thus knowing and intentional.

not "prodded" and that his admission was "spontaneous"?

* * *

MR. JUSTICE BLACKMUN, with whom MR. JUSTICE WHITE and MR. JUSTICE REHNQUIST join, dissenting.

* * *

What the Court chooses to do here, and with which I disagree, is to hold that respondent Williams' situation was in the mold of *Massiah v. United States,* **[m]** that is, that it was dominated by a denial to Williams of his Sixth Amendment right to counsel after criminal proceedings had been instituted against him. The Court rules that the Sixth Amendment was violated because Detective Leaming "purposely sought during Williams' isolation from his lawyers to obtain as much incriminating information as possible." I cannot regard that as unconstitutional *per se.*

[m] A basic question, not finally settled by this case, is whether it is ever possible for police to interview a suspect without his or her lawyer present after formal charges.

First, the police did not deliberately seek to isolate **[n]** Williams from his lawyers so as to deprive him of the assistance of counsel. *** The isolation in this case was a necessary incident of transporting Williams to the county where the crime was committed.

[n] Do the first two points made by Justice Blackmun pass the "giggle test"?

Second, Leaming's purpose was not solely to obtain incriminating evidence. The victim had been missing for only two days, and the police could not be certain that she was dead. Leaming, of course, and in accord with his duty, was "hoping to find out where that little girl was," *** but such motivation does not equate with an intention to evade the Sixth Amendment. ***

Third, not every attempt to elicit information should be regarded as "tantamount to interrogation." *** **[o]** I am not persuaded that Leaming's observations and comments, made as the police car traversed the snowy and slippery miles between Davenport and Des Moines that winter afternoon, were an interrogation, direct or subtle, of Williams. *** In summary, it seems to me that the Court is holding that *Massiah* is violated whenever police engage in any conduct, in the absence of counsel, with the subjective desire to obtain information from a suspect after arraignment. Such a rule is far too broad. Persons in custody frequently volunteer statements in response to stimuli other than interrogation. *** When there is no interrogation, such statements should be admissible as long as they are truly voluntary. ***

[o] This case can be added to *Rhode Island v. Innis* and *Arizona v. Mauro* to determine what constitutes the functional equivalent of express questioning. The majority held that Detective Leaming's speech was the functional equivalent of interrogation; the dissenters disagree. If Justice Blackmun is correct, what police statement, short of a direct question, could ever be the functional equivalent of express questioning?

* * *

present, as long as there is an *express* waiver of the right to counsel. After *Patterson,* the analogy between a suspects's invocation of counsel in *Edwards* (a Fifth Amendment situation) and when a person has been formally charged is weaker. Dissenters in *Patterson* wanted the Court to impose additional warnings to the four required by *Miranda* for suspects who have been formally charged, but the majority refused to do so.

Justice Stevens, dissenting in *Patterson,* raised a different point: that it is *unethical* for investigators or prosecutors during trial preparation to go behind the backs of their adversaries and communicate with a defendant. In his view, since it is a breach of professional ethics for an *attorney* to communicate with an opposing party without the knowledge of opposing counsel, the *Massiah* rule also "suggest[s] that law enforcement personnel may not bypass counsel in favor of direct communications with an accused." The majority did not accede to this view.

The Court further limited *Massiah* rights in *McNeil v. Wisconsin* (1991). A defendant who invokes the right to counsel for one crime (and cannot be questioned about it) is not automatically protected against police questioning for another crime. The Court held that the Sixth Amendment right to counsel is *offense-specific,* unlike the right to counsel created by the Supreme Court in *Miranda* to protect Fifth Amendment rights. The reason for this distinction is that the purpose of the Sixth Amendment right to counsel is to protect the unaided layperson at a critical confrontation. The purpose of the *Miranda-Edwards* rule is to protect a suspect's desire to deal with police only through counsel.

A strong example of Rehnquist Court activist-conservative reasoning is found in *Michigan v. Harvey* (1990) which held that a statement taken in violation of one's *Massiah* rights under *Michigan v. Jackson* can be used at a trial to impeach the defendant should he or she choose to testify. Since a violation of *Jackson* seems to be a direct violation of a suspect's Sixth Amendment rights, it is difficult to see how a statement gotten by a blatant violation of *Massiah* and *Jackson* could be used in any proceeding. Chief Justice Rehnquist, writing for the majority, achieved this goal by muddying the clear distinction between Fifth and Sixth Amendment rights which Justice Potter Stewart had worked to achieve in cases like *Spano, Massiah.* and *Brewer v. Williams.* His opinion minimized the difference between *Miranda* and *Massiah*, arguing that although *Michigan v. Jackson* "is based on the Sixth Amendment" . . . its roots lie in this Court's decisions in *Miranda v. Arizona* and succeeding cases." It is difficult to comprehend the cause and effect since *Massiah* (1964) *preceded Miranda* (1966) by two years. The Court reasoned that *Michigan v. Jackson,* borrowed its a bright-line rule from *Edwards v. Arizona,* a *Miranda* case. By this reasoning, the Court held that the rights announced in *Michigan v. Jackson* were mere *prophylactic rules,* and so could be used to impeach the defendant.

Justice Stevens dissented (joined by Justices Brennan, Marshall, and Blackmun). He noted that the right to counsel is much *more pervasive* than other rights "because it affects the ability of the accused to assert any other rights he may have." Because of this, rules for waiving counsel are extremely stringent. Further, in Justice Stevens's view, the majority argument was a ploy to confuse the true basis of a *Massiah* right. In this case, Harvey's right to counsel (to see his lawyer) was violated by a police officer who told a confused Harvey that he didn't have to see his lawyer. He virtually accused the majority's recharacterization of the facts of this case as one "involving nothing more than the violation of a 'prophylactic' rule" as a smokescreen that undermines the rule of *Massiah* and a suspect's primary right to counsel.

Justice Stevens added a practical reason for excluding all use of evidence obtained in violation of *Massiah* rights:

> The police would have everything to gain and nothing to lose by repeatedly visiting with the defendant and seeking to elicit as many comments as possible about the pending trial. Knowledge that such conversations could not be used affirmatively would not detract from the State's interest in obtaining them for their value as impeachment evidence.

Michigan v. Harvey is also an example of Justices' decision-making in criminal cases that reflect the "crime control" and the "due process" models of criminal justice discussed in Chapter 1.

Undercover Policing and the Right to Counsel

In *Illinois v. Perkins* (1990), discussed earlier, under the use of deception under *Miranda,* the Court allowed undercover policing to proceed without the need to warn individuals that they were suspects, because incriminating statements made to false friends are not compelled. Deception is not a substitute for coercion. *Massiah,* on the other hand, seems to rule out this kind of deception once a person has been formally charged and is clothed with the right to counsel. The Court has maintained, but softened, the *Massiah* rule to some degree when agents or informants are planted in a suspect's jail cell to listen for incriminating statements.

JAIL CELL CASES An incriminating statement made by a suspect in a jail cell to an informant in *United States v. Henry* (1980) was thrown out as a *Massiah* violation, because the informant *"deliberately elicited"* the statement from Henry by engaging in conversations that resulted in the incriminating statement. On the other hand, in *Kuhlman v. Wilson* (1986), a jail informant placed in a cell with Wilson did not deliberately elicit the incriminating evidence. The informant did not initiate any conversations about the crime but "only listened" to Wilson and took notes later. The rule, then, is that the police can place a *passive listener* in a cell who acts like a *listening device,* which is allowable in a jail setting, as long as the cellmate does not start conversations that are likely to lead the suspect to incriminate himself. This ruling, favorable to the prosecution, does not take into account the human tendency of an inmate to talk to a cellmate, increasing the likelihood of making incriminating statements.

UNDERCOVER INFORMANT *Maine v. Moulton* (1985) is factually similar to *Massiah* and restates the jail case rules in the context of undercover policing. Colson, a codefendant of Moulton, agreed to obtain information for the police in return for the state dropping charges against him.[28] Both

Moulton and Colson, out on bail, got together to plan trial strategy during which Moulton made incriminating statements. The Supreme Court held that the statements were barred by the *Massiah* rule:

> The Sixth Amendment guarantees the accused, at least after the initiation of formal charges, the right to rely on counsel as a 'medium' between him and the State. . . . [T]his guarantee includes the State's affirmative obligation not to act in a manner that circumvents the protections accorded the accused by invoking this right. . . . Thus, the Sixth Amendment is not violated whenever—by luck or happenstance—the State obtains incriminating statements from the accused after the right to counsel has attached. . . . However, *knowing exploitation* by the State of an opportunity to confront the accused without counsel being present is as much a breach of the State's obligation not to circumvent the right to the assistance of counsel as the intentional creation of such an opportunity. (*Maine v. Moulton,* 1985, emphasis added)

The majority agreed that handing up an indictment does not prevent the police from continuing to investigate a case or from investigating the defendant for other crimes. However, they must not obtain evidence surreptitiously from an indicted defendant in a way that cuts the defendant off from the defense lawyer. Therefore, the majority made it clear that if the police are investigating a suspect for Crime B, and the suspect has already been indicted for Crime A, an undercover agent may investigate the suspect for Crime B for which the suspect has not been charged. Evidence obtained by the undercover agent pertaining to Crime A may not be admitted. Only evidence for the new crime (Crime B) is admissible.

LAW IN SOCIETY: THE SOCIAL REALITY OF CONFESSIONS

The Acceptance of *Miranda*[29]

Despite its bitter reception by police and others in 1966, the ruling has since been accepted by the legal and law enforcement communities. Chief Justice Warren Burger stated in 1980, "The meaning of *Miranda* has become reasonably clear and law enforcement practices have adjusted to its strictures; I would neither overrule *Miranda,* disparage it, nor extend it at this late date." (*Rhode Island v. Innis,* 1980). This signaled that *Miranda*'s opponents could now live with it, in part because the case did not undermine effective policing. Chief Justice Burger also wanted to avoid another round of appeals designed to clarify a major legal revolution in established and well-known confessions rules.

Many police see *Miranda,* and the study of constitutional law in general, as enhancing the professional status of policing. Some officers accept that without legal strictures, their crime-fighting behavior could turn to lawlessness. Others have internalized the *Miranda* rules and are happy to apply them to the extent that they accord with what the officers believe is "fair and decent" behavior.[30] In this light, it is important to be clear that "*Miranda* has not failed to achieve its limited goals"[31]—which was *not* to eliminate interrogation and confessions, completely equalize the power relationship between a suspect and the police, or lower confession rates. *Miranda* was designed to reduce the compulsion of the interrogation process. Understanding this, police are happy to follow the letter of *Miranda* decision if the goals of law enforcement can be generally realized.[32] This has resulted in police *adaptation* to the *Miranda* requirements.

Police Interrogation Today: Adapting to *Miranda*

What do we know about how custodial interrogation is conducted? "During the first few years after *Miranda,* empirical studies suggested that *Miranda*'s impact was minimal."[33] Few studies of *Miranda*'s effect appeared for some time, but since 1996 several have enlarged our understanding of *Miranda* and some have generated a lively debate over the "costs" to law enforcement of the need to warn interrogated suspects of their rights.

HOW ARE INTERROGATIONS CONDUCTED? As a routine practice, "third degree" tactics—the use and threats of beatings—have disappeared as police interrogation techniques. Police, today, use sophisticated psychological techniques to "persuade" recalcitrant defendants to admit their guilt. A study by Richard Leo of 182 interrogations observed in three California police departments in 1992 and 1993 provided a picture of contemporary interrogation. Most of the suspects were young working-class African-American males. Seventy percent of the primary detectives conducting the questioning were white and ninety percent were males. In sixty-nine percent of the cases, interrogation was conducted by one officer, and in thirty-one percent, two officers interrogated. Forty three percent of the cases were for robberies, twenty-four percent were for assault, twelve percent were for homicide and the other twenty-one percent were for burglaries, thefts, and other crimes.

Only twenty-two percent of the suspects invoked their *Miranda* rights after they were read. Suspects with prior felony records invoked their rights more often (thirty percent) than those with no record (eight percent) or prior misdemeanor involvement (eleven percent) in the criminal justice system. Thirty-six percent of the suspects made no incriminating statement, twenty-two percent made an incriminating statement, eighteen percent made a partial admission, and twenty-four percent made a full confession.

Thirty-five percent of the interrogations lasted less than thirty minutes, thirty-sixty percent lasted thirty to sixty minutes, twenty-one percent lasted for one to two hours and eight percent lasted more than two hours.[34] Leo concluded that under legal criteria, only four out of 182 cases, or two percent, "rose to the level of 'coercion.'"[35]

Professor Leo provides six in-depth vignettes from the cases he observed. In each, the officers use a variety of *psychological ploys* to get confessions. A suspect accused of smashing in a car window and stealing its contents was told that several witnesses saw him do this. "The detective was, of course, fabricating evidence against the suspect, but the suspect did not know this."[36] The interrogation lasted more than an hour; the suspect admitted breaking into the car and, on a plea bargain, received a one-year sentence. Another suspect, a twenty-one-year-old Hispanic male, was accused of kidnapping a fourteen-year-old girl from a party and brutally raping and anally and orally sodomizing her before returning the girl to the party with a warning that he would shoot her if she spoke. The victim immediately told a friend who called the police. A swift medical examination confirmed severe physical injury. During the interrogation, the detective, an Hispanic female, "went from somewhat formal language (which it appeared he didn't understand) to slang, crude even profane language to ask him questions about the sexual acts." He appeared nervous, but "she quickly put her hand on his in a friendly gesture, smiled, and told him to trust her, that she wouldn't be embarrassed by anything he told her. . . ." The suspect invoked counsel, ending the interrogation after thirty-four minutes. He pled guilty to statutory rape and received a one-month sentence plus four years of "formal probation."[37] This indicates that failure to obtain confessions in some cases may allow guilty parties to go free or receive less than adequate punishment.

WHY DO SUSPECTS WAIVE THEIR *MIRANDA* RIGHTS? Observations of police interrogation practices show that a variety of psychological methods are used to get suspects to talk. If the police follow the spirit of *Miranda,* then they would at least deliver the warnings in a neutral way at the beginning of an interrogation session. Some do. But many others de-emphasize the importance of *Miranda* waivers in several ways. They may indicate that the waiver is an unimportant bureaucratic detail (a mere formality) or build rapport and engage in small talk before mentioning *Miranda.* Another "selling" technique is to stress the importance of the suspect "telling his side of the story."[38] A more insidious technique is to weave the warnings into questions and answers over a long period of time so that the suspect waives rights, and after this is read the warnings in a block—a method dubbed *"participating Miranda"* by Professors Peter Lewis and Harry Allen.[39]

Leo describes the process by characterizing police interrogation as a "confidence game." Like a "con man," or perhaps any good salesperson, the police interrogator must psychologically "size up" and figure out how to manipulate the suspect. This requires knowledge of the crime, the victim, and the suspect. Unlike a true confidence man, a police interrogator cannot select or "qualify" the "mark." The officer "cultivates" the suspect by projecting a friendly and sincere image, offering coffee, and engaging in light banter. Simultaneously, the barren interrogation room, the thick case folder with the suspect's name prominently attached, and various interrogation techniques, such as pitting the suspect against a shadowy but fearsome prosecutor or judge and jury, are designed to raise the suspect's anxiety. The police frame their questions with admonitions about telling the truth; telling the truth will "make it go better" for the suspect and make him feel better. To elicit a confession, the police draw on various techniques of persuasion, deception, and neutralization: contradicting false statements, minimizing the immoral nature of what was done, posing false statements, and many more. Finally, the officers, knowing that the confessions will be attacked once defense lawyers come into the case, "cool the mark" by complimenting the suspect for the honesty and cooperation and maintaining a neutral tone and positive reaction to the defendant to the end.[40]

INTERROGATION/CONFESSIONS "OUTSIDE" *MIRANDA* A troubling interrogation practice is known as interrogation "outside *Miranda.*" This occurs when a suspect demands to see a lawyer. Instead of terminating the questioning, under *Edwards v. Arizona* (1981), the officer continues to question and may even tell the suspect that what is said after that point cannot be used in court to convict the suspect. This is correct. What the suspect is not told is that under *Harris v. New York* (1971), an incriminating statement can be used to impeach the suspect should he testify at a trial. If the case proceeds, the existence of an admission "outside *Miranda*" will improve the prosecutor's plea bargaining position, or alternately will hamper the defense lawyer's trial strategy.[41]

THE BENEFITS OF *MIRANDA* Professor Leo asserts that *Miranda* has had four positive long-range social effects. In his view, conservative critics of the 1980s were wrong to contend that *Miranda* has undermined effective law enforcement, and liberals have been shortsighted in saying that Miranda's effects have been more symbolic than real.[42] (1) "*Miranda* has exercised a civilizing influence on police behavior inside the interrogation room" by accelerating a process that was in place in 1966. This has helped to make the police more professional by establishing objective and written standards of police behavior. As a result,

"American police in the last thirty years have, by necessity, become more solicitous of suspects' rights, more respectful of their dignity, and more concerned with their welfare inside the interrogation room."[43] (2) *Miranda* "has transformed the culture—the shared norms, values and attitudes—of police . . . by fundamentally re-framing how police talk and think about the process of custodial interrogation."[44] (3) *Miranda* has increased public awareness of constitutional rights. (4) "*Miranda* has inspired police to develop more specialized, more sophisticated and seemingly more effective interrogation techniques with which to elicit inculpatory statements from custodial suspects."[45] Thus, *Miranda* is part of a larger and longer term trend in Western society in which government power is "more controlling of its subjects" but at the same time "more subject to control itself legal institutions, professional standards, and social norms."[46]

IMPROVING *MIRANDA:* VIDEOTAPING This does not mean that police interrogation is without its problems. As will be explored later, numerous false confessions raise concerns about how interrogation is conducted. To ensure that interrogation becomes more professional and effective, Professor Leo, borrowing from a 1993 Department of Justice study, has urged that courts mandate the videotaping of interrogations as a matter of due process.[47] There are many good reasons for videotaping interrogations: (1) It creates an "objective, reviewable record of custodial questioning that protects [police] against false accusations—accusations such as "softening up" a suspect prior to *Miranda,* failing to correctly read the *Miranda* warnings, or eliciting a confession through improper inducements." (2) It is "likely to improve the quality of police work and thus contribute to more professional and more effective interrogation practices. Officers and detectives who know they will be videotaped are more likely to prepare their strategies beforehand and to be more self-conscious about their conduct during questioning." (3) Tapes can be used for training. (4) Videotaping can increase law enforcement effectiveness for it "facilitates the identification, prosecution, and conviction of guilty offenders." For example, it "preserves the details of a suspect's statement that may not have been initially recorded in a detective's notes but may subsequently become important." (5) Videotapes are believed to have helped prosecutors negotiate a higher percentage of guilty pleas and obtain longer sentences because they provide "a more complete record with which to better assess the state's case against the accused" including "the demeanor and sophistication of the suspect." As a result, some defense attorneys oppose videotaping confessions because it makes it more difficult to challenge the stories of detectives, although high caseload public defenders appreciate videotapes because it helps them to more quickly cut through clients' lies so as to produce accurate guilty pleas more quickly.

Why Do Innocent People Confess?

The English common law harbors a traditional distrust of confessions (found in the rule that uncorroborated confessions are inadmissible in court) out of fear that psychological manipulation would induce innocent persons to confess. This problem still exists, despite *Miranda,* and requires precautions in how interrogation is conducted. As improbable as it may seem, when police use modern "psychological interrogation" rather than torture (e.g., *Brown v. Mississippi,* 1936), they still get innocent parties to confess.

HOW INNOCENT PEOPLE CONFESS Recent scholarship by Professors Richard Ofshe and Richard Leo, drawing on prior scholarship regarding false confessions and on their own inquiry, has explored many cases of false confessions. In one article, they review sixty cases of allegedly false confessions, and after examining available court and news media records, classify them into (i) thirty-four confessions that were proven false, (ii) eighteen highly probable false confessions and (iii) eight probable false confessions.[48] In other writings, Ofshe and Leo acknowledge that the actual number of false confessions cannot be known because (a) police do not keep complete records of interrogations, making it difficult to evaluate the reliability of the interrogation or whether there was any undue pressure; (b) no criminal justice agency keeps records or collects statistics on the number or frequency of interrogations, and (c) many cases of false confession are not reported.[49] Nevertheless, there are so many documented cases just in the past decade that false confessions must be seen as an important policy area to be addressed.[50]

Ofshe and Leo have intensively explored false confessions in a lengthy article which relies heavily on field data—transcripts of both true and false confessions—to display how certain processes lead to false confessions by the innocent.[51] They classify four types of false confessions. (1) *Stress-Compliant False Confessions.* The modern psychological interrogation is stressful by design and for some individuals—especially those with an abnormal reactivity to stress, who may be phobic, or with intellectual limitations who cope by becoming submissive—the pressure requires alleviation by saying, "I did it." (2) *Coerced-Compliant False Confessions.* This often results from the familiar "accident scenario technique," or "maximization/minimization." This is a subtle promise and threat (traditionally outlawed in England) by which the police convince the suspect that what he did was not all that serious, because there is a legal excuse or mitigation and that by confessing, he will receive lenient treatment. (3) and (4) *Voluntary and Involuntary Persuaded False Confessions.* These are instances where, after a good deal of interviewing and subtle or not so subtle badgering, the innocent person becomes so confused that confidence in his own memory is shattered. He reports that despite no overt memory of committing the crime, he agrees that the interrogators' recitation of events and (fabricated) "facts" must mean he is guilty.[52]

Ofshe and Leo do not suggest that confessions be abolished. They recommend safeguards because the process by which the innocent confess is very close to the process by which investigators obtain confessions from guilty persons. The steps by which confessions are obtained in the era of psychological interrogation shows why this is so. Detectives have two categories of suspects, "likely suspects, for whom there exists solid evidence suggesting their guilt; and possible suspects, which includes everyone whose name comes up during an investigation." Interrogation is superficially the same for both types. The detective may begin with an interview rather than interrogation format, especially for a possible suspect, to gain rapport and lull the interviewee into forgetting the adversarial nature of the encounter. Once *Miranda* warnings are read, neither "an innocent nor a guilty party is likely to appreciate the full significance of the . . . warnings." The innocent person thinks that he or she has nothing to hide. At that point, the tone and content of the interaction become confrontational and demanding. To get the suspect to say, "I did it," an investigator must strongly reject denials and insist that objective evidence points to guilt. At this point, a truly innocent person "is likely to experience considerable shock and disorientation . . . because he is wholly unprepared for the confrontation and accusations that are the core of the process, and will not understand how an investigator could possibly suspect him." The tragedy of wrongful confessions occur because the response to questioning by the guilty and the innocent "are often indistinguishable to an investigator." The investigator must now convince the suspect that his arrest is immanent and get the suspect to make an admission—get him to say, "I did it." Once this watershed is crossed, the investigator then moves the process toward obtaining a full confession.[53]

AN EXAMPLE OF A FALSE CONFESSION In 1986, Thomas F. Sawyer, a thirty-six-year-old groundskeeper, was charged with the murder of his next door neighbor, a single twenty-five-year-old woman, in Clearwater, Florida, on the basis of a confession. Janet Staschak was found strangled, nude, face down on her bed with wire and tape marks on her ankles. Sawyer, a recovering alcoholic, was extremely shy, suffered from bouts of anxiety, and often turned red and sweated profusely in ordinary social situations. When Sawyer was initially questioned by police officers, they noted his odd mannerisms and targeted him as a suspect. However, hair and blood samples obtained from Sawyer before his interrogation did not match samples found on the dead woman.

Although there was no corroborating evidence, two Clearwater detectives, John Dean and Peter Fire, obtained a confession from Sawyer. Before, during, and after the interrogation, Sawyer maintained his innocence. Then, how or why would an innocent person confess?[54]

Understanding Sawyer's confession in this case is aided by the transcript of what occurred during the entire taped sixteen-hour interrogation session, which stretched from 4:00 P.M. to 8:00 A.M., with time out for a ninety-minute nap. After several hours of questioning, the detectives asked Sawyer to pretend he was a police officer and to suggest methods and motives for the crime. Later during the questioning, they would take his statements and say that he knew too much about the crime to have guessed about the state of the room and the way in which the crime was carried out. Yet, police officers had for some time before the questioning been back and forth between Sawyer's and Staschak's apartment, and he may have heard a good deal about the crime; furthermore, the transcript, at this point, included a good deal of prompting by the detectives.

At about 8:00 P.M., four hours after the questioning began in a small room at the police station, the officers warned Sawyer of his rights, an example of "participating *Miranda*":

DEAN: All right. We got this squared away. Now Tom, because this is a criminal investigation, obviously, what we've been doing—There's a new phase we have to enter into now. And before I do that, I have to read you your rights. You watch television. You know. So just let me read you these.

DEAN: You have the right to remain silent. Do you understand that?

SAWYER: Uh-huh.

DEAN: Anything you say can and will be used against you in a court of law. Do you understand that? *[Sawyer nods.]*

FIRE: You got to go "yes."

SAWYER: Yes.

FIRE: Okay.

DEAN: You have the right to talk to a lawyer—

FIRE: No, wait a minute. You don't *have* to say yes. You answer the way you want to answer, but we have to hear you. I know you're saying yes with your nod, okay? You nodded yes, but—Okay?

SAWYER: Yeah. Okay.

DEAN: You have the right to talk to a lawyer. Have him present with you while you are being questioned. Do you understand that?

SAWYER: Yes.

DEAN: If you can't afford to hire a lawyer, one will be appointed to represent you before any questioning if you wish. Do you understand that?

SAWYER: Say it again. I wasn't—

DEAN: Okay. If you cannot afford to hire a lawyer, one will be appointed to represent you before any questioning if you wish. Do you understand that?
SAWYER: Yes.
DEAN: Okay. You can decide at any time to exercise your rights and not answer any questions or make any statements. Do you understand that?
SAWYER: Yes.
DEAN: Okay.
FIRE: Okay. So you understand everything. Okay. Listen, Tom. John and I—we've been talking to you all evening about this. Right? Okay? So why don't you tell us what happened. Tell us what happened.

This was followed by continuous denials by Sawyer and insistent statements by Dean and Fire that Sawyer was guilty.

SAWYER: I didn't do it.
FIRE: Tommy, it's not the truth.
SAWYER: Yes, it is.
FIRE: No it's not. Tom. Tell me the truth. Tell me what happened. It was an accident, Tom. I know it was. I know it was an accident. I need for you to tell me what happened.
SAWYER: I was never there. I never did it.
FIRE: Tom.
SAWYER: I'll look you in the eye and say that all night.
FIRE: I know, we got all night.

Throughout the session, Sawyer believed that his hair samples matched those found on Janet Staschak, and that a polygraph test indicated he was lying.[55] Playing on this, the detectives suggested to Sawyer that he had "blacked out" during the crime and committed it, although he did not remember anything. Throughout the session, Dean and Fire told Sawyer that he was an intelligent and good person; that the crime was not premeditated; that he would feel a great sense of relief if he confessed. Worn down, Sawyer finally confessed not only to a murder, but also to having raped Janet Staschak when in fact there was no physical evidence of sexual penetration. Many of the facts he admitted to were stated only after several false starts with persistent prompting by Fire and Dean. He made his confession conditional on the physical evidence: "The only reason I believe I did it is if my hairs were in her car and on her body and in her apartment."

At the preliminary examination, the trial court, lacking corroborating physical evidence, threw out the confession in a detailed decision. By fastening onto the closest possible suspect, the police apparently did not diligently follow up possible leads. Staschak had taken in roommates to help pay her rent; at first a heterosexual couple who were dealing drugs and later a homosexual couple. Both pairs had been evicted by her, and both had left her in some fear. It seems likely that by fastening on Sawyer, the Clearwater officers let the real culprits escape. The trial judge described the interrogation session as an intellectual wrestling match. The Florida Court of Appeals agreed and upheld the suppression of the confession.

PREVENTING FALSE CONFESSIONS As noted above, Ofshe and Leo do not recommend abolishing police interrogation. They do have recommendations to lessen the possibility of false confessions. One recommendation, discussed earlier, is that custodial interrogations be videotaped. A lengthy interrogation contains so many subtle, forward-moving points of persuasion-threat-coercion, such as maximization-minimization techniques that "is it beyond human ability to remember just what happened." Since interrogators are zealous in achieving their goals of obtaining confession, they are naturally biased and simply will not see that they did anything that might induce a false confession.

Ofshe and Leo's central point is that false confessions come about when commonplace interrogation methods (including the verbal fabrication of "evidence") are used improperly, inappropriately, or ineptly.[56] Therefore, police training is critical to avoiding false confessions. Police need to be educated in the facts of false confessions and to understand that they do occur. Since there is a subtle difference between the proper and improper use of the psychological interrogation, the most important factor is for police to be aware that when they have a possible suspect, as opposed to a likely suspect, they should seek corroborating evidence. "If police and prosecutors recognized that the mere admission "I did it" is not necessarily a true statement, they would be far less likely to arrest and prosecute suspects who give false confessions."[57]

The last recommendation is that trial judges "should evaluate the reliability of confession statements," as they do hearsay statements, to determine whether they should be allowed into evidence. "Oddly, the constitutional law of criminal procedure has no substantive safeguards in place to specifically prevent the admission of even demonstrably false confessions." The constitutional rules for confessions under the Fifth and Sixth amendments are designed to insure procedural regularity but not reliability, and the same has become true under the due process voluntariness test. Given this constitutional vacuum, it is critically important for judges to perform this task. The stakes for fairness are high: "It has been shown that placing a confession before a jury is tantamount to an instruction to convict, even when the confession fails to accurately describe the crime, fails to produce corroboration, and is contradicted by considerable evidence pointing to a suspect's innocence." Therefore, judges should demand that confessions display a minimal level of reliability. This can be done without any change in statutes or court rules. Judges routinely rule on admissibility and would, for example, not allow a jury to see a photograph that had been doctored. "A false confession is analogous to a doctored photograph. The mechanism for creating it is the ancient technology of human influence carried forward into the interrogation room."

A short decade ago, there was at best a vague awareness that false confessions were a rare and tragic, human failing. Recent scholarship has brought the problem to the forefront. Judges, prosecutors, leaders of the bar, and police officials have no reason to claim ignorance. It remains to be seen if the legal world will respond to this challenge.

SUMMARY

All persons questioned by police have a general obligation to cooperate and to answer questions truthfully. An exception is the right against self-incrimination guaranteed by the Fifth Amendment which prevents a person having to face the cruel trilemma of self-accusation, perjury, or contempt. When applicable, the privilege against self-incrimination is an absolute bar against the use of compelled testimony taken from natural persons. Physical evidence is not covered by the Fifth Amendment right.

Prior to 1966, confessions or admissions were inadmissible if they were not voluntary. Force or undue psychological pressure was held to constitute violations of due process under the voluntariness test. Judicial displeasure with the subjectivity of the voluntariness test led the Supreme Court to seek a more concrete rule. In 1963 and 1964, the Supreme Court incorporated the Sixth Amendment right to the assistance counsel and the privilege against self-incrimination. In *Escobedo v. Arizona* (1964), the Court held a confession taken by police violated the right to counsel when a suspect's attorney was deliberately prevented from seeing his client.

Miranda v. Arizona (1966) applied the Fifth Amendment right against self-incrimination to confessions instead of the Sixth Amendment right to counsel. All custodial interrogation by police was deemed inherently coercive, requiring that police inform suspects of their rights in order to dispel the coercive atmosphere of police custody. The four warnings or rights are: that the person has a right to remain silent; that any statement made may be used as evidence against him; that he has a right to the presence of an attorney; and, that if he cannot afford an attorney one will be appointed. A defendant may waive these rights if the waiver is made voluntarily, knowingly, and intelligently.

After the *Miranda* decision, a more conservative Supreme Court made a series of rulings that declared that the *Miranda* warnings were part of a "new rule" designed to protect the underlying Fifth Amendment right against self-incrimination. Because the warnings themselves were not constitutional rights, admissions or confessions taken in violation of *Miranda* could be used to impeach the defendant to lead to other evidence, including subsequent confessions taken after proper warnings had been issued. Under this rule a public safety exception was created, allowing the admission into evidence of unwarned statements made in answers to questions designed to protect the safety of arresting officers and other persons in the immediate area (*New York v. Quarles,* 1984).

Despite this, in *Dickerson v. United States* (2000), the Supreme Court held that the *Miranda* warnings were constitutional rules that could not be overridden by a Congressional statute purporting to reinstate the voluntariness test as the sole measure of the constitutionality of confessions in federal cases. The Supreme Court recognized that *Miranda* had become so widely accepted that the concerns of precedent *(stare decisis)* compelled a recognition of the rule as being constitutional.

The Fourteenth Amendment due process voluntariness test still exists, but as a back-stop to, and not a replacement for, the *Miranda* rule. Just as a waiver is not proper if coerced, so are coerced statements inadmissible even if taken after proper *Miranda* warnings and a waiver of rights.

Miranda was followed by many cases designed to clarify the meaning of its provisions. Thus, the warnings need not be given in the precise language found in the case as long as the correct understanding of the warnings is conveyed. Police do not have to add anything to the warnings such as the consequences of confessing or their knowledge that the suspect may have committed crimes that is not the immediate subject of the questioning. The prosecution has the burden of proving that a waiver is made voluntarily. A waiver is not presumed from silence, and an oral waiver is allowable as long as it was made expressly and is shown on the record. Written waivers are the common form of proving that the right to silence and counsel were waived voluntarily.

Police must cease questioning a suspect who has waived his or her rights and indicates during interrogation the wish to terminate the interrogation. However, police may resume questioning at a later time if the resumption is reasonable. It was held reasonable in *Michigan v. Mosley* (1975) where the suspect was questioned for an entirely separate crime, after a lapse of time, and was again read *Miranda* warnings.

Police must cease questioning a suspect who personally and clearly invokes a desire to see an attorney and not another kind of counselor. The police may not thereafter resume questioning unless it is initiated by the suspect (*Edwards v. Arizona,* 1981). This rule is violated if an officer in a department re-interrogates such a suspect in ignorance of his prior request for an attorney. Simple consultation with a lawyer does not dispel *Edwards* protection; a defendant has a right, after invoking counsel, to be questioned by police or prosecutors only with counsel present.

A person is in *Miranda* custody if the circumstances or surroundings are objectively coercive. Depending upon the circumstances, interviews in one's home, at a police station, or by a probation officer may not be coercive. Interrogation in prison, even for a crime unrelated to the original crime, require *Miranda* warnings. Questioning by a patrol officer after a routine traffic stop is generally not custodial because this kind of common detention is in public and lacks the coercive atmosphere of the police station. Questions designed to produce an incriminating answer or questions asked after a person has been arrested at the roadside constitute custodial interrogation.

Interrogation consists of express questioning or its functional equivalent: words or actions on the part of the police (other than normally attendant to arrest and custody) that the police should know are reasonably likely to elicit an incriminating response from the suspect. Deception by police interrogators is allowed. Undercover agents, in or out of jail, are not required to give Miranda warnings when they ask incriminating questions because the interrogation is not conducted in a coercive atmosphere.

Once a person has been formally arraigned, the police may not question a suspect without a lawyer present, or eavesdrop on a suspect. A suspect may waive this Sixth Amendment right after being read *Miranda* warnings. This rule was violated in *Brewer v. Williams* (1977) when an officer made the functional equivalent of an interrogation designed to elicit a response by delivering a "Christian Burial" speech to an isolated mental patient. Undercover agents who investigate a person who has been formally charged must not ask any questions or initiate conversations likely to generate incriminating statements. They may, however, listen for such statements which are then admissible.

LEGAL PUZZLES

LEGAL PUZZLES: HOW HAVE COURTS DECIDED THESE CASES?

8–1. Police, suspecting that a car driver was involved in a drug transaction, stopped him for driving without a rear license plate. The driver, Murray, appeared to be hiding something. He was ordered out of the car and some crack cocaine and a gun were found during a legal search. Murray was placed in the back seat of the squad car and asked a few questions without being read *Miranda* warnings. He made an incriminating statement. Should the statement be suppressed? *United States v. Murray,* 89 F.3d 459 (7th Cir. 1996).

8–2. Garibay, stopped at Customs while entering the U.S. from Mexico, was asked in Spanish to open the trunk of his vehicle. Marijuana was discovered in a hidden compartment. An hour later Customs agents asked Garibay in English if he understood English. Garibay said "yes." An agent orally read him *Miranda* rights in English. Garibay indicated that he understood. He waived his rights and made incriminating statements during the interrogation. Garibay was not offered the option of conducting the interrogation in Spanish, although Spanish-speaking agents were available at that time. The agent had to rephrase questions when Garibay did not seem to comprehend what was said to him. Garibay's primary language is Spanish; he understands only a few things in English. He attended a U.S. high school where he received D+ grades in eleventh and twelfth grade English. He never graduated. The agent did not inquire into Garibay's English proficiency. Did Garibay lawfully waive his right to remain silent knowingly? *United States v. Garibay,* 143 F.3d 534 (9th Cir. 1997).

8–3. Carrillo, a suspected drug dealer, was arrested. Before being transported to the detention facility, an officer searched him. Prior to the search, the officer asked Carrillo if he had any drugs or needles on his person. Carrillo responded, "No, I don't use drugs, I sell them." The officer asked no further questions. No *Miranda* warnings were given. Is the statement admissible? *United States v. Carrillo,* 16 F.3d 1046 (9th Cir. 1994).

8–4. Kyger was stopped and then arrested at a pizzeria because he fit the description of a robber. He was taken to the police station and later read his *Miranda* rights and asked if he understood them. He replied: "I'd just as soon have an attorney [']cause, you know ya'll say there's been a shooting involved and that's a serious charge." The officer continued to talk to and question Kyger. Kyger then signed a waiver and made incriminating statement. Were Kyger's rights violated? *United States v. Kyger,* 146 F.3d 374 (6th Cir. 1998).

ANSWERS TO LEGAL PUZZLES

8–1. NO. This was still a traffic stop. Murray was not placed under formal arrest prior to questioning. The time elapsed between the initial stop, and the questioning was brief. The encounter took place on a lighted street in an urban area in public view. The officers did not engage in conduct that could have overborne Murray's will. Murray was not "in custody" for *Miranda* purposes simply because he was questioned while seated in the back of the squad car A reasonable person in Murray's position would not have considered the brief questioning at the scene to be a custodial interrogation. He was in custody *after* the questioning when police announced he was under arrest and put him in handcuffs.

8–2 NO. A knowing and intelligent waiver implies a rational choice based upon some appreciation of the consequences of the decision. Language difficulties are a factor to consider in determining the validity of a waiver. There was no justification for the agents' failure to ask Garibay whether he preferred Spanish or English nor for their failure to seek the assistance of bilingual agents. The agents' oversight is particularly glaring given that Garibay's primary language is Spanish as well as the other available facts.

8–3. YES. The statement comes under the public safety exception. The officer's question stemmed from an objectively reasonable need to protect himself from immediate danger. The risk differs from that presented by a gun, as in *New York v. Quarles,* but the danger of transmission of disease or contact with harmful substances is real and serious enough. The lack of further questions by the officer is evidence that he was concerned with his safety and was not seeking to elicit incriminating statements.

8–4. YES. His statement that he would "just as soon have an attorney" was a request for counsel. To continue questioning after his request violated his rights; admitting his interrogation statements was unconstitutional under *Edwards v. Arizona* (1981). If Kyger's request was equivocal, the subsequent statement by the police ("Now, if you've got something to hide, I can understand you not wanting to sign that. If you ain't got nothing to hide, you know, you can answer our questions.") was an inappropriate pressure on Kyger to answer, rather than an appropriate attempt to get Kyger to clarify his response under *Davis v. United States* (1994) which approved the use of clarifying questions

FURTHER READING

R. H. Helmholz, et al., *The Privilege Against Self-Incrimination: Its Origins and Development* (Chicago: University of Chicago Press, 1997)

Liva Baker, Miranda: *Crime, Law and Politics* (New York: Atheneum, 1985)

Richard A. Leo and George C. Thomas III, *The Miranda Debate: Law, Justice and Policing* (Boston: Northeastern University Press, 1998)

ENDNOTES

1. See, e.g., Charles E. O'Hara and Gregory O'Hara, *Fundamentals of Criminal Investigation,* 5th ed. (Springfield, Ill.: Charles C. Thomas, 1988).
2. See, e.g., N.J. Stat. §2C:104–6 (2000).
3. R.H. Helmholz, "Introduction," in R.H. Helmholz, et al., *The Privilege Against Self-Incrimination: Its Origins and Development* (Chicago: University of Chicago Press, 1997), p. 1.
4. John H. Langbein, *Torture and the Law of Proof: Europe and England in the Ancien Régime* (Chicago: University of Chicago Press, 1977); Edward Peters, *Torture* (Oxford: Basil Blackwell, 1985).
5. Richard S. Frase, REVIEW ESSAY: The Search for the Whole Truth About American and European Criminal Justice— *Trials Without Truth: Why Our System of Criminal Trials Has Become an Expensive Failure and What We Need to Do to Rebuild It* (New York: New York University Press, 1999) By William T. Pizzi. *Buffalo Criminal Law Review* 3:785–849 (2000).
6. Charles H. Whitebread and Christopher Slobogin, *Criminal Procedure: An Analysis of Cases and Concepts, Fourth Edition* (New York: Foundation Press, 2000), p. 379.
7. Project, "Twenty-Fifth Annual Review of Criminal Procedure," *Georgetown Law Journal* 84(1996):641, pp. 1212–13 (footnotes omitted).
8. Project, "Twenty-Ninth Annual Review of Criminal Procedure," *Georgetown Law Journal* 88:879, pp. 1431–32 (footnotes omitted) (2000).
9. P. W. Valentine, "Woman, Jailed for Contempt, Freed After 7 Years; Md. Mother Failed to Reveal Son's Location," *Washington Post,* Nov, 1, 1995, p. D1; "Mother Ends 7-Year Jail Stay, Still Silent About Missing Child," *New York Times,* Nov. 2, 1995, p. A18 (byline AP).
10. Delmar Karlen, *Anglo-American Criminal Justice* (New York: Oxford University Press, 1967), p. 121; David J. Bodenhamer, *Fair Trial: Rights of the Accused in American History* (New York: Oxford University Press, 1992), pp. 53–4.
11. Karlen, note 10, p. 122.
12. See Samuel Walker, *Popular Justice: A History of American Criminal Justice* (New York: Oxford University Press, 1980), pp. 173–75, 189, 231. Richard Leo, *Police Interrogation in America: A Study of Violence, Civility, and Social Change* (unpublished Ph.D. Dissertation, University of California at Berkeley, 1995), pp. 12–66, examined the third degree and suggested that the practice declined because of increasing police professionalism, changing attitudes, and changes in legal doctrine.
13. Bodenhamer, note 10, p. 101.
14. Richard C. Cortner, *The Supreme Court and the Second Bill of Rights* (Madison: University of Wisconsin Press, 1981), p. 150.
15. Note, "Developments in the Law of Confessions," *Harvard Law Review* 79(1966):935, pp. 963–83 (emphasis added).
16. Fred P. Graham, *The Due Process Revolution: The Warren Court's Impact on Criminal Law* (New York: Hayden Book Co., 1970), p. 154.
17. Graham, note 16, p. 155.
18. Graham, note 16, pp. 153–93; Liva Baker, *Miranda: Crime, Law and Politics* (New York: Atheneum, 1985).
19. Baker, note 18, pp. 191–94, 408–09.
20. Baker, note 18, pp. 221–324.
21. A. L. Galub, *The Burger Court 1968–1984: The Supreme Court in American Life,* Vol. 9 (Millwood, N.Y.: Associated Faculty Press, 1986); Charles M. Lamb and Stephen C. Halpern, eds., *The Burger Court: Political and Judicial Profiles* (Urbana: University of Illinois Press, 1991).

22. 428 N.W.2d 406 (Minn. App. 1988).
23. Richard Harris, *The Fear of Crime* (New York: Praeger, 1969), p. 58.
24. Joseph Grano, *Confessions, Truth and the Law* (Ann Arbor: University of Michigan Press, 1993), quote at pp. 197–98. Professor Grano lays out the argument for overruling at pp. 199–222. The articles of a leading supporter of Miranda are collected in Yale Kamisar, *Police Interrogation and Confessions: Essays in Law and Policy* (Ann Arbor: University of Michigan Press, 1980). A recent compilation of essays: Richard A. Leo and George C. Thomas III, eds., *The Miranda Debate: Law, Justice and Policing* (Boston: Northeastern University Press, 1998).
25. *United States v. Dickerson,* 166 F.3d 667 (4th Cir. 1999). The critical analysis can be found at: Office of Legal Policy, (Truth in Criminal Justice Series), The Law of Pretrial Interrogation, *University of Michigan Journal of Law Reform* 22:437–572 (1989).
26. Roger Parloff, "Miranda on the Hot Seat," *New York Times Magazine,* Sept. 26, 1999, Section 6, p. 84.
27. 834 S.W.2d 265 (Tenn. 1992).
28. Not the same Colson in the *Massiah* case.
29. An issue not discussed here is the complex debate over the impact of *Miranda* on admissions and clearance rates. Leo first suggested that the "accepted wisdom" that *Miranda* had little effect on such rates may not be solidly grounded. R. Leo, The Impact of *Miranda* Revisited, *Journal of Criminal Law & Criminology* 86:621–692 (1996). Professor Paul Cassell and colleagues attempt to demonstrate that *Miranda* did lower confessions and clearance rates. P.G. Cassell, *Miranda's* Social Costs: an Empirical Reassessment, *Northwestern University Law Review* 90:387 (1996); P. G. Cassell and R. Fowles, "Handcuffing the Cops? A Thirty-Year Perspective on Miranda's Harmful Effects on Law Enforcement," *Stanford Law Review* 50:1055 (1998). Their methodology has been sharply criticized: G. C. Thomas III, "Plain Talk about the *Miranda* Empirical Debate: a "Steady-state" Theory of Confessions," *UCLA Law Review* 43:933–59 (1996); R. A. Leo and W. S. White, "Adapting to *Miranda:* Modern Interrogators' Strategies for Dealing With the Obstacles Posed by *Miranda,*" *Minnesota Law Review* 84:397–472 (1999), pp. 402–07. The criticisms seem well founded, but proper analysis require a detailed review that is beyond the scope of this text.
30. T. Jacoby, "Fighting Crime by the Rules," *Newsweek,* July 18, 1988, p. 53, reviewing *Tempered Zeal* by R. Uviller.
31. Leo, *Police Interrogation,* note 12, p. 335.
32. Leo, *ibid.* note 12, p. 336–42.
33. Richard A. Leo and Welsh S. White, "Adapting to *Miranda:* Modern Interrogators' Strategies for Dealing With the Obstacles Posed by *Miranda,*" *Minnesota Law Review* 84:397–472 (1999), p. 402, n. 18 lists some of the early studies.
34. Leo, *Police Interrogation,* note 12, pp. 258–68, 276–77. Leo's dissertation has been published in several articles: Inside the Interrogation Room, *Journal of Criminal Law and Criminology* 86: 266–303 (1996); Richard A. Leo, Miranda's Revenge: Police Interrogation as a Confidence Game, *Law & Society Review* 30:259–88 (1996).
35. Leo, note 12, p. 271.
36. Leo, note12, p. 191.
37. Leo, note 12, pp. 212–20.
38. Leo & White, "Adapting to *Miranda,*" note 33 pp. 431–47.
39. P. W. Lewis and H. E. Allen, "'Participating *Miranda*': An Attempt to Subvert Certain Constitutional Safeguards," *Crime and Delinquency* 23(1):75–80 (1977).
40. See Leo, note 12, pp. 230–51; D. Simon, *Homicide: A Year on the Killing Streets* (Boston: Houghton Mifflin, 1991).
41. Charles D. Weisselberg, "Saving *Miranda,*" *Cornell Law Review* 84:109 (1998); Leo & White, Adapting to *Miranda*, note 33, pp. 447–50.
42. Leo, *ibid.* note 12, p. 354.
43. Leo, *ibid.* note 12, pp. 357–59.
44. Leo, *ibid.* note 12, pp. 359–60.
45. Leo, *ibid.* note 12, pp 361–63.
46. Leo, *ibid.* note 12, p. 416.
47. Richard Leo, "The Impact of Miranda Revisited," *Journal of Criminal Law & Criminology* 86:621–692 (1996), pp. 683–84, relying on William A. Geller, U.S. Department of Justice, *Videotaping Interrogations and Confessions* (Mar. 1993).
48. Richard A. Leo and Richard J. Ofshe, "The Consequences of False Confessions: Deprivations of Liberty and Miscarriages of Justice in the Age of Psychological Interrogation," *Journal of Criminal Law and Criminology* 88:429–96 (1998).
49. Richard A. Leo and Richard J. Ofshe, "Missing The Forest for The Trees: A Response to Paul Cassell's "Balanced Approach" to the False Confession Problem," *Denver University Law Review* 74:1135 (1997).
50. In Jim Dwyer, Peter Neufeld, and Barry Scheck, *Actual Innocence* (New York: Doubleday, 2000), pp. 78–106, the law professors who operate the "innocence project" list false confessions as one of several problems that contribute to what DNA testing has disclosed to be a major problem of convicting the innocent.
51. Richard J. Ofshe and Richard A. Leo, "The Decision to Confess Falsely: Rational Choice and Irrational Action," *Denver University Law Review* 74:979–1122 (1997).
52. Ofshe & Leo, ibid, pp. 997–1000.
53. Ofshe & Leo, ibid, pp. 986–94.
54. The information on the Sawyer case is derived from a 292-page transcript of the police interrogation. The secondary sources used that reprinted parts of the transcript are found in: "Readings: [Transcript] True Confession?," *Harper's,* (Oct. 1989), pp. 17–20+ and Philip Weiss, "Untrue Confessions," *Mother Jones* (Sept. 1989), pp. 18–24+.
55. The lie detector examination was given during the evening when he was under great stress. A later polygraph examination indicated that Sawyer's denial of the murder was truthful.
56. Leo & Ofshe, "Missing The Forest," note 49.
57. Ofshe & Leo, "The Decision to Confess Falsely," note 51, pp. 1119–1120.

JUSTICES OF THE SUPREME COURT

NIXON'S CONSERVATIVES
BURGER—REHNQUIST

President Nixon had the good political fortune to name four justices during his first term in office and thus was able to significantly mold the Court's direction. He attacked the Warren Court as a campaign issue in 1968, and was only too happy to fill retiring Chief Justice Warren's seat with Warren Burger, an outspoken critic of the Warren Court's criminal procedure rulings. Justice Rehnquist, appointed in 1972 from a position in the Justice Department, has been the most consistently conservative justice over the next three decades.

The Burger Court's output, while more conservative than that of the Warren Court, did not achieve a radical conservative counter-revolution contemplated by the extreme Right. Thus, the Burger Court supported gender equality, was moderately supportive of prisoner's rights, and did not significantly inhibit freedom of expression. Indeed, the Court's 1973 abortion rights decision has been a constant lightning rod for criticism from conservatives. Its criminal procedure cases were generally conservative; they halted the expansion of suspects' rights without overruling Warren Court decisions. On the whole, the Supreme Court probably reflects a nation that may be better described as moderate (or perhaps vacillating), rather than strictly conservative, in social issues.

Justice Rehnquist was elevated to Chief Justice in 1986, upon Warren Burger's retirement, only the third sitting associate justices to have been so promoted. (The other two were Edward D. White and Harlan Fisk Stone. Charles Evans Hughes, a retired associate justice, was later named chief justice). Although a chief justice has only one vote among nine, when in the majority he appoints the writer of the opinion, and thus has an additional opportunity to shape the emphasis of American constitutional law.

WARREN EARL BURGER

Virginia 1907–1995

Republican

Appointed by Richard Nixon as Chief Justice

Years of Service: 1969–1987

Collection of the Supreme Court of the United States. Photographer: Robert S. Oakes

LIFE AND CAREER Burger, a Minnesota native, was graduated *magna cum laude* from the St. Paul College of Law, and practiced with a substantial St. Paul law firm from 1931 to 1956. Active in political affairs, he supported governor Harold Stassen's bid for the presidential nomination on the Republican ticket in 1948. At the 1952 nominating convention, Burger played a key role in swinging Stassen's delegates to Eisenhower, ensuring his nomination over Ohio's Senator Taft. Thereafter, President Eisenhower's attorney general, Herbert Brownell, brought Burger to the Justice Department as an assistant attorney general. He was appointed to the U.S. Court of Appeals for the District of Columbia in 1956 where he gained recognition as a highly competent jurist who was outspoken in criticizing the Warren Court's expansion of the rights of criminal suspects. This reputation was an important factor in Burger's nomination by Richard Nixon, whose 1968 presidential campaign included sharp criticism of the liberal Supreme Court's criminal decisions.

CONTRIBUTION TO CRIMINAL PROCEDURE He was quite conservative, calling for abolition of the exclusionary rule and limiting its scope wherever possible (e.g., noncoerced statements obtained in violation of *Miranda* could be used to impeach a witness; the exclusionary rule is not a constitutional right but merely a Court-created police deterrent).

On the other hand, in *Chadwick* (1977), he upheld the plain text of the Fourth Amendment by ruling that a warrant was required to search a footlocker.

Signature Opinion Dissent in *Bivens v. Six Unknown Named Agents* (1971). The Court, in an opinion by Justice Brennan held, for the first time, that a person whose Fourth Amendment rights are violated by federal law enforcement officers may bring a civil, tort lawsuit in federal court against such officers. Chief Justice Burger dissented, arguing that the Fourth Amendment itself created no such lawsuit and that under the separation of powers, the Court should not authorize such a suit but wait for Congress to establish a federal civil remedy. In his opinion, he wrote broadly on the exclusionary rule, trying to narrow its scope by characterizing it as resting only "on the deterrent rationale—the hope that law enforcement officials would be deterred from unlawful searches and seizures" if the products of such searches were suppressed.

Assessment In other areas, the Chief Justice was often moderate to conservative and pragmatic. In First Amendment law, he broadened the scope of what is considered obscenity but struck down a gag order on the press in criminal trials. In civil rights, he upheld busing to integrate deliberately segregated school systems but not where segregation was not intended; he upheld the denial of federal tax credits to schools that discriminate but voted against holding that inequitable school taxes violated the Equal Protection Clause. He concurred in *Roe v. Wade* (1973)(abortion rights) and in *United States v. Nixon* (1974) wrote for a unanimous Court that President Nixon's claim of executive privilege did not override a court order to turn over tapes of his Watergate conversations. He was not known as an especially effective leader as chief justice, and during his tenure Justices Brennan, Rehnquist, and Powell were more influential with their fellow justices. In 1987, Burger stepped down to head the national celebration of the bicentennial of the Constitution, a fitting role after eighteen years of service as chief justice of the United States.

Further Reading

Charles M. Lamb, "Chief Justice Warren E. Burger: A Conservative Chief for Conservative Times," in *The Burger Court: Political and Judicial Profiles,* edited by Charles M. Lamb and Stephen C. Halpern, pp. 129–162 (Urbana: University of Illinois Press, 1991).

William H. Rehnquist

Arizona 1924–

Republican

Appointed by Richard Nixon and Ronald Reagan

Years of Service: Associate Justice: 1972–1986; Chief Justice: 1986–

Collection of the Supreme Court of the United States. Photographer: Dane Penland.

Life and Career Rehnquist was born in Milwaukee, Wisconsin, and attended Stanford University after service during World War II. His very conservative views were formed early in his life. He received a master's degree in political science and graduated first in his class from Stanford Law School. He clerked for Justice Robert Jackson, and practiced law in Phoenix, Arizona, from 1953 to 1969, was active in conservative Republican politics, and in 1969 became an assistant attorney general in the Nixon administration. He was appointed to the Court at the relatively young age of 47, and at that time was the most conservative member of the Court. He faced strong opposition in his initial appointment, and again in 1986 when President Reagan nominated Rehnquist to the position of chief justice.

Contribution to Criminal Procedure Justice Rehnquist has been a prolific opinion writer in criminal procedure cases and has helped to shape a very conservative view of Fourth Amendment rights. His majority opinions have restricted Fourth Amendment standing to those with property-like interests; replaced the two-prong rule for accepting the hearsay of a secret informant to obtain a search warrant, with the more lenient "totality of the circumstances" test; held that *Miranda* warnings were only protective devices and not themselves constitutionally rights protected rights; created a "public safety exception" to the *Miranda* rule; expanded *Terry* stops to crimes of possession based on hearsay; limited the right to counsel on second appeals; and held that drug courier profiles constituted reasonable suspicion for a stop. More recently, he has held that prosecuting a higher proportion of African Americans for possession of crack cocaine, which carries a heavier penalty than powdered cocaine, is not selective prosecution; that a law which allows the forfeiture of a wife's interest in her car, which her husband used for a tryst with a prostitute, does not violate due process; that a lawyer's failure to object to an aggravating factor at a death penalty trial does not prejudice the defendant.

Signature Opinion *Dickerson v. United States* (2000). Chief Justice Rehnquist, for a 7–2 majority, upheld the *Miranda* ruling, calling it "a constitutional rule that Congress may not supersede legislatively." His adroit opinion seemed to go against his many earlier opinions that established the rule that "The prophylactic *Miranda* warnings therefore are not themselves rights protected by the Constitution but are instead measures to insure that the right against compulsory self-incrimination is protected"—Rehnquist's own words in the majority opinions of *Michigan v. Tucker* (1974) and *New York v. Quarles* (1984). Indeed, *Dickerson*'s reasoning, while plausible in some respects, did not easily square with the earlier pronouncements of the Chief Justice and the Court. How can this be explained? The answer seems to be that Rehnquist saw the institutional role of the Supreme Court as outweighing doctrinal purity in this case. The nation had come to rely on *Miranda* warnings to such an extent that they "have become part of our national culture." As such, the dictates of *stare decisis,* a doctrine that Rehnquist never thought was paramount in constitutional adjudication, nevertheless carried the day here.

Assessment Justice Rehnquist's judicial philosophy dictates the outcome of many of his cases. He believes that American federalism requires the Court to play a small role in the affairs of the states and of other branches of government. He disfavored the incorporation doctrine and would prefer that the states make their own decisions in regard to defendants' rights. He has written that the Supreme Court does not have a special position as the ultimate guardian of individual rights because that was not a role intended by the Framers of the Constitution. Rehnquist's constitutional philosophy of strict federalism and deference to the elected branches of government can be seen as democratic in giving the majority a greater voice, while reducing the Court's role as a "guardian" of minorities.

Further Reading

Sue Davis, *Justice Rehnquist and the Constitution* (Princeton, N.J. : Princeton University Press, 1989).

CHAPTER 9

Identification of Suspects: Lineups and Showups

Law enforcement may have the elements of a contest about it, but it is not a game.

—Justice Byron White, dissenting in *Massiah v. United States*, 377 U.S. 201, 213 (1964)

CHAPTER OUTLINE

KEY TERMS AND PHRASES

Cross-examination
Eyewitness identification
Lineup
Showup
Suggestibility
Testimonial evidence

Introduction: The Persistence of Mistaken Identification

Eyewitness identification is the most important source of truth in most criminal cases and, ironically, the leading source of error that results in the prosecution, conviction, imprisonment, and even the execution of innocent persons. The need to use eyewitnesses at every stage of the criminal process is self-evident. A victim of a street mugging sits in a police car and is asked whether an apprehended suspect matches her description. A store clerk at a police station **lineup** is asked whether each person presented to him in a lineup is or is not the armed robber. At a trial, a householder sitting in the witness box is asked to identify the burglar; she raises her arm, points to the person sitting next to the defense lawyer, and says, "That's the man; I'd know him anywhere."

The possibility of honestly mistaken identification is part of common-sense psychology. This understanding has been institutionalized in use of **cross-examination** in the common-law criminal trial. During cross-examination, the opposing attorney asks the eyewitness common-sense questions to cast doubt on the accuracy of the witness' assertions of identification: For how long did the witness observe the perpetrator? Was the witness wearing prescription lenses? What were the lighting conditions? The legal system places great faith in the ability of cross-examination to ferret out the truth. A century ago, Dean Henry Wigmore (1863–1943) of Northwestern University Law School called cross-examination "the greatest legal engine ever invented for the discovery of truth" and the United States Supreme Court said that "cross-examination is the principal means by which the believability of a witness and the truth of his testimony are tested" (*Davis v. Alaska,* 1974).[1]

Nevertheless, for a century it has been known that human identification is fraught with error. Classroom experiments by German psychologist Hugo Münsterberg were published in 1908 and dramatically demonstrated that human recall of recent events is filled with errors.[2] In 1932, Yale Law Professor Edwin Borchard published the book, *Convicting the Innocent: Sixty-five Actual Errors of Criminal Justice,* which details cases of individuals who were found guilty of felonies and were later proven to be completely innocent.[3] The largest number of these miscarriages of justice were caused by mistaken eyewitness identification. In some cases, prosecutorial malfeasance took place. The released individuals were often given monetary compensation by special acts of state legislatures. A similar book appeared in 1957 by Jerome Frank and Barbara Frank, with thirty-four documented instances of innocents convicted in American courts.[4] According to a 1996 book by Huff, Rattner, and Sagarin, the number of wrongful convictions is estimated at almost 10,000 annually—a count which is based on responses to questionnaires which were given to Ohio judges and criminal justice officials. Another estimate is that "more than 4,250 Americans per year are wrongfully convicted due to sincere, yet woefully inaccurate eyewitness identifications."[5] Although the actual number cannot be known with certainty, 94% of the respondents in the Huff, Rattner, and Sagarin study estimated that wrongful convictions sometimes occur.[6] Hugo Bedeau and Michael Radelet conducted an exhaustive and systematic study to identify every case where an innocent person was convicted of a crime carrying the death penalty or "potentially capital cases."[7] They found 350 such wrongful convictions between 1900 and 1985 in all American jurisdictions, with no indication that the justice system is becoming progressively more accurate.[8]

These studies confirm the astonishing regularity with which such cases are reported in the news media. In 1985, a New York assistant prosecutor was charged with attempted rape before a look-alike confessed.[9] In another New York case in 1974, a person was held for a year for armed robbery based on a photo identification. Police knew he had an accent but did not ask the victim. A year later, a probation officer, after hearing the defendant's thick West Indian accent, asked the victim whether the robber spoke with an accent and subsequently discovered the wrong man was held.[10] "Freedom for Another Dallas Prisoner" a newspaper story reported that five innocent persons convicted in Dallas within a few years had been freed.[11] A Roman Catholic priest, Father Bernard Pagano, was mistaken for the "gentleman robber" in Delaware.[12] Lenel Geter, a young African-American engineer, was convicted of a fast-food franchise robbery, although co-workers testified he was at work, fifty miles from the robbery site, and he bore little resemblance to the robber's description. There was "intense national publicity, including a feature story on CBS's *60 Minutes*" before Geter was released.[13] Randall Dale Adams, convicted of the murder of Dallas police officer Robert Wood in 1977, had his case brought to light by a riveting documentary film, *The Thin Blue Line*, produced by Errol Morris. The film exposed a combination of prosecutorial overzealousness and witness incompetence that generated the conviction and elicited a virtual confession from David Harris, who appears to have been the actual killer.[14] Recent books have detailed the nationally famous convictions, later shown to be false, of Sam Sheppard and Rubin "Hurricane" Carter.[15]

A cursory review of news stories over a three month period in 2000 disclosed that

- in Houston, Texas, DNA tests cleared two men who were wrongfully convicted of rape on the basis of faulty eyewitness testimony;
- in Orange County, California, eighteen-year-old Arthur Carmona spent two years in prison for a robbery that he did not commit; his conviction was based on eyewitnesses who later recanted their testimonies,
- in Norfolk, Virginia, a judge threw out a drug prosecution of a man identified by an undercover informant as a drug seller who was in jail on the day of the alleged sale, leading state authorities to drop thirty-seven other cases based on the informer's identification;
- a Boston, Massachusetts man was freed on the basis of DNA tests after spending ten years in prison for a rape he did not commit;
- in another Boston case, Marlon Passley was released after prosecutors admitted that his murder conviction had been obtained on the basis of mistaken eyewitness identification—Passley had just lost an appeal after spending four years in prison;
- and to return to Orange County, California, three other men were released from prison for serious crimes, two after decades.[16]

In June 2000, Jennifer Thompson, a rape victim, wrote a moving article in the *New York Times* detailing her experience of positively identifying the wrong man, after making efforts to recall her assailant. DNA tests identified another man who later confessed to the crime. Thompson wrote, "If anything good can come out of what Ronald Cotton suffered because of my limitations as a human being, let it be an awareness of the fact that eyewitnesses can and do make mistakes."[17] Thompson urged that the planned execution of Gary Graham in Texas be halted. Graham was convicted of murder largely on the testimony of a single witness who said she saw him from thirty to forty feet away through her car windshield. There was no physical evidence linking Graham to the crime. Tests showed that the gun he was carrying was not the murder weapon, and two other witnesses who were never called to testify at trial said they had seen the killer—and it was not Graham. He was represented at trial by a court-appointed lawyer who failed to mount a meaningful defense.[18] Despite these substantial indications of doubt, the governor of Texas resisted calls from people requesting that he intervene in the pardon process, asserting that "there has not been one innocent person executed since I've been governor" in the one hundred thirty-five executions he had presided over. Gary Graham was executed on June 22, 2000.

What can be done to reduce the incidence of wrongful convictions? There are two general avenues of attack: administrative and legal. Administrative changes in the way in which police investigate cases, interview witnesses, and conduct lineups would logically have the greatest effect. The ability of cross-examination to correct errors of mistaken eyewitness testimony is limited. By the 1960s, the basic problems with eyewitness identification were sufficiently known to be a concern among justice scholars and some members of the legal community. Nevertheless, very little action had been taken by courts or police departments to systematically investigate the question and take appropriate action. As a result, the Warren Court responded to constitutional challenges and, for the first time, held that certain deficiencies in the identification process amounted to violations of the rights of defendants. Three distinct constitutional areas were explored by the Court: (1) the Sixth Amendment right to counsel during a lineup; (2) the Fifth Amendment rights against self-incrimination of a suspect during a lineup or showup; and (3) the Fifth and Fourteenth amendment due process rights of lineup and showup participants.

It may be argued that refined legal procedures, such as providing an attorney at lineups, are marginally helpful in reducing mistaken eyewitness identification. However, these procedures do not get at the heart of the problem—the psychology of perception—that mostly leads to the misidentification of defendants. On the other hand, given the lack of action on the part of the criminal justice system, the Supreme Court's involvement had at least raised the visibility of this issue.

For the first time, beginning in the late 1990s, serious attention is being focused on changing the way in which the police identification process is conducted with goals to improve accuracy. The most convincing evidence of this change was the publication in late 1999 of a National Institute of Justice report, *Eyewitness Evidence: A Guide for Law Enforcement*, which suggested specific guidelines for the conduct of initial reports, the composition of mug books, procedures for interviewing witnesses, the conduct of field identifications procedures **(showups),** and the conduct of lineups. The two major incentives for this have been (1) substantial bodies of theoretical and practical research by psychologists of perception that have added greatly to the store of knowledge about identification procedures and (2) the stunning revelations about wrongful convictions that were generated by the growing use of DNA testing in forensic investigations. The Innocence Project, run by Professors Barry Scheck and Peter Neufeld at Cardozo Law School,[19] the freeing of half of the death row inmates in Illinois,[20] and the publication of a National Institute of Justice report detailing the phenomenon of "Convicted by Juries, Exonerated by Science" have brought home to the criminal justice system its responsibility to improve the process of identification.[21] These developments will be discussed in the Law in Society section of this chapter.

IDENTIFICATION AND THE RIGHT TO COUNSEL

The Supreme Court turned its attention to the issue of lineup identification in 1967, just four years after *Gideon v. Wainwright* and one year after *Miranda v. Arizona*. The tide of the Court's due process revolution was still riding high, and the lineup cases were an understandable sequel to the burgeoning right to counsel cases. Yet, the cases startled the legal community because of the novelty of the issue. Unlike search and seizure, confessions, and the right to appointed counsel, which had been the subject of constitutional litigation for decades and which rested on ancient legal principles, the lineup rules were the creation of imaginative lawyers who, imbued with the innovative spirit of the due process revolution, took a hand at suggesting ways of expanding the frontiers of the Bill of Rights. This annoyed jurists who did not favor such innovations. Judge Warren Burger of the United States Court of Appeals for Washington D.C. said in 1965, four years prior to his elevation to chief justice of the United

States: "Such 'Disneyland' contentions as that absence of counsel at the police line-up voids a conviction are becoming commonplace."[22]

The Right to Counsel at Postindictment Lineups

The Court in 1967 decided identification cases of *United States v. Wade, Gilbert v. California,* and *Stovall v. Denno. Wade* and *Gilbert* were companion cases that presented the same issue, holding that a postindictment lineup is a *critical stage* and that the right to counsel is violated if a postindictment lineup in federal (under the Sixth amendment) and state cases (under the Sixth and Fourteenth amendments) was conducted without a defense attorney being present. *Stovall* held that the lineup right to counsel was not retroactive to earlier cases in which such a violation had occurred. *Stovall* was also a due process case and is reviewed in the following section.

Does *Wade* require that a lawyer be present when police apprehend a suspect immediately after a crime based on a

• CASE & COMMENTS •

United States v. Wade
388 U.S. 218, 87 S.Ct. 1926, 18 L.Ed.2d 1149 (1967)

MR. JUSTICE BRENNAN delivered the opinion of the Court.

The question here is whether courtroom identifications of an accused at trial are to be excluded from evidence because the accused was exhibited to the witnesses before trial at a postindictment lineup conducted for identification purposes without notice to and in the absence of the accused's appointed counsel. **[a]**

[In September, 1964, a federally insured bank was robbed by a man with a small strip of tape on each side of his face who forced a teller and bank officer, at gunpoint, to fill a pillowcase with money. He escaped with an accomplice who had been waiting in a stolen car outside the bank. In March 1965, Wade and two others were indicted for conspiracy and bank robbery.] **[b]** Wade was arrested on April 2, and counsel was appointed to represent him on April 26. Fifteen days later an FBI agent, without notice to Wade's lawyer, arranged to have the two bank employees observe a lineup made up of Wade and five or six other prisoners and conducted in a courtroom of the local county courthouse. **[c]** Each person in the line wore strips of tape such as allegedly worn by the robber and upon direction each said something like "put the money in the bag," the words allegedly uttered by the robber. Both bank employees identified Wade in the lineup as the bank robber.

At trial, the two employees, when asked on direct examination if the robber was in the courtroom, pointed to Wade. The prior lineup identification was then elicited from both employees on cross-examination. **[d]** At the close of testimony, Wade's counsel moved for a judgment of acquittal or, alternatively, to strike the bank officials' courtroom identifications on the ground that conduct of the lineup, without notice to and in the absence of his appointed counsel, violated his Fifth Amendment privilege against self-incrimination and his Sixth Amendment right to the assistance of counsel. The motion was denied, and Wade was convicted. The Court of Appeals for the Fifth Circuit reversed the conviction and ordered a new trial at which the in-court identification evidence was to be excluded, holding that, though the lineup did not violate Wade's Fifth Amendment rights, "the lineup, held as it was, in the absence of counsel, already chosen to represent appellant, was a violation of his Sixth Amendment rights. . . ." **[e]** *** We reverse the judgment of the Court of Appeals and remand to that court with direction to enter a new judgment vacating the conviction and remanding the case to the District Court for further proceedings consistent with this opinion.

[a] This narrow statement of the issue is tailored to the requirements of the "remedy" which is stated in Part V of the Court's opinion. In fact, there are other legal issues in the case.

[b] Wade's indictment prior to the lineup may seem like an inconsequential detail. In later cases, it became an important factor in determining the scope of the right to counsel.

[c] This statement does not include all of the facts of the *Wade* and *Gilbert* lineups. In Part IV, the Court embellishes the facts of the lineup. The facts of a case are frequently scattered throughout an opinion.

[d] These were novel constitutional challenges raised for the first time in the Supreme Court.

[e] Although the Supreme Court reversed the court of appeals, it did not agree with the trial court that Wade had no right to counsel at the lineup. The court of appeals took an absolute approach, but the Supreme Court's ruling on the remedy is more complex (see Part V).

• CASE & COMMENTS •

I

[The Court ruled that no Fifth Amendment violation occurred by requiring Wade to participate in the lineup, or by placing strips of tape on his face or by repeating what was said at the robbery. **[f]** Providing physical evidence of one's identity is not the kind of "testimonial evidence" protected by the privilege against self-incrimination.]

[f] This issue is examined in the next section of the text.

II

[The assistance of counsel is indispensable to protect the right to a fair trial. Justice Brennan, responding to the dissent's argument that lawyers never participated in lineups and have no proper role to play there, noted that "The Framers of the Bill of Rights envisaged a broader role for counsel than under the practice then prevailing in England of merely advising his client in "matters of law," and eschewing any responsibility for 'matters of fact.'" The operative Sixth Amendment rule is that counsel is required at any critical stage of the criminal proceedings, and thus the Court must "analyze whether potential substantial prejudice to defendant's rights inheres in the particular confrontation and the ability of counsel to help avoid that prejudice."]

III

The Government characterizes the lineup as a mere preparatory step in the gathering of the prosecution's evidence, not different—for Sixth Amendment purposes—from various other preparatory steps, such as systematized or scientific analyzing of the accused's fingerprints, blood sample, clothing, hair, and the like. **[g]** We think there are differences which preclude such stages being characterized as critical stages at which the accused has the right to the presence of his counsel. Knowledge of the techniques of science and technology is sufficiently available, and the variables in techniques few enough, that the accused has the opportunity for a meaningful confrontation of the Government's case at trial through the ordinary processes of cross-examination of the Government's expert witnesses and the presentation of the evidence of his own experts. The denial of a right to have his counsel present at such analyses does not therefore violate the Sixth Amendment; they are not critical stages since there is minimal risk that his counsel's absence at such stages might derogate from his right to a fair trial.

[g] The science of taking and analyzing physical evidence is well-established and errors can be ascertained by cross-examination; therefore, it is not a *critical stage*. Errors in fluid and potentially suggestive identification procedures cannot be reconstructed by cross-examination. Thus, all the justices believe it is absurd and constitutionally unnecessary to require defense lawyers to accompany fingerprint technicians, but a majority believe that lineups are essentially different from scientific evidence gathering.

IV

But the confrontation compelled by the State between the accused and the victim or witnesses to a crime to elicit identification evidence is peculiarly riddled with innumerable dangers and variable factors which might seriously, even crucially, derogate from a fair trial. The vagaries of eyewitness identification are well-known; the annals of criminal law are rife with instances of mistaken identification. *** **[h]** A major factor contributing to the high incidence of miscarriage of justice from mistaken identification has been the degree of suggestion inherent in the manner in which the prosecution presents the suspect to witnesses for pretrial identification. A commentator has observed that "[t]he influence of improper suggestion upon identifying witnesses probably accounts for more miscarriages of justice than any other single factor—perhaps it is responsible for more such errors than all other factors combined." *** Suggestion can be created intentionally or unintentionally in many subtle ways. And the dangers for the suspect are particularly grave when the witness' opportunity for observation was insubstantial, and thus his susceptibility to suggestion the greatest.

[h] Justice Brennan asserts the basis of eyewitness misidentification as not just human fallibility but suggestibility by state officials, establishing a constitutional basis for imposing the Sixth Amendment counsel requirement.

Moreover, "[i]t is a matter of common experience that, once a witness has picked out the accused at the line-up, he is not likely to go back on his word later on, so that in practice the issue of identity may (in the absence of other relevant evidence) for all practical purposes be determined there and then, before the trial." **[i]**

[i] The identification process is a "critical stage" because what transpires there can influence the outcome of the trial. Are you convinced by Justice Brennan's

The pretrial confrontation for purpose of identification may take the form of a lineup, also known as an "identification parade" or "showup," as in the present case, or presentation of the suspect alone to the witness. *** It is obvious that risks of suggestion attend either form of confrontation and increase the dangers inhering in eyewitness identification. But as is the case with secret interrogations, there is serious difficulty in depicting what transpires at lineups and other forms of identification confrontations. * * * For the same reasons, the defense can seldom reconstruct the manner and mode of lineup identification for judge or jury at trial. Those participating in a lineup with the accused may often be police officers; in any event, the participants' names are rarely recorded or divulged at trial. The impediments to an objective observation are increased when the victim is the witness. Lineups are prevalent in rape and robbery prosecutions and present a particular hazard that a victim's understandable outrage may excite vengeful or spiteful motives. In any event, neither witnesses nor lineup participants are apt to be alert for conditions prejudicial to the suspect. And if they were, it would likely be of scant benefit to the suspect since neither witnesses nor lineup participants are likely to be schooled in the detection of suggestive influences. Improper influences may go undetected by a suspect, guilty or not, who experiences the emotional tension which we might expect in one being confronted with potential accusers. Even when he does observe abuse, if he has a criminal record he may be reluctant to take the stand and open up the admission of prior convictions. Moreover, any protestations by the suspect of the fairness of the lineup made at trial are likely to be in vain; the jury's choice is between the accused's unsupported version and that of the police officers present. In short, the accused's inability effectively to reconstruct at trial any unfairness that occurred at the lineup may deprive him of his only opportunity meaningfully to attack the credibility of the witness' courtroom identification.

opinion that without an attorney to record what happened at a lineup it would be difficult for a defendant to assert improprieties at the trial?

* * *

The potential for improper influence is illustrated by the circumstances, insofar as they appear, surrounding the prior identifications in the three cases we decide today. **[j]** In the present case, the testimony of the identifying witnesses elicited on cross-examination revealed that those witnesses were taken to the courthouse and seated in the courtroom to await assembly of the lineup. The courtroom faced on a hallway observable to the witnesses through an open door. The cashier testified that she saw Wade "standing in the hall" within sight of an FBI agent. Five or six other prisoners later appeared in the hall. The vice president testified that he saw a person in the hall in the custody of the agent who "resembled the person that we identified as the one that had entered the bank."

[j] Justice Brennan now recites the facts of the lineups in *Wade* and *Gilbert* to demonstrate how it is possible that witnesses were "contaminated" in forming their opinions by the way in which Wade was presented by the police, or by the opportunity for cross-talk and influencing witnesses in the *Gilbert* situation.

The lineup in *Gilbert*, [a companion case], was conducted in an auditorium in which some 100 witnesses to several alleged state and federal robberies charged to Gilbert made wholesale identifications of Gilbert as the robber in each other's presence, a procedure said to be fraught with dangers of suggestion. And the vice of suggestion created by the identification in *Stovall, supra*, was the presentation to the witness of the suspect alone handcuffed to police officers. It is hard to imagine a situation more clearly conveying the suggestion to the witness that the one presented is believed guilty by the police. ***

The few cases that have surfaced therefore reveal the existence of a process attended with hazards of serious unfairness to the criminal accused and strongly suggest the plight of the more numerous defendants who are unable to ferret out suggestive influences in the secrecy of the confrontation. We do not assume that these risks are the result of police procedures intentionally designed to prejudice an accused. Rather we assume they derive from the dangers inherent in eyewitness identification and the **suggestibility** inherent in the context of the pretrial identification. *** **[k]** "[T]he fact that the police themselves have, in a given case, little or no doubt that the man put up for identification has committed the offense, and that their chief pre-occupation is with the problem of getting sufficient proof, because he has not 'come clean,' involves a danger that this persuasion may communicate itself even in a doubtful case to the witness in some way . . . ." ***

[k] This kind of "silent suggestion" is so well known that in medical trials experimental drugs are dispensed in a "double blind" procedure so that the person dispensing the drugs cannot suggest whether a drug or placebo is being administered.

*** [E]ven though cross-examination is a precious safeguard to a fair trial, it cannot be viewed as an absolute assurance of accuracy and reliability. Thus in the present context, where so many variables and pitfalls exist, the first line of defense must be the prevention of unfairness and the lessening of the hazards of eyewitness identification at the lineup itself. The trial which might determine the accused's fate may well not be that in the courtroom but that at the pretrial confrontation, with the State aligned against the accused, the witness the sole jury, and the accused unprotected against

• CASE & COMMENTS •

the overreaching, intentional or unintentional, and with little or no effective appeal from the judgment there rendered by the witness—"that's the man."

[l] Since it appears that there is grave potential for prejudice, intentional or not, in the pretrial lineup, which may not be capable of reconstruction at trial, and since presence of counsel itself can often avert prejudice and assure a meaningful confrontation at trial, there can be little doubt that for Wade the postindictment lineup was a critical stage of the prosecution at which he was "as much entitled to such aid [of counsel] . . . as at the trial itself." *** Thus both Wade and his counsel should have been notified of the impending lineup, and counsel's presence should have been a requisite to conduct of the lineup, absent an "intelligent waiver." *** No substantial countervailing policy considerations have been advanced against the requirement of the presence of counsel. Concern is expressed that the requirement will forestall prompt identifications and result in obstruction of the confrontations. As for the first, we note that in the two cases in which the right to counsel is today held to apply, counsel had already been appointed and no argument is made in either case that notice to counsel would have prejudicially delayed the confrontations. Moreover, we leave open the question whether the presence of substitute counsel might not suffice where notification and presence of the suspect's own counsel would result in prejudicial delay. And to refuse to recognize the right to counsel for fear that counsel will obstruct the course of justice is contrary to the basic assumptions upon which this Court has operated in Sixth Amendment cases. *** In our view counsel can hardly impede legitimate law enforcement; on the contrary, for the reasons expressed, law enforcement may be assisted by preventing the infiltration of taint in the prosecution's identification evidence. That result cannot help the guilty avoid conviction but can only help assure that the right man has been brought to justice.

[l] The Court assumes that the presence of a defense attorney will reduce the instances of police suggestion. This may be true as to purposeful suggestion but may have little impact on unintentional suggestion.

Legislative or other regulations, such as those of local police departments, which eliminate the risks of abuse and unintentional suggestion at lineup proceedings and the impediments to meaningful confrontation at trial may also remove the basis for regarding the stage as "critical." **[m]** But neither Congress nor the federal authorities have seen fit to provide a solution. What we hold today "in no way creates a constitutional straitjacket which will handicap sound efforts at reform, nor is it intended to have this effect." ***

[m] Justice Brennan openly notes that legislatures and the criminal justice system have failed to take action to make the identification process more fair. This is only beginning to happen at the start of the twenty-first century.

V

We come now to the question whether the denial of Wade's motion to strike the courtroom identification by the bank witnesses at trial because of the absence of his counsel at the lineup required, as the Court of Appeals held, the grant of a new trial at which such evidence is to be excluded. **[n]** We do not think this disposition can be justified without first giving the Government the opportunity to establish by clear and convincing evidence that the in-court identifications were based upon observations of the suspect other than the lineup identification. *** Where, as here, the admissibility of evidence of the lineup identification itself is not involved, a *per se* rule of exclusion of courtroom identification would be unjustified. *** A rule limited solely to the exclusion of testimony concerning identification at the lineup itself, without regard to admissibility of the courtroom identification, would render the right to counsel an empty one. **[o]** The lineup is most often used, as in the present case, to crystallize the witnesses' identification of the defendant for future reference. We have already noted that the lineup identification will have that effect. The State may then rest upon the witnesses' unequivocal courtroom identification, and not mention the pretrial identification as part of the State's case at trial. Counsel is then in the predicament in which Wade's counsel found himself—realizing that possible unfairness at the lineup may be the sole means of attack upon the unequivocal courtroom identification, and having to probe in the dark in an attempt to discover and reveal unfairness, while bolstering the government witness' courtroom identification by bringing out and dwelling upon his prior identification. Since counsel's presence at the lineup would equip him to attack not only the lineup identification but the courtroom identification as well, limiting the impact of violation of the right to counsel to exclusion of evidence only of identification at the lineup itself disregards a critical element of that right.

[n] This Part concerns the remedy. The Court first tries to be fair to the prosecution. Even if the lineup identification must be excluded because counsel was not present, the prosecution is allowed to have the witnesses identify the defendant at the trial if it can show, by the high standard of "clear and convincing evidence," that the witness' memory was based on observations of the crime incident and not on the lineup.

[o] On the other hand, the remedy is fair to the defendant: If courtroom identification is based on memory of the lineup, the courtroom identification will be disallowed, possibly causing the prosecution to collapse.

• CASE & COMMENTS •

We think it follows that the proper test to be applied in these situations is that quoted in *Wong Sun v. United States*, [1963], "'[W]hether, granting establishment of the primary illegality, the evidence to which instant objection is made has been come at by exploitation of that illegality or instead by means sufficiently distinguishable to be purged of the primary taint.' ***" *** **[p]** Application of this test in the present context requires consideration of various factors; for example, the prior opportunity to observe the alleged criminal act, the existence of any discrepancy between any pre-lineup description and the defendant's actual description, any identification prior to lineup of another person, the identification by picture of the defendant prior to the lineup, failure to identify the defendant on a prior occasion, and the lapse of time between the alleged act and the lineup identification. **[q]** It is also relevant to consider those facts which, despite the absence of counsel, are disclosed concerning the conduct of the lineup.

[p] What is the "primary illegality" in the lineup situation? What is the "exploitation of that illegality"?

[q] These factors are guides to the judge to try to assess the basis of the witness' memory. Do you think it is possible to determine the basis of a person's memory?

We doubt that the Court of Appeals applied the proper test for exclusion of the in-court identification of the two witnesses. *** [The judgment of the Court of Appeals was vacated and the case remanded for further proceedings].

[Chief Justice Warren and Justices Black, Douglas, and Fortas concurred, but believed that compelling Wade to wear tape and speak at the lineup violated his Fifth Amendment privilege against self-incrimination. Justice Clark concurred in the majority opinion.]

MR. JUSTICE BLACK, dissenting in part and concurring in part.

[Justice Black agreed that a lineup is a critical stage at which counsel is required. However, he found fault with the Court's remedy (in Part V) on both practical and constitutional grounds. He would have allowed the witness to identify the defendant at the trial and voted to uphold the conviction.] **[r]**

In the first place, even if this Court has power to establish such a rule of evidence, I think the rule fashioned by the Court is unsound. The "tainted fruit" determination required by the Court involves more than considerable difficulty. I think it is practically impossible. How is a witness capable of probing the recesses of his mind to draw a sharp line between a courtroom identification due exclusively to an earlier lineup and a courtroom identification due to memory not based on the lineup? What kind of "clear and convincing evidence" can the prosecution offer to prove upon what particular events memories resulting in an in-court identification rest? How long will trials be delayed while judges turn psychologists to probe the subconscious minds of witnesses? All these questions are posed but not answered by the Court's opinion. ***

[r] In addition to this critique, Justice Black attacked the majority for exercising what he believed was unconstitutional power under the Due Process Clause to make new law.

MR. JUSTICE WHITE, whom MR. JUSTICE HARLAN and MR. JUSTICE STEWART join, dissenting in part and concurring in part.

* * *

I share the Court's view that the criminal trial, at the very least, should aim at truthful factfinding, including accurate eyewitness identifications. **[s]** I doubt, however, on the basis of our present information, that the tragic mistakes which have occurred in criminal trials are as much the product of improper police conduct as they are the consequence of the difficulties inherent in eyewitness testimony and in resolving evidentiary conflicts by court or jury. I doubt that the Court's new rule will obviate these difficulties, or that the situation will be measurably improved by inserting defense counsel into the investigative processes of police departments everywhere.

[s] This, in effect, means that there is no "state action" on which to base a constitutional rule.

But, it may be asked, what possible state interest militates against requiring the presence of defense counsel at lineups? After all, the argument goes, he *may* do some good, he *may* upgrade the quality of identification evidence in state courts and he can scarcely do any harm. Even if true, this is a feeble foundation for fastening an ironclad constitutional rule upon state criminal procedures. Absent some reliably established constitutional violation, the processes by which the States enforce their criminal laws are their own prerogative. ***

Beyond this, however, requiring counsel at pretrial identifications as an invariable rule trenches on other valid state interests. **[t]** One of them is its concern with the prompt and efficient enforcement of its criminal laws. Identifications frequently take place after arrest but before an indictment is returned or an information is filed. The police may have arrested a suspect on probable cause but may still have the wrong man. Both the suspect and the State have every interest in a prompt

[t] The dissenters here display "Crime Control Model" reasoning, with an emphasis on efficiency in the criminal process. They foresee a

• CASE & COMMENTS •

identification at that stage, the suspect in order to secure his immediate release and the State because prompt and early identification enhances *accurate* identification and because it must know whether it is on the right investigative track. Unavoidably, however, the absolute rule requiring the presence of counsel will cause significant delay and it may very well result in no pretrial identification at all. Counsel must be appointed and a time arranged convenient for him and the witnesses. Meanwhile, it may be necessary to file charges against the suspect who may then be released on bail, in the federal system very often on his own recognizance, with neither the State nor the defendant having the benefit of a properly conducted identification procedure.

Nor do I think the witnesses themselves can be ignored. They will now be required to be present at the convenience of counsel rather than their own. Many may be much less willing to participate if the identification stage is transformed into an adversary proceeding not under the control of a judge. Others may fear for their own safety if their identity is known at an early date, especially when there is no way of knowing until the lineup occurs whether or not the police really have the right man.

delay and an impairment of the criminal justice system. With the greater number and availability of lawyers today, and with the growth of defenders' systems, this fear may no longer be a strong concern.

* * *

victim's description and show the stopped suspect to the victim or witness? This standard practice has the dual benefit of immediately exonerating innocent look-alikes and presenting an identification opportunity when recall is the strongest. To delay such a showup until a lawyer can be secured can multiply injustices for both the victim and the defendant.[23] Faced with the unpalatable possibility of extending the right to counsel rule to on-the-street situations, the liberal United States Court of Appeals for the District of Columbia Circuit in 1969 carved out an exception to the right to counsel for immediate postarrest showups.[24] The need for such an exception became unnecessary after the Supreme Court dealt with the timing of the right to counsel issue in a more systematically in *Kirby v. Illinois* (1972).

When Does the Right to Counsel at Lineups Attach?

The lineup in *Wade* occurred after Wade had been indicted. The issue in *Kirby* was whether the right to counsel applied to a lineup that was conducted before a suspect was indicted. There is little doubt that had the same Court that decided *Wade* decided this issue, the right to counsel would have been extended to preindictment lineups. As noted in Chapter 1, a holding of a case is the rule of the case that is controlled by its essential facts. Was the timing of the lineup an essential fact of *Wade?* Justice Brennan, who wrote the majority opinion in *Wade* and dissented in *Kirby,* said no. The majority in *Kirby* disagreed. What had changed between the years 1967 and 1972 was the composition of the Court. A more conservative Supreme Court, bent on reversing or limiting the individual rights advanced by the Warren Court, set to work in *Kirby* and like cases, to limit, if not overrule, expansive Warren Court rulings.

The facts of *Kirby* were simple. Willie Shard, a robbery victim, was asked to identify two suspects who were detained in a police station two days after the incident. The victim immediately identified the suspects, Kirby and Bean, who had been found with the victim's travelers' checks and Social Security card. No lawyer was present during the identification; the suspects did not ask for a lawyer, nor were they advised of any right to the presence of counsel. Six weeks later, the suspects were indicted for the robbery. At trial, Shard identified Kirby and Bean and testified to his police station identifications. The Illinois Supreme Court upheld the legality of this identification process. Kirby argued that the benefits of counsel to dispel or record suggestive action by police officers is equally important in a preindictment lineup as in a postindictment lineup. The Supreme Court upheld Kirby's conviction.

Justice Stewart, who dissented in *Wade,* wrote the majority opinion in *Kirby*. The *Wade-Gilbert* right to counsel was based on the Sixth Amendment, and not the Fifth Amendment as was *Miranda v. Arizona* (1966). All previous Sixth Amendment cases held that the right to counsel "attaches at the time of arraignment" or the "initiation of judicial criminal proceedings." The right to counsel in *Miranda* was based on vindicating the privilege against self-incrimination. Therefore, the right of counsel does not apply to preindictment lineups but only to lineups and showups "at or after the time that adversary judicial proceedings have been initiated against him."

To justify the decision, Justice Stewart noted that:

> The initiation of judicial criminal proceedings is far from a mere formalism. It is the starting point of our whole system of adversary criminal justice. For it is only then that the government has committed itself to prosecute, and only then that the adverse positions of government and defendant have solidified. It is then that a defendant finds himself faced with the prosecutorial forces of organized society, and immersed in the intricacies of substantive and procedural criminal law. (*Kirby v. Illinois*, pp. 689–90)

If any abuses were alleged to occur during a preindictment lineup or showup, the defendant could urge a court to apply the due process rule which was announced in *Stovall v. Denno* (discussed later in this text). The majority opinion was joined by each of the justices who were appointed by President Nixon: Chief Justice Burger and Justices Blackmun, Powell, and Rehnquist. Justice Powell issued a one sentence concurrence simply saying that he "would not extend the *Wade-Gilbert per se* exclusionary rule." Thus, the concept that the Sixth Amendment right to counsel can never apply to a procedure that occurs before an indictment is not a constitutional rule; Justice Powell, nevertheless, made clear his dislike of exclusionary rules.

Justice Brennan's dissent in *Kirby* argued that the right to counsel is designed to ensure a fair trial. Having a lawyer present at a police station showup is necessary to prevent the suggestibility that influences a witness and thus is crucial to a fair trial. Therefore, the essence of the *Wade-Gilbert* rule is that an attorney be present at a *pretrial* identification confrontation. The unfairness of suggestibility can equally infect a preindictment or a postindictment showup or lineup. In this regard, "an abstract consideration of the words 'criminal prosecutions' in the Sixth Amendment" should not limit the extension of the right to counsel at all stationhouse-identification procedures. Justice Brennan virtually accused the majority of willfully misconstruing the real meaning of the *Wade* and *Gilbert* cases by inflating the importance of the fortuitous circumstance that the lineups in those cases occurred after indictments. Indeed, "every United States Court of Appeals that has confronted the question has applied *Wade* and *Gilbert* to preindictment confrontations," as well as the appellate courts of thirteen states. Against this, only five states at that time ruled, as did Illinois, that the *Wade* rule applied only to postindictment lineups. Justice Brennan was joined not only by liberal Justices Douglas and Marshall but also by Justice Byron White, who had dissented in *Wade*. Justice White confirmed Justice Brennan's hint that the *Kirby* majority was motivated by conservative ideological activism by briefly noting that *Wade* and *Gilbert* "govern this case and compel reversal of the judgment below." Justice White was expressing the judicial conservatism of *stare decisis* in his vote.

Kirby displayed the Burger Court's discontent with the *Wade* rule, but an unwillingness or inability to completely overturn it. The Court nevertheless stood by the *Kirby* rule as seen in *Moore v. Illinois* (1977). A rape victim gave a description of the rapist to the police. In the week following the crime, the victim examined two sets of photographs and whittled possible suspects down to two or three from 200 photographs. One of these was of Moore. He was arrested and presented at a preliminary examination (to determine whether he should be formally charged by the grand jury) the next day. The police accompanied the victim to the preliminary examination during which she was to view Moore and to "identify him if she could." She positively identified him and the detectives had her sign a complaint that named Moore as her assailant. Moore, unrepresented by a lawyer at this point, was bound over.

Moore argued that the preliminary hearing "marked the initiation of adversary judicial criminal proceedings against him. Hence, under *Wade, Gilbert,* and *Kirby,* he was entitled to the presence of counsel at that confrontation." The Supreme Court agreed with Moore. *Kirby* applied the *Wade* counsel rule not only after *indictment,* but "at or after the initiation of *adversary judicial criminal proceedings,*" including proceedings instituted "by way of formal charge [or] *preliminary hearing*." Thus, not only did the showup in the *Moore* case fall within the direct rule of *Kirby,* it was obviously a *critical stage:* Moore faced a state prosecutor at the hearing; it was a hearing where the charges could have been dismissed; the state had to produce evidence against the defendant at that point; and, of course, the defendant was identified at that proceeding.

In addition, the Court made it absolutely clear that the *Wade-Gilbert-Kirby* rules apply to a *showup,* as well as a *lineup,* of several look-alikes:

> Although *Wade* and *Gilbert* both involved lineups, *Wade* clearly contemplated that counsel would be required in both situations. *** Indeed, a one-on-one confrontation generally is thought to present greater risks of mistaken identification than a lineup. . . . There is no reason, then, to hold that a one-on-one identification procedure is not subject to the same requirements as a lineup. (*Moore v. Illinois,* p. 229).

Finally, the prosecution argued that the victim's identification testimony should be automatically introduced at trial because there was an "independent source" for it. That is, the victim said she thought she had seen Moore at a neighborhood bar. The Supreme Court rejected this argument. It ruled that the prosecution cannot violate the *Wade-Gilbert* rules and then simply allow the defendant to be identified in the case-in-chief based on the theory that the identification was not based on the showup at the preliminary examination, but on the crime or other encounter. Instead the case was remanded to determine if the victim's memory was based on the incident or the showup. Justice Rehnquist grudgingly concurred, noting that he would prefer that *Wade-Gilbert*'s *per se* exclusionary rule of the lineup/showup identification be replaced with a totality of the circumstances approach. In conclusion, although the Supreme Court erected a somewhat artificial distinction in *Kirby*, it maintained the doctrinal integrity of the *Kirby* rule in *Moore v. Illinois*.

Does the Right to Counsel Apply to Photographic Identification?

Showing photographs from a "mug book" of individuals resembling the description of a suspect (usually consisting of previously arrested persons) is a common identification procedure. The issue in *United States v. Ash* (1973) was whether the *Wade* and *Kirby* rules would apply to photographic identification. The Supreme Court ruled (6–3) that, as a matter of Sixth Amendment law, an attorney is never required at a photographic identification process, even if the process occurred after an indictment.

In *Ash*, an informant told FBI agents that Charles J. Ash, Jr. had been involved in a bank robbery. Prior to pressing formal charges, the agents "showed five black-and-white mug shots of Negro males of generally the same age, height, and weight, one of which was of Ash, to four witnesses. All four made uncertain identifications of Ash's picture." Prior to trial, after Ash had been formally charged, the prosecutor "decided to use a photographic display to determine whether the witnesses he planned to call would be able to make in-court identifications. Shortly before the trial, an FBI agent and the prosecutor showed five color photographs to the four witnesses who previously had tentatively identified the black-and-white photograph of Ash. Three of the witnesses selected the picture of Ash, but one was unable to make any selection." Ash claimed that this process violated his right to counsel at a *critical stage* of the prosecution. The trial judge denied this claim. At trial, the three witnesses who had been inside the bank identified Ash as the gunman, but they were unwilling to state that they were certain of their identifications. The trial judge ruled that all five color photographs would be admitted into evidence. The jury convicted Ash. The Court of Appeals applied the *Wade-Gilbert* rule and held that Ash's right to counsel was violated when his attorney was not given the opportunity to be present at the postindictment, pretrial photographic displays.

Justice Blackmun's majority opinion for the United States Supreme Court noted that the core purpose of the Sixth Amendment counsel guarantee was to assure assistance of counsel *at trial,* when the accused was confronted with both the intricacies of the law and the advocacy of the public prosecutor. Later developments led the Court to recognize that "assistance" would be less than meaningful if it were limited *only* to the formal trial itself:

> This extension of the right to counsel to events before trial has resulted from changing patterns of criminal procedure and investigation that have tended to generate pretrial events that might appropriately be considered to be parts of the trial itself. At these newly emerging and significant events, the accused was confronted, just as at trial, by the procedural system, or by his expert adversary, or by both. (*United States v. Ash,* p. 310)

This reasoning acknowledged that the Sixth Amendment right to counsel is a "dynamic" (i.e., expandable) right that applies to procedures other than the trial itself, and could have led the Court to extend the right to counsel to photographic identification. Having confronted the fact that the Court had in the past extended the right to the assistance of counsel to pretrial stages—and especially to postindictment lineups in *Wade* and *Gilbert*—the majority now must explain why it does not apply the right to photographic identification. How did the majority distinguish the *Ash* case from the *Wade* and *Gilbert* holdings?

First, the majority stated that in all cases where the right to counsel was extended "to trial-like confrontations, the function of the lawyer has remained essentially the same as his function at trial. In all cases considered by the Court, counsel has continued to act as a spokesman for, or advisor to, the accused." This is a slight mischaracterization of counsel's role at a lineup, but accurately depicts counsel's role at the preliminary examination or at a pretrial conference between the prosecutor and the defendant. What was left unsaid by the majority's justices was that many felt that *Wade* was a mistake in the first place, but the majority was unable or unwilling to overrule this precedent.

Next, the Court noted that although the lineup is not a procedure in which the defendant is confronted with the type of legal questions a lawyer is qualified to deal with, "the lineup offered opportunities for prosecuting authorities to take advantage of the accused." The majority in *Wade* found that at a lineup the defendant was not in a good position to notice any suggestive influences while an attorney was so placed. In his concurrence Justice Stewart added that because the defendant was required to "act" at a lineup, there were "numerous and subtle possibilities for . . . improper suggestion."

Justice Stewart, in his concurrence, answered this point by asserting that any suggestiveness in a photographic identification could be corrected by cross-examination at the trial (while this was not feasible in regard to lineups).

> A photographic identification is quite different from a lineup, for there are substantially fewer possibilities of

> impermissible suggestion when photographs are used, and those unfair influences can be readily reconstructed at trial. It is true that the defendant's photograph may be markedly different from the others displayed, but this unfairness can be demonstrated at trial from an actual comparison of the photographs used or from the witness' description of the display. Similarly, it is possible that the photographs could be arranged in a suggestive manner, or that by comment or gesture the prosecuting authorities might single out the defendant's picture. But these are the kinds of overt influence that a witness can easily recount and that would serve to impeach the identification testimony. In short, there are few possibilities for unfair suggestiveness — and those rather blatant and easily reconstructed. Accordingly, an accused would not be foreclosed from an effective cross-examination of an identification witness simply because his counsel was not present at the photographic display. For this reason, a photographic display cannot fairly be considered a "critical stage" of the prosecution. (*United States v. Ash,* Stewart, J., concurring, pp. 324–25)

Although Justice Blackmun's majority opinion agreed with this, the main thrust of its argument was that photographic identification is simply not a trial-like confrontation that requires the presence of defense counsel to equalize the fairness of the procedure to the defendant. "[T]he accused himself is not present at the time of the photographic display, and asserts no right to be present [and so] no possibility arises that the accused might be misled by his lack of familiarity with the law or overpowered by his professional adversary." Instead, the photographic identification is more like "the prosecutor's trial-preparation interviews with witnesses," an aspect of case preparation that the Court would not include within the right of a defense counsel to be present. The majority noted that the defense could arrange for its own photographic identification session with witnesses. In short, to extend the right to counsel to a photographic identification session would require a "substantial departure from the historical test" of the right to counsel.

Justice Brennan dissented, joined by Justices Douglas and Marshall. His first point was that "as in the lineup situation, the possibilities for impermissible suggestion in the context of a photographic display are manifold." Suggestion, intentional or unintentional, could stem from three possible sources: (1) differences in the photographs themselves that highlight the defendant, (2) "the manner in which the photographs are displayed to the witness" by, for example, emphasizing the suspect's photograph by leaving it out longer, arraying it in a way to point it out, and so forth, and (3) by "gestures or comments of the prosecutor at the time of the display [that] may lead an otherwise uncertain witness to select the 'correct' photograph." In this regard, Justice Brennan touched on the powerful psychological effect that is conveyed even by unintentional cues: "More subtly, the prosecutor's inflection, facial expressions, physical motions, and myriad other almost imperceptible means of communication might tend, intentionally or unintentionally, to compromise the witness' objectivity" (*United States v. Ash,* Brennan, J., dissenting, p. 334).

Justice Brennan next asserted that it is usually impossible for the defense to reconstruct the way in which the photographic identification session was carried out, which is not captured by the mere physical retention of the identification photographs themselves. Also, the fact that the defendant was not present means that a possible witness to irregularities is missing. The dissenters and the majority thus disagreed, not on a point of law, but on a factual understanding of the nature of perception. The dissent, therefore, argued that a photographic identification procedure is essentially the same as a lineup when it comes to suggestibility. Justice Brennan concluded this part of his dissent by stating that "considerations of logic, consistency, and, indeed, fairness compel the conclusion that a pretrial photographic identification, like a pretrial corporeal identification, is a critical stage of the prosecution at which [the accused is] as much entitled to such aid [of counsel] . . . as at the trial itself" (*United States v. Ash,* Brennan, J., dissenting, p. 338, internal quotation marks omitted).

Since the studies of the psychology of perception tend to favor the views of the three dissenting justices, the majority's reliance on the nature of the procedure as not being essentially trial-like, formed a stronger legal basis for the *Ash* holding. Justice Brennan's reply to this was that the Court's logic was "a triumph of form over substance," because in past instances where the Court found that a critical stage existed, requiring the presence of counsel, the essential point was that the stage of the criminal process was one in which unfairness would undermine the fairness of the trial itself. Since, in the view of the dissenters, the uncorrectable suggestibility of the photographic identification would taint the trial, it was a critical stage.

United States v. Ash (1975) is a clear example of a case in which expansive Warren Court rulings, favoring the rights of suspects, were trimmed back by the more conservative Burger Court. The reasoning of the justices clearly marked the "Crime Control" and the "Due Process" models of constitutional analysis specified by Professor Herbert Packer, noted in Chapter 1. The majority did not attempt to overrule the *Wade-Gilbert* rule, but clearly held it to its facts. The majority was concerned that any extension of *Wade-Gilbert* might interfere with the ability of prosecutors to prepare cases without defense counsel being present. The dissenters displayed greater concern with the overall fairness of the process and were willing to make the investigation process less efficient for the purpose of reducing the possibility of wrongful convictions.

Identification and the Fifth Amendment

United States v. Wade held that "Neither the lineup itself nor anything shown by this record that Wade was required to do in the lineup violated his privilege against self-incrimination." This holding can be divided into two rules. The first rule is that the simple display of a person at trial or at a lineup so that she can be identified as a suspect does not violate the Fifth Amendment privilege against self-incrimination. It appears that the Court unanimously supported this rule. The Fifth Amendment prohibits the compulsion of **testimonial evidence.**

> We have no doubt that compelling the accused merely to exhibit his person for observation by a prosecution witness prior to trial involves no compulsion of the accused to give evidence having testimonial significance. It is compulsion of the accused to exhibit his physical characteristics, not compulsion to disclose any knowledge he might have. (*United States v. Wade*, p. 222).

Wade raised a more refined argument that was accepted by four dissenting justices: Justice Black in a separate dissent, and Justice Fortas in a dissent joined by Chief Justice Warren and Justice Douglas. Wade was required to wear strips of tape on each side of his face, as had the robber, and to speak words which were spoken by the robber. The second part of the Court's Fifth Amendment ruling is that this kind of compelled behavior, which goes beyond the simple display of a suspect's face, does not violate the privilege against self-incrimination.

Justice Brennan relied on the precedent of *Schmerber v. California* (1966). Blood was drawn from Schmerber by medical personnel after he had been arrested for a drunk driving fatality. The Supreme Court held that the principle of the Fifth Amendment was to protect individuals from divulging information "of a *communicative* nature." Generally speaking, this means that the Fifth Amendment prohibits the state from forcing a person to admit to guilt by spoken words, actions that convey meaning, or writings that convey a sense of guilt. On the other hand, the state, in enforcing the law, may have access to any *physical evidence* that is probative and that may be obtained without violating other constitutional protections, such as the Fourth Amendment. The *Schmerber* principle has allowed the use of different kinds of physical evidence, including blood samples; handwriting exemplars to show that the handwriting of the defendant matched that of an incriminating note;[25] voice exemplars;[26] and body evidence such as fingerprints, photographs, hair samples, and cell scrapings from which DNA tracers can be identified; and one's name.[27]

In summary, the majority in *Wade* ruled that speaking words (for identification purposes) and wearing an item that was worn at the crime, constitutes physical rather than testimonial evidence. The dissenters noted that although Wade could be compelled to show his face at the trial, he could not be forced to say anything or wear any identifying clothing. To do so would lead to a mistrial.

The dissenters thought that what Wade was required to do "is more than passive, mute assistance to the eyes of the victim or of witnesses. It is the kind of volitional act—the kind of forced cooperation by the accused—which is within the historical perimeter of the privilege against compelled self-incrimination." Nevertheless, as Justice Brennan pointed out, the precedent of *Holt v. United States* (1910), authored by Justice Holmes, upheld the right of the state to require a suspect at a lineup to wear an article of clothing that was worn at the crime.

Due Process and Eyewitness Identification

The Supreme Court, in *Stovall v. Denno* (1967) ruled that the suggestiveness of a lineup or showup must be guided by the Due Process Clause because unnecessarily suggestive pretrial identification procedures are *fundamentally unfair*. The test of whether a procedure violates the Due Process Clauses of the Fifth (applicable to the federal government) or Fourteenth (applicable to the states) amendments based on it being unfair, is a *flexible* test that requires a court to examine the *totality of the circumstances*. A due process rule, therefore, is more a *general standard* than a clear-cut or *bright-line* rule. As a result, in due process litigation, the Court frequently is faced with finely differentiated fact situations that require careful examination. The Court has examined the due process rule in five cases.

Stovall v. Denno (1967) demonstrates that the requirement of non-suggestive identification procedures is not absolute. The necessities of law enforcement may override the absolute purity of the identification process. In this case a physician, Dr. Behrendt, was stabbed to death in the kitchen of his home at midnight of August 23. His wife, also a physician, entered the kitchen and jumped at the assailant. He knocked her to the floor and stabbed her eleven times. Physical clues led the police to Stovall and he was arrested on the afternoon of August 24. The wife was hospitalized for major surgery to save her life that same day.

> The police, without affording [Stovall] time to retain counsel, arranged with her surgeon to permit them to bring petitioner to her hospital room about noon of August 25, the day after the surgery. Petitioner was handcuffed to one of five police officers who, with two members of the staff of the District Attorney, brought him to the hospital room. [Stovall] was the only Negro in the room. Mrs. Behrendt identified him from her hospital bed after being asked by an officer whether he

> "was the man" and after petitioner repeated at the direction of an officer a "few words for voice identification." None of the witnesses could recall the words that were used. Mrs. Behrendt and the officers testified at the trial to her identification of the petitioner in the hospital room, and she also made an in-court identification of petitioner in the courtroom. (*Stovall v. Denno,* p. 295).

Stovall's conviction was upheld by state courts. However, a federal appellate court, on a habeas corpus petition, reversed the conviction on the ground that the eyewitness identification violated Stovall's right to counsel. Since the Court decided in *Stovall* that the rule of *Wade* and *Gilbert* did not apply retroactively, the Court dealt with the issue of whether the conviction should be overturned because the identification procedure "was so unnecessarily suggestive and conducive to irreparable mistaken identification that he was denied due process of law."

The Supreme Court ruled against Stovall without specifically evaluating whether the showup was suggestive. Instead, the Court held that the totality of circumstances include the exigency of law enforcement and it offered as an explanation the following quote from the Court of Appeals opinion:

> "Here was the only person in the world who could possibly exonerate Stovall. Her words, and only her words, 'He is not the man' could have resulted in freedom for Stovall. The hospital was not far distant from the courthouse and jail. No one knew how long Mrs. Behrendt might live. Faced with the responsibility of identifying the attacker, with the need for immediate action and with the knowledge that Mrs. Behrendt could not visit the jail, the police followed the only feasible procedure and took Stovall to the hospital room. Under these circumstances, the usual police station line-up, which Stovall now argues he should have had, was out of the question." (*Stovall v. Denno,* p. 302, quoting the Court of Appeals decision.)

From this it can be inferred that the showup in *Stovall was* suggestive. Nevertheless, under the circumstances—which included the reasonable possibility that the only eyewitness to the serious crime might soon die, the impossibility to construct a lineup, and the fact that the suspect was not chosen at random but was tied to the crime scene by physical evidence—the choice was between a suggestive identification procedure or none at all. These circumstances resulted in the conclusion that the showup in this case was not fundamentally unfair.

Perhaps the clearest example of a lineup that violated due process was *Foster v. California* (1969). Foster, a thin, six-foot-tall robbery suspect, wearing a leather jacket similar to the robber's, was placed in a lineup with two other men who were approximately five-foot-five and were not wearing leather jackets. Despite these discrepancies, the witness could not identify Foster, so he was brought into a room with the witness and made to speak. "Even after this one-to-one confrontation [the witness] still was uncertain whether petitioner was one of the robbers: 'Truthfully—I was not sure,' he testified at trial." In a second lineup a week later, Foster was the only individual from the first lineup. At this point, the witness was convinced. Justice Fortas's opinion, finding that due process was violated, relied on the element of *reliability:* "The suggestive elements in this identification procedure made it all but inevitable that [the witness] would identify [Foster] whether or not he was in fact 'the man.' In effect, the police repeatedly said to the witness, 'This is the man.' . . . This procedure so undermined the reliability of the eyewitness identification as to violate due process" (*Foster v. California,* p. 443).

On the other hand, *Simmons v. United States* (1968) is an example of a case where the Court found no due process violation. Snapshots of Simmons, a bank robbery suspect, were shown to five bank employees who had witnessed the robbery. This was not a photographic array (i.e., a "photographic lineup") with pictures of similar looking persons added. The witnesses identified Simmons at trial and he was convicted. Simmons argued that his pretrial identification by means of the photographs was so unnecessarily suggestive, prejudicial, and conducive to misidentification as to deny him due process of law. In the alternative, Simmons argued that the Supreme Court should reverse the conviction in the exercise of its supervisory power over the lower federal courts.

The Supreme Court in *Simmons* recognized that the showing of photographs can lead to incorrect identification, especially where only the photographs of the suspect/defendant are shown to witnesses. The Court first refused to establish a bright-line rule prohibiting the use of identifying photographs:

> Despite the hazards of initial identification by photograph, this procedure has been used widely and effectively in criminal law enforcement, from the standpoint both of apprehending offenders and of sparing innocent suspects the ignominy of arrest by allowing eyewitnesses to exonerate them through scrutiny of photographs. The danger that use of the technique may result in convictions based on misidentification may be substantially lessened by a course of cross-examination at trial which exposes to the jury the method's potential for error. We are unwilling to prohibit its employment, either in the exercise of our supervisory power or, still less, as a matter of constitutional requirement. Instead, we hold that each case must be considered on its own facts, and that convictions based on eyewitness identification at trial following a pretrial identification by photograph will be set aside on that ground only if the photographic identification procedure was so

> impermissibly suggestive as to give rise to a very substantial likelihood of irreparable misidentification. (*Simmons v. United States,* p. 384)

The Court went on to find that the use of the photographs was not suggestive in this case. First, Simmons was still a fugitive and it "was essential for the FBI agents swiftly to determine whether they were on the right track, so that they could properly deploy their forces in Chicago and, if necessary, alert officials in other cities." Second, the facts and circumstances of this case made it unlikely that the use of the photographs would lead to misidentification:

> The robbery took place in the afternoon in a well-lighted bank. The robbers wore no masks. Five bank employees had been able to see the robber later identified as Simmons for periods ranging up to five minutes. Those witnesses were shown the photographs only one day later, while their memories were still fresh. At least six photographs were displayed to each witness. Apparently, these consisted primarily of group photographs, with Simmons . . . appearing several times in the series. Each witness was alone when he or she saw the photographs. There is no evidence to indicate that the witnesses were told anything about the progress of the investigation, or that the FBI agents in any other way suggested which persons in the pictures were under suspicion.
>
> . . . Notwithstanding cross-examination, none of the witnesses displayed any doubt about their respective identifications of Simmons. Taken together, these circumstances leave little room for doubt that the identification of Simmons was correct, even though the identification procedure employed may have in some respects fallen short of the ideal. We hold that in the factual surroundings of this case the identification procedure used was not such as to deny Simmons due process of law or to call for reversal under our supervisory authority. (*Simmons v. United States,* pp. 385–86)

The last two due process cases decided by the Supreme Court have established the rule that identification resulting from a suggestive showup may be allowed into evidence if there are strong indicia of reliability.

Neil v. Biggers (1972) concerned a rape conviction based on evidence consisting in part of the victim's visual and voice identification of Biggers at a station-house showup seven months after the crime. The victim had been in her assailant's presence for fifteen minutes to a half hour and had directly observed him indoors and under a full moon outdoors. She testified that she had "no doubt" that Biggers was her assailant. She previously had given the police a description of the assailant. Over a period of seven months the victim viewed suspects in her home or at the police station, some in lineups and others in showups, and was shown between thirty and forty photographs, but did not identify any of these. The police called her to identify the suspect at the police station who was being held on another charge; they could not locate individuals at the city jail or the city juvenile home fitting Biggers' unusual physical description, so they conducted a showup instead.

On federal habeas corpus, the lower federal courts held that the confrontation was so suggestive as to violate due process. The Supreme Court reversed and held that the evidence had properly been allowed to go to the jury. The Court in *Biggers* summed up earlier cases to establish *general guidelines* concerning the due process rules concerning identification.

> . . . It is, first of all, apparent that the primary evil to be avoided is "a very substantial likelihood of irreparable misidentification." [*Simmons*] While the phrase was coined as a standard for determining whether an in-court identification would be admissible in the wake of a suggestive out-of-court identification, with the deletion of "irreparable" it serves equally well as a standard for the admissibility of testimony concerning the out-of-court identification itself. It is the likelihood of misidentification which violates a defendant's right to due process, and it is this which was the basis of the exclusion of evidence in *Foster*. Suggestive confrontations are disapproved because they increase the likelihood of misidentification, and unnecessarily suggestive ones are condemned for the further reason that the increased chance of misidentification is gratuitous. But as *Stovall* makes clear, the admission of evidence of a showup without more does not violate due process.
>
> What is less clear from our cases is whether, as intimated by the district court, unnecessary suggestiveness alone requires the exclusion of evidence. While we are inclined to agree with the courts below that the police did not exhaust all possibilities in seeking persons physically comparable to respondent, we do not think that the evidence must therefore be excluded. The purpose of a strict rule barring evidence of unnecessarily suggestive confrontations would be to deter the police from using a less reliable procedure where a more reliable one may be available, and would not be based on the assumption that in every instance the admission of evidence of such a confrontation offends due process. . . . (*Neil v. Biggers,* pp. 198–199)

With this in mind the Court turned to evaluating the totality of circumstances in *Biggers* to determine whether his due process rights to fundamentally fair procedures had been followed.

> [T]he factors to be considered in evaluating the likelihood of misidentification include the opportunity of the witness to view the criminal at the time of the crime, the witness' degree of attention, the accuracy of the witness' prior description of the criminal, the level of certainty demonstrated by the witness at the confrontation, and the length of time between the crime and the confrontation. (*Neil v. Biggers,* pp. 199–200)

On one hand, the procedure was suggestive; the police were not fully diligent in searching for lineup participants, and seven months elapsed between the crime and the positive identification. On the other hand, the victim had ample opportunity to observe her assailant under good light; she was a practical nurse by profession, which implies that she was trained to make accurate observations; her description to the police was complete, including the assailant's approximate age, height, weight, complexion, skin texture, build, and voice; and over the seven-month lapse she had "made no previous identification at any of the showups, lineups, or photographic showings" indicating that her "record for reliability was . . . a good one, as she had previously resisted whatever suggestiveness inheres in a showup." On balance, the identification did not violate Biggers' right to due process in an identification.

The final case in this series, *Manson v. Brathwaite* (1977), generated somewhat more specific criteria for evaluating the *Biggers* factors. The facts in *Manson* were that Glover, a narcotics undercover police officer, and Brown, an informant, went to a suspected apartment building in Hartford, Connecticut, during daylight, to make a controlled narcotics buy. Glover and Brown were observed by backup Officers D'Onofrio and Gaffey. Glover and Brown knocked on a third-floor door in an area illuminated by natural light from a window in the hallway. A man opened the door; Brown asked for "two things" of narcotics; Glover handed over a ten-dollar bill and observed the man in the apartment; the door closed; a moment later, the man opened the door and handed Glover two glassine bags of heroin; Glover was within two feet of the seller and observed his face.

At headquarters, Glover, who is an African American, described the seller to D'Onofrio as "a colored man, approximately five feet eleven inches tall, dark complexion, black hair, short Afro style, and having high cheekbones, and of heavy build. He was wearing at the time blue pants and a plaid shirt." D'Onofrio thought that Brathwaite might be the seller and left a photograph of him at Glover's office. Two days later, Glover viewed the photograph for the first time and identified Brathwaite as the seller. At the trial, eight months after the sale, the identification photograph was received in evidence without defense objection. Glover said he had no doubt that the person in the photograph was the seller, and he made an in-court identification. No explanation was offered by the prosecution for the failure to utilize a photographic array or to conduct a lineup.

The Connecticut Supreme Court upheld Brathwaite's conviction, saying that no "substantial injustice resulted from the admission of this evidence." On a habeas corpus petition appeal, the federal Court of Appeals ruled that the photograph should have been excluded, regardless of reliability, because the examination of the single photograph was unnecessary, suggestive, and possibly unreliable. The Supreme Court reversed. In this case the viewing of the single photograph left for Glover was suggestive and unnecessary, since D'Onofrio could have prepared a photographic array. The Court noted that the showup in *Biggers* also had been suggestive and unnecessary, and continued to rule that this alone did not require the *per se* exclusion of such identifications. The Court did recognize, indeed, that a *per se* exclusionary rule would tend to make identification more reliable and lessen the opportunity of mistaken identification. The more lenient totality of circumstances approach, while possibly allowing more instances of injustice, was nevertheless supported by the policy rationale of flexibility in allowing suggestive identifications to be considered. The *per se* approach was more likely to deter improper police procedures, but the totality rule also guards against impropriety, since a suggestive showup or lineup might be excluded. Finally, the *per se* approach made it more likely that a guilty party would go free. On balance, the Court continued to uphold the due process totality of circumstances approach in evaluating the admissibility of suggestive identification procedures.

The Court then analyzed each of the *Biggers* factors and found that the "indicators of Glover's ability to make an accurate identification are hardly outweighed by the corrupting effect of the challenged identification itself."

1. The opportunity to view. The facts indicated that Glover had natural lighting and two to three minutes to observe Brathwaite from two feet away.
2. The degree of attention. Glover was a trained on-duty, police officer specializing in narcotics enforcement, was an African American and could be expected "to pay scrupulous attention to detail, for he knew that subsequently he would have to find and arrest his vendor" and testify about this in court.
3. The accuracy of the description. Glover's description was given to D'Onofrio within minutes after the transaction and included the vendor's race, height, build, the color and style of his hair, and the high cheekbone facial feature. It also included clothing the vendor wore. D'Onofrio reacted positively, and two days later, when Glover was alone, he viewed the photograph and identified its subject as the narcotics seller.
4. The witness' level of certainty. Glover, in response to a question whether the photograph was that of the seller, testified: "There is no question whatsoever."
5. The time between the crime and the confrontation-identification was very short. The Court concluded that "we cannot say that under all the circumstances of this case there is 'a very substantial likelihood of irreparable misidentification.'

LAW IN SOCIETY

REDUCING THE ERROR OF EYEWITNESS IDENTIFICATION

The obligation that police, prosecutors, judges, and juries have to detect, prosecute, and convict the guilty carries an obligation not to convict innocent persons. Studies persistently show that eyewitnesses are frequently mistaken in their identifications of suspects and half of the wrongfully convicted are victims of mistaken eyewitness identification.[28] The criminal justice system has perennially accepted wrongful convictions based on misidentification as the inevitable failing of a human system. Lawyers believed, with some justification, that properly conducted criminal trials kept mistaken identification to a minimum. An experienced defense attorney with sufficient time and resources to investigate a case prior to trial, and skillful in cross-examining witnesses, was sufficient to ferret out the truth. This faith might have been justified up to the beginning of the twentieth century. The growing findings of modern scientific psychological research, however, demonstrate the variability of human memory and legal scholars have become more aware that an alarming number of completely innocent people are wrongfully convicted.[29]

By the 1960s, this knowledge led the Warren Court to augment the legal protections of the common-law jury trial with constitutional rules meant to prevent wrongful conviction. This effort had limited success as the more conservative Burger Court restricted the right to counsel at identification procedures (*Kirby v. Illinois,* 1972; *United States v. Ash,* 1973). Of greater significance, the right to counsel during identification procedures and due process rules concerning suggestiveness are crude tools to prevent and correct misidentification.

Since the 1960s, several factors have laid a foundation for a major breakthrough in the "disease" of wrongful conviction. First, extensive research by psychologists has led to better explanations of human identification and misidentification, establishing a scientific foundation for improvements. They have also designed studies to find out which kinds of questioning and identification procedures are more likely to provide accurate identification. This research has been disseminated to the legal community, making it more aware of its shortcomings, although prosecutors believe in the accuracy of eyewitnesses far more than do defense lawyers.[30] At the same time, celebrated cases of wrongful conviction, such as those of Rubin "Hurricane" Carter, Dr. Sam Shepard, or Randall Adams, and the dramatic moratorium on executions by Illinois governor George Ryan after half of those on death row were exonerated, have sensitized the wider public to the fact that misidentification is a persistent problem.

The factor that has made the greatest impression since 1990 has been DNA testing. It has revealed that the worst fears of critics have been justified: an unacceptably high proportion of people who are charged with crimes and convicted are innocent. The DNA breakthrough is not a prescription for complacency. The authors of *Actual Innocence,* who run the Innocence Project at Cardozo Law School, write:

> Most of the lessons of the DNA era have nothing to do with high-tech gizmos or biotechnical wizardry. "Jurors should get innocence training," says Kevin Green [a wrongly convicted man]. They need to be told: "'You're doing this because we have to find the truth. The police haven't necessarily found the truth. The district attorney hasn't found the truth. Only you can.'"[31]

The authors note that England established "an official Criminal Case Review Commission that investigates claims of innocence."[32] Barry Scheck and Peter Neufeld, attorney's who have done as much as anyone to force authorities to allow inmates with credible claims to have DNA tests, warn that these tests are not a panacea for correcting wrongful convictions:

> In a few years, the era of DNA exonerations will come to an end. The population of prisoners who can be helped by DNA testing is shrinking, because the technology has been used widely since the early 1990s, clearing thousands of innocent suspects before trial. Yet blameless people will remain in prison, stranded because their cases don't involve biological evidence. . . .
>
> From Borchard's review of cases stretching back to the dawn of the American republic, all the way to the dawn of the twenty-first century, the causes of wrongful conviction remain the same. Clarity is manufactured about moments of inherent confusion. Witnesses swear they can identify the man who held the gun or knife. Police officers then coax or force confessions from suspects they believe guilty. Prosecutors bury exculpatory evidence and defense lawyers sleep on the job. . . . [33]

Thus, steps can and should be taken to improve the accuracy of identification throughout the investigation and trial process. Before a sound program of accurate identification can be put in place, a foundation of scientific knowledge about the nature of memory and recall is required.

Understanding Memory and Recall

Research has generated a better understanding of human perception, memory, and recall than "common sense," even if an integrated theory of perception has not been fully developed.[34] This information helps us better understand eyewitness testimony.

An important starting point is the wide agreement in perception research that eyewitness testimony is often unreliable. This contradicts the beliefs of many people and the experience of jurors:[35] Under experimental conditions such as a staged crime before a class "witnesses have been proven to be remarkably inaccurate."[36] An experiment by Buckhout had a New York television news program run a staged robbery for twelve seconds. A six-man lineup was then shown, and viewers were invited to call in to pick out the perpetrator. Over two thousand viewers called in and only 14.1% picked the correct man, a result that was no better than a random guess.[37] Because psychological experiments can modify the elements of perception and recall, the percent of accurate recall in various experiments has varied from no better than chance to 90%.[38]

A field experiment by Brigham and colleagues assessed the accuracy of facial recall in a real-life setting.[39] Two men, one white and one African American, entered seventy-three convenience food stores within five minutes of one another, posing as customers. One paid for a pack of cigarettes entirely with pennies and asked for directions. The other asked for directions after fumbling around for change. Two hours later two men pretending to be law interns asked the clerk to identify each "customer" from two photo arrays, one of six whites and one of six African Americans. The overall rate of accurate identifications was 34.2%, which increased to 46.8% when instances of "no identification" were omitted. This is significantly higher than the 16.7% rate (one out of six) that would be expected by random guessing, but it also confirms a large number of incorrect identifications. The correct recall of convenience store clerks fell to chance when the "law interns" presented the photo arrays more than twenty-four hours after the "customers" left the store.

This study also found, in accord with other research, that identification accuracy of a person of *one's own race* is higher and that the ability of white clerks to identify the African-American "customer" was significantly related to the amount of cross-racial experience of the white clerk. The African-American clerks in this study had higher accuracy rates than the white clerks: they were 13% more accurate in identifying the white "customer" and 23% more accurate in identifying the African-American "customer." As expected, recognition was higher for the "customers" who were more attractive or distinctive and from lineups using larger pictures.

Elizabeth Loftus' summary of research findings first notes that the memory process is *selective*. Humans do not simply record events like a videotape recorder but *process* information at the *acquisition* stage when the event is perceived, during the *retention* stage, and again at the *retrieval* stage during which a person recalls stored information.[40] A complex event consists of a vast amount of information; an individual's sensory mechanism selects only certain aspects of the visual stimulus. People are therefore much better at remembering salient facts of an event than peripheral details.[41]

Acquisition is affected by *event factors:* retention time and frequency (the longer or more frequently something is viewed, the more information is stored) and the type of fact observed (people have great difficulty in assessing speed and time; violent and emotional events produce lower accuracy of memory).[42] "Studies also show that the amount of time perceived as going by is overestimated under conditions of danger and that the overestimation tends to increase as the stress increases."[43] *Witness factors* also affect observation. The "role that stress plays at the time a witness is perceiving a complex event is captured in the Yerkes-Dodson Law[:] . . . that strong motivational states such as stress or other emotional arousal facilitate learning and performance up to a point, after which there is a decrement."[44] Much social-psychological research demonstrates that individual bias affects perception, whether the bias is a result of situational expectations, personal or cultural prejudice, or expectations from past experience.[45]

The *retention stage* is affected by the time lapse between the event and recall. More unnerving, the memory of an event can *change*. "Postevent information can not only enhance existing memories but also change a witness's memory and even cause nonexistent details to become incorporated into a previously acquired memory."[46] This underlines the danger of suggestibility, so prominent in the *Wade-Gilbert-Stovall* trilogy of cases. Studies have shown that: (1) the *likelihood of recall* of an event is enhanced simply by mentioning it; (2) *postevent suggestion* can cause the memory to compromise between what was originally seen and what is reported; and (3) mentioning a *nonexistent object* to a witness can cause the witness to later report having seen it. Not only simple facts, but also subjective recollections about the violence of an event can be modified by postevent suggestion.

Verbal cues subtly influence retention. Subjects shown a filmed traffic accident were asked if they saw broken glass, although there was none. Seven percent of those asked about cars that "hit" reported broken glass compared to sixteen percent of those asked about cars that "smashed" into each other. Both *original* information and *external* information acquired *after the event* become merged into one memory. Labeling a situation influences memory as does the practice of witnesses guessing at information if they are not sure of their original memory. The dangers of inaccuracy during memory retention are worsened by a *freezing effect:* A person who makes a statement about an event, tends to more strongly remember the *statement* at a later time; and this applies to objectively true elements of the original event as well as false information.[47]

Similar memory modification occurs during the *retrieval stage*. Accuracy of recall is increased when a person relays it in a familiar and comfortable setting and in a narrative form rather than answering controlled questions. Increased status of the questioner enhances the quantity and accuracy of responses. The wording of questions influences responses. An experiment demonstrated that more witnesses asked to describe "the" event said they saw something not present in a film compared to those asked about "an" event.[48]

Toward More Accurate Identification

It is utopian to believe that wrongful convictions can be entirely eliminated. Nevertheless, practical knowledge exists that can be applied by police agencies to substantially reduce this injustice. As noted earlier in this chapter, the National Institute of Justice of the United States Department of Justice issued a report in late 1999, *Eyewitness Evidence: A Guide for Law Enforcement.* This forty-four page booklet was compiled by a group of law enforcement personnel, defense lawyers, and psychologists. It does not provide the background research but, rather, lists precise procedural suggestions for law enforcement agencies. The *Guide* goes a long way toward establishing national criteria, although it has some weaknesses. Professor Donald Judges' thorough review of the *Guide,* states that it is "the most faithful to research findings in its recommendations to avoid instruction bias."[49] On the other hand he faults it for not recommending double-blind and sequential line up procedures.[50]

The *Guide* offers recommendations to police in five areas: taking the *initial report* of a crime; preparing *mug books* and composites and instructing witnesses who view them, procedures for *follow up interviews* of witnesses, field identification *(showup)* procedure, and *lineup* procedures for eyewitness identification of suspects. Under *lineups,* procedures are recommended for composing photo and live lineups, instructing witnesses prior to lineups, and conducting identification procedures. The *Guide* indicates that the NIJ is planning a second phase of the eyewitness project to produce training criteria for these procedures. It notes that no validation studies have been authorized and that changes may be recommended in the future.

In general terms, the *Guide*'s recommendations are designed to improve the accuracy of police interviewing and identification. In regard to the initial interviews and follow-up interviews with witnesses, the *Guide* adopts many research findings of what is known as the cognitive interview.[51] Police are instructed to ask open-ended questions and augment answers with closed-ended questions, to avoid asking suggestive or leading questions, to separate witnesses, to instruct witnesses to avoid discussing details of the incident with other witnesses, to encourage the witness to volunteer information without prompting, to encourage the witness to report all details, even if they seem trivial, to caution the witness not to guess, avoid interrupting the witness, and so forth. According to Professor Judges, the *Guide* misses some points.

> For example, in its statements of principle or policy, the Guide does not explicitly state the concepts underlying the components of the cognitive interview, including the witness-centered control of information. Other specific recommendations from CI [Cognitive Interview] are either lacking or only obliquely referred to, such as inviting narrative presentation, witness-compatible questioning (i.e., tailoring questions to witnesses' mental representation of the event, such as a witness who viewed the perpetrator from the side or rear only), and the varied-retrieval method (e.g., having the witness recall the event in reverse chronological order).[52]

In the remainder of this section, some methods which experts have proposed to improve lineups are reviewed.

Improving Lineups

ESTABLISH DOUBLE-BLIND PROCEDURES The dangers of suggestibility or contamination of witnesses by even subtle or unintended emphasis is very well established and uniformly supported by psychological research.[53] Professor Judges urges that "eyewitness identification procedures should be conducted only by persons who are ignorant of which lineup member is the suspect. . . .

Use of 'double-blind' procedures—which has long been standard practice in human-subject research—would preclude the possibility of contamination even from inadvertent or subtle feedback cues from the investigator."[54]

CONDUCT LINEUPS IN A SEQUENTIAL MANNER, NOT SIMULTANEOUSLY The problem with the more typical simultaneous lineup, where all the individuals are viewed while standing together is that it forces the witness to engage in relative (comparative) judgment ("does this person look more like the suspect than that person"), instead of absolute judgment ("that is the man").

> A review of research found that "critical tests of this hypothesis have consistently shown that a sequential procedure produces fewer false identifications than does a simultaneous procedure with little or no decrease in rates of accurate identification." This manipulation, because it directly addresses the cognitive source of the problem, is an especially important component of the set of recommendations advanced by researchers in this area for reducing the risk of false identifications.[55]

UTILIZE "LINEUP CONTEXT CUES" They improve the accuracy of lineup identifications. Cutler and Penrod recommend:

> that lineup procedures should ensure the use of voice samples and should show the lineup members from three-quarter poses and, whenever possible and appropriate, allow the

witness to watch the lineup members walking in and out of the observation room. Such cues should also be taken into consideration when photographs are taken for the purpose of mug books.[56]

CONSTRUCT LINEUPS FAIRLY This seems to be axiomatic, but police in the past have been tempted to construct the lineup so that the suspect stands out. The *Guide* urges fairness. Lindsay and Wells note that as nonsuspects ("foils") in a lineup come to resemble the suspect more, more witnesses can be expected to erroneously identify the foils, suggesting a trade-off between a high probability of selecting the suspect in unfair (low-similarity) lineups and a high probability of selecting an innocent person in high-similarity lineups. Using experimental lineups with a "criminal" present and a "criminal" absent, Lindsay and Wells found that the choice of a "guilty" suspect fell from 71% in unfair lineups to 58% in fair ones in the criminal-present mode. However, choosing the "innocent suspect" (a look-alike to the "criminal") fell from 70% to 31% in the criminal-absent mode. Lindsay and Wells developed diagnosticity ratios that indicated mathematically that the fair lineups improve the relative quality of both identifications and no identifications over the unfair lineups. The practical value of this experiment is to dissuade police from setting up unfair lineups in the hope of highlighting suspects who they are "certain" are guilty.[57] After all, since the selection and conviction of an innocent person leaves the real criminal at large, law enforcement and prosecution have as real a desire to make lineups more fair as do defendants.

THE OFFICER WHO CONSTRUCTS A LINEUP SHOULD BE THE SAME RACE AS THE SUSPECT Research shows that same-race identification tends to be more accurate than recognition of other-race faces. If other-race faces tend to look similar, there is a risk that, e.g., a white officer who constructs a lineup of a black suspect and black foils for black witnesses may construct a lineup of faces that look alike to him but will appear dissimilar to the witnesses.[58] This point is conjectural and has not yet been subject to rigorous research.

USE EXPERT WITNESSES OR CLOSING ARGUMENTS TO REBUT ERRORS ABOUT EYEWITNESS IDENTIFICATION This has been strenuously resisted by prosecutors for fear that experts would undermine juror confidence in eyewitnesses. Courts and scholars are split on whether to allow experts to testify. Huff, Rattner, and Sagarin would always allow expert witnesses on the issue of reliability, while Donald Judges is skeptical of its value.[59] Lisa Steele urges attorneys to utilize closing statements to inform jurors about eyewitness identification. The two specific points raised by Steele in which research contradicts common sense is witness certainty and accuracy of a prior description. Thus, many studies show little or no correlation between the confidence that witnesses express in their certainty and the accuracy of their observations, while others do.[60] The common finding of no confidence-accuracy correlation is counterintuitive; in fact, the Supreme Court in *Neil v. Biggers* (1972) and *Manson v. Brathwaite* (1977) relied on confidence as one of five indicia of certainty, thus possibly injecting an element of factual injustice into some cases. An expert could be useful in bringing this to the attention of a jury, as well as alerting them to other possibly relevant issues.

This list does not exhaust all of the ways in which identification procedures can be made more accurate. The *Guide* is only a first step, and it has flaws. It is probably the case that very few law enforcement departments conduct lineups in a double-blind fashion, and given the disruption of routine, it is not expected that many will change rapidly. The hopeful sign is that for the first time serious national attention has been given to the issue. Time will tell whether real advances will be made in making the identification process more accurate or whether these efforts will be soon forgotten.

SUMMARY

Eyewitness identification is an important source of truth in the justice process but is often mistaken and leads to the unwarranted conviction of innocent persons. Legal rules are of limited value in preventing mistaken eyewitness identification.

Identification can be made on a one-to-one basis, a procedure called a showup, or by a live or photographic lineup. A lineup is a police identification procedure in which a witness views a suspect in to the crime whose presence or likeness is mixed in with a number of other people with similar physical characteristics.

The Supreme Court has ruled in three distinct areas of eyewitness identification; its justification for its constitutional rulings rests on the state action of suggestiveness in these procedures by police officers.

In *United States v. Wade* (1967), the Supreme Court held that a suspect is entitled to counsel during a police lineup after he has been indicted under the Sixth Amendment. The role of counsel at lineup is to prevent suggestiveness, or to detect and record it. If a postindictment lineup occurs without counsel being present the witnesses may not offer that identification into testimony. In such case the witness may identify the defendant at trial only if the prosecution can show that the memory of the witness is based on observations made at the time of the crime. In *Kirby v. Illinois* (1972), the Court limited this right to counsel only to postindictment stages of the criminal process and held that suspects are entitled to counsel only after an adversary judicial proceeding has been directed against them. "It is then that a defendant finds himself faced with the prosecutorial forces of organized society, and immersed in the intricacies of substantive and procedural criminal law." The Court continues to recognize the pre/postindictment distinction. In *Moore v. Illinois* (1977), the defendant was identified at an uncounseled showup during a preliminary examination where the formal adversary process had begun. This violated Moore's Sixth Amendment rights.

The *Wade* right to counsel rule does not apply at photographic identification procedures because a photo array is determined not to present the same dangers of suggestibility as a lineup.

There is no Fifth Amendment protection against the requirement that suspects allow the identification of physical characteristics; the right against self-incrimination protects a suspect from divulging testimonial evidence. In addition to simply being viewed, a suspect in a lineup can be required to speak for voice identification purposes, to wear certain items of clothing, and to make movements that were made at the time of the crime.

There is a due process right that identification procedures be conducted fairly. The due process rule is a totality of the circumstances test; the Court has rejected a narrower *per se* rule. In deciding whether a defendant's due process rights have been violated, the necessity to conduct a showup may be taken into account. A showup is justified if a witness may die. Pictures of a lone suspect may be shown to witnesses prior to arrest to aid in apprehension. Identification after a grossly unfair lineup in which the suspect is made to stand out violates due process and results in the suppression of the identification. In *Manson v. Brathwaite* (1977), the Court listed five factors to be taken into account in determining whether an identification that has been tainted by an unfair identification procedure, such as a single-suspect showup, should be admitted: (1) the opportunity the witness had to view the suspect at the scene of the crime; (2) the witness's degree of attention; (3) the accuracy of the witness's original description; (4) the witness's level of certainty; and (5) the time elapsed between the crime and the identification procedure.

LEGAL PUZZLES

LEGAL PUZZLES: HOW HAVE COURTS DECIDED THESE CASES?

9–1. Christenbury identified Townes, who was charged with murder, at a postindictment lineup where Townes did not have counsel present. Townes had previously gone to Christenbury's home to purchase a pistol of the type used in the murder. Christenbury and Townes were alone in his kitchen, carrying on a conversation, for at least ten minutes. May Christenbury identify Townes at trial? *Townes v. Murray,* 68 F.3d 840 (4th Cir. 1995).

9–2. Three witnesses to a bank robbery identified LaPierre at a postindictment lineup. LaPierre's attorney arrived at the police department fifteen minutes before the lineup and was told by an FBI agent to wait on a bench outside the hallway leading to the lineup room. LaPierre was taken to the lineup room. The FBI agents who entered the lineup room with the witnesses, were aware that his attorney was waiting outside. The lineup began, with witnesses separated from the suspect and foils by a one-way window, and two lineup members were paraded for review before an FBI agent noticed that counsel was not in the viewing area. The agent and attorney returned while the third lineup member was being presented. LaPierre was the fourth member of the lineup. The attorney was present for the rest of the lineup, including the presentation of LaPierre. Did this violate LaPierre's Sixth Amendment rights? *United States v. LaPierre,* 998 F.2d 1460 (9th Cir. 1993).

9–3. Joe Emanuele was convicted of two bank robberies. Lorraine Woessner, a teller, observed the robber for several minutes at close range in the well-lit bank lobby. Shown a six-photo array that included a photograph of the defendant shortly after the crime, Woessner was unable to identify the robber. The one fingerprint taken from the Waterworks Bank did not match that of defendant. Woessner and the tellers at the other robbed bank were subpoenaed by the government to testify, and after checking in at the United States Attorney's office, they were directed to sit outside the courtroom. There, the tellers saw defendant led from the courtroom in manacles by United States marshals. Though later Woessner could not remember for certain who had spoken first, outside the courtroom the two tellers talked to each other about the defendant, telling each other "it has to be him." Was Woessner's in-court positive identification of Emanuele admissible? *United States v. Emanuele,* 51 F.3d 1123 (3rd Cir. 1995).

9–4. Williams was wanted for several robberies of photo booths; the robber was identified by different victim-employees as a "Mexican," as "dark-complexioned, possibly Mexican," as "Puerto Rican in appearance," and as "Spanish, Cuban, or Mexican in race." All identified the robber as having dark, curly hair, a moustache, and driving a green car. Williams was arrested as the suspect and placed in a lineup. Williams was the only African American in the lineup; the others in the lineup were Hispanic who had similar skin tone and facial characteristics as Williams. Did this lineup violate Williams's due process right? *Williams v. Weldon,* 826 F.2d 1018 (11th Cir. 1987) *cert. denied,* 485 U.S. 964 (1988).

ANSWERS TO LEGAL PUZZLES

9–1. YES. *United States v. Wade* allows courts to determine whether an in-court identification has an independent origin other than a "tainted" lineup identification. In this case, the length of time of the conversation between Christenbury and Townes provided a sufficient independent basis for the trial court to have permitted his in-court identification.

9–2. YES. *United States v. Wade* requires that counsel be present. The rule is not overridden by a good faith error of the government. The state has an affirmative obligation to ensure counsel's presence at the lineup, which was not met here. The lawyer did not act unreasonably; he arrived on time and let the agents know he was there. He made a professional judgment not to enter a restricted area unbidden; the government was responsible for beginning the lineup without counsel present. The lawyer's presence in the building while LaPierre was being presented is not relevant. The witnesses viewed the lineup as a whole; from the very beginning LaPierre was within view of the witnesses. LaPierre's right to counsel attached at the moment he and the other lineup members were within the sight of the witnesses.

9–3. NO. A government identification procedure violates due process when it is "unnecessarily suggestive" and creates a "substantial risk of misidentification." A confrontation caused by the government, albeit inadvertently, where a defendant in shackles and with a United States marshal at each side walks before the key identification witnesses is impermissibly suggestive. The conversation between the tellers may have overwhelmed any doubts Woessner retained after observing the defendant in the hallway. Woessner could not, despite her opportunity to observe the robber, recognize him in a photo array. That failure, coupled with the highly suggestive viewing of the defendant in conditions reeking of criminality, bolstered by the comments of another witness, rendered the in-court identification unreliable. There clearly was a substantial risk of misidentification. This was not harmless error because there was no other physical evidence against Emanuele. The error was significant in relation to everything else the jury considered.

9–4. NO. Simply being of a different race or ethnic group from others placed in a lineup does not necessarily make that lineup impermissibly suggestive, especially where, as here, the other individuals in the lineup had roughly the same characteristics and features as the accused.

FURTHER READING

Elizabeth Loftus, *Eyewitness Testimony* (Cambridge: Harvard University Press, 1979).

C. Ronald Huff, Arye Rattner and Edward Sagarin, *Convicted But Innocent: Wrongful Conviction and Public Policy* (Thousand Oaks: Sage, 1996).

Edward Connors, Thomas Lundregan, Neal Miller, and Tom McEwen, *Convicted by Juries, Exonerated by Science: Case Studies in the Use of DNA Evidence to Establish Innocence After Trial* (National Institute of Justice, June 1996, NCJ 161258).

ENDNOTES

1. 5 John H. Wigmore, *Evidence in Trials at Common Law* § 1367 (John H. Chadbourn rev. ed. 1974).
2. Noted in James Marshall, *Law and Psychology in Conflict* (Indianapolis: Bobbs-Merrill, 1966).
3. Edwin M. Borchard, *Convicting the Innocent: Sixty-five Actual Errors of Criminal Justice* (New York: Garden City Publishing Company, 1932).
4. Jerome Frank and Barbara Frank, *Not Guilty* (Garden City: Doubleday, 1957).
5. Andre A. Moenssens et al., *Scientific Evidence in Civil and Criminal Cases* § 9.15, at 1171–72 (4th ed. 1995), cited in Laurie L. Levenson, Eyewitness Ids, *The National Law Journal*, July 10, 2000, p. A20
6. C. R. Huff, A. Rattner and E. Sagarin, *Convicted* But *Innocent: Wrongful Conviction and Public Policy* (Thousand Oaks: Sage, 1996).
7. H. A. Bedeau and M. L. Radelet, Miscarriages of Justice in Potentially Capital Cases, *Stanford Law Review* 40:21, pp. 31–36 (1987). The authors use a conservative definition of "miscarriage of justice," limiting it essentially to cases where "the defendant was legally or physically uninvolved in the case."
8. *Ibid.,* p. 38. Of these 350 cases, 116 resulted in death sentences, and 23 innocent persons were actually convicted. For an updated and more narrative account of this research see Michael Radelet, Hugo Bedau and Constance Putnam, *In Spite of Innocence* (Boston: Northeastern University Press, 1992).
9. S. Raab, "Man Wrongfully Imprisoned by New York to Get $600,000," *New York Times,* Jan. 18, 1985, p. 1.
10. R. Hermann, "The Case of the Jamaican Accent," *New York Times Magazine,* Dec. 1, 1974, p. 30.
11. *New York Times,* Feb. 16, 1990, p. A10, (nat. ed.).
12. Mentioned in E. Loftus, "Trials of an Expert Witness," *Newsweek,* June 29, 1987, p. 10.
13. C. R. Huff, A. Rattner, and E.Sagarin, "Guilty Until Proven Innocent: Wrongful Conviction and Public Policy," *Crime and Delinquency* 32(4):518–44 (1986).
14. P. Applebome, "Overturned Murder Conviction Spotlights Dallas-Style Justice," *New York Times,* Mar. 7, 1989, p. 11 (nat. ed.); R.D. Adams, with W. Hoffer and M. M. Hoffer, *Adams v. Texas* (New York: St. Martin's, 1991).
15. Cynthia L. Cooper and Sam Reese Sheppard, *Mockery of Justice* (Boston: Northeastern University Press, 1995); James S. Hirsch, *Hurricane* (Boston: Houghton Mifflin, 2000).

16. Lisa Teachey and Amy Raskin, DNA tests clear 2 of rape; New questions raised about eyewitness testimony, *Houston Chronicle,* September 30, 2000, p. A1; Stuart Pfeifer, Jack Leonard, and Jeff Gottlieb, Youth to Be Freed as Judge Voids Conviction, *Los Angeles Times,* Aug. 22, 2000, p. B1; Matthew Bruun, More rely on miracle' of DNA test; Power to convict, exonerate, *Sunday Telegram* (Worcester, Mass.), July 16, 2000, p. B1; Sacha Pfeiffer, after Serving 4 Years, Man Is Exonerated in '95 Slaying, *Boston Globe,* Sept. 14, 2000, p. B6; Hector Becerra, Yet Another Reversal with a Witness Issue, *Los Angeles Times,* August 22, 2000, Part A; Part 1; p. 18 (Orange County Edition).
17. Jennifer Thompson, 'I Was Certain, but I Was Wrong,' *New York Times,* June 18, 2000, Sec. 4, p. 15
18. Editorial, Irreversible Error in Texas, *New York Times,* June 23, 2000, p. A22; Jim Yardley, In Death Row Dispute, a Witness Stands Firm, *New York Times,* June 16, 2000, p. A22.
19. Barry Scheck, Peter Neufeld, and Jim Dwyer, *Actual Innocence* (New York: Doubleday, 2000).
20. Dirk Johnson, Illinois, Citing Faulty Verdicts, Bars Executions, *New York Times,* Feb. 1, 2000, p. A1 (noted that "13 men had been sentenced to death in Illinois since 1977 for crimes they did not commit, before ultimately being exonerated and freed by the courts").
21. Edward Connors, Thomas Lundregan, Neal Miller, and Tom McEwen, *Convicted by Juries, Exonerated by Science: Case Studies in the Use of DNA Evidence to Establish Innocence After Trial* (National Institute of Justice, June 1996, NCJ 161258).
22. The quote is from *Williams v. United States,* 345 F.2d 733, 736 (D.C. Cir. 1965), reprinted in F. P. Graham, *The Due Process Revolution* (New York: Hayden Books Co., 1970) (originally *The Self-Inflicted Wound*), p. 223.
23. Graham, *Due Process,* pp. 236–37, referring to the unreported case of *United States v. Beasley.*
24. *Russell v. United States,* 408 F.2d 1280 (D.C. Cir. 1969); see comments on this case in Graham, *Due Process,* p. 238.
25. *Gilbert v. California* (1967); *United States v. Mara* (1973).
26. *United States v. Dionisio* (1973).
27. *California v. Byers* (1971), upholding a law that required drivers involved in an accident to stop and leave their names; such activity does not provide testimonial or communicative evidence.
28. Jennifer L. Devenport, Steven D. Penrod, and Brian Cutler, Eyewitness Identification Evidence: Evaluating Commonsense Evaluations, *Psychology, Public Policy and Law,* 3:338–58 (1997).
29. Donald P. Judges. Two Cheers for the Department of Justice's Eyewitness Evidence: A Guide for Law Enforcement, *Arkansas Law Review* 53:231–97, pp. 283–91 (2000).
30. J.C. Brigham and M. P. Wolfskiel, Opinions of Attorneys and Law Enforcement Personnel on the Accuracy of Eyewitness Identifications, *Law and Human Behavior,* 7:337–39 (1983).
31. Scheck, et al., note 19, p. 245.
32. Scheck, et al., note 19, p. 246.
33. Scheck, et al., note 19, p. 250.
34. See, for example, E. F. Loftus, *Eyewitness Testimony* (Cambridge, Mass.: Harvard University Press, 1979); A. D. Yarmey, *The Psychology of Eyewitness Testimony* (New York: The Free Press, 1979); John C. Yuille, "A Critical Examination of the Psychological and Practical Implications of Eyewitness Research," *Law and Human Behavior* 4(4):335–45 (1980).
35. Loftus, *Eyewitness,* note 34, p. 19.
36. Yuille, "Critical Examination,"note 34, p. 336.
37. R. Buckhout, "Nearly 2,000 Witnesses Can Be Wrong," in Loftus, *Eyewitness,* note 34, pp. 135–36.
38. Woodhead, *et al.*, n.d., recounted in Loftus, *Eyewitness,* note 34, pp. 166–70.
39. J. Brigham, A. Maass, L. Snyder, and K. Spaulding, "Accuracy of Eyewitness Identifications in a Field Setting," *Journal of Personality and Social Psychology* 42(4):673–81 (1982).
40. Loftus, *Eyewitness*, note 34, p. 21 (citations omitted).
41. *Ibid.,* pp. 21, 25–27.
42. *Ibid.,* pp. 23–32.
43. Yarmey, *Psychology,* p. 52.
44. Loftus, *Eyewitness,* note 34 p. 33.
45. *Ibid.,* pp. 32–51.
46. *Ibid.,* p. 55.
47. *Ibid.,* pp. 52–87.
48. *Ibid.,* pp. 88–104.
49. D. Judges, note 29, p. 277.
50. D. Judges, note 29, pp. 238–39, 253, 262–63, 270.
51. Warren E. Leary, "Novel Methods Unlock Witnesses' Memories," *New York Times,* Nov. 15, 1988, p. 25 (nat. ed.).
52. D. Judges, note 29, p. 274.
53. Gary L. Wells and Eric P. Seelau, Eyewitness Identification: Psychological Research and Legal Policy on Lineups, *Psychology, Public Policy & Law* 1:765 (1995); other sources noted in D. Judges, footnote 29.
54. D. Judges, note 29, p. 270.
55. D. Judges, note 29, p. 263, citing Wells and Seelau, note 53.
56. Brian Cutler and Steven Penrod, "Improving the Reliability of Eyewitness Identification: Lineup Construction and Presentation," *Journal of Applied Psychology* 72(2):281–90, p. 289 (1988).
57. R. C. L. Lindsay and Gary L. Wells, "What Price Justice? Exploring the Relationship of Lineup Fairness to Identification Accuracy," *Law and Human Behavior* 4(4):303–13 (1980).
58. John C. Brigham, "Perspectives on the Impact of Lineup Composition, Race, and Witness Confidence on Identification Accuracy," *Law and Human Behavior* 4(4):315–21, p. 318 (1980).
59. Huff, Rattner, and Sagarin, *Convicted* But *Innocent,* note 6, p. 151 ; D. Judges, note 29, pp. 289–90.
60. Yarmey, *Psychology,* note 34, pp. 150–51, 156; Loftus, *Eyewitness,* note 34, pp. 100–101; Brigham *et al.,* "Accuracy," note 39.

JUSTICES OF THE SUPREME COURT

The Nixon-Ford Moderates
Blackmun—Powell—Stevens

To a significant degree, these moderate justices really defined the agenda of the Burger Court. With staunch liberal (Douglas, Brennan, and Marshall) and conservative (Burger and Rehnquist) wings, and with Justice White joining various alignments depending upon the issue, Blackmun, Powell, and Stevens were often the "swing" votes that determined the outcome of cases in the 1970s and 1980s. At the beginning of his career on the Supreme Court, it appeared that Justice Blackmun would be a clone of the Chief Justice Burger (they were irreverently dubbed "the Minnesota twins"). But in the late-1970s, his voting patterns began to shift away from the Court's conservative wing, and he often voted with Brennan and Marshall, but not so consistently to have been labeled a liberal. Roe v. Wade, *his abortion rights opinion in 1973, blocking state laws from prohibiting first trimester abortions, was by far the most controversial liberal decision in the past decades.*

In civil liberties areas including obscenity, school prayer, public religious displays, and free press, the Burger Court did not decide cases in ways favored by the extreme Right. In these and in civil rights cases, Justices Blackmun, Powell, and Stevens took moderate or liberal positions. On the other hand, Justice Powell tended generally to rule for the prosecution in criminal cases, with Blackmun and Stevens voting for defendants more often than Powell but not as often as Brennan and Marshall. In the affirmative action decisions, the Court was so evenly balanced that Justice Powell's compromise opinions became the law of the land.

This kaleidoscope of opinions should make it abundantly clear that it is a gross oversimplification to label the Supreme Court at a particular time as liberal or conservative in general. Even in specific areas of law, it is more meaningful to pay close attention to the reasoning of the Justices in order to obtain a better understanding of the Court's work.

Harry A. Blackmun

Minnesota 1908–1999

Republican

Appointed by Richard Nixon

Years of Service: 1970–1994

Collection of the Supreme Court of the United States. Photographer: Joseph D. Lavenburg

Life and Career A lifelong friend of Warren Burger, Harry Blackmun graduated *summa cum laude* as a mathematics major from Harvard University and from Harvard Law School in 1931. He clerked for a federal judge and practiced estate and tax law from 1934 to 1950 with a Minneapolis firm; he also engaged in public service and taught law. He was resident counsel for the Mayo Clinic in Rochester, Minnesota during the 1950s, an association that may have influenced his famous *Roe v. Wade* (1973) abortion rights decision. Appointed to the U.S. Court of Appeals for the Eighth Circuit (Missouri, Minnesota, Arkansas, Iowa, Nebraska, South Dakota, and North Dakota) in 1959, he developed a reputation as a conservative but not inflexible judge, usually denying a criminal defendant's claims but holding that whipping inmates was cruel and unusual punishment. In the turbulent Vietnam War era, he expressed dismay at the militant anti-establishment views of many young people.

Contribution to Criminal Procedure It is difficult to characterize Blackmun's position because although he was at first a moderate-conservative on criminal procedure issues after 1988 he began to shift to the left, and by 1992 his votes put him on the liberal wing of a Court that was growing progressively more conservative. On the conservative side, he joined Chief Justice Burger's campaign to overturn the exclusionary rule, holding that illegally seized evidence need not be excluded from civil proceedings (*United States v. Janis,* 1976); ruled that the right to counsel does not extend to photographic identification procedures after a defendant was formally charged (*United States v. Ash,* 1973); ruled against a juvenile defendant's right to a jury trial (*McKeiver v. Pennsylvania,* 1971); and dissented in the "Christian Burial Speech" case, claiming that police could interrogate a formally charged suspect without his lawyers being present.

He began to diverge from a solidly conservative position by joining the dissenters in three cases that upheld aerial surveillance by fixed-wing aircraft and helicopters. His decisions regarding confessions were mixed, agreeing that a confession made while an attorney was trying to contact her client is admissible (*Moran v. Burbine,* 1986), but joining the dissent in *Arizona v. Mauro,* (1987) (taped conversation between husband-suspect and wife after the murder of their child constituted an interrogation). He wrote the dissent protesting the decision that upheld the law allowing the confiscation of funds used for the payment of attorney fees. Shortly before his retirement, his growing concern over the application of the death penalty led him to hold that it was not possible to apply the death penalty in a constitutional manner, and he would henceforth vote against every application of capital punishment (*Callins v. Collins,* 1994).

SIGNATURE OPINION *California v. Acevedo* (1991). For a 6–3 majority, Blackmun ruled that police having probable cause could search a container in an automobile without a warrant. Although Blackmun generally upheld an individual's Fourth Amendment right of privacy in the home, he ruled in such a way as to defer to the needs of police in automobile searches, giving them a bright-line rule that allowed the opening of containers whether probable cause extended to the entire car or to the specific container.

ASSESSMENT Despite his pro-prosecution rulings in the 1970s, a generally conservative stance in free speech and obscenity cases, and inconsistent positions in equal protection cases, Justice Blackmun produced several major surprises. He authored three opinions that upset the older "commercial speech" doctrine which said that First Amendment protections do not apply to commercial speech. He was the author of *Roe v. Wade* (1973), the abortion rights decision, the most controversial opinion of the Burger Court and an issue that has continued to spark public, political, and legal contention.

FURTHER READING

Stephen L. Wasby, "Justice Blackmun and Criminal Justice: A Modest Overview," *Akron Law Review* 28:125–186 (1995).

LEWIS F. POWELL, JR.

Virginia 1907–1998

Democrat

Appointed by Richard Nixon

Years of Service: 1972–1987

Collection of the Supreme Court of the United States. Photographer: Joseph Bailey

LIFE AND CAREER Lewis Powell, from a well-to-do background in Norfolk, Virginia, graduated first in his class at Washington and Lee College where he was class president; completed a three-year law program at Washington and Lee in two years, again graduating first; and after studying law at Harvard University for a year, entered the private practice of law in Richmond, Virginia. His practice was primarily in corporate law, representing some of the nation's largest businesses. During World War II, he served as an Air Force intelligence officer in North Africa. Powell was always involved in substantial public and professional service activities. While serving as president of the Richmond School Board from 1952 to 1961, his moderation and leadership fostered the peaceful racial integration of the public schools. He served as president of the American Bar Association, the American College of Trial Lawyers, the Virginia State Board of Education, and was a member of President Johnson's Crime Commission in the late 1960s.

CONTRIBUTION TO CRIMINAL PROCEDURE Justice Powell generally voted in favor of the state. In *Stone v. Powell* (1976), he ruled that federal habeas corpus should not be open to state defendants who argued the issues before state courts, thus cutting off access of a large group of cases to the Supreme Court. He ruled against an absolute right to counsel at probation revocation hearings but allowed for a due process totality of circumstances rule that would require counsel if special circumstances existed (*Gagnon v. Scarpelli,* 1973). If core values of the Bill of Rights were attacked, he would rule against the government; he ruled that the President cannot issue electronic eavesdropping orders without a warrant (*United States v. U.S. District Court,* 1972)

SIGNATURE OPINION In *United States v. Calandra* (1974), Justice Powell raised the theory that the purpose of the exclusionary rule is primarily to deter police misconduct. While this arguably misread the intent of *Mapp v. Ohio* (1961), it was a potent approach that gave the Burger and Rehnquist courts the intellectual ammunition to curtail the scope of the exclusionary rule which paved the way to the *Leon* exception, which allowed illegally seized evidence to be introduced into evidence if it was seized by police relying in good-faith on a bad search warrant.

ASSESSMENT At the time he retired, Justice Powell was called the most powerful man in America because he often provided the deciding vote in important Supreme Court cases. Outside of his generally conservative stance in criminal procedure, he tended to be a nondoctrinaire judge. Under the Equal Protection Clause, he voted against gender inequality or laws that imposed extra fiscal burdens on indigents. He precisely analyzed competing interests in cases. In a First Amendment case, for example, he ruled that a shopping mall did not have to allow the distribution of leaflets because, unlike in a company town, the leaflet distributors could find other places to make their views known.

His greatest "balancing act" was in the *Bakke* (1978) medical school admissions affirmative action case. Affirmative action programs posed an explosive issue for the Court. If racial quotas were upheld, a white backlash could wipe out the programs, while a finding of unconstitutionality could produce resentment and even violence in parts of the minority community. In *Bakke,* eight justices split in each of these liberal and conservative directions. Justice Powell's opinion split the difference by ruling that numeric quotas were unconstitutional but that race could legitimately be taken into account in admissions decisions in order to achieve the laudable goals of affirmative action. This statesmanlike decision legitimated affirmative action programs in a way designed to be most acceptable to the entire society.

FURTHER READING

John C. Jeffries, Jr., *Justice Lewis F. Powell, Jr.* (New York: Charles Scribner's Sons, 1994).

JOHN PAUL STEVENS

Illinois 1920–

Republican

Appointed by Gerald Ford

Years of Service: 1975–

Collection of the Supreme Court of the United States. Photographer: Joseph Bailey

LIFE AND CAREER Born into a wealthy Chicago household, Stevens graduated Phi Beta Kappa from the University of Chicago, served as a naval officer during World War II, graduated first in his class from Northwestern University Law School, clerked for Supreme Court Justice Wiley Rutledge, and practiced law in Chicago from 1948 to 1970. His expertise in antitrust law led to his service as an advisor on antitrust reform to Congress and the U.S. Attorney General. He published several articles on antitrust law and taught courses at the University of Chicago and Northwestern University Law schools. Appointed to the United States Court of Appeals for the Seventh Circuit in 1970, he gained a reputation as one of the best appellate judges in the country. His first written opinion—a dissent urging that a legislature could not use its contempt power to summarily imprison one who disrupted a legislative session—was adopted by the Supreme Court, which held that due process required a hearing before imprisonment. One reason that President Ford nominated Stevens was the correct perception that he was centrist; after the resignation of President Nixon, Ford was not in a political position to appoint a sharply conservative person to the Court.

CONTRIBUTION TO CRIMINAL PROCEDURE By joining with liberal and moderate justices, Stevens prevented the dismantling of the major features of the due process revolution: the Fourth Amendment exclusionary rule and the *Miranda* rule. Compared to a staunch liberal such as Justice Brennan, Stevens would be considered a moderate, but in recent years has been viewed as liberal on criminal procedure issues. During the Burger Court era, he voted for the prosecution in forty-four percent of criminal cases. These included his majority opinion extending the automobile search exception to closed containers where the police have probable cause to search the entire vehicle (*United States v. Ross,* 1982);

allowing police to detain the owner of premises while executing a search warrant (*Michigan v. Summers,* 1981); and holding that in cases of multiple representation the Sixth Amendment does not require a trial judge to inquire into the possibility of a conflict of interest (*Burger v. Kemp,* 1987).

However, Justice Stevens has often written or voted in favor of the defendant in dissent: ambiguous *Miranda* (1966) warnings violate a suspect's rights (*California v. Prysock,* 1981); the "public safety" exception to *Miranda* violates a suspect's rights (*New York v. Quarles,* 1984); police should not be able to stop a person on the basis of a barely corroborated anonymous telephone call (*Alabama v. White,* 1990). His dissent in *Moran v. Burbine* (1986), arguing that confessions taken after an attorney attempts to contact a suspect should be inadmissible, is a masterful essay on the fundamental attributes of our adversarial system of justice.

SIGNATURE OPINION *Payton v. New York* (1979), held that an arrest warrant is a prerequisite to a lawful entry of a person's home in order to arrest him. "In this case . . . neither history nor this Nation's experience requires us to disregard the overriding respect for the sanctity of the home that has been embedded in our traditions since the origins of the Republic."

ASSESSMENT Justice Stevens has hewed an independent course not easily identified as either liberal or conservative. He often writes separate concurring opinions to clearly state his position and seems more interested in staking out an independent position than in modifying his views to build coalitions. In First Amendment religion cases he was a reliable liberal, but less so in freedom of expression cases. In cases concerning protection for underprivileged or vulnerable groups, such as aliens, illegitimate children, or prisoners, he tends to find in favor of the rights of the underdog.

FURTHER READING

Bradley G. Canon, "Justice John Paul Stevens: The Lone Ranger in a Black Robe," in *The Burger Court: Political and Judicial Profiles,* edited by Charles M. Lamb and Stephen C. Halpern, pp. 343–374 (Urbana: University of Illinois Press, 1991).

CHAPTER 10

ENTRAPMENT

"Fidelity" to the commands of the Constitution suggests balanced judgment rather than exhortation. The highest "fidelity" is not achieved by the judge who instinctively goes furthest in upholding even the most bizarre claim of individual constitutional rights, any more than it is achieved by a judge who instinctively goes furthest in accepting the most restrictive claims of governmental authorities. The task of this Court, as of other courts, is to "hold the balance true." . . .

—Justice William H. Rehnquist in *Illinois v. Gates,* 462 U.S. 213, 241 (1986)

CHAPTER OUTLINE

KEY TERMS AND PHRASES

Agent Provacateur
Covert facilitation
Criminal Law Approach
Criminal procedure approach
Decoy
Due process defense
Encouragement
Entrapment
Hypothetical person test
Inducement
Objective test
Outrageous conduct test
Predisposition
Subjective test
Supervisory power

INTRODUCTION

Entrapment is a complete defense to a crime; if a court or jury concludes that a defendant was entrapped, the indictment is dismissed or the defendant is acquitted. It seems a strange rule, because the absolved defendant did indeed "commit" the crime charged. Nevertheless, the defendant is released under the law when it appears to judge or jury that police used tactics that planted the idea of the crime in the defendant's mind. The rule is not based on the Constitution. Therefore, each state is free to adopt its own entrapment rule or to have no entrapment rule. It is fair to say that, although the defense of entrapment is not based directly on the Due Process Clauses of the Fifth or Fourteenth amendments, it originated in a sense of common decency and fair play that is akin to the due process notion of fundamental fairness. The entrapment defense announces that there is a limit to what the police will be allowed to do in order to ferret out crime.

Classification and Origins of the Entrapment Defense

Entrapment differs from other criminal procedure doctrines, because it is classified as a rule of substantive criminal law (as a defense to crime) *and* as a rule of criminal procedure.[1] How can this be? Entrapment was created as a criminal law defense by state supreme court decisions in the late nineteenth and early twentieth centuries. They interpreted criminal statutes to declare that the legislature intended to criminalize only persons whose criminal intent was not conceived by the police. As this criminal law defense is clearly concerned with restraining excessive police action, it is also properly a subject of criminal procedure. Entrapment is a uniquely American rule that is not the product of the English common law and has had no counterpart in Roman/civil law (e.g., the German or French legal systems), although this may be changing.[2]

As a criminal law defense, lawyers argued that where police overreached their responsibility and drew the defendant into crime, courts should "condemn excessive police encouragement [and] completely absolve any individuals who commit the encouraged acts."[3] Some sympathetic courts, at first, simply condemned police manipulation that led weak persons into crime, but upheld the convictions. Other courts felt that a defendant who gave in to temptation—even if manufactured by the police—should not have a criminal defense.[4] In 1878, the Michigan Supreme Court in *Saunders v. State,*[5] was the first in the nation to recognize, in dictum, that an entrapment defense existed. A lawyer improperly asked a police officer to leave a courtroom unlocked so that he could have access to certain records. The officer, instead of refusing, laid a trap. The court held that this was not entrapment, but rather only furnished an opportunity to commit the crime. Nonetheless, it ruled that evidence of the "entrapment context of the crime ought to be available to the jury."[6] In a proper case, therefore, a jury could acquit a person, because government officers caused the defendant to commit a crime. A concurring justice in *Saunders* noted that "human nature is frail enough at best, and requires no encouragement in wrong-doing."[7] Over time, state supreme courts went from condemning extreme police encouragement to adopting entrapment as a defense. In the century after *Saunders,* every state had adopted a form of entrapment defense either by court ruling or by statute.

The distinction between whether entrapment is a rule of criminal law or criminal procedure (or both) is important, because it suggests different *theories of entrapment.* Under the **criminal law approach,** the main purpose of entrapment is to protect the essentially innocent. This, the **"subjective" theory** or the **subjective test,** emphasized whether the defendant was **predisposed** to commit the crime in the first place or whether the defendant was *induced* into the commission of the crime by police acts. To those who favor the **criminal procedure approach,** the essence of entrapment lies in the *control of excessive police activity.* This **"objective" theory** (also known as the **objective test**) requires courts to determine when police participation goes too far, whether or not the defendant was predisposed. The debate is not entirely theoretical; different approaches can result in more or fewer entrapment acquittals or dismissals for different sorts of defendants. Under either classification, entrapment belongs in the study of criminal procedure, because it concerns the control of police activity that infringes on personal liberty and involves issues of fairness in the administration of criminal justice.[8]

An important limit on the entrapment defense is that it "is unavailable when causing or threatening bodily injury is an element of the offense."[9] Entrapment is most often claimed as a defense in vice crimes (drug dealing and manufacture, prostitution, loan sharking, liquor bootlegging); bribery and various forms of corrupt practices (e.g., a prison guard smuggling contraband into prison; kickbacks in awarding government contracts); political subversion cases; buying or selling stolen property, extortion, counterfeiting; many white collar crimes; money laundering, and the like. No cases appear to involve crimes of violence.

Before continuing to explore the entrapment defense, we will review police encouragement tactics, and whether police undercover investigation, out of which entrapment claims arise, is constitutional.

Covert Policing: Encouragement and Undercover Agents

Encouragement and undercover investigation are lawful and necessary police functions. Because they involve deception, however, they are prone to abuses. Entrapment, for example, occurs when police undercover agents or informants go too far in using techniques of encouragement. Covert techniques are most useful in enforcing such crimes as drug dealing or bribery, where the perpetrator and victim are willing participants in an illicit business transaction that they conceal from public scrutiny. It may be impossible to penetrate organized or white collar crime without covert policing techniques.

"Encouragement," also called **covert facilitation,** is:

> [T]he activity of the police officer or police agent (a) who acts as a victim; (b) who intends, by his actions, to encourage a suspect to commit a crime; (c) who actually communicates this encouragement to the suspect; and (d) who has thereby some influence upon the commission of the crime. Encouragement does not usually consist of a single act but a series of acts, part of the normal interplay between victim and suspect.[10]

A police **decoy** who poses as a "street person" or a taxi cab driver, and makes an arrest when attacked by a mugger or a cab robber, plays the role of a potential victim and thus provides the opportunity for a crime, but aside from this deception, provides no or little encouragement. An undercover officer who poses as a prostitute, who buys drugs from a dealer, or who offers a bribe to a public official, goes further to encourage a targeted suspect to commit a specific crime. The undercover officer communicates to the target that the officer is a willing participant in an illicit transaction and thus influences the target to engage in the illegal act. Undercover officers engage in a double lie about their identity and the true motives of their transaction.

Encouragement, though lawful and necessary to make arrests in secretive crimes, is inherently unethical conduct that can only be justified by a concept of the "greater good." Some officers who regularly engage in deceit may lie about the specifics of the suspect's behavior in borderline cases in order to make questionable arrests "stick" (see *Law in Society* section, Chapter 3). Courts, therefore, become suspicious of overzealous police officers who convince suspects to commit crimes they would not have otherwise initiated. At this point, encouragement slips over to entrapment: The criminal intent is implanted in the mind of an otherwise law-abiding citizen.

Consider, for example, the common scenario of a female police officer dressed as a "lady of the evening." She pretends to be a consenting participant in the "victimless" crime of prostitution. If a potential "customer" approaches her, and she accepts an illicit offer, her behavior is lawful encouragement because it only provides the opportunity. On the other hand, if the officer actively solicits males walking by and arrests one who accepts her advances, the officer's actions might be considered entrapment by a judge or jury, because it cannot be shown that the passerby *otherwise* would have agreed to engage in sex for hire had he not been approached. It is true that the "John" made the illegal offer, but it may be that he had no prior intention to do the illegal act until he was tempted by the officer's active solicitation. The real danger is that police entrapment *manufactures* crime. Entrapment also results when the police use *civilian* undercover informers to play the role of criminal participants in return for money, nonprosecution, or other benefits.

UNDERCOVER AGENTS AND INFORMERS *Hoffa v. United States* (1966) held that no provision of the Constitution is violated by the simple use of undercover agents. Jimmy Hoffa, national Teamsters Union president, was on trial in Nashville, Tennessee, on federal charges related to union matters. During the trial, Edward Partin, a local Teamsters official in criminal trouble with the federal government, spent time at Hoffa's Nashville apartment with the knowledge and support of federal agents. During this espionage, Partin learned that Hoffa was engaged in jury tampering. In exchange for leniency in his own case and payments to his wife, Partin divulged jury tampering information to federal agents. In a subsequent criminal prosecution against Hoffa for jury tampering, Hoffa claimed that this use of an undercover agent violated his Fourth, Fifth, Sixth, and Fourteenth amendment rights, and that Partin's evidence should therefore be excluded.

The Court, in an opinion by Justice Potter Stewart, held that the entry of an undercover agent into a home does not violate the search and seizure amendment. Applying the pre-*Katz* (1967) "constitutionally protected area" doctrine, it found that no interest protected by the amendment was violated. "Neither this Court nor any member of it has ever expressed the view that the Fourth Amendment protects a wrongdoer's misplaced belief that a person to whom he voluntarily confides his wrongdoing will not reveal it" *(Hoffa v. United States)*. Clearly, even under the *Katz* "expectation of privacy" doctrine, the misplaced confidence in a *false friend* does not violate the right to be free from illegal search and seizure.[11]

Nor does an undercover agent violate the right to be free from *self-incrimination*. The Fifth Amendment prohibits the government from *compelling* a person to testify. The statements in *Hoffa* were *wholly voluntary*. The deception maintained by undercover agents is not a substitute for Fifth Amendment compulsion. Neither was Hoffa's Sixth Amendment *right to counsel* violated, because Hoffa could not prove that Partin heard incriminating statements during Hoffa's sessions with his lawyer. The right to counsel does include "the right of a defendant and his counsel to prepare for trial without intrusion upon their confidential relationship by an agent of the Government, the defendant's trial adversary." However, Partin's mere presence in the apartment while Hoffa conferred with his lawyers did not violate the Constitution. The Court also ruled that the government has no obligation to arrest a person as soon as it has enough evidence to support probable cause, so as to protect the right to counsel. "There is no constitutional right to be arrested." An investigation may continue after the police have probable cause to arrest so as to gather more convincing evidence for use at a trial.

Finally, the Court rejected Hoffa's claim that using an undercover agent violated his Fourteenth Amendment due process right to fundamental fairness because (1) the use of informers is an odious practice and (2) given Partin's motives, there was a high probability that he would commit perjury. Quoting Learned Hand, a renowned federal judge, the Court said, "Courts have countenanced the use of informers from time immemorial; in cases of conspiracy, or in other cases when the crime consists of preparing for another crime, it is usually necessary to rely upon them or upon accomplices because the criminals will almost certainly proceed covertly. . . ."[12] As for the second point, the Court noted that any possible perjury by Partin could be uncovered through cross-examination. Informers are bound by the legal and constitutional restrictions that apply to all witnesses and governmental agents. But "the use of secret informers is not *per se* unconstitutional" (*Hoffa v. United States* 1966).

Chief Justice Warren, perhaps disturbed by Attorney General Robert Kennedy's personal vendetta to indict Hoffa, dissented.[13] He did not seek an absolute ban on undercover police work, but a reversal of the conviction under a flexible rule whereby a court could throw out evidence obtained by an undercover agent in specific cases "in order to insure that the protections of the Constitution are respected and to maintain the integrity of federal law enforcement." (*Hoffa v. United States* 1966). The Chief Justice argued that the Court should use its *supervisory power* over federal criminal justice to exclude evidence or order new trials in flagrant circumstances. No other justice joined him in this view.

THE SUBJECTIVE AND OBJECTIVE TESTS OF ENTRAPMENT

Development of Federal Entrapment Law

As with state cases, an 1878 federal case stated *in dictum* that a court should not "lend its countenance to a violation of positive law, or to contrivances for inducing a person to commit a crime."[14] For the first time, in 1915, a federal appeals court held that a conviction was obtained by entrapment. In *Woo Wai v. United States,*[15] federal undercover agents, who had no reason to believe that Woo Wai was smuggling aliens into the United States, nevertheless spent several months pressuring him to assist them in bringing Chinese aliens into the United States from Mexico. He continually resisted their pleas, saying that to do so was illegal. He finally relented and was convicted. The Ninth Circuit Court of Appeals overturned the conviction, saying, "We are of the opinion that it is against public policy to sustain a conviction obtained" in this way "and a sound public policy can be upheld only by denying the criminality of those who are thus induced to commit acts which infringe the letter of the law."[16]

The Supreme Court first adopted the entrapment defense in *Sorrells v. United States* (1932). *Sorrells* is especially important because its majority and concurring opinions clearly enunciated the subjective and objective theories that continue to frame legal analysis of entrapment. The subjective-predisposition-**inducement** theory was explained by Chief Justice Charles Evans Hughes writing for the majority: a defendant not predisposed to commit a crime may claim entrapment as a defense if the idea for the crime was implanted by the police. An undercover Prohibition agent, pretending to be an out of town business man, was introduced to Sorrells by a third person. They visited at Sorrells' home for an hour and a half, sharing their mutual war experiences. The agent, four or five times, said he would like to bring home some whiskey. Sorrells said he "did not fool with whiskey." After repeated requests, however, he left his home and returned a half hour later with a half-gallon of liquor, which he sold to the "business man." There was no evidence that Sorrells was a professional "rum runner."

Chief Justice Hughes ruled that, although the National Prohibition Law contained no statutory defense of entrapment, it was within the authority of the Court to *interpret the statute* to find such a defense. To read the statute literally would produce a clear injustice. "We are unable to conclude that it was the intention of Congress in enacting this statute that its processes of detection and enforcement should be abused by the instigation by government officials of an act on the part of persons otherwise innocent in order to lure them to its commission and to punish them."[17] Merely using an "artifice or stratagem" to catch criminals by enabling law enforcement to "reveal the criminal design" is legal and often necessary. However, "[a] different question is presented when the criminal design originates with the officials of the Government, and they implant in the mind of an innocent person the disposition to commit the alleged offense and induce its commission in order that they may prosecute." In such case, the defendant may raise to the jury the defense that she was entrapped and be acquitted on that ground.

Justice Owen Roberts, concurring, joined by Justices Brandeis and Stone, argued vigorously for a different theory as the basis for entrapment. He criticized the majority's reasoning that Congress intended to create an entrapment defense in a Prohibition statute that was silent on the subject. "This seems a strained and unwarranted construction of the statute; and amounts, in fact, to judicial amendment. It is not merely broad construction, but addition of an element not contained in the legislation." He then proposed, as the true basis of entrapment, a judicial policy of fair law enforcement:

> The doctrine rests, rather, on a fundamental rule of public policy. The protection of its own functions and the preservation of the purity of its own temple belongs only to the courts. It is the province of the court and of the court alone to protect itself and the government from such prostitution of the criminal law. The violation of the principles of justice by the entrapment of the unwary into crime should be dealt with by the court no matter by whom or at what stage of the proceedings. . . . Proof of entrapment, at any stage of the case, requires the court to stop the prosecution, direct that the indictment be quashed, and the defendant set at liberty. If in doubt as to the facts it may submit the issue of entrapment to a jury for advice. But whatever may be the finding upon such submission the power and the duty to act remain with the court and not with the jury," (*Sorrells v. United States,* 1932)

Twenty-five years later, the Court clarified the *Sorrells* doctrine in *Sherman v. United States* (1956), in which a majority of the Court again upheld the entrapment defense based on the subjective theory, while a concurring minority urged the objective theory. The debate was not over the existence of the entrapment defense, but its rationale.

• CASE & COMMENTS •

Sherman v. United States

356 U.S. 369, 78 S.Ct. 819, 2 L.Ed.2d 848 (1958)

MR. CHIEF JUSTICE WARREN delivered the opinion of the Court.

The issue before us is whether petitioner's conviction should be set aside on the ground that as a matter of law the defense of entrapment was established. **[a]** Petitioner was convicted under an indictment charging three sales of narcotics in violation of 21 U.S.C. sec. 174. *** [P]etitioner's defense was a claim of entrapment: an agent of the Federal Government induced him to take part in illegal transactions when otherwise he would not have done so.

In late August 1951, Kalchinian, a government informer, first met petitioner at a doctor's office where apparently both were being treated to be cured of narcotics addiction. Several accidental meetings followed, either at the doctor's office or at the pharmacy where both filled their prescriptions from the doctor. From mere greetings, conversation progressed to a discussion of mutual experiences and problems, including their attempts to overcome addiction to narcotics. Finally Kalchinian asked petitioner if he knew of a good source of narcotics. He asked petitioner to supply him with a source because he was not responding to treatment. From the first, petitioner tried to avoid the issue. Not until after a number of repetitions of the request, predicated on Kalchinian's presumed suffering, did petitioner finally acquiesce. Several times thereafter he obtained a quantity of narcotics which he shared with Kalchinian. **[b]** Each time petitioner told Kalchinian that the total cost of narcotics he obtained was twenty-five dollars and that Kalchinian owed him fifteen dollars. The informer thus bore the cost of his share of the narcotics plus the taxi and other expenses necessary to obtain the drug. After several such sales Kalchinian informed agents of the Bureau of Narcotics that he had another seller for them. On three occasions during November 1951, government agents observed petitioner give narcotics to Kalchinian in return for money supplied by the Government.

At the trial the factual issue was whether the informer had convinced an otherwise unwilling person to commit a criminal act or whether petitioner was already predisposed to commit the act and exhibited only the natural hesitancy of one acquainted with the narcotics trade. The issue of entrapment went to the jury, and a conviction resulted. Petitioner was sentenced to imprisonment for ten years. ***

In *Sorrells v. United States,* 287 U.S. 435 (1932), this Court firmly recognized the defense of entrapment in the federal courts. The intervening years have in no way detracted from the principles underlying that decision. The function of law enforcement is the prevention of crime and the apprehension of criminals. Manifestly, that function does not include the manufacturing of crime.

[a] If the Federal statute cited contained no specific entrapment defense, how can entrapment be established "as a matter of law"? Criminal law defenses involve either a lack of criminal intent (e.g., insanity, infancy) or an impairment of criminal knowledge because of a mistake of fact. Do such considerations apply to entrapment?

[b] Why are the facts recited at such length? Are Kalchinian's actions effective narcotics law enforcement?

• CASE & COMMENTS •

Criminal activity is such that stealth and strategy are necessary weapons in the arsenal of the police officer. **[c]** However, "A different question is presented when the criminal design originates with the officials of the Government, and they implant in the mind of an innocent person the disposition to commit the alleged offense and induce its commission in order that they may prosecute." *** Then stealth and strategy become as objectionable police methods as the coerced confession and the unlawful search. Congress could not have intended that its statutes were to be enforced by tempting innocent persons into violations. **[d]**

However, the fact that government agents "merely afford opportunities or facilities for the commission of the offense does not" constitute entrapment. Entrapment occurs only when the criminal conduct was "the product of the *creative* activity" of law-enforcement officials. *** To determine whether entrapment has been established, a line must be drawn between the trap for the unwary innocent and the trap for the unwary criminal. The principles by which the courts are to make this determination were outlined in *Sorrells.* On the one hand, at trial the accused may examine the conduct of the government agent; and on the other hand, the accused will be subjected to an "appropriate and searching inquiry into his own conduct and predisposition" as bearing on his claim of innocence. ***

We conclude from the evidence that entrapment was established as a matter of law. In so holding, we are not choosing between conflicting witnesses, nor judging credibility. Aside from recalling Kalchinian, who was the Government's witness, the defense called no witnesses. We reach our conclusion from the undisputed testimony of the prosecution's witnesses.

It is patently clear that petitioner was induced by Kalchinian. **[e]** The informer himself testified that, believing petitioner to be undergoing a cure for narcotics addiction, he nonetheless sought to persuade petitioner to obtain for him a source of narcotics. In Kalchinian's own words we are told of the accidental, yet recurring, meetings, the ensuing conversations concerning mutual experiences in regard to narcotics addiction, and then of Kalchinian's resort to sympathy. One request was not enough, for Kalchinian tells us that additional ones were necessary to overcome, first, petitioner's refusal, then his evasiveness, and then his hesitancy in order to achieve capitulation. Kalchinian not only procured a source of narcotics but apparently also induced petitioner to return to the habit. Finally, assured of a catch, Kalchinian informed the authorities so that they could close the net. *** Although he was not being paid, Kalchinian was an active government informer who had but recently been the instigator of at least two other prosecutions. Undoubtedly the impetus for such achievements was the fact that in 1951 Kalchinian was himself under criminal charges for illegally selling narcotics and had not yet been sentenced. It makes no difference that the sales for which petitioner was convicted occurred after a series of sales. **[f]** They were not independent acts subsequent to the inducement but part of a course of conduct which was the product of the inducement. In his testimony the federal agent in charge of the case admitted that he never bothered to question Kalchinian about the way he had made contact with petitioner. ***

The Government sought to overcome the defense of entrapment by claiming that petitioner evinced a "ready complaisance" to accede to Kalchinian's request. Aside from a record of past convictions *** the Government's case is unsupported. There is no evidence that petitioner himself was in the trade. When his apartment was searched after arrest, no narcotics were found. There is no significant evidence that petitioner even made a profit on any sale to Kalchinian. The Government's characterization of petitioner's hesitancy to Kalchinian's request as the natural wariness of the criminal cannot fill the evidentiary void. **[g]**

[CHIEF JUSTICE WARREN next stated that Sherman's conviction for narcotics sale in 1942 and another for possession in 1946 "are insufficient to prove petitioner had a readiness to sell narcotics at the time Kalchinian approached him. ***"]

[c] Was Sherman "otherwise innocent" in August 1951? Was he still "otherwise innocent" in November 1951 when he sold the heroin? Suppose his motive was to ease the pain and suffering of his new friend Kalchinian: is good motive a valid defense to a felony?

[d] If the statute is silent about entrapment, how can the Chief Justice be so certain about the intent of Congress? Compare Chief Justice Warren's bald statement in this regard to Justice Frankfurter's criticism of this "legal fiction" below.

[e] Inducement appears to be the deciding factor in making out entrapment. The Court does not assert its supervisory power as the basis of this defense. Thus, it appears that the Court finds entrapment to be a defense "inherent" in the statute. Is the defense inherent in all criminal statutes? Suppose that during the heyday of the late 1960s, a "freelance" government informer infiltrated a radical group made up of immature and volatile persons aged eighteen to twenty-one with no previous history of violence and convinced them to commit violent crimes such as arson, kidnapping, or assaults? Would entrapment be inherent in the arson, kidnapping or assault statutes?

[f] This says that the government *caused* the crime.

[g] Prior criminal activity is relevant to establish that the defendant was predisposed to commit the crime. Do these convictions only go to show that Sherman has been a heroin addict for a long time?

• CASE & COMMENTS •

The case at bar illustrates an evil which the defense of entrapment is designed to overcome. **[h]** The government informer entices someone attempting to avoid narcotics not only into carrying out an illegal sale but also into returning to the habit of use. Selecting the proper time, the informer then tells the government agent. The set-up is accepted by the agent without even a question as to the manner in which the informer encountered the seller. Thus the Government plays on the weaknesses of an innocent party and beguiles him into committing crimes which he otherwise would not have attempted. Law enforcement does not require methods such as this.

[CHIEF JUSTICE WARREN went on to reject the position of the dissent, that the case should be decided on the grounds put forward by Justice Roberts in the *Sorrells* case]. ***

Reversed and remanded.

MR. JUSTICE FRANKFURTER, whom MR. JUSTICE DOUGLAS, MR. JUSTICE HARLAN, and MR. JUSTICE BRENNAN join, concurring in the result. **[i]**

Although agreeing with the Court that the undisputed facts show entrapment as a matter of law, I reach this result by a route different from the Court's.

*** [T]he basis of this defense, affording guidance for its application in particular circumstances, is as much in doubt today as it was when the defense was first recognized over forty years ago, although entrapment has been the decisive issue in many prosecutions. The lower courts have continued gropingly to express the feeling of outrage at conduct of law enforcers that brought recognition of the defense in the first instance, but without the formulated basis in reason that it is the first duty of courts to construct for justifying and guiding emotion and instinct.

Today's opinion does not promote this judicial desideratum, and fails to give the doctrine of entrapment the solid foundation that the decisions of the lower courts and criticism of learned writers have clearly shown is needed. *** **[j]**

It is surely sheer fiction to suggest that a conviction cannot be had when a defendant has been entrapped by government officers or informers because "Congress could not have intended that its statutes were to be enforced by tempting innocent persons into violations." **[k]** In these cases raising claims of entrapment, the only legislative intention that can with any show of reason be extracted from the statute is the intention to make criminal precisely the conduct in which the defendant has engaged. That conduct includes all the elements necessary to constitute criminality. Without compulsion and "knowingly," where that is requisite, the defendant has violated the statutory command. If he is to be relieved from the usual punitive consequences, it is on no account because he is innocent of the offense described. In these circumstances, conduct is not less criminal because the result of temptation, whether the tempter is a private person or a government agent or informer.

The courts refuse to convict an entrapped defendant, not because his conduct falls outside the proscription of the statute, but because, even if his guilt be admitted, the methods employed on behalf of the Government to bring about conviction cannot be countenanced. *** Insofar as they are used as instrumentalities in the administration of criminal justice, the federal courts have an obligation to set their face against enforcement of the law by lawless means or means that violate rationally vindicated standards of justice, and to refuse to sustain such methods by effectuating them. **[l]** They do this in the exercise of a recognized jurisdiction to formulate and apply "proper standards for the enforcement of the federal criminal law in the federal courts," *McNabb v. United States,* 318 U.S. 332, 341 (1943), an obligation that goes beyond the conviction of the particular defendant before the court. Public confidence in the fair and honorable administration of justice, upon which ultimately depends the rule of law, is the transcending value at stake.

[h] Is the "evil" the method used by the government to obtain a conviction, or that it preyed on the victim's weakness? Would the evil be the same if Sherman regularly sold small quantities of heroin to support a habit? Would it be the same if he sold larger quantities to supplement his income? What if he sold as much heroin as he could to become rich?

[i] This lineup of justices includes two liberals and two conservatives—two who opposed the incorporation doctrine and two who formulated the due process revolution. Labeling justices has limited uses.

[j] It is the function of the Supreme Court to establish general rules for the guidance of lower courts, not simply to decide individual cases.

[k] This may be true, but legal fictions often serve a useful policy purpose. It is probably the case that it was easier for courts to establish entrapment by resorting to the notion of a criminal law defense than to base its decision on its supervisory power over federal police.

[l] Justice Frankfurter thus believes that the Court should exercise its *supervisory power* to establish entrapment. Is this an appropriate practice for the Court to pursue? If deceptive practices such as undercover agents are necessary, how are courts to distinguish between legitimate and illegitimate techniques? Might the public be upset with the courts "tying the hands" of the police?

• CASE & COMMENTS •

The formulation of these standards does not in any way conflict with the statute the defendant has violated, or involve the initiation of a judicial policy disregarding or qualifying that framed by Congress. **[m]** A false choice is put when it is said that either the defendant's conduct does not fall within the statute or he must be convicted. The statute is wholly directed to defining and prohibiting the substantive offense concerned and expresses no purpose, either permissive or prohibitory, regarding the police conduct that will be tolerated in the detection of crime. A statute prohibiting the sale of narcotics is as silent on the question of entrapment as it is on the admissibility of illegally obtained evidence. **[n]** It is enacted, however, on the basis of certain presuppositions concerning the established legal order and the role of the courts within that system in formulating standards for the administration of criminal justice when Congress itself has not specifically legislated to that end. Specific statutes are to be fitted into an antecedent legal system.

[m] Justice Frankfurter here attempts to head off the criticism that his "objective" approach involved "judicial legislation"—an undermining of congressional authority and a violation of the separation of powers doctrine.

[n] The Rule of Law, the philosophical basis of our legal system, here is suggested as a specific, practical basis for the exercise of the Court's power. Perhaps a majority of the Court did not adopt Justice Frankfurter's formulation out of caution that it is difficult to put limits on the Rule of Law as an operational principle.

* * *

The crucial question, not easy of answer, to which the court must direct itself is whether the police conduct revealed in the particular case falls below standards, to which common feelings respond, for the proper use of governmental power. **[o]** For answer it is wholly irrelevant to ask if the "intention" to commit the crime originated with the defendant or government officers, or if the criminal conduct was the product of "the creative activity" of law-enforcement officials. Yet in the present case the Court repeats and purports to apply these unrevealing tests. Of course in every case of this kind the intention that the particular crime be committed originates with the police, and without their inducement the crime would not have occurred. But it is perfectly clear from such decisions as the decoy letter cases in this Court, *** where the police in effect simply furnished the opportunity for the commission of the crime, that this is not enough to enable the defendant to escape conviction.

[o] This is a candid admission that the "objective" test rests on the Court's evaluation of popular feelings of justice. This is akin to Justice Frankfurter's "shocks the conscience" test in *Rochin v. California* (1952).

The intention referred to, therefore, must be a general intention or predisposition to commit, whenever the opportunity should arise, crimes of the kind solicited, and in proof of such a predisposition evidence has often been admitted to show the defendant's reputation, criminal activities, and prior disposition. The danger of prejudice in such a situation, particularly if the issue of entrapment must be submitted to the jury and disposed of by a general verdict of guilty or innocent, is evident. The defendant must either forego the claim of entrapment or run the substantial risk that, in spite of instructions, the jury will allow a criminal record or bad reputation to weigh in its determination of guilt of the specific offense of which he stands charged. **[p]** Furthermore, a test that looks to the character and predisposition of the defendant rather than the conduct of the police loses sight of the underlying reason for the defense of entrapment. No matter what the defendant's past record and present inclinations to criminality, or the depths to which he has sunk in the estimation of society, certain police conduct to ensnare him into further crime is not to be tolerated by an advanced society. **[q]** And in the present case it is clear that the Court in fact reverses the conviction because of the conduct of the informer Kalchinian, and not because the Government has failed to draw a convincing picture of petitioner's past criminal conduct. Permissible police activity does not vary according to the particular defendant concerned; surely if two suspects have been solicited at the same time in the same manner, one should not go to jail simply because he has been convicted before and is said to have a criminal disposition. ***

[p] Another weakness with the majority's approach is that it drags a defendant's prior criminal history into the trial; this is usually forbidden by rules of evidence because of its powerful prejudicial effect. Such a rule also detracts from the focus on improper police activity.

[q] Justice Frankfurter offers a "police conduct" test of entrapment. What is the standard for improper police conduct? Does it depend on outrage expressed in the public media? on public opinion polls? on the feelings of the judge who is hearing a case? It seems that there are subjective elements to the "objective rule."

• CASE & COMMENTS •

This does not mean that the police may not act so as to detect those engaged in criminal conduct and ready and willing to commit further crimes should the occasion arise. Such indeed is their obligation. **[r]** It does mean that in holding out inducements they should act in such a manner as is likely to induce to the commission of crime only these persons and not others who would normally avoid crime and through self-struggle resist ordinary temptations. This test shifts attention from the record and predisposition of the particular defendant to the conduct of the police and the likelihood, objectively considered, that it would entrap only those ready and willing to commit crime. **[s]** It is as objective a test as the subject matter permits, and will give guidance in regulating police conduct that is lacking when the reasonableness of police suspicions must be judged or the criminal disposition of the defendant retrospectively appraised. It draws directly on the fundamental intuition that led in the first instance to the outlawing of "entrapment" as a prosecutorial instrument. The power of government is abused and directed to an end for which it was not constituted when employed to promote rather than detect crime and to bring about the downfall of those who, left to themselves, might well have obeyed the law. Human nature is weak enough and sufficiently beset by temptations without government adding to them and generating crime.

[r] This is the "hypothetical person" test.

[s] This appears to be the source of the labels "objective test" for the position of the concurring justices and "subjective test" for the majority position.

* * *

[JUSTICE FRANKFURTER concluded by noting that under an objective test that focuses on police conduct, the issue would be decided before a judge in a hearing before trial, rather than being submitted to the more emotional arena of a jury trial.]

The Entrapment Tests in Action

The subjective and objective tests overlap. Both are concerned with police conduct and both seek "to determine whether the government's involvement is the principal cause of the crime."[18] This meshing of concerns is observed in *Jacobson v. United States* (1992), the most recent Supreme Court entrapment case. The Court, 5–4, reversed the conviction of Keith Jacobson, "a 56-year-old veteran-turned-farmer who supported his elderly father in Nebraska" finding that he was entrapped into receiving literature depicting minors engaged in sexually explicit conduct. The objective test was not urged by any of the justices; four dissenters argued that Jacobson was not entrapped.

In 1984, Jacobson lawfully purchased two magazines through the mails that contained photographs of nude preteen and teenage boys, but did not contain displays of sexual conduct. Three months after this purchase, Congress enacted the Child Protection Act of 1984, which criminalizes the knowing receipt through the mails of a "visual depiction [that] involves the use of a minor engaging in sexually explicit conduct." To enforce this law, the Postal Service and the Customs Service set up several fictitious organizations as sting operations to prosecute purchasers of child pornography. These Services obtained Jacobson's name from a mailing list from his 1984 purchase. For two and a half years, they sent him a stream of information from phony front organizations such as the "American Hedonist Society," "Midlands Data Research," and "Heartland Institute for a New Tomorrow" (HINT). These mailings did not contain advertisements or solicitations to purchase "kiddy porn." Instead, the sting operations enrolled Jacobson in a group that purported to support the First Amendment right to purchase sexually oriented material. Jacobson mailed back several questionnaires indicating that he "enjoyed" sexual materials involving "pre-teen sex" but that he was opposed to pedophilia. One agent began to write to Jacobson as a pen-pal, who "mirrored" Jacobson's interests. Jacobson wrote to him twice and then discontinued the correspondence. Finally, after twenty-six months of this, Jacobson was twice sent catalogues advertising magazines with photographs of young boys engaging in sex. Jacobson twice purchased such magazines from the fictitious businesses run by the government. A search of Jacobson's home turned up no pornography other than that which had been mailed by the government agency.

In overturning Jacobson's conviction, the Court added several important rules to the federal law of entrapment under the subjective-predisposition theory. First, the Court noted that if Jacobson had simply been sent a catalogue and had purchased child pornography, this would be lawful encouragement and not illegal entrapment. It is true that he was predisposed to purchase these materials in March of 1987 when he responded to the sting. But it is not clear that he was predisposed to do so in 1985 when the government sting went after him. There was no evidence that he had purchased child pornography from other sources while the government was bombarding him with information and questionnaires from supposed civil rights organizations. Therefore, the issue of predisposition must be assessed "at the moment of the government's *first contact,* rather than at the moment the government induces the defendant to commit the crime."[19] Justice White, writing for the majority, stated, "it is our view that the Government did not prove that this predisposition was independent and not the product of the attention that the Government had directed at petitioner since January 1985" (*Jacobson v. United States,* p. 550).

Second, the Court placed that the *burden of proof* on the government to "prove beyond reasonable doubt that the defendant was disposed to commit the criminal act prior to first being approached by Government agents." Third, *Jacobson* held that the evidence of predisposition has to be based on past *criminal* acts which are *substantially similar* to the act for which the prosecution is based. The government relied on Keith Jacobson's 1984 purchases of magazines with pictures of nude boys, "[b]ut this is scant if any proof of petitioner's predisposition to commit an illegal act, the criminal character of which a defendant is presumed to know. It may indicate a predisposition to view sexually oriented photographs that are responsive to his sexual tastes; but evidence that merely indicates a generic inclination to act within a broad range, not all of which is criminal, is of little probative value in establishing predisposition" (*Jacobson v. United States,* p. 550).

Justice O'Connor, dissenting, argued strenuously against the rule that predisposition must be determined at the outset of the government's contact with a suspect. She feared such a rule "has the potential to be misread by lower courts as well as criminal investigators as requiring that the Government must have sufficient evidence of a defendant's predisposition *before it ever seeks to contact him*" (*Jacobson v. United States,* p. 557, emphasis added). In the dissent's view, Jacobson made a purchase the first time one was offered, and this was merely offering him the opportunity to commit the crime, not entrapment.

Although *Jacobson* reaffirms the subjective test, the case shows a preoccupation with the heavy-handed practices of the two federal agencies. "[W]hat is new in *Jacobson* is the extent to which the Court was willing to take its disapproval of police methods as authorization to immunize the defendant."[20] Justice White dwelled on the facts of government excess in this case: twenty-six months of repeated mailings; phony front organizations; and appeals to genuine First Amendment rights to snag a person who, despite his sexual inclinations, was not otherwise a purchaser of child pornography. The government claimed that the sting "resulted in 147 convictions, of which 35 cases 'disclosed evidence of ongoing or past child sexual abuse.'... There were also four suicides in this group, including another Nebraska farmer and a Wisconsin man who left a note saying he had been 'cursed with a demon for a sexual preference.'"[21] The Court said that the government cast its net too broadly.

PROOF OF PREDISPOSITION A major preoccupation with the subjective test is *proving* predisposition. Some courts have tended to rule that it is not necessary to prove that the defendant intended to commit the *specific* crime charged at a specific time and place. These courts say that the defendant's general intent or purpose to commit *a* crime when the opportunity was provided is sufficient: "[i]t is sufficient if the defendant is of a frame of mind such that once his attention is called to the criminal opportunity, his decision to commit the crime is the product of his own preference and not the product of government persuasion." Other courts have ruled that the predisposition must be to commit the specific crime charged.[22]

The kind of evidence needed to prove predisposition generally falls into six categories: (1) the defendant's character or reputation, including any prior criminal record; (2) whether the government agent was the first to suggest criminal activity; (3) whether the defendant was engaged in the criminal activity for profit; (4) whether the defendant evidenced reluctance to commit the offense, overcome only by repeated government inducement or persuasion; (5) the nature of the inducement or persuasion supplied by the police; and (6) whether the defendant has the ability to carry out the crime.[23]

These factors are not mechanically applied. For example, from the totality of the evidence in *United States v. Sherman* (1956), it was apparent that Sherman's two past drug convictions that were several years old showed only that he was an addict, and not that he was engaged in the illicit business of drug selling. Also, in *Jacobson* (1992), the Supreme Court made it clear that the relevant inquiry is to prior crimes, not to prior acts. As for willingness to commit the crime, a federal court held that expressing a willingness to deal in stolen property was not so similar to the crime of dealing in firearms that the prosecution could introduce those remarks in a firearms case.[24] Sophistication about how to commit a crime is a good measure of predisposition, but the inability to carry out a crime is not an infallible gauge of lack of predisposition.[25]

An example of the objective test is the Florida case of *Cruz v. State.*[26] A police decoy, posing as a drunken "skid row bum," smelling of alcohol, had $150 sticking out of a pocket. Cruz passed by and noticed the money. He returned after fifteen minutes, took the cash, and was arrested. Although the decoy was placed in a high-crime Tampa neighborhood, there was no specific problem with drunks being "rolled" there. The amount of money protruding from the decoy's pocket was said by the Florida Supreme Court to be *too tempting*. It was large enough to create a substantial risk that an ordinary person who would not usually seek to rob drunks would be tempted to take the money.

Both the subjective and objective tests of entrapment have weaknesses. The legislative intent basis of the subjective test is a legal fiction, that is "extraordinarily tenuous considering that the defendant has, in fact, engaged in legislatively proscribed conduct."[27] More importantly, a criminal law-subjective approach does not rest logically on the concept of moral blameworthiness, a bedrock principle of substantive criminal law. If a person commits a crime and can show no predisposition to commit it, but was induced into the crime by a *private person,* this is no defense. Yet, the identical inducement by an undercover police agent does constitute a defense. This clearly indicates that even the subjective test is mainly concerned with improper government action.[28]

The objective test focuses on how extensive or egregious the conduct of the police is. As Justice Frankfurter's concurring opinion in *Sherman* honestly noted, this determination cannot be made with scientific exactitude: "The crucial question, not easy of answer, to which the court must direct itself is whether the police conduct revealed in the particular case falls below standards, to which common feelings respond, for the proper use of governmental power."

The objective test was adopted by the *Model Penal Code* in this formulation:

> A public law enforcement official or a person acting in cooperation with such an official perpetrates an entrapment if for the purpose of obtaining evidence of the commission of an offense, he induces or encourages another person to engage in conduct constituting such offense by either:
> (a) making knowingly false representations designed to induce the belief that such conduct is not prohibited; or
> (b) employing methods of persuasion or inducement that create substantial risk that such an offense will be committed by persons other than those who are ready to commit it.[29]

Part (b) is known as the **hypothetical person test.** Justice Frankfurter stated in *Sherman* that police encouragement should be of such a nature "as is likely to induce to the commission of crime only these persons [who are ready and willing to commit the crime] and not others who would normally avoid crime and through self-struggle resist ordinary temptations." Otherwise, the government has the resources to offer such lavish temptations that morally weaker persons—who were not bent on crime—would succumb. The objective test also avoids the problem of having to introduce potentially prejudicial evidence to the jury about the defendant's past crime in order to prove predisposition.

The objective test, though, has some flaws. First, police actions may be declared objectively to be such that would entrap a hypothetical person, and lead to the acquittal of defendants who are clearly predisposed—ready, willing, and able to commit crimes. Next, trying to determine whether particular police encouragement would entrap a "hypothetical person" is highly speculative and may be determined more by the predilection of the judges than by any objective standard. The Court's focus on police operations in most cases tends to show that "separation of the objective and subjective approaches is unworkable. Inducement cannot be considered in isolation from predisposition."[30] This points the way to the consideration of other approaches to entrapment.

Other Tests: Due Process and Outrageous Conduct

In recent years, both federal and state courts have considered alternatives to the subjective and objective tests. In 1971, for the first time, a federal court threw out the conviction of predisposed, professional manufacturers of bootleg whiskey because for two and a half years a government agent acted as a business collaborator with them. The Ninth Circuit Court of Appeals did not give a statutory or constitutional rationale for its holding; it obviously was offended by **outrageous governmental conduct** that violated the court's sense of justice.[31]

The issue of whether an outrageous conduct test existed as a matter of due process was twice considered by the Supreme Court in the 1970s. In both cases, the Court's majority (1) applied the subjective test and found the defendants were predisposed, and (2) announced that a **due process defense** was theoretically possible in cases of outrageous governmental conduct. In *United States v. Russell* (1973), a federal undercover narcotics agent, Joe Shapiro, got to know three men (Richard Russell and John and Patrick Connolly) who had an operating methamphetamine laboratory. Shapiro offered to supply the defendants with the chemical phenyl-2-propanone—a legal, but hard to get essential ingredient in manufacturing methamphetamine—in return for one-half of the drug produced. Shapiro said he had to see a sample of the drug which they were making and the laboratory where it was being produced. Shapiro supplied the chemical and watched the methamphetamine being made in the laboratory. The five-justice majority, applying the subjective test, found no entrapment because the defendants were predisposed. Further, the Court reversed the Ninth Circuit Court of Appeals, which had overturned Russell's conviction on grounds of "an intolerable degree of governmental participation in the criminal enterprise." The Circuit Court decision was based on two theories. First, that entrapment existed whenever the government *furnished contraband* to a suspect.[32] The second rationale was not entrapment but what has come to be called the outrageous government conduct test: "because a government investigator was so enmeshed in the criminal activity . . . the prosecution of the defendants was . . . repugnant to the American criminal justice system."[33] The Circuit Court said that both rationales "are premised on fundamental concepts of due process and evince the reluctance of the judiciary to countenance overzealous law enforcement."[34]

Justice Rehnquist, writing for five justices, upheld the *Sherman* predisposition test. He argued that the facts showed that the chemical could have been obtained by the defendants from other sources and, therefore, they could not benefit from the Circuit Court's rule. (This fact was disputed in Justice Stewart's dissent). His opinion disapproved of the discretion that the due process rule would place in the hands of judges:

> [T]he defense of entrapment *** was not intended to give the federal judiciary a "chancellor's foot" veto over law enforcement practices of which it did not approve. The execution of the federal laws under our Constitution is confided primarily to the Executive Branch of the Government, subject to applicable constitutional and statutory limitations and to judicially fashioned rules to enforce those limitations. We think that the decision of the Court of Appeals in this case quite unnecessarily introduces an unmanageably subjective standard which is contrary to the holdings of this Court in *Sorrells* and *Sherman.* (*United States v. Russell,* 1973, p. 435)

On the other hand, the majority opinion also stated, "While we may some day be presented with a situation in which the conduct of law enforcement agents is so outrageous that due process principles would absolutely bar the government from invoking judicial processes to obtain a conviction, . . . the instant case is distinctly not of that breed" (*United States v. Russell* (1973), pp. 431–32). "This 'some day' dicta, as the passage has come to be known, has been so widely cited in connection with the outrageous government conduct defense that it has effectively become a battle cry for the defense's proponents."[35] Subsequently, Justice Rehnquist tried, but failed, to kill the possibility of the Court ever adopting a due process entrapment defense.

In *Hampton v. United States* (1976), the Court once again refused to apply a due process theory of entrapment. Hampton was convicted of selling heroin to two Drug Enforcement Administration (DEA) agents. The sale was set up by DEA informant Hutton, who was an acquaintance of Hampton. The two were shooting pool when Hampton noticed "track" (needle) marks on Hutton's arms. Hampton said that he needed money and knew where he could get some heroin. Hutton said he could find a buyer and Hampton suggested that he "get in touch with those people." Hutton then called a DEA officer and arranged a sale. Hampton made two sales—for $145 and $500—to DEA agents posing as dealers. The government claimed that Hampton obtained the drugs on his own. Hampton claimed that Hutton introduced him to a pharmacist who manufactured a legal counterfeit drug; that he and Hutton were supplied with this supposedly counterfeit drug; and that they sold this to another person before selling it to the DEA agents.

Hampton was convicted by a jury. The judge refused to instruct the jury they must acquit whenever the government supplies drugs to a suspect before arresting him. The Supreme Court upheld the conviction. The lineup of votes was important to the continued existence of a due process-outrageous conduct entrapment test. There was no majority opinion in *Hampton.* Justice Rehnquist, writing the plurality opinion for himself, Chief Justice Burger and Justice White, stated that in *Russell,* "We ruled out the possibility that the defense of entrapment could ever be based upon governmental misconduct in a case, such as this one, where the predisposition of the defendant to commit the crime was established." Justice Rehnquist tried to reverse the meaning of the 'some day' dicta in *Russell.* He asserted that the difference between *Hampton* and *Russell* was only one of degree, despite the fact that the government supplied Hampton with illegal drugs, which "constituted the *corpus delicti* for the sale," while the substance supplied to Russell was a legal chemical. The difference was unimportant because the defendants in both cases were predisposed and, under the subjective test, a predisposed defendant cannot claim entrapment.

> The limitations of the Due Process Clause of the Fifth Amendment come into play only when the Government activity in question violates some protected right of the *defendant.* Here, as we have noted, the police, the Government informant, and the defendant acted in concert with one another. If the result of the governmental activity is to "implant in the mind of an innocent person the disposition to commit the alleged offense and induce its commission," * * * the defendant is protected by the defense of entrapment. If the police engage in illegal activity in concert with a defendant beyond the scope of their duties the remedy lies, not in freeing the equally culpable defendant, but in prosecuting the police under the applicable provisions of state or federal law. * * * But the police conduct here no more deprived defendant of any right secured to him by the United States Constitution than did the police conduct in *Russell* deprive Russell of any rights. (*Hampton v. United States,* 1976, pp. 490–91)

If taken seriously, this would mean that no matter how outrageous the police conduct, a defendant could never claim a due process violation unless it could be proven that his or her rights under the Fourth, Fifth, or Sixth amendments were violated.

This attempt to close off the due process defense failed because a total of five justices disagreed.[36] Justice Powell, joined by Justice Blackmun, concurred in upholding the conviction, agreeing in this case that the government conduct was not outrageous. But they felt that *Russell* did not foreclose the Court's use of its supervisory power in future cases "to bar conviction of a predisposed defendant because of outrageous police conduct." Three dissenting justices (Brennan, Stewart and Marshall) (a) would have adopted the objective theory of entrapment, (b) found that Hampton was entrapped under the subjective approach, (c) agreed with Justice Powell that the Court can exercise its supervisory power or due process principles to dismiss convictions of predisposed defendants "where the conduct of law enforcement authorities is sufficiently offensive," and (d) found that the police activity was outrageous in this case because the police supplied contraband and because the government was too heavily involved in the case. It was a set-up:

> The beginning and end of [the two drug sales] coincided exactly with the Government's entry into and withdrawal from the criminal activity involved in this case. * * * Where the Government's agent deliberately sets up the accused by supplying him with contraband and then bringing him to another agent as a potential purchaser, the Government's role has passed the point of toleration. * * * The Government is doing nothing less than buying contraband from itself through an intermediary and jailing the intermediary. * * * There is little, if any, law enforcement interest promoted by such conduct; plainly it is not designed to discover ongoing drug traffic. Rather, such conduct deliberately entices an individual to commit a crime. That the accused is "predisposed" cannot possibly justify the action of government officials in purposefully creating the crime. * * * (*Hampton v. United States,* 1976, pp. 498–500)

After *Hampton,* the due process approach has been successfully used on rare occasions by lower federal courts, although it has been rejected in principle by some circuits.[37] In *United States v. Twigg,*[38] a convicted methamphetamine manufacturer, Robert Kubica, agreed to apprehend illegal drug dealers for the DEA in order to have a four-year prison sentence reduced. Kubica contacted an old friend, Henry Neville, to discuss setting up a "speed" laboratory. Neville expressed interest. Over several months, Kubica and Neville spoke many times as arrangements were made to set up the laboratory. Neville assumed primary responsibility for raising capital and arranging for distribution of the product, while Kubica undertook the acquisition of the necessary equipment, raw materials, and a production site. DEA agents supplied Kubica with: two and a half gallons of phenyl-2-propanone at a cost of $475.00, although the chemical could retail for twice as much; twenty percent of the glassware needed; and a rented farmhouse in which to set up the laboratory. DEA officials made arrangements with chemical supply houses to facilitate the purchase of the materials by Kubica under a phony business name. Kubica personally bought almost all of the supplies with approximately $1500.00 supplied by Neville. About seven months after this episode began, Neville introduced Kubica to William Twigg who got involved in the operation to repay a debt to Neville. Twigg accompanied Kubica on a trip to several chemical supply houses and was at the laboratory set up at the farmhouse. The laboratory operated for one week, producing approximately six pounds of methamphetamine hydrochloride. Kubica was completely in charge of the laboratory. Neville and Twigg provided minor production assistance at Kubica's direction. Twigg often ran errands for groceries or coffee, while Neville spent much of his time away from the farmhouse. At the end of a week of manufacture, Kubica notified the DEA agents who arrested Neville as he was driving from the farmhouse, and they found a suitcase containing six pounds of methamphetamine hydrochloride, a Lysol can containing cocaine, and some more speed. Twigg was arrested at the farmhouse.

A two-judge majority of the three-judge federal Court of Appeals panel reversed the convictions and concluded that "the nature and extent of police involvement in this crime was so overreaching as to bar prosecution of the defendants as a matter of due process of law. Although no Supreme Court decision has reversed a conviction on this basis, the police conduct in this case went far beyond the behavior found permissible in previous cases" (*Twigg,* p. 377). This court noted that the Supreme Court left the door open to a due process appeal and that the government involvement in the manufacture of methamphetamine was much greater in this case than it was in *Russell.* Essentially, the government set up a criminal enterprise, actively worked at it, and then prosecuted its collaborators (*Twigg,* p. 379). Significantly, the criminal scheme was initiated by the government through a convicted felon seeking to reduce the severity of his sentence. A major factor in the case was that the government supplied a substantial amount of the funds and materials for the laboratory when it was not clear that the parties had the means to obtain the chemicals on their own. Indeed, the DEA made arrangements with chemical suppliers to circumvent regulations needed to get controlled chemicals. "Neither defendant had the know-how with which to actually manufacture methamphetamine. The assistance they provided was minimal and then at the specific direction of Kubica" (*Twigg,* p. 381). Although Neville and Twigg were predisposed, it does not appear that they would have gotten into the business of drug manufacture if Kubica had not proposed the scheme. In conclusion, the court said: "This egregious conduct on the part of government agents generated new crimes by the defendant merely for the sake of pressing criminal charges against him when, as far as the record reveals, he was lawfully and peacefully minding his own affairs. Fundamental fairness does not permit us to countenance such actions by law enforcement officials and prosecution for a crime so fomented by them will be barred" (*Twigg,* p. 381).

THE ENTRAPMENT DEFENSE IN THE STATES

Selecting the Subjective and Objective Tests

Because the entrapment defense is not derived from the United States Constitution, the states are free to develop their own rules. Most have remained with the subjective theory. A minority of states have adopted the objective standard of entrapment, and a few combine both tests into various forms of hybrid tests.

The Ohio Supreme Court gave three reasons for affirmatively selecting the subjective test in *State v. Doran* (1983).[39] First, the objective test can result in convicting "otherwise innocent" people if the police activity is not objectively outrageous, although it actually induces the criminal acts. Second, "real" (predisposed) criminals who regularly engage in criminal behavior can be released under the objective test. Third, in practice, the objective test can lead to difficulties of proof and "swearing contests" as to what the police really did, because the acts that lead to claims of entrapment usually occur in private. Although the subjective test posed fewer problems, the Ohio court did express concern about the use of reputation evidence, standing alone, as proof of predisposition.

Alaska was the first jurisdiction to adopt the objective test in *Grossman v. State* (1969),[40] saying that "unlawful entrapment occurs when a public law enforcement official, . . . in order to obtain evidence of the commission of an offense, induces another person to commit such an offense by persuasion or inducement which would be effective to persuade an average person other than the one who is ready and willing, to commit such an offense." Examples of objective entrapment include "extreme pleas of desperate illness, appeals based primarily on sympathy, pity or close personal friendship, and offers of inordinate amounts of money."[41] The Alaska Supreme Court, nevertheless, included a concern that is part of the subjective approach: "we do not intend that entrapment should become a ready escape hatch for those who are engaged in a course of criminal enterprise. But, under standards of civilized justice, there must be some control on the kind of police conduct which can be permitted in the manufacturing of crime."[42]

The Michigan Supreme Court, in *People v. Turner* (1973),[43] adopted the objective approach. In 1967, Partridge, a part-time sheriff's deputy and truck driver, befriended Turner, an antique dealer who had no adult criminal record. Six months after they met, Turner sold Partridge legal caffeine pills. The two maintained a casual friendship for three years. Partridge told the state police that he suspected that Turner was selling drugs. An undercover agent, Ewers, posing as a truck driver, joined Partridge in 1969 in his meetings with Turner. On several occasions, Partridge asked Turner to sell him drugs. Turner replied that he did not know anything about them and lectured Partridge on the harmful effects of marijuana and heroin. Partridge invented a story about a good-looking girlfriend who was a heroin addict and would leave Partridge if he did not get some heroin for her. Turner ultimately obtained twenty dollars worth of heroin from a friend in Detroit who had become an addict, which Turner sold to Partridge at cost, but refused further requests to purchase drugs for Partridge. At Partridge's urging, he drove Partridge and Ewers to Detroit and introduced them to his addict friend, from whom they purchased heroin. Turner was convicted of these two sales and received a minimum prison sentence of twenty years. A majority of the Michigan court held that this was entrapment as a matter of law and adopted the objective formulation of the concurring justices in *Sorrells* and *Sherman.* "This is the type of overreaching by the police condemned by our Court in *Saunders v. People* (1878). . . ."

A Mississippi case has established an objective rule for one kind of situation although the state otherwise adheres to the subjective test. When one state agent furnishes drugs to a defendant and another buys the drugs from the defendant, *Epps v. State* (1982) held that this is repugnant and *per se* entrapment in Mississippi law.[44] This ruling drew on similar cases from New Jersey and Illinois and did not follow the reasoning of the Supreme Court's majority rule in the *Russell* and *Hampton* decisions.[45] This state ruling echoes Justice Brennan's dissent in *Hampton* (1976) that the "Government is doing nothing less than buying contraband from itself through an intermediary and jailing the intermediary." *Epps* is an interesting case because it shows that a state supreme court can create situation-specific entrapment rules to deal with persistent problems of police overreaching.

Even states that adopt the objective rule by statute do not always establish clear rules. Pennsylvania, for example, adopted an entrapment definition based on the Model Penal Code in 1973, that in effect defined entrapment as police activity that would draw a hypothetical person into crime.[46] Nevertheless, Pennsylvania courts interpreted the statute inconsistently, with some cases following a subjective test and others the objective test.[47] To make matters worse, another section of the Pennsylvania code on the burden needed to prove entrapment injected a subjective element. The defendant has the burden to show that his or her behavior was *actually* caused by the inducement, making the lack of predisposition important.[48] This level of confusion concerning the entrapment test is not unique to Pennsylvania.[49]

Because the subjective and objective tests have some drawbacks, several states have tried to improve their entrapment rules by combining both tests into hybrid rules.

The Hybrid Approach

A state can combine the subjective and objective tests into a *composite* hybrid approach, where a defendant has to prove entrapment both under the subjective *and* the objective approaches, or into a *discrete* hybrid approach, where a defendant has to prove entrapment either under the subjective *or* the objective approach in order to be released.[50] The composite hybrid approach is unfair because it forces a genuinely non-predisposed defendant to show that the nature of the police inducement would also lead a hypothetical person into crime. The benefit of the objective test in disallowing prejudicial evidence of the defendant's past is negated by the composite approach, because past crimes are still allowed into evidence.[51] This was the result of the New Jersey Supreme Court's interpretation of a statute intended to prevent governmental misconduct in *State v. Rockholt.*[52] Thus, instead of benefitting the defendant as New Jersey had intended, the hybrid elements of its entrapment defense favors the state.[53]

The *discrete hybrid approach* "gives a defendant greater latitude to assert an entrapment defense while reducing the burden of persuasion. It provides the non-predisposed defendant with a defense against the government's overwhelming power to coerce, and also gives the non-predisposed defendant a defense against egregious police conduct."[54] Florida adopted the discrete hybrid approach in *Cruz v. State,*[55] (the decoy case discussed previously) to describe an example of the objective approach. The Florida court improved on the two tests by adding two policy issues into a determination of whether entrapment existed as a matter of law: (1) Is the police activity aimed at interrupting *specific ongoing criminal activity?* (2) Have the police utilized *means reasonably tailored* to apprehend those involved in ongoing criminal activity? If the answer to either of these questions is negative, the effect of the undercover work is to *create crimes* where none of that type had been occurring. The state also must provide some evidence of the likelihood of predisposition.

The Entrapment Scoreboard

A 1993 article estimated that every state had adopted an entrapment test with the majority favoring the subjective approach.[56] According to this count, twenty states had adopted the subjective approach by case decisions and another thirteen by statute.[57]

A more recent count by Kenneth Lord notes that twelve states currently follow the objective test: Alaska, Arkansas*, Colorado, Hawaii*, Iowa, Kansas, Michigan, New York, Pennsylvania*, Texas*, Utah*, and Vermont (* adopted the test by statute, typically based on the *Model Penal Code*). North Dakota had adopted the objective test but its legislature added a subjective element in 1993, creating a hybrid approach.[58] Texas, however, appears to have adopted a hybrid test in 1994.[59]

Six states have adopted hybrid tests of entrapment. Indiana, New Hampshire and New Jersey have adopted a composite ("and") hybrid approach. Florida, New Mexico and North Dakota follow the discrete ("or") hybrid test.

Recommendation

A close examination of the actual implementation of entrapment in the states, and even in the federal system in a case such as *Jacobson* (1992), shows that subjective (predisposition) and objective (nature of the inducement) factors often become intertwined. After analyzing entrapment cases, Kenneth Lord concluded "most jurisdictions in the United States are operating under a dual system of defenses in which the subjective approach to entrapment is augmented by the outrageous government conduct defense."[60] The goal of the entrapment defense is to minimize unfair government activity when it is necessary for police officers or their civilian agents (who may be criminals themselves) to use undercover techniques of encouragement. At the same time, there is sense in not allowing entrapment to become an easy escape hatch for committed criminals regularly involved in a criminal enterprise. To achieve these goals, Lord recommends that:

> courts . . . retain the flexibility to conduct a dual subjective/objective inquiry. Under such a dual inquiry, the judge or jury first engages in an objective examination into whether the government's actions were either outrageous or would cause an otherwise innocent person to engage in the crime charged, depending on the applicable law of the jurisdiction. If this inquiry fails, the jury can then proceed with a subjective inquiry to determine whether the defendant was an unwary innocent induced into committing a crime by the government. . . . [U]sing an objective approach as a backstop allows courts to provide explicit guidance to police agencies concerning the appropriateness of their actions in undercover operations.

This is a reasonable recommendation. Years of experience since *Sherman* (1958) demonstrate that the concerns of all the justices were valid, and that neither the subjective nor the objective theory, standing alone, is complete. A state that adopts a dual approach should make the first test an outrageous conduct test. This gives the courts greater flexibility to determine whether police techniques in question are beyond what is necessary to deal with a particular crime problem, whether they are likely to sweep many innocent people into the state's net, and whether they are particularly offensive to the sense of justice.

LAW IN SOCIETY: UNDERCOVER POLICING AND ITS CONTROL

Undercover police work is fascinating. It includes dangerous tactics by courageous officers to uncover major crimes, sleazy and routine vice enforcement, and questionable tactics where the police manufacture crime. Undercover work often includes encouragement (also called covert facilitation)[61] but may involve spying as the officer or informant gathers information about crime. Undercover policing is an essential tool of law enforcement for detecting covert consensual forms of crime (e.g., vice, white collar crime) or organized crime. Yet, it poses so many undesirable side effects that it must be carefully monitored by police agencies.

The Nature and Growth Policing

According to Professor Gary Marx's comprehensive study, undercover policing has three major functions: intelligence, prevention, and facilitation. "*Intelligence* operations use covert and deceptive tactics to gather information about crimes that" have occurred, might be planned, or are in progress. For example, a police agent befriending a suspect in order to gather more information and get a confession.[62] This happened in *Arizona v. Fulminante* (1991) when Anthony Sarivola—an ex-cop prisoner—played a mobster in prison and befriended Fulminante to gain a confession to the murder of his stepdaughter (see Chapter 8). This was not entrapment, but the confession was coerced because of the implied threats to Fulminante's life. Intelligence gathering includes police putting snitches in jail cells. *Prevention* occurs when police infiltrate an organization, such as an extremist political group, and convinces its members to refrain from acts of violence. The classical counterpoint to this is the **agent provocateur** who tries to stir up violent protest in order to arrest members of the organization. *Facilitation* is encouragement and the form of undercover policing most likely to result in entrapment. In using facilitative techniques, agents can pose either as victims (e.g., decoys) or as co-conspirators.[63]

Prior to 1975, most undercover activity focused on vice: public solicitation for prostitution, operating after-hours bars, selling drugs, and the like, although FBI monitoring and infiltration of radical political organizations occurred.[64] Since the 1970s, undercover police activity has expanded to many new areas. Decoy officers dress and act as potential victims, such as "skid row bums" or elderly people who are prey to muggers. In New York City, decoy officers drove taxi cabs after a rash of cabdriver robbery-murders. Sting operations became popular. Police set up fictitious criminal enterprises to do business with criminals such as burglars or car thieves. Police have posed as major drug dealers, selling to or buying from wholesale drug traffickers. Undercover operations develop in response to a changing society. The rapid growth of Internet use has spawned computer crime. A particularly odious form—sexual predation of minors by pedophiles—has been met by police officers going online and posing as young teens on sexually oriented chat lines. According to a news account, between 1998 and 2000 the "number of Illinois law enforcement agencies dedicating an officer or unit to investigate computer sex crimes has jumped from six to 50 [and] arrests and convictions of cyber pedophiles have nearly doubled."[65]

Since the 1970s, undercover work has grown enormously and has shifted in focus to target white-collar crime, organized crime, and political corruption.[66] Justice Department appropriations for undercover activities increased from one million dollars in 1977 to twelve million dollars in 1984.[67] Professor Marx estimated that in 1982 "the proportion of all police arrests involving undercover work has roughly doubled in the last 15 years."[68] The number of federal undercover operations investigating political corruption in the United States jumped from fifty in the late 1970s to 463 in 1981.[69] This trend has continued. Between 1985 and 1995, federal spending on informers alone increased from twenty-five million dollars to about one hundred million dollars a year[70]—a figure that does not include local law enforcement expenditures.

Organized crime, long thought immune from infiltration, has been penetrated by government agents, including the famous seven-year undercover operation of FBI Agent Joseph Pistone who as "Donnie Brasco" infiltrated the leadership of the Bonanno crime family.[71] Undercover work can be part of a larger strategy to disrupt organized crime by intelligence gathering, electronic surveillance, and coordinated police and prosecution strategies.[72] A 1990 FBI operation known as Cat-com (for catch communications), for example, put a dent in cocaine importation. For three years federal agents infiltrated a Miami communications shop used as a meeting point for drug dealers. Hidden video cameras gathered evidence that led to the break up of the drug importation ring, the arrest of sixty-eight suspects, the seizure of several millions of dollars in cash and property, and the seizure of drugs worth several hundreds of millions of dollars. The operation, which generated 800 reports, gave federal authorities a better picture of Colombian cocaine trafficking patterns.[73]

Since the Watergate scandal in the early 1970s, federal investigation of local government corruption has become routine. Rumors of judicial corruption in Chicago, for example, led to an astonishing investigation: "Operation Greylord." A downstate Illinois judge was transferred to Chicago and "wired" to record incriminating statements of corrupt fellow judges. This resulted in the conviction of nine local Chicago judges, thirty-seven attorneys, and nineteen court officers and clerks by mid-1988.[74] Integrity testing is also important in police and correctional agencies to insure that police and correctional officers do not succumb to the temptations that regularly come their way. The Detroit Police Department recently inaugurated integrity testing, after officers were found guilty of selling the drugs that they took during raids. The tests include police supervisors leaving cash and drugs in drug houses to see if officers sent there turn them in. Such integrity testing has been used in cities such as New York, Washington, D.C., and New Orleans, and it seems to have had positive effects.[75]

The most extensive corruption probe was *Abscam* (short for Abdul scam—1978 to 1980). It began when an informant, during a stolen art sting, told investigators that the mayor of Camden, New Jersey, was taking bribes. The FBI set up a fictitious company, "Abdul Enterprises, Ltd.," furnished with offices and a yacht, that played on the then popular theme of oil-rich Arabian sheiks with vast wealth seeking to buy favors. The "sheik" (FBI agent Anthony Amoroso) worked with Melvin Weinberg, a convicted "con man," who made connections with politicians. The FBI allowed Weinberg to design what, in effect, became a major integrity testing program. The Abscam players, in the course of discussing supposedly legitimate investment and immigration matters, offered huge sums of money to political figures and operatives. Camden's mayor, for example, was videotaped receiving $125,000 in return for promising to help get permission for "Abdul Ltd." to open a casino in Atlantic City. The sting operation snowballed. Congressmen were to be paid $50,000 to introduce private bills to allow fictitious "sheiks" refugee status.[76] Abscam middlemen spread tales about huge sums of money available for returning favors. "The operation was finally forced to shut down due to the large number of minor politicians seeking bribe money from the sheik."[77] By 1980, "six United States congressmen, one United States senator, a United States Immigration Service official, three members of the Philadelphia City Council, the mayor of Camden, New Jersey, and assorted bagmen, middlemen, and corrupt lawyers" were exposed by Abscam.[78] Was Abscam entrapment? The courts said no, and upheld the conviction of the politicians and middlemen. Some appellate judges expressed concern that the huge sums offered, "in excess of real-world opportunities," might have created crimes.[79] Most judges, however, saw this as creating a grapevine to which corrupt and greedy politicians responded.[80]

White-collar crime milks billions of dollars from consumers and honest business firms, creates dangers that cause injuries and deaths, and undermines public confidence in business. Past violations were treated as administrative errors, and even after prosecution, penalties were light.[81] After the Watergate scandal, which included revelations of illegal business payoffs to politicians, local and federal prosecutors began to prosecute white-collar crimes with greater vigor—judicial sentences included prison terms for corporate executives. In this climate of opinion, the government has utilized undercover agents in some unusual areas.

For example, an elaborate FBI operation to investigate corruption in the Chicago Board of Trade (the "Merc") ran from 1987 to 1989.[82] Suspicion arose that traders were overcharging customers, not paying full proceeds of sales, and using knowledge of customers' orders to first trade for themselves. Archer-Daniels-Midland Company, a large agricultural concern, complained about abuses and aided the FBI sting by "hiring" two agents to work for the company's trading subsidiary. Getting information was difficult because Merc traders formed tight-knit cliques where much depended on mutual trust. Over a two-year period, four undercover agents lived the fast-paced lives of Chicago futures traders with false identities, fabricated college degrees (verified by cooperating universities), expensive apartments and cars, memberships in trendy health clubs, and seats on the Merc so they could work regularly as traders. They infiltrated the trader culture so as to win other traders' confidence. "Once into the sting operation, the agents tape recorded traders in restaurants, at parties, in health clubs and on the noisy floors of the exchanges themselves." At the conclusion of the operation, the agents had sufficient incriminating evidence to subpoena fifty traders and others for various securities violations and frauds.

White-collar sting operations can be expensive to run and can involve immense stakes. At times, they expose links between big business and political corruption. Some investigations have international repercussions, and prosecution plans may become entangled with conflicting policies of the State Department, the Commerce Department, and even the White House.[83] In other white-collar stings, big business mixes with ordinary crime. The flamboyant automobile entrepreneur, John Z. DeLorean, desperately needed ten million dollars to finance a sinking enterprise to build sports cars in Ireland. He was approached by a former neighbor—a narcotics dealer and FBI informant—with the prospect of raising money through a cocaine deal. When DeLorean could not raise the cash for the drug deal, the agent proposed that he sign over his company as collateral. DeLorean may have been convicted if the subjective test of entrapment had been adhered to strictly, but he was acquitted. The jury apparently disapproved of the government's unrelenting tactics and the singling out of the defendant because of his high visibility.[84]

Problems with Covert Policing

Undercover work is subject to abuses and unintended consequences, aside from entrapment. First, despite the heroic TV and movie image of undercover work, some officers are *psychologically or physically damaged* by the high-stress effort required to play a negative role, thus raising moral dilemmas that often go unresolved. In extreme cases, agents cannot return to normal work; some turn criminal. Covert work puts greater than ordinary strains on officers' family lives. Undercover police are sometimes mistaken for real criminals and mistreated by uniformed officers. In an extreme example, a Detroit robbery decoy unit set up in the late 1960s resulted in three officers and sixteen civilians being killed before the unit was disbanded.[85] Recently, New York City was rocked by the killing of a completely innocent man in a reverse sting. Patrick Dorismond, twenty-six, father of two, and an off-duty security guard was hailing a cab outside a midtown Manhattan bar when he was rushed by an undercover police officer who wanted to buy marijuana. Dorismond, offended, brushed him off. They argued, scuffled, and the undercover detective called for backup. In a moment, Dorismond, who was African American, was shot and killed.[86]

Higher rates of entrapment can be expected, for example, when police use notoriously unreliable drug informants to make unobserved buys.[87] Informants may be motivated by revenge and are sometimes paid for their work. Police recruits may be selected because they are not known to local criminals. To ensure their credibility and the lack of a "police attitude," they are put on the street before entering the academy with virtually no training or briefing. Since these agents may remain on the street for many months, making hundreds of buys before terminating their covers, the dangers of lost evidence and misidentification are multiplied.[88] Unfortunately, undercover officers have been known to falsify drug purchase reports by not including information that could clear a defendant; since they work in secret, this form of perjury is hard to detect. Some studies show that officers' *reports* adhere to the letter of the law even if their *actions* do not.[89]

Overuse of sting operations, such as a fictitious business buying stolen goods from burglars, raises serious *cost-benefit questions* beyond issues of entrapment. These operations are costly, and there should be an administrative determination of whether the total costs of running the operation are worth it in terms of the amount of property recovered. Another issue, which is difficult to measure, is whether a sting operation increases the quantity of crime. A new sting operation might stimulate people with no record as burglars to commit crimes when they hear that there is money to be made at this "new outlet."[90]

Undercover work poses risks to citizens as a result of administrative bungling. A chilling example was documented by R. E. Payne, a Covington, Louisiana, newspaper reporter.[91] Payne went to the FBI with a tip about an organized crime murder of a tow-truck operator and agreed to go undercover to detect a political corruption connection. He met with a businessman, K. T. Fogg, who was a local official and requested a bribe for silence about incriminating information. Payne was not wired for sound; what he did not know was that Fogg had become an undercover operative for a *separate* FBI political corruption unit and was wearing a recording device. As a result of their conversation, Payne was indicted for conspiracy, and his FBI handler refused to acknowledge that Payne was working undercover! Payne was saved from conviction when his attorney obtained a memorandum proving his undercover status. As undercover work expands, more *administrative mismanagement,* leading to botched cases and gross injustice, can occur. Close administrative supervision is essential in any espionage work, whether it involves national security or civilian criminal justice.

Covert policing carries political risks to democratic government. For most of the twentieth century, the FBI has used informers to infiltrate not only foreign espionage cells, but to spy on citizens' groups with extremist political views. In the turbulent days of the late 1960s, FBI *agents provocateurs,* often criminals, infiltrated groups of anti-war protesters to provoke violent incidents that would lead to arrests. The worst case involved an informer in the Chicago Black Panther Party who provided a diagram of the Panthers' apartment, indicating where everyone slept. The FBI passed it to a Chicago police unit and persuaded it to make the 1969 predawn raid in which Fred Hampton, the local leader, was killed in his bed by a hail of police bullets. The FBI role was not discovered for several years.[92]

Despite the risks of abuse, poorly defined benefits, and dangers of generating crime and entrapment, undercover policing is necessary. It would be impossible or outrageously expensive to police criminal behavior that is secret and where victims do not come forward to complain. The question, then, is how to appropriately control abuses.

Judicial and Administrative Control of Undercover Policing

There are limits to the judicial control of undercover work. The entrapment defense, useful in marking the outer limits of covert facilitation, does not provide appropriate guidance of undercover policing. Some scholars advocate further legal and judicial control of undercover: that police not engage in covert facilitation unless reasonable suspicion or probable cause exists to believe that known or unknown suspects are engaged in the crime targeted by the covert facilitation and that a judge has approved the covert facilitation "for only one integrity test."[93] These suggestions are misplaced. Undercover policing is not a search, so warrants are not Constitutionally required.[94] Even if created by statute, undercover probable cause warrants would go beyond traditional judicial case-by-case reasoning. Judges would have to enter into administrative oversight and pass on the wisdom of police work, a task for which they are not trained. Courts have assumed administrative control of prisons and other executive agencies only in extreme cases to preserve the constitutional rights of inmates. The quasi-administrative role of supervising undercover work could tarnish the judicial role. Conversely, judicial involvement can hamper proper undercover work: some judges might unnecessarily restrict creative policing while others would rubber-stamp unwise stings. Judge shopping can cause even greater inconsistencies.

Undercover policies and operations are best directed by police agencies that should adopt administrative standards and guidelines for encouragement techniques. General standards can be mandated by law, but operations should be planned at high levels in police departments and the reason for each general undercover program should be well thought out. For example, Irvin Nathan, the Abscam coordinator, suggested guidelines for federal agencies before they undertake corruption stings: "(A) the corrupt nature of the activity is reasonably clear to potential subjects; (B) there is reasonable indication that the undercover operation will reveal illegal activities; and (C) the nature of any inducement is not unjustifiable in view of the character of the illegal transaction in which the individual is invited to engage." Before commencing, anti-corruption stings would be approved by an agency review board.[95]

The effective use of guidelines ensures that law enforcement controls an essential function, assures the public that abuses will be kept to a minimum, and avoids overreliance on the entrapment defense, which is not well suited to the routine guidance of police undercover work.

SUMMARY

Entrapment is a complete defense to crime based on the concept that the idea for the crime was implanted in the defendant's mind by police. It is both a criminal law defense and a doctrine of criminal procedure. It is not a constitutional defense, but is a judge-made doctrine of statutory interpretation. The defense is not applied to crimes of violence.

Covert police work, encouragement and undercover policing, involve the lawful use of deception. Undercover police pretend to be victims or participants in crime. They may or may not use the technique of encouragement. Encouragement is police activity in which an undercover agent pretends to be a participant in crimes and furnishes an opportunity for a person to engage in crime. Undercover work does not, in itself, violate any provision of the Constitution.

There are two theories of entrapment. The subjective test—favored by a majority of states and the federal courts—views entrapment as occurring when a law enforcement officer implants a criminal idea into the mind of a person who otherwise would not have engaged in an illegal act. A person predisposed to commit a crime cannot claim entrapment. Proof of entrapment allows the introduction into evidence of prejudicial facts: prior criminal acts. The objective test—favored by a minority of Supreme Court justices and a few states—holds that entrapment occurs when government agents perform acts that would tend to draw average persons into crime. Both the subjective and objective tests are concerned with predisposition and excessive police behavior.

Another test, suggested by the United States Supreme Court and applied by a few courts, is that particularly outrageous law enforcement action used to draw a person into crime violates the defendant's due process rights. In some states, outrageous conduct occurs when the police sell drugs to a suspect and buy them back. The Supreme Court has held such policing does not constitute entrapment if the defendant is predisposed.

Most states follow the subjective test. Several have adopted hybrid tests that combine the subjective and objective tests. A composite hybrid approach requires a defendant to prove that entrapment occurred under both the subjective and the objective approaches; the discrete hybrid approach allows the defense where a defendant proves entrapment under either the subjective or the objective approach.

The entrapment rules deemed the most fair to both the state and to defendants is one in which courts first determine whether the police conduct was outrageous; if not, the defendant is then free to offer to the jury or judge evidence of the lack of predisposition to show entrapment under the subjective test.

LEGAL PUZZLES

HOW HAVE COURTS DECIDED THESE CASES?

11–1. The FBI employed Helen, a known prostitute, heroin user, and fugitive from Canadian justice, to infiltrate the business of Darrel, a suspected drug dealer. She did so and, over a period of time, was having sexual relations with Darrel and using heroin. This was known by the FBI. Was the FBI's activity in manipulating Helen into becoming an informer and continuing to use her while she was sleeping with Darrel and using heroin so outrageous as to be a violation of Darrel's due process rights? *United States v. Simpson,* 813 F.2d 1462 (9th Cir), *cert. denied,* 108 S.Ct. 233 (1987).

11–2. An FBI informant told the IRS that Frank Coyle, a stockbroker, was involved in money laundering. An IRS undercover agent, Monaghan, contacted and met with Coyle who identified Val King as a friend who "could legitimize any kind of money" for a fee of twenty–five percent. Undercover agent Monaghan provided money for "laundering, and when he met King he made it clear that he got the money from selling cocaine. King immediately began to set up a fictitious business to launder sums of money and carried the plan through." Was the government's behavior outrageous and entrapment in fact? *United States v. Payne,* 962 F.2d 1228 (6th Cir. 1992).

11–3. Ray told George he would give him fifty dollars if he could find a woman with whom Ray could have sexual intercourse. George told the police. Lianne, an undercover female police officer, wearing an electronic transmitter was introduced to Ray. In their ten-minute conversation, Lianne repeatedly asked Ray variations of the question, "What's the deal?" Ray did not immediately declare that he wanted sex in return for money. When questioned by Lianne, he said he wanted "good lay, . . . companionship, a little loving." There was more questioning before he said he was prepared to pay for sex and he would give in return "a lot of loving and money." Ultimately, Ray and Lianne agreed they would meet the following morning and the defendant would pay "a hundred bucks for the day." Ray was then arrested. Was this entrapment? *Vermont v. George,* 157 Vt. 580, 602 A.2d 953 (1991).

11–4. Wells, a part-time employee at Avis, was living in a condemned house in dire poverty. An informant working with a police stolen-car investigation befriended Wells and suggested that Wells sell stolen cars. Wells, at first, refused but after some importuning agreed to do so and sold three stolen cars to the undercover informant. When Wells got a full-time job with Avis, he stopped dealing in stolen cars. In the past, a government informer had tried to get Wells to deal in drugs, but he had refused. Was Wells induced into selling the stolen cars? *State v. Wells,* 731 S.W.2d 250 (Missouri, en banc 1987).

ANSWERS TO LEGAL PUZZLES

11–1. NO. The Ninth Circuit held that for government activity to violate a defendant's due process rights, it would have to be violent or physically abusive, noting that the government's informer did not manufacture the defendant's crime.

11–2. NO. Unlike the situation in *Jacobson v. United States* (1992), there was reasonable suspicion to believe that Coyle was involved in money laundering, and Coyle led the government to King. Unlike Jacobson, King was not continuously importuned before he engaged in money laundering but became a willing participant after only one telephone call from Coyle, providing evidence that King and Coyle had prior conversations about money laundering. Finally, Agent Monaghan's role-playing as a drug dealer and supplying the case was not excessive government activity; it merely gave the defendants the opportunity to commit the crime of money laundering. The defendants supplied the fictitious account in which to deposit the laundered money, accepted the cash and converted it into checks without filing a currency transaction report, and established a fictitious business in order to issue checks back to the fictitious account previously set up to accept the laundered cash.

11–3. NO. The police did not create a trap for the random citizen. They responded to information received from an informant that the defendant was seeking to commit the crime. Although Lianne was persistent in her questioning of the defendant to elicit the statements later used to prove his guilt, a reasonable juror could find that what she sought was in fact only clarification of the relationship Ray was seeking to establish. Indeed, Ray first made reference to sex, and he raised the subject of money.

11–4. YES. The state supreme court ruled there were sufficient facts to believe that the informer overcame Wells's reluctance to sell the cars by appealing to his financial burdens. This indicates a lack of predisposition and willingness to engage in such conduct that was overcome by the acts of the government.

FURTHER READING

Gary Marx, *Undercover: Police Surveillance in America* (Berkeley: University of California Press, 1988).

David Wise, *The American Police State: The Government Against the People* (New York: Random House, 1976).

Scott Turow, *Personal Injuries* (Toronto: HarperCollins, 1999).

ENDNOTES

1. The subject is found in criminal law and criminal procedure textbooks: W. LaFave and A. W. Scott, Jr., *Handbook on Criminal Law* (St. Paul: West Publishing, 1972), pp. 369–74; C. Whitebread and C. Slobogin, *Criminal Procedure* (New York: Foundation Press, 2000), pp. 503–20.
2. Paul Marcus, "The Development of Entrapment Law," *Wayne Law Review* 33:5–37 (1986), pp. 5–9; Comment, C. Robton Perelli-Minetti, "Causation and Intention in the Entrapment Defense," *UCLA Law Review* 28:859–905 (1981); George

Fletcher, *Rethinking Criminal Law* (Boston: Little, Brown, 1978), p. 541.

Mark M. Stavsky, "The 'Sting' Reconsidered: Organized Crime, Corruption and Entrapment," *Rutgers Law Journal* 16 (1985):937–89, notes that, in New Zealand, entrapment may result in the exclusion of evidence and Canadian dictum indicates that entrapment is a legitimate defense.

A recent account reported the first successful entrapment defense in Scottish history. A female undercover officer, failing to catch major drug dealers, led a nightclub disc jockey to believe that they were romantically involved. To secure her "love," he obtained the drug 'Ecstasy' for her. The trial judge ruled that the entrapment violated the European Convention on Human Rights. Stephen Rafferty, "Ecstasy Case Man Cleared after Entrapment Claim," *The Scotsman,* February 29, 2000, p. 4.

3. Stavsky, "The 'Sting,'" p. 949.
4. *Board of Commissioners v. Backus,* 29 How. Pr. 33, 42 (New York, 1864), quoted in Marcus, "Development," p. 9.
5. 38 Mich. 218 (1878), commented on by Marcus, "Development." The Michigan Supreme Court was one of the most highly respected state supreme courts in the mid- to late-19th century, under Chief Justice Thomas M. Cooley, a leading legal scholar.
6. Marcus, "Development," p. 10.
7. Justice Marston in *Saunders v. Michigan,* 38 Mich. 218 (1878), commented on by Marcus, "Development."
8. See Stavsky, "The 'Sting,'" pp. 942, 969–89.
9. Model Penal Code sec. 2.13(3).
10. Lawrence P. Tiffany, Donald M. McIntyre, Jr., and Daniel L. Rotenberg, *Detection of Crime* (Boston: Little, Brown, 1967), Part III, Encouragement and Entrapment, pp. 207–82, quotation at p. 210. In this text, illegal *entrapment* is distinguished from lawful *encouragement.* The Model Penal Code and some state statutes, however, use these terms synonymously.
11. This was made clear when the Court upheld the use of evidence obtained with a body microphone without the need for a warrant, *United States v. White* (1971).
12. *Hoffa v. United States* (1966), quoting from *United States v. Dennis,* 183 F.2d 201, 224 (2d Cir. 1949) (prosecution of leaders of the American Communist Party).
13. Victor Navasky, *Kennedy Justice* (New York: Atheneum, 1971).
14. *United States v. Whittier,* 28 F. Cas. 591 (C.C.E.D. Mo. 1878) (No. 16,688), discussed in Marcus, "Development," p. 12.
15. 223 F. 412 (9th Cir. 1915), reported in Marcus, "Development," pp. 12–13.
16. *Ibid.*
17. *Sorrells v. United States* (1932).
18. Kenneth Lord, "Entrapment and Due Process: Moving Toward a Dual System of Defenses," *Florida State University Law Review,* 25:463–517, p. 465 (1998).
19. Lord, "Entrapment and Due Process," p. 473; *Jacobson v. United States,* p. 549 (emphasis added).
20. Nancy Y. T. Hanewicz, Comment, "*Jacobson v. United States:* The Entrapment Defense and Judicial Supervision of the Criminal Justice System," *Wisconsin Law Review* 1993: 1163–93, p. 1191.
21. Ruth Marcus, "Fair Sting or Foul Trap?; Child Pornography Investigation Challenged," *Washington Post,* Nov. 6, 1991, p. A1.
22. Lord, "Entrapment and Due Process," pp. 475–76; general intent: see *State v. Houpt,* 504 P.2d 570 (Kan. 1972); *United States v. Williams,* 705 F.2d 603, (2d Cir. 1983); specific intent: *United States v. Ortiz,* 804 F.2d 1161 (10th Cir. 1986); *United States v. Perez-Leon,* 757 F.2d 866 (7th Cir. 1985); *Jacobson v. United States* (1992).
23. Lord, "Entrapment and Due Process," pp. 478, 489–90, citing *United States v. Kaminski,* 703 F.2d 1004 (7th Cir. 1983).
24. Lord, "Entrapment and Due Process," pp. 479–80, citing United *States v. Swiatek,* 819 F.2d 721 (7th Cir. 1987).
25. Lord, "Entrapment and Due Process," pp. 489–90, citing *Gossmeyer v. State,* 482 N.E.2d 239 (Ind. 1985); *United States v. Aikens,* 64 F.3d 372 (8th Cir. 1995) (defendant predisposed—demonstrated skill and sophistication selling crack cocaine to undercover officer); *United States v. Hernandez,* 31 F.3d 354 (6th Cir. 1994) (by giving sophisticated advice to undercover officer about cocaine trafficking, defendant demonstrated he was not innocent dupe); *Collins v. State,* 520 N.E.2d 1258 (Ind. 1988); *United States v. Hollingsworth,* 27 F.3d 1196 (7th Cir. 1994) (en banc).
26. 465 So.2d 516 (Fla. 1985); see Kelly M. Haynes, Casenote, "Criminal Law—Florida Adopts a Dual Approach to Entrapment—*Cruz v. State,* 465 So. 2d 516 (Fla. 1985)," *Florida State University Law Review* 13(1986): 1171–89.
27. Lord, "Entrapment and Due Process," p. 490.
28. Lord, "Entrapment and Due Process," pp. 465, 489–90.
29. American Law Institute, *Model Penal Code,* sec 2.13 (Philadelphia, 1985).
30. Hanewicz, "The Entrapment Defense," p. 1182.
31. Greene v. U.S., 454 F.2d 783 (9th Cir. 1971); Lord, "Entrapment and Due Process," pp. 504–05.
32. The Supreme Court cited two decisions that were decided on this basis: *United States v. Bueno,* 447 F.2d 903 (5th Cir. 1971); *United States v. Chisum,* 312 F.Supp. 1307 (C.D. Cal. 1970).
33. United States v. Russell, p. 428.
34. Ibid., internal quotation marks eliminated.
35. Lord, "Entrapment and Due Process," p. 509.
36. Eight justices participated: Justice Stevens took no part in the consideration or decision of the case.
37. United States v. Tucker, 28 F.3d 1420 (6th Cir. 1994).
38. 588 F.2d 373 (3rd Cir. 1978).
39. 5 Ohio St. 3d 187, 449 N.E.2d 1295 (1983), commented on in Margaret Baker, Comment, "Criminal Law: Entrapment in Ohio," *Akron Law Review* 17(1984):709–15.
40. 457 P.2d 226 (Alaska 1969). In this case, the Alaska Supreme Court did not make a decision whether the facts amounted to

entrapment but instead remanded the case to the trial court to reconsider the conviction.

41. *Ibid.*
42. *Ibid.*
43. 390 Mich. 7, 210 N.W.2d 336 (1973).
44. See John S. Knowles, III, Casenote, "Criminal Procedure—Entrapment as a Matter of Law: Contraband Supplied to Defendants by Government Agents—*Epps v. State,* 417 So. 2d 543 (Miss. 1982), *Mississippi College Law Review* 4(1983): 99–111, pp. 105–7.
45. *Ibid.;* New Jersey: *State v. Talbot,* 71 N.J. 160, 364 A.2d 9 (1976); Illinois: *People v. Strong,* 21 Ill. 2d 320, 172 N.E.2d 765 (1961).
46. Brian Victor, Comment, "The Citizen and the Serpent: *State v. Rockholt* and Entrapment in New Jersey," *Rutgers Law Review* 38(1984):589–617.
47. George, "Entrapment," pp. 121–24.
48. *Pennsylvania Crimes Code,* section 313(b), reprinted in *ibid.,* p. 120.
49. George, "Entrapment," pp. 130–31.
50. Lord, "Entrapment and Due Process," pp. 498–504.
51. Ibid, pp. 498–501.
52. 96 N.J. 570, 476 A.2d 1236 (1984); see Victor, "The Citizen," p. 589.
53. Victor, "The Citizen," pp. 611–16.
54. Lord, "Entrapment and Due Process," p. 502.
55. 465 So.2d 516 (Fla. 1985); see Kelly M. Haynes, Casenote, "Criminal Law—Florida Adopts a Dual Approach to Entrapment—*Cruz v. State,* 465 So. 2d 516 (Fla. 1985)," *Florida State University Law Review* 13(1986): 1171–89.
56. The summary of the state entrapment tests is found in Erich Weyand, Comment, "Entrapment: From Sorrells to Jacobson—The Development Continues," *Ohio Northern University Law Review* 20(1993):293–317, pp. 299, 303–04.
57. Case law states: Arizona, Idaho, Louisiana, Maine, Maryland, Massachusetts, Minnesota, Mississippi, Nebraska, Nevada, New Mexico, North Carolina, Ohio, Oklahoma, Rhode Island, South Carolina, South Dakota, Virginia, Wisconsin, and Wyoming. Statutory adoption states: Alabama, Connecticut, Delaware, Georgia, Illinois, Indiana, Kansas, Kentucky, Missouri, Montana, Oregon, Tennessee, and Washington.
58. Lord , "Entrapment and Due Process," pp. 496, 498, 502.
59. The "Texas Court of Criminal Appeals significantly changed" the entrapment test in *England v. State,* 887 S.W.2d 902 (Tex. Cr. App. 1994) (5–4 en banc). "The *England* Court . . . determined that the legislature actually enacted a mixed objective/subjective test for entrapment" in Texas Penal Code §8.06. Barbara A. Belbot, *Guide to Criminal Law for Texas: A Supplement to Joel Samaha's Criminal Law,* Sixth Edition (Wadsworth 1999) p. 87.
60. Lord , "Entrapment and Due Process," p. 516.
61. John Braithwaite, Brent Fisse and Gilbert Geis, "Covert Facilitation and Crime: Restoring Balance to the Entrapment Debate," *Journal of Social Issues,* 43:5–41 (1987).
62. Gary Marx, *Undercover: Police Surveillance in America* (Berkeley: University of California Press, 1988), p. 61.
63. Marx, *Undercover,* pp. 60–65.
64. Tiffany, McIntyre, and Rotenberg, *Detection of Crime.* The data for this study were collected in Detroit, Milwaukee, and Topeka in the 1950s. For FBI infiltration of the Communist Party or the Ku Klux Klan under J. Edgar Hoover see Richard Gid Powers, *Secrecy and Power: The Life of J. Edgar Hoover* (New York: Free Press, 1987).
65. F. Main, A. Pallasch, and D. Rozek, "Stings netting online deviants; Arrests, convictions of pedophiles soar," *Chicago Sun-Times,* February 27, 2000, p. 1.
66. Stavsky, "The Sting," p. 955: white-collar crimes include tax evasion, bribery, embezzlement of pension funds, and some forms of political corruption; much organized crime includes intimidation-type crimes such as protection rackets, loan-sharking, blackmail, or simple extortion, which are often "invisible crimes" because victims are reluctant to come forward. This new focus was due in large measure to the FBI's changed priorities after the death of J. Edgar Hoover in 1972, Powers, *Secrecy and Power.*
67. Whelan, "Lead Us Not," p. 1194, n. 6, citing a 1984 congressional subcommittee report.
68. See Gary T. Marx, "Who Really Gets Stung? Some Issues Raised by the New Police Undercover Work," in Gerald M. Caplan, ed., *ABSCAM Ethics: Moral Issues and Deception in Law Enforcement* (Washington, D.C.: Police Foundation, 1983), pp. 65–99.
69. Stavsky, "The 'Sting,'" p. 956; David Katz, "The Paradoxical Role of Informers Within the Criminal Justice System: A Unique Perspective," *University of Dayton Law Review* 7(1981):51–71, pp. 55–56, reports that in the late 1970s the FBI engaged 2,800 "operators" and paid nearly $ 1.5 million dollars to informants, resulting in 2,600 arrests. James B. Stewart, *The Prosecutors: Inside the Offices of the Government's Most Powerful Lawyers* (New York: Simon and Schuster/Touchstone, 1987), p. 91.
70. Stephen Labaton, "The Nation; The Price Can Be High For Talk That's Cheap," *New York Times,* Apr. 2, 1995, §4, p. 3.
71. Howard Abadinsky, *Organized Crime,* 2nd ed. (Chicago: Nelson-Hall, 1988), p. 295; Robert P. Rhodes, *Organized Crime: Crime Control vs. Civil Liberties* (New York: Random House, 1984); Arnold H. Lubasch, "F.B.I. Infiltrator Says Mob Chief Told of Slayings," *New York Times,* August 4, 1982, p. B 1.
72. Ralph Blumenthal, "New Technology Helps in Effort to Fight Mafia," *New York Times,* Nov. 24, 1986, p. B3.
73. Jeff Gerth, "A Covert and Major Victory Is Reported in the Drug War," *New York Times,* Apr. 23, 1990, p. 1 (nat. ed.).
74. Tuohy and Warden, *Greylord.*

75. Darren A. Nichols, "Cops divided on sting testing: They react to plan to test honesty of Detroit force." *The Detroit News,* Feb. 3, 2000, p. D1.
76. *Ibid.,* pp. 1200–1203; Stavsky, "The 'Sting,'"pp. 956–61.
77. Stavsky, "The 'Sting,'" p. 957.
78. Whelan, "Lead Us Not," p. 1200.
79. *United States v. Kelly,* 707 F.2d 1460 (D.C. Cir. 1983), by Judge Ruth Bader Ginsburg.
80. *United States v. Kelly,* 707 F.2d 1460 (D.C. Cir. 1983), by Judge MacKinnon. A spirited defense of the Abscam operation is presented by its Justice Department coordinator: Irvin B. Nathan, "ABSCAM: A Fair and Effective Method for Fighting Public Corruption," in Caplan, ed., *ABSCAM Ethics,* pp. 1–16.
81. Gilbert Geis, *White-Collar Criminal: The Offender in Business and the Professions* (New York: Atherton Press, 1968).
82. "F.B.I. Commodities 'Sting': Fast Money, Secret Lives," *New York Times,* Jan. 30, 1989, p. 1 (nat. ed).
83. Stewart, *The Prosecutors,* p. 92, discussing a sting of corporate executives of Hitachi, Ltd., a major Japanese manufacturer, who were attempting to illegally purchase IBM secrets regarding the design of new computers.
84. Whelan, "Lead Us Not," pp. 1197–1200.
85. Marx, *Undercover,* pp. 159–79.
86. Judy Mann, "War on Drugs Can't Help but Run Amok," *Washington Post,*
87. Stavsky, "The 'Sting,'" p. 953.
88. George I. Miller, "Observations on Police Undercover Work," *Criminology* 25(1987):27–46.
89. *Ibid.,* pp. 39–40; the other studies referred to are Jerome Skolnick, *Justice without Trial* (New York: Wiley, 1975) and Peter K. Manning, "Police Lying," *Urban Life and Culture* 3(1974):283–306.
90. See Marx, "Who Really Gets Stung?"
91. Andrew Radolf, "Lesson Learned: Working Undercover for the FBI Nearly Lands a Louisiana Reporter in Jail; Articles by a Columnist for Another Paper Help Him Beat Extortion Rap," *Editor and Publisher,* Sept. 24, 1988, pp. 9–11.
92. Nelson Blackstock, *Cointelpro: The FBI's Secret War on Political Freedom* (New York: Vintage Books, 1975), pp. 12–13; John Kifner, "The Nation—Informers: A Tale in Itself," *New York Times,* Jan. 22, 1995, §4, p. 4.
93. Braithwaite, Fisse and Geis, "Covert Facilitation," pp. 9–10; Whelan, "Lead Us Not," pp. 1216–1218.
94. Lawrence W. Sherman, "Reinventing Probable Cause: Target Selection in Proactive Investigations," *Journal of Social Issues,* 43:87–94 (1987).
95. Nathan, "ABSCAM," p. 15.

JUSTICES OF THE SUPREME COURT

REAGAN'S CONSERVATIVE LEGACY
O'CONNOR—SCALIA—KENNEDY

Ronald Reagan's presidency capped off a dramatic political shift whereby the conservative wing of the Republican Party became dominant and sought to transform American politics as deeply as had President Roosevelt in the 1930s. Although the Senate was controlled by Republicans at the onset of the Reagan years, the Congress reverted to Democratic hands, and the sweep of the Reagan revolution was not complete. The greatest Reagan victories were in economic deregulation and a military buildup. The ideologically far-right social agenda of some conservatives has never been fully achieved. Still, the shift to the right has been felt in the Supreme Court to which Reagan appointed three justices—including the first female justice, Sandra Day O'Connor.

President Reagan's three successful Supreme Court nominees joined the Burger Court, which was better described as moderate than conservative. Justice Antonin Scalia was a brilliant academic and judicial supporter of conservative economic theories before being named to the Court. Justice Anthony Kennedy was a low-keyed and popular nominee after President Reagan's tumultuous failed attempts to have Judge Robert Bork and then Judge Douglas Ginsberg named to the Court.

Justices O'Connor, Scalia, and Kennedy are highly rated for their judicial craft and acuity. While each has voted for the prosecution far more often than for the defense, they do not vote in lockstep, and each has displayed independence in evaluating the facts and doctrines of criminal procedure cases, leading each to decide specific cases for the individual on the basis of carefully reasoned criteria.

SANDRA DAY O'CONNOR

Arizona 1930–

Republican

Appointed by Ronald Reagan

Years of Service: 1981–.

Collection of the Supreme Court of the United States. Photographer: Dane Penland

LIFE AND CAREER Justice O'Connor holds the distinction of being the first woman appointed to the Supreme Court. She graduated magna cum laude from Stanford University and was third in the 1952 Stanford Law School class in which William Rehnquist graduated first. Despite her academic attainments, she received no offers from private firms because of the gender bias of that era. She worked as a county attorney in San Mateo, California, as a civilian attorney for the Army while her husband served, and in private practice while raising a family in Phoenix, Arizona. Active in civic and political activities—and described as a "mainstream pragmatic Republican"—O'Connor served as assistant attorney general of Arizona from 1965 to 1969. She was appointed and then elected twice to the Arizona Senate, rising to Senate majority leader before becoming judge of the Maricopa County Superior Court in 1974 and judge of the Arizona Intermediate Court of Appeals in 1979.

CONTRIBUTION TO CRIMINAL PROCEDURE Her position is generally conservative. In right to counsel cases, she found no constitutional violation by the forfeiture of funds to pay for counsel (*Caplin & Drysdale v. United States* 1989). Her opinion in *Moran v. Burbine* held that the fact that an attorney has been retained and is attempting to reach a suspect does not affect the voluntariness of a confession given after

Miranda warnings have been read and the suspect has waived the right to remain silent.

In *Illinois v. Krull* (1987), O'Connor dissented from a ruling that evidence of an illegal search based on the good-faith reliance on a statute is admissible. Although she joined the conservative majority in *Leon* (1984), holding illegal evidence seized in a good faith reliance on a bad warrant is admissible, her experience as a legislator led her to distinguish a warrant from a statute. A legislature's "unreasonable authorization may affect thousands or millions," while a magistrate's error only affects the individual involved, and legislators are more subject to "political pressures that may threaten Fourth Amendment values" than are judges.

SIGNATURE OPINION *Strickland v. Washington* (1984). While holding that a defendant's Sixth Amendment right to counsel can be violated by the ineffective assistance of counsel, she formulated a weak standard which requires a defendant to show a serious deficiency in an attorney's performance and also requires that this performance was responsible for the verdict or sentence.

ASSESSMENT She came to the Supreme Court with a moderate to conservative record, supporting the death penalty, having a mixed position on abortion, and in favor of the Equal Rights Amendment and other proposals to equalize the legal position of women. In general, these policies have characterized her votes as a justice. Her judicial philosophy downplays broad ideological positions. As a *judicial* conservative, she seeks to avoid constitutional issues where possible and changes the law in incremental steps. This lawyer-like approach has anchored the law in precedent and to the facts of cases and prevented a radical conservative legal revolution that Justices Scalia and Thomas would be willing to lead. O'Connor often influences the law through concurring opinions, by joining the conservative majority in high-visibility areas such as abortion, the death penalty, and church-state relations, but preventing it from establishing sweeping doctrines. For example, she has voted to allow the states to place some restrictions on abortions but has voted against overturning *Roe v. Wade* (1973). In the church-state area, her concept that Christmas season displays that are predominantly secular are permissible under the First Amendment has become the Court's position.

FURTHER READING

Nancy Maveety, *Justice Sandra Day O'Connor: Strategist on the Supreme Court* (Lanham, Md.: Rowman & Littlefield, 1996).

ANTONIN SCALIA

New Jersey 1936–

Republican

Appointed by Ronald Reagan

Years of Service: 1986–.

Collection of the Supreme Court of the United States. Photographer: Joseph Lavenburg

LIFE AND CAREER Antonin Scalia, the son of a Sicilian immigrant and professor of romance languages at Brooklyn College, was a superb student, graduating first in his class from Xavier High School and Georgetown University. He was an editor on the *Harvard Law Review* and received his law degree from Harvard Law School in 1960. His strong conservative beliefs were pronounced even as a schoolboy. He practiced corporate law, taught at the University of Virginia Law School, and from 1971 to 1977, held several key appointments on legal advisory staffs to Presidents Nixon and Ford, including assistant attorney general in charge of the Justice Department's Office of Legal Counsel. He spent a year as scholar-in-resident at the American Enterprise Institute, a conservative think tank, four years as law professor at the University of Chicago, and was appointed to U.S. Court of Appeals for the District of Columbia in 1982.

Scalia was a leading conservative spokesperson on issues of law and economics, asserting the power of the executive branch, favoring judicial restraint, and backing deregulation of the marketplace; he blasted judicially supported affirmative action programs. These positions were evident in many of his opinions on the Court of Appeals. His opinions were forceful, and when he was appointed to replace Justice Rehnquist (who was elevated to the office of Chief Justice) it was thought that his charm and powers of persuasion would solidify a conservative court that would overturn *Roe v. Wade.* His nomination sailed through the Senate and he was confirmed by a 98-to-0 vote.

CONTRIBUTION TO CRIMINAL PROCEDURE His position in criminal procedure has proven to be something of a surprise. While hardly a liberal—most of his criminal law votes favor the prosecution—he has, on several occasions, taken positions where the logic of the law lead him to support the defendant. These include his opinion in *Arizona v. Hicks* (1987) (a slight movement of property to view a serial number constitutes a search), and dissenting opinions in *Nat'l Treasury Emp. Union v. Von Raab* (1989) (automatic drug testing of every customs officer is not based on a real need but on political motivations and violates Fourth Amendment) and *Maryland v. Craig* (1990) (placing a screen between a defendant and an accuser who is a minor violates the Sixth Amendment confrontation clause).

His many pro-prosecution opinions include *Wyoming v. Houghton* (1999) (police can search handbag of passenger of stopped car, where probable cause to search car exists, despite lack of suspicion against the passenger); *Whren v. U. S.* (1996) (pretext search of automobile upheld); and *Vernonia School District 47J v. Acton* (1995) (special needs allows drug testing of every public high school student athlete).

SIGNATURE OPINION *California v. Hodari D.* (1991). A youth fleeing from the police threw away drugs before being tackled. For the Court, Scalia wrote that there was no stop or arrest before the youth was physically seized; the drugs were therefore abandoned and admissible into evidence. To reach this result, he set aside the existing rule that a person is seized when they reasonably believe they are not free to leave and replaced it with the physical restraint standard.

ASSESSMENT Scalia is a leading intellectual on the Court and has been instrumental in the Court reviving the rights of property owners against government regulation. His votes are generally conservative in First Amendment and other civil rights areas, although less so than Rehnquist and Thomas. He is known for his opinions and writings that argue that the plain text of statutes should be the leading principle as to their interpretation and wary of legislative history as a guide to statutory interpretation. He has been a lone dissenter on the question of the separation of powers where he believes that sharp lines must be drawn between the branches of government and thus voted against the constitutionality of the U.S. Sentencing Commission on which judges and executive appointees join to set policy.

FURTHER READING

David A. Schultz and Christopher E. Smith, *The Jurisprudential Vision of Justice Antonin Scalia* (Lanham, Md: Rowman & Littlefield, 1996).

ANTHONY KENNEDY

California 1936–

Republican

Appointed by Ronald Reagan

Years of Service: 1988–.

Collection of the Supreme Court of the United States. Photographer: Joseph Bailey

LIFE AND CAREER A Sacramento, California, native, Kennedy graduated from Stanford University (member of Phi Beta Kappa) and graduated cum laude from Harvard Law School in 1961. He practiced law in San Francisco and took over his father's Sacramento law and lobbying practice in 1963. His approach to law practice was scholarly, and for twenty-three years he taught law part-time at the McGeorge School of Law. He came to Governor Reagan's attention in 1971 by drafting a tax-limitation amendment that was the forerunner of California's famous Proposition 13. On Reagan's recommendation, he was appointed to the Ninth Circuit Court of Appeals in 1975 by President Ford.

Kennedy was a respected federal judge, who upheld precedent, carefully considered all sides of a case before rendering a decision, and who, in civil rights cases generally did not find in favor of women, minorities, or homosexuals. His decision declaring the "legislative veto" unconstitutional (i.e., Congress delegates power to administrative agencies to overrule agency rules) was upheld by the Supreme Court.

He was quickly confirmed as associate justice after the monumental battle that blocked President Reagan's nomination of Robert Bork to the Supreme Court and the failed attempt to have a second nominee, Judge Douglas Ginsburg, approved.

CONTRIBUTION TO CRIMINAL PROCEDURE In most cases, Kennedy votes for the government and against the individual. He has voted to uphold the drug courier profile as a basis for a *Terry* stop; to find that ambiguity in a *Miranda* warning does not void a confession; that a judge can deny a defendant's free choice of attorney on grounds of conflict of interest over the defendant's objections; that a helicopter overflight of residential backyard is not a search. In *Skinner v. Railway Labor*

Executives' Association (1989) and *National Treasury Employees Union v. Von Raab* (1989) he upheld drug testing on the basis of the special needs doctrine.

SIGNATURE OPINION *Powers v. Ohio* (1991). A prosecutor used peremptory challenges to keep seven blacks off the jury in a murder trial. For the majority, Justice Kennedy held that a white defendant could object. He wrote, "Jury service is an exercise of responsible citizenship by all members of the community, including those who otherwise might not have the opportunity to contribute to our civic life."

ASSESSMENT Aside from criminal procedure cases, Justice Kennedy is a conservative moderate who is often aligned with O'Connor and Souter and not with the most conservative wing of the Court (Rehnquist, Scalia and Thomas). In a pivotal abortion case, he wrote a joint opinion with O'Connor and Souter upholding a woman's right to choose based on the concept of precedent. He held that the burning of the American flag during a protest was protected speech and could not be criminal because the result was compelled by the Constitution. In a case involving the solicitation of funds and distribution of leaflets by members of Hare Krishna at an airport, he joined the moderates on the Court holding that while the solicitation could be banned, the leafleting was protected by the First Amendment. And in *Romer v. Evans* (1996), he wrote for a majority that struck down a state referendum that specifically stated that homosexual orientation could not be a basis for heightened anti-discrimination protection. Kennedy viewed this law as violating the Equal Protection Clause because it singled out a certain class of citizens for disfavored legal status or general hardships.

FURTHER READING

Akhil Reed Amar, "Justice Kennedy and the Ideal of Equality," *Pacific Law Journal* 28:515–32 (1997).

CHAPTER 11

THE PRETRIAL PROCESS

It may be that it is the obnoxious thing in its mildest and least repulsive form; but illegitimate and unconstitutional practices get their first footing in that way, namely, by silent approaches and slight deviations from legal modes of procedure. This can only be obviated by adhering to the rule that constitutional provisions for the security of person and property should be liberally construed. A close and literal construction deprives them of half their efficacy, and leads to gradual depreciation of the right, as if it consisted more in sound than in substance. It is the duty of courts to be watchful for the constitutional rights of the citizen, and against any stealthy encroachments thereon.

— Justice Joseph P. Bradley in *Boyd v. United States,* 116 U.S. 616, 635 (1886)

CHAPTER OUTLINE

KEY TERMS AND PHRASES *(CONTINUES ON NEXT PAGE)*

Adversary system
Arraignment
Bail
Bail bond
Bail bondsman
Bind-over decision
Charging
Deposit bond
Discovery
Facial attack
Formal charges
Grand jury

Immunity	Preventive detention	Transactional immunity
Indictment	Release on recognizance	Trial *de novo*
Information	Screening	True bill
Initial appearance	Selective prosecution	Unindicted coconspirator
Motions	Separation of powers doctrine	Use immunity
Multiple-district prosecutions	Subpoena	Venue
Preliminary examination	Subpeona power	Vindictive prosecution

INTRODUCTION

After arrest, a defendant is thrown into the bewildering world of the courts. What happens before trial is critically important to her. There is a fifty-fifty chance that a prosecutor will dismiss her case. A few cases will be screened out by a grand jury or a judge after a preliminary hearing, although it is more likely that an indictment will be handed up or the defendant will be bound over for trial. Pretrial release, by bail or personal recognizance, will determine whether the defendant sits in jail or goes free before trial. A lawyer appointed during this process can work for a dismissal, for a satisfactory negotiated plea, or prepare for trial. Counsel can bring pretrial motions that challenge the admissibility of evidence obtained by unconstitutional methods.

Pretrial Justice

Pretrial **screening** goes back to the common law. The **grand jury,** (or the "jury of presentment,") is a panel of citizens that dates back to the origin of trial by jury in the thirteenth century. If it refuses to indict a suspect, the suspect goes free. The value of quickly screening out innocent suspects eliminates "easy" cases from trial dockets and relieves innocent suspects from further expense, inconvenience, and fear. Preliminary examinations were created by statute in early modern times. They were designed to secure information of the crime immediately after an arrest. Professor John Langbein reports that when an arrested thief was brought before a London justice of the peace (magistrate) in the late seventeenth century, preliminary examination procedure required the magistrate to question the suspect and any material witnesses, and bind them over to appear at the trial. The magistrate reduced the examination to writing and transmitted it to the trial court. In some instances, the magistrate would appear before the trial judge to describe the evidence.[1] The modern preliminary examination also acts as a screen to dismiss cases in which the state cannot establish probable cause or a prima facie case.

The pretrial process in America has become lengthy and complex process; a typical felony case takes on average from six months to a year from arrest to adjudication. Some critics say that the heavy reliance on pretrial settlement by guilty plea has undermined the **adversary system.**[2] In contrast, Professor Malcolm Feeley suggests that despite the decline in the number of trials, the expanded use of pretrial procedures actually strengthens the adversary system:

> Probable cause hearings, bills of particulars, motions to suppress evidence, and the like, all shape the criminal process prior to trial and formal adjudication of guilt or innocence. In many cases, pretrial hearings—or for that matter negotiations in the shadow of the law—can become mini-trials. Whether the early review of the evidence reveals a strong or weak case or whether the testimony of a particular witness or the introduction of a specific piece of evidence will or will not be admitted into the record can make or break a case, and depending on the conclusion reached, charges may be dropped, reduced, or the accused may plead guilty or take his case to trial. So, while we have witnessed the demise of the trial, we have at the same time experienced an increase in pretrial opportunities to review in adversarial context some of the same types of issues that once were *less* carefully considered by the jury at trial.[3]

The modern pretrial process thus provides a defendant with fair treatment. An attorney is provided early in the process. Weaker cases are removed, by dismissal or plea, leaving trials for closely contested cases or more serious crimes. This chapter focuses on the defendant's rights at the bail decision, prosecutorial charging, the preliminary examination, and the grand jury. The chapter begins with a brief overview of the major elements of the pretrial process.

Steps in the Pretrial Process

A suspect's progress through the court system differs sharply depending upon whether the charge is a misdemeanor or a felony. For a misdemeanor, usually carrying a maximum sentence of no longer than one year in jail, the proceedings are quicker and less formal than proceedings for felonies. A misdemeanor defendant is tried in a court of limited jurisdiction, often called a district, magistrate, police, or municipal court, where jury trials are rarely held. In some jurisdictions, a person charged with a misdemeanor can plead guilty and have the case disposed of at the initial appearance before a judge. A felony defendant is initially processed through the same lower court that disposes of misdemeanors. In a felony case, the magistrate conducts a variety of preliminary legal procedures short of conducting a trial. This chapter focuses on pretrial felony processing. The procedures described as follows are basically the same in each state, although details may vary.

INITIAL APPEARANCE A suspect must be brought before a magistrate within twenty-four to forty-eight hours of arrest. A typical **initial appearance** takes a few minutes, during which several important things happen. The initial charges are read to the defendant; he or she is informed of his or her constitutional rights and the right to a preliminary examination; indigents are assigned a lawyer or a public defender; and bail or other mode of pretrial release is arranged or denied. A felony defendant is not allowed to plead guilty at this point and is most likely to be bound over for further proceedings. *Gerstein v. Pugh* (1975) (Chapter 5) ruled that a prosecutor's or police officer's decision to arrest and detain a person must be reviewed quickly by a magistrate. This prevents abuses, especially lengthy and secret detention in order to "work on" a suspect to obtain a confession (see Chapter 8).

BAIL/PRETRIAL RELEASE DECISION A defendant's pretrial liberty status is first determined at the initial appearance, most commonly by cash bail or **release on recognizance,** but also on the signing of a property bond. Suspects who are denied bail or those who cannot raise the bail amount may reapply for bail or move for a reduction of the bail amount later in the process. The prosecutor can move to increase the bail amount or to revoke release if the defendant has violated a condition of release. Bail may be denied to defendants who are charged with a capital crime; who are known flight risks; or who have threatened witnesses.[4]

PROSECUTORIAL CHARGING Prosecutors have great discretion in deciding whether to charge a person, and if so, with which crimes. Half of all felony arrests are dismissed by the prosecutor in many jurisdictions.[5] There is more variation in the charging process than there is in other pretrial procedures. In some jurisdictions, for example, prosecuting attorneys frame charges in the complaint prior to the initial appearance, but in other places, prosecutors do not become involved until after that stage.

Formal charges drafted by the prosecutor are either **indictments** or **informations.** Formal charges are important because they tell the defendant that he or she will stand trial only on the crimes charged. If new facts come to light, the prosecutor can charge a defendant with additional "counts" (specific crimes) in an *amended* indictment approved by the grand jury or an amended information approved by a judge. In states where prosecution must be commenced by a grand jury, the prosecutor drafts the proposed bills of indictment for the grand jury. In states that do not use grand jury indictments, the prosecutor draws up official charges in an information. Indictments and informations are short documents that name the penal code sections that the defendant is accused of committing and include a brief recital of the facts of the crime.

GRAND JURY PROCEEDINGS In federal prosecutions and approximately one-third of the states, formal charges are approved by a grand jury.[6] This body consists of from twelve to twenty-three citizens (depending on the state) who are brought together to review relevant evidence and decide *in secret,* by majority vote, whether there is sufficient evidence—probable cause or a *prima facie* case—to justify a trial. The prosecutor presents the grand jury with charges in an indictment and presents subpoenaed witnesses to establish the facts sufficient to indict. Most states that do not require indictment by grand jury, allow the prosecutor to convene a citizens' grand jury to investigate a crime, typically in large-scale investigations of organized or white-collar crime. The grand jury **subpoena** powers are useful to investigators. Grand juries may also be called in politically sensitive cases, as when criminal charges are brought against high elected officials.

PRELIMINARY EXAMINATION The **preliminary examination,** or preliminary hearing, is a public, trial-like hearing, held before a magistrate, to determine whether sufficient evidence exists to justify a trial. The prosecutor puts witnesses on the stand to establish probable cause that the defendant committed the alleged crime. The defense has the right to question these witnesses, but rarely calls defense witnesses. If there is sufficient evidence, the judge will **bind over** the defendant to the felony court for trial. In some states, a defendant who is indicted by a grand jury may also have a preliminary examination, while in others, a grand jury indictment cuts off the statutory right to a preliminary examination. In addition to its bind-over function, a preliminary examination is useful to the lawyers to get a sense of the strength of the evidence and witnesses.

PRETRIAL MOTIONS This text has examined the constitutionality of arrests, searches, confessions, and lineups. Before trial, the defense attorney makes **motions**—applications or requests to a judge to obtain a ruling or order—asking for a hearing to determine whether evidence has been obtained illegally. A motion can be made by the prosecutor or defense at any time before trial, but the usual practice is for courts to set aside a special day of the week to present motions. Depending upon the nature of the motion and the complexity of the facts, a separate hearing may be granted to inquire into the merits of the motion. Motion hearings are open to the public (*Waller v. Georgia,* 1984). Motion practice is extremely important in regard to procedural and substantive fairness in the trial process. Motions for a change of **venue,** for example, may play a vital role in avoiding local prejudice. At times when prosecutors are not forthcoming with factual evidence, a defense motion for **discovery** can compel the prosecutor to divulge facts that were found during the police investigation and that are helpful to the defense (*Brady v. Maryland,* 1963). There is no theoretical limit on the nature of motions—an attorney can fashion a new motion to deal with a specific issue. There are a large number of standard motions. Some of the more common motions include those to obtain continuances (adjournments); to request psychiatric services; to lower the amount of bail; to waive filing fees on the ground of indigence; for a competency hearing; to be tried by jury; to strike redundant counts of an indictment; to join or sever codefendants or charges in the same or separate trials, and so forth.

PROSECUTOR-DEFENSE CONFERENCES In recent years, because of case pressure and trial delays, judges have required the prosecutor and defense counsel to meet in order to either prepare for the trial or to establish the grounds for a negotiated plea agreement. In a sense, pretrial conferences formalize what for many years has been an informal process of meetings between attorneys. If the case is going to trial, the conference is an opportunity for the defense lawyer to request evidence from the prosecutor and to inform the prosecutor that certain defenses will be used that require preparation before trial.[7] Otherwise, the attorneys review the facts of the case to determine whether it is appropriate for the defendant to plead guilty, and if so, to determine an acceptable arrangement. In the latter case, the defense attorney must convey the gist of the negotiations to his or her client before proceeding.

ARRAIGNMENT The **arraignment** is a brief procedure where the charges are read to the defendant who is then given the opportunity to plead guilty, not guilty, *nolo contendere,* or to remain mute. The practice has ancient roots in the common law. The arraignment bolsters due process by giving the defendant explicit notice of the charges on which he or she is to be tried. It is held in open court. As the pretrial process has become so complex, and the defendant has many opportunities to learn of the charges, the arraignment is now conducted in a *pro forma* manner. In fact, a failure to comply with arraignment procedure is a technical error that usually will not lead to the reversal of a conviction (*Garland v. Washington,* 1914). In many jurisdictions, defendants plead guilty at the arraignment hearing if a plea bargain has already been worked out with the prosecutor. The term *arraignment,* incidentally, is used in different ways that can cause confusion. In some states, arraignment refers to the reading of charges at the initial appearance; in others, it refers to the initial appearance and to the "arraignment on the information or indictment." The formal arraignment can take place immediately after the preliminary examination or grand jury proceeding, immediately before trial, or at any time between those two points.

The Bail Decision: Pretrial Release

The Eighth Amendment states: "Excessive bail shall not be required. . . ." This does not guarantee pretrial release in every case, but reflects a policy favoring the pretrial freedom of a criminal suspect. It supports the presumption of innocence. The bail provision reflects the traditional method of balancing individual freedom with the state's need to ensure that defendants will return to court to stand trial. **Bail** is the release of a defendant before trial based on that defendant's promise to return. The promise is *secured* by some form of collateral, such as money, that the defendant agrees to transfer to the court if he or she does not show up for the trial. However, appellate courts have held that in extreme circumstances, where it appears that no amount of bail will be sufficient to compel a defendant to return to court for trial, bail may be refused.[8]

This legal device has become a business. A **bail bondsman** receives a portion of the bail amount from the defendant, usually ten percent and in return posts a **bail bond** with the court, promising to pay the full bail amount if the defendant does not show. This results in pretrial freedom for the defendant, an income for the bail bondsman, and some assurance to the court that the defendant will show up. If the defendant defaults by "skipping town," the bail bondsman must pay the full amount of the bail to the court and then find and sue the defendant for that money. Courts have the power to forgive part or all of the forfeited amount. Whereas this discretion may be fair in some instances, it is also an obvious source of corruption.

The Eighth Amendment and the Right to Bail

The Eighth Amendment does not absolutely guarantee pretrial release. Under common law and in most American states, capital crimes punishable by death are not bailable. The modern approach to bail in capital cases is to establish a *presumption* against bail where "the proof is evident or the presumption of guilt is great." Thus, even a capital suspect may obtain bail if a magistrate determines that the prosecutor's case has weaknesses.

In the leading case of *Stack v. Boyle* (1951), twelve defendants, Communist Party leaders, were charged with advocating the violent overthrow of the American government (Smith Act). The bail amount for each defendant was set at fifty thousand dollars. They appealed the amount of bail as excessive under the Eighth Amendment. The Supreme Court found that there was little evidence of the defendants' having a history of or intention of fleeing prosecution. The typical bail amount for persons charged with crimes carrying a maximum penalty of five years imprisonment and a ten thousand-dollar fine was usually much lower than fifty thousand dollars. There was no support for the prosecution's belief that the defendants would "jump bail" because they were allegedly involved in a conspiracy with worldwide communist powers. The Supreme Court held that the high bail amount was arbitrary and a violation of the Eighth Amendment. In reaching this decision Chief Justice Fred Vinson said, "Unless this right to bail before trial is preserved, the presumption of innocence, secured only after centuries of struggle, would lose its meaning."

Modern Forms of Pretrial Release

Bail practice was for many years criticized as discriminatory, confining persons who were otherwise good risks to return for trial, simply because they lacked sufficient funds. Since the 1960s most states and the federal government have established release mechanisms designed to increase release before trial of suspects who are likely to return.

RELEASE ON RECOGNIZANCE (ROR) A court officer interviews the defendant to determine whether personal characteristics make him a good prospect to return to court for additional hearings or trial. Objective characteristics include home stability, living with a family member, having a job or attending school, and prior history of escapes. If the suspect receives a high score indicating a likelihood of returning, eligibility is established for release without posting any kind of security, but by making a formal promise to return to court when summoned.

CONDITIONS OF RELEASE Modern laws allow a judge to place restrictions on a suspect released before trial, in addition to bail or part of ROR, to ensure the suspect's return to court for further proceedings. The Federal Bail Reform Act of 1984, which applies only to federal courts, includes that the defendant follow these conditions:

1. report to a police, pretrial release, or probation officer or other court agency on a regular basis;
2. stay away from certain people (e.g., victim or witnesses) or places (e.g., airports, bars);
3. be under the custody or care of a specific individual or treatment program that can ensure the defendant will appear and not endanger the community;
4. maintain employment or schooling;
5. comply with a curfew;
6. not possess a deadly weapon;
7. refrain from alcohol or drug use;
8. undergo medical, psychiatric, or drug treatment;
9. agree to forfeit property or money on failure to appear;
10. execute a bail bond; and/or
11. be jailed in the evening and on weekends.

These conditions must be reasonably related to facilitating the defendant's return and be tailored to the defendant's circumstances

DEPOSIT BOND A few states, to end to what is thought to be the unsavory business of bail bondsmen and to ensure equal treatment for indigents, have created the **deposit bond** as a bail bond substitute. If a judge believes that ROR is not appropriate, a bail amount is set and the defendant raises ten percent of the bail amount to win release. The ten percent is not paid to a bail bondsman but to the court. If the defendant fails to appear he or she becomes liable for the entire amount. Defendants who return to court, on the other hand, receive the deposit amount less a one percent retention fee. The Illinois deposit bond law was challenged as a due process and equal protection violation but was upheld in *Schilb v. Kuebel* (1971), which referred to bail bondsmen in harsh terms. The Supreme Court rejected the argument that the one percent fee ultimately retained was discriminatory against indigents. The Court noted that the fee was reasonable and the statute also had an ROR provision that the judge could use as a release mechanism for indigent defendants who were good risks, thus avoiding any discrimination. This decision, in addition to upholding the deposit bond system, displays faith in the nation's trial court judges to fairly administer pretrial release.

PREVENTIVE DETENTION The pro-defendant, Due Process Model, theory of bail is that the *only* reason to detain arrested suspects before trial is to ensure their return for the trial and other legal proceedings, and that bail amounts should be set only with this in mind. On the other hand, bail practice has also reflected the pro-prosecution, Crime Control Model, theory that bail serves other functions. Therefore, it is widely known that judges often set high bail to detain a suspect feared likely to commit crimes while on bail, attempt to destroy evidence, or intimidate witnesses. Denying bail for these reasons is referred to as **preventive detention.** Congress, believing that preventive detention can be constitutional when accompanied by procedural safeguards, authorized its use in the *Bail Reform Act of 1984.*[9] The constitutionality of the act was upheld in *United States v. Salerno* (1987).

• CASE & COMMENTS •

United States v. Salerno
481 U.S. 739, 107 S.Ct. 2095, 95 L.Ed.2d 697 (1987)

CHIEF JUSTICE REHNQUIST delivered the opinion of the Court.

The Bail Reform Act of 1984 (Act) allows a federal court to detain an arrestee pending trial if the Government demonstrates by **[a]** clear and convincing evidence after an adversary hearing that no release conditions "will reasonably assure . . . the safety of any other person and the community." *** We granted certiorari because of a conflict among the Courts of Appeals regarding the validity of the Act. **[b]** We hold that, as against the **facial attack** mounted by these respondents, the Act fully comports with constitutional requirements. ***

[a] Clear and convincing is a high standard of proof. See Table 4–1.

[b] A statute can be challenged as applied or on its face (hence facial attack). A facial attack is a broad attack on the constitutionality of the entire section of the law being challenged.

I

[The Act is a response to "the alarming problem of crimes committed by persons on release." **[c]** Section 3141(a) gives the "judicial officer" discretion to order the pretrial detention of an arrestee; section 3142(e) allows pretrial detention if the judge "finds that no condition[s] will reasonably assure the appearance of the person as required and the safety of any other person and the community." Section 3142(f) establishes procedural safeguards, including the presence of counsel and the right to testify, present witnesses, proffer evidence, and cross-examine other witnesses. Under sections 3142(i) and (f), if the judge finds that no release conditions "can reasonably assure the safety of other persons and the community," the findings of fact must be stated in writing, supported by "clear and convincing evidence."]

[c] The statute requires a judge to *predict* a defendant's future behavior. This is an error-prone task (a person who would not have committed a crime while on bail could be held, while a person could be released who does commit a crime while on pretrial release). Do you think judges are equipped to do this accurately?

The judicial officer is not given unbridled discretion in making the detention determination, [but must consider several statutory factors: **[d]** (1) the nature and seriousness of the charges, (2) the substantiality of the government's evidence against the arrestee, (3) the arrestee's background and characteristics, and (4) the nature and seriousness of the danger posed by the suspect's release. Section 3142(g). If pretrial detention is ordered,] the detainee is entitled to expedited appellate review of the detention order. §§3145(b), (c).

[d] How do these factors limit discretion? Do the first three factors, which are merely formal, add much of a check on the prosecutor?

[Salerno, charged with racketeering, was believed to be a high ranking "boss" in an organized crime "family" who had participated in two murder conspiracies. The district court believed these allegations and granted the government's detention motion.] **[e]**

[The court of appeals reversed, concluding that due process prevented the detention of persons merely because they were thought to present a danger to the community.] It reasoned that our criminal law system holds persons accountable for past actions, not anticipated future actions. Although a court could detain an arrestee who threatened to flee before trial, such detention would be permissible because it would serve the basic objective of a criminal system—bringing the accused to trial. ***

[e] The district court views the law from the "Crime Control Model" of criminal justice; the Court of Appeals from the "Due Process Model."

II

A facial challenge to a legislative Act is, of course, the most difficult challenge to mount successfully, since the challenger must establish that no set of circumstances exists under which the Act would be valid. **[f]** The fact that the Bail Reform Act might operate unconstitutionally under some conceivable set of circumstances is insufficient to render it wholly invalid. *** We think respondents have failed to shoulder their heavy burden to demonstrate that the Act is "facially" unconstitutional.

[f] If the Act were seen to apply disproportionately to, say, gang members, or to racial minorities, a defendant might have been able to challenge the Act "as applied.'

* * *

A

* * *

Respondents first argue that the Act violates substantive due process because the pretrial detention it authorizes constitutes impermissible punishment before trial. *** The Court of Appeals assumed that pretrial detention under the Bail Reform Act is regulatory, not penal, and we agree that it is. **[g]**

As an initial matter, the mere fact that a person is detained does not inexorably lead to the conclusion that the government has imposed punishment. *** To determine whether a restriction on

[g] In this case, detention—a physical state—can be either "punishment" (not allowed before

• CASE & COMMENTS •

liberty constitutes impermissible punishment or permissible regulation, we first look to legislative intent. *** Unless Congress expressly intended to impose punitive restrictions, the punitive/regulatory distinction turns on "'whether an alternative purpose to which [the restriction] may rationally be connected is assignable for it, and whether it appears excessive in relation to the alternative purpose assigned [to it].'" ***

We conclude that the detention imposed by the Act falls on the regulatory side of the dichotomy. The legislative history of the Bail Reform Act clearly indicates that Congress did not formulate the pretrial detention provisions as punishment for dangerous individuals. *** Congress instead perceived pretrial detention as a potential solution to a pressing societal problem. *** There is no doubt that preventing danger to the community is a legitimate regulatory goal.

Nor are the incidents of pretrial detention excessive in relation to the regulatory goal Congress sought to achieve. **[h]** The Bail Reform Act [is] carefully limit[ed] *** to the most serious of crimes[:] *** crimes of violence, offenses for which the sentence is life imprisonment or death, serious drug offenses, or certain repeat offenders. The arrestee is entitled to a prompt detention hearing, *** and the maximum length of pretrial detention is limited by the stringent time limitations of the Speedy Trial Act. *** Moreover, *** the conditions of confinement envisioned by the Act "appear to reflect the regulatory purposes relied upon by the" Government [requiring] that detainees be housed in a "facility separate, to the extent practicable, from persons awaiting or serving sentences or being held in custody pending appeal." *** We conclude, therefore, that the pretrial detention contemplated by the Bail Reform Act is regulatory in nature, and does not constitute punishment before trial in violation of the Due Process Clause.

[The Court goes on to note that there is no absolute due process prohibition on confinement for regulatory purposes, citing the detention of: **[i]** persons believed to be dangerous in time of war, potentially dangerous resident aliens pending deportation proceedings, mentally unstable individuals who present a danger to the public, dangerous defendants who become incompetent to stand trial, dangerous arrested juveniles before trial, and an arrestee who presents a risk of flight, or a danger to witnesses. There are enough exceptions to the "general rule" of freedom under substantive due process to provide precedent for the Act.]

*** The Bail Reform Act *** narrowly focuses on a particularly acute problem in which the Government interests are overwhelming. **[j]** The Act operates only on individuals who have been arrested for a specific category of extremely serious offenses. *** Congress specifically found that these individuals are far more likely to be responsible for dangerous acts in the community after arrest. *** **[g]**

[Chief Justice Rehnquist recognizes the individual's strong interest in liberty, but holds that given the carefully delineated law, individual liberty must be "subordinated to the greater needs of society." He concluded this section by holding that the procedures of the Bail Reform Act were] "adequate to authorize the pretrial detention of at least some [persons] charged with crimes," *** As we stated in *Schall* [*v. Martin,* 467 U.S. 253 (1984)], "there is nothing inherently unattainable about a prediction of future criminal conduct." ***

B

*** We think that the Act survives a challenge founded upon the Eighth Amendment.

The Eighth Amendment addresses pretrial release by providing merely that "[e]xcessive bail shall not be required." This clause, of course, says nothing about whether bail shall be available at all. Respondents nevertheless contend that this Clause grants them a right to bail calculated solely upon considerations of flight. They rely on *Stack v. Boyle.* *** In respondents' view, since the Bail Reform Act allows a court essentially to set bail at an infinite amount for reasons not related to the risk of flight, it violates the Excessive Bail Clause. Respondents concede that the right to bail they have discovered in the Eighth Amendment is not absolute. **[k]** A court may, for example, refuse bail in capital cases. And, as the Court of Appeals noted and respondents admit, a court may refuse bail when the defendant presents a threat to the judicial process by intimidating witnesses. Respondents

trial) or "regulation" (allowed before trial). Can Congress and the Court simply label pretrial detention as a "regulation" to get around inconvenient legal obstacles? Civil impositions, such as taxes or fees, are regulatory, not punitive. What makes a loss a "punishment?" The Court provides several legal tests that include the intent of Congress and whether there is a reasonable regulatory purpose.

[h] There are two "punishment" arguments: first, whether preventive detention *is* punishment, and second, whether preventive detention is so excessive a means to achieve the regulatory purpose of preventing crime by releasees as to violate due process.

[i] Are these examples close enough to the situation of a person held before trial to prevent crime or can they be "distinguished?"

[j] Studies have placed the pretrial crime rate at about five percent. Is this an acute problem that requires preventive detention? [note - footnote 10 goes here]

[k] This is a clear weakness in Salerno's argument. If the law allows one restriction on bail (e.g.,

• CASE & COMMENTS •

characterize these exceptions as consistent with what they claim to be the sole purpose of bail—to ensure the integrity of the judicial process.

*** [W]e reject the proposition that the Eighth Amendment categorically prohibits the government from pursuing other admittedly compelling interests through regulation of pretrial release. ***

*** Nothing in the text of the Bail Clause limits permissible government considerations solely to questions of flight. The only arguable substantive limitation of the Bail Clause is that the government's proposed conditions of release or detention not be "excessive" in light of the perceived evil. Of course, to determine whether the government's response is excessive, we must compare that response against the interest the government seeks to protect by means of that response. Thus, when the government has admitted that its only interest is in preventing flight, bail must be set by a court at a sum designed to ensure that goal, and no more. *** We believe that when Congress has mandated detention on the basis of a compelling interest other than prevention of flight, as it has here, the Eighth Amendment does not require release on bail.

no bail in capital offenses) why not another? What is Salerno's argument?

* * *

JUSTICE MARSHALL, with whom JUSTICE BRENNAN joins, dissenting.

This case brings before the Court for the first time **[l]** a statute in which Congress declares that a person innocent of any crime may be jailed indefinitely, pending the trial of allegations which are legally presumed to be untrue, if the Government shows to the satisfaction of a judge that the accused is likely to commit crimes, unrelated to the pending charges, at anytime in the future. Such statutes, consistent with the usages of tyranny and the excesses of what bitter experience teaches us to call the police state, have long been thought incompatible with the fundamental human rights protected by our Constitution. Today a majority of this Court holds otherwise. Its decision disregards basic principles of justice established centuries ago and enshrined beyond the reach of governmental interference in the Bill of Rights.

[l] Part of the force of Salerno's attack on the Act is its novelty—preventive detention of this kind had never been part of American law. Does Justice Marshall's liberalism make him a conservative when it comes to accepting legal changes to deal with a problem?

* * *

II

* * *

[Justice Marshall first attacked the conclusion that detention under the Bail Reform Act is regulatory and not punitive.] The ease with which the conclusion is reached suggests the worthlessness of the achievement. ***

This argument does not demonstrate the conclusion it purports to justify. **[m]** Let us apply the majority's reasoning to a similar, hypothetical case. After investigation, Congress determines (not unrealistically) that a large proportion of violent crime is perpetrated by persons who are unemployed. It also determines, equally reasonably, that much violent crime is committed at night. From amongst the panoply of "potential solutions," Congress chooses a statute which permits, after judicial proceedings, the imposition of a dusk-to-dawn curfew on anyone who is unemployed. Since this is not a measure enacted for the purpose of punishing the unemployed, and since the majority finds that preventing danger to the community is a legitimate regulatory goal, the curfew statute would, according to the majority's analysis, be a mere "regulatory" detention statute, entirely compatible with the substantive components of the Due Process Clause.

[m] Is Justice Marshall's shocking hypothesis clearly applicable under the reasoning of the majority? Does the fact that the Act applied to *arrested* persons make the hypothesis weak, or does the fact that it applies to persons presumed to be innocent make the hypothesis a logical consequence of the majority's ruling?

[Justice Marshall claims that the majority simply redefined punishment as regulation, and so allows a clear violation of the due process rights of detainees.]

* * *

*** [Justice Marshall next suggested that the Court failed to consider whether the Eighth Amendment flatly prohibits the denial of bail for future dangerousness.] The majority does not ask, *** if there are any substantive limits contained in both the Eighth Amendment and the Due Process Clause which render this system of preventive detention unconstitutional. The majority does not ask because the answer is apparent and, to the majority, inconvenient.

• CASE & COMMENTS •

III

The essence of this case may be found, ironically enough, in [another] provision of the Act to which the majority does not refer, [p]rovid[ing] that "[n]othing in this section shall be construed as modifying or limiting the presumption of innocence." But the very pith and purpose of this statute is an abhorrent limitation of the presumption of innocence. The majority's untenable conclusion that the present Act is constitutional arises from a specious denial of the role of the Bail Clause and the Due Process Clause in protecting the invaluable guarantee afforded by the presumption of innocence.

* * *

[Justice Marshall posed this puzzle: if an indicted person is detained under the act and is later acquitted, she must be released. Otherwise,] that would allow the Government to imprison someone for uncommitted crimes based upon "proof" not beyond a reasonable doubt. *** But our fundamental principles of justice declare that the defendant is as innocent on the day before his trial as he is on the morning after his acquittal. Under this statute an untried indictment somehow acts to permit a detention, based on other charges, which after an acquittal would be unconstitutional. The conclusion is inescapable that the indictment has been turned into evidence, if not that the defendant is guilty of the crime charged, then that left to his own devices he will soon be guilty of something else. ***

* * *

As Chief Justice Vinson wrote for the Court in *Stack v. Boyle,* [this volume] "Unless th[e] right to bail before trial is preserved, the presumption of innocence, secured only after centuries of struggle, would lose its meaning." ***

* * *

[Justice Stevens dissented].

In *United States v. Montalvo-Murillo* (1990), Montalvo was held in jail while his bail hearing was delayed for almost two weeks. Bail was set at fifty thousand dollars plus conditions because the magistrate ruled that Montalvo was a flight risk. The government sought review of the bail decision in the federal district court. The district court agreed with the government that there was no condition or combination of conditions that reasonably would ensure the respondent's appearance; nevertheless, it ordered Montalvo's release because the detention hearing, in violation of federal law, was not held on the "first appearance." Montalvo fled and was still at large while his attorneys pursued the bail issue in the Supreme Court.

The Supreme Court held (6–3) (per Kennedy, J.) that the failure to comply with the statutory requirement that "the hearing shall be held immediately upon the person's first appearance" did *not* require the individual's release. The theory of the Bail Reform Act of 1984 is to provide fair bail procedures while protecting the safety of the public and assuring the appearance at trial of defendants found likely to flee. "Automatic release contravenes the object of the statute."

Justice Stevens, dissented. He felt that the government broke the law by imprisoning Montalvo without a timely hearing. "In its haste to ensure the detention of respondent, the Court readily excuses the Government's prior and proven violation of the law. I cannot agree." Justice Stevens believed that primary *constitutional* rule favors liberty before guilt is proven. Since the Bail Reform Act's preventive detention is an *exception* to this fundamental constitutional preference, the act must be strictly enforced. As in *United States v. Salerno,* the differing opinions of the conservative majority and liberal dissenters closely match the Crime Control and the Due Process models of criminal justice.

PROSECUTORIAL CHARGING

The prosecutor, an executive branch officer, is typically an elected county official. Prosecutors' offices range in size from a single, part-time attorney in rural counties to metropolitan offices with hundreds of assistant prosecuting attorneys. The prosecutor is the pivotal actor in the pretrial and trial process, having virtually unlimited discretion over the vital function of determining the charges on which the suspect will stand trial.

Charging is a discretionary function because every state penal code allows prosecutors to choose among a variety of criminal complaints carrying different penalties. For example, a serial rapist can be charged with multiple counts of rape or brought to trial on only one; the defendant may be charged with assault instead of rape because of difficulties in proving the crimes. A rape conviction would result in a longer sentence, but the possibility of acquittal may be higher in a rape trial. Prosecutors may bring charges against all individuals involved in a crime or only one or two; co-defendants can be charged jointly so that they can be tried together, or they can be charged separately. The charging power gives the prosecutor substantial leverage in positioning a case to the state's advantage at trial or in plea bargaining.

Because the prosecutor is an elected official, charging cannot be entirely divorced from politics. Whereas most cases are processed according to legal standards, in certain cases, political factors, such as reelection, may weigh in the charging decision. The positive side of the prosecutor being an elected official is that his or her policies and practices are more open to public input; on occasion a prosecutor who pursues an unpopular course may be removed by the ballot box. The negative side is that political consideration may warp the decision to charge, which ideally is made evenhandedly according to legal criteria. Even if political considerations are not visible, critics accuse prosecutors of using their discretion to routinely *overcharge* defendants so that they will be forced into disadvantageous plea bargains. Prosecutors reply that they frame charges by fitting the facts to the definitions of the penal law. In rebuttal, defense-oriented critics maintain that statutory criminal penalties are unrealistically harsh.

Thus, charging, is not a mechanical process. Prosecutors need give no reasons for dismissing a case. As noted above, as many as half of all felony arrests are dismissed by prosecutors. Many cases are dismissed on *legal* grounds such as: lack of evidence; a belief there is reasonable doubt about guilt; or because the prosecutor believes that the police acted illegally. Other cases are dismissed for reasons of *equity:* a belief that in a specific case the harm caused by the crime is negligible; the defendant is genuinely remorseful and/or promises to make restitution; the complainant does not wish to bring charges or is considered unreliable.[11]

In states where the grand jury does not routinely hand up indictments, the formal charges on which the defendant will stand trial are drawn up by the prosecutor in a formal document known as the prosecutor's information. This document is considered at a preliminary hearing before a court of limited jurisdiction. A trial is held if, after the preliminary hearing, a magistrate finds probable cause to support the charges in the information.

Discretion and the Separation of Powers Doctrine

The prosecutor's broad power to decide whether to charge an arrestee exists as long as there is probable cause to believe that the suspect committed a crime (*United States v. Batchelder,* 1979; *Wayte v. United States,* 1985). This discretion includes which crimes with which to charge a defendant (*Ball v. United States,* 1985), whether or not to plea-bargain,[12] when to bring charges (*United States v. Lovasco,* 1977), and whether to grant immunity to one or more defendants in a case.[13]

The 1963 civil rights era case of *United States v. Cox,*[14] from the Court of Appeals for the Fifth Circuit, tested these principles. A federal judge in Mississippi determined that African-American defendants lied in testifying that a local registrar refused to give them voting registration applications. He referred their case to a grand jury, which proceeded to hand up indictments for perjury. The United States attorney (i.e., the federal prosecutor) in that district, on orders of the Attorney General of the United States, refused to sign the indictment. The federal district court judge held the United States attorney in contempt and threatened to hold the attorney general in contempt. The case was quickly appealed to the Court of Appeals, which reversed the trial court, saying:

> The discretionary power of the attorney for the United States in determining whether a prosecution shall be commenced or maintained may well depend upon matters of policy wholly apart from any question of probable cause. Although as a member of the bar, the attorney for the United States is an officer of the court, he is nevertheless an executive officer of the Government, and it is as an officer of the executive department that he exercises a discretion as to whether or not there shall be a prosecution in a particular case. It follows, as an incident of the constitutional separation of powers, that the courts are not to interfere with the free exercise of the discretionary powers of the attorneys of the United States in their control over criminal prosecutions. (*Cox v. United States,* 5th Cir. 1963).

The Court of Appeals recognized the basic rule of *prosecutorial autonomy* from judicial control in the charging function, which is now well established.[15] It is based on the **separation of powers doctrine,** which limits the interference of one branch of government into the proper sphere of another. Despite the prosecutor's autonomy, there is a limited place for judicial control over charging: when prosecutors abuse their discretion through selective or vindictive prosecution.

Selective Prosecution

Selective prosecution occurs when a defendant is singled out for charging on impermissible grounds, such as race, religion, political beliefs, or for exercising constitutional rights. For example, a selective prosecution claim can be raised if, after a fatal robbery, a prosecutor charged an African-American defendant with capital murder while charging white coconspirators with second-degree murder, unless a rational factor distinguished the African-American codefendant. Similarly, selective prosecution might occur if a district attorney brought felony charges against all people who requested a public defender while allowing those who agreed to waive their right to counsel to plead to a misdemeanor. The classic case of selective prosecution, deemed to violate the *equal protection of the law* under the Fourteenth Amendment, was *Yick Wo v. Hopkins* (1886). Without a waiver from the board of supervisors, a San Francisco ordinance required laundries to operate in brick or stone buildings. The board granted permits to operate laundries in wooden buildings to all white applicants except one, but it denied such permits to two hundred Chinese applicants. This blatant racial discrimination in the enforcement of a law, which was essentially fair if it had been applied uniformly, was held to violate the Equal Protection Clause.

The contours of selective prosecution were explored in *Wayte v. United States* (1985), involving a prosecution for failure to register for the draft. Under the Selective Service Act, (the military draft law) the president issued a proclamation requiring twenty-year-old males to register with the Selective Service System (SSS, or the draft), in case the military draft were to be reinstated. Wayte fell within the class of eligible twenty-year-old males but did not register. Instead, he wrote letters to government officials, including the president, stating that he would not register on the grounds of conscience. He received no reply, but continued to write to government officials notifying them that he was not registering and that he would encourage resistance to draft registration. The SSS adopted a policy of "passive enforcement": it would enforce the law against only those resisters who advised the SSS they were not registering, instead of actively investigating to find all who failed to register. The SSS wrote to Wayte and other known violators, to inform them of their duty to register, request that they comply or explain why not, and warn that a violation could result in criminal prosecution and specified penalties.

A year later, the SSS sent the names of one hundred thirty-four young men, including Wayte, to the Department of Justice (DOJ) for investigation and potential prosecution under its passive enforcement system. The DOJ screened out more names and referred the rest to the FBI for further investigation and to the United States Attorneys for prosecution. Instead of immediate prosecution, FBI agents were sent to interview nonregistrants in an effort to persuade them to change their minds; this was known as the "beg" policy. After six months, the DOJ instructed United States attorneys not to initiate prosecutions under the act. Instead, the president announced a grace period to give nonregistrants a further opportunity to register without penalty. Wayte still did not register.

Wayte moved to dismiss his prosecution on the grounds that he was being targeted for prosecution (out of an estimated 674,000 nonregistrants) for exercising his First Amendment rights and because of discriminatory prosecution policy. Approximately 8.3 million men registered out of the 9 million who were required to do so; the SSS referred 286 nonregistrants to the Department of Justice, and of them, sixteen were indicted. Those not indicted were exempt from the draft, could not be found, or were still under investigation. The district court dismissed the prosecution because it found that others similarly situated to Wayte were not prosecuted and further that Wayte was selected for prosecution on the discriminatory ground of exercising First Amendment rights. The Court of Appeals reversed. It agreed that prosecuting thirteen out of 674,000 nonregistrants was a discriminatory choice, but it found that the basis for this discrimination was reasonable. The government did not prosecute Wayte because of his protest activities but rather because of his nonregistration; he was identified because the identities of nonreported nonregistrants were not known, and nonregistrants who expressed their refusal to register made clear their willful violation of the law. This was so, according to the Court of Appeals, even though the DOJ was aware that its passive enforcement policy was more likely to result in the prosecution of protesters than that of nonprotesters.

The United States Supreme Court affirmed the decision of the Court of Appeals. It reaffirmed the rule that in "our criminal justice system, the Government retains broad discretion' as to whom to prosecute." One reason for the wisdom of the rule is that "the decision to prosecute is particularly ill-suited to judicial review. Such factors as the strength of the case, the prosecution's general deterrence value, the Government's enforcement priorities, and the case's relationship to the Government's overall enforcement plan are not readily susceptible to the kind of analysis the courts are competent to undertake." The Court also expressed the fear that judicial supervision of charging would cause delays that would make prosecution less effective.

The Court also recognized that some *constitutional* checks on prosecutorial discretion exist, including "selectivity in the enforcement of criminal laws." The doctrine of selective prosecution under the Equal Protection Clause standards requires a showing of both *discriminatory effect* and *discriminatory purpose.* The Court denied that either rule had been violated by the government. In this case, Wayte could show that under the passive enforcement program some, but not all, of those who exercised their First Amendment rights to protest draft registration were prosecuted. Some men who had *not* protested were indicted. The Court reasoned that Wayte "has not shown that the enforcement policy selected nonregistrants for prosecution on the basis of their speech. Indeed, he could not have done so given the way the "beg" policy was carried out." The facts of the case "demonstrate that the Government treated all reported nonregistrants similarly. It did not subject vocal nonregistrants to any special burden. Indeed, those prosecuted in effect selected themselves for prosecution by refusing to register after being reported and warned by the Government." Therefore, the Court found no discriminatory effect.

As for discriminatory purpose, the most that could be said was that "the Government was aware that the passive enforcement policy would result in prosecution of vocal objectors and that they would probably make selective prosecution claims." Discriminatory purpose, however, implies more than awareness of consequences. "It implies that the decisionmaker . . . selected or reaffirmed a particular course of action at least in part 'because of,' not merely 'in spite of,' its adverse effects upon an identifiable group." This could not be shown in the present case. As a result, the Supreme Court rejected Wayte's selective prosecution claim.

Justice Marshall dissented, joined by Justice Brennan, on the grounds that Wayte had a right to an evidentiary hearing to discover government documents relevant to his claim of selective prosecution. Wayte claimed that the suppressed evidence supported his claim that the government had designed a prosecutorial scheme that purposefully discriminated against those who had chosen to exercise their First Amendment rights to oppose draft registration. Justice Marshall's lengthy analysis concluded that Wayte met the legal criteria for an evidentiary hearing and that it was, therefore, an abuse of discretion for the appeals court to not allow an evidentiary discovery hearing. Since Wayte was entitled to additional evidence that the government withheld, his claim could not be rejected on the merits until he was granted access to those records.

In a case that provoked much controversy, *United States v. Armstrong* (1996), the Supreme Court held that the defendants failed to make a preliminary showing that the government singled out African Americans for "crack" cocaine prosecution. The issue arose against a background of laws that punish the possession and distribution of crack cocaine (cocaine base) *one hundred times* more severely than powdered cocaine. "The distribution of 50 grams of crack is thus punishable by the same mandatory minimum sentence of 10 years in prison that applies to the distribution of 5,000 grams of powder cocaine."[16] The case did not settle the explosive political and social issue of whether the drug penalty disparity is racially motivated. In 1996, "about 90 percent of those convicted in Federal court for crack offenses are black; for powdered cocaine, 29.7 percent last year were black, 25.9 percent were white and the rest were Hispanic."[17] And neither did it resolve the question of whether the federal prosecutor for the central district of California targeted cocaine defendants on a racial basis. Instead, the Supreme Court ruled (8–1) that Armstrong had not made a preliminary showing that the prosecutor engaged in racially selective prosecution.

Armstrong raised the issue of selective prosecution by showing that in 1991, each of twenty-four defendants represented by the local federal defender in cocaine cases were African Americans. He also submitted hearsay evidence that an equal number whites use and deal crack cocaine as African Americans and that many non-African Americans are prosecuted in state court for crack offenses. The government responded that this did not show that African Americans were singled out for prosecution. The federal district court, however, ordered the government to produce a three-year list of all cocaine cases, identifying defendants by race. The government argued that a DEA report concluded that large-scale crack manufacture trafficking is controlled by Jamaicans, Haitians and African-American street gangs. The Ninth Circuit Court of Appeals, *en banc,* affirmed the district court.

The Supreme Court reversed. Chief Justice Rehnquist, writing for the Court, noted that prosecutorial decisions are supported by a *presumption of regularity.* Courts cannot second-guess prosecutors unless there is *clear evidence* that a prosecutor's decision violated the Equal Protection Clause (for state prosecution) or the equal protection idea that exists in the Fifth Amendment Due Process Clause (for federal prosecution). To establish a preliminary showing of an equal protection violation a defendant first "must show that *similarly situated* individuals of a different race were not prosecuted." This standard was not met by the evidence provided to the district court. The case was remanded, however, giving Armstrong and other defendants an opportunity to prove that the prosecutor's office was discriminatory in effect *and* in intent.

Although "[t]he similarly situated requirement does not make a selective-prosecution claim impossible to prove," it is a demanding standard that is difficult to establish. The Court expressed its Crime Control Model inclination by stating that its decision "also stems from a concern not to *unnecessarily impair* the performance of a core executive constitutional function. As in *Wayte,* the Court expressed concern that judicial oversight would delay and weaken law enforcement. To establish a selective enforcement claim based on racial disparity, a defendant claiming anti-black bias must make a "credible showing" that *similarly situated* persons "who were not black, could have been prosecuted for the offenses for which respondents were charged, but were not so prosecuted." The Court ruled that Armstrong cannot rely on a *presumption* "that people of all races commit all types of crimes." Thus, while proof of racial disparity in sentencing amounting to an equal protection violation is possible, it must be established by clear proof.

Vindictive Prosecution

Vindictive prosecution occurs when new and more serious charges are brought simply because a defendant has exercised her statutory or constitutional rights. For example, if a defendant wins a new trial after appealing a conviction for breaking and entering, it is illegally vindictive behavior for a prosecutor to recharge the more serious crime of burglary. Increasing the charge might be interpreted as the prosecutor "getting even" with the defendant for exercising the legal right to appeal. The United States Supreme Court ruled on discriminatory prosecution in two cases that create subtle but real distinctions.

In *Blackledge v. Perry* (1974), Perry was found guilty of a misdemeanor and sentenced to six-month's incarceration. Under North Carolina's two-tiered trial system, he had a **trial *de novo*** in the superior court, where "the slate is wiped clean, the prior conviction annulled, and the prosecution and defense begin anew." The prosecutor charged Perry with the felony of assault with a deadly weapon. He was convicted and sentenced to a term of five to seven years in prison. Justice Stewart held that the prosecutor's enhancement of the charges constituted a due process violation for "vindictiveness." It was not necessary to show that the prosecutor was motivated by ill will or bad faith, only that the harsher charge was in response to the defendant's exercise of a *legal* right. The basis of the vindictiveness rule is "the fear that such vindictiveness may unconstitutionally deter a defendant's exercise of the right to appeal his first conviction . . . ." Due process requires that "a defendant be freed of the apprehension of such a retaliatory motivation" on the part of the prosecutor. In this instance, "[a] person convicted of an offense is entitled to pursue his statutory right to a trial *de novo* without apprehension that the State will retaliate by substituting a more serious charge for the original one thus subjecting him to a significantly increased potential period of incarceration."

A factual distinction in *United States v. Goodwin* (1982) produced a different result. Goodwin was charged with a misdemeanor assault but *before trial* requested a jury trial. The case was transferred from a magistrate's court, which had no authority to try felonies, to a felony level court. The United States attorney obtained a felony assault indictment. After conviction, Goodwin claimed that the enhanced charge amounted to vindictiveness under the rule of *Blackledge.* The Court disagreed and found no vindictiveness.

> There is good reason to be cautious before adopting an inflexible presumption of prosecutorial vindictiveness in a pretrial setting. In the course of preparing a case for trial, the prosecutor may uncover additional information that suggests a basis for further prosecution or he simply may come to realize that information possessed by the State has a broader significance. At this stage of the proceedings, the prosecutor's assessment of the proper extent of prosecution may not have crystallized. In contrast, once a trial begins—and certainly by the time a conviction has been obtained—it is much more likely that the State has discovered and assessed all of the information against an accused and has made a determination, on the basis of that information, of the extent to which he should be prosecuted. Thus, a change in the charging decision made after an initial trial is completed is much more likely to be improperly motivated than is a pretrial decision.

Therefore, a defendant's request for a jury trial over a bench trial does not trigger a presumption of vindictiveness when charges are thereafter increased.

A case decided by the District of Columbia Court of Appeals, *United States v. Meyer,*[18] indicates that, depending on the facts, prosecutorial vindictiveness may exist *before* trial. In this case, two hundred political demonstrators were arrested outside the White House and charged with "demonstrating without a permit." Those charged could either pay fifty dollars or go to trial. For those who chose trial, the maximum penalty was a five-hundred-dollar fine and six months in jail. Demonstrators who demanded a trial were additionally charged with "obstructing a sidewalk." In the pretrial proceedings, the prosecutor agreed to drop the second charge if the defendants pled guilty; if the second charge was dropped, the defendants would lose their right to a jury trial. The prosecutor then informed the trial-demand defendants that he would dismiss one charge and recommend probation if they would plead guilty. Defense counsel then demanded a jury trial.

In *Meyer,* the Court of Appeals agreed that this constituted vindictive prosecution. The *Meyer* case differed from *Goodwin,* where a pretrial increase in charges after defendants demanded a trial was not vindictive, because in *Meyer,* those who elected to go to trial were treated differently from those who did not. In this case, a hearing to determine vindictiveness caused the prosecutor to try to drop the second charge in order to eliminate a jury trial, perhaps because a jury trial would raise complex First Amendment issues.

The Court of Appeals also ruled that in deciding whether vindictiveness existed, the trial court may examine the likely motives of the entire prosecutor's office or the entire government side, and is not limited to examining the bad motives of individual prosecuting attorney. "To do otherwise would be to ignore that the desire to punish defendants for exercising their legal rights arises more often from institutional than from personal wellsprings." The appellate court also ruled that it was not an abuse of discretion for the trial court to *dismiss* the *entire prosecution* against the jury-demanding defendants, rather than dismissing only the additional charge. If the trial court is limited to striking down only the additional charge, the prosecutor would have nothing to lose by acting vindictively, and the *Blackledge* rule would lose its deterrent effect.

THE GRAND JURY

The grand jury is one of the oldest common-law institutions of justice, dating back to the reign of Henry II (1154–1189). As a local arm of royal administration, a group of local knights would be called together to inform traveling royal circuit judges which crimes had been committed and who ought to be brought to trial. During the seventeenth century, grand juries gained popular respect by refusing to indict popular figures who were political opponents of the crown. Resistance to British authorities by grand juries made them popular in the American colonies. As a result, each new American state and the federal government required that criminal prosecutions be initiated by grand jury. Federal grand juries for federal prosecutions were guaranteed in the Bill of Rights' Fifth Amendment in 1791.

In mid-nineteenth century, over half of the states eliminated the grand jury indictment requirement because grand juries were costly and cumbersome, and elected prosecutors could be trusted to charge defendants fairly by information. A constitutional challenge to this reform failed. The Supreme Court ruled in *Hurtado v. California* (1884) that the Fifth Amendment requirement that "[n]o person shall be held to answer for a capital, or otherwise infamous crime, unless on a presentment or indictment of a Grand Jury" is not so fundamental to liberty and justice as to be an element of due process under the Fourteenth Amendment. Thus, the grand jury requirement has not been incorporated (see Chapter 2). However, almost all of the states that had dropped the indictment requirement retain grand juries by statute and allow them to be called by a prosecutor in special cases. These tend to be complex white-collar, organized crime, or government corruption cases where grand jury secrecy and its subpoena powers prove useful. Therefore, the grand jury continues to play an important role in American criminal justice.

It is composed of a body of citizens, usually numbering between twelve and twenty-three, formally convened by the court or the sheriff to investigate crimes and to determine whether there is probable cause to hold a suspect for trial. The citizens' grand jury may also investigate government corruption or misfeasance. As a body of citizens, the grand jury is not administratively or legally situated within any of the three branches of government. It does, however, work with both the executive branch as represented by the prosecutor and the judicial branch as represented by the court. Thus, the prosecutor presents cases to the grand jury and generally guides its activities, whereas the court is responsible for deciding evidentiary questions that may arise during grand jury proceedings.

Grand juries sometimes sit for extended periods of time—up to several months. The term of a federal grand jury is eighteen months with six-month extensions. In practice, federal grand jury service lasts for a month. Then, although the grand jurors no longer meet, the grand jury retains its "legal" existence. This is important because a person who is granted **immunity** by a grand jury but refuses to testify can be held in contempt and jailed during the entire life of the grand jury, even if the jury is not actively sitting.

Grand Jury Composition

The Supreme Court has consistently held that racial bias in the selection of members of a grand jury results in the automatic reversal of the indictment (*Ex Parte Virginia,* 1880; *Cassell v. Texas,* 1950). Legal objections to a grand jury's racial composition ordinarily must be brought before the case goes to trial. If an objection was not possible before the trial began, however, it is still possible for the indictment to be reversed even though the defendant was found guilty beyond a reasonable doubt by an unbiased petit jury. This rule was applied in *Vasquez v. Hillary* (1986). The appellant's conviction occurred *twenty-four years* prior to the appeal being filed, but as Justice Marshall, writing for the majority, pointed out, a conviction does not erase all the damage that a biased grand jury can inflict:

> The grand jury does not determine only that probable cause exists to believe that a defendant has committed a crime, or that it does not. In the hands of the grand jury lies the power to charge a greater offense or a lesser offense; numerous counts or a single count; and perhaps most significant of all, a capital offense or a noncapital offense—all on the basis of the same facts . . . Once having found discrimination in the selection of a grand jury, we simply cannot know that the need to indict would have been assessed in the same way by a grand jury properly constituted.

The underlying policy of unbiased grand jury selection was forcefully stated in Justice Blackmun's opinion in *Rose v. Mitchell* (1979):

> Selection of members of a grand jury because they are of one race and not another destroys the appearance of justice and thereby casts doubt on the integrity of the judicial process. The exclusion from grand jury service of Negroes, or any group otherwise qualified to serve, impairs the confidence of the public in the administration of justice. As this Court repeatedly has emphasized, such discrimination "not only violates our Constitution and the laws enacted under it but is at war with our basic concepts of a democratic society and a representative government."

The Supreme Court has held that discrimination in the selection of the grand jury's *foreperson* does not require the dismissal of an indictment if the foreperson was selected from among the grand jury by its own members, as long as the grand jury pool was selected in an unbiased manner from among a cross-section of the community (*Hobby v. United States,* 1984). A federal grand jury foreperson is not in a position to sway the outcome of a case. On the other hand, in *Rose v. Mitchell* (1979), the foreman was not selected from among the local grand jury but instead from outside of it by a judge. Furthermore, the foreman had significant power in issuing subpoenas that could be influence the substance of an indictment. This did constitute a due process violation.

Grand Jury Functions and Powers

The grand jury operates as a *"sword,"* to *investigate* crime with broad subpoena powers, and a *"shield,"* to *screen* cases brought by the prosecutor by determining whether or not there is sufficient evidence to prosecute. If the jury finds, by a majority vote, that probable cause exists it votes a **true bill** of indictment, specifying the charges on which the defendant must stand trial. The function of a pretrial screen is to prevent oppressive, unjust, hasty, malicious, or ill-founded prosecutions.

GRAND JURY INVESTIGATION The grand jury has several *powers* that give it enormous advantages in conducting investigations. In theory, its independent citizens can investigate any crime or government misdeed that comes to its attention. In practice, the grand jury is dependent upon the prosecutor to bring cases and gather evidence, and its powers make the prosecutor more effective. "Runaway" grand jury investigations of issues that a prosecutor does not want investigated are almost unheard of.

SUBPOENA The grand jury has, under the court's authority, **subpoena power** to require individuals to testify (subpoena *ad testificandum*) or to bring papers and evidence (subpoena *duces tecum*) in an effort to further a criminal investigation. There is a general obligation to obey grand jury subpoenas. In *Branzburg v. Hayes* (1972), the Supreme Court held that a news reporter does not have a First Amendment privilege to withhold information or to avoid testifying before a grand jury when the reporter promised not to reveal a sources who may have been involved in criminal activity. The Court made it clear that if a grand jury was called as a pretext to harass a reporter, federal courts could act to protect them under the First Amendment. Failure to obey a subpoena can be punished with a contempt of court charge. Testimony before the grand jury is under oath, so false or contradictory statements can be used later to impeach the witness or be used as a basis for a perjury prosecution. A grand jury does not need probable cause that a witness or evidence is necessary to the case in order to subpoena someone, but courts may overrule a subpoena if (1) the requested evidence is not relevant to the investigation or (2) the request for documents is too vague or unreasonable.[19]

IMMUNITY A related power of the grand jury is the ability to grant **immunity** to witnesses who refuse to testify on Fifth Amendment self-incrimination grounds (Chapter 8). Immunity granted by a state court or grand jury also prohibits federal prosecution, and federal immunity prevents state prosecution (*Murphy v. Waterfront Commission,* 1964). The *scope* of immunity may be either narrow or broad. Prosecutors in *Counselman v. Hitchcock* (1892) granted a limited form of **use immunity** to grand jury witnesses. This prevents the use and derivative use of testimony in future prosecutions, but does not bar future prosecutions of the defendant if evidence is obtained from an *independent source.* The Supreme Court held in 1892, that such immunity was not sufficient to protect the witness's privilege against self-incrimination. In response to *Counselman,* Congress adopted a **transactional immunity** statute that provided that a witness required to testify was granted immunity "for or on account of any transaction, matter, or thing concerning which he may testify or produce evidence." The Court began to shift its ground in *Murphy v. Waterfront Commission* (1964), leading Congress to again narrow its immunity statute. The Supreme Court upheld the constitutionality of the narrower use immunity in *Kastigar v. United States* (1972). This narrow reading of the privilege against self-incrimination is another indication of the Burger Court reflecting the Crime Control Model of criminal justice.

SECRECY Another grand jury power is *secrecy.* Lawyers of witnesses and suspects are barred, as is the general public. The Supreme Court gives five reasons for grand jury secrecy:

1. to prevent the escape of indicted persons,
2. to ensure great freedom of deliberation for grand jurors,
3. to prevent witness tampering,

4. to encourage the free testimony of persons with information about the crime, and
5. to protect the identity of an innocent suspect who is exonerated (United States v. Procter & Gamble Co., 1958).

Under the Federal Rules of Criminal Procedure,20 grand jury information (except for the jury deliberations and vote of specific grand jurors) may be released automatically to other prosecutors or law enforcement personnel to assist them in their official duties. Otherwise, grand jury information may be released only upon a court order, with or without a request by the defendant.

GRAND JURY SCREENING To determine whether probable cause exists for an indictment, the grand jury meets in secret with only the prosecutor, a stenographer, and one witness present at a time. The presentation of evidence to a grand jury is nonadversarial, and a witness has no right to have an attorney present in the grand jury room, although a legal advisor may be present in the courthouse to confer with the witness during recesses about whether a question may be declined on self-incrimination grounds. Witnesses need not be given *Miranda* warnings (*United States v. Mandujano,* 1976), nor told that they are the targets of the grand jury investigation if warnings have been given (*United States v. Washington,* 1977). Although witnesses have the privilege not to incriminate themselves, they may voluntarily testify to matters that may lead to their prosecution (*United States v. Monia,* 1943). Evidentiary rules generally do not apply to grand jury proceedings. Under the Federal Rules of Criminal Procedure, if one grand jury refuses to indict, a prosecutor may later submit the same evidence to another grand jury.

EVIDENCE THAT CAN BE CONSIDERED BY THE GRAND JURY Consistent with the probable cause standard of proof, a grand jury may indict on the basis of *hearsay* evidence, such as summarizations of testimony by government agents rather than the direct testimony of witnesses (*Costello v. United States,* 1956). Justice Black, writing for the majority in *Costello* said that nothing in the Fifth Amendment disallows hearsay. He also noted that if indictments were open to challenge, great delay and duplication would result. As noted in Chapter 3, the Supreme Court in *United States v. Calandra* (1974) held that grand jury questions may be based on *illegally seized evidence.* In deciding not to extend the exclusionary rule to grand jury questions, the Court took the history and function of that institution into account. According to Justice Powell, "[t]raditionally the grand jury has been accorded wide latitude to inquire into violations of criminal law. No judge presides to monitor its proceedings. It deliberates in secret and may alone determine the course of its inquiry. The grand jury may compel the production of evidence or the testimony of witnesses as it considers appropriate, and its operation generally is unrestrained by the technical procedural and evidentiary rules governing the conduct of criminal trials." Given this background, and considering the majority's view of the exclusionary rule as a protective device to curb police illegality, the Court declined to impose a rule that would weaken the efficacy of the grand jury. The *Calandra* Rule makes it considerably easier for prosecutors to gain indictments.

Misuse of the Grand Jury and the Calls for Reform

The grand jury has come under severe criticism in America in recent years, with some calling for its abolition or reform. In fact, the grand jury was abolished in England in 1933 on the grounds that it was a cumbersome institution that did little to protect defendants from improper prosecution.

A major criticism is that the grand jury is not an independent citizen's body any more; it has become a rubber stamp for the prosecutor, who values it only for its secrecy and enormous powers of compelling testimony. The prosecutor controls the information about the crime that the grand jurors receive. The prosecutor drafts the indictments, calls the witnesses, and acts as the grand jury's legal advisor. "It is the rare grand jury that thinks itself of indicting, or is led by someone other than the prosecutor to indict."[21] Further, it has been used to oppress witnesses: "The opportunity to bully, to harass, to intimidate is surely present in the grand jury room, and it has surely been exploited on too many occasions."[22]

During the Nixon administration (1969–1974), there was widespread abuse of the federal grand jury process against anti-war activists and peaceful dissidents by the Justice Department's Internal Security Division. National jurisdiction gave federal prosecutors the ability to subpoena witnesses, on short notice, ordering them to appear before a grand jury located clear across the nation. Witnesses were picked up in the morning; flown across the country to a locale where they were total strangers; became increasingly disoriented and afraid; and would then be asked to tell a grand jury about *every association* they had over a period of years with any number of people. In one case, the teenage son of the presidential advisor suspected of leaking the "Pentagon Papers" was subpoenaed and taken into custody at his home at 7:30 one morning to testify about his father two hours later.[23] With the resignation of President Nixon and conviction of Attorney General John Mitchell in the Watergate scandal, and the winding down of the Vietnam War, political tensions of the late 1960s and early 1970s abated; and abuses of the federal grand jury process subsided. This temporary aberration from the normally even-handed, if vigorous, approach to federal prosecution is a reminder that the grand jury lends itself to abuses of power.

A grand jury can become abusive by issuing a report to the public which smears individuals as **unindicted coconspirators,** that is, persons who appear to be as guilty as those indicted, but who for some reason are not charged. Ironically, President Nixon suffered this same treatment at the hands of the Watergate grand jury. Aside from the special circumstance of reluctance to indict a sitting president, the practice of naming unindicted coconspirators in grand jury reports subjects people "to an accusation of criminality without any opportunity to disprove it. As a result, reputations are damaged and employment opportunities lost."[24] The American Bar Association recommended that grand juries not issue reports naming unindicted coconspirators or otherwise criticize an individual who is not indicted. Other proposed reforms are aimed at weakening or eliminating all or most of the powers that a grand jury has to investigate criminal conspiracies. Such proposals are based on the view of some that the occasional abuses of the grand jury outweigh its usefulness.[25]

In 1973, a federal judge recommended abolition of federal grand juries, but such a move, requiring a constitutional amendment, is highly unlikely.[26] However, numerous reform proposals, have been made. Perhaps the strongest is that witnesses' attorneys be allowed in the grand jury room during testimony to advise their clients on the legality of questions, but not be allowed to offer substantive challenges. This makes sense because people subpoenaed before a grand jury often are accompanied by their attorneys to the courthouse; once there, the attorneys are not allowed in the jury room. If a witness is unsure whether a question should be answered, he or she must request frequent delays to confer with counsel. This is cumbersome and can be used excessively to disrupt proper grand jury functioning. Furthermore, not allowing counsel to be present, tends to intimidate the witness. Today, about fifteen states allow counsel to be brought into their grand jury hearings.[27]

Another reform allows the "target" of the grand jury investigation to testify voluntarily and present evidence before an indictment has been handed up. While such a procedural change may make a grand jury hearing resemble a trial or preliminary hearing, a number of states are moving in the direction of requiring more rigorous evidentiary standards in grand jury hearings. Today, about ten states require evidence standards approaching the requirements imposed at trial.[28]

Other proposals include requiring federal prosecutors to present every proposed indictment to superiors in the United States attorney's office, with a memorandum explaining the evidentiary and policy basis for the prosecution. Additionally, targets of grand jury investigation would be informed that they are likely indictees and would be allowed to address the grand jury if they so wish.[29]

In opposition to reforms, experienced lawyers concede that the federal grand jury is a tool of the prosecutor, but argue that (1) its power is not usually abused and (2) it is an important cog in the government's investigatory machinery. Without the grand jury, prosecutorial charging followed by preliminary examinations in complex white-collar crime cases could lead to hearings occupying weeks of judicial time. Also, questions asked by grand jurors often help the prosecutor to sharpen the focus of the indictment or decide to terminate further investigation. As the movement for grand jury abolition has waned, the strengthening of the grand jury and instituting some procedural reform seem appropriate courses for the federal and state governments.

THE PRELIMINARY EXAMINATION

The preliminary examination is a trial-like adversary hearing. It is not guaranteed by the Constitution but is a statutory right in every jurisdiction.[30] Under the Federal Rules of Criminal Procedure, the preliminary examination must be held within ten days after the initial appearance if the defendant is in custody or within twenty days if the defendant had been released.[31]

The Right to a Preliminary Examination

The preliminary examination is primarily a screening device to determine whether there is sufficient evidence to hold the defendant for trial. If the judge finds probable cause to believe the defendant committed the crime charged, the defendant is bound over to the trial court. If the evidence is not sufficient, the case is dismissed without jeopardy attaching—the prosecutor may recharge the defendant and resubmit new evidence at a later time.

The screening function overlaps with the grand jury's screening role, setting the stage for an interesting controversy. In jurisdictions that initiate prosecutions by a grand jury indictment, the general rule is that once the indictment is handed up, the defendant no longer has a right to a preliminary examination. This rule was inserted into the Federal Rules of Criminal Procedure in 1972: "the preliminary examination shall not be held if the defendant is indicted or if an information against the defendant is filed in district court before the date set for the preliminary examination."[32] It confirmed what many courts had held, that a grand jury indictment makes a preliminary examination redundant.[33] However, defense attorneys object to "quick indictments" by prosecutors because the defendants lose access to the other valuable functions of the preliminary examination (discussed later in this text). The effect of this rule has been to virtually eliminate the preliminary examination in some federal district courts.[34]

A case of unfair manipulation regarding this rule occurred when a federal prosecutor sought to adjourn a preliminary examination because the defense obtained permission to inspect an FBI agent's field notes. The adjournment was supposedly to allow the agent to delete irrelevant material from the notes. The prosecutor, however, quickly obtained an indictment and moved to dismiss the preliminary examination. The district court chastised the prosecutor for deliberately misleading the defense and "creating . . . a feeling that the search for probable cause in a preliminary examination amounts to no more than a game in which the government can never lose, regardless of what the evidence reveals." Nevertheless, because the defendant did not lose any formal rights, the court granted the dismissal of the hearing.[35]

In some states, especially where formal charges are brought by information, courts have held that a defendant is entitled to a preliminary hearing even after a grand jury indictment.[36] Although this may appear to be needless duplication, it provides an independent determination of probable cause and acknowledges the existence of important informal functions of the preliminary examination.

A defendant may waive his or her right to a preliminary examination. This is often inadvisable, especially if a defendant waives the examination at the initial hearing, before consulting with an attorney. If counsel believes a preliminary examination favors the prosecutor, a waiver may be a wise course. For example, defense counsel may want to avoid giving prosecution witnesses an opportunity to become practiced and at ease in the courtroom. Prosecutors in many jurisdictions can insist upon a preliminary examination even if the defendant waives it.

Preliminary Examination Procedures

A preliminary examination is conducted much like a trial—it is open to the public and held in a courtroom before a magistrate or judge; witnesses may be called and cross-examined; and a transcript is made of the proceedings. The defendant must be present and be represented by an attorney. The preliminary examination is noticeably different than the grand jury, which operates in strict secrecy.

There are major differences between a preliminary examination and a trial. First, the goal of the preliminary examination—to determine whether probable cause exists—means that the testimony elicited by the prosecutor is more limited than that presented at trial, where the prosecutor must prove a defendant guilty beyond a reasonable doubt. Thus, the magistrate may restrict the scope of the questioning or the cross-examination if, for example, she believes that the cross-examination goes beyond an attempt to undermine probable cause and becomes a quest for discovery.[37] Also, in most states, evidence may be admitted in a preliminary examination that is not admissible at the trial. Although the probable cause standard is the most common evidentiary basis for the bind-over decision, some states require the higher standard of a *prima facie* case (see Table 4–1).

A preliminary examination must be *open to the public.* In *Press Enterprise Co. v. Superior Court* (1986), a forty-one-day preliminary examination was held in a case where the defendant was charged with the murder of twelve people by the administration of a heart drug. The magistrate refused to release the transcript of the hearing to the Press Enterprise news company because a release of the manuscript to the public might prejudice the defendant's right to a fair trial. The Supreme Court reversed, holding that the plaintiff's First Amendment right guaranteed access to the preliminary examination. Chief Justice Burger reasoned that a preliminary examination is sufficiently like a trial; therefore, First Amendment rules applicable to a trial also apply to a preliminary examination. Furthermore, "public access plays a significant positive role in the functioning" of the preliminary examination, which is often the only public airing of a criminal prosecution. In the absence of a jury, the presence of the public helps prevent corrupt or overzealous prosecution, or compliant, biased, or eccentric judges. A magistrate can legally bar the public from a preliminary examination if he or she makes a specific, on-the-record finding that demonstrates that closure is essential to preserve "higher values," such as the fairness of the trial, and is narrowly tailored to serve that interest.

Although the defendant has a right to present witnesses at the preliminary examination, this is rarely done. If the defendant has evidence that will positively clear him or her, it may be a wise strategy to bring this out at the preliminary examination so that the case will be dismissed. More typically, the defense probes the prosecutor's claim of probable cause by cross-examination. The defendant has little to gain by introducing evidence, since that simply raises issues clouding the proof of guilt that has to be resolved at trial. Another strategic reason for the defendant not to show any more of his defense than is necessary is that it alerts the prosecutor to evidence and approaches that will be used trial if the case is not dismissed.

At the conclusion of the preliminary examination, a transcript must be made if requested by a party and ordered by the magistrate. Under federal practice, an indigent defendant may receive a free transcript. However if the defendant has available an informal alternative that appears to be substantially equivalent to a transcript, the transcript need not be provided (*Britt v. North Carolina,* 1971).

THE RIGHT TO COUNSEL The Supreme Court held that the preliminary examination is a critical stage of the criminal prosecution, requiring that counsel be present under the Sixth Amendment, unless waived (*Coleman v. Alabama,*

1970). Under *Powell v. Alabama* (1932), counsel must be provided to indigents, as an incident of due process, if the lack of counsel would prove to *undermine* the defendant's right to a *fair trial.* Thus, the question is whether the defendant would be *prejudiced* by not having counsel at the preliminary examination, in the sense that evidence introduced at the examination would tend to prove the defendant's guilt at trial. To answer the issue, the Court described a lawyer's functions at the preliminary hearing:

> First, the lawyer's skilled examination and cross-examination of witnesses may expose fatal weaknesses in the State's case that may lead the magistrate to refuse to bind the accused over. Second, in any event, the skilled interrogation of witnesses by an experienced lawyer can fashion a vital impeachment tool for use in cross-examination of the State's witnesses at the trial, or preserve testimony favorable to the accused of a witness who does not appear at the trial. Third, retained counsel can more effectively discover the case the State has against his client and make possible the preparation of a proper defense to meet that case at the trial. Fourth, counsel can also be influential at the preliminary hearing in making effective arguments for the accused on such matters as the necessity for early psychiatric examination or bail. The inability of the indigent accused on his own to realize these advantages of a lawyer's assistance compels the conclusion that the Alabama preliminary hearing is a "critical stage" of the State's criminal process at which the accused is 'as much entitled to such aid [of counsel] . . . as at the trial itself.' *Powell v. Alabama.*" (*Coleman v. Alabama,* 1970)

Coleman demonstrated that having counsel at the preliminary examination was as crucial to a defendant's interests in a fair defense as it was at the actual trial.

The Functions of the Preliminary Examination

The preliminary examination serves functions other than its primary screening role that are not explicitly recognized by statutes and generally have lower legitimacy in the eyes of many judges. The least controversial "covert" function is to *preserve testimony* in the transcript of the examination. Because witnesses are under oath and subject to cross-examination, the transcripts may be used to *impeach* the testimony of a witness during trial. The inconsistencies of a witness who testifies differently at the preliminary examination and at trial can be used to discredit him or her.

Statements on the transcript of a preliminary examination may be introduced into evidence if a witness is *unavailable* for trial due to death, disability, or disappearance. This is a recognized hearsay rule exception. In *California v. Green* (1970), the defendant was charged with furnishing marijuana to Porter, a minor. On the witness stand, Porter became evasive and uncooperative and claimed a lapse of memory when asked about receiving marijuana from Green. The prosecutor then introduced the preliminary hearing transcript to prove that Porter had received illegal substances from Green. The Supreme Court upheld the practice. First, the Sixth Amendment Confrontation Clause was not violated by the introduction of testimony made during a prior hearing because the witness was *subject* to cross-examination, even if he had *not actually* been cross-examined. The fact that preliminary examination questioning is not usually as intense as cross-examination at trial does not alter the rule. Second, the witness was unavailable for *constitutional* purposes. "As in the case where the witness is physically unproducible, the State here has made every effort to introduce its evidence through the live testimony of the witness; it produced Porter at trial, swore him in as a witness, and tendered him for cross-examination. Whether Porter then testified in a manner consistent or inconsistent with his preliminary hearing testimony, claimed a loss of memory, claimed his privilege against compulsory self-incrimination, or simply refused to answer, nothing in the Confrontation Clause prohibited the State from also relying on his prior testimony to prove its case against Green" (*California v. Green,* 1970).

A more controversial function is the defense using the examination as a discovery device to gather information and assess the strength of the prosecution's case. This purpose is less important in jurisdictions where prosecutors fully and promptly share factual information with the defense. On the other hand, prosecutors who keep information from the defense for tactical reasons (e.g., obtaining a favorable guilty plea despite weak evidence) encourage the covert use of the preliminary examination by opposing counsel. A few judges support discovery as a proper preliminary examination function, but most believe that discovery is subordinate to the primary bind-over function. A magistrate may, therefore, limit cross-examination by the defense if it appears to be aimed at only discovering information in the hands of the prosecutor and sheds no light on the existence of probable cause.

Another important function of the preliminary examination is its role in plea bargaining. Placing prosecution witnesses on the stand makes the prosecutor's case graphically clear to the defendant and to the counsel. Observing a strong case may provide the needed stimulus to the defendant to agree to plead guilty. On the contrary, where prosecution testimony is weak, the defense may have a basis to suggest a reduction of charges. If a case does go to trial, the prosecution may benefit by having given witnesses an "audition" where they become more familiar with the courtroom setting and with their "lines." If they later testify at trial, they are less apt to show nervousness and are likely to display greater confidence in the delivery of their testimony.

LAW IN SOCIETY

PROSECUTORIAL MISCONDUCT

Prosecutors are the most powerful actors in the criminal justice process, with virtually unreviewable power to dismiss a case or to prosecute a criminal suspect. They decide how to charge a defendant, whether to accept a plea, or whether to recommend sentencing leniency. In states with capital punishment, prosecutors decide whether or not to seek the death penalty. Since the 1970s, "[p]rosecutors have become central figures in America's fight against crime, wielding more power than ever before."[38] The stated ideal of a prosecutor is not simply to win cases but to do justice.[39] Achieving justice, to a great degree, depends on the integrity as well as the technical competence of prosecuting attorneys. Prosecutorial misconduct undermines the ability to achieve justice in the courts and weakens "the public perception of the integrity of our criminal justice system."[40]

Supreme Court Rulings

The Supreme Court has issued clear rulings that collectively say that prosecutorial misconduct, which increases the risk of the wrongful conviction of innocent defendants, violates due process.

- The first important ruling was *Mooney v. Holohan* (1935), which ruled that "a deliberate deception of court and jury by the presentation of testimony known to be perjured" violated the defendant's due process rights. This case arose out of the conviction of a well-known labor radical, Tom Mooney, for setting off a bomb during a pro-military parade in San Francisco in 1916 that killed ten people and seriously injured forty. There was strong exonerating evidence, but it was a period of anti-radical hysteria and the prosecutor relied on "eyewitnesses" who were known liars. Mooney was pardoned soon after the Supreme Court's ruling.[41]
- Dr. Sam Sheppard was convicted of killing his wife in 1956, in a Cleveland trial that took place in a "circus atmosphere," with great misconduct committed by the press, who convicted Sheppard in the headlines well before trial; the police who broadcast their evidence; and the judge who failed to control the situation. But at the heart of the wrongs in the case was the prosecutorial suppression of evidence contradictory to its case. A defense demand for files and records, was ignored. A forensic examination of the crime scene brought out evidence favorable to Sheppard which the prosecutor ignored.[42] In 1966, the Supreme Court reversed the case, and in a retrial with a more vigorous and focused defense counsel, F. Lee Bailey, Sheppard was acquitted on a powerful presentation of forensic evidence.[43]
- In *Brady v. Maryland* (1963) the Supreme Court tried to ensure that the travesties of justice that occurred in the Mooney and Sheppard cases would not reoccur. It required, as a matter of due process, that the prosecution turn over *factual evidence* that is *favorable* to the defendant when the evidence is *material* to guilt or punishment. In *Brady,* the prosecutor withheld a statement by Brady's co-defendant who admitted to actually doing the killing. The *Brady* principle does *not* require the prosecutor to turn over evidence that is neutral or unfavorable to the defendant, that is available to the defendant from other sources, or that the defendant already possesses. The government must also turn over *requested information* that tends to *impeach* witnesses, such as deals that the government makes not to prosecute a witness or to pay the witness for evidence (*Giglio v. United States,* 1972; *United States v. Bagley,* 1985). A *Brady* violation is a deprivation of due process even if the prosecutor acted without a malicious motive. Brady and its subsequent cases have done much to make the prosecution function far more fairly than in the past.

Recent Examples of Misconduct

These terrible cases occurred decades ago. Surely, with improved training and awareness, the level of prosecutorial misconduct must now be a rare occurrence. Unfortunately, while this text does not claim that prosecutorial misconduct is routine, there have been a disturbing number of instances of this problem in recent years.

- David Pardue, in jail awaiting a perjury trial, told an inmate he wanted to silence a witness. The jailbird told the authorities who set up a sting. An FBI agent posed as a hit man. David had his twenty-year-old son, Michael, a college student, deliver $250 to the "hit man" as a down payment. When Pardue was released, he forgot about the "contract." Nine weeks later the FBI staged a phony death scene, with the "hit man" claiming he completed the contract and asking for his money. This terrified Michael and his grandfather who feared a cold-blooded professional killer. They payed the demanded fee and were then charged with conspiracy to commit murder. A federal district court judge threw out the case against Michael, the son, seeing this as *outrageous* prosecutorial conduct. The Eighth Circuit Court of Appeals reinstated the prosecution because it seemed that Michael Pardue was willing to go along with his father's plans, even though concocted in part by the government, and had committed the *actus reus* of the crime by the payment. Whatever the appellate ruling, it seems that the prosecutor manufactured a case against twenty-year-old Michael who then faced life imprisonment for being manipulated into playing a role in a convincing government play.

- In a notorious case, U.S. District Judge Edward Rafeedie acquitted Mexican physician Humberto Alvarez Machain, of participating in the torture killing of United States drug agent Enrique "Kiki" Camarena. Federal agents had Dr. Machain abducted in Mexico and brought to the United States for trial (see Chapter 7). Judge Rafeedie accused federal prosecutors of hiding an informant's story that another doctor, not Alvarez Machain, had committed the crime.[44]
- A heavy-handed federal weapon is **multiple-district prosecutions,** where the federal government prosecutes a business in many different districts where the enterprise does business. Given the large resources of the Justice Department and the United States Attorneys, they can bankrupt a business simply by forcing it to defend the same case in different federal courts. Until 1987 Justice Department guidelines discouraged this tactic, except in the most serious cases.[45] The Reagan administration's zealous attack on pornography distributors, led by Attorney General Edwin Meese, "encouraged" multiple prosecution in such cases. The Department hired two lawyers who previously worked for an private anti-pornography group, the Citizens for Decency Through Law (CDL), which was founded and funded by conservative Arizona financier Charles H. Keating Jr., (who was later convicted of massive fraud in the savings and loan scandal). The Justice Department worked closely with the CDL and brought prosecutions in the most conservative states in the Union against P.H.E., Inc., a distributor of materials that included *Playboy* magazine and *The Joy of Sex.* This indicates a narrow, *politically motivated* prosecution policy combined with multiple-district prosecutions.

  Nevertheless, federal prosecutors backed off of this case after a North Carolina state jury acquitted P.H.E. The jury foreman told the press that "It just seems like the government is trying too hard to regulate what we look at . . . We just felt like the whole deal was politically motivated." Thereafter, P.H.E. president Phillip D. Harvey said in a trade publication that he would not give in to federal pressure from Utah federal prosecutor Rich Lambert, who had aggressively pursued multiple-district prosecutions. The following year, Lambert again brought charges, saying that Harvey was a major distributor of pornography and that "he was personally offended by Harvey's comments in the magazine interview." This indicates that a prosecutor can go after people in part out of *personal vindictiveness.*

  Fearing prosecutions in Kentucky and Utah, Harvey, in July 1990, obtained a restraining order from United States District Judge Green in Washington, prohibiting charges in more than one district at a time. As of 1993, three federal courts had condemned the multiple-district prosecution tactic.
- A federal judge in Chicago, calling his decision tragic and painful, reversed the convictions of seven members of the notorious Chicago "El Rukns" street gang, because federal prosecutors suppressed key evidence and suborned perjury, which denied defendants a fair trial. Prosecutors allowed illegal drug use by imprisoned, cooperating witnesses and allowed them improper favors (e.g., conjugal visits in federal offices) in an effort to keep the witnesses favorable.[46]
- *A case of overzealous prosecution.*[47] In 1986, federal bribery convictions were secured against a lobbyist for the company Recognition Equipment Inc. (REI), and a high ranking postal official in connection with selling REI scanners to the post office. Joseph B. Valder, an experienced federal career prosecutor in the District of Columbia, targeted REI president William G. Moore, Jr., believing he must have known of the bribery. A grand jury indicted Moore. Nevertheless, federal Judge George H. Revercomb, a Reagan appointee who had served as associate deputy attorney general, "could not detect even the skeleton of a criminal case." He "found the case so weak . . . that he stopped the trial after six weeks and acquitted Moore . . . without hearing any defense witnesses."

How could this happen? Moore charged Valder, in a civil suit, with misleading the grand jury by not presenting exculpatory, as well as incriminating, evidence. For example, Valder pressured William Spartin, a conspirator in the first bribery case who was not prosecuted in return for giving evidence, to finger Moore. Valder threatened to revoke the deal and send Spartin to prison. "Spartin said 19 times that he never heard the illegal payments being discussed with [Moore]. 'Everybody is beating me up on this issue,' he told the inspector. . . . I wish I could give them REI. . . . I'll be damned if I can do it and I'm not going to lie." Valder also questioned REI executive Frank Bray for days and reduced Bray's statements to a twenty-two page memorandum. Bray felt the summary inaccurately incriminated Moore and wanted to change it, but Valder refused, threatening Bray with grand jury "grilling" that would leave Bray open to perjury charges.

Valder maintained he did nothing wrong. He acknowledged that there was no direct evidence against Moore but argued that sophisticated business leaders can engage in bribery without leaving traces of evidence. As for misleading the grand jury, Valder said, "[I]t's not the prosecutor's obligation . . . to make defense arguments to the grand jury," and

"[T]he Justice Department's Office of Professional Responsibility (OPR) found that there had been a 'rational basis' for seeking the indictment and that no 'serious misconduct' by the prosecutor had occurred, but that Valder had 'exercised poor judgment' in his handling of a grand jury witness. . . ." Although acquitted, "the indictment cost Moore his job at REI, which spent more than $ 9 million in legal fees defending the case (the company also was indicted and acquitted), and he now operates a private consulting firm in Texas."

Bennett L. Gershman, in a leading text, finds many reported cases of prosecutorial misconduct:

- "Courts have consistently condemned prosecutors' attempts to create an impression on the jury by *innuendoes* in questions when no supporting evidence exists."[48]
- "Prosecutors are well aware of the devastating impact of *lie detector* proof on the minds of jurors, and in cases when the verdict hinges on the credibility of witnesses, have committed reversible error by eliciting that the defendant failed the test, or that the witness passed the test, or indirectly eliciting that the witness took the test, leaving the inescapable inference that the witness passed."[49]
- "Appeals by the prosecutor to the *jurors' fears, passions, and biases* are a common tactic not only in argument to the jury but also in presentation of evidence."[50]
- "A prosecutor waved before the jury a pair of men's undershorts, misrepresenting them as blood-stained, when they were actually stained with red paint."[51]
- "Prosecutors sometimes elicit evidence that is not only irrelevant and inadmissible but deliberately *inflammatory.* Examples abound."[52]
- "Cross-examination into prior acts of misconduct of the witness [] is proper when the prosecutor's aim is to show bias. By contrast, badgering a witness with baseless and humiliating questions about prior acts of misconduct was reversible error when the witness was crucial to the defense. The trial court in such situations has a responsibility to ascertain that the prosecutor's questions are in good faith."[53]
- "Prosecutors have in various ways frustrated defense attempts to locate and interview witnesses before trial."[54]
- "Prosecutors have engaged in unprofessional behavior sometimes amounting to constitutional error by instructing witnesses not to talk to defense counsel."[55]
- ". . . prosecutors have *intimidated witnesses* and prevented them from giving exculpatory testimony for the defendant by threatening them with perjury or other substantive charges."[56]
- "When courts and commentators talk about prosecutorial misconduct, they usually are referring to the prosecutor's argument to the jury. A random survey of law reports shows that one of the most common contentions on appeal is that the prosecutor's *oratory was excessive,* improper, and prejudicial."[57]
- "A prosecutor must not use arguments calculated to inflame the passions or prejudices of the jury."[58] Categories of *inflammatory remarks* include law and order appeals, name calling and abuse, imputing to the defendant violence and threats against a witness, appeals to racial prejudice, appeals to national and religious prejudice, appeals to patriotism, appeals to wealth and class bias, and appeals to jurors as parents.[59]

Reasons for Prosecutorial Misconduct

ATTITUDE AND THE WAR ON CRIME Why does the extent of prosecutorial misconduct appear high today? It is always difficult for honest prosecutors to walk the fine line between effective and overzealous prosecution. An experienced prosecutor, Kenneth Bresler, warns against the *attitude* of many prosecutors that leads them to "count wins," calling it egotistical, unprofessional, and a misplacement of fundamental values.[60] Beyond this "background" of prosecutorial zeal, a journalist who has followed this issue suggests that the problem is aggravated by the contemporary political preoccupation with crime:

> Public pressure to combat rising crime, 12 years of conservative administrations, and a "law and order" Supreme Court majority have transformed the U.S. criminal justice system and vastly expanded the powers of federal prosecutors over the past decade.
>
> The changes can be measured in numbers: The Justice Department's budget grew from $ 2.3 billion in 1981 to $ 9.3 billion today, while the number of department lawyers and assistant U.S. attorneys has nearly doubled, to 7,881.
>
> At the same time, Justice Department policies and Supreme Court rulings have given prosecutors more flexibility than ever before in pursuing convictions, and made it increasingly difficult for courts or aggrieved individuals to hold federal prosecutors accountable for tactics that once were considered grounds for case dismissal or disciplinary action.[61]

VAGUE STANDARDS An important reason for seemingly widespread prosecutorial misconduct is that the standards and rules designed to guide prosecutors are vague. A leading authority notes, "[p]rosecutors, like police officers, often act intuitively based on their sense of fairness and duty. Unlike police, however, the prosecutor is an attorney who has the luxury of foresight."[62] Not only are the standards vague, but there are a variety of standards in existence, and it is not always clear which standard applies in a particular case. Furthermore, the "lack of enforcement [of standards of prosecutorial behavior] may be traced in part to the diffusion of regulatory authority."[63] This dilemma is seen in the case of "John Doe," an Assistant United States Attorney (AUSA) practicing in the District of Columbia and licensed to practice by the New Mexico Bar. In a 1988 prosecution, Doe violated the *District of Columbia Code of Professional Responsibility* by contacting a defendant without knowledge of the defendant's lawyer. The defense lawyer filed a motion to dismiss. The District of Columbia court rejected the motion but referred the matter to the district's bar's Board of Professional Responsibility. That body referred the case to the New Mexico Disciplinary Board. New Mexico Chief Disciplinary Counsel, Virginia Ferrera, filed charges against Doe for violating ethical rules. Doe tried to have the case removed to federal courts in New Mexico and the District of Columbia. The federal court in New Mexico remanded the case back to the New Mexico Disciplinary Board. In the District of Columbia federal court, the United States Justice Department argued that its internal ethics rules allowing an AUSA to contact a defendant overrode the state ethics rules under the Supremacy Clause. A temporary injunction blocked state action, but the District of Columbia court ultimately held that an agency directive is not "law" and allowed New Mexico to resume the disciplinary investigation.[64]

This case not only displays the confusion over the sources of prosecutorial discipline but also shows that the Justice Department has been playing "hardball" and has sought to insulate itself from external review.

Controlling Prosecutorial Misconduct

What measures exist to sanction and control prosecutorial misconduct? Sanctions may be formal or informal. Formal sanctions include appellate reversal of a conviction, finding the prosecutor in contempt of court, referring the prosecutor to a bar association grievance committee, removing the prosecutor from office, and filing civil suits.[65] For the most part, these formal sanctions have had limited effect. The previously noted case of Michael Pardue is an example of a growing trend: federal judges, including many conservative, tough-on-crime Reagan and Bush appointees, have been appalled by prosecutorial misconduct but cannot dismiss the prosecution because the Supreme Court has consistently sided with prosecutors on these issues. In the issue raised in the case of William Moore, the former president of REI, the Supreme Court ruled in 1992, in *United States v. Williams,* that federal courts do not have supervisory power to require prosecutors to present substantial evidence of innocence to grand juries. Thus, regardless of whether the action of prosecutor Valder was or was not unethical or overbearing, he was, under Supreme Court rules, allowed to disregard evidence of innocence in presenting his case to the grand jury.

Civil suits against prosecutors are difficult but not impossible. The Supreme Court has ruled that a state prosecutor has absolute immunity in a suit brought under the Civil Rights Act, 42 *United States Code* §1983 in initiating a prosecution and in presenting the state's case (*Imbler v. Pachtman,* 1976). But the Court has limited absolute immunity to only functions that are within the scope of prosecutorial duties. Thus, a prosecutor has absolute immunity for actions that occurred while participating in a probable cause hearing, but not for giving legal advice to the police (*Burns v. Reed,* 1991). Recently, the Court has clarified the standard to be applied to determine if a prosecutor has absolute immunity, that is, whether an action was within the prosecutorial function. The standard to be applied to draw the line between "advocacy" and "investigation" is that "a prosecutor neither is, nor consider himself to be, an advocate before he has probable cause to have anyone arrested" (*Buckley v. Fitzsimmons,* 1993). In *Buckley* the Court held that this standard does not offer a prosecutor absolute immunity for making false statements to the press or for fabricating evidence during the investigation prior to an arrest.

Because of the limited effectiveness of formal sanctions, some attention should be given to "the importance of informal judicial controls."[66] Professor Bruce Green, who believes "that critics exaggerate the prevalence and seriousness of prosecutorial misconduct," writes:

> The power of a court to "discipline" a prosecutor for misconduct that comes to its attention by issuing unfavorable scheduling and discovery orders and evidentiary rulings is not to be underestimated. Indeed, some might argue that, in deference to judicial authority, prosecutors are more apt to be underzealous than overzealous. Of equal importance is the judge's ability to call misconduct to the attention of a prosecutor's supervisors and to seek assurances from them that appropriate measures will be taken. Because a prosecutor's office, as an institution, appears repeatedly before the court, it has a greater incentive than other law offices to respond appropriately to such requests.[67]

Others call for greater prosecutor education in ethical standards.[68] Despite Professor Green's well-taken point, prosecutorial misconduct seems to be a real problem that the justice system does not appear to be adequately dealing with at the present time. It is time for prosecutors to take to heart a judge's charge to a jury: "The government always wins when justice is done, regardless of whether the verdict be guilty or not guilty."[69]

Summary

The pretrial process contains numerous steps; involves important constitutional rights; and adds substantial complexity and due process to the prosecution of crimes. The trade-off for this complexity is that cases are thoroughly screened so that, ideally, only those that are based on solid evidence and are deserving of prosecution go forward to trial. Consequently, the government is able to give more formal attention to serious and important cases.

The important processes that occur before trial include: initial appearance, bail hearings, prosecutorial charging, plea negotiations, grand jury and/or preliminary hearings, and pretrial motion hearings. The decisions rendered at each of these stages can influence prosecutorial discretion to bring a case forward or to forgo further criminal prosecution.

A critical pretrial process is the pretrial release, or bail decision. *Stack v. Boyle* held that defendants are entitled to "reasonable" bail that is not out of line with current practices. Disparity in who gets released has led some jurisdictions to develop such reform programs as release on recognizance for indigents who are good risks, and court-run deposit bond systems designed to lower the cost of bonds and eliminate the need for bail bondsmen. At the same time, the federal government passed a preventive detention statute under which suspects may be held without bail prior to trial if they are considered to be a danger to society. In *United States v. Salerno* (1987), the Supreme Court upheld the legality of such measures if there are hearings and proper procedural guidelines to maintain the due process rights of persons held without bail on the prediction that they may commit crimes while on pretrial release.

Prosecutors have great discretion in bringing criminal charges. As a general rule, courts cannot dismiss charges that they think are unwise, but can dismiss where there is selective or vindictive prosecution. Selective prosecution occurs when a defendant is prosecuted on impermissible grounds, such as race, religion, political beliefs, or for exercising constitutional rights, where the prosecutor's intent is discriminatory. For a dismissal on vindictive prosecution grounds, discriminatory intent need not be proven. It occurs when more serious charges are preferred against a defendant who exercised his or her constitutional rights.

The grand jury is a citizen's institution originated in the common law. It meets in secret to investigate charges and decide whether to indict suspects. It may issue subpoenas to compel persons to testify or supply evidence and request immunity for witnesses who plead the privilege against self-incrimination. Grand juries are criticized for meeting in secret and for being the prosecutor's rubber stamp. The federal constitutional guarantee of prosecution only on indictment by grand jury is not applicable to the states. Proposals for the reform of grand jury procedures include the right of counsel to attend as witness's advisors and the right of a target of investigation to attend and voluntarily address the grand jury.

The preliminary examination consists of the presentation of prosecution witnesses before a lower court judge to determine if probable cause exists to bind the defendant over for trial. Preliminary hearings are open to the public; prosecution witnesses can be cross-examined; and defendants have a right to counsel. The preliminary hearing preserves testimony for trial if a witness should become unavailable and may be a way for the defense to discover the strengths and weaknesses of the prosecutor's case as well as factual information.

LEGAL PUZZLES

LEGAL PUZZLES: HOW HAVE COURTS DECIDED THESE CASES?

11–1. Ibrahim El-Gabrowny was indicted, with others, for the February 1993 World Trade Center bombing in New York City. In March 1993, he assaulted officers who were searching his home with a warrant, and was arrested. At that time, he held five fraudulent Nicaraguan passports. After the arrest he was ordered not to wash his hands in order to test them for traces of chemicals used in the bombing. While using the bathroom, he plunged his hands into the toilet bowl, to expose them to uric acid to eliminate any chemical traces. Bail was denied because he posed a risk of flight and a threat of danger. Were his *eighteen months* in custody a due process violation? *United Stated v. El-Gabrowny,* 35 F.3d 63 (2d Cir. 1994).

11–2. Gordon, an African American, was indicted for voter fraud. He sought governmental information to show that the government chose to prosecute him and other African-American political leaders in Alabama's black-majority "Black Belt" counties for voting fraud, while not prosecuting county residents who were members of a rival white-dominated political party and who committed similar election offenses. Gordon presented a prejudiced statement by a Justice Department spokesperson and some numeric data. His motion for information about the prosecutor's motive in charging was denied. Was the denial proper? *United States v. Gordon,* 817 F.2d 1538 (11th Cir. 1987) (per curiam), *vacated in part on other grounds,* 836 F.2d 1312 (1988).

11–3. The federal district court for the Eastern District of Michigan, in order to ensure that the percentage of African Americans in the federal jury pool for ("qualified jury wheel") was equivalent to the proportion of adult eligible African-American jurors in the district, and to fulfill the mandate of the Jury Selection and Service Act that a jury be drawn from a fair cross section of the community, and finding that in the district white jury pool members were over-represented, ordered, under a District Jury Selection plan, that one in five non-African Americans were selected at random to be removed from the jury wheel simply because of their racial status. In the selection of the grand jury pool from which petitioners' grand jury was drawn, at least fourteen Hispanics and 863 other individuals who were not African Americans were removed from the jury wheel. Petitioners moved for dismissal on the grounds that the District Plan biased the grand jury that indicted them by underrepresenting Hispanic jurors. Was the Jury Plan constitutional? *United States v. Ovalle,* 136 F.3d 1092 (6th Cir. 1998).

11–4. William John, on federal parole for a sexual assault conviction, was convicted by a New Mexico court for a rape committed while on parole. After serving several years under the New Mexico conviction, he was released. The federal Parole Commission thereafter revoked his federal parole without a hearing. John filed a habeas corpus petition arguing that under *Morrissey v. Brewer* (1972) before parole is revoked a parolee is entitled to a preliminary hearing and a revocation hearing. He wished to call and cross-examine the victim of his initial 1986 rape conviction to determine if there were mitigating factors that favor parole. Is he constitutionally entitled to cross-examine witnesses at the equivalent of a preliminary examination? *John v. United States Parole Commission,* 122 F.3d 1278 (9th Cir. 1997).

ANSWERS TO LEGAL PUZZLES

11–1. NO. The Constitution is not violated simply because of long detention. The government contributed to the delay by opposing his request for severance of his trial; but the delay was justified by the importance and complexity of the case and the extensive evidence, including numerous tapes in Arabic, reasonably requiring a lengthy period for pretrial preparation. If convicted, he would face a long period of imprisonment and that, coupled with his forged passports, indicated a great incentive and inclination to flee. The trial was scheduled to begin a month after the bail reduction request. All the factors taken together justified continued detention.

11–2. NO. Ordinarily, the prosecutor's discretion is beyond court challenge. However, whenever there is evidence of selective prosecution based on discrimination, and the defendant raises some credible information to support the charge, the court must allow the party to pursue the issue.

11–3. NO. "The implementation of the jury selection plan is clearly not race neutral. Individuals were eliminated from consideration for jury service on the basis of their race. Any non-African-American had a chance of being eliminated from the jury wheel solely based on race." The Plan was adopted to meet a compelling governmental interest (representative jury wheels), but it is not narrowly tailored to meet this end. Alternative methods of broadening membership in the jury pool could have been utilized. The appellants did not win relief because they did not raise their claims prior to trial.

11–4. YES. John was entitled to identify circumstances in mitigation during the parole revocation. The Parole Commission was compelled by *Morrissey* to abide by the requirements of accurate factfinding to satisfy the minimum requirements of due process, including the right to confront and cross-examine adverse witnesses, unless the hearing officer specifically finds good cause for not allowing confrontation. Since a hearing officer did not find good cause, John had the right to cross-examine the victim. Also, recent Supreme Court cases have ruled that the mere fact of a state conviction is not automatic grounds for a federal parole revocation.

FURTHER READING

Milton Heumann, *Plea Bargaining: The Experience of Prosecutors, Judges, and Defense Attorneys* (Chicago: University of Chicago Press, 1979).

Jim McGee and Brian Duffy, *Main Justice: The Men and Women Who Enforce the Nation's Criminal Laws and Guard Its Civil Liberties* (New York: Simon and Schuster, 1996).

H. Richard Uviller, *Virtual Justice: The Flawed Prosecution of Crime in America* (New Haven: Yale University Press, 1996).

ENDNOTES

1. John H. Langbein, The Criminal Trial Before the Lawyers, *University of Chicago Law Review* 45:263–316, pp. 280–81 (1978).
2. Albert W. Alschuler, Implementing the Criminal Defendant's Right to Trial: Alternatives to the Plea Bargaining System, *University of Chicago Law Review* 50:931–1050 (1983).
3. Malcolm M. Feeley, "Plea Bargaining and the Structure of the Criminal Process," *Justice System Journal* 7:338–55 (1982).
4. See Roy B. Flemming, *Punishment Before Trial: An Organizational Perspective of Felony Bail Processes* (New York: Longman, 1982); John Goldcamp, *Two Classes of Accused: A Study of Bail and Detention in American Justice* (Cambridge: Ballinger, 1979); Paul B. Wice, *Freedom for Sale: A National Study of Pretrial Release* (Lexington: Lexington Books, 1974).
5. President's Commission on Law Enforcement and Administration of Justice, *Task Force Report: Science and Technology* (Washington, D.C.: U.S. Government Printing Office, 1967), p. 60; Brian Forst, Judith Lucianovic, and Sarah J. Cox, *What Happens After Arrest?* (Washington, D.C.: INSLAW, 1978), pp. 17, 67–70; Vera Institute of Justice, *Felony Arrests: Their Prosecution and Distribution in New York City's Courts*, rev. ed. (New York: Longman, 1981), p. 1.
6. Deborah Emerson, *Grand Jury Reform: A Review of Key Issues* (Washington D.C.: Dept. of Justice, National Institute of Justice, 1983).
7. The most common are the insanity defense where time for a psychiatric examination is needed, and the alibi defense, where time to investigate the witnesses and the circumstances is needed.

8. *United States v. Abrahams*, 575 F.2d 3 (1st Cir. 1978).
9. 18 *U.S.C.* §§ 3141–3150.
10. Michael Gottfredson, Empirical Analysis of Pretrial Release Decisions, *Journal of Criminal Justice* 2:287 (1974).
11. See Frank W. Miller, *Prosecution: The Decisions to Charge a Suspect with a Crime* (Boston: Little, Brown, 1969); Elizabeth Anne Stanko, "The Impact of Victim Assessment on Prosecutors' Screening Decisions: The Case of the New York County District Attorney's Office," *Law & Society Review* 16:225–38 (1982).
12. *United States v. Williams*, 47 F.3d 658 (4th Cir. 1995).
13. *United States v. Schweihs*, 971 F.2d 1302 (7th Cir. 1992).
14. 342 F.2d 167 (5th Cir. 1965).
15. *United States v. Armstrong* (1996); *Town of Newton v. Rumery* (1987).
16. *United States v. Armstrong* (1996) (Stevens, J., dissenting).
17. Linda Greenhouse, "Supreme Court Roundup: Race Statistics Alone Do Not Support a Claim of Selective Prosecution, Justices Rule," *New York Times*, May 14, 1996, p. A20.
18. 810 F.2d 1242 (D.C. Cir. 1986).
19. *United States v. Gurule*, 437 F.2d 239 (10th Cir. 1970).
20. Rule 6(e)(3).
21. *Ibid.*, p. 53.
22. Marvin E. Frankel and Gary P. Naftalis, *The Grand Jury: An Institution on Trial* (New York: Hill & Wang, 1977), p. 108.
23. Barry Winograd and Martin Fassler, "The Political Question," *Trial Magazine*, Jan./Feb. 1973, pp. 16–20.
24. Frankel and Naftalis, *The Grand Jury,* p. 93.
25. American Bar Association Section of Criminal Justice, "Proposed ABA Grand Jury Principles," *Criminal Justice* 4(4):5 (Winter 1977); American Bar Association, *ABA Grand Jury Policy and Model Act,* 2d ed. (Chicago: American Bar Association, 1982).
26. William J. Campbell, "Eliminate the Grand Jury," *Journal of Criminal Law and Criminology* 64(1973):174.
27. Bureau of Justice Statistics, *Report to the Nation on Crime and Justice,* 2d ed. (Washington, D.C.: U.S. Department of Justice, 1988), p. 72.
28. *Ibid.,* p. 72.
29. Thomas P. Sullivan and Robert D. Nachman, "If It Ain't Broke, Don't Fix It: Why the Grand Jury's Accusatory Function Should Not Be Changed," *Journal of Criminal Law and Criminology* 75:1047–69 (1984).
30. See Federal Magistrate's Act, 18 U.S.C. § 3060; Rules 5 and 5.1 of the Federal Rules of Criminal Procedure.
31. Rule 5(d). The conduct of the preliminary examination is guided by Rule 5.1.
32. *Federal Rules of Criminal Procedure* 5(d).
33. *Sciortino v. Zampano,* 385 F.2d 132 (2d Cir. 1967); *United States v. Quinn,* 357 F. Supp. 1348 (N.D. Ga. 1973), holding that if an indictment is obtained *during* the preliminary examination, the examination must be terminated.
34. Yale Kamisar, Wayne R. LaFave, and Jerold H. Israel, *Modern Criminal Procedure,* 6th ed. (St. Paul: West Publishing, 1986), p. 944.
35. *United States v. Quinn,* 357 F. Supp. 1348 (N.D. Ga. 1973).
36. *People v. Duncan,* 201 N.W.2d 629 (Mich. 1972).
37. *Coleman v. Burnett,* 477 F.2d 1187 (D.C. Cir. 1973).
38. Lyn Morton, "Seeking the Elusive Remedy for Prosecutorial Misconduct: Suppression, Dismissal, or Discipline?" *Georgetown Journal of Legal Ethics* 7:1083–1116 (1994), p. 1085.
39. *Berger v. United States* (1935); see American Bar Association, *Standards Relating to the Administration of Criminal Justice,* Chapter 3: The Prosecution Function (1972).
40. *Young v. United States* ex rel. *Vuitton et Fils S.A.* (1987), p. 811.
41. Richard H. Frost, *The Mooney Case* (Stanford: Stanford University Press, 1968).
42. Cynthia L. Cooper and Sam Reese Sheppard, *Mockery of Justice: The True Story of the Sheppard Murder Case* (Boston: Northwest University Press, 1995), pp. 83–93.
43. *Sheppard v. Maxwell* (1966); Cooper and Sheppard, *Mockery,* pp. 117–26.
44. Jim McGee, "War on Crime Expands U.S. Prosecutors' Powers; Aggressive Tactics Put Fairness at Issue," (Series: The Appearance of Justice, Part 1 of 6), *Washington Post,* Jan. 10, 1993, p. A1.
45. The information and quotes for this segment are from Jim McGee, "U.S. Crusade Against Pornography Tests the Limits of Fairness," (Series: The Appearance of Justice, Part 2 of 6), *Washington Post,* Jan. 11, 1993, p. A1.
46. Morton, "Seeking," p. 1084.
47. Jim McGee, "Courts Losing Options in Prosecutor Misdeeds," (Series: The Appearance of Justice, Part 4 of 6), *Washington Post,* Jan. 13, 1993, p. A1.
48. Bennett L. Gershman, *Prosecutorial Misconduct* (Deerfield, Ill.: Clark Boardman Callaghan, 1995) § 9.4(a).
49. Gershman, *Prosecutorial Misconduct* § 9.4(b).
50. Gershman, *Prosecutorial Misconduct* § 9.5.
51. Gershman, *Prosecutorial Misconduct* § 9.5. *Miller v. Pate* (1967)—the prosecutor's misconduct hid police due process errors in obtaining a false confession.
52. Gershman, *Prosecutorial Misconduct* § 9.5(b). Examples of irrelevant facts introduced: racially biased statements of the defendant to prejudice black jurors, defendant and homicide victim had homosexual relationship, and defendant a known pedophile.
53. Gershman, *Prosecutorial Misconduct* § 9.6(b).
54. Gershman, *Prosecutorial Misconduct* § 9.10(b)(2). Examples include: withholding addresses in violation of a court order, keeping a witness in custody, subpoenaing a witness and keeping her incommunicado, dismissing charges against an

informant knowing he would flee the jurisdiction, paying a witness to leave the jurisdiction, knowingly giving the defense a false address of a witness.

55. Gershman, *Prosecutorial Misconduct* § 9.10(b)(3).
56. Gershman, *Prosecutorial Misconduct* § 9.10(b)(4).
57. Gershman, *Prosecutorial Misconduct* § 10.1.
58. Gershman, *Prosecutorial Misconduct* § 10.2.
59. Gershman, *Prosecutorial Misconduct* § 10.24(a)–(h).
60. Kenneth Bresler, "'I Never Lost a Trial': When Prosecutors Keep Score of Criminal Convictions," *Georgetown Journal of Legal Ethics* 9:537–46 (1996).
61. Jim McGee, "War on Crime Expands U.S. Prosecutors' Powers; Aggressive Tactics Put Fairness at Issue," (Series: The Appearance of Justice, Part 1 of 6), *Washington Post,* Jan. 10, 1993, p. A1.; Morton, "Seeking," pp. 1085–86; Bennett L. Gershman, "The New Prosecutors," *University of Pittsburgh Law Review* 53:393 (1992).
62. Gershman, *Prosecutorial Misconduct,* p. viii.
63. Bruce A. Green, "Policing Federal Prosecutors: Do Too Many Regulators Produce Too Little Enforcement?" *St. Thomas Law Review* 8(1995):69–95, p. 91.
64. Morton, "Seeking," pp. 1105–06.
65. Gershman, *Prosecutorial Misconduct* Chapter 13, §§ 13.1—13.7(c).
65. Green, "Policing Federal Prosecutors," p. 70.
66. Green, "Policing Federal Prosecutors," p. 71.
68. Bresler, "'I Never Lost a Trial,'" p. 544.
69. Cited in Bresler, "'I Never Lost a Trial,'" p. 539.

JUSTICES OF THE SUPREME COURT

The Twenty-First Century Court
Souter—Thomas—Ginsburg—Breyer

Each of these justices previously served as federal judges, although David Souter, a New Hampshire supreme court judge, had barely taken his federal appointment to the First Circuit Court of Appeals before his elevation to the Supreme Court, and Clarence Thomas had only one year of judicial experience. These appointments of President George Bush replaced the most enduring liberals on the Court—Brennan and Marshall. Many thought that these appointments would mark the end of the politically inflammatory abortion rights decision, Roe v. Wade. This was not to be. In the criminal procedure area, however, the new appointments did not change the generally pro-prosecution cast of the Court. What was lost with the retirement of Brennan and Marshall was a strong liberal voice, even if in dissent. Justice Souter aligned with the moderate conservative center of the court and Justice Thomas joined the extreme conservatives on these issues.

President Bill Clinton, appointing the first Democrats to the Court since 1967 (Thurgood Marshall), disappointed some supporters by not naming liberals to offset the distinctive conservatism of Justices Scalia and Thomas. Justices Ginsburg and Breyer both had reputations as extremely competent and moderate federal judges. Ruth Bader Ginsburg had been a leading litigator in womens' rights cases before the Supreme Court in the 1970s and was viewed as liberal on some issues. Justice Breyer had a national reputation as an original thinker on issues of economic regulation and as a member of the federal Sentencing Commission. Neither of them, replacing Justices Blackmun and White, were expected to modify the Court's position on criminal procedure. Indeed, they have proven to be centrists. This reflects the national mood and President Clinton's position as moderately conservative on crime issues.

Oddly, then, the only sitting justice who might fairly be called a criminal procedure liberal is Justice Stevens, who migrated to the position from a centrist posture. The Court at the outset of the twenty-first century can best be described as moderate to conservative on criminal procedure issues. The general framework of incorporation, a legacy of the Warren Court's "due process revolution," has endured; but it has been weakened by decisions that block access to federal courts (i.e., standing and habeas corpus) and by decisions that interpret such categories as due process, reasonable suspicion, probable cause, and cruel and unusual punishment in ways that are favorable to the state. Defendants have been able to prevail on issues associated with property rights (e.g., asset forfeiture) or race discrimination (peremptory challenges to remove jurors). Recent decisions holding that auto checkpoints for crime control purposes violate the Fourth Amendment or that a bare anonymous tip does not sustain reasonable suspicion may indicate that even a very conservative Supreme Court has reached a point beyond which individual rights under the Constitution cannot be denied without eroding the fabric of American liberty.

David H. Souter

New Hampshire 1939–

Republican

Appointed by George Bush

Years of Service: 1990– .

Collection of the Supreme Court of the United States. Photographer: Joseph Bailey

Life and Career Souter's pre-Court record was so obscure that he was dubbed the "stealth" candidate, after the radar-avoiding airplane. This politically prudent choice by President Bush put a candidate with no known views on the abortion issue before the Senate, which had blocked Judge Robert Bork's 1987 appointment because of his outspoken and radically conservative views. Justice Souter's smooth nomination proved the wisdom of this choice.

A native of New Hampshire, Souter attended Harvard College, spent two years at Oxford University as a Rhodes Scholar, and after graduating from Harvard Law School practiced law for two years in Concord, New Hampshire. He served as deputy state attorney general under Warren Rudman and was then appointed state attorney general. In 1978, he became a trial judge and in 1983, Governor John Sununu, on the recommendation of Senator Warren Rudman, named Souter to the New Hampshire Supreme Court. In 1990, Souter was appointed to the federal Circuit Court of Appeals but was soon after nominated to the Supreme Court, clearly on the recommendation of President Bush's White House chief of staff, John Sununu.

Contribution to Criminal Procedure By replacing Justice Brennan, the most liberal justice on the Court, Souter at first swung the Court's criminal procedure jurisprudence generally in favor of the state. In his first year on the Court, he voted with the majority in every case, almost always for the prosecution argument. By 1995, he began to shift to a more moderate stance, in his majority opinion holding that a state appellate court on collateral review must grant a new trial to the defendant if a prosecutor withheld relevant evidence (*Kyles v. Whitely,* 1995). Although he still votes more often for the prosecution, in some cases he has joined what passes for a liberal bloc, for example, in joining Justice Stevens' dissent in *Illinois v. Wardlow* (2000) (flight from police constitutes reasonable suspicion), along with Ginsburg and Breyer.

Signature Opinion Dissenting opinion in *Pennsylvania Board of Probation And Parole v. Scott* (1998) In a formulaic opinion by Justice Thomas, the Court's majority held that evidence seized in violation of a parolee's Fourth Amendment rights (parole agents entered his home without a warrant or exigent circumstances) is not excluded under the exclusionary rule. Souter's dissent (joined by Stevens, Ginsburg and Breyer) relied on a functional analysis of the work of parole officers to demonstrate that they are subject to similar motives as police and that the deterrent rationale of the exclusionary rule should therefore apply to them.

Assessment Souter is a part of the moderate-conservative center of the Court. In *Planned Parenthood v. Casey* (1992), he joined with O'Connor and Kennedy, in upholding *Roe v. Wade* (by a narrow 5–4 vote) on the basis of *stare decisis. Casey* signaled that the most extreme conservative interpretations of the Constitution, espoused by Chief Justice Rehnquist and Justices Scalia and Thomas, would not become the law of the land. In today's world of extremely partisan politics, Souter has become a lightening rod for conservative ire. "No more Souters!" has become a slogan of conservatives frustrated that the Reagan-Bush appointees on the Supreme Court have not been able to overturn a woman's right to choose abortion, *Miranda,* and the ban on school-prayer under the First Amendment.

Further Reading

David Garrow, "Justice Souter Emerges," *The New York Times Magazine,* September 25, 1994.

Clarence Thomas

Virginia 1948–

Republican

Appointed by George Bush

Years of Service: 1991– .

Collection of the Supreme Court of the United States. Photographer: Joseph Bailey

Life and Career Thomas was born into a poor family in segregated Savannah, Georgia. He was raised by his grandparents, who instilled in him a sense of pride and discipline, self-reliance and hard work, commitment to black solidarity through the NAACP, and a determination that education was the key to a better life. He attended Catholic school and experienced blatant racism of fellow students in a Missouri seminary. He graduated from Holy Cross College and Yale Law School, where he developed a dislike for affirmative action. After graduation in 1974, he worked as an assistant attorney-general in Missouri, as a corporate lawyer, and as legislative assistant to Senator Danforth of Missouri in Washington.

As one of few African-American conservatives during the Reagan administration he became chairman of the Equal Employment Opportunity Commission (EEOC), an agency to which the administration was hostile. Thomas handled this difficult assignment by ultimately abandoning the agency's affirmative action agenda and class-action suits and focused instead on individual discrimination cases. Many criticized his EEOC leadership as failing to effectively support claims of minorities, women and the elderly. He was nominated to the U.S. Court of Appeals for the Washington, D.C. Circuit in 1989, an appointment which was viewed as a stepping stone to the Supreme Court.

Thomas' confirmation process, when nominated by President Bush to the Supreme Court to replace retiring Justice Thurgood Marshall, was extremely controversial. He was lambasted for his conservatism, his lack of high judicial qualifications, and his opposition to *Roe v. Wade.* Many thought that George Bush cynically manipulated the "black seat" on the Court to make it difficult for African Americans to oppose a black candidate. And this was *before* the sensational story broke that he had sexually harassed Anita Hill, a former employee and a law professor. The hearings on Professor Hill's testimony and Judge Thomas' impassioned defense were televised and was the scandal of the hour. Thomas denied the allegations and called the ordeal "a high-tech lynching for uppity blacks." His nomination was affirmed by a 52 to 48 vote of the Senate.

Contribution to Criminal Procedure From 1991 to 1995, Thomas was second only to Chief Juste Rehnquist in conservative voting in criminal procedure cases, supporting individuals in only nineteen percent of cases. Although he is a solid conservative on a conservative court, he has little influence because he is not given opportunities to write majority opinions for the Court in important cases, but typically writes majority opinions only when the justices share a strong consensus, as was the case in holding that the "knock-and-announce" rule of search warrant execution is a constitutional rule (*Wilson v. Arkansas,* 1995). He is the most conservative justice in death penalty, habeas corpus, and Eighth Amendment cases.

Signature Opinion Dissenting opinion in *Hudson v. McMillan* (1992) The court held that excessive force by a prison guard (the beating alleged was deliberate and resulted in minor bruises, facial swelling, loosened teeth, and a cracked dental plate) may constitute cruel and unusual punishment even though the inmate does not suffer serious injury. Justice Thomas said "In my view, a use of force that causes only insignificant harm to a prisoner may be immoral, it may be tortious, it may be criminal, and it may even be remediable under other provisions of the Federal Constitution, but it is not 'cruel and unusual punishment.'"

Assessment He applied the theory of originalism more rigidly than Justice Scalia, and although he expresses confidently that he knows the intent of the framers of the Constitution, it was noted that he "has shown little familiarity with the most recent scholarship about" the origin of the Fourteenth Amendment, where he seems to have mistakenly asserted that its framers intended to create a "color-blind" Constitution, a position that supports his votes.

Further Reading

Christopher E. Smith, "Clarence Thomas: A Distinctive Justice," *Seton Hall Law Review* 28:1–28 (1997).

Ruth Bader Ginsburg

New York 1933 –

Democrat

Appointed by William Clinton

Years of Service: 1993– .

Collection of the Supreme Court of the United States. Photographer: Richard Strauss

Life and Career Ruth Bader grew up in Brooklyn, New York, in a Jewish, lower-middle-class family. An excellent student, she won a scholarship to Cornell University, and decided to pursue a career in the law with her husband, Martin Ginsburg. Following Martin's army service and the birth of their first child, she entered Harvard Law School a year after Martin did. She was one of only nine women in a class of 500 students. Martin was diagnosed with cancer and underwent radiation therapy while Ruth took notes in his classes as well as her own, and typed his third-year paper while caring for their child. Martin recovered, obtained a position with a New York law firm, and Ruth transferred to Columbia Law School. Justice Ginsburg was the first woman to have served on two law reviews.

After graduation, sexism prevented her from being hired by a law firm. She clerked for a state judge. She joined the Rutgers Law School faculty in 1963; in 1972 she became the first tenured woman law professor at Columbia Law School. Between 1972 and 1978 Ginsburg argued six and won five gender-equality cases before the Supreme Court, on the basis that sex-role stereotypes violated the Equal Protection Clause. Some have called her "the Thurgood Marshall of womens' rights." In 1980, she was appointed to the U.S. Court of Appeals for the District of Columbia, where she developed an excellent reputation as a leading centrist judge.

Contribution to Criminal Procedure Ginsburg's votes in criminal cases are liberal to moderate. She has been described as pragmatic. She has sided with the government in upholding drug testing of school athletes, pretext searches, gaining consent to search cars without informing drivers of their rights, the forfeiture of a wife's interest in a car which was confiscated after her husband was found guilty of soliciting prostitution, and ordering non-suspicious passengers out of stopped cars.

However, she has joined with liberal and moderate justices to support individual rights in dissent where fleeing from an officer has been held to constitute reasonable suspicion, where a car was seized for forfeiture without a warrant, where parole officers entered a parolee's home without a warrant, and where police searched the handbag of a non-suspicious automobile passenger. She, along with Justice Stevens, has attacked the way in which *Michigan v. Long* (1983) has applied the adequate and independent state grounds doctrine, arguing in *Arizona v. Evans* (1995) that the Court should not overturn state court decisions that expand defendants constitutional rights.

SIGNATURE OPINION *Florida v. J.L.* (2000) For a unanimous Court, Ginsburg held that an anonymous phone call "that a young black male standing at a particular bus stop and wearing a plaid shirt was carrying a gun" does not in itself establish reasonable suspicion to conduct a *Terry* stop if all that the police know is that a person at the described place fits the description given by the caller. The ruling indicates that the Court has become wary of extending the reach of police powers that clearly go beyond constitutional protections: "an automatic firearm exception to our established reliability analysis would rove too far."

ASSESSMENT She is a moderate liberal and takes a dynamic approach to the complex issues of legal process. The major themes of her writings include the ideal of a person's day in court, court efficiency, and judicial integrity, including *stare decisis* and procedural regularity. In *United States v. Virginia* (1996), she wrote the majority opinion holding that the Virginia Military Institute could not lawfully exclude women students.

FURTHER READING

Elijah Yip and Eric K. Yamamoto, "Justice Ruth Bader Ginsburg's Jurisprudence of Process and Procedure," *Hawaii Law Review* 20:647–698 (1998).

STEPHEN G. BREYER

Massachusetts 1938 –

Democrat

Appointed by William Clinton.

Years of Service: 1994– .

Collection of the Supreme Court of the United States. Photographer:Richard Strauss

LIFE AND CAREER Raised in San Francisco, Breyer's father, a lawyer, brought him to a voting booth when he was young and helped to impart "a love for the possibilities of democracy." His mother was active in local Democratic politics and the League of Women Voters and instilled in Stephen a sense that intellectual activity had to be balanced by an ability to work with and help people. He was Boy Scout, worked as a delivery boy, and dug ditches for a local utility company. He graduated from Stanford University with highest honors, earned another degree at Oxford University in philosophy, politics and economics, and was graduated magna cum laude from Harvard Law School in 1964.

After law school, Breyer clerked for Justice Goldberg. He thereafter was an antitrust lawyer in the Justice Department and a Harvard Law School professor. He developed a sophisticated but pragmatic theory of the regulatory state and believes that economic regulation should maximize competition and not burden the private sector with unnecessary government restraints. He also served as an assistant on the Watergate Special Prosecution force that helped to topple President Nixon, and as counsel to the Senate Judiciary Committee. In 1980, he was appointed to the First Circuit Court of Appeals. He was a coalition builder on that court. In 1985, Judge Breyer was appointed to the United States Sentencing Commission, which was designed to rationalize federal sentencing practices.

CONTRIBUTION TO CRIMINAL PROCEDURE As an expert in economic regulation, Breyer has written few major opinions in the criminal procedure area. His voting pattern is middle-of-the road. He voted for the government in *United States v. Armstrong* (1996)(not selective prosecution to charge a disproportionate percentage of African Americans for crack cocaine offenses); *Carlyle v. United States* (1996) (motion for judgment of acquittal cannot be granted if filed one day beyond time limit); *Lewis v. Fletcher* (1996) (no violation of rights from inadequate law library unless actual injury shown); *Wyoming v. Houghton* (1999) (police can search handbag of a non-suspicious automobile passenger); and *Bond v. United States* (2000)(traveler has no expectation of privacy "that strangers will not push, pull, prod, squeeze, or otherwise manipulate his luggage" on an inter-city bus). He has, on occasion, joined liberal and moderate justices: in dissent where fleeing from an officer has been held to constitute reasonable suspicion; in dissent where parole officers entered a parolee's home without a warrant, and in dissent where wife's interest in car was forfeited for her husband's crime.

Signature Opinion Dissenting opinion in *Apprendi v. New Jersey* (2000) The majority held that a factual element of the crime used to enhance a sentence must be submitted to a jury and proved beyond a reasonable doubt. Breyer, dissenting, stated that "the real world of criminal justice cannot hope to meet" the ideal that "juries, not judges, determin[e] the existence of those facts upon which increased punishment turns." "It can function only with the help of procedural compromises, particularly in respect to sentencing."

Assessment In *United States v. Lopez* (1995), the Court struck down a federal law based on the commerce clause—making it a federal crime to possess a weapon within one hundred feet of a local school—for the first time since the 1930s. Breyer wrote a sharp and detailed dissent, joined by Justices Stevens, Souter and Ginsburg, defending federal authority to pass such a law.

Further Reading

Walter E. Joyce, "The Early Constitutional Jurisprudence of Justice Stephen G. Breyer: a Study of the Justice's First Year on the United States Supreme Court," *Seton Hall Constitutional Law Journal* 7:149–163 (1996).

CHAPTER 12

THE TRIAL PROCESS

[T]here are principles of liberty and justice, lying at the foundation of our civil and political institutions, which no State can violate consistently with that due process of law required by the Fourteenth Amendment in proceedings involving life, liberty, or property.

—Justice John Marshall Harlan I, dissenting, *Hurtado v. California,* 110 U.S. 516, 546 (1884)

CHAPTER OUTLINE

KEY TERMS AND PHRASES

Abuse of discretion
Accusatorial trial system
Adversarial trial system
Adverse comment
Challenge for cause
Common law trial system
Compulsory process
Confrontation Clause
Cross-examination
Expert witness
Fair cross-section
Hearsay evidence
In camera
Inquisitorial trial system
Inquisitorial trial
Invidious discrimination
Jury deliberation
Jury nullification
Jury pool
Jury trial
"Key Man" method
Master jury list
Peremptory challenges
Petty crime
Presumption of innocence
Reasonable doubt
Sequestering a jury
Subpoena
Venire
Verdict
Voir dire

THE IDEAL OF THE FAIR TRIAL

Almost all cultures seek to balance public safety with justice. When the question arises of who is responsible for a serious misdeed, human societies create institutions that satisfy two needs. The first is to ascertain the culprit in a practical and efficient manner, in accord with local cultural understandings of what it means to find facts. The second is to provide a formal setting that solemnizes the conclusion that *this* person is guilty and must be punished. In the Anglo-American legal tradition, this institution is the **jury trial.**[1] Trial by jury is the product of a distinct English history; many have argued that it is not the most efficient or effective method of separating out who is guilty from who is not. Nevertheless, it is solidly embedded in American culture and is guaranteed by Article III of the United States Constitution and the Sixth and Seventh amendments, as well as by the constitution of every state.

The English jury trial and the European **inquisitorial trial** began developing into their modern forms after the Roman Catholic Church, in the Fourth Lateran Council of 1215, forbade priests from conducting trials by ordeal. Both forms of trial were a great advance over the superstitious and brutal methods of trial by ordeal and trial by battle (which later fell into disuse). In later centuries, and especially after the seventeenth century, the common law criminal jury trial was extolled as a guarantor of liberty—a body of citizens that could resist dictatorial government pressure by acquitting political opponents who were unfairly prosecuted by the state.[2] On the other hand, the jury trial has been criticized as inefficient and error-prone.[3] Professor John Langbein notes that the conduct of English criminal trials before lawyers regularly defended suspects (before the mid-eighteenth century) left much to be desired. In these criminal trials, the defendant had to defend himself. The jury often sat through twenty trials a day, each typically lasting not more than half an hour, and made decisions on groups of cases in open court. The judge dominated the jury and could openly influence its **verdict.**[4]

But even in this kind of trial—that does not hold up to modern standards of due process—a sense of fair play prevailed. The English maxim—*it is better that twenty guilty go free than one innocent be convicted*—sums up the common law attitude to criminal justice. Thus, for example, the English common law trial did not utilize torture, unlike continental inquisitorial trials prior to the eighteenth century. At the core of the **adversarial trial** is the idea of a fair fight, one in which the defendant is given a full opportunity to challenge the state, to present witnesses, to confront the accusers, to cross-examine them, and present the case to an impartial group of legal equals. The state, furthermore, has a very high burden of proof—proof beyond a reasonable doubt—and the forum of the trial court before an impartial judge is one where the prosecutor is simply another party. Later in this Chapter, we will see that currently the jury is in crisis—that for all of its procedural strengths designed to accurately assess guilt and ensure to the greatest extent possible that an innocent person is not convicted, it is failing on both sides of this equation.

Barton Ingraham notes that in the **common law** and the **inquisitorial systems** of justice, trials are generally *open to the public* and play an expressive as well as a functional role:

> Legal systems to determine guilt are fundamentally different from administrative methods of determining facts, which can be carried out secretly, but with accuracy and impartiality, by police or other investigators. Legal proceedings, however, must give the appearance of being fair and accurate, and the best way—perhaps the only way—to give that appearance is by allowing the community either to witness the process through which the decision is made or to participate in some way. This lends the proceeding legitimacy, avoids suspicion and rumor of official prejudice and arbitrariness, and gives the public a feeling of security. In the second place, public adjudication proceedings perform an important function in the administration of criminal justice which cannot be achieved by administrative fact-finding: they dramatize moral issues and inform the public of the sad consequences which attend violation of the law. Through their public ceremonies adjudication proceedings condemn, educate, and deter.[5]

A better understanding of important features of the jury trial can be gleaned by a brief comparison with some features of the inquisitorial trial.

COMPARING ADVERSARIAL AND INQUISITORIAL TRIALS The key features of the English and American jury trial—part of the "common law" system of justice—contrast with the classic features of European trials, which derive from the "civil" or "Roman" system of justice. Common law trials are **accusatorial** or adversarial while civil law trials, which originated in continental Europe and now are the norm in most countries of the world except for those that have been colonized by England, are said to be **inquisitorial,** although they no longer have the cruel attributes of medieval inquisitorial practice, that included torture as a legal method of getting to the truth in a difficult case.[6] (1) The most obvious difference is that in the common law trial a group of ordinary citizens, the jury, chosen to hear one or a few cases, makes the key determination as to what happened, and then disperse back into the population. They are the sole triers of fact. In the inquisitorial mode of trial, both the law and the facts are decided by trained professional judges, although in recent times European countries have allowed citizens to participate in assisting judges in fact finding. (2) Another difference is that English and American judges are drawn from the ranks of practicing lawyers while inquisitorial judges are highly-trained, lifelong career professionals. (3) Common law trials are based primarily on oral testimony that, ideally, should be heard in a continuous process. Written or physical evidence has to be introduced with testimony as to its authenticity. Inquisitorial trials allow the introduction of written or documentary evidence to a greater extent. In minor cases in the inquisitorial system, it is possible to try cases largely upon documentary evidence. (4) In the inquisitorial trial, the judge is the central actor. The judge "runs' the trial, conducts most of the questioning, and shapes the introduction of evidence. The common law judge is more of a referee, who decides whether the lawyers are in error and occasionally supplements the questions of attorneys with his or her own. (5) The privilege against self-incrimination strictly protects the defendant against speaking or having negative inferences drawn from silence. The days of torture, of course, are over in continental trials. For example, in French trials a defendant enjoys the right of not participating as a witness. Negative inferences, however, may be drawn from this silence. (6) An old distinction no longer holds. In the common law trial, the burden of proof is always on the state, and the defendant is presumed innocent. In an older inquisitorial trial system, the presumption differed. In modern European judicial systems, the burden of proof rests on the state and a presumption of innocence prevails.

An important distinction between the systems is the centrality of the *search for the truth.* In the modern inquisitorial system, the search for the truth is paramount, while the adversarial trial is multipurposed. Professor Ingraham notes that the accusatorial system is unique in "the degree to which the question of guilt or innocence is left to the game-playing skills of two adversary lawyers."[7] Because the adversarial jury system supports goals other than the truth of the case, (e.g., suppressing illegally seized evidence in order to deter police and prosecutorial misconduct) it is a better counterweight to political oppression and is better able to ensure that an innocent person will not be convicted. The role of the common law judges as umpires tends to foster a less partisan attitude in the courtroom, thus ensuring a greater sense of evenhandedness and fairness among citizens at large.[8]

Steps in the Jury Trial

JURY SELECTION There are two major phases of jury selection. First, the court or a jury commission determines how many jurors will be needed over a long time period, selected from among all eligible jurors in the jurisdiction. That group of names is placed on a **master jury list.** From this list, smaller groups of citizens—the **venire**—are chosen. The venire is summoned to court on assigned days and, from the venire, **jury pools** are chosen. The actual jury is then selected from this pool. Today, attempts are made to select the master jury list in a manner that produces a statistically accurate cross-section of the community. Second, when a jury pool of, say, forty prospective jurors is seated, the process of **voir dire** allows the judge or attorneys to question jurors to determine if they are biased. An unlimited number of **challenges for cause** are permitted to eliminate those individuals shown to be biased in the case. A limited number of **peremptory challenges** are granted to each side that allows the attorneys to eliminate jurors for any or no reason, except for the deliberate elimination of jurors on the grounds of race or gender.

OPENING STATEMENTS Each lawyer outlines the main points of the case to the jury, putting the best interpretation on the case. Both in voir dire and in opening statements, lawyers also try to make good personal impressions on jurors.

PROSECUTOR'S CASE-IN-CHIEF The heart of the case is the presentation of witnesses who testify as to their personal observations. **Expert witnesses,** on the other hand, are allowed to offer opinions in the area of their expertise. A witness may also introduce documents or physical evidence. After each witness testifies, the defense may **cross-examine** the witness in an attempt to discredit the testimony or credibility with the jury. The prosecutor may then ask questions on redirect which are limited to clarifying or rehabilitating the witness on the points specifically raised by cross-examination. The job of the prosecutor is to establish guilt at the end of the case. The defense may make motion at the conclusion of the prosecutor's case-in-chief to dismiss the case on the grounds that proof of guilt has not been established. The motion is typically denied, but may succeed if the prosecutor has not offered proof as to an essential element of the crime. The job of the defense attorney is to raise a **reasonable doubt** as to guilt, and if the defense believes that this has been established through its cross-examination, it may rest its case without calling any witnesses.

DEFENSE CASE-IN-CHIEF Like the prosecutor, the defense calls witnesses, including expert witnesses. Another type of witness, who may give opinion evidence, is a character witness who may relate the defendant's general reputation for good character. The prosecutor may cross-examine each witness, and redirect is available to the defense.

PROSECUTION REBUTTAL The prosecutor may offer evidence to refute or contradict evidence that is initially presented by the defendant, most typically evidence of an alibi or insanity.

CLOSING STATEMENTS The defense attorney first addresses the jury, followed by the prosecutor. The prosecutor has the last word because of the heavy burden of proof. The attorneys bring together the various pieces of testimony and evidence, weaving it together in a coherent and convincing narrative that explains why the evidence indicates that—of the prosecutor—the defendant is guilty beyond a reasonable doubt and why—for the defense—reasonable doubt exists. Perhaps the most pithy and famous example of reasonable doubt is Johnny Cochran's exhortation to the jury in the O. J. Simpson murder trial—if the glove doesn't fit, you must acquit.

JURY INSTRUCTIONS Following the presentation of evidence and closing statements, the judge instructs the jurors on the law by defining and explaining the definitions of the crime's charges, the rules of evidence, and the possible verdicts that are allowed.

JURY DELIBERATIONS Jurors are sworn to follow the law as instructed by the judge and deliberate in private to review and vote on the case.

VERDICT The result of deliberations is the jury's verdict. For each count of the indictment, the jury must enter either a verdict of guilty or not-guilty. The verdict must be unanimous, except in states that allow a verdict based on a supermajority vote such as 11–1. If a jury is deadlocked, and the vote is lopsided, the judge will admonish holdout jurors not to be rigid, and to reasonably review the evidence as viewed by the majority. If further deliberations do not change the vote, the court declares a hung jury and the case may be retried.

POST-VERDICT MOTIONS The defense can submit a motion notwithstanding the verdict or motion in arrest of judgment, arguing that the jury could not have reasonably convicted the defendant based on the evidence presented. The defense can also file a motion for a new trial based on the judge's errors in admitting evidence. Such motions are rarely successful.

An actual trial involves more complex preparation, strategy analysis, psychological penetration, and dramatic human action than this list can show.[9]

Important Constitutional Trial Rights

The trial is guided by many complex rules of criminal procedure and evidence law. This section presents an overview of some important constitutional trial rights.

The Right to Be Present

A defendant's right to be present at the trial is based on the **Confrontation Clause** of the Sixth Amendment (*Diaz v. United States,* 1912) and on due process considerations. A defendant has the right to accompany the jury if it leaves the courtroom briefly to view the scene of the crime. However, in *United States v. Gagnon* (1985), there was no Sixth Amendment violation when a judge met with a juror and the defense attorney (out of the defendant's presence) in regard to a juror's nervousness caused by the fact that the defendant drew sketches of the jurors during the trial. The defendant's presence at the meeting was not required to ensure fundamental fairness or a reasonable opportunity to conduct the defense. The *Gagnon* rule applies to cases where the defendant is excluded from pretrial evidence suppression hearings.

Secret trials ("kangaroo courts," "star chamber proceedings") are anathema to the accusatorial system and have been eliminated from United States jurisprudence. The celebrated 1989 trial of Oliver North—for lying to Congress regarding the secret sale of arms to Iran and covert support of the Nicaraguan Contras with the sales proceeds—involved a law designed to avoid secret trials. The Classified Information Procedures Act of 1980 was designed to balance the open trial guarantee with the need to protect government secrets in espionage and other prosecutions where classified information was vital evidence. Under the law, the defense is not barred from using classified material, but it must notify the prosecutor in advance as to which secrets will be used. The government is then given the opportunity to submit edited statements in place of the disputed documents. If the judge is not satisfied that these statements are fair to the defense, the prosecution is then given the option of allowing the documents to be made public or to drop the charges that bring the secrets to light in the courtroom.[10]

DISRUPTIVE DEFENDANTS A defendant who behaves in a loud, obnoxious, and disruptive manner cannot force the state to delay or dismiss a case. In *Illinois v. Allen* (1970), Justice Black stated:

> It is essential to the proper administration of criminal justice that dignity, order, and decorum be the hallmarks of all court proceedings in our country. The flagrant disregard in the courtroom of elementary standards of proper conduct should not and cannot be tolerated. We believe trial judges confronted with disruptive, contumacious, stubbornly defiant defendants must be given sufficient discretion to meet the circumstances of each case. No one formula for maintaining the appropriate courtroom atmosphere will be best in all situations. We think there are at least three constitutionally permissible ways for a trial judge to handle an obstreperous defendant like Allen: (1) bind and gag him, thereby keeping him present; (2) cite him for contempt; (3) take him out of the courtroom until he promises to conduct himself properly. (*Illinois v. Allen* 1970)

A trial judge must first be patient with and admonish a disruptive defendant, explaining that obstructionist tactics will not work, before taking the drastic steps of binding or removal. As communications technology improves, defendants forcibly removed from the courtroom are able to view the trial and communicate with his or her lawyer from a jail cell by interactive video links.

ABSCONDING DEFENDANTS A defendant who skips out in the middle of a trial forfeits the right to be present, and the trial may continue in his or her absence. The Supreme Court has rejected the argument that in such a case the judge must explicitly warn a defendant about a right to be present before the trial can continue *in absentia.*

> It is wholly incredible to suggest that petitioner, who was at liberty on bail, had attended the opening session of his trial, and had a duty to be present at the trial, . . . entertained any doubts about his right to be present at every stage of his trial. It seems equally incredible to us, . . . "that a defendant who flees from a courtroom in the midst of a trial—where judge, jury, witnesses and lawyers are present and ready to continue—would not know that as a consequence the trial could continue in his absence" (*Taylor v. United States,* 1973).

The Right to Compulsory Process

The Sixth Amendment guarantee "to have **compulsory process** for obtaining witnesses in his favor"—the **subpoena** right—is meant to eliminate barriers to relevant testimony that the defendant wishes to offer. A trial would be grossly unfair if only the state, and not the defense, had such power. The right was incorporated into the Fourteenth Amendment Due Process Clause in *Washington v. Texas* (1967). Washington was charged with murder for a killing that occurred during an argument. His defense was that he was trying to persuade Fuller, the actual killer, to leave and was not in the room when the gun went off. Fuller had been convicted and was willing to testify in Washington's defense. The state blocked his testimony by relying on a Texas law that forbade an accomplice to testify for another. The Supreme Court held that this law violated the Compulsory Process Clause. A state may prevent some defense testimony under ordinary rules of evidence (e.g., on the grounds that the testimony is irrelevant or incompetent), but may not disallow relevant evidence.

In *Webb v. Texas* (1972), the defendant's only witness was subpoenaed from prison where he was serving a sentence. The trial judge threatened the witness with heavy-handed warnings against committing perjury and said that lying would extend the witness's prison term and be counted against him by the parole board. As a result, the witness refused to testify. The Supreme Court ruled that the trial judge's unnecessarily emphatic warning "drove the witness off the stand." This due process violation tended to undermine the subpoena right. In recent years, the Supreme Court has weakened the right to compulsory process.

In *United States v. Valenzuela-Bernal* (1982), the Supreme Court held that the government could deport illegal immigrants before a trial in which they might be called as defense witnesses concerning their being smuggled into the United States. The defense attorney did not even have an opportunity to interview them. The Court felt that the government's legal obligation to swiftly deport aliens, the financial costs of prolonged detention, and the human costs to the detainees were more important that a defendant's Sixth Amendment right to subpoena witnesses.

In *Pennsylvania v. Ritchie* (1987), a father charged with incest sought to subpoena records from Children and Youth Services (CYS), a protective service agency, claiming that the records were necessary for the defense to cross-examine witnesses. Pennsylvania courts granted the defense request to fully examine the contents of CYS files on the basis of the defendant's confrontation and compulsory process rights. The United States Supreme Court reversed, in part, noting that the Confrontation Clause "does not include the power to require the pretrial disclosure of any and all information that might be useful in contradicting unfavorable testimony." Since the defense counsel was able to cross-examine all prosecution witnesses fully, there was no violation of the Confrontation Clause. Also, Justice Powell, writing for the majority, noted that Pennsylvania law allowed a court to disclose parts of a youth's record. The Court agreed that Ritchie was entitled to have a trial judge, but not the defense lawyer, review the CYS records to determine which were material. In this way, the defendant's compulsory process right was balanced with "the Commonwealth's compelling interest in protecting its child abuse information." The *Ritchie* rule places much discretion and trust in the judge's hands, but undermines the adversary system of justice that is premised on the understanding that the lawyers are better able to detect favorable facts in a record because they are motivated to do so.

Prosecutorial Misconduct and False Evidence

As noted in Chapter 11, a defendant's right to due process and a fair trial is violated if a prosecutor deliberately introduces *perjured testimony* (*Mooney v. Holohan,* 1935). Post-*Mooney* cases highlight the importance to the fairness of the adversary system of honest prosecutors who check their facts. Prosecutors must have an evenhanded attitude and a desire to achieve the truth rather than to get a conviction at any price. The cases show that cross-examination is effective as a truth-getting device only if trials are conducted honestly.

MISLEADING TESTIMONY The *Mooney* principle was applied in *Alcorta v. Texas* (1957), which held that due process is violated by introducing evidence that creates a *false impression* regarding a *material fact,* if it was *elicited by the prosecutor with knowledge of its inaccuracy. Alcorta* was a prosecution of a jealous husband for murdering his cheating wife. Before the trial, the wife's lover told the prosecutor that he and Alcorta's wife had been sexually intimate. The prosecutor told him not to volunteer such evidence but to answer questions put to him at trial truthfully. At trial, the lover testified that he had not kissed the deceased woman on the night she died, and that he only had a casual affair with her. The truth was disclosed after the defendant was convicted of first-degree murder. This violated Alcorta's due process right to a fair and meaningful trial, even though the prosecutor's actions were not as deliberate as those in *Mooney* and affected the *level* of guilt and punishment rather than a determination of guilt or innocence.

WITNESS CREDIBILITY In *Napue v. Illinois* (1959), a prosecution witness testified on direct examination that he received no promise of consideration for his testimony. The prosecutor knew this was false and made no effort to correct the falsehood. The lie was not directly material to the issue of guilt, but it undermined the ability of the defense to properly cross-examine by impeaching the witness's credibility. This violated due process.

MISCHARACTERIZING EVIDENCE In *Miller v. Pate* (1967), an innocent taxi driver was convicted of the rape and murder of a young girl on the basis of red-stained underpants found near the murder scene and a confession that was obtained under duress. At trial, the prosecutor held up the garment and referred to it as "bloody shorts." Only after a lengthy appeal process, during which Miller spent years on Illinois' death row, did forensic tests by the defense disclose that the red stains were paint and not blood. Miller was freed from his decade-long ordeal by a Supreme Court finding that the prosecutor's trial oratory violated due process. The prosecutor must be accurate and check facts.

The rule against the prosecutor injecting false or misleading evidence is strengthened by the pretrial discovery rule of *Brady v. Maryland* (1963) (discussed in Chapter 11) which requires the prosecution to turn over material factual evidence that is favorable to the defendant.

Due Process and the Preservation of Evidence

Closely related to the *Brady* rule is what may be called the "constitutionally guaranteed access to evidence" (*United States v. Valenzuela-Bernal,* 1982). In two cases, the Supreme Court has ruled against defendants seeking to make the *preservation of evidence* by police a due process requirement. More specifically, the Court has held that breathalyser and semen evidence that has not been preserved may nevertheless be introduced into evidence against a defendant. In neither case was there any evidence of bad faith on the part of the police in trying to evade the rule that requires the prosecution to turn over factual evidence to the defendant. At the worst, the police were negligent in failing to preserve the evidence.

In *California v. Trombetta* (1984), defendants, convicted on evidence of breath alcohol readings, challenged their convictions on the ground that their pretrial requests for preserved samples of their breath (which is technically feasible) was denied. The police departments replied that they do not ordinarily preserve breath samples, and made no effort to do so. Trombetta argued that if he had a sample of the test, he could impeach the accuracy of the test. The Court ruled that the introduction of the results of the breathalyser tests did not violate a defendant's due process right to a fair trial. An important factor for the holding is that "the chances are extremely low that preserved samples would have been exculpatory." The breathalyser test is relatively routine, and, if administered properly, there is a low probability that it is inaccurate. Prior cases held that a defendant's due process rights were not violated when evidence was admitted based on preliminary field notes taken by FBI agents (used to prepare a formal report) that were inadvertently destroyed (*Killian v. United States* 1961). The Court noted that the accuracy of breathalyser tests can be generally challenged by defendant counsel. There was a hint that for the Court to impose an administrative requirement on all police departments bordered on the Court exercising its supervisory power.

A more difficult case arose in *Arizona v. Youngblood* (1988). Youngblood was identified by the victim in a photo lineup nine days after the abduction and anal sodomy of a 10-year-old boy. Shortly after the assault, a physical at a hospital collected evidence using a "sexual assault kit," including samples of the boy's saliva, blood, and hair, and swabs from the boy's rectum and mouth. Microscopic slides of the samples were made but not examined at any time. The police placed the kit in a secure refrigerator at the police station. At the hospital, the police also collected the boy's underwear and T-shirt. This clothing was not refrigerated or frozen. Ten days after the attack, a state criminalist examined the kit, but not the clothing, to determine that sexual contact had occurred; as a matter of routine, he did not perform any other tests, including a blood group test. Prior to Youngblood's trial, examination of the materials in the kit indicated that the samples were insufficient to supply a saliva comparison or to detect any blood group substances. Approximately fourteen months later, the boy's clothing was examined and two semen stains were found. Because the clothing had not been refrigerated, the semen stains could not yield information as to the blood type of the semen depositor under tests that were available at that time. At his trial, Youngblood argued that the victim's identification was inaccurate, and that he could have proven his innocence if the clothing had been properly refrigerated.

As in *Trombetta,* the state courts in *Youngblood* found that "when identity is an issue at trial and the police permit the destruction of evidence that could eliminate the defendant as the perpetrator, such loss is material to the defense and is a denial of due process." The United States Supreme Court reversed. Again, there was no bad faith attempt by the police to hide evidence from the defendant in order to get around his *Brady* right to disclosure. Although the semen evidence, if properly preserved, might have exonerated Youngblood, the majority noted that the Court had in the past been reluctant to say that the fundamental fairness idea of due process imposed "on the police an undifferentiated and absolute duty to retain and to preserve all material that might be of conceivable evidentiary significance in a particular prosecution" (citing *Lisenba v. California,* 1941). Justice Stevens concurred: because the police had no reason to hide accurate information of the crime, their actions were negligent and not deliberate, and the jury was instructed that they could take the missing evidence into account, but they still found Youngblood guilty.

Justice Blackmun dissented, joined by Justices Brennan and Marshall. The main points of his dissent were that (1) The *Brady* line of cases did *not* rest on a prosecutor's bad faith i.e., any failure to provide evidence was a constitutional wrong, whether done maliciously or negligently; (2) The real test of whether a trial is *fundamentally unfair* is whether the non-available evidence was "*constitutionally material;*" (3) The *Trombetta* decision relied on the high accuracy level of breathalyser tests, so that the breath samples were not constitutionally material; (4) A preserved semen stain could have identified a blood type marker that could clearly have exonerated Youngblood if his semen blood type marker did not match that of the semen on the victim's clothing; (5) Therefore, semen evidence is constitutionally material. Justice Blackmun noted that due process must take the burdens on law enforcement into account. In a case such as this, the state could have had the proper and available tests conducted in a timely fashion or could notify the defense that it intends to discard the original evidence and thus, given the defense time to have the evidence tested.

The Youngblood case underscores the vital importance of proper police procedures in preserving evidence. In the 1990s, DNA testing became available allowing tests on small samples of dry body evidence. A DNA test on the preserved semen stain on the unrefrigerated clothing in the Youngblood case showed that he could not have been the attacker of the ten-year-old boy. Youngblood was released from custody in August 2000. One journalist speculated that social prejudice may have played a role in the initial conviction of a "black, one-eyed, homosexual rapist who claimed it was a case of mistaken identity. P.S.: He also walked with a limp." Jane Siegel Greene, executive director of the Innocence Project at the Cardozo School of Law in New York City, commenting on *Youngblood* case noted: "What the case says is that the state has no duty to preserve evidence, and they've based that law, now, on somebody who is actually innocent. So now he's freed, but how many other people like him—because of case law just like Arizona vs. Youngblood—have no access to their evidence."[11]

Right to Silence

The Fifth Amendment right to not "be compelled in any criminal case to be a witness against himself" was held to mean in *Griffin v. California* (1965) (overruling *Adamson v. California,* 1947) that if a defendant in a state trial chooses not to testify, the Constitution strictly forbids the judge or prosecutor from making a comment that allows a jury to draw an adverse inference. This was the federal rule (*Wilson v. United States,* 1893). **Adverse comment** on silence "is a penalty imposed by our courts for exercising a constitutional privilege. It cuts down on the privilege by making its assertion costly. . . . What the jury may infer given no help from the court is one thing. What they may infer when the court solemnizes the silence of the accused into evidence against him is quite another." Further, a prosecutor cannot introduce evidence that a defendant remained silent after being read *Miranda* warnings to impeach him (*Doyle v. Ohio,* 1976). This due process violation is inconsistent with the implied guarantee that silence in response to the *Miranda* warnings will carry no penalty.

Carter v. Kentucky (1978) ruled, however, that a trial judge, when *requested* by the *defense, must* instruct the jury that the defendant's silence does not lead to a negative inference. Justice Potter Stewart noted in *Carter* that a trial judge has "an affirmative constitutional obligation" to instruct the jury: "No judge can prevent jurors from speculating about why a defendant stands mute in the face of a criminal accusation, but a judge can, and must, if requested to do so, use the unique power of the jury instruction to reduce that speculation to a minimum." On the other hand, *Lakeside v. Oregon* (1978) held that the trial judge can constitutionally give such a protective instruction, *over the objection* of the defense, if he or she believes that not to do so would lead to an *unfair trial.* This ruling places great faith in the ability of trial judges to control their courtrooms and to ensure fair trials.

Confrontation, Hearsay, and Cross-examination

INCORPORATION The Confrontation Clause was incorporated into the Due Process Clause of the Fourteenth Amendment in *Pointer v. Texas* (1965). *Pointer* held that a witness's statement taken at a preliminary hearing, at which there was no adequate opportunity for cross-examination (because the defendant had no lawyer at that point), could not be introduced in the trial. To do so violated Pointer's Sixth Amendment rights. The right to confront witnesses means, among other things, that the defendant must have an opportunity to meaningfully *challenge* the witnesses' assertions, whenever they are made, through the time-honored method of cross-examination. The confrontation right is fulfilled when the *opportunity* to cross-examine exists. If a defense attorney decides not to cross-examine at a preliminary hearing for tactical reasons, the right is fulfilled. Evidence obtained from a witness who is later unavailable is admissible at trial (*Ohio v. Roberts,* 1980). Also, there is no confrontation violation if the defense attorney failed to counter a hearsay statement at the preliminary examination by not calling the speaker of the statement to the witness stand at the examination (*Dutton v. Evans,* 1970).

CONFRONTATION, HEARSAY AND CROSS-EXAMINATION *Pointer* demonstrates the strong relationship between the confrontation guarantee, the evidentiary rule against **hearsay evidence,** and the chief common law device of ascertaining the truth: cross-examination. The primary reason for the common law rule excluding hearsay evidence (where a witness testifies to something that the witness did not personally observe) from the trial is not its inherent unreliability but the problem that the opposing counsel cannot subject the original witness to cross-examination—the defendant cannot confront the one who made the damaging statement.

THE PURPOSE OF CROSS-EXAMINATION The heart of the adversarial truth-seeking method is cross-examination:

> The purpose of cross-examination is to weaken the testimony the witness has given, or, at best, negate it, or, less spectacularly but highly useful, to do no more than clarify ambiguous responses. The cross-examiner seeks to show inadequacy of observation, confusion, bias, inconsistency, even contradiction. The dramatic interest, of course, arises mainly from the contest between the witness bent on maintaining his position and a lawyer bent on destroying it. The audience, at a real trial or a fictional one, loves the plangent clash and wants to see the witness bleed, or the lawyer bleed, or, even better, both. The contest can be good-humored, or at least courteous, but it is often drenched in hostility. The cross-examined witness is typically a cross examined witness.
>
> The fight is fine; it suits the adversary system. But it should stay cool, and its function kept in mind. Petty triumph is not the goal. . . . The lawyer should do nothing whose aim is personal gratification.[12]

SECRET WITNESSES *Rovario v. United States* (1957) held that the government may not conceal the *identity* of an informer who testifies at a trial. The police testified exclusively about what agent "John Doe" did but did not want to produce him at trial. John Doe was Rovario's one material witness. His opportunity to cross-examine the police officer "was hardly a substitute for an opportunity to examine the man who had been nearest to him and took part in the transaction. Doe had helped to set up the criminal occurrence and had played a prominent part in it. His testimony might have disclosed an entrapment. He might have thrown doubt upon petitioner's identity or on the identity of the package. . . . The desirability of calling John Doe as a witness, or at least interviewing him in preparation for trial, was a matter for the accused rather than the Government to decide." *Rovario* was decided on the basis of the Court's supervisory power over federal cases. Nevertheless, the "*Rovario* rule" stands for the proposition that confrontation includes the right to know the identity of one's accusers. The rule forces prosecutors, in cases involving undercover police agents or informants, to lift the agent's "cover" in order to bring a prosecution. If the prosecutor believes it is more important to preserve the informant's anonymity, the prosecution must be dropped. This creates tough choices for prosecutors, but a different rule is not compatible with the unconstitutionality of secret trials.

A similar Confrontation Clause issue arises when the trial court or the prosecutor, for one reason or another, *withholds information* from the defense that may be of value in the cross-examination. When this has occurred, the Supreme Court has required that the information be made available. For example, the refusal of an undercover narcotics officer to give his *real name* at trial violates the defendant's constitutional rights because it does not give the defense a full opportunity to gather information that might cast a shadow on the witness's credibility (*Smith v. Illinois,* 1968). In another case, the Court said that withholding the fact that a witness was on probation for juvenile delinquency, when that fact was relevant to the witness's possible bias, unconstitutionally weakened the defendant's ability to cross-examine the witness (*Davis v. Alaska,* 1974).

Confrontation in Child Sex Abuse Cases

One of the most difficult and sensitive tasks confronting prosecutors and defense counsel is the examination of child witnesses in sexual abuse cases. The onslaught of sex abuse cases has made this a major area of social and legal concern, raising four issues: the competence of children as witnesses, their credibility, the rights of children, and the rights of defendants.[13] This section focuses on a few Supreme Court cases that have dealt with confrontation rights in such cases.

The reliance on cross-examination as the underpinning of the Confrontation Clause was underscored in *Kentucky v. Stincer* (1987). Stincer, charged with child sexual abuse against children eight, seven, and five years of age, was excluded from **in camera** (in chambers) proceedings where the judge questioned the children to determine if the two younger children were competent to testify. Stincer's lawyer was present. The Supreme Court held that Stincer's Sixth Amendment Confrontation Clause was not violated. It noted that this practice did not preclude effective cross-examination by defense counsel. Any background questions relevant to the trial could be repeated on direct examination of the child-witnesses in court. "[T]he critical tool of cross-examination was available to counsel as a means of establishing that the witnesses were not competent to testify, as well as a means of undermining the credibility of their testimony" (*Stincer,* 1987). Justice Marshall, dissenting (joined by Blackmun and Stevens), wrote, "Although cross-examination may be a primary means for ensuring the reliability of testimony from adverse witnesses, we have never held that standing alone it will suffice in every case. . . . Physical presence of the defendant enhances the reliability of the factfinding process" (*Stincer* 1987).

Stincer must be distinguished from the issue of *face-to-face confrontation* at the trial itself. More recent cases deal with attempts by the states to make it more likely for child witnesses to testify by shielding them from the direct gaze of defendants. The state's argument is that actual face-to-face confrontation may undermine the entire prosecution by making the child witness unable to testify out of undue psychological pressure. The defendant's argument is that this is one basic purpose of the right to confront one's witnesses. Indeed, among the real cases of child sexual abuse there has been a wave of improbable prosecutions against totally innocent people who worked in day care centers which are based on public hysteria reminiscent of the Salem witch trials of 1692.[14] It is in such cases that shielding the testifying child from the view of the defendant may cause profound injustices. Trial procedure has evolved over the centuries to create a sober atmosphere in the courtroom where a search for the truth can be conducted, removed from prejudice and the popular passions of the day. When procedures to protect the defendant—presumed to be innocent—are weakened, the worst injustices can occur. This is troubling in its own right, but also because it diverts attention from the real problem of child abuse, which more often is inflicted by family members or personal acquaintances.

In *Coy v. Iowa* (1988), the Supreme Court struck down a state rule that allowed two fifteen-year-old sexual abuse victims to testify from behind a *screen* so as to avoid eye-to-eye contact with the defendant. This violated the Confrontation Clause. The majority did go so far as to say that eye-to-eye contact was absolutely required by the Sixth Amendment. It held that a "legislatively imposed presumption of trauma," without requiring "individualized findings that these particular witnesses needed special protection . . ." allowed a legislative presumption to override a constitutional right. Concurring, Justice O'Connor noted that while only Iowa provided for a screen in the courtroom in sensitive cases, by 1988, half the states had trial rules that allowed the presentation of testimony in child sex abuse cases by one- or two-way closed-circuit television. She suggested that the *Coy* ruling did not prevent the use of such devices. Justice Blackmun, dissenting, asserted that the requirements of live testimony and cross-examination were fulfilled in this case and that, therefore, there was no violation of the Confrontation Clause.

The issue left open in *Coy* was resolved in *Maryland v. Craig* (1990), which upheld (5–4) the use of *one-way closed-circuit television* to transmit the testimony of a child witness where certain *procedural safeguards* were established. Under Maryland law, closed-circuit testimony is used only where absolutely necessary and only on a case-by-case basis. The trial court had to establish that the *specific witness,* in this case a six-year-old allegedly victimized by the owner of a child care center, would suffer serious *emotional distress* such that she could *not reasonably communicate* in a face-to-face confrontation. The closed-circuit television hookup had to allow the defendant to observe the demeanor of the witness during examination and cross-examination, and the defendant was in electronic communication with her defense counsel at all times. Counsel retained the right to object to any questions.

Justice O'Connor, for the majority, held that the Sixth Amendment does *not* guarantee an *absolute* right to a face-to-face meeting at the trial. Instead, "[t]he central concern of the Confrontation Clause is to ensure the reliability of the evidence against a criminal defendant by subjecting it to rigorous testing in the context of an adversary proceeding before the trier of fact. The word 'confront,' after all, also means a clashing of forces or ideas, thus carrying with it the notion of adversariness" (*Maryland v. Craig,* 1990). She noted that while face-to-face confrontation is an important aspect of the right, there are other protections found in the Maryland practice: (1) the witness must testify under *oath,* to impress on her the seriousness of the procedure and to establish the perjury penalty for lying; (2) *cross-examination,* the "greatest legal engine ever invented for the discovery of truth" is allowed; and (3) that the jury observes the witness's demeanor so as to assess her credibility. It is these factors together that satisfy the right of confrontation. The defendant's rights had to be balanced against the important state interest of protecting minor victim-witnesses from further trauma and psychological harm.

Justice Scalia, writing for four dissenters, noted:

> Seldom has the Court failed so conspicuously to sustain a *categorical* guarantee of the Constitution against the tide of prevailing current opinion. . . . The purpose of enshrining [the Confrontation Clause] protection in the Constitution was to assure that none of the many policy interests from time to time pursued by statutory law could overcome a defendant's right to face his or her accusers in court. . . .
>
> . . . [The Court's] reasoning abstracts from the right to its purposes, and then eliminates the right. It is wrong because the Confrontation Clause does not guarantee reliable evidence; it guarantees specific trial procedures that were thought to *assure* reliable evidence, undeniably among which was "face-to-face" confrontation. Whatever else it may mean in addition, the defendant's constitutional right "to be confronted with the witnesses against him" means, always and everywhere, at least what it explicitly says: the "right to meet face to face all those who appear and give evidence at trial" (*Maryland v. Craig,* 1990, emphasis added).

On the day the Court decided *Maryland v. Craig,* it held in *Idaho v. Wright* (1990) (5–4) that the hearsay testimony of a pediatrician about what child sex-abuse victims said, did not have "circumstantial guarantees of trustworthiness" and was therefore inadmissible as a Confrontation Clause violation. A physician interviewed victimized children, aged two-and-one-half and five-and-one-half at the time of the crimes charged, but failed to keep a picture that he drew during the interview and did not keep detailed notes recording changes in the children's affects or attitudes. The Idaho Supreme Court ruled that the admission of the pediatrician's hearsay violated the Sixth Amendment because the testimony did not fall within a recognized hearsay exception, which provides a traditional standard of trustworthiness, and the interview lacked procedural safeguards. Unlike standard hearsay exceptions, such as the business-records exception that inherently provides an index of trustworthiness, the physician's statements were admitted under a "residual hearsay exception." In affirming the state court, Justice O'Connor expressed the concern that were the Court to say that statements under the residual hearsay exception were automatically admissible, this would grant every statutory hearsay exception "constitutional stature, a step this Court has repeatedly declined to take."

Maryland v. Craig and *Idaho v. Wright,* taken together, indicate a willingness on the part of the Court to allow state law to water down the traditional Sixth Amendment rule of face-to-face confrontation for a child witness in sex abuse cases, as long as this expansion of prosecutorial power is used only where necessary and is limited with procedural safeguards.

Presumption of Innocence and Proof Beyond A Reasonable Doubt

Two fundamental and closely linked rules that are central to the fairness of the common law are (1) that a defendant is clothed with the **presumption of innocence** and, (2) that the state must prove the defendant guilty of every element of the crime charged by proof beyond a reasonable doubt. Neither rule is found in the text of the Constitution, probably because they were so fundamental that it was assumed that they were part of the constitutional guarantee of trial by jury. Indeed, the Supreme Court did not have to confront the issue until 1970, when it firmly held in *In re Winship,* a juvenile delinquency adjudication, that a defendant's right to not be deprived of life, liberty, or property in a criminal matter without due process of law included the reasonable doubt standard.

A more difficult task is defining reasonable doubt, an elusive concept, with constitutional certainty. A judge may constitutionally instruct a jury on reasonable doubt without defining the term, but if the judge does define it, although no special form or words are required, "taken as a whole, the instructions [must] correctly convey the concept of reasonable doubt to the jury" (*Holland v. United States,* 1954). The danger to the defendant's due process right is that the judge might define the term in a way that makes the defendant's task of establishing a reasonable doubt more difficult than what the Constitution requires.

The Supreme Court has ruled that a judge's instruction violates due process for this reason only once, in *Cage v. Louisiana* (1990). The judge in *Cage* gave the jury the following instruction:

> " '[A reasonable doubt] is one that is founded upon a real tangible substantial basis and not upon mere caprice and conjecture. *It must be such doubt as would give rise to a grave uncertainty,* raised in your mind by reasons of the unsatisfactory character of the evidence or lack thereof. A reasonable doubt is not a mere possible doubt. *It is an actual substantial doubt.* It is a doubt that a reasonable man can seriously entertain. What is required is not an absolute or mathematical certainty, but a *moral certainty.*' " (*Cage v. Louisiana,* emphasis in original)

The highlighted words, "substantial" and "grave," as they are commonly understood, suggest a *higher* degree of *doubt* than is required for acquittal under the reasonable doubt standard. The Court stated that "When those statements are then considered with the reference to 'moral certainty,' rather than evidentiary certainty, it becomes clear that a reasonable juror could have interpreted the instruction to allow a finding of guilt based on a degree of proof below that required by the Due Process Clause." In other words, a judge's instruction that tends to make a juror think that the defendant must raise an almost certain doubt, lowers the prosecutor's burden of proof.

In *Estelle v. McGuire* (1991), the Court held that the test of whether a jury instruction violated due process in properly defining reasonable doubt is not whether the instruction "could have" been applied in an unconstitutional manner, but whether there is a *reasonable likelihood* that the jury *did* so apply the instruction.

The Supreme Court tacked the definition of reasonable doubt again in *Victor v. Nebraska* (1994), which consolidated two cases from Nebraska (*Victor*) and California (*Sandoval*), and in both found that the instructions did not violate the defendants' due process rights. There were two main issues: the "moral certainty" language and the phrase "substantial doubt."

In *Sandoval,* the following instruction was given:

> "Reasonable doubt is defined as follows: It is *not a mere possible doubt;* because everything relating to human affairs, and *depending on moral evidence,* is open to some possible or imaginary doubt. It is that state of the case which, after the entire comparison and consideration of all the evidence, leaves the minds of the jurors in that condition that they cannot say they feel an abiding conviction, *to a moral certainty,* of the truth of the charge."

The use of the terms "moral evidence" and "moral certainty" goes back to the eighteenth century, where it essentially meant probabilistic evidence and certainty as opposed to absolute evidence and certainty. Thus, James Wilson, a founder of the nation, a key framer of the Constitution, one of the great American lawyers, and a justice of the Supreme Court from 1789 to 1798, wrote "In moral evidence, we rise, by an insensible gradation, from possibility to probability, and from probability to the highest degree of moral certainty." Therefore, in upholding the instruction in *Sandoval* Justice O'Connor wrote: "We recognize that the phrase 'moral evidence' is not a mainstay of the modern lexicon, though we do not think it means anything different today than it did in the 19th century. The few contemporary dictionaries that define moral evidence do so consistently with its original meaning." This is all well and good, but Justice Kennedy, concurring, had the better argument:

> . . . California's use of "moral evidence" is the most troubling, and to me seems quite indefensible. The derivation of the phrase is explained in the Court's opinion, but even with this help the term is a puzzle. And for jurors who have not had the benefit of the Court's research, the words will do nothing but baffle.
>
> I agree that use of "moral evidence" in the California formulation is not fatal to the instruction here. I cannot understand, however, why such an unruly term should be used at all when jurors are asked to perform a task that can be of great difficulty even when instructions are altogether clear. The inclusion of words so malleable, because so obscure, might in other circumstances have put the whole instruction at risk. (*Victor v. Nebraska,* 1994, Kennedy. J., concurring)

The second issue was the use of "substantial doubt" in the *Victor* instruction, which read in part:

> You may be convinced of the truth of a fact beyond a reasonable doubt and yet be fully aware that possibly you may be mistaken. You may find an accused guilty upon the *strong probabilities of the case,* provided such probabilities are strong enough to exclude any doubt of his guilt that is reasonable. A reasonable doubt is an *actual and substantial doubt* arising from the evidence, from the facts or circumstances shown by the evidence, or from the lack of evidence on the part of the state, as distinguished from a doubt arising from mere possibility, from bare imagination, or from fanciful conjecture" (*Victor v. Nebraska,* 1994, emphasis in original).

Did the equating of reasonable doubt with a "substantial doubt" overstate the degree of doubt necessary for acquittal? The Court said no, but noted that it was a close question:

> We agree that this construction is somewhat problematic. On the one hand, "substantial" means "not seeming or imaginary"; on the other, it means "that specified to a large degree." *** The former is unexceptionable, as it informs the jury only that a reasonable doubt is something more than a speculative one; but the latter could imply a doubt greater than required for acquittal under *Winship.* Any ambiguity, however, is removed by reading the phrase in the context of the sentence in which it appears: "A reasonable doubt is an actual and substantial doubt . . . *as distinguished from* a doubt arising from mere possibility, from bare imagination, or from fanciful conjecture" (*Victor v. Nebraska,* 1994, emphasis in original).

The inclusion of the latter phrase, telling jurors that a substantial doubt does not mean "fanciful conjecture" distinguishes *Victor* from *Cage.*

It is likely that the justices were not happy with the instructions in these cases, but decided not to interfere with them, in part, because they did not want to impose a rigid rule on the states. In a useful concurrence, Justice Ginsburg offered a better instruction drafted by the Federal Judicial Center:

> "Proof beyond a reasonable doubt is proof that leaves you firmly convinced of the defendant's guilt. There are very few

> things in this world that we know with absolute certainty, and in criminal cases the law does not require proof that overcomes every possible doubt. If, based on your consideration of the evidence, you are firmly convinced that the defendant is guilty of the crime charged, you must find him guilty. If on the other hand, you think there is a real possibility that he is not guilty, you must give him the benefit of the doubt and find him not guilty" (*Victor v. Nebraska,* 1994, Ginsburg, J., concurring).

THE JURY

> In all criminal prosecutions, the accused shall enjoy the right to a speedy and public trial, by an impartial jury of the State and district wherein the crime shall have been committed, which district shall have been previously ascertained by law, and to be informed of the nature and cause of the accusation; to be confronted with the witnesses against him; to have compulsory process for obtaining witnesses in his favor, and to have the Assistance of Counsel for his defence.
>
> —Sixth Amendment, United States Constitution

Note that the Sixth Amendment includes eight distinct rights.

Constitutional Requirements

CONSTITUTIONAL FOUNDATION Trial by jury is guaranteed by Article III of the Constitution (1789) (in criminal cases) and by the Sixth (criminal) and Seventh (civil) amendments of the Bill of Rights (1791). In 1968, the Supreme Court *incorporated* the Sixth Amendment right to a jury trial in criminal cases into Fourteenth Amendment due process, giving the Supreme Court the constitutional authority to establish the constitutional parameters of state jury trials:

> Because we believe that trial by jury in criminal cases is fundamental to the American scheme of justice, we hold that the Fourteenth Amendment guarantees a right of jury trial in all criminal cases which—were they to be tried in federal court—would come within the Sixth Amendment guarantee. (*Duncan v. Louisiana,* 1968)

Duncan held that a person actually sentenced to less than six months imprisonment is entitled to a jury trial if the crime carries a potential penalty of two years.

The Court, however, has ruled that under the Sixth Amendment, federal jury requirements can differ from those imposed on the states. Federal juries adhere to the traditional common law requirements of twelve persons who render verdicts of "guilty" or "not guilty" by unanimous decisions. State criminal juries, on the other hand, have been held by the Supreme Court to differ in several regards, thus weakening the idea that incorporation (see Chapter 2) establishes identical rights for state and federal defendants. The Seventh Amendment right to a federal jury in civil cases has never been incorporated.

THE PETTY CRIME-SERIOUS CRIME DISTINCTION The Court in *Duncan* feared that requiring a jury in "all crimes" would saddle the states with added expense and delay if jury trials were demanded in **petty crimes.** *Duncan* reaffirmed the long-established view that so-called "petty offenses" may be tried without a jury. What this meant was tested in *Baldwin v. New York* (1970), which held that "no offense can be deemed 'petty' for purposes of the right to trial by jury where imprisonment for *more than six months* is authorized." A New York City ordinance that disallowed juries in crimes with penalties up to *one year* in prison was held unconstitutional. Justices Black and Douglas disagreed with this part of the case: they felt that the Sixth Amendment, by its terms, guaranteed a jury trial in "*all* criminal prosecutions." Thus, the prime criterion of what distinguished a serious crime from a petty crime was the length of the maximum penalty.

In *Blanton v. City of North Las Vegas* (1989), the Court held that a crime punishable by up to six months incarceration is still "petty" even though it carries *additional penalties* such as a minimum jail stay and community service. *Blanton,* however, left open the possibility that additional statutory penalties could be so severe that a crime carrying a maximum jail sentence of less than six months might still require a jury trial. (The likelihood of the Court following the hint in *Blanton* appears slim.) *Lewis v. United States* (1996) held that a defendant who is prosecuted in a single trial for multiple petty crimes and whose total punishment could amount to more than six months of imprisonment is not entitled to a jury trial. The Court adhered strictly to the notion that a petty crime depends on the legislative judgment in setting the authorized maximum penalty for the offense. The actual term of imprisonment meted out is not the criterion by which the petty-serious distinction is judged. The one exception to this rule is that the actual aggregate jail term for a *criminal contempt of court,* where the maximum is not fixed by the legislature, determines whether a jury is legally required (*Codispoti v. Pennsylvania,* 1974).

Four justices disagreed with the majority in *Lewis.* Justice Kennedy concurring, wrote: that the "holding both in its doctrinal formulation and in its practical effect is one of the most serious incursions on the right to jury trial in the Court's history, and it cannot be squared with our precedents." He pointed out that the "primary purpose of the jury in our legal system is to stand between the accused and the powers of the State. Among the most ominous of those is the power to imprison." In summary, then, the concurring and the dissenting justices (Stevens and Ginsburg) were profoundly disturbed by a policy that allows the state to imprison a person for years without the protection afforded by a citizen's jury.

THE SIZE OF THE JURY *Williams v. Florida* (1970) held that a *six-person felony jury* did not violate the Sixth Amendment, reversing an eight-hundred-year common law tradition requiring twelve jurors. Justice White relied on *functional analysis* to support this decision:

> The purpose of the jury trial . . . is to prevent oppression by the Government. . . . Given this purpose, the essential feature of a jury obviously lies in the interposition between the accused and his accuser of the common-sense judgment of a group of laymen, and in the community participation and shared responsibility which results from this group's determination of guilt or innocence. The performance of this role is not a function of the particular number of the body which makes up the jury. To be sure, the number should probably be large enough to promote group deliberation, free from outside attempts at intimidation, and to provide a fair possibility for obtaining a representative cross section of the community. But we find little reason to think that these goals are in any meaningful sense less likely to be achieved when the jury numbers six, than when it numbers 12—particularly if the requirement of unanimity is retained. And, certainly the reliability of the jury as a fact-finder hardly seems likely to be a function of its size. . . .
>
> Similarly, while in theory the number of viewpoints represented on a randomly selected jury ought to increase as the size of the jury increases, in practice the difference between the 12-man and the six-man jury in terms of the cross section of the community represented seems likely to be negligible. (*Williams v. Florida,* 1970)

Justice White based these views on a handful of social science studies then available that supported his conclusions.

The Court drew the line on the constitutionally permissible size of a felony jury by striking down a five-person jury in *Ballew v. Georgia* (1978); henceforth, juries must contain at least six members. *Ballew* contained a subtle admission that the functional analysis of *Williams* was premature. Justice Blackmun's opinion noted that (1) recent studies cast doubt on the accuracy of small jury verdicts, (2) the defense seems to be hurt by small juries, (3) minority group representation decreases in smaller juries, and (4) there are no significant gains in cost or efficiency in a five-person jury. Nevertheless, the *Williams* rule still stands. Only a dozen states still require twelve-person juries in felony trials.

THE VOTING REQUIREMENT: MAJORITY VERSUS UNANIMITY The common law requires a *unanimous* jury verdict. A single holdout juror can cause a "hung jury," blocking a verdict either of guilt or acquittal. The government may order a retrial after a hung jury. Several states authorize felony verdicts based on less than unanimous votes. The Supreme Court has upheld such laws under the Sixth Amendment if they require a *super-majority* vote for a guilty verdict, allowing guilty verdicts by votes of eleven-to-one and ten-to-two in *Apodaca v. Oregon* (1972). In *Johnson v. Louisiana* (1972), the Court approved a law authorizing a nine-to-three verdict under the Fourteenth Amendment Equal Protection Clause. Justice White, in *Apodaca,* again relied on functional analysis: a "requirement of unanimity . . . does not materially contribute to the exercise of [the] commonsense judgment" of a group of laymen. "Requiring unanimity would obviously produce hung juries in some situations where nonunanimous juries will convict or acquit. But in either case, the interest of the defendant in having the judgment of his peers interposed between himself and the officers of the State who prosecute and judge him is equally well served." Such majority verdicts did not undermine the reasonable doubt standard.

Justice Douglas, dissented, expressing strong misgivings. "The diminution of verdict reliability flows from the fact that nonunanimous juries need not debate and deliberate as fully as must unanimous juries. As soon as the requisite majority is attained, further consideration is not required . . . even though the dissident jurors might, if given the chance, be able to convince the majority." Justice Douglas cited an empirical study to show that such reversals by persuasion occurred in ten percent of all jury deliberations.[15] Additionally, deadlocks usually occur because one, two, or three jurors hold out. Since the majority favors the prosecutions in most deadlocked cases, the majority vote rule upsets a traditional common law protection of defendants.

Concern for this point led the Court to prohibit nonunanimous verdicts in six-person misdemeanor juries. A law allowing guilty verdicts by five out of six jurors in crimes carrying less than six months of imprisonment was declared unconstitutional by a unanimous Supreme Court in *Burch v. Louisiana* (1979). Justice Rehnquist reasoned that "lines must be drawn somewhere if the substance of the jury trial right is to be preserved." Only two states at that time allowed majority verdicts in six person juries, thus indicating the national view favored unanimity.

WAIVER OF THE RIGHT TO A JURY Defendants may have strategic reasons to waive a jury trial and opt for a "bench trial" or "waiver trial" with a judge as the sole trier of fact. They may believe that a jury would be prejudiced and unlikely to render a fair decision, or that a trained judge is better able to find reasonable doubt than a lay jury. A defendant's waiver to surrender the right to a jury trial must be express and intelligent (*Patton v. United States,* 1930). Under federal law, the jury trial is considered the standard mode of adjudication, and waiver requires *agreement of the judge and prosecutor* as well as the defendant.[16] The

Supreme Court ruled, in an opinion by Chief Justice Warren, that "[a] defendant's only constitutional right concerning the method of trial is to an impartial trial by jury. . . . The Constitution recognizes an adversary system as the proper method of determining guilt, and the Government, as a litigant, has a legitimate interest in seeing that cases in which it believes a conviction is warranted are tried before the tribunal which the Constitution regards as most likely to produce a fair result" (*Singer v. United States,* 1965). Some states, on the other hand, view the jury primarily as a protection to the defendant, and the defendant has the last word as to whether the trial will be held before a judge or a jury.

THE JURY RIGHT IN JUVENILE DELINQUENCY HEARINGS The Supreme Court has ruled, in *McKeiver v. Pennsylvania* (1971), that a jury trial is *not* constitutionally required in juvenile delinquency proceedings. The decision surprised juvenile justice experts because it halted a trend of decisions between 1966 and 1971 granting juvenile offenders legal rights equal to adults under due process in delinquency adjudications. *Kent v. United States* (1966) imposed the due process requirements of *notice* and *counsel* if a juvenile was to be transferred to the adult court system for a criminal trial. The Supreme Court in *In re Gault* (1967), noting that a delinquency determination could result in state confinement much like a criminal conviction, held that the essentials of due process and fair treatment in juvenile delinquency adjudications included *notice* of charges, the right to *trial, confrontation* of witnesses and *cross-examination,* and the right against *self-incrimination.* And *In re Winship* (1970) held that "the constitutional safeguard of proof beyond a *reasonable doubt* is as much required during the adjudicatory stage of a delinquency proceeding as are those constitutional safeguards applied in *Gault.*"

Nevertheless, the Court (5–3) refused to extend the jury right to juvenile delinquency adjudication proceedings. The Court noted in *McKeiver* that, although juvenile delinquency trials are due process hearings requiring procedural safeguards, they are not Sixth Amendment criminal prosecutions where the jury right would automatically apply. Relying on a more flexible, policy-oriented approach under the Due Process Clause, Justice Blackmun noted that despite criticisms of the juvenile court system, its existence represented the view that juveniles should be processed less formally than adults, in special proceedings that allow consideration of social factors not related to factual guilt. A jury requirement would be the final blow to this concept, bringing formality, legalism, and delay which are incompatible with the ideals of the juvenile court. *McKeiver* also supported federalism, deferring to the needs of the states. Justice Blackmun expressed a desire not to impose a single national standard but to allow the states to experiment with advisory juries, if they wished, in juvenile adjudication.

TRIALS DE NOVO Some states maintain a trial *de novo* system—a two-stage process whereby a minor crime is first heard before a magistrate without any right to a jury. If found guilty, the defendant can have the case tried anew, as if it had never been adjudicated before, in a court where jury trial is available. In *Ludwig v. Massachusetts* (1976), the Supreme Court upheld a state trial *de novo* law, even though it seemed to be designed to improve efficiency by discouraging the use of juries. The Massachusetts system did not unconstitutionally subvert the right to a jury trial; the Court said that the added cost and time involved in trying the case over again was not constitutionally relevant and that there was no danger of vindictively harsher sentences.

CONTEMPT OF COURT HEARINGS Judges have broad authority to enforce order in their courtrooms through the contempt power. Hearings are required for contempts that result in criminal-type penalties, and the right to a jury in such hearings is similar to that in trials for statutory crimes. The issue of when a jury is required, though, is not as clear because the scope of the penalty for contempt is typically not laid out concretely in statutes. Although the Supreme Court has not precisely defined when a jury is required, it has clarified the law by a series of rulings. Thus, *no jury is required* where the maximum statutory penalty for contempt is ten days in jail and a fifty-dollar fine (*Dyke v. Taylor Implement Mfg. Co.,* 1968), where the maximum penalty is less than six months' imprisonment but up to five years' probation (*Frank v. United States,* 1969), and where a ten thousand-dollar fine is issued against a labor union (*Muniz v. Hoffman,* 1975). On the other hand, *the right to a jury exists* in contempt cases where the defendant was sentenced to twenty-four months, there were no statutory limits (*Bloom v. Illinois,* 1968), and where the aggregate of jail sentences amounts to more than six months, although no single contempt sentence is more than six months. (*Codispoti v. Pennsylvania,* 1974)

Selecting an Unbiased Jury

Selecting an unbiased, impartial jury takes two steps. First, a jury pool is selected from among eligible jurors in the citizenry that reflects a representative cross-section. Second, the actual jurors in a case are selected in a process known as voir dire to weed out jurors with actual or potential biases. The mechanics of jury selection involve a unit of government, typically a county, compiling a master jury list (also called a jury wheel or master wheel) of eligible jurors from among the citizenry. From this list, a venire—jury pool—is selected and summoned to appear for jury service. (These terms are often interchanged.) At the court house, jury panels are drawn from the entire venire. The panel then undergoes voir dire and the twelve or six jurors, plus alternates, are selected.

Prior to the Federal Jury Selection Act of 1968, methods used to select the master jury list did not guarantee a representative cross-section. Indeed, some methods were designed to select an elite. Since the passage of the Act, the more egalitarian ideal that the jury master list and venire be a representative cross-section of eligible jurors is attained, first, by supplementing voter lists as a source of eligible jurors with drivers' license lists, city or telephone directories, and the like. Next, rigorous statistical methods are applied to ensure unbiased selection.[17] The Supreme Court has ruled on various challenges to laws and practices which in the past have fostered racial and gender discrimination in the makeup of juries under two distinct constitutional provisions.

THE EQUAL PROTECTION CASES The Fourteenth Amendment (1868) was designed to promote basic rights and political equality of African Americans. Jury service, along with voting, is a primary method by which American citizens express their sovereign political influence. Preventing groups of citizens from serving on juries or voting was meant to cripple their political participation and influence. The Equal Protection Clause declares: "No State shall . . . deny to any person within its jurisdiction the equal protection of the laws." Relying on this clause, the Supreme Court, in *Strauder v. West Virginia* (1880), held that a statute that *explicitly* excluded African Americans from jury service was unconstitutional. The following year, the Court held that a *practice* that excluded African Americans from juries under a neutral statute was unconstitutional (*Neal v. Delaware,* 1881).

The malign power of Jim Crow segregation made a mockery of these rulings in the South. For example, facially race-neutral laws requiring jury members be property holders eliminated minorities from juries. In fact, blacks were denied the right to serve on juries (and to vote) in the South for a century after the Civil War. These rights were gained after the struggles of the civil rights movement of the 1950s to the 1970s. In 1935, the Court in *Norris v. Alabama* at last recognized that virtual *exclusion* of African Americans from juries violated equal protection. Despite *Norris,* blacks continued to be underrepresented on juries. The *Norris* rule was weak, and under it a bare showing that African Americans made up nearly seven percent of grand jury panels in a Texas county where they comprised over fifteen percent of the population was held *not* to be discrimination *per se* (*Cassell v. Texas,* 1950). In *Avery v. Georgia* (1953), the fact that *not one* African American was selected for a jury panel of sixty people, where five percent of the jury list was African American, was held in itself *not* sufficient to establish discrimination. On the other hand, *Avery* held there was an equal protection violation only because color-coded jury ballots demonstrated *actual* discrimination, normally very hard to prove.

In the 1960s, the Supreme Court was slow to extend the social insights of its desegregation rulings to jury selection. *Swain v. Alabama* (1965) held that, while the exclusion of a prospective juror on account of race violated the defendant's equal protection rights, there was *no* violation where twenty-six percent of the eligible voters in a county were African American, while over the period of a year only ten to fifteen percent of the jury panels consisted of black jurors. The Court was blind to the fact that this statistical pattern was nearly impossible in a fair selection system.[18] Instead, noting that Alabama did not totally exclude African Americans from jury venire panels, and that a defendant is not entitled to a petit jury or a panel on which a proportionate number of her race sit, Justice White stated that "[n]either the jury roll nor the venire need be a perfect mirror of the community or accurately reflect the proportionate strength of every identifiable group."

The Supreme Court finally began to recognize that a *statistically significant imbalance* had to be the product of **invidious discrimination.**

- *Whitus v. Georgia* (1967): there is a prima facie case of purposeful discrimination where three of thirty-three prospective grand jurors and seven of ninety in the petit jury venire were African Americans in a county where forty-three percent of males over twenty-one years old were African Americans.
- *Turner v. Fouche* (1970): there is prima facie discrimination where, in a county with sixty percent African American population, thirty-seven percent of the grand jury list was African American and 171 of the 178 persons disqualified for lack of "intelligence" or "uprightness" were African American.
- *Alexander v. Louisiana* (1972): a prima facie case of discrimination existed where there was less than seven percent African American representation on grand jury panels, although nearly fourteen percent of grand jury questionnaires were submitted by African Americans, and the county was twenty-one percent African American.

Casteneda v. Partida (1977), involving under-representation of Hispanics on grand juries, specified a three-step process for deciding an equal protection claim. (1) The under-represented group must be a recognizable, *distinct class.* (2) The *degree* of under-representation must be proved by *comparing* the proportion of the group in the total population to the proportion of the group called to serve as grand jurors over a *significant period of time.* (3) "A *selection procedure* that is *susceptible to abuse* or not racially neutral supports the presumption of discrimination." Once a prima facie case is made, the burden shifts to the government to rebut discrimination. In *Casteneda,* a prima facie case was made by showing that, in a county that was seventy-nine percent Mexican-American, between thirty-nine and fifty percent of the grand jurors had Spanish surnames and that the **"key man" method** of selection (whereby the district judge selects three to five jury commissioners who in turn select fifteen to twenty persons known to them in the county) was not neutral. The prima facie case was not rebutted by the district judge's bare assertion that there were no prejudicial motives in the selection process. Nor was the prima facie discrimination rebutted by the theory that discrimination is impossible where the recognizable group constitutes a "governing majority" in the jurisdiction.

THE SIXTH AMENDMENT: AN IMPARTIAL JURY A Sixth Amendment challenge to jury that is not impartial is far broader than an equal protection challenge. Under the Equal Protection Clause, a defendant can claim that a jury was selected to discriminate against *that person's* ethnic or racial group or gender. *Every* defendant, on the other hand, has a right to an impartial jury. Once the impartial jury provision was incorporated in *Parker v. Gladden* (1966), the way was clear for application in jury selection.[19]

Thus, a *white male* defendant is entitled to a jury system that does not systematically exclude *blacks* (*Peters v. Kiff,* 1972), and a *male* defendant is entitled to a jury drawn from a selection process that does not suppress the number of *females* who might otherwise serve (*Taylor v. Louisiana,* 1975). These cases constitutionalized the right "to a jury drawn from a venire constituting a **fair cross section** of the community" (*Taylor,* 1975). Justice White, in *Taylor v. Louisiana,* explained that:

> The purpose of a jury is to guard against the exercise of arbitrary power—to make available the common sense judgment of the community as a hedge against the overzealous or mistaken prosecutor and in preference to the professional or perhaps overconditioned or biased response of a judge. This prophylactic vehicle is not provided if the jury pool is made up of only special segments of the populace or if large, distinctive groups are excluded from the pool. Community participation in the administration of the criminal law, moreover, is not only consistent with our democratic heritage but is also critical to public confidence in the fairness of the criminal justice system. Restricting jury service to only special groups or excluding identifiable segments playing major roles in the community cannot be squared with the constitutional concept of jury trial.

Taylor eliminated a practice whereby a woman who wanted to serve on a jury had to file a written declaration of her desire. Incidentally, women constitute a distinctive segment of the population for purposes of jury service (a federal rule: *Ballard v. United States,* 1946), even though they do not respond to issues as a class any more than do men. The Court rejected the argument of Louisiana that women play a distinctive role in society that is deterred by jury service. The Victorian notion that women have to be "protected" from jury service is simply passé in an era when women have almost reached numerical parity with men in the legal profession.

The Court expanded the *Taylor* rule in *Duren v. Missouri* (1979), holding that the gross underrepresentation of women on jury venires (fifteen out of fifty-four percent of the population) as a result of rules that made it very easy for women to decline jury service (for example by not showing up) constituted a prima facie violation of the Sixth Amendment rule that juries constitute a fair cross-section of the population. *Duren* ruled that a prima facie case of discrimination requires a showing that: (1) the excluded group is "distinctive" in the community; (2) the group is statistically underrepresented in venires, and (3) the underrepresentation is due to systematic exclusion of the group in the jury selection process.

Aside from minority groups and women, federal courts have not upheld defendants' claims that various subgroups of the population constitute "distinctive groups" under *Duren*: blue-collar workers, college students, less-educated people, young adults, rural inhabitants, persons who chose not to register to vote, jurors with last names beginning with M to Z, persons over the age of seventy, and jurors with absolute scruples against imposing the death penalty.[20] Several lower courts have held that absolute disparities of *more than ten percent* constitutes unfair representation and have refused to accept smaller disparities as discrimination.[21] Lower courts have also ruled that the systematic-exclusion prong of the *Duren* rule was held not to apply to rules that allow certain professionals such as doctors, lawyers, and sole proprietors, to be excluded from jury service upon request. This was seen as a rational accommodation to the community's needs.[22] In recent years, the laws and rules of many states have disallowed such exclusion as the one-day, one-trial practice has become common.

Voir Dire and Fairness

Voir dire is a process of questioning prospective jurors for bias. There are an unlimited number of challenges for cause—all jurors who say they cannot be fair or are shown to be biased must be excused by the judge as a matter of fundamental fairness and the impartial jury requirement of the

Sixth Amendment. The trial judge has discretion in conducting the voir dire, most importantly as to the extent to which the judge asks the questions as opposed to allowing the lawyers to conduct voir dire. Judges who conduct voir dire may allow attorneys to submit questions they wish the judge to ask prospective jurors. Judges do not have to ask such questions—to conserve time or to prevent a "slant" to the case. An attorney can appeal a judge's refusal to ask or allow a question, but the high legal standard is whether the denial amounts to an **abuse of discretion.**

In *Ham v. South Carolina* (1973), the Supreme Court held that it was a due process violation for the judge to disallow questions regarding *racial prejudice* in a prosecution of a bearded, African American, civil rights worker for possession of marijuana. On the other hand, *Ristaino v. Ross* (1976) held there was no constitutional error when a judge refused to allow questions about prejudice regarding the defendant's beard in a robbery case where the defendant was black and the victim white. In this case, the possible prejudice regarding the defendant's beard was tenuous. More importantly, *Ristaino* held that the Constitution does not require such questions whenever the defendant is black and the victim white. There were no factors of racial tension or animosity in *Ristaino* that raised a real need for a special instruction.

An exception is made to the *Ristaino* rule in death penalty cases. "[A] capital defendant accused of an interracial crime is entitled to have prospective jurors informed of the race of the victim and questioned on the issue of racial bias"(*Turner v. Murray,* 1986). Justice White's rationale for the decision was that because the jury has *greater discretion* in the sentencing phase of a capital case than in the guilt-finding phase, the death sentence should not stand where the *voir dire* did not inquire into race prejudice. The Supreme Court also held (6–3) that in a death penalty case, a requested voir dire question about a juror's propensity to automatically impose the death penalty even if mitigating factors existed, had to be asked. (*Morgan v. Illinois,* 1992)

Mu'Min v. Virginia (1991) was a murder case with substantial pretrial publicity. The judge on voir dire questioned prospective jurors about whether they had read or heard about the case and whether they had formed an opinion based on outside information. However, the judge refused to question prospective jurors about the *content* of their information, as requested by the defense. The Supreme Court held this did *not* violate due process. Justice Marshall, dissenting, argued it is constitutionally unfair to not allow content questions because they (1) determine whether the type and extent of pretrial publicity would disqualify the juror as a matter of law, (2) give "legal depth" to the trial court's finding of impartiality, and (3) facilitate accurate trial court fact finding.

PEREMPTORY CHALLENGES In addition to unlimited challenges for cause, both sides in a criminal prosecution have a *limited* number of peremptory challenges, whereby a juror is excused without a stated cause or reason. These are often based on an attorney's "hunch" that the individual will prove unsympathetic to a client's cause. Where several defendants are tried together, each is entitled to peremptory challenges while the prosecutor may be limited to a smaller number. (In recent years, defendants protested that the use of peremptories by prosecutors to deliberately produce racially unbalanced juries is unconstitutional). In 1986, the Supreme Court responded positively to this claim, making an important change in the law regarding peremptory challenges.

• CASE & COMMENTS •

Batson v. Kentucky
476 U.S. 79, 106 S.Ct. 1712, 90 L.Ed.2d 69 (1986)

JUSTICE POWELL delivered the opinion of the Court.

This case requires us to reexamine that portion of *Swain v. Alabama* (1965), **[a]** concerning the evidentiary burden placed on a criminal defendant who claims that he has been denied equal protection through the State's use of peremptory challenges to exclude members of his race from the petit jury.

[a] The basic rule is not in issue, but rather how a defendant must *prove* that peremptory challenges were improperly based on race.

I

Petitioner, a black man, was indicted in Kentucky on charges of second-degree burglary and receipt of stolen goods. [At the trial,] the judge conducted *voir dire* examination of the venire, excused certain jurors for cause, and permitted the parties to exercise peremptory challenges. The prosecutor used his peremptory challenges to strike all four black persons on the venire, and a jury composed

• CASE & COMMENTS •

only of white persons was selected. [b] [Counsel claimed] that the prosecutor's removal of the black veniremen violated petitioner's rights under the Sixth and Fourteenth Amendments to a jury drawn from a cross section of the community, and under the Fourteenth Amendment to equal protection of the laws. [The judge denied the motion, observing] that the parties were entitled to use their peremptory challenges to "strike anybody they want to." ***

[Batson's conviction was upheld by the Kentucky Supreme Court, which relied on *Swain:*] a defendant alleging lack of a fair cross section must demonstrate systematic exclusion of a group of jurors from the venire. *** We granted certiorari, ***and now reverse.

[b] Batson raised a Sixth Amendment as well as a Fourteenth Amendment challenge because he was not sure he could win on equal protection grounds.

II

In *Swain v. Alabama,* this Court recognized that a "State's purposeful or deliberate denial to Negroes on account of race of participation as jurors in the administration of justice violates the Equal Protection Clause." [c] *** This principle has been "consistently and repeatedly" reaffirmed, ***in numerous decisions of this Court both preceding and following *Swain.* We reaffirm the principle today.

[c] The substantive *Swain* rule of equality means little if it almost impossible for a defendant to prove a racially biased exercise of the prosecutor's peremptories.

A

[The Court stated the rule of *Strauder v. West Virginia*: that exclusion of blacks from jury service violates the Equal Protection Clause of the Fourteenth Amendment.]

In holding that racial discrimination in jury selection offends the Equal Protection Clause, the Court in *Strauder* recognized, however, that a defendant has no right to a "petit jury composed in whole or in part of persons of his own race." [d] *** "The number of our races and nationalities stands in the way of evolution of such a conception" of the demand of equal protection. *** But the defendant does have the right to be tried by a jury whose members are selected pursuant to nondiscriminatory criteria. *** The Equal Protection Clause guarantees the defendant that the State will not exclude members of his race from the jury venire on account of race, ***or on the false assumption that members of his race as a group are not qualified to serve as jurors.

[d] This remains an appropriate rule; a fair selection process cannot guarantee that a member of one's own race is on the jury but purposeful exclusion of jurors on a racial basis is inherently discriminatory.

Purposeful racial discrimination in selection of the venire violates a defendant's right to equal protection because it denies him the protection that a trial by jury is intended to secure. [e] "The very idea of a jury is a body . . . composed of the peers or equals of the person whose rights it is selected or summoned to determine; that is, of his neighbors, fellows, associates, persons having the same legal status in society as that which he holds." The petit jury has occupied a central position in our system of justice by safeguarding a person accused of crime against the arbitrary exercise of power by prosecutor or judge. *** Those on the venire must be "indifferently chosen," to secure the defendant's right under the Fourteenth Amendment to "protection of life and liberty against race or color prejudice." ***

[e] As a matter of law "peers" are persons having the same *legal* status, i.e., other eligible prospective jurors; informally, however, many sense that a jury should include a diverse mix of people to include some who may match the defendant in terms of race, age, or social class,

* * *

The harm from discriminatory jury selection extends beyond that inflicted on the defendant and the excluded juror to touch the entire community. [f] Selection procedures that purposefully exclude black persons from juries undermine public confidence in the fairness of our system of justice. Discrimination within the judicial system is most pernicious because it is "a stimulant to that race prejudice which is an impediment to securing to [African Americans] that equal justice which the law aims to secure to all others."

[f] The Court acknowledges that the issues in this case go beyond the defendant's specific rights but implicates the fairness of the entire trial system.

B

[The Court finds that prior cases require that the Equal Protection Clause apply not only to the selection of the jury pool and venire, but also to the selection of the jury itself, i.e., a jury selection practice that is neutral on its face cannot be used in a discriminatory manner].

Accordingly, the component of the jury selection process at issue here, the State's privilege to strike individual jurors through peremptory challenges, is subject to the commands of the Equal Protection Clause. [g] Although a prosecutor ordinarily is entitled to exercise permitted peremptory challenges "for any reason at all, as long as that reason is related to his view concerning the

[g] This states a general rule; the Court has not yet gotten to the

• CASE & COMMENTS •

outcome" of the case to be tried, ***the Equal Protection Clause forbids the prosecutor to challenge potential jurors solely on account of their race or on the assumption that black jurors as a group will be unable impartially to consider the State's case against a black defendant.

procedures by which purposeful exclusion of jurors on account of race can be detected and prevented.

III

*** A recurring question in [the jury selection] cases, as in any case alleging a violation of the Equal Protection Clause, was whether the defendant had met his burden of proving purposeful discrimination on the part of the State. *** That question also was at the heart of the portion of *Swain v. Alabama* we reexamine today.

A

*** While the Constitution does not confer a right to peremptory challenges, *** those challenges traditionally have been viewed as one means of assuring the selection of a qualified and unbiased jury. *** **[h]** To preserve the peremptory nature of the prosecutor's challenge, the Court in *Swain* declined to scrutinize his actions in a particular case by relying on a presumption that he properly exercised the State's challenges.***

*** Since this interpretation of *Swain* has placed on defendants a crippling burden of proof, prosecutors' peremptory challenges are now largely immune from constitutional scrutiny. For reasons that follow, we reject this evidentiary formulation as inconsistent with standards that have been developed since *Swain* for assessing a prima facie case under the Equal Protection Clause.

[h] In other words, a defendant who believed that the prosecutor in *his* case was discriminating in exercising peremptory challenges can do *nothing* about it unless he can prove that this was part of a pattern in past cases.

B

[In equal protection cases regarding selection of the jury panel (venire) since *Swain,* the Court has required a finding of "a racially discriminatory purpose" in order to find unconstitutional discrimination. **[i]** The burden of proving this is on the defendant. But once the defendant "has carried his burden of persuasion," even by circumstantial evidence, the court "must undertake 'a sensitive inquiry'" into the direct and circumstantial evidence.]

*** Once the defendant makes the requisite showing, the burden shifts to the State to explain adequately the racial exclusion. *** The State cannot meet this burden on mere general assertions that its officials did not discriminate or that they properly performed their official duties. *** Rather, the State must demonstrate that "permissible racially neutral selection criteria and procedures have produced the monochromatic result." ***

*** [A] defendant may make a prima facie showing of purposeful racial discrimination in selection of the venire by relying solely on the facts concerning its selection *in his case.* "*** A single invidiously discriminatory governmental act" is not "immunized by the absence of such discrimination in the making of other comparable decisions." *** For evidentiary requirements to dictate that "several must suffer discrimination" before one could object, *** would be inconsistent with the promise of equal protection to all.

[i] Section B specifies modern procedures and rules for disclosing invidious discrimination in the selection of the jury pool or venire. These procedures form the template for procedures and rules applied to discover whether an Equal Protection Clause violation exists in the prosecutor's exercise of peremptory challenges.

C

*** [A] defendant may establish a prima facie case of purposeful discrimination in selection of the petit jury solely on evidence concerning the prosecutor's exercise of peremptory challenges at the defendant's trial. **[j]** To establish such a case, the defendant first must show that he is a member of a cognizable racial group *** and that the prosecutor has exercised peremptory challenges to remove from the venire members of the defendant's race. Second, the defendant is entitled to rely on the fact, as to which there can be no dispute, that peremptory challenges constitute a jury selection practice that permits "those to discriminate who are of a mind to discriminate." *** Finally, the defendant must show that these facts and any other relevant circumstances raise an inference that the prosecutor used that practice to exclude the veniremen from the petit jury on account of their race. This combination of factors in the empaneling of the petit jury, as in the selection of the venire, raises the necessary inference of purposeful discrimination.

[j] The simple act of a prosecutor striking a black prospective juror does not in itself prove, or even raise an inference of discrimination. The defendant must show "other relevant circumstances" that tend to show *why* the striking of jurors of the defendant's distinct class is discriminatory. Some examples are given in the next paragraph.

• CASE & COMMENTS •

In deciding whether the defendant has made the requisite showing, the trial court should consider all relevant circumstances. For example, a "pattern" of strikes against black jurors included in the particular venire might give rise to an inference of discrimination. Similarly, the prosecutor's questions and statements during *voir dire* examination and in exercising his challenges may support or refute an inference of discriminatory purpose. These examples are merely illustrative. We have confidence that trial judges, experienced in supervising *voir dire,* will be able to decide if the circumstances concerning the prosecutor's use of peremptory challenges creates a prima facie case of discrimination against black jurors.

Once the defendant makes a prima facie showing, the burden shifts to the State to come forward with a neutral explanation for challenging black jurors. **[k]** Though this requirement imposes a limitation in some cases on the full peremptory character of the historic challenge, we emphasize that the prosecutor's explanation need not rise to the level justifying exercise of a challenge for cause. *** But the prosecutor may not rebut the defendant's prima facie case of discrimination by stating merely that he challenged jurors of the defendant's race on the assumption—or his intuitive judgment—that they would be partial to the defendant because of their shared race. *** Just as the Equal Protection Clause forbids the States to exclude black persons from the venire on the assumption that blacks as a group are unqualified to serve as jurors, *** so it forbids the States to strike black veniremen on the assumption that they will be biased in a particular case simply because the defendant is black. **[l]** The core guarantee of equal protection, ensuring citizens that their State will not discriminate on account of race, would be meaningless were we to approve the exclusion of jurors on the basis of such assumptions, which arise solely from the jurors' race. Nor may the prosecutor rebut the defendant's case merely by denying that he had a discriminatory motive or "affirm[ing] [his] good faith in making individual selections." *** If these general assertions were accepted as rebutting a defendant's prima facie case, the Equal Protection Clause "would be but a vain and illusory requirement." *** The prosecutor therefore must articulate a neutral explanation related to the particular case to be tried. The trial court then will have the duty to determine if the defendant has established purposeful discrimination.

[k] The defendant's showing does not end the matter—it raises an inference of discrimination that the prosecutor now may rebut for offering a race-neutral explanation for striking members of the distinct class to which the defendant belongs.

[l] The Court touches on the ethical and political core of the case—whatever the sociological tendency of individuals to have group leanings, as individuals every eligible juror is presumed to be fit to evaluate that facts of a case in an impartial way and follow the judge's instructions as to the law.

IV

The State *** argues that the privilege of unfettered exercise of the challenge is of vital importance to the criminal justice system. **[m]**

[m] The majority desires to keep the peremptory challenge alive, but to modify it so that it will not be used in a way that constitutes racial discrimination.

While we recognize, of course, that the peremptory challenge occupies an important position in our trial procedures, we do not agree that our decision today will undermine the contribution the challenge generally makes to the administration of justice. The reality of practice, amply reflected in many state- and federal-court opinions, shows that the challenge may be, and unfortunately at times has been, used to discriminate against black jurors. By requiring trial courts to be sensitive to the racially discriminatory use of peremptory challenges, our decision enforces the mandate of equal protection and furthers the ends of justice. In view of the heterogeneous population of our Nation, public respect for our criminal justice system and the rule of law will be strengthened if we ensure that no citizen is disqualified from jury service because of his race. ***

[The case was remanded.]

JUSTICE MARSHALL, concurring.

I join JUSTICE POWELL's eloquent opinion for the Court, which takes a historic step toward eliminating the shameful practice of racial discrimination in the selection of juries. **[n]** *** I nonetheless write separately to express my views. The decision today will not end the racial discrimination that peremptories inject into the jury-selection process. That goal can be accomplished only by eliminating peremptory challenges entirely.

[n] Justice Marshall's radical solution would deprive prosecutors and defense counsel of peremptory challenges in cases where race is not a factor. Is his remedy worth the price?

I

* * *

Misuse of the peremptory challenge to exclude black jurors has become both common and flagrant. ***

• CASE & COMMENTS •

II

*** Cases . . . illustrate the limitations of the [Court's] approach. First, defendants cannot attack the discriminatory use of peremptory challenges at all unless the challenges are so flagrant as to establish a prima facie case. This means, in those States, that where only one or two black jurors survive the challenges for cause, the prosecutor need have no compunction about striking them from the jury because of their race. *** Prosecutors are left free to discriminate against blacks in jury selection provided that they hold that discrimination to an "acceptable" level. **[o]**

Second, when a defendant can establish a prima facie case, trial courts face the difficult burden of assessing prosecutors' motives. *** Any prosecutor can easily assert facially neutral reasons for striking a juror, and trial courts are ill equipped to second-guess those reasons. ***

Nor is outright prevarication by prosecutors the only danger here. "[I]t is even possible that an attorney may lie to himself in an effort to convince himself that his motives are legal." *** A prosecutor's own conscious or unconscious racism may lead him easily to the conclusion that a prospective black juror is "sullen," or "distant," a characterization that would not have come to his mind if a white juror had acted identically. . . .

[o] Justice Marshall points suggest that the Court's rule in this case will be of more symbolic than real value to defendants who believe that the prosecutor is unjustly striking jurors.

III

The inherent potential of peremptory challenges to distort the jury process by permitting the exclusion of jurors on racial grounds should ideally lead the Court to ban them entirely from the criminal justice system. * * * [Therefore, neither should defendants be allowed peremptory challenges because they can also "engage in racial discrimination in jury selection."]

* * *

CHIEF JUSTICE BURGER, joined by JUSTICE REHNQUIST, dissenting.

[Chief Justice Burger's dissent raised several points: (1) the peremptory challenge serves an important function in assuring that the jury will decide a case on the basis of the evidence; (2) unlike the *Strauder* rule, which properly finds an equal protection violation when *classes* of persons are excluded from the venire, this case attacks a procedure involving a discrete decision tailored to the circumstances of a particular case; (3) the majority's equal protection rule applies only to race and not to other equal protection grounds such as sex, religious or political affiliation, mental capacity, or profession, and (4) since the rule is based on equal protection rather than Sixth Amendment principles, it must be applied to *defendants,* denying them of the use of peremptory challenges when they believe a class of jurors are racially biased.

[Further, the Chief Justice argued that the procedural requirements of *Batson,* including the need for a prosecutor to offer a race-neutral explanation to defendants' attacks, the truly peremptory nature of a peremptory challenge will be destroyed. He felt that it was impossible to apply the rule of the case]

*** I am at a loss to discern the governing principles here. A "clear and reasonably specific" explanation of "legitimate reasons" for exercising the challenge will be difficult to distinguish from a challenge for cause. . . . Apparently the Court envisions permissible challenges short of a challenge for cause that are just a little bit arbitrary—but not too much. While our trial judges are "experienced in supervising *voir dire,*" *** they have no experience in administering rules like this.

Batson's Aftermath

The Equal Protection Clause rule of *Batson* has been held to limit the use of peremptory challenges to other categories of cases.

- *White defendant*—has *third-party standing* to challenge a *prosecutor's peremptory challenge* to remove an African American from the jury (*Powers v. Ohio,* 1991). "A prosecutor's discriminatory use of peremptory challenges harms the excluded jurors and the community at large."
- *Civil lawsuits—Batson* rule applies to all parties; the necessary *state action* predicate for an equal protection violation lies in the *judge's* action of dismissing a challenged juror on a party's request. (*Edmonson v. Leesville Concrete Co.,* 1991)
- *Hispanic Jurors*—The *Batson* rule extends to the exclusion of Hispanic jurors on account of their ethnicity. (*Hernandez v. New York,* (1991)
- *Criminal Defendant's Peremptory*—"A criminal defendant's exercise of peremptory challenges in a racially discriminatory manner inflicts the harms addressed by *Batson*." It erodes *public confidence* in a fair and impartial jury. (*Georgia v. McCollum,* 1992)
- *Gender*—Neither male nor female jurors can be stricken by use of peremptory challenges solely on the basis of their sex. The equal protection violation lay in the assumption that men and women "hold particular views simply because of their gender," and this stereotype reflects and reinforces patterns of historical discrimination. (*J.E.B. v. Alabama,* 1994)

Prosecutors' *race-neutral explanations* for exercising peremptory challenges against *Batson* categories have been readily accepted:

- A prosecutor's exclusion of Latino jurors, on the grounds that there was some reason to believe specific Spanish speaking jury panel members would not automatically accept that the official translator's version of testimony given in Spanish, was deemed race-neutral by the Supreme Court. (*Hernandez v. New York,* 1991)
- A prosecutor eliminated two African-American jurors, and when challenged under *Batson* said they were excluded not because of their race, but because each had long unkempt hair, a mustache, and a goatee. The Supreme Court remanded to consider whether this was a race-neutral reason. (*Purkett v. Elem* (1995)
- The Supreme Court tilted procedures to favor prosecutors' race-neutral explanations. *Purkett v. Elem* (1995) held that *any* race-neutral explanation for striking a juror must at first be accepted by a trial judge. Then, the burden shifts to the opponent of the peremptory strike to *prove* that the proffered explanation is an *implausible* or *fantastic justification* that is a *pretext* or cover for purposeful discrimination. In *Purkett,* the Court said the lower court acted too quickly in rejecting the peremptory challenge.

Professor Charles J. Ogletree, reviewing the application of *Batson* in lower courts, concluded that "trial judges' acceptance of prosecutors' facially neutral explanations for peremptory strikes have undermined the protection *Batson* was meant to offer against discriminatory peremptory strikes."[23] Several authors have suggested, as correctives, (i) requiring that some minority jurors be seated in the trial of a minority defendant, (ii) race-conscious change-of-venue statutes, (iii) increasing the number of minorities on the jury venire, (iv) seating minority jurors who are struck by peremptories, and (v) reducing the number of prosecutors' peremptory challenges.[24] Professor Ogletree adds: (1) dismissing a prosecution where a prosecutor violates *Batson,* or (2) eliminate prosecution, but not defense, use of peremptory challenges. This last seemingly unbalanced proposal is based on a concern that a total elimination of peremptories would empower trial judges to seat biased jurors. It is unlikely that the current Supreme Court or state legislatures would adopt any of these extremely pro-defendant or racially based rules. These suggestions, however, point to serious problems with the administration of the *Batson* rule.

Law in Society: The Jury in Crisis?

High-visibility jury trials in recent years have raised doubts about the ability of juries to render fair or accurate verdicts.

Outrageous Verdicts?

Outrageous jury verdicts in high profile cases seem to have increased. Much criticism is a consequence of polarized racial or gender views, either of the jurors or of observers.

- The Dan White "Twinkie" Defense Case In 1978, Dan White, a former San Francisco Supervisor entered city hall through a window to avoid a metal detector and deliberately killed political rivals Mayor George Moscone and Supervisor Harvey Milk, a prominent gay activist. Gays were striken from the jury in White's homicide trial. He was portrayed as a decent person who acted out of depression brought on, in part, by consuming junk food. The jury returned a manslaughter verdict. White served only four-and-a-half years. Outraged gays in San Francisco rioted after the verdict was announced.[25]
- John Hinckley: The Reagan Assassination Attempt On November 30, 1981, John W. Hinckley, Jr. shot President Ronald Reagan and two others on a Washington, D.C., street. The lonely, directionless young man fantasized that

this would draw the attention of actress Jodie Foster. In June 1982, a jury found him not guilty by reason of insanity, even while expressing criticism of their verdict. Hinckley remains confined under court order at St. Elizabeth's Hospital in Washington. The verdict produced a wave of outrage, and many states eliminated the insanity defense or created "guilty but mentally ill" verdicts.[26]

- Ronald Ebens/Vincent Chin In June 1982, Chinese-American Vincent Chin was beaten to death with a baseball bat outside a bar near Detroit by auto worker Ronald Ebens. Ebens mistook Chin for a Japanese person at a time of extreme hostility to the Japanese in the "Motor City," whose main product was undercut by better-built Japanese cars. Ebens pled guilty to manslaughter and received a probation sentence. An outraged Chinese-American community demanded justice, and Ebens was prosecuted in federal court for violating Chin's civil rights. A jury of ten whites and two blacks acquitted Ebens of civil rights charges in May 1987.
- Bernhard Goetz: The Subway Vigilante[27] In December 1984, a white gunman shot four "underclass" black teenagers in a New York City subway car and then disappeared. The news media portrayed the youths as potential muggers and lionized the shooter as the "subway vigilante," which appealed to a public that was fed up with crime. Bernhard Goetz soon emerged as the shooter and, in the glow of a positive aura, a grand jury refused to indict him. After the public mood—sensing racism—turned on Goetz, an indictment was secured. The trial began in 1987 before a mixed-race jury. The defense portrayed the youths shot by Goetz as predators, and in June 1987, the jury acquitted Goetz of all attempted murder charges. He served a few months for illegal weapons possession. In April 1996, a Bronx, New York jury awarded Darrell Cabey, one of the four youths—who was paralyzed for life by Goetz—forty-three million dollars in civil damages.[28]
- The Central Park Jogger Case In August 1990, three black teens were found guilty in New York City for the rape and beating of a white woman, an investment banker, who had been jogging in Central Park one evening. She was left for dead and was in a state of amnesia for months. The youths, from middle-class families, were accused of "wilding" in the park. The jury included four whites, four blacks, three Hispanics, and one Asian; it deliberated "bitterly" for ten days, but at the end, the jurors praised one another for staying focused on the evidence, including confessions,[29] although no eyewitnesses or no physical evidence directly linked the defendants to the victim. "Throughout the trial the Manhattan courthouse at 111 Centre Street has been the scene of frequent and volatile demonstrations, most by people protesting that the trial was grounded in racism, that the defendants were falsely accused and that they could not get a fair trial."[30]
- The Marion Barry Crack-Cocaine Trial Federal law enforcement paid a woman who was a former acquaintance of Washington, D.C. mayor Marion Barry to lure him to a hotel room to smoke crack cocaine. The sordid episode was taped. Barry seemed more interested in sex, but the informer coaxed him into smoking the illegal substance. The prosecutor believed that the evidence was overwhelming. Nevertheless, in an August 1990 trial, a Washington, D.C., jury consisting entirely of African Americans, sensing entrapment, acquitted Barry of all serious charges. Barry served a six-month sentence for a misdemeanor drug conviction, went through rehabilitation, and was reelected mayor in 1994.
- Middle East Nationalism: Meir Kahane/El Sayyid Nosair In November 1990, the extremist Jewish nationalist leader Rabbi Meir Kahane was gunned down as he ended a speech in a New York City hotel. Several witnesses saw El Sayyid Nosair with a gun. As he fled, Nosair shot seventy-two year-old Irving Franklin who tried to stop him, got away by holding a pistol to the head of taxi driver Franklin Garcia, and shot and wounded uniformed officer Carlos Acosta. The .357 Magnum used by Nosair was the same gun that was used to kill Kahane. Radical defense lawyer, William Kunstler, kept Jews off the jury and alluded to tales of Jewish conspiracies as an explanation for the killing. The jury acquitted Nosair in December 1991 of all charges of killing Kahane. He was convicted on the other assaults and sentenced to the maximum seven-and-a-half to twenty-two years. Demonstrations of nationalistic Jews followed in Israel and New York, and Nosair was burned in effigy in front of the courthouse.
- The William Kennedy Smith Rape Trial While barhopping with his famous uncle, Senator Edward Kennedy, in Palm Beach, Florida, medical student William Kennedy Smith picked up a woman who returned with him to the Kennedy family compound. They had sex; she claimed that Smith raped her. The Kennedy family spent at least one million dollars to defend Smith, including high-priced jury consultants. In a televised trial made famous by the "fuzzy ball" that hid the victim's face, the country saw expert witnesses examine every aspect of the case. The jury deliberated two hours before acquitting William Kennedy Smith of sexual battery against Patricia Bowman in December 1991. Many feminists were outraged at the verdict.
- The Mike Tyson Rape Trial In July 1991, heavyweight boxer Mike Tyson had a late night date with Desiree Washington, a contestant at the Miss Black America beauty pageant in Indianapolis. As in the William Kennedy Smith case, she claimed she was raped, and Tyson said they

voluntarily had sex. Tyson's case drew much media attention, and like Smith, he had an excellent lawyer. Nevertheless, Tyson was convicted in February 1992 and sent to prison. Was Tyson convicted because he was black? Perhaps. Professor George Fletcher notes, however, that Tyson appeared before an Indiana grand jury and made statements that were inconsistent with later testimony. Florida, on the other hand, had no grand jury procedure so Smith's lawyer could focus more attention on inconsistencies in Patricia Bowman's testimony. Tyson was released in March 1995 and resumed his boxing career. In June 1995, Tyson quietly settled a civil suit brought against him by Desiree Washington for an undisclosed amount.

- The Lozano Miami Police Shooting Case In January 1989, Hispanic police officer William Lozano shot and killed two African Americans riding on a motorcycle in Miami. Riots broke out. In December 1989, Lozano was convicted of manslaughter in Miami. In June 1991, a Florida appellate court overturned the verdict, ruling that the trial judge committed error by not considering Lozano's change of venue motion. From April 1992 to May 1993, the case bounced back and forth between Orlando and Tallahassee at least four times before being tried in Orlando where a jury of three whites, two Hispanics, and one black acquitted Lozano in May 1993. This unseemly spectacle exposed politicized, racialized justice, as African-American pressure on the prosecution sought a venue favorable to blacks and the defense played for a venue favorable to Hispanics.[31]

- The "Rodney King"/Simi Valley Trial In March 1991, black motorist Rodney King was stopped for speeding, resisted arrest, and was beaten by three Los Angeles police officers for at least eighty-six seconds, as captured on videotape. The tape was released to the public and caused an international uproar. The trial was moved to Simi Valley in Ventura County. A jury of ten whites, a Hispanic, and an Asian acquitted the officers in April 1992. The nation was shocked by the verdict and by the rioting in the African-American community of South Central Los Angeles that resulted in fifty deaths. While the defense attorneys skillfully projected a version of the case from the law enforcement officers' perspectives, few doubted that the decisive element in the case that rocked the nation was the change of venue from Los Angeles, where it is likely that several African Americans would sit as jurors. A year later, Officer Powell and Sergeant Koon were convicted in federal court for violating King's civil rights.

- The Crown Heights Riot Murder Trial[32] In August 1991, a car escorting a leading Hasidic Rabbi careened onto a sidewalk killing Gavin Cato, an African American child in the Crown Heights section of Brooklyn, New York. A mob formed, and three days of the worst racial rioting in New York since World War II followed in the largely black neighborhood that also houses about fifteen thousand Lubavitch. The rioting was marked by frequent anti-Semitic remarks, indicating a history of community friction between the groups. An hour after the automobile accident, Yankel Rosenbaum, a twenty-nine year old Hasidic scholar from Australia, encountered a group of ten or fifteen black youths; minutes later he was stabbed four times in the chest. Police arrested a youth, Lemrick Nelson, Jr., at the scene. Nelson was identified as the assailant by Rosenbaum before he died of the wounds. A knife covered with the victim's type of blood was found in Nelson's pocket. He confessed but then recanted his confession. During the trial, the defense lawyer raised points of police incompetence as a basis for reasonable doubt but also suggested that Rosenbaum was a member of a Jewish defense unit. In October 1992, a jury with no Jews acquitted Nelson of all charges in the killing of Rosenbaum.[33] Later, jury members went partying with Nelson to celebrate the acquittal. Nelson was later tried by federal authorities for violating Rosenbaum's civil rights and was found guilty.[34] The police handling of the riot led to a state investigation and was a factor in the defeat of Mayor David Dinkins, New York City's first black mayor, by Rudolph Giuliani in the next election.

- Damian Williams/Reginald Denny: Los Angeles Riot Trial In the riots that followed the Simi Valley acquittal (the "Rodney King" case), news cameras took video pictures of Damian Williams beating truck driver Reginald Denny with a concrete block and then doing a little victory dance. Williams was black and Denny white, and the pictures seemed to epitomize the sense of black rage and revenge that fueled the Los Angeles riots. Denny's life was saved by other African Americans who pulled him to safety and took him to a hospital. Williams's lawyer skillfully depicted the defendants as "the victims of racism, riot contagion, and other forces beyond their control."[35] A Los Angeles jury acquitted Williams of attempted murder in October 1993. Williams was sentenced to a maximum ten-year term after he pled guilty to a reduced charge of felony mayhem.

- The Menendez Brothers' Parent Killing Trial In August 1989, Erik and Lyle Menendez, aged eighteen and twenty-one, drove to San Diego from their home in Los Angeles in a new sports car given to them by their parents, purchased a shotgun, and a few days later killed their parents with the gun while their parents were watching television. Their trial for first-degree murder, conducted before two separate juries, began in July 1993. The juries heard convincing tales of a life of sexual abuse, although no physical evidence to support this was ever produced. In January 1994, both juries deadlocked on murder charges. Retrial began on August 23, 1995, and in June 1996, the brothers were each found guilty of murder and given life sentences. Professor Fletcher treats the Menendez brothers' defense with contempt. It involved blaming the victim; generating a defense with virtually no support except, perhaps, good acting ability both by the defendants and by Leslie Abramson, Erik's attorney; and an unwise extension of the victim-of-abuse defense under circumstances where the brothers could easily have escaped from their parents' supposed abuse.[36] The public reaction to this case is interesting. At first, the public was fascinated by the soap opera-like "plot" of the case and was sympathetic to the brothers. After the hung jury in the first case, the public, seemingly fed up with excuses, appeared to favor their convictions.

- Lorena and John Bobbitt Domestic Violence Trials In a case that amused as well as shocked the nation and became grist for the television talk show mill, Lorena Bobbitt cut off her husband's penis in a domestic fight in June 1993. In November of that year, a jury in Manassas, Virginia, acquitted John Wayne Bobbitt of sexual marital abuse. In January 1994, Lorena Bobbitt was found not guilty by reason of insanity on a charge of malicious wounding. She was released from a state institution a month later and directed to seek up to six months of counseling. Both parties could have been found guilty of serious violent crimes, but both successfully competed "for the status of victim."[37]
- The O. J. Simpson Murder Trial The June 1994 murder of Nicole Brown and Ronald Goldman quickly became a bizarre media and celebrity spectacle when O. J. Simpson seemingly tried to flee in his white Bronco which was driven by a friend. An unprecedented amount of media attention was given to the case as it dragged out from jury selection in September 1994 to the not guilty verdict in October 1996. The instantly televised reactions of black law students and white observers powerfully pictured a nation divided.

Jury Nullification

Some of these cases may have been correctly decided on the evidence available to the jury. In others, the overwhelming opinion of most observers is that the jury made real blunders and was swayed by inappropriate factors. Part of the concern about these cases is that they may reflect **jury nullification** run amok.[38] Jury nullification is the *power,* but not the *right,* of juries to disregard the judge's instructions regarding the law and return a verdict based on their own sense of justice or what the law should be. Jury nullification can be used for evil purposes as well as for good purposes. Nullification has allowed juries to defy the crown's attempt to crush liberty, as in *Bushell*'s case (1670) when jurors acquitted William Penn in a political prosecution by the British government for preaching in public. A New York jury that acquitted John Peter Zenger in 1735 of charges of seditious libel immeasurably advanced the freedom of the press.[39] But jury nullification also explains thousands of hideous cases of white jurors in the old segregated South exonerating the murderers of African Americans, as occurred after the killing of civil rights leader Medgar Evars in the 1960s.

Some critics have argued that jury nullification should be legitimated. If judges were allowed to instruct juries that they may impose their own interpretation of the law, it would make incoherent the very concept of uniform law applicable equally to all, and would create a form of "legal anarchy." The critics argue that this occurs in any event. However, telling juries they may decide the law and disregard factual evidence will break down the discipline that keeps a jury true to their oaths to decide cases according to the evidence and the law. Paul Butler, for example, advocated jury nullification by African Americans in victimless crimes (but not in violent crimes) for purposes of community solidarity and to focus on ways of dealing with social problems outside of the criminal justice system.[40] Professor David Brody has pointed out that a form of jury nullification actually exists in a few jurisdictions and argues that empirical evidence in those jurisdictions shows that jury nullification instructions can safely be issued without causing "legal anarchy."[41]

These intriguing radical proposals for jury nullification are unlikely to make much headway with the legislatures or courts. Jury nullification surely exists. A "classic" form of jury nullification was at work in the three acquittals of Dr. Jack Kevorkian for assisting in the suicide of suffering patients before he was ultimately convicted for a televised euthanasia (mercy killing).[42] But it seems that in the heated atmosphere that followed the O. J. Simpson case, any adoption of a jury nullification standard would only inflame the divisiveness that has marked many of the cases listed above.

Reforming Jury Service

Attacks on the jury have occurred at a time of heightened jury reform. Judith Kaye, chief judge of New York, has led the way in improving the conditions of jury service. This includes improving computer technology to implement the *one day/one trial* jury service model, abolishing automatic exemptions to jury service, eliminating mandatory **sequestering the jury** (which was unique to New York), increasing jury pay, reducing the number of peremptory challenges, and upgrading jury waiting rooms.[43] Massachusetts law requires employers to pay employees' full salaries for the first three days of jury service; for the fourth day and beyond, the state pays a jury fee of fifty dollars per day.[44] New York set up a juror complaint hotline directly connected to the Office of Court Administration. It experimented with a juror ombudsman.[45] Professor James Levine, reviewing the great stress associated with jury sequestration, points out that it can often undermine a fair trial and should, as a general matter, not be used.[46]

In order to make the ideal of the cross-sectional jury a reality, many changes have occurred. One is the elimination of *automatic exemptions* by a person's profession or by practices that allow lawyers, physicians, corporate executives, and even judges to absent themselves from service. Stephen J. Adler, critical of juries, notes that in the past, jury service was limited to elites, but now, ironically, it has become limited to persons who know the least about what is going on.[47] Another reform is to expand the lists from which jurors are selected. Voting lists include citizens who are more willing to participate in government but, given the dismal record of Americans when it comes to voting, may exclude up to half of eligible jury members and tends to exclude younger people and members of ethnic minorities. More controversial methods include the stratified selection of jurors to restore to jury venires the racial or ethnic diversity that is sometimes missing from original source lists and color-conscious jury selection.[48]

Several observers, from the late Justice Marshall—one of the most experienced trial lawyers on the Supreme Court—to *Wall Street Journal* editor Stephen Adler, have recommended eliminating the peremptory challenge. Adler notes that this would destroy the only means through which lawyers can

> "get a jury you like the look of." . . . [I]t would also mean destroying the huge market for jury consultants who promise not only to pack juries but to do so scientifically. It would mean the end of primers, courses, and conferences on how to assemble a winning jury. And it would mean that decades of stereotypes about how people of various ethnic groups are likely to vote would become moot.[49]

Other reforms are designed to improve the actual operation of the jury. These include giving jurors *printed jury instructions* at the beginning of the trial so they can hear the testimony in the context of the law. Another suggestion, now widely adopted, is to allow jurors to *take notes.* Some courts allow jurors to ask questions of witnesses by writing them down and submitting them to the judge for approval.[50] Another reform that has become glaringly obvious after the O. J. Simpson trial is the need for trials to be conducted as swiftly as possible with the needs of the jury in mind. The extreme length of some California trials, such as the McMartin school case, may reflect local norms. But there can be little doubt that Judge Lance Ito seriously erred. Professor Barbara Allen Babcock writes that

> a jury should be assembled once for a single purpose, that it should be composed of strangers who know each other only through their deliberations. This fundamental feature of a jury was violated in the Simpson case by a star-struck judge who lost control of the situation. He caused the jury to spend many hours waiting while he heard and reheard lawyers' arguments, took time off to engage celebrities, and through it all patronized the jurors, conveying by his tone and manner that their time was not important. He should have taken drastic measures to move the trial along, for instance by hearing motions in the evenings or holding court on Saturdays. Instead, by his leisurely approach, he violated the very premise of the jury system and opened up the possibility that this jury would become a little band with its own agenda.[51]

A highly controversial reform touted in the aftermath of O. J. Simpson's acquittal is for states to adopt a rule allowing *nonunanimous verdicts.*[52] The concern with a supermajoritarian jury verdict is that it reduces or eliminates the need for **jury deliberation.** The jury does not merely vote; it deliberates. It reviews the evidence, and when differences arise, as they typically do in human affairs, jurors with different views of the evidence must try to persuade one another. If jurors change their minds, they come to realize that they were wrong. When the jury works well, and it often does, it is a sober exercise in self-government and the collective judgment of ordinary citizens. Any human system, of course, is subject to human frailties. Some jurors are obstinate, some cave in to pressure against their better judgment, and others reach compromise verdicts. Jeffrey Abramson writes, "[a]bolishing the unanimous verdict would weaken the conversations through which laypersons educate one another about their common sense of justice."[53] It is well worth keeping in mind, before advocating radical changes in the jury's method of operation, that the notorious cases reviewed above may not reflect the average reality of jury service. One recent work suggests that juries do, in fact, dispense commonsense justice.[54]

The recent outpouring of scholarly research on the jury indicates more than a deep disquiet about the functioning of a component of the justice system. The jury is the most unique aspect of American justice. As the embodiment of popular justice, it reflects the best and the worst of American life.[55] The jury is not a branch of government: it is a pure element of direct democracy. The deeper concern about the jury is that its failure may spell the failure of democracy in a rapidly changing world. If juries are seen to fail because jurors who are separated by race, or gender, or religion, or age, or class cannot come together to resolve difficult cases, can the larger society bridge these divides? The situation regarding the jury is not hopeless. A combination of physical, administrative, and operational changes, guided by a sense of purpose about the proper functioning of the jury, may make the odd verdicts of the 1990s a passing episode and result in a stronger jury system.

SUMMARY

The common law jury trial is a central legal institution in America that has great symbolic and functional importance to support and ensure justice in the processing of criminal suspects. Unlike the trial practices of civil law nations, the common law trial is marked by the unique power of the citizen jury to be the final arbiter of the facts of the case and by the extent to which the trial is conducted by attorneys rather than by the judge.

The jury trial of a felony consists of many steps and involves numerous rights enumerated in the Sixth Amendment. After jury selection, the prosecutor and defense counsel may make opening statements. The prosecution enters evidence that is subject to cross-examination by the defense. The defense may then introduce evidence that is subject to the prosecutor's cross-examination, or it may rest without introducing evidence. A defendant has a constitutional right to be present at all phases of the trial unless the defendant voluntarily absents himself or acts disruptively. This right does not include every conference between the judge and the attorneys, in-camera competence hearings, or brief meetings with witnesses or jurors where the meetings are not unfair and the defense attorney is on hand. It does include such aspects of the trial as a visit to the scene of the crime. Compulsory process to subpoena witnesses is another important right that supports a fair trial.

The Fifth Amendment right against self-incrimination requires that the prosecutor and the judge refrain from commenting on the defendant's absolute right not to testify, unless so requested by the defendant. If the prosecutor makes prejudicial statements in closing arguments, they may be the basis for a reversal of the conviction. A mistrial or reversal must be ordered if the prosecutor knowingly allows false evidence to be introduced into the trial. The prosecution may conceal the identity of an informant before a trial, but if the informant testifies, his or her identity must be disclosed to the defense. There is no due process right that the police preserve evidence, as long as evidence is not destroyed in bad faith.

Confrontation is central to the common law trial because it affords the defendant the opportunity to cross-examine the prosecution's witnesses. Cross-examination is the central method used in the trial to elicit the truth; in cross-examination, the lawyer tests the credibility of the witness and the strength of the testimony. A defense attorney seeks to establish a reasonable doubt by cross-examination. The elimination of eye-to-eye contact in the trial itself has been held to be a violation of the Confrontation Clause, unless special circumstances are proven.

Proof of guilt must be beyond a reasonable doubt, a standard of evidence inherent in due process. No specific constitutional definition of reasonable doubt exists; a judge's instruction to the jury on reasonable doubt is constitutional if, taken as a whole, it correctly conveys the idea of reasonable doubt. An instruction that defines it as a "doubt as would give rise to a *grave uncertainty,*" standing alone, violates due process because it suggests a higher degree of doubt than is required for acquittal under the reasonable doubt standard. On the other hand, an instruction to the jury that "A reasonable doubt is an *actual and substantial doubt* arising from the evidence, . . . as distinguished from a doubt arising from mere possibility, from bare imagination, or from fanciful conjecture" does not violate due process because it is tied to real facts. A jury instruction using the archaic phrase "moral certainty" does not automatically violate due process.

The jury is guaranteed by the Sixth Amendment in the criminal trial of all but petty crimes and is not required in juvenile delinquency hearings. Some constitutional variations are allowed between the federal common law jury, which requires twelve members and a unanimous verdict, and state juries, some of which consist of fewer than twelve persons and allow verdicts by a "super majority" (e.g., nine to three).

A fair jury is required under (1) the Equal Protection Clause of the Fourteenth Amendment—persons cannot be excluded from the jury because they share the race, ethnicity or gender of the defendant, or (2) the Sixth Amendment requirement of an impartial jury—any jury must be selected from a panel that reflects a fair cross-section of the community, whatever the relation between the defendant's race, etc. and the characteristics of jury pool members.

The jury itself, because of its small size, need not reflect a fair cross-section of the community, but if the prosecutor uses peremptory challenges to excuse prospective jurors because of their race, ethnicity or gender, *Batson v. Kentucky* (1986) holds that the Equal Protection Clause requires that the conviction be reversed, unless a race-neutral explanation of the peremptory is accepted. Post-*Batson* cases have extended its rule to civil trials and criminal defendants, and to the categories of gender and ethnicity. The Court has been lenient in accepting race-neutral explanations for striking minorities from juries.

LEGAL PUZZLES

LEGAL PUZZLES: HOW HAVE COURTS DECIDED CASES?

12–1. Taylor and Ortiz were charged with the first degree murder of Andrew Sweet. Ortiz successfully moved to sever the defendants and separate trials were ordered. Taylor moved to have his trial after Ortiz' trial, submitting an affidavit by Ortiz stating that he (Ortiz) would assert his Fifth Amendment privilege until after his trial, but that after his conviction or acquittal, he would provide exculpatory testimony at Taylor's trial. This request was denied, Taylor was prosecuted before Ortiz and convicted. Did the trial judge's refusal to schedule Taylor's trial after Ortiz violate his Sixth Amendment right to compulsory process in order to call a witness whose testimony is both material and favorable to the defense? *Taylor v. Singletary,* 122 F.3d 1390 (11th Cir. 1997)

12–2. Michael Monus was convicted of over 100 counts of fraud arising out of the operation of a retail discount drugstore chain that he owned. Monus pointed out that prosecutors commented on his decision not to testify at trial, and this prosecutorial misconduct required a reversal on all the counts. During cross-examination witness Pat Finn was asked when Monus knew he had to falsify records. Finn replied: "A. That'll be something you will have to ask [Monus] because it was his decision." During closing arguments, the defense lawyer argued that Finn's replies to the cross-examination were illogical. In response, the prosecutor told the jury in his closing argument that the defense attorney was trying to impose his conception of what's logical upon the facts. "And if you remember, after an hour of this [on cross examination] Pat Finn finally said, well, is it logical or reasonable what is going on, you have to ask [defendant]. I'm just telling you what happened." Was this a veiled comment on the fact that Monus did not testify? Did if violate Monus' right against self-incrimination and require a new trial? *United States v. Monus,* 128 F.3d 376 (6th Cir. 1997)

12–3. Melvin Joe, a Native American living on the Navajo Indian Reservation in New Mexico, was tried for murder. The prosecutor exercised a peremptory challenge of the only Native American juror on the venire. Did this violate Joe's right to equal protection under the Fourteenth Amendment? *United States v. Joe,* 8 F.3d 1488 (10th Cir. 1993)

12–4. Melvin Johnson, an African American, was tried for the murder, robbery, burglary, theft, and aggravated assault of an elderly white man and his sister. The male victim was known to have solicited sexual favors from young black boys over a period of time prior to his death. After five white women and one white man had been seated as jurors, the prosecutor used peremptory strikes to exclude the only three African Americans in the venire. In a *Batson* challenge, he explained that the jury would learn that a victim had solicited sexual favors from young black boys and that the stricken black jurors might be more sympathetic to the defendant and less sympathetic to the victims than would a white juror. Is this a race-neutral explanation? *Johnson v. Love,* 40 F.3d 658 (3d Cir. 1994)

ANSWERS TO LEGAL PUZZLES

12–1. YES. The prosecutor told the jury that both Ortiz and Taylor murdered Sweet and offered evidence that placed Taylor at Sweet's apartment. Ortiz's testimony, had it been offered, could have substantially impacted the judgment of the jury with respect to witnesses who identified Taylor and would have correlated with Taylor's statements that might have exonerated him or reduced the severity of his crime. "In short, Taylor's inability to call Ortiz essentially precluded him from putting on a defense."

12–2. YES. NO. Under rules established by Sixth Circuit precedent, improper statements by a prosecutor do not constitute reversible error unless the violation of defendant's rights was flagrant. The prosecutor's comment, which did call attention to the defendant's failure to testify was isolated, was not intended to mislead the jury, and was relevant to the inquiry at hand. Further, the overall evidence against the defendant was strong. The error was not flagrant.

12–3. NO. The defendant must show that he is a member of a cognizable racial group and that the prosecution has exercised peremptory challenges to remove members of a particular race from the venire because of their race. The court decided that Native Americans constitute a cognizable racial group under *Batson* and that striking the only Native American juror on the venire raised an inference that she was excluded on account of her race. The court ruled that Joe's rights were not violated because it accepted the prosecutor's race-neutral explanation of the strike: the juror was an artist, was only twenty-five years of age, and failed to respond on a questionnaire whether she owned or rented a home. The prosecutor believed that artists tended not to be progovernment, and given the serious nature of a murder charge, the prosecutor was concerned about the juror's life experiences and maturity level.

12–4. NO. On its face, this explanation for striking the prospective jurors is not race-neutral. The assumption that an African American juror would be prejudiced against the victim because of his pederasty is indistinguishable in principle from assuming her objectivity would be impaired because the defendant is black—an assumption the Equal Protection Clause forbids. Both assumptions are based on a stereotypical view or intuition that black people, because of their race, will relate to other black persons in a way that may preclude them from basing a verdict solely on the relevant evidence.

Further Reading

Jeffrey Abramson, *We, the Jury: The Jury System and the Ideal of Democracy* (New York: Basic Books, 1994).

George P. Fletcher, *With Justice for Some: Victims' Rights in Criminal Trials* (Reading, Mass.: Addison-Wesley, 1995).

Barry Scheck, Peter Neufeld and Jim Dwyer, *Actual Innocence: Five Days to Execution, and Other Dispatches From the Wrongly Convicted* (New York: Doubleday, 2000).

Endnotes

1. See Charles Rembar, *The Law of the Land: The Evolution of Our Legal System* (New York: Touchstone Books, 1980).
2. William Blackstone, *Commentaries on the Laws of England, Vol. 4, Of Public Wrongs* (1769 facsimile, Chicago: University of Chicago Press, 1979), pp. 342–43.
3. See Jerome Frank, *Courts on Trial: Myth and Reality in American Justice* (New York: Atheneum, [1949] 1963); Stephen J. Adler, *The Jury: Disorder in the Courts* (New York: Doubleday, 1994).
4. John H. Langbein, "The Criminal Trial before the Lawyers," *University of Chicago Law Review* 45:263–316 (1978); Malcolm M. Feeley, "Plea Bargaining and the Structure of the Criminal Process," in George F. Cole, ed., *Criminal Justice: Law and Politics*, 5th ed. (Pacific Grove, CA: Brooks/Cole, 1988), pp. 467–82.
5. Barton L. Ingraham, *The Structure of Criminal Procedure: Law and Practice of France, the Soviet Union, China, and the United States* (New York: Greenwood Press, 1987) p. 86.
6. See Rene David and John E. C. Brierly, *Major Legal Systems in the World Today,* 3d ed. (London: Stephens & Sons, 1985); Rene David and Henry P. de Vries, *The French Legal System: An Introduction to Civil Law Systems* (New York: Oceana Publications, 1958); Richard J. Terrill, *World Criminal Justice Systems: A Survey* (Cincinnati: Anderson, 1984).
7. Ingraham, *Criminal Procedure,* p. 85.
8. See Thurman Arnold, *The Symbols of Government* (New Haven: Yale University Press, 1935), pp. 134–48.
9. From among a vast and fascinating literature, see Stephen Phillips, *No Heroes, No Villains* (New York: Random House, 1977); Marshall Houts, *King's X; Common Law and the Death of Sir Harry Oaks* (New York: Morrow, 1972); Paul and Shirley Eberle, *The Abuse of Innocence: The McMartin Preschool Trial* (Buffalo, NY: Prometheus Books, 1993).
10. S. Engleberg, "At Storm's Eye, a Law About Secrets," *New York Times,* Feb. 13, 1989, p. 6 (nat. ed.).
11. Tim O'Brien, "Reasonable Doubt and DNA," *Washington Post,* Sept. 7, 2000, p. A25; Associated Press, "Innocence Proved; Case Was Source of Adverse Evidence Preservation Ruling," *Associated Press State & Local Wire,* Aug. 10, 2000.
12. Charles Rembar, *The Law of the Land: The Evolution of Our Legal System* (New York: Touchstone Books, 1980), p. 337.
13. Nancy Walker Perry and Lawrence S. Wrightsman, *The Child Witness: Legal Issues and Dilemmas* (Newbury Park, CA: Sage, 1991).
14. A poignant case is that of Kelly Michaels, a young woman working at a day care center, charged with lurid instances of sexual abuse. A reporter thought that the case was fishy and wrote an article that led attorneys to exonerate her. See Dorothy Rabinowitz, "From the Mouths of Babes to Jail Cells, Child Abuse and the Abuse of Justice: A Case Study," *Harper's Magazine,* May 1990, pp. 52–63, and Nancy Hass, "Margaret Kelly Michaels Wants Her Innocence Back," *New York Times Magazine,* Sept. 10, 1995, p. 37. See Eberle, *Abuse of Innocence* (describing the McMartin Preschool trial, one of the longest on record, that ultimately exonerated the school owners, but effectively destroyed their lives). See Timothy Egan, "Pastor and Wife Are Acquitted on All Charges in Sex-Abuse Case," *New York Times,* Dec. 12, 1995, p. A11 (Wenatchee, Washington case). See Michael Granberry, "Case Illustrates Flaws in Child Abuse Trials; Courts: Dale Akiki's Acquittal Was a Stinging Rebuke to The System That Arrested And Tried Him. Some Question The Prominence of Social Workers And Therapists in Obtaining Testimony," *Los Angeles Times,* Nov. 29, 1993, p. A3. The danger of false accusations, with devastating effect, also extends to physical, nonsexual abuse, Debra West, "Cleared of Child Abuse, but the Anguish Lingers," *New York Times,* Oct. 19, 1995, p. A12. See Martha M. Young, "The Salem Witch Trials 300 Years Later: How Far Has the American Legal System Come? How Much Further Does It Need to Go?" *Tulane Law Review* 64:235–58 (1989).
15. Harry Kalven and Hans Zeisel, *The American Jury* (Boston: Little, Brown, 1966), p. 490.
16. Federal Rules of Criminal Procedure 23(a).
17. See Hiroshi Fukurai, Edgar W. Butler and Richard Krooth, *Race and the Jury* (New York: Plenum Press, 1993).
18. Michael Finkelstein, "The Application of Statistical Decision Theory to the Jury Discrimination Cases," *Harvard Law Review* 80:338 (1966).
19. See Henry J. Abraham, *Freedom and the Court: Civil Rights and Liberties in the United States,* 4th ed. (New York: Oxford University Press, 1982), p. 76.
20. Cases collected in "Project: Twenty-Fifth Annual Review of Criminal Procedure," *Georgetown Law Journal* 76:713–1530 (1996), p. 1145, n. 1714.
21. *United States v. Hafen,* 726 F.2d 21 (1st Cir. 1984); *United States v. Rodriguez,* 776 F.2d 1509 (11th Cir. 1985); *United*

States v. Pepe, 747 F.2d 632 (11th Cir. 1984); *State v. McCarthy,* 496 A.2d 513 (Conn. 1985).

22. *United States v. Arnett,* 342 F. Supp. 1255 (D. Mass. 1970).
23. Charles J. Ogletree, "Just Say No!: A Proposal to Eliminate Racially Discriminatory Uses of Peremptory Challenges," *American Criminal Law Review* 31(1994):1099–151, p. 1100.
24. *Ibid.,* pp. 1113–16.
25. George P. Fletcher, *With Justice for Some: Protecting Victims' Rights in Criminal Trials* (Reading, MA: Addison–Wesley, 1996), pp. 9–36.
26. *Washington Post,* Apr. 1, 1981, p. A1; *Washington Post,* June 9, 1982, p. A1; *Washington Post*, June 25, 1982, p. A3; *New York Times,* June 24, 1982, p. D21.
27. See George P. Fletcher, *A Crime of Self Defense: Bernard Goetz and the Law on Trial* (New York: Free Press, 1988).
28. Adam Nossiter, "Bronx Jury Orders Goetz to Pay $43 Million to Shooting Victim," *New York Times,* Apr. 26, 1996, p. A1.
29. Ronald Sullivan, "Jogger Trial Jury Relied on Physical Evidence, Not Tapes," *New York Times,* Dec. 13, 1990, p. B1.
30. Ronald Sullivan, "3 Youths Guilty of Rape And Assault of Jogger," *New York Times,* Aug. 19, 1990, § 1, p. 1.
31. Marvin Zalman and Maurisa Gates, "Rethinking Venue in Light of the 'Rodney King' Case: An Interest Analysis," *Cleveland State Law Review* 41:215–77 (1993), pp. 274–76.
32. Fletcher, *With Justice,* pp. 86–106.
33. See Patricia Hurtado, "Crown Heights Jury: Why It Didn't Add Up; Murder Trial Was Marred by Missteps," *Newsday,* Nov. 8, 1992, p. 7.
34. Editorial, A Second Crown Heights Verdict, *New York Times,* Feb. 11, 1997, p. A20.
35. Fletcher, *With Justice,* p. 244.
36. Fletcher, *With Justice,* 140–48, *passim.*
37. Fletcher, *With Justice,* p. 244.
38. For a review of jury nullification, see Abramson, *We, the Jury,* pp. 57–95.
39. See Paul Butler, "Racially Based Jury Nullification: Black Power in the Criminal Justice System," *Yale Law Journal* 105(1995):677–725, pp. 701–703; Thomas A. Green, *Verdict According to Conscience: Perspectives on the English Criminal Trial 1200–1800* (Chicago: University of Chicago Press, 1985), pp. 249–64.
40. Butler, *Racially Based Jury Nullification,* pp. 715–25.
41. David C. Brody, "*Sparf* and *Dougherty* Revisited: Why the Court Should Instruct the Jury of Its Nullification Right," *American Criminal Law Review* 33(1995):89–122.
42. Kevorkian was acquitted in Wayne County, Michigan on May 2, 1993, on charges of violating a temporary state law banning assisted suicide in the suicide of Thomas Hyde; he was acquitted on March 8, 1996, of statutory assisted suicide charged in the cases of Merian Frederick and Ali Khalili in Oakland County Circuit Court; and he was acquitted on May 14, 1996, in Oakland County Circuit Court of charges of violating a common law crime of assisted suicide in cases involving the suicides of Marjorie Wantz and Sherri Miller. Earlier, charges of murder were dismissed by the judge in the cases of Ms. Wantz and Ms. Miller.
43. Judith S. Kaye, "It Is Time to Reform the Jury System," *New York Law Journal,* Jan. 25, 1995, p. S1.
44. G. Thomas Munsterman, "A Brief History of State Jury Reform Efforts," *Judicature* 79(5):216–19 (Mar.-Apr. 1996).
45. *Ibid.*
46. James Levine, "The Impact of Sequestration on Juries," *Judicature* 79(5):266–72 (Mar.-Apr. 1996).
47. Adler, *The Jury,* pp. 218–21.
48. Nancy J. King and G. Thomas Munsterman, "Stratified Jury Selection: A Cross-section By Design," *Judicature* 79(5): 273–78 (Mar.-Apr. 1996); Albert Alschuler, "Would Color-Conscious Jury Selection Help—Yes: A Racially Diverse Jury Is More Likely to Do Justice," *ABA Journal*, p. 36 (Dec. 1995); Randall L. Kennedy, "Would Color-Conscious Jury Selection Help—No: Drawing Racial Lines Has a Toxic Effect on Society," *ABA Journal,* p. 37 (Dec. 1995).
49. Adler, *The Jury,* p. 224.
50. Adler, *The Jury,* pp. 224–40; B. Michael Dann and George Logan III, "Jury Reform: The Arizona Experience," *Judicature* 79(5):280–86 (Mar.-Apr. 1996).
51. Barbara Allen Babcock, "In Defense of the Criminal Jury," pp. 160–67, in Jeffrey Abramson, ed., *Postmortem: The O. J. Simpson Case—Justice Confronts Race, Domestic Violence, Lawyers, Money, and the Media* (New York: BasicBooks, 1996), pp. 163–64.
52. Akhil Reed Amar and Vikram David Amar, "Unlocking the Jury Box," *Policy Review,* pp. 38–44 (May-June 1996).
53. Abramson, *We, the Jury*, p. 205.
54. Paul Reidinger, Book Review of Norman J. Finkel, *Commonsense Justice: Jurors' Notions of the Law* (Cambridge, Mass.: Harvard University Press, 1995) in *ABA Journal,* p. 100 (Nov. 1995).
55. Samuel Walker, *Popular Justice: A History of American Criminal Justice* (New York: Oxford University Press, 1980).

Selected Provisions of the Constitution of the United States

We the People of the United States, in Order to form a more perfect Union, establish Justice, insure domestic Tranquility, provide for the common defence, promote the general Welfare, and secure the Blessings of Liberty to ourselves and our Posterity, do ordain and establish this Constitution for the United States of America.

Article I

Section 1. All legislative Powers herein granted shall be vested in a Congress of the United States, which shall consist of a Senate and House of Representatives.

Section 2. The House of Representatives shall be composed of Members chosen every second Year by the People of the several States, and the Electors in each State shall have the Qualifications requisite for Electors of the most numerous Branch of the State Legislature.

No Person shall be a Representative who shall not have attained to the Age of twenty five Years, and been seven Years a Citizen of the United States, and who shall not, when elected, be an Inhabitant of that State in which he shall be chosen.

[Representatives and direct Taxes shall be apportioned among the several States which maybe included within this Union, according to their respective Numbers, which shall be determined by adding to the whole Number of free Persons, including those bound to Service for a Term of Years, and excluding Indians not taxed, three fifths of all other Persons.][1] The actual Enumeration shall be made within three Years after the first Meeting of the Congress of the United States, and within every subsequent Term of ten Years, in such Manner as they shall by Law direct. The number of Representatives shall not exceed one for every thirty Thousand, but each State shall have at Least one Representative; and until such enumeration shall be made, the State of New Hampshire shall be entitled to chuse three, Massachusetts eight, Rhode Island and Providence Plantations one, Connecticut five, New York six, New Jersey four, Pennsylvania eight, Delaware one, Maryland six, Virginia ten, North Carolina five, South Carolina five, and Georgia three.

When vacancies happen in the Representation from any State, the Executive Authority thereof shall issue Writs of Election to fill such Vacancies.

The House of Representatives shall chuse their Speaker and other Officers; and shall have the sole Power of Impeachment.

Section 3. The Senate of the United States shall be composed of two Senators from each State, [chosen by the Legislature thereof,][2] for six Years; and each Senator shall have one Vote.

Immediately after they shall be assembled in Consequence of the first Election, they shall be divided as equally as may be into three Classes. The Seats of the Senators of the first Class shall be vacated at the Expiration of the second Year, of the second Class at the Expiration of the fourth Year, and of the third Class at the Expiration of the sixth Year, so that one third may be chosen every second Year; [and if Vacancies happen by Resignation, or otherwise, during the Recess of the Legislature of any State, the Executive thereof may make temporary Appointments until the next Meeting of the Legislature, which shall then fill such Vacancies.][3]

No Person shall be a Senator who shall not have attained to the Age of thirty Years, and been nine Years a Citizen of the United States, and who shall not, when elected, be an Inhabitant of that State for which he shall be chosen.

The Vice President of the United States shall be President of the Senate, but shall have no Vote, unless they be equally divided.

The Senate shall chuse their other Officers, and also a President pro tempore, in the Absence of the Vice President, or when he shall exercise the Office of President of the United States.

The Senate shall have the sole Power to try all Impeachments. When sitting for that Purpose, they shall be on Oath or Affirmation. When the President of the United States is tried, the Chief Justice shall preside: And no Person shall be convicted without the Concurrence of two thirds of the Members present.

Judgment in Cases of Impeachment shall not extend further than to removal from Office, and disqualification to hold and enjoy any Office of honor, Trust or Profit under the United States: but the Party convicted shall nevertheless be liable and subject to Indictment, Trial, Judgment and Punishment, according to Law.

Section 4. The Times, Places and Manner of holding Elections for Senators and Representatives, shall be prescribed in each State by the Legislature thereof; but the Congress may at any time by Law make or alter such Regulations, except as to the Places of chusing Senators.

The Congress shall assemble at least once in every Year, and such Meeting shall be [on the first Monday in December,][4] unless they shall by Law appoint a different Day.

Section 5. Each House shall be the Judge of the Elections, Returns and Qualifications of its own Members, and a Majority of each shall constitute a Quorum to do Business; but a smaller Number may adjourn from day to day, and may be authorized to compel the Attendance of absent Members, in such Manner, and under such Penalties as each House may provide.

Each House may determine the Rules of its Proceedings, punish its Members for disorderly Behaviour, and, with the Concurrence of two thirds, expel a Member.

Each House shall keep a Journal of its Proceedings, and from time to time publish the same, excepting such Parts as may in their Judgment require Secrecy; and the Yeas and Nays of the Members of either House on any question shall, at the Desire of one fifth of those Present, be entered on the Journal.

Neither House, during the Session of Congress, shall, without the Consent of the other, adjourn for more than three days, nor to any other Place than that in which the two Houses shall be sitting.

Section 6. The Senators and Representatives shall receive a Compensation for their Services, to be ascertained by Law, and paid out of the Treasury of the United States. They shall in all Cases, except Treason, Felony and Breach of the Peace, be privileged from Arrest during their Attendance at the Session of their respective Houses, and in going to and returning from the same; and for any Speech or Debate in either House, they shall not be questioned in any other Place.

No Senator or Representative shall, during the Time for which he was elected, be appointed to any civil Office under the Authority of the United States, which shall have been created, or the Emoluments whereof shall have been encreased during such time; and no Person holding any Office under the United States, shall be a Member of either House during his Continuance in Office.

Section 7. All Bills for raising Revenue shall originate in the House of Representatives; but the Senate may propose or concur with Amendments as on other Bills.

Every Bill which shall have passed the House of Representatives and the Senate, shall, before it becomes a Law, be presented to the President of the United States; If he approve he shall sign it, but if not he shall return it, with his Objections to that House in which it shall have originated, who shall enter the Objections at large on their Journal, and proceed to reconsider it. If after such Reconsideration two thirds of that House shall agree to pass the Bill, it shall be sent, together with the Objections, to the other House, by which it shall likewise be reconsidered, and if approved by two thirds of that House, it shall become a Law. But in all such Cases the Votes of both Houses shall be determined by yeas and Nays, and the Names of the Persons voting for and against the Bill shall be entered on the Journal of each House respectively. If any Bill shall not be returned by the President within ten Days (Sundays excepted) after it shall have been presented to him, the Same shall be a Law, in like Manner as if he had signed it, unless the Congress by their Adjournment prevent its Return, in which Case it shall not be a Law.

Every Order, Resolution, or Vote to which the Concurrence of the Senate and House of Representatives may be necessary (except on a question of Adjournment) shall be presented to the President of the United States; and before the Same shall take Effect, shall be approved by him, or being disapproved by him, shall be repassed by two thirds of the Senate and House of Representatives, according to the Rules and Limitations prescribed in the Case of a Bill.

Section 8. The Congress shall have Power To lay and collect Taxes, Duties, Imposts and Excises, to pay the Debts and provide for the common Defence and general Welfare of the United States; but all Duties, Imposts and Excises shall be uniform throughout the United States;

• CONSTITUTION OF THE UNITED STATES •

To borrow Money on the credit of the United States;

To regulate Commerce with foreign Nations, and among the several States, and with the Indian Tribes;

To establish an uniform Rule of Naturalization, and uniform Laws on the subject of Bankruptcies throughout the United States;

To coin Money, regulate the Value thereof, and of foreign Coin, and fix the Standard of Weights and Measures;

To provide for the Punishment of counterfeiting the Securities and current Coin of the United States;

To establish Post Offices and post Roads;

To promote the Progress of Science and useful Arts, by securing for limited Times to Authors and Inventors the exclusive Right to their respective Writings and Discoveries;

To constitute Tribunals inferior to the supreme Court;

To define and punish Piracies and Felonies committed on the high Seas, and Offenses against the Law of Nations;

To declare War, grant Letters of Marque and Reprisal, and make Rules concerning Captures on Land and Water;

To raise and support Armies, but no Appropriation of Money to that Use shall be for a longer Term than two Years;

To provide and maintain a Navy;

To make Rules for the Government and Regulation of the land and naval Forces;

To provide for calling forth the Militia to execute the Laws of the Union, suppress Insurrections and repel Invasions;

To provide for organizing, arming, and disciplining, the Militia, and for governing such Part of them as may be employed in the Service of the United States, reserving to the States respectively, the Appointment of the Officers, and the Authority of training the Militia according to the discipline prescribed by Congress;

To exercise exclusive Legislation in all Cases whatsoever, over such District (not exceeding ten Miles square) as may, by Cession of particular States, and the Acceptance of Congress, become the Seat of the Government of the United States, and to exercise like Authority over an Places purchased by the Consent of the Legislature of the State in which the Same shall be, for the Erection of Forts, Magazines, Arsenals, dock-Yards and other needful Buildings;—And

To make all Laws which shall be necessary and proper for carrying into Execution the foregoing Powers, and all other Powers vested by this Constitution in the Government of the United States or in any Department or Officer thereof.

Section 9. The Migration or Importation of such Persons as any of the States now existing shall think proper to admit, shall not be prohibited by the Congress prior to the Year one thousand eight hundred and eight, but a Tax or duty may be imposed on such Importation, not exceeding ten dollars for each Person.

The Privilege of the Writ of Habeas Corpus shall not be suspended, unless when in Cases of Rebellion or Invasion the public Safety may require it.

No Bill of Attainder or ex post facto Law shall be passed.

No Capitation, or other direct, Tax shall be laid, unless in Proportion to the Census or Enumeration herein before directed to be taken.[5]

No Tax or Duty shall be laid on Articles exported from any State.

No Preference shall be given by any Regulation of Commerce or Revenue to the Ports of one State over those of another: nor shall Vessels bound to, or from, one State, be obliged to enter, clear, or pay Duties in another.

No Money shall be drawn from the Treasury, but in Consequence of Appropriations made by Law, and a regular Statement and Account of the Receipts and Expenditures of all public Money shall be published from time to time.

No Title of Nobility shall be granted by the United States: And no Person holding any Office of

Profit or Trust under them, shall, without the Consent of the Congress, accept of any present, Emolument, Office, or Title, of any kind whatever, from any King, Prince, or foreign State.

Section 10. No State shall enter into any Treaty, Alliance, or Confederation; grant Letters of Marque and Reprisal; coin Money; emit Bills of Credit; make any Thing but gold and silver Coin a Tender in Payment of Debts; pass any Bill of Attainder, ex post facto Law, or Law impairing the Obligation of Contracts, or grant any Title of Nobility.

No State shall, without the Consent of the Congress, lay any Imposts or Duties on Imports or Exports, except what may be absolutely necessary for executing it's inspection Laws: and the net Produce of all Duties and Imposts, laid by any State on Imports or Exports, shall be for the Use of the Treasury of the United States; and all such Laws shall be subject to the Revision and Controul of the Congress.

No State shall, without the Consent of Congress, lay any Duty of Tonnage, keep Troops, or Ships of War in time of Peace, enter into any Agreement or Compact with another State, or with a foreign Power, or engage in War, unless actually invaded, or in such imminent Danger as will not admit of delay.

Article II

Section 1. The executive Power shall be vested in a President of the United States of America. He shall hold his Office during the Term of four Years, and, together with the Vice President, chosen for the same Term, be elected, as follows

Each State shall appoint, in such Manner as the Legislature thereof may direct, a Number of Electors, equal to the whole Number of Senators and Representatives to which the State may be entitled in the Congress: but no Senator or Representative, or Person holding an Office of Trust or Profit under the United States, shall be appointed an Elector.

[Sections on electoral college and amendments omitted.]

The Congress may determine the Time of chusing the Electors, and the Day on which they shall give their Votes; which Day shall be the same throughout the United States. No Person except a natural born Citizen, or a Citizen of the United States, at the time of the Adoption of this Constitution, shall be eligible to the Office of President; neither shall any person be eligible to that Office who shall not have attained to the Age of thirty five Years, and been fourteen Years a Resident within the United States.

[In Case of the Removal of the President from Office, or of his Death, Resignation, or Inability to discharge the Powers and Duties of the said Office, the Same shall devolve on the Vice President, and the Congress may by Law provide for the Case of Removal, Death, Resignation or Inability, both of the President and Vice President, declaring what Officer shall then act as President, and such Officer shall act accordingly, until the Disability be removed, or a President shall be elected.][6]

The President shall, at stated Times, receive for his Services, a Compensation, which shall neither be increased nor diminished during the Period for which he shall have been elected, and he shall not receive within that Period any other Emolument from the United States, or any of them.

Before he enter on the Execution of his Office, he shall take the following Oath or Affirmation:—"I do solemnly swear (or affirm) that I will faithfully execute the Office of President of the United States, and will to the best of my Ability, preserve, protect and defend the Constitution of the United States."

Section 2. The President shall be Commander in Chief of the Army and Navy of the United States, and of the Militia of the several States, when called into the actual Service of the United States; he may require the Opinion, in writing, of the principal Officer in each of the executive Departments, upon any Subject relating to the Duties of their respective Offices, and he shall have Power to grant Reprieves and Pardons for Offenses against the United States, except in Cases of Impeachment.

He shall have Power, by and with the Advice and Consent of the Senate, to make Treaties, provided two thirds of the Senators present concur; and he shall nominate, and by and with the Advice and Consent of the Senate, shall appoint Ambassadors, other public Ministers and Consuls, Judges of the supreme Court, and all other Officers of the United States, whose Appointments are not herein otherwise provided for, and which shall be established by Law: but the Congress may by Law vest the Appointment of such inferior Officers, as they think proper, in the President alone, in the Courts of Law, or in the Heads of Departments.

The President shall have Power to fill up all Vacancies that may happen during the Recess of the Senate, by granting Commissions which shall expire at the End of their next Session.

Section 3. He shall from time to time give to the Congress Information of the State of the Union, and recommend to their Consideration such Measures as he shall judge necessary and expedient; he may, on extraordinary Occasions, convene both Houses, or either of them, and in Case of Disagreement between them, with Respect to the Time of Adjoumment, he may adjourn them to such Time as he shall think proper; he shall receive Ambassadors and other public Ministers; he shall take Care that the Laws be faithfully executed, and shall Commission all the Officers of the United States.

Section 4. The President, Vice President and all civil Officers of the United States, shall be removed from Office on Impeachment for, and Conviction of, Treason, Bribery, or other high Crimes and Misdemeanors.

Article III

Section 1. The judicial Power of the United States, shall be vested in one supreme Court, and in such inferior Courts as the Congress may from time to time ordain and establish. The Judges, both of the supreme and inferior Courts, shall hold their Offices during good Behaviour, and shall, at stated Times, receive for their Services, a Compensation, which shall not be diminished during their Continuance in Office.

Section 2. The judicial Power shall extend to all Cases, in Law and Equity, arising under this Constitution, the Laws of the United States, and Treaties made, or which shall be made, under their Authority;—to all Cases affecting Ambassadors, other public Ministers and Consuls;—to all Cases of admiralty and maritime Jurisdiction;—to Controversies to which the United States shall be a Party;—to Controversies between two or more States;—[between a State and Citizens of another State;—] between Citizens of different States,—between Citizens of the same State claiming Lands under Grants of different States, [and between a State, or the Citizens thereof, and foreign States, Citizens or Subjects.][7]

In all Cases affecting Ambassadors, other public Ministers and Consuls, and those in which a State shall be Party, the supreme Court shall have original Jurisdiction. In all the other Cases before mentioned, the supreme Court shall have appellate Jurisdiction, both as to Law and Fact, with such Exceptions, and under such Regulations as the Congress shall make.

The Trial of all Crimes, except in Cases of Impeachment; shall be by Jury; and such Trial shall be held in the State where the said Crimes shall have been committed; but when not committed within any State, the Trial shall be at such Place or Places as the Congress may by Law have directed.

Section 3. Treason against the United States, shall consist only in levying War against them, or in adhering to their Enemies, giving them Aid and Comfort. No Person shall be convicted of Treason unless on the Testimony of two Witnesses to the same overt Act, or on Confession in open Court.

The Congress shall have Power to declare the Punishment of Treason, but no Attainder of Treason shall work Corruption of Blood, or Forfeiture except during the Life of the Person attainted.

Article IV

Section 1. Full Faith and Credit shall be given in each State to the public Acts, Records, and judicial Proceedings of every other State; And the Congress may by general Laws prescribe the Manner in which such Acts, Records and Proceedings shall be proved, and the Effect thereof.

Section 2. The Citizens of each State shall be entitled to all Privileges and Immunities of Citizens in the several States.

• CONSTITUTION OF THE UNITED STATES •

A Person charged in any State with Treason, Felony, or other Crime, who shall flee from Justice, and be found in another State, shall on Demand of the executive Authority of the State from which he fled, be delivered up, to be removed to the State having Jurisdiction of the Crime.

[No Person held to Service or Labour in one State, under the Laws thereof, escaping into another, shall, in Consequence of any Law or Regulation therein, be discharged from such Service or Labour, but shall be delivered up on Claim of the Party to whom such Service or Labour may be due.][8]

Section 3. New States may be admitted by the Congress into this Union; but no new State shall be formed or erected within the Jurisdiction of any other State; nor any State be formed by the Junction of two or more States, or Parts of States, without the Consent of the Legislatures of the States concerned as well as of the Congress.

The Congress shall have Power to dispose of and make all needful Rules and Regulations respecting the Territory or other Property belonging to the United States; and nothing in this Constitution shall be so construed as to Prejudice any Claims of the United States, or of any particular State.

Section 4. The United States shall guarantee to every State in this Union a Republican Form of Government, and shall protect each of them against Invasion; and on Application of the Legislature, or of the Executive (when the Legislature cannot be convened) against domestic Violence.

Article V

The Congress, whenever two thirds of both Houses shall deem it necessary, shall propose Amendments to this Constitution, or, on the Application of the Legislatures of two thirds of the several States, shall call a Convention for proposing Amendments, which, in either Case, shall be valid to all Intents and Purposes, as Part of this Constitution, when ratified by the Legislatures of three fourths of the several States, or by Conventions in three fourths thereof, as the one or the other Mode of Ratification may be proposed by the Congress; Provided that no Amendment which may be made prior to the Year One thousand eight hundred and eight shall in any Manner affect the first and fourth Clauses in the Ninth Section of the first Article; and that no State, without its Consent, shall be deprived of it's equal Suffrage in the Senate.

Article VI

All Debts contracted and Engagements entered into, before the Adoption of this Constitution, shall be as valid against the United States under this Constitution, as under the Confederation.

This Constitution, and the Laws of the United States which shall be made in Pursuance thereof; and all Treaties made, or which shall be made, under the Authority of the United States, shall be the supreme Law of the Land; and the Judges in every State shall be bound thereby, any Thing in the Constitution or Laws of any State to the Contrary notwithstanding.

The Senators and Representatives before mentioned, and the Members of the several State Legislatures and all executive and judicial Officers, both of the United States and of the several States, shall be bound by Oath or Affirmation, to support this Constitution; but no religious Test shall ever be required as a Qualification to any Office or public Trust under the United States.

Article VII

The Ratification of the Conventions of nine States, shall be sufficient for the Establishment of this Constitution between the States so ratifying the Same.

Done in Convention by the Unanimous Consent of the States present the Seventeenth Day of September in the Year of our Lord one thousand seven hundred and Eighty seven and of the Independence of the United States of America the Twelfth In Witness whereof We have hereunto subscribed our Names, [signers omitted].

• CONSTITUTION OF THE UNITED STATES •

Amendments To The Constitution of The United States of America

Amendment I[9]

Congress shall make no law respecting an establishment of religion, or prohibiting the free exercise thereof; or abridging the freedom of speech, or of the press, or the right of the people peaceably to assemble, and to petition the Government for a redress of grievances.

Amendment II

A well regulated Militia, being necessary to the security of a free State, the right of the people to keep and bear Arms, shall not be infringed.

Amendment III

No Soldier shall, in time of peace be quartered in any house, without the consent of the Owner, nor in time of war, but in a manner to be prescribed by law.

Amendment IV

The right of the people to be secure in their persons, houses, papers, and effects, against unreasonable searches and seizures, shall not be violated, and no Warrants shall issue, but upon probable cause, supported by Oath or affirmation, and particularly describing the place to be searched, and the persons or things to be seized.

Amendment V

No person shall be held to answer for a capital, or otherwise infamous crime, unless on a presentment or indictment of a Grand Jury, except in cases arising in the land or naval forces, or in the Militia, when in actual service in time of War or public danger; nor shall any person be subject for the same offence to be twice put in jeopardy of life or limb, nor shall be compelled in any criminal case to be a witness against himself, nor be deprived of life, liberty, or property, without due process of law; nor shall private property be taken for public use without just compensation.

Amendment VI

In all criminal prosecutions, the accused shall enjoy the right to a speedy and public trial, by an impartial jury of the State and district wherein the crime shall have been committed; which district shall have been previously ascertained by law, and to be informed of the nature and cause of the accusation; to be confronted with the witnesses against him; to have compulsory process for obtaining witnesses in his favor, and to have the assistance of counsel for his defence.

Amendment VII

In Suits at common law, where the value in controversy shall exceed twenty dollars, the right of trial by jury shall be preserved, and no fact tried by a jury shall be otherwise reexamined in any Court of the United States, than according to the rules of the common law.

Amendment VIII

Excessive bail shall not be required, nor excessive fines imposed, nor cruel and unusual punishments inflicted.

Amendment IX

The enumeration in the Constitution of certain rights shall not be construed to deny or disparage others retained by the people.

Amendment X

The powers not delegated to the United States by the Constitution, nor prohibited by it to the States, are reserved to the States respectively, or to the people.

Amendment XI[10]

The Judicial power of the United States shall not be construed to extend to any suit in law or equity, commenced or prosecuted against one of the United States by Citizens of another State, or by Citizens or Subjects of any Foreign State.

Amendment XII

[Amends procedures for selection of the President, superseded in part by the 20th Amendment]

Amendment XIII[11]

Section 1. Neither slavery nor involuntary servitude, except as a punishment for crime whereof the party shall have been duly convicted, shall exist within the United States, or any place subject to their jurisdiction.

Section 2. Congress shall have power to enforce this article by appropriate legislation.

Amendment XIV[12]

Section 1. All persons born or naturalized in the United States and subject to the jurisdiction thereof, are citizens of the United States and of the State wherein they reside. No State shall make or enforce any law which shall abridge the privileges or immunities of citizens of the United States; nor shall any State deprive any person of life, liberty, or property, without due process of law; nor deny to any person within its jurisdiction the equal protection of the laws.

Section 2. Representatives shall be apportioned among the several States according to their respective numbers, counting the whole number of persons in each State, excluding Indians not taxed. But when the right to vote at any election for the choice of electors for President and Vice President of the United States, Representatives in Congress, the Executive and Judicial officers of a State, or the members of the Legislature thereof, is denied to any of the male inhabitants of such State, being twenty-one years of age, and citizens of the United States, or in any way abridged, except for participation in rebellion, or other crime, the basis of representation therein shall be reduced in the proportion which the number of such male citizens shall bear to the whole number of male citizens twenty-one years of age in such State.

Section 3. No person shall be a Senator or Representative in Congress, or elector of President and Vice President, or hold any office, civil or military, under the United States, or under any State, who, having previously taken an oath, as a member of Congress, or as an officer of the United States, or as a member of any State legislature, or as an executive or judicial officer of any State, to support the Constitution of the United States, shall have engaged in insurrection or rebellion against the same, or given aid or comfort to the enemies thereof. But Congress may by a vote of two-thirds of each House, remove such disability.

Section 4. The validity of the public debt of the United States, authorized by law, including debts incurred for payment of pensions and bounties for services in suppressing insurrection or rebellion, shall not be questioned. But neither the United States nor any State shall assume or pay any debt or obligation incurred in aid of insurrection or rebellion against the United States, or any claim for the loss or emancipation of any slave; but all such debts, obligations and claims shall be held illegal and void.

Section 5. The Congress shall have power to enforce, by appropriate legislation, the provisions of this article.

• CONSTITUTION OF THE UNITED STATES •

Amendment XV[13]

Section 1. The right of citizens of the United States to vote shall not be denied or abridged by the United States or by any State on account of race, color, or previous condition of servitude.

Section 2. The Congress shall have power to enforce this article by appropriate legislation.

[Amendments 16 to 27 omitted]

NOTES

1. Changed by section 2 of the Fourteenth Amendment.
2. Changed by the Seventeenth Amendment to allow popular election of Senators.
3. Changed by the Seventeenth Amendment.
4. Changed by section 2 of the Twentieth Amendment.
5. Sixteenth Amendment to allow for an income tax.
6. Changed by the Twenty-Fifth Amendment.
7. Changed by the Eleventh Amendment to prohibit suits against state governments without their consent.
8. Changed by the Thirteenth Amendment.
9. The first ten Amendments (Bill of Rights) were ratified effective December 15, 1791.
10. The Eleventh Amendment was ratified February 7, 1795.
11. The Thirteenth Amendment was ratified December 6, 1865.
12. The Fourteenth Amendment was ratified July 9, 1868.
13. The Fifteenth Amendment was ratified February 3, 1870.

SUMMARY INFORMATION ABOUT SELECTED SUPREME COURT JUSTICES

JUSTICE	PRESIDENT APPOINTING	YEARS OF SERVICE	POLITICAL PARTY	POSITIONS AND NOTED ACTION IN CRIMINAL PROCEDURE
John M. Harlan (I)	Hayes	1877–1911	Rep.	Championed total incorporation of Bill of Rights to apply to the states.
Oliver W. Holmes	Roosevelt, T.	1902–1932	Rep.	*Moore v. Dempsey* - apply due process to state errors; *Olmstead* dissent.
Louis Brandeis	Wilson	1916–1939	Rep.	*Olmstead* dissent - classic statement of Rule of Law.
William H. Taft, CJ	Harding	1921–1930	Rep.	Conservative. *Olmstead:* wiretapping not covered by Fourth Amendment.
George Sutherland	Harding	1922–1938	Rep.	*Powell v. Alabama:* Scottsboro case: due process violated by lack of counsel.
Harlan Fiske Stone	Coolidge	1925–1941	Rep.	Moderate. *Carolene Products* (1938) footnote 4 pointed to a civil rights agenda.
Edward Sanford	Harding	1923–1930	Rep.	Wrote opinions incorporating First Amendment rights, advanced incorporation.
Benjamin Cardozo	Hoover	1932–1938	Dem.	Blocked advance of incorporation in *Palko* (1937).
Hugo Black	Roosevelt, F.	1937–1971	Dem.	Championed incorporation; dissent in *Adamson;* right to counsel - *Gideon.*
Stanley Reed	Roosevelt, F.	1938–1957	Dem.	Opposed incorporation; majority opinion in *Adamson*
Felix Frankfurter	Roosevelt, F.	1939–1962	Ind.	Conservative-moderate. Opposed incorporation; favored due process approach.
William Douglas	Roosevelt, F.	1939–1975	Dem.	Liberal. Favored incorporation.
Frank Murphy	Roosevelt, F.	1940–1949	Dem.	Liberal. Favored incorporation.
Harlan Fiske Stone, CJ	Roosevelt, F.	1941–1946	Rep.	Moderate-liberal. Championed freedom of belief in flag-salute cases.
Robert Jackson	Roosevelt, F.	1941–1954	Dem.	New deal liberal. Close to Frankfurter in criminal procedure.
Wiley Rutledge	Roosevelt, F.	1943–1949	Dem.	Liberal. Favored incorporation. Classic definition of probable cause in *Brinegar* (1949).
Harold Burton	Truman	1945–1958	Rep.	Stalwart Conservative.
Fred Vinson, CJ	Truman	1946–1953	Dem.	Stalwart Conservative.
Tom Clark	Truman	1949–1967	Dem.	Conservative-moderate. Wrote majority in *Mapp v. Ohio* (1961).
Sherman Minton	Truman	1949–1956	Dem.	Stalwart Conservative.
Earl Warren, CJ	Eisenhower	1953–1969	Rep.	Liberal. Authored *Miranda, Terry.*
John Harlan (II)	Eisenhower	1954–1971	Rep.	Conservative-moderate. Opposed incorporation.
William Brennan	Eisenhower	1956–1990	Dem.	Liberal. Active writing liberal dissents in Burger & Rehnquist Court eras.

SUMMARY INFORMATION ABOUT SELECTED SUPREME COURT JUSTICES

JUSTICE	PRESIDENT APPOINTING	YEARS OF SERVICE	POLITICAL PARTY	NOTED ACTION IN CRIMINAL PROCEDURE
Charles Whittaker	Eisenhower	1957–1962	Rep.	Stalwart Conservative.
Potter Stewart	Eisenhower	1958–1981	Rep.	Moderate-conservative. Wrote many criminal procedure opinions.
Byron White	Kennedy	1962–1993	Dem.	Mixed. Wrote many criminal procedure opinions.
Arthur Goldberg	Kennedy	1962–1965	Dem.	Liberal. Opinion in *U.S. v. Ventresca* (1965) - preference for search warrant.
Abe Fortas	Johnson, L.	1965–1969	Dem.	Liberal. Major opinions for juvenile rights: *In re Gault* (1967).
Thurgood Marshall	Johnson, L.	1967–1991	Dem.	Liberal. Active writing liberal dissents in Burger & Rehnquist Court eras.
Warren Burger, CJ	Nixon	1969–1986	Rep.	Conservative. Initially opposed the exclusionary rule.
Harry Blackmun	Nixon	1970–1994	Rep.	Changed from conservative to liberal over time.
Lewis Powell	Nixon	1972–1987	Dem.	Conservative. Opinions limited access to courts on 4th Amend. Issues.
William Rehnquist	Nixon	1972–1986	Rep.	Conservative. Wrote many criminal procedure opinions.
John Paul Stevens	Ford	1975–	Rep.	Moderate. Has swung to liberal in criminal procedure.
Sandra Day O'Connor	Reagan	1981–	Rep.	Conservative. Can join moderate, pro-defendant decisions.
Antonin Scalia	Reagan	1986–	Rep.	Conservative. Originalist. Favors defendant regarding Confrontation Clause.
William Rehnquist, CJ	Reagan	1986–	Rep.	Conservative. Continues to write many criminal procedure opinions.
Anthony Kennedy	Reagan	1988–	Rep.	Conservative. Can join moderate, pro-defendant decisions.
William Souter	Bush	1990–	Rep.	Moderate-conservative. Appears to be moving to more liberal position.
Clarence Thomas	Bush	1991–	Rep.	Conservative. Originalist.
Ruth Bader Ginsburg	Clinton	1993–	Dem.	Moderate-liberal.
Steven Breyer	Clinton	1994–	Dem.	Moderate-liberal. Takes conservative position in some cases.

Glossary

Abuse of discretion A high standard for an appellate court to reverse the decision of a lower court where the trial court was lawfully invested with discretion. It does not imply an intentional wrong or bad faith, but the exercise of discretion was clearly against logic.

Accusatorial trial system The Anglo-American or common-law system of adjudication. Its key elements include: judge is an impartial referee; lawyers control the presentation of evidence; witnesses are cross-examined; innocence is presumed; prosecutor must prove guilt beyond a reasonable doubt; privilege against self-incrimination protects the defendant from testifying; facts conclusively determined by a citizen jury.

Actual border For purposes of border search cases, stops that are made at or very near to the actual border between the United States and a neighboring nation; border searches may also take place further inland either at fixed checkpoints or by roving patrols.

Actual mobility The automobile exception to the search warrant requirement applies to vehicles that are actually capable of being driven.

Actual imprisonment rule Counsel is an absolute Sixth Amendment requirement for the trial of a misdemeanor only if the defendant has been actually imprisoned after conviction.

Adequate and independent state grounds A state court ruling concerning the rights of a suspect that is based exclusively on state constitutional grounds cannot be disturbed by a federal court as long as the state constitutional ruling does not fall below the minimum standards of the Fourteenth Amendment Due Process Clause. To determine if a state ruling is based on state or federal grounds, where the ruling discussed both federal and state law, the Supreme Court examines it to determine if the holding is based on adequate and independent state grounds. See *judicial federalism.*

Ad hoc "For this"; for a special purpose without application to a general purpose; for example, an *ad hoc* rule is intended to apply to only the particular circumstances at hand and is not intended to be a general rule.

Adjudicate To judge a case; to resolve an issue in the exercise of judicial authority.

Administrative search The entry and search of premises by a governmental officer who is enforcing a governmental regulation regarding public health or safety, rather than a police search for persons or items in relation to the enforcement of the criminal law.

Admission Statements made by a party that acknowledge the existence of certain facts. See *confession.*

Adversary or Adversarial [trial] system Same as *accusatorial [trial] system.*

Adverse comment A comment by the judge or prosecutor to a jury in a criminal case, pointing out that the defendant did not take the witness stand.

Advisory opinion An opinion issued by a court at the request of the government or a party indicating how it would rule on an issue were it to arise in litigation. Some state supreme courts issue advisory opinions. The United States Supreme Court does not issue such opinions because its jurisdiction is limited in Article III, section 2, of the Constitution to various "cases and controversies."

Affiant The person who makes and subscribes an affidavit.

Affidavit A written declaration or statement of facts made voluntarily and confirmed by oath before a person with the authority to take such an oath.

Affirm An appellate court that upholds the ruling of a lower court is said to affirm the ruling.

Anticipatory warrants Search warrants authorized by the Federal Rules of Criminal Procedure that may be issued on probable cause that evidence will be located in a particular place on the date of execution. See *controlled delivery.*

Antifederalists Those opposed to the ratification of the Constitution in 1788 on the grounds that it created too much central power.

Appearance bond See *bail bond.*

Appellate decision The outcome of an appellate court; an appellate court may affirm, modify, reverse, and/or remand the decisions of the lower court.

Appellate opinion An opinion is the explanatory essay written by an appellate judge explaining the decision.

Appointed counsel A lawyer for an indigent defendant may be appointed by the court on an informal basis, through organized lists established by a local bar association, or by the court; the lawyer is paid by the county according to a fee schedule for work performed. Same as *assigned counsel.*

Arraignment The procedure whereby a defendant is brought before a court to plead to a criminal charge.

Arrest To deprive a person of liberty by legal authority; an arrest occurs in law when a person is taken into custody by government officers, even if the purpose is for investigation or harassment. It is not necessary for a booking to occur for an arrest to be made. An arrest may be made with or without a warrant.

Arrest warrant Judicial warrant concluding that probable cause exists supporting the belief that a crime has been committed and that the named person has committed it, and authorizing law enforcement to take the suspect into custody; the warrant is required, except for an exigency, if officers must enter the home of the person to be arrested.

Asset forfeiture Laws that authorize the forfeiture of non-contraband assets used in and moneys derived from the commission of certain crimes. The assets may be seized as of the time the crime was committed and thus be denied to lawyers representing defendants whose assets are forfeited.

Assigned counsel See *appointed counsel.*

Assize A name for general trial courts in England and France.

Attenuation rule An exception to the "fruit-of-the-poisonous-tree doctrine." It comes into play when the link between the initial illegality and the evidence sought to be introduced has become so weak or tenuous that the "fruit" has become "untainted."

Authorized imprisonment rule A position that counsel should be absolutely guaranteed by the Sixth Amendment in all misdemeanor trials where the statutory penalty allows for imprisonment; this rule was rejected by the Supreme Court.

Automobile search An exception to the requirement that a search of an effect be authorized in advance by a judicial search warrant, based on the exigency of a mobile vehicle and on the lower expectation of privacy accorded to automobiles, as long as the officer has probable cause to believe there is contraband in the automobile. Also known as the vehicle exception.

Bail To procure the release of a person charged with a crime by ensuring his or her further attendance in court; this is done by having the person pledge or deposit something of value that will be returned when he or she appears in court and/or by having a third party agree to be responsible for the return of the person.

Bail bond A bond (an "instrument" or writing promising to pay money) that is executed by a third party promising to forfeit money to the court if the defendant who is released on bail does not appear for further criminal proceedings; also known as an "appearance bond."

Bail bondsman A business person who receives a portion of the bail amount from a defendant, usually ten percent, and posts a bail bond with the court promising to pay the full bail amount if the defendant does not show; is responsible for ensuring the appearance of the defendant in court.

Balancing of interests See *balancing test.*

Balancing test A widely used phrase in criminal procedure, especially in Fourth Amendment adjudication, referring to appellate courts attempting to balance the needs of effective law enforcement against the privacy rights of individuals.

Bench In law, a term for the court or the judge. For an appellate court, the bench consists of all the judges on the court or who are sitting on a panel of the court.

Bench trial A trial without a jury; the judge (who sits on the "bench") is the trier of both the facts and the law. In a jury trial the judge is the finder only of legal issues and the jury finds the facts. See *waiver trial.*

Beeper An electronic device that emits a signal indicating its location; it may be used by agents to track the movement of a vehicle or object.

Bill of attainder A special act of a legislature passing the death penalty or other penalty on a person without recourse to standard judicial proceedings; in England, attainder led to the entire estate of a person convicted of a felony or treason being forfeited to the crown. The United States Constitution (Art. I, secs. 9 and 10) forbids the federal government and the states from passing bills of attainder.

Bill of particulars A form of discovery in which the prosecution sets forth the time, place, manner, and means of the commission of the crime as alleged in the complaint or indictment.

Bill of Rights A designation for the first ten amendments to the United States Constitution.

Bind-over decision The decision of the judge, at the conclusion of the preliminary examination, as to whether there is sufficient evidence to establish probable cause that the defendant committed the crime and "bind the defendant over," that is, require him or her to go to trial.

***Bivens* suit** A federal tort suit by a person against federal officers alleged to have violated the person's Fourth Amendment rights; created in *Bivens v. Six Unknown Agents* (1971).

Body cavity search Procedure whereby authorized law enforcement or correctional personnel conduct a visual inspection of oral, genital, or anal areas for contraband. Also called *strip search.*

Booking An administrative process conducted by police officials that typically follows an arrest and includes the taking of the suspect's name and identifying information, photographing, fingerprinting, searching, and inventorying of personal property.

Border The international boundary of a nation; for purposes of law, immigration, and customs searches, the border includes international airports, inland ports, and fixed checkpoints remote from the actual boundary.

Border search A search at the national border by immigration officers for illegal immigrants and by customs officers for contraband, criminals, fugitives, and terrorists.

Brevity requirement Rule under *Terry v. Ohio* (1968) that a "stop and frisk" be concluded quickly, or in just enough time for an officer to confirm or dispel whether the officer's reasonable suspicion constitutes probable cause; strictly interpreted by the Supreme Court.

Brief A brief is a written argument presented to a trial or appellate court by a lawyer to support the attorney's position on legal issues.

Briefing a case This refers to notes taken by law students that abstract the essential points of an appellate opinion, especially the facts, legal issues, holding, and reasons for the holding.

Bright-line rule A clear-cut and easy-to-apply standard established by a court to distinguish legal categories.

Bug An electronic listening device that is placed surreptitiously to overhear conversations.

Burger Court The Supreme Court during the period that Warren Burger was Chief Justice of the United States, (1969 to 1986).

Capital crime In common law, a crime punishable with death; today, in some states, it includes crimes punishable with life imprisonment. Under the laws of some states, bail may be denied to persons charged with capital crimes.

Case of first impression A law case in which the issue to be decided has never been resolved by an appellate court.

Case law See *common law.*

Caveat A warning to be careful.

Certiorari A writ used by the United States Supreme Court to determine in its discretion which filed cases it will hear and decide.

Challenge for cause In the *voir dire,* the ability of one of the sides to request the judge to dismiss a prospective juror because the juror has indicated a bias; the number of challenges for cause are unlimited.

Chancery English court established under the king's chancellor to do equity or to decide cases according to rules of justice rather than under formal writs of common-law courts of Common Pleas and King's Bench. Over time, chancery courts became part of the common-law court system. Common-law courts render money judgments as legal remedies whereas equity or chancery courts grant "equitable relief," i.e., orders requiring that a party perform or cease some activity. Most American states merged courts of law and equity; a few still have separate chancery or equity courts. See *equity.*

Charging The process by which the prosecutor decides which offenses to formally prefer or "charge" against a suspect, either in a prosecutor's information or an indictment.

Checks and balances A political and constitutional doctrine for maintaining balanced government by giving different branches of government the power to limit the authority of other branches in specified ways; closely related to the separation of powers doctrine.

Citizen's arrest An arrest made by a person who is not a law enforcement officer; if the arrest is in error (i.e., no crime was committed or the wrong person was arrested), the citizen who made the arrest is subject to a civil suit for false arrest even if probable cause existed.

Civil law system The legal system of the nations of Europe, Latin America, Africa, and Asia (except for England and former British colonies) that is found primarily in codes; civil-law trials follow the inquisitorial model; it is contrasted to the common-law system.

Civil rights function Criminal-procedure law has two broad functions: to facilitate prosecution and, simultaneously, to protect the civil rights of suspects and defendants.

Civil War amendments The Thirteenth, Fourteenth and Fifteenth amendments, ratified in 1866, 1868, and 1870 respectively. Also called the *Reconstruction amendments.*

Collateral proceeding Not a direct appeal from a conviction on a point of law, but instead a second "appeal," not of right; habeas corpus proceedings are collateral proceedings.

Common law In England, America, and other common-law countries, law is created by judges, mostly by "appellate courts," in written essays called "opinions," which the judges issue to explain their decision of the legal issues. Also called *case law* or *precedent* (because the rule established in one case becomes a binding precedent on later courts). The term arose because the law created by royal judges was common to all of England.

Common-law trial system Same as *accusatorial system.*

Companion case A case decided along with another case. *Sibron v. New York* (1967) and *Peters v. New York* (1967) were companion cases to *Terry v. Ohio* (1967). Companion cases may be consolidated into one case; *Miranda v. Arizona* (1966) also decided the companion cases of *Vignera v. New York* (1996), *Westover v. United States* (1966), and *California v. Stewart* (1966).

Compulsion A person is protected by the Fifth Amendment against being "compelled in any criminal case to be a witness against himself." The Fifth Amendment applies only if evidence is obtained by compulsion, as by a court order or grand jury subpoena. Fifth Amendment compulsion in law of confessions, under *Miranda,* supplied by in-custody police interrogation, which is inherently compelling. See *self-incrimination rule.*

Compulsory process A subpoena to produce witnesses or real evidence; a right guaranteed to defendants by the Sixth Amendment.

Confession A statement made by one person to another admitting guilt of an offense and disclosing facts about the crime and the suspect's role in it; may include inculpatory or exculpatory statements. See *admission.*

Conflict of interest In regard to the right to counsel, a conflict of interest most typically arises when, as a result of multiple representation, an attorney must sacrifice a defense technique for one defendant in order to better defend another defendant. See *multiple representation.*

Confrontation Clause The provision of the Sixth Amendment that in all criminal prosecutions, "the accused shall enjoy the right . . . to be confronted with the witnesses against him."

Consent The voluntary agreement of one person who has the capacity to make an agreement of free will to do an act proposed by another. In the administration of criminal justice, a suspect or defendant can consent to cooperate with police or prosecutors. See *waiver.*

Consent search A search made by a police officer after a person has given consent to the search; consent to search validates a warrantless search or a search made without probable cause.

Constitutionalism A political theory of balanced government; modern constitutionalism includes the concepts of civil rights and the rule of law.

Contempt of court An act which is calculated to embarrass, hinder, or obstruct a court in the administration of justice; may be punished by a judge with fine or imprisonment.

Continuance A delay in legal proceedings granted by the judge.

Contraband Any property that is illegal either to produce or possess, such as controlled substances or untaxed, smuggled goods.

Controlled delivery A law enforcement technique by which contraband is intercepted and then delivered to the suspected criminal party under police surveillance. "Anticipatory warrants" may be issued in cases where controlled deliveries are set up.

Counsel, right to This word is used interchangeably with "lawyer," "attorney," and "attorney-at-law."

Court of general jurisdiction A trial court with jurisdiction to try all matters, including felonies; typically called a superior or circuit court.

Court of limited jurisdiction A trial court whose jurisdiction is limited by statute to certain matters; usually to civil cases where the amount in dispute is below a certain amount (e.g., $10,000), to the dispositions of misdemeanors, and to conducting the preliminary phases of a felony case before binding over the case to a court of general jurisdiction for trial.

Covert facilitation Same as *encouragement.*

Crime Control Model A theory developed by Herbert Packer which suggests that within a constitutional system of criminal justice there are two general attitudes; the Crime Control Model stresses crime control, efficiency, a "presumption of guilt, and finality; See *Due Process Model.*

Crime scene investigation exception Supreme Court has refused to create Fourth Amendment exception to allow police, without warrant, to remain beyond the time of the exigency, on the premises where a crime has been committed, for purposes of conducting an investigation of the premises.

Criminal law approach In the law of entrapment, the majority rule, known also as the *subjective test.* Based on legal fiction that legislature did not intend statute to apply to persons who were not predisposed to commit the crime but were induced by police.

Critical stage The point in criminal proceedings when counsel is constitutionally required because, at that point, rights may be lost, defenses waived, or privileges claimed or waived that can affect the outcome of the case.

Cross-examination The examination of a witness at a trial or hearing by the party opposed to the side that produced the witness, after direct examination, to test the truth of the witness, to further develop the evidence, or for other purposes.

Cruel trilemma A witness who is asked a question that may prove to be incriminating faces three negative consequences: self-accusation, perjury, or the risk of being held in contempt of court for refusing to testify.

Curtilage Area protected by Fourth Amendment under eaves of the main house; various small structures that are near the main house, such as a garage, shed, or smokehouse, and the fenced-in area around a house. See *open fields.*

Custodial arrest When a police officer arrests a person for a crime which authorizes the officer to take the suspect into custody, the officer may perform a complete search incident to arrest.

Custody The keeping, guarding, care, watch, inspection, preservation or security of a thing or person. The custody of a person is a prerequisite for a Fourth Amendment seizure under *California v. Hodari D.* (1991).

Damages Monetary compensation awarded by a court in a civil case to compensate a party for losses.

Decoy In entrapment law and practice, an officer who poses as a potential victim (usually of a crime of violence such as street robbery) waiting to be attacked, in order to arrest a perpetrator.

Deficient performance The first prong of the rule that the ineffective assistance of counsel in a criminal trial violates the Sixth Amendment rights of the defendant. Deficient performance of an attorney is an objective standard determined by what constitutes reasonably effective assistance according to prevailing norms of legal practice.

Democracy A political philosophy that emphasizes the participation of all citizens in government decisions on an equal basis either directly or by representation; it is a value that underlies constitutional criminal procedure.

De novo review A rehearing of an issue that does not take into consideration findings made at an earlier hearing.

***De novo* trial (or trial *de novo*)** A second or new trial that is held as if no decision had been previously rendered. A trial *de novo* is not an appeal because the facts are relitigated.

Deposit bond A bail bond that is executed by the defendant; under the laws of several states, the defendant puts up ten percent of the bail amount, which is returned, except for a one percent fee, when the defendant returns to court for the trial.

Derivative evidence In the Fourth and Fifth amendment context, evidence that police obtain on the basis of illegally seized evidence; under the "fruit-of-the-poisonous-tree doctrine," such derivative evidence must be excluded from a trial to prove the guilt of a defendant.

Dictum An abbreviated form of *obiter dictum,* a "remark by the way," that is, a remark by a judge in a written opinion, commenting on the legal rule of the case, that is not essential to the determination of the holding or decision and, therefore, does not have weight as precedent.

Discovery A set of practices in both civil and criminal trial procedure that allows both sides to obtain factual evidence in the possession of the other side; it is designed to encourage settlements or prevent surprises at the trial so as to avoid delays.

Disgorgement The theory of jurisprudence that a person who has wrongfully obtained goods should be made to give them up.

Disseised To be dispossessed of one's land, in English medieval land law. See *novel disseisin.*

Diversity of citizenship jurisdiction Article III of the Constitution allows federal courts to hear cases between "citizens" of different states.

Domestic tranquillity A phrase in the Preamble to the Constitution of the United States; it recognizes that maintaining public safety is a fundamental purpose of government.

Dossier A bundle of papers (French); a report on an individual.

Drug courier profile A set of behavioral characteristics developed by the Drug Enforcement Agency (DEA) to determine whether a person fits the model of a person surreptitiously transporting illegal drugs; the profile itself, even if it consists entirely of innocent actions, constitutes a basis for finding that reasonable suspicion exists.

Due Process Clause The Fifth Amendment and the Fourteenth Amendment include such clauses, the first applying against the federal government and the second against state governments, saying that no person shall be deprived of life, liberty or property without due process of law.

Due process approach In constitutional criminal procedure, this term designates a philosophy on the part of Supreme Court justices that errors in state criminal procedure that constitutes grossly unfair and unjust proceedings can be reviewed by the federal courts under the Due Process Clause of the Fourteenth Amendment. The term also conveys the idea that a decision made under this approach does not necessarily produce bright-line rules, because every case is decided on the totality of its facts and circumstances.

Due process defense In entrapment law, the theory that entrapment may be established by police conduct that was so outrageous as to violate the Due Process Clause.

Due Process Model A theory developed by Herbert Packer suggests that within a constitutional system of criminal justice there are two general attitudes; the due process model stresses an insistence on formal, adjudicative, adversary factfinding, the prevention and elimination of mistakes, a stress on legal (as opposed to actual) guilt, and viewing the presumption of innocence to mean that every suspect must be treated as if he were innocent; See *Crime Control Model.*

Due Process Revolution The period from 1961 to 1969 when most of the criminal provisions of the Bill of Rights were incorporated. See *incorporation doctrine.*

Egalitarianism A political theory that supports the eradication of legal and social distinctions between citizens; it is an ideal of American republicanism and has been a force behind the expansion of rights such as the right of all citizens to serve on juries; it is a value that underlies constitutional criminal procedure. See *equality.*

En banc An appellate case heard and decided by the entire appellate bench rather than by a panel of judges drawn from the entire bench.

Encouragement A term describing a range of police investigatory activity designed to create a criminal opportunity for offenders who commit crimes that are difficult to detect, but without inducing them to commit the crimes. See *entrapment.*

Enhancement device Mechanism that is used to enhance the natural senses of a law enforcement officer to detect contraband; may include flashlights, binoculars, and sophisticated electronic listening and thermal detection devices.

Entrapment Act of police officers or government agents inducing a person to commit a crime for the purpose of arresting and prosecuting the person; a defense to conviction. See *encouragement.*

Equality See *egalitarianism.*

Equal Protection Clause Section 1 of the Fourteenth Amendment guarantees that "No state shall . . . deny to any person within its jurisdiction the equal protection of the laws." This right can be enforced by federal courts and by congressional legislation.

Equity See *chancery.*

Exclusionary rule A legal rule that illegally obtained evidence may not be used in legal proceedings; may be created by common law (e.g., as to coerced confessions), constitutional adjudication (e.g., the Fourth Amendment exclusionary rule established in *Weeks v. United States* 1914), or by statute (e.g., the exclusionary rule for illegal electronic eavesdropping).

Exculpatory statement A statement that tends to justify, excuse, or clear the defendant from alleged fault or guilt.

Exigency exception Generally, an emergency requiring immediate action; pressing; urgent. In Fourth Amendment law, an exigency is an emergency that gives rise to an exception to the warrant requirement.

Ex parte On one side only. A judicial hearing is *ex parte* when it occurs at the request of one party without the other party being present.

Expectation of privacy The basis for determining the existence of Fourth Amendment rights under *Katz v. United States* (1967).

Expert witness A witness who, by reason of specialized education or experience, possesses superior knowledge regarding a subject about which persons having no particular training are incapable of forming an accurate opinion; a witness who is qualified as an expert is allowed to assist the jury in understanding complicated or technical subjects and may be allowed to answer hypothetical questions.

Ex post facto law A criminal law passed after the occurrence of an act which retrospectively changes the legal consequences by making an innocent act criminal, by increasing the penalty for an act, or by changing rules of evidence that make it easier to obtain a conviction; prohibited by the United States Constitution, Art. I, §§ 9 and 10 to the federal and state governments.

Extraterritorial Beyond the physical and juridical boundaries of a particular state or nation; laws may have extraterritorial effect.

Eyewitness One who saw the act, fact, or transaction to which one testifies. It may be distinguished from an ear-witness (*auritus*); but, for purposes of the law of identification, similar rules apply.

Facial attack A legal challenge to the constitutionality of a statute is either (1) a facial attack, which means that the statute is challenged "on its face" or in every way in which it may be applied, or (2) "as applied," a narrower attack that the statute is unconstitutional only if applied in a certain way.

Facilitating function Criminal-procedure law has two broad functions: to facilitate prosecution and, simultaneously, to protect the civil rights of suspects and defendants

Fair cross-section In jury selection, the larger groups of prospective jurors on the jury master list or jury wheel, or the venire must be selected in a manner to be most likely to statistically represent the larger community under federal law and constitutional standards of equal protection. The particular jury panel (or venire) from which the petit jury is selected, and the jury itself, need not be a representative sample.

False arrest An arrest that is not based upon probable cause; evidence seized as the result of a false arrest is inadmissible. A false arrest is a basis for a civil action against a peace officer who made the arrest.

Federalism The division and relationship of power between the state and federal governments.

Federalists Those favoring the ratification of the Constitution in 1788. This group emerged as the political party of Presidents George Washington and John Adams; those favoring a strong federal government; Chief Justice John Marshall was a prominent Federalist.

Field interrogation Police practice of ordering persons to briefly stop and answer questions in regard to suspicious behavior.

Fixed checkpoint In border search law, a search of automobiles at a fixed checkpoint on a road within one hundred miles from the U.S. border for illegal aliens; an investigative stop of a car slowed at such a point must be based on reasonable suspicion.

"Fleeing felon" rule A common-law rule that allows a police officer to shoot to kill any fleeing felon, whether or not the felon had used deadly force. The rule was brought under the Fourth Amendment by *Tennessee v. Garner* (1985)—an officer may now lawfully shoot at a fleeing felon only if the suspect is reasonably believed to be armed and dangerous.

Footnote 4 The most famous footnote in a Supreme Court case was Footnote 4 in *United States v. Carolene Products Co.* (1938), which outlined a post-New Deal Court agenda focusing on: (1) cases involving the Bill of Rights, (2) laws that restrict the normal political process, and (3) laws aimed at "discrete and insular" religious, national, or racial minorities.

Formal charge rule The right to counsel at a lineup or showup attaches only after the defendant has been formally charged with a crime. In these procedures the Supreme Court has not applied the *critical stage* rule.

Formal charges A suspect is informally charged with an offense by a police officer's report or arrest warrant or other initial charging document issued by the magistrate after an initial appearance; formal charges are the charges upon which the state intends to prosecute the defendant and typically are the prosecutor's information that has been found by a magistrate to establish probable cause in a bindover proceeding, or an indictment that has been voted on by a grand jury. Formal charges can only be amended with the approval of a court.

Formal rights In the history of the incorporation doctrine, prior to 1961 the designation of rights located in the Bill of Rights as "formal" (as opposed to fundamental) meant that they were not incorporated into the Fourteenth Amendment Due Process Clause.

Framers Term used collectively to include the men involved in the drafting of the United States Constitution and Bill of Rights; narrower term than "founders," which refers to individuals who led the rebellion from England and the founding of the federal republic of the United States.

Frisk A colloquial term used to describe a police search of a person who is stopped; it consists of a "pat down" of the outer clothing to determine if the person stopped has a weapon.

Fruit of the poisonous tree doctrine A Fourth Amendment doctrine that states that evidence derived from illegally seized evidence cannot be used by the prosecution; it applies to confessions if an otherwise valid confession is obtained from a suspect who is illegally detained.

Fundamental fairness A meaning attached to due process, i.e., a procedure violates due process if the procedure is deemed by a court to be fundamentally unfair. Another way of stating the "due process approach," so that for a court to decide if a procedure is fundamentally unfair, it must examine the totality of the circumstances.

Fundamental rights test The test by which it is decided whether a right located in the Bill of Rights is to be incorporated into the Due Process Clause of the Fourteenth Amendment by a process of *selective incorporation* and made applicable to the states; a right that is "fundamental" must be incorporated, but one deemed "formal" is not.

General-reasonableness construction In Fourth Amendment jurisprudence, a conservative doctrine that emphasized the idea that the constitutionality of a search and seizure is to be decided by whether it is reasonable.

General warrant A search warrant without limit; a general warrant violates the particularity requirement of the Fourth Amendment. The term was used at the time of the Revolution by Americans to describe the writs of assistance issued by colonial governors.

Grand jury A jury summoned to hear charges against persons accused of crime to determine whether there is enough evidence for the persons to stand trial; the common-law grand jury (i.e., the "large" jury) consists of twenty-three persons and decides whether to indict by a majority vote.

Habeas corpus, writ of A judicial writ requiring that a person claiming illegal detention be brought to court forthwith to determine the legality of detention.

Hearsay evidence A statement, other than one made by the declarant while testifying at the trial or hearing, offered in evidence to prove the truth of the matter asserted. In ordinary affairs, hearsay evidence may be reliable, but a hearsay statement cannot be subject to cross-examination. The general rule of evidence is that hearsay statements are not admissible, but there are numerous exceptions to the hearsay evidence rule.

Hierarchy of courts Courts may be ranked by their authority to declare precedent, with a supreme court establishing common-law rules, which must be followed by all courts "below" it, and an intermediate appellate court having such authority over trial courts.

Hierarchy of law The relative authority of law derives from the body that creates it; thus constitutional law is superior to legislation, which may in turn abolish or modify court-made common law.

Hierarchy of rights The Burger Court's rulings in criminal procedure have tended to be more supportive of Fifth and Sixth amendment rights in comparison to the Fourth amendment, especially the Fourth Amendment exclusionary rule, which is treated as a right of lesser status.

Hot pursuit A common-law right of a police officer to follow a felon across jurisdictional lines or to enter a house or other area protected by a Fourth Amendment expectation of privacy to make an arrest if the officer is in hot pursuit, that is, closely following the felon.

Human rights A special class of rights held by a person simply by virtue of being human; moral rights grounded in the equal moral dignity of each person, that can and should be made legally binding in national, regional, or international law.

Hypothetical person test In entrapment law, an element of the "objective test"—where the inducement offered by the government agent is so great as to persuade persons other than those who are ready and willing to commit the crime.

Identification parade British terminology for a lineup.

Illegal arrest An arrest that is made by an officer who has no legal authority or jurisdiction to make such an arrest, e.g., where an officer arrests a person in a foreign state. Where a suspect is brought into the jurisdiction of a court on the basis of an illegal arrest, the court does not thereby lose jurisdiction to try the case.

Immunity In criminal law, this refers to a person being immune from prosecution for a crime as a result of a binding promise by the government, allowed by statute, to not prosecute in return for the person's testimony in another prosecution; it is granted to override the person's privilege against self-incrimination. See *transactional immunity* and *use immunity.*

Impanel a jury A process whereby the clerk of court makes up a list of the jurors selected for a particular trial.

Impeach To impeach a witness is to challenge the truthfulness of the witness by presenting evidence that tends to contradict the testimony or to show that for some other reason the witness might have lied.

Impoundment To seize and take an item, such as an automobile, into lawful custody of a court or law enforcement agency. An impoundment is a prelude to an inventory search, and the rules of many police departments require an inventory search following an impoundment.

In camera Hearings held in the judge's chamber, away from the public and the jury.

Incompetent evidence Evidence that is relevant to prove an issue but is not allowed to be used in the trial because of other policy considerations; examples are hearsay or unconstitutionally seized evidence; generally, inadmissible evidence.

Incorporation by reference The method of making one document of any kind become a part of separate document by referring to the former in the latter.

Incorporation doctrine The constitutional doctrine by which provisions of the Bill of Rights become "incorporated" (in a rough analogy to the legal concept of *incorporation by reference*) into the Fourteenth Amendment and thus made applicable to the states.

Incorporation plus The incorporation doctrine plus the ability of courts to apply the due process approach where a specific right in the Bill of Rights does not apply.

Inculpatory statement A statement that tends to establish guilt or incriminate.

Independent source rule An exception to the "fruit-of-the-poisonous-tree doctrine." It comes into play when the evidence in question also was obtained in a lawful manner via an independent source.

Index crime Eight felonies counted by the FBI to construct a "crime index." They include murder or non-negligent manslaughter, rape, robbery, aggravated assault, burglary, automobile theft, larceny, and arson.

Indictment A formal, written criminal accusation voted on by a grand jury setting out the charges (crimes) for which the defendant must stand trial.

Indigent Needy; poor; an indigent defendant is a person without funds to hire a lawyer for the defense and is entitled to appointed counsel by operation of the Sixth and Fourteenth amendments.

Inducement In entrapment law, the benefits offered to commit a crime that is posed by the undercover agent.

Inevitable discovery rule A Fourth Amendment doctrine that overlooks unconstitutional police acts so as not to exclude evidence if the evidence would have been discovered in any event.

Inferior courts Lower courts; for example, trial courts, which are "below" appellate courts in the judicial hierarchy.

Information A formal, written, criminal accusation drawn up by a prosecutor setting out the charges (crimes) for which the defendant must stand trial; this replaces the indictment in many states and often follows the bind-over decision.

In loco parentis The doctrine that a school teacher stands in the place of a parent and may exercise parental authority; the Supreme Court has ruled that this in *not* a basis for a search of a public school student under the Fourth Amendment.

Initial appearance The hearing before a magistrate that occurs typically within twenty-four hours after a defendant's arrest; the purposes of the hearing are to inform the defendant of the charges, take an initial plea, set bail, and determine whether a defendant has an attorney; known as the "arraignment on the [arrest] warrant" in some states.

Injunction A court order requiring that a party perform some act or refrain from some act; a remedy in an action in a court of equity or in a court with equitable powers.

In personam jurisdiction The jurisdiction a court has over a person in its custody; a court does not lose *in personam* jurisdiction if a defendant was brought into the court's custody as the result of an illegal arrest.

In presence rule In the law of arrest, the general common-law rule is that a police officer can arrest a person for a misdemeanor only if the crime was committed in the officer's presence; exceptions for traffic violations and domestic violence have been created by statute.

Inquisitorial trial system European system of adjudication based on Roman law in civil-law countries. Distinguishing features include: cases are developed by civil service prosecutors operating under judicial instruction; defendants are under a general obligation to answer some questions in the preliminary stages but need not answer at trial; defendants' silence may be used against them; the judge plays an active role in the trial by questioning witnesses; there is no independent jury; and jurors may advise the professional judges.

Internal passport In some countries, residents must carry official personal identification at all times; under the Fourth Amendment there can be no general obligation to carry an internal passport or to provide identification without an arrest or stop.

Interrogation Generally, to interrogate is to question; in criminal procedure, it refers more specifically to the process of questions posed by the police to a suspect or a witness in an effort to solve a crime. Interrogation may also include the functional equivalent of questioning whereby actions by the police are designed to elicit incriminating statements from a suspect.

Inventory and return A sworn document prepared by law enforcement officers who have been issued and have executed a search warrant, indicating the execution and itemizing the items seized.

Inventory search A search made for the purpose of making an inventory, that is, a detailed list of articles of property.

Investigative stop Same as a *Terry* stop; forceful stopping of a person for field questioning when reasonable suspicion exists to believe the person is involved in criminal activity.

Invidious discrimination The kind of distinction based on race, gender or other irrational factor that allows a court to determine that a distinction caused by law violates the rights of a person to the "equal protection of the laws" under the Fourteenth Amendment; not every legal distinction between persons is invidious.

Ipse dixit He himself said it; a bare assertion resting on the authority of the individual.

Irrelevant evidence Evidence that does not logically pertain to the issue to be decided.

Judicial craft The quality of a judge's opinions, based on the level of judge's legal scholarship, the judge's understanding of issues, and the quality of the judge's writing style.

Judicial federalism In constitutional criminal procedure, the interaction between federal and state constitutional rights; the Fourteenth Amendment establishes a "constitutional floor" of minimum standards of rights that cannot be violated by a state; above this "floor" a state may grant additional rights under its own constitution or statutes. See *adequate and independent state grounds.*

Judicial independence The right and the actual ability of a court to decide cases on the basis of the facts and its interpretation of law without interference from other branches of the government; a vital aspect of the rule of law. Judicial independence is made more certain by the appointment of judges for good behavior and by the provision of Article III that the compensation of federal judges shall not be diminished.

Judicial philosophy An aspect of *judicial statesmanship*—whether a judge favors judicial restraint or judicial activism.

Judicial policy An aspect of *judicial statesmanship*—what particular policy views a judge may hold on any issue. For example, in criminal procedure, some justices are identified by their voting patters as being "pro-prosecution," others as "pro-defense" and others as "middle of the road."

Judicial restraint A philosophy of the judicial function which holds that judges should not make broad rulings that have legislative effect.

Judicial review The authority of a court to review a statute and declare it null and void if the statute is in conflict with a provision of the state or federal constitution.

Judicial statesmanship The ability of Supreme Court justices to write opinions that properly guide the nation.

Jurisdiction Legal power or authority.

Jury deliberation In deciding on a verdict, a jury is supposed to discuss the evidence, and not simply take a vote.

Jury independence The right of a jury to determine the facts of a case independently without judicial interference; this right was held to be a part of the common-law jury process in *Bushell's* case (1670).

Jury nullification The idea that a jury may disregard the legal instruction of the judge and render a verdict purely on the basis of conscience or feelings; although this happens, it is not usually authorized by legal doctrine.

Jury panel The group of prospective jurors called to the courthouse from which juries are chosen.

Jury trial The trial of a matter before a jury as opposed to a judge (or bench) trial; guaranteed by the United States Constitution Art. III, § 2, and by the Sixth and Seventh amendments.

Jury wheel A physical device or electronic system for the storage and random selection of the names or identifying numbers of prospective jurors.

Just Compensation Clause The Fifth Amendment states: "nor shall private property be taken for public use without just compensation." This provision was in effect incorporated as a due process right that federal courts applied against state takings (*Chicago, Burlington & Quincy Rr. Co. v. Chicago,* 1897) in an era when personal rights were not incorporated, thus creating a double standard.

Justice The term used for a judge of the Supreme Court; generally interchangeable with judge.

"Key man" method A method of selecting members of petit or grand juries whereby a judge picks a small number of jury commissioners known to him personally, and the commissioners in turn select persons known to them for the grand jury; this method, which dates back to the nineteenth century and tends to perpetuate established power relationships in county government while keeping minorities or new residents from jury service, is no longer used.

Knock and announce rule The common law rule that before an officer may open or break in the door to a premises to execute a search warrant, the officer must announce the presence of police and demand entry; declared to be a constitutional rule in *Wilson v. Arkansas* (1995). See *no-knock* warrant.

Law A body of written rules issued by legitimate sources of order in a state (e.g., the legislature) and designed to guide and control the actions of citizens. Law also derives from the text of a written constitution and, in common-law jurisdictions, from the opinions of appellate judges.

Law of the land A phrase in the Magna Carta, indicating that no peer could be punished except by "the law of the land"; believed to express the concept of due process.

Least intrusive means When a constitutional liberty collides with a state action required to maintain order, courts at times require that the state's intrusion be done in a manner that intrudes the least on individual privacy. Such a rule has not been applied to arrest or stop under the Fourth Amendment.

Legal doctrine The common-law process of case interpretation results in the development of rules that arise from the decisions of numerous similar, but not identical, cases. The rules in a related body of law are formed into legal doctrines. Over time, the rationales for such doctrines often change or erode. Thus, many legal doctrines of the common law often have a life cycle of birth, a period of growth and utility, change, and decline.

Legal fiction A legal doctrine or assumption that may not be true but that is adopted in order to achieve a beneficial end. The idea that entrapment is a defense to a crime that is inferred by the legislature is a legal fiction adopted by judges who first announced the doctrine.

Legal reasoning The mental process of ratiocination by a judge, by which the rules of an earlier case are discerned and applied to a case at hand; legal reasoning is not a mechanical process and is considered a branch of jurisprudence or legal philosophy. See *precedent.*

Legislative history The background and events, including committee reports, hearings, and floor debates, leading up to the enactment of a law (including constitutional provisions). Such history is important to courts when they are required to determine the legislative intent of a particular statute.

Liberty A political theory which undergirds republicanism, as it implies that the purpose of government is to allow individuals maximum freedom to pursue their individual and collective goals within the rule of law; it is a value that underlies constitutional criminal procedure.

Lineup A police identification procedure by which the suspect in a crime is exhibited before the victim or witness to determine if he committed the offense. In a lineup, the suspect is lined up with other individuals for purposes of identification.

Locke, John (1632–1704) Political philosopher whose social contract theory of government undermined the notion of royal absolutism; his ideas of the inherent equality of all and a fundamental right of each person to liberty, bound only by law made by mutual consent, had a profound influence on English constitutionalism and the United States Constitution.

Magistrate The term can apply to (1) an inferior (i.e., lower) judicial officer, (2) any judge, or (3) any public civil officer with executive or judicial authority.

Magna Carta (1215) A charter of liberties sworn by King John of England to his barons; its *law of the land* clause is believed to be the forerunner of due process.

Mandamus, writ of A judicial writ ordering a government officer to perform some "ministerial act," that is, an act required by law over which the officer has no discretion to not carry out.

Master jury list Also called a jury wheel; the master list compiled by a county or district jury commission from the most widely available lists of eligible voters, including voting registration lists, driver's license and state identification lists, and city directories. Jury venires are drawn from the master jury list.

Media ride-along A practice of some police departments to invite news reporters and/or photo or video journalists to accompany the police during the execution of warrants; held to violate the Fourth Amendment rights of householders in *Wilson v. Layne* (1999).

Merchant's privilege A statutory right enacted in most states that allows security personnel to conduct brief investigatory detentions of suspected shoppers that would be tortious or criminal if carried out by ordinary citizens.

Missouri Compromise A compromise measure adopted by Congress in 1820 declaring that slavery could not be introduced into new states north of the southern boundary of Missouri. The compromise paired the admission of new free and slave states into the union as a way of maintaining parity between the North and the South. It was designed to preserve the Union and prevent sectional conflicts from erupting into disunion or civil war. An 1850 extension was declared unconstitutional in *Scott v. Sandford* (1857), hastening the Civil War.

Mistaken arrest An arrest that is based on probable cause but results in the arrest of a person who is not, in fact, the suspect. A police officer who makes such an arrest is protected against civil liability; a private person who makes a mistaken citizen's arrest, is subject to a tort action for false imprisonment. A statutory exception exists, see *merchant's privilege.*

Mixed question of law and fact A question depending for solution on questions of both law and fact, but is really a question of either law or fact to be decided by either judge or jury.

Motion An application made to a court to obtain an order requiring some act to be done in the favor of the applicant.

Multiple-district prosecution A practice of federal prosecutors whereby an enterprise is simultaneously prosecuted in several districts in which the enterprise does business; generally viewed as an unfair prosecution tactic.

Multiple representation A situation where one attorney represents two or more defendants in the same matter; the defendants may be tried in the same or in different (severed) trials. See *conflict of interest.*

Neutral and detached magistrate Phrase from *Johnson v. United States* (1948) explaining rationale for Fourth Amendment search warrant—that a judicial officer is less partisan than a police officer in deciding whether probable cause exists on the basis of the institutional role and traditions of the judicial officer.

No-knock warrant A warrant that explicitly authorizes police to enter a premises without knocking and announcing their presence, based on probable cause to believe that the occupants are likely to immediately destroy contraband or pose a threat of deadly violence to police executing the warrant. See *knock and announce rule.*

Non-incorporation era A period designated in this text as falling between the ratification of the Bill of Rights in 1791 to the ratification of the Civil War amendments in 1870, when it was clear doctrine that the Bill of Rights was not intended to be applied to the states; thereafter, the issue became contested.

Novel Disseisin A medieval English writ that set up an efficient procedure to determine the rightful possession of land taken by force; it utilized a precursor to the modern jury to determine facts.

Nulla poena sine lege No punishment without law.

Nullum crimen sine lege No crime without law.

Objective test In entrapment law, the view held by a minority of Supreme Court justices and a minority of the states, that entrapment should be based on whether the conduct of the police fell to such a level as would induce a hypothetical person to engage in the criminal behavior.

Open fields Private land not protected against police trespass under the Fourth Amendment. See *curtilage.*

Opinion The statement by a judge or court of the decision reached in a case tried before them, expounding the law as applied to the case and detailing the reasons upon which the judgment is based.

Order When contrasted to liberty, it implies the lawful limits placed on the freedom of individuals necessary to maintain the "domestic tranquillity" that is a necessary function of government; the contrast cannot be complete because public order is necessary for individuals and groups to enjoy their liberty.

Ordered liberty Resonant phrase found in *Palko v. Connecticut* (1938) and other cases, that encapsulates the tension between two fundamental aspects of American governance.

Originalism A theory of constitutional interpretation that holds that judges must apply the Constitution in accordance with the true intent of the framers. The theory is based on the principle of separation of powers and the idea that judges should not "make" law. Opponents argue that the true intent of the framers cannot be known with certainty in regard to broad constitutional rights (e.g., due process) and that changing conditions require justices to interpret provisions to meet contemporary needs.

Outrageous conduct test In entrapment law, same as *due process defense.*

Overrule When an appellate court finds that one of its prior opinions was incorrect or unsound, it may overrule the prior case and replace it with a different ruling; thus, strictly speaking, an appellate court is not bound by its own precedent; See *reverse.*

Parallel right Prior to the incorporation of the Bill of Rights the Supreme Court established certain rights under the Due Process Clause which were parallel to rights found in the Bill of Rights, but not applied with the same level of certainty. An example is the Sixth Amendment rule stating that counsel was automatically required in every federal felony trial, unless waived, whereas due process held states to provide counsel for indigents only if special circumstances existed.

Parliamentary supremacy The English system in which the statute (a declaration of the legislature) is superior to any written or unwritten constitutional provision or custom.

Particularity requirement The requirement, drawn from the Fourth Amendment, that search warrants "particularly describ[e] the place to be searched, and the persons or things to be seized." The opposite are *general warrants* that the Fourth Amendment was designed to abolish.

Pattern and practice suit A review of a local police department by the U.S. Justice Department for discriminatory patterns and practices; under the law passed in 1994, a special master can be appointed to oversee modifications in the training and supervision provided by the local police department.

Peer In England, a member of the nobility; originally, "jury of peers" meant that non-nobles could not sit on juries to judge the guilt of peers. In modern usage, the term refers to equals. A "jury of peers" in America is composed of fellow citizens, without regard to class, gender, race/ethnicity, economic status, or other irrelevant attribute.

Pen register A device that electronically registers the telephone numbers from or to which a particular telephone makes calls, without recording the contents of the conversations.

Peremptory challenge In the voir dire, each side has a limited number of challenges that may be used to excuse a prospective juror even though the person has not exhibited any clear bias; recently, the Supreme Court has limited the ability of parties to exercise peremptory challenges in ways that are based primarily on race or gender. See *voir dire.*

Persuasive authority When an appellate court follows the reasoning of another court, even though the other court has no power to set binding precedent for the appellate court, the opinion followed is called "persuasive authority".

Pervasively regulated industry In the law of administrative searches, an administrative warrant is *not* required to search the place of a "pervasively regulated" industry.

Petit jury The common-law, twelve-person trial jury that has the authority to determine the facts and render a verdict in criminal trials; *"petit"* is the French word for "small" and refers to the size of the jury in contrast to the twenty-three-person grand jury.

Petty crime The designation of a crime as "petty" carries the constitutional consequence that it may be tried without a jury.

"Plain feel" rule The concept that evidence seized in plain view includes evidence lawfully felt by police and that is immediately apparent as contraband.

Plain statement The United States Supreme Court will not disturb a state court criminal procedure ruling if the state opinion includes a plain statement that the ruling is based on adequate and independent state gorunds.

Plain view doctrine Contraband that is located in a public place or in a private place where an officer has a right to be present may be seized "in plain view" without a search warrant.

Police officer expertise In *Terry v. Ohio* (1968) the traditional rule that a Fourth Amendment seizure of a person may be based only on probable cause was eased to allow a temporary stop on the basis of reasonable suspicion in part on the fact that the on-the-street situation was evaluated by a police officer applying his or her special expertise. This element of *Terry* was dropped when the Court decided that reasonable suspicion could be based on the hearsay statement of an informant.

Police power A concept of constitutional law that state governments have plenary or general authority to pass laws for the health, safety, morals, general welfare, and good ordering of the people.

Precedent In law, an adjudged case or decision of a court that furnishes authority for an identical or similar case that arises afterward on a similar question of law. See *legal reasoning.*

Predisposition In entrapment law, a defendant's state of mind that is inclined toward the commission of the crime in question prior to the police "encouragement" activity,

Prejudice This commonly means bias. In appellate procedure, it means that an error that occurred at the trial or pretrial stage was the likely cause of the guilty verdict; in some instances, a conviction will not be overturned unless the appellate court finds prejudice in this sense.

Prejudice the case The second prong of the rule stating that the ineffective assistance of counsel in a criminal trial violates the Sixth Amendment rights of the defendant. Prejudice in this sense is made out by a reasonable probability that, absent the errors, the factfinder would have had a reasonable doubt respecting guilt.

Preliminary examination or hearing A hearing before a magistrate to determine whether the prosecution can present sufficient evidence to establish probable cause to show that the defendant committed a crime; if so, the judge binds the defendant over for trial.

Presentment Instead of an indictment, a formal accusation based on the personal knowledge of the grand jurors themselves; this is rare or nonexistent today. An accusation initiated by the grand jury; an instruction to the prosecutor to prepare an indictment.

Presumption of innocence A feature of the common-law trial that is guaranteed by the Due Process Clause; it requires that the burden of proof of guilt of every element of a crime is placed on the prosecution and that the burden is proof beyond a reasonable doubt.

Pretext search *Whren v. United States* (1996) held that a search of an automobile made by an officer who stopped the car on the objectively correct basis of a traffic violation is valid even if the traffic stop was made for the real purpose of searching the automobile for drugs.

Preventive detention Confinement of a defendant before trial; the formal denial of bail on the grounds that the defendant is likely to commit a crime while awaiting trial.

Private law Involves the rights and disputes of private individuals, groups, and corporations; subject matter areas include contracts, property, torts (the law of injuries), commercial law, and civil procedure; in contrast to public law.

Privilege In law, a particular benefit or a right or immunity against or beyond the course of law. Thus, the privilege against self-incrimination allows a person to refuse to testify despite the general legal obligation that a person has to testify when summoned to a court.

Privileges or Immunities Clause Clause in Section 1 of the Fourteenth Amendment, stating that "No state shall make or enforce any law which shall abridge the privileges or immunities of citizens of the United States. . . ." This clause was thought to be the basis of the idea of "total incorporation." The clause was interpreted in such a manner as to render it a virtual nullity by the *Slaughter-house Cases* (1873).

Probable cause A standard to determine whether sufficient evidence exists that allows a prudent person to conclude that other facts exist; the standard for the validity of an arrest, a lawful search, and the holding of a person for trial.

Pro bono publico For the good of the public; attorneys take a certain number of cases without fee to represent indigents *pro bono.*

Procedural law Prescribes the methods of enforcing rights that are breached and includes rules of jurisdiction and the serving of legal process (e.g., a summons) and rules that guide the conduct of a trial.

Pro forma As a matter of form; a decision made *pro forma* is made not because it is right but merely to facilitate further proceedings.

Property theory In Fourth Amendment jurisprudence, the concept that Fourth Amendment rights are based on an individual's legal claims over private property; this theory has been superseded by the *expectation of privacy* concept.

***Pro se* defense** Self-representation, Latin meaning, "for himself."

Prosecutor's information Formal document charging a defendant with crimes on which the defendant must stand trial; replaces the grand jury indictment in states that allow informations; used in jurisdictions with grand juries in cases in which the defendant waives the grand jury.

Protective sweep "A quick and limited search of a premises, incident to an arrest and conducted to protect the safety of police officers or others. It is narrowly confined to a cursory visual inspection of those places in which a person might be hiding." *Maryland v. Buie* (1990).

Public defender A full time, paid position as a defense attorney for indigent defendants. Caseloads of public defenders tend to be high.

Public law Law that concerns the powers of governmental bodies and involves disputes between governmental departments or between private persons and government. Public law includes such subjects as constitutional law, administrative law, tax law, substantive criminal law, and criminal procedure.

Quash To annul, make void; e.g., to quash an indictment.

Radical Republicans The ascendant wing of the Republican Party which, in the aftermath of the Civil War, pushed for legislation that supported the full civil rights of African Americans and imposed punitive measures on the South.

Radio bulletin Information transmitted by radio from one police department to others notifying them that a specified individual is wanted for a crime; evidence seized in a search incident to an arrest made on the basis of such a report is admissible even if there was no probable cause for the initial report; it has the effect of a mistaken arrest.

Real evidence Physical evidence.

Reasonable doubt The standard of evidence sufficiency for a verdict of guilt in a criminal case; a doubt that would cause a prudent person to hesitate before acting in a matter of personal importance; not a fanciful doubt.

Reasonable force Police may use reasonable force to make an arrest, as determined by all the facts and circumstances.

Reasonableness clause The first part of the Fourth Amendment that prohibits "unreasonable searches and seizures." It is the basis of the *general-reasonableness construction.*

Reconstruction amendments See *Civil War amendments.*

Recoupment The process by which the state or unit of local government later recovers the cost of providing assistance of counsel to a formerly indigent defendant.

Rehnquist Court The Supreme Court during the period that William Rehnquist has been Chief Justice of the United States, from 1986 to the present.

Release on recognizance Pretrial release of a defendant without the posting of a bail bond or other security but only on the promise of the defendant to return to court for trial or further proceedings.

Remand An action of an appellate court sending all or part of a case back to the lower court without overturning the lower court's ruling but with instructions for further proceedings that may range from conducting a new trial to entering a proper judgment.

Remedial law Law that determines the actual benefits or remedies that a successful party to a lawsuit will receive. In criminal law the "remedy" is the punishment meted out. In constitutional criminal procedure, the exclusion of evidence after a court has decided that evidence has been seized in violation of a person's constitutional protections is deemed a "remedy."

Reparation Repayment; remedy designed to restore the injured party to his or her position before the injury occurred.

Republicanism Political theory that government is instituted for benefit of all the people; formal classes, nobility, or monarchy inconsistent with republicanism. As a result, for example, jury of peers means a jury of citizens.

Retained counsel A lawyer hired by and paid for by the defendant.

Reverse An appellate court is said to reverse the decision of a lower court when it disagrees with the decision and orders the lower court to change it to be in conformity with the appellate court ruling. See *overrule.*

Roadblock An automobile that crashes into a police roadblock effectively arrests the driver; injuries that result from such a crash may be the basis of police liability for effecting the arrest with excessive force if the placement of the roadblock was unreasonable.

Roving patrol Refers to a stop of a vehicle being driven on the highway by border patrol agents within one hundred air miles of the U.S. border; distinguished from a fixed checkpoint stop.

Rule application A major function of trial courts—to decide cases in accord with the law; contrasted with *rule making.*

Rule of Law The political and legal principle that the government must act in accordance with established law and that governmental officers must not exceed their authority; also known as the "principle of legality."

Rule making A process of interpretation of prior cases, statutes or constitutional provisions by appellate courts by which rules of common law are developed. See *legal reasoning* and *precedent.*

Scope of search incident to arrest Police may search the area within an arrested person's immediate control to ensure officer safety and to secure evidence from destruction; the scope may include an area to which the arrested person may reach, but does not authorize the search of an entire premises.

Screening device The preliminary hearing and grand jury are pretrial screening devices. They screen out cases where probable cause cannot be established in order to prevent hasty or oppressive prosecutions.

Search incident to arrest A search of an individual and the arrested person's immediate surroundings that takes place immediately upon or after the arrest; the search is a part of the arrest process. The search is for weapons (to protect the arresting officer and others) and for incriminating evidence.

Secret informant A person who supplies evidence of probable cause to obtain a search warrant but whose identity is not divulged to the magistrate in order to maintain the security of an investigation; may be an undercover police agent or a paid "snitch."

***Section 1983* suit** A civil lawsuit in federal court against a state officer or municipality who has violated the federal or constitutional rights of an individual; established under 42 U.S.C. §1983. Enacted in 1871 as a civil rights act designed to curb the terrorism of the Ku Klux Klan. Also called a "constitutional tort" suit.

Sectional conflict Political, economic, or social friction between different sections of the nation; specifically, the conflict between the North and the South before the Civil War.

Seditious libel A writing that has the intent of inciting the people to overthrow the government by force. It was long a political crime in Great Britain.

Seizure of the person An arrest or stop constitutes a seizure under the Fourth Amendment.

Selective incorporation The concept that individual provisions of the Bill of Rights may become incorporated into the Fourteenth Amendment due process doctrine if the Supreme Court finds that such provisions are fundamental to our system of ordered liberty. See *total incorporation.*

Selective prosecution Occurs when a defendant is singled out for charging on impermissible grounds, such as race, religion, political beliefs, or for exercising constitutional rights.

Self-incrimination rule The constitutional doctrine that a criminal defendant is privileged to remain silent in the face of an accusation, whether made in court or before; the right extends to all persons questioned in official hearings where what they say may "incriminate" them. The right is based on the constitutional provision in the Fifth Amendment that "No person . . . shall be compelled in any criminal case to be a witness against himself. . . ." See *compulsion.*

Self-representation A situation where a defendant waives the right to appointed counsel and conducts his or her own defense.

Separation of powers A political and constitutional doctrine that states that the essential functions of one branch of government are not to be exercised by another.

Sequester a jury Require a jury to be removed from the community during the period of a trial so as to avoid the contaminating influences of news accounts or discussions with friends, relatives and strangers about a crime; it was required in the early common law and is now infrequent.

Shocks the conscience test Formula for the due process test to determine when police action is so egregious during arrest and/or search activity to violate the Due Process Clause; it excludes the notions of the application of the Fourth Amendment and its exclusionary rule.

Showup One-to-one confrontation between the suspect and a witness to a crime. It is a form of pretrial identification procedure in which the suspect is confronted by or exposed to the victim of or witness to a crime.

Silver platter doctrine Rules established by the United States Supreme Court under its supervisory power prior to *Mapp v. Ohio* (1961) that forbade federal officers from supplying state officers with illegally seized evidence, and then testifying as to the evidence in state court, or from receiving illegally seized evidence from state officers.

Sobriety checklane A roadblock set up by police for purpose of determining whether drives are under the influence of intoxicants is not a stop for a criminal investigation, and therefore such a temporary detention without individualized suspicion does not violate the Fourth Amendment.

Source city An element of the drug courier profile is that the place from which the stopped person has traveled from is a "source city" for drugs.

Source of law Law is made by a specific human institution: courts develop rules of common law; legislatures and governors fashion legislation, and constitutions are made by "the people" in special constitutional conventions or by special rules for amending constitutions.

Sovereign immunity Legal doctrine that prevents a party from suing a government unless the government by law allows itself to be sued.

Special circumstances rule Rule of *Powell v. Alabama* (1932) that due process requires a state to pay for lawyer for an indigent defendant only if special circumstances exist.

"Special needs" doctrine A doctrine developed by Supreme Court constitutional adjudication which allows government agents to search without a warrant, and possibly without individualized suspicion where searches are conducted for "special needs beyond the normal need for law enforcement," such the search of the bags of public school students suspected of carrying items banned under school rules.

Standby counsel Counsel appointed at the discretion of the trial judge to advise a pro se defendant and to ensure that the defendant's rights are not undermined.

Standing A plaintiff has standing to sue in a court when there is an actual case or controversy between the plaintiff and a defendant that a court may hear and decide; the party must have a real stake in the outcome of the case.

Stare decisis Doctrine of precedent.

Status quo ante The existing state of things before a given time.

Stop The temporary restraint of a person's mobility by a police officer where the officer has reasonable suspicion to believe that the person stopped has just committed, is committing, or is about to commit a crime; practice declared constitutional in *Terry v. Ohio* (1968).

Stop and frisk The colloquial term for a *Terry* stop. Also called an *investigative stop.*

Strip search See *body cavity search.*

Subjective test or theory The majority rule of entrapment law. The theory that entrapment exists when police activity plants the idea of the crime in a person who is otherwise not predisposed to commit it.

Subpoena A command of a court to a witness to appear at a certain time and place to give testimony; a grand jury also has subpoena power. If the subpoena is not obeyed, the person refusing to appear may be held in contempt of court and fined or jailed until she agrees to cooperate with the legal process. The word derives from the Latin, meaning under (*sub*) the penalty (*poena*) of law.

Subpoena *ad testificandum* A subpoena to testify.

Subpoena *duces tecum* A subpoena to produce documents, books, papers, and other matters for inspection in a case.

Sub rosa Confidential, secret.

Substantive due process The concept that the due process clause includes substantive rights that limit the power of government to legislate. Applied to property rights by the Supreme Court before the New Deal. The right to privacy that supports the abortion rights case, *Roe v. Wade* (1973), is a substantive due process concept. Contrast to procedural due process.

Substantive law Establishes, defines, and governs rights, powers, obligations, and freedoms. Rules of substantive law, for example, establish contractual obligations, property rights, or the right to recovery for personal injuries (torts). Substantive criminal law defines crimes such as homicide and theft and defenses such as insanity.

Suggestibility A term for the human process by which the subtle reactions of one person can influence the thinking of another; in *U. S. v. Wade* (1967) it was the legal basis for the Supreme Court to determine that state action existed as the basis for its holding.

Sui generis Of its own kind or class, i.e., unique, the only one of its kind.

Sumptuary law A law designed to regulate habits primarily on moral or religious grounds but justified for the health or welfare of the community; *sumptuary crimes* is synonymous with "vice" or "victimless crimes."

Supervisory authority The power of higher courts to require lower courts to act within their jurisdiction; the power is sometimes used by the United States Supreme Court as a way of enforcing appropriate standards on federal law enforcement agencies.

Supremacy Clause Article VI, paragraph 2, of the United States Constitution, which declares that the Constitution, laws, and treaties of the federal government are the "Supreme Law of the Land"; that is, that they supersede state laws when there is a conflict between state and federal law.

Telephonic warrant A search warrant allowed by the Federal Rules of Criminal Procedure and the laws of some states, that allows a magistrate to receive an affidavit from an officer by telephonic means.

***Terry* stop** See *stop* and *stop and frisk.*

Testimonial evidence Evidence elicited from a witness to prove a fact, as opposed to documentary evidence or real (i.e., tangible) evidence.

Thermal imaging An advanced technology utilized by law enforcement to detect whether an unusually high amount of heat is emanating from a premises; may indicate the presence of the commercial growing of marijuana indoors.

Third degree The process of securing a confession of information from a suspect or prisoner by prolonged questioning, the use of threats, or actual violence.

Tort A private or civil wrong or injury, other than breach of contract, for which the court will provide a remedy in the form of an action for damages.

Total incorporation The concept that the privileges and immunities clause or the due process clause of the Fourteenth Amendment intended to make the first eight amendments of the Bill of Rights applicable to the states upon ratification in 1868. See *selective incorporation.*

Totality of circumstances See *due process approach.*

Transactional immunity A blanket immunity against prosecution for the crimes about which the immunized witness is testifying; broader protection than use immunity.

Treason Clause Provisions of United States Constitution, Art. 3, Sec. 3 that limit the definition and punishment of treason against the United States; such limitation implies that republican government intended to be liberal and restrained and operate within the Rule of Law.

Trespass A common law tort; the wrongful interference with property rights.

Trial *de novo* Same as *de novo trial.*

True bill An indictment that has not yet been signed by the prosecuting attorney; when the grand jury votes to indict an accused person, it issues a "true bill"; when it votes against indicting an accused, it votes a "no bill."

Two-pronged test In Fourth Amendment law, a test to be applied by a magistrate on whether or not to issue a warrant where information has been supplied by a secret informant; the test requires that the affidavit to indicate the basis of the informant's knowledge and a basis for accepting the informant's veracity. The test has been supplanted by a totality of the circumstances test.

Undercover agent A police officer who lies about his or her identity in order to pose as a victim or criminal for the purposes of law enforcement investigation.

Unenumerated Rights Clause The Ninth Amendment to the constitution: "The enumeration in the Constitution of certain rights shall not be construed to deny or disparage others retained by the people." The Supreme Court has yet to decide a case that declares an unenumerated right to be protected by the Court.

Unindicted coconspirator A person so named by a grand jury is one against whom there may be a *prima facie* case of guilt, but for some reason is not indicted.

Use immunity This form of immunity prohibits the witness's compelled testimony or its fruits from being used in any way to prosecute the witness; however, the witness may be prosecuted on the basis of independently obtained evidence; narrower protection than transactional immunity.

Universal Declaration of Human Rights A formal document promulgated by the United Nations in 1948 which attempts to codify all human rights; many provisions are borrowed from or parallel to provisions of the Bill of Rights—the first ten amendments to the United States Constitution.

Vagrancy statute A law making it a crime to loiter; older vagrancy statutes prior to *Papachristou v. City of Jacksonville* (1972) were quite vague and gave police discretion to arrest whom they would; modern vagrancy statutes are closely tailored to describe particular types of vagrancy such as house prowling or streetwalking prostitution.

Venire In jury practice, the list of jurors summoned to serve during a particular court term; from the Latin word meaning "to come"; to appear in court.

Venue The locality or place where a trial is to be held; the usual rule is that it is to be held in the locality (often the county) where the crime was committed; it may be changed if there is so much publicity in the locality as to make it impossible to select an unbiased jury.

Verdict The decision of a jury or judge as finder of fact in a criminal case: guilty or not guilty of the charges.

Vindictive prosecution Occurs when new and more serious charges are brought simply because a defendant has exercised statutory or constitutional rights.

Voir dire The process of jury selection involving the questioning of prospective jurors in order to determine biases; after questioning, the juror is either selected or dismissed for cause or for no reason under the peremptory challenge. See *challenges for cause* and *peremptory challenge.*

Voluntariness test A common law rule developed in the eighteenth and nineteenth centuries claiming that any confession obtained by violence, threats, or promises is involuntary and is excluded from evidence; the rule was adopted as a due process rule that the Supreme Court applied to state cases. The rule still exists as a backup to the *Miranda* rule.

Waiver The waiver of a Fifth or Sixth amendment right must be an "intelligent relinquishment or abandonment of a known right or privilege." See *consent.*

Waiver of counsel A defendant can waive the right to the assistance of counsel if the decision is made with full knowledge of the right; a trial judge cannot require that a defendant be represented by counsel if the defendant can do a minimally competent job of defending himself or herself.

Waiver trial Same as a bench trial; the defendant waives the right to a jury and opts to be tried by a sole judge.

Warrant Generally, the command of an authority; in criminal procedure, it refers to a written order issued by a judge or magistrate. A search warrant authorizes police officers to search a premises where there is probable cause to believe contraband is hidden. An arrest warrant authorizes officers to arrest a named person where there is probable cause to believe that the person committed a crime.

Warrant clause The second clause of the Fourth Amendment specifying rules concerning a search warrant.

Warrantless search A search conducted by an officer without having obtained a search or arrest warrant

Warrant-preference construction A liberal construction of Fourth Amendment rights that holds that a search is presumptively unreasonable if it is not accompanied by a search warrant unless there exists a narrowly drawn exception to the warrant requirement.

Warren Court The Supreme Court during the period that Earl Warren a Chief Justice of the United States (1953 to 1969).

Whig party Political party in the United States in the first half of the nineteenth century; it was absorbed by the Republican Party in the 1850s.

Wiretap (Tap) A means of listening in on telephone conversations by electronically intercepting the conversations at some point outside the place where the telephone is located.

Writs of assistance General search warrants issued by British colonial governors in America to enforce the hated Stamp Act; these writs and their enforcement became political issues that helped to ignite the American Revolution.

TABLE OF CASES

[Case & Comments in boldface; citations to Legal Puzzles not included]

Sitz v. Michigan State Police, 443 Mich. 744, 506 N.W.2d 209 (1993) . . . 210
Skinner v. Railway Labor Executives' Association, 409 U.S. 602, 109 S.Ct. 1402, 103 L.Ed.2d 639 (1989) . . . 69, 122, 253, 255–6, 409
Slaughterhouse Cases, 16 Wall. (83 U.S.) 36, 21 L.Ed. 394 (1873) . . . 41–2
Smith v. Bennett, 365 U.S. 708, 81 S.Ct. 895, 6 L.Ed.2d 39 (1961) . . . 303
Smith v. Illinois, 390 U.S. 129, 88 S.Ct. 748, 19 L.Ed.2d 956 (1968) . . . 450
Smith v. Illinois, 469 U.S. 91, 105 S.Ct. 490, 83 L.Ed.2d 488 (1984) . . . 332
Smith v. Ohio, 494 U.S. 541, 110 S.Ct. 1288, 108 L.Ed.2d 464 (1990) . . . 67–8
Soldal v. Cook County, 506 U.S. 56, 113 S.Ct. 538, 121 L.Ed.2d 450 (1992) . . . 121, 237–8
Sorrells v. U.S., 287 U.S. 435, 53 S.Ct. 210, 77 L.Ed. 413 (1932) . . . 387–9, 404
South Carolina v. Gathers, 490 U.S. 805, 109 S.Ct. 2207, 104 L.Ed.2d 876 (1989) . . . 50–1
South Dakota v. Opperman, 428 U.S. 364, 96 S.Ct. 3092, 49 L.Ed.2d 1000 (1976) . . . 234, 245– 7
Spano v. U.S., 360 U.S. 315, 79 S.Ct. 1202, 3 L.Ed.2d 1265 (1959) . . . 314, 339
Spies v. Illinois, 123 U.S. 131, 8 S.Ct. 22, 31 L.Ed. 80 (1887) . . . 42
Spinelli v. U.S., 393 U.S. 410, 89 S.Ct. 584, 21 L.Ed.2d 637 (1969) . . . Case & Comments 129–31, 134, 136, 158, 160, 225
Stack v. Boyle, 342 U.S. 1, 72 S.Ct. 1, 96 L.Ed. 3 (1951) . . . 164–5, 415, 417, 419, 434
Stanford v. Texas, 379 U.S. 476, 85 S.Ct. 506, 13 L.Ed.2d 431 (1965) . . . 113
Stansbury v. California, 511 U.S. 318, 114 S.Ct. 1526, 128 L.Ed.2d 293 (1994) . . . 335
State v. Aplaca, 837 P.2d 1298 (Hawaii 1992) . . . 296
State v. Berry, 391 So.2d 406; op. at 396 So.2d 880 (La. 1980) . . . 99
State v. Crump, 834 S.W.2d 265 (Tenn. 1992) . . . 331
State v. Doran, 5 Ohio St. 3d 187, 449 N.E.2d 1295 (1983) . . . 397
State v. Hazley, 428 N.W.2d 406 (Minn. App. 1988) . . . 326
State v. Houpt, 504 P.2d 570 (Kan. 1972) . . . 404
State v. McCarthy, 496 A.2d 513 (Conn. 1985) . . . 472
State v. Marsala, 216 Conn. 150, 579 A.2d 58 (1990) . . . 84
State v. Rockholt, 96 N.J. 570, 476 A.2d 1236 (1984) . . . 398
State v. Talbot, 71 N.J. 160, 364 A.2d 9 (1976) . . . 405
State v. Tucker, 626 So.2d 707 (La. 1993) . . . 204
Steagald v. U.S., 451 U.S. 204, 101 S.Ct. 1642, 68 L.Ed.2d 38 (1981) . . . 183
Stewart v. California, 384 U.S. 436, 86 S.Ct. 1602, 16 L.Ed.2d 694 (1966) . . . 316
Stewart v. Lubbock County, 767 F.2d 153 (5th Cir. 1985) . . . 160
Stone v. Powell, 428 U.S. 465, 96 S.Ct. 3037, 49 L.Ed.2d 1067 (1976) . . . 50, 77, 80, 90, 381
Stoner v. California, 376 U.S. 483, 84 S.Ct. 889, 11 L.Ed.2d 856 (1964) . . . 121, 148–9
Stovall v. Denno, 388 U.S. 293, 87 S.Ct. 1967, 18 L.Ed.2d 1199 (1967) . . . 360, 362, 369–70, 374
Strauder v. West Virginia, 100 U.S. 303, 25 L.Ed. 664 (1880) . . . 457, 460
Strickland v. Washington, 466 U.S. 668, 104 S.Ct. 2052, 80 L.Ed.2d 674 (1984) . . . Case & Comments 291–5, 297, 408
Stromberg v. California, 283 U.S. 359, 51 S.Ct. 532, 75 L.Ed. 1117 (1931) . . . 37, 44, 303
Swain v. Alabama, 380 U.S. 202, 85 S.Ct. 824, 13 L.Ed.2d 759 (1965) . . . 457, 459–60

Tague v. Louisiana, 444 U.S. 469, 100 S.Ct. 652, 62 L.Ed.2d 622 (1980) . . . 330
Taylor v. Alabama, 457 U.S. 687, 102 S.Ct. 2664, 73 L.Ed.2d 314 (1982) . . . 68
Taylor v. Louisiana, 419 U.S. 522, 95 S.Ct. 692, 42 L.Ed.2d 690 (1975) . . . 458
Taylor v. U.S., 414 U.S. 17, 94 S.Ct. 194, 38 L.Ed.2d 174 (1973) . . . 447
Tennessee v. Garner, 471 U.S. 1, 105 S.Ct. 1694, 85 L.Ed.2d 1 (1985) . . . 172, 177
Terry v. Ohio, 392 U.S. 1, 88 S.Ct. 1868, 20 L.Ed.2d 889 (1967) . . . 24, 67, 118, 124–6, 139, 157, 169–70, 173, 186, 188, Case & Comments 191–5, 198, 200, 202, 204–5, 208, 212, 221, 268, 482
Texas v. Brown, 460 U.S. 730, 103 S.Ct. 1535, 75 L.Ed.2d 502 (1983) . . . 146
Texas v. White, 423 U.S. 67, 96 S.Ct. 304, 46 L.Ed.2d 209 (1975) . . . 235–6
Thomas v. Arn, 474 U.S. 140 , 106 S.Ct. 466, 88 L.Ed.2d 435 (1985) . . . 22
Thompson v. Utah, 170 U.S. 343, 118 S.Ct. 620, 42 L.Ed. 1061 (1898) . . . 43
Thurman v. City of Torrington, 595 F.Supp. 1521 (D.Conn 1984) . . . 215
Townsend v. Sain, 372 U.S. 293, 83 S.Ct. 745, 9 L.Ed.2d 770 (1963) . . . 314
Trupiano v. U.S., 344 U.S. 699, 68 S.Ct. 1229, 92 L.Ed. 1663 (1948) . . . 185
Turner v. Fouche, 396 U.S. 346, 90 S.Ct. 532, 24 L.Ed.2d 567 (1970) . . . 457
Turner v. Murray, 476 U.S. 28, 106 S.Ct. 1683, 90 L.Ed.2d 27 (1986) . . . 459
Twining v. New Jersey, 211 U.S. 78, 29 S.Ct. 14, 53 L.Ed.2d 97 (1907) . . . 26, 36, 38, 43, 47, 276

U.S. v. 12 200–Ft. Reels of Film, 413 U.S. 123, 93 S.Ct. 2665, 37 L.Ed.2d 500 (1973) . . . 265
U.S. v. Abrahams, 575 F.2d 3 (1st Cir. 1978) . . . 436
U.S. v. Aikens, 64 F.3d 372 (8th Cir. 1995) . . . 404
U.S. v. Alvarez-Machain, 504 U.S. 655, 112 S.Ct. 2188, 119 L.Ed.2d 441 (1992) . . . 50, 176
U.S. v. Alvarez-Sanchez, 511 U.S. 350, 114 S.Ct. 1599, 128 L.Ed.2d 319 (1994) . . . 327
U.S. v. Armstrong, 517 U.S. 456, 116 S.Ct. 1480, 134 L.Ed.2d 687 (1996) . . . 422–3, 441

INDEX

Note: Pages in italic indicate a table is on that page.

D

E

F